THE PRINCIPLES OF THE LAW OF RESTITUTION

THE PRINCIPLES OF

THE LAW OF RESTITUTION

Third Edition

GRAHAM VIRGO

OXFORD
UNIVERSITY PRESS

OXFORD
UNIVERSITY PRESS

Great Clarendon Street, Oxford, OX2 6DP,
United Kingdom

Oxford University Press is a department of the University of Oxford.
It furthers the University's objective of excellence in research, scholarship,
and education by publishing worldwide. Oxford is a registered trade mark of
Oxford University Press in the UK and in certain other countries

First published 1999
Third published 2015
First published in paperback 2016

Published in the United States of America by Oxford University Press
198 Madison Avenue, New York, NY 10016, United States of America

British Library Cataloguing in Publication Data
Data available

Library of Congress Cataloging in Publication Data
Data available

ISBN 978–0–19–872638–8 (Hbk.)
ISBN 978–0–19–872639–5 (Pbk.)

PREFACE

The Law of Restitution is like a mountain. From a distance it may appear somewhat insignificant; indeed, some have dismissed it simply as a hill, a minor bump on the legal landscape. But, on closer inspection, it is definitely a mountain. It is big and complex, and it is very easy to get lost on its slopes. It has been explored many times in the recent past. Some explorers have recorded the mountain's features in great detail. Others have sought to understand how the mountain was formed and why its various features have developed. Others have simply tried to find the safest and quickest routes to the summit. But, although many explorers have visited the mountain recently, it has been inhabited for a much longer time. These inhabitants know the mountain well, even though they may not understand all its features, because they work on it every day. They know the quick routes to the summit. The explorers have created new routes, which may be better. But for explorers and inhabitants alike, there is only one true objective: to reach the summit safely. This book seeks to provide a map for those who are trying to climb to the top of the mountain. In doing so, it attempts to identify the best routes to the summit, where restitutionary remedies can be awarded to the conqueror. But it also seeks to explain the features which are passed on the way and identify the holes and swamps which will catch the unwary. Usually the route to the summit will be well established and well signposted. Sometimes, however, the most convenient route is one that goes along the byways—along paths which have been forgotten or are rarely used. Occasionally, the map-maker must cut across new country, forging a new route. Maybe others will follow, and the authorities may eventually recognize that route as legitimate, as giving those who come later a right of way, but they are unlikely to do so if there is another perfectly serviceable route nearby.

This book owes a great deal to those who have explored the English Law of Restitution before, particularly Lord Goff of Chieveley, Professor Gareth Jones, Professor Andrew Burrows, and the late Professor Peter Birks. It does not seek to describe the law in an encyclopaedic way as Goff and Jones did in each of the seven editions of their seminal work *The Law of Restitution*, and the way it continues in the *Law of Unjust Enrichment*, under the editorship of Professor Charles Mitchell, Professor Paul Mitchell, and Dr Stephen Watterson. Nor does it solely seek to identify a theoretical structure to assist in the organization of the subject, particularly if such a structure has not been expressly recognized in the cases. This is what Birks sought to do in his books *An Introduction to the Law of Restitution* and *Unjust Enrichment*. Rather, this book seeks both to state the law and to identify a coherent and consistent structure which assists in the understanding and explanation of the subject. As with the previous editions, this book does not seek to concentrate wholly on the theory and policy behind the law, but seeks to adopt a balance between identification, analysis, and justification of the rules themselves and how they operate in practice, through the distillation of principle from the authorities. A particular problem for any textbook writer is whether he or she should simply seek to follow the law, by stating it as it is, or seek to lead it on by suggesting the direction which the law should take. It is both an advantage and disadvantage of the approach adopted by Birks in particular that he was prepared to lead the judges on. If he was dissatisfied with the analysis adopted in the cases, he was prepared to develop his own analysis and make the cases fit, and, if they did not, they were rejected. But sometimes he took this too far and he created theories of restitution which are inconsistent with the cases. A further advantage of the approach adopted by Birks, seen in its purest form in his *Unjust Enrichment*, was that his analysis of the subject was elegant and pure. But the law of restitution is not a work of art, something to be looked at and admired. It is a body of law which must operate in the real world. Elegance and function do not always go together. Far better that the body of law works, even if it has some rough edges. Consequently, some of the conclusions reached in this book lack the elegance of those of Birks, but if they work and, equally importantly, are likely to be recognized and adopted by the judges, the loss of elegance is a small price to pay.

When the first edition of this book was published in 1999 I proposed a tripartite structure to the Law of Restitution, whereby restitutionary remedies are triggered by unjust enrichment, wrongdoing, and the vindication of property rights. Subsequent developments in the courts have, for the most part, vindicated this approach. Consequently, the basic structure of this book remains unchanged. But the rapid development of the law since the last edition was published in 2006, the sophisticated analysis of commentators, and the development of my own thinking, have meant that every single chapter has had to be substantially rewritten. I have also introduced a new chapter on legal basis as a bar to claims in unjust enrichment. The growing complexity of the subject and rapid expansion of the literature means that the focus on principles is more important to understand the Law of Restitution than ever before. Whilst others have decided to focus their attention on the Law of Unjust Enrichment, my view remains unchanged that, although there is a recognizable body of law called the Law of Unjust Enrichment, it forms only part, albeit a significant part, of a larger body of law called Restitution and much is lost if the connections with that larger body of law are cut.

This book could not have been written without the help and support of many friends and colleagues. My interest in the subject was first triggered at Oxford by Professor Andrew Burrows, Sir Jack Beatson and Professor John Cartwright. At Cambridge that interest was nurtured by Professor Gareth Jones. I have had the privilege of teaching The Law of Restitution at Cambridge on the LLM and as part of the undergraduate courses 'Aspects of the Law of Obligations' and 'Equity' with the best of colleagues, and I particularly wish to thank Dr Janet O'Sullivan, Professor Richard Nolan, Dr David Fox, Professor Steve Hedley, Professor Craig Rotherham, Dr Rebecca Williams, Amy Goymour, Dr Stephen Watterson, Dr Peter Turner, Dr Jonathan Morgan, Professor Sarah Worthington, and Paul Davies for their critical interest, support, and assistance. A substantial portion of this edition was written and rewritten whilst I was a Miegunyah Distinguished Visiting Fellow at the Law School, University of Melbourne. I am especially grateful to Professor Elise Bant, Dr Matthew Harding, Professor Michael Bryan, Julian Sempill, and Dr Katy Barnett for their support, advice, and encouragement whilst I was in Australia. I also want to express my thanks to all those students who have helped me formulate my ideas about the subject, often without knowing it. I am also grateful for the support and encouragement of the Fellows and students at Downing College. I particularly wish to express my thanks to the following students, friends, and colleagues who have always been willing to answer my questions and from whom I have learned a great deal: Professor Stephen Pitel, Dr Eoin O'Dell, Professor Hang Wu Tang, Rachel Leow, Dr Chris Hunt, Rajiv Shah, Dr Oke Odudu, Roger Kaye QC, and Clare Stanley QC. Finally, the support of my friends and family throughout the period I have been working on this edition is something for which I am most grateful. The Gamlingay Players provided a refuge of normality. My children, Elizabeth and Jonathan, have become ever more interested in the subject and have supported me throughout. My wife, Cally, has remained a constant source of encouragement and strength, particularly at a time of especial challenge for her. I dedicate this book to her. To you all, thank you.

I have attempted to state the law as of 5 January 2015 but it has been possible to incorporate references to some more recent developments.

Graham Virgo
The Old Schools, Cambridge
1 June 2015

CONTENTS

Table of Cases   xv
Table of Legislation   xl

PART I THE FUNDAMENTAL PRINCIPLES
OF THE LAW OF RESTITUTION

1. THE ESSENCE OF RESTITUTION   3

1. What is the Law of Restitution About?   3
2. What is the Nature of Restitutionary Remedies?   3
3. When Will Restitutionary Remedies Be Awarded?   7
4. What is the Justification for Recognizing an Independent
   Law of Restitution?   17
5. The Principal Types of Restitutionary Remedy   18

2. THEMES AND CONTROVERSIES   34

1. The Relevance of Fault   34
2. Risk-Taking   36
3. Respecting Autonomy   37
4. The Nature of the Relationship Between the Parties   38
5. The Principle Against Fictions   39
6. The Role of Public Policy   39
7. The Relationship Between Law and Equity   40
8. Rules Versus Discretion   41

PART II UNJUST ENRICHMENT

3. THE PRINCIPLE OF UNJUST ENRICHMENT   45

1. A Brief History of the Law of Unjust Enrichment   45
2. Justifying the Unjust Enrichment Principle   51
3. The Function of the Unjust Enrichment Principle   55
4. The Role of the Unjust Enrichment Principle in Practice   58

4. ENRICHMENT   62

1. The Relevance of Enrichment   62
2. Particular Types of Enrichment   73
3. Methods of Defeating Subjective Devaluation   78
4. Restitution Without Enrichment   90
5. Part Performance of a Contract   94
6. The Valuation of the Enrichment   95

5. AT THE EXPENSE OF THE CLAIMANT   104

   1. General Principles   104
   2. Direct and Indirect Enrichment   105
   3. Correspondence of Gain and Loss   116

6. PRINCIPLES UNDERLYING THE RECOGNITION
  OF THE GROUNDS OF RESTITUTION   120

   1. Claimant-Oriented Grounds of Restitution   121
   2. Defendant-Oriented Grounds of Restitution   122
   3. Policy-Oriented Grounds of Restitution   124
   4. Four Additional Considerations   125
   5. Absence of Basis   127

7. LAWFUL BASES   133

   1. Contract   133
   2. Discharge of a Debt   144
   3. Statutory Authority   146
   4. *Res Judicata*   147
   5. Natural Obligations   147
   6. Gifts   148
   7. Voluntary Transfers   149

8. IGNORANCE   152

   1. Is Ignorance a Ground of Restitution?   152
   2. Relying on Ignorance as a Ground of Restitution   153
   3. Election Between Principles   155
   4. The Role of Ignorance as a Ground of Restitution   156

9. MISTAKE   157

   1. General Principles   157
   2. Mistake as a Ground of Restitution   165
   3. Relief from Transactions Entered into Under Mistake   192

10. COMPULSION   203

   1. General Principles   203
   2. Duress   206
   3. Undue Pressure   229
   4. Legal Compulsion   233
   5. Threats to Secure the Performance of a Statutory Duty   253

11. EXPLOITATION   255

   1. General Principles   255
   2. Undue Influence   257
   3. Abuse of Fiduciary Relationships of Confidence   275
   4. Unconscionable Conduct   278
   5. The Parties Are Not *Par Delictum*   286

12. NECESSITY   289

   1. General Principles   289
   2. Necessitous Intervention by a Stranger   296
   3. Agency and Other Pre-Existing Legal Relationships   301
   4. Necessity in the Context of Maritime Adventures   305

13. FAILURE OF BASIS   308

   1. General Principles   308
   2. Establishing Total Failure of Basis   313
   3. The Operation of Total Failure of Basis   332
   4. Partial Failure of Basis   355
   5. Void Transactions   367

14. INCAPACITY   379

   1. General Principles   379
   2. The Categories of Incapacity   381

15. RESTITUTION FROM PUBLIC AUTHORITIES   389

   1. General Issues   389
   2. The Grounds of Restitution   394
   3. Particular Statutory Provisions   406
   4. Defences   408

PART III RESTITUTION FOR WRONGS

16. GENERAL PRINCIPLES   415

   1. The Essence of Restitution for Wrongs   415
   2. The Principles Underlying the Award of Restitutionary Remedies
      for Wrongs   420
   3. The Types of Gain-Based Remedy for Wrongdoing   424
   4. Causation and Remoteness   434
   5. The Relationship Between Gain-Based and Compensatory
      Remedies for Wrongdoing   438
   6. The Available Defences for Restitution for Wrongs   441
   7. Recommendations for Reform   443

17. RESTITUTION FOR TORTS   444

   1. General Principles   444
   2. Torts for Which Gain-Based Remedies are Available   453
   3. Is There a General Principle in Favour of the Award of Gain-Based
      Remedies for Torts?   466

18. RESTITUTION FOR BREACH OF CONTRACT   468

   1. General Principles   468
   2. Should Gain-Based Remedies Generally Be Available for
      Breach of Contract?   481

19. RESTITUTION FOR EQUITABLE WRONGDOING | 486

  1. General Principles | 486
  2. The Categories of Equitable Wrongdoing | 488

20. CRIMINAL OFFENCES | 526

  1. General Principles and Policies | 526
  2. Restitutionary Claims Brought by the Victim | 526
  3. Restitutionary Claims Brought by the State | 534
  4. Denial of Benefits Arising from the Commission of Crimes | 542

PART IV PROPRIETARY RESTITUTIONARY CLAIMS

21. ESTABLISHING PROPRIETARY RESTITUTIONARY CLAIMS | 557

  1. The Nature of Proprietary Restitutionary Claims | 557
  2. Identification of the Proprietary Interest | 569
  3. Following and Tracing | 607

22. RESTITUTIONARY CLAIMS AND REMEDIES TO VINDICATE PROPERTY RIGHTS | 631

  1. General Principles | 631
  2. Proprietary Claims and Remedies | 632
  3. Personal Claims and Remedies | 641

23. THE DEFENCE OF *BONA FIDE* PURCHASE | 656

  1. The Function of the Defence | 656
  2. Ambit of the Defence | 657
  3. Conditions for Establishing the Defence | 658
  4. Operation of the Defence | 659

PART V GENERAL DEFENCES TO RESTITUTIONARY CLAIMS

24. FUNDAMENTAL PRINCIPLES | 663

  1. The Function and Ambit of General Defences | 663

25. DEFENCES ARISING FROM CHANGES IN THE DEFENDANT'S CIRCUMSTANCES | 666

  1. Estoppel by Representation | 666
  2. Transfer of a Benefit by an Agent to His or Her Principal | 674
  3. Change of Position | 678

26. PASSING ON AND MITIGATION OF LOSS | 702

  1. Passing On | 702
  2. Mitigation of Loss | 705

27. ILLEGALITY — 708

1. General Principles — 708
2. The Policies Underpinning the Illegality Defence — 713
3. Defining Turpitude — 716
4. Mechanisms for Excluding the Illegality Defence — 717
5. Serious Criminal Culpability — 723
6. The Preferred Approach — 724

28. INCAPACITY — 726

1. Questions of Policy — 726
2. Minority — 727
3. Mental Incapacity — 730
4. Institutional Incapacity — 731
5. Should a Defence of Incapacity Be Recognized? — 733

29. LIMITATION PERIODS AND LACHES — 734

1. Limitation Periods — 734
2. Laches — 741
3. Reform of the Law on Limitation Periods — 743

Bibliography — 745
Index — 761

TABLE OF CASES

21st Century Logistic Solutions Ltd v
Madysen Ltd [2004] EWHC 231
(QB), [2004] 2 Lloyd's Rep 92 722
R v A-G of England and Wales [2003]
UKPC 22 (PC) 207–8, 216, 260,
265, 267
A v B plc [2003] QB 195 . . . . 464, 516
A v Bottrill [2002] UKPC 44, [2003] 1
AC 449 432
AB v South West Water Services Ltd [1993]
QB 507 437
ACES System Development Pte Ltd v Yenty
Lily [2013] SGCA 53. 449
AIB Group (UK) plc v Redler [2014] UKSC
58, [2014] 3 WLR 1367. 419
Abbott, Re [1900] 2 Ch 326 593
Abbott v Abbott [2007] UKPC 53 589
Abbotts v Barry (1820) 2 Brad and B 369,
129 ER 1009 463
Aberdeen Railway Company v Blaikie Bros
(1854) 1 Macq 461 493
Abou-Rahmah v Abacha [2006] EWCA Civ
1492, [2007] 1 All ER (Comm)
827. . . . . 180, 523,
650, 692
Adam Opel GmbH v Mitras Automotive
(UK) Ltd [2007] EWHC 3481
(QB) 218, 219, 221
Adras Building Material Ltd v Harlow and
Jones GmbH (1988) 42 (1) PD (Israeli
Supreme Court) 483, 484
Agip (Africa) Ltd v Jackson [1991]
Ch 265. . . . . .613, 616, 617, 642, 646,
647, 648, 675, 677
Agip (Africa) Ltd v Jackson [1991] Ch 547
(CA) 613, 615, 616, 617, 647
Ahmad; Fields [2014] UKSC 36, [2015]
AC 299 . . . . 537, 539, 540
Ahmed Angullia bin Hadjee Mohamed
Sallah Angullia v Estate and Trust
Agencies (1927) Ltd [1938]
AC 624 481
Aiken v Short (1856) 1 H and N 210, 156 ER
1180. . . . . 146, 165, 173, 174, 191
Air Canada v British Columbia (1989) 59
DLR (4d) 161 (Supreme Court
of Canada). 162, 398, 703
Air Jamaica v Charlton [1999] 1 WLR
1399. . . . . 583, 593, 595
Alberta v Elder Advocates of Alberta Society
2011 SCA 23, [2011] 2 SCR 261 (Supreme
Court of Canada) 392, 489

Alec Lobb (Garages) Ltd v Total Oil Great
Britain Ltd [1983] 1 WLR 87 281
Alec Lobb (Garages) Ltd v Total Oil Great
Britain Ltd [1985] 1 WLR 173 (CA). 283
Alev, The [1989] 1 Lloyd's Rep
138. 207, 221, 225, 226
Alexander v Rayson [1946] 1 KB 169. . .353, 720
Alfred McAlpine Construction Ltd v
Panatown [2001] 1 AC 518 476
Allcard v Skinner (1887) 36 Ch
D 145. . . . . .256, 258, 259, 261, 263, 265,
267, 268, 282, 580, 735, 741, 742
Alliance Bank JSC v Aquanta Corp [2011]
EWHC 3281 (Comm). 636
Allpress [2009] EWCA Crim 8, [2009] 2 Cr
App R (S) 399 . . . . .536, 540
Aluminium Industrie Vassen RV v Romalpa
Aluminium Ltd [1976] 1 WLR 676 572
Amalgamated Investment and Property Co
Ltd v Texas Commerce International Bank
Ltd [1982] QB 84 .90
Amec Developments v Jury's Hotel
Management [2001] EGLR 81 471
American Cyanamid Co v Ethicon Ltd
(No 1) [1975] AC 396. 441
Ames' Settlement, Re [1946]
Ch 217. . . . . .311, 593
Amicable Society for a Perpetual Life
Assurance Office, The v Bolland (183)
4 Bligh (NS) 194, 5 ER 70. 544
Amministrazione delle Finanze dello Stato v
SpA San Giorgio [1983] ECR 3595
(European Court of Justice) 119, 391, 400,
409, 411, 703, 705
Amontilla Ltd v Telefusion plc (1987) 9
Constr LR 139. 738
Ancona v Rogers (1876) 1 Ex D 285 540
Anderson v McPherson (No 2) [2012]
WASC 19 (Supreme Court of Western
Australia). 308
Andrew v St Olave's Board of Works [1898]
1 QB 775. 243
Anfield (UK) Ltd v Bank of Scotland [2010]
EWHC 2374 (Ch), [2011] 1 WLR
2414. . . . . .636, 641
Anglia Television Ltd v Reed [1972] 1 QB
60. 468
Annulment Funding Co Ltd v Cowey [2010]
EWCA Civ 711 258
Anson v Anson [1953] 1 QB 636 241
Appleby v Myers (1867) LR 2
CP 651. 90, 96, 342, 362

Arab Monetary Fund v Hashim (No 9)
[1993] 1 Lloyd's Rep 543 525

Archbolds (Freightage) Ltd v Spanglett
Ltd [1961] QB 374 717

Argyll (Duchess) v Argyll (Duke) [1967]
1 Ch 302 712

Armstrong v Jackson [1917] 2 KB 822. 495

Armstrong DLW GmbH v Winnington
Networks Ltd [2012] EWHC 10 (Ch),
[2013] Ch 156. . . . . . .105, 529, 599, 600, 641,
643, 650, 658, 691, 692, 696

Aroso v Couuts and Co [2001] 1 WTLR
797. 588

Arris and Arris v Stukley (1677) 2
Mod 260; 86 ER 1060 . . . . .114, 154

Arthur v Attorney-General of the Turks and
Caicos Islands [2012] UKPC 30. . . 646, 648, 650

Ashburn Anstalt v Arnold [1989] Ch 1 603

Ashbury Railway Carriage and Iron Co Ltd v
Riche (1875) LR 7 HL 653 731

Asher v Wallis (1707) 11 Mod 146; 88
ER 956. 154

Ashwell, R v (1885) 16 QBD 190 . . . . . .574, 575

Askey v Golden Wine Co Ltd [1948] 2 All
ER 35. 722

Assicurazioni Generali v Arab Insurance
Group [2002] EWCA Civ 1642, [2003] 1
All ER (Comm) 140 198

Associated Japanese Bank (International)
Ltd v Credit du Nord SA [1989] 1
WLR 255. 193

Aster Healthcare Ltd v Shefi [2014] EWCA
Civ 1350 . . . . .294, 299

Astley v Reynolds (1731) 2 Stra 915, 93 ER
939. . . . . 205, 208, 212, 226, 720

Atlantic Baron, The [1979] QB
705. . . . . 204, 212, 213, 214, 220, 228

Atlas Express Ltd v Kafco (Importers
and Distributors Ltd) [1989]
QB 833 . . . . .220, 225

Attorney-General v Blake [1998] Ch 439
(CA) 427, 433, 436, 492, 501, 502, 542

Attorney-General v Blake [2001] 1 AC 268 . . . 19,
312, 332, 417, 421, 424, 425, 427, 428, 429,
433, 440, 441, 451, 453, 465, 468, 469, 473,
474, 475, 476, 477, 478, 480, 481, 482, 483,
484, 485, 517, 542, 543

Attorney-General v Goddard (1929) 98 LJKB
743. 500

Attorney-General v Guardian Newspapers Ltd
(No 2) [1990] 1 AC 109 . . . . 421, 435,
492, 501, 514, 515, 516, 519, 526

Attorney-General v Nissan [1970] AC 179 . . .48

Attorney-General for Hong Kong v Humphreys
Estate (Queen's Garden Ltd) [1987]
AC 114 . . . . .350, 520

Attorney-General for Hong Kong v Reid
[1994] 1 AC 324 (PC). 436, 511, 512,
513, 514, 528, 531

Attorney-General v Wilts United Dairies
Ltd (1921) 37 TLR 884 (CA) 389

Attorney-General v Wilts United Dairies
Ltd (1922) 127 LT 822 (HL). 389

Attorney-General's Reference (No 1 of 1983)
[1985] QB 182. 576

Attwood v Small (1836) 6 Cl and F 232, 7
ER 684. 198

Auckland Harbour Board v R [1924] AC
318 (PC) 387, 390, 579

Australasian Steam Navigation Co v Morse
(1872) LR 4 PC 222 . . . . .292, 293

Australia and New Zealand Banking Group
Ltd v Westpac Banking Corp (1988) 164
CLR 662 (High Court of Australia) . . . 676, 678

Australian Competition and Consumer
Commission v CG Berbatis [2003] HCA
18, (2003) 214 CLR 51 (High Court of
Australia). 280, 286

Australian Competition and Consumer
Commission v Samton Holdings Pty Ltd
[2002] 117 FCR 301 (Federal Court of
Australia). 286

Australian Elizabeth Theatre Trust, Re (1991)
102 ALR 681 (Federal Court of Australia) . . .594

Australian Financial Services and Leasing
Pty Ltd v Hills Industries Ltd [2014]
HCA 14 (High Court of
Australia). 41, 54, 55, 679, 683, 687

Autologic Holdings plc v IRC [2005] UKHL
54, [2006] 1 AC 118 405

Avon County Council v Howlett [1983]
1 WLR 605 . . . . 162, 668, 669, 670, 671,
672, 673, 686

Avon Finance Co Ltd v Bridger [1985]
2 All ER 281 196

Awwad v Geraghty and Co [2001]
QB 570 . . . . .332, 721

Ayers v South Australian Banking Corp
(1871) LR 3 PC 548 578

Ayerst v Jenkins (1873) LR 16 Eq 275 712

B and S Contracts and Design Ltd v
Victor Green Publications Ltd [1984]
ICR 419. . . . . .225, 227

BA Peters Ltd, Re [2008] EWCA Civ
1604, [2010] 1 BCLC 142 623

BCCI v Aboody See Bank of Credit and
Commerce International (BCCI) SA v Aboody

BCCI (overseas) v Jan See Bank of Credit and
Commerce International (Overseas) Ltd v Jan

BCL Old Co Ltd v Aventis SA [2005]
CAT 2 466

BMP Global Distribution Inc v Bank of
Nova Scotia [2009] SCC 15 (Supreme
Court of Canada) 127, 616

BP Exploration Co (Libya) Ltd v Hunt (No 2)
[1979] 1 WLR 783. . . . . .48, 62, 65, 73, 75, 76,
77, 79, 96, 97, 99, 357, 358, 359, 360, 361,
362, 363, 364, 537, 678

BP Exploration Co (Libya) Ltd v Hunt (No 2)
[1981] 1 WLR 232 (CA)...... 357, 363, 364
BP Exploration Co (Libya) Ltd v Hunt (No 2)
[1983] 2 AC 352 (HL)........ 364, 365, 736
BP Oil International Ltd v Target Shipping
Ltd [2012] EWHC 1590 (Comm), [2012]
2 Lloyd's Rep 245 ....177, 178
BRB (Residuary) Ltd v Connex South Eastern
Ltd [2008] EWHC 1172 (QB), [2008] 1
WLR 2867.........................248
Backhouse v Backhouse [1978] 1
WLR 243........................280, 285
Bainbrigge v Browne (1880) 18 Ch D 188 . . .264
Baines and Ernst Ltd v Commissioners of
Customs and Excise [2004] UKVAT
V18769 .... 408, 703, 717
Baker, Re (1881) 20 Ch D 230 734
Baker v Courage and Co [1910] 1
KB 56............................185, 736
Baker (GL) Ltd v Medway Building and
Supplies Ltd [1958] 1 WLR 1216 . . . . 644, 741
Baldwyn v Smith [1900] 1 Ch 588 381
Baltic Shipping Co v Dillon (1992) 176 CLR
344 (High Court of
Australia)................ 40, 312, 313, 319
Bank of America v Arnell [1999] Lloyd's
Rep 399........................599, 617
Bank of Credit and Commerce International
(BCCI) SA v Aboody [1990] 1 QB 923 260,
261, 262, 267, 268, 275, 276, 277, 502,
503, 504
Bank of Credit and Commerce International
(Overseas) Ltd v Akindele [2001]
Ch 437............. 648, 649, 650, 653, 698
Bank of Credit and Commerce International
(Overseas) Ltd v Jan (unreported) 11
November 1999.......................741
Bank of New South Wales v Murphett [1983]
VR 489 (Supreme Court of Victoria).....189
Bank of Scotland v Bennett [1997]
1 FLR 801 267
Bank Melli Iran v Samadi-Rad [1995]
2 FLR 367 271
Bankers Trust Co v Shapira [1980] 1 WLR
1274..............................599
Banner Homes Group plc v Luff
Developments Ltd [2000] Ch 372........597
Banque Belge pour l'Etranger v Hambrouck
[1912] 1 KB 321 ....153, 603, 613, 615,
616, 657
Banque Financière la Cité v Parc (Battersea)
Ltd [1999] 1 AC 221.......7, 8, 9, 15, 16, 18,
20, 21, 24, 41, 51, 54, 60, 104, 106, 107,
116, 120, 171, 172, 179, 234, 563, 636,
637, 638, 639, 655
Barber v NWS Bank plc [1996] 1
WLR 641.........................319, 333
Barclay and Co Ltd v Malcolm and Co
(1925) 133 LT 512....................166

Barclays Bank plc v Caplan [1998] 1 FLR
532...............................274
Barclays Bank plc v Kalamohan [2010]
EWHC 1383 (Ch).....................691
Barclays Bank plc v O'Brien [1994] 1
AC 180 ....199, 200, 210, 259, 264, 266,
270, 658
Barclays Bank Ltd v Quistclose Investments
Ltd [1970] AC 567 ....593, 594, 595
Barclays Bank Ltd v WJ Simms, Son and
Cooke (Southern) Ltd [1980]
QB 677 ..... 48, 126, 135, 145, 150, 166, 170,
171, 174, 175, 189, 190, 192, 224, 235,
252, 329, 574, 678
Barlow Clowes International Ltd v
Eurotrust International Ltd [2005]
UKPC 37, [2006] 1 WLR 1476......522, 523
Barlow Clowes International Ltd v Vaughan
[1992] 4 All ER 22 622
Barnes, Re (1861) 4 LTNS 60.............236
Barnes v Eastenders Cash and Carry plc
[2014] UKSC 26, [2015] AC 1 ...17, 120, 139,
140, 308, 310, 311, 323, 328, 329, 537
Barons Finance Ltd v Kensington Mortgage
Co Ltd [2011] EWCA Civ 1592.........685
Barrett v Barrett [2008] EWHC 1061
(Ch), [2008] 2 P & CR 17..........589, 718
Barros Mattos Junior v MacDaniels Ltd
[2004] EWHC 1188 (Ch), [2005] 1
WLR 247....... 642, 684, 685, 693, 694, 711
Barton v Armstrong [1976]
AC 104 ....175, 204, 206, 207,
209–10, 211, 212, 219, 222
Bathurst CC v PWC Properties Pty Ltd (1998)
195 CLR 566 (High Court of Australia)...605
Baylis v Bishop of London [1913] 1
Ch 127........ 9, 54, 166, 664, 675, 679, 681
Beaman v ARTS Ltd [1948] 2 All
ER 89.........................442, 739
Beaney, Re [1978] 1 WLR 770 ....381, 382
Beckton Dickinson UK Ltd v Zwebner
[1989] QB 208.......................241
Bell v Lever Bros Ltd [1932]
AC 161 .... 193, 194, 200
Bell Group Ltd v Westpac Banking
Corporation (No. 9) [2008] WASC 239
(Supreme Court of Western Australia) ...286
Belmont Finance Corp Ltd v Williams
Furniture Ltd (No 2) [1980] 1 All ER 393 ...648
Belshaw v Bush (1851) 11 CB 190, 138
ER 444...........................235
Belvoir Finance v Stapleton [1971] QB 210 . . . 579
Benedetti v Sawiris [2010] EWCA
Civ 1427 ....19, 79
Benedetti v Sawiris [2013] UKSC 50, [2014]
AC 938 ....7, 9, 46, 65, 66, 67, 69, 70, 71, 72,
74, 78, 85, 91, 96, 97, 98, 99, 101, 117, 123,
134, 135, 332, 344, 345, 454, 538, 663,
664, 680

Benourad v Compass Group plc [2010]
    EWHC 1882 (QB)....................344
Beresford v Royal Insurance Co Ltd [1937]
    2 KB 197.....................544, 548
Beresford v Royal Insurance Co Ltd [1938]
    AC 586 .... 543, 544, 545, 550, 713
Berezovsky v Edmiston [2010] EWHC
    1883 (Comm), [2010] CLC 126 135
Berg v Sadler and Moore [1937] 2
    KB 158.....................330, 718, 720
Berghoff Trading Ltd v Swinbrook
    Developments Ltd [2008] EWHC
    1785 (Comm) 239
Berkeley Applegate (Investment
    Consultants) Ltd, Re [1989] Ch 32.....63, 80
Bernard v Reese (1794) 1 Espinasse 91, 170
    ER 290............................711
Beswick v Beswick [1968] AC 58 441
Bhullar v Bhullar [2003] EWCA Civ 424,
    [2003] 2 BCLC 241 497
Bigos v Bousted [1951] 1 All ER
    92.................. 287, 353, 355, 720
Bilbie v Lumley (1802) 2 East 469; 102
    ER 448............................161
Binions v Evans [1972] Ch 359 603
Binstead v Buck (1777) 2 Black W 1117,
    96 ER 660 ....290, 300
Birkley v Presgrave (1801) 1 East 220, 102
    ER 86.............................307
Birse Construction Ltd v Haiste Ltd [1996]
    1 WLR 675 248
Bishopsgate Investment Management Ltd
    v Homan [1995] Ch 211...... 624, 625, 628
Bishopsgate Investment Management Ltd
    v Maxwell (No 2) [1994] 1 All ER 261....487
Bishopsgate Motor Finance Corp v
    Transport Brakes Ltd [1949] 1 KB 322 ...657
Black v F S Freedman and Co (1910) 12
    CLR 105 (High Court of Australia) 600
Blomley v Ryan (1956) 99 CLR 362 (High
    Court of Australia) 280, 379
Bloomsbury International Ltd v Sea Fish
    Industry Authority [2009] EWHC 1721
    (QB), [2010] 1 CMLR 12 ...... 392, 410, 690
Bloxsome v Williams (1824) 3 B and C
    232, 107 ER 720 330
Blue Haven Enterprises Ltd v Tully [2006]
    UKPC 17 (PC) 520
Boake Allen Ltd v IRC [2006] EWCA Civ 25,
    [2006] STC 606.....................10
Boardman v Phipps [1967] 2 AC 46 ... 426, 486,
              493, 497, 498, 499, 507, 509, 511, 519,
                                      534, 606
Bodega Co Ltd, The, Re [1904]
    1 Ch 276 ....165, 188
Bofinger v Kingsway Group Ltd [2009]
    HCA 44 (High Court of Australia)....21, 637
Boissevain v Weil [1950] AC 327......722, 732
Bolkiah v KPMG [1999] 2 AC 222........515

Bolton v Mahadeva [1972] 1 WLR
    1009.................. 338, 341, 342, 343
Bonner v Tottenham and Edmonton
    Permanent Investment Building Society
    [1899] 1 QB 161 242
Boomer v Muir 24 P 2d 570 (1933) (District
    Court of Appeal of California) 101, 335
Borden (UK) Ltd v Scottish Timber Products
    Ltd [1981] Ch 25...................623
Borelli v Ting [2010] UKPC 21
    (PC)........... 208, 217, 218, 220, 232, 233
Boscawen v Bajwa [1996] 1 WLR
    328........ 557, 558, 611, 613, 617, 621, 625,
          626, 627, 633, 635, 636, 637, 638, 639,
                          645, 655, 656, 696, 697
Bossevain v Weil [1950] AC 327 48
Boston Deep Sea Fishing and Ice Co v
    Ansell (1888) 39 Ch D 339............340
Boulter v Peplow (1850) 9 CB 493, 137
    ER 984............................247
Boulton v Jones (1857) 2 H and N 564; 157
    ER 232.........................71, 158
Boustany v Piggott (1993) 69 P & CR 298
    (PC)..........................280, 281
Bowmakers Ltd v Barnet Instruments
    Ltd [1945] 1 KB 65...............618, 723
Box v Barclays Bank [1998] Lloyd's LR
    Bank 185..........................593
Boyd and Forrest v Glasgow and South
    Western Railway Co [1915] SC (HL) 20 ...27
Boyter v Dodsworth (1796) 6 TR 682; 101
    ER 770.................. 113, 114, 436
Bracewell v Appleby [1975] Ch 408........471
Bradshaw v Beard (1862) 12 CB (NS)
    344, 142 ER 1175 297
Brasserie du Pêchuer SA v Federal Republic
    of Germany (Joined Cases C-46/93
    and C-48/93) [1996] QB 404 (ECJ) 390
Bray v Ford [1896] AC 44 ....493, 500
Brennan v Bolt Burdon [2004] EWCA Civ 1017,
    [2005] QB 303 ....143, 164, 177, 179,
                  184, 192, 193, 194, 195, 197
Brewer Street Investments Ltd v Barclays
    Woollen Co Ltd [1954] 1 QB
    428.................. 91–2, 345, 348, 349
Bridgeman v Green (1755) 2 Ves Sen 627,
    28 ER 399 526
Bridgeman v Green (1757) Wilm 58, 97
    ER 22.............................526
Bridgewater v Griffiths [2000] 1
    WLR 524............................86
Briess v Woolley [1954] AC 333.......197, 198
Briggs v Gleeds [2014] EWHC 1178 (Ch),
    [2014] 3 WLR 1469...................667
Brisbane v Dacres (1813) 5 Taunt 143,
    128 ER 641 .... 144, 161, 177
Bristol and West Building Society v
    Mothew [1998] Ch 1......487, 488, 489, 491,
                  492, 493, 496, 602, 613, 629

Bristow v Eastman (1794) 1 Esp 172, 170 ER
317 . . . . .727, 729
British American Continental Bank v
British Bank for Foreign Trade [1926]
1 KB 328 134
British Steel Corp v Cleveland Bridge and
Engineering Co Ltd [1984] 1 All
ER 504 . . . . 48, 102, 345, 346
British Steel Corp v Commissioners of Customs
and Excise [1997] 2 All ER 366 405
Brittain v Rossiter (1879) 11
QBD 123 . . . . .135, 144
Brocklebank Ltd v R [1925] 1 KB 52 396
Brocklehurst, Re [1978] Ch 14 . . . . .265, 269
Brook's Wharf and Bull Wharf Ltd v
Goodman Brothers [1937] 1
KB 534 . . . . 47, 62, 236, 242
Broome v Cassell and Co Ltd [1972]
AC 1027 432
Brotherton v Aseguradora Cobeguros (No 2)
[2003] EWCA Civ 705, [2003] 3 All ER
(Comm) 298 23
Brown v Bennett [1999] 1 BCLC
649 . . . . .646, 647
Brown v IRC [1965] AC 244 496
Brown & Davies Ltd v Galbraith [1972] 1
WLR 997 142
Brown Jenkinson and Co Ltd v Percy
Dalton (London) Ltd [1957] 2 QB 621 . . .717
Buller v Harrison (1777) 2 Cowp 565, 98
ER 1243 . . . . .675, 676
Burgess v Rawnsley [1975] Ch 429 310
Bush v Canfield (1818) 2 Conn 485 (Supreme
Court of Errors, Connecticut) 335
Butler v Rice [1910] 2 Ch 277 639
Butterworth v Kingsway Motors Ltd [1954]
1 WLR 1286 320
Byfield, Re [1982] 1 All ER 249 105
CF Partners (UK) LLP v Barclays
Bank plc and another [2014] EWHC
3049 (Ch) 517
CIBC Mortgages plc v Pitt [1994] 1
AC 200 . . . . 261, 262, 263, 268, 276, 277,
503, 504
CMS Dolphin Ltd v Simonet [2001] EWHC
415 (Ch), [2001] 2 BCLC
704 . . . . 434, 476, 492, 497, 498, 510
CPS v Jennings [2008] UKHL 29, [2008] 1 AC
1046 535
CPS Nottinghamshire v Rose [2008] EWCA
Crim 239 536
CTN Cash and Carry Ltd v Gallaher Ltd
[1994] 4 All ER 714 . . . . .38, 57, 125, 130,
131, 203, 215, 216, 217, 220, 232, 279
Cadogan Petroleum Holdings Ltd v Global
Process Systems [2013] EWHC 214
(Comm) 337
Cadogan Petroleum plc v Tolley [2011]
EWHC 2286 (Ch) 512

Cain v Clarica Life Insurance Co (2005) 263
DLR (4th) 368 (Court of Appeal
of Alberta) 286
Cairns v Modi [2012] EWCA Civ 1382,
[2013] 1 WLR 1015 467
Calland v Loyd (184) 6 M and W 26, 151
ER 307 . . . . .153, 573
Callaway, Re [1956] Ch 559 551
Campbell v Hall (1774) 1 Cowp 204, 98
ER 1245 397
Campbell v Mirror Group Newspapers Ltd
[2004] UKHL 22, [2004] 2 AC 457 . . .464, 515
Campden Hill Ltd v Chakrani [2005]
EWHC 911 (Ch) 599, 618, 624, 684
Canadian Aero Services Ltd v
O'Malley (1973) 40 DLR (4th) 371
(Supreme Court of Canada) 498
Cantor Index Ltd v Shortall [2002] All ER
(D) 161 223
Capital Finance Co Ltd v Stokes [1969]
1 Ch 261 640
Car and Universal Finance Co Ltd v
Caldwell [1965] 1 QB 525 . . . . .23, 28, 580
Carillion Construction Ltd v Felix (UK)
Ltd [2001] BLR 1 . . . . .218, 223
Carl-Zeiss Stiftung v Herbert Smith (No 2)
[1969] 2 Ch 276 659
Carr-Saunders v Dick McNeil Associates Ltd
[1986] 2 All ER 888 461
Cattley v Pollard [2006] EWHC 3130 (Ch),
[2007] Ch 353 742
Cave v Cave (1880) 15 Ch D 639 . . . . . .611, 657
Cavenagh Investment Pte Ltd v Rajiv
[2013] SGHC 45, [2013] 2 SLR 543
(High Court of Singapore) 693
Cawley v Lillis [2011] IEHC 515 (Irish
High Court) 549
Central London Property Trust v High
Trees House [1947] KB 130 520
Chagos Islanders v Attorney-General [2003]
EWHC 2222 283
Challinor v Bellis [2015] EWCA
Civ 59 . . . . 73, 578, 593, 691
Chalmers v Pardoe [1963] 1 WLR 677 521
Chambers v Miller (1862) 13 CBNS 125,
143 ER 50 574
Chan Yuen Lan v See Fong Mun [2014]
SGCA 36 (Singapore Court of Appeal) . . .583
Chandler v Webster [1904] 1 KB 493 356
Chandler Bros Ltd v Harding [1936] 3 All
ER 179 333
Chaplin v Leslie Frewin (Publishers) Ltd
[1966] Ch 71 . . . . .379, 386, 579
Charles Terence Estates Ltd v Cornwall
County Council [2011] EWHC
2542 (QB) 689
Chase Manhattan Bank NA v Israel-British
Bank (London) Ltd [1981] Ch 105 . . . 16, 104,
116, 179, 563, 575, 576, 598, 599, 601, 602

Chater v Mortgage Agency Services
    Number Two Ltd [2003] EWCA Civ
    490, [2004] 1 P & CR 4 . . . . 260, 266
Cheese v Thomas [1994] 1 WLR 129 . . . . 23, 26,
                        28, 257, 267, 272, 273, 685
Chellew v Royal Commission on the Sugar
    Supply [1921] 1 KB 627 307
Cheltenham and Gloucester plc v Appleyard
    [2004] EWCA Civ 291 . . . . .636, 637–8,
                             639, 640, 655
Chesworth v Farrar [1967] 1 QB 407 442,
                        444, 446, 460, 739
Chichester Diocesan Fund and Board of
    Finance Inc v Simpson [1944] AC 341 617
Chief Constable of Kent v V [1983] 1
    QB 3 629
Chief Constable of Leicestershire v M [1989]
    1 WLR 20 . . . . 421, 436, 529, 530
R v Chief National Insurance Commissioner,
    ex p Connor [1981] 1 QB 758 . . . . . . 546, 548
Child v Morley (1800) 8 TR 610, 101 ER
    1574. 247
Chillingworth v Chambers [1898] 1
    Ch 685. 247
Chillingworth v Esche [1924] 1
    Ch 97. . . . . 311, 316, 338, 347, 348, 377
China Pacific SA v Food Corp of India (The
    Winson) [1982] AC 939 . . . . . . .293, 294, 301,
                             303, 304, 305
Choko Star, The [1990] 1 Lloyd's
    Rep 516. 303
Chrastny (No 2) [1991] 1 WLR 1385. 539
Church, R v [1966] 1 QB 59. 546
R v Church (1970) 55 Cr App R 65 528
Cia de Seguros Imerio v Health (REBX) Ltd
    [2001] 1 WLR 112. 740
Citibank NA v Brown Shipley and Co Ltd
    [1991] 2 All ER 690 . . . . 169, 574
Citigroup v National [2012] NSWCA 381,
    82 NSWLR 391 (New South Wales Court
    of Appeal) 683
City Bank of Sydney v McLaughlin (1909)
    9 CLR 615 (High Court of Australia). 235
City Electrical Supply Nominees Ltd v Thorn
    EMI Retail Ltd (1991) 63 P & CR 143 236
City Index Ltd v Gawler [2007] EWCA Civ
    1382, [2008] Ch 313 . . 248, 250, 251, 651, 652
City of New Orleans v Fireman's Charitable
    Association (1891) 9 Sol 486 (Supreme
    Court of Louisiana). 474
Clark v Woods, Smith and Cooper (1848) 2
    Ex 395, 154 ER 545. 211
Clarke v Dickson (1858) EB and E 148; 120
    ER 463. 25
Clarke v Guardians of the Cuckfield Union
    (1852) 21 LJ (QB) 349 80
Clarke v Shee and Johnson (1774) 1 Cowp
    197, 98 ER 1041 . . . . . . .49, 53, 153, 560, 573,
                             642, 657, 659, 660

Clarke Boyce v Mouat [1994] 1 AC 428. 496
Clay v Yates (1856) 1 H and N 73, 156
    ER 1123. 717
Clayton's Case, Re (1817) 1 Mer 572, 35
    ER 781. 621–3
Cleadon Trust Ltd, Re [1939] Ch 286 . . . .85, 88
Cleaver v Mutual Reserve Fund Life
    Association [1892] 1 QB 147 . . .543, 545, 546,
                             547, 548, 550, 551
Cleveland Bridge UK Ltd v Multiplex
    Construction (UK) Ltd [2010] EWCA
    Civ 139 340
Clough v London and North Western Rly Co
    (1871) LR 7 Exch 26. . . . . 23, 28, 576
Clugas v Penaluna (1791) 4 Term Reports
    466, 100 ER 1122 .711
Coatsworth v Johnson (1886)
    54 LT 520 712
Cobbold v Bakewell Management Ltd [2003]
    EWHC 2289 (Ch). 176, 177, 604
Coco v AN Clark (Engineers) Ltd [1969]
    FSR 415. 515
Collier v Collier [2002] EWCA Civ 1095,
    [2002] BPIR 1057 . . . . 354, 589, 591, 720
Collings v Lee [2001] 2 All ER 332. 195
Collins v Blantern (1767) 2 Wils 347, 95
    ER 859. . . . . 545, 715
Colonial Bank v Exchange Bank of Yarmouth,
    Nova Scotia (1885) 11
    App Cas 84 . . . . 105, 111, 166, 173
Commercial Bank of Australia v Amadio
    (1983) 151 CLR 447 (High Court of
    Australia). 278, 280, 285
Commercial Union Assurance Co Ltd
    v Hayden [1977] QB 804 247
Commerzbank AG v Gareth Price-Jones
    [2003] EWCA Civ 1663, [2005] 1 Lloyd's
    Rep 298. . . . . 681, 688, 689, 694, 699
Commerzbank AG v IMB Morgan plc [2004]
    EWHC 2771 (Ch), [2005] 1 Lloyd's
    Rep 298. . . . . 599, 622
Commissioner for Stamp Duties (Queensland)
    v Livingston [1965] AC 694 (PC). . . . 618, 644
Commissioner of State Revenue v Royal
    Insurance Australia Ltd (High Court
    of Australia) (1994) 126 ALR 1 703
Commonwealth of Australia v Burns
    (Supreme Court of Victoria, Australia)
    [1971] VR 825. . . . . 387, 388
Constable of the Greater Manchester Police
    v Wigan Athletic AFC Ltd [2008] EWCA
    Civ 1449, [2009] 1 WLR 1580 . . . 77, 86, 88, 122
Continental Caoutchouc and Gutta Percha
    Co v Kleinwort Sons (1904) 90 LT 474,
    (1904) 20 TLR 403 . . . . 676, 677
Cook v Deeks [1916] 1 AC 554
    (PC). 498, 510
Cook v Lister (1863) 13 CB (NS) 543, 143
    ER 215. 236

Cooper v Phibbs (1867) LR 2 HL 149 162
Cooper v Twynam (1823) Turn and R 424,
   37 ER 1164 247
Co-operative Insurance Society Ltd v
   Argyll Stores (Holdings) Ltd [1998]
   AC 1 .... 441, 483, 484
Corpe v Overton (1833) 10 Bing 252, 131
   ER 901.............................385
Costello v Chief Constable of Derbyshire
   Constabulary [2001] EWCA Civ 387,
   [2001] 1 WLR 1437..............600, 641
Cotnam v Wisdom (1907) 104 SW 164
   (Supreme Court of Arkansas)...........93
Cotronic (UK) Ltd v Dezonie [1991]
   BCLC 721 369
Coulthard v Disco Mix Club Ltd [2000] 1
   WLR 707...........................740
Countrywide Communications Ltd v ICL
   Pathway Ltd [2000] CLC 324 349
County of Carleton v City of Ottawa (1965)
   52 DLR (2d) 220 (Supreme Court of
   Canada)............................80
Courage Ltd v Crehan (Case C-453/99)
   [2002] QB 507 (ECJ)................720
Couturier v Hastie (1856) 5 HL Cas 673 194
Coventry v Lawrence [2014] UKSC 13,
   [2014] AC 822......................462
Cowan de Groot Property Ltd v Eagle
   Trust plc [1992] 4 All ER 700..........648
Cowern v Nield [1912] 2 KB 419 ......727, 728
Cox v Prentice (1815) 3 M and S 344, 105
   ER 641.............................676
Crabb v Arun District Council [1976]
   Ch 179..........................520, 521
Craig, Re [1971] Ch 95.................265
Crantrave Ltd v Lloyds Bank plc [2000]
   QB 917 235
Craven-Ellis v Canons Ltd [1936] 2 KB
   403..................... 68, 80, 81, 370
Crédit Lyonnais Bank Nederland NV v
   Burch [1997] 1 All ER 144 .....265, 266, 268,
                    269, 279, 281, 283
Credit Suisse (Monaco) SA v Attar [2004]
   EWHC 374 (Comm).................684
Crescendo Management Pty Ltd v Westpac
   Banking Corp (1988) 19 NSWLR 40
   (New South Wales Court of
   Appeal) 208, 209, 210, 222,
                    227, 232
Cressman v Coys of Kensington (Sales) Ltd
   [2004] EWCA Civ 47, [2004] 1 WLR
   2775.............................130
Cresswell v Potter [1978] 1 WLR 255n 283
Criterion Properties plc v Stratford UK
   Properties LLC [2002] EWCA Civ 1783,
   [2003] 1 WLR 2108..............649, 650
Criterion Properties plc v Stratford UK
   Properties LLC [2004] UKHL 28, [2004]
   1 WLR 1846 .... 22, 646, 649, 650, 654

Cross v Kirby [2000] EWCA
   Civ 426 ....715, 719, 722
Crossco No 4 Unlimited v Jolan Ltd [2011]
   EWCA Civ 1619.....................597
Crown Dilmun v Sutton [2004] EWHC 52,
   [2004] 1 BCLC 468...... 422, 498, 499, 651
Crown House Engineering Ltd v Amec
   Projects Ltd (1989) 48 BLR 37 103
Cundy v Lindsay (1878) 3 App
   Cas 459 ....197, 574, 576
Cunigunda (otherwise Cora) Crippen
   (deceased), In the Estate of [1911] P 108... 550
Currey (1994) 16 Cr App R (S) 421........535
Customs and Excise Commissioners v
   McMaster Stores (Scotland) Ltd [1995]
   STC 846.......................407, 703
Customs and Excise Commissioners v
   National Westminster Bank plc [2002]
   EWHC 2204, (Ch) [2003] 1 All ER
   (Comm) 327 ....190, 235
D and C Builders v Rees [1966] 2 QB
   617...........................213, 220
DO Ferguson v Sohl (1992) 62
   BLR 92........................313, 324
DPP for Northern Ireland v Lynch [1975]
   AC 653 ....206, 227, 292
DSND Subsea Ltd v PGS Offshore
   Technology AS [2000] BLR 530 .... 213, 218,
             219, 221, 223, 224, 225, 226, 228
DWS, Re [2001] Ch 568.................552
Daily Telegraph Newspaper Co Ltd v
   McLaughlin [1904] AC 776 383
Dale v IRC [1954] AC 11................508
Dale v Sollet (1767) 4 Burr 2133; 98
   ER 112.............................53
Daly v Sydney Stock Exchange (1986) 65
   ALR 193 (High Court of Australia) 602
Daniel v Drew [2005] EWCA Civ 507,
   [2005] WTLR 807................258, 261
Daraydan Holdings Ltd v Solland
   International Ltd [2004] EWHC 622
   (Ch), [2005] Ch 119 .... 501, 510, 511
Darjan Estate Co plc v Huxley (No 2) [2012]
   EWHC 189 (Ch), [2012] 1 WLR 1782....271
David Securities Pty Ltd v Commonwealth
   Bank of Australia (1992) 175 CLR 353
   (High Court of Australia)....54, 60, 145, 149,
             162, 173, 189, 191, 321, 322, 324,
                    679, 683, 687, 688
Davies v London and Provincial Marine
   Insurance Co (1878) 8 Ch D 469........205
Davis Contractors Ltd v Fareham Urban
   District Council [1956] AC 696 356
Davey [2013] EWCA Crim 1662 537
Davitt v Titcumb [1990] Ch 110 549
Day v Day [2013] EWCA Civ 280, [2014]
   Ch 114.............................21
De Bernardy v Harding (1853) 8 Exch 821,
   155 ER 1586 ....137, 333

De Bussche v Alt (1878) 8 Ch D 286 304
De Medina v Grove (1846) 10 QB 152, 116
ER 59. 147
De Molestina v Ponton [2002] 1 All ER
(Comm) 587 271
Debtor, Re a [1937] Ch 156 241
Deering v Earl of Winchelsea (1787) 2 Bos
and Pul 270, 126 ER 1276. . . . . . 234, 247, 712
Deglman v Guaranty Trust of Canada [1954]
3 DLR 785, [1954] SCR 725 (Supreme
Court of Canada) 57, 351
Delaney v Pickett [2011] EWCA Civ 1532,
[2012] 1 WLR 2149. 722
Demerara Bauxite Co Ltd v Hubbard [1923]
AC 673 . . . . 276, 496, 503
Derry v Peek (1889) 14 App Cas 337 . . . 187, 197
Deutsche Bank (London Agency) v Beriro
and Co (1895) 73 LTR (ns) 669 166,
668, 671
Deutsche Morgan Grenfell Group plc v IRC
[2006] UKHL 49, [2007] 1 AC 558 . . . . 7, 36,
37, 60, 96, 127, 130, 133, 146, 164, 172,
174, 177, 178, 179, 180, 182, 183, 186,
188, 392, 394, 401, 403, 412
Devaux v Connolly (1849) 8 CB 640, 137
ER 658. 321
Devenish Nutrition Ltd v Sanofi-Aventis SA
(France) [2008] EWCA Civ 1086, [2009]
Ch 390. . . . . . 420, 440, 448, 453, 465, 466, 475
Dew v Parsons (1819) 2 B and Ald 562,
106 ER 471 . . . . 396, 397
Dextra Bank and Trust Co v Bank of Jamaica
[2001] UKPC 50, [2002] 1 All ER (Comm)
193. . . . . 163, 172, 681, 689, 691, 694
Dies v British and International Mining and
Finance Co Ltd [1939] 1 KB 724 . . . . 337, 338
Dillwyn v Llewelyn (1862) 4 De GF and
J 157, 54 ER 1285 521
Dimond v Lovell [2002] 1 AC 384 . . . . . 352, 732
Dimskal Shipping Co SA v International
Transport Workers Federation, The
Evia Luck [1992] 2 AC 152. . . . . 204, 206,
212, 213, 218, 219, 222, 223, 227, 442
Diplock's Estate, Re [1948] Ch 465 566,
580, 607, 611, 612, 616, 617, 618, 620, 621,
623, 624, 626, 627, 628, 633, 635, 639,
644, 657, 696, 735, 741
Docker v Somes (1834) 2 My and K 655, 39
ER 1095. 426
Doe v Kersey (1795) (CP) quoted in Bower's
Law Dictionary (1839) 604
Dominion Securities Inc v Dawson (1994)
111 DLR (4th) 230 (Newfoundland Court
of Appeal) 698
Donoghue v Stevenson [1932] AC 562. 174
Dorchester upon Medway City Council v
Kent CC (1998) The Times, 5 March. 375
Douglas v Hello! Ltd (No 3) [2005] EWCA
Civ 595, [2006] 1 QB 125 . . . . . . 464, 516, 519

Downer Enterprises Ltd, Re [1974] 1 WLR
1460. 239
Dowson and Mason Ltd v Potter [1986] 2 All
ER 418. 516
Doyle v Olby (Ironmongers) Ltd [1969]
2 QB 158. 198
Dubai Aluminium Co Ltd v Salaam [2002]
UKHL 48, [2003] AC 366. . . . . 248, 524,
597, 650, 651, 652, 653, 692
Duggan v Governor of Full Sutton Prison
[2004] EWCA Civ 78, [2004]
1 WLR 1010 581
Duke de Cadaval v Collins (1836) 4 Ad and
E 858, 111 ER 1006. . . . . . . 211, 446, 527, 577
Duke of Norfolk v Worthy (1808) 1 Camp
337, 170 ER 977 675
Duke of Norfolk's Settlement Trust, Re
[1982] Ch 61. 80
Dunbar v Plant [1998] Ch 412 . . . . 544, 546,
547, 549, 553, 554, 590, 712
Dunbar Bank plc v Nadeem [1998] 3 All ER
876. . . . . 22, 25, 26, 260, 261, 267
Durrant v The Ecclesiastical Commissioners
for England and Wales (1880) 6 QBD 234 . . . 687
EIC Services Ltd v Phipps [2003] EWHC
1507, [2003] 1 WLR 2360. 194
ENE Kos 1 Ltd v Petroleo Brasileiro SA
(No 2) [2012] UKSC 17, [2012] 2 AC
164. 289, 302, 304, 305
Eagle Star Insurance Co Ltd v Karasiewicz
[2002] EWCA Civ 940 . . . . 21, 637
Eagle Trust plc v SBC Securities Ltd [1993] 1
WLR 484. 648
Eagle Trust plc v SBC Securities Ltd (No 2)
[1996] 1 BCLC 121. 648
Earl of Aylesford v Morris (1873) LR 8 Ch
App 484. . . . . 274, 278, 281, 284
Earl of Chesterfield v Janssen (1751) 2 Ves
Sen 125, 28 ER 82. 278
Edelsten v Edelsten (1863) 1 De GJ and Sm
185, 46 ER 72 . . . . 460, 461
Edinburgh Corp v Lord Advocate See Lord
Provost of Edinburgh v Lord Advocate
Edgington v Fitzmaurice (1880) 25 Ch
D 459. . . . . 175, 187, 197, 198
Edmunds v Wallingford (1885) 14
QBD 811. . . . . 236, 239, 240, 241, 245
Edwards, Re [2014] VSC 392 (Supreme Court
of Victoria, Australia). 545, 547
El Ajou v Dollar Land Holdings plc [1993] 3
All ER 717, [1993] BCLC 735. . . . . . . 24, 587,
603, 613, 615, 616, 617, 618, 628
Eldan Services Ltd v Chandag Motors Ltd
[1990] 4 All ER 459. 575
Elders Pastoral Ltd v Bank of New Zealand
[1989] 2 NZLR 180 (New Zealand Court
of Appeal). 617
Elek v Bar-Tur [2013] EWHC 207 (Ch),
[2013] EGLR 159 . . . . 137, 138, 334

Ella Constance, The (1864) 33 LJ
Adm 189 293

Ellis v Braker (1870) LR 7 Ch App 104 264

Ellis v Goulton [1893] 1 QB 350 675

Elsayed [2014] EWCA Crim 333, [2014] 1
WLR 3916 . . . . .66, 538

Emery's Investment Trusts, Re [1959]
Ch 410 589

Empirnall Holdings Pty Ltd v Machon Paull
Partners Pty Ltd (1988) 14 NSWLR 523
(New South Wales Court of Appeal) 135

England v Marsden (1866) LR 1 CP 529 240

English v Dedham Vale Properties Ltd [1978] 1
WLR 93 . . . . 488, 490, 491

Enimont Overseas AG v Rojugotanker Zadar
(The Olib) [1991] 2 Lloyd's Rep 108 228

Equitas Ltd v Walsham Bros & Co Ltd [2013]
EWHC 3264 (Comm). 32, 736

Equus Corp Pty Ltd v Haxton [2012] HCA 7,
[2012] 86 ALJR 296 (High Court of
Australia). 111, 332, 377, 714, 721, 722

Erlanger v New Sombrero Phosphate Co
(1878) 3 App Cas 1218 . . . 23, 25, 26, 327, 741

Esso Petroleum Co Ltd v Hall Russell and Co
Ltd [1989] AC 643 . . . . . . .142, 234, 235, 241,
242, 244

Esso Petroleum Co Ltd v Niad Ltd [2001]
All ER (D) 324 477

Eugena Ltd v Gelande Corp Ltd [2004]
EWHC 3273 (QB). 346

Euro-Diam Ltd v Bathurst [1990]
QB 1 . . . . 544, 545, 710, 714

Evans v Llewllin (1787) 1 Cox 333, 29
Ex 1191 283

Evans v Lloyd [2013] EWHC 1725 (Ch) 278

Everet v Williams (1725) (unreported) 715

Evia Luck, The, See Dimskal Shipping Co SA v
International Transport Workers Federation
(The Evia Luck)

Exall v Partridge (1799) 8 TR 303, 101 ER
1405. . . . . .77, 80, 145, 236, 239, 240, 245, 301

Experience Hendrix LLC v PPX Enterprises
Inc [2003] EWCA Civ 323, [2003] 1 All ER
(Comm) 830 . . . . .417, 424, 429, 469, 473,
478, 479, 484, 518

F (Mental Patient: Sterilisation), Re [1990]
2 AC 1 . . . . 289, 293, 294

FHR European Ventures LLP v Cedar Capital
Partners LLC [2014] UKSC 45, [2015]
AC 250 . . . . 42, 110, 419, 433, 470, 487,
565, 604, 607, 470, 487, 512, 513,
519, 531, 565, 596, 598, 604,
607, 613, 635, 646

FJ Chalke Ltd v The Commissioners for Her
Majesty's Revenue and Customs [2009]
EWHC 952 (Ch), [2009] STC 2007 60

Faccenda Chicken v Fowler [1987] Ch 117 . . . 515

Fairfield Sentry Ltd v Migani [2014]
UKPC 9 . . . . 133, 145, 190, 237

Falcke v Scottish Imperial Insurance (1886)
34 Ch D 234 . . . . 36, 37, 85, 87, 88, 289,
290, 295, 300, 301, 306

Farah Construction Pty Ltd v Say-Dee Pty
Ltd [2007] HCA 22 (High Court of
Australia). 54, 646, 653

Farepak Food and Gifts Ltd, Re [2006]
EWHC 3272 (Ch) 313, 599, 600, 604

Federal Sugar Refining Co v US Sugar
Equalization Board Inc (1920) 268 F 575
(Southern District of New York) 466

Fell v Whittaker (1871) LR 7 QB 120. 212

R v Ferguson [1970] 1 WLR 1246 528

Fibrosa Spolka Akcyjna v Fairbairn Lawson
Combe Barbour Ltd [1943] AC 32 . . . . . . 4, 7,
8, 46, 47, 49, 51, 53, 62, 188, 308, 310,
318, 321, 356, 357

Field Common Ltd v Elmbridge BC [2008]
EWHC 2079 (Ch) .454

Filby v Mortgage Express (No 2) Ltd [2004]
EWCA Civ 759 . . . 20, 107, 636, 638, 640, 655

Financial Institutions Services Ltd v Negril
Holdings Ltd [2004] UKPC 40. 275

Fiona Trust & Holding Corp v Privalov
[2010] EWHC 3199 (Comm) 523

Fitzalan-Howard (Norfolk) v Hibbert
[2009] EWHC 2855 (QB) 601

Flett v Deniliquin Publishing Co Ltd [1964–5]
NSWLR 383 (New South Wales) 99

Flood v Irish Provident Assurance Co (1912)
46 ILT 214. 731

Flower v Sadler (1882) 10 QBD 572. 230

Foran v Wright (1989) 64 ALJR 1 (High
Court of Australia) 135

Force India Formula One Team Ltd v 1
Malaysia Racing Team Sdn Bhd [2012]
EWHC 616 (Ch) 429, 430, 480, 517

Forsyth-Grant v Allen [2008] EWCA
Civ 505 462

Foskett v McKeown [1998] Ch 265
(CA) 14, 568, 625, 633, 635

Foskett v McKeown [2001] 1 AC 102
(HL). 7, 11, 12, 13, 14, 16,
34, 557, 559, 561, 562, 563, 564, 565, 566,
568, 569, 573, 580, 596, 608, 609, 610,
611, 612, 613, 620, 621, 625, 626, 628,
629, 632, 633, 634, 635, 643, 656, 696, 697

Foster Bryant Surveying Ltd v Bryant [2007]
EWCA Civ 200, [2007] 2
BCLC 239 . . . . 492, 498

Francisco v Diedrick (1998) The Times,
3 April. 547

Freeman v Jeffries (1869) LR 4 Exch 189. . . .736

French's Estate, Re (1887) 21 LR Ir 283
(Ireland) 611

Friends' Provident Life Office v Hillier Parker
May and Rowden (a firm) [1997]
QB 85 . . . . 161, 162, 248, 249, 250, 377

Fry v Lane (1888) 40 Ch D 312 . . . . . . .281, 283

Fuller v Happy Shopper Markets Ltd [2001]
  1 WLR 1681 736
Fyffes Group Ltd v Templeman [2000]
  2 Lloyd's Rep 643 . . . . . . .421, 426, 440, 507,
                                        511, 525
Gafford v Graham [1999] 7 P & CR 73 471
Galambos v Perez 2009 SCR 48, [2009] 3
  SCR 247 (Supreme Court of Canada). 490
Galbraith v Mildenhall Estates [1965] 2
  QB 478 339
Gamerco SA v ICM/Fair Warning (Agency)
  Ltd [1995] 1 WLR 1226 . . . . .358, 359
Garland v Consumers' Gas Distributors Inc
  [2004] 1 SCR 629 (Supreme Court of
  Canada). 41, 57, 127, 132
Gascoigne v Gascoigne [1918] 1 KB 223 589
Gaudet v Brown (1873) LR 5 PC 134. 302
Gebhardt v Saunders [1892] 2 QB
  452. . . . . 235, 242, 298
Geismar v Sun Alliance and London
  Insurance Ltd [1978] QB 383 544
George Whitechurch Ltd v Cavanagh [1902]
  AC 117 671
Ghana Commercial Bank v Chandiram [1960]
  AC 732 639
Ghosh, R v [1982] QB 1053 523
Gibb v Maidstone and Tunbridge Wells
  NHS Trust [2010] EWCA Civ 678. . . . .58, 78
Gibbon v Mitchell [1990] 1 WLR 1304 201
Gibbons v Wright (1954) 91 CLR 423 (High
  Court of Australia) 382, 383, 384
Giedo van der Garde BV v Force India
  Formula One Team Ltd [2010] EWHC
  2373 (QB) 309, 313, 317, 319, 321, 322,
                   323, 324, 325, 429, 479, 480, 484
Gilbert Partners v Knight [1968] 2 All ER
  248. 135
Giles (deceased), Re [1972] Ch 544 . . . .546, 548
Giles v Edwards (1797) 7 Term Rep 181,
  101 ER 920 .317, 333
Giles v Thompson [1994] 1 AC 142. 716
Gillett v Holt [2001] Ch 210. 520
Gillette UK Ltd v Edenwest Ltd [1994]
  RPC 279 461
Gillingham Bus Disaster Fund, Re [1958]
  Ch 300. 584
Girardy v Richardson (1793) 1 Esp 13, 170
  ER 265. 716
Glasgow Corp v Lord Advocate 1959 SC 203
  (Court of Session, Scotland) 391
Goldcorp Exchange plc, Re [1995] 1 AC 74
  (PC). 489, 490, 570, 571,
                   577, 581, 600, 601, 603, 606, 624, 628
Goldsworthy v Brickell [1987]
  Ch 338. . . . . .264, 265
Gondall v Dillon Newspapers Ltd [2001]
  RLR 221. 428
Goodchild v Bradley [2006] EWCA Civ
  1868. 267

Goodman v Pocock (1850) 15 QB 576,
  117 ER 577 . . . . .68, 314
Gordon v Chief Commissioner of
  Metropolitan Police [1910] 2 KB 1080. . . .711
Gore v Gibson (1843) 13 M and W 623,
  153 ER 260 383
Goring, The [1987] QB 687 . . . . .295, 306
Goss v Chilcott [1996] AC
  788. . . . . 321, 322, 324, 328, 375, 695
Gray v Barr [1970] 2 QB 626 . . . . .545, 546
Gray v Barr [1971] 2 QB 554 (CA). 545, 546, 548
Gray v Thames Trains Ltd [2009] UKHL 33,
  [2009] 1 AC 1339 . . . . .709, 710, 716, 718,
                                        722, 723
Grayson v United Kingdom (2008) 48
  EHRR 722 536
Great Northern Railway Company v Swaffield
  (1874) LR 9 Ex 132. . . . . 291–2, 302, 305
Great Peace Shipping Ltd v Tsavliris Salvage
  (International) Ltd [2002] EWCA Civ 1407,
  [2003] AC 679. . . . . 22, 29, 160, 193, 194, 272
Great Western Railway v Sutton (1869) LR
  4 HL 226. . . . . .253, 254
Green [2008] UKHL 30, [2008] 1 AC 1053. . . 538
Green v Portsmouth Stadium Ltd [1953]
  QB 190 288
Greenwood v Bennett [1973] QB 195 82,
           83, 84, 126, 158, 169, 173, 632, 657
Greenwood v Martins Bank Ltd [1932]
  1 KB 371 (CA) 672
Greenwood v Martins Bank Ltd [1933]
  AC 51 (HL). 669, 671, 672
Gribbon v Lutton [2001] EWCA Civ 1956,
  [2002] QB 902. . . . . .313, 333
Griffiths, Re [2009] Ch 162. 163
Grimaldi v Chameleon Mining NZ (No 2)
  [2012] FCAFC 6, (2012) 200 FCR 296
  (Federal Court, Australia). 513, 604, 605
Grist v Bailey [1967] Ch 532 . . . . .195, 272
Groves v Groves (1829) 3 Y and J 163,
  148 ER 1136 712
Guardian Ocean Cargoes Ltd v Banco de
  Brasil SA [1991] 2 Lloyd's Rep 68 . . .235, 311
Guardian Ocean Cargoes Ltd v Banco de
  Brasil SA (No 2) [1994] 2 Lloyd's
  Rep 152. 736
Guildford BC v Hein [2005] EWCA
  Civ 979 . . . . .300, 303
Guinness plc v Saunders [1990]
  2 AC 663. . . . . .47, 48, 134, 314, 369,
           370, 426, 486, 507, 508, 509, 718
Guinness, Mahon and Co Ltd v Kensington
  and Chelsea Royal London Borough
  Council [1999] QB 215. . . . 127, 317, 374, 376
Gwembe Valley Development Co Ltd v Koshy
  (No 3) [2003] EWCA Civ 1478, [2004]
  1 BCLC 131. . . . . 494, 506, 651
H (deceased), Re [1990] 1 FLR
  441. 545, 546, 547, 554

H Dakin and Co Ltd v Lea [1916] 1 KB 566....341
HIH Casualty and General Insurance v
    Chase Manhattan Bank [2003] UKHL 6,
    [2003] 2 Lloyd's Rep 6 199
Hain SS Co Ltd v Tate and Lyle Ltd [1936]
    3 All ER 597 341
Halifax Building Society v Thomas [1996]
    Ch 217..... 415, 421, 436, 437, 446, 463, 464,
            527, 528, 529, 530, 531, 595, 596, 597
Halifax plc v Omar [2002] EWCA Civ 21,
    [2002] 2 P & CR 377...............21, 637
Hall, In the Estate of [1914] P 1...........546
Hall v Hebert [1993] 2 SCR 159 (Supreme
    Court of Canada) 713
Hallett's Estate, Re (1880) 13
    Ch D 696..........613, 616, 617, 618, 619,
                    620, 622, 624, 634
Halley v The Law Society [2003] EWCA
    Civ 97 599
Halpern v Halpern (No 2) [2006] EWHC
    1728 (Comm), [2007] QB 88 23
Halpern v Halpern (Nos 1 and 2) [2007]
    EWCA Civ 291, [2008] QB 195 ...... 25, 26,
                            27, 204
Hambly v Trott (1776) 1 Cowp 371, 98 ER
    1136......................... 416, 442, 466
Hammond v Osborn [2002] EWCA Civ 885,
    [2002] WTLR 1125....... 258, 266, 267, 269
Handayo v Tjong Very Sumito [2013]
    SGA 44 (Singapore Court of Appeal).....565
Hardy v Motor Insurers' Bureau [1964] 2
    QB 745 544
Harris v Digital Pulse Pty Ltd (2003) 56
    NSWLR 298 (New South Wales Court of
    Appeal) 432
Harris v Williams-Wynne [2006] EWCA
    Civ 104, [2006] P & CR 27............449
Harrison v Halliwell Landau [2004] EWHC
    1316 (QB) 217, 232
Harrison v Madjeski and Coys of
    Kensington [2014] EWCA
    Civ 361 .... 10, 71, 81, 692
Harry v Tate and Lyle Refineries Ltd [1982]
    2 Lloyd's Rep 416 ....265, 283
Harry Parker Ltd v Mason [1940] 2
    KB 590.............................720
Hart v O'Connor [1985] AC 1000
    (PC).......... 262, 279, 280, 281, 282, 382
Hartog v Colin and Shields [1939] 3 All
    ER 566.............................197
Haseldine v Hoskin [1933] 1 KB 822.......544
Hassard v Smith (1872) IR 6 Eq 429
    (Ireland) 382
Hatch, Re [1919] 1 Ch 351...............161
Hatch v Hatch (1804) 9 Ves 292, 32
    ER 615.............................264
Haugesund Kommune v Depfa ACS Bank
    [2010] EWCA Civ 579, [2012] QB 549 ... 46,
                368, 373, 375, 377, 695, 722, 732

Haugesund Kommune v Depfa ACS Bank
    [2011] EWCA Civ 33, [2011]
    3 All ER 655 ....9, 104
Hazell v Hammersmith and Fulham London
    Borough Council [1992] AC 1 ... 372, 393, 732
Hedley Byrne and Co Ltd v Heller and
    Partners Ltd [1964] AC 465 198
Hemming (t/a Simply Pleasure Ltd) v The
    Lord Mayor and Citizens of Westminster
    [2013] EWCA Civ 591, [2015] UKSC 25,
    [2015] 2 WLR 1271....... 109, 402, 405, 737
Henderson v Folkestone Waterworks Co
    (1885) 1 TLR 329 162
Henderson v Merrett Syndicates Ltd [1995]
    2 AC 145...........................491
Hennessy v Craigmoyle and Co Ltd [1986]
    ICR 461...........................221, 225
Hewett v First Plus Financial plc [2010]
    EWCA Civ 312, [2010] 2 FLR 177.......261
Hewison v Meridian Shipping Pte Ltd
    [2002] EWCA Civ 1821, [2003]
    ICR 766................... 710, 714, 724
Heywood v Wellers (a firm) [1976]
    QB 446 313
Hickey v Roche [1993] RLR 196..........482
Hicks v Hicks (1802) 3 East 16, 102
    ER 502.............................371
Hill v Perrott (1810) 3 Taunt 274, 128
    ER 109.............................462
Hillesden Securities Ltd v Ryjak Ltd [1983]
    2 All ER 184 460
Hillsdown plc v Pensions Ombudsman
    [1997] 1 All ER 862 ....57, 648
Hilton v Barker, Booth and Eastwood [2005]
    UKHL 8, [2005] 1 WLR 567........491, 496
Hinks, R v [2001] AC 241 50
R v Hinks [2001] AC 241................561
Hirachand Punamchand v Temple [1911] 2
    KB 330.............................236
Hobbs v Marlowe [1978] AC 16........20, 636
Hochster v De La Tour (1852) 2 E and B
    678, 118 ER 922 68
Hodgson v Marks [1971] Ch 892..........583
Hoenig v Isaacs [1952] 2 All ER 176 ... 341, 342
Holder v Holder [1968] 1 Ch 353 495
Holiday v Sigil (1826) 2 Car and P 177, 172
    ER 81..............................572
Holland v Russell (1863) 4 B and S 14, 122
    ER 365.........................676, 677
Holman v Johnson (1775) 1 Cowp 341, 98
    ER 1120............. 47, 186, 187, 287, 532,
            544, 589, 693, 709, 710, 711, 712,
                            718, 719
Holmes v Payne [1930] 2 KB 301.........143
Holt v Markham [1923] 1 KB
    504................... 9, 176, 668, 671
Home and Colonial Insurance Co Ltd v
    London Guarantee and Accident Co
    Ltd (1928) 45 TLR 134............165, 166

Horsford v Bird [2006] UKPC 3
  (PC). 430, 431, 454, 455, 459
Hospital Products International Ltd
  v United States Surgical Corp
  (1984) 156 CLR 41 (High Court of
  Australia). 470, 490
Hospitality Group Pty Ltd v Australian
  Rugby Football Union Ltd [2001] FCA
  1040 (Federal Court of Australia). 481
Houghton, Re [1915] 2 Ch 173 546
Houghton v Fayers [2000] 1 BCLC 511 648
Hounga v Allen [2014] UKSC 47,
  [2014] 1 WLR 2889. . . . . 708, 709, 713,
                                       718, 719, 724
Hovenden and Sons v Millhof (1900) 83
  LT 41. 501
Howard v Shirlstar Container Transport
  Ltd [1990] 1 WLR 1292 710
Howard v Wood (1679) 2 Lev;
  83 ER 540, 2 Shaw KB 21;
  89 ER 767 . . . . 114, 154
Howe v Smith (1884) 27 Ch D 89 . . . . . . 36, 338
Howes Percival LLP v Page [2013] EWHC
  4104 (Ch) 136, 137, 334
Huffer v Allen (1867) LR 2 Ex 15. 147
Hughes v Liverpool Victoria Legal Friendly
  Society [1916] 2 KB 482 187
Huguenin v Baseley (1807) 14 Ves Jun 273,
  33 ER 526 258
Hunter v Moss [1994] 1 WLR 452 . . . . . 571, 581
Hurley v Darjan Estate Co plc [2012]
  EWHC 189 (Ch), [2012] 1 WLR 1782. . . . 258
Hussey v Palmer [1972] 1 WLR 1286 . . . 521, 598
Huyton SA v Peter Cremer GmbH [1999]
  1 Lloyd's Rep 620 . . . . 209, 210, 215,
                                 218, 219, 223, 225, 229
Hyundai Heavy Industries Co Ltd v
  Papadopoulos [1980] 1 WLR 1129. 318
Ibrahim v Barclays Bank plc [2011]
  EWHC 1897 (Ch), [2012] 1 BCLC 33 636
Ibrahim v Barclays Bank plc [2012] EWCA
  Civ 640, [2013] Ch 400. . . . . . . 236, 239, 244
Ilich, R v (1987) 69 ALR 231, 162 CLR 110
  (High Court of Australia). 155, 572, 574,
                                 575, 576, 657, 659
Imperial Loan Co v Stone [1892]
  1 QB 599. . . . . 382, 383
In Plus Group Ltd v Pyke [2002] EWCA
  Civ 370, [2002] 2 BCLC 201. . . . . 492, 498
Inche Noriah v Shaik Alli Bin Omar [1929]
  AC 127 269
Indata Equipment Supplies Ltd v ACL
  Ltd [1998] FSR 248. 515
Independent Trustee Service Ltd v GP
  Noble Trustees Ltd [2012] EWCA Civ
  196, [2013] Ch 91 660
Industrial Development Consultants Ltd v
  Cooley [1972] 1 WLR 443 . . . . 425, 498
Ingram v Little [1961] 1 QB 31 195

Inverugie Investments Ltd v Hackett [1995]
  1 WLR 713 (PC). 428, 431, 449, 456
Investment Trust Companies v HMRC [2012]
  STC 1150, [2015] EWCA Civ 82 . . . . . . 9, 56,
                                       104, 108, 109, 110,
                                       111, 139, 140
Investment Trust Companies v HMRC
  (No 2) [2013] EWHC 665 (Ch), [2013]
  STC 1129. . . . . 400, 403, 404
Investment Trust Companies v HMRC [2015]
  EWCA Civ 82. . . . . 108, 109, 110, 393,
                                 404, 407, 564, 637
Inwards v Baker [1965] 2 QB 29 521
Ionides v Pender (1874) LR 9 QB 531 21
R v IRC, ex p Woolwich Equitable Building
  Society [1990] 1 WLR 1400 . . . . 398, 404
Irvani v Irvani [2000] 1 Lloyd's Rep 412 281
Islam, R v [2009] UKHL 30, [2009] AC
  1076. 538
Islamic Republic of Iran v Barakat Galleries
  Ltd [2009] QB 22 600
Island Export Finance Ltd v Umunna
  [1986] BCLC 460 498
Island Records Ltd v Tring International
  plc [1996] 1 WLR 1256. . . . . 438, 439, 440
Item Software (UK) Ltd v Fassihi [2004]
  EWCA Civ 1244, [2005] ICR 450. 342
J Lauritzen AS v Wijsmuller (The Super
  Servant Two) [1990] 1 Lloyd's Rep 1 356
J S Bloor Ltd v Pavillion Developments Ltd
  [2008] EWHC 724 (TCC). 79
Jacob v Allen (1703) 1 Salkeld 27,
  91 ER 26 114
Jaggard v Sawyer [1995] 1 WLR 269 429,
                                       437, 471, 473
James, ex p (1803) 8 Ves 337 495
James v British General Insurance Co Ltd
  [1927] 2 KB 311 544
James v Williams [2000] Ch 1 . . . . 603, 741
James Roscoe (Bolton) Ltd v Winder
  [1915] 1 Ch 62 624
Jarvis (deceased), Re [1958] 1 WLR
  815. . . . . 425, 426
Jebara v Ottoman Bank [1927] 2 KB 254. . . . 301
Jegon v Vivian (1871) LR 6 Ch App 742 424
Jenkins v Tucker (1788) 1 H Bl 91,
  126 ER 55 . . . . 296, 297, 300
Jennings v Cairns [2003] EWCA Civ 1935,
  [2004] WTLR 361. 269
Jennings and Chapman Ltd v Woodman
  Matthews and Co [1952] 2 TLR
  409. . . . . 92, 345, 348
Jeremy D Stone Consultants Ltd v National
  Westminster Bank [2013] EWHC 208
  (Ch). 73, 675, 691, 693, 700
John Alexander's Clubs Pty Ltd v White City
  Tennis Club Ltd [2010] HCA 19, (2010)
  241 CLR 1 (High Court of Australia). 605
Johnson v Agnew [1980] AC 367. . . . . . . 68, 136

Johnson v Clark [1908] 1 Ch 303 379

Johnson v Gore-Wood and Co [2002] 2 AC
1, [2001] 2 WLR 72 673

Johnson v Royal Mail Steam Packet Co
[1867] LR 3 CP 38 239

Jon Beauforte (London) Ltd, Re [1953]
Ch 131 380

Jones v Churcher [2009] EWHC 722 (QB),
[2009] 2 Lloyd's Rep 94 . . . . 111, 691, 692

Jones v Kernott [2011] UKSC 53, [2012]
1 AC 776 597

Jones v Morgan [2001] EWCA Civ
995 . . . . 280, 281, 286

Jones v Powys Local Health Board [2008]
EWHC 2562 (Admin) 405

Jones v Ricoh Ltd [2010] EWHC 1743
(Ch) 480, 481

Jones v Ruth [2011] EWCA Civ 804, [2012]
1 WLR 1495 . . . . 454, 455

Jones (RE) Ltd v Waring and Gillow Ltd
[1926] AC 670 . . . . 166, 171, 189, 191,
574, 667, 668, 672

Jorden v Money (1854) 5 HL Cas 185, 10
ER 868 673

Jyske Bank (Gibraltar) Ltd v Spjeldnaes
(unreported) 23 July 1997 625

K (deceased), Re [1985] Ch 85 549

K (deceased), Re [1986] Ch 180
(CA) 543, 546, 553, 554

K v P [1993] Ch 140 248

Kakavas v Crown Melbourne Ltd [2013]
HCA 25 (High Court of Australia) 281

Kali and Burlay v Chawla [2007] EWHC
2357 (Ch) 635

Karak Rubber Co Ltd v Burden (No 2)
[1972] 1 WLR 602 648

Kaufman v Gerson [104] 1 KB 591 230

Kearley v Thompson (1890) 24 QBD
742 . . . . 353, 719, 723

Keech v Sandford (1726) Sel Cas t King 61,
25 ER 223 . . . . 497, 498, 510

Kellar v Williams [2004] UKPC 30 (PC) 716

Kelly v Cooper [1993] AC 205 496

Kelly v Solari (1841) 9 M and W 54, 152
ER 24 . . . . 53, 129, 150, 165, 166,
170, 171, 176, 179, 181, 694

Kennedy v Kennedy [2014] EWHC 4129
(Ch) 21, 28, 29, 201, 202

Kerr v Baranow; Vanasse v Seguin [2011]
SCC 10, [2011] 1 SCR 269 (Supreme
Court of Canada) 70, 132

Kerrison v Glynn, Mills, Currie and Co
(1911) 81 LJKB 465 . . . . 166–7, 171

Khan v Malik [2011] EWHC 1319 (Ch) 336

King v Alston (1848) 12 QB 971, 116
ER 1134 114

Kingstreet Investments Ltd v New Brunswick
(Finance) [2007] 1 SCR 3 (Supreme Court
of Canada) 5, 118, 146, 392, 703

Kiriri Cotton Co Ltd v Dewani [1960] AC 192
(PC) 287, 288, 532, 720

Kleinwort Benson Ltd v Birmingham City
Council [1997] QB 380 . . . . 105, 118,
373, 465, 703, 704, 706

Kleinwort Benson Ltd v Glasgow City Council
[1999] 1 AC 153 . . . . 7, 46, 61, 250

Kleinwort Benson Ltd v Lincoln City Council
[1999] 2 AC 349 . . . . 7, 9, 50,
120, 130, 133, 146, 150, 161, 162, 163,
172, 174, 176, 177, 183, 184, 185, 186,
188, 190, 191, 374, 378, 394, 412, 574,
578, 586, 667

Kleinwort Benson Ltd v Sandwell BC [1994]
4 All ER 890 . . . . 372, 376

Kleinwort Benson Ltd v South Tyneside
Metropolitan Borough Council [1994] 4
All ER 972 . . . . 704, 736, 738

Kleinwort Benson Ltd v Vaughan [1996]
CLC 620 236

Kleinwort Sons and Co v Dunlop Rubber Co
(1907) 97 LT 263 . . . . 166, 171, 675, 676, 678

Kuddus v Chief Constable of Leicestershire
[2001] UKHL 29, [2002] 2 AC 122 432

Kuwait Airways Corp v Iraqi Airways Co
(Nos 4 and 5) [2002] UKHL 19, [2002]
2 AC 883 . . . . 15, 641, 693

Kuwait Airways Corp v Iraqi Airways Co
(No 6) [2004] EWHC 2603, Comm 460

Kwei Tek Chao v British Traders and
Shippers Ltd [1954] 2 QB 459 314

LAC Minerals Ltd v International Corona
Resources Ltd (1989) 61 DLR (4th) 14
(Supreme Court of Canada) 519

Lacey, ex p (1802) 6 Ves 625 495

Lady and Kid v Skatteministeriet (Case
C- 398/09) [2012] STC 854
(ECJ) 408, 411, 703, 705

Lady Hood of Avalon v Mackinnon [1909]
1 Ch 476 . . . . 160, 200

Lamare v Dixon (1873) LR 6 HL 414 22

Lamb v Bunce (1815) 4 M and S 275, 105
ER 836 . . . . 86, 298

Lamine v Dorrell (1701) 2 Ld Raym 1216;
92 ER 303 460

Lampson (Australia) Pty Ltd v Fortescue
Metals Group Ltd (No 3) [2014] WASC
162 (Supreme Court of Western
Australia) 55

Lancashire Loans Ltd v Black [1934] 1
KB 380 264

Lane v O'Brien Homes Ltd [2004] EWHC
303 (QB) 471, 472

Larner v London County Council [1949] 2
KB 683 . . . . 167, 168, 670, 671, 678

Laskar v Laskar [2008] EWCA Civ 347,
[2008] 1 WLR 2695 . . . . 588, 589

Latimer v IRC [2004] UKPC 14, [2004] 1
WLR 1466 594

Lavin v Toppi [2015] HCA 4 (High Court
    of Australia) 246, 247
Lawford v Billericay Rural District Council
    [1903] 1 KB 772 85
Leaf v International Galleries [1950] 2
    KB 86. . . . . .38, 743
Leeder v Stevens [2005] EWCA
    Civ 50 . . . . 265, 267
Lee-Parker v Izzett (No 2) [1972] 1 WLR
    775. 521
Legal and General Assurance Society Ltd v
    Drake Insurance Co Ltd [1992] QB 887. . .246
Lehman Brothers International (Europe) Ltd,
    Re [2009] EWHC 3228 (Ch), [2010] 2
    BCLC 301 630
Lehman Commercial Mortgage Conduit
    Ltd v Gatedale Ltd [2012] EWHC
    848 (Ch) 636, 639
Leigh v Dickeson (1884) 15 QBD 60 . . . . .85, 86
Leigh and Sillivan Ltd v Aliakmon Shipping
    Co Ltd [1986] AC 785 653
Les Laboratoires Servier v Apotex [2012]
    EWCA Civ 593, [2013] Bus LR 80 709,
                                            713, 724
Les Laboratoires Servier v Apotex [2014]
    UKSC 55, [2015] AC 430 . . . . . .187, 708, 709,
                     715, 716, 717, 718, 722, 724
Leslie (J) Engineers Co Ltd, Re [1976]
    1 WLR 292 . . . . 644, 660
Leslie (R) Ltd v Shiell [1914] 3 KB 607 727,
                                            728, 729
Lever v Goodwin (1887) 36 Ch D 1 460
Liberian Insurance Agency Inc v Mosse
    [1977] 2 Lloyd's Rep 560 233
Liberty Mutual Insurance Co (UK) Ltd v
    HSBC Bank plc [2002] EWCA
    Civ 691 . . . . 636, 640
Liddle v Cree [2011] EWHC
    3294 (Ch) 286
Liggett (Liverpool) Ltd v Barclays Bank
    Ltd [1928] 1 KB 48 . . . . 236, 252
Lindsay Petroleum Co v Hurd (1874) LR 5
    PC 221. . . . . 742, 743
Lipkin Gorman (a firm) v Karpnale Ltd
    [1991] 2 AC 548 . . . . .7, 13, 45, 48, 49, 50,
                  53–4, 110, 153, 158, 409, 442, 527,
                  558, 560, 561, 572, 573, 600, 611,
                  613, 614, 642, 643, 653, 659, 660, 672, 674,
                  679, 680, 681, 682, 685, 687, 688, 690,
                  691, 692, 693, 695, 696, 698, 701
Lissack v Manhattan Loft Corporation Ltd
    [2013] EWHC 128 (Ch) 309, 310
Lister and Co v Stubbs (1890) 45 Ch
    D 1. . . . . 510, 511, 512
Littlewoods Retail Ltd v HMRC [2010]
    EWHC 1071 (Ch), [2010] STC
    2072. . . . . 118, 409, 410, 693
Littlewoods Retail Ltd v HMRC (Case
    C-591/10) [2012] STC 1714 (ECJ) 407

Littlewoods Retail Ltd v HMRC [2015]
    EWCA Civ 515 . . . . 32, 69,
                                      74, 389, 407
Lloyd's Bank Ltd v Brooks (1950) 6 Legal
    Decisions Affecting Bankers 161 667
Lloyd's Bank Ltd v Bundy [1975] QB
    326. . . . . .229, 232, 233,
                     260, 261, 265, 266,
                     276, 278, 279, 284, 395
Lloyds Bank plc v Independent Insurance
    Co Ltd [2000] QB 110 . . . . . . 9, 145, 146, 190
Load v Green (1846) 15 M and W 216, 153
    ER 828. 580
Lodder v Slowey [1904] AC 442
    (PC). 94, 101, 137, 335
Loftus (deceased), Re [2006] EWCA Civ
    1124, [2007] 1 WLR 591. . . . . 741, 742
Logicrose Ltd v Southend United Football
    Club Ltd [1988] 1 WLR 1256. 501
London Allied Holdings v Lee [2007]
    EWHC 2061 (Ch) 603, 606
London Wine Co (Shippers) Ltd (1986)
    PCC 121 570
Lonrho plc v Fayed (No 2) [1992] 1
    WLR 1. 603
Lord Napier and Ettrick v Hunter [1993]
    AC 713 20
Lord Provost of Edinburgh v The Lord
    Advocate (1879) 4 App Case
    823 (HL Sc). 623, 634
Louth v Diprose [1992] 75 CLR 621 (High
    Court of Australia) 256, 280, 281
Lovell and Christmas v Beauchamp [1894]
    AC 607 384
Lowson v Coombes [1999] Ch 373. 590
Lumbers v W Cook Builders Pty Ltd (in liq)
    [2008] HCA 27, (2008) 232 CLR 635
    (High Court of Australia) 54, 142, 330
Lunn Poly Ltd v Liverpool and Lancashire
    Properties Ltd [2006] EWCA Civ 430,
    [2006] 2 EGLR 29. . . . . 429, 430
Lupton v White (1808) 15 Ves Jun 432,
    33 ER 817 619
Lusty v Finsbury Securities Ltd (1991)
    58 BLR 66 137
Luxe Holding Ltd v Midland Resources
    Holding Ltd [2010] EWHC 1908 (Ch). . . .480
Lyell v Kennedy (1889) 14 App Cas 437 154
MCC Proceeds Inc v Lehman Bros
    International (Europe) [1995]
    4 All ER 675 . . . . 40, 653
MSM Consulting Ltd v United Republic of
    Tanzania [2009] EWHC 121 (QB). . . .99, 349
McCarthy v McCarthy and Stone plc
    [2007] EWCA Civ 664 242
MacDonald Dickens and Macklin v Costello
    [2011] EWCA Civ 930, [2012]
    QB 244 . . . . .10, 36, 100, 105, 108, 127,
                                      142, 330

McDonald v Coys of Kensington [2004]
EWCA Civ 47, [2004] 1 WLR 2775 . . . 65, 71,
78, 81, 84, 86, 87, 88, 89, 684, 691
McDonald v Dennys Lascelles (1933) 48
CLR 457 (High Court of Australia) 338
Macclesfield Corp v Great Central Railway
[1911] 2 KB 528 . . . . .151, 290
Mackenzie v Royal Bank of Canada [1934]
AC 468 24
Mackle, R v [2014] UKSC 5, [2014] AC
678. 540
Macmillan Inc v Bishopsgate Investment
Trust plc (No 3) [1995] 1
WLR 978. . . . . 416, 570, 658
Macmillan Inc v Bishopsgate Investment
Trust plc (No 3) [1996] 1 WLR
387(CA). 13, 561, 573
Madden v Quirk [1989] 1 WLR 702 248
Maersk Air Ltd v Expeditors International
(UK) Ltd [2003] 1 Lloyd's Rep 491 180,
650, 691
Magee v Pennine Insurance Co Ltd [1969]
2 QB 507. 195
Mahesan s/o Thambiah v Malaysia
Government Officers' Co-operative
Housing Society Ltd [1976]
AC 374 . . . . 438, 440, 501, 525
Mahmoud and Ispahani [1921] 2 KB 716 . . .717
Mahoney v Purnell [1996] 3 All ER 61 257,
274, 275, 277, 487
Mainwaring, Re [1937] Ch 96 247
Malone v Commissioner of Police of the
Metropolis [1980] QB 49 542
Manifest Shipping Co Ltd v Uni-Polaris
Insurance Co Ltd (The Star Sea) [2001]
UKHL 1, [2003] 1 AC 469 22
Marine Trade SA v Pioneer Freight Futures Co
Ltd [2009] EWHC 2656 (Comm), [2010] 1
Lloyd's Rep 631. .178
Marks and Spencer plc v BNP Paribas
Securities Services Trust Co (Jersey) Ltd
[2013] EWHC 1279 (Ch) 323, 329
Marks and Spencer plc v Commissioners of
Customs and Excise [2005] UKHL 53,
[2005] STC 1254. . . . . .118, 703
Marks and Spencer plc v Commissioners
of Customs and Excise (Case 309/06)
(ECJ) 408
Marks and Spencer plc v Freshfields
Bruckhaus Deringer (a firm) [2004]
EWHC 1137 (Ch), [2004] 1 WLR 2331 . . .496
Marley v Rawlings [2014] UKSC 2, [2015]
AC 129 21
Marsh v Keating (1834) 1 Bing NC 198, 131
ER 1094. . . . . 153, 573, 614
Marston Construction Ltd v Kiglass
Ltd (1989) 15 Con LR 116 . . . . .79, 84
Maskell v Horner [1915] 3 KB 106. 149,
212, 225, 240, 395

Mason v New South Wales (1959) 102
CLR 108 (High Court of Australia) 150,
231, 395, 703
Matheson v Smiley [1932] 2 DLR 787
(Manitoba Court of Appeal). 93, 299
Matthews v Baxter (1873) LR 8 Exch 132 . . .383
May, R v [2008] UKHL 28, [2008] 1 AC
1028. . . . . 534, 535, 536, 537, 538, 539
Mayson v Clouet [1924] AC 980 338
Mediana, The [1900] AC 113. 428
Menelaou v Bank of Cyprus plc [2013]
EWCA Civ 1960, [2014] 1 WLR 854 20,
109, 234, 636
Merry v Green (1841) 7 M and W 623, 151
ER 916. 572
Metallgesellschaft v IRC (Cases C-397/98
and C-410/98) [2001] Ch 620 (ECJ). . . 30, 403
Metall und Rohstoff AG v Donaldson,
Lufkin and Jenrette Inc [1990] 1
QB 391 . . . . 596, 597, 603
Metropolitan Bank v Heiron (1880) LR
5 Ex D 319 . . . . 510, 511
Middleton, R v (1873) LR 2 CCR 38 . . .570, 574
Midland Bank plc v Brown Shipley and Co
Ltd [1991] 2 All ER 690 . . . . .174, 194
Midland Bank plc v Greene [1994] 2
FLR 82. 272
Midland Bank Trust Co Ltd v Green [1981]
AC 513 308
Mihalios Xilas, The [1979] 1 WLR 1018 323
Miles v Wakefield Metropolitan District
Council [1987] AC 539. . . . . .339, 342
Millar's Machinery Co Ltd v David Way and
Son (1935) 40 Com Cas 204. 313
Miller v Miller [2011] HCA 9, (2011) 242
CLR 446 (High Court of Australia) 721
Miller v Race (1758) 1 Burr 452, 97 ER
398. 657
Ministre du Budget, des Comptes Publics et
de la Fonction Publique v Accor SA
(Case C-310/09) [2012] STC 438
(ECJ) 411, 705
Ministry of Defence v Ashman [1993] EGLR
102, (1993) 66 P & CR 195. . . . . . . 37, 65, 70,
416, 427, 447, 457, 458
Ministry of Defence v Thompson [1993] 40
EG 148, [1993] 2 EGLR 107. . . . . . . .457, 458
Ministry of Health v Simpson (sub nom
Re Diplock) [1951] AC 251 . . . . 48, 155,
644, 645, 660, 679
Mitchell v Homfray (1881) 8 QBD 587 264
Mitchell v James [2001] 1 All ER 116 281
Moffat v Kazana [1968] 3 All ER 271. 572
Mohamed v Alaga and Co (a firm) [2000]
1 WLR 1815 .331, 721
Molton v Camroux (1849) 4 Ex 17, 154
ER 117. 383
Monks v Poynice Pty Ltd (1987) 11 ACLR 637
(Supreme Court of New South Wales). 81

Monnickendam v Leanse (1923) 39
    TLR 445. . . . . 36, 315, 338, 351
Monro v HMRC [2008] EWCA Civ 306,
    [2009] Ch 69. 406
Montagu's Settlement Trust, Re [1987]
    Ch 264. 648
Moody v Cox and Hatt [1917] 2
    Ch 71. . . . . 275, 276, 495, 496, 503
Moore v Vestry of Fulham [1895] 1
    QB 399 150
Moorgate Tobacco Co Ltd v Philip Morris
    Ltd (No 2) (1984) 156 CLR 414 (High
    Court of Australia) 464, 515
Morgan, R v [2013] EWCA Crim 1307,
    [2014] 1 WLR 3450. 537
Morgan v Ashcroft [1938] 1 KB 49 144,
                                        168, 169, 186, 377
Morgan v Palmer (1824) 2 B and C 729,
    107 ER 584 396
Morgan Guaranty Trust Co of New York
    v Lothian Regional Council 1995 SLT
    299 (Inner House of the Court of Session
    in Scotland). 162
Morley v Laughnan [1893] 1 Ch 736 260
Morris v Tarrant [1917] 2 QB 143 416
Morrison v Coast Finance Ltd (1965) 55
    DLR (2d) 710 (British Columbia Court
    of Appeal) 278
Moses v Macferlan (1760) 2 Burr 1005, 97
    ER 676. . . . . .4, 8, 41, 45, 46, 53,
                        54, 120, 147, 309, 664, 665, 679
Moule v Garrett (1872) LR 7 Exch
    101. 236, 239, 241, 242
Mowlem plc v Stena Line Ports Ltd [2004]
    EWHC 2206 . . . . .134, 314
Moynes v Cooper [1956] 1 QB 439 . . . .575, 576
Muckleston v Brown (1801) 6 Ves Jun 52,
    31 ER 934 . . . . .709, 711
Multiservice Bookbinding Ltd v Marden
    [1979] Ch 84. . . . . .281, 285
Munro v Butt (1858) 8 E and B 738, 120
    ER 275. . . . . .340, 342
Munro v Willmott [1949] 1 KB 295. . . . .82, 304
Murad v Al-Saraj [2005] EWCA Civ 959,
    [2005] WTLR 1573 . . . . . . .423, 425, 426, 434,
        492, 494, 495, 499, 500, 504, 505, 506, 507
Muschinski v Dodds (1985) 160 CLR 583
    (High Court of Australia) 604, 605
Mutual Finance Ltd v John Wetton and Sons
    Ltd [1937] 2 KB 389. . . .204, 207, 217, 230, 231
My Kinda Town Ltd v Soll and Grunts
    Investments [1982] FSR 147. . . . 425, 434, 461
My Kinda Town Ltd v Soll and Grunts
    Investments [1983] RPC 407 (CA). 434
NEC Semi-Conductors v IRC [2006]
    EWCA Civ 25, [2006] STC 606 405
Nash v Inman [1908] 2 KB 1 299
National Bank of Egypt International Ltd
    v Oman Housing Bank SAOC [2002]

EWHC 1760 (Comm), [2003] 1 All ER
    (Comm) 246 . . . . 380, 675, 684, 731
National Carriers Ltd v Panalpina (Northern)
    Ltd [1981] AC 675 356
National Commercial Bank (Jamaica) Ltd
    v Hew [2003] UKPC 51 . . . . .24, 25, 257, 258,
                            259, 264, 266, 270, 271
National Crime Agency v Robb [2014]
    EWHC 4384 (Ch), [2015] EWCA
    Civ 515 . . . . 21, 542, 588, 602, 603, 622
National Motor Mail-Coach Co Ltd, Re
    [1908] 2 Ch 515 244
National Pari-Mutuel Association Ltd v
    R (1930) 47 TLR 110 398
National Provincial Building Society v
    UK [1997] STC 1466 394
National Westminster Bank Ltd v Barclays
    Bank International Ltd [1975] QB 654. . . 667,
                                        669, 671
National Westminster Bank plc v Morgan
    [1985] AC 686. . . . . .258, 263, 264, 265,
                            266, 267, 276, 279
National Westminster Bank plc v Somer
    International (UK) Ltd [2001] EWCA Civ
    970, [2002] 1 All ER 198. . . . . .673, 681, 685,
                                        698, 700
Nayyar v Denton Wilde Sapte [2009]
    EWHC 3218 (QB). 716
Neate v Harding (1851) 6 Exch 349, 155
    ER 577. 572
Nelson, R v [2009] EWCA Crim 1573,
    [2010] QB 678. 536
Nelson v Larholt [1948] 1 KB 339 153,
                    573, 580, 629, 658, 660
Nelson v Nelson (1995) 70 ALJR 47, (1995)
    184 CLR 538 (High Court of
    Australia). 712, 714, 721
Nelson v Rye [1996] 1 WLR 1378 734,
                                    739, 742, 743
Nesté Oy v Lloyd's Bank plc [1983] 2
    Lloyd's Rep 658. .600
Newall v Tomlinson (1871) LR 6 CP 405. 675
Newland Shipping and Forwarding Ltd v
    Toba Trading FZC [2014] EWHC 661
    (Comm). 141, 337
Nichols v Jessup [1986] 1 NZLR 226
    (Court of Appeal of New
    Zealand) 280–1, 282
Nichols v Jessup (No 2) [1986] 1 NZLR
    237 (High Court, New Zealand). 282
Nicholson v Chapman (1793) 2 Hy Bl 254,
    126 ER 536 . . . . 290, 291, 300, 301, 396
Niru Battery Manufacturing Co v Milestone
    Trading Ltd [2002] EWHC 1425 (Comm),
    [2002] 2 All ER (Comm) 705 180,
                            650, 676, 678, 691
Niru Battery Manufacturing Co v Milestone
    Trading Ltd [2003] EWCA Civ 1446,
    [2004] QB 985. . . . . 180, 650, 681, 692

Niru Battery Manufacturing Co v Milestone
 Trading Ltd (No 2) [2004] EWCA Civ 487,
 [2004] 2 All ER (Comm) 289 . . . 243, 249, 694
Nisbet and Pott's Contract, Re [1906]
 1 Ch 386 658
Nocton v Lord Ashburton [1914]
 AC 932 . . . . 487, 504
North British and Mercantile Insurance Co
 v London, Liverpool and Globe Insurance
 Co (1876) 5 Ch D 569 247
Norreys v Zeffert [1939] 2 All ER 187 231–2
Norton v Haggett (1952) 85 A 2d 571
 (Vermont Supreme Court) 238
Norwich Union Fire Insurance Society Ltd
 v Price [1934] AC 455 . . . . 168, 169, 194
Nott and Cardiff Corp, Re [1918] 2
 KB 146. 242
Nottingham University v Fishel [2000]
 ILRL 471 507
Novoship (UK) Ltd v Mikhaylyuk [2014]
 EWCA Civ 908, [2015] 2 WLR 526 435,
                            504, 524, 525, 645, 646
Nu Line Construction Group Pty Ltd v
 Fowler [2014] NSWCA 51 (Court of
 Appeal of New South Wales) 736
Nurdin and Peacock plc v DB Ramsden and
 Co Ltd [1999] 1 WLR 1249 176
OBG Ltd v Allan [2007] UKHL 21, [2008]
 AC 1 . . . . 515, 519, 529, 632, 641, 646
OEM plc v Schneider [2005] EWHC 1072
 (Ch). 642
Oatway, Re [1903] 2 Ch 356. . . . . 620, 622
Ocular Sciences Ltd v Aspect Vision Care
 Ltd [1997] RPC 289 . . . . .511, 519
Official Custodian of Charities v Mackey
 (No 2) [1985] 1 WLR 1308. . . . . 112, 113
Ogilvie v Littleboy (1897) 12 TLR 399
 (CA) 201
Ogilvie v Littleboy (1899) 15 TLR 294
 (HL). 201
O'Kelly v Davies [2014] EWCA Civ
 1606. 718
Ollins v Walters [2008] EWCA Civ 782,
 [2009] Ch 212. 603
O'Neil v Gale [2013] EWHC 644 (Ch). 693
O'Neil v Gale [2013] EWCA Civ 1554
 (CA) 693
One Step (Support) Ltd v Morris-Garner
 [2014] EWHC 2213 (QB). 429, 430,
                                       478, 481
Oom v Bruce (1810) 12 East 225, 104
 ER 87. . . . . .187, 358
Orakpo v Manson Investments Ltd [1978]
 AC 95 . . . . 20, 48, 636, 641
O'Rorke v Bolingbroke (1877) 2 App Cas
 814. 284
O'Sullivan v Management Agency and
 Music Ltd [1985] QB 428 . . . . . .256, 257, 265,
             273, 277, 327, 486, 507, 508, 534

Owen and Co v Cronk [1895] 1 QB
 265. 677
Owen and Gutch v Homan (1853) 4 HLC
 997, 10 ER 752 280
Owen v Tate [1976] QB 402. . . . . . .36, 150, 151,
                      234, 236, 244, 245, 298
Oxley v Hiscock [2004] EWCA Civ 546,
 [2005] QB 211. 597
P v P [1916] 2 IR 400 (Ireland) 311
Pacific National Investments Ltd v Corp of
 the City of Victoria [2004] SCC 75
 (Supreme Court of Canada) 127, 132
Padden v Bevan Ashford (a firm) [2012]
 1 WLR 1759, [2011] EWCA Civ 1616 271
Pagel v Farman [2013] EWHC 2210
 (Comm). 182
Palaniappa Chettiar v Amnasalam Chettiar
 [1962] AC 294. 589
Palmer v Temple (1839) 9 Ad and E 508,
 112 ER 1304 .36, 338
Pan Atlantic Insurance Co Ltd v Pine Top
 Insurance Co Ltd [1995] 1 AC 501 200
Pan Ocean Shipping Co Ltd v Creditcorp Ltd
 (The Trident Beauty) [1994] 1 WLR
 161. . . . . .36, 61, 135, 141, 142, 314,
                                315, 329, 336
Pankhania v Hackney London Borough
 Council [2002] EWHC 2441 (Ch) 197
Pao On v Lau Yiu Long [1980] AC 614
 (PC). 38, 212, 213, 214, 221, 224, 225, 233
Papamichael v National Westminster Bank
 plc [2003] 1 Lloyd's Rep 341 180,
         599, 601, 602, 650, 656, 691, 692, 696
Papous v Gibson-West [2004] EWHC 396 . . . 262
Paragon Finance plc v DB Thakerar and Co
 (a firm) [1999] 1 All ER 400. 524,
                       597, 651, 737, 740, 743
R v Parker [1970] 2 All ER 458 528
Parkingeye Ltd v Somerfield Stores Ltd [2012]
 EWCA Civ 1338, [2013] QB 840 709,
                                     717, 724
Parkinson v College of Ambulance [1923]
 2 KB 1 . . . . . .187, 320, 331, 711, 715, 716, 721
Parsons Bros Ltd v Shea (1968) 53 DLR (2d) 86
 (Newfoundland, Canada) 361
Pascoe v Turner [1979] 1 WLR 431. 521
Patel, R v [1999] EWCA Crim 2268, [2000]
 2 Cr App R (S) 10. . . . . .535, 538
Patel v Mirza [2014] EWCA Civ 1047,
 [2015] 2 WLR 405. . . . . .140, 141, 331,
            354, 355, 591, 718–19, 720, 723–4
Pavey and Matthews Pty Ltd v Paul (1986) 162
 CLR 221 (High Court of Australia) 54,
         99, 102, 144, 315, 351, 352, 353
Paynter v Williams (1833) 1 C and M
 810, 149 ER 626 86
Peacock, Re [1957] Ch 310. 551
Pearce v Brain [1929] 2 KB 310 . . . . . . .369, 385
Pearce v Brooks (1866) LR 1 Ex 213 717

Pearson v Lehman Brothers Finance
  SA [2010] EWHC 2914 (Ch) 581
Peco Arts Inc v Hazlitt Gallery Ltd [1999]
  2 AC 349. 737
Pell Frischmann Engineering Ltd v Bow
  Valley Iran Ltd [2009] UKPC 45, [2011]
  1 WLR 2370 (PC). 429, 430, 480, 484
Penarth Dock Engineering Co Ltd v
  Pounds [1963] 1 Lloyd's Rep 359. 428,
                                    453, 459, 471
Pendlebury v Walker (1841) 4 Y and C Ex
  424, 160 ER 1072 247
Pennell v Deffell (1853) 4 De GM & G
  372, 43 ER 551 622
Peso-Silver Mines Ltd v Cropper (1966)
  58 DLR (2d)1 (Supreme Court of
  Canada). 500
Pesticcio v Niersmans [2004] EWCA Civ
  372, [2004] WTLR 699. . . . . .259, 269
Peter Pan Manufacturing Corp v Corsets
  Silhouette Ltd [1964] 1 WLR 96. . . . .517, 519
Peter Persaud v Pln Versailles
  (1971) 17 WIR 105 (Court of Appeal
  of Guyana) 45
Petrotrade Inc v Smith [2000] 1 Lloyd's
  Rep 486. . . . . 440, 500, 501, 525
Pettkus v Becker [1980] 2 SCR 834 (Supreme
  Court of Canada), (1980) 117 DLR (3d)
  257. . . . . 57, 127, 604
Philip Collins Ltd v Davis [2000] 3 All
  ER 808. . . . . 682, 683, 690, 698
Phillips v Brooks Ltd [1919] 2 KB 243. . .27, 195
Phillips v Homfray (1871) LR 6 Ch App
  R 770. 450
Phillips v Homfray (1883) 24 Ch
  D 439. . . . . .450, 452
Phillips v Homfray [1892] 1 Ch 465 452
Phillips v Phillips (1862) 4 DE GF and
  J 208, 45 ER 1164 602
Phoenix Life Assurance Co, Re (1862) 2 J
  and H 441, 70 ER 1131. 731
Photo Production Ltd v Securicor
  Transport Ltd [1980] AC 827. 136
Pitt v Coomes (1835) 2 Ad and E 459, 111
  ER 478. 211
Pitt v Holt [2010] EWHC 45 (Ch), [2010]
  1 WLR 1199 160
Pitt v Holt; Futter v Futter [2013] UKSC 26,
  [2013] 2 AC 108 . . . . . . .7, 159, 160, 163, 172,
            177, 179, 180, 182, 188, 200, 201, 202
Pitts, Re [1931] 1 Ch 546 546
Pitts v Hunt [1991] 1 QB 24. . . . . .709, 724
Planché v Colburn (1831) 5 Car and P 58,
  172 ER 876, (1831) 8 Bing 14, 131
  ER 305. . . . . 68, 69, 92, 99, 137
Pollard v Bank of England (1871) LR 6 QB
  623. 146
Pollock, Re [1941] 1 Ch 219. 551

Polly Peck International plc (No 2), Re
  [1998] 3 All ER 812 . . . . . . 566, 596, 603, 604
Polly Peck International plc v Nadir (No 2)
  [1992] 4 All ER 769 658
Port Caledonia and the Anna, The [1903]
  P 184. 284
Porter v Latec Finance (Qld) Pty Ltd (1964)
  111 CLR 177 (High Court of
  Australia). 191
Portman Building Society v Dusangh
  [2000] EWCA Civ 142, [2000] 2 All
  ER (Comm) 221 . . . . .280, 281, 283
Portman Building Society v Hamlyn Taylor
  Neck [1998] 4 All ER 202. . . . . . .22, 135, 678
Potisk (1973) 6 SASR 389. 575
Powell v Thompson [1991] 1 NZLR 597
  (High Court, New Zealand) 604
Prager v Blatspiel, Stamp and Heacock
  Ltd [1924] 1 KB 566. . . . . 302, 303, 304
President of India v La Pintada Compania
  Navigacion SA [1985] AC 104 30
Prickett v Badger (1856) 1 CB (NS) 296;
  140 ER 123 . . . . .68, 92
Primary Group (UK) Ltd v Royal Bank
  of Scotland plc [2014] EWHC 1082
  (Ch). 429, 465, 516, 517
Primlake Ltd (In Liquidation) v Matthews
  Associates [2006] EWHC 1227 (Ch),
  [2007] 1 BCLC 666. . . . . .375, 510
Proactive Sports Management Ltd v Rooney
  [2010] EWHC 1807 (QB). 352
Procter and Gamble Philippine
  Manufacturing Corp v Peter Cremer
  GmbH and Co (The Manila) [1988]
  3 All ER 843 78
Professional Cost Management Group Ltd
  v Easynet Ltd, 9 July 2012. 123
Progress Bulk Carriers Ltd v Tube City
  IMS LCC [2012] EWHC 273 (Comm);
  [2012] 1 Lloyd's Rep 501
  (Comm). 208, 216, 218, 220, 232, 233
Prudential Assurance Co Ltd v HMRC
  [2013] EWHC 3249 (Ch), [2014] 2
  CMLR 10. . . . . 31, 32, 404, 406, 409, 695
Pulbrook v Lawes (1876) 1 QBD 284. . .312, 351
Pullan v Koe [1913] 1 Ch 9 659
Q v Q [2008] EWHC 1874 (Fam), [2009] 1
  FLR 935. 591
Quarter Master UK Ltd v Pyke [2005] 1
  BCLC 245 . . . . 497, 498, 508
Queens of the River Steamship Co Ltd v The
  Conservators of the River Thames (1899) 15
  TLR 474. 397
Queensland Mines Ltd v Hudson [1978] 52
  ALJR 379 (PC) 500
RBC Dominion Securities Inc v Dawson
  (1994) 111 DLR (4th) 230 (Newfoundland
  Court of Appeal). 674, 684, 686

RTS Flexible Systems Ltd v Molkerai Alois
    Müller GmbH [2010] UKSC 14,
    [2010] 1 WLR 753 135
Radcliffe v Price (1902) 18 TLR 466 264
Ramsden v Dyson (1866) LR 1 HL 129 520
Ramzan v Brookwide Ltd [2010] EWHC
    2453 (Ch), [2011] 2 All ER 38 . . . . . 453, 454,
                                           455, 459
Randall v Randall [2004] EWHC 2258
    (Ch) 265, 269
Rasmanis v Jurewitsch [1968] 2 NSWLR 166
    (New South Wales) 549
Ratcliffe v Barnard (1871) LR 6 Ch App
    652 659
Reading v Attorney-General [1951] AC
    507 . . . . 48, 470, 500, 528
Receiver for the Metropolitan Police District
    v Croydon Corp [1957] 2 QB 154 242
Redgrave v Hurd (1881) 20 Ch D 1 . . . . . 28, 198
Redwood Music Ltd v Chappell and
    Co Ltd [1982] RPC 109 461
Rees v Hughes [1946] KB 517 296
Reese Silver Mining Co v Smith (1869) LR 4
    HL 64 23
Regal (Hastings) Ltd v Gulliver [1967] 2
    AC 134n 494, 497, 498, 505
Regalian Properties plc v London Docklands
    Development Corp [1995] 1 WLR
    212 . . . . 36, 92, 96, 141, 345, 346, 347
Regional Municipality of Peel v Her Majesty
    the Queen in Right of Canada (1993)
    98 DLR (4th) 180 (Supreme
    Court of Canada) 57, 58, 78, 80, 127
Registered Securities Ltd, Re [1991] 1 NZLR
    545 (New Zealand Court of Appeal) 622
Reid v Rigby [1894] 2 QB 40 642
Reid-Newfoundland Co v Anglo-American
    Telegraph Co [1912] AC 555 (PC) 470
Relfo Ltd v Varsani [2014] EWCA Civ 360,
    [2015] 1 BCLC 14 . . . . 107, 109, 153,
                                           564, 607, 625
Renard Constructions (ME) Pty Ltd v
    Minister for Public Works (1992) 26
    NSWLR 234 (New South Wales Court
    of Appeal) 100, 101, 335
Rhodes, Re (1890) 44 Ch D 94 . . . . 36, 80,
                                           294, 299, 300, 730
Riverlate Properties Ltd v Paul [1975]
    Ch 133 197
Robinson v Harman (1848) 1 Ex 850, 154
    ER 363 468
Robinson v Lane [2010] EWCA Civ
    385 . . . . 338, 347
Roche v Sherrington [1982] 1 WLR 599 276
Rogers v Price (1829) 3 Y and J 28, 148
    ER 1090 297
Rolled Steel Products (Holdings) Ltd v
    British Steel Corp [1986] Ch 246 648

Rookes v Barnard [1964] AC 1129 432,
                                           444, 467
Rose v AIB Group (UK) plc [2003]
    EWHC 1737 (Ch), [2003] 1 WLR 2791 . . . 684
Rosenfeldt v Olson (1986) 25 DLR (4th) 472
    (British Columbia Court of Appeal) 532–3
Rover International Ltd v Cannon Film
    Sales Ltd (No 3) [1989] 1 WLR 912 . . 84, 101,
    102, 126, 158, 188, 317, 318, 320, 337, 369, 679
Rowe, Re [1904] 2 KB 483 235
Rowe v Vale of White Horse District
    Council [2003] EWHC 388 (Admin)
    [2003] 1 Lloyd's Rep 418 . . . 77, 78, 81, 86, 87,
                            88, 120, 122–3, 124, 130, 177
Rowland v Divall [1923] KB 500 . . . . 106, 319, 320
Roxborough v Rothmans of Pall Mall
    Australia Ltd [2001] HCA 68, (2001)
    208 CLR 516, [2002] 185 ALR 335,
    (2002) 76 ALJR 203 (High Court of
    Australia) 41, 53, 54, 118,
                            138, 139, 140, 321, 326, 466, 703
Roy v Kensington and Chelsea and
    Westminster Family Practitioner
    Committee [1992] 1 AC 624 405
Royal Bank of Australia, Robinson's
    Executors, Re (1856) 6 De G M and G
    572, 43 ER 1356 247
Royal Bank of Scotland v Etridge (No 2)
    [2001] UKHL 44, [2002] 2 AC 773 184,
    199, 200, 256, 257, 258, 259, 260, 261, 262,
                            263, 264, 266, 267, 269, 271
Royal Boskalis Westminster NV v
    Mountain [1999] QB 674 207
Royal Brompton Hospital NHS Trust v
    Hammond [2002] UKHL 14, [2002] 1
    WLR 1397 . . . . 249, 250
Royal Brunei Airlines Sdn Bhd v Tan
    [1995] 2 AC 378 (PC) 522, 523, 651
Royse, Re [1985] Ch 22 . . . . 546, 551
Ruabon Steamship Company Ltd v London
    Assurance Company Ltd [1900] AC 6 114
Rural Municipality of Storthoaks v Mobil
    Oil Canada Ltd (1975) 55 DLR (3d) 1
    (Supreme Court of Canada) 679, 685, 687
Russell v Smith [1958] 1 QB 27 575
Russell-Cooke Trust Co v Prentis
    [2002] EWHC 2227 (Ch), [2003] 2 All
    ER 478 622
Ruxley Electronics and Construction Ltd v
    Forsyth [1996] AC 344 476
S, Re [1996] 1 WLR 235 554
S and W Process Engineering Ltd v
    Cauldron Foods Ltd [2005] EWHC 153
    (TCC) 134–5, 314
Sabemo Pty Ltd v North Sydney Municipal
    Council [1977] 2 NSWLR 880 (New
    South Wales) 91, 92, 99, 348
Sachs v Miklos [1948] 2 KB 23 303

Sadler v Evans (1766) 4 Burr 1984, 98
     ER 34. . . . . .53, 675
Safeway Stores Ltd v Twigger [2010]
     EWHC 11 (Comm), [2012] 2 Lloyd's
     Rep 39 716
Sale, R v [2013] EWCA Crim 1306,
     [2014] 1 WLR 663. 538
Salvation Army Trustee Co Ltd v West
     Yorkshire Metropolitan County Council
     (1980) P & CR 179 . . . . 90, 350, 520, 521
Sandher v Pearson [2013] EWCA Civ
     1822. . . . . 135, 636, 718
Sandvik Australia Pty Ltd v Commonwealth
     of Australia (1989) 89 ALR 213 (Federal
     Court of Australia) 387
Sargeant v National Westminster Bank plc
     (1990) 61 P & CR 518. 495
Sargood Bros v The Commonwealth (1910)
     11 CLR 258 (High Court of Australia). . . .396
Saronic Shipping Co Ltd v Huron Liberian
     Co [1979] 1 Lloyd's Rep 341 171
Saronic Shipping Co Ltd v Huron Liberian
     Co [1980] 2 Lloyd's Rep 26 (CA). 171
Satnam Investments Ltd v Dunlop Heywood
     and Co Ltd [1999] 3 All ER 652. . . . . 519, 646
Saunders v Anglia Building Society [1971]
     AC 1004 196
Saunders v Edwards [1987] 1 WLR 1116. . . .710
Saunders and Co (a firm) v Hague [2004]
     2 NZLR 475 (New Zealand High
     Court) 694
Saunders v Vautier (1841) 4 Beav 115; 49
     ER 282. 19
Scarisbrick v Parkinson (1869) 20 LT
     175. . . . . 97, 99, 351, 353
Scottish Equitable plc v Derby [2000] 3 All
     ER 793. . . . . .681, 683
Scott v Pattison [1923] 2 KB 723 351
Scottish Equitable plc v Derby [2001]
     3 All ER 818 (CA). . . .639, 681, 682, 683, 684,
                    687, 690, 698, 682, 683, 684,
                    687, 690, 698, 699
Seager v Copydex Ltd (No 1) [1967] 1 WLR
     923, [1967] 2 All ER 415. . . 425, 517, 518, 519
Seager v Copydex Ltd (No 2) [1969] 1 WLR
     809. . . . . .517, 518
Sebel Products Ltd v Commissioners of
     Customs and Excise [1949] Ch 409 . . .141, 405
R v Secretary of State for Transport, ex parte
     Factortame [2000] 1 AC 524 390
R (Child Poverty Action Group) v Secretary
     of State for Work and Pensions
     [2010] UKSC 54, [2011] 2 AC 15. 388
Securities and Exchange Commission v
     Chenery Corp (1943) 318 US 80
     (United States Supreme Court). 491
Selous Street Properties Ltd v Oronel
     Fabrics Ltd (1984) 270 EG 643. 241

Semco Salvage and Marine Pte Ltd v
     Lancer Navigation Co Ltd [1997]
     AC 455 306
Sempra Metals Ltd v IRC [2007] UKHL 34,
     [2008] 1 AC 561 . . . . .7, 30, 31, 32, 41, 61,
                    66, 67, 69, 71, 73, 74, 75, 97,
                    116, 118, 128, 130, 146, 172, 188
Serious Fraud Office v Lexi Holdings plc
     [2008] EWCA Crim 1443, [2009] QB
     376. . . . . .537, 623
Serious Organised Crime Agency v Perry
     [2012] UKSC 35, [2013] 1 AC 182. 535,
                    537, 542
Severn Trent Water Ltd v Barnes [2004]
     EWCA Civ 570 . . . . 428, 449, 454
Shadrokh-Cigari, R v [1988] Crim LR 465. . .576
Shallcross v White (1850) 12 Beav 558, 50
     ER 1174. 299
Shalson v Russo [2003] EWHC 1637 (Ch),
     [2005] Ch 281 . . . . .22, 600, 602, 603,
                    604, 608, 613, 623, 625, 626, 628
Sharab v Prince Al-Waleed Bin Talal
     Bin Abdul-Aziz Al-Saud [2012] EWHC
     1798 (Ch), [2012] 2 CLC 612 . . . . . . 123, 135
Sharma v Simposh Ltd [2011] EWCA Civ
     1383, [2013] Ch 23 . . . 333, 338, 339, 347, 377
Sharpe, Re [1980] 1 WLR 219 604
Sharpley v Louth and East Coast Ry Co
     (1876) 2 Ch D 663 .28
Shaw v Shaw [1965] 1 WLR 537 330
Shilliday v Smith 1998 SLT 976 (Scottish
     Court of Sessions). .45
Shogun Finance Ltd v Hudson [2003]
     UKHL 62, [2004] 1 AC 919 195
Siboen and the Sibotre, The [1976] 1 Lloyd's
     Rep 293 . . . . 212, 213, 221, 224, 468
Sidney Balson Investment Trust Ltd v E
     Karmios and Co (London) Ltd [1956]
     1 QB 529 667
Sigsworth, Re [1935] 1 Ch 89 . . . . .548, 551
Silverwood v Silverwood (1987) 74 P &
     CR 453. 590, 591, 719
Simmons v Wilmot (1800) 3 Esp 91, 170
     ER 549. 298
Simons, R v (1993) 98 Cr App R 100. 538
Simpson v Eggington (1855) 10 Ex 845,
     156 ER 683 235
Simpson v Simpson [1989] Fam
     Law 20. . . . . 381, 382, 383
Simpson v Simpson [1992] 1 FLR 601 266
Sims and Co v Midland Railway Co [1913]
     1 KB 103 304
Sinclair v Brougham [1914] AC 398. 16,
                    46, 48, 372, 373, 374, 540, 563, 585,
                    602, 612, 613, 616, 620, 621, 732
Sinclair Investment Holdings SA v Versailles
     Trade Finance Ltd [2005] EWCA Civ
     722. 599

Sinclair Investment Holdings SA v
    Versailles Trade Finance Ltd [2011]
    EWCA Civ 347, [2012]
    1 AC 776 . . . .497, 506, 511, 512, 523, 619, 658
Sine Nomine, The [2002] 1 Lloyd's Rep
    805. 478
Singh v Ali [1960] AC 167 579
Singlar v Bashir [2002] EWHC 883 (Ch). . . .281
Sivaraman, R v [2008] EWCA Crim 1736,
    [2009] 1 Cr App R (S) 469 537
Skeate v Beale (1841) 11 Ad and E 983, 113
    ER 688. 212
Skibinski v Community Living British
    Columbia [2010] BCSC 1500, (2010)
    BCLR (5th) 271 (Supreme Court of
    British Columbia) 299
Skyring v Greenwood (1825) 4 B and C
    281, 107 ER 1064 669
Slater v Burnley Corp (1888) 59 LT
    636. 396
Sledmore v Dalby (1996) 72 P & CR
    196. 521
Smalley v Bracken Partners [2003] EWCA
    Civ 1875, [2004] WTLR 599. . . . . . . .567, 570
Smith, R v [2013] EWCA Crim 502, [2014]
    1 WLR 898 541
Smith v Bromley (1760) 2 Doug 696n, 99
    ER 441. . . . . .287, 714
Smith v Charlick (William) Ltd (1924) 34
    CLR 38 (High Court of Australia) . . . 215, 233
Smith v Cooper [2010] EWCA Civ 722,
    [2010] 2 FLR 1521 . . . . 271, 272
Smith v Cuff (1817) 6 M and S 160, 105 ER
    1203. . . . . .287, 720
Smith v Hughes (1871) LR 6 QB 597. 197
Smith v Jenkins (1969) 119 CLR 397 (High
    Court of Australia) 709
Smith New Court Securities Ltd v Citibank
    NA [1997] AC 254 463
Smith New Court Securities Ltd v
    Scrimgeour Vickers (Asset
    Management) Ltd [1994] 1 WLR 1271,
    [1994] 2 BCLC 212 (CA) 22, 24, 25, 26
Smith New Court Securities Ltd v Scrimgeour
    Vickers (Asset Management) Ltd [1997] AC
    254 (HL) 21, 26, 197, 327
Snowden, ex p (1881) 17 Ch D 44 248
Snowdon v Davis (1808) 1 Taunt 359, 127
    ER 872. 676
Société des Hôtels Réunis v Hawker (1913)
    29 TLR 578 230
Solle v Butcher [1950] 1 KB 671. . . . . . .195, 272
Somes v British Empire Shipping Co (1860) 8
    HLC 838, 11 ER 459. 212
Sopov v Kane Constructions Pty Ltd (No 2)
    [2009] VSCA 141 (Supreme Court of
    Victoria) 98, 102, 137, 334
Sorrell v Finch [1977] AC 728 675
Sorrell v Paget [1950] 1 KB 252 . . . . . . .300, 306

South Australian Cold Stores Ltd v Electricity
    Trust of South Australia (1957) 98 CLR 65
    (High Court of Australia) 54
South of Scotland Electricity Board v
    British Oxygen Co Ltd (No 2) [1959]
    1 WLR 587 . . . . .253, 398
South Tyneside Metropolitan BC v Svenska
    International plc [1995] 1 All ER
    545. . . . . 58, 388, 674, 689, 691, 694, 698
Space Investments Ltd v Canadian Imperial
    Bank of Commerce Trust Co (Bahamas)
    Ltd [1986] 1 WLR 1072 (PC) 617, 627
Spanish Government v North of England
    Steamship Co Ltd (1938) 54 TLR 852 212
Spaul v Spaul [2014] EWCA Civ 679. 182,
    308, 310
Spectrum Plus Ltd, Re [2005] UKHL 41,
    [2005] 2 AC 680 .184
Spence v Crawford [1939] 3 All
    ER 271. . . . . 23, 25, 26
Spiers and Pond Ltd v Finsbury Metropolitan
    Borough Council (1956) 1 Ryde's Rating
    Cases 219. 678
Spiers and Son Ltd v Troup (1915) 84
    LJKB 1986. 246
Springform Inc v Toy Brokers
    [2002] FSR 776 440
Springer v Great Western Railway Co
    [1921] 1 KB 257 .304
St John Shipping Corp v Joseph Rank Ltd
    [1957] 1 QB 267 . . . . 526, 545, 547, 715
Stack v Dowden [2007] UKHL 17, [2007] 2
    AC 432 . . . . 583, 588, 589, 597
Stadium Capital Holdings v St Marylebone
    Properties Co plc [2010] EWCA
    Civ 952 . . . . 453, 454, 459
Standard Chartered Bank v Pakistan
    National Shipping Corp (No 2) [2003]
    1 AC 959. 198
Stapylton Fletcher Ltd, Re [1994] 1
    WLR 1181. . . . . 566, 570, 571
Starglade Properties Ltd v Nash [2010]
    EWCA Civ 1314 .523
State Bank of New South Wales v Swiss
    Bank (1995) 39 NSWLR 350 (New South
    Wales Court of Appeal) 683
Steam Saw Mills Co Ltd v Baring Bros Co
    Ltd [1922] 1 Ch 244 134
Steele v Tardiani (1946) 72 CLR 386 (High
    Court of Australia) 342
Steele v Williams (1953) 8 Ex 625, 155
    ER 1502. . . . . .205, 398
Steenkamp and Steenkamp, ex p (1952)
    (1) SA 744 (T) (South Africa). 548
Steeples v Lea [1998] 1 FLR 138. 268
Steinberg v Scala (Leeds) Ltd [1923] 2
    Ch 452. 148, 384, 385
Stenia v Hutchinson [2006] EWCA Civ 1551,
    [2007] ICR 445 670

Stephens v Avery [1988] Ch 449 . . . . . . 464, 515

Stilk v Meyrick (1809) 2 Camp 317, 170
    ER 1168. 214

Stockloser v Johnson [1954] 1 QB 476. 339

Stocks v Wilson [1913] 2 KB 235. . . . . .599, 729

Stocznia Gsanska SA v Latvian Shipping
    Co [1998] 1 WLR 574. . . . . .310, 315, 316,
        317, 318, 324, 328, 333

Stoke-on-Trent City Council v W and J
    Wass Ltd [1988] 1 WLR 1406 . . .447, 449–50,
        461, 465, 466

Stone and Rolls Ltd v Moore Stephens
    [2009] UKHL 39, [2009] AC 1391. . . .709, 716,
        718, 719, 724

Strand Electric and Engineering Co Ltd v
    Brisford Entertainments Ltd [1952]
    QB 246 . . . . 428, 449, 459, 460

Straton v Rastall (1788) 2 Term Rep 366, 100
    ER 197. 41

Strickland v Turner (1852) 7 Ex 208, 155
    ER 919. 196

Strydom v Vendside Ltd [2009] EWHC
    2130 (QB) 281, 285

Sumpter v Hedges [1898] 1 QB 673. 69,
        95, 340, 341, 342

Surrey CC v Bredero Homes Ltd [1993] 1
    WLR 1361. . . . . . . 422, 468, 470, 473, 482, 484

Sutherland v Caxton [1936] Ch 323. 438

Sutton v Mischon de Reya [2003] EWHC
    3166 (Ch) 716

Swindle v Harrison [1997] 4 All ER
    705. 419, 487, 504, 505

Swordheath Properties Ltd v Tabet [1979]
    1 WLR 285 . . . . .458, 459

TFL Management Services Ltd v Lloyds TSB
    Bank plc [2013] EWCA Civ 1415,
    [2014] 1 WLR 2006. . . . . . . 109, 111, 114, 115

TH Knitwear (Wholesale) Ltd, Re [1988]
    Ch 275. 636

TRA Global Pty Ltd v Kebakoska [2011]
    VSC 480 (Victoria) 666

TSB Bank plc v Camfield [1995] 1
    WLR 430. . . . . 23, 24, 28, 271, 272

Tahar Benourad v Compass Group plc
    [2010] EWHC 1882 (QB). 345, 349

Tang Man Sit v Capacious Investments Ltd
    [1996] AC 514 (PC) 438, 439, 440, 445

Tappenden v Randall (1801) 2 Bos and Pul
    467, 126 ER 1388 723

Target Holdings Ltd v Redferns (a firm)
    [1996] AC 421. . . . . .419, 487

Tate v Williamson (1866) LR 2 Ch
    App 55. . . . . .276, 502

Taylor v Bhail [1996] CLC
    377. . . . . 47, 330, 331, 723

Taylor v Blakelock (1886) 32 Ch D 560. 659

Taylor v Bowers (1876) 1 QBD 291 . . . .353, 719

Taylor v Chester (1868–69) LR 4
    QB 309 718

Taylor v Laird (1856) 25 LJ Exch 320 38,
        76, 124, 301

Taylor v Plumer (1815) 3 M and S 562, 105
    ER 721. 615

Taylor Fashions Ltd v Liverpool Victoria
    Trustees Co Ltd [1982] QB 133 520

Taylor (Robert) v Motability Finance Ltd
    [2004] EWHC 2619 (Comm). 100, 134,
        136, 137, 140, 311, 314, 316, 328, 334,
        335, 336

Teacher v Calder [1899] AC 451 468

Telemachus, The [1957] P 47. 306

Tennent v The City of Glasgow Bank
    and Liquidators (1879) 4 App Cas 615 27

Test Claimants in the FII Group Litigation v
    HMRC [2008] EWHC 2893 (Ch), [2009]
    STC 254. . . . . 409, 410, 693

Test Claimants in the FII Group Litigation v
    HMRC [2010] EWCA Civ 103, [2010]
    STC 1251. 693

Test Claimants in the FII Group Litigation
    v HMRC [2012] UKSC 19, [2012] 2
    AC 337 . . . . 7, 9, 120, 128, 130, 389, 390, 400,
        401–2, 403, 404, 406, 408, 409, 411,
        693, 737

Test Claimants in the FII Group Litigation
    v Commissioners for HMRC (No 2) [2014]
    EWHC 4302 (Ch). . . . 12, 32, 60, 74, 185, 390,
        391, 392, 401, 408, 409, 410, 682, 683,
        688, 690, 693, 695, 696

Test Claimants in the FII Group Litigation
    v HMRC (Case C-362/12) [2014]
    2 CMLR 33 . . . . 409, 737

Test Claimants in the FII Group Litigation v
    IRC (Note) (Case C-446/04) [2012] 2 AC
    436 (ECJ). 403

Thackwell v Barclays Bank plc [1986]
    1 All ER 676 710

Thomas v Brown (1876) 1 QBD 714 . . . 315, 351

Thomas v Houston Corbett and Co [1969]
    NZLR 151 (Court of Appeal, New
    Zealand) 694

Thomas Witter Ltd v TBP Industries Ltd
    [1996] 2 All ER 573 . . . . 27, 199

Thompson v Foy [2009] EWHC 1076 (Ch),
    [2010] 1 P & CR 16 . . . . .261, 264

Thomson, Re [1930] 1 Ch 203 493

Thomson v Clydesdale Bank [1893]
    AC 282 659

Thomson v Eastwood (1877) 2 App
    Cas 215 496

Thorne v Motor Trade Association [1937]
    AC 797 . . . . .207, 229

Thorner v Major [2009] UKHL 18, [2009]
    1 WLR 776 . . . . .581, 606

Tilley's Will Trusts, Re [1967] 1 Ch
    1179. . . . . 619, 620, 625

Ting Siew May v Boon Long Choo [2014]
    SGCA 28 (Singapore Court of Appeal) . . .724

Tinker v Tinker [1970] P 136..... 589, 591, 712

Tinline v White Cross Insurance
  Association Ltd [1921] 3 KB 327 544

Tinsley v Milligan [1992] Ch 310 (CA) 714

Tinsley v Milligan [1994] 1 AC 340
  (HL).... 16, 331, 557, 582, 583, 588, 589, 590,
      591, 592, 693, 710, 712, 713, 714, 718,
      719, 723, 725

Tito v Waddell (No 2) [1977] Ch 106 429,
      469, 471, 493, 495

Tomlinson v Bentall (1826) 5 B and C 737,
  108 ER 738 298

R v Tower Hamlets LBC, ex p Chetnik
  Developments Ltd [1988] AC 858 .... 48, 161

Townson v Wilson (1808) 1 Camp 396, 170
  ER 997.............................676

Transvaal and Delagoa Bay Investment Co
  Ltd v Atkinson [1944] 1 All ER 579..... 675,
      676, 677

Transvaal Land Co v New Belgium
  (Transvaal) Land and Development
  Co [1914] 2 Ch 488 504

Tribe v Tribe [1996] Ch 107............. 133,
      353, 355, 589, 591, 714, 719, 720

Trident Beauty, The, See Pan Ocean
  Shipping Co Ltd v Creditcorp Ltd

Trustee of the Property of FC Jones and Sons
  (a firm) v Jones [1997] Ch 159...40, 557, 561,
      613, 614, 615, 629, 632, 642, 643

Trustor AB v Smallbone (No 2) [2001] 1
  WLR 1177......................646, 647

Tufton v Sperni (1952) 2 TLR 516........279

Turkey v Awadh [2005] EWCA Civ 382,
  [2005] 2 P & CR 29 ....263, 265, 267

Turriff Construction Ltd v Regalia Knitting
  Mills [1972] EG (Dig) 257 350

Turvey v Dentons (1923) Ltd [1953]
  1 QB 218............................179

Twentieth Century Fox Film Corporation v
  Harris [2013] EWHC 159 (Ch) 461

Twinsectra Ltd v Yardley [2002] UKHL
  12, [2002] 2 AC 164 ....522, 523, 524,
      583, 594, 595, 651, 652, 653, 710

Twyford v Manchester Corp [1946]
  Ch 236.........................208, 396

Tyrrell v Bank of London (1862) 10 HL
  Cas 26 511

UCB Corporate Services Ltd v Williams
  [2002] EWCA Civ 555, [2003]
  1 P & CR 12 261

UCB Group Ltd v Hedworth [2003] EWCA
  Civ 1717 261

Ultraframe (UK) Ltd v Fielding [2005]
  EWHC 1638 (Ch), [2006] FSR 16 .... 493, 498,
      500, 522, 525, 646, 651

United Australia Ltd v Barclays Bank Ltd
  [1941] AC 1 ....39, 46, 47, 170, 331, 337,
      438, 444, 445, 446, 447, 452, 460, 466, 728

United Overseas Bank v Jiwani [1976] 1
  WLR 964...................667, 670, 671

United Pan-Europe Communications NV
  v Deutsche Bank AG [2002] 2 BCLC
  461............................505, 519

Unity Joint Stock Mutual Banking
  Association v King, The (1858) 25
  Beav 72, 53 ER 563 521

Universe Tankships Inc of Monrovia v
  International Transport Workers Federation
  (The Universe Sentinel) [1983] 1 AC
  366................143, 204, 206, 207, 213,
      216, 218, 219, 222, 224, 225, 227, 442

Universe Sentinel, The See above Universe
  Tankships Inc of Monrovia v International
  Transport Workers Federation

University of Canterbury v Attorney-General
  [1995] 1 NZLR 78 (High Court of New
  Zealand) 173, 181

University of Nottingham v Fishel [2001]
  RPC 367 478

Unwin v Leaper (184) 1 Man and G 747,
  133 ER 533 231

Uren v First National Home Finance Ltd
  [2005] EWHC 2529 (Ch) 58, 60, 104, 130

Uzinterimpex JSC v Standard Bank
  plc [2008] EWCA Civ 819 647

Vadasz v Pioneer Concrete (SA) Pty Ltd
  (1995) 184 CLR 102 (High Court of
  Australia)...........................271

Vale v Armstrong [2004] EWHC 1160;
  [2004] WTLR 1471...............267, 269

Valencina v Llupar [2012] EWCA
  Civ 396........................345, 346

Valentini v Canali (1889) 24 QBD
  166.....................369, 386, 387

Van den Berg v Giles [1979] 2 NZLR 111
  (New Zealand High Court)..............86

Vandervell v IRC [1967] 2 AC 291.........583

Vandervell's Trusts (No 2), Re [1974]
  Ch 269.............................592

Vaughan, ex p (1884) 14 QBD 25 436

Vedatech Corp v Crystal Decisions (UK)
  Ltd [2002] EWHC 818 (Ch).............54

Vellino v Chief Constable of Greater
  Manchester Police [2001] EWCA Civ
  1249, [2002] 1 WLR 218...............724

Ventura v Kyle 214 WL 6687499
  (Minnesota District Court).............467

Vercoe v Rutland Fund Management Ltd
  [2010] EWHC 424 (Ch) 430, 480, 515,
      517, 518

Verschures Creameries Ltd v Hull and
  Netherlands Steamship Co Ltd [1921]
  2 KB 608 447

Vestergaard Fradsen A/S v Bestnet Europe
  Ltd [2013] UKSC 31, [2013] 1 WLR
  1556.......... 464, 515, 516, 519, 522, 650

Vita Food Products Inc v Unus Shipping
  Co Ltd [1939] AC 277 711
Vyse v Foster (1872) 8 Ch App 309 432
WWF World Wide Fund for Nature v
  World Wrestling Federation
  Entertainment Inc [2002] FSR 32. 478
WWF World Wide Fund for Nature v
  World Wrestling Federation Entertainment
  Inc [2007] EWCA Civ 286, [2008] 1 WLR
  445. . . . . 425, 429, 478, 479, 484
Wacker, R v [2003] QB 1207 . . . . .330, 711
Waikato Regional Airport Ltd v Attorney-
  General [2003] UKPC 50, [2004]
  3 NZLR 1 (PC) 402
Walford v Miles [1992] AC 128 349
Walker, Re [1905] 1 Ch 160 381
Walker v Boyle [1982] 1 WLR 495. 199
Walsh v Shanahan [2013] EWCA
  Civ 411 . . . . 464, 465, 515, 518
Walsh v Singh [2009] EWHC
  3219 (Ch) 150
Walstab v Spottiswode (1846) 15 M and
  W 501, 153 ER 952 312
Walter v James (1871) LR 6 Exch 124 . . . 238, 252
Walter J Schmidt & Co, Re 298 F 314, 316
  (1923) (New York) 622
Waltons Stores (Interstate) Ltd v Maher
  (1988) 164 CLR 387 (High Court of
  Australia). 350, 520
Wambo Coal Co Pty Ltd v Ariff [2007]
  NSWSC 589 (Supreme Court of New
  South Wales). 599
Ward and Co v Wallis [1900] 1 QB 675 . . . .73, 162
Warman v Southern Counties Car Finance
  Co Ltd [1949] 2 KB 576 319
Warman International Ltd v Dwyer (1995)
  182 CLR 544, (1995) 128 ALR 201 (High
  Court of Australia) 426, 427, 435, 438,
                  487, 502, 505, 507, 509, 515
Wasada Pty Ltd v State Rail Authority of New
  South Wales (No 2) [2003] NSWSC 987
  (Supreme Court of New South Wales). . . .120
Watson, Laidlaw and Co Ltd v Pott, Cassels
  and Williamson (1914) 31 RPC 104. 422,
                  425, 428, 437, 439
Way v Latilla [1937] 3 All ER 759 100
Waya, R v [2012] UKSC 51, [2013] 1 AC
  294. . . . . 535, 537, 538
Waymell v Reed (1794) 5 Term Rep 599,
  101 ER 335 711
Weatherby v Banham (1832) 5 Car and P
  228; 172 ER 950 86
Webb v Chief Constable of Merseyside
  Police [2000] All ER 209. 542
Wee Chiaw Sek Anna v Ng Li-Ann
  Genevieve [2013] SGCA 36 (Singapore
  Court of Appeal). 124, 599
Wehner v Dene Steam Shipping Co [1905]
  2 KB 92 323

Welby v Drake (1821) 1 C and P 557, 171
  ER 1315. 236
Weld-Blundell v Synott [1940] 2 KB
  107. . . . . 166, 179, 667
Westdeutsche Landesbank Girozentrale v
  Islington London Borough Council [1994]
  4 All ER 890 . . . . 371, 372,
                  375, 377, 388, 397, 694, 735
Westdeutsche Landesbank Girozentrale v
  Islington London Borough Council [1994] 1
  WLR 938 (CA) 372, 373, 375,
                  377, 397, 618, 732
Westdeutsche Landesbank Girozentrale v
  Islington London Borough Council [1996]
  AC 669 (HL). 7, 16, 30, 31, 46, 47, 53, 56,
    61, 328, 350, 373, 374, 524, 530, 552, 563,
    567, 571, 578, 578, 579, 581, 582, 583,
    585, 588, 595, 598, 599, 600, 601, 602,
    603, 604, 605, 617, 654, 655, 728,
                  732, 735
Westminster Bank Ltd v Lee [1956]
  Ch 7. 602
West Sussex Constabulary's Widows,
  Children and Benevolent Fund
  [1971] Ch 1. 593
Whelpdale's case (1605) 5 Co Rep 119a 21, 204
Whincup v Hughes (1871)
  LR 6 CP 78 . . . . 321, 323, 324, 357, 358
White v Jones [1995] 2 AC 207 491
White v Shortall [2006] NSWSC 1379
  (New South Wales Court of Appeal) 581
Whitham v Bullock [1939] 2 KB 81 239
Whittaker v Campbell [1984] QB
  318 (CA) 24, 48
Whittle Movers Ltd v Hollywood Express
  Ltd [2009] EWCA Civ 1189 . . . . .135, 344
Wild v Simpson [1919] 2 KB 544. 712
Wilkes v Spooner [1911] 2 KB 473 660
Wilkinson v Lloyds (1854) 7 QB 25, 115
  ER 398. 335
William Lacey (Hounslow) Ltd v Davis
  [1957] 1 WLR 932. . . . . 46, 91, 136, 345
William Sindall plc v Cambridgeshire
  CC [1994] 1 WLR 1016 . . . . 195, 199, 274
William Whiteley Ltd v R (1910) 101 LT
  741. 395
Williams v Bayley (1866) LR 1 HL
  200. . . . . 229, 230, 231, 233
Williams v Central Bank of Nigeria
  [2014] UKSC 10, [2014]
  AC 1189 . . . . .522, 524, 597,
                  645, 650, 651, 692, 740, 741
Williams v Roffey Bros and Nicholls
  (Contractors) Ltd [1991] 1 QB 1 . . 214–15, 484
Willis Faber Enthoven (PTY) Ltd v Receiver
  of Revenue 1992 (4) SA 202 (A)
  (Appellate Division of the Supreme
  Court of South Africa) 162
Willmott v Barber (1880) 15 Ch D 96 90

Wilson v First County Trust Ltd (No 2)
[2003] UKHL 40, [2004] 1 AC 816 . . . . .352, 732
Wilson v Hurstanger Ltd [2007] EWCA
Civ 299, [2001] 1 WLR 2351 23
Wilson v Ray (1839) 10 Ad and E 82, 113
ER 32. 287
Winson, The, See China Pacific SA v Food
Corp of India (The Winson)
Woolwich Equitable Building Society v Inland
Revenue Commissioners [1993] AC
70. . . . . 7, 57, 61, 127, 149, 205, 206, 231,
253, 371, 380, 390, 393, 394, 395, 396, 398,
399, 400, 401, 402, 403, 404, 406, 408, 409,
410, 411, 412, 579, 693, 695, 703, 705, 731
Wrexham, Mold and Connah's Quay
Railway Co [1899] 1 Ch 440. 655
Wright v Carter [1903] 1 Ch 27 . . .256, 264, 269,
275, 502, 503
Wright v National Westminster Bank plc
[2014] EWHC 3158 (Ch) 201, 202
Wrotham Park Estate Co Ltd v Parkside
Homes Ltd [1974] 1 WLR 798. . . 429, 453, 471,
472, 473, 474, 477, 479, 483, 518, 748
Wuhan Guoyu Logistics Group Co Ltd v
Emporiki Bank [2013] EWCA Civ 1679,
[2014] 1 Lloyd's Rep 273 134

Yam Seng Pte Ltd v International Trade
Corporation Ltd [2013] EWHC 111
(QB) 349
Yardley v Arnold (1842) Car and M 434,
174 ER 577 114
Yaxley v Gotts [2000] Ch 162. 597
Yearworth v North Bristol NHS Trust
[2009] EWCA Civ 37, [2010] QB 1 305
Yeoman Credit Ltd v Apps [1962] 2
QB 508 320
Yeoman's Row Management Ltd v
Cobbe [2008] UKHL 55,
[2008] 1 WLR 1752. . . . . 7, 37,
59, 60, 76, 99, 126, 312, 333,
345, 348, 597
Yorkshire Bank plc v Tinsley [2004] EWCA
Civ 816, [2004] 1 WLR 2380 260,
272, 280, 282
Zamet v Hyman [1961] 1 WLR 1442. 28,
268, 271
Zinga, R v [2014] EWCA Crim 52, [2014]
1 WLR 2228 535
Zouch de Abbot v Parsons (1763) 3 Burr
1794, 97 ER 1103 385
Zuhal K and Selin, The [1987]
Lloyd's Rep 151. .298

TABLE OF LEGISLATION

AUSTRALIA

Builders Licensing Act 1971 144
Crimes Act 1958
  s 9AD 547
New South Wales Frustrated Contracts Act
  1978 360
South Australian Frustrated Contracts Act
  1988 360

CANADA

British Columbian Frustrated Contracts Act
  1974 . . . . .360, 367
  s 5(1) 367
  s 5(3) 367
  s 5(4) 367
Newfoundland Frustrated Contracts
  Act 1956 361

EUROPE

European Convention of Human
  Rights 394, 516, 532, 536
  Art 6 542
  Art 6(2) 532
First Protocol, Art 1 . . . . .411, 537

INTERNATIONAL INSTRUMENTS

International Convention on Salvage 1989
  art 23(1) 736
UNIDROIT Principles of International
  Commercial Contracts (2010)
  art 3.2.7(1)(a) 286

ISRAEL

Contract Law (General Part) 1973
  s 31 725

NEW ZEALAND

Illegal Contracts Act 1970
  s 7 725
Judicature Act 1908
  s 94A 162

  s 94B 679, 687, 694
Judicature Amendment Act 1958
  s 2 . . . . .162, 679

UNITED KINGDOM

Administration of Estates Act 1925 552
Apportionment Act 1870 342–3
  s 2 342
Annuity Act 1777 371
Annuity Act 1813 371
Bill of Rights 1689 .390
  Art 4 389
Bribery Act 2010 716
  s 2 528
Civil Evidence Act 1968
  s 11 547
Civil Jurisdiction and Judgments Act 1982 . .250
Civil Liability Contribution Act
  1978 .248–51, 736
  s 1(1) 248
  s 1(2) 249
  s 1(3) 249
  s 1(4) 249
  s 2(1) 248
  s 2(2) 248
  s 6(1) 248, 249
Civil Procedure Rules 1998 (SI 1998/3132)
  r 54(3)(2) 405
  r 54(5)(3) 405
Common Law Procedure Act 1852 45
  s 3 58
Companies Act 2006
  s 39(1) 731
  s 40 380
  s 51(1) 369
  s 175(1) 493
  s 175(2) 496, 497
Competition Act 1998 716
  s 47A 466
  s 58A 466
Consumer Credit Act 1974 . . . . .286, 352
  s 140(b)(2)(9) 286
  s 140A 286
  s 140B(1)(a) 286
Consumer Credit Act 2006 286
Consumer Rights Act 2015 367
  s 2(3) 367
  s 20(10) 367
  s 20(11) 367
  s 21 367

Copyright, Designs and Patents Act 1988
  s 96(2) 460
  s 97(1) 461
  s 229(2) 460
  s 233(1) 461
Coroners and Justice Act 2009
  Pt 7 .... 533, 541, 543
  ss 54–56 546
  s 59 546
  s 155 541
  s 155(2) 541
  s 156(2) 541
  s 160(2) 541
  s 160(3) 541
  s 162(3) 541
  s 163(1) 541
  s 163(4) 541
Criminal Justice Act 1993
  Part V 331
  s 52 720
Criminal Law Act 1967
  s 5(1) 230
Criminal Procedure (Insanity) Act 1964
  s 1 546
Equality Act 2010
  s 199 589
Estates of Deceased Persons (Forfeiture
    Rule and Law of Succession)
    Act 2011 552
Family Law Reform Act 1969
  s 1 .... 384, 727
Finance Act 1985 398
Finance Act 1989
  s 29 406
  s 29(3) 703
Finance Act 2004
  s 320 .... 409, 737
Finance (No. 2) Act 2005
  s 3(11) 406
Finance Act 2007
  s 107 .... 409, 737
Finance Act 2009
  Sch 52(1) 406
Forfeiture Act 1870 545
Forfeiture Act 1982 .... 545, 546, 548, 552–4
  s 1 545
  s 1(2) 553
  s 2(1) 553
  s 2(2) 553
  s 2(4)(a) 553
  s 2(4)(b) 553
  s 2(5) 553
  s 5 552
  s 7(4) 553
Fraud Act 2006 .... 527, 530, 717
  s 2 592
  s 3 592
Gambling Act 2005 .... 148, 377
  s 335 .... 144, 148
Gaming Act 1845 377

  s 18 168
Homicide Act 1957
  s 2 546
  s 4 546
Human Rights Act 1998 532
Infants' Relief Act 1874 .... 384, 386
Inheritance (Provision of Family and
    Dependants) Act 1975 551
Inheritance Tax Act 1984
  s 241 406
Insolvency Act 1986
  s 278 614
  s 306 614
Judicature Acts 1873–1875 40
Law of Property (Miscellaneous Provisions)
    Act 1989
  s 2 .... 59, 76, 351
Law Reform (Frustrated Contracts) Act
    1943 .... 29, 48, 62, 65, 96,
                    193, 318, 325, 355, 356, 357,
                    359, 361, 362, 366, 735
  s 1(1) 357
  s 1(2) 325, 357, 358, 359,
                    360, 363, 364, 365, 679
  s 1(3) 95, 101, 325, 357,
                    359, 360, 361, 362, 363, 364,
                    365, 537, 679
  s 1(3)(a) 362, 363
  s 1(3)(b) 362, 363, 365
  s 1(4) 358
  s 2(3) 358
  s 2(5) 356
Law Reform (Miscellaneous Provisions) Act
    1934 450
Law Reform (Miscellaneous Provisions) Act 1970
  s 3(2) 311
Limitation Act 1623
  s 3 735
Limitation Act 1980 .... 250, 734, 735,
                    738, 739, 740, 742
  s 2 738
  s 2(1)(a) 735
  s 3(1) 740
  s 3(2) 740
  s 4(1) 740
  s 5 .... 735, 738
  s 9 735
  s 10(1) 736
  s 10(2)–(4) 736
  s 15 740
  s 17 740
  s 21(1)(a) 739, 741
  s 21(1)(b) 741
  s 21(3) 739, 741
  s 22(a) 741
  s 23 739
  s 28 737
  s 29(5) 738
  s 32(1)(a) 737, 739
  s 32(1)(b) 737

s 32(1)(c) 185, 394, 403, 409, 737, 739
s 36(1) 735, 740
s 36(2) 741
s 38 739
s 38(2) 737

Marine Insurance Act 1906
s 66(1) 307
s 66(2) 307

Marine Shipping Act 1995
s 224 736
Sch 11 736

Mental Capacity Act 2005
s 2(1) 381
s 2(2) 381
s 3(1) 381
s 7 . . . . 300, 383
s 7(2) 299
s 16(2) 381
Sch 6 730

Merchant Shipping Act 1995
s 73(2) 306

Minors' Contracts Act 1987 . . . . . . 351, 369, 384
s 3 632
s 3(1) 380, 579, 730
s 3(3) 299
s 4(2) 384

Misrepresentation Act 1967
s 1 199
s 2(1) 198
s 2(2) 199, 274

Official Secrets Acts 1911 and 1920 493
s 1 474

Patents Act 1977
s 61(1) 461
s 61(1)(d) 460
s 62(1) 461

Police (Property) Act 1897 528

Powers of Criminal Courts (Sentencing) Act
        2000 528
s 130 528
s 148 528

Proceeds of Crime Act 2002 534,
                        535, 537, 538, 541, 547
Pt V 529, 542
s 6 535
s 6(4)(b) 536
s 6(4)(c) 536
s 6(6) 529
s 7(1) 536
s 7(2) 536
s 9(1) 536
s 9(1)(b) 541
s 10 536
s 75 536
s 76(4) 536, 537
s 76(5) 537
s 76(7) 536
ss 79–80 536
s 79(2) 536
s 80(2) 536

s 80(3) 536
s 84(1) 537
s 84(2)(h) 540
s 281 542
s 327 540

Public Health (Control of Disease) Act 1984
s 46(5) 297

Road Traffic Act 1988
s 1 547

Road Traffic Act 1991
s 1 547

Sale of Goods Act 1979 570
s 3(2) 300, 383, 727, 730
s 16 570
s 17 570
s 30(1) 342
s 30(3) 86, 100

Sale of Goods (Amendment) Act 1995 571
s 1(2) 570
s 1(3) 571

Senior Courts Act 1981
s 35A 29
s 35A(1) 32

Social Security Administration Act 1992
s 71 388

Statute of Frauds 1677 351

Taxes Management Act 1970 406
s 33(1) 162
Sch 1AB 406
Sch 1AB 2 406
Sch 1AB 3(1) 406

Theft Act 1968
s 1 574
s 4(1) 529
s 5(4) 574
s 21 . . . . 207, 229, 527
s 28 527

Torts (Interference with Goods) Act 1977 83
s 3(2) 642
s 3(3) 632
s 3(3)(a) 433
s 6(1) 83
s 7(4) 245
s 12 304
s 13 304
Sch 1 304

Trustee Act 1925
s 68(7) 741
s 68(17) 739

Unfair Contract Terms Act 1977 141
s 3 141

Unfair Terms in Consumer Contract
        Regulations 1999 (SI 1999/2083) 141

Value Added Tax Act 1994 . . . . 406, 407
s 78 407
s 80 406–7
s 80(3) 407, 408, 411, 703
s 80(4) 407
s 80(7) 407

Wills Act 1837 552

PART I

THE FUNDAMENTAL PRINCIPLES OF THE LAW OF RESTITUTION

1

THE ESSENCE OF
RESTITUTION

1. WHAT IS THE LAW OF RESTITUTION ABOUT?

Before the principles and rules which form the law of restitution are examined, it is important to identify what this body of law is actually about. The answer is simple, but it is an answer which has rarely been articulated by judges or commentators. The law of restitution is concerned with the award of a generic group of remedies which arise by operation of law and which have one common function, namely to deprive the defendant of a gain rather than to compensate the claimant for loss suffered.[1] These are called the restitutionary remedies.[2] Whilst there is a great deal more to the subject than the identification of an appropriate remedy, since it is also vital to determine what circumstances will trigger the award of restitutionary remedies, it is only because there are a group of remedies which have a common function of depriving defendants of gains that we are able to assert that there is an independent body of law which can be called the law of restitution, a body of law which is concerned with the defendant's liabilities to orders made by the court.[3] To understand what these remedies are, how they operate, and when they are available requires examination of a complex body of law. To assist in the understanding of this law it is necessary to identify and analyse the principles which underlie the rules. That is the aim of this book.

2. WHAT IS THE NATURE OF RESTITUTIONARY REMEDIES?

(A) THE CATEGORIES OF RESTITUTIONARY REMEDY

The restitutionary remedies themselves fall into two distinct categories.

---

[1] See Lord Wright of Durley, *Legal Essays and Addresses* (Cambridge: Cambridge University Press, 1939), 36; K Barker, 'Rescuing Remedialism in Unjust Enrichment Law: Why Remedies are Right' (1998) 57 CLJ 301.

[2] The range of restitutionary remedies is considered at p 18, below.

[3] On the relevance of liabilities to the law of restitution see S Smith, 'The Restatement of Liabilities in Restitution' in C Mitchell and W Swadling (eds), *The Restatement Third: Restitution and Unjust Enrichment—Critical and Comparative Essays* (Oxford: Hart Publishing, 2013), ch 10; S Smith, 'A Duty to Make Restitution' (2013) 26 *Canadian Journal of Law and Jurisprudence* 157. Emphasizing the liability of the defendant to make restitution, which depends on the court making an order, rather than a primary duty to make restitution, explains why the defendant is not liable to pay damages for a failure to make restitution. See S Smith, 'Unjust Enrichment: Nearer to Tort Than Contract' in R Chambers, C Mitchell, and J Penner (eds), *Philosophical Foundations of the Law of Unjust Enrichment* (Oxford: Oxford University Press, 2009), ch 7.

(i) Personal Restitutionary Remedies

These remedies restore to the claimant the value of a benefit which the defendant has received. They are said to operate *in personam*. This means that the defendant is liable to pay the value of the benefit to the claimant rather than transfer the benefit itself. Consequently, the claimant has a right against the defendant, rather than against the specific benefit which was transferred. So, for example, if the claimant pays £1,000 to the defendant by mistake, the defendant will be liable to repay the amount of £1,000 to the claimant, even if the defendant no longer has the money which he or she received from the claimant.[4] It follows that the award of a personal restitutionary remedy creates a relationship of creditor and debtor between the parties, since the defendant owes money to the claimant. Crucially, this category of remedy does not depend on the defendant retaining the benefit which he or she had received from the claimant.

(ii) Proprietary Restitutionary Remedies

The function of these remedies[5] is to enable the claimant to assert his or her property rights in an asset which is held by the defendant. These remedies are said to operate *in rem*. There are two types of proprietary restitutionary remedy: first, remedies by virtue of which the claimant can recover the asset which is held by the defendant; secondly, remedies which recognize that the claimant has a security interest in an asset which is held by the defendant. The key advantage of both types of remedy is that, since the claimant has a proprietary interest in an asset which is held by the defendant, the claimant's claim to the asset ranks above other creditors of the defendant, with the result that the claimant is more likely to recover the asset or its value if the defendant becomes insolvent. The particular advantage of the first type is that the claimant can gain the benefit of any increase in the value of the asset. Crucially, the award of proprietary restitutionary remedies depends on the defendant retaining the asset in which the claimant has a proprietary interest.[6]

(B) THE CHARACTERISTICS OF RESTITUTIONARY REMEDIES

(i) Restoring What the Claimant Lost

Since restitutionary remedies are assessed by reference to the defendant's gain, they operate in a very different way from compensatory remedies, where the measure of relief is assessed by reference to the claimant's loss. Despite this, in many cases the effect of a restitutionary remedy will be to restore to the claimant what he or she has lost, because the extent of the defendant's gain will reflect precisely what the claimant lost. 'Restitutionary' is clearly the most appropriate word to describe such remedies, since their function is to restore to the claimant the value of the thing, the thing itself, or its substitute, which the claimant had lost.

The award of such restitutionary remedies to the claimant can be justified on the ground that, where the defendant has obtained a benefit at the claimant's expense, justice demands that this should be restored to the claimant.[7] This is known as 'corrective justice'.[8]

---

[4] Subject to the application of defences, such as change of position. See Chapter 25.
[5] See Chapter 22.   [6] See Chapter 21.
[7] See *Moses v Macferlan* (1760) 2 Burr 1005, 1012; 97 ER 676, 681 (Lord Mansfield) and *Fibrosa Spolka Akcyjna v Fairbairn Lawson Combe Barbour Ltd* [1943] AC 32, 61 (Lord Wright).
[8] See K Barker, 'Understanding the Unjust Enrichment Principle in Private Law: A Study of the Concept and its Reasons' in J Neyers, M McInnes, and S Pitel (eds), *Understanding Unjust Enrichment* (Oxford: Hart

As Bastarache J recognized in *Kingstreet Investments Ltd v New Brunswick (Finance)*:[9] 'Restitution is a tool of corrective justice. When a transfer of value between two parties is normatively defective, restitution functions to correct that transfer by restoring parties to their pre-transfer positions.'

The importance of restitutionary remedies as a mechanism for correcting injustice between the parties was recognized by Fuller and Perdue:

> If, following Aristotle, we regard the purpose of justice as the maintenance of an equilibrium of goods among members of society, the restitution interest presents twice as strong a claim to judicial intervention as the reliance interest, since if A not only causes B to lose one unit but appropriates that unit to himself, the resulting discrepancy between A and B is not one unit but two.[10]

The essence of corrective justice is that, where it can be shown that it is just for the defendant to make restitution to the claimant, legal rules are required to impose an obligation of restitution on the defendant. The award of restitutionary remedies consequently operates as a mechanism to secure corrective justice by rectifying an imbalance between the claimant and the defendant, by requiring the defendant to give back what has been received from the claimant.

(ii) Disgorgement

In some cases the remedy awarded, although it is still assessed by reference to the defendant's gain, results in the claimant obtaining something of value which he or she never had before. For example, the defendant may have obtained some money from a third party in breach of duty to the claimant. In such circumstances the claimant may be able to make a claim in respect of the money,[11] but, since it has not been taken from the claimant, it is inappropriate to describe the remedy which enables the claimant to obtain this money as literally restitutionary, because it is not possible to restore to the claimant what he or she never had in the first place. It is more appropriate, therefore, to describe the function of such remedies as requiring the defendant to disgorge benefits to the claimant, rather than to restore to the claimant what he or she has lost.[12] Even though the description of these disgorgement remedies as 'restitutionary' is not always felicitous, it is still appropriate to treat them as falling within the law of restitution, simply because the remedy is assessed by reference to a gain made by the defendant, albeit that the defendant is required to give this gain up rather than give it back.[13]

Publishing, 2004); E Weinrib, 'Correctively Unjust Enrichment' in R Chambers, C Mitchell, and J Penner (eds), *Philosophical Foundations of the Law of Unjust Enrichment* (Oxford: Oxford University Press, 2009), ch 2; E Weinrib, *The Idea of Private Law* (Oxford: Oxford University Press, 2012); LD Smith, 'Restitution: The Heart of Corrective Justice' (2001) 79 Tex LR 2115.

[9] [2007] 1 SCR 3, [32].

[10] LL Fuller and WR Perdue, 'The Reliance Interest in Contract Damages' (1936–37) 46 *Yale LJ* 52, 56. See Aristotle, 'Nichomachean Ethics', Book V, ch 2, 4.   [11] See Part III, below.

[12] LD Smith, 'The Province of the Law of Restitution' (1992) 71 CBR 672, 696; J Edelman, *Gain-Based Damages: Contract, Tort, Equity and Intellectual Property* (Oxford: Hart Publishing, 2002).

[13] Birks suggested that the description of these remedies as restitutionary is justified because the 'underlying Latin "*restituere/restitutio*" indicates that the word can include both 'give up' and 'give back': 'Equity in the Modern Law: An Exercise in Taxonomy' (1996) 26 Univ WALR 1, 28. See also F Giglio, 'Gain-Related Recovery' (2008) OJLS 501, 518.

The award of such disgorgement remedies can be justified on a different basis to that of literal restitutionary remedies. Justice demands that the defendant should disgorge gains obtained as a result of breach of a duty because of a fundamental principle of the law of restitution that no defendant should profit from his or her wrongdoing. So disgorgement remedies have a deterrent or distributive function.[14] But disgorgement remedies can also be justified on the basis that they operate as a mechanism to secure corrective justice between the parties. This is because the claimant is the victim of a wrong, and requiring the defendant to disgorge gains obtained as a result of committing the wrong is an appropriate mechanism for protecting the claimant's rights.[15]

(iii) Giving Up Rights and Reinstatement of Obligations

Lodder[16] has identified an additional category of restitutionary remedy. He distinguishes between two types of enrichment, namely factual enrichment, which involves the receipt of a valuable benefit, and legal enrichment, which arises where the defendant has gained a right or has had an obligation discharged as a result of the claimant's action. Where the defendant is enriched in this legal sense the remedy which is awarded operates either to defeat the right obtained or to reinstate the obligation discharged. For example, a right may have been created under a contract and the remedy which might be awarded arises from the vitiation of the contract so that the right is destroyed. Lodder considers such remedies to be restitutionary because removing a right or restoring an obligation involves the removal of a gain from the defendant.

The effect of this interpretation of gain-based remedies is to expand the ambit of the law of restitution to encompass remedies which may not have pecuniary conse-quences, such as the rescission of an executory contract[17] or rectification[18] of a contract. This is controversial but, if correct, it means that the principles on which the award of restitutionary remedies is founded must also be used to explain when restitution of legal enrichment will be available and, if those principles are found wanting, they may need to be adapted to provide for this type of restitutionary remedy. Crucially, however, this type of restitutionary remedy can also be justified by reference to corrective justice, since the effect of the remedy is to correct an injustice between the claimant and the defendant. Although the extinction of a right appears not to give anything back to the claimant, the existence of the defendant's right curtails the enjoyment of the claimant's rights. Consequently, the extinction of a right can be considered to involve the depriv-ation of a benefit enjoyed by the defendant and a corresponding enhancement of the claimant's own rights, meaning that the extinction of the right can legitimately be described as a restitutionary remedy, in that there is both a giving up of the defendant's right and a consequent removal of the burden which would otherwise be suffered by the claimant. Similarly, where an obligation is reinstated, this involves the reversal of a benefit which had been enjoyed by the defendant, namely the extinction of a liability, and a corresponding benefit to the claimant, who now has a right which can be vindicated against the defendant.

---

[14] K Barker, 'Understanding the Unjust Enrichment Principle in Private Law: A Study of the Concept and its Reasons' in J Neyers, M McInnes, and S Pitel (eds), *Understanding Unjust Enrichment* (Oxford: Hart Publishing, 2004), 101.

[15] K Barker, 'Unjust Enrichment: Containing the Beast' (1995) 15 OJLS 457, 473.

[16] AVM Lodder, *Enrichment in the Law of Restitution and Unjust Enrichment* (Oxford: Hart Publishing, 2012), ch 3. See also R Chambers, 'Two Kinds of Enrichment' in R Chambers, C Mitchell, and J Penner (eds), *Philosophical Foundations of the Law of Unjust Enrichment* (2009), ch 9, who distinguishes between enrich-ments as value and as rights.

[17] See p 22, below.   [18] See p 21, below.

3. WHEN WILL RESTITUTIONARY REMEDIES BE AWARDED?

Although the policy of corrective justice can be relied on to justify the award of restitutionary remedies, it is too uncertain to operate as an underlying principle on which the law of restitution can be built. For, if the question of whether restitutionary remedies can be awarded depended simply on whether it was just to require the defendant to give back or give up to the claimant what the defendant had gained, the law of restitution would be unpredictable and unworkable such that it would effectively be void for uncertainty. Consequently, it is necessary to identify more specific principles which provide the basis for determining whether the claimant may obtain restitutionary relief. It is important to recognize that, for the purposes of this book, a principle (as distinct from a policy or a value) is a generalized rule of law which has explanatory force in synthesizing complex policies and doctrines in a simple pithy statement.[19]

The key question concerns when the law will recognize that the claimant has a right which can be vindicated by means of restitutionary remedies. Orthodox learning suggests that there is only one principle on which the law of restitution is dependent, namely the principle of unjust enrichment.[20] This equation of the law of restitution with the principle of reversing the defendant's unjust enrichment has been recognized by the judiciary.[21] But it was not until the decisions of the House of Lords, first in *Lipkin Gorman (a firm) v Karpnale Ltd*[22] and then in *Woolwich Equitable Building Society v IRC*,[23] that we could be certain that there is a body of law which exists to secure the reversal of unjust enrichment.[24] Probably the most important *dictum* of the modern law of restitution is that of Lord Goff in *Lipkin Gorman*, who recognized that:

> The recovery of money in restitution is not, as a general rule, a matter of discretion for the court. A claim to recover money at common law is made as a matter of right; and even though the underlying principle of recovery is the principle of unjust enrichment, nevertheless, where recovery is denied, it is denied on the basis of legal principle.[25]

Despite the recognition by the House of Lords that the law of restitution equates with the reversal of the defendant's unjust enrichment, such an interpretation of the law is in

---

[19] For a jurisprudential analysis of 'principle' see J Gardner, 'Ashworth on Principles' in L Zedner and J Roberts (eds), *Principles and Values in Criminal law and Criminal Justice: Essays in Honour of Andrew Ashworth* (Oxford: Oxford University Press, 2012), 25.

[20] See C Mitchell, P Mitchell, and S Watterson (eds), *Goff and Jones: The Law of Unjust Enrichment* (8th edn, London: Sweet and Maxwell, 2011), 5; AS Burrows, *The Law of Restitution* (3rd edn, Oxford: Oxford University Press, 2011), 4.

[21] Notably by Lord Wright in *Fibrosa Spolka Akcyjna v Fairbairn Lawson Combe Barbour Ltd* [1943] AC 32, 61. See further p 47, below.

[22] [1991] 2 AC 548. See in particular Lord Bridge, 558, Lord Templeman, 559, and Lord Goff, 578.

[23] [1993] AC 70, 197 (Lord Browne-Wilkinson).

[24] See also *Westdeutsche Landesbank Girozentrale v Islington LBC* [1996] AC 669, 710 (Lord Browne-Wilkinson); *Kleinwort Benson Ltd v Glasgow CC* [1999] 1 AC 153, 167 (Lord Goff) and 185 (Lord Clyde); *Banque Financière de la Cité v Parc (Battersea) Ltd* [1999] 1 AC 221; *Kleinwort Benson Ltd v Lincoln CC* [1999] 2 AC 349, 373 (Lord Goff), 406 (Lord Hope); *Foskett v McKeown* [2001] 1 AC 102; *Deutsche Morgan Grenfell Group plc v IRC* [2006] UKHL 49, [2007] 1 AC 558; *Sempra Metals Ltd v IRC* [2007] UKHL 34, [2008] 1 AC 561; *Yeoman's Row Management Ltd v Cobbe* [2008] UKHL 55, [2008] 1 WLR 1752; *Test Claimants in the FII Group Litigation v HMRC* [2012] UKSC 19, [2012] 2 AC 337; *Pitt v Holt* [2013] UKSC 26, [2013] 2 AC 108; *Benedetti v Sawiris* [2013] UKSC 50, [2014] AC 938.

[25] *Lipkin Gorman (a firm) v Karpnale Ltd* [1991] 2 AC 548, 578.

fact too simplistic and does not accurately reflect the true operation of the law of restitution.[26] Careful analysis of the case law suggests that the law of restitution is not founded upon one principle but rather is founded on three different principles, namely:

(1) the reversal of unjust enrichment;

(2) the prevention of a wrongdoer from profiting from his or her wrong; and

(3) the vindication of property rights with which the defendant has interfered.

Restitutionary remedies are available in respect of each of these three principles, but it is vital that they are kept separate and are not brought together within one general principle of unjust enrichment, for the award of restitutionary remedies involves very different considerations depending on which principle the claimant relies. Each of these three principles requires careful description at the outset.

(A) THE REVERSAL OF UNJUST ENRICHMENT

The reversal of the defendant's unjust enrichment is the most important principle in the law of restitution, since it underlies the award of restitutionary relief in a wide variety of cases. It is therefore crucial to determine exactly what unjust enrichment means. Two different senses of the phrase can be identified and it is the failure to distinguish between them that has resulted in the assumption by many that the reversal of unjust enrichment is the only principle on which the award of restitutionary remedies is dependent.

(i) The Descriptive Sense of Unjust Enrichment

Unjust enrichment may be relied upon simply to describe a state of affairs where the defendant can be said to have been enriched in circumstances of injustice. Since restitutionary remedies will only be awarded where the defendant has received some sort of benefit in circumstances where he or she is required to transfer that benefit or its value to the claimant, this descriptive notion of unjust enrichment can be treated as underlying the whole of the law of restitution. Indeed, it is this idea of unjust enrichment which was recognized by Lord Wright in the *Fibrosa* case, who equated it with what 'conscience' demands,[27] and which had earlier been adopted by Lord Mansfield in *Moses v Macferlan*,[28] who recognized that 'the gist of this kind of action is, that the defendant, upon the circumstances of the case, is obliged by the ties of natural justice and equity to refund the money'. This descriptive sense of unjust enrichment was also acknowledged by Lord Clyde, who said that the unjust enrichment principle 'is equitable in the sense that it seeks to secure a fair and just determination of the rights of the parties concerned in the case'.[29]

Whilst the award of restitutionary remedies can be justified after the event on the ground that it is fair and just to require the defendant to make restitution, unjust enrichment in this descriptive sense can hardly be considered to be a legal principle which is sufficiently certain to determine when restitutionary remedies should be awarded. Indeed, the assumption in a number of cases that the award of restitutionary remedies was dependent simply on whether or not the defendant had been enriched in

---

[26] That the law of restitution should not be equated solely with the unjust enrichment principle was also recognized by Birks: PBH Birks, 'Misnomer' in W Cornish, R Nolan, J O'Sullivan, and G Virgo (eds), *Restitution: Past, Present and Future* (Oxford: Hart Publishing, 1998), 7. See also PBH Birks, *Unjust Enrichment* (2nd edn, Oxford: Oxford University Press, 2005), 4.

[27] *Fibrosa Spolka Akcyjna v Fairbairn Lawson Combe Barbour Ltd* [1943] AC 32, 61. See p 47, below.

[28] (1760) 2 Burr 1005, 1012; 97 ER 676, 681.

[29] *Banque Financière de la Cité v Parc (Battersea) Ltd* [1999] 1 AC 221, 237.

circumstances of injustice was one of the main obstacles to the recognition of the law of restitution as an independent body of law. This is illustrated by the *dictum* of Hamilton LJ in *Baylis v Bishop of London*[30] that the judges 'are not now free in the twentieth century to administer that vague jurisprudence which is sometimes attractively styled "justice as between man and man"'.

(ii) The Substantive Sense of Unjust Enrichment

Alternatively, and much more acceptably, unjust enrichment has been relied on as a substantive principle which can be used to determine when restitutionary remedies should be available. To establish this substantive sense of unjust enrichment it is now recognized that four separate questions need to be considered:[31]

(a) the defendant must have been benefited or received an enrichment;[32]

(b) the enrichment must have been received at the claimant's expense;[33]

(c) the enrichment must have been received in circumstances of injustice, meaning that the claim falls within one of the recognized grounds of restitution;[34]

(d) the defendant is not able to rely on a defence which defeats or reduces liability.[35]

If the first three requirements are satisfied, and the defendant does not have a defence which removes liability, a restitutionary remedy will be awarded to enable the claimant to recover the value of any enrichment which had been received by the defendant. The only remedies which are available for actions founded on the reversal of unjust enrichment are restitutionary and, even then, only personal restitutionary remedies are available.

These four questions are increasingly treated as a formula which needs to be applied to determine whether the defendant is liable to make restitution by virtue of unjust enrichment. But caution has sometimes been expressed about the nature of this formula. For example, in *Investment Trust Companies v HMRC*,[36] Henderson J characterized this conceptual structure as involving 'broad headings for ease of exposition' which 'should not be approached as if they had statutory force'. But this is an unfortunate approach to the essential elements of the unjust enrichment claim, since it may lead back to a

---

[30] [1913] 1 Ch 127, 140. See also *Holt v Markham* [1923] 1 KB 504, 513 where Scrutton LJ described the history of restitution as a 'history of well-meaning sloppiness of thought'.

[31] *Banque Financière de la Cité v Parc (Battersea) Ltd* [1999] 1 AC 221, 227 (Lord Steyn), 234 (Lord Hoffmann); *Haugesund Kommune v Defra ACS Bank* [2011] EWCA Civ 33, [2011] 3 All ER 655, [69] (Rix LJ); *Investment Trust Companies v HMRC* [2012] EWHC 458 (Ch), [38] (Henderson J); *Benedetti v Sawiris* [2013] UKSC 50, [2014] AC 938, [10] (Lord Clarke). The determination of the appropriate remedy is sometimes considered to be a fifth question which needs to be examined. See *Lloyds Bank plc v Independent Insurance Co Ltd* [2000] QB 110, 123 (Waller LJ), referring to P Millett, 'Restitution and Constructive Trusts' in W Cornish, R Nolan, J O'Sullivan, and G Virgo (eds), *Restitution: Past, Present and Future* (Oxford: Hart Publishing, 1998), 208. Birks, *Unjust Enrichment* (2nd edn), 39, identified a fifth question concerning whether the claimant acquired a personal or a proprietary right. The preferable view, though, is that only personal rights are acquired as a result of unjust enrichment, so this is a redundant question. In *Banque Financière de la Cité v Parc (Battersea) Ltd* [1999] 1 AC 221, 234 Lord Hoffmann stated that a further question was whether there were any reasons of policy for denying a remedy. This is preferably dealt with through the elements of the claim and the defences which are available to it.

[32] See Chapter 4.   [33] See Chapter 5.

[34] See Part II. These are sometimes called 'unjust factors'. See *Banque Financière de la Cité v Parc (Battersea) Ltd* [1999] 1 AC 221, 227 (Lord Steyn); *Kleinwort Benson v Lincoln CC* [1999] 2 AC 349, 363 (Lord Browne-Wilkinson), 386 (Lord Goff), 395 (Lord Lloyd), 409 (Lord Hope); *Test Claimants in the FII Group Litigation v HMRC* [2012] UKSC 19, [2012] 2 AC 337, [81] (Lord Walker). 'Grounds of restitution' is the preferred expression in this book, simply for reasons of elegance.

[35] See Part V.   [36] [2012] EWHC 458 (Ch), [39].

more normative approach to the identification of unjust enrichment, with consequent uncertainty and unpredictability. It is far better to assert that a claim in unjust enrichment can only be established if each of the first three questions are answered affirmatively. Then attention can focus on whether the defendant has a complete or partial defence to the claim.

Although the four questions which constitute the unjust enrichment formula can now be considered to be orthodox, they should not be considered to be comprehensive in identifying what needs to be proved to establish an unjust enrichment claim. Increasingly, in both the academic literature but also in decisions of the courts, a fifth question is examined, although it is rarely acknowledged that it needs to be considered separately. This fifth question is whether there is a valid legal basis for the defendant to have received the enrichment. If there is such a legal basis, which is sometimes called a 'juridical base', then a claim in unjust enrichment should fail, since awarding restitution in such circumstances would undermine the legal legitimacy of the defendant's receipt. So, for example, if the claimant has transferred a benefit to the defendant in fulfilment of a valid contractual obligation, the defendant's receipt is valid and the defendant's gain is legitimate. Similarly, if the defendant has received an enrichment which discharges a valid statutory obligation or it has been transferred as a valid gift. The significance of recognizing this fifth part of the unjust enrichment formula is considered further in Chapter 7. This fifth question has previously been hidden away in the identification of a relevant ground of restitution. But then it can be missed. It is vital that is drawn out explicitly with reference to a separate question in the unjust enrichment formula.

It follows that a claim in unjust enrichment should only be established where it can be shown that (i) the defendant was enriched; (ii) at the claimant's expense; (iii) a recognized ground of restitution is engaged; (iv) there was no valid legal basis for the defendant's receipt; and (v) there is no defence to the claim. Where liability in unjust enrichment is established, the remedy which is awarded is limited to a personal remedy assessed with reference to the value of the enrichment received by the defendant. A claim for unjust enrichment is not a claim for compensation for loss.[37] Despite this, sometimes the restitutionary remedy to reverse unjust enrichment has been described inappropriately as 'compensation'[38] or 'damages'.[39] To the extent that this suggests a focus on the loss suffered by the claimant, such language should be avoided.[40]

(B) THE DEPRIVATION OF BENEFITS FROM A WRONGDOER

(i) The Nature of Restitution for Wrongs

In certain cases the victim of a wrong may be able to bring a restitutionary claim to recover the value of the benefit obtained by the defendant as a result of the wrongdoing.[41] For example, where the defendant commits a tort against the claimant, the remedial response is not necessarily assessed by reference to the claimant's loss, but may be assessed by reference to the defendant's gain.[42] A similar response may also arise in respect of benefits accruing to the defendant as a result of a breach of contract,[43] the commission of equitable wrongs such as breach of fiduciary duty,[44] and even the commission of criminal offences.[45]

---

[37] *Boake Allen Ltd v HMRC* [2006] EWCA Civ 25, [2006] STC 606, [175] (Mummery LJ).
[38] *MacDonald Dickens and Macklin v Costello* [2011] EWCA Civ 930, [2012] QB 244, [31] (Etherton LJ).
[39] *Harrison v Madjeski and Coys of Kensington* [2014] EWCA Civ 361, [3] (Etherton C).
[40] Although see further p 116, below.   [41] See Part III.   [42] See Chapter 17.
[43] See Chapter 18.   [44] See Chapter 19.   [45] See Chapter 20.

Although some commentators have argued that the restitutionary response in such circumstances arises because the defendant has been unjustly enriched at the claimant's expense,[46] this is only correct to the extent that unjust enrichment is used in its descriptive and not its substantive sense. But, where the defendant has received a benefit as a result of the commission of a wrong, it is not possible to say that the defendant has been unjustly enriched in any substantive sense for two reasons.[47] First, because the claimant's restitutionary claim will succeed even though the defendant's benefit was not obtained from the claimant, so it is not possible to show that the defendant has been enriched at the claimant's expense, save in the most artificial sense that the benefit was obtained from the commission of a wrong against the claimant. Secondly, because it is not necessary to show that the restitutionary claim falls within one of the recognized grounds of restitution. It is sufficient that the defendant has committed a wrong against the claimant, and that this wrong is of a type which has been recognized as triggering a restitutionary response. It is this wrongdoing, and not unjust enrichment on a particular ground, which constitutes the cause of action for which the relevant remedy may be restitutionary.[48]

(ii) The Nature of the Restitutionary Remedy

Where the claimant seeks a restitutionary remedy in respect of a wrong committed by the defendant, that remedy will usually be personal. There are, however, cases where the defendant has been awarded a proprietary restitutionary remedy and where the event which triggered this was a wrong, invariably an equitable wrong.[49] In such cases there is clearly an overlap between the principle of restitution for wrongs and the principle of vindicating property rights. It is preferable, however, to treat such claims as ultimately founded on the wrong, since it is the commission of the wrong which triggers the recognition of the claimant's proprietary right.

The justification for the award of restitutionary remedies where the defendant has committed a wrong is the fundamental principle that wrongdoers should not be allowed to profit from their wrongdoing.[50]

(C) THE VINDICATION OF PROPERTY RIGHTS WITH WHICH THE DEFENDANT HAS INTERFERED

(i) The Nature of Restitutionary Claims Founded on the Vindication of Property Rights

Where the claimant has a proprietary right to an asset which has been received by the defendant, the claimant may seek to obtain a restitutionary remedy to vindicate that right,[51] regardless of whether it previously existed or has been created by operation of law. Such proprietary restitutionary claims may take two forms.

---

[46] See Burrows, *The Law of Restitution* (3rd edn), 12, where he considers restitution for wrongs to be founded on the principle against unjust enrichment. See also the report of the Law Commission, *Aggravated, Exemplary and Restitutionary Damages* (Law Com No 247, 1997), 51. Birks at one time shared this view (PBH Birks, *An Introduction to the Law of Restitution* (rev edn, Oxford: Clarendon Press, 1989), 26) but he subsequently changed his mind: Birks, 'Misnomer', 14.

[47] See LD Smith, 'The Province of the Law of Restitution' (1992) 71 CBR 672, 683.

[48] Although Burrows stills clings to the theory which awards restitutionary remedies only where the defendant is unjustly enriched, he acknowledges that, for restitution for wrongs, the underlying cause of action is the wrong rather than unjust enrichment: *The Law of Restitution* (3rd edn), 12.

[49] See Chapter 19. [50] See Chapter 16.

[51] *Foskett v McKeown* [2001] 1 AC 102, 129 (Lord Millett).

(1) Where the defendant received property in which the claimant has a proprietary interest and the defendant has retained that property or its proceeds, the claimant can obtain a proprietary restitutionary remedy in respect of that property itself, the cause of action being the vindication of the claimant's continuing property rights.

(2) Where the defendant received property in which the claimant had a proprietary interest at the time of receipt but that interest has since been lost, the only restitutionary remedy available to the claimant is a personal one, representing the value of the property which the defendant has received. But the cause of action can still be the vindication of property rights, since the claimant can show that he or she had a proprietary interest in the property received by the defendant at the time of the receipt.

(ii) Is a Proprietary Restitutionary Claim Founded on the Unjust Enrichment Principle?

It has often been assumed that, where the claimant seeks to recover property in which he or she has a proprietary interest, the recovery of that property or its proceeds can be justified only by reference to the principle that the defendant has been unjustly enriched at the expense of the claimant. But this is only true to the extent that 'unjust enrichment' is used in a trivial, descriptive sense to indicate that the defendant has property which it is just for him or her to return to the claimant.[52] 'Unjust enrichment' in its substantive sense is completely irrelevant in this context, because the action to vindicate property rights forms part of the law of property and has nothing to do with the principle of reversing the defendant's unjust enrichment.[53] Once it has been shown that the defendant has received or has retained property in which the claimant has a proprietary interest, nothing else needs to be proved to establish the claimant's cause of action. If the defendant has the claimant's property he or she should return it, or its value, to the claimant, without the claimant first having to establish that the defendant has been unjustly enriched at his or her expense.

This analysis of proprietary restitutionary claims was adopted by the House of Lords in *Foskett v McKeown*.[54] It remains, however, a controversial analysis and has been criticized by a number of commentators,[55] especially as regards claims to property which is substituted for the original property received, such as where the defendant receives money and uses it to buy a car. For these commentators enrichment is readily established because the receipt of an asset will typically be characterized as an enrichment which cannot be devalued by the defendant.[56] Further, if the claimant had a proprietary interest in the property which can be identified in the substitute, this shows that the property was received at the claimant's expense. But the stumbling block with this analysis relates to the identification of the ground of restitution. The commentators who seek to explain proprietary claims with reference to unjust enrichment are forced to identify artificial grounds of restitution to explain the decided cases. But such artifice is completely unnecessary. The reported cases do not use

---

[52] Ibid, 115 (Lord Hoffmann).

[53] See Chapter 21. See also RB Grantham and CEF Rickett, 'Property and Unjust Enrichment: Categorical Truths or Unnecessary Complexity?' [1997] 2 NZ Law Rev 668. See also *Test Claimants in the FII Group Litigation v Commissioners for HMRC* [2014] EWHC 4302 (Ch), [348] (Henderson J).

[54] [2001] AC 102.

[55] See especially Birks, *Unjust Enrichment* (2nd edn), 34–6; AS Burrows, 'Proprietary Restitution: Unmasking Unjust Enrichment' (2001) 117 LQR 412; C Mitchell, P Mitchell, and S Watterson (eds), *Goff and Jones: The Law of Unjust Enrichment* (8th edn, London: Sweet and Maxwell, 2011), ch 7.

[56] See further p 81, below.

such reasoning and they have no need to do so, simply because it is sufficient to establish that the defendant has received property in which the claimant has a proprietary interest.

Even before the decision of the House of Lords in *Foskett v McKeown* a number of cases were consistent with the theory that proprietary restitutionary claims are not founded on unjust enrichment. For example, in *Macmillan v Bishopsgate Investment Trust plc (No 3)*,[57] the claimant wished to recover shares from the defendants which had been transferred to them by a third party in breach of trust. The defendants pleaded the defence that they were *bona fide* purchasers for value.[58] The issue before the court concerned the choice of law rule for this type of action. It was agreed that the claim should be characterized as restitutionary, and the argument then related to whether it was based on an obligation or property right. The Court of Appeal unanimously held that it was a matter of property and so proprietary choice of law rules were applicable. The importance of this case is that the court implicitly recognized that a cause of action could be restitutionary even though the action was not founded upon the reversal of an unjust enrichment. For example, Auld LJ emphasized that the issue in the case was essentially a proprietary one and stated that 'it is difficult to see what unjust enrichment the [defendants] have had'.[59] Further, the result, but not the analysis, of the leading case of *Lipkin Gorman (a firm) v Karpnale Ltd*[60] is consistent with the proprietary restitutionary claim theory. Although the House of Lords, following the lead of Lord Goff, agreed that all restitutionary claims are founded on the unjust enrichment principle, this was not in fact an unjust enrichment case, save in the broadest and least useful descriptive sense of the defendant having received a benefit which should be returned as a matter of justice. Rather, *Lipkin Gorman* was primarily concerned with the vindication of the claimant's proprietary rights. This explains why none of the judges expressly identified all of the elements which are required to establish that the defendant has been unjustly enriched, most notably the ground for restitution, an omission which has been a serious cause of concern for some commentators.[61] This is not a problem if the basis for awarding restitutionary remedies was the vindication of property rights rather than the reversal of unjust enrichment, because where the claimant wishes to vindicate property rights it is only necessary to identify the property right and not a ground of restitution.

Lipkin Gorman concerned a partner of the claimant firm of solicitors who had stolen money from the firm over a period of time and used this money to gamble at the defendant casino. The claimant brought a restitutionary claim to recover the value of the money received by the defendant. The claimant's action succeeded. Both Lords Templeman and Goff emphasized the claimant's continuing proprietary interest in the money from the moment it was stolen by the partner until it, or its substitute, was received by the defendant.[62] Consequently, a continuing proprietary interest was clearly recognized and appears to have proved vital to the success of the claim.[63] If this analysis is correct we are left with a nice irony. Whilst the decision of the House of Lords in *Lipkin Gorman* is of

---

[57] [1996] 1 WLR 387. See GJ Virgo, 'Reconstructing the Law of Restitution' (1996) 10 TLI 20 and WJ Swadling 'A Claim in Restitution?' [1996] LM CLQ 63 for further discussion of this case.

[58] See Chapter 23.

[59] *Macmillan v Bishopsgate Investment Trust plc (No 3)* [1996] 1 WLR 387, 409.

[60] [1991] 2 AC 548.

[61] See PBH Birks, 'The English Recognition of Unjust Enrichment' [1991] LMCLQ 473, E McKendrick, 'Restitution, Misdirected Funds and Change of Position' (1992) 55 MLR 377 and Burrows, *The Law of Restitution* (3rd edn), 414.

[62] *Lipkin Gorman (a firm) v Karpnale Ltd* [1991] 2 AC 548, 560 (Lord Templeman), 572 (Lord Goff).

[63] See further Chapter 3.

prime importance as the leading case where the unjust enrichment principle was first formally recognized as constituting part of English law, that case should not be regarded as authority for the application of the unjust enrichment principle on the facts.

That this is the proper conclusion was confirmed by the decision of the House of Lords in *Foskett v McKeown*,[64] where the majority recognized a fundamental distinction between the law of unjust enrichment and the law of property, and held that a claim to recover substitute property in which the claimant asserted a proprietary interest depended on the vindication of property rights and not unjust enrichment. *Foskett v McKeown* concerned a claim brought by the beneficiaries of a trust to recover part of the proceeds of a life insurance policy. One of the trustees had misappropriated money from the trust fund to pay the fourth and fifth annual premiums for a life assurance policy, with the earlier premiums being paid from his own money.[65] After the fifth premium of £10,220 had been paid, the trustee committed suicide and his children were entitled to receive a payment of just over £1 million under the policy. The beneficiaries of the trust claimed a proportionate share of this sum, amounting to £400,000, on the basis that trust money had been used to pay two of the premiums which contributed to the receipt of the death benefit by the children. The Court of Appeal[66] had confined the beneficiaries to a lien on the proceeds of the policy to secure payment of the amount which had been misappropriated from the trust, amounting to £20,440. The House of Lords held by a bare majority that the beneficiaries' claim for a proportionate share of the £1 million should succeed. The importance of the decision for present purposes is the recognition that the restitutionary claim of the beneficiaries fell within the law of property and was concerned with the vindication of property rights rather than with whether the defendant was unjustly enriched at the expense of the claimant.[67]

Almost as important was the clear rejection by most of the judges of a normative approach to proprietary restitutionary claims, by virtue of which the identification and vindication of proprietary rights would depend on the discretion of the court. This rejection was forcefully expressed by Lord Millett:[68] 'Property rights are determined by fixed rules and settled principles. They are not discretionary. They do not depend upon ideas of what is "fair, just and reasonable". Such concepts, which in reality mask decisions of legal policy, have no place in the law of property.'[69]

Lord Browne-Wilkinson also recognized that proprietary claims do not depend on any discretion vested in the court; it was 'a case of hard-nosed property rights'.[70] The approach of the court could not have been clearer: where the claimant is seeking a proprietary restitutionary remedy the claim is founded on the claimant's rights in the property held by the defendant rather than the defendant's unjust enrichment.

---

[64] [2001] AC 102.

[65] Although it was unclear whether the third premium was paid from the trustee's own money or from the trust fund.

[66] *Foskett v McKeown* [1998] Ch 265.

[67] *Foskett v McKeown* [2001] AC 102, 109 (Lord Browne-Wilkinson), 115 (Lord Hoffmann), 118 (Lord Hope), and 129 (Lord Millett). Lord Steyn concluded that the children were not unjustly enriched because the payment of the premiums did not constitute an enrichment: ibid, 112.

[68] Ibid, 127.

[69] Cf Lord Hope who said, ibid, 120, that, since there was no principle or authority to assist with the division of the mixed substitution in this case, it should be divided in such proportions as were equitable, having regard to the terms of the life insurance policy and the equities affecting each party.

[70] Ibid, 109.

(iii) Criticisms of the Vindication of Property Rights Principle

The recognition of a vindication of property rights principle as distinct from an unjust enrichment principle has been criticized on three grounds.

The first criticism is that, whereas unjust enrichment is an event for which restitutionary remedies are available, it is not possible to treat proprietary rights as an event and so it is not possible to contrast unjust enrichment and property rights as triggers of restitutionary remedies.[71] This argument stems from the writings of Birks who drew a fundamental distinction[72] between events and responses. According to Birks, in the law of civil obligations it is necessary to identify an event before the appropriate response can be considered. The law, he asserted, recognizes four events, namely consent, wrongs, unjust enrichment, and other events. Where the event of unjust enrichment can be established, the only response is restitution. Vindication of property rights is not an event and so, he concluded, restitution cannot respond to it. As he said:

> The key point is that the law of property is not formed in answer to a question about causative events: 'How do rights arise?' It is formed in response to the quite different question: 'Against whom are rights exigible?'[73]

He concluded: 'It is an error of logic to force a choice between the law of property and the law of unjust enrichment.'

But this choice between the law of property and the law of unjust enrichment is not the relevant choice which should be made. The use of the phrase 'property rights' is neutral and does not suggest that any event has occurred. But the crucial feature of the vindication of property rights principle is that the defendant has interfered with the claimant's property rights by not allowing the claimant the exclusive benefit of his or her rights. It is this interference which justifies the award of restitutionary remedies and which can be analysed as the appropriate event.[74]

A second related criticism is that unjust enrichment and the vindication of property rights cannot be considered to be distinct principles because the claimant's property right might be created as a result of the defendant being unjustly enriched at the claimant's expense. This was particularly the view of Birks, who argued that both personal and proprietary rights might be triggered as a response to unjust enrichment.[75] But, with one potential exception,[76] no case has expressly recognized that property rights can arise as a

---

[71] Birks, *Unjust Enrichment* (2nd edn), 33; AS Burrows, 'Proprietary Restitution: Unmasking Unjust Enrichment' (2001) 117 LQR 412. In *Kuwait Airways Corpn v Iraqi Airways Co (Nos 4 and 5)* [2002] UKHL 19, [2002] 2 AC 883, 1093, Lord Nicholls of Birkenhead, in the context of the tort of conversion, characterized the vindication of the claimant's property rights as involving unjust enrichment.

[72] See especially PBH Birks, 'Equity in the Modern Law: An Exercise in Taxonomy' (1996) 26 Univ WALR 1, 8–10; 'Property, Unjust Enrichment and Tracing' [2001] CLP 231.   [73] Ibid, 241.

[74] See RB Grantham and CEF Rickett, 'Property and Unjust Enrichment: Categorical Truths or Unnecessary Complexity?' [1997] NZ Law Rev 668, 680; RB Grantham and CEF Rickett, 'Property Rights as a Legally Significant Event' (2003) CLJ 717.

[75] Birks, *Unjust Enrichment* (2nd edn), 33; Birks, 'Misnomer'.

[76] In *Banque Financière de la Cité v Parc (Battersea) Ltd* [1999] 1 AC 221 the House of Lords awarded the remedy of subrogation in response to the defendant's unjust enrichment. This has been treated in some later cases as involving a proprietary remedy being awarded to reverse an unjust enrichment, although the nature of the remedy in that case was somewhat idiosyncratic. See further p 637, below. Further, this case did not consider claims of the claimant to recover property transferred to the defendant. That was considered by the House of Lords in *Foskett v McKeown* two years later, without linking the remedy to the reversal of unjust enrichment.

result of the defendant being unjustly enriched at the claimant's expense. Birks[77] con-sidered that *Foskett v McKeown*[78] was such a case, even though the majority judgments clearly contradict this, and that there were other cases which were consistent with this approach, including *Sinclair v Brougham*,[79] but this has been overruled,[80] and *Chase Manhattan Bank v Israel-British Bank*,[81] but this case was subsequently reinterpreted by the House of Lords.[82] Further, none of these cases explicitly recognizes that property rights, as opposed to security rights,[83] can derive from unjust enrichment. There is simply no empirical evidence to support the assertion that property rights can derive from the defendant's unjust enrichment. Also, there is no need to rely on the substantive unjust enrichment principle to explain why the claimant has an interest in property. It is sufficient that the claimant's case falls within one of the recognized categories of case by virtue of which property rights arise, and none of these cases requires the claimant to establish specifically that the defendant has been unjustly enriched at the expense of the claimant.[84] It follows that the substantive unjust enrichment principle should be con-sidered as triggering only personal and not proprietary rights.

A final criticism of the vindication of property rights principle is the use of the word 'vindication'. Certainly, the use of that word can be criticized on the technical ground that vindication refers to a specific remedy by virtue of which property, which is in the possession of the defendant but belongs to the claimant, is restored to the claimant. This *vindicatio* is not recognized at Common Law, and even in Equity it is not the only remedy where the defendant has interfered with the claimant's property rights,[85] so it could be concluded that it is not appropriate to refer to the vindication of property rights, since property rights are not necessarily vindicated. Nevertheless, the use of the word 'vindication' does serve a useful function. This is because it describes, albeit in general terms, the nature of the remedy where property rights have been interfered with by the defendant. The word 'vindication' relates to the phrase 'property rights' in the same way that the word 'reversal' relates to 'unjust enrichment'.[86] Because of the technical meaning of vindication, an alternative word could be suggested, such as 'protection', but this too lacks precision since it suggests that the restitutionary remedy will be awarded before the proprietary right has been interfered with, to ensure that such interference does not occur, whereas typically the property right has already been interfered with, hence the need for a restitutionary remedy. Consequently, the word 'vindication' will be used in this book, as the most useful word to describe the award of restitutionary remedies where the defendant has interfered with the claimant's property rights.[87]

(iv) Justifying the Award of Restitutionary Remedies to Vindicate Property Rights

The justification for the award of restitutionary remedies to vindicate the claimant's property rights stems from the fundamental principle of English law that property rights are of such importance that they are deserving of particular protection.[88] But, despite this,

---

[77] Birks, *Unjust Enrichment* (2nd edn), 35.   [78] [2001] 1 AC 102.   [79] [1914] AC 398.
[80] *Westdeutsche Landesbank Girozentrale v Islington LBC* [1996] AC 669.
[81] [1981] Ch 105.
[82] *Westdeutsche Landesbank Girozentrale v Islington LBC* [1996] AC 669. See p 598, below.
[83] As in *Banque Financière de la Cité v Parc (Battersea) Ltd* [1999] 1 AC 221. See p 637, below.
[84] See Chapter 21.   [85] See Chapter 22.
[86] The equivalent word for wrongdoing would be 'remedy'.
[87] The use of the word 'vindication' does have some judicial support: see, for example, *Tinsley v Milligan* [1994] 1 AC 340, 368 (Lord Lowry) and *Foskett v McKeown* [2001] AC 102, 129 (Lord Millett).
[88] See Chapter 21.

it might be thought that it does not matter whether the restitutionary claim is analysed with reference to the vindication of property rights or unjust enrichment. It is certainly true that in many cases the same result will be achieved regardless of how the claim is analysed. But the proper analysis can matter for practical reasons, such as whether the defence of change of position should apply,[89] what the elements of the respective causes of action might be and which remedies are potentially available. It also matters for intellectual reasons, since it is the legitimacy of the vindication of property rights principle which has become the battleground for vital theoretical discussion amongst commentators and increasingly judges about the proper classification of rights and remedies both at Law and in Equity.

(D) SUMMARY OF THE KEY PRINCIPLES

The consequence of the analysis adopted in this book and developments in the case law is that the law of restitution should properly be analysed in the following way. The law of restitution is concerned with all claims where the remedy which the claimant seeks is assessed with reference to the defendant's gain. Such remedies are available in three situations: first, where it can be shown that the defendant has been unjustly enriched—here the only remedies which are available are personal restitutionary remedies; secondly, where the defendant has committed a wrong for which restitutionary relief may be available—here the remedy may be restitutionary, but it can also be compensatory; finally, where the claimant wishes to vindicate his or her property rights—here the remedy is typically restitutionary and, depending on whether or not the defendant retains property in which the claimant has a proprietary interest, the restitutionary remedy will either be proprietary or personal.

4. WHAT IS THE JUSTIFICATION FOR RECOGNIZING AN INDEPENDENT LAW OF RESTITUTION?

When the law of restitution was equated with the law of unjust enrichment, the justification for recognizing an independent body of law called the law of restitution was clear, since it was a distinct subject different from contract, tort, and the law of property. But, once it is accepted that the law of restitution is not confined to the law of unjust enrichment, but is simply a body of law concerning a common category of remedies which may be awarded in particular circumstances, the justification for recognizing an independent law of restitution is more difficult to find. It might be thought better to stop talking about and studying the law of restitution and, instead, concentrate our efforts on the law of unjust enrichment[90] and, where relevant, wrongdoing and vindication of proprietary rights. This would be a mistake. Significantly, the American Law Institute in its *Restatement Third: Restitution and Unjust Enrichment*,[91] retains the word 'Restitution' and, whilst it includes core unjust enrichment liabilities, it also encompasses

---

[89] See Chapter 25.

[90] As Birks did in *Unjust Enrichment* and the editors of *Goff and Jones* have done in renaming the book *The Law of Unjust Enrichment*. See also *Barnes v Eastenders Cash and Carry plc* [2014] UKSC 26, [2015] AC 1, [100] (Lord Toulson), who emphasized that it is the content of the law which matters, rather than what it is called.

[91] *Restatement Third: Restitution and Unjust Enrichment* (St Paul, MN: American Law Institute Publishing, 2011).

proprietary restitutionary claims and restitution for wrongs, albeit that in both cases unjust enrichment is considered to underpin the claim. As the Restatement proves, there is much to be gained from this holistic treatment of the law of restitution.

The main reason for identifying any legal category, such as contract, Equity, or company law, is that, by grouping together cases which are concerned with the same legal issues, common principles can be identified which assist in the better understanding and prediction of the law. This is true of the law of restitution as well. There are a number of common principles and questions of policy which relate to all restitutionary claims regardless of the cause of action.[92] So, for example, there are important questions of relevance to all restitutionary claims concerning how restitutionary remedies should be assessed. Similarly, there are defences which are generally applicable to all restitutionary claims regardless of the principle on which that claim is founded. Also, as a mechanism for analysis of the law, the law of restitution remains a useful hook on which to hang disparate areas of law. It forces us to make connections which might otherwise be ignored, so the subject remains of great benefit for the purposes of legal exposition. So, for example, when determining the role of fault,[93] the way fault is interpreted in one part of the law of restitution will be of importance when considering the issue in another area.[94] For all of these reasons much is to be gained by recognizing the law of restitution as an independent body of law in its own right, where the only common characteristic is that it concerns the award of remedies which are assessed by reference to the benefit obtained by the defendant.

5. THE PRINCIPAL TYPES OF RESTITUTIONARY REMEDY

There are a number of different restitutionary remedies which will be examined through-out this book. At this stage it is sufficient to identify the most important ones. Whilst the remedy which is available for a particular restitutionary claim will vary according to the circumstances of the case, the function of all restitutionary remedies is 'to effect a fair and just balance between the rights and interests of the parties concerned'.[95]

(A) MONEY HAD AND RECEIVED

This is a Common Law restitutionary remedy which is applicable where the claimant simply wishes to recover money which had been paid to the defendant. It is a personal remedy which enables the claimant to recover the value of the money received by the defendant rather than the actual notes and coins transferred.

(B) REASONABLE VALUE OF PROPERTY AND SERVICES

Where the claimant has transferred property to the defendant, or has provided a service for the benefit of the defendant, and the claimant successfully brings a restitutionary claim in respect of these benefits, the typical remedy which he or she will be awarded is a pecuniary one, assessed by reference to the value of the benefit received by the defendant.

---

[92] These are identified and examined in Chapter 2.   [93] See Chapter 2.

[94] See GJ Virgo, 'The Role of Fault in the Law of Restitution' in AS Burrows (ed), *Mapping the Law of Obligations* (Oxford: Oxford University Press, 2006).

[95] *Banque Financière de la Cité v Parc (Battersea) Ltd* [1999] 1 AC 221, 237 (Lord Clyde).

Where the claim is for the reasonable value of the property transferred, this is called a *quantum valebat*, and where the claim is for the reasonable value of services, this is called a *quantum meruit*, which literally translated means 'as much as he deserves'.[96] The question of valuation of goods and, particularly, services is one which is fraught with difficulty.[97]

(C) ACCOUNT OF PROFITS

Where the defendant has committed a wrong against the claimant, such as a breach of fiduciary duty, and the defendant makes a profit as a result, one of the restitutionary remedies which may be awarded is that of an account of profits.[98] This involves an account being taken to ascertain the profit made by the defendant as a result of the wrongdoing, which the defendant is then liable to pay to the claimant. This is a personal remedy, since the defendant is only required to transfer the value of the profit made.[99]

(D) RESTITUTIONARY DAMAGES

Whereas an account of profits can only be awarded where the defendant has profited from the commission of a wrong, there may be circumstances where the defendant has benefited from wrongdoing by saving expenditure and it is appropriate to deprive him or her of this benefit by means of a restitutionary remedy. An appropriate name for this remedy is 'restitutionary damages'.[100] In *Attorney-General v Blake*,[101] however, Lord Nicholls rejected this name in favour of 'account of profits'. It appears that this was due to a sense that the word 'damages' only relates to a compensatory remedy which arises where the claimant has suffered a loss as a result of the commission of a wrong. Whilst it is true that 'damages' usually does have a compensatory connotation, if the prefix 'restitutionary' is used there is no obvious objection to the name of this remedy. Further, it is clear that this type of remedy does need to be recognized to deal with the situation where the benefit obtained by the defendant involves money saved rather than profit gained. Consequently, the term 'restitutionary damages' will be used in this book, but only to name the remedy concerned with restitution of a negative benefit, whereas account of profits will be used where the defendant has obtained a positive benefit as a result of the commission of a wrong.

(E) RECOGNITION OF A BENEFICIAL INTEREST

Where the defendant has received and retains property in which the claimant has a continuing equitable proprietary interest, the defendant may be required to hold that property on trust for the claimant, who has a beneficial interest in it.[102] This means that the claimant can call for the return of the property whenever he or she wishes.[103] This type of proprietary restitutionary remedy involving the transfer of property is not available at Common Law. Consequently, if the defendant has property in which the claimant has retained a legal proprietary interest, the claimant is only able to obtain the value of the property and is not able to recover the property itself.

---

[96] *Benedetti v Sawiris* [2010] EWCA Civ 1427, [2] (Arden LJ).   [97] See Chapter 4.

[98] See Chapter 16.

[99] The profit may, however, be held on constructive trust so that the claimant has an equitable proprietary interest in the profit. See Chapter 19.

[100] See Chapter 16 and *Aggravated, Exemplary and Restitutionary Damages* (Law Com No 247, 1997), 51.

[101] [2001] 1 AC 268.   [102] See Chapter 22.

[103] See *Saunders v Vautier* (1841) 4 Beav 115, 49 ER 282.

(F) EQUITABLE CHARGE

Where the defendant has property in which the claimant has an equitable proprietary interest, an alternative restitutionary remedy to that of recognizing that the claimant has a beneficial interest in it is for the courts to impose an equitable charge over it.[104] This is a proprietary restitutionary remedy, since it recognizes that the claimant has a proprietary interest in the property to secure repayment of what the defendant owes to the claimant. Consequently, although the claimant cannot compel the defendant to transfer the property to him or her, the claimant's claim for repayment is given priority over the claims of unsecured creditors of the defendant.

(G) SUBROGATION

Subrogation[105] is a restitutionary remedy which is designed to ensure 'a transfer of rights from one person to another... by operation of law'.[106] Essentially, the function of subrogation is to enable the claimant to rely on the rights of a third party against a defendant, or the rights of a defendant against a third party. This will be a particularly useful remedy where, for example, the claimant lends money to the defendant in circumstances where the claimant thinks that the loan is secured by a charge so that he or she has priority over the defendant's other creditors. If the charge is invalid the claimant would simply be an unsecured creditor and so will not have priority over other creditors. In such a case the claimant could be subrogated to the rights of another secured creditor of the defendant, even where that security has already been discharged. The security in such circumstances is treated as though it had been assigned to the claimant,[107] so that he or she is able to rely on it as against the defendant and so gain priority over the defendant's unsecured creditors. Since subrogation is a restitutionary remedy, this notional assignment of the charge is only effective as against a defendant who is liable to make restitution to the claimant.

In *Banque Financière de la Cité v Parc (Battersea) Ltd*[108] the House of Lords acknowledged that there are two forms of subrogation which are recognized in English law.

(i) Contractual

The first type of subrogation arises by virtue of the express or implied intentions of the parties, as occurs in contracts of insurance where a term is implied that insurers are subrogated to the rights of the assured against the party who caused loss.[109] Since this right to subrogation arises by virtue of contract, it has nothing to do with the law of restitution.[110]

(ii) Restitutionary

The other type of subrogation is the equitable restitutionary remedy which is available by operation of law specifically to reverse the defendant's unjust enrichment.[111] It may also

---

[104] See Chapter 22.

[105] See C Mitchell and S Watterson, *Subrogation: Law and Practice* (Oxford: Oxford University Press, 2007).

[106] *Orakpo v Manson Investments Ltd* [1978] AC 95, 104 (Lord Diplock).

[107] *Banque Financière de la Cité v Parc (Battersea) Ltd* [1999] 1 AC 221, 236 (Lord Hoffmann).

[108] [1999] 1 AC 221.

[109] See, for example, *Lord Napier and Ettrick v Hunter* [1993] AC 713.

[110] *Hobbs v Marlowe* [1978] AC 16, 39 (Lord Diplock).

[111] *Banque Financière de la Cité v Parc (Battersea) Ltd* [1999] 1 AC 221, 231 (Lord Hoffmann); *Filby v Mortgage Express (No 2) Ltd* [2004] EWCA Civ 759; *Menelaou v Bank of Cyprus plc* [2013] EWCA Civ 1960, [2014] 1 WLR 854.

be used to *prevent* the defendant's unjust enrichment.[112] Although the matter was not discussed by the House of Lords, subrogation should also be available where the claimant's restitutionary claim is founded on the vindication of property rights, and is in fact most likely to arise in such circumstances.[113] Whilst the remedy is in principle available where the claim is founded on the commission of a wrong, there are no cases where such a remedy has been awarded, and it is difficult to conceive of a case where such a remedy would be appropriate.

(H) RECTIFICATION

Rectification is an equitable remedy which enables the court to amend a written document where that document does not reflect the common intention of the parties, or where it does not reflect the intention of one of them and the other knows that it does not do so.[114]

In many cases rectification will not involve a valuable benefit or right being given up by the defendant, but will simply ensure that contractual documentation reflects the intentions of the parties. But there will be cases where rectification will effect restitution. For example, the effect of rectification may be to extinguish rights which would otherwise be enjoyed by the defendant according to the face of the contract, with corresponding expansion of the rights enjoyed by the claimant.[115] Rectification may also enable the claimant to recover property which had been transferred to the defendant, by ensuring that the restitutionary claim is not barred by the operation of the contract.[116] This is illustrated by *Day v Day*,[117] where a written conveyance was rectified as a consequence of there being a common mistake relating to its legal effect. Property had been settled on trust. The settlor had intended the property to be used simply as security to enable the defendant to raise funds, whereas the effect of the settlement was to give the defendant a beneficial interest in the property. The effect of rectification was to enable the settlor's estate to recover the property which had been mistakenly transferred to the defendant.

(I) RESCISSION

(i) The Nature of Rescission

Where a transaction, usually a contract,[118] is voidable for fraudulent misrepresentation,[119] duress,[120] or non-disclosure in respect of contracts of insurance or guarantee,[121] the claimant can set it aside at Common Law. Where it is voidable for fraudulent[122]

---

[112] *Banque Financière de la Cité v Parc (Battersea) Ltd* [1999] 1 AC 221, 231 (Lord Hoffmann).

[113] *Halifax plc v Omar* [2002] EWCA Civ 21, [2002] 2 P and CR 377; *Eagle Star Insurance Co Ltd v Karasiewicz* [2002] EWCA Civ 940. See also *Bofinger v Kingsway Group Ltd* [2009] HCA 44. See Chapter 22.

[114] See generally *Marley v Rawlings* [2014] UKSC 2, [2015] AC 129. The test is whether the document accords with intent rather than motive: *Kennedy v Kennedy* [2014] EWHC 4129 (Ch), [43] (Etherton C).

[115] See AVM Lodder, *Enrichment in the Law of Restitution and Unjust Enrichment* (Oxford: Hart Publishing, 2012), 138.

[116] Thus, avoiding the bar of a lawful basis to the restitutionary claim. See Chapter 7.

[117] [2013] EWCA Civ 280, [2014] Ch 114.

[118] But the transaction may also be a deed or a voluntary disposition to a trust.

[119] *Smith New Court Securities Ltd v Scrimgeour Vickers (Asset Management) Ltd* [1997] AC 254.

[120] *Whelpdale's case* (1605) 5 Co Rep 119a.   [121] *Ionides v Pender* (1874) LR 9 QB 531.

[122] *The National Crime Agency v Robb* [2014] EWHC 4384 (Ch), which also held that a transaction is voidable for fraud even though the transaction was initially legitimate and the fraud arose subsequently.

or non-fraudulent misrepresentation[123] or undue influence,[124] the transaction can be set aside in Equity.[125] Both at Law and in Equity the mechanism for setting the transaction aside is rescission.[126] Once a transaction is rescinded it is nullified and everything which has been done under it is liable to be undone,[127] so that the parties are restored to their original position; there is a giving and a taking back on both sides.[128] This is effected by reference to the law of restitution rather than the law of contract.[129]

Rescission has been described as a remedy,[130] and it can be considered to have restitutionary consequences since a function of rescission is that the claimant can recover 'the property with which he has parted under the contract and [must return] the benefit which he received' to the defendant.[131] This restitutionary consequence is available once the claimant has satisfied the conditions for setting the transaction aside, as recognized by Millett LJ in *Portman BS v Hamlyn Taylor and Neck*:[132]

> The obligation to make restitution must flow from the ineffectiveness of the transaction under which the money was paid and not from a mistake or misrepresentation which induced it . . . If the payer exercises his right of rescission in time and before the recipient deals with the money in accordance with his instructions, the obligation to make restitution may follow.

Rescission does not necessarily have restitutionary consequences. For example, sometimes the court may order rescission on terms, such as requiring the parties to enter into a new, more appropriate contract.[133] Usually, however, rescission will have restitutionary consequences. For example, money paid by a claimant pursuant to a voidable transaction can be recovered as a consequence of rescission. This restitutionary consequence follows automatically from the rescission of the transaction, but it is also a condition of rescission, since the transaction cannot be set aside if the parties cannot be restored to their original position. Even where an executory contract is rescinded it can be considered to have restitutionary consequences, since the defendant is required to give up those rights against the claimant which derived from the contract, with a corresponding benefit to the claimant.[134]

---

[123] *Lamare v Dixon* (1873) LR 6 HL 414.

[124] *Dunbar Bank plc v Nadeem* [1998] 3 All ER 876. See Chapter 11.

[125] Following *Great Peace Shipping Ltd v Tsavliris Salvage (International) Ltd* [2002] EWCA Civ 1407, [2003] AC 679 the equitable jurisdiction to grant rescission for common mistake has been rejected.

[126] See generally D O'Sullivan, S Elliott, and R Zakrzewski, *The Law of Rescission* (Oxford: Oxford University Press, 2007); N Andrews, M Clarke, A Tettenborn, and G Virgo, *Contractual Duties: Performance, Breach, Termination and Remedies* (London: Sweet and Maxwell, 2012), chs 1–4.

[127] *Manifest Shipping Co Ltd v Uni-Polaris Insurance Co Ltd (The Star Sea)* [2001] UKHL 1, [2003] 1 AC 469, [51] (Lord Hobhouse).

[128] *Shalson v Russo* [2003] EWHC 1637 (Ch), [2005] Ch 281, [122] (Rimer J).

[129] *Manifest Shipping Co Ltd v Uni-Polaris Insurance Co Ltd (The Star Sea)* [2001] UKHL 1, [2003] 1 AC 469, [51] (Lord Hobhouse).

[130] *Dunbar Bank plc v Nadeem* [1998] 3 All ER 876, 884 (Millett LJ).

[131] *Smith New Court Securities Ltd v Scrimgeour Vickers (Asset Management) Ltd* [1994] 1 WLR 1271, 1280 (Nourse LJ).

[132] [1998] 4 All ER 202, 208.   [133] See p 28, below.

[134] NY Nahan, 'Rescission: A Case For Rejecting the Classical Model?' (1997) 27 Univ WALR 66, 72; AVM Lodder, *Enrichment in the Law of Restitution and Unjust Enrichment* (Oxford: Hart Publishing, 2012), 117. Cf *Criterion Properties plc v Stratford UK Properties LLC* [2004] 1 WLR 1846, 1855 where Lord Scott recognized that the creation of contractual rights through an executory contract does not constitute the receipt of an asset and therefore cannot constitute an enrichment.

(ii) The Process of Rescission

The method by which the claimant rescinds a transaction depends on whether rescission occurs at Law or in Equity.[135]

(1) Rescission at Law

Where the claimant wishes to rescind a transaction at Law he or she can do so without obtaining a court order.[136] Consequently, rescission at Law is a self-help mechanism.[137] Where the claimant wishes to rescind a transaction it is usually necessary that he or she communicates this wish to the defendant, either through words or conduct.[138] But in certain exceptional circumstances such direct communication is not required. For example, in *Car and Universal Finance Co Ltd v Caldwell*[139] the claimant wanted to rescind a contract to sell a car, but he could not trace the purchaser of the vehicle. It was held to be sufficient to rescind the contract that he had notified both the Automobile Association and the police that he wished them to assist him in finding the car. Alternatively, if there is a dispute about the right to rescind, and the claimant commences judicial proceedings to resolve the matter, the statement in the particulars of claim that the transaction has been or should be set aside will in itself be sufficient to rescind the transaction.[140]

(2) Rescission in Equity

Rescission in Equity is a form of equitable relief which is determined and effected by the court in the exercise of judicial discretion.[141] Although a claimant must still elect for the contract to be rescinded, this is simply a decision made by the claimant as to whether an application should be made to the court. Once the order of the court has been obtained, rescission will operate retrospectively to the date when the claimant commenced proceedings.[142] The judge has a discretion both as to whether to order rescission and, if so, as to the nature and extent of that relief which may, for example, be subject to conditions.[143]

(iii) Restitution Following Rescission

The restitutionary consequences which follow rescission can be justified with reference either to the principle of vindicating property rights or the unjust enrichment principle, depending on whether the consequence of rescission is proprietary or personal.

(1) Proprietary

The proprietary consequences of rescission will be that, if the transaction is rescinded at Law, legal title to property will be revested in the claimant.[144] Where the claimant rescinds

---

[135] See J O'Sullivan, 'Rescission as a Self-help Remedy: A Critical Analysis' (2000) 59 CLJ 509.

[136] *Car and Universal Finance Co Ltd v Caldwell* [1965] 1 QB 525, 532 (Lord Denning MR); *Brotherton v Aseguradora Cobeguros (No 2)* [2003] EWCA Civ 705, [2003] 3 All ER (Comm) 298, [27] (Mance LJ).

[137] *Halpern v Halpern (No 2)* [2006] EWHC 1728 (Comm), [2007] QB 88, [26] (Nigel Teare QC).

[138] *Clough v London and North Western Railway Co* (1871) LR 7 Ex 26, 34 (Mellor J).

[139] [1965] 1 QB 525.

[140] *TSB Bank plc v Camfield* [1995] 1 WLR 430, 438 (Roch LJ).

[141] *Erlanger v New Sombrero Phosphate Co* (1878) 3 App Cas 1218, 1278 (Lord Blackburn); *Spence v Crawford* [1939] 3 All ER 271, 288 (Lord Wright).

[142] *Reese Silver Mining Co v Smith* (1869) LR 4 HL 64.

[143] *Cheese v Thomas* [1994] 1 WLR 129, 137 (Sir Donald Nicholls V-C); *Wilson v Hurstanger Ltd* [2007] EWCA Civ 299, [2001] 1 WLR 2351, [48] (Tuckey LJ).

[144] *Car and Universal Finance Co Ltd v Caldwell* [1965] 1 QB 525. Cf WJ Swadling, 'Rescission, Property and the Common Law' (2005) 121 LQR 123 who argues that rescission at Common Law should not have any proprietary consequences. See p 580, below.

the transaction in Equity, the consequence will be that the property which the claimant transferred to the defendant will be held on trust for the claimant who will have an equitable proprietary interest in it.[145] In either case the claimant will be able to bring a proprietary restitutionary claim to vindicate his or her property right.

(2) Personal

Where the claimant has transferred property to the defendant under a voidable transaction which is rescinded, the defendant may not have retained the property or its traceable substitute, so that a proprietary restitutionary claim will not be available. The claimant will, however, be able to recover the value of the benefits transferred. This restitutionary response can be justified on the basis that, if the defendant was not required to make restitution to the claimant, the consequence of the claimant setting the transaction aside will be that the defendant is unjustly enriched at the claimant's expense.[146] This is because the defendant will have obtained a benefit from the claimant in circumstances where the defendant's retention of that benefit is unjust, since the claimant had not intended the defendant to receive the benefit in those circumstances. Consequently, the real significance of the unjust enrichment principle for the purposes of rescission is that it has a negative function to ensure that the consequence of rescission is that the defendant will not be unjustly enriched.[147] This was explicitly recognized by Robert Goff J in *Whittaker v Campbell*[148] who said: 'The remedy of rescission, by which the unjust enrichment of the [defendant] is prevented . . . is a straightforward remedy in restitution.'

Regardless of whether the transaction is rescinded at Law or in Equity, once it has been rescinded there will be mutual restitutionary consequences since the claimant can recover 'the property with which he has parted under the contract and [must return] the benefit which he received' to the defendant.[149] The policy of the law is to return the parties to the position which they occupied before entering into the transaction. Consequently, the defendant will be obliged to return to the claimant the value of all benefits which he or she received under the transaction, and the claimant must make counter-restitution to the defendant.[150] This restitution is typically in monetary form.[151]

---

[145] *El Ajou v Dollar Land Holdings plc* [1993] 3 All ER 717, 734 (Millett LJ).

[146] *National Commercial Bank (Jamaica) Ltd v Hew* [2003] UKPC 51, [43].

[147] That the unjust enrichment principle can function in this negative way was recognized by the House of Lords in *Banque Financière de la Cité v Parc (Battersea) Ltd* [1999] 1 AC 221 where the remedy of subrogation was awarded to prevent the defendant from becoming unjustly enriched.

[148] [1984] QB 318, 327.

[149] *Smith New Court Securities Ltd v Scrimgeour Vickers (Asset Management) Ltd* [1994] 1 WLR 1271, 1280 (Nourse LJ).

[150] *TSB Bank plc v Camfield* [1995] 1 WLR 430, 434–5 (Nourse LJ). English law only requires the parties to the transaction in question to make restitution to each other. If a third party has received a benefit under the transaction, as will be the case where a bank has lent money to a third party as a result of the claimant agreeing to act as surety, the guarantee can be rescinded even though the bank cannot recover what it had lent to the third party: *Mackenzie v Royal Bank of Canada* [1934] AC 468, 476 (Lord Atkin). But, if the restitutionary consequence is founded on unjust enrichment, it should be subject to the defence of change of position, which would mean that the defendant would not be required to make restitution if he or she had transferred a benefit to a third party. See P Watts, 'Rescission of Guarantees for Misrepresentation and Actionable Damages' (2002) 61 CLJ 301; M Chen-Wishart, 'Unjust Factors and the Restitutionary Response' (2000) OJLS 557. See p 273, below.

[151] This is sometimes described as pecuniary rescission: PBH Birks, 'Unjust Factors and Wrongs: Pecuniary Rescission for Undue Influence' [1997] RLR 72. This is misleading. Rescission involves setting aside the transaction; the pecuniary element relates to restitution following rescission.

(iv) Bars to Rescission

The claimant's right to rescind a voidable transaction may be barred in certain circumstances.

Various bars to rescission have been recognized which generally apply regardless of the ground for rescission and regardless of whether rescission occurs at Law or in Equity, although the bars are interpreted differently depending on the jurisdiction for rescission, with the bars being interpreted more restrictively in Equity than at Law.

(1) Restoration of the Defendant Impossible

Rescission will be barred if it is not possible to restore the defendant to the position which he or she was in before the contract was made.[152] This is also called the bar of *restitutio in integrum* being impossible, or the obligation to make counter-restitution.[153] The justification for this bar is both to ensure that the claimant is not unjustly enriched at the expense of the defendant,[154] which would occur if the claimant was able to recover the value of benefits from the defendant but was not required to restore to the defendant the value of benefits received, and also to protect the defendant from being in a worse position following the rescission of the contract than he or she was in before the contract was made.[155] Although *restitutio in integrum* is often described as requiring both parties to be restored to their pre-transaction position,[156] the doctrine only operates as a bar to rescission when the defendant cannot be restored.[157] The fact that a claimant cannot be restored to his or her pre-transaction position will not bar rescission,[158] presumably because the claimant has elected to rescind the contract and takes the risk of not being restored precisely to that position. The bar will not operate to defeat rescission where a contract is executory, since the effect of rescission will simply be to terminate future contractual obligations and the claimant will not have received any benefit from the defendant, so that there is nothing tangible to return.[159]

The orthodox view has been that rescission will be barred whenever counter-restitution cannot be made exactly.[160] Consequently, it has been held that, where the claimant has consumed or disposed of property which was received from the defendant under a voidable contract, the claimant will be barred from rescinding the contract because counter-restitution is not possible.[161] So, for example, if the claimant has received documents under a contract which have then been destroyed, rescission will be barred.[162] In *Smith New Court Securities Ltd v Scrimgeour Vickers (Asset Management) Ltd*[163] the claimant had been induced to buy shares as a result of the defendant's fraudulent misrepresentation. The Court of Appeal held that the claimant was unable to rescind

---

[152] *Spence v Crawford* [1939] 3 All ER 271, 288–9 (Lord Wright); *Smith New Court Securities Ltd v Scrimgeour Vickers (Asset Management) Ltd* [1994] 1 WLR 1271, 1280 (Nourse LJ).

[153] *Dunbar Bank plc v Nadeem* [1998] 3 All ER 876, 884 (Millett LJ).

[154] *Spence v Crawford* [1939] 3 All ER 271, 288–9 (Lord Wright).

[155] See E Bant, *The Change of Position Defence* (Oxford: Hart Publishing, 2009), 118.

[156] See, for example, *Erlanger v The New Sombrero Phosphate Co* (1878) 3 App Cas 1218, 1278 (Lord Blackburn).

[157] *Spence v Crawford* [1939] 3 All ER 271, 289 (Lord Wright).

[158] Ibid, 279 (Lord Thankerton); *Halpern v Halpern* [2007] EWCA Civ 291, [2008] QB 195, [75] (Carnwath LJ).

[159] *National Commercial Bank (Jamaica) Ltd v Hew* [2003] UKPC 51, [43].

[160] *Spence v Crawford* [1939] 3 All ER 271, 288–9 (Lord Wright); *Smith New Court Securities Ltd v Scrimgeour Vickers (Asset Management) Ltd* [1994] 1 WLR 1271, 1280 (Nourse LJ) and *Dunbar Bank plc v Nadeem* [1998] 3 All ER 876, 884 (Millett LJ).

[161] *Clarke v Dickson* (1858) EB and E 148, 120 ER 463.

[162] *Halpern v Halpern* [2007] EWCA Civ 291, [2008] QB 195.   [163] [1994] 1 WLR 1271.

the contract and recover the full purchase price of the shares from the defendant, because the claimant had sold the shares to a third party and so was unable to make 'substantial restitution in specie of the property' which it had received.[164]

This requirement to make precise restitution has proved to be a greater obstacle to rescission at Law[165] than in Equity, because Equity does not require precise restoration; it is sufficient that the defendant can be restored substantially to his or her pre-transaction position, by reference to a more flexible criterion of 'practical justice'.[166] It follows that the *restitutio in integrum* bar is of more limited significance in Equity. Equity effects this substantial restitution by directing accounts and making allowances.[167] Rescission should only be denied where it is not possible to value the benefit which has been provided. This is illustrated by *Erlanger v New Sombrero Phosphate Co*,[168] where the claimant wished to rescind a contract for the purchase of a phosphate mine on the ground of non-disclosure of a material fact by the defendant. The problem was that the claimant had worked the mine and obtained some benefit from it. The House of Lords held that the claimant was able to rescind the contract, as long as it returned the mine to the defendant and accounted for the profits it had made from working the mine. As Lord Blackburn said, a court of Equity will grant relief 'whenever, by the use of its powers, it can do what is practically just, though it cannot restore the parties precisely to the state they were in before the contract'.[169]

The consequence of such decisions is that rescission will hardly ever be defeated in Equity by the bar of counter-restitution not being possible, since restitution can be made in respect of virtually all benefits received if the benefit can be valued, even if it is not possible to return the specific benefit to the defendant.[170] It is, however, most unfortunate that a similar approach to pecuniary restitution was not recognized for rescission at Law by the Court of Appeal in *Smith New Court Securities Ltd v Scrimgeour Vickers (Asset Management) Ltd*.[171] Surely, it would have been sufficient for the claimant to pay the value of the shares to the defendant or to buy substitute shares which could be returned to the defendant. This was, in fact, recognized by Lord Browne-Wilkinson when the case was heard on appeal, although the question of rescission was not specifically considered by that court. Lord Browne-Wilkinson said that:

> if the current law in fact provides (as the Court of Appeal thought) that there is no right to rescind the contract for the sale of quoted shares once the specific shares purchased have been sold, the law will need to be closely looked at hereafter. Since in such a case other, identical, shares can be purchased on the market, the defrauded purchaser can offer substantial *restitutio in integrum* which is normally sufficient.[172]

---

[164] Ibid, 1280 (Nourse LJ). This issue was not raised on appeal before the House of Lords.

[165] Ibid.

[166] *Erlanger v New Sombrero Phosphate Co* (1878) 3 App Cas 1218, 1278 (Lord Blackburn); *Spence v Crawford* [1939] 3 All ER 271, 279 (Lord Thankerton), 288 (Lord Wright); *Halpern v Halpern* [2007] EWCA Civ 291, [2008] QB 195, [61] (Carnwath LJ).

[167] *Cheese v Thomas* [1994] 1 WLR 129, 136 (Sir Donald Nicholls V-C).

[168] (1878) 3 App Cas 1218.

[169] Ibid, 1278. In the exercise of this power the court will also be prepared to grant the defendant an allowance in respect of the deterioration in value of any property which is returned to him or her.

[170] See *Dunbar Bank plc v Nadeem* [1998] 3 All ER 876, 888 where Morritt LJ contemplated that, on the exceptional facts of that case, counter-restitution would not be possible.

[171] [1994] 2 BCLC 212.

[172] *Smith New Court Securities Ltd v Scrimgeour Vickers (Asset Management) Ltd* [1997] AC 254, 262.

This is surely the more just approach. In *Halpern v Halpern*[173] Carnwath LJ expressed a willingness to adopt a more flexible approach to rescission at Law, an approach which would appear to be consistent with that which is adopted in Equity. Consequently, in all cases of rescission it should be sufficient that the claimant can restore the defendant substantially to the position he or she occupied before the transaction was made.[174] It should follow that the bar of not being able to make counter-restitution should only be relevant where the benefit obtained cannot be valued[175] or where counter-restitution is impractical. For example, in *Thomas Witter Ltd v TBP Industries Ltd*[176] rescission was barred where a company had been sold to the claimant but the nature of the business changed from being the operator of licensed premises to a property holding company and there had been numerous changes of staff.

(2) Third-Party Rights

Rescission is also traditionally barred at Law where the effect of rescinding the transaction entered into by the claimant and the defendant would be to interfere with the rights of third parties.[177] In particular, the right of rescission will be barred if a third party subsequently acquires a legal[178] interest in property which was transferred to the defendant under a voidable contract, where the third party acquired the property for value and without notice of the defect which provided the reason for the claimant wishing to rescind it. The fact that a third party has acquired an interest in property will not, however, defeat rescission in Equity as between the claimant and the defendant. So, for example, where the defendant has sold the property which was transferred under the voidable contract to a third party, the claimant can still rescind the contract and obtain the proceeds of sale from the defendant, but this will have no effect on the validity of the sale to the third party.

The existence of the third-party rights bar is difficult to defend. Whilst it is correct that, if a third party has acquired proprietary rights in good faith and for value, the claimant should not be able to bring a claim against the third party to recover the property, it does not necessarily follow that the acquisition of third-party proprietary rights should prevent the claimant from rescinding the contract with the defendant[179] and so protect the defendant. Although an effect of rescission is traditionally to revest title in property to the claimant, it would not be appropriate for rescission to have this effect where a third party has acquired rights in the property transferred for value; the security of the third-party's receipt is then paramount. But there is no reason why this should bar rescission completely, since rescission has other consequences, such as to avoid future contractual obligations and to recover the value of the property transferred to the defendant, but leave the third party's proprietary right unaffected.[180]

(3) Affirmation

The claimant cannot rescind a transaction which he or she has affirmed. Two conditions must be satisfied before the transaction can be considered to have been affirmed. First, the claimant must know of the circumstances which enable him or her to rescind the

---

[173] [2007] EWCA Civ 291, [2008] QB 195, [74].   [174] Ibid, [76] (Carnwath LJ).

[175] See R Halson, 'Rescission for Misrepresentation' [1997] RLR 89, 91.

[176] [1996] 2 All ER 573, 587 (Jacob J). See also *Boyd and Forrest v Glasgow and South Western Railway Co* [1915] SC (HL) 20 (land could not be restored to its original condition).

[177] *Tennent v The City of Glasgow Bank and Liquidators* (1879) 4 App Cas 615, 621 (Earl Cairns LC).

[178] *Phillips v Brooks Ltd* [1919] 2 KB 243.

[179] NY Nahan, 'Rescission: A Case For Rejecting the Classical Model?' (1997) 27 Univ WALR 66, 74.

[180] B Häcker, 'Rescission and Third Party Rights' [2006] RLR 21, 36.

transaction, as will be the case where the claimant discovers that he or she was induced to enter into the contract by virtue of the defendant's misrepresentation.[181] But rescission will not be barred if the claimant merely had the means of discovering that there was a ground for rescinding the transaction, even if this could have been discovered with due diligence.[182]

Secondly, the claimant must unequivocally show by words or conduct that he or she has decided not to rescind the contract.[183] It is not necessary for the claimant to communicate this affirmation to the defendant.[184] So, for example, in *Sharpley v Louth and East Coast Railway Co*[185] the claimant was induced by a misrepresentation of the defendant company to purchase shares in that company. The claimant sought to rescind the contract but was unable to do so because, having discovered that the defendant's representations had been untrue, he continued to act as a shareholder, for example by attending general meetings of the company. This was conduct which was considered to show that he intended to affirm the contract.

(4) Lapse of Time

The claimant will also be barred from rescinding a transaction if a reasonable period of time has elapsed before he or she has attempted to rescind it.[186] What constitutes a reasonable period of time is a question of fact which depends on the particular circumstances of the case. This bar is often difficult to distinguish from the bar of affirmation since, if the claimant delays unnecessarily before seeking to rescind the transaction, this may be treated as affirmation of it.[187]

(v) Partial Rescission and Rescission on Terms

A contract can only be rescinded in its entirety and not partially,[188] and it is also not possible to rescind a transaction on terms, such as by setting aside the whole transaction and substituting a new one for it.[189] This is illustrated by *TSB Bank plc v Camfield*,[190] where it was held that a mortgage would be set aside completely as a result of a husband's misrepresentation and it would not be treated as valid to the extent of the maximum liability which the wife had actually accepted.

The apparent reason for the courts' refusal to allow partial rescission or rescission on terms stems from the perceived nature of rescission itself. Rescission is not considered to be a form of relief to which terms can be attached, but is a form of self-help. The claimant rescinds the transaction and the only role for the courts is to determine whether he or she has rescinded the transaction or is entitled to do so.[191] There is consequently no scope for any halfway house; either the claimant is or is not entitled to rescind the transaction in question. But, as has been seen, this is only true of rescission at Law, whereas rescission in Equity does indeed depend on the intervention of the court. In fact, rescission on terms has been recognized in Equity, such as where a claimant wishes to rescind a transaction for undue influence.[192] There will also be circumstances where it is appropriate to exercise judicial discretion in Equity to impose terms as a condition of rescission. So, for example,

---

[181] *Car and Universal Finance Co Ltd v Caldwell* [1965] 1 QB 525.
[182] *Redgrave v Hurd* (1881) 20 Ch D 1.
[183] *Clough v London and North Western Railway Co* (1871) LR 7 Exch 26.
[184] *Car and Universal Finance Co Ltd v Caldwell* [1965] 1 QB 525.   [185] (1876) 2 Ch D 663.
[186] *Leaf v International Galleries* [1950] 2 KB 86.
[187] *Clough v London and North Western Railway Co* (1871) LR 7 Exch 26.
[188] *Kennedy v Kennedy* [2014] EWHC 4129 (Ch), [46] (Etherton C).
[189] *Zamet v Hyman* [1961] 1 WLR 1442.   [190] [1995] 1 WLR 430. See p 271, below.
[191] See ibid, 438 (Roch LJ).   [192] *Cheese v Thomas* [1994] 1 WLR 129. See p 272, below.

if the claimant entered into a transaction as a result of misrepresentation, thinking that he or she had entered into a surety transaction for £5,000 but in fact the transaction was for £50,000, the surety transaction should be rescinded but terms be imposed that a £5,000 surety transaction should be substituted, since this is the amount which the claimant had actually consented to guarantee.

It has been recognized that it is possible to rescind a self-contained and severable part of a non-contractual voluntary transaction, such as a disposition to a trust made by a deed which is voidable for mistake.[193] This has been justified on the unconvincing ground that in such a transaction there is no need to restore both parties to their original position, since, being a voluntary disposition, only the recipient will have received a benefit.

(vi) The Future of Rescission

Rescission in Equity is much more adaptable than rescission at Law. Increasingly, the limitations of rescission at Law are difficult to defend. It would be preferable if the equitable approach to rescission should prevail,[194] so that all rescission should be effected by means of a judicial order to which terms can be attached if necessary, rather than be treated simply as a self-help remedy. This was recognized by the Court of Appeal in *Great Peace Shipping Ltd v Tsavliris Salvage Ltd*:[195]

> An equitable jurisdiction to grant rescission on terms where a common fundamental mistake has induced a contract gives greater flexibility than a doctrine of common law which holds the contract void in such circumstances. Just as the Law Reform (Frustrated Contracts) Act 1943 was needed to temper the effect of the common law doctrine of frustration, so there is scope for legislation to give greater flexibility to our law of mistake than the common law allows.

It is unfortunate that the Court felt that this creativity had to be a matter for Parliament rather than being developed by the courts.

(1) The Award of Interest

Since it is a function of restitutionary remedies that the defendant should be deprived of those gains obtained as a result of being unjustly enriched, having committed a wrong or receiving property in which the claimant has a proprietary interest, it should follow automatically that whenever pecuniary restitutionary remedies are awarded the claimant should also be awarded interest. This is because, immediately the defendant has received a benefit which he or she is liable to restore to the claimant, the defendant is not entitled to the benefit and so should pay the claimant for its use until it, or its value, is given up to the claimant. The law of restitution recognizes this argument, and so the defendant is liable to pay the claimant for the use of the benefit by means of the award of interest.

But, when it comes to assessing the interest which the defendant is liable to pay to the claimant, the law becomes much more controversial. Should simple or compound interest be awarded? Simple interest may be awarded by virtue of section 35A of the Senior Courts Act 1981. This is awarded on the amount of money which is owed by the defendant to the claimant. Compound interest has traditionally been awarded in Equity where money has been obtained or retained by fraud or where money has been withheld

---

[193] *Kennedy v Kennedy* [2014] EWHC 4129 (Ch), [46] (Etherton C).

[194] J O'Sullivan, 'Rescission as a Self-help Remedy: A Critical Analysis' (2000) 59 CLJ 509, 528.

[195] [2002] EWCA Civ 1407, [2003] AC 679, [161].

or misapplied by a fiduciary.[196] Compound interest is awarded both on the amount of money which is owed by the defendant to the claimant and on the amount of interest which is already due to the claimant. Consequently, the award of compound interest is more favourable to the claimant. The usual rate of compound interest which is awarded in the Commercial Court is the Bank of England base rate + 1% compounded monthly.

In *Westdeutsche Landesbank Girozentrale v Islington LBC*[197] the issue for the House of Lords was whether compound interest was available in respect of all restitutionary claims. A majority of the judges decided that, since the jurisdiction to award compound interest was equitable, compound interest could only be awarded in respect of equitable restitutionary claims. Consequently, where the claim was for money had and received the claimant could only obtain simple interest because this was a Common Law claim.

In two very strong dissenting judgments, Lords Goff and Woolf asserted that, since the policy of the law of restitution was to remove benefits from the defendant, compound interest should be available in respect of all restitutionary claims, regardless of whether they arise at Law or in Equity.[198] This argument can be illustrated by the following example. In the straightforward case where the claimant pays money to the defendant by mistake and the defendant is liable to repay that money, the liability arises from the moment the money is received by the defendant, who has the use of it and so should pay the claimant for the value of that benefit. This was accepted by all the judges in the case. The difficulty relates to the valuation of this benefit. If the defendant were to borrow an equivalent amount of money from a financial institution, he or she would typically be liable to pay compound interest to that institution. It follows that the defendant has saved that amount of money and so this is the value of the benefit which the defendant should restore to the claimant, in addition to the value of the money which the defendant received in the first place.[199] If it could be shown that, had the defendant borrowed the equivalent amount of money, the institution would only have paid simple interest, it would be appropriate for the interest awarded to the claimant to be simple rather than compound.[200] Usually, however, the interest awarded in commercial transactions will be compound interest.

The approach of the minority is much more attractive than that of the majority, since the award of compound interest is consistent with the fundamental principles underlying all restitutionary claims, especially that, where the defendant has obtained a benefit from the claimant in circumstances where the claimant can bring a restitutionary claim, the defendant should be required to make full restitution of all benefits obtained, regardless of the nature of the cause of action. The essential question relating to the award of interest turns on the valuation of the benefit which the defendant has obtained. Where the defendant has been saved paying compound interest to a financial institution as a result of receiving a benefit from the claimant, it is entirely appropriate that this benefit should be valued by reference to what the defendant has saved, namely a liability to pay compound interest.

The approach of the minority in *Westdeutsche* to the valuation of interest was adopted by the House of Lords in *Sempra Metals Ltd v IRC*.[201] That case arose from a decision of the European Court of Justice (ECJ) that the denial of group income tax relief to corporate taxpayers, who had paid dividends to parent companies resident in a Member State of the EU other than the United Kingdom, was discriminatory and unlawful.[202] The effect of this

---

[196] *President of India v La Pintada Compania Navigacion SA* [1985] AC 104, 116 (Lord Brandon).
[197] [1996] AC 669.   [198] Ibid, 696 (Lord Goff), 736 (Lord Woolf).
[199] Ibid, 719 (Lord Woolf).   [200] Ibid, 728 (Lord Woolf).
[201] [2007] UKHL 34, [2008] 1 AC 561.
[202] Case C-410/98 *Metallgesellschaft Ltd v IRC; Hoechst v IRC* [2001] Ch 620.

denial of relief was that the taxpayers had paid corporate tax earlier than they would otherwise have done had the relief been available and a group income election been made. As a result of the decision of the ECJ, the United Kingdom was required to provide a remedy for the taxpayers who had been denied the group relief. It was accepted that this remedy was to be assessed through the application of a rate of interest for the period during which the tax had been paid prematurely, although it should be noted that here interest was only being used as a measure to value the defendant's enrichment and so determine the principal sum owed to the claimant, and not as an ancillary award on the principal sum.[203] In *Sempra Metals* the majority affirmed that the appropriate measure of the Revenue's enrichment was compound interest, but the Court went further and recognized that compound interest should be generally available for unjust enrichment claims as of right at Common Law.[204] Simple interest was not considered to be an appropriate measure of the time value of an enrichment because it is an artificial construct which has no relation to business reality.[205]

In assessing the compound interest in *Sempra Metals* the majority considered what it would have cost the Government to borrow an equivalent amount of money. A normal borrower would have paid compound interest at the market rate, this being the conventional interest rate for ordinary commercial borrowings.[206] Since, however, the Government would have been able to borrow an equivalent amount of money at a lower rate of interest, this rate was used as the measure of its enrichment.[207]

In *Sempra Metals* compound interest was used to value the defendant's enrichment arising from its premature use of the tax payment, which was assessed from the date of the payment until the date when the taxpayer would have paid the money to discharge its tax liability had it been able to make the group income election. At that time the defendant's liability to the claimant to make restitution of the value of its benefit would have crystallized.[208] From the time when this liability had been incurred until its later discharge, the defendant should also be liable to pay interest to the claimant. How should this interest be determined? The claimant had conceded that interest for this period from liability incurred until liability discharged should be assessed as simple interest.[209] However, Lords Nicholls and Walker contemplated the possibility of compound interest being awarded for this subsequent period too, because 'the Inland Revenue continued to derive interest benefits from the benefits it had already obtained from having use of the [tax] payments'.[210] This must be correct as being consistent with the analysis of compound interest being the measure for the defendant's use value of the money, since this is what the imposition of interest for the period following liability accruing is seeking to do.

---

[203] See further p 66 below, for consideration of the identification and assessment of this principal sum.

[204] So effectively overruling *Westdeutsche Landesbank Girozentrale v Islington LBC* [1996] AC 669: *Sempra Metals Ltd v IRC* [2007] UKHL 34, [2008] 1 AC 561, [36] (Lord Hope), [112] (Lord Nicholls), although that decision was not formally overruled: [109] and [111] (Lord Nicholls).

[205] Ibid, [33] (Lord Hope).   [206] Ibid, [13] (Lord Hope).   [207] See further p 66, below.

[208] This liability was actually incurred on a daily basis whilst the defendant had the improper use of the money paid prematurely, but the final liability for use crystallized at the point when the defendant's receipt could be considered to be legitimate, namely when the claimant would have discharged its tax liability had it been able to make a group income election.

[209] *Sempra Metals Ltd v IRC* [2007] UKHL 34, [2008] 1 AC 561, [114] (Lord Nicholls).

[210] Ibid, [129] (Lord Nicholls), [156] (Lord Walker). Such an award was made by Henderson J in *Prudential Assurance Co Ltd v HMRC* [2013] EWHC 3249 (Ch), [2014] 2 CMLR 10, [246], because 'the Revenue remains enriched until the date of actual repayment'.

As regards the identification of the date from which liability to pay interest arises, it has been suggested that this is from the date of the defendant's receipt of the enrichment.[211] The preferable view, however, is that interest should only accrue from the date when the cause of action crystallizes,[212] for the defendant will only be liable to the claimant from that point. Normally, the cause of action will crystallize at the time the enrichment is received. But this will not always be the case, such as where the claimant pays money to the defendant subject to a condition and that condition only fails subsequently.[213] In such circumstances, the liability to pay interest should only be triggered once the condition has failed. Lord Nicholls in *Sempra Metals* recognized that compound interest should be assessed until the date of judgment,[214] whereas in *Littlewoods Retail Ltd v HMRC*[215] Henderson J indicated that interest should run until the date when the loss of use is fully restored to the claimant, which is consistent with the rationale behind the award of interest in the law of restitution, namely to ensure that the defendant does not profit from the receipt of the benefit in any way. In the Court of Appeal[216] it was assumed that Henderson J had recognized that interest should run until the date of judgment, rather than until the principal sum had been repaid. In fact, a distinction needs to be drawn between the valuation of the enrichment and interest awarded on the sum due. In a case where the claimant has paid tax which was not due the defendant is enriched by the opportunity to use the money paid. The value of this enrichment can be assessed with reference to compound interest until the date of the judgment. This is what Lord Nicholls was referring to in *Sempra Metals*. Once the judgment has been entered the defendant is liable to pay interest on the judgment debt until the debt is discharged. This is what Henderson J went on to consider.

The state of the law on the award of interest for restitutionary claims, following the decision of the House of Lords in *Sempra Metals*, can be summarized as follows:

(1) Interest can be used as the measure of the defendant's enrichment from his or her use of money,[217] both where the claimant has paid money to the defendant or where the defendant's use relates to money which he or she is required to pay the claimant on receipt from a third party.[218] The award of interest in such circumstances does not involve the exercise of the court's discretion. Rather it constitutes the measure of the enrichment and so constitutes part of the remedy to which the claimant is entitled.[219]

(2) In addition to interest being used to value the principal sum due to the claimant, interest can also be awarded as an ancillary award on the principal sum, since the defendant remains enriched until the principal liability is discharged.[220]

(3) Regardless of whether the claim is characterized as arising at Law or in Equity, either simple or compound interest will be available.

---

[211] M Yip, 'The Use Value of Money in the Law of Unjust Enrichment' (2010) LS 586, 607.

[212] Which is consistent with the approach to the award of simple interest: Senior Courts Act 1981, s 35A(1).

[213] See p 310, below.

[214] Which is consistent with the award of simple interest: Senior Courts Act 1981, s 35A(1).

[215] [2014] EWHC 868 (Ch), [450]. See also *Test Claimants in the FII Group Litigation v HMRC* [2014] EWHC 4302 (Ch), [434] (Henderson J). In *Littlewoods Ltd v HMRC* [2015] EWCA Civ 515 the Court of Appeal interpreted Henderson J as holding that interest should run until the date of judgment. In fact this refers to the valuation of the defendant's enrichment, arising from the defendant's use of the payment of tax. The defendant's enrichment is assessed up until the judgment. Interest is charged thereafter.

[216] [2015] EWCA Civ 515, [204].   [217] See further p 73, below.

[218] *Equitas Ltd v Walsham Bros & Co Ltd* [2013] EWHC 3264 (Comm).

[219] *Prudential Assurance Co Ltd v HMRC* [2013] EWHC 3249 (Ch), [2014] 2 CMLR 10, [221] (Henderson J); *Littlewoods Retail Ltd v HMRC* [2014] EWHC 868 (Ch), [417] (Henderson J); [2015] EWCA Civ 515.

[220] *Prudential Assurance Co Ltd v HMRC* [2013] EWHC 3249 (Ch), [2014] 2 CMLR 10, [246].

(4) When determining whether simple or compound interest applies it is appropriate to consider what type and rate of interest the defendant would have had to pay to borrow an equivalent amount of money from a third party, in order to determine the benefit to the defendant from the use of the money.

(5) The preferable view is that interest on the principal sum owed to the claimant should be assessed from the date when the defendant's liability arose, since there will then be a debt in respect of which interest is due, until the date when that liability is discharged.

(6) Where the restitutionary claim is founded on a Common Law wrong, such as a tort or breach of contract, compound interest is now available.

(7) Where the restitutionary claim is founded on an equitable wrong or involves an equitable proprietary claim for which a personal remedy is awarded,[221] compound interest continues to be available in the exercise of the equitable jurisdiction to award such interest, but it can now be rationalized on the basis that the function of compound interest is to identify and value the defendant's benefit derived from the receipt of a benefit.

---

[221] See p 644, below.

2

THEMES AND CONTROVERSIES

The previous chapter was concerned with identifying the bare bones of the law of restitution, by establishing the essential structure of the subject. This chapter is concerned with putting some flesh on those bones, by identifying key principles and policies which affect the operation and structure of the law of restitution. These principles and policies affect the whole of the law of restitution, but their application will vary depending on the principle on which the restitutionary claim is founded. This chapter will also identify some of the issues about which there is particular controversy, the resolution of which is decisive for the future development of the subject.

1. THE RELEVANCE OF FAULT

(A) FAULT IS GENERALLY IRRELEVANT

One of the most important issues concerning the structure of the law of restitution relates to the role of fault of both the claimant and the defendant in determining whether restitutionary remedies should be awarded. The orthodox approach is that restitutionary claims are generally ones of strict liability. In other words, the defendant will be liable to make restitution to the claimant without any need to show fault on the part of the defendant. This is generally true of claims founded on the reversal of the defendant's unjust enrichment, where the claim can succeed once it has been established that the defendant has been enriched at the claimant's expense in circumstances which fall within one of the recognized grounds of restitution, and it is not necessary to show that the defendant was at fault in any way.[1] So, for example, if the claimant pays money to the defendant mistakenly believing that he or she is liable to do so, in circumstances where the defendant has done nothing to encourage this belief, and might even share it, the defendant is liable to repay the claimant.[2] Similarly, where the restitutionary claim is founded on the vindication of property rights, the defendant will be liable to make restitution to the claimant regardless of the defendant's fault.[3]

But the apparent simplicity of this orthodox analysis of restitutionary claims, where the difficulties involving the definition and proof of fault do not appear to intrude, is misleading. In fact, issues of fault, and notions of culpability or blameworthiness, are highly significant to many different aspects of the law of restitution.

---

[1] PBH Birks, *Unjust Enrichment* (2nd edn, Oxford: Oxford University Press, 2005), 7.
[2] See Chapter 9.   [3] *Foskett v McKeown* [2001] 1 AC 102.

(B) CIRCUMSTANCES WHERE THE FAULT OF EITHER PARTY IS RELEVANT

Fault is relevant in the law of restitution in a number of different circumstances.[4]

(1) Where the claimant wishes to found a restitutionary claim on the commission of a wrong, the fault of the defendant may be important when considering whether the defendant has committed a wrong. But, whether fault needs to be proved, and, if it does, the degree of fault required, will depend on the nature of the wrong which has been committed. Some wrongs can be committed without proof of fault, such as breach of contract or breach of fiduciary duty. Other wrongs, especially some torts and serious criminal offences, will only be committed if the defendant was at fault in some way.

(2) Some of the defences which apply to restitutionary claims will only succeed if the claimant was acting in good faith. So, for example, if the defendant acted in bad faith he or she will not be able to rely on the defences of change of position[5] or *bona fide* purchase.[6] What is meant by bad faith for these purposes is a matter of controversy, but certainly neither defence will be available to a defendant who knew of or suspected the existence of the restitutionary claim.

(3) In the context of certain restitutionary claims founded on the reversal of the defendant's unjust enrichment, the fault of both the claimant and the defendant may be relevant when considering whether a ground of restitution can be established. For example, some grounds of restitution will only be established if the defendant is considered to be more blameworthy than the claimant.[7] For other grounds of restitution, whilst it might appear on the face of the ground that it is not necessary to prove that the defendant was at fault, fault is implicit in the nature of the ground, such as where the defendant has compelled the claimant to transfer a benefit[8] or the defendant has exploited the claimant's weaker position.[9] The fault of the defendant may also be a relevant consideration when identifying and valuing an enrichment.[10] Sometimes, whether the claimant was at fault in some way will also be relevant when establishing a ground of restitution. So, if a claimant knew or suspected that money had been incorrectly transferred to the defendant, the claimant will not be able to establish that he or she had been mistaken.[11]

(4) Where a restitutionary claim arises in Equity the question of fault is often explicit. For example, where the defendant has received property which has been transferred in breach of trust, he or she may be liable to the beneficiary of the trust in an action for knowing receipt. But this will depend on the claimant proving that the defendant had acted unconscionably in receiving the property.[12] The meaning of unconscionability for these purposes is a matter of some controversy, but it is clear that it requires proof of fault on the part of the defendant before restitutionary liability can be established.

---

[4] PBH Birks, 'The Role of Fault in the Law of Unjust Enrichment' in GH Jones and WS Swadling (eds), *The Search for Principle* (Oxford: Oxford University Press, 1999), 235–75; GJ Virgo, 'The Role of Fault in the Law of Restitution' in AS Burrows (ed), *Mapping the Law of Obligations* (Oxford: Oxford University Press, 2006).

[5] See Chapter 25.   [6] See Chapter 23.

[7] Such as the ground of the defendant being more responsible for participation in an illegal transaction than the claimant. See Chapter 11.   [8] See Chapter 10.

[9] See Chapter 11.   [10] See Chapter 4.   [11] See Chapter 9.   [12] See Chapter 22.

2. RISK-TAKING

It is a fundamental principle of the law of restitution that, where the claimant has taken a risk in transferring a benefit to the defendant, any restitutionary claim must fail. This is sometimes expressed in the aphorism that restitution will not assist a volunteer or a claimant who has acted officiously.[13] The claimant will generally be considered to have acted officiously where he or she transferred a benefit to the defendant in circumstances in which the defendant had not requested the benefit to be transferred.[14] So, for example, in *Re Rhodes*,[15] a nephew paid for his aunt, who was of unsound mind, to be kept in a lunatic asylum. Since there was no evidence that the nephew intended to be repaid, there was no restitutionary liability as against the aunt's estate after she had died. Restitutionary relief was unavailable because the nephew had acted voluntarily in paying for the upkeep of his aunt.

Where the claimant can be considered to have taken the risk either that the transfer of the benefit to the defendant was valid or that the defendant might pay for the benefit without being obliged to do so, it is not for the law of restitution to reallocate the risks so that the defendant is required to make restitution to the claimant.[16] This will particularly be the case where the risk of something going wrong with the transaction is considered to have been allocated by contract.[17] Whether the risk has been allocated by the contract will turn on all the evidence, including the nature of any bargaining between the parties, but such a conclusion should only be drawn where the risk has clearly been allocated to the claimant. Whether the risk has been allocated is especially well illustrated by the cases which consider whether a payment from the claimant can be characterized as a non-refundable deposit or simply an advance payment. If it is the former, it follows that the payer takes the risk of his or her default in the performance of the contract but does not take the risk of the defendant's default.[18] If it is an advance payment, the claimant does not bear the risk of any default.[19] Similarly, where the claimant transfers a benefit to the defendant pursuant to an agreement which is subject to contract, this operates to exclude the right to restitution as a general rule, because the inclusion of the phrase 'subject to contract' allocates the risk of a contract not being made to the person who transfers a benefit before a contract is made.[20]

Whilst this risk-taking principle has clearly been recognized in English law,[21] its ambit remains a matter of great uncertainty and its existence a matter of controversy. Wilmot-Smith,[22] for example, has criticized analysis of restitutionary claims with reference to risk-taking because he considers that such analysis is circular, ambiguous, inconclusive, incapable of explaining all the decided cases, and unnecessary. It is certainly the case

---

[13] See EW Hope, 'Officiousness' (1929) Cornell LQ 25 and JW Wade, 'Restitution for Benefits Conferred Without Request' (1966) Vanderbilt LR 1183. See also W Evans, 'An Essay on the Action for Money Had and Received' [1998] RLR 1, 8.   [14] See *Owen v Tate* [1976] QB 402.

[15] (1890) 44 Ch D 94.

[16] See *Pan Ocean Shipping Co Ltd v Creditcorp Ltd* [1994] 1 WLR 161, 166 (Lord Goff of Chieveley).

[17] See further Chapter 7.

[18] *Howe v Smith* (1884) 27 Ch D 89; *Monnickendam v Leanse* (1923) 39 TLR 445. See p 338, below.

[19] *Palmer v Temple* (1839) 9 Ad and E 508, 112 ER 1304.

[20] See, for example, *Regalian Properties plc v London Docklands Development Corporation* [1995] 1 WLR 212. See p 346, below.

[21] See, for example, *Falcke v Scottish Imperial Insurance* (1886) 34 Ch D 234, 248 (Bowen LJ); *MacDonald Dickens and Mackin v Costello* [2011] EWCA Civ 930, [2012] QB 244, [21] (Etherton LJ). See also *Deutsche Morgan Grenfell v IRC* [2006] UKHL 49, [2007] 1 AC 558, [27] (Lord Hoffmann). See p 177, below.

[22] F Wilmot-Smith, 'Replacing Risk-Taking Reasoning' (2011) LQR 610.

that the jurisprudence relating to risk-taking is undeveloped, such that the meaning of risk-taking is unclear and, where the language of risk is adopted by the courts, there appears to be a tendency to hide behind an assertion that the claimant was a risk-taker to deny restitution, without any analysis. There are also cases where the claimant appears to have taken a risk as regards the validity of the transfer of an enrichment to the defendant, but restitution is still awarded.[23]

But Wilmot-Smith does not suggest that risk-taking reasoning is irrelevant to restitutionary claims, particularly claims grounded on unjust enrichment. He simply incorporates such reasoning within the definition of particular grounds of restitution, such that the definition of the ground makes provision for a claimant who is a risk-taker not being able to establish the ground. A key question which will need to be considered throughout this book is whether the denial of restitution on the ground of the claimant having taken a risk that there might not be a valid basis for the transfer of a benefit should be dealt with in the definition of the elements of the claim or explicitly as bar to the claim.[24] If risk-taking is recognized as a distinct bar to restitution, it would then be necessary to consider whether the taking of a risk should be determined objectively or subjectively. The preferable view is that it is to be assessed objectively.[25] So it is not a matter of whether the relevant party believed that he or she was taking a risk, but whether, on the facts of the case, the party is deemed to have taken the risk.

3. RESPECTING AUTONOMY

It is a particularly significant principle of the law of restitution that the autonomy of those who might be affected by the law of restitution is respected. Autonomy focuses on the freedom of actors to choose how to act. But the autonomies of different actors will inevitably interact and contradict each other; that is when the law of restitution is needed to resolve the conflict.

Various parts of the law of restitution can be explained as operating to respect the autonomy of the claimant. The law of unjust enrichment, for example, can be justified on the ground that it is needed to vindicate the claimant's right to self-determination, such that, where the claimant's decision to act can be considered to have been impaired in some way, it is appropriate to award restitution to vindicate that right.[26]

But aspects of the law of restitution can also be explained by reference to the need to respect the autonomy of the defendant. So, for example, if the defendant receives goods or a service from the claimant which was not requested by the defendant, he or she will not generally be required to pay for it.[27] As Bowen LJ recognized in *Falke v Scottish Imperial Insurance Co*:[28] 'Liabilities are not to be forced upon people behind their backs any more than you can confer a benefit on a man against his will.'

Where the defendant is not given a free choice about the receipt of a particular benefit, it is perfectly legitimate for the defendant to say that he or she did not value it. Even if the

---

[23] See, for example, *Yeoman's Row Management Ltd v Cobbe* [2008] UKHL 55, [2008] 1 WLR 1752. See p 348, below.

[24] As advocated, for example, by J Goodwin, 'Failure of Basis in the Contractual Context' [2013] RLR 24, 28.

[25] As recognized for mistake by Lord Hoffmann in *Deutsche Morgan Grenfell v IRC* [2006] UKHL 49, [2007] AC 558, [25].

[26] See JM Nadler, 'What Right does Unjust Enrichment Protect?' (2008) OJLS 245.

[27] See p 69, below.

[28] *Falke v Scottish Imperial Insurance Co* (1886) 34 Ch D 234, 248. See also *Ministry of Defence v Ashman* [1993] 40 EG 144, 147 (Hoffmann LJ).

defendant used what had been received, it does not necessarily follow that he or she valued it, because '[if the claimant] cleans another's shoes, what can the other do but put them on?'[29] Similarly, if the claimant has paid money to the defendant by mistake, and the defendant spent that money in good faith, not being aware of the mistake, the defendant will not be required to make restitution through the operation of the defence of change of position, which exists to protect the defendant's autonomy to lose the enrichment without being subjected to a continuing liability to make restitution. Where, however, the claimant paid money to the defendant by mistake, such that the claimant's intention to transfer the money freely can be considered to have been vitiated, the defendant will be required to make restitution if he or she has retained the money, because then, as between the claimant and the defendant, respecting the claimant's autonomy prevails over that of the defendant.

Another significant operation of the principle in favour of autonomy relates to the respect given to contractual bargains. For, if the parties have entered into a contract to govern their relationship, the law of restitution should respect the choices which they have made.[30]

4. THE NATURE OF THE RELATIONSHIP BETWEEN THE PARTIES

In certain circumstances the nature of the relationship between the parties may influence the court's decision to award restitutionary relief. The most important circumstance is whether the relationship between the parties can be characterized as commercial. This will be significant in two particular circumstances where the commercial characterization means that restitutionary claims are less likely to succeed.

(A) RELEVANCE TO UNJUST ENRICHMENT CLAIMS

The nature of the relationship between the claimant and the defendant may determine whether one of the recognized grounds of restitution is applicable. So, for example, in the context of the grounds of duress and undue influence, restitution is much more likely to be awarded where the claimant is a consumer and the defendant a commercial trader, than if both parties are trading companies which have entered into arm's length commercial transactions.[31] The law of restitution is much more reluctant to intervene where the parties have entered into commercial transactions, because of the fear that this will introduce undesirable uncertainty into the commercial bargaining process and could 'enable *bona fide* settled accounts to be reopened when parties to commercial dealings fall out'.[32] This was recognized by the Privy Council in *Pao On v Lau Yiu Long*,[33] where Lord Scarman held that 'justice requires that men, who have negotiated at arm's length, be held to their bargains unless it can be shown that their consent was vitiated by fraud, mistake or duress'. Even so, exceptionally, restitution is prepared to intervene in such commercial transactions, primarily because the nature of the defendant's conduct is so

---

[29] *Taylor v Laird* (1856) 25 LJ Ex 320, 332 (Pollock CB). Cf where the defendant uses and retains a particular piece of property rather than the benefit of a service. See p 81, below.

[30] See p 133, below.

[31] See, in particular, *CTN Cash and Carry Ltd v Gallaher Ltd* [1994] 4 All ER 714.

[32] Ibid, 719 (Steyn LJ).   [33] [1980] AC 614, 634.

unconscionable that restitution is appropriate to protect the claimant from unscrupulous exploitation.[34]

(B) RELEVANCE TO THE IDENTIFICATION OF FIDUCIARY RELATIONSHIPS

Where a defendant owes fiduciary duties to the claimant and breaches those duties, the defendant will typically be liable to make restitution to the claimant of any benefits obtained as a result of the wrongdoing. It is consequently important to determine whether the defendant owes fiduciary duties to the claimant. But the courts are generally reluctant to recognize that parties to a purely commercial transaction are subject to such duties.[35] Although it does not necessarily follow that, just because the relationship between the parties is purely commercial, one of the parties will not owe fiduciary duties to the other, such a fiduciary relationship will, however, only be recognized in exceptional circumstances.

5. THE PRINCIPLE AGAINST FICTIONS

For a long time the law of restitution was founded on the fiction of the implied contract, whereby the right to obtain a restitutionary remedy depended on whether or not it was possible to imply a contract between the claimant and the defendant.[36] This fiction has now been abandoned,[37] and it is essential that such fictions do not reappear. There is, however, evidence that the judges do still rely on fictions to achieve what they perceive to be the just result. The best example of this is the way the courts have been prepared to identify fiduciary relationships between the parties as a means of securing restitutionary remedies.[38]

Reliance on fictions is dangerous because it results in muddled thinking and uncertainty. Also, once the original reason for the fiction has been forgotten, it is an easy step to treating a fiction as a requirement which must be satisfied before restitutionary remedies can be awarded, rather than simply as a means to an end. It is far better that the award of restitutionary remedies is transparent, founded on clear principles, and does not happen behind the smoke-screen of a fiction. If the law of restitution is founded on a clear theoretical basis, there should be no need to rely on fictions to secure the desired result.[39]

6. THE ROLE OF PUBLIC POLICY

It is the basic thesis of this book that there are a number of principles which underlie the law of restitution and, once they have been identified, it is possible to predict whether or not restitutionary remedies will be available. But it would be foolish to assert that the law of restitution is absolutely principled, both because many of these principles are poorly developed and lack explicit judicial recognition, and also because the decision to award restitutionary remedies is often affected by policy decisions. Numerous examples of this

---

[34] See Chapters 10 and 11.   [35] See Chapter 19.   [36] See Chapter 3.

[37] *United Australia Ltd v Barclays Bank Ltd* [1941] AC 1.   [38] See Chapters 18 and 20.

[39] See JH Baker, 'The History of Quasi-Contract in English Law' in W Cornish, R Nolan, J O'Sullivan, and G Virgo (eds), *Restitution: Past, Present and Future* (Oxford: Hart Publishing, 1998) and JJ Langbein, 'The Later History of Restitution' in W Cornish, R Nolan, J O'Sullivan, and G Virgo (eds), *Restitution: Past, Present and Future* (Oxford: Hart Publishing, 1998), 41 and 57–8.

policy-oriented approach can be identified throughout the law of restitution. So, for example, the law is reluctant to assist a claimant who is party to an illegal transaction.[40] The law also seeks to encourage the highest standard of behaviour on the part of those people who are in a relationship of trust and confidence with the claimant.[41] There is also a general policy in favour of depriving wrongdoers of the benefits obtained from the commission of their wrongdoing.[42]

7. THE RELATIONSHIP BETWEEN LAW AND EQUITY

The administration of Law and Equity was fused into a single system as a result of the Judicature Acts 1873–1875, but this did not result in the fusion of the substantive law. Consequently, the substantive rules of Law and Equity remain distinct, and this has proved to be highly significant within the law of restitution. It follows that it is still often necessary to consider whether a claim is brought in Equity or at Law, since the applicable rules are subtly, sometimes even fundamentally, different. This difference between legal and equitable claims is probably most important in the context of restitutionary proprietary claims. For the purposes of such claims it is vital to determine whether the claimant is seeking to vindicate a legal or equitable proprietary interest, since this will affect the claimant's ability to trace his or her proprietary right into substitute assets[43] and will also affect the nature of the claim and the remedy which is available.[44]

One of the most important challenges facing the contemporary law of restitution is to determine to what extent the disparate approaches of Law and Equity to the award of restitutionary remedies can and should be assimilated. Such assimilation is particularly difficult because of the different policies, principles, and terminology in these different areas, but there is a growing recognition that assimilation is vital. This was recognized by Deane and Dawson JJ in the decision of the High Court of Australia in *Baltic Shipping Co v Dillon*:[45]

> In a modern context where common law and equity are fused with equity prevailing, the artificial constraints imposed by the old forms of action can, unless they reflect coherent principle, be disregarded where they impede the principled enunciation and development of the law. In particular, the notions of good conscience, which both the common law and equity recognised as the underlying rationale of the law of unjust enrichment, now dictate that, in applying the relevant doctrines of law and equity, regard be had to matters of substance rather than technical form.

Such assimilation of legal and equitable regimes is increasingly being advocated in this country, most notably in the context of the tracing rules for the identification of the claimant's proprietary interest in substitute assets.[46] There is also evidence that assimilation is taking place in discrete pockets of the law. For example, the old rule that compound

---

[40] See Chapter 27.   [41] See Chapter 19.   [42] See Part IV.   [43] See Chapter 21.

[44] See *MCC Proceeds Inc v Lehman Bros International (Europe)* [1995] 4 All ER 675 where it was held that the claimant could not sue the defendant for the tort of conversion where the defendant had interfered with the claimant's equitable proprietary right, whereas such a claim would have been available had there been interference with a legal proprietary right.   [45] (1992) 176 CLR 344, 376.

[46] See, for example, *Trustee of the Property of FC Jones and Sons (a firm) v Jones* [1997] Ch 159, 170 (Millett LJ). See Chapter 21. For a note of caution see K Barker, 'Equitable Title and Common Law Conversion: The Limits of the Fusionist Ideal' [1998] RLR 150, 156.

interest was only available for equitable claims has now been rejected, so that compound interest is available regardless of whether the claim originates at Law or in Equity.[47]

But the demands for assimilation go further than this, with Burrows in particular advocating complete assimilation.[48] There is, however, a danger that rapid assimilation of rules which have existed for a long time will mean that the deep-rooted nuances and subtleties of the different parts of the law will be lost. Where there is no need for separate rules then assimilation is appropriate, but often the historical roots of the rules remain valid even today.[49]

A further controversy relating to the law of restitution arises from the growing perception that much, if not all, of the law of restitution can be considered to be equitable. This has proved to be particularly significant in Australia[50] and Canada[51] with the focus being placed on conscience and unconscionability, but equitable notions have also been emphasized in England as well.[52] Clearly substantive notions of Equity are relevant to restitution for wrongs, where the relevant wrong is equitable, and as regards the vindication of equitable property rights. When considering the unjust enrichment principle there has certainly been an equitable influence in the development of the principle,[53] but using the language of Equity today when describing unjust enrichment creates the danger that the law of restitution is perceived to be discretionary and dependent on the exercise of the judge's arbitrary choice, when in fact it is highly principled.

8. RULES VERSUS DISCRETION

One of the most controversial questions facing the modern law of restitution concerns exactly how this body of law should be formulated. In particular, should the law be formulated as rules, with consequent certainty and predictability but also inflexibility, or should it be formulated in such a way as to give the judge a discretion as to the appropriate result, with consequent flexibility but also uncertainty.

This question has been particularly important in the context of determining how restitutionary remedies should be formulated,[54] and especially whether the remedial constructive trust should be recognized in English law, as it is in other jurisdictions, notably Australia and Canada. Currently, English law recognizes the institutional constructive trust where the defendant's conduct falls within one of the recognized categories of unconscionable behaviour which gives rise to such a trust, with the result that the defendant holds property on trust for the claimant by operation of law.[55] Although the circumstances in which such a trust is recognized may be poorly defined, it is at least clear

---

[47] *Sempra Metals Ltd v IRC* [2007] UKHL 34, [2008] 1 AC 561. See p 30, above.

[48] AS Burrows, *Hochelga Lectures, Fusing Common Law and Equity: Remedies, Restitution and Reform* (2002); AS Burrows, 'We Do This At Common Law But That In Equity' (2002) 22 OJLS 1.

[49] See further GJ Virgo, 'Restitution Through the Looking Glass: Restitution Within Equity and Equity Within Restitution' in J Getzler (ed), *Rationalizing Property, Equity and Trusts: Essays in Honour of Edward Burn* (London: Lexis Nexis, 2003), 106.

[50] *Roxborough v Rothmans of Pall Mall Australia Ltd* (2002) 185 ALR 335; *Australian Financial Services and Leasing Pty Ltd v Hills Industries Ltd* [2014] HCA 14.

[51] *Garland v Consumers' Gas Distributors Inc* [2004] 1 SCR 629.

[52] See, for example, *Banque Financière de la Cité v Parc (Battersea) Ltd* [1999] 1 AC 221, 237 (Lord Clyde).

[53] See *Moses v Macferlan* (1760) 2 Burr 1005, 1012; 97 ER 676, 681 (Lord Mansfield); *Straton v Rastall* (1788) 2 Term Rep 366, 370 (Buller J). See Virgo, 'Restitution Through the Looking Glass', 87–94.

[54] See especially PD Finn, 'Equitable Doctrine and Discretion in Remedies' in W Cornish, R Nolan, J O'Sullivan, and G Virgo (eds), *Restitution: Past, Present and Future* (Oxford: Hart Publishing, 1998), ch 17.

[55] See Chapter 21.

that the judge's decision that the defendant holds property on constructive trust derives from the application of rules rather than the exercise of the judge's discretion.[56] But some judges and commentators have suggested that a remedial constructive trust should be recognized, the consequence of which would be that the recognition that the defendant holds property on constructive trust for the claimant would arise from the exercise of the judge's discretion rather than operation of law.[57]

The approach which is adopted in this book is that the law of restitution should be as principled as possible. Certainty and predictability of the law is a virtue. There are a number of advantages in having a principled law of restitution, notably it makes exposition of the law clearer and encourages settlement out of court rather than litigation. But the exercise of judicial discretion is not necessarily unprincipled. Hart[58] recognized that discretion is fundamentally different from arbitrary choice: discretion is 'a certain kind of wisdom or deliberation guiding choice',[59] so that a decision which is not susceptible to principled justification is not an exercise of discretion at all. Hart rejected arbitrary choice as a basis for judicial decision-making. He was right to do so. Whilst the role of judicial discretion involves a choice and is essential to ensure that justice is achieved, if the resort to justice is to be defensible and predictable, there need to be identifiable principles or recognized factors to guide that discretion and to ensure that like cases are treated alike, for the benefit of the parties, their advisers and, if the case goes to trial, the judge. Consequently, giving the judge a discretion to determine the application of the rules of law on the facts of the case is defensible, as long as clear principles can be identified to justify the exercise of that discretion. It follows, for example, that there is no reason why the remedial constructive trust should not be recognized in English law, but only if clearly defined principles can be identified to enable judges to exercise their discretion when determining whether property received by the defendant should be held on constructive trust for the claimant.[60]

Ultimately, the proper formulation of the law of restitution involves a balancing exercise between certain rules and flexible discretions. Throughout this book it will be seen that the law of restitution is constantly trying to balance these two objectives. The only way it can do so properly is through the identification of clear principles which underpin the subject.

---

[56] *FHR European Ventures Ltd v Mankarious* [2014] UKSC 45, [2015] AC 250. See p 512, below.
[57] See Chapters 19 and 21.
[58] HLA Hart, 'Discretion', written in 1956 and published in (2013) Harvard Law Review 652.
[59] Ibid, 658.   [60] See further p 595, below.

PART II
UNJUST ENRICHMENT

3

THE PRINCIPLE OF UNJUST ENRICHMENT

1. A BRIEF HISTORY OF THE LAW OF UNJUST ENRICHMENT

The unjust enrichment principle was first recognized by the House of Lords in *Lipkin Gorman (a firm) v Karpnale Ltd.*[1] Although this book is not the place for a detailed exposition of the history of the law of unjust enrichment,[2] the essential features of that history remain of vital importance to a proper understanding of the modern law, particularly because this explains why the principle was only recognized relatively late in England and Wales.[3]

(A) THE CONCEPTION OF THE UNJUST ENRICHMENT PRINCIPLE

The seeds of unjust enrichment can be traced back to the old forms of action, especially the action of *indebitatus assumpsit* which was developed in the seventeenth century. The conception of what would eventually become the modern principle of unjust enrichment can be identified in the judgment of Lord Mansfield in *Moses v Macferlan.*[4] But it took 230 years for the unjust enrichment principle to be recognized explicitly by the House of Lords. Two reasons can be identified for this. First, the development of the law occurred within four forms of action: money had and received to the defendant's use; money paid to the defendant; *quantum valebat* to recover the reasonable value of goods; and *quantum meruit* to recover the reasonable value of services. This artificial division of claims prevented their unification in a single unjust enrichment principle. The artificiality of the distinction became even more marked following the abolition of the forms of action by the Common Law Procedure Act 1852. But the language of the forms of action continued to be used, and they still appear to rule us from their graves.[5]

The second reason for the late recognition of unjust enrichment was the implied contract theory. The old forms of action originally required the claimant to prove that the defendant owed money to the claimant and had promised to repay this money.

---

[1] [1991] 2 AC 548.

[2] For detailed analysis of the history of what is now unjust enrichment see RM Jackson, *The History of Quasi-Contract in English Law* (Cambridge: Cambridge University Press, 1936). See also JH Baker, 'The History of Quasi-Contract in English Law' in W Cornish, R Nolan, J O'Sullivan, and G Virgo (eds), *Restitution: Past, Present and Future* (Oxford: Hart Publishing, 1998), ch 3 and D Ibbetson, *A Historical Introduction to the Law of Obligations* (Oxford: Oxford University Press, 1999), Part IV.

[3] The unjust enrichment principle was recognized in other Common Law jurisdictions before it was recognized in England. See, for example, *Peter Persaud v Pln Versailles* (1971) 17 WIR 105 (Court of Appeal of Guyana). For the recognition of unjust enrichment in Scotland see *Shilliday v Smith* 1998 SLT 976.

[4] (1760) 2 Burr 1005.   [5] See p 59, below.

Although initially the defendant's promise to repay the claimant had to be proved
expressly, increasingly it was implied from the circumstances of the case, so that the
promise became a fiction.[6] This was recognized by Barry J in *William Lacey (Hounslow)
Ltd v Davis*[7] who said:

> In these quasi-contractual cases the court will look at the true facts and ascertain from
> them whether or not a promise to pay should be implied, irrespective of the actual views or
> intentions of the parties at the time when the work was done or the services rendered.

In fact the award of restitution in these cases can, in retrospect, be justified by reference to
the principle of unjust enrichment. But, until the middle of the twentieth century, the
claim depended on whether it was possible to imply a promise by the defendant to repay
the claimant. If the facts of the case were inconsistent with the implication of such a
promise, it followed that the restitutionary claim must fail. So, for example, restitutionary
remedies could not be awarded where there was an express contract in existence which
prevented a contract from being implied or where one of the parties was incapacitated
from making a contract.[8]

It was this emphasis on promise to pay and the notion of an implied contract that
proved to be the main obstacle to the recognition of a distinct law of unjust enrichment.
Analysis in terms of implied promises meant that the question whether a restitutionary
remedy was available was treated simply as an appendix to the law of contract, as was
reflected by the fact that such restitutionary liability was characterized as quasi-
contractual.[9] The law of unjust enrichment has, however, been emancipated from its
reliance on contract. This occurred in the important case of *United Australia Ltd v
Barclays Bank Ltd*,[10] where Lord Atkin memorably said:

> These fantastic resemblances of contracts invented in order to meet requirements of the
> law as to forms of action which have now disappeared should not in these days be allowed
> to affect actual rights. When these ghosts of the past stand in the path of justice clanking
> their medieval chains the proper course for the judge is to pass through them undeterred.[11]

The implied contract approach to restitutionary awards for unjust enrichment was
'unequivocally and finally' rejected by the House of Lords in *Westdeutsche Landesbank
Girozentrale v Islington LBC*,[12] and this has since been confirmed by the Supreme Court.[13]
It follows that unjust enrichment claims will succeed even though it is not possible to
imply a contract between the parties. This was recognized by the decision of the Court of
Appeal in *Haugesund Kommune v Depfa ACS Bank*.[14] The case involved a bank which had
lent money to Norwegian public authorities in circumstances where the authorities lacked
the capacity to borrow the money. It followed that the bank was unable to sue on the
contract of loan, which was void. It was held, however, that the bank could recover the
amount lent by a claim founded on the unjust enrichment principle. The fact that it was

---

[6] See *Sinclair v Brougham* [1914] AC 398, 452 (Lord Sumner); *Fibrosa Spolka Akcyjna v Fairbairn Lawson
Combe Barbour Ltd* [1943] AC 32, 63 (Lord Wright).
[7] [1957] 1 WLR 932, 936.   [8] *Sinclair v Brougham* [1914] AC 398.
[9] An expression which had been recognized by Lord Mansfield in *Moses v Macferlan* (1760) 2 Burr 1005,
1008; 97 ER 976, 978.
[10] [1941] AC 1.   [11] Ibid, 28.
[12] [1996] AC 669, 710 (Lord Browne-Wilkinson), 718, (Lord Slynn), 720 (Lord Woolf), 738 (Lord Lloyd).
See also *Kleinwort Benson Ltd v Glasgow CC* [1999] 1 AC 153.
[13] *Benedetti v Sawiris* [2013] UKSC 50, [2014] AC 938, [148] (Lord Reed).
[14] [2010] EWCA Civ 579.

not possible to imply a promise to repay the money, because that would contradict the public authority's lack of contractual capacity, was considered to be irrelevant.

This rejection of the implied contract theory does not prevent a claimant from suing the defendant on an implied contract. The effect of the *United Australia* case is to remove the fiction of an implied contract from English law, but it does not prevent the implication of a contract from the facts where the evidence is consistent with such an implication.[15] Where, however, there is insufficient evidence to imply a contract, relief can still be obtained by operation of law, by reference to principles such as unjust enrichment.[16]

The legacy of the fictional implied contract does unfortunately live on, since judges still sometimes consider whether a contract can be implied when determining whether restitutionary relief should be available to the claimant. One of the most blatant contemporary examples of such reliance on the implied contract principle is contained in the judgment of Millett LJ in *Taylor v Bhail*.[17] One of the questions for the court in that case was whether a builder could recover the reasonable value of his building work from a customer after the builder had inflated the estimated price of the work to enable the customer to defraud his insurance company. This inflation of the price made the transaction illegal and, since the courts will not enforce illegal transactions,[18] the claimant's action on the contract failed. But Millett LJ also concluded that the claimant's restitutionary claim should fail because '[t]he illegality renders any implied promise to pay a reasonable sum unenforceable—just as it renders the express promise to pay the contract price unenforceable'.

Such reliance on quasi-contractual reasoning should have no part to play in the modern law of restitution. The obligation to make restitution is imposed as a matter of law and does not involve enforcement of any fictional promise made by the defendant.[19]

The rejection of the implied contract theory opened the way for the recognition of a unified unjust enrichment principle. In fact, the first recognition of unjust enrichment in the House of Lords occurred two years after the decision in *United Australia*, in the judgment of Lord Wright in *Fibrosa Spolka Akcyjna v Fairbairn Lawson Combe Barbour Ltd*:[20]

> It is clear that any civilised system of law is bound to provide remedies for cases of what has been called unjust enrichment or unjust benefit, that is to prevent a man from retaining the money of or some benefit derived from another which it is against conscience that he should keep. Such remedies in English law are generically different from remedies in contract or tort, and are now recognised to fall within a third category of the common law which has been called quasi-contract or restitution.

Lord Wright had clearly been influenced in his recognition of unjust enrichment by the work of Seavey and Scott in the United States, who had used the principle as the foundation of the American Law Institute's *Restatement of the Law of Restitution, Quasi-Contracts and Constructive Trusts*, promulgated in May 1936.[21] In November 1937 Lord

---

[15] See further p 135, below.   [16] Cf S Hedley, 'Implied Contract and Restitution' (2004) CLJ 435.

[17] [1996] CLC 377. See also *Guinness plc v Saunders* [1990] 2 AC 663, 689 (Lord Templeman).

[18] *Holman v Johnson* (1775) 1 Cowp 341, 98 ER 1120. See Chapter 27.

[19] This view has been endorsed in the House of Lords in *Westdeutsche Landesbank Girozentrale v Islington LBC* [1996] 2 AC 669, 710 (Lord Browne-Wilkinson).

[20] [1943] AC 32, 61. See also *Brook's Wharf and Bull Wharf Ltd v Goodman Bros* [1937] 1 KB 534, 545 where, as the Master of the Rolls, he referred to an obligation arising by operation of the law where the defendant was 'unjustly benefited at the cost of the plaintiffs'.

[21] *Restatement of the Law of Restitution, Quasi-Contracts and Constructive Trusts* (St Paul, MN: American Law Institute Publishing, 1937).

Wright delivered a lecture to the Cambridge University Law Society[22] on *Sinclair v Brougham*,[23] which he explained as giving relief:

> to prevent unjust enrichment, or to achieve restitution, if we accept the useful term which has been employed in the recently published American Restatement of the Law of Restitution. The word itself is only an echo of the language which will be found in English judgments...It is therefore important not merely to recognise the existence of this separate head in the law (in which word I include law and equity) but to enumerate, to classify and to distinguish.[24]

Although the course seemed to be set for the assimilation of the unjust enrichment principle into English law by the House of Lords,[25] this did not occur. In *Reading v Attorney-General*[26] Lord Norman stated that the 'exact status of the law of unjust enrichment is not yet assured'. Further, Lord Diplock in *Orakpo v Manson Investments*[27] stated that 'there is no general doctrine of unjust enrichment recognised in English law. What it does is to provide specific remedies in particular cases of what might be classified as unjust enrichment in a legal system that is based on the civil law'.

(B) THE BIRTH OF THE UNJUST ENRICHMENT PRINCIPLE

It is not much of an exaggeration to say that the modern unjust enrichment principle was created by Lord Goff and that it was strongly influenced by his own writings as a jurist and his subsequent judgments. The seminal *Law of Restitution*, written with Gareth Jones, was published in 1966 and established that the recognition of the unjust enrichment principle by the courts was a natural development for English law to take. When Robert Goff became a judge he used the unjust enrichment principle to explain the operation of the Law Reform (Frustrated Contracts) Act 1943.[28] On elevation to the House of Lords he had an opportunity to recognize formally the unjust enrichment principle in *Lipkin Gorman (a firm) v Karpnale*.[29]

Although this decision is of profound significance to the recognition and subsequent development of the unjust enrichment principle, it was an inappropriate vehicle for its recognition and should not be considered to be a case about unjust enrichment at all. Rather, it concerns the vindication of property rights.[30] One of the partners of the claimant firm of solicitors, Cass, had authority to draw on the firm's client bank account on his signature alone. Cass was a compulsive gambler who stole over £300,000 from the

---

[22] RA Wright, '*Sinclair v Brougham*' (1938) 6 CLJ 305.

[23] *Sinclair v Brougham* [1914] AC 398.

[24] Wright, '*Sinclair v Brougham*', 306. See also Lord Wright, '*United Australia Ltd v Barclays Bank Ltd*' (1941) 57 LQR 184 and A Denning, 'The Recovery of Money' (1949) 65 LQR 37, 48.

[25] Although it was also recognized by Lord Pearce in *Attorney-General v Nissan* [1970] AC 179, 228.

[26] [1951] AC 507, 513–14.

[27] [1978] AC 95, 104. Other sceptics included Lord Radcliffe in *Bossevain v Weil* [1950] AC 327, 341; Lord Simonds in *Ministry of Health v Simpson* [1951] AC 251, 275; and Lord Templeman in *Guinness plc v Saunders* [1990] 2 AC 663, 689, although the latter changed his mind soon afterwards in *Lipkin Gorman v Karpnale* [1991] 2 AC 548.

[28] *BP Exploration Co (Libya) Ltd) v Hunt (No 2)* [1979] 1 WLR 783, 799. See p 357, below. See also *Barclays Bank v WJ Simms (Southern) Ltd* [1980] QB 677, 697 (restitution of mistaken payment, where the language of unjust enrichment was not used but restitution was); *British Steel Corporation v Cleveland Bridge and Engineering Co Ltd* [1984] 1 All ER 504, 511 (anticipated contract); and in the Court of Appeal in *Whittaker v Campbell* [1984] QB 318, 327 (rescission preventing unjust enrichment).

[29] [1991] 2 AC 548, 578. This had been prefigured in *R v Tower Hamlets LBC, Ex p Chetnik Developments Ltd* [1988] AC 858, 882.   [30] See p 13, above.

account, which he used to fund his gambling habit at the defendant casino. On discovering what had happened, the firm sought to recover the stolen money from the club. The House of Lords held that the claim against the club for money had and received should succeed because it had been unjustly enriched, although the liability to make restitution was reduced to the extent that the club had changed its position. The unjust enrichment principle was recognized as underpinning the claim for money had and received, with specific reference to the judgment of Lord Wright in *Fibrosa Spolka Akcyjna v Fairbairn Lawson Combe Barbour Ltd.*[31] But surprisingly little was said about the elements of this principle, other than that the defendant's enrichment must have been obtained at the claimant's expense; a ground of restitution was not identified. Further, the defendant's enrichment was not directly at the expense of the claimant.[32] Lord Goff did, however, emphasize that the principle did not enable the court to reject a claim simply because it was considered to be unfair or unjust.

In fact, the reason why the House of Lords considered that the defendant casino should make restitution was because the money which had been stolen from the client account belonged to the claimant firm of solicitors. So Lord Templeman recognized that[33] 'in a claim for money had and received by a thief, the plaintiff victim must show that money belonging to him was paid by the thief to the defendant and that the defendant was unjustly enriched and remained unjustly enriched'.

The claim should properly be analysed as being based on the vindication of the firm's property rights in the money and was in fact analysed in this way by both Lords Templeman and Goff. Lord Templeman's analysis was rather unsophisticated. He asserted that the claim depended on the defendant's retention of the money, although this appeared to reflect confusion about the role of the defence of change of position. In fact, Lord Goff emphasized that the claim for money had and received did not depend on the club's retention of any money; it was a personal claim which turned on whether the club had received money in which the firm had a continuing proprietary interest at the time of the defendant's receipt. Lord Goff acknowledged that the firm needed to establish a basis on which it was entitled to the money and it could do so by showing that the money was its legal property. Particular reliance was placed on the decision of Lord Mansfield in *Clarke v Shee and Johnson*,[34] where the claimant recovered money which had been stolen by his servant, who had used it to buy lottery tickets. The claimant successfully sued the defendants who ran the lottery. Crucially, Lord Mansfield specifically recognized that the claimant sued 'for his identified property'.[35] The significance of this to Lord Goff was that the claim was 'founded simply on the fact that, as Lord Mansfield said, the third party cannot in conscience retain the money—or, as we say nowadays, for the third party to retain the money would result in his unjust enrichment at the expense of the owner of the money'.[36]

Now it is true that Lord Goff used the unjust enrichment principle to justify restitution in that case, but he did not need to do so, because the claim turned on the vindication of a property right. That is why in *Lipkin Gorman* itself, rather than searching for a recognized reason why the enrichment was unjust, Lord Goff focused instead on showing that the defendant had received money which belonged to the firm at Law. He held that the firm did not have any proprietary rights in the money which was credited to the client bank account because Cass had authority to draw money from the account. However, he concluded that, since the bank owed the money to the firm, the firm owned a chose in

[31] [1943] AC 32, 61.   [32] See further p 105, below.
[33] *Lipkin Gorman (a firm) v Karpnale* [1991] 2 AC 548, 559–60.   [34] (1774) 1 Cowp 197, 98 ER 1041.
[35] Ibid, 200–1; 1043.   [36] *Lipkin Gorman (a firm) v Karpnale* [1991] 2 AC 548, 572.

action at law which it could trace into the cash drawn from the bank account by the solicitor and into the money received by the club. But this does not satisfactorily deal with the fact that the money drawn by Cass belonged to him because he had authority to draw on the account. True, his act of drawing the money constituted theft, because he had interfered with another's property rights dishonestly, but this did not render the with-drawal unauthorized. Lord Goff's analysis was half-hearted, and he seemed almost too ready to reach the desired result of allowing restitution, but without providing convincing reasons, especially as to how it was possible to identify a continuing proprietary interest in money which clearly belonged to the thief.[37]

The reasoning of the House of Lords could have been much clearer without the distraction of unjust enrichment. If, instead, the focus had been on the vindication of property rights at law, it would have been clear that the firm had to show that it had title to the money paid to the defendant. It could not have shown this and so the claim should have failed.[38]

In addition to the recognition of the unjust enrichment principle, the most significant aspect of *Lipkin Gorman* was the recognition of the change of position defence, which has been vital to the future development of the law of unjust enrichment. It is only because such a defence was recognized that it has been possible to expand the unjust enrichment principle itself, as Lord Goff acknowledged would be the case.[39] The essence of that principle is that the defendant is liable without proof of any wrongdoing or bad faith; liability is strict. This would make the award of restitutionary remedies difficult to justify if, for example, the claimant has made a mistake which was not induced by the defendant, for why should the defendant be required to make restitution when the claimant was to blame? But the award of a restitutionary remedy in such circumstances is much easier to justify if innocent changes in the defendant's position can be taken into account to reduce or negate the defendant's liability, and so enable the defendant's autonomy to be respected. If the defendant's position has not changed then it is clearly much more appropriate that the defendant should make restitution to the claimant, in order to return the parties to their original position, as the corrective justice principle dictates.[40] With the defence firmly in place, despite its ambit being left unclear, the courts could confidently expand the grounds of restitution which are available.[41]

(C) THE US INFLUENCE

It is clear that the United States has had a significant influence on the development of the unjust enrichment principle in England. Whilst the raw materials for what became unjust enrichment were developed in England from the eighteenth century in particular, it was jurists in the United States in the late nineteenth century who first sought to explain these disparate rules with reference to the language of restitution and unjust enrichment.[42] This was developed significantly by the publication of Seavey and Scott's first *Restatement of the Law of Restitution, Quasi-Contracts and Constructive Trusts*, which undoubtedly had a dramatic effect on the development of the law of restitution in England and beyond,

---

[37] That a thief can be guilty of a crime whilst still obtaining property rights has been explicitly recognized by the House of Lords: *Hinks* [2001] AC 241.

[38] See further p 560, below.   [39] *Lipkin Gorman (a firm) v Karpnale* [1991] 2 AC 548, 581.

[40] See p 4, above.

[41] Especially the abolition of the bar on the recovery for mistake of law: *Kleinwort Benson Ltd v Lincoln CC* [1999] 2 AC 349, 371–2 (Lord Goff). See p 162, below.

[42] See A Kull, 'James Barr Ames and the Early Modern History of Unjust Enrichment' (2005) OJLS 297.

influencing both commentators—particularly Goff and Jones, who acknowledged the influence explicitly in the preface to the first edition of *The Law of Restitution*—and judges. A second Restatement was abandoned. *Restatement Third: Restitution and Unjust Enrichment* was published in 2011 and this constitutes the most important survey of the US law of restitution for over 70 years. Reference will be made to it where appropriate throughout this book. The influence of US law on the development of English law has been much reduced recently, however. Restitution and unjust enrichment are generally not taught specifically in US law schools, but are covered in courses on contracts or remedies.[43] It is to be hoped that the publication of *Restatement Third* will rejuvenate interest in the subject in the United States. *Restatement Third* has been influential in England, with the publication of Burrows' *A Restatement of the English Law of Unjust Enrichment.*[44] Whilst this is the personal view of Professor Burrows as to the state of the English law of unjust enrichment, albeit advised by a group of academics, judges, and practitioners, it is a significant contribution to the understanding of the English law and again references will be made as appropriate to it throughout this book.

2. JUSTIFYING THE UNJUST ENRICHMENT PRINCIPLE

Even though the unjust enrichment principle has been clearly recognized at the highest level in England, the location of that principle within the law of obligations and the identification of its function still require careful justification.

(A) THE PLACE OF UNJUST ENRICHMENT WITHIN THE LAW OF OBLIGATIONS

The unjust enrichment principle has a vital and distinct role within the law of obligations.[45] Whenever it can be shown that the defendant has been unjustly enriched at the expense of the claimant the defendant will be obliged, by operation of law, to restore to the claimant the value of the benefit which the defendant has received. Consequently, liability for unjust enrichment is properly regarded as falling within the law of obligations and it should be treated as being on a par with the law of tort and law of contract.[46] But, crucially, liability for unjust enrichment is very different from these other aspects of the law of obligations, hence the justification for treating it separately. The law of tort is concerned with the identification of wrongdoing, whereas liability for unjust enrichment does not depend on proof of any wrong. Equally, whereas liability for breach of contract arises from the agreement itself, liability for unjust enrichment is imposed by operation of law and does not depend on any agreement having been made between the parties. Indeed, liability for unjust enrichment will be excluded if a contract between the parties is subsisting.[47]

---

[43] See J Langbein, 'The Later History of Restitution' in W Cornish, R Nolan, J O'Sullivan, and G Virgo (eds), *Restitution: Past, Present and Future* (Oxford: Hart Publishing, 1998), 60–2.

[44] Hart Publishing, 2012.

[45] AS Burrows, 'Contact, Tort and Restitution—A Satisfactory Division or Not?' (1983) LQR 217.

[46] This was recognized by Lord Wright in *Fibrosa Spolka Akcyjna v Fairbairn Lawson Combe Barbour Ltd* [1943] AC 32, 61. See also *Banque Financière de la Cité v Parc (Battersea) Ltd* [1999] 1 AC 221, 227 (Lord Steyn) and *Restatement Third: Restitution and Unjust Enrichment* (American Law Institute, 2011), 3.

[47] See p 134, below.

(B) ALTERNATIVE THEORIES

Even though the unjust enrichment principle has clearly been recognized in English law, its validity and usefulness continue to be a source of controversy. Some commentators and jurisdictions have rejected unjust enrichment and suggest that restitutionary liability should be based on a different theoretical foundation.

(i) Proprietary Theory

A significant critique of the unjust enrichment principle was made by Stoljar, who advocated a proprietary theory of the law of restitution.[48] The essence of this theory is that restitution is justified where the defendant received property which belonged to the claimant. Stoljar's recognition of a proprietary theory of restitution is consistent with the principle of vindicating proprietary rights, where the claimant is able to obtain restitution if he or she can establish a continuing proprietary interest in property which was received and retained by the defendant.[49] But Stoljar took his proprietary theory much further, since he considered that it even encompassed unjust enrichment claims. But this is unacceptable for the following reasons.

(1) In most cases where the claimant transfers property to the defendant, the claimant cannot be said to have a proprietary interest in the property once it is received by the defendant, since the claimant's title to the property will usually have passed to the defendant at the time of receipt.[50] It follows that the restitutionary claim cannot be based on the fact that the defendant has received property which belongs to the claimant, because, at the point of receipt, the property no longer belongs to the claimant. It is for this reason that there is a role for the unjust enrichment principle, since this does not depend on proof that the claimant has retained a proprietary interest in the property which was received by the defendant.

(2) The fact that the defendant received property which belonged to the claimant before it was transferred is hardly a convincing justification for the award of restitutionary remedies where the consequence of the receipt is that the property then belongs to the defendant. Something else needs to be shown to justify the award of such remedies, such as the application of one of the grounds of restitution for the purposes of a claim founded on the defendant's unjust enrichment.

(3) Stoljar's proprietary theory also does not explain how restitutionary remedies can be awarded where the defendant is enriched by the receipt of services, since the claimant has no proprietary interest in the provision of a service. Although Stoljar accepted that his theory did not cover such claims, he adopted an alternative explanation, namely that a remedy is awarded to the claimant in respect of the services which he or she had provided to the defendant on the basis of the claimant's loss rather than the defendant's gain, this being called the principle of 'unjust sacrifice'.[51] But this is highly artificial, particularly when the principle of reversing the defendant's unjust enrichment explains why restitutionary remedies can be available where the defendant has benefited from the claimant's services.

---

[48] SJ Stoljar, *The Law of Quasi-Contract* (2nd edn, Sydney: The Law Book Co, 1989), 9–10 and 250. See also P Jaffey, *The Nature and Scope of Restitution* (Oxford: Hart Publishing, 2000), ch 9.

[49] See Part IV.   [50] See Chapter 21.

[51] SJ Stoljar, 'Unjust Enrichment and Unjust Sacrifice' (1987) 50 MLR 603. See Chapter 4 for further discussion of this principle.

(ii) No Unifying Principle of Unjust Enrichment

An alternative critique of the unjust enrichment principle is that it is of little or no utility to our understanding of when restitutionary remedies will be awarded.[52] This is both because unjust enrichment is not sufficiently recognized by the courts and also because the principle is artificial in bringing together disparate areas of the law which are not sufficiently similar, so that it is not possible to identify a coherent independent body of law founded on the reversal of the defendant's unjust enrichment. This rejection of the unjust enrichment principle can itself be rejected on two grounds. First, because the principle has now been explicitly recognized in a number of decisions of the House of Lords and the Supreme Court.[53] Secondly, because the unjust enrichment principle does indeed have an important, but not a universal, function in explaining when restitutionary remedies can be awarded. It is a principle which explains earlier cases and can be used to predict results in future cases. It also enables disparate areas of the law to be brought together. The proof of the usefulness of the unjust enrichment principle will be found in the remaining chapters of this Part.

(iii) Unconscionable Retention

There is a sense, amongst certain members of the judiciary and certain academics, that the young upstart 'unjust enrichment', created by the Common Law, is seeking to take over the long established principles of Equity and subvert them.[54] This has been recognized by Gummow J in *Roxborough v Rothmans of Pall Mall Australia Ltd*,[55] a decision of the High Court of Australia, who said that the recognition of the unjust enrichment principle 'may distort well settled principles in other fields, including those respecting equitable doctrines and remedies, so that they answer the newly mandated order of things. Then various theories will compete, each to deny the others.'[56]

In Australia, as a result of this concern, the High Court has rejected the unjust enrichment principle in favour of restitution being awarded where the defendant's retention of a benefit can be characterized as unconscionable. This locates the law of restitution firmly within the Equity jurisdiction of the Chancery court, where the prime justification for equitable intervention is conscience, either of the defendant or the judge.

Even in England the origins of what is now called unjust enrichment can be traced back to the notion that the defendant's retention of a gain would be against conscience.[57] In *Sadler v Evans*[58] Lord Mansfield recognized that the action for money had and received was 'founded upon large principles of equity, where the defendant can not conscientiously hold the money'. The significance of conscience to the law of restitution was emphasized subsequently. In *Kelly v Solari*[59] it was recognized that money paid by mistake could be recovered, even though the claimant had made the mistake negligently, because it would be against conscience for the payee to retain it. Even in *Lipkin Gorman (a firm) v Karpnale*

---

[52] See especially PS Atiyah, *The Rise and Fall of Freedom of Contract* (Oxford: Clarendon Press, 1979), 768 and S Hedley, *Restitution: Its Division and Ordering* (London: Sweet and Maxwell, 2001).

[53] See p 7, above.

[54] In *Westdeutsche Landesbank Girozentrale v Islington LBC* [1996] AC 669, 685 Lord Goff referred to the tension between the aims and perceptions of restitution lawyers and 'equity lawyers'.

[55] [2002] 185 ALR 335.   [56] Ibid, 355.

[57] Most famously, Lord Mansfield in *Moses v Macferlan* (1760) 2 Burr 1007, 1011; 97 ER 676, 680.

[58] (1766) 4 Burr 1984, 1986; 98 ER 34, 35. See also *Dale v Sollet* (1767) 4 Burr 2133, 2134; 98 ER 112, 113; *Clarke v Shee and Johnson* (1774) 1 Cowp 197, 199; 98 ER 1041, 1042.

[59] (1841) 9 M and W 54, 58; 152 ER 24, 25 (Parke B). See also *Fibrosa Spolka Akcyjna v Fairbairn Lawson Combe Barbour Ltd* [1943] AC 32, 61 (Lord Wright), p 47, above.

Ltd[60] Lord Goff explicitly related the defendant's unjust enrichment to Lord Mansfield's contention that it would be against conscience for the defendant to retain the money in such circumstances.

But the award of restitution is not tied to vague notions of conscience, enabling the judge to exercise an arbitrary choice depending on perceived notions of justice on the facts of the case.[61] Instead the unjust enrichment formula is applied.[62] Since *Lipkin Gorman* the language of conscience is rarely used when examining unjust enrichment, although there are limited exceptions.[63]

In Australia the law of restitution has taken a different course, albeit from a starting point similar to the modern English approach.[64] In *Pavey and Matthews Pty Ltd v Paul*[65] the High Court explicitly recognized unjust enrichment. Refinement of principle followed. But it was Justice Gummow in particular, in *Roxborough v Rothmans of Pall Mall Australia Ltd*,[66] who put the Australian law of restitution on a different course. In rejecting the role of unjust enrichment as a unifying principle, he emphasized instead the equitable origins of restitution in *Moses v Macferlan,* from which he concluded that the law of restitution should be founded on the defendant's unconscionable retention of a benefit. Confirmation of this approach followed in a number of decisions.[67] In *Australian Financial Services and Leasing Pty Ltd v Hills Industries Ltd*[68] the plurality recognized[69] that 'the concept of unjust enrichment is not the basis of restitutionary relief in Australian law'. Rather, the 'enquiry is conducted by reference to equitable principles', namely whether the retention of monies paid to the defendant can be considered to be unconscionable. The difficulty with this approach relates to the identification of when the defendant's retention can be considered to be unconscionable. The plurality recognized that 'conscience' does not involve the judge's subjective evaluation of the justice of the case,[70] and purported to identify equitable principles to assess what conscience demands. But the only indication as to what these principles are involved reference to 'a construct of standards and values',[71] or, as Chief Justice French recognized,[72] a legal standard 'informing guiding criteria for particular classes of case'. But there was no attempt to identify what these standards, values, or criteria might be.

But might the unjust enrichment principle have an appropriate role in constructing what conscience demands? On the same day that the High Court handed down judgment in *Hills Industries*, Edelman J in the Western Australian Supreme Court handed down

[60] [1991] 2 AC 548, 572.

[61] A concern of Hamilton LJ in *Baylis v Bishop of London* [1913] 1 Ch 127, 140.

[62] *Banque Financière de la Cité v Parc (Battersea) Ltd* [1999] 1 AC 221, 227 (Lord Steyn).

[63] See, for example, *Vedatech Corp v Crystal Decisions (UK) Ltd* [2002] EWHC 818 (Ch), [74] (Jacob J). In *Banque Financière de la Cité v Parc (Battersea) Ltd* [1999] 1 AC 221, 237 Lord Clyde described the action as equitable but emphasized that it was did not follow that it was entirely discretionary in its application.

[64] See W Swain, 'Unjust Enrichment and the Role of Legal History in England and Australia' (2013) 36 UNSWLJ 1030.

[65] (1987) 162 CLR 221. See also *David Securities Pty Ltd v Commonwealth Bank of Australia* (1992) 175 CLR 353.

[66] (2002) 185 ALR 335, 355. See also *South Australian Cold Stores Ltd v Electricity Trust of South Australia* (1957) 98 CLR 65, 75 (Dixon CJ, McTiernan, Williams, Webb, and Taylor JJ); J Dietrich, *Restitution: A New Perspective* (Sydney: The Federation Press, 1998); IM Jackman, *The Varieties of Restitution* (Sydney: The Federation Press, 1998); B Kremer 'Restitution and Unconscientiousness: Another View' (2003) 119 LQR 188; M Bryan, 'Unjust Enrichment and Unconscionability in Australia: A False Dichotomy?' in JW Nyers, M McInnes, and SGA Pitel (eds), *Understanding Unjust Enrichment* (Oxford: Hart Publishing, 2004), ch 4.

[67] Including *Farah Construction Pty Ltd v Say-Dee Pty Ltd* (2007) 230 CLR 89 and *Lumbers v W Cook Builders Pty Ltd (in liq)* (2008) 232 CLR 635.

[68] [2014] HCA 14.   [69] Ibid, [78].   [70] Ibid, [76].   [71] Ibid.   [72] Ibid, [16].

judgment in *Lampson (Australia) Pty Ltd v Fortescue Metals Group Ltd (No 3)*,[73] and sought to preserve a role for unjust enrichment in the light of what was said in *Hills Industries*. He considered that unjust enrichment is not a direct source of liability in Australia, but has a useful function as a taxonomic category in assisting understanding, in the same way as 'torts' is a useful descriptive category but does not identify the underlying cause of action of a particular tort. Nevertheless, Edelman J went on to identify the core features of the unjust enrichment formula, involving enrichment which is unjust and at the plaintiff's expense, which provides the reason for restitution to be awarded. Surely this involves the recognition of unjust enrichment as a principle. If the test for restitution is to be whether the defendant's retention of a benefit is unconscionable, some principle needs to be identified to guide the court in determining unconscionability. The principle of unjust enrichment would serve that purpose, but then that is elevating unjust enrichment beyond a mere 'label', 'concept', or 'notion' to something else which gives meaning to what is unconscionable. That still preserves the equitable foundation of the claim, but makes sense of it by incorporating an unjust enrichment principle.

As a matter of form, the divide between English and Australian restitution law seems more significant than ever following the decision of the High Court in *Hills Industries*, with England relying on unjust enrichment and Australia on conscience. But, as a matter of substance, the difference is vanishingly small. In England unjust enrichment operates to establish whether the receipt of the enrichment is unconscionable in a principled sense, whereas in Australia unconscionability can only be interpreted in a principled way with reference to unjust enrichment. As French CJ rightly said,[74] 'legal principles of restitution or unjust enrichment can be equated with seminal equitable notions of good conscience'. It follows that, if it is necessary to explain the law of restitution with reference to conscience, it is vital that the principle of unjust enrichment be used to justify what conscience demands. The language of conscience might be considered to have no useful function in this context, so it can be ignored, as now occurs in England. But if it is retained in Australia there is a significant danger that conscience will be interpreted as allowing the judge to exercise an arbitrary choice on the facts about what is the just response. The exercise of judicial discretion can only be rendered principled if it is constrained within the bounds of unjust enrichment.[75]

3. THE FUNCTION OF THE UNJUST ENRICHMENT PRINCIPLE

(A) POSSIBLE FUNCTIONS OF THE UNJUST ENRICHMENT PRINCIPLE

Now it has been recognized that there is a principle of unjust enrichment in English law, it is necessary to determine the function of that principle. It can be interpreted as having two alternative functions, which can usefully be called the 'formulaic' and the 'normative' functions.

(i) The Formulaic Function

According to the formulaic function, the defendant will only be considered to have been unjustly enriched where the circumstances of the case satisfy the formula for unjust

---

[73] [2014] WASC 162.
[74] *Australian Financial Services and Leasing Pty Ltd v Hills Industries Ltd* [2014] HAC 14, [16].
[75] See p 42, above, for examination of the proper interpretation of judicial discretion.

enrichment, namely that the defendant has received an enrichment at the expense of the claimant and in circumstances which fall within one of the recognized grounds of restitution. Crucially, restitutionary relief will only be available to the claimant according to this interpretation of the principle if restitutionary liability has previously been recognized in similar circumstances.

(ii) The Normative Function

According to the normative function of the principle, the defendant can be considered to have been unjustly enriched whenever the court considers that the circumstances of the enrichment were unjust. The normative function is much more discretionary, involving the judge considering the facts of the case without regard to whether restitutionary relief has previously been awarded in similar circumstances.[76]

(B) THE APPROACH ADOPTED BY ENGLISH LAW

English law considers the unjust enrichment principle to have a formulaic rather than a normative function. Consequently, the defendant will be considered to have been unjustly enriched only where the circumstances of the enrichment fall within one of the recognized grounds of restitution. It follows that whether the defendant will be found to have been unjustly enriched is determined by reference to principle rather than to vague notions that, as a matter of justice, the defendant ought to return a benefit to the claimant.

It has been recognized, however, that this formula of unjust enrichment should not be treated as though it has statutory force.[77] It is unclear what this means, other than to state the obvious that unjust enrichment is judge-made law. But, if this denial of statutory force suggests that judges are to be given significant discretion to determine whether the formula is satisfied on arbitrary grounds, this unacceptably confuses the formulaic and normative functions of the unjust enrichment principle.

(C) SHOULD THE UNJUST ENRICHMENT PRINCIPLE HAVE A NORMATIVE FUNCTION?

Although the unjust enrichment principle has traditionally been treated as having a formulaic function, there is some evidence that the principle may be shifting towards a more normative function. The trigger for this shift may be an important dictum of Lord Goff in *Westdeutsche Landesbank Girozentrale v Islington LBC*[78] where he recognized that:

> An action of restitution appears to me to provide an almost classic case in which the jurisdiction should be available to enable the courts to do full justice... The seed is there, but the growth has hitherto been confined within a small area. That growth should now be permitted to spread naturally elsewhere within this newly recognised branch of the law. No genetic engineering is required, only that the warm sun of judicial creativity should exercise its benign influence rather than remain hidden behind the dark clouds of legal history.

---

[76] For an extreme version of the normative approach see H Dagan, *The Law and Ethics of Restitution* (Cambridge: Cambridge University Press, 2004), who adopts a 'contextual normative inquiry' to the law of unjust enrichment, 36. Consequently, for Dagan the unjust enrichment principle does not have a unifying function because the appropriate result depends on the particular context of the case.

[77] *Investment Trust Companies v HMRC* [2012] EWHC 458 (Ch), [39] (Henderson J).

[78] [1996] AC 669, 697.

Whilst it cannot follow from this that we must throw away the recognized principles which underlie the award of restitutionary relief, this dictum does suggest that there is a shift of emphasis away from a backward-looking, principled approach towards a forward-looking approach, which is much more prepared to enter new territory and award restitutionary relief in circumstances where such relief has not been awarded before. Is this desirable?

Such an approach has been adopted in Canada, where the courts have been much more prepared to award restitutionary remedies by reference to a general notion of unjust enrichment rather than the pre-existing grounds of restitution.[79] But such an approach is surely unsatisfactory. The virtually unconstrained discretion of the judge to decide whether or not the receipt of an enrichment was in circumstances of injustice will result in great uncertainty. Such discretion is alien to the Common Law tradition where judges reach their decision by reference to what has gone before. The introduction of such a discretion would mean that judges would be more concerned with the circumstances of the case and balancing the conduct of the parties to see where the balance of justice lies. This danger is particularly well illustrated by the decision of Knox J in *Hillsdown plc v Pensions Ombudsman*[80] who said:

> As to its being unjust...one only has to compare the position of Hillsdown who successfully wielded a big but misguided stick with that of the members of the...scheme who were never told anything of what was being done as regards the payment of surplus to Hillsdown to see which way the scales of justice fall.

Although judges must be allowed a degree of discretion when determining whether the defendant should be liable to make restitution and what the nature of the restitutionary remedy should be, this discretion must never be at the expense of principle.

(D) THE MIDDLE WAY

It does not, however, follow from this emphasis on principle rather than discretion that the grounds of restitution are closed. The recognized grounds of restitution need to be adaptable and, if necessary, new grounds of restitution must be recognized to ensure that the law of restitution remains relevant to the demands of the late twentieth century.[81] There is, in fact, evidence that the law of restitution is able to adapt by developing the notion of what constitutes injustice for the purposes of the unjust enrichment principle. This is exemplified by the decision of the House of Lords in *Woolwich Equitable Building Society v IRC*,[82] where the claimant was able to recover overpaid tax from the Inland Revenue by reference to the newly recognized ground that a public authority was not authorized to receive such an *ultra vires* payment.

There is, therefore, a middle way between the formulaic and normative functions of the unjust enrichment principle. That principle cannot be allowed to be a strait-jacket to restitutionary claims, but it needs to adapt to changing circumstances. But this adaptation must be by reference to the established principles, rather than simply by referring to the

---

[79] See, in particular, *Deglman v Guaranty Trust of Canada* [1954] SCR 725 and *Pettkus v Becker* [1980] 2 SCR 834, both decisions of the Supreme Court of Canada. See also GB Klippert, 'The Juridical Nature of Unjust Enrichment' (1980) 30 University of Toronto LJ 356. Cf *Peel v Canada* (1993) 98 DLR (4th) 180, and *Garland v Consumers' Gas Distributors Inc* [2004] 1 SCR, considered at p 132, below.

[80] [1997] 1 All ER 862, 903.

[81] *CTN Cash and Carry Ltd v Gallaher Ltd* [1994] 4 All ER 714, 720 (Sir Donald Nicholls V-C).

[82] [1993] AC 70. See Chapter 15.

justice of the case. This 'middle way' has been expressly recognized by the Supreme Court of Canada in *Peel v Canada*[83] where McLachlin J said: '[W]e must choose a middle path; one which acknowledges the importance of proceeding on general principles but seeks to reconcile the principles with the established categories of recovery.'[84]

This notion of a 'middle path' is reflected in English law as well.[85] It is vital that new grounds of restitution are recognized, or that the existing grounds are reinterpreted where it is appropriate to do so, and also that the definition of enrichment and at the claimant's expense are open to development, but this recognition and development should always occur with great care and be continuously informed by the existing and well-established principles relating to the elements of the unjust enrichment formula.

4. THE ROLE OF THE UNJUST ENRICHMENT PRINCIPLE IN PRACTICE

It is one thing to recognize the unjust enrichment principle as a means of analysing certain types of restitutionary claim, but how does this principle operate in practice? Most importantly, how does the claimant plead a restitutionary claim founded on unjust enrichment? This raises a further question, namely what is the cause of action when the claim is founded on unjust enrichment?

(A) CURRENT PRACTICE

In practice, where the claimant wishes to bring a restitutionary claim founded on the defendant's unjust enrichment that claim will still be pleaded with reference to the old forms of action, known as the common counts, even though they were abolished in the nineteenth century.[86] There are four types of action:

(1) the action for money had and received by the defendant to the use of the claimant;

(2) the action for money paid to the defendant;

(3) *quantum valebat* to recover the reasonable value of goods which had been transferred to the defendant; and

(4) *quantum meruit* to recover the reasonable value of services which the defendant had received from the claimant.

Which action is pleaded depends on the type of enrichment which the claimant alleges the defendant has received and the circumstances in which it has been received. Even though the restitutionary claim is formulated in terms of the old form of action, it does not follow that it is unrelated to the unjust enrichment principle. In fact, the forms of action are explicable today only by reference to that principle. This was recognized by Clarke J in *South Tyneside MBC v Svenska International plc*,[87] who accepted that the recognition of unjust enrichment does not constitute the recognition of a new cause of action different from that of money had and received and the other forms of action. Rather, unjust enrichment 'is simply another way of describing the same thing'.

---

[83] (1993) 98 DLR (4th) 140.   [84] Ibid, 153.

[85] *Uren v First National Home Finance Ltd* [2005] EWHC 2529 (Ch), [17] (Mann J); *Gibb v Maidstone and Tunbridge Wells NHS Trust* [2010] EWCA Civ 678, [27] (Laws LJ).

[86] By s 3 of the Common Law Procedure Act 1852.

[87] [1995] 1 All ER 545, 557.

The continued inclusion of the old forms of action in pleadings is liable to confuse, especially because this indicates that the underlying cause of action is, for example, the action for money had and received. If the language of the old forms of action is to be retained, they should be treated as describing the remedy which is awarded rather than the underlying claim.[88] In fact, because of the liability to confuse, the language of the old forms of action should be rejected completely. The need for this is clearly illustrated by the decision of the House of Lords in *Yeoman's Row Management Ltd v Cobbe*.[89] Although the case was primarily concerned with an unsuccessful claim founded on proprietary estoppel, a claim for restitution succeeded. What makes the case so controversial is that three distinct causes of action were recognized, when in fact each cause of action was a different way of describing the same thing. The claimant had entered into an oral agreement in principle with the defendant to buy the defendant's land. No written contract was made. The claimant successfully made an application for planning permission to develop the land, at significant expense in preparing plans and submitting the application. Negotiations for purchase of the land broke down. The claimant was unable to sue for breach of contract, because contracts for the sale of land must be in writing,[90] so the claimant sought a restitutionary remedy from the defendant. This claim succeeded on the basis that the defendant had obtained the benefit of the planning permission.[91] Lord Scott recognized that there were three causes of action available to the claimant:

(1) unjust enrichment—on the basis that the defendant had obtained a benefit at the expense of the claimant;

(2) *quantum meruit*—on the basis that the defendant's benefit consisted of the provision of the claimant's services in obtaining planning permission;

(3) failure of consideration[92]—on the basis that the claimant had expected to obtain the land in respect of which the planning permission had been obtained and this was not forthcoming.

That the claimant could obtain a personal restitutionary remedy in these circumstances is not controversial; that the claimant had three distinct ways to obtain this remedy is. The only claim available was one in unjust enrichment, for which the only appropriate remedy would have been *quantum meruit* (the reasonable value of the services provided) and for which the unjust element would be satisfied by showing that there had been a total failure of basis, in that the claimant had received nothing from the defendant. In identifying three distinct claims Lord Scott was simply describing one claim but from three different perspectives: the underlying principle, the remedy, and the ground of restitution.

The most worrying aspect of Lord Scott's analysis was the proposition that *quantum meruit* was a cause of action in its own right. But that cause of action was abolished in 1852. Even if the cause of action could still be considered to exist in its own right, what are the elements of the claim which need to be established? Lord Scott gave no indication of this and it is difficult to see what would be required, other than that the defendant had benefited from the receipt of the services provided by the claimant and that there was a reason why the defendant should be required to pay for this service. But that is what unjust enrichment establishes. There is a growing body of law on the identification and valuation

---

[88] See further Chapter 1.   [89] [2008] UKHL 55, [2008] 1 WLR 1752.
[90] Law of Property (Miscellaneous Provisions) Act 1989, s 2.
[91] As to the identification and valuation of this enrichment, see p 76, below.
[92] What in this book is called 'failure of basis'. See Chapter 13.

of enrichment, which has been contributed to by the decision in *Yeoman's Row*, and reliance on a recognized ground of restitution shows why a remedy should be awarded. Nothing can be gained by simply asserting a claim in *quantum meruit*.

(B) IDENTIFICATION OF THE CAUSE OF ACTION IN UNJUST ENRICHMENT CLAIMS

Rather than the pleadings formulating a claim for restitution with reference to the old forms of action, it would be preferable to formulate the claim with explicit reference to the unjust enrichment principle. Unjust enrichment cannot, however, be pleaded as a cause of action in its own right,[93] since it is too vague to be acceptable.[94] Rather, the unjust enrichment principle consists of a number of different causes of action, distinguished by reference to particular grounds of restitution, such as the cause of action for total failure of basis and that for the recovery of money paid under a mistake.[95] It follows that the pleading of a claim in unjust enrichment operates in a similar way to the pleading of a claim in tort. Tort as such is not a cause of action, but a category of related causes of action connected by wrongdoing. It would never be acceptable for the claimant simply to sue the defendant in tort; the particular tort and its constituent elements need to be identified. The same is true of unjust enrichment; the particular claim within unjust enrichment and its constituent elements need to be identified.

This analysis of the cause of action in unjust enrichment is consistent with the other two principles which trigger restitutionary remedies. So, where the restitutionary claim is founded on the defendant's wrongdoing, it is not sufficient merely to say that the claim is founded on a wrong; it is necessary to identify the particular type of wrongdoing which is alleged. Similarly, where the claim is founded on the vindication of property rights, it is necessary to identify the right which the claimant seeks to vindicate and sometimes to formulate the claim with some precision, as is the case where, for example, the claim is founded on the action for unconscionable receipt.[96]

(C) ESTABLISHING THE CLAIM IN UNJUST ENRICHMENT

The claimant bears the burden of proving the elements of the unjust enrichment claim, namely that the defendant has been enriched at the claimant's expense and one of the recognized grounds of restitution apply.[97] Once this has been established, the burden then shifts to the defendant to establish a defence to the claim. Analysis of the different burdens borne by the claimant and the defendant has been assisted by Mitchell and Goudkamp, who draw a significant distinction between denials and defences.[98] A denial is an assertion by a defendant that an element of the cause of action is not established, whereas defences only arise once the cause of action has been established to

---

[93] *Uren v First National Home Finance Ltd* [2005] EWHC 2529 (Ch), [16] (Mann J).

[94] As was recognized by Dawson J in *David Securities Pty Ltd v Commonwealth Bank of Australia* (1992) 175 CLR 353, 406.

[95] *F J Chalke Ltd v The Commissioners for Her Majesty's Revenue and Customs* [2009] EWHC 952 (Ch), [2009] STC 2007, [127] (Henderson J); *Test Claimants in the FII Group Litigation v Commissioners for HM Revenue and Customs* [2014] EWHC 4302 (Ch), [248]. See also *Deutsche Morgan Grenfell Group plc v IRC* [2006] UKHL 49, [2007] 1 AC 558, [17] (Lord Hoffmann).   [96] See Chapter 22.

[97] *Banque Financière de la Cité v Parc (Battersea) Ltd* [1999] 1 AC 221, 227 (Lord Steyn).

[98] C Mitchell and J Goudkamp, 'Denials and Defences in the Law of Unjust Enrichment' in C Mitchell and W Swadling (eds), *The Restatement Third: Restitution and Unjust Enrichment* (Oxford: Hart Publishing, 2013), ch 6.

indicate a reason why the defendant should not be liable or the liability should be reduced in some way. So, for example, if the defendant argues that there was a legal basis for the receipt of an enrichment, this is properly characterized as a denial of the claim, because the claimant bears the burden of proving that there was no legal basis for the enrichment.[99] If however, the defendant argues that his or her position has changed after the enrichment has been received, this is a defence, which the defendant bears the burden of proving, because the change of position is only considered to be relevant after the cause of action has been established.[100]

(D) THE LAW OF UNJUST ENRICHMENT

The creation and nurturing of the unjust enrichment principle is the most significant legal development in English private law of the late twentieth and early twenty-first century. It is noteworthy that in its early years the judges, notably Lord Goff, spoke of the law of restitution rather than a law of unjust enrichment.[101] Unjust enrichment used to be thought of as a concept,[102] but we should now recognize that we have a distinct law of unjust enrichment.[103] Unjust enrichment still operates as a legal principle rather than a cause of action, but the different rules relating to unjust enrichment are now sufficiently well developed that it is possible to identify a distinct body of law which is appropriately called unjust enrichment.

---

[99] See Chapter 7.   [100] See Chapter 25.

[101] See, for example, *Woolwich Equitable Building Society v IRC* [1993] AC 70, 163; *Pan Ocean Shipping Co Ltd v Creditcorp Ltd, The Trident Beauty* [1994] 1 WLR 161, 164; and *Westdeutsche Landesbank Girozentrale v Islington LBC* [1996] AC 669, 697, where he spoke of an action of restitution. See also Lord Hutton in *Kleinwort Benson Ltd v Glasgow City Council* [1999] 1 AC 153, 186.

[102] See *Woolwich Equitable Building Society v IRC* [1993] AC 70, 197 (Lord Browne-Wilkinson).

[103] As Lord Hope described it in *Sempra Metals Ltd v IRC* [2007] UKHL 34, [2008] 1 AC 561, [8].

4

ENRICHMENT

1. THE RELEVANCE OF ENRICHMENT

The identification of an enrichment goes to the heart of a restitutionary claim which is founded on reversal of the defendant's unjust enrichment, for until an enrichment has been identified and valued it is not possible to ascertain exactly what should be restored to the claimant. Usually, the need to identify an enrichment causes no difficulty for the claimant. So, in a typical claim where the defendant has received money from the claimant, the defendant is always regarded as enriched by that money, since it is the measure of value.[1] But where the claimant seeks to recover the value of non-money benefits, such as goods or services, the identification of an enrichment and its valuation is a matter of some complexity. It must not be forgotten that, even though it can be shown that the defendant has been enriched, it does not follow that the restitutionary claim will necessarily succeed, since it must also be established that the enrichment was received at the claimant's expense[2] and that one of the recognized grounds of restitution is applicable.

When considering the definition of enrichment for purposes of the law of unjust enrichment it is vital to distinguish clearly between the process of identifying the enrichment and, once this has been done, the valuation of that enrichment. Although, as will be seen, identification and valuation of enrichments share common principles, the interpretation and application of those principles sometimes differ.

(A) UNJUST ENRICHMENT OR UNJUST BENEFIT?

Whilst the principle of reversing unjust enrichment clearly assumes that it is a precondition of liability that the defendant has been enriched, sometimes the restitutionary action is analysed in terms of whether or not the defendant has been unjustly benefited rather than enriched. For example, in *Fibrosa Spolka Akcyjna v Fairbairn Lawson Combe Barbour Ltd*[3] Lord Wright referred to the principles of both unjust enrichment and unjust benefit. The Law Reform (Frustrated Contracts) Act 1943[4] uses the word 'benefit' in the context of a statutory scheme which comes into operation once a contract has been frustrated and which exists to reverse the defendant's unjust enrichment.[5] Does it make any difference whether 'enrichment' or 'benefit' is used, or can these words be used interchangeably?

Linguistically there is an important difference between 'enrichment' and 'benefit', and consequently the word which is used may have an important effect upon the ambit of the restitutionary claim. This is because 'enrichment' could be interpreted as being limited to

---

[1] See p 73, below.   [2] See Chapter 5.
[3] [1943] AC 32, 61. See also *Brook's Wharf and Bull Wharf Ltd v Goodman Brothers* [1937] 1 KB 534, 545 (Lord Wright MR).   [4] See Chapter 13.
[5] *BP Exploration Co (Libya) Ltd v Hunt (No 2)* [1979] 1 WLR 783, 799 (Robert Goff J).

those benefits which can be assessed only in terms of monetary value, so that the defendant will only be enriched when he or she has received money or money's worth. Consequently, Beatson[6] has assumed that enrichment equates with wealth and concludes that a defendant will only be enriched where he or she received something which has an exchange value, so that, on receipt of the enrichment, the defendant is financially better off than he or she would have been had he or she not received the enrichment. This may be acceptable as an economic definition of what constitutes an enrichment, but is it really acceptable as a legal definition? Colloquially, a defendant may say that he or she was enriched even though he or she has not received something which itself has an exchange value. This is particularly relevant where the defendant has received a 'pure service', namely a service which leaves no marketable residuum,[7] such as attendance at a concert or receiving a massage. Beatson, by virtue of his rigorously economic approach to the definition of enrichment, concludes that pure services cannot be treated as enrichments, save where the service anticipates expenditure which the defendant would necessarily have incurred.[8]

But the recipients of pure services can, and often will, say that they were enriched by what they had received even though they were not left with anything of any value. There will often be a demand for pure services in the market where reasonable people are prepared to pay for the service, so this suggests that the service is a valuable benefit.[9] It is for this reason that 'benefit' is a better expression than 'enrichment', since it emphasizes that the unjust enrichment principle should not be limited by the artificial restrictions of economic analysis.[10]

The fact that 'benefit' is a more flexible and wider expression than 'enrichment' has been noted before. For example, Fuller and Perdue in their essay on 'The Reliance Interest in Contract Damages'[11] recognized that 'enrichment' is a narrower term than benefit, which, if it is used, will have the effect of restricting the potential ambit of the restitutionary response.

Despite this preference for the use of 'benefit', the terms 'enrichment' and 'benefit' will be used interchangeably throughout this book for two reasons. First, this reflects the practice in the cases, where the words are used indiscriminately without any obvious intention that they have different senses. Secondly, the word 'enrichment' is explicitly incorporated in the principle of reversing unjust enrichment. It is too late now to rename this 'the principle for reversing unjust benefit', even though this would be more accurate. But where 'enrichment' is referred to, it must always be remembered that it should be given a wide interpretation; one which is not constrained by economic definitions of wealth, so that it should include pure services.[12]

---

[6] J Beatson, *The Use and Abuse of Unjust Enrichment* (Oxford: Clarendon Press, 1991), 29 ff.

[7] A marketable residuum will be left where the effect of the service is to leave a valuable end product, for example a service which improves the defendant's property and so increases its value.

[8] Beatson, *The Use and Abuse of Unjust Enrichment*, 32

[9] In *Re Berkeley Applegate (Investment Consultants) Ltd* [1989] Ch 32, Edward Nugee QC sitting as a Deputy High Court Judge apparently rejected Beatson's contention when, at 50, he said that the suggestion that services would constitute an enrichment only where the work added to the assets of the defendant was 'too narrow a view of the principles'. See also PBH Birks, 'In Defence of Free Acceptance' in AS Burrows (ed), *Essays on the Law of Restitution* (Oxford: Clarendon Press, 1991), 134.

[10] AVM Lodder, *Enrichment in the Law of Unjust Enrichment and Restitution* (Oxford: Hart Publishing, 2012), 34, considers 'benefit' to refer to anything which has the quality of value.

[11] LL Fuller and WR Perdue, 'The Reliance Interest in Contract Damages' (1936) 46 Yale LJ 52, 72.

[12] Lodder, *Enrichment in the Law of Unjust Enrichment and Restitution*, 45, considers enrichment to be a more technical term than benefit, but concludes that there is no basis for the linguistic connection between enrichment and economic value.

(B) DIFFERENT SENSES OF ENRICHMENT

Lodder in *Enrichment in the Law of Unjust Enrichment and Restitution*[13] has drawn a fundamental distinction between what he calls factual and legal enrichment. Factual enrichment relates to the identification of benefits which have an economic value and which can be restored to the claimant through the payment of money. Legal enrichment, on the other hand, relates to the acquisition of a specific right by the defendant or the discharge of a specific obligation owed by the defendant. Here the enrichment is reversed either through the negation of the right or the reinstatement of the obligation. Crucially, legal enrichment does not need to be valued.

Whilst Lodder recognizes that both forms of enrichment are relevant to the identification of an unjust enrichment, his analysis can be considered to be consistent with the fundamental division in the law of restitution as advocated in this book. Since factual enrichments are valued in money, the restitutionary remedy is personal. Legal enrichments, involving the negation of rights or the reinstatement of obligations, might trigger proprietary responses in order to vindicate the claimant's proprietary rights.[14]

The recognition of legal enrichment as being a relevant enrichment for the purposes of the law of restitution is controversial,[15] but for the purposes of this chapter it is unnecessary to consider such issues, since the focus is on what Lodder calls 'factual enrichment', this being the relevant enrichment for purposes of the law of unjust enrichment which triggers a personal restitutionary remedy.

(C) THE ESSENCE OF ENRICHMENT

The essential feature of a factual enrichment is that it must be capable of being measured in money. The need to value the enrichment is vital since, as the remedy for unjust enrichment is personal, the claimant will only be able to recover the value of the enrichment from the defendant and this remedy can only be expressed in monetary terms. Resorting to value as the indicator of enrichment does not mean that Beatson's notion of exchange value is being recognized. This is because something may be regarded as valuable without necessarily having an exchange value. For example, a pure service may be valuable, in that reasonable people would pay for it, even though the defendant is left with nothing of any exchange value. It follows, however, that benefits which cannot be valued, such as happiness, will not count for purposes of the law of unjust enrichment.

Much of the uncertainty concerning the definition of enrichment has stemmed from lack of consensus about where the analysis should start. Essentially, there are two options available. Either we start with an objective test, ascertained by asking whether reasonable people would consider the defendant to have received something of value, or we start with a subjective test, by considering whether the defendant considers that he or she has received something of value. Whilst the use of the words 'objective' and 'subjective' might be considered to be ambiguous, they are useful shorthand for complex ideas. Subjective notions of value involve focusing on the particular value of the enrichment to the defendant. Lodder has called this 'idiosyncratic value'.[16] He calls the other notion of value 'relational value', this being an abstract value which enables the value of different

---

[13] See also R Chambers, 'Two Kinds of Enrichment' in R Chambers, C Mitchell, and J Penner (eds), *Philosophical Foundations of the Law of Unjust Enrichment* (Oxford: Oxford University Press, 2009).

[14] See, for example, the analysis of the resulting trust and subrogation at p 582 and p 636, below.

[15] See p 6, above.

[16] Lodder, *Enrichment in the Law of Unjust Enrichment and Restitution*, 15.

things to be compared in relation to each other. An example of this relational value is the market value of goods.

Whilst both objective and subjective tests are relevant to the identification of an enrichment, the better view is that it is the objective test which should always be considered first,[17] for four reasons.

(1) It makes practical sense for the claimant to establish that the defendant has received an objective benefit and then for the burden to shift to the defendant to disprove this, by arguing that he or she did not subjectively value what had been received. To require the claimant at the outset to show that the defendant actually valued what was received is difficult and illogical.

(2) The emphasis on the objective test is justified by the fact that the subjective test of enrichment has usually been formulated in terms of the principle of subjective devaluation,[18] whereby the defendant is allowed to show that he or she did not value the benefit which had been received. But, for the principle of subjective devaluation to work, the defendant must first be shown to have received an objective benefit; otherwise there is nothing to devalue.

(3) The objective test is generally relied on when valuing the enrichment and so, for consistency, that test should also be adopted, at least initially, when identifying the enrichment.[19]

(4) Finally, the objective test is adopted in practice as the starting point to identify an enrichment. So, for example, it is the objective test which is adopted for the purposes of determining whether the defendant has received a valuable benefit under a frustrated contract.[20] It has now been adopted explicitly by the Supreme Court in *Benedetti v Sawiris*.[21]

(i) The Objective Test of Enrichment
(1) The Nature of the Objective Test
The objective test of enrichment was carefully analysed by the Supreme Court in *Benedetti v Sawiris*,[22] where Lord Reed distinguished between the 'ordinary market value' and the 'objective value of the benefit'.[23] The former is the price which would have been agreed in the market in the absence of some unusual characteristic of the purchaser, whereas the latter is the value of the benefit to the reasonable person in the position of the defendant which would have been taken into account by the market and which may be higher or lower than the ordinary market value. Usually, both values will be the same, and it will be sufficient to assess what it would have cost a reasonable person to acquire the goods or services elsewhere in the market. This will depend on the specific circumstances operating at a particular place and time.[24] So, to use an example suggested by Lord Reed, in *Vanity Fair*[25] Becky Sharp sells her horse in Brussels following the battle of Waterloo, at a time when the inhabitants fear that Napoleon and his army is approaching. Consequently,

---

[17] This passage was approved by Lord Clarke in *Benedetti v Sawiris* [2013] UKSC 50, [2014] AC 938, [15].

[18] As recognized by the Court of Appeal in *Ministry of Defence v Ashman* [1993] EG 144, 147 (Hoffmann LJ); *McDonald v Coys of Kensington* [2004] EWCA Civ 47, [2004] 1 WLR 2775, 2787 (Mance LJ); *Benedetti v Sawiris* [2013] UKSC 50, [2014] AC 938.

[19] See *Benedetti v Sawiris* [2013] UKSC 50, [2014] AC 938.

[20] By virtue of the Law Reform (Frustrated Contracts) Act 1943. See *BP Exploration Co (Libya) Ltd v Hunt (No 2)* [1979] 1 WLR 783, 802 (Robert Goff J).

[21] [2013] UKSC 50, [2014] AC 938.   [22] Ibid.   [23] Ibid, [108].   [24] Ibid, [105].

[25] By William Makepeace Thackeray, first published in 1847–48.

horses are exceptionally valuable, but the exorbitant price she obtains can still be considered to be the ordinary market value, objectively determined and assessed by the horse market in Brussels at that time. Lord Reed[26] recognized that there were some goods or services which are so tailored to the preferences of a particular recipient that the idea of a reasonable recipient other than the actual recipient becomes unrealistic, such as costumes designed for the stage performance of a pop star. But even here the value of the costumes is not assigned by the recipient but is ascertained on the basis of objective evidence of the market value.

The objective value of the benefit may be higher or lower than the ordinary market value by virtue of the defendant's position, so it is necessary to consider what aspects of the defendant's position would be taken into account by the market.[27] The defendant's position does not include characteristics such as his or her generous or parsimonious personality,[28] but will include, for example, the defendant's buying power in the market which enables him or her to negotiate a lower price, the defendant's credit rating and even, according to Lord Reed,[29] the defendant's age, gender, occupation, and state of health. For example, a famous film star who wishes to purchase a designer dress might obtain a significant discount because of the publicity generated if she wears it on the red carpet. Consequently, the fact that she is famous is an aspect of her position which affects the objective value of the benefit. Lord Neuberger considered that the claimant's position might also be relevant to determine the objective value, such as where the claimant has particular expertise or experience, if this would have been reflected in the market.[30] This approach to the analysis of objective valuation was considered to be consistent with the decision of the House of Lords in *Sempra Metals Ltd v IRC*,[31] a case arising from the payment of tax which had been unlawfully levied prematurely. The claimant had paid tax due to the Revenue in circumstances where it should have been allowed to elect to defer payment for a period of time. Once the mistake was discovered, the claimant could not recover the money paid because it had discharged a legitimate tax liability,[32] but the claimant successfully argued that the Government, through the Revenue, had been enriched from its use of the money during the period from when the money was actually paid until it would have been paid had the election for deferred payment been made. The starting point for valuing the Government's benefit from the use of the money was to identify the objective value of the benefit, namely the reasonable cost of borrowing an equivalent amount of money,[33] which was to be assessed by reference to compound interest, this being the conventional interest for ordinary commercial borrowings.[34] This was considered by the Supreme Court in *Benedetti* to be the ordinary market value of the use of the money. It was presumed by the majority in *Sempra Metals v IRC*[35] that the Government did benefit from the receipt of the money in that, if it had not been paid, it would have borrowed an equivalent amount from a different source. In determining the objective market value of this benefit it was appropriate to have regard to a person in the position of the defendant, namely the Government, which was able to borrow on more favourable terms at a lower interest rate. So the objective market value was the public

---

[26] *Benedetti v Sawiris* [2013] UKSC 50, [2014] AC 938, [102].

[27] A similar approach is adopted when identifying the benefit obtained from a crime for purposes of the statutory confiscation regime. See *Elsayed* [2014] EWCA Crim 333, [2014] 1 WLR 3916, p 538, below.

[28] *Benedetti v Sawiris* [2013] UKSC 50, [2014] AC 938, [17] (Lord Clarke).

[29] Ibid, [101].   [30] Ibid, [184].   [31] [2007] UKHL 34, [2008] 1 AC 561. See p 30, above.

[32] See p 146, below.

[33] *Sempra Metals Ltd v IRC* [2007] UKHL 34, [2008] 1 AC 561, [116] (Lord Nicholls).

[34] See further p 31, above.

[35] [2007] UKHL 34, [2008] 1 AC 561, [33] (Lord Hope), [102] (Lord Nicholls), [180] (Lord Walker).

sector borrowing rate,[36] which was less than the interest which would have been charged to a commercial organization. The public sector borrowing rate is relevant to the objective value of the enrichment, since it is a factor which would be taken into account by the market in determining the value of the enrichment. Although there are dicta in *Sempra Metals* which appears to be consistent with the majority adopting a subjective valuation of the enrichment,[37] they were considered by the Supreme Court in *Benedetti v Sawiris*[38] to be ambiguous. All the Justices in *Benedetti* recognized that *Sempra Metals* actually involved objective valuation of the enrichment, having regard to the defendant's position as a public body able to borrow at a lower rate of interest. Logically, as Lord Reed recognized, if the defendant has a poor credit rating and so could only borrow at a rate above the market rate, the objective value of the enrichment will increase.

It follows that *objective* devaluation and over-valuation of the market value of the enrichment have both been recognized by the Supreme Court. Whether the defendant's circumstances should be characterized as affecting objective or subjective valuation will be a matter of judgment since, as Lord Clarke recognized, the line between them is narrow. Essentially the difference will depend on whether the defendant's position would have been taken into account by the market in determining the value of the enrichment. If it would, it is relevant to the objective value. This matters because it affects the burden of proof, since the claimant bears the burden of proving objective enrichment. However, in *Sempra Metals* the majority recognized a presumption that the Government had been enriched by the receipt of the tax, in that it had the opportunity to use the money paid by the claimant rather than to borrow an equivalent amount from elsewhere. It was not necessary for the claimant to prove that the Government had relied on the receipt of the money in any way. The minority considered this to be a wholly conceptual benefit and wanted the claimant to bear the burden of proving that the defendant had actually relied on the receipt of the money. The approach of the majority is preferable, since it is appropriate to assume that the defendant has relied on the money in some way, since the defendant is in the best position to show there was no reliance on the receipt, for example because it was put in a box under a bed or credited to a non-interest bearing current account. Consequently, the majority presumed that the Government had been enriched, since if the money had not been paid prematurely it would have borrowed an equivalent amount from another source.

The recognition by the Supreme Court in *Benedetti* of the distinction between ordinary market value and the objective value of the benefit with regard to the defendant's position means in effect that the law recognizes a core objective valuation with reference to the relevant market, but this can be objectively devalued or over-valued with reference to the effect of the defendant's position on the market valuation.[39]

(2) Positive and Negative Enrichment

The objective enrichment may take many forms. Often it will be positive, such as where the defendant receives a chattel or benefits from a service which increases the value of the defendant's property. Alternatively, a defendant may be negatively enriched, for example where he or she has been saved an expense which would otherwise have been incurred.

---

[36] Ibid, [50] (Lord Hope).   [37] Ibid, [119] (Lord Nicholls), [49] (Lord Hope), and [184] (Lord Walker).

[38] [2013] UKSC 50, [2014] AC 938, [22] (Lord Clarke), [127] (Lord Reed).

[39] In *Benedetti v Sawiris* [2013] UKSC 50, [2014] AC 938 Lord Reed, [108], recognized that there is room for argument as to whether the variation in value by reference to the defendant's position is an aspect of market value or a departure from it. The preferable view is that it is an aspect of market value, since the defendant's position is only objectively relevant if it would have influenced the market value.

This is illustrated by the facts of *Craven-Ellis v Canons Ltd*,[40] where the claimant director of the defendant company provided services to that company. These services were described as necessary to the running of the company, and so it is possible to conclude that the company had been enriched by them, because it had been saved money which it would otherwise necessarily have incurred had the claimant not provided the services.

(3) Receipt of Enrichment

The defendant cannot be considered to have been enriched objectively unless he or she has actually received a benefit. It is not sufficient for the claimant simply to have supplied a benefit to the defendant which has not been received. This follows logically from the essential nature of restitutionary claims, where the remedy is assessed by reference to the value of the benefit obtained by the defendant. This will be particularly important where the claimant argues that the defendant has been enriched by a service. Even where the alleged benefit takes the form of pure services, the defendant can only be considered to be benefited if he or she received the service. So, for example, if the defendant goes to a concert, he or she can only be considered to have been benefited by the musicians' services if he or she actually heard the music.

It follows from the receipt requirement that the defendant cannot be considered to have been enriched simply because the claimant commenced work in providing a service. But not every case is consistent with this principle. This is illustrated by the difficult case of *Planché v Colburn*,[41] where the claimant had entered into a contract with the defendant to write a book on the history of costume and ancient armour for £100, to be published by the defendant in a series called *The Juvenile Library*. After the claimant had commenced research for the book, by visiting museums and consulting reference books, and had started to write it, but before he had delivered any part of the manuscript, the defendant abandoned the series in breach of contract and refused to pay the claimant for the work which he had done. The claimant successfully sued the defendant and recovered a sum representing the reasonable value of his work, amounting to £50. The court apparently stressed that the remedy was a *quantum meruit* and that this was not awarded for breach of contract.[42] It appears, therefore, that the claimant was awarded a restitutionary remedy by virtue of which the defendant was required to pay for the reasonable value of the services provided by the claimant. But this cannot have been a case where the remedy was awarded to reverse the defendant's unjust enrichment, since the defendant had not received any benefit. At the time the doctrine of an anticipatory breach of contract, which enables a party to terminate the contract and recover compensatory damages, was not recognized. Since such a doctrine is now recognized,[43] as is the fact that acceptance of a repudiatory breach discharges a contract rather than renders it void *ab initio*,[44] it follows that, if the facts of *Planché v Colburn* arose today, the claimant would be able to sue for the anticipatory breach of contract and recover compensatory damages for expenditure incurred and the value of his services. Alternatively, the award of a restitutionary remedy might be justified if it was possible to estop the defendant from denying

---

[40] [1936] 2 KB 403. See p 81, below.

[41] (1831) 5 Car and P 58, 172 ER 876. For the history of the case see C Mitchell and P Mitchell, 'Planché v Colburn (1831)' in P Mitchell and C Mitchell (eds), *Landmark Cases in the Law of Restitution* (Oxford: Hart Publishing, 2006), ch 4. See also *Prickett v Badger* (1856) 1 CB (NS) 296, 140 ER 123.

[42] See Tindal CJ in *Planché v Colburn* (1831) 5 Car and P 58, 61; 172 ER 876, 877 (in argument). See also *Goodman v Pocock* (1850) 15 QB 576, 582–3, 117 ER 577, 580 (Patteson J).

[43] See, for example, *Hochster v De La Tour* (1852) 2 E and B 678, 118 ER 922.

[44] *Johnson v Agnew* [1980] AC 367.

that he or she had received a benefit,[45] although this would be difficult to establish on the facts, even if estoppel was recognized in this context. The preferable view, however, is that the defendant should only be considered to be enriched where the benefit was received. *Planché v Colburn* should not be treated as an obstacle to this principle, because today such a case would be decided by reference to the law of contract.

(ii) The Subjective Test of Enrichment

Once the claimant has established that the defendant had received an objective benefit, the burden shifts to the defendant to show that he or she did not want the benefit so that he or she cannot be considered to be enriched. This is the subjective test of enrichment which is called the principle of 'subjective devaluation', and which was formally recognized by a majority in *Benedetti v Sawiris*,[46] who held that the objective value of the benefit may be negated or reduced with reference to the defendant's own personal preferences and idiosyncratic views as to the value of the enrichment. Lord Clarke recognized that, whilst the burden of adducing evidence of the objective value is borne by the claimant, it shifts to the defendant to establish subjective devaluation.[47] It follows that subjective devaluation is properly analysed as a defence to a claim in unjust enrichment,[48] rather than a denial of an element of that claim, and it was recognized as such by Henderson J in *Littlewoods Retail Ltd v HMRC*.[49] But it is not sufficient for the defendant simply to assert that he or she did not value the benefit at its market value; there will need to be 'an objective manifestation of the defendant's subjective views'.[50] This manifestation could occur either before or after the enrichment had been received, although subsequent conduct is unlikely to carry much evidential weight.

Usually the defendant will accept that an objective enrichment is valuable to him or her so that there is no scope for subjective devaluation.[51] But there may be circumstances where, although the defendant acknowledges that he or she had received something of objective value, he or she wishes to argue that he or she did not want it and so should not be required to pay for it. That the defendant can deny the enrichment was recognized by Collins LJ in *Sumpter v Hedges*:[52] 'the circumstances must be such as to give an option to the defendant to take or not to take the benefit of the work done'. This is founded on the principle of autonomy,[53] which respects the defendant's freedom to choose whether or not he or she wants the benefit received from the claimant,[54] as was explicitly recognized by Lord Clarke in *Benedetti v Sawiris*.[55]

---

[45] See p 90, below. Birks, 'In Defence of Free Acceptance', 141, considered that a defendant should be deemed to be enriched if he or she requested the work, regardless of whether it was received.

[46] *Benedetti v Sawiris*, [21] (Lord Clarke). See also *Sempra Metals Ltd v IRC*, [48] (Lord Hope), 116 (Lord Nicholls), and 180 (Lord Walker).

[47] See also Lord Neuberger in *Benedetti v Sawiris* [2013] UKSC 50, [2014] AC 938, [181].

[48] See further p 663, below.

[49] [2014] EWHC 868 (Ch), [384]. For the distinction between defence and denial, see p 60, above. See also M Garner, 'The Role of Subjective Benefit in the Law of Unjust Enrichment' (1990) OJLS 42, 45; M Yip, 'The Use Value of Money in the Law of Unjust Enrichment' (2010) LS 586, 604.

[50] *Benedetti v Sawiris* [2013] UKSC 50, [2013] 3 WLR 351, [23].

[51] Alternatively the defendant might acknowledge that a valuable benefit had been received, but might wish to argue that he or she does not value it at the market value. See further p 97, below.

[52] [1898] 1 QB 673, 676.   [53] See p 37, above.

[54] This freedom will be qualified where the defendant requested or accepted the benefit or where the enrichment is considered to be incontrovertibly beneficial. See p 78, below.

[55] [2013] UKSC 50, [2014] AC 938, [18].

The recognition of the principle of subjective devaluation has proved to be controversial. Lodder[56] has argued that there is no role for such a principle when identifying and valuing an enrichment. He argues that the focus should simply be placed on whether the defendant has received an objective benefit, and then it is only necessary to consider whether the defendant had chosen the benefit or whether it can be regarded as incontrovertibly beneficial. Lord Reed went further in *Benedetti* in rejecting subjective devaluation completely, with the focus being placed on the determination of objective value only. Although he acknowledged that it was important to respect the defendant's right to choose to pay for a benefit which had not been requested, he considered that this was a normative question which related to whether the enrichment was unjust, rather than to its identification and valuation.[57] This is dangerous, however, because, despite Lord Reed's assertion that this would 'not entail a descent into unstructured reasoning about injustice',[58] such normative reasoning could easily become unprincipled and unclear.[59]

Whilst Lord Clarke in the majority recognized subjective devaluation and Lord Reed rejected it, Lord Neuberger, who gave the final judgment in the case, expressed no concluded view as to which approach he preferred. He did recognize, however, that in most cases both approaches will lead to the same outcome, at least where the defendant had requested or voluntarily accepted the benefit, with the only difference being one of procedural analysis as to which part of the unjust enrichment formula is engaged. For example, if a kitchen fitter mistakenly enters the defendant's house, rips out his kitchen and installs a new one, when she should have installed it in a neighbour's house, it is surely right that the defendant should not be required to pay for the kitchen, because he should be free to choose whether he wants a new kitchen. But what is the best method for achieving such a result? It might be concluded, with Lord Reed, that the defendant's enrichment was not unjust, but this changes the accepted understanding of most grounds of restitution being claimant-focused, without regard to the defendant's circumstances when establishing the claim.[60] Those circumstances are usually only taken into account at the defence stage, particularly through the defence of change of position, but the defendant cannot be considered to have changed his position in this situation. Surely it is preferable to conclude that the defendant has simply not been enriched. Whilst he had clearly received something of objective value, he should be allowed to say that he did not value it at all, because he wanted to spend his resources on something else. If the defendant was contemplating purchasing a new kitchen, but would only have done so at a significant discount in the sales, it is appropriate to take this into account in reducing the objective value. This respects the defendant's autonomy, but does so at the enrichment stage of the unjust enrichment inquiry.

The preferable view, therefore, is that there is a proper role for subjective devaluation when determining whether the defendant has been enriched. It is essential that the

---

[56] Lodder, *Enrichment in the Law of Unjust Enrichment and Restitution*, 49.

[57] *Benedetti v Sawiris* [2013] UKSC 50, [2014] AC 938, [117]. Relating freedom of choice to the unjust part of unjust enrichment has also been adopted in Canada: *Kerr v Baranow* [2011] 1 SCR 269 at [37], [41], and [45].

[58] *Benedetti v Sawiris* [2013] UKSC 50, [2014] AC 938, [118].

[59] Lord Reed also considered, ibid, [134], that the question of the defendant's freedom of choice to accept the benefit might be dealt with through the operation of the defence of change of position, but this is likely to be relevant only in exceptional cases where the receipt of the benefit has prevented the defendant from acquiring an equivalent benefit which would have been cheaper, as in *Ministry of Defence v Ashman* (1993) 66 P and CR 195. See p 457, below. This application of the change of position defence is unlikely to be relevant where the defendant does not value the benefit at all.

[60] See p 121, below.

defendant is given the opportunity to state whether or not he or she wanted the enrichment. If he or she did not want it, it is legitimate for the defendant to assert that he or she did not value it at all. This is consistent with the analysis of enrichment through the use of money in *Sempra Metals*.[61] It was recognized by the majority in that case that, if a defendant had received money but had made no use of it, the defendant cannot be considered to have been enriched at all. So, for example, if the defendant received money and put it into a non-interest bearing bank account or simply placed it in a box under her bed, the defendant will not have used the money and so should not be considered to have been enriched, even though she had the opportunity to enrich herself through the use of the money but chose not to do so. Rather than calling this subjective *de*valuation, which suggests that the defendant's valuation is reduced rather than eliminated, this might more accurately be called subjective *no*-valuation, to reflect the essential feature that the defendant does not value the enrichment at all.

The defendant may subjectively devalue an objective benefit for a variety of reasons, including a simple wish to be perverse. For example, if the claimant had washed the defendant's dirty windows without being requested to do so, the reasonable person would consider this to be an objective benefit, but the defendant, for some reason, might have preferred the windows to remain dirty.[62] Consequently, the objective enrichment will be defeated by subjective devaluation.[63] Another motive for subjective devaluation is that the defendant might have a different priority for expenditure. For example, if the claimant installed a fitted kitchen in the defendant's house which should have been fitted in the house next door, the defendant would presumably acknowledge that the fitted kitchen was an objective benefit, but might not wish to pay for it because he was saving to buy a new car, something which he considered to be a much more urgent expenditure.

One of the best examples of subjective devaluation in operation arises from the facts of *Boulton v Jones*.[64] In this case the defendant ordered and received a quantity of pipe. This pipe was supplied by the claimant, although the defendant had not made a contract with the claimant but with his predecessor in title. Consequently, when the claimant sued the defendant under the contract for the price of the pipe, his action was defeated because there was no contract between the claimant and the defendant. No restitutionary liability would have arisen on these facts either. Although the defendant was objectively enriched by the receipt of the pipe, he did not actually value it. This was because the predecessor in title of the claimant owed money to the defendant. The defendant had ordered the pipe from the claimant's predecessor in title in the expectation that he would be able to set off what was due to him against the price of the pipe. Since the money was still due from the predecessor in title, the defendant could legitimately say that he had not actually been enriched by the receipt of the pipe from the claimant.[65]

The operation of subjective devaluation following the decision of the Supreme Court in *Benedetti* has proved to be difficult. This is particularly illustrated by *Harrison v Madejski and Coys of Kensington*.[66] In this case, Harrison, through his son, bid at auction for a Jaguar car, which belonged to Sir John Madejski, chairman of Reading Football Club.

---

[61] [2007] UKHL 34, [2008] 1 AC 561. See p 73, above. See *Littlewoods Retail Ltd v HMRC* [2015] EWCA Civ 515, [187].

[62] Garner, 'The Role of Subjective Benefit in the Law of Unjust Enrichment', 44.

[63] Subject to the limitations on the operation of subjective devaluation. See p 78, below.

[64] (1857) 2 H and N 564, 157 ER 232.

[65] Although the defendant might have freely accepted the benefit. See p 85, below.

[66] [2014] EWCA Civ 361, the facts of which are very similar to *McDonald v Coys of Kensington* [2004] EWCA Civ 43, [2004] 1 WLR 2775, see p 81, below.

Madejski's car had a personal registration number, known as a Cherished Mark, which was 'JM2'. When Madejski decided to auction his car he wanted to retain the right to the Mark and so he requested that it should not be sold along with the car. Despite this, the Mark was sold with the car to Harrison, who had submitted the highest bid and who then registered the Mark in his own name. Madejski sued Harrison in unjust enrichment, on the basis that the Mark was mistakenly transferred to him. One of the key issues concerned the identification and valuation of the enrichment. It was clear that the right to the Mark was an objectively valuable enrichment, since there is a market for such Marks and this one was valued at £50,000. However, Harrison had told his son that the maximum bid for the car should be £100,000 if the Mark was not included, and £130,000 if the Mark was included. Believing that the Mark came with the car, the son successfully bid £130,000. Consequently, Harrison argued that he subjectively devalued the objective market value of the Mark to £30,000, since that was what he was willing to pay for it. Even though this appears to be a clear case of subjective devaluation, the Court of Appeal held that the fact that Harrison was only willing to pay £30,000 did not mean that that should be the value of the enrichment, because there was nothing to suggest that there were any personal considerations of Harrison which indicated that the Mark was worth anything less to him. But this is to confuse the different components of the enrichment test in *Benedetti*. The objective value of the Mark was £50,000. There were no personal circumstances of Harrison which would be taken into account by the market to reduce that objective value. But it was still open to Harrison to seek to devalue that enrichment subjectively. Although the Court of Appeal went on to conclude that any resort to subjective devaluation should be defeated for other reasons, notably that the Mark was readily returnable and so the failure to return it meant that Harrison must value it,[67] this only serves to establish that Harrison could not argue that he had not received anything of value. But Harrison never argued that. He acknowledged that he did value it, he just did not value it at the full market value. That argument should have succeeded on the facts of the case.

If we are prepared to adopt a subjective test to ascertain whether the defendant has been enriched, should this test be confined to the defendant's own perception of the value of what he or she has received, or should the claimant's perception of the value of what he or she has provided also be taken into account? For example, imagine a case where the defendant has taken the claimant's ring without consent. This ring is actually cheap cosmetic jewellery, but it was given to the claimant by his mother who has recently died and so it is of great sentimental value. The defendant has lost the ring and so the claimant seeks to recover its value. Should the claimant's perception of the value of the ring be taken into account in assessing whether, and the extent to which, the defendant has been enriched? The answer must be 'no', for the simple reason that it is not the function of the law of restitution to assess relief by reference to the claimant's loss.[68] The law of restitution assesses restitutionary remedies only by reference to the defendant's gain. Therefore, in assessing that particular gain, the claimant's own valuation is irrelevant. It is the function of compensatory remedies to take into account the claimant's particular circumstances and compensation is not a function of the law of restitution.[69]

---

[67] See further p 81, below.

[68] Save to the extent that the defendant's gain must have been obtained at the expense of the claimant, but, for that purpose, the claimant's loss is determined objectively. See Chapter 5.

[69] Approved by Lord Clarke in *Benedetti v Sawiris* [2013] UKSC 50, [2014] AC 938, [16].

2. PARTICULAR TYPES OF ENRICHMENT

Enrichments may take many different forms, but generally they fall into one of four categories, which reflect the historic division between the four common counts, namely the actions for money had and received, *quantum valebat* (the reasonable value of property), *quantum meruit* (the reasonable value of services), and money paid to a third party on behalf of the defendant.

(A) MONEY

(i) Exchange Value

Most restitutionary claims involve the claimant seeking to recover money from the defendant to whom the claimant has paid it. In these circumstances the enrichment question is not of critical importance, because money is always regarded as an enrichment. This was recognized by Robert Goff J in *BP Exploration Co (Libya) Ltd v Hunt (No 2)*,[70] where he stressed that, because money is the universal medium of exchange, it always constitutes an enrichment.[71] Consequently, it is never possible for defendants to rely on the subjective devaluation principle and argue that they do not value the money which has been received. In the vast majority of cases 'money' refers to coins and notes which are legal tender. But 'money' may also include a sum credited to the account of the defendant. This is deemed to be equivalent to a payment[72] and will similarly always be regarded as an enrichment.

In assessing whether the defendant has been enriched by the receipt of money it is necessary to have regard to the net transfer of value. So, where there have been payments between the claimant and the defendant, the net amount will constitute the enrichment. Further, any consequent liabilities which might negate the enrichment also need to be taken into account. So, for example, in *Jeremy D Stone Consultants Ltd v National Westminster Bank*[73] it was recognized that a bank was not enriched by a payment made to it by the claimant for the account of a customer, even though the bank became beneficially entitled to the money, because the increase in the bank's assets was matched by an immediate balancing liability in the form of the debt which it owed to its customer. In such circumstances the claimant should sue the customer rather than the bank.

In *Challinor v Bellis*[74] it was recognized that, where money is transferred by the claimant to the defendant who holds the money on trust for a third party, the defendant trustee should not be considered to be enriched because the money belonged beneficially to the third party. But this confuses the factual and legal interpretations of enrichment. If the trustee retains the money he or she should be liable to make restitution to the claimant if a ground of restitution can be identified. If the trustee has transferred the money to the beneficiary any claim for restitution against the trustee should be defeated by the defence of change of position.[75]

(ii) Use Value

It was recognized by the House of Lords in *Sempra Metals Ltd v IRC*[76] that a defendant who has received money may also be enriched by the opportunity to use this money, what

---

[70] [1979] 1 WLR 783, 789.   [71] In other words, it is an incontrovertible benefit. See p 78, below.
[72] *Ward and Co v Wallis* [1900] 1 QB 675, 679 (Kennedy J).   [73] [2013] EWHC 208 (Ch).
[74] [2015] EWCA Civ 59, [113] (Briggs LJ).   [75] See Chapter 25.
[76] [2007] UKHL 34, [2008] 1 AC 561. See p 30, above.

has also been described as 'the time value of money'.[77] This is a negative enrichment in the sense that it relates to what the defendant has saved by not having to borrow an equivalent amount of money from elsewhere. In *Sempra Metals*, where the claimant had mistakenly paid tax to the Revenue prematurely, the majority presumed that the Government had been enriched by the receipt of the money because it had the opportunity to use this money from the time of payment until the time when the tax liability would have been discharged had the taxpayer been able to delay payment. It was not necessary for the claimant to prove that the Government would necessarily have borrowed an equivalent amount from elsewhere had it not received the money from the taxpayer. The minority considered that a restitutionary remedy should only be available where the defendant has obtained an 'actual benefit' and not where the benefit was 'assumed'.[78] So, if the defendant could be shown to have decided not to borrow money because of the receipt of the tax from the claimant, the actual interest saved would be a benefit,[79] but the fact that the Revenue might have saved interest by not having to borrow money from elsewhere was not considered to be an enrichment, because it was not proved to be an actual benefit. The key difference between the majority and the minority does not concern the definition of an enrichment, but how it is established. Ultimately, this difference of approach turns on the role of assumptions and allocation of the burden of proof. The judges in the majority were willing to infer that receipt of the money must have benefited the defendant. Whether or not it did so could, however, be taken into account when valuing the benefit. The approach of the majority is to be preferred, since it is appropriate to assume that the defendant has relied on the receipt of the money in some way and he or she is in the best position to show that no use had been made of the money. In other words, it is open to the defendant to establish that he or she 'subjectively devalued' the use of the money.[80] Although Lord Nicholls used the language of subjective devaluation to explain this result, he did also suggest that this might involve the operation of the change of position defence,[81] although it is difficult to see how failure to rely on the money received can be considered to involve any change in the defendant's position, since the defendant's position remains the same. Further, the operation of defences only arises once the unjust enrichment claim has crystallized. The key issue in *Sempra Metals* concerned the identification and valuation of an enrichment rather than the operation of a defence.[82]

An additional issue in *Sempra Metals* was how the Government's presumed use of the premature payment of tax should be valued. Following the analysis of the decision in *Benedetti v Sawiris*,[83] the ordinary market value of the use of the money was considered to be what a reasonable person would have had to pay to borrow an equivalent amount of money, namely compound interest at ordinary commercial rates. This objective value was, however, reduced, because the Government could borrow at a lower rate of interest.

This analysis of the use value of money as an enrichment was applied in *Littlewoods Retail Ltd v HMRC*,[84] another case which involved the premature payment of tax, but also

---

[77] *Sempra Metals Ltd v IRC* [2007] UKHL 34, [2008] 1 AC 561, [10] (Lord Hope). Birks correctly described this as a non-money benefit: PBH Birks, *Unjust Enrichment* (2nd edn, Oxford: Oxford University Press, 2005), 53. It follows that it is possible subjectively to devalue the benefit.

[78] *Sempra Metals Ltd v IRC* [2007] UKHL 34, [2008] 1 AC 561, [132] (Lord Scott), [231] (Lord Mance).

[79] Ibid, [143] (Lord Scott).   [80] See further p 71, above.

[81] See also *Test Claimants in the FII Group Litigation v HMRC* [2014] EWHC 4302 (Ch), [414] (Henderson J).

[82] *Sempra Metals Ltd v IRC* [2007] UKHL 34, [2008] 1 AC 561, [48] and [49] (Lord Hope), [233] (Lord Mance).

[83] [2013] UKSC 50, [2014] AC 938. See p 66, above.

[84] [2015] EWCA Civ 515.

the payment of tax which was not due. The Court of Appeal recognized that the Government had been enriched by its opportunity to use the money paid. The trial judge had recognized that the market value of the use of money is normally measured by compound interest and that the defendant should be treated as if he or she had received a loan of money on ordinary commercial terms for a borrower in his or her objective position.[85] This normal measure will, however, be displaced if the defendant can establish that the receipt did not have its ordinary commercial use value for him or her, or that it had no value at all. This could be established, for example, if the defendant can show that he or she would never have borrowed the money from elsewhere, or if the defendant had placed the money received in a non-interest bearing bank account. The Court of Appeal emphasized that this second stage involves a subjective test of devaluation, with regard to a defendant-focused rate of interest rather than the market valuation. On the facts of the case, as in *Sempra Metals* itself, the Court could see no scope for an argument that the Government had subjectively devalued its use value of the money received.

The court's recognition in *Sempra Metals* that there is a claim in unjust enrichment for the defendant's use of money means that most claimants will have two claims relating to the transfer of money to the defendant. So, for example, where the claimant has paid money to the defendant by mistake, the defendant will be enriched both by the value of the money transferred and by the defendant's presumed use of that money, save where the defendant can rebut that presumption.

(B) PROPERTY

Generally, where the defendant receives property, such as land or chattels, he or she would acknowledge that the property is a valuable benefit and so constitutes an enrichment. But it is possible subjectively to devalue property. This will especially be the case where the defendant argues that he or she would not have chosen to spend money on that property, preferring instead to spend the money on something which was of more use to him or her. For example, if the defendant already has a car and is given another car by the claimant by mistake, the defendant could rely on subjective devaluation and assert that she did not value the car. Such subjective devaluation would, however, be subject to those principles which operate to limit its application.[86] Whereas money has both an intrinsic value and a use value, property can only be valued either by reference to its exchange value or its use value and not both,[87] because, for example, the exchange value of the property will reflect its use value as well.

(C) SERVICES

The issue of when the receipt of services constitutes an enrichment for the purposes of the law of unjust enrichment is highly controversial. The reason for this was identified by Robert Goff J in *BP Exploration Co (Libya) Ltd v Hunt (No 2)*[88] when he stressed that services, unlike money, cannot be restored and 'the identity and value of the resulting benefit to the recipient may be debatable'.[89] A particular problem relating to the determination of whether the receipt of services constitutes an enrichment arises where the

---

[85] [2014] EWHC 868 (Ch), [2014] STC 1761, [369] (Henderson J).   [86] See p 78, below.

[87] Lodder, *Enrichment in the Law of Unjust Enrichment and Restitution*, 98.

[88] [1979] 1 WLR 783, 799.

[89] Robert Goff J recognized that a similar problem arises with the provision of goods where the goods are consumed or transferred to somebody else.

services were provided without being requested by the defendant. In such circumstances the defendant might be able subjectively to devalue the service if he or she had no choice but to accept it.[90]

Whether a particular service constitutes an enrichment will depend upon the type of service which is being provided. Essentially, the provision of services falls into two categories depending on whether or not the effect of the service is to produce a valuable end product.

(i) Services Resulting in an End Product

Where the service results in the receipt of a valuable end product by the defendant, should the enrichment be identified as the service or the end product? For example, if the claimant provides a service which results in an increase in the value of the defendant's property, this increase in value could be considered to be the relevant enrichment, since this is the benefit which was actually received by the defendant. Alternatively, the true enrichment might be considered to be the service itself,[91] because it is the service rather than the end product which was received from the claimant. This difficulty can be resolved by asking what enrichment was received by the defendant as a result of the transfer from the claimant. In other words, what benefit was caused by the claimant's intervention? If the effect of the service provided by the claimant is to improve the defendant's property and so increase its value, the total value of the property cannot be considered to be the benefit, because the original value of the property is not causatively linked to the unjust enrichment.[92]

This was recognized by the House of Lords in *Cobbe v Yeoman's Row Management Ltd*.[93] The claimant had entered into an oral agreement in principle with the defendant to purchase some flats for redevelopment. No written contract was made. The claimant, believing that the property would be sold to him, spent time and money preparing to make an application for planning permission to develop the land. This application was successful. The defendant withdrew from the agreement and, since the agreement was not in writing, it was not possible to sue for breach of contract.[94] The claimant sought instead a restitutionary remedy from the defendant for the value of his services, since the value of the defendant's land had substantially increased following the grant of planning permission. This increase in value was considered by the trial judge to be the measure of the enrichment, but this was rejected by the House of Lords which concluded that the relevant enrichment was the service and not the end product. Lord Scott drew an analogy with a locked cabinet which is believed to contain valuables, but the key is missing. If the claimant locksmith makes a key which enables the defendant to unlock the cabinet and obtain the valuables inside, the defendant can only be considered to be enriched by the cost of the key and not by the value of the valuables, because everything which is inside the cabinet is already owned by the defendant. So, in *Yeoman's Row* Lord Scott concluded that the planning permission did not 'create the developmental potential of the property; it unlocked it'.[95] In other words, the increase in value was inherent in the property and could

---

[90] *Taylor v Laird* (1856) 25 LJ Ex 329, 332 (Pollock CB).
[91] See *BP Exploration Co (Libya) Ltd v Hunt (No 2)* [1979] 1 WLR 783, 801 (Robert Goff J).
[92] See R Stevens, 'Three Enrichment Issues' in AS Burrows and Lord Rodger of Earlsferry (eds), *Mapping the Law* (Oxford: Oxford University Press, 2006), 54.
[93] [2008] UKHL 55, [2008] 1 WLR 1752.
[94] Law of Property (Miscellaneous Provisions) Act 1989, s 2.
[95] *Cobbe v Yeoman's Row Management Ltd* [2008] UKHL 55, [2008] 1 WLR 1752, [41].

not be attributed to the claimant's services. Rather, the true benefit was simply what the defendant had saved in not having to apply for planning permission.

This is a significant decision on the law of enrichment since it shows that the defendant can only be considered to be enriched to the extent that the claimant has caused the defendant to be benefited. It follows that, where for example, a claimant has explored for and discovered oil on the defendant's land, the oil itself cannot be considered to be the enrichment, since the defendant already owned it and did not obtain it at the claimant's expense. Rather, the enrichment was the ability of the defendant to exploit the oil after it had been found, which would be assessed by reference to the value of the claimant's services in finding the oil. Where, however, the claimant has improved the defendant's property, the relevant enrichment should be the increase in the value of the property, since this was the benefit which can be attributed to the claimant, such that it was obtained at the claimant's expense. So, if the claimant restored and improved the defendant's car, which was worth £1,000 before the work was done and afterwards was worth £3,000, the defendant should be considered to have been enriched by £2,000, but only if this increase in value can be attributed to the claimant's work rather than to the intrinsic potential value of the car.

(ii) Pure Services

An alternative category of services is those which leave no end product, known as 'pure services', such as the provision of lessons and entertainments. Beatson has argued that, because of the absence of an end product, such services cannot constitute an enrichment, except where the defendant has been saved a necessary expense.[96] But this is to adopt a highly artificial definition of enrichment, grounded upon economic principles, which is contrary to common sense.[97] The provision of pure services can be objectively beneficial since reasonable people are prepared to pay for them, and so they should be regarded as an objective enrichment,[98] although this will be subject to subjective devaluation. Pure services which leave no end product have been recognized as a relevant enrichment, such as the removal of sewage[99] and the policing of a football match.[100]

(D) RELEASE OF OBLIGATIONS

Where the claimant has secured the release of an obligation owed by the defendant to a third party it is legitimate to consider the defendant to be enriched. So, for example, if the defendant owes money to the third party and the claimant pays off this debt, then, to the extent that this payment discharges the debt,[101] this will constitute an objective benefit to the defendant, since reasonable people would regard this as valuable.[102] So, for example, if the claimant pays £100 which is credited to the defendant's bank account, which is overdrawn by £200, the effect of the payment will be to reduce the defendant's overdraft owed to the bank and, to that extent, the defendant will be enriched. Such a benefit is a non-money benefit, because it is the effect on the defendant and not the third party which

---

[96] Beatson, *The Use and Abuse of Unjust Enrichment*, 23. [97] See p 63, above.

[98] See *BP Exploration Co (Libya) Ltd v Hunt (No 2)* [1979] 1 WLR 783, 801–2 (Robert Goff J).

[99] *Rowe v Vale of White Horse DC* [2003] EWHC 388 (Admin), [2003] 1 Lloyd's Rep 418.

[100] *Constable of the Greater Manchester Police v Wigan Athletic AFC Ltd* [2008] EWCA Civ 1449, [2009] 1 WLR 1580.

[101] The question of when a debt is discharged is discussed in Chapter 11.

[102] See, for example, *Exall v Partridge* (1799) 8 TR 303, 101 ER 1405.

characterizes its nature. This benefit could be regarded as a service,[103] but, since it concerns the payment of money albeit to a third party, it is useful to examine it separately from the provision of services, and it was traditionally kept separate from the provision of services in the common counts. The count for the provision of services was a *quantum meruit*, whereas that for payments made to third parties fell specifically within the action for money paid. Since this enrichment is characterized as a non-money benefit it may be subjectively devalued by the defendant if, for example, the defendant could have relied on a set off or a counterclaim to negate his or her liability to the third party.

(E) FORGOING A CLAIM

An enrichment has also been held to include where the claimant has forgone a valid claim against the defendant, such as a claim for compensation for unfair dismissal.[104]

3. METHODS OF DEFEATING SUBJECTIVE DEVALUATION

If the defendant pleads the defence of subjective devaluation, it is open to the claimant to defeat this defence, either by proving that the defendant had received an incontrovertible benefit or by establishing that the defendant had requested or freely accepted the benefit.[105]

(A) INCONTROVERTIBLE BENEFIT

The principle of incontrovertible benefit has been explicitly recognized in English law as a means to defeat the subjective devaluation principle.[106] The essence of incontrovertible benefit was identified by McLachlin J in *Regional Municipality of Peel v Her Majesty the Queen in Right of Canada*,[107] a decision of the Supreme Court of Canada, where she described it as:

> an unquestionable benefit, a benefit which is demonstrably apparent and not subject to debate and conjecture. Where the benefit is not clear and manifest it would be wrong to make the defendant pay, since he or she might well have preferred to decline the benefit if given the choice.

Consequently, incontrovertible benefit defeats the defendant's reliance on subjective devaluation because it identifies those circumstances where it can be irrebutably presumed that the defendant would not have declined the benefit even if he or she had been given the choice to do so. In other words, the defendant will be incontrovertibly benefited where the only possible conclusion is that the defendant had received a valuable benefit. Treating the defendant as enriched in these circumstances will not infringe the defendant's autonomy by making the defendant pay for a benefit he or she did not want since, by definition, the

---

[103] This was how the benefit was characterized in *Procter and Gamble Philippine Manufacturing Corp v Peter Cremer GmbH and Co (The Manila)* [1988] 3 All ER 843.

[104] *Gibb v Maidstone and Tunbridge Wells NHS Trust* [2010] EWCA Civ 678, [30] (Laws LJ).

[105] *Benedetti v Sawiris* [2013] UKSC 50, [2014] AC 938, [25] (Lord Clarke).

[106] See especially *Rowe v Vale of White Horse DC* [2003] EWHC 388 (Admin), [2003] 1 Lloyd's Rep 418; *McDonald v Coys of Kensington* [2004] EWCA Civ 43, [2004] 1 WLR 2775, 2789 (Mance LJ).

[107] (1993) 98 DLR (4th) 140, 159.

defendant must acknowledge that an incontrovertible benefit is a valuable enrichment to him or her. Obviously proof of incontrovertible benefit is not sufficient in its own right to establish unjust enrichment, since the other elements of the claim must also be identified;[108] the incontrovertible benefit principle is simply relevant to the identification of an enrichment.

Whether the defendant can be considered to have been incontrovertibly benefited will require careful analysis of the facts. For example, in *J S Bloor Ltd v Pavillion Developments Ltd*[109] it was held that the building of a road by the claimant, in circumstances where the defendant was contractually required to build it, was not incontrovertibly beneficial because, even though the defendant was benefited, it also suffered a detriment arising from the fact that it had not been able to design the road to its own specifications and had not negotiated the cost. In *Benedetti v Sawiris*[110] Arden LJ had recognized that a defendant could not be incontrovertibly benefited by the receipt of services if the defendant never expected to pay for them. But this confuses the distinct questions of whether the defendant had been enriched and whether this enrichment is unjust. If the defendant did not expect to pay for the service, this would not prevent that service from being incontrovertibly beneficial, but it might indicate that there was no ground of restitution, since the basis for the performance of the service might be that it was to be paid for by somebody other than the defendant.[111]

Although the determination of whether a benefit can be characterized as incontrovertible is ultimately a question of fact, five tests can be identified which will assist in the characterization of the benefit.

(i) Money

The simplest and most common example of an incontrovertible benefit is the receipt of money, because no reasonable person would ever regard this as anything other than beneficial.[112] It is with the non-money benefits that the greatest difficulties arise. What need to be identified are those non-money benefits which are so unequivocally enriching that their receipt can be treated as equivalent in effect to the receipt of money. It is consequently important to distinguish between the intrinsic value of money and the use value of money, since it is possible to devalue the use value of money where the defendant can show that he or she did not rely on it any way.[113]

(ii) Anticipation of Necessary Expenditure

Where the defendant receives a benefit which saves him or her from incurring expenditure which would otherwise necessarily have been incurred, the defendant should be treated as incontrovertibly benefited. Such a defendant cannot convincingly argue that he or she did not value what had been received, since he or she would have paid for the particular benefit anyway had the claimant not provided it. Because of the circumstances of necessity, the defendant has no choice as to whether or not to accept the benefit and therefore treating the defendant as enriched does not infringe the autonomy principle.

The circumstances of necessity may arise in two different ways.

---

[108] It appears that this was ignored in *Marston Construction Ltd v Kigass Ltd* (1989) 15 Con LR 116.

[109] [2008] EWHC 724 (TCC).

[110] [2010] EWCA Civ 1427. This was not considered by the Supreme Court on appeal.

[111] See further p 142, below.

[112] *BP Exploration Co (Libya) Ltd v Hunt* [1979] 1 WLR 783, 799 (Robert Goff J).

[113] See p 73, above.

(1) By Operation of Law

The expenditure which the defendant needed to incur may arise by operation of law. For example, in *Exall v Partridge*[114] the claimant's carriage, which was on the defendant's premises, was distrained by the defendant's landlord because the defendant's rent was in arrears. To recover his carriage, the claimant was compelled to pay the outstanding rent to the landlord. He then successfully recovered this money from the defendant. Clearly the defendant was enriched, since the money paid to the landlord discharged the debt which the defendant owed. The defendant could never argue that he did not value this benefit because, if the claimant had not paid the money, the defendant would have been legally obliged to pay the landlord and so the expenditure would necessarily have been incurred.[115] Similarly, in *County of Carleton v City of Ottawa*,[116] a decision of the Supreme Court of Canada, the claimant, thinking that a destitute woman was resident within its boundaries, paid for board, lodging, and medical assistance to be provided to her. In fact, the woman was resident within the defendant's boundaries, so the defendant was liable to make provision for her. It was held that the defendant was liable to repay the claimant. The defendant was incontrovertibly benefited since the claimant had discharged the defendant's legal liability. If the defendant is to be characterized as incontrovertibly benefited by the discharge of a liability, this must have been a legal rather than a moral liability.[117]

(2) Factually Necessary Expenditure

Alternatively, the expenditure may be factually necessary. This will arise where, although the defendant is not compelled by law to incur the expenditure, he or she would have incurred it had the claimant not provided the benefit. So, for example, if, whilst the defendant is on holiday, burglars break into his house and break a window, the claimant, who is a neighbour, may arrange for the window to be replaced to ensure that the property is protected. When the defendant returns from holiday he will be obliged to reimburse the claimant. The defendant cannot argue that he was not benefited by what the claimant did, because if the claimant had not replaced the window, the defendant would inevitably have done so.[118] This is illustrated by *Re Berkeley Applegate (Investment Consultants) Ltd*,[119] where services provided by a liquidator in administering trust property were held to have been of substantial benefit to the beneficiaries, because 'if the liquidator had not done this work, it is inevitable that the work, or at all events a great deal of it, would have had to be done by someone else, and on application to the court a receiver would have been appointed whose expenses and fees would necessarily have had to be borne by the trust assets'.

Other examples of factually necessary expenditure being anticipated by the claimant arise in the context of the supply of necessaries to the incapacitated, such as infants and the mentally disturbed.[120] By the very definition of 'necessaries', their supply constitutes

---

[114] (1799) 8 TR 308; 101 ER 1405. See p 239, below.

[115] On the question of the ground for restitution, see Chapter 11.   [116] (1965) 52 DLR (2d.) 220.

[117] *Regional Municipality of Peel v Her Majesty the Queen in Right of Canada* (1993) 98 DLR (4th) 140, 156 (McLachlin J).

[118] See Chapter 12 for consideration of the relevant ground of restitution in such circumstances.

[119] [1989] Ch 32, 50 (Edward Nugee QC). See also *Craven-Ellis v Canons Ltd* [1936] 2 KB 403, 412 (Greer LJ); *Re Duke of Norfolk's Settlement Trusts* [1982] Ch 61.

[120] See, for example, *Re Rhodes* (1890) 44 Ch D 94. See also *Clarke v The Guardians of the Cuckfield Union* (1852) 21 LJ (QB) 349, concerning the supply of toilets to a work-house, which were held to be necessary.

an incontrovertible benefit. In *Rowe v Vale of White Horse DC*[121] it was recognized that the supply of services by a council to remove sewage from properties was incontrovertibly beneficial, presumably because it was factually necessary.

One specific problem which arises in respect of factually necessary expenditure relates to the determination of what is meant by 'necessary' in this context. This is not a problem for legally necessary expenditure, since the law either requires the expenditure to be incurred or it does not. But in the context of factual necessity it might be possible for the defendant to carry on without incurring the expenditure. If so, the benefit received should not be regarded as incontrovertibly beneficial. But, when considering whether the expenditure was necessary, unrealistic or fanciful possibilities of the defendant doing without the enrichment should be ignored; the key test should be whether the expenditure would reasonably have been incurred.[122] For example, in *Craven-Ellis v Canons Ltd*,[123] it was recognized that the services of the managing director of a company were necessary to the company;[124] although it might have been argued that the company could have continued to function without the managing director's services, this would be unrealistic. As long as it can be shown that, in the ordinary course of events the defendant would have incurred the expenditure, the defendant should be considered to have been incontrovertibly benefited.

(iii) Failure to Return Property

In *McDonald v Coys of Kensington*[125] the Court of Appeal recognized another way of establishing incontrovertible benefit. Coys had sold a car to McDonald on behalf of the executors of Mr TA Cressman. This car carried the personalized registration mark 'TAC 1'. It was an express term of the contract of sale that the purchaser was not buying the right to the personalized mark, known as a Cherished Mark, but Coys mistakenly failed to retain the right to it. Consequently, when the car was delivered to McDonald, he was entitled to have the car registered in his name with that Mark, which he did. McDonald refused to transfer the Mark to the executors when requested to do so. Having settled with the estate, Coys sought restitution of the Mark or its value from McDonald. The objective enrichment in this case was the right to the Cherished Mark itself, which had a market value of £15,000. But the defendant sought to rely on subjective devaluation by stating that it was of no intrinsic value to him, as his initials were different and he had no intention of selling it. The Court created a new category of incontrovertible benefit to defeat this reliance on the subjective devaluation principle, namely where property has been received which is readily returnable without substantial difficulty or detriment. Since McDonald could easily have transferred the right to register the Mark when requested to do so, but had not done so, he must have considered the retention of the Mark to be valuable and so was enriched. This is a legitimate extension of the notion of an incontrovertible benefit. Where property has been received and the defendant could easily return it but decides not to do so, it is appropriate to conclude that the defendant's decision indicates that he or she did value the benefit.

The application of this principle of a readily returnable benefit is likely to be of limited use within unjust enrichment claims, since it only applies in respect of property. It will not

---

[121] [2003] EWHC 388 (Admin), [2003] 1 Lloyd's Rep 418.

[122] Birks, *Unjust Enrichment* (2nd edn), 60. See *Monks v Poynice Pty Ltd* (1987) 11 ACLR 637, 640 (Supreme Court of New South Wales).

[123] [1936] 2 KB 403.   [124] Ibid, 412 (Greer LJ).

[125] [2004] EWCA Civ 47, [2004] 1 WLR 2775. See also *Harrison v Madejski and Coys of Kensington* [2014] EWCA Civ 361, p 71, above.

apply to money, which is always beneficial, or to the use value of money where the defendant can show that he or she did not rely on the money received,[126] and it will not apply to services which, by their nature, cannot be returned.

(iv) Benefit Realized in Money

If the defendant has received a benefit which is then realized in money, the defendant should be considered to be incontrovertibly benefited. In such circumstances the defendant should not be allowed subjectively to devalue the benefit, because its value has been converted into money and the receipt of money is always an enrichment. So, for example, if the claimant restores and improves the defendant's damaged car, which is then sold by the defendant, the defendant will be regarded as enriched to the extent that the car has increased in value as a result of the claimant's services and the effect of that service has been realized in money.

Some support for the notion that the defendant can be incontrovertibly benefited by realizing a benefit in money can be identified in the decision of the Court of Appeal in *Greenwood v Bennett*.[127] This is a difficult case to analyse since, although the award of a restitutionary remedy appears to have been considered, the court assumed without comment that the recipient of the benefit was objectively enriched and there was no apparent reliance on subjective devaluation. Despite this, the facts of the case provide a useful scenario for analysis of the incontrovertible benefit principle. Bennett, who managed a car dealership, sent one of his cars to be repaired. The repairer drove the car and crashed it. He then sold it to Harper, who bought the car thinking that he had acquired good title to it. Harper repaired and improved the car and sold it on to a finance company, which let it on hire purchase. The police recovered the car and then brought proceedings to ascertain who had the better claim to it. Essentially the dispute boiled down to one between Bennett, who claimed the car, and Harper, who wished to be paid for his work in repairing and improving it. The trial judge held that Bennett had a better claim to the car and so ordered it to be restored to him, without making any order for Harper to be reimbursed for his services. Harper appealed to the Court of Appeal. Before that appeal was heard, Bennett sold the car. The Court of Appeal affirmed that Bennett had the better title to the car, but held that, as a condition of recovery, Harper should be reimbursed for the cost of the repairs and improvements.

The imposition of the condition that Harper should be reimbursed for his services can be interpreted either as compensating Harper for his loss or ensuring that Bennett made restitution of a gain. But if this restitutionary analysis is to succeed, it would need to be established that Bennett had been unjustly enriched. This raises three separate questions.

(1) Identification of an Enrichment

Bennett had clearly been objectively enriched by Harper's work in repairing and improving the car, and he could be prevented from subjectively devaluing this benefit by means of establishing an incontrovertible benefit. In considering the application of this principle, it is necessary to draw a subtle but important distinction between the different types of work which Harper had undertaken. In respect of the repairs needed to restore the car to its original condition before the crash, Bennett can be regarded as incontrovertibly benefited since Harper had presumably anticipated expenditure which Bennett would necessarily have incurred once he had regained possession of the vehicle. Bennett was a commercial dealer in cars and presumably would have repaired the car so that he could have sold it,

---

[126] See p 73, above.   [127] [1973] QB 195. See also *Munro v Willmott* [1949] 1 KB 295.

which he did once the car had been recovered. Harper also improved the car. This cannot be regarded as necessary expenditure, because there was nothing to suggest that Bennett would have improved the car once he had recovered it. But the improvement could still be considered to have incontrovertibly benefited Bennett because he had realized the value of the improvement by selling the car.[128] The difficulty with this analysis is that, when the case came before the trial judge, it was not open to him to say that the value of the improvement had been realized, since at that point the car had not been sold. Perhaps, therefore, it is sufficient that the value of the services would be realized in the ordinary course of events.[129] This is a fair conclusion on the facts since, as Bennett was in the motor trade, he would be expected to sell the car at some stage.

(2) Identification of a Ground of Restitution

Once it could be shown that Bennett had been enriched at Harper's expense, Harper would need to identify a ground of restitution before Bennett could be considered to have been unjustly enriched. This could easily be established since Harper had mistakenly believed that the car belonged to him, and, had he not made this mistake, he would not have undertaken the work on the car.[130]

(3) Passive or Active Claim?

Even though Harper could have established that Bennett was unjustly enriched, he was not bringing a claim to recover the value of the services which he had provided. Rather, Harper's restitutionary claim was passive, since it took the form of a condition that he should be reimbursed before Bennett could recover the car. This passive claim was recognized by all three members of the Court of Appeal. But the more controversial question is whether Harper could have brought an active restitutionary claim on these facts. For example, if Bennett had recovered possession of the car without recourse to the courts, could Harper have instigated an action against him to recover the value of his services? Although Cairns LJ expressly rejected such a claim,[131] Lord Denning MR was adamant that such a claim could be brought.[132] Surely Lord Denning was correct. Harper could have established that Bennett had been unjustly enriched and so should have been able to recover the reasonable value of the services which he had provided.

Since the decision of the Court of Appeal in *Greenwood v Bennett*, the law has been clarified to some extent by the enactment of the Torts (Interference with Goods) Act 1977. The gist of this statute is to create a new tort of wrongful interference with goods, which covers the torts of conversion, trespass, and negligence as they apply to goods. Section 6(1) of this statute makes specific provision for a passive restitutionary claim. By virtue of this provision, when the court is assessing the damages which are due for the tort of wrongful interference with goods, it must award the defendant an allowance in respect of his or her work in improving the goods, as long as the defendant did so in the honest belief that he or she had title to the goods. This allowance is assessed by reference to the increase in the value of the goods which is attributable to their improvement by the defendant. This statute would not, however, have resolved the dispute in *Greenwood v Bennett* since Bennett did not recover damages but recovered his car, and section 6(1) of the 1977 Act only applies where the claimant is awarded damages. Also the statute, illogically, only

---

[128] Also, presumably, the improvement increased the value of the car rather than unlocked its value. See p 77, above.

[129] See p 84, below.   [130] See Chapter 9.   [131] *Greenwood v Bennett* [1973] QB 195, 203.

[132] Ibid, 202. Phillimore LJ agreed with Denning LJ, but did not expressly consider whether an active restitutionary claim could be brought.

provides for a passive restitutionary claim. What is needed now is either statutory reform or express judicial recognition that a person who repairs and improves property belonging to somebody else, mistakenly thinking that the property belongs to him or her, can recover the value of the services from the owner where it can be shown that the owner has been incontrovertibly benefited by realizing the value of the service. There is some evidence for the existence of such an active claim in the decision of the Court of Appeal in *Rover International Ltd v Cannon Film Sales Ltd (No 3)*,[133] where the claimant successfully recovered the value of its services which had mistakenly been provided for the benefit of the defendant. Counsel for the defendant had conceded that the defendant had received a benefit and this concession was correctly made because, as Kerr LJ recognized, the services provided by the claimant had generated money for the defendant. In other words, the defendant had been incontrovertibly benefited since the value of the services provided by the claimant had been realized in money.[134]

(v) Benefit Realizable in Money

It remains unclear whether it is appropriate to consider a defendant to have been incontrovertibly benefited where the claimant has improved the defendant's property, and so increased its value, but the defendant has not realized that benefit in money. Burrows considers that a benefit which is potentially realizable in money should be treated as an incontrovertible benefit, but only if it was reasonably certain that the defendant would realize the benefit.[135] Judge Bowsher QC in *Marston Construction Co Ltd v Kigass Ltd*[136] accepted that a realizable benefit can be considered to be an incontrovertible benefit.[137] This approach appears to have been supported by the Court of Appeal in *McDonald v Coys of Kensington*,[138] although Burrows' qualification of the realization being reasonably certain was rejected as being too restrictive.[139]

But the conclusion that the defendant has been incontrovertibly benefited simply because he or she has received something which could be sold is generally unacceptable,[140] because it unnecessarily subverts the autonomy principle. Analysis of all the other categories of incontrovertible benefit shows that, with the exception of the test of whether the benefit is realizable in money, the principle does not subvert the autonomy of the individual which underlies the principle of subjective devaluation. This is because, where it is proved that the defendant has received an incontrovertible benefit within one of these other categories, it is clear that either the defendant has no free choice to exercise as to whether to accept the benefit, as in the category of anticipation of necessary expenditure, or had exercised that choice, where the benefit has been realized in money or where the defendant has received property which he or she could return. The difficulty with the test of whether the benefit is realizable in money arises precisely because in that situation the defendant does have a free choice whether or not to accept the benefit, and there is no acceptable basis on which we can exercise that choice on the defendant's behalf. Therefore, the better view is that this test of incontrovertible benefit should be rejected save, perhaps, where it is inevitable that the defendant will realize the benefit, for in such a situation there

---

[133] [1989] 1 WLR 912.   [134] Ibid, 922.

[135] AS Burrows, *The Law of Restitution* (3rd edn, Oxford: Oxford University Press, 2011), 49. See also DA Verse, 'Improvements and Enrichments: A Comparative Analysis' [1998] RLR 85, 96.   [136] (1989) 15 Con LR 116, 129.

[137] It might also be used to explain the initial success of the passive restitutionary claim in *Greenwood v Bennett* [1973] QB 195. See p 83, above.

[138] [2004] EWCA Civ 47, [2004] 1 WLR 2775, 2789.   [139] Ibid, 2790.

[140] See Birks, *Unjust Enrichment* (2nd edn), 61.

will be no free choice to exercise. Such inevitability will, however, be virtually impossible to prove.

(B) REQUEST

Since the subjective devaluation defence operates to respect the defendant's autonomy, such that the defendant is free to decide that he or she does not value the benefit which the claimant has transferred, it must follow that the defendant cannot rely on the defence where he or she requested the benefit in the first place.[141] Proof of the request must mean that the defendant wanted the benefit and so valued it. The existence of a request by the defendant must, however, be treated with caution, since it may provide the basis for implying a contract to pay for the benefit.[142] Where such a contract can be implied, the defendant will be liable on the contract rather than in the law of unjust enrichment.[143]

Whether the defendant had requested the benefit will require careful analysis of the facts. In *Re Cleadon Trust Ltd*[144] the secretary of the defendant company had requested the claimant, a director of the company, to pay a sum of money to meet the financial obligations of two of the defendant's subsidiaries. The claimant paid the money which was due, on the footing that his payment was a loan to the defendant.[145] A meeting of the defendant's board of directors purported to confirm that the money had been paid at the defendant's request. The defendant was wound up, and the claimant sought to recover the loan. His claim was unsuccessful because the directors' meeting, which purported to confirm that the money had been paid at the company's request, was inquorate. This meant that there was no organ of the company which was capable of requesting the benefit. It was, however, accepted that if the directors' meeting had been quorate then the claim would have succeeded by reason of the defendant's acceptance of the benefit.[146]

(C) FREE ACCEPTANCE

Where the defendant had an opportunity to reject proferred services and failed to do so, knowing that the claimant expected to be paid for those services, the defendant can be considered to have freely accepted the benefit.[147] Such a principle defeats the defendant's reliance on the subjective devaluation principle since the defendant will have been exercising a voluntary choice in deciding not to reject the benefit. Consequently, the fact that the defendant freely accepted the benefit is consistent with the principle of the autonomy of the individual to decide that he or she wants the benefit which has been received. The defendant can be considered to have freely accepted a benefit even though he or she had not requested it, since it is sufficient that the defendant knowingly acquiesced in the provision of the benefit.[148]

At the outset it is important to recognize that the doctrine of free acceptance is sometimes regarded as having a dual function in the law of restitution. This was at one

---

[141] *Benedetti v Sawiris* [2013] UKSC 50, [2014] AC 938, [25] (Lord Clarke). See also *Lawford v The Billericay RDC* [1903] 1 KB 772.

[142] See p 135, below.   [143] See p 134, below.   [144] [1939] Ch 286.

[145] This was not money paid to the defendant, which would have been an incontrovertible benefit, but money paid on behalf of and for the benefit of the defendant, so it was possible for the defendant to subjectively devalue it.

[146] *Re Cleadon Trust Ltd* [1939] Ch 286, 298 (Sir Wilfrid Greene MR).

[147] This term was first coined by R Goff and G Jones, *The Law of Restitution* (1st edn, London: Sweet & Maxwell, 1966), 30. See also Birks, *Unjust Enrichment* (2nd edn), 56.

[148] See *Leigh v Dickeson* (1884) 15 QBD 60; *Falcke v Scottish Imperial Insurance* (1886) 34 Ch D 234.

stage the view of Birks,[149] and Goff and Jones also agree.[150] This dual function involves free acceptance operating both to establish an enrichment and as a ground of restitution in its own right. This dual function is highly controversial, but unfortunately it has been recognized judicially.[151] The preferable view, however, is that there is no role for free acceptance as a ground of restitution in its own right, since the ground of failure of basis adequately does the work which it is thought can be done by free acceptance and without incorporating any element of fault.[152] But this does not affect the validity of free acceptance as an important principle to assist in the identification of whether or not the defendant has been enriched.

Although the principle of free acceptance has been recognized explicitly by the courts,[153] the features of the principle were influential in a number of earlier decisions, even though that principle was not recognized by name. For example, some judges referred to the fact that the defendant stood by whilst the claimant was providing the benefit.[154] In *Leigh v Dickeson*[155] the claimant sought to recover rent from the defendant who was initially the claimant's tenant but then became a co-owner with the claimant of a house. The defendant counterclaimed for money spent to the use of the claimant in respect of repairs to the house. The counterclaim failed, essentially because, although the claimant had received an objective benefit by virtue of the repairs, which were considered to be reasonable and proper, the defendant's expenditure had been incurred voluntarily and it could not be shown that the claimant valued it. In other words, the claimant resorted to subjective devaluation which the defendant was unable to defeat. In reaching this conclusion, Brett MR identified the essence of free acceptance. He emphasized[156] that if a person receives a benefit in circumstances where there is an option to adopt or decline it, and the recipient adopts the benefit, the expenditure incurred by the other party must be repaid. If the recipient declines the benefit, he or she will not be liable to make restitution to the other party. But if the recipient has no choice but to accept the benefit, the recipient will not be liable to the other party. Since on the facts the claimant had no choice but to accept the benefit, because she continued to live in the house, she was not liable to the defendant who had incurred the expenditure.[157] This is a perfect example of a case where it was not possible to defeat reliance on subjective devaluation, simply because

---

[149] See, for example, PBH Birks, *Restitution—The Future* (Sydney: The Federation Press, 1992), 98–9.

[150] C Mitchell, P Mitchell, and S Watterson (eds), *Goff and Jones: The Law of Unjust Enrichment* (8th edn, London: Sweet & Maxwell, 2011), Ch 17.

[151] *Rowe v Vale of White Horse DC* [2003] EWHC 388 (Admin), [2003] 1 Lloyd's Rep 418, 422 (Lightman J). See p 122, below.   [152] See Chapter 6.

[153] See especially *Bridgewater v Griffiths* [2000] 1 WLR 524; *Rowe v Vale of White Horse DC* [2003] EWHC 388 (Admin), [2003] 1 Lloyd's Rep 418; *McDonald v Coys of Kensington* [2004] EWCA Civ 47, [2004] 1 WLR 2775; *Constable of the Greater Manchester Police v Wigan Athletic AFC Ltd* [2008] EWCA Civ 1449, [2009] 1 WLR 1580. It has also been recognized in New Zealand: *Van den Berg v Giles* [1979] 2 NZLR 111, 120 (Jeffries J). The principle is also implicitly recognized by certain statutory provisions. For example, s 30(3) of the Sale of Goods Act 1979 states that, where a vendor delivers more goods to the purchaser than the vendor had contracted to sell and the purchaser accepts all of the goods delivered, the purchaser will be liable to pay for all of the goods.

[154] See, for example, *Weatherby v Banham* (1832) 5 Car and P 228, 172 ER 950; *Lamb v Bunce* (1815) 4 M and S 275, 105 ER 836; *Paynter v Williams* (1833) 1 C and M 810, 149 ER 626.

[155] (1884) 15 QBD 60.   [156] Ibid, 64.

[157] But since the repairs had been considered to be necessary and proper it could have been concluded that the claimant had been incontrovertibly benefited since she had been saved a factually necessary expenditure. See p 80, above.

there was no evidence that the recipient of the benefit had chosen it and so it could not be concluded that the recipient valued the benefit.

In *Falcke v Scottish Imperial Insurance Co*[158] the claimant, having paid premiums on a life assurance policy mistakenly believing that he had acquired an interest in it, sought to recover the expenditure from the defendant who did have an interest in the policy. Clearly the defendant had received an objective benefit, since the claimant's payments preserved the policy,[159] but there was insufficient evidence to defeat the defendant's reliance on arguments of subjective devaluation. In particular, the defendant was unaware of the claimant's payments, so she could not be regarded as having chosen to accept the benefit. But it was expressly recognized that, if the defendant had been aware of the payments and had then failed to intervene, she would have been liable to reimburse the claimant.[160]

The free acceptance principle was explicitly recognized by Lightman J in *Rowe v Vale of White Horse DC*,[161] although it could not be established on the facts. The defendant council had provided sewerage services for some of its tenants who occupied council houses. These tenants were not charged separately for these services, the cost of which was included in the rents paid by the tenants. Many tenants bought their council houses and, in some cases, no provision was made for the payment of sewerage charges and the defendant did not claim payment for these services. Eventually the council demanded payment for the provision of the services for the previous six years. Rowe challenged the legitimacy of this demand in judicial review proceedings and the council claimed restitution. The key question was whether the service could be considered to be an enrichment.[162] It was accepted that, if Rowe had freely accepted the services, the claim for restitution would have succeeded, but this could not be established on the facts because he did not reasonably expect to pay for them, since the council had perpetuated the belief that no payment was required, and because Rowe did not have an opportunity to reject them. In other words, he had not acquiesced in the supply of services. Even more significantly, in *McDonald v Coys of Kensington*[163] the Court of Appeal was willing to apply the free acceptance principle, although it did not do so in the end because it was possible to show that the receipt of the right to a personalized registration mark constituted an incontrovertible benefit.[164] Mance LJ recognized that the defendant could not be considered to have freely accepted the Mark when the car was delivered, but he did suggest that the defendant might have freely accepted it when he registered the Mark in his own name, since at that point he was aware of the seller's mistake and so acted unconscientiously or reprehensibly in registering it. But this argument can only be right if the benefit is considered to be the registration of the Mark in the defendant's name, rather than the right to register the Mark which was received on delivery. This is a novel conclusion since it suggests that events subsequent to receipt may convert a benefit which has been legitimately subjectively devalued into an enrichment. This might be considered to undermine the principle that the enrichment is identified and valued when the unjust enrichment claim is crystallized,[165] which was presumably when the car was delivered to

---

[158] (1886) 34 Ch D 234.

[159] Again, it could have been concluded that the defendant had been incontrovertibly benefited by the claimant's expenditure, which constituted a necessary expense to preserve the insurance policy.

[160] *Falcke v Scottish Imperial Insurance Co* (1886) 34 Ch D 234, 249 (Bowen LJ).

[161] [2003] EWHC 388 (Admin), [2003] 1 Lloyd's Rep 418.

[162] It was conceded that the service was an incontrovertible benefit, see p 81, above, but it was still necessary to consider free acceptance to identify a ground of restitution. See p 122, below.

[163] [2004] EWCA Civ 47, [2004] 1 WLR 2775.

[164] See p 81, above.   [165] See p 9, above.

the defendant. Subsequent events are only relevant through the operation of defences, such as change of position. Nevertheless, if it is possible to recognize a realized benefit as an incontrovertible benefit after an objective enrichment has been received,[166] there is no reason why free acceptance cannot operate in the same way. This does not undermine the rule about events occurring after crystallization of the cause of action, but is actually consistent with it. This is because the unjust enrichment claim should be considered to have crystallized only when the defendant has received an objective enrichment and a ground of restitution can be identified. It is then open to the defendant to plead the defence of subjective devaluation and, in order to defeat this defence, the claimant should be able to rely on facts arising after the enrichment has been received in order to defeat that defence.

(i) The Elements of Free Acceptance

Three conditions need to be satisfied before it can be concluded that the defendant has freely accepted the benefit.

(1) Since free acceptance depends on the defendant having chosen to accept the benefit, it is vital that the defendant had the opportunity to reject it before it was provided.[167] A defendant cannot be considered to have freely accepted the benefit if he or she lacked the capacity to accept it.[168]

Having the opportunity to reject the benefit proved to be decisive in *Chief Constable of the Greater Manchester Police v Wigan Athletic AFC Ltd.*[169] A police authority claimed restitution for its services in policing football matches, which were more extensive than required by statute. It was held that the defendant football club could not be considered to have freely accepted the additional services because they were not in a position to reject those services alone.

(2) The defendant will only be considered to have freely accepted the benefit if the defendant was aware that the claimant either expected to receive something in return for the benefit, typically payment for it,[170] or was aware that the claimant thought he or she was doing something of benefit to him or herself rather than the defendant, such as where the claimant improves the defendant's property in the mistaken belief that he or she owns it.[171] This is a subjective test since it depends on the defendant being aware that the benefit was not provided gratuitously.[172] Such a test is consistent with the true function of free acceptance, namely to prevent the defendant from relying on the principle of subjective devaluation where the defendant can be considered to have actually valued the benefit.

(3) The final condition is that, even though the defendant had the opportunity to reject the benefit and was aware that it was not provided gratuitously, he or she failed to reject it.

---

[166] See p 82, above.
[167] *Rowe v Vale of White Horse DC* [2003] EWHC 388 (Admin), [2003] 1 Lloyd's Rep 418, 422 (Lightman J).
[168] See *Re Cleadon Trust Ltd* [1939] Ch 286.
[169] [2008] EWCA Civ 1449, [2009] 1 WLR 1580.
[170] *Rowe v Vale of White Horse DC* [2003] EWHC 388 (Admin), [2003] 1 Lloyd's Rep 418, 421 (Lightman J).
[171] See *Ramsden v Dyson* (1866) LR 1 HL 129.
[172] See especially *Falcke v Scottish Imperial Insurance Co* (1886) 34 Ch D 234, 249 (Bowen LJ); *Re Cleadon Trust Ltd* [1939] Ch 286; *McDonald v Coys of Kensington* [2004] EWCA Civ 47, [2004] 1 WLR 2775.

How the principle of free acceptance operates in practice is illustrated by the following example, suggested by Birks.[173] If the claimant cleans the defendant's windows, without having been requested to do so, the reasonable person would presumably regard the defendant as having received an objective benefit, since this is the type of service which is commonly paid for and so it has a market value. The defendant, however, might subjectively devalue this benefit, perhaps because he or she cleans the windows him or herself and does not see the need to pay somebody else to do it. The claimant would then have to find some way of defeating the defendant's reliance on the subjective devaluation principle. The defendant does not appear to have been incontrovertibly benefited, save if it could be shown that he or she was about to pay somebody to clean the windows and so had been saved a factually necessary expense.[174] If this cannot be established, the claimant's only hope is to prove that the defendant had freely accepted the benefit. This would be established if the claimant can show that, when he or she was cleaning the windows, the defendant was in the house, was aware of what the claimant was doing and that the claimant expected to be paid for the service, and had failed to make it clear to the claimant that he or she did not want the windows to be cleaned by the claimant.

Although this example illustrates how the free acceptance principle might operate in practice, it should be emphasized that, even if the defendant had freely accepted the benefit, it does not follow that restitution will be awarded. Indeed, it is most unlikely that the restitutionary claim would succeed, because there is no apparent ground for restitution and, most importantly, the claimant took the risk that the defendant might not pay for the window cleaning. It is a fundamental principle of the law of restitution that risk-taking claimants should not be able to obtain restitutionary remedies.[175]

(ii) The Function of Free Acceptance

Although the principle of free acceptance has been recognized in English law, its very existence and function remains controversial. Some commentators have rejected the legitimacy of recognizing such a wide principle, asserting that a much narrower principle should be recognized instead, the function of which is to ascertain that the defendant positively valued the benefit which was received by showing that he or she had reprehensibly sought it out.[176] But other commentators, notably the editors of Goff and Jones,[177] support the recognition of the free acceptance principle and assert that it has a negative function, namely to defeat the defendant's reliance on the principle of subjective devaluation. Both approaches were recognized by Mance LJ in *MacDonald v Coys of Kensington*,[178] who concluded that both would have been satisfied on the facts to establish free acceptance, although he did not express a preference between them.

To assess which approach is to be preferred, it is necessary to examine what the function of free acceptance actually is. Whether the defendant had freely accepted the benefit is only significant where the defendant seeks to argue that he or she did not value the benefit. It follows that the function of the principle is not to show that the defendant did positively value the benefit but, rather, to prevent the defendant from subjectively

---

[173] PBH Birks, *An Introduction to the Law of Restitution* (rev edn, Oxford: Clarendon Press, 1989) 265.

[174] Interpreting what constitutes 'necessary' expenditure broadly, as was examined at p 81, above.

[175] See p 36, above.

[176] For example, Burrows, 'Free Acceptance and the Law of Restitution' (1988) 104 LQR 576; Burrows, *The Law of Restitution* (3rd edn), 57–8. See also Garner, 'The Role of Subjective Benefit in the Law of Unjust Enrichment'.

[177] *Goff and Jones: The Law of Unjust Enrichment* (8th edn), 92. See also Birks, *Unjust Enrichment* (2nd edn), 56.

[178] [2004] EWCA Civ 47, [2004] 1 WLR 2775.

devaluing it. Consequently, it has a negative function of preventing the defendant from relying on the subjective devaluation principle because the defendant can be considered to have acted unconscionably in indicating that he or she did not value the benefit after freely accepting it.[179] Where the defendant does freely accept the benefit and then says that he or she did not value it, the defendant's conduct deprives him or her of the opportunity to assert individual autonomy by devaluing the benefit.

This analysis of free acceptance as a principle which is triggered by the defendant's unconscionable conduct and which prevents the defendant from relying on the subjective devaluation principle, implies that free acceptance is actually a form of estoppel.[180] By freely accepting the benefit the defendant is estopped from asserting that he or she did not value it. This also justifies the assertion that free acceptance is triggered by the defendant's unconscionable conduct, since such conduct underlies the recognition of estoppel.[181] It should follow that free acceptance should only be available where the claimant has relied on the defendant's acceptance. Whilst reliance has not been expressly recognized as a component of the free acceptance principle, it is certainly consistent with it. For example, where the claimant has cleaned the defendant's windows without being requested to do so, but the defendant stood by knowing that the claimant expected to be paid for the service, it might be concluded that the defendant's conduct satisfied the requirements of free acceptance, but the claimant, not having relied on the defendant's representation or acquiescence, should not be able to obtain restitutionary relief because he or she is a risk-taker. Consequently, the absence of reliance by the claimant on the defendant's free acceptance establishes that the claimant was a risk-taker.

4. RESTITUTION WITHOUT ENRICHMENT

Although it seems obvious that if the claimant is to obtain restitutionary relief by virtue of the defendant's unjust enrichment it must be established that the defendant has indeed been enriched, there are two situations where it might be possible to conclude that the claim for restitution should succeed even though the defendant has not been enriched.

(A) THE DEFENDANT IS ESTOPPED FROM DENYING THE ENRICHMENT

(i) The Function of Estoppel

Although the defendant may not have received an objective benefit, it might still be possible to show that the defendant has been enriched where he or she is estopped from asserting that he or she has not received a benefit at the claimant's expense. If estoppel is being used to establish enrichment, it does not automatically establish the cause of action, since it will still be necessary for the claimant to establish that one of the recognized grounds of restitution is applicable. Rather, the function of the estoppel is simply to enable the claimant to pursue a restitutionary cause of action by negating one of the required elements of that action.[182]

---

[179] See Birks, *Restitution—The Future*, 97.

[180] See Birks, *An Introduction to the Law of Restitution*, 276.

[181] See Chapter 21. See *Appleby v Myers* (1867) LR 2 CP 651, 659–60 (Blackburn J); *Willmott v Barber* (1880) 15 Ch D 96; and *Salvation Army Trustee Co Ltd v West Yorkshire Metropolitan CC* (1980) P and CR 179, 198.

[182] See Brandon LJ in *Amalgamated Investment and Property Co Ltd v Texas Commerce International Bank Ltd* [1982] QB 84, 131–2.

(ii) The Conditions for Establishing an Estoppel

Three conditions need to be satisfied before the defendant could be estopped from denying that he or she had been enriched.

(1) The defendant must have represented to the claimant that he or she wanted to receive the benefit and would pay the claimant for it. Evidence of a request will typically satisfy this condition. But passive acquiescence in the provision of the service should also be sufficient.

(2) The claimant must have acted to his or her detriment in reliance upon the defendant's representation that he or she would pay for the benefit.

(3) The defendant must have falsified the representation in some way. This establishes that the defendant was to blame and provides the justification for preventing the defendant from denying that he or she was enriched.[183] The defendant should not be estopped from denying the enrichment if the representation is falsified without blame on the part of the defendant. So where, for example, the defendant encourages the claimant to incur expenditure in anticipation of a contract and no contract is made simply because the parties are unable to agree, the defendant is not at fault and so should not be estopped from denying that he or she had been enriched.[184]

(iii) The Application of the Estoppel Principle

Although the estoppel principle has not been clearly recognized as a way of satisfying the claimant's need to establish that the defendant was enriched,[185] the operation of this principle can be discerned in a few cases. Its most important role will be in those cases where the claimant has spent time and money in doing work which has not yet been received by the defendant, or where the claimant has done work on behalf of the defendant which has been received by a third party. In both situations the defendant has not received any benefit, so a restitutionary claim founded on the reversal of the defendant's unjust enrichment can only succeed if he or she is estopped from denying that he or she has been enriched.

The most important context where this estoppel principle can be used to justify the award of restitutionary remedies is where the claimant has acted in anticipation of a contract which is not forthcoming.[186] In some of these cases the defendant received an objective benefit which he or she would have been unable subjectively to devalue because it was incontrovertibly beneficial or had been freely accepted.[187] In other cases, however, the claimant was awarded a restitutionary remedy even though there was no evidence that the defendant had received an objective benefit. This is particularly well illustrated by *Brewer*

---

[183] The requirement of fault has been stressed in a number of cases. See, in particular, *Brewer Street Investments Ltd v Barclays Woollen Co Ltd* [1954] 1 QB 428 and *Sabemo Pty Ltd v North Sydney Municipal Council* [1977] 2 NSWLR 880.

[184] *Sabemo Pty Ltd v North Sydney Municipal Council* [1977] 2 NSWLR 880, 880 and 901 (Sheppard J). See also 903.

[185] Although Lord Clarke in *Benedetti v Sawiris* [2013] UKSC 50, [2014] AC 938, [29], did acknowledge the possible role of estoppel in establishing enrichment by the provision of a service even though the defendant had not obtained any benefit. See also Lord Neuberger, ibid, [199], who contemplated that the defendant might be liable for the additional value above the objective market value, where the defendant led the claimant to believe that he was willing to pay more for the benefit and the claimant reasonably and foreseeably relied on this representation, by virtue of estoppel. See further p 98, below.

[186] See Chapter 13.

[187] See, for example, *William Lacey (Hounslow) Ltd v Davis* [1957] 1 WLR 932.

Street Investments Ltd v Barclays Woollen Co Ltd,[188] where the defendant had been negotiating with the claimant for a lease of the claimant's property. Before a contract had been signed, the defendant requested the claimant to do some work on the property, which the claimant did. No contract was ever signed, and so the claimant brought a restitutionary claim against the defendant to recover the value of the work which it had done. The claim succeeded. The problem with this case is that the defendant had not received any benefit from the claimant's work, because the work had occurred on the claimant's own property and the defendant had never entered into possession of it, but the defendant was still held liable to pay the claimant for the reasonable value of its services. A majority of the Court of Appeal explained this restitutionary liability by virtue of the fact that no contract had been made because of the defendant's conduct,[189] namely the defendant's insistence on the granting of an option when it knew at the outset that the claimant would never do so. Although none of the judges stated that the defendant was estopped from denying enrichment, the language they used is consistent with that principle. The defendant had requested the claimant to do the work, the claimant had done so in reliance on this request and the failure to make the contract was due to the fault of the defendant. It followed that the defendant could not deny that he had been enriched.

Similarly, in the Australian case of *Sabemo Pty Ltd v North Sydney Municipal Council*,[190] the defendant had requested the claimant to do some work for it in anticipation of a contract being made. This contract was not forthcoming due to the fault of the defendant, in that it unilaterally decided to drop the proposal.[191] So, even though the trial judge held that the defendant had not been unjustly enriched since it had not received a benefit,[192] the restitutionary remedy which was awarded could still be justified by reference to the principle of unjust enrichment, with the enrichment being assumed, since the defendant's conduct, on which the claimant had relied, estopped it from denying that it had been enriched.

In *Jennings and Chapman Ltd v Woodman Matthews and Co*,[193] on the other hand, although the facts were similar to those of *Brewer Street*, restitution was denied. The preferable explanation for this is simply that in *Jennings* the reason why no contract was forthcoming was because of a mutual breakdown in negotiations; there was no evidence that the defendant was at fault in any way and so there was no basis for preventing the defendant from denying that it had been enriched.[194]

This estoppel principle might also be relevant to explain the difficult case of *Planché v Colburn*.[195] In that case the claimant had contracted with the defendant to research and write a book, but the defendant terminated the contract after the claimant had done much of the research and writing but before anything had been received by the defendant. The claimant successfully brought an action to recover the reasonable value of his services. Although the claimant's action would today be founded on breach of contract, it is still

---

[188] [1954] 1 QB 428.

[189] This was the conclusion of both Somervell and Romer LJJ. Denning LJ did not find that the defendant was at fault, though he did find that the defendant had agreed to take responsibility for the claimant's work: ibid, 437.   [190] [1977] 2 NSWLR 880.

[191] Ibid, 901 where Sheppard J said that 'the defendant's decision to drop the proposal is the determining factor'.

[192] Ibid, 897.   [193] [1952] 2 TLR 409.

[194] See also *Regalian Properties plc v London Dockland Development Corporation* [1995] 1 WLR 212 where Rattee J specifically distinguished *Sabemo Pty Ltd v North Sydney Municipal Council* on the basis that in that case the anticipated contract failed to materialize because of the defendant's conduct, whereas in *Regalian* no contract was forthcoming due to a mutual inability to agree a price.

[195] (1831) 8 Bing 14, 131 ER 305. See p 68, above. See also *Prickett v Badger* (1856) 1 CB (NS) 296, 140 ER 123.

possible to justify the award of a restitutionary remedy by reference to the estoppel principle. This is because the defendant had requested the claimant's performance on the understanding that the claimant would be paid for it, the claimant had acted in reliance on this request and the defendant by his own act falsified the representation that the performance would be paid for under the contract by terminating it.[196] Consequently, even though the defendant had not received an enrichment, it might still have been possible to assume that the defendant had been enriched because he would have been estopped by his conduct from denying that this was the case.

(B) UNJUST SACRIFICE

(i) The Significance of Recognizing the Unjust Sacrifice Principle

It has sometimes been suggested that, where a claimant has suffered a loss without the defendant necessarily obtaining a benefit, the claimant should be able to obtain a remedy without founding an action in contract or tort. Rather, liability should be founded on the unjust sacrifice principle.[197] If such liability exists, clearly it cannot be founded on the principle of reversing unjust enrichment, because of the lack of an enrichment. Also the remedies consequent upon such liability could not be termed restitutionary, since if the defendant has not been enriched, and cannot be assumed to have been enriched, there is no actual or deemed benefit which the defendant can restore to the claimant. It might, therefore, be thought that analysis of unjust sacrifice has no place in a textbook on the law of restitution. Its analysis can be justified, however, because if such a principle is recognized it would have an important influence on the question of how enrichment is defined. For if unjust sacrifice liability does exist, it will not be so important to adopt a wide definition of enrichment to ensure that the claimant obtains a remedy. Equally, if the notion of enrichment is defined widely, as has been argued in this chapter, there is little, if any role, for unjust sacrifice liability to play.[198]

(ii) Is the Principle Recognized in English Law?

The unjust sacrifice principle has not been expressly recognized in any English decision. Many of the situations which might be covered by such a principle are better regarded as falling within the principle of unjust enrichment, essentially because of the wide interpretation of incontrovertible benefit. For many of the cases which have been relied on to establish the unjust sacrifice principle involve the supply of necessaries or discharge of the defendant's liability and are better analysed as cases where the defendant has been incontrovertibly benefited.[199]

(iii) Should the Unjust Sacrifice Principle Be Recognized in English Law?

Despite the absence of case law support for the unjust sacrifice principle, can a case be made for its recognition? Stoljar provides an example of a situation in which this principle would have a useful role to play, namely where the claimant attends to the defendant's child injured in an accident, but the child dies.[200] Clearly, the defendant cannot be regarded as benefited by the claimant's services in these circumstances, so a restitutionary remedy cannot lie. But should the defendant be held liable to recompense or reimburse the

---

[196] See, in particular, the report of the case at (1831) 1 LJCP 7.
[197] See especially SJ Stoljar, 'Unjust Enrichment and Unjust Sacrifice' (1987) 50 MLR 603.
[198] Birks, *Restitution—The Future*, 103.   [199] See p 78, above.
[200] Stoljar, 'Unjust Enrichment and Unjust Sacrifice', 612. See, for example, *Cotnam v Wisdom* (1907) 104 SW 164 and *Matheson v Smiley* [1932] 2 DLR 787.

claimant for the reasonable value of these services? Stoljar suggests the answer is 'yes', as long as those services were provided in the expectation that they would be paid for and were 'manifestly necessary or urgent or useful' for the defendant, so that the provision of those services cannot be regarded as officious.[201] Stoljar's justification for the defendant's liability in these circumstances is that the claimant's non-gratuitous provision of services requires protection as though it were his or her property. But this justification is not convincing. Where the defendant has not been benefited, why should he or she be required to recompense the claimant? Where the claimant has attempted to save the life of the defendant's child but failed, perhaps this was due to the fault of the claimant. Also, where the defendant has not received any benefit at all, it is difficult to conclude that the claimant's officiousness has been displaced. Although we presumably want people to try to save the lives of children, we must not be misled by the emotive nature of this example. Where the defendant has not been benefited in any way, no obligation to pay the claimant should be imposed, despite the policy that society wishes to encourage intervention in an emergency. It is for this reason that the unjust sacrifice principle should be rejected.

5. PART PERFORMANCE OF A CONTRACT

There is an additional problem which relates to the identification of an enrichment, where the claimant has done some of the work which is required to be done under a contract, but did not complete it. Can the defendant in such circumstances be regarded as enriched so that the claimant can recover the reasonable value of the work which he or she has done in a claim grounded on unjust enrichment? It should be emphasized that the restitutionary claim will only be relevant once the contract has been discharged for whatever reason, because of the principle that restitutionary claims are always subordinate to contractual claims.[202]

Where the defendant has received the benefit of the claimant's partial performance of the contract, the defendant will typically have received an objective benefit. So, for example, if the claimant agreed to build a house for the defendant and, after having done half of the work, the claimant fails, for whatever reason, to complete the house, the defendant is in receipt of a benefit, namely half a house, which is of some objective value. But, because the defendant wanted a whole house, it would be perfectly appropriate for him or her subjectively to devalue the benefit which had been received. Will it be possible for the claimant to defeat the defendant's reliance on this principle? This will depend on the circumstances of the case, and five different circumstances need to be considered.

(A) THE DEFENDANT COMPLETED THE WORK

If the defendant has completed the work which had been started by the claimant, this adoption of the benefit should defeat the defendant's reliance on subjective devaluation. For the defendant's voluntary acceptance of the benefit shows that he or she values what the claimant provided, so it is inconsistent for the defendant then to say that he or she did not value what the claimant had done.[203]

---

[201] Stoljar, 'Unjust Enrichment and Unjust Sacrifice', 613.

[202] See Chapter 7. See also Chapter 13 for examination of the ground of restitution where a contract has been discharged after the claimant has partly performed it.

[203] See *Lodder v Slowey* [1904] AC 442.

(B) THE DEFENDANT PREVENTED THE CLAIMANT FROM PERFORMING

If the defendant has prevented the claimant from completing the performance, this should be sufficient to prevent the defendant from subjectively devaluing the benefit.[204] But it would be difficult to show that the defendant had freely accepted the benefit, since it does not necessarily follow from the fact that the defendant has prevented the claimant from continuing to perform that the defendant values what the claimant has already done. It might be concluded that the defendant should be considered to be enriched because he or she had requested the claimant to do the work in the first place,[205] but the defendant's request only shows that he or she valued the whole and not necessarily the part performance. Despite this, it should still be possible to establish that the defendant was enriched in these circumstances by virtue of the estoppel principle.[206] This principle will be applicable because the defendant had represented that he or she would pay for the benefit, the claimant detrimentally relied on this representation , and the defendant's representation was falsified because it was the defendant who prevented the claimant from performing the contract.

(C) THE CLAIMANT BREACHED THE CONTRACT

Where the reason why the claimant failed to perform the contract was that he or she breached it, it will be very difficult to prevent the defendant from relying on the subjective devaluation principle, save where it can be shown either that the defendant had voluntarily accepted the benefit despite the breach, or that the benefit was incontrovertibly beneficial.

(D) THE CONTRACT WAS FRUSTRATED

Where the claimant was unable to perform his or her side of the bargain because the contract was frustrated, it will still be possible to establish that the defendant has been enriched by virtue of the statutory regime under the Law Reform (Frustrated Contracts) 1943, s 1(3).[207]

(E) ENTIRE CONTRACT

Where the contract is entire, meaning that the defendant is not liable to pay until the claimant has fully performed his or her side of the bargain, then, even though the defendant can be considered to have been enriched by the part performance of the contract, the claimant's restitutionary claim will fail.[208] This is because the effect of making the contract entire is that the claimant takes the risk of not fully performing it, so the right to obtain restitution is effectively excluded by the contract.[209]

6. THE VALUATION OF THE ENRICHMENT

Once it has been shown that the defendant has received an enrichment, it is necessary to value it. This value forms the basis for assessing the restitutionary remedy which is

---

[204] Birks, 'In Defence of Free Acceptance', 140.
[205] Burrows, 'Free Acceptance and the Law of Restitution', 586.   [206] See p 90, above.
[207] See Chapter 13.   [208] *Sumpter v Hedges* [1898] 1 QB 673.   [209] See p 141, below.

awarded to reverse the defendant's unjust enrichment. A number of questions need to be examined when valuing the defendant's enrichment.

(A) TIMING OF THE VALUATION

In order to value the defendant's enrichment it is first necessary to consider when this valuation should take place. In particular, should the enrichment be valued at the time of receipt or the time of the trial? This is an important question, since the test of timing which is adopted could have a profound effect upon the value which is actually restored to the claimant. The importance of the timing question is illustrated by *Appleby v Myers*,[210] where the claimant partly performed a contract to build machinery for the defendant, but before he was able to complete the work the machinery was destroyed by fire, so frustrating the contract. If the enrichment was valued at the time it was received it would have been a substantial amount, but if the enrichment was valued at the time of the trial it would have been worth nothing, since the enrichment no longer existed.

English law recognizes that the enrichment should be valued at the time when it was received by the defendant.[211] It would be more accurate, however, to say that the enrichment should be valued when all the elements of the unjust enrichment claim have been satisfied, for only then will the claim be crystallized.[212] Normally, the claim will crystallize when the enrichment is received because the ground of restitution will also be established at that point. So, for example, if money has been paid by mistake, all the elements of the claim will be satisfied at the time of payment, so long as it can be shown that the money would not have been paid at that time had the claimant known the true state of the facts or the law.[213] Where, however, the claimant transfers a benefit to the defendant on the basis, for example, that a benefit will be transferred by the defendant in return on some future occasion, and no benefit is transferred, the ground of restitution will only arise when the basis fails, so that the enrichment should be valued at that point at which the claim crystallizes.

Once the unjust enrichment claim has crystallized, subsequent events which affect the enrichment should not be taken into account, save to the extent that the defendant can satisfy the conditions for the defence of change of position,[214] which will operate to reduce or extinguish the restitutionary liability, or if the claimant seeks to defeat the defendant's reliance on the defence of subjective devaluation.[215]

This timing question was considered by Rattee J in *Regalian Properties plc v London Docklands Development Corp*,[216] who assumed that the defendant had not been enriched by the claimant's preparatory work, relating to the redevelopment of the defendant's land, because property values had fallen after negotiations for a contract had collapsed so that no-one would wish to develop the defendant's land. Consequently, the claimant's preparatory work was ultimately worthless.[217] This decision might be criticized on the ground that events subsequent to receipt of the enrichment should only be taken into account by virtue of the defence of change of position and, since it was not possible to

---

[210] (1867) LR 2 CP 651. The case would today be governed by the Law Reform (Frustrated Contracts) Act 1943. See Chapter 13.

[211] *BP Exploration Co (Libya) Ltd v Hunt* [1979] 1 WLR 783, 802 (Robert Goff J); *Benedetti v Sawiris* [2013] UKSC 50, [2014] AC 938, [14] (Lord Clarke).

[212] See Stevens, 'Three Enrichment Issues', 58.

[213] *Deutsche Morgan Grenfell Group plc v IRC* [2006] UKHL 49, [2007] 1 AC 558, [59] (Lord Hope).

[214] See Chapter 25.   [215] See further p 78, above.   [216] [1995] 1 WLR 212.

[217] Ibid, 225.

establish a link between the receipt of the enrichment and the later failure to redevelop the land, this defence could not have been established. In fact the judge's conclusion about the timing of valuation can be defended by focusing on when the claim crystallized. For the reason why the unjust enrichment claim actually failed was because the agreement between the parties was subject to contract, which meant that the claimant bore the risk of no concluded contract materializing. Had the agreement not been subject to contract the unjust enrichment claim would have crystallized at the point when negotiations for the contract collapsed, at which point there was a total failure of basis. Since, however, the claimant bore the risk of the negotiations failing, there was no failure of basis for the services and so the claim in unjust enrichment had not crystallized. Consequently, it was appropriate to take into account the subsequent fall in property values which meant that the claimant's work was ultimately worthless, so that the defendant was no longer enriched.

(B) THE TEST OF VALUATION

The question of valuing the enrichment usually does not cause any difficulty. So, for example, where the benefit conferred on the defendant consists of the receipt of money, the defendant is benefited by the amount received and it is this amount which must be repaid to the claimant.[218] This does not mean that there can never be valuation problems when the enrichment is money received, since there may be particular problems relating to inflation, the valuation of foreign currency[219] and the payment of interest.[220]

These problems are nothing, however, when compared with those which can arise in connection with the valuation of non-money benefits. The general test of valuation which should be adopted is an objective test,[221] namely the reasonable value of the benefit received, since this is the basic test which is relied on when identifying whether or not the defendant has actually been enriched.[222] This reasonable value is ascertained by reference to the market value, which is the price which a reasonable person in the position of the defendant would have had to pay for the services.[223]

Although the objective test of valuation will initially be used to value the enrichment, that test may be qualified by the subjective devaluation principle, whereby the defendant can prove that he or she valued the benefit at less than the market value.[224] This principle is recognized by virtue of the need to protect the defendant's autonomy.[225] So, for example, the defendant may have received a benefit and acknowledges that it is valuable, but is free to argue that he or she valued it less than the objective value. But, in the same way that the principle of subjective devaluation may be defeated by the principles of incontrovertible benefit, request, and free acceptance for the purpose of identifying an enrichment, the defendant's reliance on subjective devaluation should be circumscribed for the purposes of valuing the enrichment. This means that, if it can be shown that the defendant had been incontrovertibly benefited or had requested or freely accepted the

---

[218] Subject to the operation of the general defences.

[219] *BP Exploration Co (Libya) Ltd v Hunt* [1979] 1 WLR 783, 839–41 (Robert Goff J).

[220] See Chapter 1.

[221] *Benedetti v Sawiris* [2013] UKSC 50, [2014] AC 938, [16] (Lord Clarke).

[222] See p 65, above.

[223] *Benedetti v Sawiris* [2013] UKSC 50, [2014] AC 938, [17] (Lord Clarke).

[224] Ibid, [18] (Lord Clarke). So subjective devaluation applies both to the identification and the valuation of the enrichment. See also *Scarisbrick v Parkinson* (1869) 20 LT 175, 177 (Kelly CB); *Sempra Metals Ltd v IRC* [2007] UKHL 34, [2008] AC 561, [48] (Lord Hope), [116] (Lord Nicholls), and [180] (Lord Walker).

[225] *Benedetti v Sawiris* [2013] UKSC 50, [2014] AC 938, [18] (Lord Clarke). See p 37, above.

benefit, the objective value of the benefit should be adopted and the defendant's own valuation of it should be considered to be irrelevant.

In the context of identifying the appropriate test for valuing benefits there are three issues which require particular consideration.

(i) Subjective Over-Valuation

It might be considered to follow logically from the recognition of the subjective devaluation principle that a principle of subjective over-valuation[226] should also be recognized, such that the value of the enrichment should be increased above its objective value if the defendant valued it more highly. However, none of the Justices in *Benedetti v Sawiris*[227] recognized this principle, although Lord Clarke, with whom Lords Kerr and Wilson agreed, did reserve the possibility of recognizing it in exceptional circumstances, but without identifying what they might be.[228] Subjective over-valuation was not considered to be necessary to protect the defendant's autonomy to choose and value the benefit,[229] it being sufficient that the defendant restored to the claimant no more than the objective value of the benefit, for then the enrichment would be considered no longer to be unjust.[230] So, for example, if the defendant asked the claimant to decorate his house in execrable taste, the enrichment would be the objective value of the claimant's service, which will not be increased by reference to the fact that the defendant valued this service more than the reasonable person would do.[231] It followed, on the facts of *Benedetti*, that the defendant was not liable to pay the claimant more than the objective market value of the services provided by the claimant, even though the defendant had offered the claimant a larger sum to settle the proceedings. Even if this offer reflected the defendant's perception that the services were worth more than their objective value, and it is doubtful whether an offer made to settle proceedings really can be regarded as evidence of the defendant's personal valuation of the service, it was not relevant to the valuation of the enrichment.

The crucial consequence of the decision of the Supreme Court in *Benedetti* is that, whilst the objective value of an enrichment may be reduced by the defendant's personal valuation, it cannot be increased by reference to the defendant's valuation.

(ii) Valuing Services

Where the claimant has provided a service which the defendant is unable subjectively to devalue, the objective value of the benefit will be adopted. Where the benefit takes the form of services it should follow that the defendant's enrichment should be assessed as the reasonable value of those services by reference to the market. Determining the market value for services involves an assessment of the necessary costs incurred in doing the work, plus a reasonable profit margin assessed by reference to the relevant industry rates and practices.[232]

---

[226] Garner, 'The Role of Subjective Benefit in the Law of Unjust Enrichment', 43 called this 'subjective revaluation', but 'over-valuation' better reflects the nature of the principle.

[227] [2013] UKSC 50, [2014] AC 938, [29] (Lord Clarke), [115] (Lord Reed), [195] (Lord Neuberger).

[228] Lord Neuberger, ibid, [199], also contemplated that the defendant might be liable for the additional value above the objective market value where the defendant led the claimant to believe that he was willing to pay more for the benefit and the claimant reasonably and foreseeably relied on this representation. He considered that the subjective revaluation would be relevant by virtue of estoppel (see p 90, above), but it is just as likely to be covered by a contractual claim.

[229] Ibid, [29] (Lord Clarke).   [230] Ibid, [196] (Lord Neuberger).   [231] Ibid, [121] (Lord Reed).

[232] See *Sopov v Kane Constructions Pty Ltd (No 2)* [2009] VSCA 141.

In *Cobbe v Yeoman's Row Management Ltd*[233] the value of the claimant's service in obtaining planning permission was valued as including his outgoings in applying for and obtaining planning permission, which was presumed to have been reasonably incurred unless the defendant could prove otherwise, and a fee for the service, which was to be assessed at the rate charged by an experienced property developer.

The reasonable profit margin will vary according to the circumstances, having regard to the margins which are typical in the industry, the nature and quality of the work, and the level of competition. So, for example, in *MSM Consulting Ltd v United Republic of Tanzania*[234] a claim of £250 per hour, for the provision of services involving the identification of property for the defendant to purchase, was considered to be too high since the claimant had no surveying or valuation qualifications. £125 was considered to be a more appropriate rate for the particular claimant's work.

(iii) Estoppel

Where the defendant is estopped from denying that he or she has been enriched, it follows that he or she is deemed to have received a benefit. Since no benefit will have actually been received, the measure of the enrichment should be assessed by reference to the market value of the claimant's work.[235] So, in a case such as *Planché v Colburn*,[236] if the estoppel principle is adopted to identify an enrichment, the value of the defendant's deemed benefit should be assessed by reference to the objective value of the claimant's work in researching and preparing the manuscript.

(C) THE ROLE OF THE CONTRACT IN THE VALUATION OF THE ENRICHMENT

One of the most controversial matters relating to the valuation of benefits, and one which is closely related to the question whether a subjective or an objective test of valuation should be adopted, concerns the effect of a contract upon the valuation of a benefit. If the defendant receives a benefit under a contract, and that contract is subsequently set aside so that the claimant is forced to sue the defendant in unjust enrichment rather than on the contract, should the value of the benefit be assessed by reference to its market value or to the price which the parties had agreed in the contract?

In determining the relevance of the contract price to the value of the benefit it is important first to emphasize that the price agreed by the parties is likely to constitute significant evidence of both the market value of the benefit and also, to the extent that it is different, its objective value.[237] There are a number of situations where the contract price has been taken into account in valuing the benefit which the defendant had received, such as where the contract itself was unenforceable.[238] Where the claimant delivers more goods to the defendant than the claimant had contracted to sell and the defendant accepts these

---

[233] [2008] UKHL 55, [2008] 1 WLR 1752, [42].   [234] [2009] EWHC 121 (QB).

[235] This was the test of valuation which was adopted in *Sabemo Pty Ltd v North Sydney Municipal Council* [1977] 2 NSWLR 880, 903.

[236] (1831) 8 Bing 14, 131 ER 305. See p 68, above.

[237] *Benedetti v Sawiris* [2013] UKSC 50, [2014] AC 938, [56] (Lord Clarke). This was also the view of Robert Goff J in *BP Exploration Co (Libya) Ltd v Hunt (No 2)* [1979] 1 WLR 783 as regards the valuation of the just sum for benefits in kind which have been provided under a contract subsequently frustrated. See p 364, below. See also *Flett v Deniliquin Publishing Co Ltd* [1964–5] NSWLR 383, 386 (Herron CJ).

[238] *Scarisbrick v Parkinson* (1869) 20 LT 175 and *Pavey and Matthews Pty v Paul* (1987) 162 CLR 221.

goods, the excess will be valued at the contract price.[239] Even if the parties have not agreed on a specific price for work done or property transferred, the course of the parties' negotiations has been of considerable assistance in determining the value of the benefit received. As Lord Atkin said in *Way v Latilla*, albeit in a case concerning the implication of a term of a contract about payment:[240]

> [the] court may take into account the bargainings between the parties, not with a view to completing the bargain for them, but as evidence of the value which each of them puts upon the services. If the discussion had ranged between three per cent. on the one side and five per cent. on the other, all else being agreed, the court would not be likely to depart from somewhere about those figures, and would be wrong in ignoring them altogether and fixing remuneration on an entirely different basis, upon which, possibly, the services would never have been rendered at all.

But there will be some situations where the price agreed by the parties will be higher or lower than the objective value of the benefit, because, for example, the market value may have changed by the time the benefit was provided. Where the contract price is higher than the objective value, there is no reason to increase that valuation to enable the claimant to recover outside of a claim for breach of contract more than the objective value of the benefit.

But where the contract price is less than the objective value, the contract price might be considered to be more significant. This is because the claimant will be considered to have entered into a 'bad bargain' and, it might be argued, should be restricted to the bargain which had been made, with the contract price operating as a ceiling on the value of the benefit. There are mixed views in the cases and amongst commentators as to the relevance of the contract price in valuing benefits.

(i) The Contract Price Should Operate as a Ceiling to the Valuation of the Benefit

In *Taylor v Motability Finance Ltd*,[241] Cooke J, held, albeit *obiter*, that there is never a justification for the claimant to recover in excess of the contract price. He considered that allowing the claimant to recover more than the contractual ceiling 'would be unjust since it would put the innocent party in a better position than he would have been if the contract had been fulfilled'.[242] Similarly, in *MacDonald Dickens and Macklin v Costello*[243] Etherton LJ recognized that it is appropriate that the contract price should operate as a ceiling on the valuation of the benefit, since the claimant should not be allowed to escape from a bad bargain by resorting to a claim in unjust enrichment.[244]

This emphasis on the contract price as being a ceiling on the value of the defendant's benefit is consistent with the subjective devaluation principle when valuing benefits.[245] Once it has been recognized that the defendant can argue that he or she did not value the benefit as much as its objective value, it is necessary for the defendant to produce evidence

---

[239] Sale of Goods Act 1979, s 30(3).
[240] *Way v Latilla* [1937] 3 All ER 759, 764. In *Renard Constructions (ME) Pty Ltd v Minister for Public Works* (1992) 26 NSWLR 234, Meagher JA regarded the contract price as strong evidence but not conclusive evidence of the value of the benefit.
[241] [2004] EWHC 2619 (Comm), [26].
[242] Ibid.   [243] [2011] EWCA Civ 930, [2012] QB 244, [31].
[244] See also the relevance of a bad bargain when considering whether restitution should be available for a failure of basis. See p 326, below.   [245] Birks, *Unjust Enrichment* (2nd edn), 59.

to support that valuation. The contract price as contained in the contract agreed by the parties is very strong evidence of the defendant's own valuation.[246]

(ii) The Contract Price Should Not Operate as a Ceiling to the Valuation of the Benefit

It has sometimes been recognized, however, that the contract price should not be used to restrict the valuation of the enrichment received by the defendant.[247] *Rover International Ltd v Cannon Film Sales Ltd (No 3)*[248] involved a claim to recover the value of services provided in respect of a contract for the dubbing and distribution of films in Italy. The contract was void *ab initio* since it was made before the claimant company had been incorporated. Counsel for the defendant conceded that the claim could be established, so the only remaining issue related to the valuation of the benefit. Kerr LJ, with whom Nicholls LJ concurred,[249] held that the valuation of the benefit received by the defendant was not constrained by the amount which the claimant would have received under the contract for the provision of the service. Kerr LJ provided three reasons for this conclusion.[250]

(1) It would not be just for the defendant to rely on the contract to restrict the valuation of the benefit when it was the defendant who had initially relied on the invalidity of the contract to discontinue its performance. In other words, the defendant's conduct had been such that it could not ignore the contract at one stage of the proceedings and rely on its terms when it was in its own interest to do so.[251]

(2) If the contract terms did constitute a ceiling on the restitutionary claim this would result in undesirable inconsistency in the law of restitution, particularly because when relief is awarded following the frustration of a contract the contract terms do not restrict the restitutionary claim.[252]

(3) It would be unprincipled to rely on the contract to restrict the restitutionary claim when that contract was null and void. Since such claims arise from the fact that the contract was non-existent, it would be illogical then to rely on that contract when valuing the benefit.

The first two of the judge's reasons are unconvincing. The first reason, concerning the relative merits of the parties' conduct, should not be relevant when considering the role of the contract in valuing the benefits provided, for that is the route to palm-tree justice and consequent uncertainty.[253] As regards the second reason, any inconsistency with the law concerning frustrated contracts may be undesirable but might be inevitable, since the implications of a contract being frustrated is now governed by statute. But the third reason is surely relevant in concluding that the claim should not have been circumscribed by the contract price. If the contract is null and void then how can its terms be relevant to the

---

[246] See *Benedetti v Sawiris* [2013] UKSC 50, [2014] AC 938, [56] (Lord Clarke).
[247] *Lodder v Slowey* [1904] AC 442. See also *Boomer v Muir* 24 P 2d 570 (1933); *Renard Constructions (ME) Pty Ltd v Minister for Public Works* (1992) 26 NSWLR 234.
[248] [1989] 1 WLR 912.   [249] The other judge, Dillon LJ, did not consider the matter.
[250] Ibid, 927–8.
[251] See also *Renard Constructions (ME) Pty Ltd v Minister for Public Works* (1992) 26 NSWLR 234, 278 (Meagher JA).
[252] Law Reform (Frustrated Contracts) Act 1943, s 1(3). See Chapter 13.
[253] See the rejection of relative fault when considering the operation of the defence of change of position: p 694, below.

restitutionary claim? This explains why in *Pavey and Matthews Pty Ltd v Paul*[254] the High Court of Australia held that the contract price operated as a ceiling on the restitutionary claim, because in that case the contract was merely unenforceable and not void, so the contract price continued to be relevant.

That the contract price should never be relevant to the assessment of the value of a service, even where the contract was not void, has sometimes been justified on the ground that, when a claim is founded on unjust enrichment, the contractual regime no longer applies. This was the approach adopted by the Court of Appeal of Victoria in *Sopov v Kane Constructions Pty Ltd (No 2)*.[255] Even though that court was persuaded by the argument that the termination of the contract did not mean that the contractual regime ceased to apply completely, the judges felt bound by previous authority to conclude that the claim for a *quantum meruit* is based on a fiction that the contract ceases to exist *ab initio*, so that it cannot limit the *quantum meruit*.[256] But such fictions have no role to play in a modern law of unjust enrichment. Where a contract has been terminated for breach it is certainly the case that the claimant can opt to pursue a claim in unjust enrichment rather than for breach of contract,[257] but it does not follow that the contract necessarily has no part to play in the unjust enrichment claim. It has already been noted that the contract may provide factual evidence of the objective value of the enrichment. Similarly, there is no reason of policy or precedent why the agreed contract price should not limit the claim as a matter of law, save where the contract was null and void, for then there is no contract price to limit the valuation of the benefit. Even then the price which the parties purported to agree may still be considered to be reliable evidence of the value of the benefit. This will depend on why the contract was void. If, for example, the contract was void because of the incapacity of the defendant, the contract price should be treated as unreliable evidence of how the defendant valued the benefit, since the defendant lacked capacity to enter into the contract and so cannot be considered to have consented to any of its terms. Where, however, the contract was void because of the claimant's incapacity, as was the case in *Rover International*, it is much more difficult to justify the failure to treat the contract price as evidence of the defendant's valuation of the benefit, since the defendant had the capacity to enter into the contract and did so voluntarily. Ultimately, whether the contract price is taken into account should depend on how reliable it is as evidence of either the objective value of the benefit or the defendant's valuation of the benefit.

(D) INADEQUATE PERFORMANCE

Where the claimant provides a service to the defendant but it is performed inadequately or late,[258] should this be a matter which is taken into account when valuing the benefit received by the defendant? As a matter of principle the answer should be 'yes', since the defendant should be able subjectively to devalue the benefit which was received. Consequently, if the defendant considers the service to be less valuable because it was poorly performed or was performed late so that the defendant incurred additional expense or liabilities to third parties, this should be taken into account when valuing the service. Of course, if the defendant had freely accepted the service or the enrichment was treated as

---

[254] (1987) 162 CLR 221.
[255] [2009] VSCA 141.   [256] Ibid, [21].   [257] See p 332, below.
[258] As occurred in *British Steel Corporation v Cleveland Bridge and Engineering Co Ltd* [1984] 1 All ER 504. The question of whether a deduction should be made for inadequate performance was not considered because the parties had agreed the reasonable value of the services.

incontrovertibly beneficial, the objective value of the benefit should be adopted. Some judicial support for this approach can be found in the decision of the Court of Appeal in *Crown House Engineering Ltd v Amec Projects Ltd.*[259] Although Bingham LJ said[260] that he was agnostic on the point, he suggested that the courts should have regard to the claimant's acts or omissions in the provision of the service if they depreciated or even eliminated the value of the services to the defendant. This is an entirely appropriate response to the problem, since it is consistent with the fundamental principles concerning the identification and valuation of an enrichment.

---

[259] (1989) 48 BLR 37.

[260] Ibid, 58. Slade LJ, ibid, 54, described this as 'a difficult question' but did not provide any assistance as to how to resolve it.

5

AT THE EXPENSE OF
THE CLAIMANT

1. GENERAL PRINCIPLES

Where the claimant wishes to obtain restitution from the defendant on the ground of unjust enrichment it is not enough simply to show that the defendant has been enriched in circumstances which fall within one of the grounds of restitution; the claimant must also establish that this enrichment was obtained at the claimant's expense. This requires the claimant to establish a connection or nexus between the receipt of an enrichment by the defendant and the claimant's loss, so as to justify the restitutionary claim against the defendant.[1] This essentially requires proof of some form of causative link between the defendant's gain and the claimant's loss,[2] and is justified by the corrective justice principle, by which liability in unjust enrichment is imposed to correct the injustice of the claimant losing a benefit and the defendant gaining it.[3] This requirement is usually easily established, especially where the defendant's enrichment involves money paid by the claimant. For example, if the claimant pays £1,000 directly to the defendant by mistake, it is obvious that the defendant was enriched at the claimant's expense, because the money was obtained directly from the claimant and the defendant's gain mirrors the claimant's loss exactly. There are, however, certain categories of case in which the question whether the benefit was obtained at the claimant's expense is much more difficult to answer and raises some fundamentally important questions about the ambit of the unjust enrichment principle. The most important questions are, first, whether the benefit obtained by the defendant must have been obtained directly from the claimant or can be obtained indirectly via a third party, and, secondly, whether the benefit gained by the defendant must be reflected exactly by a corresponding loss suffered by the claimant.

---

[1] See *Chase Manhattan NA v Israel British Bank (London) Ltd* [1981] Ch 105, 125 (Goulding J); *Banque Financière de la Cité v Parc (Battersea) Ltd* [1999] 1 AC 221, 237 (Lord Clyde); *Uren v First National Home Finance Ltd* [2005] EWHC 2529 (Ch), [23] (Mann J); *Investment Trust Companies v HMRC* [2012] EWHC 458 (Ch), [2012] STC 1150, [71] (Henderson J). In *Haugesund Kommune v Depfa ACS Bank* [2011] EWCA Civ 33, [2011] 3 All ER 655 Rix LJ recognized, [70], that loss for the purposes of a claim in unjust enrichment does not necessarily equate with loss for the purposes of a claim for breach of contract or in tort.

[2] See generally GJ Virgo, 'Causation and Remoteness in the Law of Restitution' in S Degeling and J Edelman (eds), *Unjust Enrichment in Commercial Law* (Sydney: Lawbook Co, 2008), ch 8.

[3] See p 4, above.

2. DIRECT AND INDIRECT ENRICHMENT

(A) DIRECT ENRICHMENT

If the requirement that an enrichment was obtained at the expense of the claimant is interpreted strictly, the claimant can only establish that the defendant has been unjustly enriched where the defendant has obtained a benefit directly from the claimant.[4] It follows that, where the defendant obtains a benefit indirectly via a third party, the defendant will not have been enriched at the claimant's expense. So, for example, if the claimant pays £1,000 to X intending that X will pay that money to Y, but the money is mistakenly paid by X to the defendant, the defendant would be enriched at the expense of X rather than at the expense of the claimant, even though the defendant's gain is mirrored by an equivalent loss suffered by the claimant.

This strict interpretation of the 'at the claimant's expense' requirement appears to be generally recognized as a fundamental principle of unjust enrichment claims.[5] It follows that the claimant can only bring an unjust enrichment claim against the direct recipient of a benefit, although restitutionary claims founded on other principles might be available against the indirect recipient. This principle of direct enrichment was recognized by Etherton LJ in *MacDonald Dickens and Macklin v Costello*,[6] who held that the defendants, who were directors and shareholders of a company, could not be considered to have been enriched at the claimant's expense where the claimant had provided a service to the company, because the enrichment to the defendant would only have been provided indirectly by the claimant. The principle which prevents the claimant from suing the defendant who has been indirectly enriched can be called the 'rule against leapfrogging'.

The reason for the imposition of this requirement of direct connection between the defendant's gain and the claimant's loss is fundamental to our understanding of the action to reverse the defendant's unjust enrichment. Crucially, where the claimant seeks to obtain restitution for unjust enrichment the action depends on the claimant showing that he or she has a stronger claim to the value received by the defendant than the defendant has to retain that value. But where, for example, the claimant pays money to a third party who pays the same amount to the defendant, the claim for restitution is much weaker. The enrichment obtained by the defendant would then have been obtained directly from the third party, and so the defendant will have been enriched at that party's expense rather than the claimant.[7] Consequently, as a general rule, the claimant will not be able to establish standing to sue the defendant because the defendant's enrichment can be characterized as being too remote from the claimant.

In an important contribution to the understanding of this need for direct connection, Tettenborn has provided a further explanation of why a defendant who has received a benefit from a third party should not generally be required to make restitution to the claimant,[8] namely that the defendant will have lawfully received the benefit from the third party when the benefit was the unencumbered property of that person.[9] It follows that,

---

[4] *Re Byfield* [1982] 1 All ER 249, 256 (Goulding J); *Kleinwort Benson Ltd v Birmingham CC* [1997] QB 380, 394 (Saville LJ), 400 (Morritt LJ); *Armstrong DLW GmbH v Winnington Networks Ltd* [2012] EWHC 10 (Ch), [2013] Ch 156, [97] (Stephen Morris QC).

[5] See, in particular, *The Colonial Bank v The Exchange Bank of Yarmouth, Nova Scotia* (1885) 11 App Cas 84, 85 (Lord Hobhouse).

[6] [2011] EWCA Civ 930, [2012] QB 244, [20].

[7] See P Millett, 'Tracing the Proceeds of Fraud' (1991) 107 LQR 71, 79.

[8] A Tettenborn, 'Lawful Receipt—A Justifying Factor?' (1997) 5 RLR 1. [9] Ibid, 12.

where the defendant has lawfully received a benefit, he or she cannot be considered to be unjustly enriched. The recognition of this principle of lawful receipt is to be welcomed, both because it explains why a requirement of direct connection should generally be recognized and also because it is consistent with a policy of general application in English law, namely that it is important to encourage transactional security by protecting those who are involved in permissible activities.[10] Ultimately, where the defendant has lawfully obtained a benefit from a third party, albeit that it was derived indirectly from the claimant, it is not for the law of restitution to unsettle the defendant's security in the lawful receipt of the benefit. Further, Tettenborn's thesis is consistent with the fundamental principle that, where there is a legal basis for the defendant's receipt, a claim in unjust enrichment will be barred.[11] If no ground of restitution can be established as regards the transfer between third party and defendant, it follows that the defendant will not be unjustly enriched. If such a ground of restitution can be identified, such as where the third party paid the money to the defendant by mistake, the defendant will be unjustly enriched but at the expense of the third party and not the claimant.

Whether the defendant has directly received a benefit from the claimant may require careful analysis of the facts, especially where the enrichment is a non-money benefit. This is illustrated by the facts of *Rowland v Divall*,[12] where the vendor purported to sell a car to the purchaser, when the car actually belonged to a third party. After the purchaser had used the car for a few months, he discovered that the vendor had not been able to transfer title to him and he successfully recovered the purchase price from the vendor. At first sight it seems that the vendor might have had a restitutionary claim against the purchaser, who had clearly benefited from the use of the car, and this benefit appears to have been obtained directly at the vendor's expense, simply because the car had been obtained directly from the vendor. But that is not strictly correct. The benefit had in fact been obtained at the expense of the true owner, since it was the true owner of the car who suffered the real loss through the purchaser's use of the car.

Sometimes the defendant may be considered to have received a non-money benefit directly from the claimant even though the claimant only dealt with a third party. The best example of this is where the claimant has discharged the defendant's liability to a third party by paying off a debt owed by the defendant to that party. As long as this payment was effective to discharge the debt,[13] the defendant can be considered to have been enriched directly at the claimant's expense, even though the defendant had not received any money from the claimant. This is because the relevant enrichment is the discharge of liability rather than the receipt of payment, such that the discharge of the defendant's liability can be considered to be a direct result of the claimant's payment.

The question whether an enrichment was received directly or indirectly at the expense of the claimant when a debt is discharged is particularly well illustrated by the decision of the House of Lords in *Banque Financière de la Cité v Parc (Battersea) Ltd*.[14] The claimant had entered into a refinancing transaction involving the payment of a sum of money to the chief financial officer of a holding company, which was transmitted to a subsidiary of that company to discharge a debt owed by the subsidiary. It was conceded that the discharge of this debt enriched the defendant, another subsidiary of the holding company which was also owed money by the first subsidiary, because the discharge of the first debt meant that the defendant's debt was more likely to be repaid.[15] One of the questions for the House of

---

[10] Ibid, 7.   [11] See Chapter 7, below.   [12] [1923] 2 KB 500. See further p 319, below.

[13] This is discussed at p 235, below.   [14] [1999] 1 AC 221.

[15] The first debt was secured by a first legal charge over the subsidiary's property and the defendant's debt was secured by a second legal charge over the same property. Consequently, the discharge of the first debt meant that the defendant's charge became the first legal charge so that the defendant's position was much more secure.

Lords was whether this enrichment could be considered to have been at the claimant's expense, when the money paid by the claimant had been paid to the chief financial officer rather than to the first subsidiary directly. The reason the transaction had been structured in this way was to avoid the need to report the transaction to the Swiss financial authorities. Consequently, the court was prepared to consider the realities of the case and the role of the financial officer was ignored, so that the benefit obtained by the defendant, namely the reduction of the other subsidiary's liabilities, was considered to have been obtained directly at the claimant's expense.[16]

(B) INDIRECT ENRICHMENT

The requirement of direct connection between the claimant's gain and the defendant's loss has, however, been qualified. Some of these qualifications are clear exceptions to the direct enrichment principle, but others, when analysed carefully, do not qualify that principle but are consistent with it.

(i) Economic Reality

Restricting restitution to a claim against the direct recipient of a benefit has been criticized. For example, Watterson[17] has criticized the language of 'direct transfer' because it has no natural or agreed meaning; he considers it to be a blunt way of constraining unjust enrichment claims and argues that it has doubtful normative foundations. Instead, he argues that the key test should simply be one of 'but for causation', such that the claimant can sue an indirect recipient of an enrichment if it can be shown that, but for the claimant enriching a third party, the defendant would not have been enriched. He modifies this test of causation, however, where two claimants pay a third party who then transfers the payments to the defendant. In such circumstances it is sufficient that the claimants' payments were a sufficient cause rather than needing to be a necessary cause of the payment to the defendant.

This focus on causation alone does, however, cause difficulties. For if A has paid money to B who then pays it to C, in circumstances where A does not have a proprietary claim to the money, B's independent and voluntary decision to pay C might be characterized as a *novus actus* which breaks the chain of causation between A and C. In fact, although the courts have retained the general principle of direct enrichment, they are starting to acknowledge that even an indirect enrichment can be considered to be at the claimant's expense, but something more than but for causation needs to be established to show that B's actions have not breached the chain of causation, which requires focus on the economic reality of the case.[18] This test is clearly influenced by the decision of the House of Lords in *Banque Financière de la Cité v Parc (Battersea) Ltd*,[19] because, even though it was held that the defendant company was directly enriched at the expense of the claimant, the court reached that conclusion specifically with reference to the realities of the case.

---

[16] See also *Filby v Mortgage Express (No 2) Ltd* [2004] EWCA Civ 759, [62] (May LJ).

[17] S Watterson, 'Direct Transfers in the Law of Unjust Enrichment' (2013) CLP 435. See also C Mitchell, 'Liability Chains in Unjust Enrichment' in S Degeling and J Edelman (eds), *Unjust Enrichment in Commercial Law* (Sydney: Lawbook Co, 2008), ch 7.

[18] *Relfo Ltd v Varsani* [2014] EWCA Civ 360, [2015] 1 BCLC 14, [72] (Arden LJ).

[19] [1999] 1 AC 221. See p 106, above.

The significance of examining the economic realities of the case was identified in the very important decision of *Investment Trust Companies v HMRC*,[20] where the Court of Appeal affirmed the analysis of Henderson J,[21] who had recognized that, although there is no rule which automatically excludes unjust enrichment claims against indirect recipients, there is a general requirement of direct connection to which there are limited exceptions. In determining these exceptions the following principles were identified:[22]

(1) There needs to be a close causal connection between the transfer from the claimant and the enrichment of the indirect recipient.

(2) The claimant should be required to exhaust his or her remedies against the direct recipient to avoid any risk of double recovery.

(3) Any conflict with contracts between the parties should be avoided and there should in particular be no leapfrogging over an immediate contractual counterparty so as to undermine the contract. What this means, for example, is that if there is a contractual claim between the claimant and the party who directly transferred the enrichment to the defendant, the law of unjust enrichment should not be used to subvert this contract.[23]

(4) The remedy will be confined to so-called 'disgorgement of undue enrichment' and will not encroach into the territory of compensatory damages.

In the *Investment Trust Companies* case a claim founded on unjust enrichment was recognized even though the defendant had only been indirectly benefited at the expense of the claimant. In that case VAT had been paid directly to the defendant tax authority by the suppliers of fund management services in circumstances where this tax was not due because the supply of the services was exempt from VAT. The full economic burden of the tax had been borne by the customers from whom the value of the tax had been collected by the suppliers. The suppliers had been able to recover from the defendant some of the unlawful tax which had been paid and had passed this on to their customers, but the suppliers had not been able to recover all of the tax which had been paid, partly because of a statutory limitation period of three years, which did not apply to a Common Law claim for restitution. It was held in principle that the customers should be able to recover the remaining tax from the defendant, even though the defendant had only been indirectly enriched at their expense. Crucially, the Court of Appeal considered that there was a sufficient causal connection between the payment of money by the customers and the receipt of VAT by the defendant, even though the tax liability was that of the suppliers of the services and the liability of the customers was a contractual one between them and the suppliers. But Henderson J and the Court of Appeal emphasized the economic rather than the legal realities of the transactions, since, in reality, VAT was a tax on the consumer of the services, collected by the supplier and accounted for by them to the tax authority. Consequently, the nexus between the customers and the tax authority was considered to be close and strong, albeit indirect and, in economic terms, the unlawful tax was indubitably paid at the expense of the customers.

This is an important decision which undoubtedly modifies the strict requirement of there being a direct connection between the claimant's loss and the defendant's gain, although that principle is still affirmed as the norm. The exceptions to it are founded on

---

[20] [2015] EWCA Civ 82.   [21] [2012] EWHC 458 (Ch), [2012] STC 1150, [67].
[22] Ibid, [68].
[23] See *MacDonald Dickens and Macklin v Costello* [2011] EWCA Civ 930, [2012] QB 244, [20] (Etherton LJ). See further p 142, below.

the need to establish a connection between the claimant's loss and the defendant's gain with reference to the economic realities of the transactions, even though a strict causal connection cannot be established.[24] This was recognized by the Court of Appeal, which noted that the suppliers' duty to account for the VAT operated regardless of whether the VAT was contractually due as between the customers and the suppliers. On the facts of the *Investment Trust Companies* case the recognition that the tax authority was enriched at the expense of the customers appears correct, because the tax authority had undoubtedly been unjustly enriched at the direct expense of the suppliers, but, for a technical statutory reason, the suppliers could not obtain full restitution. By recognizing an exceptional principle of indirect connection, the customers' claims for restitution of tax were not avoided on a technicality, especially because the tax authority should not have received the tax in the first place and restitution was required by EU law.[25] A remaining concern, however, is that this might be the thin end of the wedge, such that increasingly claimants will be able to seek restitution from indirect recipients. Whilst it is to be hoped that the principles identified by Henderson J, and confirmed by the Court of Appeal, will serve to confine the principle of indirect connection to the most exceptional facts, where the economic reality is that the defendant's gain was so closely connected to the claimant's loss that it is acceptable to conclude that the defendant was enriched at the claimant's expense, other cases suggest that the indirect enrichment principle will be interpreted expansively.

This is exemplified by the decision of the Court of Appeal in *Menelaou v Bank of Cyprus plc*,[26] where the defendant was considered to have been indirectly enriched at the expense of a bank, after the bank mistakenly promised to release charges on one property which enabled the defendant to purchase another property. The defendant was considered to have been enriched at the bank's expense because, as a matter of economic reality, there was a transfer of value from the bank to the defendant through the release of the charges, since, had this not occurred, funds would not have become available to enable the defendant to purchase the other property.

Even more significantly, in *Relfo Ltd v Varsani*[27] Arden LJ suggested that the law was moving towards the recognition of some general principle in favour of indirect enrichment, although the other two members of the Court of Appeal were reluctant to recognize such a principle in that case. It was, however, explicitly recognized that one of the exceptions to the direct enrichment rule involves having regard to substance rather than form with reference to the commercial or economic reality of the transactions. So, in that case, it was possible to look behind the corporate structures through which money had been transferred, to identify the commercial or economic reality of the case and conclude that the true nature of the transaction involved a direct payment from the claimant to the defendant, albeit via artificial corporate structures.

It remains unclear, however, what precisely is meant by looking at the economic reality of the case. Possibly this should turn on identifying the intentions of the parties, particularly the claimant and the third party. So, for example, if from the outset it is intended that money which is paid from A to B is to be paid on to C, it is appropriate to treat C as having been enriched at A's expense. This is what happened in *Relfo*, where it was intended from

---

[24] *Investment Trust Companies (in liquidation) v HMRC* [2015] EWCA Civ 82, [69] (Patten LJ).
[25] See p 390, below.
[26] [2013] EWCA Civ 1960, [2014] 1 WLR 854. See also *Hemming (trading as Simply Pleasure Ltd) v The Lord Mayor and Citizens of Westminster* [2013] EWCA Civ 591, [129] (Beatson LJ) and *TFL Management Services Ltd v Lloyds TSB Bank plc* [2013] EWCA Civ 1415, [57] (Floyd LJ).
[27] [2014] EWCA Civ 360.

the start that money would be transferred from the claimant to the defendant via a complex corporate structure. The *Investment Trust Companies* case is more complex, because the money was actually paid by the suppliers to the defendant and might only have been recouped by the suppliers from the customers subsequently by virtue of the contractual arrangements between them. But the contracts between the suppliers and customers provided for the burden of the tax liability to be borne by the customers, so the intention of the suppliers and customers was clear that the loss was to be borne by the customers such that there was a sufficient nexus with the defendant's gain. But if the focus is to be placed on the intention behind the transfer of the enrichment from the claimant, it is clear from the *Investment Trust Companies* case that the intention of the defendant is irrelevant, since the defendant tax authority was not party to the contract. What if the claimant was unaware that the money paid to the third party was intended by both the third party and the defendant to be transferred by the defendant? Should that be sufficient to treat the defendant as enriched at the claimant's expense, with regard to the economic realities of the case? Perhaps in these circumstances the third party's act in paying the defendant should be regarded as sufficient to break the chain of causation, so that the defendant is not enriched at the claimant's expense. It follows that, if the claimant pays money to a third party as the result of fraud of which the claimant was unaware, and the third party transfers that money to the defendant as was intended by them from the start, the defendant should not be considered to be enriched at the claimant's expense. It does not follow that the claimant has no restitutionary claim against the defendant in such circumstances,[28] it is just that there is no claim in unjust enrichment.

(ii) Restitutionary Claims to Vindicate the Claimant's Proprietary Rights

Where the defendant has received property in which the claimant retains a proprietary interest, the claimant will be able to bring a restitutionary claim against the defendant even though the defendant received the benefit indirectly. In fact, most claims involving the vindication of proprietary rights are brought against the indirect recipients of property. This is illustrated by the decision of the House of Lords in *Lipkin Gorman (a firm) v Karpnale Ltd*,[29] where a partner in the claimant firm of solicitors stole money from the firm, which he then used to gamble at the defendant's casino. The restitutionary claim against the defendant succeeded, even though the defendant had not received the benefit directly from the claimant. But this is not an exception to the direct enrichment requirement simply because the restitutionary claim to vindicate property rights should not be considered to be founded on the unjust enrichment principle.[30]

(iii) Restitutionary Claims Founded on Wrongdoing

Where the restitutionary claim is founded on a wrong it is irrelevant that the defendant obtained a benefit indirectly from the claimant, it being sufficient that the enrichment arose from the commission of a wrong by the defendant against the claimant, without there being any need to show that the benefit necessarily represents a loss suffered by the claimant. So, for example, where the defendant owes fiduciary duties to the claimant and receives a bribe from a third party to induce him or her to act in breach of those duties, the claimant can claim disgorgement of this money even though he or she has not suffered any loss.[31] But, again, this is not an exception to the direct enrichment principle simply

---

[28] There might, for example, be a claim grounded on the vindication of property rights. See Chapter 21.
[29] [1991] 2 AC 546.   [30] See p 48, above.
[31] See *FHR European Ventures LLP v Cedar Capital Partners* LLC [2014] UKSC 45, [2015] AC 250.

because restitution in such circumstances is not founded on the reversal of unjust enrichment, but on the wrongdoing itself.[32]

(iv) Agency

Where a benefit is transferred from the claimant to the defendant by the claimant's agent, the claimant will be able to bring a restitutionary claim against the defendant even though he or she is an indirect recipient of the enrichment.[33] This is simply a function of the law of agency, whereby the agent acts on behalf of his or her principal and so the transfer is deemed to have been directly at the claimant's expense. Similarly, where the benefit is received by the defendant's agent directly from the claimant and is then transmitted to the defendant, the claimant can bring a restitutionary claim against the defendant, simply because the benefit received by the defendant's agent with authority to receive it is deemed to have been received by the defendant directly from the claimant.[34] This is a true exception to the direct enrichment principle, since the defendant is considered to have been enriched at the claimant's expense even though the enrichment was received directly from a third party.

The agency exception might have been deployed to recover the indirect enrichment in *Investment Trust Companies v HMRC*.[35] Whilst, strictly, the suppliers were not acting as agents for the tax authorities, since they were statutorily liable in their own right to pay the tax, with the customers being contractually liable to reimburse them, the suppliers were effectively collecting the tax and accounting for it to the tax authorities on behalf of the customers, since it was the supply of services to the customers which triggered the liability to pay and account for the VAT. Henderson J did, however, specifically reject the agency analysis, preferring to examine the economic reality of the case.[36]

(v) Assignment of Right to Restitution

In *Equuscorp Pty Ltd v Haxton*[37] the High Court of Australia held that the right to restitution is assignable where the assignee has a genuine commercial interest in the dispute. Where the right to restitution is properly assigned, the assignee will have a claim for restitution against the defendant even though the defendant will not have been enriched directly at the expense of the assignee.[38] But this is not a true exception to the direct enrichment principle, since the defendant will have been enriched directly at the expense of the assignor, and the effect of the assignment is simply to enable the assignee to stand in the assignor's shoes such that the defendant can be considered to have been enriched directly at the assignee's expense.

(vi) Interceptive Subtraction

In some cases the defendant may be indirectly enriched where a third party purports to transfer a benefit to the claimant which is intercepted by the defendant before the claimant receives it.[39] This will be treated as a benefit obtained at the claimant's expense if, had the

---

[32] See Chapter 19.

[33] *Colonial Bank v Exchange Bank of Yarmouth, Nova Scotia* (1885) 11 App Cas 84, 90 (Lord Hobhouse).

[34] *Jones v Churcher* [2009] EWHC 722 (QB), [2009] 2 Lloyd's Rep 94, [48] (Judge Havelock-Allen QC).

[35] [2012] EWHC 458 (Ch), [2012] STC 1150.

[36] Ibid, [50].   [37] [2012] HCA 7, [2012] 86 ALJR 296.

[38] See *TFL Management Ltd v Lloyds Bank plc* [2013] EWCA 1415, [2014] 1 WLR 2006, p 114, below.

[39] See PBH Birks, *Unjust Enrichment* (2nd edn, Oxford: Oxford University Press, 2005), 75–8. This principle is examined rigorously and critically by LD Smith, 'Three-Party Restitution: A Critique of Birks's Theory of Interceptive Subtraction' (1991) 11 OJLS 481. See also M McInnes, 'Interceptive Subtraction, Unjust Enrichment and Wrongs—A Reply to Professor Birks' (2003) CLJ 697.

defendant not intervened, the benefit would have been received by the claimant. Consequently, the claimant should be able to bring a restitutionary claim against the defendant in respect of the benefit which has been intercepted if the claimant can establish that one of the recognized grounds of restitution is applicable.[40] This principle of interceptive subtraction is founded on there being a sufficient causative link between the claimant's loss and the defendant's gain since, but for the defendant's interception, the claimant would have received the benefit.

The advantage of recognizing the principle of interceptive subtraction is that it avoids multiplying proceedings, as recognized by Nourse J in *Official Custodian for Charities v Mackey (No 2)*,[41] who said that the rationale for restitution in these cases is to avoid circuity of actions, in order to ensure that the person who is ultimately entitled to receive the money can recover it directly. So, rather than the claimant suing the third party for what was due to the claimant, and the third party then suing the defendant to recover the enrichment, the claimant is allowed to sue the defendant directly.

(1) Establishing Interceptive Subtraction

Two conditions must be satisfied before the claimant can establish that the defendant has been indirectly enriched at the claimant's expense by means of the principle of interceptive subtraction.

(a) Inevitability of Receipt

It must first be shown that the benefit received by the defendant would inevitably have come to the claimant had the defendant not intervened, for otherwise it is not possible to conclude that the defendant's enrichment had effectively been subtracted from the claimant so that the claimant suffered a consequential loss. This notion of inevitability of receipt may be interpreted in two separate ways.

(1) Where the third party was under a legal obligation to transfer the benefit to the claimant and this benefit was intercepted by the defendant, the defendant will have been enriched at the claimant's expense simply because, had the defendant not intervened, it would have been inevitable that the claimant would have received the benefit. The third party's obligation to transfer the benefit to the claimant may have arisen by operation of law or by agreement between the parties.

(2) Where the third party was not obliged to transfer the benefit to the claimant but it can be established that, had the defendant not intervened, the benefit would definitely have been received by the claimant, it might also be possible to conclude that the defendant has been enriched at the claimant's expense. This factual test of inevitability was recognized by Birks,[42] although he acknowledged that the claimant bears a heavy onus in establishing the inevitability of receipt in such circumstances.

In fact, the proper interpretation of the notion of inevitable receipt is limited to that of legal inevitability, as was recognized by Nourse J in *Official Custodian for Charities v Mackey (No 2)*:[43]

[A] defendant, intervening without right between the claimant and a third party, renders himself accountable to the claimant for the sum which he receives from the third party. It

---

[40] Ignorance or failure of basis would typically be most appropriate. See Chapters 8 and 13 respectively.
[41] [1985] 1 WLR 1308, 1315.   [42] Birks, *Unjust Enrichment* (2nd edn), 76.
[43] [1985] 1 WLR 1308, 1314.

seems to me that it is of the essence of all [such] cases … that there is a contract or some other current obligation between the third party and the claimant on which the defendant intervenes …

The application of this test of legal inevitability is particularly well illustrated by the *Mackey* case itself. The claimant landlord had forfeited a lease and then sought to recover rent which had mistakenly been paid by sub-tenants to receivers on behalf of the tenant's mortgagee. Since the sub-tenants were liable to pay the claimant mesne profits whilst they occupied the premises after the lease had been forfeited, the claimant sued the receivers in an action for money had and received to recover the money which had been paid to them by the sub-tenants. The claimant's action failed on the ground that it could not be assumed that the mesne profits which the sub-tenants were liable to pay to the claimant were precisely equivalent to the rent which the sub-tenants had paid to the receivers. Although Nourse J did not refer specifically to the principle of subtractive interception, his analysis is consistent with that principle. For the claimant's restitutionary claim to succeed it had to be shown that the money paid by the sub-tenants to the receivers would inevitably have been paid to the claimant had the receivers not intervened. It was not possible to show this, simply because the sub-tenants were not liable to pay rent to the claimant but were only liable to pay mesne profits and, crucially, the sub-tenants were not liable to pay this sum until the claimant had sued for it and judgment had been entered against them.

(b) The Defendant Must Not Have Earned the Benefit

The claimant will not be able to rely on the interceptive subtraction principle if the defendant who received the benefit from the third party had earned it, since in such a case the defendant cannot be considered to have deprived the claimant of the benefit but will instead have received it in his or her own right. This is illustrated by *Boyter v Dodsworth*.[44] The claimant had been appointed to the office of Sexton of Salisbury Cathedral for life. He did not receive any regular fees for this office, but it was usual for him to be paid by visitors for whom he gave a tour of the Cathedral. The defendant usurped the claimant's office and was paid by visitors for guided tours. The claimant then brought an action for money had and received to recover these fees. This claim failed on the ground that the money paid to the defendant had taken the form of gratuities for the services that he had provided and which the visitors were not obliged to pay to him. The money paid to the defendant had therefore been paid as a result of the work which he had done and it could not be shown that the claimant would necessarily have received this money if he had shown visitors round the Cathedral.

(2) Application of the Principle

The principle of interceptive subtraction has been applied in a number of different contexts. In each one the ground of restitution may be a matter of some controversy, although typically restitution can be justified on the ground of ignorance.[45]

Where the claimant is entitled to receive fees from a third party by virtue of the claimant's office and the defendant has collected this money by usurping that office, the claimant has an action for money and received to recover what had been paid to the defendant, even though this money was received directly from the third party rather than the claimant. Such an action will succeed, so long as it can be shown that the fees were certain and were annexed

---

[44] (1796) 6 TR 682, 101 ER 770.   [45] See Chapter 8.

to the discharge of duties relating to the office.[46] Clearly, where it is certain that the money received by the defendant would have been received by the claimant had the defendant not intervened, these cases illustrate the principle of interceptive subtraction. That these cases relate to the award of restitutionary remedies is supported by *King v Alston*,[47] where it was recognized that the claimant could recover the money which had actually been paid to the defendant usurper but had no claim against the defendant in respect of any greater sum which the claimant might have earned had the defendant not intervened. In other words, the claimant's claim is confined to the amount which the defendant had gained rather than what the claimant had lost.

The principle of interceptive subtraction can be identified in other contexts as well. So, for example, in *Jacob v Allen*[48] the defendant had acted as administrator of the deceased's estate until the deceased's will was found. Whilst acting as administrator the defendant had received money from the estate. The claimant executor of the estate then sued the defendant in an action for money had and received and successfully recovered this money. Similarly, where a defendant acts as an executor *de son tort* he or she is liable to the rightful representatives of the deceased for what the defendant had received from the estate.[49] In both situations, money which was properly due to the claimant was received by the defendant who was then liable to pay it to the claimant.

(C) INCIDENTAL BENEFITS

Even where the defendant can be considered to have been enriched as a direct result of something done by the claimant, this enrichment might not be considered to be at the claimant's expense where it is characterized as an incidental benefit. A benefit will be characterized as incidental where the claimant was acting primarily out of self-interest to benefit him or herself, but, in doing so, the defendant is also benefited, even though this was not intended by the claimant. It has been a matter of some controversy as to whether a restitutionary claim should be defeated where the defendant's benefit is incidental. Birks argued that such a bar should be recognized to deal with the following hypothetical problem.[50] A spends money heating his ground floor flat and the heat rises, incidentally benefiting B in the flat above, so that B does not need to turn on her own heating. Birks correctly concluded that A will not be able to claim restitution from B in such circumstances, but the reason is that there is no obvious ground of restitution on which A can rely,[51] rather than artificially concluding, as Birks did, that B's incidental benefit was a gift from A.

Although there are dicta in some cases which might be consistent with the recognition of the incidental benefit bar in English law,[52] it was expressly rejected by the Court of Appeal in *TFL Management Ltd v Lloyds Bank plc*.[53] In that case a company had spent £550,000 on legal fees in a claim to recover a debt. The claim failed, but the Court of

---

[46] *Boyter v Dodsworth* (1796) 6 TR 682, 683, 101 ER 770, 771 (Lord Kenyon CJ). See also *Arris v Stukley* (1677) 2 Mod 260, 86 ER 1060; *Howard v Wood* (1679) 2 Lev 245; 83 ER 540; and *Jacob v Allen* (1703) 1 Salkeld 27, 91 ER 26.

[47] (1848) 12 QB 971, 116 ER 1134.   [48] (1703) 1 Salkeld 27, 91 ER 26.

[49] *Yardley v Arnold* (1842) Car and M 434, 174 ER 577.

[50] Birks, *Unjust Enrichment* (2nd edn), 158.

[51] The hypothetical problem caused Birks particular problems because he had rejected the need to identify particular grounds of restitution to establish unjust enrichment, it being sufficient that there was no basis for the transfer. See further p 127, below.

[52] See, for example, *Ruabon Steamship Company Ltd v London Assurance Company Ltd* [1900] AC 6, 12 (Lord Halsbury LC).

[53] [2013] EWCA 1415, [2014] 1 WLR 2006.

Appeal held that the debt was actually owed to the defendant. Subsequently, the defendant entered into a settlement with the debtor, relying on this judgment. The company's rights having been assigned to the claimant, it sued the defendant in unjust enrichment on the ground that the company had incurred legal costs which conferred a valuable benefit on the defendant as a result of the company's mistaken belief that the money was owed to it rather than to the defendant. Although the issue for the Court of Appeal in the *TFL Management* case was whether the claim for restitution had any prospect of success on the assumption that the facts as pleaded could be proved, the Court held that the fact the benefit to the defendant was incidental did not necessarily defeat the claim. The court held that it was not compelled to recognize the incidental benefit bar as a matter of authority, and, because there was no clear conceptual basis for denying restitution where the claimant had acted selfishly, the court refused to recognize the bar. But the court did emphasize that, where the benefit obtained by the defendant was incidental, there is likely to be difficulty in establishing the components of the unjust enrichment formula. So, for example, on the facts of the *TFL Management* case, it would be difficult to establish that the defendant had been enriched. Whilst the defendant had been able to enter into a settlement with the debtor, all the judgment obtained by the company had done was to procure a declaration that the defendant had a right to be paid the debt. That right was not created by the declaration; it existed already. The only possible enrichment was what the defendant had saved in legal expenses in not having to bring the claim in the first place. But, even if the defendant had commenced proceedings, it would presumably have been able to recover its costs from the debtor. The majority concluded that the defendant might have been saved other costs following the company's proceedings, but these would be significantly less than the money it received following the settlement. Although this money would not have been obtained directly at the expense of the company, it was considered to be arguable that there was a sufficient causal connection between the company's legal proceedings and anything which the defendant had saved. Finally, the only possible ground of restitution would be that of mistake, but this would also be difficult to establish because the company might be characterized as having taken a risk in commencing litigation.[54] Although it would be difficult for the claimant in such a case to establish a claim in unjust enrichment, the effect of the Court of Appeal's refusal to recognize a limiting principle of incidental benefit means that it is possible, in principle at least, that the claimant will obtain restitution even though he or she had been acting selfishly. That is surely right. If the elements of the unjust enrichment formula can be established, there is then no reason to defeat the claim on the ground that the claimant was acting in his or her own interests rather than specifically to benefit the defendant. But, where the claimant is motivated by self-interest, it will be very difficult to establish the elements of the claim. So, for example, if the claimant has spent money removing a tree from his land which has the incidental benefit of dramatically improving the view from the defendant's land, with a consequent increase in the value of the defendant's property, it should be possible to say that the defendant has been enriched and this was at the claimant's expense, but there is no obvious ground of restitution to make the enrichment unjust.

(D) CONSEQUENTIAL BENEFITS

Analysing the 'at the claimant's expense' requirement as embodying a test of causation provides a ready solution to the difficult problem of whether a defendant who has been

---

[54] See p 177, below.

unjustly enriched is also liable for benefits resulting from the receipt of the original benefit from the claimant. If, for example, the claimant pays the defendant £100 by mistake and the defendant spends that money on National Lottery tickets, one of which wins the £10 million jackpot, is the claimant confined to a claim to recover £100, or is it possible to recover the £10 million as being a gain made at the claimant's expense?[55] If the claimant can establish a proprietary claim to the money paid by mistake, it might be possible to claim the jackpot.[56] But, as regards a claim in unjust enrichment, the defendant's decision to purchase the National Lottery tickets should be considered to be a voluntary decision which breaks the chain of causation, such that the jackpot cannot be considered to be obtained at the expense of the claimant. In other words, purchasing the tickets is a distinct transaction which breaks the chain of causation, even if it can be shown that, had the defendant not received the money paid by mistake, she would not have purchased the tickets. This is another reason why reliance on a 'but for' test of causation is not by itself sufficient to explain when a benefit is properly treated as being obtained at the expense of the claimant.[57]

3. CORRESPONDENCE OF GAIN AND LOSS

(A) THE CORRESPONDENCE PRINCIPLE

The requirement that the defendant's enrichment must have been received at the claimant's expense serves to show that the defendant's gain is reflected by a loss suffered by the claimant.[58] But it is a matter of particular controversy as to whether it is necessary to show an exact correspondence between the claimant's gain and the defendant's loss. On one view[59] it is not necessary to show an exact correspondence, because the function of the requirement that the benefit was obtained at the claimant's expense is simply to show that there is a causal link between the claimant's loss of an enrichment and the defendant's gain. Once this causal link has been established it is no longer necessary to consider the 'at the claimant's expense' requirement, since the law of restitution is only concerned with the identification and valuation of the benefit which was received by the defendant and is not concerned with compensating the claimant's loss. It follows that, if the defendant's gain is greater than the claimant's loss, the claimant can still recover the full amount of the defendant's gain. This was expressly recognized by Lord Hope in *Sempra Metals Ltd v IRC*,[60] who emphasized that the defendant in that case had to give back the whole of the benefit it had received from the claimant without regard to the extent of the claimant's loss, and that the process was 'one of subtraction, not compensation'.

The alternative view is that the claimant's restitutionary claim is limited by the need to show an exact correspondence of gain and loss.[61] The justification for this interpretation

---

[55] If the correspondence principle is recognized, whereby the defendant's gain is capped by the claimant's loss, the claimant will anyway be limited to claiming the money paid. See below.

[56] See Chapter 21.   [57] See further p 107, above.

[58] See *Chase Manhattan NA v Israel British Bank (London) Ltd* [1981] Ch 105, 125 (Goulding J) and *Banque Financière de la Cité v Parc (Battersea) Ltd* [1999] 1 AC 221, 237 (Lord Clyde).

[59] See Birks, *Unjust Enrichment* (2nd edn), 78–86; M Rush, *The Defence of Passing On* (Oxford: Hart Publishing, 2006), 172.

[60] [2007] UKHL 34, [2008] 1 AC 561, [31].

[61] See LD Smith, 'Restitution: The Heart of Corrective Justice' (2001) 79 Texas LR 2115; McInnes, 'Interceptive Subtraction, Unjust Enrichment and Wrongs—A Reply to Professor Birks', 708; RB Grantham and CEF Rickett, 'Disgorgement for Unjust Enrichment?' (2003) CLJ 159; A Simester, 'Correcting Unjust Enrichment' (2010) OJLS 579, 594. See also Lord Wright, '*Sinclair v Brougham*' (1938) 6 CLJ 305, 306. See also *Relfo Ltd v Varsani* [2014] EWCA Civ 360, [2015] 1 BCLC 14, [98] (Arden LJ).

of the 'at the claimant's expense' requirement is founded on the notion of corrective justice which underpins the unjust enrichment principle.[62] The significance of corrective justice is that the defendant is liable to make restitution to the claimant, without proof of fault, because the gain obtained by the defendant is reflected by a loss suffered by the claimant. The function of the law of unjust enrichment is not the giving up of enrichment but the reversal of transactions.[63] For some commentators on the law of unjust enrichment the validity of this correspondence principle is highly significant because of the wide definition they give to unjust enrichment, particularly encompassing proprietary claims. The correspondence principle is, however, much less significant for the law of unjust enrichment as interpreted in this book. It is not necessary to consider how the correspondence principle affects claims to recover property and substitute property, because such issues are covered by the vindication of property rights principle, which does not require the claimant to establish that the defendant was unjustly enriched at the claimant's expense.[64] Similarly, it is not relevant to claims for restitution for wrongs, since such claims are founded on the commission of the wrong and not unjust enrichment. Even as regards the unjust enrichment principle as interpreted in this book the correspondence principle is not particularly important. Most unjust enrichment claims involve the receipt of money from the claimant. In such cases the benefit gained by the defendant will usually correspond precisely with the loss suffered by the claimant. Similarly, where the enrichment is goods, the claimant's objective loss will usually correspond precisely with the defendant's gain. Recognition of the correspondence principle may, however, be significant where the defendant has received services which are worth more to the defendant than the loss suffered by the claimant. Even here the correspondence principle is much less likely to be relevant following the decision of the Supreme Court in *Benedetti v Sawiris*,[65] which has expanded the scope of objective valuation of services by reference to the market value of the service, including particular circumstances of the defendant which would be taken into account by the market, so that the objective value of the claimant's loss is much more likely to correspond precisely with the objective value of the defendant's gain. If the defendant is able to devalue subjectively the service, so that it is valued less than the claimant's loss, whether or not the correspondence principle is recognized will make no difference because the defendant's liability will inevitably be capped by the value of the enrichment on either approach. If the principle of subjective over-valuation was recognized, such that the defendant's gain was greater than the claimant's loss, then whether the correspondence principle was recognized would matter, because the effect of that principle would be to cap the defendant's gain at the value of the claimant's loss. The Supreme Court in *Benedetti v Sawiris*, however, refused to recognize the subjective over-valuation principle, so this problem cannot arise.[66]

There may, however, be certain very exceptional circumstances where the objective value of the defendant's enrichment might be greater than the claimant's loss. For example, if the claimant mistakenly transfers a vase to the defendant worth £10,000, and the defendant already owns that vase's identical twin, such that the value of having both vases is £30,000, the claimant's loss would be £10,000 but the defendant's gain would be £20,000, consisting of the value of the second vase and the marriage value arising from possessing the pair. In such circumstances, should the defendant be required to make restitution of the gain of £20,000 or should this be capped at the claimant's loss of £10,000?

---

[62] See p 4, above.
[63] C Mitchell, 'The New Birksian Approach to Unjust Enrichment' [2004] RLR 265, 267.
[64] See further Chapter 21.   [65] [2013] UKSC 50, [2014] AC 938. See Chapter 4.
[66] See p 98, above.

This requires a decision to be made as to whether the correspondence principle should be recognized. The preferable view is that the restitutionary remedy should indeed be capped by the claimant's loss, by virtue of the recognition of the principle of corrective justice. That principle justifies the award of a restitutionary remedy to correct the injustice arising from the defendant's unjust gain being at the claimant's expense. But this injustice can be corrected simply by requiring the defendant to ensure that the loss suffered by the claimant is removed. It is not necessary for any additional gain obtained by the defendant to be transferred to the claimant, since this would over-correct any injustice.

Despite the logic of the use of the corrective justice principle to justify the recognition of the correspondence principle in the law of unjust enrichment, there have been some indications in the cases that the defendant should be required to give up all gains even though this exceeds the loss suffered by the claimant. So, for example, where the defendant's enrichment involves benefiting from the use value of the money paid by the claimant, the defendant's objective gain might be greater than the claimant's loss, particularly having regard to the defendant's particular circumstances which would mean that it would cost more for the defendant to borrow an equivalent amount of money than the claimant, meaning that the defendant's gain from the use of the money would be greater than the claimant's loss in not having the use of the money.[67] It has been recognized that in such circumstances the claimant can still recover the value of the defendant's benefit, contrary to the correspondence principle.[68] But, even in this context, where the value of the defendant's gain is greater than the value of the claimant's loss, the restitutionary remedy should be capped by the claimant's loss.

(B) THE DEFENCE OF PASSING ON

If the correspondence principle is recognized it might be considered to follow that, where the claimant has paid money to the defendant but the claimant has passed this loss on to a third party, for example by increasing the purchase price of goods, the reduction in the claimant's loss should operate to reduce the defendant's liability to make restitution. However, English law does not generally recognize a defence of passing on,[69] although in *Marks and Spencer plc v Commissioners of Customs and Excise*[70] Lord Walker of Westingthorpe recognized that it is a possible defence to any restitutionary claim. This was, however, *obiter* and anyway questionable because his Lordship cited *Roxborough v Rothmans of Pall Mall Australia Ltd*[71] in support of this conclusion, even though that decision expressly rejected the passing on defence in Australia.

The rejection of the passing on defence might be considered to undermine the correspondence principle, since it suggests that the law of unjust enrichment is not concerned with the loss suffered by the claimant. But the rejection of the passing on defence is not necessarily incompatible with the correspondence principle, since the rejection of the defence simply means that the law of unjust enrichment is not concerned with whether the claimant's loss continues after the defendant has been enriched, but simply whether the

---

[67] See p 66, above.

[68] *Littlewoods Retail Ltd v HMRC* [2010] EWHC 1071 (Ch), [2010] STC 2072, [145]–[147] (Vos J). See also *Sempra Metals Ltd v IRC* [2007] UKHL 34, [2008] 1 AC 561, [31] (Lord Hope).

[69] *Kleinwort Benson Ltd v Birmingham CC* [1997] QB 380. Australia has also rejected the passing on defence: *Roxborough v Rothmans of Pall Mall Australia Ltd* (2002) 76 ALJR 203; as has Canada: *Kingstreet Investments Ltd v New Brunswick (Finance)* [2007] 1 SCR 3. See Chapter 26. The passing on defence is, however, recognized in EU law where the claimant seeks to recover taxes paid in breach of EU law. See p 411, below.

[70] [2005] UKHL 53, [2005] STC 1254, [25].   [71] (2002) 76 ALJR 203.

claimant suffered an initial loss which corresponds with the defendant's gain at the time when the unjust enrichment claim crystallized.[72] In other words, it is only necessary to show that the defendant's gain is causatively linked to a loss suffered by the claimant. The fact that the claimant's loss is subsequently reduced or dissipated does not affect whether the defendant's gain can be considered to have been obtained at the claimant's expense, because reduction or removal of the loss suffered by the claimant after the defendant has been enriched is not causatively linked to the defendant's enrichment.[73] It arises from a distinct transaction, a *novus actus interveniens*, between the claimant and a third party, and is not directly linked to the defendant's receipt of the enrichment.[74]

[72] See also the defence of change of position which is concerned with changes in the defendant's position following receipt of the enrichment. See Chapter 25.

[73] Or it may simply be described as too remote. See M McInnes, 'At the Plaintiff's Expense—Quantifying Restitutionary Relief' (1998) 57 CLJ 472, 479.

[74] Other reasons have been given for not recognizing the defence of passing on, notably that it is virtually impossible to show that the transaction with a third party will have involved the passing on of a loss from the claimant to the third party. See *Amministrazione delle Finanze dello Stato v SpA San Giorgio* [1983] ECR 3595, 3629. See also R Stevens, 'Three Enrichment Issues' in AS Burrows and Lord Rodger of Earlsferry (eds), *Mapping the Law* (Oxford: Oxford University Press, 2006), 53; Rush, *The Defence of Passing On.*

6

PRINCIPLES UNDERLYING THE RECOGNITION OF THE GROUNDS OF RESTITUTION

The orthodox analysis of the law of unjust enrichment is that, once it has been established that the defendant has been enriched at the expense of the claimant, the defendant is only liable to make restitution if the receipt of the enrichment can be considered to be unjust. This is not simply an opportunity for judges to exercise their discretion to determine what justice requires. Rather, specific grounds of restitution have been recognized within which the claim must fall.[1] The recognition of these so-called 'unjust factors'[2] provides what has been described as 'a principled ground for granting a restitutionary remedy'.[3] It is vital to be aware of what the grounds of restitution are and also why they have been recognized. Although the particular grounds of restitution are now generally well established, the reason for their recognition remains controversial, especially following Birks' radical reconsideration of the unjust enrichment claim.[4]

The nature of the grounds of restitution was usefully identified by Lord Toulson in *Barnes v Eastenders Cash and Carry plc*.[5] He recognized that they are a 'generalisation of all the factors which the law recognizes as calling for restitution'[6] and emphasized that the reasons why the defendant's enrichment will be characterized as unjust varies between different sets of cases. It follows, he said, that the law of unjust enrichment is more like the law of torts, where a variety of reasons are recognized why the defendant is liable to compensate the claimant for harm suffered, rather than the law of contract, which is embodied by a single principle, namely that 'expectations engendered by binding promises must be fulfilled'.

The main grounds of restitution were recognized by Lord Mansfield in *Moses v Macferlan*:[7]

> [This action of money had and received] lies for money paid by mistake; or upon a consideration which happens to fail; or for money got through imposition, (express or implied) or extortion; or oppression; or an undue advantage taken of the plaintiff's situation, contrary to laws made for the protection of persons under those circumstances.

---

[1] *Rowe v Vale of White Horse DC* [2003] EWHC 388 (Admin), [2003] 1 Lloyd's Rep 418, 422 (Lightman J).

[2] *Banque Financière de la Cité v Parc (Battersea) Ltd* [1999] 1 AC 221, 227 (Lord Steyn); *Kleinwort Benson Ltd v Lincoln CC* [1999] 2 AC 349, 363 (Lord Browne-Wilkinson), 386 (Lord Goff), 395 (Lord Lloyd), 409 (Lord Hope); *Test Claimants in the FII Group Litigation v HMRC* [2012] UKSC 19, [2012] 2 AC 337, [81] (Lord Walker).

[3] *Banque Financière de la Cité v Parc (Battersea) Ltd* [1999] 1 AC 221, 227 (Lord Steyn).

[4] See p 127, below.   [5] [2014] UKSC 26, [2015] AC 1, [102].

[6] Referring to the judgment of Campbell J in *Wasada Pty Ltd v State Rail Authority of New South Wales (No 2)* [2003] NSWSC 987, [16].   [7] (1760) 2 Burr 1005, 1012; 97 ER 676, 681.

This list proved highly significant to the subsequent rationalization of the law by jurists, notably William Evans in 1801.[8] These are still the main grounds of restitution for purposes of establishing liability for unjust enrichment. But why have these grounds of restitution been recognized? The answer is that the receipt of a benefit by the defendant in the circumstances recognized by Lord Mansfield can be considered to be unjust. According to the orthodox view of the law of unjust enrichment, originally advocated by Birks,[9] this notion of injustice derives from three different principles, which can usefully be summarized as claimant-oriented, defendant-oriented, and policy-oriented. Every ground of restitution can be explained by reference to at least one of these principles.

1. CLAIMANT-ORIENTED GROUNDS OF RESTITUTION

Most of the grounds of restitution are claimant-oriented in the sense that, to determine whether the receipt of a benefit by the defendant can be considered to be unjust, it is necessary to consider the circumstances from the perspective of the claimant. Usually, what this means is that a ground of restitution will only be applicable where the circumstances of the transfer are such that the claimant's intention to transfer the benefit to the defendant can be considered to be absent, vitiated, or qualified. Where the claimant's intention has been affected in some way, he or she cannot be considered to have voluntarily transferred a benefit to the defendant and so the defendant's enrichment can be considered to be unjust.

(A) ABSENCE OF INTENTION

The simplest grounds of restitution to explain are those where the defendant received a benefit in circumstances in which the claimant had no intention that the defendant should receive it. This absence of intention may arise as a matter of fact, as where the benefit was stolen from the claimant without his or her knowledge,[10] or it may arise as a matter of law, as where the claimant is incapable of forming the necessary intention because of incapacity.[11]

(B) VITIATED INTENTION

The best example of a ground of restitution which operates where the claimant's intention can be considered to be vitiated is mistake. Where the claimant transfers a benefit to the defendant as a result of an operative mistake, the claimant's intention to transfer the benefit is considered to have been vitiated by virtue of the mistake.[12] Similarly, where the claimant is compelled to transfer a benefit to the defendant, the claimant is not able to exercise a free choice by virtue of the compulsion, and so again his or her intention to transfer the benefit will be considered to have been vitiated.[13]

(C) QUALIFIED INTENTION

Where the claimant has transferred a benefit to the defendant on the basis that a condition will be satisfied, such as the receipt of a benefit in return, the claimant's intention that the

---

[8] W Evans, 'An Essay on the Action for Money Had and Received' [1998] RLR 1.
[9] See PBH Birks, 'No Consideration: Restitution after Void Contracts' (1993) 23 Univ WALR 195, 206.
[10] See Chapter 8. [11] See Chapter 14. [12] See Chapter 9. [13] See Chapter 10.

defendant should receive the benefit has been qualified. Consequently, if the condition fails, the claimant's intention can be considered to have been negated by the failure and this will constitute the ground of restitution, which is called total failure of basis.[14]

The crucial distinction between vitiated intention and qualified intention is that the claimant's intention can only be vitiated by the circumstances which exist when the defendant received the benefit, whereas, where the claimant's intention is qualified, the question of whether a ground of restitution can be established arises after the receipt of the benefit by the defendant.

2. DEFENDANT-ORIENTED GROUNDS OF RESTITUTION

Grounds of restitution can be considered to be defendant-oriented if it is necessary to consider the defendant's conduct or intention when considering whether the defendant received a benefit in circumstances of injustice.

(A) EXPLOITATION

The best examples of defendant-oriented grounds of restitution are those which are founded on the principle of exploitation, such as undue influence and unconscionable conduct.[15] Whether these grounds of restitution are defendant-oriented has proved to be a particularly controversial matter, since it has sometimes been suggested that, where the defendant has exploited the claimant, the claimant's intention to benefit the defendant can be considered to be vitiated.[16] The better view is that these grounds of restitution are both claimant- and defendant-oriented, because the effect of the exploitation is to vitiate the claimant's intention, but this requires proof that the defendant had actually exploited the claimant's weaker position or can be presumed to have done so. The same is also true of those grounds of restitution which are founded on compulsion, which require proof that the defendant compelled the claimant to transfer a benefit.

(B) FREE ACCEPTANCE

It has sometimes been suggested that there is another ground of restitution which can only be characterized as defendant-oriented, namely free acceptance or, a more accurate description, unconscionable receipt.[17] Such a ground of restitution would be established where the defendant accepted a benefit, knowing that the claimant expected to be paid for it and in circumstances where the defendant had an opportunity to reject it.[18] Whether such a ground of restitution should be recognized is a highly contentious matter, particularly because, if it exists, its characteristics are very different from the majority of the other grounds of restitution, since it is wholly defendant-oriented and depends upon proof of fault, namely that the defendant had acted unconscionably. In *Rowe v Vale of White Horse DC*,[19] however, Lightman J specifically recognized that free acceptance was a ground of

---

[14] See Chapter 13.   [15] See Chapter 11.   [16] See p 259, below.

[17] See, for example, PBH Birks, *An Introduction to the Law of Restitution* (rev edn, Oxford: Clarendon Press, 1989), ch 8; C Mitchell, P Mitchell, and S Watterson (eds), *Goff and Jones: The Law of Unjust Enrichment* (8th edn, London: Sweet and Maxwell, 2011), ch 17.

[18] *Rowe v Vale of White Horse DC* [2003] EWHC 388 (Admin), [2003] 1 Lloyd's Rep 418.

[19] Ibid. See p 87, above. Free acceptance was also assumed to be a ground of restitution in *Chief Constable of Greater Manchester Police v Wigan AFC* [2008] EWCA Civ 1449, [2009] 1 WLR 1580.

restitution in its own right, although it was not established on the facts. In that case the council had provided sewerage services for Rowe without charge. Eventually the council sought restitution in respect of the provision of these services on the basis that Rowe had freely accepted them. Lightman J recognized that free acceptance was relevant both to establishing an enrichment and as a ground of restitution. Free acceptance was not, however, established because Rowe had not reasonably expected to pay for the services and had not been given an opportunity to reject them. Consequently he could not be considered to have acted unconscionably. Further, in *Benedetti v Sawiris*[20] Lord Reed referred to free acceptance as a ground of restitution. Whilst he did not endorse its recognition, he did not deny that it could operate as a ground of restitution.

The strongest proponent of free acceptance as a ground of restitution was Birks in some of his earlier writings, but he subsequently tempered his views and recognized that many of the cases which he once argued were explicable by reference to free acceptance are better explained as cases where there was a failure of basis.[21] So, for example, where the defendant has requested the claimant to transfer a benefit to her and the claimant does so on the condition that the defendant would pay for it but she fails to do so, the ground of restitution will be failure of basis because the recognized condition for the transfer of the benefit to the defendant has failed.[22]

Where, however, the claimant transfers a benefit to the defendant in the hope or expectation that the defendant will pay for it, but without any request from the defendant or previous communication between the parties, it will not be possible for the claimant to ground a claim on failure of basis.[23] Consequently, Birks argued that it is in this limited context that there is a role for free acceptance as a ground of restitution. He called this the 'secret acceptance' case. It is characterized by the facts that the defendant had the opportunity to reject the benefit and knew that the claimant expected to be paid for it, but the claimant was not aware that the defendant knew this.[24] The operation of this principle can be illustrated by reference to Birks's notorious example of the window cleaner who cleans the defendant's windows without being requested to do so.[25] If the defendant was in the house at the time, knew that the claimant expected to be paid for cleaning the windows and failed to stop the claimant from continuing with the work, even though the defendant had the opportunity to do so, Birks concluded that the defendant had received the benefit unconscionably and restitution should follow. Unconscionable receipt would only be established in such a case if the defendant believed that the claimant would have stopped cleaning had the defendant said that he or she would not pay for the work,[26] and as long as the defendant had decided at the time of the cleaning that he or she would not pay the claimant.

---

[20] [2013] UKSC 50, [2014] AC 938, [117]. See also *Sharab v Prince Al-Waleed Bin Talal Bin Abdul-Aziz Al-Saud* [2012] EWHC 1798 (Ch), [2012] 2 CLC 612, [68] (Sir William Blackburne) and *Professional Cost Management Group Ltd v Easynet Ltd*, 9 July 2012, [90].

[21] PBH Birks, 'In Defence of Free Acceptance' in AS Burrows (ed), *Essays on the Law of Restitution* (Oxford: Clarendon Press, 1991), 111. See also A Simester, 'Unjust Free Acceptance' [1997] LMCLQ 103, 104. Free acceptance had no part to play in Birks's later scheme of absence of basis, as expounded in his *Unjust Enrichment* (2nd edn, Oxford: Oxford University Press, 2005). See p 127, below.

[22] See Chapter 13; Birks, 'In Defence of Free Acceptance', 111.

[23] The conditions for establishing failure of basis are examined at p 314, below.

[24] Birks, 'In Defence of Free Acceptance', 118.

[25] Birks, *An Introduction to the Law of Restitution*, 265.

[26] Birks, 'In Defence of Free Acceptance', 121. It is for this reason that the defendant who refuses to put money in a busker's hat after listening to the busker's music cannot be regarded as unconscionably receiving a benefit, since the busker would have carried on playing music even if he or she knew that the defendant would not pay.

Two arguments can be identified for rejecting free acceptance as a ground of restitution. First, because the claimant took the risk that the defendant would not pay for the work.[27] It is a fundamental principle of the law of restitution that the claimant who is a risk-taker should not be able to obtain restitutionary relief.[28] Burrows has correctly argued that the claimant's risk-taking cancels out the shabbiness of the defendant's behaviour in unconscionably accepting the benefit. Consequently, there is no injustice in the law of restitution failing to require the defendant to pay for the benefit in such circumstances. This argument is consistent with a number of cases which recognize that a claimant who provides a benefit which has not been requested by the defendant, should not be able to obtain restitution if none of the other recognized grounds of restitution are applicable.[29] Indeed, the failure to establish free acceptance on the facts of *Rowe v Vale of White Horse DC*[30] is consistent with the principle of risk-taking barring the claim. For the council in that case had deliberately decided not to inform the householder that sewerage charges were payable, because the council was unsure whether it was able to demand such payments. This prevented it from relying on the ground of mistake,[31] but also indicates why free acceptance was not available either.

A further criticism of free acceptance as a ground of restitution is that liability will be imposed on the defendant for his or her failure to act, and this is contrary to the general approach of English law which is opposed to imposing liability for omissions, save in the most exceptional and well-defined circumstances where it is possible to conclude that the defendant was under a duty to act.[32] This general rejection of liability for omissions is consistent with the autonomy principle.[33]

It follows that the preferable view, despite the decision in *Rowe v Vale of White Horse DC*[34] and *dicta* in other cases, is that free acceptance should not be recognized as a ground of restitution.[35] Failure of basis and other grounds of restitution should be available in many of the cases where the claimant has provided a non-money benefit to the defendant and, to the extent that the claimant is a risk-taker, the award of restitutionary remedies cannot be justified anyway.

3. POLICY-ORIENTED GROUNDS OF RESTITUTION

Some of the recognized grounds of restitution can be justified on the basis that the defendant's receipt of the enrichment is unjust for reasons of policy. Examples of this type of ground of restitution include necessity[36] and recovery of *ultra vires* payments from public authorities.[37]

This justification for the recognition of grounds of restitution is clearly open to criticism for vagueness. There is a particular danger that all grounds of restitution may ultimately be justified by reference to policy, and this would lead to unjust enrichment being interpreted as a normative principle, since restitution would be justified whenever the

---

[27] AS Burrows, 'Free Acceptance and the Law of Restitution' (1988) 104 LQR 576, 578.

[28] See p 36, above.   [29] See, for example, *Taylor v Laird* (1856) 25 LJ Ex 329, 332 (Pollock CB).

[30] [2003] EWHC 388 (Admin), [2003] 1 Lloyd's Rep 418.   [31] See p 177, below.

[32] See G Mead, 'Free Acceptance: Some Further Considerations' (1989) 105 LQR 460 and Simester, 'Unjust Free Acceptance' [1997] LMCLQ 103, 116–20.

[33] See p 37, above.   [34] [2003] EWHC 388 (Admin), [2003] 1 Lloyd's Rep 418.

[35] In *Wee Chiaw Sek Anna v Ng Li-Ann Genevieve* [2013] SGCA 36 the Singapore Court of Appeal, [108], noted the controversy about recognizing free acceptance as a ground of restitution, because unjust enrichment is considered to be claimant-focused and does not focus on the fault of the defendant.

[36] See Chapter 12.   [37] See Chapter 15.

circumstances of receipt were considered to be unjust. To guard against this argument, it is vital to identify with some precision the policy which is being fulfilled in respect of each ground of restitution which is considered to be policy-oriented. So, for example, necessity constitutes a ground of restitution because of the policy of encouraging people to help those who are in urgent need of assistance. Similarly, recovery of *ultra vires* payments from public authorities is justified because of the constitutional principle that a public authority cannot legitimately receive a benefit unless it is authorized to do so.

4. FOUR ADDITIONAL CONSIDERATIONS

(A) THE DANGER OF OVER-SIMPLIFICATION

Although it is useful to identify the three different rationales for the recognition of grounds of restitution, there is a great danger of over-simplification of analysis,[38] for some of the existing grounds of restitution can be explained by reference to more than one of these principles. So, for example, the ground of undue influence, which applies where the defendant has exploited a relationship of influence between him or her and the claimant, should be treated as both a claimant- and a defendant-oriented ground of restitution.[39] This is because, to establish undue influence, it is necessary to show both that the claimant's intention to transfer a benefit to the defendant can be treated as vitiated and that the defendant's conduct can be considered to be exploitative in some way. Similarly, the necessity principle can be analysed as both claimant- and policy-oriented.[40] It is important that this overlap between the principles is acknowledged, otherwise the principles become artificial straitjackets to the proper analysis of each ground of restitution.

(B) THE GROUNDS OF RESTITUTION ARE NOT CLOSED

In *CTN Cash and Carry Ltd v Gallaher Ltd*[41] Sir Donald Nicholls V-C recognized that the grounds of restitution are not closed. This is exemplified by the explicit judicial creation of two grounds of restitution, namely the recovery of *ultra vires* payments from public authorities[42] and absence of basis.[43] There is nothing to stop new grounds of restitution being recognized in the future, but it is vital that the existence and definition of such grounds can be justified by reference to at least one of the three underlying rationales which justify the recognition of grounds of restitution.

(C) THE RELEVANCE OF THE TYPE OF ENRICHMENT

One issue which has proved to be particularly controversial is whether each ground of restitution should be applicable regardless of the type of enrichment which is involved, or whether certain grounds of restitution are only applicable to particular types of enrichment. This issue has proved to be particularly significant in respect of restitutionary claims which are founded on failure of basis,[44] where traditionally the ground has only been applicable in respect of claims to recover money. The issue is also significant in respect of claims grounded on mistake.

---

[38] See Simester, 'Unjust Free Acceptance', 120. [39] See Chapter 11. [40] See Chapter 12.
[41] [1994] 4 All ER 714, 720. [42] See Chapter 15. [43] See Chapter 13.
[44] Ibid.

Whilst every ground of restitution clearly applies to money claims, there has been some doubt whether every ground of restitution can apply where the claimant seeks restitution of a non-money benefit. This is largely because judicial analysis of restitutionary claims in respect of non-money benefits has been restricted by excessive reliance on the old forms of action. Typically, the decision to award restitutionary remedies is expressed simply in terms of granting a *quantum valebat* for goods or a *quantum meruit* for services.[45] The incantation of these Latin phrases avoids the need for rigorous legal analysis. But it is not acceptable for a principled law of restitution to rely on such an approach. It is vital to identify the ground of restitution involved, since the simple fact that the defendant has received a non-money benefit from the claimant does not in itself provide any reason why the restitutionary claim should or should not succeed.

There is no reason why the application of any of the grounds of restitution should depend on the nature of the enrichment which the defendant has received.[46] In fact, careful analysis of those cases where a *quantum valebat* or *quantum meruit* was awarded suggests that the court could have awarded the claimant a restitutionary remedy by reference to one of the recognized grounds of restitution, such as mistake[47] or failure of basis. Indeed, the House of Lords in *Yeoman's Row v Cobbe*[48] has unequivocally recognized that a restitutionary claim for services can be grounded on failure of basis. There is no reason now to think that the application of any of the grounds of restitution depends on the nature of the enrichment.

(D) RESTITUTION AND THIRD PARTIES

Although the usual case of unjust enrichment will involve the defendant having received a benefit from the claimant in circumstances where the ground of restitution operates between the claimant and the defendant, this is not necessarily the case. Although the defendant must have received the benefit from the claimant, either directly or exceptionally indirectly,[49] the ground of restitution may relate to a third party. It should be irrelevant that the defendant is not tainted by the ground of restitution, so long as the defendant has been enriched at the claimant's expense and the claimant can establish that one of the grounds of restitution is applicable as regards the transfer of the enrichment to the defendant. So, for example, in *Barclays Bank Ltd v WJ Simms, Son and Cooke (Southern) Ltd*[50] the claimant paid money to the defendant in the mistaken belief that it had been authorized to do so by a third party. The claimant was able to recover the money from the defendant on the ground of mistake, even though the mistake related to the authorization by the third party. This principle is also applicable where the grounds of restitution are duress or undue influence. So, where the claimant was compelled or unduly influenced by a third party to transfer a benefit to the defendant, restitution founded on reversing the defendant's unjust enrichment should be available.[51] Similarly, where the claimant transfers a benefit to the defendant which is conditional on the performance of a third party, if this is not forthcoming the claimant will be able to recover from the

---

[45] See p 58, above.

[46] PBH Birks, *Restitution—the Future* (Sydney: The Federation Press, 1992), 87.

[47] See, for example, *Greenwood v Bennett* [1973] QB 195 and *Rover International Ltd v Cannon Film Sales Ltd (No 3)* [1989] 1 WLR 912.

[48] [2008] UKHL 55, [2008] 1 WLR 1752.   [49] See Chapter 5.

[50] [1980] QB 677, see p 171, below.

[51] But, as regards undue influence by a third party, the defendant's liability to make restitution will depend on him or her having notice of the undue influence. See p 269, below. The same is true where the claimant has transferred a benefit to the defendant as the result of a misrepresentation by the third party. See p 199, below.

defendant by virtue of the failure of basis. Where, however, the claimant provides a benefit to the defendant in the expectation of being paid by a third party and such payment is not forthcoming, the claimant will not be able to bring a restitutionary claim against the defendant on the ground of failure of basis, at least where the third party was contractually liable to pay the claimant, because the existence of the contract will defeat any claim against the defendant which is grounded on unjust enrichment.[52]

5. ABSENCE OF BASIS

Although Birks was the main proponent of the principled analysis of particular grounds of restitution, with reference to their being either claimant-, defendant, or policy-oriented, he subsequently advocated a radical reinterpretation of the unjust element of unjust enrichment.[53] He argued that the identification of a specific ground of restitution from a list of recognized grounds was unreliable, cumbersome, and could produce the wrong results.[54] He concluded that it should be rejected in favour of a civilian approach,[55] whereby there should be one single ground of restitution, namely that there was no explanatory basis for the defendant's receipt of an enrichment.[56] If there was no such basis, the receipt should be considered to be unjust. There would be a basis for receipt if, for example, the enrichment was transferred to discharge a contractual or other obligation or was a valid gift.[57]

Whether this absence of basis approach should be adopted in English law remains a matter of controversy. That it does not yet reflect the state of English law is clear, even though Birks considered it to have been accepted implicitly by cases which had recognized that money paid pursuant to void contracts could be recovered simply because the transaction was void.[58] In *Deutsche Morgan Grenfell v IRC*[59] all the judges in the House of Lords analysed the unjust enrichment principle with reference to the need to establish specific grounds of restitution, and none adopted the absence of basis analysis in respect of a claim relating to mistaken payment of tax. Lord Walker did, however, acknowledge the

---

[52] *MacDonald Dickens and Macklin v Costello* [2011] EWCA Civ 930, [2012] QB 244, discussed at p 142, below.

[53] Birks, *Unjust Enrichment* (2nd edn). See especially Chapters 5 and 6. See also T Baloch, 'The Unjust Enrichment Pyramid' (2007) LQR 636.

[54] Birks, *Unjust Enrichment* (2nd edn), 160.

[55] Building on the work of Meier: S Meier, 'Restitution after Executed Void Contracts' in P Birks and F Rose (eds), *Lessons from the Swaps Litigation* (London: Informa Law, 2000), 168; S Meier, 'Unjust Factors and Legal Grounds' in D Johnston and R Zimmermann (eds), *Unjustified Enrichment: Key Issues in Comparative Perspective* (Cambridge: Cambridge University Press, 2002), 37. See also F Zimmermann, 'Unjustified Enrichment: The Modern Civilian Approach' (1995) 15 OJLS 403; S Meier and F Zimmermann, 'Judicial Development of the Law, Error Iuris and the Law of Unjust Enrichment' (1999) 115 LQR 556; J du Plessis, 'Toward a Rational Structure of Liability for Unjustified Enrichment: Thoughts From Two Mixed Jurisdictions' (2005) 122 South African LJ 142; F Giglio, 'A Systematic Approach to "Unjust" and "Unjustified" Enrichment' (2003) 23 OJLS 455; HLE Verhagen, 'Absence of Basis and Unjustified Enrichment in Dutch Law' [2004] RLR 132.

[56] Birks, *Unjust Enrichment* (2nd edn), chs 5 and 6. This approach had been specifically rejected by Lord Goff in *Woolwich Equitable Building Society v IRC* [1993] AC 70, 172. Cf Canada where 'no juristic basis' has been recognized by the Supreme Court: *Pettkus v Becker* [1980] 2 SCR 834; *Peel v Canada* (1993) 98 DLR (4th) 140; *Garland v Consumers' Gas Distributors Inc* [2004] 1 SCR 629; *Pacific National Investments v Victoria* [2004] SCC 75. Note, however, *BMP Global Distribution Inc v Bank of Nova Scotia* [2009] SCC 15 where the Supreme Court of Canada explicitly relied on the ground of mistake to justify the restitutionary claim.

[57] Birks, *Unjust Enrichment* (2nd edn), 104.

[58] See especially *Guinness, Mahon and Co Ltd v Kensington and Chelsea Royal LBC* [1999] QB 215.

[59] [2006] UKHL 49, [2007] 1 AC 558.

persuasiveness of Birks's approach and recognized that it might be appropriate to consider its reception into English law at a future date:[60]

> The recognition of 'no basis' as a single unifying principle would preserve ... the purity of the principle on which unjust enrichment is founded, without in any way removing (as this case illustrates) the need for careful analysis of the content of particular 'unjust factors' such as mistake.

But no decision subsequently has recognized absence of basis instead of the orthodox grounds of restitution. Indeed, in *Test Claimants in the FII Group Litigation v HMRC*[61] Lord Walker, when deciding that a claimant could recover overpaid tax from the Revenue even when this had not been demanded, considered that this would not be a decisive step towards the recognition of the absence of basis principle instead of the traditional grounds of restitution. Lord Sumption[62] in the same case emphasized that English law had still not recognized the principle that liability would be imposed simply because money had been paid which was not due to the defendant.

Even so, it is important to consider whether analysis with reference to absence of basis is preferable to the traditional analysis of specific grounds of restitution.

(A) NO EXPLANATORY BASIS

Birks explored the meaning of 'basis' in some detail. He drew a key distinction[63] between situations where the claimant participated in the transfer of the enrichment and where he or she had no control over the transfer. Where the claimant did participate, two distinct explanatory bases for the transfer might be identified. First, where the claimant transferred the enrichment to discharge an obligation, such as a contractual or other liability, including a court judgment.[64] If the obligation was valid, an explanatory basis for the transfer could be identified. If there was no valid obligation, there would be no explanatory basis for the enrichment. Secondly, where the claimant voluntarily transferred the enrichment to achieve a purpose, such as to make a contract, constitute a trust or as a gift. If this purpose was not fulfilled, there would be an absence of basis for the transfer. So, for example, if the claimant transferred a benefit with a view to make a contract but no contract was made, there would be no explanatory basis for the transfer, although in such circumstances the restitutionary claim would probably be defeated because the claimant was a risk-taker.[65]

Alternatively, where the enrichment has been transferred involuntarily,[66] such as where it has been stolen or the claimant is powerless to prevent the transfer, there would be no explanatory basis for the transfer, save where the defendant had legal authority to acquire the enrichment.

Although Birks described the absence of basis principle as having a 'surgical simplicity',[67] it is neither as simple nor as radical as might first be thought. This is because he accepted that many of the traditional grounds of restitution remain relevant when

---

[60] Ibid, [158] (Lord Walker). Lord Hoffmann also made reference to this absence of basis analysis: [28]. See also Lord Hope in *Sempra Metals Ltd v IRC* [2007] UKHL 34, [2008] 1 AC 561, [25], who did refer to 'no legal ground' as the ground of restitution, although he had earlier accepted that the ground was mistake of law. Lord Mance left the point open: ibid, [192].

[61] [2012] UKSC 19, [2012] 2 AC 337, [81].   [62] Ibid, [162].

[63] Birks, *Unjust Enrichment* (2nd edn), 129.

[64] Ibid, 140. Birks considered that the vast majority of cases would be of this type: ibid, 130.

[65] See p 36, above.   [66] Birks, *Unjust Enrichment* (2nd edn), 154.   [67] Ibid, 160.

identifying whether there is an absence of basis. Birks adopted a pyramidal structure to his analysis of the 'unjust factor' part of the unjust enrichment principle.[68] At the base of the pyramid are the existing grounds of restitution which identify whether the claimant intended the defendant to be enriched,[69] as well as other considerations which identify that the transfer of the enrichment was invalid, such as the invalidity of a contract. Establishing any of these grounds or considerations will determine whether there was an absence of basis for the transfer, which is at the second level of the pyramid, and, once this absence of basis has been identified, it can be concluded that the enrichment was unjust; which is at the top of the pyramid. Birks's shift of focus from positive grounds of restitution to absence of basis remains significant, however, since, once the claimant has established the absence of a basis for the transfer of a benefit to the defendant, the unjust element has been established and the burden would then shift to the defendant to show that there was no valid basis for the transfer.[70] It follows from Birks's thesis that much of the work which is normally done within the law of unjust enrichment would be done outside of it.[71] Often there would need to be a prior determination of whether there was a legal basis for the transfer of the enrichment, within the law of contract or gift for example, and only once it has been decided that there is no such basis would the law of unjust enrichment be engaged.

(B) CRITICISMS OF ABSENCE OF BASIS

In most cases it will not matter whether the unjust enrichment claim is analysed as involving positive grounds of restitution or absence of basis, as reflected by the fact that Birks was able to reach the same result in many of the cases which relied on these specific grounds by resorting to his absence of basis analysis. Indeed, in *Kelly v Solari*,[72] one of the leading cases on restitution for mistake, Parke B adopted a dual analysis. He concluded that insurers, who had mistakenly paid money under an insurance policy which had lapsed, were able to obtain restitution, both because the defendant was not entitled to receive the money and because the insurers' mistaken belief as to the liability to pay meant that they did not intend the defendant to receive the money.

Even so, Birks was adamant that a choice had to be made between the two approaches, both as a matter of principle and also because sometimes different results would be achieved depending on which approach was adopted. It is therefore necessary to decide whether the absence of basis approach is preferable to that which requires the identification of specific grounds of restitution. The preference is most definitely for the latter approach, for a number of reasons.[73]

---

[68] Ibid, 104.   [69] But not 'policy-motivated' grounds of restitution.

[70] This is preferably analysed as a denial rather than as a defence, see p 60, above, because absence of basis would constitute an essential component of the cause of action.

[71] RB Grantham, 'Absence of Juristic Reason in the Supreme Court of Canada' [2005] 13 RLR 102, 105; AS Burrows, 'Absence of Basis: The New Birksian Scheme' in AS Burrows and Lord Rodgers (eds), *Mapping the Law: Essays in Memory of Peter Birks* (Oxford: Oxford University Press, 2006), 36.

[72] (1841) 9 M&W 45, 59; 152 ER 24, 26 (Parke B). See p 165, below.

[73] See also HW Tang, 'Natural Obligations and the Common Law of Unjust Enrichment' (2006) 6 OUCLJ 133; D Sheehan, 'Unjust Factors or Restitution of Transfers *Sine Causa*' (2008) Oxford University Comparative Law Forum 1; GJ Virgo, 'Demolishing the Pyramid—the Presence of Basis and Risk-Taking in the Law of Unjust Enrichment' in A Robertson and HW Tang (eds), *The Goals of Private Law* (Oxford: Hart Publishing, 2009), 477.

(i) State of the Authorities

Birks felt compelled to reconstruct his treatment of the grounds of restitution because he considered that recent decisions of the English courts meant that the absence of basis analysis was the only way of satisfactorily explaining the law. This was primarily because of the tranche of cases which he interpreted as recognizing that money paid pursuant to void interest rate swap transactions could be recovered simply by virtue of the fact that the transaction was void.[74] But absence of basis analysis has never been recognized by the courts and, despite Birks's assertions to the contrary, the swaps cases do not compel its recognition.[75] Indeed, the orthodox approach requiring positive grounds of restitution to be established by the claimant has been specifically affirmed by the courts.[76] Most importantly, this was affirmed by the House of Lords in *Deutsche Morgan Grenfell v IRC*,[77] where the identification of a mistake was vital to the claim for restitution to enable the claimant to benefit from the extended limitation period under the Limitation Act 1980.[78]

(ii) Different Results

There are circumstances where a basis, as defined by Birks, can be identified but restitution is still appropriate. This is illustrated by cases where the claimant has been legally compelled to discharge a debt owed by the defendant and the defendant is liable to make restitution.[79] In such cases the defendant's liability cannot be analysed in terms of absence of basis, because the claimant has discharged a real legal liability owed to the defendant's creditor, so that there was a basis for the transfer, as against the creditor, but restitution is still awarded, as against the defendant debtor.

The emphasis on absence of basis creates other dissonances with the common law by identifying cases where restitution should have been awarded even though it was rejected on the facts. For example, in *CTN Cash and Carry Ltd v Gallaher Ltd*[80] the claimant was unable to obtain restitution from the defendant, which had mistakenly demanded payment and had threatened to withdraw credit facilities in the future if the money was not forthcoming. In such a case the money which the claimant had paid to the defendant was not due to it, but the Court of Appeal held that the claim for restitution failed because the requirements for economic duress could not be established, since it was lawful for the defendant to withdraw credit facilities in respect of future dealings.[81] If absence of basis was recognized, however, restitution should be awarded, simply because there was no basis for the payment to be made. But this raises serious concerns about the extension of the law of unjust enrichment which would undermine the security of transactions, especially in a commercial context.

(iii) Analytical Complexity

A significant problem with Birks's 'absence of basis' thesis is that it suggests something elegant when in fact it is unwieldy.[82] The analogy with a pyramid is misplaced. The better

---

[74] See p 372, below.
[75] R Stevens, 'The New Birksian Approach to Unjust Enrichment' [2004] 12 RLR 260, 271.
[76] See *Kleinwort Benson Ltd v Lincoln CC* [1999] 2 AC 349, 408–9 (Lord Hope); *Rowe v Vale of White Horse DC* [2003] EWHC 388 (Admin), [2003] 1 Lloyd's Rep 418, 422 (Lightman J); *Cressman v Coys of Kensington (Sales) Ltd* [2004] EWCA Civ 47, [2004] 1 WLR 2775; *Uren v First National Home Finance Ltd* [2005] EWHC 2529 (Ch), [17] (Mann J); *Sempra Metals Ltd v IRC* [2007] UKHL 34, [2008] 1 AC 561; *Test Claimants in the FII Group Litigation v HMRC* [2012] UKSC 19, [2012] 2 AC 337.
[77] [2006] UKHL 49, [2007] 1 AC 558.   [78] See further p 403, below.
[79] See p 239, below.   [80] [1994] 4 All ER 714.   [81] Ibid, 717 (Steyn LJ). See p 216, below.
[82] See also Burrows, 'Absence of Basis: The New Birksian Scheme', 45.

analogy is with an iceberg, where nine-tenths of the object is hidden below the surface. This is because focusing on absence of basis alone cannot be sufficient to justify restitution. Where there is a potential basis for a transfer, the grounds of restitution still need to be examined to determine whether the basis was valid. Even as regards the void swaps cases, Birks acknowledged[83] that it would still be necessary to consider whether the claimant was mistaken when paying the money to the local authorities, since this would indicate that the claimant had not willingly taken the risk that the money was not due. But this emphasis on risk-taking, which appears to incorporate aspects of the law concerning the established grounds of restitution, undermines the elegant structure of Birks' approach to absence of basis. For, as regards his analysis of the swaps cases, he asserted that the unjust enrichment claim could be grounded simply on the invalidity of the underlying transaction. Absence of basis is then established at the top of the pyramid, but we need to return to the base of the pyramid to determine risk-taking with express reference to mistake. Now it may be easy to show in such a case that the claimant was not a risk-taker, but it is still a factor which needs to be taken into account. The role of risk within the law of unjust enrichment is significant and difficult, but the absence of basis approach does not make it any easier. For Birks, risk-taking is an implicit part of the absence of basis question,[84] but it can be easily missed. Risk-taking needs to be brought out explicitly as a bar in its own right to unjust enrichment claims.[85]

(iv) Too Much Restitution

The generally restrictive approach to the interpretation of the law of unjust enrichment means that the defendant's receipt of the benefit is secure save in the exceptional cases where the claimant establishes that the defendant's enrichment is unjust. This principle of security of receipt is important to the law of restitution, especially in the commercial field where parties generally need to be certain that benefits have been effectively transferred and will not be upset too readily. It is consequently consistent with the principle of respecting the parties' autonomy, which is particularly important because unjust enrichment liability is strict.[86] A move to an absence of basis approach might destabilize commercial transactions by allowing for too much restitution.[87] Birks recognized this and, for that reason, he considered that identifying an absence of basis only means that a prima facie case for restitution has been established.[88] The emphasis then shifts to the defences. But his analysis of the defences was much wider than the orthodox exposition and much of his analysis was too vague to be commercially acceptable.

(v) Uncertainty as to Basis

A theory where the award of a restitutionary remedy depends on there being no basis for a transfer can only work effectively if the range of bases can be defined clearly and comprehensively. There is, however, a lack of clarity about the range and definition of particular bases. This is particularly exemplified by the difficulty in defining gift, a basis of particular significance to the Birksian scheme. For example, must a gift involve the transfer of property or can it include the provision of services? What is the mental state of the donor to establish a gift? Further evidence of uncertainty about the range of bases derives from the Canadian experience, where there is a 'no juristic basis' test and where there has been a tendency to incorporate factors such as public policy or legitimate

---

[83] Birks, *Unjust Enrichment* (2nd edn), 132.   [84] Ibid, 133.   [85] See p 36, above.
[86] See p 37, above.
[87] See also the analysis of *CTN Cash and Carry Ltd v Gallaher Ltd* [1994] 4 All ER 714, at p 130, above.
[88] Birks, *Unjust Enrichment* (2nd edn), 263.

expectations of the parties to determine whether there was a basis for the receipt of an enrichment.[89] This is too uncertain to provide a workable test of basis.

Consequently, Birks's absence of basis theory should be rejected, since it is not supported by authority, principle or policy. But it certainly does not follow that the notion of absence of basis is alien to the law of unjust enrichment. In fact it forms a very important part of it and has long done so. The preferable view is that, once one of the recognized grounds of restitution has been identified, it is then necessary to determine whether there was a legitimate legal basis for the defendant's receipt of the enrichment, the existence of which will operate to defeat the restitutionary claim. This legal basis principle is considered in the next chapter.

---

[89] *Garland v Consumers' Gas Distributors Inc* [2004] 1 SCR 629; *Pacific National Investments v Victoria* [2004] SCC 75; *Kerr v Baranow; Vanasse v Seguin* [2011] SCC 10, [40] (Cromwell J).

7

LAWFUL BASES

It was concluded in the last chapter that Birks's absence of basis analysis of the unjust element of the unjust enrichment claim should be rejected in favour of the orthodox identification of particular grounds of restitution. Nevertheless, there is much in Birks's theory which makes sense in that, if there is a lawful basis for the defendant's receipt of an enrichment, restitution should be denied because there is no reason why the law of restitution should undermine a lawful transfer. It is consequently preferable to recognize that if there is a legally effective basis for the transfer of a benefit to the defendant a claim in unjust enrichment should be denied. Indeed, this was specifically recognized by Lord Hope in *Kleinwort Benson v Lincoln CC*:[1]

> the payee cannot be said to have been unjustly enriched if he was entitled to receive the sum paid to him. The payer may have been mistaken as to the grounds on which the sum was due to the payee, but his mistake will not provide a ground for its recovery if the payee can show that he was entitled to it on some other ground.

So, for example, where the claimant has transferred a benefit to the defendant pursuant to a valid statutory obligation, such as a valid tax demand, restitution will not lie because there is a legal basis for the defendant's receipt.[2] Where there is a legally effective basis for the receipt of an enrichment by the defendant, this can usefully be called the 'presence of basis' bar. The bar should be treated as functioning as a denial of the unjust enrichment claim rather than a defence, so that the burden is placed on the claimant to prove that there was no lawful basis for the transfer once the bar has been pleaded by the defendant.[3] This is consistent with the analysis of Millett LJ in *Tribe v Tribe*[4] that the claimant bears the burden of proving that the enrichment has not been transferred by way of gift or an enforceable contract. This bar should apply where the defendant's receipt of the enrichment can be considered to be legally effective in some way, in the sense that it has a legal consequence, as will occur, for example, where the transfer has discharged an existing obligation or creates a liability other than the liability to make restitution.

A legally effective basis for a transfer of an enrichment can be identified in a variety of different ways.

1. CONTRACT

Undoubtedly the most significant lawful basis for the transfer of an enrichment arises from contract.[5] If the parties have entered into a valid agreement which is to regulate their

---

[1] [1999] 2 AC 349, 408. See also *Fairfield Sentry Ltd v Migani* [2014] UKPC 9, [18] (Lord Sumption).
[2] *Deutsche Morgan Grenfell v IRC* [2006] UKHL 49, [2007] 1 AC 558, [89] (Lord Scott).
[3] See p 60, above, for the distinction between denials and defences.   [4] [1996] Ch 107, 125.
[5] See RB Grantham and CEF Rickett, 'On the Subsidiarity of Unjust Enrichment' (2001) 117 LQR 273.

relationship it is vital that the law of unjust enrichment does not undermine what they have decided. It is only where the agreement does not operate, or has ceased to operate, that the law of unjust enrichment should have a role to play in any dispute between the parties. Consequently, the law of restitution should be considered to be subsidiary to the law of contract. Contract is relevant to the law of unjust enrichment in a variety of ways.

(A) DISCHARGE OF A CONTRACTUAL OBLIGATION

Where the claimant has provided a benefit to the defendant pursuant to a valid contract, payment for the benefit will be governed by the contract and not the law of unjust enrichment. If that contractual obligation has been discharged by the defendant, there is no scope for a further claim by the provider of the benefit in unjust enrichment. So, for example, in *Benedetti v Sawiris*[6] the claim for restitution for services failed because the defendant had already paid money to a company controlled by the claimant in respect of the claimant's services and pursuant to a contract between the parties. As Lord Reed recognized,[7] if a contract made provision for remuneration in respect of the services which had been provided, and that contract was valid, no question of unjust enrichment could arise. The payment made by the defendant completely discharged the contractual obligation such that there was no role for a residual claim in unjust enrichment.

Similarly, where the claimant owes money to the defendant under a contract and pays the money to discharge the liability, this will constitute a legally effective basis to defeat a claim for restitution of the money. For example, in *Steam Saw Mills Co Ltd v Baring Bros Co Ltd*[8] the claimant paid money due under a contract to agents of a foreign government in ignorance of the fact that a revolution had broken out which subsequently led to the downfall of the government. The money was not recoverable even though the claimant would not have made the payment had it known of the revolution, because 'the money was paid, not under a mistake of fact as to the existence of an obligation; it was paid in pursuance of an obligation which in fact existed',[9] and was effective to discharge that obligation. Where, however, the claimant paid money under a contract to the defendant in ignorance of the fact that the contract had already been repudiated by the other party, it was held that the payment was recoverable because it did not discharge any legal obligation.[10]

In *Wuhan Guoyu Logistics Group Co Ltd v Emporiki Bank*,[11] following a demand for payment in respect of a performance bond, a bank mistakenly made payment. Even though the money was not due, the nature of the performance bond meant that there was a complete and enforceable obligation to pay which arose on the demand for payment being made, such that the claim was indefeasible and it was irrelevant that the demand was made on a mistaken premise. Consequently, the discharge of the valid contractual obligation to pay prevented any recourse to a claim in unjust enrichment, because there was a legally effective basis for the defendant's receipt.

(B) CONTINUING CONTRACTUAL REGIME

Where a benefit is transferred to the defendant pursuant to a contractual obligation, the continued existence of the contract will usually defeat the restitutionary claim.[12] A contract

---

[6] [2013] UKSC 50, [2014] AC 938. See Chapter 4.
[7] *Benedetti v Sawiris* [2013] UKSC 50, [2014] AC 938, [91].   [8] [1922] 1 Ch 244.
[9] Ibid, 254.   [10] *British American Continental Bank v British Bank for Foreign Trade* [1926] 1 KB 328.
[11] [2013] EWCA Civ 1679, [2014] 1 Lloyds Rep 273.
[12] *Guinness plc v Saunders* [1990] 2 AC 663, 697–8 (Lord Goff); *Taylor v Motability Finance Ltd* [2004] EWHC 2619 (Comm), [23] (Cooke J); *Mowlem plc v Stena Line Ports Ltd* [2004] EWHC 2206; *S and W Process*

will therefore constitute a lawful basis, save where it can be shown to be void, has been rescinded or has been discharged for breach.[13] This was recognized by Millett LJ in *Portman Building Society v Hamlyn Taylor Neck*:[14]

> The continuing validity of the transaction under which the money was paid to the firm is, in my judgment, fatal to the society's claim. The obligation to make restitution must flow from the ineffectiveness of the transaction under which the money was paid and not from a mistake or misrepresentation which induced it. It is fundamental that, where money is paid under a legally effective transaction, neither misrepresentation nor mistake vitiates consent or gives rise by itself to an obligation to make restitution.

The contractual obligation to transfer the benefit to the defendant may be express or implied. So, for example, where the claimant has provided services to the defendant whilst negotiating a contract, but before the contract is completed, the courts may be able to imply a genuine contract where there is sufficient evidence to indicate what terms the parties objectively intended to agree.[15] Even where the parties have made an express contract for the provision of services, it may make no provision for remuneration. In such circumstances the law will normally imply a term into the contract that the remuneration will be reasonable in all the circumstances, this being consistent with the intention of the parties objectively ascertained.[16] This has sometimes been called a claim in *quantum meruit*. But, since the focus of the court is on identifying the objective intention of the parties, the claim lies in contract and not in unjust enrichment. The courts have, however, recognized that a contract or a term will only be implied where it is consistent with the parties' intentions. In *Whittle Movers Ltd v Hollywood Express Ltd*[17] Waller LJ emphasized that the court should not strain to find a contract where terms are still under negotiation, because, if a contract cannot be implied, it may still be possible to bring a claim in unjust enrichment. Whilst an implied contract is a useful device to respect the intentions of the parties, even where these have not been clearly expressed, a contract should only be implied where it is clear that the parties did intend the contract to be made or would have intended it to be made had they thought about the matter. If contracts are implied in circumstances beyond this, contract will become a fiction, with consequent uncertainty. It does not follow that implied contracts have no role to play in the law of obligations; clearly they do,[18] but their role must not be abused by artificial extension.

The extent to which it is appropriate to imply a contract between the parties is illustrated by *Empirnall Holdings Pty Ltd v Machon Paull Partners Pty Ltd*,[19] where the claimant architects were engaged in an extensive property development for which the defendant property developer had refused to execute a printed contract. The New South Wales Court of Appeal was able to infer that the defendant had accepted the terms of this

---

Engineering Ltd v Cauldron Foods Ltd [2005] EWHC 153 (TCC); *Berezovsky v Edmiston* [2010] EWHC 1883 (Comm), [2010] CLC 126, [70] (Field J); *Sandher v Pearson* [2013] EWCA Civ 1822. See also *Foran v Wright* (1989) 64 ALJR 1, 13 (Mason CJ).

[13] *Barclays Bank Ltd v W J Simms, Son & Cooke (Southern) Ltd* [1980] QB 677, 695 (Robert Goff J). See also *Brittain v Rossiter* (1879) 11 QBD 123, 127; *Gilbert Partners v Knight* [1968] 2 All ER 248, 250 (Harman LJ); *Pan Ocean Shipping Co Ltd v Creditcorp Ltd* [1994] 1 WLR 161, 164 (Lord Goff).

[14] [1998] 4 All ER 202, 208.

[15] *RTS Flexible Systems Ltd v Molkerai Alois Müller GmbH* [2010] UKSC 14, [2010] 1 WLR 753.

[16] *Benedetti v Sawiris* [2013] UKSC 50, [2014] AC 938, [9] (Lord Clarke).

[17] [2009] EWCA Civ 1189, [15]. See also *Sharab v Prince Al-Waleed Bin Talal Bin Abdul-Aziz Al-Saud* [2012] EWHC 1798 (Ch), [2012] 2 CLC 612, [58] (Sir William Blackburne).

[18] See S Hedley, 'Implied Contract and Restitution' (2004) 63 CLJ 435.

[19] (1988) 14 NSWLR 523.

contract by virtue of its conduct, even though it had not signed the contract. Consequently, the claimants were able to sue on the contract for the value of the benefits which had been provided. The ratio of the case can be found in a dictum of McHugh JA who said:[20]

> Where an offeree with a reasonable opportunity to reject the offer of goods or services takes the benefit of them under circumstances which indicate that they were to be paid for in accordance with the terms of the offer, it is open to the tribunal of fact to hold that the offer was according to its terms.

This case falls just above the threshold of what constitutes an acceptable implication of a contract. But this dictum shows the danger of implied contracts. Since the decision essentially turned upon an analysis of the facts of the case to identify the objective intentions of the parties, there is clearly scope for judges to manipulate the facts to secure what they believe to be the just result. This could easily escalate into the fiction of implying a contract as a matter of law where the justice of the case demands it. This is unacceptably uncertain and should be rejected. The implication of a contract to pay for benefits which have been received should be confined to those exceptional cases where it is possible to conclude that the relationship between the parties really was governed by a contract. Consequently, a contract should not be implied where the facts as found negate the existence of such a contract. For example, if two parties are negotiating a contract and the claimant, encouraged by the defendant, incurs expenditure in preparing to perform the contract, it will not be possible to imply a contractual obligation that the defendant should reimburse the claimant for this expenditure if the parties intended that the reimbursement would be paid for out of the proceeds of the contract. Nevertheless, there may still be scope for the imposition of restitutionary liability.[21]

The principle that a claim in unjust enrichment cannot be established if the contractual regime is considered to subsist is especially well illustrated by *Taylor v Motability Finance Ltd*,[22] where the defendant employer terminated an employment contract with the claimant. The claimant argued that this constituted a repudiatory breach so that a restitutionary remedy could be awarded outside of the contract for the work he had done. This argument was rejected because the claimant had fully performed the contract by providing services to the defendant and so, although the primary obligation to continue to perform had been revoked, the contractual regime subsisted in terms of the secondary obligation to pay damages for breach.[23] Cooke J said:

> Not only is it true to say that, historically, restitution has emerged as a remedy where there is no contract or no effective contract, but there is no room for a remedy outside the terms of the contract where what is done amounts to a breach of it where ordinary contractual remedies can apply and payment of damages is the secondary liability for which the contract provides.[24]

This is consistent with the presence of basis bar, in that the right to payment was considered to have already accrued under the contract before it was terminated. Where, however, a claimant has paid money to the defendant, rather than providing a service, and received nothing in return, Cooke J in *Taylor v Motability Finance* suggested that, once the

---

[20] Ibid, 535.
[21] See *William Lacey (Hounslow) Ltd v Davis* [1957] 1 WLR 932, discussed at p 345, below.
[22] [2004] EWHC 2619 (Comm). Approved in *Howes Percival LLP v Page* [2013] EWHC 4104 (Ch).
[23] See *Johnson v Agnew* [1980] AC 367; *Photo Production Ltd v Securicor Transport Ltd* [1980] AC 827.
[24] *Taylor v Motability Finance Ltd* [2004] EWHC 2619 (Comm), [23].

contract had been terminated, the contractual regime no longer applied and a restitutionary claim for the money would lie.[25] Although this difference of approach depending on whether the enrichment involves money or services is artificial and unconvincing,[26] *Taylor v Motability Finance* does at least recognize that, if the contractual regime subsists, restitution should not be available. This was acknowledged in *Howes Percival LLP v Page*[27] as being particularly significant where a solicitor had entered into a conditional contract, whereby the solicitor would only be paid if the case being pursued on behalf of the defendant was successful. The defendant repudiated the contract with the solicitor, who had already done significant work on the case. In such circumstances, if the solicitor was allowed to bring a claim for the reasonable value of his or her services, this might undermine the purpose of the contract. So, for example, if the defendant stood little chance of winning her case, it would follow that the solicitor would be unlikely to have recovered anything under the contract. This result should not be avoided by bringing a claim for restitution instead. Consequently, it was held in *Howes* that the solicitor would be confined to a claim in damages for breach of contract. If the defendant was unlikely to have won her case, then the loss suffered by the claimant might be assessed as zero. This can be justified on the ground that the conditional contractual regime should be considered to continue to operate after the contract has been breached, thus excluding a claim for restitution.

The analysis of restitutionary claims for the value of services provided under a contract which was adopted in *Taylor Motability Finance* was qualified in *Elek v Bar-Tur*.[28] The trial judge in that case reluctantly recognized that he was bound by authority to find that a claimant, who had provided services pursuant to a contract which had been repudiated following a breach by the defendant, could bring a restitutionary claim to recover the value of the services.[29] But this was considered only to apply where the claimant was unable to complete his or her contractual performance by virtue of the breach, so that the defendant's obligation to pay was not yet due. Where the claimant had fully performed and was entitled to payment under the contract, the claimant could not bring a claim for unjust enrichment, presumably because in such a situation the contractual regime would continue to apply, so the claimant could only sue for breach of the contract. This would be significant where the objective value of the service was greater than the contract price. This advantage would disappear, however, if, as seems likely, the value of the enrichment for purposes of a claim in unjust enrichment was capped by the contract price.[30]

Although it has been recognized that a claimant can bring a restitutionary claim in respect of services provided pursuant to a contract, this has been criticized. In *Sopov v Kane Constructions Pty Ltd (No 2)*[31] the Victorian Court of Appeal in Australia held that, where a building contract had been repudiated by the landowner after building work had been substantially performed, the builder could elect to claim a *quantum meruit* rather than compensatory damages, although the court only reached this decision because the judges felt bound by authority. The judges felt that the arguments in favour of confining

---

[25] Ibid, [25] (Cooke J).   [26] See further p 125, above.   [27] [2013] EWHC 4104 (Ch).
[28] [2013] EWHC 207 (Ch).
[29] *Planché v Colburn* (1831) 5 Car & P 57, 172 ER 876; *De Bernardy v Harding* (1853) 8 Exch 822, 155 ER 1586; *Lodder v Slowey*, [1904] AC 442; *Lusty v Finsbury Securities Ltd* (1991) 58 BLR 66. See further Chapter 13.   [30] See p 99, above.
[31] [2009] VSCA 141.

the claimant to compensatory damages were very powerful.[32] Similarly, in *Elek v Bar-Tur* David Donaldson QC said:[33]

> I regard the rule as conceptually unsound and fertile with unattractive consequences, [but] doctrinal purity and logic does not always win out in the common law, and if it is now to be rejected, that will have to occur at a much higher level in the judicial hierarchy than I occupy...

If, however, focus is placed on whether the contractual regime continues to apply, sense can be made of the law. Where the claimant has transferred a benefit to the defendant, whether it be money, goods, or services, pursuant to a contract which is terminated for breach, the contractual regime as a general rule should no longer be applicable, save where the claimant has fully performed under the contract so that the defendant's contractual counter-performance is then engaged before the contract is repudiated, or where the defendant's counter-performance is intended by the parties to be dependent on the claimant satisfying all relevant conditions which had not been satisfied on the facts.

Sometimes, however, it has been recognized that a claim for restitution can lie despite the continued existence of the contractual regime. If this is adopted generally, it would undermine the lawful basis bar. This problem is especially well illustrated by the decision of the High Court of Australia in *Roxborough v Rothmans of Pall Mall Australia Ltd*,[34] where the defendant was licensed as a wholesaler of tobacco products. The defendant sold those products to the claimant retailers for a price which included a licence fee, which the defendant was required by statute to pay to the State government. The statute which imposed this liability on the defendant was held to be unconstitutional. Had the defendant paid the money it had received to the government, it would have been able to recover it because the statute which authorized the licence fee was declared to be invalid, so there would have been no basis for the payment.[35] But the statute was declared invalid before the defendant had paid the money that it had received from the claimants to the Revenue. So the claimants sought restitution of the money from the defendant and their claim succeeded on the ground that the basis for the payment had failed.[36] The problem with this conclusion was that the licence fee had been paid to the defendant pursuant to a contract for the sale of tobacco which had not been set aside. The significance of this was recognized by Kirby J, who dissented partly because the contract had not been terminated. Most of the majority failed to consider the requirement that the contract must be terminated before restitution could be awarded. Callinan J did consider the point and suggested that restitution could be awarded either where performance of the contract was not possible or, if formal termination of the contract was required, the bringing of proceedings for restitution would be sufficient. But this would contradict the presence of basis bar, for, if payment is made pursuant to a valid contract this should be sufficient to defeat the restitutionary claim. Beatson has argued that there might be exceptional circumstances where restitutionary relief can be awarded even though the contract has not been terminated, but only where this would not subvert the contractual allocation of risk.[37] Even if this is correct, it could not justify the success of the restitutionary claim in *Roxborough* because there was no evidence that the risk of the liability to pay the licence fee being declared invalid had been placed on

---

[32] Ibid, [11].   [33] *Elek v Bar-Tur* [2013] EWHC 207 (Ch), [12].

[34] [2001] HCA 68, (2001) 208 CLR 516.

[35] Whether the claimants could have sued the Revenue would depend on whether the Revenue could be considered to have been indirectly enriched at the claimants' expense. See p 107, above.

[36] See Chapter 13.

[37] J Beatson, 'Restitution and Contract: Non-Cumul?' (2000) 1 Theoretical Inquiries in Law 83.

the defendant rather than the claimants. The only way that the success of the claim to recover the payment of the licence fee can be justified is on the basis that the money paid to the defendant can be apportioned between payment for the tobacco, which remained valid, and payment of the licence fee, which was invalid. Indeed, this notion of apportionment was adopted by the majority to distinguish restitution of the licence fee from restitution of the purchase price for the tobacco products, the basis for which had not failed.[38] This focus on apportionment of the constituent parts of the payment, suggests that it is possible to treat the contract as valid in part, as regards the purchase of the tobacco products, and void in part, as regards the licence fee payment.

In England a similar scenario to that in *Roxborough* arose in *Investment Trust Companies v HMRC*,[39] where customers successfully sought restitution of money which had been paid to the suppliers of services, who had accounted for this amount of money to the Revenue in discharge of their tax liability, the full amount of which was not actually due to the Revenue. The customers were able to recover some of the money paid by the suppliers from the Revenue, even though the customers had paid money to the suppliers as a result of a contractual obligation. Despite this, the Revenue conceded that the contract between the customers and the suppliers should not bar the claim against the Revenue. Had this not been conceded, it would have been possible, following the approach in *Roxborough*, to apportion the payments to the suppliers between the payment for the services which were valid and the tax component which was not.

Such apportionment was also recognized in the difficult decision of the Supreme Court in *Barnes v Eastenders Cash and Carry plc*,[40] but this case illustrates the dangers of ignoring a contract as a bar to an unjust enrichment claim. The case concerned a contractual arrangement between the Crown Prosecution Service (CPS) and the claimant receiver, whereby the CPS arranged for the receiver to manage assets of a company whilst a criminal investigation was being undertaken. The parties expected that the claimant would be remunerated for his services from the assets which he was managing, over which he had a lien. It was specifically agreed that the CPS would not indemnify the claimant if the assets were insufficient to remunerate him. The Supreme Court recognized that the receiver therefore accepted the risk that those assets might be of insufficient value to provide appropriate remuneration. The Supreme Court held, however, that the lien was invalid and that the claimant could not use the assets he was managing to recover his remuneration. But it was also held that the claimant could recover the value of his services from the CPS in an action for unjust enrichment, on the ground that the claimant expected to be paid for the services and had received nothing from them. The difficulty with this conclusion is that there was a contract between the claimant and the CPS and the claimant had accepted the risk that he would not be fully remunerated for his services. The Supreme Court did not deal with this issue explicitly. Rather, *Roxborough* was cited and the principle of what was called 'severance of the consideration' was approved. But it is unclear how that was relevant to the facts of the case, since, whereas in *Roxborough* it was necessary to apportion the money paid between the price of the goods and the licence fee, there was nothing to apportion in *Barnes*, since the claimant had provided services and had received no payment at all. Further, the award of restitution in this case appears to undermine the clear allocation of risk of non-payment, which was borne by the claimant rather than the CPS, as emphasized by the fact that the parties agreed that the CPS would not indemnify the claimant. The essence of the decision of the Supreme Court appears to

---

[38] See further p 321, below.

[39] [2015] EWCA Civ 82. See p 108, above, for analysis of how the enrichment was considered to be at the claimant's expense. [40] [2014] UKSC 26, [2015] AC 1.

be that, where the claimant has provided a service pursuant to a contract and receives no payment for that service, the beneficiary of the service will be liable in unjust enrichment, despite the existence of a contract between them. This is inconsistent with *Taylor v Motability Finance*,[41] and the claim for restitution was much stronger in that case because there had been a breach of contract by the defendant which could be treated as terminating the contractual regime. There was no breach of contract in *Barnes*.

The decision of the Supreme Court in *Barnes* is potentially important, although the judgment lacks any significant engagement with the problems arising from there being a continued contractual relationship. The preferable view remains the strict one that, where a contract continues to operate, and a benefit is transferred to the defendant pursuant to that contract, there is no role for a claim in unjust enrichment. In *Barnes* itself the contract between the parties had not been discharged, so the claimant could only have sought a remedy under the contract. Since the claimant had accepted the risk that he might not be fully remunerated for his services, it is unlikely that a claim for breach of contract could have been brought. In those circumstances it is unacceptable for the contractual allocation of risk to be subverted through the law of unjust enrichment. Further, the reference to the apportionment of payments in *Roxborough*, and acknowledged in *Barnes*, betrays an unacceptable confusion between identifying whether there has been a total failure of basis as a ground of restitution[42] and whether a contractual regime continues to operate. Consequently, even in *Roxborough* restitution should have been denied. The payment of the licence fee was a contractual requirement and recovery of that fee could only occur once the contract had been set aside. The concession of the Revenue in the *Investment Trust Companies* case, that the existence of the contractual obligation to pay the amount of tax to the suppliers, might be treated as justifiable in that that there was no contract as between the claimant and the defendant. But, as we will see,[43] the contractual bar on a claim in unjust enrichment also extends to where there is a contractual obligation between the claimant and a third party to provide a benefit to the defendant. In such circumstances the existence of the contract also defeats the claim in unjust enrichment, suggesting that the concession was incorrectly made.

It is important to emphasize, however, a significant limitation on the bar involving the continued existence of a contract, namely that it should only apply where the benefit which the claimant has transferred to the defendant has been transferred pursuant to a contractual obligation. It follows, for example, that if the claimant has paid more to the defendant than is due under the contract, the claimant can bring a claim for restitution of the excess on the ground of mistake, despite the continued existence of the contract.[44] This is because the excess payment was not transferred pursuant to a contractual obligation. *Roxborough, Investment Trust Companies* and *Barnes* were all different, because in each case the enrichment which was transferred or provided by virtue of the explicit contractual obligation to do so.

There is one further difficulty which the claimant might face in establishing that the contractual regime is no longer operative so that a claim in unjust enrichment is available. Where the claimant has transferred a benefit to the defendant pursuant to an illegal contract,[45] the contract is void so it will not appear to operate as a bar to the restitutionary claim. It has been recognized, however, that if the claimant needs to refer to illegality in his or her pleadings, the claim for restitution will be barred for reasons of public policy,[46] save

---

[41] [2004] EWHC 2619 (Comm). See p 136, above.   [42] See p 321, below.
[43] See p 142, below.   [44] See further p 144, below, concerning discharge of a debt.
[45] See p 716, below, for the definition of illegality.
[46] *Patel v Mirza* [2014] EWCA Civ 1047, [2015] 2 WLR 405, [20] (Rimer LJ). This artificial rule was rejected by Gloster LJ, ibid, [79], who considered that the question is whether illegality of necessity forms an essential part of the claimant's cause of action.

if another doctrine can be applied to avoid the operation of illegality.[47] Since the claimant will need to refer to the illegality to show that the contract no longer applies, this artificial rule operates as a significant bar to restitution, which should be rejected.[48]

(C) EXCLUSION OF RESTITUTION BY CONTRACT

If a contract excludes the possibility of the claimant obtaining restitution from the defendant, it is not for the law of restitution to subvert the contract and enable the claimant to obtain a restitutionary remedy.[49] The contract may exclude restitution expressly or impliedly. So where, for example, the claimant transfers a benefit to the defendant pursuant to an agreement which is subject to contract, this operates to exclude the right to restitution as a general rule, because the inclusion of the phrase 'subject to contract' allocates the risk of a contract not being made to the person who transfers a benefit before any contract is made.[50]

Such exclusions of the right to obtain restitution might be thought to be open to challenge by virtue of the Unfair Contract Terms Act 1977, but that Act is inapplicable to exclusions of the right to restitution. This is because the application of the Act is confined to those cases where a party has excluded his or her liability arising in contract,[51] whereas the obligation to make restitution following unjust enrichment does not arise from contract, but is an independent obligation imposed by law.[52]

(D) PROVISION FOR RESTITUTION BY CONTRACT

A contract might provide, either expressly or impliedly, for restitution of benefits transferred under the contract,[53] in which case it will be possible for the claimant to obtain what appears to be restitution from the defendant by relying on the terms of the contract. But such an apparently restitutionary claim should not be considered to fall within the law of restitution, since the obligation to make restitution does not arise by operation of law but arises simply by operation of the agreement between the parties. It is consequently the contractual regime which governs the claim. This is important because it means, for example, that the claimant does not need to establish the elements of the unjust enrichment claim. Indeed, it was recognized in *Newland Shipping and Forwarding Ltd v Toba Trading FZC*[54] that where enrichment is sanctioned by a contract it cannot be considered to be unjust.[55] It also follows that the general defences which apply to claims in unjust enrichment are not applicable to the contractual claim for restitution.

---

[47] Such as withdrawal from the illegal transaction, as operated in *Patel v Mirza* itself. See further p 719, below.   [48] See further p 719, below.

[49] *Pan Ocean Shipping Co Ltd v Creditcorp Ltd* [1994] 1 WLR 161, 164 (Lord Goff).

[50] See, for example, *Regalian Properties plc v London Docklands Development Corporation* [1995] 1 WLR 212. See Chapter 13.

[51] Unfair Contract Terms Act 1977, s 3. The Act is, however, applicable where a party has purported to exclude his or her liability in tort. Consequently, it will be relevant where the restitutionary claim is founded on the commission of a tort, the liability for which the defendant has sought to exclude.

[52] See A Tettenborn, *The Law of Restitution in England and Wales* (3rd edn, London: Cavendish Publishing Ltd, 2002), 269. Presumably the same reasoning applies to the Unfair Terms in Consumer Contracts Regulations 1999.

[53] See *Sebel Products Ltd v Customs and Excise Commissioners* [1949] Ch 409.

[54] [2014] EWHC 661 (Comm).   [55] Ibid, [87] (Leggatt LJ).

Where a claim in unjust enrichment has already crystallized, the parties may enter into a contract to provide for restitution which will then prevail over the unjust enrichment claim. That contract may itself be terminated, in which case the original unjust enrichment claim will continue to operate, save if the contract is interpreted as extinguishing the unjust enrichment claim.[56]

(E) CONTRACT WITH A THIRD PARTY

Where the claimant has transferred a benefit to the defendant pursuant to a contract between the claimant and a third party, the existence of that contract will bar a claim in unjust enrichment against the defendant.[57] This is most likely to be significant where the third party is insolvent, and thus not worth suing, and the claimant seeks recovery from another party by means of a separate claim in unjust enrichment. But, if the contract between the claimant and third party still subsists, the unjust enrichment claim will fail. This is illustrated by *MacDonald Dickens and Macklin v Costello*,[58] where the claimant had entered into a building contract with a company to build houses. The houses having been built, the company had failed to pay for the work, so the claimants sought to recover the value of their services from the defendants, who were the sole directors and shareholders of the company and who had incorporated the company for tax reasons. This claim failed, however, even though the defendants had received the benefit of the claimant's services, because it was held that the award of a restitutionary remedy would undermine the contractual arrangement between the claimant and the company, regardless of the fact that there was no such contract between the claimant and the defendants. As Etherton LJ recognized,[59] the parties had chosen to allocate the risks in the transaction by virtue of a contract between the claimant and the company, such that the obligation to pay was borne by the company alone and so that the claimant bore the risk of non-payment only by the company. He justified this conclusion as follows:[60]

> The general rule should be to uphold contractual arrangements by which parties have defined and allocated and, to that extent, restricted their mutual obligations, and, in so doing, have similarly allocated and circumscribed the consequences of non-performance. That general rule reflects a sound legal policy which acknowledges the parties' autonomy to configure the legal relations between them and provides certainty, and so limits disputes and litigation.

Etherton LJ[61] provided a further significant justification for the primacy of contract, relating to the difference between restitutionary and contractual remedies. Damages for breach of contract will be assessed with reference to the contract price and terms, whereas the restitutionary remedy will be calculated with reference to the value of the services, which may be different. If the restitutionary remedy is worth more than the contractual remedy, the claimant should not be able to avoid the bargain by resorting to a claim in unjust enrichment, at least where the contractual regime is still operative.

The primacy of the contract between a claimant and a third party is also reflected in the significant case of the High Court of Australia in *Lumbers v W Cook Builders Pty Ltd*,[62] where the claimant wished to sue a non-contracting party who had benefited from the

---

[56] Ibid, [92] (Leggatt LJ).
[57] *Pan Ocean Shipping Co Ltd v Creditcorp Ltd* [1994] 1 WLR 161. See also *Brown & Davies Ltd v Galbraith* [1972] 1 WLR 997; *Esso Petroleum v Hall Russell & Co* [1989] AC 64.
[58] [2011] EWCA Civ 930, [2012] QB 244.   [59] Ibid, [21].   [60] Ibid, [23].
[61] Ibid, [31].   [62] [2008] HCA 27.

claimant's services. The case involved an oral contract made between Lumbers and Cook and Sons Ltd ('Sons') to build a house. Without the knowledge of Lumbers, Sons entered into a sub-contract with Cook Builders Pty Ltd ('Builders'), an unlicensed builder, to do most of the building work. Sons having gone into liquidation, Builders then sued Lumbers for the value of its services. The High Court held that this claim should fail. Various reasons were suggested for this. The majority considered that the contract between Lumbers and Sons barred any restitutionary liability to Builders.[63] But it was not made clear why this contract, to which Builders was not a party, should bar the claim. As Gleeson CJ recognized, the claim should be barred because of the contract between Builders and Sons. There was indeed a contract between Lumbers and Sons which had not been terminated, but the provision of the services by Builders, which benefited Lumbers, could not be attributed to this contract. Rather, the provision of the benefit by Builders could be attributed to its contractual obligation to Sons, as a result of which Sons was contractually liable to pay Builders for this work. The continued existence of the contract between Builders and Sons meant that Builders bore the risk that Sons would not pay for the service. This was specifically recognized by Gleeson CJ:[64]

> The contractual arrangements that were made effected a certain allocation of risk; and there is no occasion to disturb or interfere with that allocation. On the contrary, there is every reason to respect it. There was no mistake or misunderstanding on the part of Builders. It was accepted on both sides in argument that in the ordinary case a building subcontractor does not have a restitutionary claim against a property owner, but must look for payment to the head contractor.

(F) SETTLEMENT AND COMPROMISE

Where the claimant settles or compromises[65] the defendant's claim for payment, the claimant will be barred from obtaining restitution from the defendant because the policy of the law is to uphold the settlement of claims, which constitute a legally effective basis for receipt of an enrichment.[66] A settlement constitutes a bargain between the parties and should only be invalidated in extreme circumstances, namely where the contractual test for mistake is satisfied,[67] or where the defendant induced the settlement by fraud, duress, undue influence, or absence of good faith.[68]

In determining whether the claimant has settled or compromised the defendant's claim, Andrews identified four key principles:[69]

(1) A settlement may consist either of an agreement to pay the defendant or actual payment in response to a claim by the defendant. Payment may itself constitute a contractual settlement of the claim, since the consideration for the settlement will be the defendant's promise to abandon the claim, at least where the defendant

---

[63] Ibid, [77] (Gummow, Hayne, Crennan, and Kiefel JJ).   [64] Ibid, [46].

[65] N Andrews, 'Mistaken Settlements of Disputable Claims' [1989] LMCLQ 431. See also S Arrowsmith, 'Mistake and the Role of the "Submission to an Honest Claim"' in AS Burrows (ed), *Essays on the Law of Restitution* (Oxford: Clarendon Press, 1991), 29–32. The terms 'settlements' and 'compromise' are not terms of art and can be used interchangeably.

[66] For analysis of the arguments in favour of the policy in favour of upholding settlements see Andrews, 'Mistaken Settlements of Disputable Claims', 432–5.

[67] *Holmes v Payne* [1930] 2 KB 301. This includes a mistake of law: see *Brennan v Bolt Burdon* [2004] EWCA Civ 1017, [2005] QB 303, p 193, below.

[68] See *The Universe Sentinel* [1983] AC 366, 387 (Lord Diplock).

[69] Andrews, 'Mistaken Settlements of Disputable Claims', 435–8 and 449.

believes that he or she has a claim against the claimant.[70] Where the defendant does not believe that he or she has a valid claim, new consideration will need to be provided for the settlement to be valid.[71] To avoid the suggestion that the claimant has settled the claim, he or she should protest at the time of paying the defendant.

(2) A settlement may exist even though the parties have not commenced litigation.[72]

(3) There may be a settlement even though the defendant could not have sustained a proper legal claim against the claimant.

(4) The parties can settle a dispute which has not yet been fully spelt out. In determining whether there has been a settlement of such a dispute, it is necessary to see whether a promise to pay or an actual payment was made by the claimant when there was some doubt as to whether the money was due, so that it was reasonable for the defendant to suppose that the payment closed the matter.

(G) UNENFORCEABLE CONTRACTS

Where a benefit has been transferred in respect of an unenforceable contract it should not be recoverable because the contract provides a continuing basis for the defendant's retention of the benefit. As Brett LJ recognized in *Brittain v Rossiter*,[73] 'the contract exists, but no one is liable on it'. The significance of this is exemplified by *Morgan v Ashcroft*,[74] where the claimant's mistaken payment to the defendant was held to be irrecoverable because it was made pursuant to an unenforceable gambling transaction.[75] It follows that restitution will only be available if the unenforceable contract can be set aside for some other reason.

There are, however, cases where restitution has been awarded even though the contract was unenforceable, most notably the decision of the High Court of Australia in *Pavey and Matthews Pty Ltd v Paul*.[76] In that case a builder had made a contract with Mrs Paul to do some building work for her. The contract was unenforceable under the Builders Licensing Act 1971. Despite that, the builder was able to recover the value of the work which had been done. This does not appear to be consistent with the 'legally effective basis' bar. Birks justified the result on the ground that the refusal of Mrs Paul to pay for the work constituted a repudiatory breach: 'It was because of the breach of that good but unenforceable contract that the basis of her enrichment failed.'[77] Assuming that the builder had accepted the breach as repudiating the contract, there was no longer any valid basis for the retention of the enrichment and so the builder should be able to establish the unjust enrichment, even though the contract was unenforceable.

2. DISCHARGE OF A DEBT

Where the claimant pays money which effectively discharges a debt,[78] this constitutes the provision of a legally effective basis which will operate to bar the unjust enrichment claim

---

[70] J Beatson, 'Duress as a Vitiating Factor in Contract' (1974) CLJ 97, 103.

[71] E MacDonald, 'Duress by Threatened Breach of Contract' (1989) JBL 460, 466.

[72] *Brisbane v Dacres* (1813) 5 Taunt 143, 160; 128 ER 641, 648 (Heath J).

[73] (1879) 11 QBD 123, 127.   [74] [1938] 1 KB 49.

[75] Gambling agreements are now enforceable following the Gambling Act 2005, s 335.

[76] (1987) 162 CLR 221.

[77] PBH Birks, *Unjust Enrichment* (2nd edn, Oxford: Oxford University Press, 2005), 127.

[78] A debt will be discharged typically where the creditor accepts payment. See D Friedmann, 'Payment of Another's Debt' (1983) 99 LQR 534, 537; PBH Birks and J Beatson, 'Unrequested Payment of Another's Debt' (1976) 92 LQR 188, 201. See further p 235, below.

against the creditor, at least to the extent of the value of the debt. This was recognized by Lord Sumption in *Fairfield Sentry Ltd v Migani*,[79] who said that a mistaken payment could not be recovered 'to the extent [it] discharges a contractual debt of the payee'. But he went on to recognize that, '[s]o far as the payment exceeds the debt properly due, then the payer is in principle entitled to recover the excess'.

This has sometimes been described as constituting a 'defence' of good consideration.[80] It is the discharge of the debt which constitutes the provision of good consideration[81] and which means that the creditor is no longer enriched at the expense of the claimant to the value of the discharged debt.[82] But the language of a good consideration defence is liable to mislead for two reasons. First, this is preferably treated as a denial of the unjust enrichment claim, because of the existence of a legally effective basis for the payment, rather than as a defence. Secondly, the language of 'consideration', with its contractual connotations of the *quid pro quo* for an enforceable promise, is not appropriate in the context of a restitutionary claim. The discharge of the debt should consequently be recognized simply as a lawful basis which should bar a claim for restitution against the creditor. Since the payment to the creditor has effectively discharged the liability, it is not for the law of unjust enrichment to reverse the transaction by recreating the debt.

Where the debt was owed by the claimant to the defendant, this will typically have arisen by virtue of a contract between them such that restitution will be barred through the operation of the contractual regime.[83] But the claimant's payment to the creditor might instead discharge a debt owed by a third party to the creditor. In such circumstances, a claim for restitution against the creditor will be barred because of the discharge of the debt, even though there was no contract between the claimant and the creditor. Since, however, the debtor will have been enriched from the discharge of the debt,[84] the claimant will have a claim in unjust enrichment against him or her. This is illustrated by *Exall v Partridge*[85] where the claimant had left his carriage on land, which was leased by the defendant, for the defendant to repair. The defendant had not paid his rent to his landlord, who entered the land and lawfully seized the claimant's carriage. The claimant was compelled to pay the rent to the landlord in order to recover his carriage. The claimant then sought restitution from the defendant. As between the claimant and landlord there was a legally effective basis for the payment, since the rent liability was discharged. As between the claimant and the defendant there was no basis and, since the defendant had been unjustly enriched at the claimant's expense, it was appropriate to award restitution.

Whether the claimant's payment will be effective to discharge a debt owed to the creditor will depend on whether it was authorized by the debtor. So in *Barclays Bank Ltd v W J Simms, Son & Cooke (Southern) Ltd*[86] the claimant bank had mistakenly paid money to the defendant in respect of a cheque drawn on a customer's account. If, which did not occur on the facts, the claimant's mistake had simply been to believe that the customer had sufficient funds in the account, it would follow that, since the customer had authorized the payment, the debt which the customer owed to the defendant would have been discharged and the claimant bank would then have to seek restitution from the

---

[79] [2014] UKPC 9, [18].
[80] *Barclays Bank Ltd v W J Simms, Son & Cooke (Southern) Ltd* [1980] QB 677, 695 (Robert Goff J). See further p 189, below.
[81] *David Securities Pty Ltd v Commonwealth Bank of Australia* (1992) 175 CLR 353, 406 (Dawson J).
[82] *Lloyds Bank plc v Independent Insurance Co Ltd* [2000] QB 110, 132 (Peter Gibson LJ).
[83] See p 134, above.   [84] See p 77, above.
[85] (1799) 8 Term Rep 308, 101 ER 1405.   [86] [1980] QB 677.

customer.[87] But, in this case the mistake related to the fact that the claimant had paid the money even though the customer had countermanded the payment. Consequently, the payment ceased to be authorized and so did not discharge the debt. It followed that the claimant could recover the money from the defendant because the payment had had no legal effect.

3. STATUTORY AUTHORITY

Where the claimant has transferred a benefit to the defendant pursuant to a valid statutory obligation, restitution will not lie because the discharge of the obligation means that there is a legally effective basis for the defendant's receipt.[88] So, for example, payment of tax pursuant to a valid tax demand cannot be recovered, because the payment is legally effective by discharging the tax liability.[89]

The identification of a valid statutory base for the receipt of tax payments by the Revenue proved to be a matter of particular controversy in *Deutsche Morgan Grenfell v IRC*,[90] where the majority allowed a restitutionary claim for the use value of tax paid prematurely, where the claimant had not been able to claim tax relief which would have delayed its liability to pay the tax which was due to the Revenue. Lord Scott dissented on the ground that, since the tax relief had not been claimed, the claimant was actually liable to pay tax to the Revenue so that the payment was lawfully due.[91] In determining whether Lord Scott was correct it is vital to remember the essential feature of this type of restitutionary claim. This was not a claim for recovery of the amount of tax which had been paid because, as was subsequently recognized in *Sempra Metals Ltd v IRC*,[92] this sum was eventually set off against the corporation tax which was lawfully due, so at that point there was a legally effective basis for the Revenue's receipt of that money. Rather, the claim for restitution related simply to the premature payment of tax in circumstances where the claimant would have wished to delay payment by means of electing to benefit from the tax relief, had it been able to do so.[93] If the focus is placed on the entitlement of the Revenue to receive the money when it did, rather than on whether the tax was actually due to the Revenue, it is much easier to understand why the Revenue was required to make restitution: because the Revenue obtained an unlawful timing advantage as the result of premature payment of the tax. During the period when the Revenue had the unlawful use of this money there was no valid legal basis for its receipt. Once, however, the tax which had been paid was set off against the taxpayer's mainstream corporation tax liability, the Revenue's receipt became lawful and so, at that point, there was a basis for this payment and so the amount of money which had been paid could not be recovered.

---

[87] See *Aiken v Short* (1856) 1 H and N 210, 156 ER 1180; *Pollard v Bank of England* (1871) LR 6 QB 623; *Kleinwort Benson Ltd v Lincoln CC* [1999] 2 AC 349, 408 (Lord Hope); *Lloyds Bank plc v Independent Insurance Co Ltd* [2000] QB 110, 132 (Peter Gibson LJ).

[88] *Deutsche Morgan Grenfell v IRC* [2006] UKHL 49, [2007] 1 AC 558, [89] (Lord Scott). See M Chowdry and C Mitchell, 'Tax Legislation as a Justifying Factor' [2005] RLR 1.

[89] In *Kingstreet Investments Ltd v New Brunswick* [2007] SCR 3, the Supreme Court of Canada recognized that it was open to the State to suspend the declaration that a tax was invalid and also to enact valid tax legislation and apply them retrospectively. In either case, receipt of the tax would become authorized.

[90] [2006] UKHL 49, [2007] 1 AC 558.

[91] See R Stevens, 'Justified Enrichment' (2005) 5 OUCLJ 141.

[92] [2007] UKHL 34, [2008] 1 AC 561.

[93] *Deutsche Morgan Grenfell v IRC* [2006] UKHL 49, [2007] 1 AC 558, [5] (Lord Hoffmann).

4. *RES JUDICATA*

When money has been paid by the claimant to the defendant as the result of a court judgment it cannot be recovered[94] unless the judgment is set aside, for the judgment constitutes a basis for the payment.[95] The judgment operates as a legally effective basis for the defendant's receipt, even if the judgment has been obtained by fraud.[96] It is only where the judgment is subsequently set aside that restitution will be awarded.[97] Similarly, where a judgment has been declared for too much money, the claimant is unable to recover the excess money paid to the defendant until the judgment has been rectified.[98]

5. NATURAL OBLIGATIONS

In *Moses v Macferlan*[99] Lord Mansfield recognized that where a claimant has discharged an obligation in circumstances where the claimant was not aware that the defendant could not have enforced the obligation, the claimant could not obtain restitution even though the money was technically not due, because the claimant was morally or naturally bound to have paid the money to the defendant. This so-called 'natural obligation' would exist where money is claimed from the claimant:

> as payable in point of honor and honesty although it could not have been recovered from him by any course of law; as in payment of a debt barred by the Statute of Limitations, or contracted during his infancy, or to the extent of principal and legal interest upon an usurious[100] contract, or for money fairly lost at play: because in all these cases, the defendant may retain it with a safe conscience, though by positive law he was barred from recovering.

If money has been paid in such circumstances it would appear that there is a basis for its receipt and so restitution will not be available.

The relevance of natural obligations today can be assessed with reference to each of Lord Mansfield's examples. First, if money is paid to discharge a debt where the claim is time barred, the claimant might assert that this was a mistaken payment, in the sense that, but for the mistake about the claim being barred the money would not have been paid. But restitution should be denied in such circumstances because the payment will still be effective to discharge the debt, regardless of the claim being time barred.[101] In other words, there is a legally effective basis for the payment, and the fact that the claim was time barred is irrelevant. The analysis would only be different if the effect of the relevant limitation statute was to discharge the debt, for then the payment would not be legally effective since the debt would not have been discharged. Usually, however, limitation periods 'bar only the remedy and not the right',[102] so there is no need to rely on a basis other than the discharge of the debt to bar the restitutionary claim.

---

[94] *Moses v Macferlan* (1760) 2 Burr 1005, 1009; 97 ER 676, 678 (Lord Mansfield).

[95] See Birks, *Unjust Enrichment* (2nd edn), 140.

[96] *De Medina v Grove* (1846) 10 QB 152, 116 ER 59; *Huffer v Allen* (1867) LR 2 Ex 15.

[97] *De Medina v Grove* (1846) 10 QB 152, 116 ER 59.   [98] *Huffer v Allen* (1867) LR 2 Ex 15.

[99] (1760) 2 Burr 1005, 1012; 97 ER 676, 681.

[100] Referring to a money-lending contract on terms which are immoral or unethical for some reason, typically for excessive rates of interest.

[101] See HW Tang, 'Natural Obligations and the Common Law of Unjust Enrichment' [2006] OUCLJ 133, 140.   [102] Ibid, 141.

Lord Mansfield's second category of natural obligations is where money is paid pursuant to a contract which is made during infancy. Restitution will be barred in such a case, but not because of some vague concept of 'natural obligation', but because the contract operates as a valid legal basis for the transfer. Contracts with minors for necessaries are valid.[103] Contracts where the minor acquires an interest of a permanent or continuous nature, such as for the acquisition of shares or land, are voidable,[104] and so remain a basis for the transfer until the contract is avoided. All other contracts with minors are unenforceable, and so constitute a legally effective basis until the contract has been set aside for some reason. So, again, the language of natural obligation is not of use here. The third category, concerning usurious money-lending contracts, no longer raise special issues. If such contracts are void they constitute no legally effective basis. If they are valid, voidable or unenforceable, they provide a legally effective basis for the payment of money. The fourth category concerning gambling contracts is now covered by the Gambling Act 2005, which renders such contracts enforceable.[105] Consequently, payments in respect of such contracts will be barred in the normal way by the existence of a valid contractual basis for payment.[106]

So, if the specific heads of natural obligation identified by Lord Mansfield can now be explained by reference to the existing heads of the legally effective basis bar, is there any need to identify a distinct 'natural obligations' head? This will depend on how 'natural obligations' should be defined. Sheehan[107] has described such obligations as arising where a claimant fulfils a duty which he or she had voluntarily agreed to undertake, even though the contract under which the claimant undertook the duty is void. But this involves a much wider notion of 'basis' than those previously encountered in this chapter, since this would not necessarily constitute a legally effective basis for the payment. Tang has adopted a narrower interpretation of the natural obligations principle, which has regard to 'whether the policies behind the doctrine or law which avoided the obligation will be furthered by allowing or denying restitution'.[108] But the crucial issue is whether restitution of a benefit which has been transferred pursuant to a void obligation should ever be barred. Application of the legally effective basis bar suggests that it should not be. For, if there is no legally effective basis for the transfer because the contract is void, there is no reason why the restitutionary claim should be defeated, save where the claimant bore the risk of invalidity.[109] Vague references to underlying policies can only cause confusion and uncertainty. Once the unjust enrichment claim has been established, and mistake of law will usually be readily identifiable as the relevant ground of restitution where there is a void obligation, restitution should follow unless there is some other legally effective basis which can be identified for the transfer. Consequently, there is no need to treat 'natural obligations' as providing a basis distinct from any of the other bases.

6. GIFTS

Where the receipt of a benefit can be characterized as a gift, this should constitute a legally effective basis for the transfer and restitution should be denied, because a gift is a legal transaction which, if valid, should not be undermined by the law of unjust enrichment.[110]

---

[103] See p 384, below.   [104] *Steinberg v Scala (Leeds) Ltd* [1923] 2 Ch 452.
[105] Gambling Act 2005, s 335.   [106] See p 144, above.
[107] D Sheehan, 'Natural Obligations in English Law' [2004] LMCLQ 172.
[108] Tang, 'Natural Obligations and the Common Law of Unjust Enrichment'.
[109] See p 36, above.
[110] Birks considered that a transfer which was intended by the claimant to be a gift could not be recovered: *Unjust Enrichment* (2nd edn), 104.

The donee should be secure in the validity of the receipt of the gift and the law of restitution should not be used to unsettle this security.

It is consequently important to be able to identify when a transfer can be considered to be a gift. But this is not straightforward because the key test turns on the nature of the claimant's mental state at the time of the transfer. Clearly, if the claimant intended the transfer to be gratuitous, this will be a gift. Birks considered that the notion of oblique intent will suffice, so that if the claimant foresaw that the defendant might receive a benefit as a virtually certain consequence without the claimant receiving anything in return, this could be considered to be gratuitous. Birks even considered that knowingly taking a risk that the claimant might not be paid for the provision of a benefit could mean that the claimant had made a gift to the defendant.[111] So, for example, the busker who wants to be paid for his music was considered by Birks to have made a gift of his services to those who chose not to pay. But it is artificial to describe the busker as a donor of his services. The real problem with buskers is that they are taking a risk as to whether anybody will pay money for the music. Risk-taking should not be treated as an implicit part of the identification of a legally effective basis, but should be a separate consideration when determining whether restitution should be awarded, albeit one that often forms part of the identification of a ground of restitution.[112] Consequently, gift as a legally effective basis for the transfer of a benefit should be interpreted restrictively to encompass only a purpose on the part of the claimant to benefit the defendant gratuitously. Where the benefit has been provided recklessly, whether restitution should be awarded should depend on the application of the different principle of risk-taking.

Where the claimant has purported to make a gift to the defendant there will not be a valid basis for the transfer where there are particular circumstances which undermine the validity of the gift, such as where the claimant was mistaken[113] or had been compelled to make the gift to the defendant.[114]

7. VOLUNTARY TRANSFERS

Where the claimant has acted voluntarily[115] in transferring a benefit to the defendant which was not due, then, even though it appears that there was no legally effective basis for the transfer, the claimant will not be able to obtain restitution. This principle was recognized by Lord Reading in *Maskell v Horner*:[116]

> If a person with knowledge of the facts pays money, which he is not in law bound to pay, and in circumstances implying that he is paying it voluntarily to close the transaction, he cannot recover it. Such a payment is in law like a gift, and the transaction cannot thereafter be re-opened.

Lord Reading's analogy with gift is consistent with the idea that a voluntary transfer can in fact be considered to be a legally effective basis in its own right which should bar the restitutionary claim, because the defendant will be considered to have waived the right of recovery.[117] The difficult issue concerns the identification of when the claimant can be considered to have acted voluntarily.

---

[111] Ibid, 130–1. [112] See p 37, above. [113] See Chapter 9. [114] See Chapter 10.
[115] *David Securities Pty Ltd v Commonwealth Bank of Australia* (1992) 175 CLR 353, 374.
[116] [1915] 3 KB 106, 118.
[117] *Woolwich Equitable Building Society v IRC* [1993] AC 70, 165 (Lord Goff).

When considering whether a ground of restitution can be identified the question of whether the claimant had acted voluntarily is generally indistinguishable from the question whether the ground of restitution vitiated the claimant's intention to transfer the benefit. For example, if the claimant was compelled to pay the defendant,[118] the claimant will only be considered to have acted voluntarily if the compulsion had not actually caused the claimant to make the payment. But if the compulsion did not cause the claimant to make the payment it cannot constitute a ground of restitution anyway. The burden is consequently on the claimant to prove that he or she acted involuntarily, in other words that the compulsion caused the payment to be made.[119] Similarly, if the claimant paid the defendant as a result of a mistake, the claimant will only be able to obtain restitution if the mistake was a sufficient cause of the payment and, if it was not, the claimant can be considered to have acted voluntarily.[120] This was recognized by Robert Goff J in *Barclays Bank Ltd v W J Simms, Son & Cooke (Southern) Ltd*,[121] when he said that restitution for mistake would be denied where 'the payor intends that the payee shall have the money at all events whether the fact be true or false, or is deemed in law so to intend'.

But even if it appears that the claimant had acted involuntarily due to mistake or compulsion, it may still be possible to characterize the transfer as voluntary for other reasons. In *Walsh v Singh*,[122] for example, it was held that the claimant could not recover the reasonable value of services which she had provided to the defendant because she had provided them voluntarily, in the hope of developing a long-term relationship with the defendant which would culminate in marriage. Similarly, where the claimant has voluntarily paid the defendant to settle a demand for payment made by the defendant, the payment cannot be recovered because the defendant who has received the payment to settle the claim should be secure in the validity of the receipt. For example, where the defendant has made an unfounded claim accompanied by a threat to sue, if the claimant mistakenly satisfies the claim he or she will not be able to obtain restitution because the payment will be deemed to be voluntary.[123] This has sometimes been called 'submission to an honest claim', but it does not depend on the defendant having made an explicit claim; the claim may be implied. Payment made in response to such compulsion is deemed as a matter of law to have been voluntary simply because the claimant was given the opportunity to contest his or her liability in proceedings, but gave way and paid the defendant.[124] It makes no difference whether the claimant thought that the money was not lawfully due to the defendant or mistakenly believed that it was due.

The voluntariness of the claimant's actions has also proved to be significant where the claimant voluntarily became the surety for the defendant's liabilities owed to a third party without being requested to do so by the defendant. If the third party compels the claimant to discharge the defendant's liability it has been held that the claimant is not able to obtain restitution from the defendant, even though the defendant had benefited from the discharge of liability and bore the ultimate liability, because the claimant voluntarily assumed the suretyship.[125] Barring restitution in such circumstances has

---

[118] See Chapter 10.   [119] *Mason v New South Wales* (1959) 102 CLR 108, 144 (Windeyer J).

[120] See Chapter 9.

[121] [1980] QB 677, 695. See also Parke B in *Kelly v Solari* (1841) 9 M and W 54, 59 and Lord Abinger CB, ibid, 58.

[122] [2009] EWHC 3219 (Ch), [65] (Judge Purle QC).

[123] *Moore v Vestry of Fulham* [1895] 1 QB 399; *Kleinwort Benson v Lincoln CC* [1999] 2 AC 349, 382 (Lord Goff).

[124] *Moore v Vestry of Fulham* [1895] 1 QB 399, 402 (Lord Halsbury).

[125] *Owen v Tate* [1976] QB 402.

been criticized.[126] A particular concern for present purposes is whether it is appropriate to treat the discharge of liability in these circumstances as akin to a gift, so that a legally effective basis for the payment can be identified. Such an analysis is not obviously consistent, however, with those cases which have recognized that voluntary actions bar restitution. So, for example, in *Owen v Tate*[127] the claimant, without consulting the defendant, deposited a sum of money with the defendant's creditor as security for a loan. The reason for this was that the defendant's previous surety wished to recover the title deeds of her property which had been surrendered to the creditor and, as a favour to her, the claimant agreed to become surety. When the defendant discovered that the claimant had become the surety it protested, but, when pressed for payment by the creditor, the defendant asked the creditor to have recourse to the money which the claimant had deposited. The claimant sought restitution from the defendant, but this claim was unsuccessful because it was held that the claimant had undertaken the risk of being sued by voluntarily becoming a surety. But it is a significant feature of *Owen v Tate* that the claimant became a surety to benefit a third party and not the defendant; if there was any intent to make a gift, it was to the third party and not the defendant. This suggests that no legally effective basis can be identified as between the claimant and the defendant who had benefited from the discharge of its liability to the creditor, and so restitution should have been awarded.[128] Similarly, in *Macclesfield Corp v Great Central Railway*[129] the defendant was under a statutory duty to repair a bridge over its canal, but refused to repair it when the claimant highway authority called upon it to do so. The claimant then did the work itself but was unable to obtain restitution of the costs incurred since it was under no legal liability to repair the bridge, and accordingly had acted as a volunteer. Again, it is difficult to characterize the claimant as having intended to make a gift to the defendant, so that it is not possible to identify an effective legal basis for the defendant's receipt of the benefit.

---

[126] See PBH Birks, *An Introduction to the Law of Restitution* (rev edn, Oxford: Clarendon Press, 1989), 311.
[127] [1976] QB 402.   [128] See further p 245, below.   [129] [1911] 2 KB 528.

8

IGNORANCE

1. IS IGNORANCE A GROUND OF RESTITUTION?

Although ignorance has never been explicitly recognized by the courts as a ground of restitution in its own right, a number of commentators have resorted to this ground to explain why restitution has been ordered in a number of cases.[1] This lack of judicial recognition is initially surprizing since it has been recognized for many years that, if a claimant has paid money to a defendant under the influence of a mistaken belief that he or she is liable to pay the defendant, the claimant will be able to obtain restitution of the money.[2] This is because the claimant's intention that the defendant should receive the money can be regarded as vitiated by the operation of the mistake. If a mistake is regarded as sufficient to vitiate the claimant's intent that the defendant should receive the money, it should be even easier to justify restitution where the defendant received the claimant's money in circumstances where the claimant was ignorant of the transfer. This is because, where the claimant mistakenly pays money to the defendant, there is at least an intention to vitiate, whereas, where the claimant is ignorant that his or her money has been transferred to the defendant, there is not even an intention that needs to be vitiated. This will occur, for example, where, unknown to the claimant, the defendant has stolen the claimant's money. In such circumstances the claimant cannot argue that he or she made any mistake in respect of the transfer to the defendant, since the claimant was unaware of the theft. But, at least as a matter of principle, the claimant should be able to recover the value of the money from the defendant because there was no intention that the defendant should receive it. In the light of this it is surprising that ignorance has not been explicitly endorsed by the judges as a ground for restitution.

Although this argument for the recognition of ignorance as a ground of restitution is superficially convincing, it is subject to a flaw which largely explains why it has not been judicially recognized and is unlikely ever to be recognized as an independent ground of restitution, save in the most exceptional circumstances. The flaw arises from the fact that, where the claimant is ignorant that his or her property has been obtained by the defendant, title in that property will remain with the claimant because of the absence of intent that the property be transferred to the defendant.[3] Hence, when the claimant wishes to recover the property, he or she has no need to resort to the principle of reversing unjust

---

[1] See, in particular, AS Burrows, *The Law of Restitution* (3rd edn, Oxford: Oxford University Press, 2011), ch 16 and PBH Birks, *An Introduction to the Law of Restitution* (rev edn, Oxford: Clarendon Press, 1989), 140–6. See also AS Burrows, *A Restatement of the English Law of Unjust Enrichment* (Oxford: Hart Publishing, 2012), article 16(1), where, in addition to ignorance, the ground of powerlessness is recognized, which applies where the claimant is powerless to prevent the conduct which enriched the defendant but was aware of that conduct, so the ground of ignorance would not be engaged. The ground of powerlessness has never been recognized in the authorities.

[2] See Chapter 9.   [3] WJ Swadling, 'A Claim in Restitution' [1996] LMCLQ 63, 65.

enrichment. The restitutionary action will instead be founded upon the vindication of the claimant's continuing proprietary interest.[4]

In many cases it will in fact make no difference whether the restitutionary claim is founded on unjust enrichment, with ignorance constituting the ground of restitution, or on the vindication of property rights, with the claimant's ignorance being used to explain why title did not pass to the defendant. For example, it will make no difference which principle is relied on where the claimant only seeks a personal remedy and where it is clear that the defendant has been enriched at the expense of the claimant, for example where the claimant's money is transferred directly to the defendant. Where, however, the claimant's property is transferred indirectly to the defendant without the claimant's knowledge, the unjust enrichment action is typically not available to the claimant, because of the general rule that the defendant's enrichment is obtained directly at the expense of the claimant, save where, as a matter of economic reality, it is possible to show that the defendant is enriched at the claimant's expense, albeit indirectly.[5] If the 'at the expense of' requirement cannot be satisfied, the claimant must then establish the claim for restitution with reference to the vindication of property rights principle.[6] This action will also be the only relevant one where the claimant seeks a proprietary restitutionary remedy, a remedy which will be particularly important to the claimant where the defendant is insolvent and so the claimant wishes to secure priority over the other creditors of the defendant, or where the property or its identifiable substitute has increased in value.

2. RELYING ON IGNORANCE AS A GROUND OF RESTITUTION

Exceptionally, it might, however, be possible for the claimant to bring a restitutionary claim founded on unjust enrichment where the ground of restitution is ignorance, in circumstances where the claimant is not able to bring a claim founded on the vindication of proprietary rights.

(A) SERVICES PROVIDED IN CIRCUMSTANCES OF IGNORANCE

In principle, if the claimant has provided a service to the defendant which constitutes an enrichment and it can be shown that the claimant was ignorant that the service was provided, the claimant should be able to bring a restitutionary claim founded on the reversal of the defendant's unjust enrichment. In such a case a claim founded on the vindication of property rights is out of the question, simply because there is no proprietary interest in the provision of a service. It would, however, be possible to establish that the defendant had been unjustly enriched at the expense of the claimant. Usually, a claimant will be aware that a service has been provided, but there will be some circumstances where

---

[4] See Chapter 21.

[5] For the general rule and its exceptions, see p 105, above. Indirect enrichment might be easier to establish following the decision of the Court of Appeal in *Relfo Ltd v Varsani* [2014] EWCA Civ 360, [2015] 1 BCLC 14, although it was suggested, p 110, above, that the economic realities may not assist the claimant in establishing indirect enrichment where the claimant was unaware of the arrangement that property would be transferred from the third party to the defendant, suggesting that ignorance might negate indirect enrichment.

[6] See, for example, *Clarke v Shee and Johnson* (1774) 1 Cowp 197, 98 ER 1041; *Marsh v Keating* (1834) 1 Bing NC 198, 131 ER 1094; *Calland v Loyd* (1840) 6 M and W 26, 151 ER 307; *Banque Belge pour l'Etranger v Hambrouck* [1912] 1 KB 321; *Nelson v Larholt* [1948] 1 KB 339; *Lipkin Gorman (a firm) v Karpnale Ltd* [1991] 2 AC 548. See Chapter 1.

the ignorant provision of a service could be established. For example, the defendant may have entered the claimant's theatre without paying and seen a play being performed. Or the claimant may have been discussing confidential research with a colleague which the defendant overheard and exploited commercially. As long as it can be shown in each of these cases that the defendant had received an enrichment,[7] it would be possible to establish that the defendant has been unjustly enriched, at the expense of the claimant who was ignorant of the fact that the defendant had received the benefit.

(B) INTERCEPTIVE SUBTRACTION

Where the defendant has intervened and taken a benefit from a third party in circumstances where that benefit was intended to be transferred to the claimant, it may be possible for the claimant to found a restitutionary claim on unjust enrichment, with the ground of restitution being ignorance. Alternatively, it might be possible, in such a case, to show that the defendant had committed a wrong in taking the benefit for him or herself, as would occur if the defendant owed fiduciary duties to the claimant, so that the claim would be founded on the wrong rather than unjust enrichment.[8] It might even be possible for the claimant to bring a proprietary claim to vindicate his or her proprietary rights in the property which was transferred to the defendant, although there might be some difficulty in the claimant establishing that he or she did indeed have a proprietary interest in the property before it was received. It certainly does not necessarily follow from the fact that the third party had intended the property to be received by the claimant that the claimant has a property interest in it when it was transferred to the defendant.[9] But, if claims founded on wrongdoing and on the vindication of property rights are unavailable, the claimant will have to base a claim on the defendant's unjust enrichment, with the ground of restitution being that the claimant was ignorant that the benefit had been transferred by the third party to the defendant. The requirement that the benefit was obtained at the claimant's expense would be satisfied by the fact that the defendant had intercepted the transfer of the benefit.[10]

In most cases of interceptive subtraction, it will, however, be possible for the claimant to establish a proprietary interest in the property which was received by the defendant, typically an equitable proprietary interest. This will particularly be the case where the defendant has obtained the money in a fiduciary capacity. This is well illustrated by *Lyell v Kennedy*,[11] where land which had been let to tenants was managed by the defendant for the landowner. The defendant received rent from the tenants, which was paid into a separate earmarked account at his own bank. After the death of the landowner, the defendant continued to receive the rent. The claimant, who was the landowner's heir, then sought to recover the rent which had been received by the defendant. The claim succeeded because it was held that, since the defendant had received the money in a fiduciary capacity, he held it on trust for the claimant. A restitutionary remedy was ordered in the form of an account of the rent and profits. The Earl of Selborne, with whom the other members of the House of Lords concurred, emphasized that the money in the account had never been the property of the defendant, so presumably on the death of the landowner it belonged to the heir, even though he was ignorant of the fact that the defendant had been receiving the money from the tenants. This proprietary analysis is also

---

[7] See Chapter 4.   [8] See Chapter 19.
[9] See *Asher v Wallis* (1707) 11 Mod 146, 88 ER 956. See also *Arris and Arris v Stukely* (1677) 2 Mod 260, 86 ER 1060 and *Howard v Wood* (1679) 2 Shaw KB 21, 89 ER 767.
[10] See p 111, above.   [11] (1889) 14 App Cas 437.

the preferable explanation of the decision of the House of Lords in *Ministry of Health v Simpson*,[12] where personal representatives had mistakenly paid money to the defendants rather than the beneficiaries, who were able to recover the value of the money which the defendants had received. Although, the beneficiaries were ignorant of the receipt by the defendants, their claim did not depend on unjust enrichment, but instead is preferably analysed as dependent on the vindication of the equitable proprietary interest which they had in the money received by the defendants.[13]

3. ELECTION BETWEEN PRINCIPLES

Where the claimant is ignorant that his or her property has been taken by the defendant so that the claimant retains legal title in it, it is clear that the claimant can bring a claim for restitution grounded on the vindication of this legal title. But can the claimant alternatively bring a claim grounded on the defendant's unjust enrichment, even though the claimant has legal title in the property? It is difficult to conceive of reasons why the claimant would wish to bring such a claim when a proprietary claim is available, save where the property has fallen in value or the claimant might simply be poorly advised and think that the only claim available is one grounded on unjust enrichment. The issue is essentially whether the claim in unjust enrichment will be barred by the fact that the claimant has retained legal title.

A number of commentators have concluded that, where the claimant does retain legal title to the property, a claim grounded on unjust enrichment is barred.[14] One suggested reason is that, where the claimant has retained title in the property he or she will not be able to establish that the defendant has been enriched.[15] This argument assumes that the notion of whether or not the defendant has been enriched is a question of law rather than fact.[16] The consequence of this is that, if the claimant continues to own the property which the defendant has received, it is not possible to conclude that the defendant has been enriched because the property does not belong to the defendant. In other words, the claimant has not lost anything. Birks, on the other hand, considered that the notion of enrichment is a factual test.[17] Consequently, it is sufficient for the claimant to establish that the defendant has received a factual benefit, which is assessed by showing that value has passed from the claimant to the defendant. If the defendant steals the claimant's car it is clear that the defendant is now in possession of a car, a valuable benefit, which he or she did not have before. It follows that the defendant should be considered to be enriched by the value of the car and this enrichment should be considered to derive from the claimant, even though the claimant has retained title to the car. The question whether the defendant is legally enriched should be of no significance to the question whether the defendant has been unjustly enriched at the expense of the claimant; it is only of significance when determining whether the claimant has title to property as a matter of law for purposes of bringing a claim to vindicate his or her property rights.

---

[12] [1951] AC 251 (sub nom *Re Diplock*).   [13] See Chapter 21.

[14] Swadling, 'A Claim in Restitution?', 65; RB Grantham and CEF Rickett, 'Property and Unjust Enrichment: Categorical Truth or Unnecessary Complexity?' [1997] NZ Law Rev 668, 682–3.

[15] RB Grantham and CEF Rickett, 'Restitution, Property and Mistaken Payments' [1997] RLR 83, 87.

[16] See RB Grantham and CEF Rickett, 'Trust Money as an Unjust Enrichment: A Misconception' [1998] LMCLQ 514, 517–18. See also *Ilich* (1987) 162 CLR 110, 140–1 (Brennan J).

[17] PBH Birks, 'Property and Unjust Enrichment: Categorical Truths' [1997] NZ Law Rev 623, 654; PBH Birks, 'On Taking Seriously the Difference Between Tracing and Claiming' (1997) 11 TLI 2, 7–8.

If it is possible to show that the defendant has received a factual enrichment, even though the claimant has retained title in the property received by the defendant, and it can be shown that the defendant had obtained this benefit directly from the claimant, it should be possible to bring a restitutionary claim founded on the reversal of the defendant's unjust enrichment so long as it can be shown that the claimant was ignorant of the transfer. It is no bar to a restitutionary claim founded on unjust enrichment that the claimant could have brought a claim founded on the commission of a wrong,[18] and neither should it matter that the claim could alternatively have been founded on the vindication of proprietary rights.

4. THE ROLE OF IGNORANCE AS A GROUND OF RESTITUTION

It follows from this analysis that there is no reason of principle or law which should prevent the claimant from bringing a claim in unjust enrichment where the ground of restitution is ignorance. But, as has been seen in this chapter, such a claim will be highly exceptional. It is no wonder that ignorance has not yet been formally recognized as a ground of restitution in its own right, simply because, where the claimant was ignorant that a benefit was transferred to the defendant, a proprietary restitutionary claim has many advantages over a claim founded on the reversal of the defendant's unjust enrichment and will typically be available as a consequence of the claimant's ignorance of the transfer.

---

[18] See Chapter 16.

9

MISTAKE

1. GENERAL PRINCIPLES

(A) THE SIGNIFICANCE OF MISTAKE AS A GROUND OF RESTITUTION

A claim to recover money mistakenly paid by the claimant to the defendant is often regarded as the paradigm example of a restitutionary claim founded on the unjust enrichment principle.[1] In such a case there is clearly an enrichment at the claimant's expense and, at least where the reason for the claimant making the payment arose from a mistaken belief that he or she was liable to pay the money to the defendant, there is a clear justification for restoring the value of the money to the claimant, since the claimant's intention to make the payment can readily be treated as vitiated by the mistake. It is, however, unfortunate that mistake is regarded as the paradigm ground of restitution, because there is a consequent tendency to underestimate the complex policy issues which arise in determining whether the defendant's enrichment really can be considered to be unjust.

The complexity of mistake as a ground of restitution arises for two reasons. First, despite certain significant recent decisions, the law remains unclear about what is the appropriate test for determining what is a mistake and when it should operate to vitiate the claimant's intention to benefit the defendant. Secondly, even where it is possible to show that the claimant's intention was vitiated by the mistake, it does not necessarily follow that restitutionary relief should be available. This is because the circumstances of the defendant's receipt of a benefit and subsequent conduct may be such that it would not be just to require the defendant to make restitution. As Birks said, 'in seeking to do justice to mistaken payers the action [for money had and received] often seems to tremble on the brink of doing injustice to the recipient of the payment'.[2] Consequently, the respective interests of the parties need to be balanced carefully when determining whether restitutionary relief is appropriate, and this requires careful consideration of issues of policy.

(B) THE KEY POLICIES WHICH DETERMINE WHEN A MISTAKE SHOULD GROUND A RESTITUTIONARY CLAIM

There are four policies which are relevant to the identification of the appropriate test for determining when mistake should operate as a ground of restitution.

---

[1] See PBH Birks, *Unjust Enrichment* (2nd edn, Oxford: Oxford University Press, 2005), 3, specifically as regards the mistaken payment of a non-existent debt.

[2] PBH Birks, 'The Recovery of Carelessly Mistaken Payments' (1972) CLP 179.

(i) Security of Transactions

Restitution for mistake should not be used to undermine transactions unnecessarily. Defendants need to have a degree of security that, when they receive benefits, they will not be required to make restitution unless there is a good reason to do so. This policy favours a restrictive interpretation of mistake as a ground of restitution.

(ii) Risk Allocation

Where the parties to a contract have expressly or implicitly allocated the risk that one or both of them may be mistaken as to particular facts, it is not for the law of restitution to intrude and subvert that allocation of risk. This policy also favours a restrictive interpretation of mistake.

(iii) Concoction of Claims

There is a danger that claimants will concoct claims that they were mistaken when they transferred a benefit. It is easy for the claimant to assert that he or she was mistaken, since this simply depends on the state of his or her mind at the time the benefit was transferred, and it is difficult for the defendant to deny this. Again, this policy favours a restrictive interpretation of mistake.

(iv) Justice for the Defendant

When determining whether it is just for the defendant to make restitution to the claimant, changes in the defendant's circumstances following the receipt of the enrichment need to be taken into account. Following the recognition of the defence of change of position,[3] it is possible to have regard to whether it is just and fair for the defendant to make restitution of the enrichment transferred by mistake in the light of events following the receipt of the enrichment. The existence of this defence favours a more expansive interpretation of mistake. As Lord Goff recognized in *Lipkin Gorman (a firm) v Karpnale Ltd*,[4] 'the recognition of change of position will enable a more generous approach to be taken to the recognition of the right to restitution'. In fact, the history of mistake as a ground of restitution is a history of development of the law from a starting point at which mistake was interpreted very restrictively to the position today where the notion of an operative mistake is interpreted much more widely. But it remains vital to ensure that this generous approach to the interpretation of mistake does not infringe the other three policies.

(C) DIFFERENT TYPES OF ENRICHMENT

Where the claimant has mistakenly paid money to the defendant, the only difficult question concerns whether the mistake was sufficient to ground restitution. There are no difficulties regarding the identification of an enrichment, since money is incontrovertibly beneficial, and, if the money has been paid directly to the defendant by the claimant, it will obviously have been received at the claimant's expense. Other types of claim will, however, raise more complex issues. So, for example, where the alleged enrichment is the receipt of goods[5] or a service provided by the claimant,[6] it will also be necessary to

---

[3] *Lipkin Gorman (a firm) v Karpnale Ltd* [1991] AC 548. See Chapter 25.

[4] *Lipkin Gorman (a firm) v Karpnale Ltd* [1991] AC 548, 581.

[5] See, for example, *Boulton v Jones* (1857) 2 H and N 564, 157 ER 232.

[6] See, for example, *Greenwood v Bennett* [1973] QB 195 and *Rover International Ltd v Cannon Film Sales Ltd (No 3)* [1989] 1 WLR 912.

consider carefully whether the defendant has actually been enriched. But the fact that the identification of the enrichment is more complicated in such cases has no effect upon the test for identifying those mistakes which are sufficient to ground restitution, since the same type of mistake will ground restitution regardless of whether the enrichment is money or benefits in kind.

(D) SIGNIFICANT DISTINCTIONS

In defining what constitutes a mistake it is important to identify a number of significant distinctions. In doing so it is important to remember that mistake as a ground of restitution focuses on the state of mind of the claimant, to establish that the claimant's intention to benefit the defendant can be vitiated. It is irrelevant that the defendant did not share the mistake.[7]

(i) Ignorance of and Mistake as to the Transfer

There is no satisfactory legal definition of what constitutes an operative mistake for the purposes of the law of restitution. Mistake could be given a very wide definition so that it even encompasses those cases which have already been treated as involving ignorance of the transfer.[8] In *Pitt v Holt*,[9] however, Lord Walker confirmed that mistake was different from ignorance or inadvertence about the transfer of the enrichment to the defendant. It is important to distinguish between those cases where the claimant is unaware of the transfer to the defendant and those cases where the claimant is aware of the transfer but makes an error in respect of what is being transferred or why it is being transferred. This is because, where the claimant is unaware of the transfer, there is no intention to transfer a benefit which needs to be vitiated before the claimant can obtain restitution.[10] Where, however, the claimant is aware of the transfer, there is an apparent intention to transfer the benefit and so, if the claimant is to obtain restitution on the ground of mistake, it must be shown that the mistake vitiated the claimant's intention.

(ii) Beliefs and Assumptions

In *Pitt v Holt*[11] Lord Walker sought to define mistake by distinguishing between three different states of mind: an incorrect conscious belief, an incorrect tacit assumption, and mere causative ignorance but for which the claimant would not have acted as he did. Lord Walker considered that only the first two can be characterized as mistake; mere causative ignorance is not a mistake.[12] Although he accepted that it might be difficult to distinguish between beliefs, assumptions and ignorance, he emphasized that the court should not shrink from drawing an 'inference of conscious belief or tacit assumption when there is evidence to support such an inference'.[13]

Consequently, if it can be shown that the claimant had an incorrect belief or acted on an incorrect assumption as to fact or law, the claimant can be considered to be mistaken. If, however, the claimant had no idea about the possible existence of a fact or law, this suggests ignorance rather than mistake, unless a tacit assumption about the fact or law can be inferred.

---

[7] Although the defendant's belief can be relevant when considering the applicability of defences, such as change of position. See Chapter 25.

[8] See Chapter 8.   [9] [2013] UKSC 26, [2013] 2 AC 108, [104].   [10] See p 152, above.

[11] [2013] UKSC 26, [2013] 2 AC 108, [108].

[12] Ibid, [108]. See also C Mitchell, P Mitchell, and S Watterson (eds), *Goff and Jones: The Law of Unjust Enrichment* (8th edn, London: Sweet and Maxwell, 2011), 258.

[13] *Pitt v Holt* [2013] UKSC 26, [2013] 2 AC 108, [108].

For example, if a donor makes a gift to a charity whilst unaware of how much it spends on administration, this would not be a mistake unless it can be established that the donor made an incorrect assumption about the charity's administration at the time of payment.

This notion of an incorrect tacit assumption proved to be significant on the facts of *Pitt v Holt* itself. The case concerned a claim to set aside a voluntary disposition made to a trust on the ground that the disposition had been made by mistake. Following a road accident in which he was seriously injured, Mr Pitt received significant compensation. His wife was appointed his receiver and she sought professional advice concerning the investment of this money. As a result of this advice she placed the money in a discretionary trust for the benefit of her husband, herself, and their children. Mr Pitt later died, and his estate was found to be liable to pay inheritance tax on the sum held on trust. This liability could have been easily avoided had the trust contained a provision that at least half of the settled property applied during Mr Pitt's lifetime would be used for his benefit, but both the professional advisers and the Court of Protection, which had approved the trust, apparently overlooked the relevant tax liability. Lord Walker considered that Mrs Pitt had made a mistake relating to the inheritance tax liability: she either had an incorrect conscious belief as regards the tax consequences of the dispositions, or a tacit assumption that it would not result in adverse tax consequences. In fact, the trial judge had held[14] that Mrs Pitt had not made any mistake because she had not considered the question of inheritance tax liability at all, relying completely on her advisers. The Supreme Court disagreed and found that she was mistaken.[15] But the trial judge's finding of fact suggests that, because Mrs Pitt had no belief as to the tax liability, she must have made an incorrect tacit assumption that there would be no such liability.

This recognition that an incorrect tacit assumption constitutes a mistake potentially expands the notion of mistake significantly. It means that if, for example, the claimant has forgotten certain facts, such that he or she has already transferred a benefit to the defendant,[16] the claimant can be considered to have acted on an assumption which was incorrect. But such circumstances of forgetfulness about particular facts could be characterized as involving mere causative ignorance. The line between assumption and ignorance is consequently unclear. It would certainly have been more straightforward for the Supreme Court to have confined mistake to an incorrect conscious belief, which is how it was previously defined. In *Great Peace Shipping Ltd v Tsavliris Salvage (International) Ltd*[17] Lord Phillips MR described a mistake as an 'erroneous belief'. Sheehan usefully defined as mistake as a 'belief in something that can, at the time it is acted upon, be proved not to be the case'.[18] It would follow that forgetfulness or ignorance about particular facts would not constitute a mistake, because they do not involve belief. After the decision of the Supreme Court in *Pitt v Holt* that does not represent the law. Whether it should is a matter of policy and pragmatism.

The inclusion of incorrect tacit assumptions within mistake should be considered to be correct for two reasons. First, where the claimant has transferred a benefit to the defendant in circumstances where, for example, the claimant had forgotten a relevant fact and so had acted on a particular assumption about the state of the world, it remains appropriate to

---

[14] *Pitt v Holt* [2010] EWHC 45 (Ch), [2010] 1 WLR 1199, [50] (Robert Engelhart QC).

[15] Since the claim concerned rescission of a deed in Equity, there were additional factors to consider before restitution could be awarded. See p 200, below.

[16] As in *Lady Hood of Avalon v Mackinnon* [1909] 1 Ch 476. See p 200, below.

[17] [2002] EWCA Civ 1407, [2003] QB 679, [28].

[18] D Sheehan, 'What is a Mistake?' (2000) 20 LS 538. See also FA Farnsworth, *Alleviating Mistakes* (Oxford: Clarendon Press, 2004), 20, who concludes that a mistake should be defined as 'flawed perception'.

conclude that the claimant's intention to benefit the defendant was vitiated, even though the claimant had not consciously considered the relevance of the fact. Secondly, and even more significantly, even if mistake was confined to incorrect conscious beliefs, it will still be a matter of some difficulty for the claimant to prove what he or she actually believed at the time of transferring the benefit. Our decisions to act, whilst conscious, are typically not so carefully reasoned that we consider all relevant facts, but rather base our decisions on tacit assumptions. By recognizing that incorrect tacit assumptions form part of the doctrine of mistake, the Supreme Court was realistically defining what is a mistake and emphasized that the determination of whether the claimant was mistaken will require careful consideration of all the evidence to determine the state of the claimant's mind.

(iii) Law and Fact

It was a fundamental rule of English law for nearly 200 years that, where the claimant has made a mistake of law, a restitutionary claim could not usually be based on the mistake.[19] It followed that only mistakes of fact would be sufficient to ground a restitutionary claim. This mistake of law bar[20] was interpreted widely. The phrase covered both cases where the claimant was ignorant of what the state of the law was and cases where the claimant had a conscious but incorrect belief as to the state of the law.[21] Mistakes of law related to all aspects of the law, including judicial decisions, the existence of statutory powers, the interpretation of statutes and the construction of covenants.[22] In *Bilbie v Lumley*[23] Lord Ellenborough CJ justified the recognition of the mistake of law bar by reference to the principle that '[e]very man must be taken to be cognisant of the law; otherwise there is no saying to what extent the excuse of ignorance might not be carried. It would be urged in almost every case.'[24]

This principle that ignorance of the law is no excuse, which also encompasses an incorrect conscious belief about the state of the law, is particularly important in the laws of tort and crime where defendants are not allowed to argue that they should be excused from liability because they were unaware of the law. But it does not follow that this principle should be interpreted to mean that a claimant's mistake of law should bar a claim for restitution, for the policies of the criminal law and the law of tort are not necessarily applicable to the law of restitution. Within the context of the criminal law, for example, it is vitally important that defendants should not be allowed to rely on their ignorance of the criminal law to excuse their liability, for otherwise many criminals could not be convicted, the complexity of the criminal law being such that many defendants are unaware that their conduct may be criminal. But there is no equivalent problem within the law of restitution. This is because, where the claimant wishes to rely on mistake of law within the law of restitution, this is not in order to excuse his or her own liability, but rather to establish the defendant's liability. Reference to the ignorance of law principle was consequently an unsatisfactory explanation of the mistake of law bar.

The distinction between mistakes of law and fact was notoriously difficult to draw, and this created much scope for manipulation of restitutionary claims to ensure that they were

---

[19] See, in particular, *Bilbie v Lumley* (1802) 2 East 469, 102 ER 448; *Brisbane v Dacres* (1813) 5 Taunt 143, 128 ER 641; *R v Tower Hamlets London Borough Council, ex p Chetnik Developments Ltd* [1988] AC 858, 876–7 (Lord Bridge); and *Friends' Provident Life Office v Hillier Parker May and Rowden (a firm)* [1997] QB 85, 97 (Auld LJ).

[20] See *Kleinwort Benson Ltd v Lincoln CC* [1999] 2 AC 349, 367–75 (Lord Goff).

[21] PH Winfield, 'Mistake of Law' (1943) 59 LQR 327.   [22] *Re Hatch* [1919] 1 Ch 351.

[23] (1802) 2 East 469, 102 ER 448.   [24] Ibid, 472, 449.

founded on a mistake of fact.[25] The mistake of law bar was also subject to a number of exceptions. For example, the claimant could claim restitution by virtue of a mistake of law where the defendant had acted in bad faith, as would be the case where the defendant knew of the claimant's mistake[26] or had fraudulently induced the mistake.[27] Even certain statutes made specific provision for restitution of money which had been paid as a result of a mistake of law.[28] It followed that a principled justification for the mistake of law bar was lacking and the courts and Parliament undermined the operation of the bar by developing exceptions to it.

In 1998 in *Kleinwort Benson Ltd v Lincoln CC*[29] the House of Lords abolished the mistake of law bar. It follows that the claimant is now able to obtain restitution of benefits transferred to the defendant on the ground of mistake regardless of whether the mistake was one of fact or of law. This brings English law into line with virtually every other Common Law country, where the bar has also been abolished.[30]

The abolition of the mistake of law bar was correct simply because the receipt of an enrichment can be considered to be unjust regardless of whether the mistake is characterized as one of law or fact.[31] This is simply because, when determining whether the claimant's mistake should ground a restitutionary claim, the crucial question with which we are concerned is whether the claimant's intention to transfer a benefit to the defendant can be considered to have been vitiated by the mistake. The claimant's intention is just as likely to be vitiated where he or she made a mistake of law as where he or she made a mistake of fact. Further, before the mistake of law bar was abolished, the state of the law concerning that rule created great uncertainty on two counts. First, it was notoriously difficult to distinguish between mistakes of law and fact, and the consequent uncertainty created much scope for manipulation of the characterization of the mistake to secure what was considered to be a just result. Secondly, the mistake of law bar was riddled with exceptions, often of uncertain ambit, and there was no identifiable principle which could be considered to underlie all of the exceptions to the bar. This meant that the law was unnecessarily complex and that there were numerous ways of avoiding the rule, making those cases where it could not be avoided even more unjust.

(iv) Mistakes and Mispredictions

Mistakes are concerned with past or present facts or laws, whereas mispredictions are concerned with possible future events.[32] If the claimant has made a mistake as to a present fact or law this will constitute a ground of restitution. Where, however, the claimant has

---

[25] See, for example, *Avon CC v Howlett* [1983] 1 WLR 65. Note also the rule that mistakes as to private rights could be characterized as mistakes of fact: *Cooper v Phibbs* (1867) LR 2 HL 149.

[26] *Ward and Co v Wallis* [1900] 1 QB 675, 678. See also *Friends' Provident Life Office v Hillier Parker May and Rowden (a firm)* [1997] QB 85, 98 (Auld LJ).

[27] *Henderson v Folkestone Waterworks Co* (1885) TLR 329.

[28] See, for example, s 33(1) of the Taxes Management Act 1970 which provides for the recovery of income tax *inter alia* which has been paid as the result of a mistake of law.

[29] [1999] 2 AC 349. See further p 183, below.

[30] The rule was abolished by the Supreme Court of Canada in *Air Canada v British Columbia* (1989) 59 DLR (4d) 161; by the High Court of Australia in *David Securities Pty Ltd v Commonwealth Bank of Australia* (1992) 175 CLR 353; by the Appellate Division of the Supreme Court of the Supreme Court of South Africa in *Willis Faber Enthoven (Pty) Ltd v Receiver of Revenue* 1992 (4) SA 202(A); and by the Inner House of the Court Session in Scotland in *Morgan Guaranty Trust Co of New York v Lothian Regional Council* 1995 SLT 299. The rule was also abolished in New Zealand by the Judicature Act 1908, s 94A, as inserted by the Judicature Amendment Act 1958, s 2.

[31] *Kleinwort Benson Ltd v Lincoln CC* [1999] 2 AC 349, 407 (Lord Hope).

[32] See W Seah, 'Mispredictions, Mistakes and the Law of Unjust Enrichment' [2007] RLR 93.

made a misprediction as to future events this will not justify restitution in its own right.[33] This distinction between mistake and misprediction was recognized by Lord Walker in *Pitt v Holt*, although he acknowledged that the distinction can be a fine one.[34] Misprediction will not constitute a ground of restitution because, where the claimant has transferred a benefit to the defendant having made a misprediction as to a future event occurring, the claimant will be considered to have taken the risk that the future event might not occur.[35] It is a fundamental principle of the law of restitution that restitutionary relief will not be available to a claimant who is a risk-taker.[36] So, for example, if the claimant cleans the defendant's windows without being asked to do so, in the hope that when the defendant sees the clean windows she will pay him for the service provided, the claimant will not be able to claim that he was mistaken if the defendant refuses to pay, since he mispredicted the defendant's future reaction rather than made any mistake as to an existing state of affairs.[37] It would be different, however, if the claimant thought incorrectly that he had entered into a contract with the defendant to clean the windows, since then the claimant would be acting under an incorrect conscious belief as to the existence of the contractual obligation. Again, if the claimant is negotiating a contract with the defendant and, anticipating that the contract will be made, spends money in preparation for performance of the contract, if no contract is signed the claimant cannot found a restitutionary claim on mistake.[38] This is because the claimant was not mistaken as to present facts but had simply made a misprediction as to what might happen in the future.

The difficulty of drawing the distinction between mistake and misprediction is illustrated by the tragic case of *Re Griffiths*,[39] where the settlor, having taken tax planning advice, declared a trust of shares which he already owned. If the settlor had lived for seven years after setting up the trust his estate would not have borne any inheritance tax liability. Eight months after the trust was declared the settlor was diagnosed with lung cancer and he died the following year. If he had not settled the shares on trust, his estate would not have borne any tax liability on them. Consequently, his executor sought to set aside the disposition on trust by virtue of mistake, namely that the settlor believed that there was a real chance that he would survive for seven years, when in fact his state of health at the time of settling the shares on trust was that he was suffering from terminal cancer of which he was unaware. This claim succeeded since, had he been aware of the true state of his health, he would not have settled the shares on trust. This was consequently considered to be a mistake as to an existing fact, rather than a misprediction as to what might happen in the future. In *Pitt v Holt*[40] Lord Walker suggested that this seemed closer to being mere causative ignorance, rather than a mistake. He also emphasized that the decision turned on the finding of fact, which he considered to be a 'hair's breadth finding', that the settlor was actually suffering from cancer at the time of the settlement. Had this not been established, the case would certainly have been treated as one of misprediction regarding the state of the settlor's health in the seven years to follow. As with the distinction between tacit assumptions and ignorance, so too the distinction between mistake and misprediction

---

[33] See *Kleinwort Benson Ltd v Lincoln CC* [1999] 2 AC 349, 398 (Lord Hoffmann) and 410 (Lord Hope); *Dextra Bank and Trust Co v Bank of Jamaica* [2002] 1 All ER (Comm) 193.

[34] *Pitt v Holt* [2013] UKSC 26, [2013] 2 AC 108, [104].

[35] Though restitution may lie even though the claimant mispredicted what the defendant would do, if the claimant can found his or her claim on another ground of restitution, such as that of total failure of basis. See Chapter 13.   [36] See p 36, above.

[37] There would also be difficulties in showing that the defendant had been enriched in such circumstances. See p 71, above.

[38] A restitutionary claim may, however, be founded on total failure of basis. See Chapter 13.

[39] [2009] Ch 162.   [40] [2013] UKSC 26, [2013] 2 AC 108, [114].

will turn on careful analysis of the evidence to determine whether the claimant's belief related to the state of affairs now or in the past, which will be a mistake, or the state of affairs in the future, which will be a misprediction.

The only qualification to this distinction between mistakes and mispredictions arises from the recognition that a mistake of law can now constitute a ground of restitution. If the claimant transferred a benefit to the defendant on the correct assumption that he or she was liable to do so by operation of law, and the law was subsequently changed by judicial decision, the effect of the declaratory theory of law-making[41] is that the claimant had indeed made a mistake when he or she transferred the benefit to the defendant.[42] This is because the subsequent judicial decision is deemed to be operating at the time the benefit was transferred, so the claimant was in fact mistaken about the liability to transfer the benefit to the defendant. This could be characterized as a misprediction, because the claimant's error related to a change in the law in the future rather than the state of the law at the time when the benefit was transferred. But this argument has been found to be incorrect because judicial changes in the law are deemed to operate retrospectively and so constitute a deemed mistake.[43] The effect of this is that the claimant was not liable to transfer the benefit when he or she did so, which is deemed to be a present mistake as to the law at the time of the transfer, rather than a misprediction of future events.

(v) Spontaneous and Induced Mistakes

Usually the claimant's mistake will arise spontaneously, but sometimes it may have been induced by the defendant.[44] It is important to distinguish between spontaneous and induced mistakes because the nature of the mistake determines the test which will be adopted to determine whether the mistake was sufficient to vitiate the claimant's intention to transfer a benefit to the defendant.

(vi) Ground of Restitution and Legally Effective Basis

Where a claimant has mistakenly transferred a benefit to the defendant, the test of mistake varies depending on the nature of the restitutionary claim. There are two routes to the recovery of such benefits. First, the claimant may have transferred a benefit to the defendant by mistake in circumstances where there was no legally effective basis for the transfer.[45] In such cases the claimant will simply need to establish that the defendant has been unjustly enriched at the claimant's expense. Alternatively, the claimant may have transferred the benefit to the defendant in circumstances where there was a basis for the transfer, such as a contractual obligation or a deed. In such cases, in addition to establishing that the defendant was unjustly enriched at the claimant's expense, the claimant will also need to establish that the basis is legally ineffective. Once this additional element has been established, restitution will follow. Typically, this will be by virtue of the mistake, but the interpretation of mistake to set aside a contract or a deed is different from how mistake is interpreted as a ground of restitution for purposes of the law of unjust enrichment. As will be seen,[46] mistake is interpreted more restrictively when an otherwise legally effective transaction is set aside, by virtue of the policy in favour of protecting the

---

[41] See p 183, below.

[42] Save where the claimant can be said to have borne the risk of the mistake. See *Brennan v Bolt Burdon* [2004] EWCA Civ 1017, [2005] QB 303.

[43] *Deutsche Morgan Grenfell v IRC* [2006] UKHL 49, [2007] AC 558, [23] (Lord Hoffmann). See further p 183, below.

[44] For analysis of the effect of induced mistakes, see p 187, below.   [45] See Chapter 7.

[46] See p 193, below.

security of such transactions. It is consequently important to distinguish mistake as a ground of restitution and mistake as a factor which vitiates an otherwise legally effective transaction.

2. MISTAKE AS A GROUND OF RESTITUTION

(A) SPONTANEOUS MISTAKES

Where the claimant wishes to recover a benefit which has been transferred to the defendant as a result of a spontaneous mistake, the appropriate test for determining which mistakes should ground a restitutionary claim has been a matter of particular controversy. Three different principal tests have been recognized at varying times as grounding such claims, namely liability mistakes, fundamental mistakes, and causative mistakes.

(i) Liability Mistakes

In the first cases to recognize that the claimant's spontaneous mistake could ground a restitutionary claim, relief was confined to where the claimant mistakenly believed that he or she was liable to pay the defendant. In such circumstances it is clear that the claimant's intention to benefit the defendant must have been vitiated by the mistake. This is because, had the claimant not mistakenly believed that he or she was liable to pay the defendant, the money would not have been paid, since there would usually be no other explanation as to why the money was paid.

It is possible to identify four different types of liability mistake which have been recognized as sufficient to justify restitution.

(1) Existing Legal Liabilities Owed to the Defendant

If the claimant can show that he or she transferred a benefit to the defendant because of a mistaken belief that he or she was subject to an existing legal liability to do so, this will ground a restitutionary claim. This was recognized in *Aiken v Short*[47] where Bramwell B said:[48]

> In order to entitle a person to recover back money paid under a mistake of fact, the mistake must be as to a fact which, if true, would make the person paying liable to pay the money; not where, if true, it would merely make it desirable that he should pay the money.

The application of this principle is illustrated by *Kelly v Solari*,[49] where the claimant insurance company had paid money to the executrix of the assured believing that it was liable to do so under a life insurance policy. In fact, there was no liability to pay this money because the policy had lapsed as a result of the assured failing to pay the premiums on the policy. Such a mistake as to the existence of the liability meant that in principle the claimant could recover the money,[50] since, as Parke B recognized, where money was paid

---

[47] (1856) 1 H and N 210, 156 ER 1180. Affirmed in *Re the Bodega Company Ltd* [1904] 1 Ch 276.

[48] *Aiken v Short* (1856) 1 H and N 210, 215; 156 ER 1180, 1182. The claim failed both because there was no mistaken belief as to a liability to pay and because the defendant had provided good consideration for the payment. See p 191, below.

[49] (1841) 9 M and W 54, 152 ER 24. See also *Home and Colonial Insurance Co Ltd v London Guarantee and Accident Co Ltd* (1928) 45 TLR 134, 135 (Wright J).

[50] A retrial was ordered to determine whether the claimant really had made a mistake.

on the assumption of certain mistaken facts which, if true, would mean that the recipient was entitled to the money, it followed that restitution should be awarded where those facts were not true.[51] It was also held to be irrelevant that the means of discovering that the policy had lapsed was available to the claimant. Consequently, the carelessness of the claimant, in failing to check whether the policy had lapsed, did not prevent it from obtaining restitution.

Usually, as in *Kelly v Solari*, the mistaken belief in liability relates to a contractual liability to pay the defendant, but this is not always the case. So, in *Baylis v Bishop of London*,[52] although the claimant's mistaken belief concerned a non-contractual liability to pay ecclesiastical tithes to the Bishop of London, restitution of the money was still ordered.

Even where the claimant has made a mistake as to the existence of a legal liability, restitution only lies if the claimant can show that, if the mistake had not been made, he or she would not have transferred the benefit to the defendant. In other words, the mistaken belief as to a liability to pay must be shown to have been the cause of the transfer being made, in the sense that, but for the mistake, the benefit would not have been transferred to the defendant. For example, in *Home and Colonial Insurance Co Ltd v London Guarantee and Accident Co Ltd*[53] the payment made by the claimant had been influenced by a mistake of law as well as one of fact. It followed that restitution was denied because the claimant could not show that his decision to make the payment had only been influenced by the mistake of fact. Of course, with the abolition of the mistake of law bar, where the claimant's mistake is both a mistake of law and one of fact, restitutionary relief would now be awarded because both types of mistake can operate as grounds of restitution.

(2) Existing Liabilities Owed to Third Parties

Whether restitution can be awarded where the claimant transfers a benefit to the defendant in the mistaken belief that he or she is under an existing legal liability to a third party to do so has been a matter of some controversy. Restitution in such circumstances has sometimes expressly been rejected on the ground that the claimant mistakenly believed that he or she was liable to a third party rather than the defendant,[54] whereas in other cases restitution has been awarded even though the claimant had such a mistaken belief.[55] The better view is that the claimant's belief that the liability was owed to a third party rather than to the defendant should not bar the restitutionary claim, since the transfer is still caused by the claimant's mistaken belief that he or she was liable to make the transfer, albeit that this liability was not owed to the recipient of the benefit.[56]

(3) Future Liabilities

Restitution has also been granted where the claimant's mistake related to a belief in a future liability to transfer a benefit to the defendant. This was the result in *Kerrison v Glyn*,

---

[51] *Kelly v Solari* (1841) 9 M and W 54, 58; 152 ER 24, 26. But Parke B did not suggest that a mistaken belief as to liability to pay the money was the only type of mistake which would ground restitution. See *Barclays Bank Ltd v WJ Simms, Son and Cooke (Southern) Ltd* [1980] 1 QB 677, 687 (Robert Goff J).

[52] [1913] 1 Ch 127.   [53] (1928) 45 TLR 134.

[54] *Deutsche Bank (London Agency) v Beriro and Co* (1895) 73 LTR 669. See also *Barclay and Co Ltd v Malcolm and Co* (1925) 133 LT 512 and *Weld-Blundell v Synott* [1940] 2 KB 107.

[55] See, for example, *Colonial Bank v Exchange Bank of Yarmouth, Nova Scotia* (1885) 11 App Cas 84; *Kleinwort, Sons and Co v Dunlop Rubber Co* (1907) 97 LT 263; *R E Jones Ltd v Waring and Gillow Ltd* [1926] AC 670; *Barclays Bank Ltd v WJ Simms, Son and Cooke (Southern) Ltd* [1980] 1 QB 677.

[56] This was the view of Robert Goff J in *Barclays Bank v Simms, Son and Cooke (Southern) Ltd* [1980] 1 QB 677.

Mills, Currie and Co,[57] where the claimant agreed with a bank that he would reimburse it in respect of any payments which were made by it on his behalf. In anticipation of such a liability arising in the future, the claimant transferred money to the defendant to be paid to the bank when the liability arose. The claimant was not, however, aware that at the time of his payment to the defendant the bank was insolvent. Consequently, the claimant sought to recover the money which he had paid to the defendant on the ground that he had made a mistake of fact, namely that no liability to reimburse the bank would have arisen subsequently. Although there was no existing liability to pay the money to the bank, it was held that the claimant could recover the amount paid to the defendant because of a mistaken belief that the liability would arise in the future.

This case does cause some serious difficulties though, since a mistaken belief that a liability to pay money would arise in the future is not a mistake at all, but is a misprediction.[58] It therefore appears that the claimant in *Kerrison* had acted voluntarily in paying the defendant, so the claimant took the risk of the bank's insolvency. Consequently, the ratio of the case that restitutionary relief should be available if the claimant's 'mistake' relates to a liability arising in the future should be rejected. It does not follow, however, that the result of the case is necessarily wrong. The success of the restitutionary claim could be justified on two alternative grounds. First, the claimant can be considered to have made a mistake as to an existing fact, namely that the bank was solvent, and this mistake caused the claimant to pay the defendant. In other words, the claimant's mistake was not a liability mistake but was simply a causative mistake, in the sense that, but for the claimant's mistake as to the solvency of the bank, the claimant would not have paid the money.[59]

Alternatively, the success of the claim might be justified on the ground that the basis for the claimant paying the defendant, namely that the defendant would pay the bank, could never be satisfied because the bank was insolvent. In other words, the claimant could have relied on an alternative ground of restitution, namely total failure of basis.[60]

(4) Moral Duties

It has sometimes been suggested that, if the claimant transferred a benefit to the defendant in the mistaken belief that there was a moral duty to do so, such a mistake will enable the claimant to recover the benefit from the defendant. So, for example, in *Larner v London County Council*[61] the Council had decided to pay its employees who had entered the armed services during the Second World War the difference between their war service pay and their civil pay. The Council made such a payment to Larner, but overpaid him because he had failed to disclose changes in his war service pay. It was held by the Court of Appeal that the Council could recover the overpayment, even though it had never believed that it was legally liable to make the payment in the first place. Denning LJ emphasized that it was sufficient, on the facts as the Council believed them to be, that there was a moral duty to pay Larner.

It remains unclear how the court in *Larner* was able to conclude that there was a moral duty to pay the defendant. There are three possible explanations of the case. The first is that the duty to pay arose from national policy at the time which sought to encourage men to engage in war service by removing some of the financial risks of doing so. But this is a vague basis for identifying a moral duty to pay. An alternative explanation of the case is that the duty arose from the fact that the Council had already promised Larner that it

---

[57] (1911) 81 LJKB 465.   [58] See p 162, above.   [59] See p 170, below.
[60] See Chapter 13.   [61] [1949] 2 KB 683.

would pay him the money.[62] So a moral duty to pay would appear to be triggered by an antecedent promise to pay, regardless of the absence of any contractual liability. But if an antecedent promise creates a moral liability to pay it follows that it would sometimes be possible to recover gifts by reason of mistake, so long as the claimant has promised to make the gift in the first place. If this were possible then it would undermine any notion of restitution being confined to liability mistakes. Consequently, *Larner* is better treated as a case where the mistake did not depend on any belief on the part of the claimant that it was liable to pay the defendant. The acceptance that the Council could recover the overpayment is much easier to justify by reference to a test that the Council's mistake had caused the Council to make the payment to Larner.

(5) Is Restitution Confined to Liability Mistakes?

Even though it is clear that, where the claimant had made a mistake as to an existing liability to pay either the defendant or a third party, this is sufficient to establish a ground of restitution, it does not follow that restitution on the ground of mistake is confined to such circumstances. It is apparent from those cases which have recognized that mistakes as to future liability or moral liabilities can ground restitutionary claims, that there must be some other test of mistake, simply because the mistakes in those cases cannot properly be characterized as liability mistakes.

(ii) Fundamental Mistakes

The test of fundamental mistake was recognized by the Court of Appeal in *Morgan v Ashcroft*,[63] where the claimant was a bookmaker whose clerk had mistakenly overpaid the defendant his winnings after he had laid bets on a horse race. The claimant sought to recover the overpayment on the ground that his clerk had made a mistake. The claim failed because betting at the time was illegal and the court would not assist a claimant to recover a benefit where he or she had participated in an illegal transaction.[64] Despite this, the judges did consider the appropriate test for determining when a mistake would ground a restitutionary claim. Whilst they accepted that a mistaken belief in a liability to pay the money would be sufficient to establish such a claim, they emphasized that the ground for recovery was not restricted to liability mistakes. Rather, the cases where restitution was awarded on the basis of a liability mistake formed part of a wider principle, namely that it was sufficient that the mistake could be characterized as fundamental.[65] On the facts of the case it was considered that the claimant's mistake could not be so characterized.

In *Morgan v Ashcroft* Sir Wilfrid Greene MR specifically relied on the decision of the Privy Council in *Norwich Union Fire Insurance Society Ltd v Price*[66] as authority for this test of fundamental mistake. In the *Norwich Union* case the defendant had claimed money from the claimant insurance company in respect of a cargo of lemons which the defendant asserted had been damaged by a peril which had been insured against, and which was subsequently sold at a loss. The claimant paid the defendant the insured value of the cargo, but it later discovered that the lemons were not sold because they had been damaged but because they were ripening, and this was a risk which was not covered by the insurance policy. The claimant recovered the money it had paid on the basis that it had made a mistake. Although the success of the claim could have been justified by virtue of the

---

[62] CA Needham, 'Mistaken Payments: A New Look at an Old Theme' (1979) 12 Univ of Brit Col LR 159, 168.
[63] [1938] 1 KB 49.
[64] By virtue of the Gaming Act 1845, s 18. For analysis of the defence of illegality see Chapter 27.
[65] *Morgan v Ashcroft* [1938] 1 KB 49, 66 (Sir Wilfrid Greene MR) and 74 (Scott LJ).
[66] [1934] AC 455.

mistaken liability principle, since the claimant mistakenly believed that it was liable to pay on the insurance policy, Lord Wright justified the result on the ground that the claimant's mistake was fundamental and such a mistake prevented there being the necessary intention to pay the money.[67]

In the *Norwich Union* case Lord Wright described a fundamental mistake as one 'in respect of the underlying assumption of the contract or transaction or as being fundamental or basic'.[68] He went on to add that '[w]hether the mistake does satisfy this description may often be a matter of great difficulty'. Despite the inherent uncertainty of the fundamental mistake test, it is possible to clarify what is meant by a mistake as to the 'underlying assumption' for the transfer of the benefit to the defendant. In *Morgan v Ashcroft* two types of fundamental mistake were identified: first, those mistakes which are concerned with the nature of the transfer—the best example of this are those cases where claimants mistakenly believed that they were liable to pay the defendant; secondly, where the mistake is one of identity—such as where the claimant pays money to the defendant mistakenly thinking that the defendant is somebody else. In both situations the claimant's intention that the defendant should receive the money is vitiated by this fundamental mistake and so restitution will lie.[69]

The operation of the fundamental mistake test is crucially different from the liability mistake test, since the former is applicable to recover gifts made by mistake regardless of the fact that the claimant did not consider that he or she was liable to make the gift to the defendant, but the mistake would have to relate either to the nature of the gift or the identity of the donee.

Although the test of fundamental mistake has been recognized as a means of establishing a ground of restitution, whether such a test should be adopted is a particularly controversial matter. The key question of principle which needs to be considered when determining the most appropriate test of mistake is what degree of vitiation of intention is considered appropriate before the mistake can operate as a ground of restitution. This in turn depends on a question of policy, namely how easy should it be for claimants to claim that they have made a mistake and so are entitled to restitutionary relief? This is something which has often been ignored by the courts in those cases which advocate the test of fundamental mistake. That restrictive test is entirely appropriate where it is necessary to vitiate a contract for mistake,[70] since a bargain should only be treated as vitiated where it can be concluded that the effect of the mistake was such that the parties cannot be considered to have truly made a bargain at all. But a test which is appropriate in the context of vitiation of contracts is not necessarily appropriate where the claimant wishes to recover benefits without needing to set a transaction aside.[71] Where a contract is set aside for mistake, what needs to be shown is that the intention to contract was vitiated by the mistake. Where the claimant simply wishes to recover benefits from the defendant, all we are concerned with is whether the claimant's intention to transfer the benefit was vitiated by the mistake. The policy of the law is very different in the two

---

[67] Ibid, 462.　　[68] Ibid, 463.

[69] *Morgan v Ashcroft* [1938] 1 KB 49, 66 (Sir Wilfrid Greene MR). Fundamental mistake as to identity may have been the ground of restitution in *Greenwood v Bennett* [1973] QB 195 where the repairer of a car, who repaired the car because he mistakenly believed that he owned it, recovered from the car's owner the value of the services he had provided in repairing and improving it. See p 82, above.

[70] See p 193, below.

[71] See *Citibank NA v Brown Shipley and Co Ltd* [1991] 2 All ER 690, 700 (Waller J). Cf PBH Birks, *An Introduction to the Law of Restitution* (rev edn, Oxford: Clarendon Press, 1989), 159, who tentatively supported the fundamental mistake test because of concerns about opening the floodgates of litigation and consequent insecurity of receipts.

contexts as well. For there is a clear reluctance to set contracts aside for mistake because of the principle that parties should be held to their bargains wherever possible. There is no similar policy in operation where the claimant wishes to recover the value of a benefit from the defendant.

One possible argument which can be used to explain why the test of fundamental mistake has been adopted as a ground of restitution, even though the claimant did not need to set a transaction aside, is founded on the implied contract theory. At a time when it was believed that restitutionary relief would only be available if it were possible to imply a contract between the parties to make restitution,[72] the contractual test of mistake would appear to have been an entirely appropriate test of mistake, even though the claimant did not seek to set a contract aside. But with the rejection of the implied contract theory,[73] any analogy drawn from the law of contract is clearly inappropriate.

The fundamental mistake test is also adopted in respect of claims to vindicate proprietary rights where such a mistake operates to prevent title to property from passing to the defendant.[74] Such a restrictive test of mistake is appropriate in that context because it is only where the effect of the mistake is to negate the claimant's intention completely that it is proper to conclude that title does not pass to the defendant, so that the claimant can rely on his or her continuing title to recover property from the direct or indirect recipient. Where, however, the claimant simply wishes to recover the value of a benefit mistakenly transferred to the defendant in a personal restitutionary claim founded on the reversal of unjust enrichment, it is not necessary to show that the mistake is so serious that it prevents title from passing. If the same test of fundamental mistake were adopted for both types of restitutionary claim there would be no need for the claimant to base his or her restitutionary claim on the principle of unjust enrichment since fundamental mistakes prevent title from passing to the defendant. Consequently, the claimant will necessarily have retained a proprietary interest whenever he or she has made a fundamental mistake and the vindication of this interest can form the basis of a restitutionary action, for which the claimant may obtain either a personal or a proprietary restitutionary remedy.[75] If there is to be an independent restitutionary action founded on the reversal of unjust enrichment where the ground of restitution is mistake, the test of mistake needs to be wider than the equivalent test for proprietary restitutionary claims.

The obvious conclusion from these arguments is that the test of mistake for the purposes of restitutionary claims founded on the unjust enrichment principle should be wider than the test of fundamental mistake,[76] and so some other test of mistake needs to be identified. That other test is the test of operating cause.

(iii) Causative Mistakes

The operating cause test of mistake will be satisfied whenever the claimant's mistake caused him or her to transfer a benefit to the defendant. In *Kelly v Solari*,[77] whilst Parke B recognized that a mistaken belief as to liability to pay the defendant would constitute a ground for restitution,[78] he did not suggest that this was the only type of mistake which would ground such claims.[79] The judgment of Rolfe B in the same case supports a very wide test for recovery, one which is not restricted to mistaken beliefs as to liability to

---

[72] See Chapter 3.   [73] See *United Australia Ltd v Barclays Bank Ltd* [1941] AC 1.
[74] See p 574, below.   [75] See Chapter 22.
[76] Robert Goff J in *Barclays Bank Ltd v WJ Simms, Son and Cooke (Southern) Ltd* [1980] 1 QB 677, 689.
[77] (1841) 9 M and W 54, 152 ER 24.   [78] Ibid, 58–9; 26.
[79] As was recognized by Robert Goff J in *Barclays Bank Ltd v WJ Simms, Son and Cooke (Southern) Ltd* [1980] 1 QB 677, 687.

transfer a benefit to the defendant. Rolfe B stated that: 'wherever [money] is paid under a mistake of fact, and the party would not otherwise have paid it if the fact had been known to him, it cannot be otherwise than unconscientious to retain it'.[80]

This requirement that the claimant would not have paid the defendant had he or she not been mistaken constitutes an implicit recognition that it is sufficient to show that the mistake had caused the claimant to pay the money.

The leading case which recognized and applied the causation test is *Barclays Bank Ltd v WJ Simms, Son and Cooke (Southern) Ltd*.[81] In this case a customer of the claimant bank drew a cheque on its account with the claimant in favour of the defendant. The customer discovered subsequently that the defendant had just entered into receivership and telephoned the claimant requesting that it stop the cheque. The receiver presented the cheque to the claimant for payment. The paying official, forgetting about the existence of the stop order, paid the money to the receiver. The bank then sought to recover the money from the defendant and succeeded because the paying official's mistake had been an operating cause of the payment, since, but for the fact that the official had forgotten about the stop order, the money would not have been paid to the defendant. Although restitution could have been awarded by reference to the liability principle, since the claimant had mistakenly believed that it was liable to pay the defendant, Robert Goff J considered that principle to be only an example of a wider principle by virtue of which it was sufficient that the mistake had caused the claimant to transfer a benefit to the defendant.

This test of operative causation was recognized by the House of Lords in *Banque Financière de la Cité v Parc (Battersea) Ltd*.[82] In this case the claimant had lent money to the debtor company, which was used to discharge a liability of the debtor to a third party. The claimant's loan to the debtor was unsecured because the claimant had received a letter of postponement which stated that the debt owed by the debtor to the claimant would be paid off in priority to any debts which were owed by the debtor to any other company in the group. The defendant was another company in the same group which was also owed money by the debtor company, but the defendant's debt was secured. This meant that the defendant's debt had priority over that of the claimant, and this was important since the debtor had gone into liquidation. The question for the House of Lords concerned the effect of the letter of postponement on the relative priorities of the claims of the claimant and the defendant. It was held that, although the letter of postponement did not bind the defendant, if the claimant could establish that the defendant had been unjustly enriched, the claimant could be subrogated to the rights of the third party against the debtor and so obtain priority over the defendant.[83] The court concluded that the defendant had been enriched at the claimant's expense,[84] because the claimant's money had been used to discharge part of the debt owed to the third party, so improving the chances of the defendant being repaid. It was then necessary to consider the ground of restitution. Whilst not all the members of the House of Lords considered this matter, those who did clearly considered the ground to be the claimant's mistake in lending the money

---

[80] *Kelly v Solari* (1841) 9 M and W 54, 152 ER 24. See also *Kleinwort, Sons and Co v Dunlop Rubber Co* (1907) 97 LT 263, 264 (Lord Loreburn LC); *Kerrison v Glyn, Mills, Currie and Co* (1911) 81 LJ KB 465, 470 (Lord Atkinson) and 471 (Lord Shaw of Dunfermline); *R E Jones Ltd v Waring and Gillow Ltd* [1926] AC 670, 679–80 (Viscount Cave LC). None of these judges specified that the claimant must have mistakenly believed that he or she was under a liability to pay the defendant.

[81] [1980] QB 677. See also *Saronic Shipping Co Ltd v Huron Liberian Co* [1979] 1 Lloyd's Rep 341, 362–6 (Mocatta J), affirmed by the Court of Appeal without reference to mistake: [1980] 2 Lloyd's Rep 26.

[82] [1999] 1 AC 221.   [83] See p 638, below, for analysis of the remedy of subrogation.

[84] See p 106, above.

to the debtor in the belief that the letter of postponement was effective to give the claimant priority over the defendant. Clearly, the claimant's mistake was not a mistake as to a liability, nor could it be considered to be a fundamental mistake. Rather, the mistake was simply an operating cause of the claimant lending the money to the debtor company. This was specifically acknowledged by Lord Hoffmann, who recognized that: 'The [claimant] advanced [the money] upon the mistaken assumption that it was obtaining a postponement letter which would be effective to give it priority over any intra-group indebtedness. It would not otherwise have done so.'[85]

Although the court did not specifically examine the different theories of the appropriate test for identifying which mistakes can ground restitutionary claims, the conclusion of the court is only consistent with the but for test of causation: *but for* its mistake the claimant would not have transferred the benefit to the defendant.

Further support for the operating cause test can be found in some of the judgments in the decision of the House of Lords in *Kleinwort Benson Ltd v Lincoln CC*.[86] The most important judgment in this respect is that of Lord Hope, who stated that:

> Subject to any defences that may arise from the circumstances, a claim for restitution of money paid under a mistake raises three questions. (1) Was there a mistake? (2) Did the mistake cause the payment? And (3) did the payee have a right to receive the sum which was paid to him?[87]

This is the clearest recognition in England at the highest level that it is sufficient that the claimant's mistake simply caused the claimant to transfer a benefit to the defendant, even though the mistake did not relate to a belief that the claimant was liable to pay the defendant. The House of Lords in *Deutsche Morgan Grenfell v IRC*[88] confirmed that the appropriate test is one of causation, in a case where Lord Hope considered that the mistake related to whether the claimant could elect to delay payment of tax rather than whether there was a liability to pay tax, although, as he acknowledged, the mistake about the availability of the election meant that the claimant believed that there was a liability to pay tax immediately. Crucially, however, he recognized that there was 'an unbroken causative link between the mistake and the payment'.[89]

The operation of the 'but for' test of causation has also been recognized by the Privy Council in *Dextra Bank and Trust Co v Bank of Jamaica*.[90] Fraudsters persuaded the claimant to draw a cheque for the defendant on the basis that the defendant wished to borrow the money and would enter into a loan agreement with the claimant. But the defendant was the victim of the same fraud and it believed that the claimant was selling US currency to it. The claimant sought restitution of the money on the ground of mistake. Two different mistakes were identified, but the claimant failed to establish both of them. The first mistake related to the claimant's failure to enter into a loan agreement with the defendant. This was characterized as a misprediction as to a future event, rather than a mistake of existing fact, and so was not relevant.[91] The second mistake related to the claimant's belief that the defendant had previously agreed to take a loan. The Privy

---

[85] *Banque Financière de la Cité v Parc (Battersea) Ltd* [1999] 1 AC 221, 234. See also Lord Steyn, 227.

[86] [1999] 2 AC 349, 358 (Lord Browne-Wilkinson), 371 (Lord Goff), 399 (Lord Hoffmann).

[87] Ibid, 407.

[88] [2006] UKHL 49, [2007] 1 AC 558, [60] (Lord Hope), [143] (Lord Walker). See also Lord Scott, ibid, [84], albeit dissenting on the facts. See also *Sempra Metals Ltd v IRC* [2007] UKHL 34, [2008] 1 AC 561 and *Pitt v Holt* [2013] UKSC 26, [2013] 2 AC 108.

[89] *Deutsche Morgan Grenfell v IRC* [2006] UKHL 49, [2007] 1 AC 558, [62]. Lords Hoffmann and Walker considered that the mistake did relate to the liability to pay tax: ibid, [32] and [143].

[90] [2002] 1 All ER (Comm) 193.   [91] See p 162, above.

Council recognized that this was a causative mistake, according to the but for test of causation, but considered it to be too remote from the payment of the money to the defendant on the facts. This is an important decision, both in its recognition of the causative mistake test and also the acknowledgement that a test of but for causation is limited by considerations of remoteness.

Developments in some Commonwealth countries show that there is a growing recognition that causation is the most appropriate test for identifying those mistakes which will ground restitutionary claims. Significantly, in the decision of the High Court of Australia in *David Securities Pty Ltd v Commonwealth Bank of Australia*[92] the test of fundamental mistake, which had previously been accepted as the appropriate test for determining which mistakes would ground restitutionary claims, was rejected in favour of a causation test. The court stressed that, where the mistake had caused the claimant to pay the defendant, the claimant's intention will have been vitiated for purposes of the law of restitution and this was all that needed to be shown. In the decision of the New Zealand High Court in *University of Canterbury v Attorney-General*,[93] the claimant recovered a gift of shares which he had transferred to an educational trust in the mistaken belief that such a gift was necessary because the trust fund had been seriously depleted, when this was not in fact the case. It was held that the claimant could recover the shares because he would not have made the gift but for the mistake.[94]

It follows from the recognition of the operative test of causation in England that those cases in which restitution was granted by reference to the alternative tests of liability mistake or fundamental mistake will still have been decided the same way. This is because it is inconceivable that cases where a benefit was transferred because the claimant believed that he or she was liable to transfer it, or because the claimant had made a fundamental mistake, could now be treated as cases where the mistaken belief was not an operating cause of the transfer. Some other cases cannot be explained by reference to liability mistake but can be explained by reference to a test of operating cause, even though the court did not articulate why the mistake constituted a ground of restitution. For example, in *Greenwood v Bennett*[95] the person who had repaired and improved a car, mistakenly believing that he owned it, succeeded in recovering the value of his services in an action where the true owner sought to recover the car, even though the repairer did not believe himself liable to make the repairs. The mistaken belief of the repairer that he owned the car might be characterized as a fundamental mistake as to the identity of the person who benefited from the work: the repairer thinking that it was himself when in fact it was the owner, but it is definitely a causative mistake, since, but for that mistake, the repairer would not have undertaken the repairs.[96]

Some of the previous cases where restitution was denied because no liability mistake had been made would typically have been decided differently if a test of operating cause had been recognized. For example, in *Aiken v Short*[97] restitutionary relief was denied because the claimant had not made any mistake as to its liability to pay money to the defendant. Rather, the claimant had made the payment because it thought that it was discharging the defendant's supposed interest in the claimant's property, when in fact the

---

[92] (1992) 175 CLR 353, 378.   [93] [1995] 1 NZLR 78.

[94] Ibid, 81 (Williamson J). Williamson J also endorsed the test of fundamental mistake, but it is difficult to see how the claimant's mistake on the facts was fundamental when it related simply to his motive for making the gift.   [95] [1973] QB 195.

[96] Another case which cannot be explained by reference to a mistaken belief as to liability to pay the defendant is *Colonial Bank v Exchange Bank of Yarmouth, Nova Scotia* (1885) 11 App Cas 84.

[97] (1856) 1 H and N 210, 156 ER 1180.

defendant did not have such an interest. This mistake was an operating cause of the payment, since if the claimant had been aware at the time of the payment that the defendant did not have an interest in the property, it would not have made the payment. This was effectively recognized by Bramwell B who, whilst concluding that the claimant had acted voluntarily because it had not satisfied the mistaken liability test, recognized that the purchase of the defendant's supposed interest in the property 'turned out to be different to, and of less value than, what [the claimant] expected'.[98] Consequently, if *Aiken v Short* was decided today, restitution would be granted, subject to argument about any defences which might be relied on by the defendant or whether there was a legal basis for the defendant's receipt of the enrichment.[99]

(1) Justifications for the Operating Cause Test

The ground of restitution for mistake has developed gradually from the core case of liability mistakes, where it is easy to conclude that the defendant was unjustly enriched, to the recognition of a general principle that it suffices that the mistake was an operating cause of the benefit being transferred. This development of the ground of mistake mirrors the development of the tort of negligence. In the same way that, before the leading case of *Donoghue v Stevenson*,[100] the tort of negligence arose in specific and limited categories, so too the ground of mistake was confined to specific categories of case where the nature of the mistake justified the award of restitutionary relief. The importance of the decision of the House of Lords in *Donoghue v Stevenson* was to extract a general principle from the disparate categories of negligence, and this general principle has been the touchstone against which all claims in negligence have been determined subsequently. If the analogy with the tort of negligence is a true one it means that the decision of Robert Goff J in *Barclays Bank v Simms* should be considered to be the *Donoghue v Stevenson* of restitution for mistake, for it was in that case that Robert Goff J extracted a general principle from the previous cases which would serve to determine when a mistake could constitute a ground of restitution. The only serious drawback with this analogy is that *Donoghue v Stevenson* was a decision of the House of Lords, whereas *Barclays Bank v Simms* was merely the decision of a trial judge, albeit one whose decisions are highly influential, but that decision has now been endorsed by the House of Lords in both *Kleinwort Benson v Lincoln CC*[101] and *Deutsche Morgan Grenfell v IRC*.[102]

The recognition of the operating cause test of mistake can, however, be justified by reference to the principles which underlie the recognition of grounds of restitution.[103] A ground of restitution serves to show that the benefit received by the defendant was unjustly received. This will be the case in the context of mistake where it is possible to conclude that the effect of the claimant's mistake is to vitiate his or her intention to transfer the benefit to the defendant.[104] But this notion of vitiation of intention must be treated with caution, because vitiation of intention is a matter of degree and the effect of the different tests of mistake is that the claimant's intention is vitiated to differing extents. So, for example, where the claimant makes a fundamental mistake as to the identity of the defendant it can be concluded that the mistake is so extreme that the claimant's intention to transfer the benefit can be considered to have been utterly negated.[105] Where the

---

[98] Ibid, 215; 1182.   [99] See p 189, below.   [100] [1932] AC 562.   [101] [1999] 2 AC 349.

[102] [2006] UKHL 49, [2007] 1 AC 558, [60] (Lord Hope).   [103] See p 121, above.

[104] This was recognized by Waller J in *Midland Bank plc v Brown Shipley and Co Ltd* [1991] 2 All ER 690, 700–1.

[105] But see G Williams, 'Mistake in the Law of Theft' (1977) 36 CLJ 62, 64, where he asserts that the notion that a fundamental mistake negatives the claimant's consent 'is in varying degrees a legal fiction: there is always

claimant makes a mistake which is not even an operating cause of the benefit being transferred, so that even if the claimant had not made the mistake the benefit would still have been transferred, the intention to make the transfer clearly outweighs any element of vitiation or qualification of intention. In the middle are those mistakes which are causative of the transfer, where the mistake is not so severe that it can be regarded as negating any intention that the benefit be transferred to the defendant, but is sufficiently important to be able to conclude that the claimant's intention to transfer the benefit was so affected by the mistake that it should be treated as vitiated in that, even though the claimant intended to transfer the benefit to the defendant, so that title passes, the effect of the mistake is such that the claimant cannot be considered to have intended to benefit the defendant in those circumstances. This distinction between complete negation and partial vitiation of intent is illustrated by *Barclays Bank v Simms*, since the mistake relating to the existence of the stop order did not negate the claimant's intention completely, so title to the money did pass to the defendant, but the mistake was sufficiently serious that, had the claimant not been mistaken, the money would not have been paid. Consequently, it was possible to conclude that the claimant's intention had been vitiated to some extent so that its claim founded on unjust enrichment was successful.

(2) Defining the Operating Cause Test

If the test of causation is adopted to determine when a mistake will ground a restitutionary claim it is then necessary to define causation for these purposes. There are two alternative tests which may be adopted.

The first test is the 'but for' test, by virtue of which the claimant's mistake will only be considered to have caused the claimant to transfer a benefit to the defendant if the claimant can show that the benefit would not have been transferred but for the mistake.[106] If the claimant would still have transferred the benefit even if he or she had not been mistaken, the mistake cannot be considered to have caused the benefit to be transferred.

The second test is the 'contributory cause' test, by virtue of which it is sufficient for the claimant to establish that the mistake contributed to his or her decision to transfer the benefit to the defendant, but it is not necessary to show that, had the claimant not been mistaken, he or she would not have transferred the benefit to the defendant. This test of causation has been adopted where the transfer of the benefit was induced by a misrepresentation of the defendant[107] or was compelled by the defendant.[108]

Where the claim is based on a mistake the appropriate test of causation is that of 'but for' cause. Any analogy with the test which is adopted where the defendant has induced the claimant's mistake or has compelled the benefit to be transferred is a false one. For in those cases a less stringent test of causation is justified by virtue of the defendant's conduct, which makes it easier to conclude that any enrichment received by the defendant was received in circumstances of injustice. But, where the claimant's mistake

---

an element of consent in the transfer'. But he goes on to recognize, at 65, that where there is a fundamental mistake 'the element of non-consent bulks so large that it seems more reasonable to deny consent rather than to affirm it'.

[106] This 'but for' test has alternatively been called the 'necessary' cause: S Arrowsmith, 'Mistake and The Role of the "Submission to an Honest Claim"' in AS Burrows (ed), *Essays on the Law of Restitution* (Oxford: Clarendon Press, 1991), 21.

[107] *Edgington v Fitzmaurice* (1885) 25 Ch D 459. See p 197, below.

[108] *Barton v Armstrong* [1976] AC 104. See Chapter 10.

occurred spontaneously, it is more difficult to establish that the defendant had been unjustly enriched. Consequently, restitution should only be awarded where the claimant would not have transferred the benefit had he or she not been mistaken. This analysis is supported by a number of cases. For example, in *Kelly v Solari*[109] Parke B stressed that restitution should be awarded because 'the money would not have been paid if it had been known to the payer that the fact was untrue'. Whereas in *Holt v Markham*[110] one reason for the denial of restitution where the claimant had paid the defendant too much money was because the claimant would have paid the money anyway, even if it had known the true facts.

The operation of the 'but for' test of causation can, however, be intellectually complicated, as is well illustrated by the difficult case of *Nurdin and Peacock plc v DB Ramsden and Co Ltd*.[111] The claimant in that case had overpaid rent following the misconstruction of a lease. It had suspected that it was not liable to pay all the money to the defendant under the lease, but it paid anyway because it believed that it would be able to recover the money if the defendant's argument about the construction of the lease was incorrect. It was held that the relevant mistake was its belief that it could recover the money if it turned out that it was not liable to pay the defendant.[112] But this is a highly artificial mistake since, logically, the existence of the mistake is dependent on the operation of the law of restitution itself. The argument proceeds as follows: the claimant paid money to the defendant suspecting correctly that it was not due, so there was no operative mistake. Since there were no other grounds of restitution available it followed that the restitutionary claim could not succeed. Because of this, the claimant's belief that it could recover the money was incorrect as a matter of law and so the claimant had therefore made a mistake of law, which did ground a restitutionary claim. But why stop at this point? Because the consequence of this argument so far is that the claimant could recover the money, it surely follows that the claimant was not mistaken, but then the claimant would be mistaken, and so on. This is artificial and unacceptable. The preferable view is that the claimant was not mistaken because, if it suspected that it was not liable to the defendant but went on to pay the money, it had taken the risk that the money might not be due to the defendant and such voluntary payments cannot be recovered.[113] If the claimant suspects that the money is not due the proper course is to resolve the dispute in the courts. By allowing the claim for restitution to succeed in this case the judge undermined the bar on restitution of voluntary payments,[114] a bar which is of crucial importance to maintain the security of receipts.

(3) Voluntariness and Risk-Taking

If the claimant voluntarily transferred a benefit to the defendant it will not be possible to establish a restitutionary claim grounded on mistake.[115] How voluntariness is defined for these purposes and why it should negate the claim have been matters of particular controversy. Three different states of mind need to be distinguished.

---

[109] (1814) 9 M and W 54, 58; 152 ER 24, 26.   [110] [1923] 1 KB 504.   [111] [1999] 1 WLR 1249.

[112] Cf *Cobbold v Bakewell Management Ltd* [2003] EWHC 2289 (Ch), where the claimants paid money to the defendant in the expectation that they would be able to recover it if an appeal pending before the House of Lords was decided in their favour. This was held not to be an operative mistake because the claimants had paid the money voluntarily with their eyes open as to the uncertainty of whether the House of Lords would have decided in their favour: ibid, [19] (Rimer J). In other words, the claimants were risk-takers.

[113] See p 177, below.   [114] See p 149, above.

[115] *Kleinwort Benson Ltd v Lincoln CC* [1999] 2 AC 349, 401 (Lord Hoffmann).

(a) Knowledge

The easiest case is where the claimant knows all of the facts. This automatically negates the mistake.[116] This applies to mistakes of law as well.[117]

(b) Suspicion

Where the claimant transfers a benefit to the defendant being suspicious of the circumstances but decides to take the risk that he or she is mistaken, the claimant may be considered to have acted voluntarily and so restitution will not be awarded.[118] This is illustrated by *Rowe v Vale of White Horse DC*,[119] where a council provided sewerage services deliberately without charge, because it was unclear whether it was able to demand payment for the provision of such services. It was held that the council could not bring a restitutionary claim founded on mistake, presumably because it had consciously taken the risk to continue to provide the service without charge until the legal position had been clarified.

Various reasons have been suggested as to why restitution should not be available where the claimant suspects that his or her belief might be mistaken. These were considered by the House of Lords in *Deutsche Morgan Grenfell v IRC*.[120] Lord Brown[121] said that suspicion negated mistake. So, for example, a claimant who paid tax suspecting that it might not be due because, for example, it was being challenged in the courts, would not have made a mistake. Other judges in *Deutsche Morgan Grenfell* considered that, whilst a suspicious claimant could still be considered to be mistaken, restitution might not be available, either because the effect of the claimant's suspicions is that the mistake may not have caused the transfer to be made,[122] because, for example, the claimant may have taken a calculated risk about the existence of a liability to pay money,[123] or simply because somebody who has taken a risk as to the existence of a basis for the payment should be barred from obtaining restitution. The latter approach was advocated by Lord Hoffmann,[124] who said:

> Contestants in quiz shows may have doubts about the answer ('it sounds like Haydn, but then it may be Mozart') but if they then give the wrong answer, they have made a mistake. The real point is whether the person who made the payment took the risk that he might be wrong. If he did, then he cannot recover the money.

He considered that whether the claimant was a risk-taker would depend on 'the objective circumstances surrounding the payment as they could reasonably have been known to both parties, including…the extent to which the law was known to be in doubt'.[125]

Lord Hoffmann's recognition of a risk-taking bar has been described as not reflecting the state of English law on mistake, but has been interpreted instead as a suggestion as to how the law might develop in the future.[126] A significant problem with Lord Hoffmann's

---

[116] *Brisbane v Dacres* (1813) 5 Taunt 143, 159–60; 128 ER 641, 647–8 (Gibbs J).
[117] *Brennan v Bolt Burdon* [2004] EWCA Civ 1017, [2005] QB 303.
[118] *Kleinwort Benson Ltd v Lincoln CC* [1999] 2 AC 349, 410 (Lord Hope).
[119] [2003] EWHC 388 (Admin), [2003] 1 Lloyd's Rep 418. In *Brennan v Bolt Burdon* [2004] EWCA Civ 1017, [2005] QB 303 it was held that a state of doubt concerning the interpretation of the law would not constitute a mistake of law. See also *Cobbold v Bakewell Management Ltd* [2003] EWHC 2289 (Ch), [19] (Rimer J).
[120] [2006] UKHL 49, [2007] 1 AC 558.   [121] Ibid, [162].   [122] Ibid, [65] (Lord Hope).
[123] Ibid, [175] (Lord Brown).   [124] Ibid, [27].   [125] Ibid, [28].
[126] *BP Oil International Ltd v Target Shipping Ltd* [2012] EWHC 1590 (Comm), [2012] 2 Lloyd's Rep 245, [245] (Andrew Smith J). Lord Hoffmann's judgment was, however, commended by Lord Walker in *Pitt v Holt* [2013] UKSC 26, [2013] 2 AC 108, [114].

approach is his adoption of an objective approach to risk-taking, an approach which, as will be seen, is inconsistent with the long-standing rule that negligence, which is also assessed objectively, on the part of the claimant does not negate reliance on mistake as a ground of restitution.[127] It is also unclear why the objective risk is assessed with reference to what both parties could reasonably have known, since this is surely inconsistent with the rationale of mistake as a ground of restitution. What we are trying to show is that the claimant's intention to transfer a benefit to the defendant was vitiated by the mistake. Whilst considerations of what the reasonable person might have contemplated may be useful evidence of what the claimant contemplated, we are ultimately only concerned with the claimant's thought process; so a subjective test of risk-taking is more appropriate. Consequently, the preferable view is that of Lord Hope: namely, that the claimant's suspicion about the true circumstances negates a claim founded on mistake because it is not then possible to establish that the mistake caused the claimant to transfer the benefit to the defendant. So, for example, where the claimant suspected that he or she might not be liable to pay the defendant, but paid anyway, this suggests that the causative link between the mistake and the payment is broken, because the evidence suggests that the claimant was content to pay regardless of whether the money was due or not.[128]

Whichever of the three approaches is adopted, however, it is clear that a claim grounded on mistake will be defeated where the claimant's suspicions about the facts or law mean that the claimant is a risk-taker. The key question then is to determine what degree of suspicion the claimant must have before it can be concluded that the claimant's mistake did not cause him or her to transfer the enrichment to the defendant. While some suspicion will not prevent recovery, the greater the suspicion the less likely it is that recovery will be ordered. In *Marine Trade SA v Pioneer Freight Futures Co Ltd*[129] Flaux J recognized that a claimant who has doubts as to the liability to pay can still be considered to be mistaken, but only if the claimant concluded that it was more likely than not that he or she was liable to pay. If the payer thought it was more likely than not that he or she was *not* liable to pay, but paid nonetheless, the claimant should not be considered to be mistaken, or, preferably, that the mistake did not cause the payment to be made. In other words, the test is one of probabilities rather than possibilities. In *BP Oil International Ltd v Target Shipping Ltd*[130] Andrew Smith J recognized that, even if the claimant did consider that he or she was probably liable to pay in circumstances where there was no such liability, it does not necessarily follow that the claimant was mistaken, because the claimant may have consciously decided to take the risk that he or she was mistaken. So conscious risk-taking may still operate to bar a claim grounded on mistake, which is consistent with the fundamental principle of the law of restitution that volunteers should not obtain restitutionary relief.[131] It was further recognized in that case that a mistake made by the claimant's agent or employee will be attributed to the claimant. But, in such circumstances, the state of mind of an employee may defeat the mistake claim if the employee was responsible for the transaction, knew or suspected that the money was not due, and did not object or prevent the transaction.

The question of risk-taking was significant to the restitutionary claim in *Deutsche Morgan Grenfell* itself. The claimant taxpayer, who was not resident in England, had

---

[127] See p 179, below.

[128] *Deutsche Morgan Grenfell v IRC* [2006] UKHL 49, [2007] 1 AC 558, [70] (Lord Hope).

[129] [2009] EWHC 2656 (Comm), [2010] 1 Lloyd's Rep 631. See also *BP Oil International Ltd v Target Shipping Ltd* [2012] EWHC 1590 (Comm), [2012] 2 Lloyd's Rep 245, [232] (Andrew Smith J).

[130] *BP Oil International Ltd v Target Shipping Ltd* [2012] EWHC 1590 (Comm), [2012] 2 Lloyd's Rep 245, [233].   [131] See p 36, above.

paid tax prematurely, since it had not been able to elect to delay payment. In 2001 the European Court of Justice had found the denial of this election to delay payment constituted breach of EU law because the election would have been available had the claimant been resident in England. The claimant then sought restitution on the ground of mistake of law. One of the issues in the case was whether the claimant could be considered to be mistaken in paying the tax when it was known that the denial of the election to defer payment of tax was being challenged before the courts. But this knowledge was not considered to negate the restitution claim, because the ability to elect to defer payment of the tax was denied to the claimant by statute, so that the claimant was not considered to have any doubt as to its tax liability at the time; the claimant simply did not consider that it could defer payment of the tax.[132] Ultimately, this appears to turn on a finding of fact that the claimant had no doubts as to its liability to pay. Lord Hoffmann did, however, accept that, if the claimant had adopted a more sophisticated approach to the law, it might have had doubts about the liability to pay it if considered that the litigation before the European Court of Justice had a good chance of succeeding such that it could be considered to have taken the risk that the money might not need to be paid at that point, but this was not established on the facts.[133]

(c) Carelessness

Where the claimant has made a mistake which would not have been made by a reasonable person, such carelessness will not bar the claimant from establishing that the mistake caused him or her to transfer the benefit to the defendant.[134] In *Kelly v Solari*[135] Parke B said that recovery was possible 'however careless the party paying may have been in omitting to use due diligence to inquire into the fact'. So, for example, if the claimant would have avoided making a mistake by making some basic inquiries about whether there was a liability to pay the defendant, which a reasonable person would have made, this will not automatically defeat the restitutionary claim.

In *Brennan v Bolt Burdon*[136] it was held that, if a party ought to have known that an issue was about to be reconsidered on appeal, this would not constitute a mistake of law. This comes very close to saying that negligence on the part of the claimant will prevent reliance on the ground of mistake, but it is inconsistent with the subsequent decision of the House of Lords in *Deutsche Morgan Grenfell v IRC*[137] where it was recognized that even an awareness that a liability was subject to legal challenge would not necessarily defeat the mistake. Consequently there is no reason to distinguish between mistakes of fact and law when determining the role of carelessness in making the mistake.

The rejection of carelessness to defeat the mistake claim is, however, controversial and unsatisfactory. Bearing in mind that we are concerned with imposing restitutionary liability on the defendant by virtue of a mistake spontaneously made by the claimant, and not induced by the defendant, is it right that the claim should succeed if the claimant could easily have avoided the mistake by making some basic inquiries? In assessing the fairness of the result, it is important to have regard to the defences available to the defendant. A significant consequence of adopting a wide test of mistake is that this

---

[132] *Deutsche Morgan Grenfell v IRC* [2006] UKHL 49, [2007] 1 AC 558, [30] (Lord Hoffmann), [61] (Lord Hope).

[133] Although Lord Brown considered that it was established: ibid, [172].

[134] *Banque Financière de la Cité v Parc (Battersea) Ltd* [1999] 1 AC 221, 235 (Lord Hoffmann); *Pitt v Holt* [2013] UKSC 26, [2013] 2 AC 108, [114] (Lord Walker). See also *Kelly v Solari* (1841) 9 M and W 54, 152 ER 24; *Weld-Blundell v Synott* [1940] 2 KB 107; *Turvey v Dentons (1923) Ltd* [1953] 1 QB 218, 224 (Pilcher J); *Chase Manhattan Bank NA v Israel-British Bank (London) Ltd* [1981] Ch 105.

[135] (1841) 9 M and W 54, 59; 152 ER 24, 26.　　[136] [2004] EWCA Civ 1017, [2005] QB 303.

[137] [2006] UKHL 49, [2007] 1 AC 558.

needs to be counter-balanced by extensive defences available to the defendant, the most significant of which is the defence of change of position.[138] That defence is available where the defendant's position has changed following receipt of the enrichment as a result of which it is not just to make restitution. The defence will not be available where the defendant changed his or her position in bad faith, which has been interpreted as including dishonesty, a failure to act in a commercially acceptable way, sharp practice falling short of outright dishonesty,[139] and wilfully and recklessly failing to make such inquiries as an honest and reasonable person would make.[140] The defence will, however, still be available where the defendant changed his or her position negligently or care-lessly.[141] For reasons of symmetry between the requirements for the claim and the requirements of defences, if carelessness does not defeat the defence of change of position, it should follow that it should not negate the mistake, save if a good reason for the difference between the claim and the defence can be identified, and it is not obvious what such reason would be. Since, however, change of position will be barred where the defendant wilfully failed to make reasonable inquiries, it should follow that the mistake claim should not be established where the claimant wilfully and recklessly failed to make the inquiries which a reasonable person would have made. This can be characterized as recklessness, to distinguish it from carelessness. So, where the claimant transferred the benefit recklessly, rather than carelessly, this should bar the mistake claim. The difficulty then is to find a way to distinguish between recklessness and carelessness. In respect of the defence of change of position[142] recklessness is defined as where the defendant failed to make inquiries which it would have been reasonable to make in the light of the defendant's belief or suspicion about the facts. This is an objective test, but one which is assessed with reference to the defendant's state of mind at the time of acting. Carelessness, however, does not have regard to the defendant's belief or suspicions about the facts, but is simply concerned with what the reasonable person would have done. It is by drawing this distinction between recklessness and carelessness that it might be possible to reconcile Lord Hoffmann's assertion in *Deutsche Morgan Grenfell*[143] that the bar of risk-taking should be assessed objectively with the orthodox rejection of carelessness barring mistake. It is also consistent with Lord Walker's observation in *Pitt v Holt*[144] that a claimant who is careless can obtain restitution, but not a claimant who deliberately ran the risk that he or she was mistaken or who 'must be taken to have run the risk'. This objective notion of risk-taking can be distinguished from carelessness if recklessness is assessed with reference to the defendant's mental state.

The difference between carelessness and recklessness is subtle and will require careful analysis of the facts of the case. It is not, however, easy to differentiate between careless-ness and recklessness in the context of a mistake. Where, for example, the claimant pays money to the defendant believing that she is liable to do so, having forgotten that she had already paid the defendant last week, this might be characterized as careless, if the reasonable person would have checked before paying, but not reckless if the claimant was unaware of any facts which, had he or she been aware of them, would have resulted in the reasonable person investigating whether the liability had already been discharged.

---

[138] See Chapter 25.

[139] *Niru Battery Manufacturing Co v Milestone Trading Ltd* [2002] EWHC 1425 (Comm), [2002] 2 All ER (Comm) 705, 741. This was endorsed in the Court of Appeal: [2003] EWCA 1446 (Civ); *Abou-Rahmah v Abacha* [2006] EWCA Civ 1492, [2007] 1 All ER (Comm) 827.

[140] *Papamichael v National Westminster Bank* [2003] Lloyd's Rep 341, 369 (Judge Chambers QC).

[141] *Maersk Air Ltd v Expeditors International (UK) Ltd* [2003] 1 Lloyd's Rep 491, 499.

[142] See p 692, below.   [143] See p 177, above.   [144] [2013] UKSC 26, [2013] 2 AC 108, [114].

Indeed, this is similar to what happened in *Kelly v Solari*,[145] where money was paid in the belief that there was a liability to do so, but the liability had lapsed, and the claimant's failure to check this did not bar the claim. If, however, the claimant makes a gift to a charity and then discovers that the charity spends 75 per cent of donations on administration, the claimant might seek restitution on the ground that he would not have made the gift had he known what was spent on administration. Such a claimant may not even be able to establish on the facts that he had been mistaken, since this might be characterized as ignorance rather than an incorrect tacit assumption.[146] Even if the claimant can be considered to be mistaken, is this is a situation where he should be considered to be merely careless in failing to investigate what the charity spends on administration, or is he reckless? Certainly the claimant is not aware of any particular facts which would make the reasonable person investigate further. Consequently, distinguishing between carelessness and recklessness in the light of what the claimant believed or suspected seems to be unworkable. Perhaps the appropriate distinction to be drawn is between incorrect conscious beliefs and incorrect tacit assumptions. If the claimant, for example, consciously believes that she is liable to pay the defendant, this might be considered to be careless but not reckless, so restitution for mistake would be available. If, however, the claimant had made a tacit assumption about the facts which turn out to be incorrect, restitution might be denied if the reasonable person would have investigated further and would have discovered that the assumption was incorrect, as a result of which the claimant could be considered to have acted recklessly. This distinction would at least preserve *Kelly v Solari* and would mean that the donor to the charity would not be able to obtain restitution for failing to make investigations which were easy to make. Although there is no authority in support of relating recklessness to tacit assumptions rather than incorrect beliefs, it does at least reflect the rule that carelessness does not bar a claim in mistake, and also produces an appropriate result, by providing a mechanism for restricting claims for restitution grounded on incorrect tacit assumptions. It does not follow that a claim for mistake can never be grounded on incorrect tacit assumptions, since restitution would still be awarded if the reasonable person would not have investigated the circumstances before transferring the benefit to the defendant. But, if the reasonable person would have investigated further and would have discovered the truth, restitution should be denied on the ground that the claimant had been reckless.

(4) Mistaken Gifts

Following the recognition of the operative test for causation it should make no difference whether the claimant mistakenly believes that he or she is liable to transfer an enrichment to the defendant or the mistake relates to a gift made to the defendant. In both cases, as long as it can be shown that, but for the mistake, the enrichment would not have been transferred, restitution should follow because the claimant's intention to transfer the benefit can be treated as vitiated. This is what happened in New Zealand in *University of Canterbury v Attorney-General*,[147] where the claimant recovered a gift of shares he had made to a trust because he would not have made the gift but for his mistake that the trust fund was depleted.[148]

But restitution of mistaken gifts raises difficult issues of policy and principle which do not arise where the mistake is as to liability. The key issue of policy is whether it should be sufficient to recover a mistaken gift, simply with reference to the but for test of causation,

---

[145] (1841) 9 M and W 54, 152 ER 24. See p 165, above.   [146] See p 159, above.
[147] [1995] 1 NZLR 78.   [148] Ibid, 81 (Williamson J).

or whether a stricter test should be adopted. There is a significant difference between cases where the claimant mistakenly believed he or she was liable to transfer the enrichment and cases where the claimant voluntarily made a gift, arising from the fact that a gift provides a basis for the transfer of the enrichment. Restitution can only follow once the gift has been set aside.[149] The key question, therefore, is whether a mere operative mistake should be sufficient to set aside the gift or whether a stricter test of mistake should be adopted. Where the gift is made by deed, it is clear that a stricter test of mistake must be satisfied before the deed can be rescinded in Equity, namely that the mistake must be serious rather than simply operative.[150] But should this stricter test also be applicable where the gift has been made without a deed, so the equitable jurisdiction to rescind for mistake is not engaged?

In *Deutsche Morgan Grenfell v IRC*[151] Lord Scott considered, *obiter*, that something more than a causative mistake must be established before a gift can be recovered, such as where the gift was made as a result of a misrepresentation by the donee. Tang[152] justifies a stricter test of mistake being adopted to recover a gift by reference to the need to protect what he calls 'the moral economy'. Following the decision of the Supreme Court in *Pitt v Holt*, where the serious mistake test is adopted to rescind in Equity a gift transferred by deed, it has been assumed without analysis that this test applies to recover gifts even if the subject matter of the gift was not transferred by deed.[153] In *Pitt v Holt* itself, however, Lord Walker was reluctant to commit to there being generally a narrower test of mistake for restitution of gifts. He referred to a variety of hypothetical problem suggested by Burrows,[154] such as:

> C gives money to D, the Friends of the Earth, not knowing that they are opposed to an additional runway at Heathrow, which C supports.

Burrows suggests that restitution might not be awarded in such a case because the necessary element of seriousness of mistake would not be satisfied. Lord Walker was not so sure, however, and stated that it was not possible to give more than a tentative answer to such a hypothetical problem because there are insufficient facts to determine whether leaving the mistaken disposition uncorrected would be unjust.[155] But the tenor of Lord Walker's analysis, whilst not explicitly endorsing the application of the serious mistake test to restitution of gifts at Common Law, is at least consistent with such an approach, albeit that that this will require careful consideration of the facts to determine whether restitution would be appropriate.

It appears, therefore, that we are moving inexorably towards the recognition of a distinct and narrower test for restitution of gifts transferred by mistake, whereby it is not sufficient that but for the mistake the transfer would not have been made; it must also be a 'serious' mistake. This might be justified by virtue of the need to protect the security of the donee's receipt where the claimant has voluntarily transferred the benefit without thinking that he or she was under a liability to do so. But that is not a convincing reason for a distinct test of mistake for gifts. Narrower tests of mistake are adopted to set aside a contract for mistake[156] or to rescind a deed.[157] This can be justified on the ground that it

---

[149] See Chapter 7.   [150] *Pitt v Holt* [2013] UKSC 26, [2013] 2 AC 108. See p 201, below.

[151] [2006] UKHL 49, [2007] 1 AC 558, [87].

[152] HW Tang, 'Restitution for Mistaken Gifts' (2004) 20 JCL 1.

[153] *Pagel v Farman* [2013] EWHC 2210 (Comm); *Spaul v Spaul* [2014] EWCA Civ 679, [52] (Rimer LJ).

[154] AS Burrows, *A Restatement of the English Law of Unjust Enrichment* (Oxford: Hart Publishing, 2012), 9, article 10(4)(a).

[155] *Pitt v Holt* [2013] UKSC 26, [2013] 2 AC 108, [126].   [156] See p 193, below.

[157] See p 200, below.

should be more difficult to regard the claimant's intention to enter into such legal transactions as vitiated, because they are significant legal instruments which should only be set aside where the mistake is particularly potent. But the same reason does not necessarily apply where the claimant has simply made a gift without using a deed. Consequently, the preferable view is that to recover a gift transferred by mistake it should be sufficient to establish that the mistake was an operative cause of the transfer. Transfer by gift should not be treated in the same way as transfer by contract or by deed. In particular, the test for rescission of a voluntary transfer made by deed involves application of the equitable jurisdiction,[158] whereas restitution of gifts not made by deed involves the operation of the Common Law test of there being an operative mistake.

(5) Identifying Mistakes of Law

Even though the effect of the decision of the House of Lords in *Kleinwort Benson Ltd v Lincoln CC*[159] should be that there is no longer any need to distinguish between mistakes of law and mistakes of fact for the purposes of identifying a ground of restitution, it is still necessary to draw such a distinction since peculiar considerations need to be borne in mind when determining whether the claimant transferred a benefit as the result of a mistake of law.

Where the claimant relies on a mistake of law to establish the claim it is sufficient that the mistake was an operative cause but for which the transfer of the enrichment would not have been made,[160] but the operation of this test creates difficulties where the claimant correctly believed that he or she was liable to transfer the benefit to the defendant but the law subsequently changes. Can this change in the law operate retrospectively to create a mistake of law? This will depend on the circumstances in which the law was changed.

As the result of a long-standing principle, known as the principle of declaratory judicial law-making, when a judge's decision effects a change in the law this is deemed to operate retrospectively, because of a fiction that judges do not purport to change the law but simply declare the law to be what it has always been. Whether the effect of this fiction is sufficient artificially to create a mistake of law was the central issue in the decision of the House of Lords in *Kleinwort Benson Ltd v Lincoln CC*. The claimant bank in that case had paid money to the defendant local authority pursuant to an interest rate swap transaction which had been made in the 1980s. In 1990 the House of Lords held that such transactions were *ultra vires* the local authorities and so were void. The claimant sought restitution of the money which it had paid to the defendant and, because of the law relating to limitation periods,[161] the claimant needed to base its claim on mistake. Although the claimant's mistake was one of law, this did not automatically defeat the claim because the House of Lords unanimously abolished the mistake of law bar. But it was still necessary for the claimant to establish that it had paid the defendant as a result of a mistake. The crucial questions for the House of Lords to decide were whether the claimant could be considered to have been mistaken and what was the effect of the principle of declaratory law-making on the identification of a mistake to ground a restitutionary claim. The court identified three different scenarios which required consideration.

---

[158] Emphasized by the fact that it is an element of this test that the defendant's retention of the gift must be considered to be unconscionable. See p 201, below.

[159] [1999] 2 AC 349.   [160] *Deutsche Morgan Grenfell v IRC* [2006] UKHL 49, [2007] 1 AC 558.

[161] See Chapter 29.

(a) *The court overrules an earlier decision.* Where the claimant relies on a judicial decision to transfer a benefit and that decision is subsequently overruled,[162] the majority held that this was sufficient to establish a mistake of law. This is because of the principle of declaratory judicial law-making. Since the consequence of that principle is that the change in the law operates retrospectively, it can be assumed that the claimant was caused to transfer a benefit to the defendant as a result of a mistake which was deemed to have been operating at the time the payment was made.[163] The courts do, however, sometimes recognize that their decisions can have prospective effect only.[164] This was recognized by the House of Lords in *Re Spectrum Plus Ltd*,[165] but only exceptionally where a decision would have gravely unfair and disruptive consequences for past transactions and events.[166] The possibility of prospective overruling is clearly significant for restitutionary claims since, if the law is only changed prospectively, it will not be possible to construct a retrospective mistake.

(b) *The court clarifies existing practice.* On the facts of *Kleinwort Benson* itself the courts had not overruled an earlier decision. There was no decision which stated that interest rate swap transactions made with local authorities were valid. Rather, practitioners had assumed that such transactions were probably valid. Consequently, when the House of Lords decided in 1990 that such transactions were void, the court was not changing the law; it was simply determining the law. The House of Lords in *Kleinwort Benson* held, however, that this was a distinction without a difference. Since the claimant had assumed that the transaction was valid, the effect of the decision of the House in 1990 was to falsify this assumption and this was sufficient to create a mistake for the purposes of the restitutionary claim.

(c) *Statutory changes of the law.* Where a statute changes the law this usually operates only prospectively, so it cannot be used to create a mistake.[167] Exceptionally a statute may change the law retrospectively, but it might make specific provision for whether restitutionary claims are available as a result of the change of the law. If no such provision is made, is it possible to recognize a mistake? Lord Goff held in *Kleinwort Benson*[168] that it was not possible to identify a mistake in such circumstances, but this is very difficult to justify because it is inconsistent with the court's approach to judicial changes in the law.

Lords Browne-Wilkinson and Lloyd in *Kleinwort Benson* rejected the decision of the majority that the claimant had paid the money to the defendant as a result of a mistake of law. The conclusion of the minority seems preferable for two main reasons. First, a significant consequence of the decision of the majority is that defendants may be liable to make restitution to the claimant by reason of mistake of law many years after the claimant had paid money to the defendant. This is because the limitation period for mistakes will only begin to run from the period when the claimant discovered the mistake

---

[162] This would also cover the case where the claimant pays money to the defendant as a result of a judgment against the claimant and that judgment is later overturned on appeal.

[163] The application of that theory to create a mistake of law was criticized in *Brennan v Bolt Burdon* [2004] EWCA Civ 1017, [2005] QB 303, [49] (Bodey J), [63] (Sedley LJ).

[164] See, for example, the decision of the House of Lords in *Royal Bank of Scotland plc v Etridge (No 2)* [2002] 2 AC 773 which only applied to future transactions. See p 267, below.

[165] [2005] UKHL 41, [2005] 2 AC 680.   [166] Ibid, [40] (Lord Nicholls).

[167] *Kleinwort Benson Ltd v Lincoln CC* [1999] 2 AC 349, 381 (Lord Goff).

[168] Ibid. Cf Lord Hoffmann, ibid, 400.

or ought reasonably to have discovered it.[169] So, for example, if the claimant paid £10,000 to the defendant in 1930 because, as the law stood at the time, he was liable to do so, if the law was subsequently changed by a decision of the Court of Appeal in 2015, it follows that the claimant had made a mistake of law in 1930. But the claimant will be able to sue the defendant for repayment of the money, plus interest, since the limitation period will not have started to run until 2015 when the claimant discovered the mistake.[170] Such a result is patently unacceptable because it undermines the security of transactions. The only restriction on restitution in such circumstances derives from the potential application of the defence of change of position, but since that defence is defined restrictively because the change of position must be extraordinary, in the sense that but for the receipt of the enrichment the defendant's position would not have changed,[171] its influence in curtailing restitutionary claims many years after a benefit has been transferred is likely to be minimal if only because of the inevitable difficulties of proving a relevant change of position. It follows that there is an urgent need for statutory reform to ensure that the security of transactions are not undermined unnecessarily. This statutory intervention should take the form of an appropriately drawn limitation statute.[172]

Secondly, the decision of the majority in treating all judicial decisions as sufficient to construct a mistake of law confuses the distinction between mistakes and mispredictions and undermines a key principle concerning mistake as a ground of restitution, namely that the mistake is to be determined at the time the benefit was transferred to the defendant.[173] By applying the principle of declaratory judicial law-making the House of Lords has condoned the artificial manufacture of a mistake at the time of transfer when the claimant was not mistaken.[174] The flaw in the opinion of the majority is that they underestimate the crucial feature of mistake as a ground of restitution, namely that it is concerned with the claimant's state of mind at the time the benefit was transferred to the defendant,[175] at least where a judicial decision changes the law rather than declares the law for the first time. So, for example, where the claimant pays money to the defendant following a judicial decision recognizing a liability to do so and that decision is subsequently overruled, it is a fiction to say that the claimant was mistaken. For, when the money was paid to the defendant, there was a liability to do so such that the claimant cannot be considered to be mistaken. Whilst the law changed subsequently, and is considered to have retrospective effect, this cannot falsify history. The claimant believed there was a liability to pay and, at that time, there was such a liability, so that he or she should not be considered to have made a mistake as to the state of the existing law. Rather, he or she had made a misprediction as to what might happen in the future.[176]

---

[169] Limitation Act 1980, s 32(1)(c). See p 737, below.

[170] It is unlikely that it will be considered that the claimant could reasonably have discovered the mistake before the decision of the court which changed the law. See *Test Claimants in the FII Group Litigation v HMRC* [2014] EWHC 4302 (Ch), [465] (Henderson J). See further p 408, below.

[171] See Chapter 25.

[172] As recommended by the Law Commission Report, *Limitation of Actions* (Law Com No 270, 2001), examined in Chapter 29.

[173] *Baker v Courage and Co* [1910] 1 KB 56.

[174] This declaratory principle of law-making has been described as a 'fairy tale in which no one any longer believes': *Kleinwort Benson Ltd v Lincoln CC* [1999] 2 AC 349, 358 (Lord Browne-Wilkinson) citing Lord Reid's article, 'The Judge as Law Maker' (1972–1973) 12 JSPTL (NS) 22. See also Lord Lloyd: [1999] 2 AC 349, 394.

[175] See, in particular, Lord Hoffmann: *Kleinwort Benson Ltd v Lincoln CC* [1999] 2 AC 349, 398.

[176] Ibid, 360 (Lord Browne-Wilkinson), 394 (Lord Lloyd).

The claimant should be considered to bear the risk that the law might change in the future and so should not be allowed to obtain restitution on the ground of mistake.

The analysis is different, however, where, as on the facts of *Kleinwort Benson* itself, no case had previously decided whether or not there was a liability to pay the defendant, but the claimant believed that there was such a liability and a case subsequently decided that the liability did not exist. In this scenario, rather than the subsequent decision of the court operating retrospectively to falsify history, the later decision of the court simply establishes what the state of the law actually was at the time when the benefit was transferred. It is consequently legitimate to conclude that the claimant was indeed mistaken as to the state of the law at the time the transfer was made. But then the award of restitution will depend on whether it is appropriate to treat the claimant as a risk-taker as regards the state of the law. Certainly, if the claimant suspects that it is more probable than not that the law will be shown to be that there was no liability to pay, the claim should not succeed.[177]

The effect of the literal application of the principle of declaratory judicial law-making means that it is possible to construct a mistake of law artificially, because the declaratory principle means that, when the claimant transferred a benefit to the defendant, the claimant's belief as to the validity of the payment was incorrect.[178] Alternatively, since we know that judges do not just declare the law but actually change it, and because the ground of mistake is concerned with the claimant's thought process at the time of the payment, the declaratory theory is a fiction which should not be used to construct a mistake,[179] at least where the judges change rather than declare the law. This distinction was not, however, recognized by the majority in *Kleinwort Benson*. In *Deutsche Morgan Grenfell v IRC* Lord Hoffmann specifically characterized mistake of law as a 'deemed mistake',[180] which is the preferable way of analysing it now. It is clear, however, that the state of English law is that, regardless of whether the claimant wrongly believes that the law requires him or her to transfer a benefit because the law is silent on the point and it is subsequently established that there is no liability, or because the law recognizes a liability and it is subsequently changed, a mistake of law can be established.

(iv) Illegality

Where the claimant transfers a benefit to the defendant in circumstances where the transfer is illegal, the illegality generally operates as a defence to the restitutionary claim.[181] Where, however, the claimant is unaware of the illegality, it is possible to bring a restitutionary claim on the ground of mistake. Such a claim will only succeed if the mistake relates to the circumstances which render the transfer of the enrichment illegal; if it does not, the illegality will still operate as a defence to the restitutionary claim.[182] The reason for this is that it is only where the claimant's mistake relates to the existence of the illegality that he or she will not be considered to have been tainted by the illegality so that the restitutionary claim is not barred, because then the illegality will not

---

[177] See p 176, above.

[178] J Finnis, 'The Fairy Tale's Moral' (1999) 115 LQR 170; D Sheehan, 'What is a Mistake?', 560; RJ Sutton, 'Mistake: Symbol, Metaphor and Unfolding' [2002] RLR 9; AS Burrows, 'The English Law of Restitution: A Ten-Year Review' in JW Neyers, M McInnes, and SGA Pitel (eds), *Understanding Unjust Enrichment* (Oxford: Hart Publishing, 2004), 17.

[179] PBH Birks, 'Mistakes of Law' [2000] CLP 205.

[180] *Deutsche Morgan Grenfell v IRC* [2006] UKHL 49, [2007] 1 AC 558, [23].

[181] See *Holman v Johnson* (1775) 1 Cowp 341, 343; 98 ER 1120, 1121 (Lord Mansfield). See Chapter 27.

[182] See *Morgan v Ashcroft* [1938] 1 KB 49.

be closely connected to the claim.[183] So, for example, in *Oom v Bruce*[184] goods, which were to be transferred from Russia to England, had been insured at a time when hostilities between England and Russia had just commenced. This made the contract of insurance illegal. But, because both parties were unaware of the outbreak of hostilities, it was held that the premiums paid under the insurance contract could be recovered by the claimant. The ground of restitution was mistake, because the mistake related to the fact that war had been declared which made the contract illegal.

(B) INDUCED MISTAKES

If the claimant transfers a benefit to the defendant as a result of a mistake which was induced by a misrepresentation by the defendant, it is not necessary to show that the mistake was a 'but for' cause of the benefit being transferred, it being sufficient that the mistake was a contributory cause,[185] at least where the misrepresentation was fraudulent since the defendant knew or suspected that the representation was untrue.[186] If the misrepresentation was negligent or innocent then, by analogy with the test where a contract is set aside for misrepresentation,[187] it may be necessary to establish that the misrepresentation was an operative 'but for' cause of the transfer. The reason for the adoption of this laxer test of causation where the claimant's mistake was induced by the defendant's fraudulent misrepresentation is that the defendant is responsible for inducing the claimant's mistake. It follows that it is easier to conclude that the benefit received by the defendant was unjustly received as a result of the mistake.

Where the claimant has mistakenly transferred a benefit to the defendant in circumstances where the transfer was illegal and the mistake was induced by the defendant's fraudulent conduct, the claimant will be able to obtain restitution despite the usual rule that participation in an illegal transaction bars a restitutionary claim.[188] This is because in such a case the defendant can be considered to be more blameworthy than the claimant for entering into the transaction.[189] Consequently, a restitutionary claim will only succeed where the claimant is considered to be less blameworthy than the defendant. This is illustrated by *Parkinson v College of Ambulance*[190] where restitution of a charitable donation was denied because, although the claimant had been induced to give the money by means of a fraudulent representation that by making the gift the defendant charity could arrange for him to receive a knighthood, the claimant knew throughout that such an arrangement was illegal. The claimant was therefore an equal participant in the illegality with the defendant, but had anyway made a misprediction as to what might happen in the future.

(C) SHOULD MISTAKE BE RECOGNIZED AS A GROUND OF RESTITUTION?

Some commentators have argued that there is no need to recognize mistake as a ground of restitution, since the ground of failure of basis is applicable in all cases of mistake.[191] The

---

[183] See *Les Laboratoires Servier v Apotex* [2014] UKSC 55, [2014] 3 WLR 1257, [22] (Lord Sumption), for recognition of this close connection test. See p 722, below.

[184] (1810) 12 East 225, 104 ER 87.

[185] *Edgington v Fitzmaurice* (1885) 29 Ch D 459.

[186] *Derry v Peek* (1889) 14 App Cas 337, 374 (Lord Herschell).   [187] See p 197, below.

[188] See *Holman v Johnson* (1775) 1 Cowp 341, 343; 98 ER 1120, 1121 (Lord Mansfield). See Chapter 27.

[189] *Hughes v Liverpool Victoria Legal Friendly Society* [1916] 2 KB 482.   [190] [1923] 2 KB 1.

[191] See, for example, P Matthews, 'Money Paid Under Mistake of Fact' (1980) 130 NLJ 587 and P Matthews, 'Stopped Cheques and Restitution' (1982) JBL 281. See also PA Butler, 'Mistaken Payments, Change of Position

ground of failure of basis will be established where the claimant transfers a benefit to the defendant which is conditional on there being subsequent performance, usually by the defendant; this is the relevant basis for the transfer. If that basis fails totally, the defendant's enrichment can be considered to be unjust.[192] So, for example, if the claimant sells a car to the defendant in the expectation that £3,000 will be paid for it, and the claimant does not receive any money at all, the basis for the transfer of the car will have failed totally. Those commentators who argue that the mistake cases are better interpreted as cases where there was a total failure of basis argue that, where the claimant transfers a benefit to the defendant mistakenly believing that certain facts exist, if those facts do not exist the expected consequence of the transfer will not be achieved and so the basis for the transfer will often have failed totally. So, for example, where the claimant pays a sum of money to the defendant in the mistaken belief that it will discharge an existing liability, if there is no such liability, the basis for the payment will have failed totally, since it is not possible to discharge a liability which does not exist.

Whilst the award of restitutionary remedies in a number of cases can be justified by reference to both total failure of basis and mistake,[193] the two grounds cannot be equated for a number of reasons.

First, the state of the case law does not support the argument that the ground of mistake should not be recognized. Mistake is clearly acknowledged as a ground of restitution in its own right, independently of the ground of total failure of basis.[194] This has been recognized explicitly by the House of Lords in *Kleinwort Benson Ltd v Lincoln CC*[195] and *Deutsche Morgan Grenfell v IRC*[196] where the success of the claim depended on the ground of mistake, for otherwise the claim would have been time barred. In the former case the claimant could not have relied on the ground of total failure of basis, because it had received some of the expected performance from the defendant,[197] and in both cases such a claim was time barred.

Secondly, the claimant cannot rely on the ground of total failure of basis where any part of the basis on which the claimant's transfer of the enrichment is conditional has been provided.[198] In such circumstances the claimant's only chance of bringing a restitutionary claim within the principle of unjust enrichment will be on the ground of mistake. Even though this ground of restitution is also limited if some counter-performance has been provided by the defendant,[199] this will only bar restitution to the extent that this performance has occurred, whereas the ground of total failure of basis will be completely barred if any part of the condition for the transfer has occurred.[200]

---

and Restitution' in P Finn (ed), *Essays on Restitution* (Sydney: The Law Book Co, 1990), ch 4; S Hedley, *Restitution: Its Division and Ordering* (London: Sweet and Maxwell, 2001), ch 1.

[192] See Chapter 13.

[193] See, for example, *Re the Bodega Company Ltd* [1904] 1 Ch 276 and *Rover International Ltd v Cannon Film Sales Ltd (No 3)* [1989] 1 WLR 912.

[194] See Lord Wright in *Fibrosa Spolka Akcyjna v Fairbairn Lawson Combe Barbour Ltd* [1943] AC 32, 61.

[195] [1999] 2 AC 349.

[196] [2006] UKHL 49, [2007] 1 AC 558. See also *Sempra Metals Ltd v IRC* [2007] UKHL 34, [2008] 1 AC 561 and *Pitt v Holt* [2013] UKSC 26, [2013] 2 AC 108.

[197] The claimant could have relied in principle on the alternative ground of absence of basis (see p 371, below) but did not wish to do so because a restitutionary claim founded on that ground of restitution would also have fallen outside the limitation period.

[198] See p 316, below. For criticism of the total failure requirement, see p 325, below.

[199] See p 189, below.

[200] See Chapter 13. If partial failure of basis is ever recognized as a ground of restitution in its own right the distinction between the grounds of mistake and failure of basis will be less apparent, since then as regards both grounds of restitution the claim will only fail to the extent that the basis has failed. See p 327, below.

Thirdly, mistake and failure of basis are recognized as grounds of restitution for very different reasons. Mistake is a ground of restitution because it operates to vitiate the claimant's intention to transfer a benefit to the defendant. Where, however, there has been a total failure of basis the claimant's intention is always valid but is qualified by the claimant's expectation that some condition will be satisfied, typically that a benefit will be provided by the defendant in return. Once it is clear that the condition has failed, the ground of restitution is established. It follows that whether the claimant has made a mistake can only be determined at the time the benefit is transferred to the defendant, whereas the question of whether there has been a failure of basis can only be determined after the claimant has transferred the benefit to the defendant.[201] Mistake and failure of basis are consequently determined at different times. They both have a significant, albeit different, role in establishing the defendant's unjust enrichment.

(D) SPECIFIC BARS TO RESTITUTIONARY CLAIMS FOUNDED ON MISTAKE

Once the claimant has established that the defendant was enriched at the expense of the claimant as a result of an operative mistake, a restitutionary remedy will be awarded. The claim for restitution will be barred, however, either where the claimant is considered to be a risk-taker,[202] or where there was a legal basis for the defendant's receipt of the enrichment.[203] There is one bar which has specifically been recognized as relevant to claims grounded on mistake, known misleadingly as 'the defence of good consideration'. It has also sometimes been suggested that specific bars should be recognized where the claim is grounded on mistake of law. It is appropriate to consider these bars here. It is important to emphasize, however, that whilst these are sometimes analysed as defences, they are preferably treated as denials of the cause of action.[204] It follows that, whilst the defendant may plead these bars, the claimant bears the burden of proving that they do not apply, for otherwise the cause of action cannot be established.

(i) Good Consideration Provided by the Defendant

In *Barclays Bank Ltd v WJ Simms, Son and Cooke (Southern) Ltd*[205] Robert Goff J recognized that the claimant would not be able to recover money on the ground of mistake if the defendant had provided consideration for the payment. 'Consideration' for these purposes refers to there being some legally effective consequence of the defendant's receipt of the enrichment, typically through the discharge of a valid debt. The use of the word 'consideration' is misleading though, because of its contractual connotations of a requirement to make a promise enforceable. The language of 'consideration' is preferably replaced with that of a legally effective basis for the enrichment. It follows that 'good consideration' is properly considered to form part of the wider principle that the presence of a legally effective basis for the receipt of the benefit will defeat the claim for restitution.[206] That this is how the principle should be

---

[201] This distinction was recognized by Lord Shaw in *Jones Ltd v Waring and Gillow Ltd* [1926] AC 670, 690: 'when ... a payment [is] made under a mistake of fact, that mistake has reference to occurrences which have taken place or things which have been done prior to or at the time of the transaction ... on the other hand the imposition of a condition upon the making of a payment ... that affects the future ...'. See also Brennan J in *David Securities Pty Ltd v Commonwealth Bank of Australia* (1992) 175 CLR 353, 390.

[202] See p 177, above.   [203] See Chapter 7.

[204] See p 60, above for the distinction between denials and defences.

[205] [1980] QB 677, 695. See also *Bank of New South Wales v Murphett* [1983] VR 489.

[206] See Chapter 7.

analysed was confirmed by Lord Hope in *Kleinwort Benson Ltd v Lincoln CC*[207] who recognized that the payee of money 'cannot be said to have been unjustly enriched if he was entitled to receive the sum paid to him'. To the extent that a payment is effective to discharge a valid liability, the claim for restitution will be defeated, even though the claimant was mistaken in making the payment. This was recognized by Lord Sumption in *Fairfield Sentry Ltd v Migani*,[208] who said that a mistaken payment cannot be recovered 'to the extent [it] discharges a contractual debt of the payee'. In *Fairfield Sentry* it was concluded, following careful interpretation of the underlying contract, that the claimant was contractually bound to make the payments which it did make and so restitution was not awarded because the payments had discharged a legal liability such that the defendant could be considered to have provided 'good consideration'. But the restitutionary claim should be defeated only to the extent that there was a legally effective basis for the defendant's receipt of it. Lord Sumption said that, '[s]o far as the payment exceeds the debt properly due, then the payer is in principle entitled to recover the excess'. So, for example, if the claimant mistakenly pays £1,000 to discharge a debt owed to the defendant which is actually only £150, the restitutionary claim will only be defeated to the extent of £150.

The most common situation in which the 'good consideration' principle is applicable is where the claimant mistakenly pays a sum of money which has the effect of discharging a debt which was owed to the defendant. The discharge of the debt means that the defendant is no longer enriched at the expense of the claimant to the value of the discharged debt.[209] Whether the claimant's payment will have discharged a debt depends on whether the payment was accepted or authorized by the debtor.[210] This is particularly important in the context of banking transactions. In *Barclays Bank Ltd v WJ Simms, Son and Cooke (Southern) Ltd*,[211] for example, the claimant bank had mistakenly paid money to the defendant in respect of a cheque drawn on a customer's account. If, which did not occur on the facts of the case, the mistake which the claimant had made was simply that the customer had sufficient funds in the account it would follow that, since the customer had authorized the payment, the debt which the customer owed to the defendant would have been discharged and the claimant would be forced to recover the money from the customer.[212] But, as occurred on the facts of the case, since the customer had countermanded the payment, it ceased to be authorized and so did not discharge the debt.[213] Consequently, the claimant was able to recover the money from the defendant by reason of the mistake. This seems perfectly fair since, as the debt was not discharged, the defendant could still sue the customer on that debt.[214] Where, however, the debt is discharged because it was an authorized, albeit mistaken, payment, the defendant is entitled to receive the payment and it is not appropriate for the defendant to make restitution of it to the claimant.[215]

---

[207] [1999] 2 AC 349, 408.   [208] [2014] UKPC 9, [18].

[209] *Lloyds Bank plc v Independent Insurance Co Ltd* [2000] QB 110, 132 (Peter Gibson LJ).

[210] *Customs and Excise Commissioners v National Westminster Bank plc* [2003] 1 All ER 327, [2002] EWHC 2204 (Ch). See p 235, below.   [211] [1980] QB 677.

[212] See, for example, *Lloyds Bank plc v Independent Insurance Co Ltd* [2000] QB 110.

[213] See also *Customs and Excise Commissioners v National Westminster Bank plc* [2003] 1 All ER 327, [2002] EWHC 2204 (Ch).

[214] *Barclays Bank Ltd v WJ Simms, Son and Cooke (Southern) Ltd* [1980] QB 677, 703 (Robert Goff J).

[215] See *Kleinwort Benson Ltd v Lincoln CC* [1999] 2 AC 349, 408 (Lord Hope); *Lloyds Bank plc v Independent Insurance Co Ltd* [2000] QB 110, 132 (Peter Gibson LJ).

A case in which the 'good consideration' principle defeated a restitutionary claim was *Aiken v Short*,[216] where the claimant bank paid money to the defendant to discharge a debt which was owed to the defendant by a third party, the bank mistakenly thinking that it was discharging an incumbrance on property which it owned. The claimant was unable to recover the money from the defendant since the third-party debtor had authorized the payment and so the debt was discharged, which was held to constitute the provision of good consideration by the defendant.[217] One point of particular importance about this case was that the discharge of the debt could not be regarded as benefiting the claimant, since, having made the payment, it discovered that it did not own the property which was the subject of the incumbrance. The true beneficiary of the payment was the third-party debtor. This does not matter, for the 'good consideration' principle is only concerned with the identification of a legally effective basis for the transfer; whether or not the claimant was benefited as a result is irrelevant.

(ii) Potential Bars to Claims Founded on Mistake of Law

Now that it has been recognized that mistake of law can constitute a ground of restitution in its own right, it is necessary to consider whether any particular bars should be recognized where the restitutionary claim is founded on a mistake of law. In *Kleinwort Benson v Lincoln CC*[218] Lord Goff recognized that 'the law must evolve appropriate defences which can, together with the defence of change of position, provide protection where appropriate for recipients of money paid under a mistake of law in those cases in which justice or policy does not require them to refund the money'.

Despite this, the House of Lords was generally reluctant to recognize any specific bars to claims founded on mistake of law. A number of potential bars to such claims have been suggested.

(1) Settled View of Law

The Law Commission has recommended that a restitutionary claim founded on mistake of law should be barred where the claimant acted in accordance with a settled view of the law which was subsequently departed from by a decision of a court or tribunal.[219] The House of Lords correctly refused to recognize such a bar, simply because a change in a settled view of the law was considered to constitute a mistake of law in its own right.[220]

(2) Defendant's Honest Receipt

In *David Securities Pty Ltd v Commonwealth Bank of Australia*[221] Brennan CJ suggested that a restitutionary claim founded on mistake of law should be barred if the defendant honestly believed that he or she was entitled to receive or retain the benefit from the claimant. The reason for advocating this bar was to maintain the security of receipts. The House of Lords in *Kleinwort Benson v Lincoln CC*[222] rejected such a bar simply because it would be so wide that it would undermine the abolition of the mistake of law bar, since in

---

[216] (1856) 1 H and N 210, 156 ER 1180. See also *Porter v Latec Finance (Qld) Pty Ltd* (1964) 111 CLR 177.

[217] See especially Pollock CB, ibid, 214; 1181. Cf *Jones Ltd v Waring and Gillow Ltd* [1926] AC 670 where the money received by the defendant from the claimant did not discharge a debt which the fraudulent third party owed to it, so there was no legally effective basis for the payment.

[218] [1999] 2 AC 349, 373.

[219] *Restitution: Mistakes of Law and Ultra Vires Public Authority Receipts and Payments* (Law Com No 227, 1994), 5.13. This was also advocated by Lord Browne-Wilkinson: *Kleinwort Benson v Lincoln CC* [1999] 2 AC 349, 364.

[220] *Kleinwort Benson v Lincoln CC* [1999] 2 AC 349, 383 (Lord Goff). See p 184, above.

[221] (1992) 175 CLR 353, 399.   [222] [1999] 2 AC 349, 384 (Lord Goff).

most cases defendants would honestly believe that they were entitled to the benefit because they would typically share the claimant's mistake of law. If it had been recognized, the bar would essentially expand the recognition of the legally effective basis bar to encompass the case where the defendant believed that there was a legally effective basis for the receipt of the enrichment. This is contrary to the rationale of the legally effective basis principle, however, since that principle turns on there being an effective basis for the enrichment as a matter of law; the fact that the defendant honestly believed that there was such a basis is irrelevant.

(3) Completed Invalid Transactions

The House of Lords also held that there was no bar that the money had been paid pursuant to an invalid transaction which had been fully performed.[223] Birks had previously suggested that, if the transaction had been completed, the force of the mistake was spent.[224] This argument was rejected, primarily because the right to restitution of benefits transferred by mistake arises at the time the benefit is transferred to the defendant. The fact that the invalid transaction is subsequently completed should not deprive the claimant of the accrued cause of action. It would be different, of course, if the transaction was legally effective, because then there would be a legitimate basis for the defendant's receipt of the enrichment.

3. RELIEF FROM TRANSACTIONS ENTERED INTO UNDER MISTAKE

Where the claimant enters into a transaction, usually a contract, under a mistaken belief and transfers a benefit to the defendant pursuant to that transaction, the claimant must first show that the transaction has been vitiated by the mistake before he or she can obtain restitution of the benefit. This is because a restitutionary claim will not be available if the claimant remains subject to a valid contractual obligation,[225] because there will be a legally effective basis for the defendant's receipt of the enrichment.[226] In order to set aside the contract for mistake, the mistake must relate to the contract rather than to the transfer of the benefit to the defendant. Although the question of the effect of mistake on the validity of the contract is a matter for the law of contract, it is still important to be aware of the doctrine of contractual mistake in a book on the law of restitution for two reasons: first, where a benefit has been transferred to the defendant pursuant to a contract which was made by mistake, the question of whether the claimant can obtain restitution of the benefit cannot be considered until it can be shown that the contract is no longer operating; secondly, the definition of mistake for the purposes of the law of contract may have some effect on how mistake should be defined as a ground of restitution.[227] Since, however, the doctrine of contractual mistake is adequately dealt with in books on contract,[228] this book will only identify the key principles in outline.

---

[223] Ibid, 387 (Lord Goff), 413 (Lord Hope).

[224] PBH Birks, 'No Consideration: Restitution after Void Contracts' (1993) 23 Univ WALR 195, 230.

[225] *Barclays Bank Ltd v WJ Simms, Son and Cooke (Southern) Ltd* [1980] 1 QB 677, 695 (Robert Goff J).

[226] See Chapter 7.

[227] This is a two-way process, since the recognition of mistake of law as a ground of restitution has influenced the law on setting asides contracts. See *Brennan v Bolt Burdon* [2004] EWCA Civ 1017, [2005] QB 303, p 194, below.

[228] For detailed examination of the law concerning the vitiation of contracts for mistake, see H Beale (ed), *Chitty on Contracts* (31st edn, London: Sweet and Maxwell, 2012), ch 5.

When analysing the circumstances when a contract can be vitiated for mistake it used to be necessary to distinguish between those cases where mistake renders the contract void *ab initio* and those where the mistake makes the contract voidable, meaning that the claimant had to rescind it before obtaining restitution.[229] Essentially this distinction derived from the different approaches of Law and Equity, with mistake at Law making a contract void and a mistake in Equity making it voidable. However, following the decision of the Court of Appeal in *Great Peace Shipping Ltd v Tsavliris Salvage (International) Ltd*,[230] it is no longer necessary to consider the equitable doctrine of mistake. After careful consideration of the equitable jurisdiction, the Court of Appeal concluded that it was not possible to distinguish it from the Common Law doctrine. It follows both that the contractual doctrine of mistake in Equity no longer exists[231] and that the effect of mistake today is only to render a contract void. The Court of Appeal did recognize, however, that the equitable jurisdiction had advantages over that of the Common Law, since the jurisdiction in Equity to grant rescission gave greater flexibility to reach the just result.[232] The Court therefore suggested that there was scope for legislation, along the lines of the Law Reform (Frustrated Contracts) Act 1943,[233] to give the law greater flexibility than simply concluding that a contract was or was not void for mistake. Where a mistake renders the contract void the claimant will normally be able to recover any benefits which have been transferred under it, with the ground of restitution being either mistake or total failure of basis.[234]

(A) TRANSACTIONS WHICH ARE VOID FOR MISTAKE

Although the Common Law recognizes that a contract may be void by virtue of mistake, either of fact or law,[235] this will occur only in exceptional circumstances.[236] This is because the policy of the law seeks to ensure that contracts once made are binding on the parties[237] for reasons of certainty and commercial convenience.[238] In certain situations, however, the claimant's mistake is so extreme that his or her intention to enter into a contract can be considered to be vitiated, so it is not possible to conclude that there was a true agreement between the parties.[239] There are two types of mistake which the law recognizes as vitiating the intention to enter into the contract, namely common mistakes and unilateral mistakes. There is a related doctrine of *non est factum* which also renders a contact void. The claimant will not, however, be able to rely on the doctrine of mistake in two circumstances: first, where there are no reasonable grounds for the claimant's mistaken belief;[240] secondly, the contract itself may expressly or impliedly state which party bears the risk of the mistake and this will exclude the operation of the doctrine.[241]

---

[229] See p 21, above.   [230] [2002] EWCA Civ 1407, [2003] QB 679.

[231] As to whether it was open to the Court of Appeal to reach such a decision see S Midwinter, 'The Great Pease and Precedent' (2003) 119 LQR 180.

[232] *Great Peace Shipping Ltd v Tsavliris Salvage (International) Ltd* [2002] EWCA Civ 1407, [2003] QB 679, 726.   [233] See p 357, below.

[234] See *Great Peace Shipping Ltd v Tsavliris Salvage (International) Ltd* [2002] EWCA Civ 1407, [2003] QB 679, 692 (Lord Phillips MR).

[235] *Brennan v Bolt Burdon* [2004] EWCA Civ 1017, [2005] QB 303.

[236] D Sheehan, 'Vitiation of Contracts for Mistake and Misprepresentation of Law' [2003] 11 RLR 26.

[237] This is traditionally expressed by reference to the Latin maxim *pacta sunt servanda*. See *Bell v Lever Brothers Ltd* [1932] AC 161, 224 (Lord Atkin); *Associated Japanese Bank (International) Ltd v Credit du Nord SA* [1989] 1 WLR 255, 268 (Steyn J).

[238] Needham, 'Mistaken Payments: A New Look at an Old Theme', 164.

[239] This is sometimes described as the parties not being *ad idem*—not of one mind.

[240] *Associated Japanese Bank (International) Ltd v Crédit du Nord SA* [1989] 1 WLR 255, 268–9 (Steyn J).

[241] Ibid, 268. See *Brennan v Bolt Burdon* [2004] EWCA Civ 1017, [2005] QB 303.

(i) Common Mistakes

Common mistakes are mistakes which are shared by the parties to the contract. The test which is adopted to identify when a common mistake will render a contract void is that of fundamental mistake.[242] In *Great Peace Shipping Ltd v Tsavliris Salvage (International) Ltd*[243] the Court of Appeal held that this means that the mistake must either render performance of the contract impossible or render the contract essentially different from what the parties intended it to be.[244] Examples of such mistakes include mistakes as to the existence of the subject matter of the contract,[245] or as to the title to the subject matter. It has also been recognized that common mistakes of law can vitiate a contract,[246] but not where there is only a shared doubt as to the relevant rules of law.[247]

In every case it is a matter of degree whether the common mistake of the parties is so important that it relates to the very foundation of the contract. If the mistake is not as serious as this it will not operate to vitiate the parties' intention to enter into the contract. This is illustrated by the decision of the House of Lords in *Bell v Lever Brothers*.[248] An employer wished to terminate the service contracts of two employees and consequently agreed to make them compensatory payments. In fact, the employer could have sacked the employees summarily without compensation because they had breached their contract of employment by working on their own account when they should have been working for the employer. The House of Lords held that the employer's mistaken assumption that it could terminate the employees' contracts only if compensation was paid, a mistake which was shared by the employees, was not a fundamental mistake. This was presumably because the mistake did not relate to the validity or operation of the contract, but merely related to the employer's motivation for entering into it. In other words, there was no mistake as to what was paid but only as to the reason for making the payment. Consequently, the employer was not able to recover the compensation payments which it had paid to the employees.

More recently this doctrine of common mistake was considered by the Court of Appeal in *Great Peace Shipping Ltd v Tsavliris Salvage (International) Ltd*.[249] The defendant offered salvage services to a vessel which was in difficulties. The defendant entered into a hire contract with the claimant to provide assistance, the defendant believing that the claimant's vessel was 35 miles away from the stricken vessel. In fact, the claimant's vessel was 410 miles away. When the defendant discovered this, it did not immediately cancel the contract but delayed doing so for a few hours until it was able to find a vessel which was closer to provide assistance. The claimant then sued the defendant for payment of five days' hire under a cancellation clause in the contract. The defendant argued that the contract was void for common mistake, by virtue of its belief that the claimant's vessel was nearest to the ship which required assistance. However, the court concluded that the mistake was not such as to render the performance under the contract substantially different from that which was bargained for, as reflected by the fact that the defendant

---

[242] *Bell v Lever Brothers Ltd* [1932] AC 161, 224 (Lord Atkin). See also *Norwich Union Fire Insurance Society Ltd v Price* [1934] AC 455; *Midland Bank plc v Brown Shipley and Co Ltd* [1991] 2 All ER 690; and *Great Peace Shipping Ltd v Tsavliris Salvage (International) Ltd* [2002] EWCA Civ 1407, [2003] QB 679.

[243] [2002] EWCA Civ 1407, [2003] QB 679. See also *EIC Services Ltd v Phipps* [2003] EWHC 1507, [2003] 1 WLR 2360.

[244] *Great Peace Shipping Ltd v Tsavliris Salvage (International) Ltd* [2002] EWCA Civ 1407; [2003] QB 679, 703.

[245] See, for example, *Couturier v Hastie* (1856) 5 HL Cas 673.

[246] *Brennan v Bolt Burdon* [2004] EWCA Civ 1017, [2005] QB 303.   [247] Ibid.

[248] [1932] AC 161.   [249] [2002] EWCA Civ 1407, [2003] QB 679.

had not cancelled the contract on discovering the mistake, but waited to see whether there was a nearer vessel. In other words, the mistake did not render the performance of the contract impossible; it was simply less desirable, so the mistake could not be characterized as fundamental.

The doctrine of common mistake will not be available in certain circumstances. For example, if one party has warranted the existence of a state of affairs, he or she bears the risk that the state of affairs might not exist.[250] Further, the non-existence of a state of affairs must not be attributable to the fault of either party,[251] although it remains unclear what constitutes fault in this context.[252] Clearly, if the claimant knew of the mistake there is no mistake shared by the claimant and the defendant.[253] If the claimant suspected a mistake had been made, he or she would also be prevented from relying on the doctrine.[254] The doctrine of common mistake of law will generally be inapplicable to set aside a contract of compromise, by virtue of the countervailing policy of protecting the stability of closed transactions and the difficulty in establishing the impossibility of performing the contractual venture.[255]

(ii) Unilateral Mistakes

A unilateral mistake renders a contract void where one party makes a fundamental mistake relating to the identity of the other party to the agreement,[256] and that other party is aware that the first party was mistaken.[257] The so-called *inter praesentes* exception applies, so that if the claimant and the defendant make a contract in each other's presence, a mistake as to identity will not vitiate it, since the parties can see with whom they are contracting.[258] Where the parties are not in each other's presence and the claimant thinks that he or she is contracting with somebody other than the defendant, the contract will be void for mistake. So, for example, in *Shogun Finance Ltd v Hudson*[259] the claimant finance company lent money to a fraudster who wanted to purchase a car by hire purchase but pretended to be a different person. The finance was arranged through the car salesman by phone. The fraudster sold the car to a third party and then disappeared. The claimant sought to assert title to the car. Since the hire purchase agreement was void[260] by virtue of a unilateral mistake as to the identity of the third party, it followed that title to the car was retained by the claimant, despite the sale to the third party.

(iii) Mutual Mistakes

A mutual mistake arises where there is a mistake in the communications between the parties to the contract so that no genuine contract is formed between them. This will be the case where there is no correspondence between the offer of one party and the acceptance of the other. So, for example, where one party offers to sell his car for £5,000

---

[250] Ibid, 703. See *William Sindall plc v Cambridgeshire CC* [1994] 1 WLR 1016, 1035 (Hoffmann LJ).

[251] Ibid. See also *Solle v Butcher* [1950] 1 KB 671, 693 (Denning LJ).

[252] *Grist v Bailey* [1967] Ch 532, 542 (Goff J).

[253] *Magee v Pennine Insurance Co Ltd* [1969] 2 QB 507, 516 (Lord Denning MR).

[254] *Brennan v Bolt Burdon* [2004] EWCA Civ 1017, [2005] QB 303.

[255] Ibid, [23] (Maurice Kay LJ), [51] (Bodey J), [59] (Sedley LJ).

[256] *Ingram v Little* [1961] 1 QB 31; *Collings v Lee* [2001] 2 All ER 332; *Shogun Finance Ltd v Hudson* [2003] UKHL 62, [2004] 1 AC 919.

[257] *Shogun Finance Ltd v Hudson* [2003] UKHL 62, [2004] 1 AC 919.

[258] *Phillips v Brooks Ltd* [1919] 2 KB 243.   [259] [2003] UKHL 62, [2004] 1 AC 919.

[260] The result would have been different had the contract only been voidable for misrepresentation, for then rescission of the contract would have been barred by virtue of the third party being a *bona fide* purchaser for value. See p 27, above.

and the other party agrees to purchase it for £2,000, there is no genuine agreement between them because offer and acceptance do not correspond, so no contract is made.

(iv) The Doctrine of *Non Est Factum*

The essence of the Common Law doctrine of *non est factum* is that a written contract will be considered to be void where one of the signatories to it was misled into signing a document which was radically different from that which he or she intended to sign. This doctrine is interpreted restrictively, since it will only apply where the claimant who wishes to rely on it can be considered to have acted reasonably in signing the document.[261] The leading case on the operation of the doctrine is the decision of the House of Lords in *Saunders v Anglia Building Society*,[262] where the claimant, an old woman, was induced to sign a deed which she thought assigned the lease of her house to her nephew, when in fact the deed assigned the lease to her nephew's business associate. Since the claimant's spectacles were broken she was unable to read the document but relied on the assignee's representation that the deed involved a gift to the nephew. The claimant claimed that the deed was void, but the claim failed for two reasons. First, because there was no radical difference between what the claimant thought she was signing and what she actually signed.[263] This was because the claimant was not mistaken in thinking that the deed assigned the lease of her house; the mistake only related to the identity of the assignee. Secondly, since the claimant could have taken the trouble to find out what the effect of the document was, her failure to do so meant that she had acted unreasonably in signing the document and so her signature was valid. It would have been different if she were blind or illiterate since then she would have been compelled to rely on someone else to explain to her the effect of the deed. The consequence of this decision is that it is very difficult for the claimant to establish that a transaction is void by virtue of the *non est factum* doctrine.

(v) The Consequences of a Contract Being Void for Mistake

Once the contract has been held to be void for mistake or by virtue of the *non est factum* doctrine, the claimant can secure restitution of any benefits transferred under it. This restitutionary claim may be founded either on the vindication of property rights, if the mistake was so fundamental that title to property did not pass to the defendant,[264] or on the reversal of the defendant's unjust enrichment. As regards the latter principle, it follows from the fact that the contract has been vitiated for mistake that any benefit which has been received by the defendant from the claimant pursuant to the transaction will have been received in circumstances of injustice, since there will be no legally effective basis for the receipt. Where, for example, the claimant has paid the defendant under a contract believing that he or she was obliged to do so, and this contract is avoided by reason of a common or unilateral mistake, it is possible to show that the defendant was enriched at the claimant's expense and the ground for restitution is usually the mistake. For if the claimant's mistake was sufficient to vitiate the contract it must follow that the claimant's mistaken belief in the validity of the contract was the operating cause of the claimant's payment to the defendant.[265]

---

[261] *Avon Finance Co Ltd v Bridger* [1985] 2 All ER 281.   [262] [1971] AC 1004.

[263] Ibid, 1017 (Lord Reid). See also Lord Hodson, ibid, 1019, who said that the difference must go to the substance of the whole consideration or to the root of the matter.

[264] See p 574, below.

[265] Alternatively the claimant may rely on the ground of total failure of basis, see *Strickland v Turner* (1852) 7 Ex 208, 155 ER 919, or absence of basis, see Chapter 13.

(B) CONTRACTS VOIDABLE FOR MISTAKE

(i) Unilateral Mistake

A unilateral mistake renders a contract voidable at Common Law where one party makes a fundamental mistake, other than relating to the identity of the other contracting party, such as a mistake as to the terms of the contract or the subject matter of the contract.[266] A contract will only be voidable for unilateral mistake where the other party to the contract knew[267] of the mistake, or had engaged in sharp practice or other unconscionable conduct,[268] such as where the negotiations are conducted in such a way that the other party will not discover the mistake.

(ii) Misrepresentation

A contract will be voidable for misrepresentation where an untrue statement or assertion is made by one party which is relied on by the representee and who is induced to enter into a contract as a result.[269]

(1) The Test of Misrepresentation

Whether a contract will be voidable[270] depends on how the misrepresentation is characterized.[271] Where the mistake was induced by a fraudulent misrepresentation the contract is voidable at Common Law.[272] Fraud for these purposes means that the representor knew that the representation was untrue, had no belief in the truth of the representation, was wilfully blind, or suspected that it might be untrue.[273] Where the misrepresentation was negligent or simply innocent the contract may still be rescinded in Equity.

The law on what constitutes a misrepresentation for these purposes is complex. Essentially, the defendant must have made a representation which is false at the time when the claimant was induced to enter into the contract.[274] The representation must relate to facts or law[275] rather than matters of opinion. A statement made by the defendant may constitute a misrepresentation where it involves a representation of the defendant's existing state of mind which is untrue. So, in *Edgington v Fitzmaurice*[276] a statement in a company's prospectus, which invited subscriptions for debentures, stated that the purpose of the debentures was to enable the company to complete building operations and to develop its trade. In fact, the real purpose of the debentures was to enable the directors to discharge pressing liabilities. The Court of Appeal held that the statement in the prospectus was a representation of fact rather than intention and, since the directors never intended to use the money raised in the way they had suggested in the prospectus, the statement constituted a misrepresentation. Usually a misrepresentation involves a false statement being made by the defendant, but misrepresentations may also arise from the

---

[266] See *Smith v Hughes* (1871) LR 6 QB 597.   [267] *Riverlate Properties Ltd v Paul* [1975] Ch 133.

[268] *Hartog v Colin and Shields* [1939] 3 All ER 566; *Riverlate Properties Ltd v Paul* [1975] Ch 133.

[269] For detailed analysis of the law see Beale (ed), *Chitty on Contracts* (31st edn), ch 6.

[270] Where the induced mistake is fundamental the contract will be void. See *Cundy v Lindsay* (1878) 3 App Cas 459.

[271] If the misrepresentation is included as a term of the contract the claimant may be able to terminate it for breach, if the breach is sufficiently serious, and in any case recover damages for loss.

[272] *Smith New Court Ltd v Scrimgeour Vickers (Asset Management) Ltd* [1997] 2 AC 554.

[273] *Derry v Peek* (1889) 14 App Cas 337, 374 (Lord Herschell).

[274] *Briess v Woolley* [1954] AC 333.

[275] *Pankhania v Hackney LBC* [2002] EWHC (Ch) 2441, [58] (Rex Tedd QC); *Brennan v Bolt Burdon* [2004] EWCA Civ 1017, [2005] QB 303, 317 (Bodey J).

[276] (1885) 29 Ch D 459.

defendant's conduct or where the defendant fails to correct a representation which was initially true but was falsified by subsequent events.[277]

A misrepresentation will only be relevant where it induced the representee to enter into the contract. This is a subjective test which has regard to the effect of the representation on the representee. Reliance will not be established where, for example, the representee knew that the representation was false by the time the contract was made, perhaps because the representor had corrected the error,[278] or had forgotten about it by the time the contract was made. The negligence of the representee in failing to discover the truth will not generally prevent him or her from rescinding the contract, regardless of whether the representation was made fraudulently or innocently,[279] save where the representee was suspicious about the truth of the representation and failed to investigate.[280] Even if the representee did investigate the representation but in a cursory way so that the truth was not discovered, he or she will not be considered to have relied on it.[281]

A fraudulent misrepresentation need only operate as a contributory cause, rather than the but for cause, of the representee entering into the contract.[282] It appears that a non-fraudulent misrepresentation will only be relevant if it was a but for cause of the contract being made, in the sense that the contract would not have been made but for the representation or would have been made on materially different terms.[283]

(2) The Consequences of Misrepresentation

Once it has been established that there is an operative misrepresentation which has induced the claimant to enter into a contract, the remedies which are available are complex and are not necessarily restitutionary. If the misrepresentation was made fraudulently or negligently, the claimant may recover damages to compensate for loss suffered either for the tort of deceit[284] or negligent misstatement.[285] There is also a statutory right to damages if the misrepresentation was made other than fraudulently, save where the misrepresentor can prove that he or she had reasonable grounds for believing, and did believe up to the time when the contract was made, that the representation was true.[286] This consequently provides for damages where the misrepresentation was negligent. There is no right to damages where the misrepresentation was innocent.[287]

The claimant may also rescind the contract, regardless of whether the representation was made fraudulently, negligently, or innocently,[288] and this is subject to the usual bars for rescission.[289] The contract can be rescinded for misrepresentation even where it has

---

[277] *Briess v Woolley* [1954] AC 333.
[278] *Assicurazioni Generali v Arab Insurance Group* [2002] EWCA Civ 1642, [2003] 1 All ER (Comm) 140, [63] (Clarke LJ).
[279] *Standard Chartered Bank v Pakistan National Shipping Corp (No 2)* [2003] 1 AC 959, 967 (Lord Hoffmann).
[280] *Redgrave v Hurd* (1881) 20 Ch D 1, 14 (Jessel MR); 23 (Baggallay LJ).
[281] *Attwood v Small* (1836) 6 Cl and F 232.
[282] *Edgington v Fitzmaurice* (1885) 29 Ch D 459, 481 (Cotton LJ).
[283] *Standard Chartered Bank v Pakistan National Shipping Corp (No 2)* [2003] 1 AC 959, 967 (Lord Hoffmann).
[284] *Doyle v Olby (Ironmongers) Ltd* [1969] 2 QB 158.
[285] *Hedley Byrne and Co Ltd v Heller and Partners Ltd* [1964] AC 465.
[286] Misrepresentation Act 1967, s 2(1).
[287] Damages may, however, be awarded in lieu of rescission in the exercise of the court's discretion. See p 199, below.
[288] See p 21, above.   [289] See p 25, above.

been performed.[290] Rescission for negligent or innocent misrepresentation[291] may be excluded by the contract, so long as the provision is clear and reasonable[292] and reasonable steps have been taken to draw the provision to the notice of the claimant. There is also one specific bar to rescission which arises where the claimant was induced to enter into a contract by the defendant's innocent or negligent misrepresentation. In such circumstances, section 2(2) of the Misrepresentation Act 1967 provides that the court may order that damages be awarded in lieu of rescission. Section 2(2) identifies certain factors which should particularly be considered by the court when deciding whether to exercise this discretion, namely the nature of the misrepresentation, the loss to the misrepresentee if the contract is not rescinded, and the loss to the misrepresentor which would arise from rescission. Consequently, the court would probably award damages in lieu of rescission where the misrepresentation can be characterized as trivial or where the harm to the misrepresentor if rescission were ordered easily outweighs any advantages of rescission to the claimant.[293] Where the court orders that damages should be awarded in lieu of rescission, the claimant's remedy will be compensatory rather than restitutionary. This power to award damages will be available even though the claimant is no longer able to rescind the contract, as long as the claimant had been able to rescind the contract at some point in the past.[294]

(3) Misrepresentation and Third Parties

Where the claimant is induced to enter into a contract by virtue of a misrepresentation but enters into a contract with a third party and not with the misrepresentor, the question whether the claimant can rescind the contract is particularly complex. This scenario has arisen most frequently where a husband makes a misrepresentation to his wife to induce her to enter into a transaction with a bank, whereby the wife agrees to act as surety for her husband's debts. Usually, this security is over the matrimonial home. Where the husband fails to pay his debts the bank will wish to enforce its security by requiring the matrimonial home to be sold. The resolution of this dispute is particularly difficult because it is between two innocent parties, the wife and the bank, with the husband not being a party to the proceedings. The policy question is therefore which of two innocent parties should bear the loss. The House of Lords decided in *Barclays Bank plc v O'Brien*[295] that the wife would be able to rescind the transaction if she could show the bank had actual or constructive notice of the misrepresentation. This is because, where the bank has notice of the wife's equity to set the transaction aside, it can be considered to be more responsible for entering into the transaction and so should bear the loss. A bank will have such constructive notice where the transaction is not on its face to the wife's advantage and there is a substantial risk that the husband had made a misrepresentation to induce the wife to enter into the transaction.[296] Where, however, the bank can show that it had taken reasonable steps to ensure that the wife had not been induced to act by a misrepresentation, it will not be bound by the wife's equity to set the transaction aside. This is because the nature of the bank's conduct is such that it should not be considered to bear the responsibility for the

---

[290] Misrepresentation Act 1967, s 1.

[291] But not fraudulent misrepresentation: *HIH Casualty and General Insurance v Chase Manhattan Bank* [2003] UKHL 6, [2003] 2 Lloyd's Rep 6, [16] (Lord Bingham of Cornhill) and [121] (Lord Scott of Foscote).

[292] *Walker v Boyle* [1982] 1 WLR 495.

[293] See *William Sindall plc v Cambridgeshire CC* [1994] 1 WLR 1016, 1036–8 (Hoffmann LJ).

[294] *Thomas Witter Ltd v TBP Industries Ltd* [1996] 2 All ER 573, 590 (Jacob J). 188. See H Beale, 'Points on Misrepresentation' (1995) 111 LQR 385.

[295] [1994] 1 AC 180. See Chapter 11.   [296] *Royal Bank of Scotland v Etridge (No 2)* [2002] AC 773.

misrepresentation. The bank will be considered to have taken reasonable steps where, for example, it receives confirmation from a solicitor that the wife has received legal advice before she entered into the transaction.[297]

Although the *O'Brien* principle has so far only been applied to cases where the relationship between the misrepresentor and the misrepresentee has been a relationship of trust and confidence, there is no obvious reason why the principle should be confined to such cases. It should be applicable in any case where the misrepresentee enters into a transaction as a result of a misrepresentation from a person who is not a party to the transaction, regardless of the nature of the relationship between the misrepresentor and misrepresentee. In all such cases it should be necessary to consider whether the other party to the transaction had actual or constructive notice of the misrepresentation. It will, of course, be much more difficult to show that that party did have notice where the relationship between the misrepresentor and misrepresentee was not based on trust and confidence and was, for example, a purely commercial relationship. But it does not follow from the fact that this will be difficult to establish that the *O'Brien* principle should be artificially restricted.

(C) NON-DISCLOSURE

Usually, a failure by the defendant to disclose material facts to the claimant will not enable the claimant to rescind the contract.[298] However, in certain limited circumstances the defendant's failure to disclose material facts will render the contract voidable at Common Law where the claimant was induced to enter into the contract by reason of the non-disclosure. There is a duty to disclose material facts in respect of contracts of insurance,[299] and in surety transactions the creditor is under a duty to disclose to the surety any unusual feature of the contract between the debtor and the creditor which makes the contract materially different in a potentially disadvantageous respect from that which the surety would naturally expect.[300]

(D) VOIDABLE VOLUNTARY TRANSFERS

The making of a gift by deed may also be rescinded in Equity by virtue of the claimant's mistake. This was recognized in *Lady Hood of Avalon v Mackinnon*,[301] where a deed was rescinded where the claimant had appointed property for the benefit of one of her daughters, forgetting that she had made provision for that daughter previously. This was regarded as a sufficiently serious mistake to enable the court to rescind the deed, since the claimant had never intended to make double provision for the daughter.

The operation of the equitable jurisdiction to rescind voluntary dispositions has been clarified by the Supreme Court in *Pitt v Holt; Futter v Futter*.[302] Lord Walker identified three interlinked elements before the equitable jurisdiction is engaged:

---

[297] Ibid. For more detailed discussion of when a bank will be deemed to have constructive notice of the wife's equity to set the transaction aside and what constitutes the taking of reasonable steps, see Chapter 11.

[298] *Bell v Lever Brothers Ltd* [1932] AC 161, 227 (Lord Atkin).

[299] See, for example, *Pan Atlantic Insurance Co Ltd v Pine Top Insurance Co Ltd* [1995] 1 AC 501.

[300] *Royal Bank of Scotland plc v Etridge (No 2)* [2002] 2 AC 773, [81] (Lord Nicholls), [186] (Lord Scott).

[301] [1909] 1 Ch 476.

[302] [2013] UKSC 26, [2013] 2 AC 108. See P Davies and G Virgo, 'Relieving Trustee's Mistakes' [2013] RLR 73.

(i) The donor must have been mistaken.[303]

(ii) The mistake was sufficiently serious.

(iii) The assertion of the donee's rights would be objectively unjust or unconscionable rendering the mistake of sufficient gravity to rescind the disposition.

The second test, that '[t]he mistake was sufficiently serious', is more stringent than the usual test of 'but for' causation, but is not as stringent as the test of fundamental mistake to rescind a contract. This appears to be because a deed is a formal legal document which should not be set aside easily but, because we are concerned with voluntary transfers, it should be easier to set it aside than a contract.

Prior to the decision of the Supreme Court, a controversial issue concerned whether a mistake as to the consequences of a voluntary transfer could constitute a relevant mistake, or whether the mistake had to relate to the legal effect of the transaction.[304] This was a significant issue since a common reason for a donor wishing to set aside a voluntary transfer was because of its adverse tax consequences, rather than the legal effect of the transfer. In *Pitt v Holt* Lord Walker rejected the need to distinguish between consequences and legal effect and focused instead on the seriousness of the mistake.[305] Crucially, he recognized that:[306]

the true requirement is simply for there to be a causative mistake of sufficient gravity; and, as additional guidance to judges in finding and evaluating the facts of any particular case, that the test will normally be satisfied only where there is some mistake either as to the legal character or nature of a transaction, or as to some matter of fact or law which is basic to the transaction.

This expands the types of mistake which might be sufficient to engage the equitable jurisdiction to set aside the deed, since a mistake as to the tax consequences of the disposition might be relevant if sufficiently serious. The distinction between effect and consequence has not disappeared completely, however, but may remain of evidential significance since, as Lord Walker recognized,[307] a mistake as to the essential nature of a transaction is likely to be more serious than a mistake as to its consequences.

The third test involves unconscionability which renders the mistake of sufficient gravity to rescind the disposition. The determination of unconscionability requires close examination of the facts, including 'the circumstances of the mistake and its consequences for the person who made the vitiated disposition', change of position, and 'other matters relevant to the exercise of the court's discretion'.[308] Lord Walker used the language of 'unconscionableness', as he called it, interchangeably with that of 'justice' and 'unfairness',[309] so that the test of gravity appears to turn simply on an assessment of fairness determined through the exercise of judicial discretion.

On the facts of *Pitt v Holt* it was held that a mistake as to the tax consequences of a disposition to a trust was sufficiently serious and grave to trigger the equitable jurisdiction to rescind the disposition for mistake.[310] In *Pitt v Holt*, Mrs Pitt's husband had been seriously injured in an accident, for which he received substantial compensation. Mrs Pitt

---

[303] See p 159, above, for the definition of mistake. In *Wright v National Westminster Bank plc* [2014] EWHC 3158 (Ch), [11], Norris J confirmed that there was no need to establish that the mistake was induced by misrepresentation or fraud.

[304] As Millett J had recognized in *Gibbon v Mitchell* [1990] 1 WLR 1304.

[305] Relying on *Ogilvie v Littleboy* (1897) 13 TLR 399, 400 (Lindley LJ). Affirmed by the House of Lords: *Ogilvie v Allen* (1899) 15 TLR 294.

[306] *Pitt v Holt* [2013] UKSC 26, [2013] 2 AC 108, [122].   [307] Ibid, [123].   [308] Ibid, [126].

[309] Ibid.   [310] See also *Kennedy v Kennedy* [2014] EWHC 4129 (Ch).

sought advice as to how best to invest this money and was advised to transfer it to a trust. This disposition was then authorized by the Court of Protection. Unfortunately the method of disposition which Mrs Pitt adopted had adverse tax consequences, which could easily have been avoided. In reaching the decision that this disposition could be rescinded, a matter of particular significance was the fact that the disposition did not form part of an artificial or abusive tax avoidance scheme and also that it had been authorized by the Court of Protection. In *Wright v National Westminster Bank plc*[311] a trust was set aside by virtue of the settlor's mistaken belief that income from the asset which was settled on trust would continue to be available to him and his wife to maintain their existing standard of living.

Had the equitable jurisdiction been invoked in *Futter v Futter*,[312] which was the other case considered by the Supreme Court with *Pitt v Holt*, Lord Walker considered that it would have been more difficult to establish that the mistake was sufficiently serious and grave to justify rescission. In that case the trustees of a discretionary trust had exercised powers of advancement on the understanding that, although this would result in a tax liability, that liability could be set off against allowable losses. The decision to exercise the power was made after the trustees had obtained advice from solicitors, but it ignored the effect of a statute which provided that the tax liability could not be set off. The settlor and the beneficiaries incurred a significant tax liability as a result of the trustees' mistake. Unlike the disposition made by Mrs Pitt, this case involved an artificial tax avoidance scheme which had gone wrong.[313] Lord Walker described such schemes as constituting 'a social evil',[314] and emphasized that the court might refuse to award equitable relief to rescind a voluntary disposition on the ground of public policy, suggesting that there are moral questions which need to be examined by the court in determining whether it is appropriate to exercise the jurisdiction to rescind the disposition. It does not appear to be unconscionable for the Revenue to keep tax paid as part of an artificial avoidance scheme entered into by mistake. It follows that many claims based upon a mistake as to the fiscal implications of a disposition seem destined to fail. Where, however, the settlor or trustees have conferred a benefit on the donees in a tax efficient manner as contemplated by statute, this will be characterized as legitimate such that it would be unconscionable not to rescind the disposition for mistake.[315]

The determination of whether a voluntary disposition should be rescinded in Equity appears to involve judicial manipulation of the most blatant kind. Confusingly, the distinction between seriousness of the mistake and its gravity assessed by reference to unconscionability is likely to merge to form a single test turning on the justice of the case. What is even more concerning is that this equitable test of mistake, which was applied in the specific context of rescission of deeds, is starting to be adopted more widely to any case where the claimant has made a gift by mistake.[316] Whilst the vagueness of the tests which have been adopted for purposes of the equitable jurisdiction are a matter of concern, their potential expansion to restitution of all mistaken gifts is unacceptable.

The real problem with the approach of Lord Walker in *Pitt v Holt* is the inclusion of a third test involving the 'unconscionableness' of the defendant's receipt. There is no need for such a test. It should be enough that the mistake is sufficiently serious before a voluntary disposition can be rescinded.

---

[311] [2014] EWHC 3158 (Ch).

[312] This point had not been invoked initially and the Supreme Court declined to permit the appellants to raise it on appeal.

[313] *Pitt v Holt* [2013] UKSC 26, [2013] 2 AC, [135].   [314] Ibid, [135].

[315] *Kennedy v Kennedy* [2014] EWHC 4129 (Ch), [39] (Etherton C).   [316] See p 182, above.

10

COMPULSION

1. GENERAL PRINCIPLES

(A) THE PRINCIPLE OF COMPULSION

Although compulsion is not a ground of restitution in its own right, it is a general principle which underlies a number of specific grounds of restitution, most notably duress. The essence of the principle of compulsion is that it arises where pressure has been placed on the claimant to transfer a benefit to the defendant. Compulsion operates in a similar way to mistake as an explanation of why the receipt of an enrichment by the defendant can be regarded as unjust, namely that the pressure is treated as vitiating the claimant's intention that the defendant should receive the enrichment. This is because, where the claimant is pressurized into transferring a benefit to the defendant, the claimant's autonomy has been interfered with to such an extent that he or she cannot be considered to have freely exercised a choice to transfer the benefit to the defendant.

(B) DIFFERENT TYPES OF ENRICHMENT

Although all of the reported cases have concerned claims for the restitution of money paid as a result of compulsion, there is no reason why restitutionary claims cannot be founded on this principle where the claimant has been compelled to transfer non-money benefits to the defendant. Where the claimant has been compelled to transfer goods or to provide services it is still possible to conclude that his or her intention to transfer the benefit has been vitiated as a result of the compulsion. Although it is usually more difficult to establish that the defendant has been enriched by the receipt of goods or services,[1] this is less so where the defendant compelled the claimant to transfer the benefit, simply because the fact of compulsion suggests that the defendant valued the benefit and so he or she will not be able to rely on the defence of subjective devaluation.[2]

(C) VITIATION OF CONTRACTS FOR COMPULSION

Whereas the definition of mistake as a ground of restitution differs depending on whether it is necessary to set aside a contract before the claimant can obtain restitution,[3] this is not the case with those grounds of restitution which are founded on compulsion. These grounds are defined in exactly the same way regardless of whether the claimant wishes to bring a pure restitutionary claim or first needs to set aside a contract for compulsion before seeking restitutionary relief.[4] This is presumably because, unlike cases where the

---

[1] See Chapter 4.   [2] See p 69, above.   [3] See Chapter 9.

[4] In *CTN Cash and Carry Ltd v Gallaher Ltd* [1994] 4 All ER 714, 717, Steyn LJ said that it did not matter, for the purposes of defining economic duress, whether the claimant had agreed to pay money to the defendant or had simply paid the money unilaterally, since the same definition of duress applied.

claimant entered into a contract as a result of a spontaneous mistake but like cases where the claimant entered into a contract as a result of an induced mistake, the defendant's conduct in compelling the claimant to enter into a contract is such that it is easier to set the contract aside. Consequently, the grounds of restitution which establish that the claimant's intention to transfer a benefit to the defendant was vitiated by the compulsion, can also be used to show that the claimant did not intend to contract with the defendant, without any different definition of compulsion or the specific grounds of restitution.

Even though the grounds of restitution are the same, it is still necessary to distinguish between those cases where the claimant transferred a benefit to the defendant pursuant to a contract and those cases where there was no contract in existence for two reasons.

(i) The Time Factor

The time at which the compulsion must have been operating depends on the nature of the claim. For the purposes of setting aside a contract, the compulsion must have been operating when the contract was made. Where, however, the claimant wishes to recover a non-contractual payment it is simply sufficient to show that the compulsion was operative at the time of the payment.

(ii) The Contract Must Cease to Be Operative Before Restitutionary Remedies Can Be Awarded

If the claimant has transferred a benefit to the defendant pursuant to a contract which he or she was compelled to enter into, the claimant cannot obtain restitution until the contract has been set aside. This is because of the fundamental principle that restitutionary relief cannot be used to subvert contractual obligations.[5] Where the defendant compels the claimant to make a contract that contract will be rendered voidable and not void.[6] Consequently, if the claimant wishes to recover benefits transferred under such a contract by reason of compulsion it is first necessary to rescind the contract at Common Law.[7] Rescission will be barred, however, if the claimant affirmed it after the compulsion had ceased to operate;[8] if rescission has been unreasonably delayed; if third-party rights have intervened; or if the claimant is unable to make counter-restitution to the defendant of any benefits which the claimant had received from the defendant.[9]

(D) THE GROUNDS OF RESTITUTION

A number of different grounds of restitution can be considered to be founded on the principle of compulsion. Chief amongst these are the grounds of duress of the person, duress of goods and economic duress, and also undue pressure and legal compulsion.

---

[5] See Chapter 7.

[6] *The Universe Sentinel* [1983] 1 AC 366, 383 (Lord Diplock) and 400 (Lord Scarman); *The Evia Luck* [1992] 2 AC 152, 168 (Lord Goff); *Halpern v Halpern* [2008] QB 195. In *Barton v Armstrong* [1976] AC 104, 120 the Privy Council found that threats to kill the claimant rendered a deed void, where the deed was entered into as a result of the threats. This decision is explicable either because of the extreme nature of the threats or, more likely, because the claimant had sought a declaration that the deed was void and the form of the declaration which was granted had not been challenged by the defendant. Cf DJ Lanham, 'Duress and Void Contracts' (1966) 29 MLR 615.

[7] *Whelpdale's case* (1605) 5 Co Rep 119a. See p 23, above.

[8] *Mutual Finance Ltd v John Wetton and Sons Ltd* [1937] 2 KB 389, 397 (Porter J). In *The Atlantic Baron* [1979] QB 705 affirmation of a contract prevented the claimant from rescinding it for economic duress.

[9] *Halpern v Halpern* [2007] EWCA Civ 291, [2008] QB 195. See p 25, above.

The compulsion principle can also be treated as underlying other grounds of restitution where the claimant has been pressurized to transfer a benefit to the defendant, but for reasons of convenience these grounds are considered in separate chapters because they are also founded on other principles. This is true of three grounds of restitution in particular.

(i) Necessity

There are cases where the claimant is compelled to provide a benefit to the defendant, not because of threats made by the defendant, but by virtue of the pressure of surrounding circumstances. This intervention by the claimant in circumstances of necessity is clearly affected by the principle of compulsion, but it deserves to be treated separately because of the complex policy issues which are raised in determining in what circumstances necessity should operate as a ground of restitution.[10]

(ii) Undue Influence

Where the claimant has transferred a benefit to the defendant as a result of undue influence, the influence may sometimes involve the exercise of pressure on the claimant to transfer the benefit. But this is not necessarily the case and consequently undue influence is more accurately analysed in terms of exploitation rather than compulsion.[11]

(iii) *Colore Officii*

The ground of *colore officii* arises where a claimant is compelled to pay the defendant to secure the performance of a public duty which the defendant should perform for nothing or for less than the sum demanded.[12] Whilst this ground of restitution is clearly founded on notions of compulsion, because it is a necessary condition that the public officer exerted illegitimate pressure to obtain the payment, it is more convenient to consider it in the context of restitutionary claims from public authorities.[13] This is primarily because recent developments in this area of the law of restitution indicate that the ground of *colore officii* has been subsumed within a general ground of restitution involving the recovery of unauthorized payments made to public authorities.[14]

(E) ILLEGALITY

Despite the general principle that the claimant's restitutionary claim will be defeated if the transfer of a benefit to the defendant was tainted by illegality,[15] the claimant will be able to bring a restitutionary claim by virtue of compulsion despite the taint of illegality. This is presumably because the defendant's misconduct in compelling the claimant to transfer the benefit makes the defendant more responsible for the circumstances of illegality than the claimant, negating the application of the illegality defence. So, for example, in *Astley v Reynolds*[16] the claimant was able to recover interest payments which he had paid to the defendant to recover his goods, which the defendant had threatened to hold onto until the interest had been paid. The ground of restitution in this case was duress of goods, and it made no difference to the claim that the interest payments were illegal. Similarly, in *Davies v London and Provincial Marine Insurance Co*[17] it was held that the claimant was able to recover money which he had been compelled to pay to the defendant as a result of the

---

[10] See Chapter 12.   [11] See Chapter 11.
[12] See, for example, *Steele v Williams* (1853) 8 Ex 625, 155 ER 1502.   [13] See Chapter 15.
[14] *Woolwich Equitable Building Society v IRC* [1993] AC 70, 198 (Lord Browne-Wilkinson).
[15] See Chapter 27.   [16] (1731) 2 Stra 915, 93 ER 939.   [17] (1878) 8 Ch D 469.

defendant's threat to prosecute the claimant, even though the transaction was illegal for stifling a prosecution.

2. DURESS

(A) THE RATIONALE OF DURESS AS A GROUND OF RESTITUTION

Essentially, duress operates as a ground of restitution where the claimant has transferred a benefit to the defendant as a result either of the exercise of illegitimate pressure or the making of an illegitimate threat. This threat may either be made expressly or implied from surrounding circumstances,[18] but it must take the form of 'do this or else . . .'.

The reason why a claimant who succumbs to the illegitimate threat or pressure by transferring a benefit to the defendant should be able to obtain restitution is usually considered to be that the effect of the threat or pressure is to vitiate the claimant's intention that the defendant should receive the benefit.[19] But this notion that the duress vitiates intent is not strictly accurate, since the claimant always has a choice whether or not to transfer the benefit to the defendant; the claimant does not need to submit to the threat or the pressure, but chooses to do so.[20] The real reason, therefore, why duress should be recognized as a ground of restitution is simply that the effect of the duress is that the claimant cannot be regarded as having exercised a free choice when he or she transferred a benefit to the defendant. In other words, the duress interferes with the claimant's autonomy to benefit whomsoever he or she wishes without constraint. This was recognized by Lord Scarman in *The Universe Sentinel*: 'The classic case of duress is . . . not the lack of will to submit but the victim's intentional submission arising from the realization that there is no other practical choice open to him.'[21]

Consequently, the claimant's intention to benefit the defendant can be considered to be vitiated, but only because the claimant did not exercise a free choice to benefit the defendant.

(B) THE ELEMENTS OF DURESS

When determining whether the claimant can rely on duress as a ground of restitution, two separate questions always need to be examined.[22]

(i) Illegitimate Threats and Pressure
Duress involves either the defendant threatening to do something unless the claimant transfers a benefit to him or her, or the actual exertion of pressure until the benefit is transferred. A useful definition of 'threats' has been suggested by Smith: 'A threat is a proposal to bring about an unwelcome event unless the recipient of the proposal does

---

[18] *Woolwich Equitable Building Society v IRC* [1993] AC 70, 165 (Lord Goff).

[19] See, for example, *Barton v Armstrong* [1976] AC 104, 121 (Lords Wilberforce and Simon).

[20] This was recognized by the House of Lords in *DPP for Northern Ireland v Lynch* [1975] AC 653. Lord Simon, ibid, 695, said that 'duress is not inconsistent with act and will, the will being deflected and not destroyed'.

[21] [1983] 1 AC 366, 400 (Lord Scarman).

[22] As was recognized by the Privy Council in *Barton v Armstrong* [1976] AC 104, 121 (Lords Wilberforce and Simon). See also *The Universe Sentinel* [1983] 1 AC 366, 400 (Lord Scarman) and *The Evia Luck* [1992] 2 AC 152, 165 (Lord Goff).

something (e.g. enter a contract), where the proposal is made because the event is unwelcome and in order to induce the recipient to do the thing requested.'[23]

It is possible to distinguish a threat from a warning, on the basis that the person making the warning does not have control over whether the unwelcome consequence will occur.[24] Similarly, a threat is different from a request, which involves the defendant asking for something. Although a theoretical distinction can readily be drawn between threats, warnings, and requests, in practice it is much more difficult to make such distinctions. Threats are normally made expressly, but they can also be implicit.[25] For example, if the defendant goes to the claimant's house accompanied by three thugs and asks for money, the implicit threat is that, unless the claimant pays the defendant, the thugs will beat him up.

Where the defendant has threatened to do something to the claimant unless the claimant transfers a benefit it is clear that duress will only be established if the threat was illegitimate,[26] but this provides little assistance since it is still necessary to determine what makes a threat illegitimate. In assessing this, both the nature of the threat and the nature of what the defendant demands need to be considered.[27]

Duress can, generally, only be established where the defendant's threat is unlawful.[28] The threat can be unlawful for two reasons. First, and most usually, because what the defendant threatens to do is unlawful. Consequently, threats to commit crimes or torts, such as threats to injure the person or to interfere with property, are unlawful, as are threats to breach a contract. Secondly, the defendant may actually be threatening to do something which is lawful, but in circumstances where the making of the threat is unlawful. The best example of this is where the threat constitutes the crime of blackmail,[29] which is defined as the making of an unwarranted demand with menaces. This offence can be committed even where what the defendant is threatening to do is lawful, such as threatening to reveal some compromising conduct, but the defendant demands money as payment for not fulfilling the threat.

Exceptionally, however, the making of a lawful threat will be sufficient to establish duress, but only where the threat can be considered to be illegitimate because it is unreasonable. This extended interpretation of a relevant threat was considered by the Privy Council in *R v Attorney-General for England and Wales*.[30] In this case the claimant, a member of the Special Air Service (the SAS), which is a celebrated regiment in the British army, was required to sign a confidentiality agreement to stop him from writing about his exploits as a member of the SAS. Failure to sign the agreement would have meant that he would have to leave the SAS and join another regiment. The claimant signed the agreement and then sought to have it set aside by virtue of duress. This argument failed because it was held that the threat to transfer him to another regiment was both lawful and legitimate, since the Ministry of Defence was entitled to conclude that anybody who failed to sign the agreement was unsuitable to remain a member of the SAS. But it was accepted that, had the threat been unreasonable, it would have been sufficient to establish duress

---

[23] S Smith, 'Contracting Under Pressure: A Theory of Duress' (1997) 56 CLJ 343, 346.

[24] Ibid.

[25] *The Alev* [1989] 1 Lloyd's Rep 138, 142 (Hobhouse J).

[26] *Barton v Armstrong* [1976] AC 104. See also *The Universe Sentinel* [1983] 1 AC 366, 384 (Lord Diplock); *R v Attorney-General of England and Wales* [2003] UKPC 22.

[27] *R v Attorney-General of England and Wales* [2003] UKPC 22, [16].

[28] *Mutual Finance Ltd v John Wetton and Sons Ltd* [1937] 2 KB 389, 395 (Porter J).

[29] Contrary to s 21 of the Theft Act 1968. See *Thorne v Motor Trade Association* [1937] AC 797, 806 (Lord Atkin).

[30] [2003] UKPC 22. See also *Royal Boskalis Westminster NV v Mountain* [1999] QB 674.

even though it was lawful.[31] Subsequently, the courts have explicitly recognized that a lawful threat can be illegitimate, particularly where it was coupled with prior unlawful conduct.[32]

It is not sufficient for the claimant to establish that the threat is either unlawful or illegitimate, since it must also be shown that what the defendant demands from the claimant is not lawfully due to the defendant. For example, if the claimant owes the defendant £1,000, and the defendant threatens to seize the claimant's property unless the debt is repaid, although the threat is unlawful the demand is not, because the debt is owed to the defendant and payment of the money will discharge the debt, so that there is a legally effective basis for the payment.[33] Duress can only be established where what the defendant seeks from the claimant is something to which the defendant is not entitled. Where some money is lawfully due to the defendant and an additional amount is paid because of duress, the claimant will only be able to recover the excess amount.[34]

Where the defendant actually exerts pressure to obtain a benefit from the defendant, rather than simply threatening to exert pressure, the pressure exerted must be illegitimate. Whether it is illegitimate is determined in a similar way to illegitimate threats. First, the pressure must involve the commission of an unlawful act, such as a crime, tort, or breach of contract. Secondly, it must be shown that what the defendant seeks from the exertion of the pressure is not lawfully due to him or her. So, for example, if the defendant falsely imprisons the claimant until she pays £1,000, which is not otherwise due to the defendant, the claimant will be able to establish that the defendant exerted illegitimate pressure.

(ii) Causation

Once it has been established that the defendant has made an illegitimate threat or exerted illegitimate pressure, the claimant must then show that he or she was induced to transfer a benefit to the defendant as a result or, where relevant, that he or she was induced to enter into a contract. This is a question of causation. It is obvious that, where the claimant has not perceived any threats made or pressure exerted by the defendant or where the claimant discounted the threats, the defendant's conduct cannot be regarded as the operative cause of any transaction entered into with the defendant.[35] But, where the claimant did perceive the threats or the pressure, the difficult question concerns what test of causation should be adopted to determine whether the duress was a sufficient cause for the claimant to transfer the benefit. In the context of spontaneous mistakes it was concluded that a mistake would be considered as constituting a ground of restitution only if the claimant could show that, but for the mistake, he or she would not have transferred a benefit to the defendant.[36] But where the mistake has been fraudulently induced by the defendant, a more lenient test of causation is adopted, namely that it is sufficient that the mistake was a contributory cause of the payment without needing to show that it was the 'but for' cause.[37] This is because, where the defendant has fraudulently induced the mistake, the defendant's conduct makes it easier to conclude that the claimant's restitutionary claim is stronger than the defendant's claim to retain the enrichment. In principle, a similar argument should apply where the

---

[31] *R v Attorney-General for England and Wales* [2003] UKPC 22, [113].

[32] *Borelli v Ting* [2010] UKPC 21; *Progress Bulk Carriers Ltd v Tube City IMS LCC* [2012] EWHC 273 (Comm); [2012] 1 Lloyd's Rep 501 (Comm), [42] (Cooke J). For criticism of this expansion of duress, see p 215, below.

[33] See p 144, above.   [34] See *Astley v Reynolds* (1731) 2 Stra 915, 93 ER 939.

[35] See *Twyford v Manchester Corporation* [1946] Ch 236 and *Crescendo Management Pty Ltd v Westpac Banking Corporation* (1988) 19 NSWLR 40.

[36] See p 170, above.   [37] See p 187, above.

defendant has compelled the claimant to transfer a benefit. The key case on causation in the context of duress, *Barton v Armstrong*,[38] has adopted such an approach, with explicit reliance on the misrepresentation cases.

In *Barton v Armstrong* the defendant wanted the claimant to buy his shares in a company of which the claimant was managing director. The defendant had made numerous threats to kill the claimant if he did not purchase the shares, but it appeared that the main reason for the claimant agreeing to the purchase was commercial expediency. Despite this, the Privy Council held that the threats to kill the claimant were sufficient to vitiate the deed for the transfer of the shares. Lord Cross for the majority said that the test of causation for the purposes of duress was the same as that where a contract was induced by fraudulent misrepresentation, namely that it was sufficient that the threat or misrepresentation was a reason the claimant executed the deed, but it did not have to be the predominant reason but for which the claimant would not have executed the deed. Consequently, the claimant was 'entitled to relief even though he might well have entered into the contract if [the defendant] had uttered no threats to induce him to do so'.[39] In other words, it was not necessary to show that but for the threats the claimant would not have agreed to buy the shares. It did not matter that the claimant would have agreed to buy the shares even if the threat had not been made, as long as it could be shown that, since the threat was made, this was a factor which influenced the claimant's decision to buy the shares. As Lord Cross said, 'in this field the court does not allow an examination into the relative importance of contributory causes'.[40] The minority, Lords Wilberforce and Simon, accepted this formulation of the test of causation for the purposes of duress, though they did not agree that the test was satisfied on the facts of the case, because the trial judge's finding of fact, namely that the threats had not even been a reason for the claimant's decision to execute the deed, meant that the claimant had been motivated only by the commercial advantages of purchasing the defendant's shareholding and was not influenced by the threat at all.

Although the test of causation for the purposes of duress appears to be the same as that for fraudulently induced mistakes, namely a test of operative rather than 'but for' cause, this test may be applied differently in two respects in the context of duress.

First, Lord Cross in *Barton v Armstrong*[41] suggested that the burden of proof is on the defendant to show that the threats did not contribute to the claimant's decision to transact with the defendant. If this is correct it means that, once the claimant has established that the defendant had exercised duress, there is a presumption that the duress caused the claimant to transact with the defendant. The defendant must then seek to rebut the presumption by showing that the duress did not contribute to the claimant's decision to transact with the defendant.[42] This would be a particularly difficult presumption to rebut, since the defendant would be required to show why the claimant entered into the transaction. Even so, this presumption of causation is justifiable, at least where the duress is particularly serious, for example where it involves the actual or threatened commission of a crime against the person. Where the defendant commits or threatens to commit such a serious unlawful act, this conduct can be characterized as so unreasonable that the test of causation for purposes of restitution should be weighted in the claimant's favour.

Secondly, *Barton v Armstrong* itself involved duress against the person, the most serious type of duress, so it is relatively easy to conclude that the defendant's conduct was

---

[38] [1976] AC 104.   [39] Ibid, 119.   [40] Ibid, 118.   [41] Ibid, 120.

[42] See *Crescendo Management Pty Ltd v Westpac Banking Corporation* (1988) 19 NSWLR 40, 46 (McHugh JA); *Huyton SA v Peter Cremer GmbH* [1999] 1 Lloyd's Rep 620.

sufficiently reprehensible to justify the recognition of a lenient test of causation. But it does not necessarily follow that the same test of causation should be adopted in respect of all types of duress. Consequently, for each type of duress it will be necessary to consider whether the test of operative causation should be adopted or whether an alternative test, such as that of 'but for' cause, is more appropriate. Indeed, in *Huyton v Peter Cremer*[43] Mance J recognized that the 'but for' test of causation applies to economic duress. This is justifiable because the threat is less serious and so a stricter test of causation is required. This is consistent with the test for induced mistakes, since it is only for fraudulent misrepresentation that the contributory cause test applies; for negligent and innocent misrepresentations it must be shown that the representation was an operative cause of the benefit being transferred or a contract being made.[44]

(C) DURESS AND THIRD PARTIES

In most cases duress will involve threats made or actual pressure exerted by the defendant who obtains a benefit as a result. But it is possible that the duress emanated from a third party and this resulted in a benefit being received by the defendant. Should this make any difference to whether the defendant is liable to make restitution to the claimant? Although this question has never been raised in any reported case, it can be answered by reference to the principles which underlie the grounds of restitution. The better view is that it should be irrelevant that the duress came from a third party. All we are concerned with is the particular effect of the threats upon the claimant's freedom of choice to transfer a benefit to the defendant, and whether the duress was exerted by the defendant or a third party has no effect on this question. Where, however, the claimant transferred a benefit to the defendant as a result of duress exerted by a third party, the liability of the defendant to make restitution may depend on whether he or she had actual or constructive notice of the duress. This would be consistent with the cases where the claimant seeks restitution of benefits transferred as a result of a third party's misrepresentation or undue influence.[45]

(D) THE HEADS OF DURESS

There are three types of duress which will operate as grounds of restitution.[46] Of these, the definition of the first two, duress against the person and against property, is not controversial since they have long been recognized and clearly involve the use of illegitimate pressure. The definition of the third type, economic duress, is controversial, however, primarily because this has only been recognized relatively recently and because the line between what is and what is not regarded as legitimate economic pressure is particularly difficult to draw.

(E) DURESS OF THE PERSON

Duress of the person involves actual or threatened unauthorized interference with the person, whether by endangering life, personal safety or liberty. The test of causation which

---

[43] [1999] 1 Lloyd's Rep 620.   [44] See p 187, above.

[45] *Barclays Bank plc v O'Brien* [1994] 1 AC 180. See p 199, above and p 269, below.

[46] In *Crescendo Management Pty Ltd v Westpac Banking Corporation* (1988) 19 NSWLR 40, 46, McHugh JA suggested that the categories of duress are not closed.

is applicable to this type of duress is clearly the test of contributory cause, as was recognized in *Barton v Armstrong*,[47] a case which involved threats to kill. Consequently, it is sufficient that the duress of the person contributed to the claimant's decision to transfer a benefit to the defendant without necessarily being a cause but for which the benefit would not have been transferred.

Usually duress of the person will take the form of the defendant threatening to interfere with the person either of the claimant or somebody else unless the claimant transfers a benefit to the defendant. These threats can take one of three different forms. In each case the threat is unlawful, either because it involves a threat to commit a crime or a tort or, usually, both.[48]

(1) *Threats to kill.* It remains unclear whether a threat made by the defendant to kill will only be relevant where the defendant threatens to kill the claimant or whether it is sufficient that the defendant simply threatens to kill some person. The better view is that the threat to kill need not be directed at the claimant, as long as it can be shown to have influenced the claimant's decision to transfer a benefit to the defendant. So, for example, if the defendant threatens to kill the claimant's wife and children if he does not pay some money to the defendant, such an extreme threat must have removed the claimant's freedom of choice as to what to do with the money.

(2) *Threats to injure.* If the defendant threatens to injure the claimant, or presumably anyone else, this will operate as a ground of restitution as long as the threat was a contributory cause of the claimant's decision to transfer a benefit to the defendant.

(3) *Threats to interfere with liberty.* Where the defendant unlawfully threatens to interfere with the liberty of the claimant, or presumably anyone else, and this influenced the claimant's decision to transfer a benefit to the defendant, this too is a form of duress of the person. This is illustrated by *Duke de Cadaval v Collins*,[49] where the claimant had been unlawfully arrested by the defendant on the ground that he owed the defendant £10,000. This was a fraudulent claim made by the defendant, but, to secure his release, the claimant paid £500 to him. The claimant then sought to recover the money in an action for money had and received and succeeded, because the arrest had been wrongful and the defendant knew that he had no legitimate claim against the claimant. This is a good example of a case where the defendant actually exerted pressure against the claimant, rather than merely threatening it, because the claimant's liberty had already been infringed and would continue to be infringed until he paid the defendant. The claimant had paid the money to remove this pressure in circumstances where the money was not due to the defendant, and this was a sufficient reason for restitution to be awarded.[50]

[47] [1976] AC 104.

[48] Consequently, there might be an alternative restitutionary claim grounded on the tort rather than unjust enrichment. See Chapter 17.

[49] (1836) 4 Ad and E 858, 111 ER 1006. See also *Pitt v Coomes* (1835) 2 Ad and E 459, 111 ER 478.

[50] *Duke de Cadaval v Collins* (1836) 4 Ad and E 858, 864; 111 ER 1006, 1009 (Lord Denman CJ). In fact, Lord Denman held that title to the money never passed to the defendant, so he regarded this as a proprietary restitutionary claim. See p 577, below. See also *Clark v Woods, Smith and Cooper* (1848) 2 Ex 395, 154 ER 545.

(F) DURESS OF PROPERTY

Where the defendant threatens to seize[51] or to retain[52] property which belongs to the claimant or in which the claimant has a proprietary interest[53] unless the claimant transfers a benefit to the defendant, the claimant is able to recover the benefit by virtue of duress of property. This is because threats to seize or retain property are unlawful, being threats to commit the tort of conversion.

But duress of property will only operate as a ground of restitution if the duress caused the claimant to transfer a benefit to the defendant. Although no case has specifically considered what the test of causation should be for this particular ground of restitution, there is no reason to suppose that the test of operative causation in *Barton v Armstrong*[54] does not apply where the ground of restitution is duress of property. This is because the reasons which justify the use of that test where the duress relates to the person are also applicable where the duress relates to property, namely that the exercise of duress by the defendant can be regarded as constituting unreasonable behaviour, even though duress of property is less serious than duress of the person. Consequently, the test of operative causation, with such causation being presumed, should be applicable even where the duress relates to property.[55]

An old rule that only duress of the person could be relied on to set aside any contract which was entered into as a result of the threats[56] no longer represents the law.[57] Consequently, the defendant's threats to seize or retain property is a sufficient ground for setting aside contracts entered into as a result of such threats, with the consequence that it is then possible to recover any benefits which were transferred under the contract.

A good example of duress of property operating as a ground of restitution is *Astley v Reynolds*,[58] where the claimant pawned silver plate to the defendant for £20 and then wished to recover his property. The claimant tendered the money to redeem the loan but the defendant refused to return the plate to him unless he paid £10 interest, which was more than the interest which was legally due. The claimant tendered £4, but the defendant refused to take it. Consequently, the claimant was forced to pay the additional £10 demanded by the defendant as well as the money to redeem the loan. He then successfully brought an action for money had and received to recover this amount, the ground of restitution being that the claimant had paid the money to the defendant because of the defendant's refusal to return the claimant's property. The claimant only recovered the amount which was not lawfully due to the defendant, since the defendant's demand for the rest of the money was lawfully made.

---

[51] *Maskell v Horner* [1915] 3 KB 106.

[52] *Spanish Government v North of England Steamship Co Ltd* (1938) 54 TLR 852, 856 (Lewis J).

[53] In *Fell v Whittaker* (1871) LR 7 QB 120 it was sufficient that the claimant had possession of the property which had been seized.   [54] [1976] AC 104.

[55] Such a presumption appears to have been in operation in *Maskell v Horner* [1915] 3 KB 106, 122 (Lord Reading CJ).

[56] *Skeate v Beale* (1841) 11 Ad and E 983, 113 ER 688.

[57] *The Siboen and The Sibotre* [1976] 1 Lloyd's Rep 293, 335 (Kerr J); *The Atlantic Baron* [1979] QB 705, 719 (Mocatta J); *Pao On v Lau Yiu Long* [1980] AC 614, 636 (Lord Scarman); *The Evia Luck* [1992] 2 AC 152, 165 (Lord Goff).

[58] (1731) 2 Stra 915, 93 ER 939. See also *Somes v British Empire Shipping Co* (1860) 8 HLC 838, 11 ER 459.

(G) ECONOMIC DURESS

(i) The Essential Features of Economic Duress

Economic duress[59] has been recognized as a ground of restitution in its own right only relatively recently[60] and the requirements for establishing it remain a matter of some controversy. Essentially, economic duress arises where the defendant resorts to illegitimate commercial pressure, whether express or implied from circumstances, in support of his or her demands, whether these demands are for payment from the claimant or that the claimant is to enter into a contract or vary an existing one.

The key issue relates to the determination of what constitutes illegitimate commercial pressure for these purposes, since it is clear that commercial pressure alone cannot constitute economic duress.[61] What is needed are threats which are unlawful, typically threats to break a contract[62] or to commit a tort.[63] So, for example, if the defendant threatens to breach a contract with the claimant unless double the agreed contract price is paid, and the claimant succumbs to this threat because she requires immediate performance of this contract to be able to perform a sub-contract, this could constitute economic duress and the claimant would be able to recover the extra amount which had been paid to the defendant by virtue of the threatened breach. It must also be shown that the threat caused the claimant to enter into the contract, to vary an existing contract or to pay money to the defendant, and it is the identification of the appropriate test of causation for these purposes which has proved to be particularly controversial.

Before the definition of economic duress is examined, it is useful to consider two preliminary matters which have a significant impact on the ambit of the economic duress doctrine in practice.

(1) Avoiding Contracts for Economic Duress

Although some of the cases which are concerned with economic duress involve non-contractual restitutionary claims, the majority of them involve a claimant entering into a contract with the defendant or renegotiating an existing contract as a result of the duress. In such circumstances, if the claimant wishes to obtain restitution from the defendant it will first be necessary to set the contract aside. This can occur in two ways. First, the claimant can specifically rely on the doctrine of economic duress to show that the contract is voidable and then rescind it. This will depend on whether it is possible to establish economic duress. The claimant might alternatively seek to establish that in the circumstances of the case there was no consideration provided by the defendant for the contract which was made as a result of the threats. This is important because, if no consideration can be identified, the contract will be void[64] and the claimant will be able to recover any money paid to the defendant pursuant to the contract by virtue of the restitutionary grounds of total failure or absence of basis.[65] This is a potentially important principle in the context of existing contracts which are renegotiated as a result of duress, where the

---

[59] JP Dawson, 'Economic Duress: An Essay in Perspective' (1947) Mich LR 253.

[60] *The Siboen and The Sibotre* [1976] 1 Lloyd's Rep 293. For analysis of the previous history see *The Atlantic Baron* [1979] QB 705, 715–16.

[61] *Pao On v Lau Yiu Long* [1980] AC 614, 635 (Lord Scarman); *DSND Subsea Ltd v PGS Offshore Technology AS* [2000] BLR 530, [131] (Dyson J).

[62] *The Atlantic Baron* [1979] QB 705.

[63] *The Universe Sentinel* [1983] AC 366; *The Evia Luck* [1992] 2 AC 152.

[64] *D and C Builders v Rees* [1966] 2 QB 617.

[65] See Chapter 13. Whether either of these grounds of restitution can be established will depend on a careful analysis of the facts of the case.

effect of the pressure placed on the claimant is that he or she agrees to pay more money to the defendant than originally agreed, but the defendant does not agree to provide any additional benefits to the claimant under the contract. If no consideration has been provided for this renegotiated contract it will be invalid so that the claimant can bring a restitutionary claim without having to establish economic duress and, bearing in mind the uncertainties as to the ambit of economic duress, this is a significant advantage to the claimant.

Whether the claimant is able to establish that the contract is void because no consideration has been provided by the defendant will depend on what is meant by consideration for these purposes. Traditionally, past consideration, such as a promise to perform an existing duty, has not been considered to be good consideration for a contract.[66] The significance of this is illustrated by the following example. The claimant and the defendant entered into a contract in which the defendant agreed to supply the claimant with building materials for a big project which the claimant was developing. After the claimant had begun building, the defendant said that she would refuse to supply any more materials unless the claimant paid twice the agreed price and, because the claimant could not find the materials anywhere else, he agreed to the defendant's demands. Since the defendant had not promised to supply anything other than what she had originally agreed to supply, no new consideration had been provided for the renegotiated contract, which would be void. The courts are, however, increasingly able to find ways of identifying consideration for the new contract,[67] with the consequence that the claimant can set the contract aside only by relying on the doctrine of economic duress. This judicial manipulation of the doctrine of consideration reached its highpoint in the decision of the Court of Appeal in *Williams v Roffey Bros and Nicholls (Contractors) Ltd*[68] where, although the Court of Appeal affirmed the basic requirement that a promise will only be enforceable if consideration is provided by the promisee, it went on to limit dramatically the function of consideration by recognizing that the receipt of practical benefits by the promisor from the promisee would constitute good consideration for a promise.

In *Williams v Roffey* the claimant, who was working for the defendant under a sub-contract to refurbish a block of flats, had set his contract price too low, making it impossible for him to make a profit and meaning that he had no incentive to complete the contract on time. If there was a delay in completing the contract, the defendant would have been liable to pay a penalty under the main contract. Consequently, to ensure that the claimant completed his work on time, the defendant promised to pay him a substantial extra amount when the work on each flat was completed. The issue before the court was whether the defendant was liable to make these additional payments. Since it was the defendant who took the initiative, it was clear that there was no ground for saying that the agreement was voidable for economic duress, since the claimant had not threatened to refuse to perform the contract unless the extra money was paid. But the Court of Appeal held that the defendant's promise to pay these extra amounts was enforceable because it had received consideration from the claimant under the contract in the form of practical benefits. It did not matter that the defendant had not received any benefits in law because the claimant was not promising to do any more than he had originally agreed to do. The practical benefits which had been provided included that the claimant continued to work and did not stop in breach of the sub-contract, that there was a much reduced risk that the

---

[66] *Stilk v Meyrick* (1809) 2 Camp 317, 170 ER 1168.
[67] *The Atlantic Baron* [1979] QB 705 and *Pao On v Lau Yiu Long* [1980] AC 614, 629.
[68] [1991] 1 QB 1. See PBH Birks, 'The Travails of Duress' [1990] LMCLQ 342, 344–7.

penalty clause would be triggered by delay and that the defendant had avoided the trouble and expense of engaging other people to complete the claimant's work.

Despite the Court of Appeal's affirmation of the requirement that the promisor must receive some benefit from the promisee for the promise to be valid, the effect of its decision is to make the requirement of consideration a very easy hurdle to overcome, at least where the parties renegotiate the price for the performance of an existing obligation, because the consideration in *Williams v Roffey* was 'the routine benefits which flow from agreeing to make an extra payment'.[69] As a result, where there is an agreement to make an additional payment for the performance of an existing obligation, this will be enforceable unless it can be avoided on the ground of economic duress. Indeed, the recognition of economic duress proved to be the main justification for the Court of Appeal's decision in *Williams v Roffey*.[70] This is because consideration is a blunt tool for setting aside renegotiated contracts. The doctrine of economic duress is a much better tool, being more sophisticated in balancing the interests of the parties.

(2) Lawful Act Duress

The requirement that the defendant must threaten to do something which is unlawful before economic duress can be established means that a threat by the defendant not to enter into a contract with the claimant will not be sufficient to establish economic duress, simply because such a threat is perfectly lawful.[71] This was the effect of the decision of the High Court of Australia in *Smith v Charlick (William) Ltd*,[72] where it was held that the defendant, the Wheat Harvest Board which occupied a monopolistic position as regards the supply of wheat in South Australia, was acting legitimately in threatening that it would refuse to supply the claimant miller with any more wheat if he refused to pay a surcharge on wheat which had already been supplied to him. This money was not lawfully due to the defendant, but the High Court held that the claimant could not recover it despite the defendant's threats.[73] Admittedly, the facts of *Smith v Charlick* were rather extreme since the defendant had a monopoly, so the claimant had no choice but to contract with the defendant on the terms which it demanded if he wished to carry on business as a miller. The defendant's monopolistic position may mean that a ground of restitution could be identified after all, not economic duress due to the absence of an unlawful threat, but rather undue pressure.[74]

In England, however, there has been gradual recognition that a threat to do a lawful act can be characterized as illegitimate pressure for purposes of economic duress, with consequent expansion of that doctrine to interfere with the ordinary commercial bargaining process. A chink in the unlawful threats armour arose in *CTN Cash and Carry Ltd v Gallaher Ltd*.[75] The defendant in that case had supplied cigarettes to the claimant for sale to the public. The defendant was the sole supplier in the United Kingdom of particular brands of cigarette, including 'Benson and Hedges' and 'Silk Cut'. The commercial arrangement between the parties was that each sale of cigarettes to the claimant was under a separate contract. The defendant had also arranged credit facilities for the claimant. The dispute between the parties arose from the supply of one particular consignment of cigarettes to the

---

[69] Birks, 'The Travails of Duress', 345. In *Huyton SA v Peter Cremer GmbH and Co* [1999] 1 Lloyd's Rep 620 consideration for a compromise arose from the mutual forbearance of the parties from pursuing their original legal rights and remedies.   [70] [1991] QB 1, 13 (Glidewell LJ), 21 (Purchas LJ).

[71] *CTN Cash and Carry Ltd v Gallaher Ltd* [1994] 4 All ER 714.   [72] (1924) 34 CLR 38.

[73] Today restitution might be awarded on the ground of unauthorized receipt by a public authority. See Chapter 15.

[74] See p 229, below.   [75] [1994] 4 All ER 714.

claimant which the defendant mistakenly delivered to the wrong warehouse. When the claimant informed the defendant of this, the defendant agreed to pick up the cigarettes and take them to the correct warehouse. But, before it was able to do this, the cigarettes were stolen. The defendant mistakenly, but honestly and reasonably, believed that title to the cigarettes had passed to the claimant so that they were at the claimant's risk at the time of the theft, so it invoiced the claimant for the price of the stolen cigarettes. The claimant refused to pay, but the defendant threatened that it would withdraw the credit facilities in respect of future transactions if the claimant failed to pay for the cigarettes. Consequently, the claimant paid the money. It then sought to recover this money on the ground of economic duress. The Court of Appeal held that this action failed, even though the money was not due, because economic duress had not been established on the facts, primarily because it was lawful for the defendant to withdraw credit facilities in respect of future dealings.[76] The court also recognized that a threat not to enter into future contracts with the claimant would have been lawful as well.[77]

The result of the *CTN Cash and Carry* case is therefore consistent with the principle that economic duress will only be established where the defendant's threats are unlawful. Steyn LJ did state, however, that 'the fact that the defendants have used lawful means does not by itself remove the case from the scope of the doctrine of economic duress'.[78] This suggests that the ground of economic duress can encompass lawful threats. Whilst Steyn LJ was reluctant to extend the notion of 'lawful act duress', as he called it, to commercial transactions which involved *bona fide* claims, for fear of unsettling bargains, he was prepared to admit that even in the commercial context 'lawful act duress' might have a role to play, although it would be more important in the field of protected relationships, such as where the dispute arose in the context of dealings between a supplier and consumer.

The notion of lawful act duress has, however, been recognized in other cases. In *R v Attorney-General of England and Wales* a lawful threat was considered to be illegitimate where it was unreasonable, although this was *obiter*.[79] Crucially, in *Progress Bulk Carriers Ltd v Tube City IMS LCC*[80] a contract was rescinded where the defendant had made a lawful threat which was considered to be illegitimate. The defendant owner of a ship had withdrawn the ship from use by the charterer in a repudiatory breach of contract. The owner gave assurances that it would substitute another ship and would reimburse the charterer for its legal costs. Eventually the owner refused to substitute a ship unless the charterer agreed to waive its claim for damages in respect of the prior breach. The charterer had no reasonable alternative, and it agreed to this variation but under protest. The charterer then sought to set the variation aside on the ground of economic duress, and succeeded. Cooke J recognized that:[81]

> 'illegitimate pressure' can be constituted by conduct which is not in itself unlawful, although it will be an unusual case where that is so, particularly in the commercial context. It is also clear that a past unlawful act, as well as a threat of a future unlawful act can, in appropriate circumstances, amount to 'illegitimate pressure'.

On the facts the threat not to vary the contract was not unlawful, because the owner was not contractually obliged to substitute one ship for the other. But that lawful threat coupled with the prior repudiatory breach of contract, which was itself an unlawful act, was sufficient to

---

[76] Ibid, 717–18 (Steyn LJ).   [77] Ibid, 718 (Steyn LJ).
[78] Ibid. See also *The Universe Sentinel* [1983] AC 366, 401 (Lord Scarman) and *R v Attorney-General for England and Wales* [2002] UKPC 22.
[79] *R v Attorney-General of England and Wales* [2003] UKPC 22, [113]. See p 207, above.
[80] [2012] EWHC 273 (Comm); [2012] 1 Lloyd's Rep 501 (Comm).   [81] Ibid, [36].

enable the judge to conclude that the owner had exerted illegitimate pressure. He considered that the owner had manoeuvred the charterer into a position where it had no reasonable alternative but to submit to the owner's demand, by the owner taking advantage of the position it was in by virtue of the prior unlawful breach of contract.

This was consequently a case where a lawful act was threatened and this was characterized as illegitimate, but this characterization was coloured by the prior unlawful act of the defendant. A similar situation arose in the earlier decision of the Privy Council in *Borelli v Ting*,[82] where a settlement agreement was set aside for economic duress. In that case the defendant had, as the Privy Council put it, 'the claimant over a barrel'. The defendant had threatened to oppose a scheme of arrangement if a settlement agreement was not made, which was a lawful act. The defendant had also committed unlawful acts of forgery and adducing false evidence to frustrate the settlement agreement. The Privy Council characterized this as unconscionable conduct which was illegitimate for the purposes of economic duress. Again, what is significant here is that the illegitimate conduct constituted a mixture of a lawful threat and prior unlawful conduct.

It follows from these recent developments that a lawful threat can ground economic duress, at least where it can be characterized as illegitimate, and prior unlawful conduct will certainly help such a characterization to be made. A significant consequence of recognizing a lawful act as being sufficient to establish duress, and so unpick a contract and secure restitution, is that the law intrudes on and unsettles the commercial bargaining process. As Steyn LJ recognized in *CTN Cash and Carry v Gallaher*,[83] it would often enable 'bona fide settled accounts to be reopened when parties to commercial dealings fell out'. The defendant may have engaged in previous unlawful conduct, but should that be sufficient to rescind a contract where the defendant has made a lawful threat? Careful analysis of these cases does suggest, however, a worrying confusion in the law. There is a separate and much more restrictive equitable doctrine which enables contracts to be rescinded where the defendant has made a lawful threat but in circumstances where the defendant's conduct can be characterize as unconscionable. This is the doctrine known as 'undue pressure'.[84] The recent cases which have recognized lawful threats as being relevant to economic duress have cited cases involving undue pressure, and some of them have used the language of unconscionability to characterize the defendant's conduct. That this is the doctrine which Steyn LJ was actually referring to in *CTN Cash and Carry* is reflected in his statement that 'the critical inquiry is not whether the conduct is lawful but whether it is morally or socially acceptable'.[85] Undue pressure would also have been unavailable on the facts of that case because there was nothing to suggest that the defendant had acted unconscionably, since it believed that its demand was lawfully made. In another case, the test for a lawful threat to be characterized as illegitimate was whether the transaction was 'manifestly disadvantageous' making it unconscionable for the defendant to retain the benefit,[86] which again uses the language of the distinct doctrine of undue pressure. Most significantly, in *Borelli v Ting*[87] the Privy Council explicitly used the language of unconscionability when characterizing the defendant's conduct as illegitimate.

---

[82] [2010] UKPC 21.   [83] [1994] 4 All ER 714, 719.   [84] See p 229, below.
[85] *CTN Cash and Carry v Gallaher* [1994] 4 All ER 714, 719. He also relied on cases which are properly analysed as involving undue pressure rather than duress, most notably *Mutual Finance Ltd v John Wetton and Sons Ltd* [1937] 2 All ER 657.
[86] *Harrison v Halliwell Landau* [2004] EWHC 1316 (QB), [97] (Judge Eccles QC).
[87] [2010] UKPC 21.

Consequently, despite the recent explicit recognition that a lawful threat can still be an illegitimate threat for economic duress, the better view is that only unlawful threats should suffice. A lawful threat may still result in restitution, but only by virtue of the equitable jurisdiction and if the more stringent test of unconscionability is satisfied. This ensures that the law does not intervene unacceptably in commercial markets. Where a defendant has obtained a benefit as a result of an unlawful threat which caused the benefit to be transferred, it is appropriate for restitution to be awarded. Where the benefit was obtained as the result of a lawful threat, it is only appropriate to award restitution where the defendant's conduct is characterized as unconscionable, and prior unlawful conduct which relates to the lawful threat in some way will be relevant to the assessment of whether the threat is unconscionable. It follows that the results in both *Progress Bulk Carriers* and *Borelli v Ting* can be justified, but with reference to the equitable doctrine of undue pressure and not economic duress.

(ii) Establishing Economic Duress

In *DSND Subsea Ltd v PGS Offshore Technology AS*[88] Dyson J identified three ingredients of economic duress, namely: (i) pressure, the practical effect of which is compulsion on, or lack of practical choice for, the victim; (ii) which is illegitimate; and (iii) which is a significant cause of inducing the claimant to act. The independent relevance of these three elements is unclear and the ingredients have been described as not constituting a 'precise analytic tool'.[89] Indeed, the first ingredient is properly treated as the conclusion: economic duress operates as a ground of restitution or a vitiating factor for contract because the victim had no practical choice.[90] It follows that there are two key ingredients of economic duress: illegitimate pressure[91] and causation.[92]

(1) Illegitimate Pressure

Although it is now clear that illegitimate pressure constitutes the first ingredient of economic duress, it is a matter of some controversy what needs to be shown to establish illegitimacy. The approach advocated in this book is that pressure is illegitimate simply by proof that the defendant's conduct is either intrinsically unlawful or a threat to do an unlawful act, such as breaching a contract or committing a tort. With the recognition,

---

[88] [2000] BLR 530, [131].

[89] *Adam Opel GmbH v Mitras Automotive (UK) Ltd* [2007] EWHC 3481 (QB), [26] (David Donaldson QC).

[90] According to Smith, in 'Contracting under Pressure: A Theory of Duress', there are two separate bases of duress, one emphasizing the defendant's wrongdoing and the other emphasizing impairment of the claimant's consent. Whilst this distinction is theoretically attractive, it does not represent the law. The distinction can, however, be used to explain the difference of approach to duress of the person and goods on the one hand and economic duress on the other. This is because it appears easier to obtain restitution for duress of the person and goods, presumably because the defendant's wrongdoing is paramount in such cases. In the context of economic duress, the defendant's wrongdoing is less obvious, and so greater emphasis is placed on the validity of the claimant's consent. This distinction can also be used to explain why different tests of causation should be adopted for duress of the person and goods on the one hand and economic duress on the other. See further p 221, below.

[91] *Universe Tankships Inc of Monrovia v International Transport Workers Federation* [1983] AC 366, 400 (Lord Scarman); *The Evia Luck* [1992] 2 AC 152; *Huyton SA v Peter Cremer GmbH* [1999] 1 Lloyd's Rep 620, 629 (Mance J); *DSND Subsea Ltd v PGS Offshore Technology AS* [2000] BLR 530, [131] (Dyson J); *Carillion Construction Ltd v Felix (UK) Ltd* [2001] BLR 1, [24] (Dyson J); *Adam Opel GmbH v Mitras Automotive (UK) Ltd* [2007] EWHC 3481 (QB), [25] (David Donaldson QC); *Borelli v Ting* [2012] UKPC 21; *Progress Bulk Carriers Ltd v Tube City IMS LCC* [2012] EWHC 273 (Comm), [2012] 1 Lloyd's Rep 501 (Comm).

[92] *The Evia Luck* [1992] 2 AC 152, 165 (Lord Goff).

however, of lawful act duress,[93] something else will need to be proved to establish that the pressure was illegitimate. Of course, if the cases which recognize lawful act duress are considered either to be wrong, or to involve an application of the distinct equitable ground of undue pressure,[94] it is not necessary to identify anything beyond the unlawful threat or pressure to establish that the pressure is illegitimate. Indeed, as Lords Wilberforce and Simon recognized in *Barton v Armstrong*,[95] whether a threat is illegitimate simply depends on whether it is 'one of a kind which the law does not regard as legitimate', rather than identifying a variety of factors to assess legitimacy.

But, if something else needs to be shown to prove illegitimacy of pressure, it is unclear what that additional element is. In *DSND Subsea Ltd v PGS Offshore Technology AS*[96] Dyson J did identify various factors to assist in the identification of illegitimate pressure, including: an actual or threatened breach of contract; the defendant's good or bad faith; whether the victim had a realistic practical alternative but to submit; whether the victim protested; and whether the victim had confirmed or sought to rely on the contract. These factors have been described by David Donaldson QC[97] as not being exhaustive and the weight to be attached to each factor depended on the circumstances of each case.[98] Whilst some of these factors are undoubtedly relevant to establishing economic duress, they are preferably treated as relevant to whether the pressure caused the claimant to act, rather than specifically to the characterization of the pressure as illegitimate.[99] The problem with the approach adopted by Dyson J is that he uses factors involving the consequences of the pressure to determine whether the pressure is illegitimate. It is much more appropriate to characterize the threat or pressure at the time it is made or exerted, and preferably simply by reference to whether it is unlawful, and then determine the effect of this pressure on the claimant by reference to factors which relate to causation.

The specific identification of the defendant's good or bad faith as a factor relevant to the illegitimacy of the threat is a matter of particular concern.[100] Bad faith is a notoriously vague concept, but Birks suggested that a defendant would be acting in bad faith if he or she 'intended to exploit the claimant's weakness rather than to solve financial or other problems of the defendant'.[101] In *Huyton v Peter Cremer*,[102] although Mance J did not dismiss this test, he considered its significance to be contentious. It is an unsatisfactory test of illegitimacy for three reasons.

(1) It would be very difficult for the claimant to show what the motive of the defendant was in making the threat.

---

[93] See p 215, above.   [94] See p 229, below.   [95] [1976] AC 104, 121.

[96] [2000] BLR 530, [131].

[97] *Adam Opel GmbH v Mitras Automotive (UK) Ltd* [2007] EWHC 3481 (QB), [26].

[98] See also *The Universe Sentinel* [1983] 1 AC 366, 385 (Lord Diplock), 391 (Lord Cross), and 400 (Lord Scarman) and *The Evia Luck* [1992] 2 AC 152, 166 (Lord Goff).

[99] See further p 221, below.

[100] Burrows regards this as the preferable test: AS Burrows, *The Law of Restitution* (3rd edn, Oxford: Oxford University Press, 2011), 274. McKendrick rejects it: 'The Further Travails of Duress' in A Burrows and Lord Rodger (eds), *Mapping the Law: Essays in Memory of Peter Birks* (Oxford: Oxford University Press), 188.

[101] PBH Birks, *An Introduction to the Law of Restitution* (rev edn, Oxford: Clarendon Press, 1989), 183. An alternative test suggested by Birks, ibid, was to distinguish between a threat and a warning and to deny restitution where the defendant was simply communicating to the claimant that he or she was subject to a pressure which was not of his or her own making, whereas restitution would lie where the defendant had 'threatened the claimant with a pressure of his own making'. This distinction between threats and warning is just a more specific attempt to identify when a defendant was acting in bad faith. Birks later said that the distinction between threats and warning was too fine and too easily abused: 'The Travails of Duress', 346.

[102] [1999] 1 Lloyd's Rep 620, 637.

(2) As Burrows correctly asserts, this test 'reverses traditional contract values in that bad faith in breaking a contract has traditionally been afforded no importance (it does not, for example, affect the measure of damages) precisely because the self-interested pursuit of profit is regarded as acceptable provided the innocent party is compensated for loss'.[103] It follows that, since the defendant's motive in breaking a contract to obtain profit has no effect on the assessment of damages, there is no reason why a different approach should be adopted where the defendant threatens to break a contract to obtain profit.

(3) By emphasizing the defendant's motives for making the threat, rather than considering the effect of the threat on the claimant, the test of bad faith is inconsistent with the majority of the other grounds of restitution which are claimant-oriented, in the sense that they are concerned with the effect of the particular ground on the claimant. This is true of mistake, for example, where we are only concerned with the question whether the claimant was mistaken, without any need to consider whether the defendant was at fault. Similarly, with duress of the person and property, where we are only concerned with whether the effect of the duress was to remove the claimant's autonomy to exercise a free choice as to whether or not to transfer a benefit the defendant. There is no reason why this approach should not be adopted in the context of economic duress as well.

The test of good and bad faith has rarely been applied in the cases. In *CTN Cash and Carry Ltd v Gallaher Ltd*[104] one reason for the failure of the claimant to establish economic duress was because the defendant had acted in good faith in claiming that the claimant was required to pay for goods which had been stolen. But the real reason why the claim failed in that case was because the defendant's threat to withdraw credit facilities was not a threat to do an unlawful act. In those cases where the threat was to commit a lawful act and duress was established,[105] the court did emphasize the improper conduct of the defendant, but that is preferably explained as relevant to establish unconscionability, which is an essential feature of the distinct equitable ground of undue pressure.[106]

Further, bad faith cannot be used to explain all the cases where economic duress has been recognized, since in a number of them restitution on the basis of economic duress was awarded even though there was nothing to suggest bad faith on the part of the defendant.[107] Consequently, bad faith should be rejected as a test to determine whether the defendant's threat was illegitimate.

It has also been suggested that the defendant might be considered to have exerted illegitimate pressure where the terms proposed by him or her are substantively unfair.[108] As with the test of bad faith, this is inherently uncertain. To determine whether there was

---

[103] Burrows, *The Law of Restitution* (3rd edn), 273.

[104] [1994] 4 All ER 714. See p 215, above. The decision of the Court of Appeal in *D and C Builders v Rees* [1966] 2 QB 617 also appears to support a good faith test. In that case the claimant was not estopped from denying that it had agreed to accept a lesser sum of money for building work, because the defendant had acted in bad faith since he knew that the claimant was facing bankruptcy and so took advantage of his stronger bargaining position by threatening to pay nothing at all unless the claimant agreed to accept a lesser amount of money for the work. But this case can just as easily, and preferably, be analysed as involving exploitation rather than compulsion, where the fault of the defendant is consequently relevant.

[105] Particularly *Borelli v Ting* [2012] UKPC 21; *Progress Bulk Carriers Ltd v Tube City IMS LCC* [2012] EWHC 273 (Comm), [2012] 1 Lloyd's Rep 501 (Comm). See p 219, above.

[106] See p 229, below.

[107] See, for example, *The Atlantic Baron* [1979] QB 705 and *Atlas Express Ltd v Kafco (Importers and Distributors) Ltd* [1989] QB 833.

[108] Burrows, *The Law of Restitution* (3rd edn), 274.

substantive unfairness it would be necessary to engage in a detailed analysis of all of the surrounding circumstances and the nature of the relationship between the parties. There is a danger that such an approach would result in unpredictability which is unacceptable in the context of commercial disputes. In addition, this test lacks any clear judicial support.

The danger of establishing illegitimate pressure without specific reference to the unlawfulness of the defendant's conduct, creates unacceptable uncertainty.[109] In the sphere of commercial transactions in particular, any test which is inherently uncertain and provides any scope for judicial value judgment[110] must be rejected as unworkable. Consequently, it is more appropriate to treat a threat as illegitimate simply because it was unlawful, such as where the pressure involves the non-performance or threat of non-performance of a contract.

(2) Causation

Once illegitimate pressure has been identified it is then necessary to determine whether the pressure was sufficiently serious to deprive the claimant of a free choice when deciding whether or not to enter into a contract with the defendant, or to renegotiate an existing contract or simply to transfer a benefit to the defendant. This requires consideration of whether the illegitimate pressure was a sufficient cause of the claimant's actions. The test which has been adopted for determining whether the pressure was a sufficient cause has sometimes been expressed by asking whether the threats coerced the claimant's will so as to vitiate his or her consent.[111] The most important statement of this coerced will principle can be found in the judgment of Lord Scarman in *Pao On v Lau Yiu Long*:[112]

> In determining whether there was a coercion of will such that there was no true consent, it is material to inquire whether the person alleged to have been coerced did or did not protest; whether, at the time he was allegedly coerced into making the contract, he did or did not have an alternative course open to him such as an adequate legal remedy; whether he was independently advised; and whether after entering the contract he took steps to avoid it. All these matters are ... relevant in determining whether he acted voluntarily or not.[113]

It is the final sentence which identifies the essential concern of the coerced will principle. If the claimant's will was coerced then he or she did not act voluntarily, but this will only be the case where the pressure was a sufficient cause of the claimant's actions. What Lord Scarman is doing in this dictum is to identify factors which should be taken into account when determining whether the illegitimate pressure exerted by the defendant really can be regarded as a sufficient cause of the claimant's conduct, so that it is possible to conclude that the claimant did not freely choose to transact with the defendant.

So, if the emphasis is on causation, what test of causation should be adopted? This raises a crucial question of policy as to whether restitution for economic duress should be defined restrictively or widely. In the most common situation of economic duress, where the defendant threatens to breach a contract, the apparent policy of the courts is

---

[109] See McKendrick, 'The Further Travails of Duress', 188.

[110] As recognized in *Adam Opel GmbH v Mitras Automotive (UK) Ltd* [2007] EWHC 3481 (QB), [26] (David Donaldson QC).

[111] *The Siboen and The Sibotre* [1976] 1 Lloyd's Rep 293, 336 (Kerr J); *Pao On v Lau Yiu Long* [1980] AC 614, 635 (Lord Scarman); *Hennessy v Craigmyle and Co Ltd* [1986] ICR 461, 468 (Sir John Donaldson MR); *The Alev* [1989] 1 Lloyd's Rep 138, 145 (Hobhouse J).

[112] [1980] AC 614, 635.

[113] Some of these factors were identified by Dyson J in *DSND Subsea Ltd v PGS Offshore Technology AS* [2000] BLR 530, [131], to establish illegitimate pressure. See p 219, above.

to adopt a restrictive interpretation of economic duress due to a fear of unsettling commercial transactions.[114] So, for example, in *The Universe Sentinel*,[115] Lord Brandon said that only '*severe* economic pressure could amount to duress in law'.[116] This restrictive approach should be reflected in the test for causation. There are four possible tests of causation which might be applicable:

(a) the illegitimate pressure was the sole cause of the claimant's actions;

(b) the pressure was a contributory cause of the claimant's actions;

(c) the 'but for' test of causation;

(d) no reasonable alternative.

(a) The Illegitimate Pressure Was the Sole Cause of the Claimant's Actions

This test would be unworkable, since it would be virtually impossible to prove that the claimant was only influenced by the pressure and nothing else. In addition, there is no obvious reason why restitutionary relief should be denied to the claimant simply because he or she was influenced in doing what the defendant demanded by factors other than the pressure, even though these factors might have had only a minor influence on the claimant's decision to transact with the defendant.

(b) The Pressure Was a Contributory Cause of the Claimant's Actions

According to this test of causation it would be sufficient that the threats were *a* cause of the claimant's actions, without necessarily being *the* 'but for' cause. This test has received some support in the academic literature[117] and it has been implicitly recognized in certain key cases where the test in *Barton v Armstrong*[118] was assumed to be applicable to economic duress.[119] But this test of causation is surely inappropriate in the context of economic duress, since it does not follow from the fact that the pressure contributed to the claimant's actions that it necessarily had a sufficiently serious effect on the claimant, as should be required if economic duress is to be restrictively interpreted as policy suggests it should be. Also, the *Barton v Armstrong* test probably incorporates a presumption that the pressure was a cause of the claimant's acts, with the burden of rebutting this being placed on the defendant.[120] This too is inappropriate in respect of economic duress, where such a presumption would result in economic duress being too easily established. The *Barton v Armstrong* presumption is justifiable where the pressure is particularly serious, as where the defendant's threats relate to the person or even property, making it acceptable to presume that those threats influenced the claimant's conduct, since this is highly likely to have been the case. But commercial or economic pressure is of a very different kind, especially because the claimant is more likely to have been influenced by other factors when deciding what the appropriate course of action should be.

Even though the contributory cause test is inappropriate to determine whether the illegitimate pressure caused the claimant to make a contract with the defendant, where the

---

[114] Although this has been undermined somewhat by the recent recognition of lawful act duress which expands the scope of economic duress potentially significantly. See p 215, above.

[115] [1983] AC 366.   [116] Ibid, 405 (emphasis added).

[117] E MacDonald, 'Duress by Threatened Breach of Contract' (1989) JBL 460, 472; Birks, 'The Travails of Duress'; McKendrick, 'The Further Travails of Duress', 186.

[118] [1976] AC 104.

[119] See, for example, Lord Goff in *The Evia Luck* [1992] 2 AC 152, 165 and McHugh JA in *Crescendo Management Pty Ltd v Westpac Banking Corporation* (1988) 19 NSWLR 40, 46.

[120] See p 209, above.

illegitimate pressure caused the claimant to make a non-contractual transfer of a benefit to the defendant, a stronger case can be made for the recognition of a test of causation which is easier to satisfy,[121] because it is not necessary to set aside a contract before seeking restitution. Different tests are adopted in the law of mistake, for example, so that it is more difficult to set a contract aside for mistake than to seek restitution of a non-contractual transfer made by mistake.[122] Similarly, the test of causation for a spontaneous mistake is the 'but for' test, whereas the test of causation for a mistake induced by fraud is a contributory cause.[123] Where the claimant has transferred a benefit to the defendant as the result of illegitimate pressure, it might be thought that the closer analogy is with fraud than a spontaneous mistake. But, even though it is argued here that illegitimate pressure involves unlawful pressure, this cannot be considered to be analogous to fraud, unlike possibly duress of the person and even goods,[124] so a contributory cause test should not suffice for economic duress and it is not necessary to distinguish between tests of duress in the contractual and non-contractual contexts. No such distinction is recognized in the case law, although that is primarily because most of the cases where restitutionary claims are involved arise where the illegitimate pressure has resulted in the claimant entering into a contract with the defendant.

(c) The 'But For' Test of Causation

The preferable test of causation is therefore the 'but for' test, where it must be shown that the claimant would not have acted in the way which he or she did if the defendant had not exerted the pressure. This test of causation was specifically recognized by Mance J in *Huyton v Peter Cremer*.[125] Its recognition means that a different test of causation is adopted for economic duress than for duress of the person or goods, but this is justifiable because economic pressure tends to be much less blameworthy than pressure involving interference with the person or property. For example, economic duress usually takes the form of a threat to break a contract. Although such a threat is unlawful, it lacks the serious wrongfulness of threats to interfere with the person or property. Consequently, something else needs to be established beyond the wrongfulness of the threat before restitution should be awarded, and that extra element is proof that, had the threat not been made, the claimant would not have acted in the way which he or she did. This stricter test of causation also fulfils the policy of the law which seeks to restrict liability for duress in commercial transactions.

Birks rejected the 'but for' test of causation because it involves 'an impossible and inscrutable inquiry into the metaphysics of the will'.[126] But, as long as the test of causation is not confined to showing that the pressure was the sole reason for the claimant's actions, it is a test which is perfectly workable, particularly because the courts have identified a number of factors to assist in determining whether the pressure was indeed a 'but for' cause of the claimant's actions. Also, this test of causation is not unique to economic duress, since it has also been recognized as applying in the context of spontaneous

---

[121] McKendrick, 'The Further Travails of Duress', 194.   [122] See Chapter 9.

[123] See p 187, above.   [124] See p 210, above.

[125] [1999] 1 Lloyd's Rep 620. In *DSND Subsea Ltd v PGS Offshore Technology AS* [2000] BLR 530, [131] Dyson J used the language of a 'significant cause'. See also *The Evia Luck* [1992] 2 AC 152, 165 (Lord Goff); *Carillion Construction Ltd v Felix (UK) Ltd* [2001] BLR 1; *Cantor Index Ltd v Shortall* [2002] All ER (D) 161. Cf D O'Sullivan, S Elliott, and R Zakrzewski, *The Law of Rescission* (Oxford: Oxford University Press, 2007), 158, who assert that a contributory test of causation should suffice, because the victim also needs to show that the threat was illegitimate and that no practical alternative was available but to submit to the threat.

[126] Birks, *An Introduction to the Law of Restitution*, 183.

mistakes,[127] where it operates perfectly satisfactorily. But the most important argument in favour of the 'but for' test of causation is that it accords with the notion of coercion of the will. For it will only be possible to conclude that a claimant's will has been coerced by the pressure where, but for the pressure, the claimant would not have acted as he or she did. It is only in this situation that it can be concluded that the claimant had no free choice as to whether or not to submit to the pressure exerted by the defendant.

The application of the 'but for' test of causation is illustrated by the decision of the Privy Council in *Pao On v Lau Yiu Long*.[128] In this case the claimant had agreed to sell its shares in a private company to a public company in exchange for shares in the public company. To ensure that it did not suffer from a fall in the value of the shares in this public company, the claimant entered into a subsidiary agreement with the defendant, who was a majority shareholder in the public company, whereby the defendant agreed to buy a majority of the allotted shares at $2.50 a share. The purpose of this subsidiary agreement was to ensure that the claimant would not suffer any loss if the value of the shares fell below $2.50. Surprisingly, the claimant had failed to realize that the effect of the agreement was such that, if the shares increased in value, the defendant would benefit since it would still be able to purchase the shares at $2.50 each. Consequently, the claimant refused to perform the main agreement unless the defendant agreed to cancel the subsidiary agreement and replace it with a guarantee to indemnify the claimant against loss. The defendant submitted to this threat because it feared that the public would lose confidence in the public company if it did not complete the agreement quickly. After the shares had been allotted, their value dropped rapidly and the claimant sought to enforce the defendant's promise to indemnify it against this loss. The defendant argued that the guarantee was voidable for economic duress, but this claim failed because it could not be shown that the commercial pressure to which the defendant had been subjected by the claimant caused it to sign the guarantee. This conclusion was reached by reference to a number of different factors, the most important of which was that the defendant had taken a calculated risk that the value of the shares would not fall.[129] Since this was a purely commercial decision it was concluded that the claimant's threats had not caused the defendant to do as the claimant demanded. Presumably the claimant's threats were taken into account by the defendant when deciding whether to agree to the guarantee, but it could not be shown that it was the 'but for' cause of the defendant's action.

In *Pao On* and the later case of *The Universe Sentinel*[130] Lord Scarman identified a number of factors which might be used to determine, as he put it, whether the claimant had no choice but to submit to the defendant's demands. These factors include protesting about the validity of the demand, either at the time of entering the contract or making the payment or shortly afterwards,[131] the failure to obtain independent advice and a declaration by the claimant that he or she would go to law to recover money paid or property transferred as a result of the duress.[132] But Lord Scarman emphasized that these are merely evidential factors, so if any are absent it does not mean that the claimant necessarily did exercise a free choice. So, for example, if the claimant failed to protest about the validity of the defendant's demand it does not follow that he or she must have

---

[127] *Barclays Bank Ltd v WJ Simms, Son and Cooke (Southern) Ltd* [1980] QB 677. See p 171, above.
[128] [1980] AC 614.   [129] Ibid, 627.   [130] [1983] AC 366, 400.
[131] See also *The Siboen and The Sibotre* [1976] 1 Lloyd's LR 293, 336 (Kerr J).
[132] In *DSND Subsea Ltd v PGS Offshore Technology AS* [2000] BLR 530, [131], Dyson J considered some of these factors to be relevant to the question whether the compulsion was illegitimate. They are preferably treated as relevant to whether the pressure caused the claimant to contract or to transfer a benefit.

acted voluntarily,[133] since the claimant may fail to protest for a number of reasons, for example, because the defendant is not available when the claimant wished to protest, or because the defendant's threats are such that the claimant is constrained from protesting.[134] As Lord Scarman memorably said in *The Universe Sentinel*:[135] 'The victim's silence will not assist the bully, if the lack of any practicable choice but to submit is proved.'

(d) No Reasonable Alternative

There is one other factor which Lord Scarman emphasized in *Pao On v Lau Yiu Long*[136] as being relevant to the assessment of whether the pressure emanating from the defendant was a sufficient cause of the claimant's actions, namely whether the claimant had a reasonable alternative course open to him or her rather than submit to the pressure.[137] For, if the claimant did have an alternative course available, he or she should have taken that course rather than submit to the pressure. This factor is of such importance to the question of whether the claimant can rely on economic duress, that it should not be treated simply as an evidential factor to assist the court in determining whether the test of causation is satisfied, but it should be characterized as a rule of substance which must be established.[138] Consequently, if the claimant did have a reasonable alternative than submit to the pressure, this in itself should prevent the claimant from relying on economic duress because, as a matter of law, the pressure will not have been a sufficient cause of the claimant's actions. It does not automatically follow, however, that, just because there was no reasonable alternative open to the claimant but to submit, economic duress will have been established, since it will still be necessary to show that the threats were the 'but for' cause of the claimant's actions, although it will be possible to prove this in most cases.

Despite the suggestion in some of the cases that the question of whether there was a reasonable alternative open to the claimant is a subjective test,[139] so that it is sufficient that the claimant thought that he or she had no choice but to submit to the pressure, the better view is that this is a matter which is to be assessed objectively, by reference to what the reasonable person would have done in the claimant's position, because of the need to restrict the application of the economic duress doctrine. This objective approach was adopted in *B and S Contracts and Design Ltd v Victor Green Publications Ltd*,[140] where Kerr LJ recognized that a threat to break a contract 'will only constitute duress if the consequences of a refusal would be serious and immediate so that there is no reasonable alternative open, such as by legal redress, obtaining an injunction, etc'.[141]

The application of this 'no reasonable alternative' principle is illustrated by *Hennessy v Craigmyle and Co Ltd*.[142] The claimant was unable to set aside an agreement, in which he had promised not to bring proceedings before an industrial tribunal in respect of his

---

[133] *Maskell v Horner* [1915] 3 KB 106, 124 (Buckley LJ); *Huyton SA v Peter Cremer GmbH* [1999] 1 Lloyd's Rep 620. In *Atlas Express Ltd v Kafco Ltd* [1989] QB 833 economic duress was established despite the absence of any protest.

[134] See R Halson, 'Opportunism, Economic Duress and Contractual Modifications' (1991) 107 LQR 649, 667–8.

[135] [1983] AC 366, 400.   [136] [1980] AC 614, 627.

[137] In *DSND Subsea Ltd v PGS Offshore Technology AS* [2000] BLR 530, [136] Dyson J described this as 'no realistic practical alternative but to concede' to the pressure.

[138] A Phang, 'Economic Duress: Recent Difficulties and Possible Alternatives' [1997] RLR 53, 59. In *Huyton SA v Peter Cremer GmbH* [1999] 1 Lloyd's Rep 620, 636 Mance J described the factor as 'not being an inflexible third essential requirement of economic duress', but he clearly recognized that it was a highly significant factor, since relief would be inappropriate if the claimant chose, unreasonably, not to pursue an alternative remedy.

[139] See, in particular, Lord Scarman in *The Universe Sentinel* [1983] 1 AC 366, 400.

[140] [1984] ICR 419.   [141] Ibid, 428. See also *The Alev* [1989] 1 Lloyd's Rep 138, 147 (Hobhouse J).

[142] [1986] ICR 461.

summary dismissal, because he had a real, albeit unattractive, alternative to signing the agreement, which was to make an immediate complaint to an industrial tribunal and draw social security benefit until his complaint was heard.

A case where there was held to be no reasonable alternative open to the claimant but to submit to the defendant's demands is *The Alev*,[143] where the owners of cargo which was being retained by ship-owners had no reasonable alternative but to pay money as demanded by the ship-owners. This was primarily because the only possible alternative course of action open to the claimants was to seek an injunction to restrain the threatened breach of contract, but this would have been of no practical use because the cargo and the ship-owners were outside the jurisdiction at the time, so this alternative course of action was objectively unreasonable.

Although the most usual alternative course of action open to the claimant is to resort to legal redress, other considerations can be taken into account in determining whether the claimant's submission to the defendant's threats was reasonable. For example, if the defendant, having entered into a contract to build an extension onto the claimant's house for £40,000, refuses to do so one week before performance is required unless the claimant pays an extra £10,000, it would not be reasonable for the claimant to pay the money if it was possible to arrange for another builder to do the work at such short notice and at no substantially greater cost than the original contract price. Similarly, if the benefit which is to be rendered to the claimant by the defendant is wholly disproportionate to the seriousness of the threat, restitution should also be denied because it would not be reasonable for the claimant to have submitted to the demand. For example, if the defendant demanded that the claimant pay him £1,000 otherwise he would refuse to deliver goods worth £100, it is surely unreasonable to have succumbed to such a demand, which is wholly disproportionate to the value of the goods, and so restitution should be denied. A different result would probably be reached if the goods were required by the claimant to satisfy a lucrative contract with a third party. In such circumstances it might be considered that the claimant did indeed have no reasonable alternative but to submit to the threat.

It is this requirement of no reasonable alternative being open to the claimant which is of such crucial importance in determining whether the defendant's threat constitutes economic duress. For, where there is no reasonable alternative but to submit to the defendant's demands, the economic pressure placed on the claimant is so extreme that he or she can be regarded as having no free choice in deciding whether to do what the defendant wanted. This is the reason why this test is not required for the other heads of duress, where restitution is available even though the claimant may have had a reasonable alternative to submission to the defendant's threats,[144] because the pressure itself can be assumed to be more significant. In the different context of economic duress, restitutionary relief should be denied to the claimant if a reasonable person would not have succumbed to the defendant's threats. This is because typically the dispute is between two commercial organizations, where the defendant's demands, usually for more money, occur in the context of a continuing contractual relationship. Where the claimant succumbs to the defendant's demands in circumstances where there is a reasonable alternative open to it, that submission should be regarded as a legitimate part of the bargaining process and the law should not interfere with such commercial

---

[143] [1989] 1 Lloyd's Rep 138.

[144] For example, in *Astley v Reynolds* (1731) 2 Stra 915, 93 ER 939, the defendant obtained restitution on the ground of duress of property even though he could have brought an action in trover rather than pay the extra money which the defendant demanded.

arrangements. It is only where the defendant can be regarded as taking unfair advantage of the claimant that the law should intervene. The key characteristic of unfair advantage is that the defendant's threats caused the claimant to pay the defendant in circumstances where he or she had no reasonable alternative but to pay. If the claimant is not a commercial organization, without the resources to challenge the defendant's threats, it would presumably be less reasonable for such a person to resort to litigation rather than submit to the defendant's demands. Consequently, the notion of what is reasonable will vary depending on who the claimant is. So the question which must be asked is what it would be reasonable for the particular claimant to have done in the circumstances.

(3) Coerced or Overborne Will

Focusing on whether the claimant's will has been coerced or overborne identifies accurately those cases where restitution should be awarded for economic duress. This approach does, however, suffer from one major drawback, arising from the very use of the terms 'coerced' or 'overborne' will, which have a tendency to mislead, since, if interpreted literally, they suggest that the claimant's intention must have been completely vitiated by the defendant's threats so that the claimant was acting involuntarily in doing what the defendant demanded.[145] If such an interpretation is adopted, economic duress would be impossible to establish, since in these cases the claimant does have a choice as to whether or not to comply with the defendant's demands. This was recognized by the House of Lords in *Lynch v DPP of Northern Ireland*,[146] which unanimously rejected the overborne will theory in respect of the operation of the defence of duress in the criminal law. This interpretation of a coerced or overborne will should be rejected for the law of restitution as well, but this does not mean that the test of a coerced will should be rejected completely, because it does have a legitimate and workable function once it is recognized that the crucial issue before the court is not whether the claimant had no choice at all but to submit to the pressure, but rather, whether the claimant's choice was freely exercised. As Dyson J recognized in *DSND Subsea Ltd v PGS Offshore Technology AS*,[147] a key ingredient of economic duress is whether the practical effect of the pressure was that the victim lacked any 'practical choice'. The preferable view is that this will be established if the defendant's threats were unlawful and were a 'but for' cause of the claimant's actions, because there was no reasonable alternative for the claimant but to submit to the defendant's demands. Whilst the use of language such as an 'overborne' or 'coerced' will might be described as over-dramatic it is perfectly intelligible,[148] although 'coercion' of the will is more accurate than the will being 'overborne'.

All of the reported cases on economic duress either recognize or are consistent with the coerced will analysis of economic duress. For example, in *B and S Contracts and Design Ltd v Victor Green Publications Ltd*[149] the claimant agreed to erect exhibition stands for the defendant. The claimant's employees, who had already received redundancy notices, demanded severance pay of £9,000 to which they were not entitled. Since the claimant was only able to offer the employees severance pay of £4,500, it threatened the defendant that, if it did not pay the remaining £4,500, the claimant would not be able to complete the

---

[145] The test was interpreted in this way by McHugh JA in *Crescendo Management Pty Ltd v Westpac Banking Corpn* (1988) 19 NSWLR 40, 45, who consequently rejected it. See also Lord Goff in *The Evia Luck* [1992] 2 AC 152, 166 and Lord Diplock in *The Universe Sentinel* [1983] 1 AC 366, 384.

[146] [1975] AC 653. See especially Lord Simon, ibid, 461. See also PS Atiyah, 'Economic Duress and the "Overborne Will"' (1982) 98 LQR 197 and Dawson, 'Economic Duress—An Essay in Perspective'.

[147] [2000] BLR 530, [131].   [148] Smith, 'Contracting under Pressure: A Theory of Duress', 365.

[149] [1984] ICR 419.

contract. Since the defendant required the stands to be erected urgently it paid the money as requested. When the defendant came to pay the claimant for its work in erecting and dismantling the stands the defendant treated the £4,500 which it had already paid to the claimant as an advance payment, and it deducted this sum from the contract price. The claimant sued to recover the £4,500 from the defendant and failed, because the Court of Appeal found that the defendant had no choice but to pay the money, since cancellation of the contract to erect the stands would have caused it severe financial harm. Therefore, it was proper to treat the money paid as an advance payment and deduct it from the contract price. The finding of economic duress on these facts was surely correct. The claimant had made a veiled threat to commit an unlawful act, namely that it would breach the contract if the defendant failed to pay the sum demanded. This threat was the 'but for' cause of the defendant making the payment, since, as Eveleigh LJ put it, the defendant had 'been influenced against [its] will to pay the money'.[150] It was also expressly found that the defendant had no reasonable alternative but to pay the money.[151] This was because there was no chance that the defendant could have found another source of labour to erect the stands and, if the stands were not erected, it would be liable to a number of exhibitors who had leased exhibition space.

Similarly, in *The Atlantic Baron*[152] a shipbuilder agreed to build a ship for a fixed price in United States dollars. After the purchaser had paid the first instalment, the dollar was devalued by 10 per cent and the builder demanded an increase of 10 per cent on the remaining instalments which were due to it, threatening to breach the contract if it did not receive the extra payments. The purchaser needed the ship urgently since it was negotiating a lucrative contract for the charter of the ship, and so it paid the additional amounts when it paid the remaining instalments to the builder. For all but one of these payments the purchaser said that the payments were made without prejudice to its right to recover the additional amount paid, although it did pay the final instalment without protest. The purchaser did not commence proceedings for restitution of the excess amounts until over two years later. It was held that the builder's threat to break the contract constituted economic duress. Clearly the builder had made an unlawful threat and this was presumably the 'but for' cause of the purchaser paying the extra amount demanded. The purchaser also had no reasonable alternative but to pay this amount because it needed the ship urgently for the purpose of the charterparty, and in the circumstances it would have been unreasonable to take the matter to arbitration because of the 'inherent unavoidable uncertainties of litigation'.[153] Despite this, the purchaser was not able to rescind the contract because its conduct in making the final payment without protest and its delay in seeking rescission were considered to constitute affirmation of the variation of the contract, so that rescission was barred.[154]

One of the best examples of the coerced will theory in operation is *Enimont Overseas AG v Rojugotanker Zadar (The Olib)*,[155] where the defendant had chartered its ship for the transport of the claimant's cargo but, once it had been transported to the nominated destination, nobody accepted delivery. The defendant told the claimant that it would sell the cargo if the claimant did not collect it and pay the sums which were outstanding. Eventually the claimant paid the sums demanded and then sought to recover them on the ground of duress. The question before the trial judge was whether the claimant had a good arguable case of economic duress, for the purposes of serving a claim form on the

---

[150] Ibid, 423.   [151] Ibid, 426 (Griffiths LJ).   [152] [1979] QB 705.   [153] Ibid, 719 (Mocatta J).
[154] See also *DSND Subsea Ltd v PGS Offshore Technology AS* [2000] BLR 530, [148] (Dyson J). See p 27, above, for analysis of the bar of affirmation.
[155] [1991] 2 Lloyd's LR 108.

defendant out of the jurisdiction. The judge held that the claimant had not established such a case for two main reasons. First, it had not shown that the defendant's threat to sell the goods was unlawful as a breach of the charterparty, because the condition of the cargo was such that immediate sale was essential, and, secondly, it had not established that the defendant's threats had induced it to make the payments. The judge's reasoning identifies the two essential features of the coerced will theory, namely the making of an unlawful threat which was the 'but for' cause of the claimant's actions.

(iii) Summary of the Law on Economic Duress

Despite the uncertainties arising from the interpretation of 'illegitimate pressure', the preferable view is that economic duress will be established where the defendant actually committed or threatened to commit an unlawful act, whether this was breach of contract, a tort or a crime, in circumstances where, but for the pressure exerted by the defendant, the claimant would not have acted in the way the defendant demanded, and this test of causation requires examination, at the very least, as to whether the claimant had no reasonable alternative open to him or her but to submit to the defendant's demands.

3. UNDUE PRESSURE

(A) THE ESSENCE OF UNDUE PRESSURE

In some circumstances the defendant might threaten the claimant that, unless the claimant contracts with the defendant on particular terms or renegotiates an existing contract or pays the defendant a sum of money which is not due, the defendant will do something which is perfectly lawful. If the claimant wishes to set the transaction aside or recover the money, he or she will generally not be able to rely on duress because the defendant is not threatening to do anything unlawful.[156] A significant exception to this arises where, although the defendant threatens to do something which is lawful, the making of the threat is itself unlawful because it constitutes the crime of blackmail.[157] Such a threat would be sufficient to found a restitutionary claim on the ground of duress. But the defendant will only commit blackmail where the threat involves the making of an unwarranted demand with menaces.[158] If the defendant thinks that there are reasonable grounds for making the demand or that the use of menaces is a proper way of reinforcing the demand, the defendant will not be guilty of blackmail and so the threat will not be unlawful. Where what is being threatened and the threat itself are lawful the claimant should not be able to obtain restitution on the ground of duress but may rely on another ground of restitution instead, namely undue pressure.

Undue pressure was first recognized by Lord Denning MR in *Lloyd's Bank Ltd v Bundy*,[159] although it is an expression which has rarely been used by the judiciary.[160] Undue pressure is a ground of restitution which is founded on the principle of compulsion, since it arises where the defendant has obtained a benefit from the claimant as a result of threats, albeit that the threats are lawful. Undue pressure should be distinguished from the

---

[156] Although the concept of 'lawful act duress' has now been recognized, so it might be possible to establish economic duress in such circumstances. See p 215, above.

[157] See *Thorne v Motor Trade Association* [1937] AC 797; *Huyton SA v Peter Cremer GmbH* [1999] 1 Lloyd's Rep 620.

[158] Theft Act 1968, s 21.   [159] [1975] QB 326, 338.

[160] It was, however, used by Lord Chelmsford in *Williams v Bayley* (1866) LR 1 HL 200, 214. See also Lord Westbury, 216.

ground of undue influence, which is founded on the principle of exploitation rather than compulsion, since undue influence does not involve the defendant obtaining a benefit as a result of making threats.[161] Despite this, the grounds of undue pressure and undue influence are closely related, because they are both equitable doctrines which are triggered because the defendant's conduct can be characterized as unconscionable.

(B) THE RECOGNIZED HEADS OF UNDUE PRESSURE

There are three particular circumstances where restitution is available on the ground of undue pressure. Although the threats which are involved in these cases relate to lawful activity, the development of the law of tort may mean that some cases which were once characterized as involving undue pressure would today be treated as economic duress, because the defendant's threats relate to what is now an unlawful tortious act.[162]

The claimant will not be able to establish undue pressure in any of these cases if the benefit which the defendant demanded from the claimant was lawfully due to the defendant,[163] since there will then be a legal basis for the defendant's receipt of the enrichment.

(i) Threats to Invoke the Criminal Process

Where the defendant has threatened to prosecute the claimant or a relative of the claimant and, as a result of this, the claimant has paid money to the defendant or entered into a contract with him or her, the money can be recovered or the contract set aside on the ground of undue pressure. Although the cases which can be used to illustrate this ground of restitution tend to refer to the ground being either duress or undue influence, the better view is that the ground of restitution is that of undue pressure because the threat will tend to be lawful, since it is generally clear that the person who might be prosecuted has committed a crime.

The application of undue pressure in this context is illustrated by *Williams v Bayley*,[164] where the defendant bankers procured the claimant to execute an equitable mortgage of his property, by threatening that, if he failed to do so, they would prosecute his son for forgery with the morally certain consequence of the son being transported for life. The mortgage was set aside because of the pressure applied by the defendant. As Lord Chelmsford said, Equity would set aside an agreement 'where there is inequality between the parties, and one of them takes unfair advantage of the situation of the other, and uses undue influence to force an agreement from him'.[165] Despite the express reference to undue influence, this case is still better treated as one involving undue pressure because the defendant had induced the claimant to enter into the mortgage as a result of a threat, albeit a lawful one.[166] Similarly, in *Mutual Finance Ltd v John Wetton and Sons Ltd*[167] a guarantee had been entered into by the defendant company for the benefit of the claimant as a result of the threats made by the claimant that it would prosecute the brother of one of

---

[161] See Chapter 11.

[162] Particularly following the recognition and development of the tort of intimidation.

[163] *Flower v Sadler* (1882) 10 QBD 572; *Mutual Finance Ltd v John Wetton and Sons Ltd* [1937] 2 KB 389. See Chapter 7.

[164] (1866) LR 1 HL 200. See also *Kaufman v Gerson* [1904] 1 KB 591 and *Société des Hôtels Réunis v Hawker* (1913) 29 TLR 578.   [165] *Williams v Bayley* (1866) LR 1 HL 200, 216.

[166] Although the actual receipt of money in return for the agreement not to disclose material information relating to a serious offence is a crime (see the Criminal Law Act 1967, s 5(1)), the threat to disclose the information is not unlawful.

[167] [1937] 2 KB 389.

the directors of the defendant company for forgery. This director signed the guarantee on behalf of the defendant because he feared that, if his sick father found out about the forgery, the shock might kill him. The judge set aside the guarantee specifically because the claimant's conduct amounted to undue influence in Equity, but again a lawful threat had been made. In this case it was recognized that the facts were not sufficient to establish duress at Common Law, because the threats in each case were lawful,[168] but this did not prevent the intervention of Equity.

It does not matter what the relationship is between the person who entered into the contract or paid the money and the person who is liable to be prosecuted. Essentially the only question before the court is whether the pressure exerted by the defendant caused a contract to be made or money to be paid. In *Mutual Finance Ltd v John Wetton and Sons Ltd*[169] Porter J held that the doctrine 'extended to any case where the persons entering into the undertaking were in substance influenced by the desire to prevent the prosecution or possibility of prosecution of the person implicated, and were known and intended to have been so influenced by the person in whose favour the undertaking was given'. This notion of substantial influence by the pressure suggests that it is sufficient that the pressure was a contributory cause of the claimant's actions, without needing to be a 'but for' cause of those actions. This lower threshold for establishing causation might be justified on the ground that the equitable doctrine of undue pressure will only be established where the defendant's conduct can be characterized as unconscionable.

(ii) Threats to Sue

Usually, where the defendant threatens to sue the claimant if he or she refuses to pay money or enter into a contract, this will not in itself constitute compulsion,[170] because the claimant is expected to resist the threat and to defend the proceedings in court.[171] In certain exceptional cases, however, a threat by the defendant to sue the claimant if money is not paid has been treated as grounding a restitutionary claim, and the ground of restitution is most appropriately characterized as undue pressure. This ground of restitution will be triggered in this category of case only where the defendant can be regarded as abusing the legal process, so the defendant's conduct can be characterized as unconscionable. So, for example, in *Unwin v Leaper*[172] it was held that the defendant had abused the legal process by threatening to bring proceedings to secure payment in respect of a matter which was unrelated to the threatened proceedings.

(iii) Threats to Publish Information

Where the defendant threatens to publish information which would detrimentally affect the claimant or someone known to the claimant, any contract which is entered into as a result of the threat may be set aside or any money paid as a result of the threat may be recovered. *Norreys v Zeffert*[173] illustrates the potential application of this head of compulsion. Zeffert was not able to discharge his gambling debts. He was interviewed by the National Turf Protection Society with a view to their securing a promise from him that he would pay his creditor. In order to induce Zeffert to make this promise his creditor threatened to report him to trade protection societies and to notify his social club of his refusal to pay. As a result of these threats Zeffert promised to pay his creditor. Although

---

[168] Ibid, 395 (Porter J).   [169] Ibid, 396.   [170] *Williams v Bayley* (1866) LR 1 HL 200.
[171] See *Mason v New South Wales* (1959) 102 CLR 108, 144 (Windeyer J). See also *Woolwich Equitable Building Society v IRC* [1993] AC 70, 165 (Lord Goff).
[172] (1840) 1 Man and G 747, 133 ER 533.   [173] [1939] 2 All ER 187.

the trial judge held that this promise was not enforceable for lack of consideration, he went on to state, *obiter*, that if Zeffert had made a legally enforceable promise to pay his creditor, this would not have been enforced by the courts because it was obtained by threats and it was irrelevant that it was lawful to divulge the information as the creditor threatened to do. As Atkinson J said, just because 'a person may have a legal right to do something which will injure another is not sufficient justification for the demand of money as the price of not doing it'.[174]

Although the money which the creditor was seeking to recover from Zeffert was actually due to it, if Zeffert had paid the money he would still have been able to recover it because the money was owed to the creditor pursuant to a gambling transaction which was unlawful, and so would not have constituted a lawful basis for the creditor's receipt. The result would be different if Zeffert's debt had arisen from a lawful commercial transaction, for then the money paid would have been lawfully due to the creditor.

Although the point has never been expressly determined, as a matter of principle this type of undue pressure should be applicable regardless of the type of information and the person to whom the information is threatened to be divulged. These issues will, however, be relevant in assessing whether the threat to divulge the information to a particular person or organization actually caused the claimant to act as the defendant had demanded.

(C) IS THERE A GENERAL GROUND OF UNDUE PRESSURE?

Although the notion of undue pressure has been implicitly recognized in these three particular circumstances, is it possible to extract a general ground of restitution which can be called undue pressure and which is applicable beyond these discrete areas? The preferable view is that there is such a general ground of restitution, as was recognized by Lord Denning in *Lloyds Bank Ltd v Bundy*.[175] Since undue pressure is an equitable doctrine it is clear that the main trigger for its application relates to the unconscionable behaviour of the defendant in threatening the claimant, without any need to show that the defendant's threats were unlawful.[176] To determine whether the defendant acted unconscionably it will be necessary to examine all the circumstances of the case, especially the nature of the relationship between the parties and whether the defendant acted in good faith. These were factors which were expressly recognized in *CTN Cash and Carry Ltd v Gallaher Ltd*,[177] although the Court of Appeal in that case assumed that they assisted in the identification of economic duress. Similarly, in those cases where economic duress was established even though the illegitimate pressure was lawful,[178] the better view is that they involved undue pressure especially because the courts had particular regard to the defendant's previous unlawful conduct which coloured the lawful pressure exerted by the defendant in a commercial context. In some of these cases the defendant's conduct was explicitly characterized as unconscionable.[179]

---

[174] Ibid, 189.   [175] [1975] QB 326, 338.

[176] This was implicitly recognized by McHugh JA in *Crescendo Management Pty Ltd v Westpac Banking Corporation* (1988) 19 NSWLR 40, 46, although the judge described the notion of unconscionable, but lawful, conduct as duress rather than undue pressure. But duress should be confined to where unlawful threats are made.   [177] [1994] 4 All ER 714, 717–18 (Steyn LJ).

[178] *Borelli v Ting* [2010] UKPC 21; *Progress Bulk Carriers Ltd v Tube City IMS LCC* [2012] EWHC 273 (Comm), [2012] 1 Lloyd's Rep 501 (Comm).

[179] Notably *Borelli v Ting* [2010] UKPC 21, [32]. See also *Harrison v Halliwell Landau* [2004] EWHC 1316 (QB), [97] (Judge Eccles QC).

The difficulty with recognizing a ground of restitution which is founded on the defendant's unconscionable conduct is that unconscionability is an inherently uncertain concept. This is unavoidable, but to mitigate the uncertainty it is vital that the application of this ground of restitution is confined to the most extreme cases of unconscionable conduct, where there is such inequality between the parties that the defendant can be considered to have taken unfair advantage of the claimant.[180] Despite the general principle that there is no doctrine of unfair use of a dominant bargaining position,[181] even in the commercial context undue pressure may be applicable, at least where the defendant is aware that there are no grounds for claiming a benefit from the claimant and where the nature of the relationship is such that the defendant can be regarded as taking unfair advantage of the claimant.[182] This might be the case, for example, where the defendant was occupying a monopolistic position and the claimant had no choice but to succumb to the defendant's threats.[183] The dual test involving consideration of the nature of the relationship between the parties and the nature of the defendant's belief as to the legitimacy of his or her claim, can also be used to explain the result in the earlier decisions where the defendant's threats involved prosecution, suing or disclosure of information.

4. LEGAL COMPULSION

(A) THE ESSENTIAL CHARACTERISTICS OF LEGAL COMPULSION

Whereas duress depends on the defendant making unlawful threats or threats to do unlawful acts and undue pressure depends on the defendant's conduct being characterized as unconscionable, there is a third and independent ground of restitution, called legal compulsion, which is also founded on the general principle of compulsion. Unlike duress and undue pressure, legal compulsion is applicable where payment is demanded by somebody to whom it is lawfully due, so that there is legal basis for that person's receipt, but where the payment benefits another party and, as between the claimant and that other party, there is no lawful basis for the receipt of the benefit.

Legal compulsion will arise where the claimant is compelled to transfer a benefit to someone in circumstances where, if the claimant had not transferred the benefit, it would have been taken by recourse to the legal process.[184] This pressure may derive, for example, from an express or implicit threat to resort to litigation or to exercise a court order or to execute a judgment. Where legal compulsion operates as a ground of restitution it does so because, as with all grounds of restitution which are founded on compulsion, the effect of the pressure is that the claimant has no free choice but to transfer the benefit. But, even though the claimant's intention to transfer the benefit may be treated as vitiated by the pressure, it does not automatically follow that the claimant can obtain restitution from the

---

[180] *Williams v Bayley* (1866) LR 1 HL 200, 214 (Lord Chelmsford), 216 (Lord Westbury); *Lloyd's Bank v Bundy* [1975] QB 326, 338–9 (Lord Denning MR).

[181] *Pao On v Lau Yiu Long* [1980] AC 614, 634.

[182] In *Lloyds Bank Ltd v Bundy* [1975] QB 326, 339 Lord Denning MR recognized that abuse of a long-standing commercial relationship might constitute an illegitimate act for the purposes of undue pressure. See also *Borelli v Ting* [2010] UKPC 21 and *Progress Bulk Carriers Ltd v Tube City IMS LCC* [2012] EWHC 273 (Comm), [2012] 1 Lloyd's Rep 501 (Comm).

[183] This could have been the justification for awarding restitution in *Smith v William Charlick Ltd* (1924) 34 CLR 38, see p 215, above. But, although the defendant realized that it had no legal right to demand payment of a surcharge on wheat which it had supplied, it thought that it had a moral right to do so and this might enable its conduct to be characterized as conscionable.

[184] This includes a foreign legal process: *Liberian Insurance Agency Inc v Mosse* [1977] 2 Lloyd's Rep 560.

recipient of the benefit. This is because the pressure to transfer a benefit to prevent the other party from having recourse to legal process is 'a normal and necessary incident of social life'.[185] Consequently, the person who receives money or property as a result of the exercise of such threats will not be considered to have been *unjustly* enriched. Also, where the effect of the payment is to discharge a liability, there will be a legal basis for the recipient's receipt. Both of these factors suggest that there can be no role for legal compulsion as a ground of restitution. But it may constitute a ground of restitution where three parties are involved. For example, where a creditor is owed money by the defendant and the claimant is lawfully compelled to discharge this liability, it is the defendant, rather than the third party, who can be considered to have been unjustly enriched at the expense of the claimant. This is because, where the claimant's payment discharges the defendant's liability to the third party,[186] the defendant will have received a negative incontrovertible benefit, since the payment has saved the defendant money which he or she would otherwise inevitably have had to pay to the third party, and this benefit was received at the claimant's expense since he or she paid the money to discharge the liability. Whether the claimant can successfully bring a restitutionary claim against the defendant in these circumstances will depend on whether the claimant can establish a ground of restitution, the most important of which is that of legal compulsion.

The claimant's restitutionary claim against the defendant may take two forms. First, where the claimant is not primarily liable to pay the creditor but the defendant is, the claimant will wish to recover from the defendant the value of the money paid to the creditor. This is called reimbursement or recoupment. Secondly, where the claimant and the defendant share a common liability to the third party, and the claimant has paid what he or she owed and also some, or all, of what the defendant owed, the claimant will wish to recover the additional amount paid on behalf of the defendant. This is called contribution. In both cases the remedy which is awarded is restitutionary, since the claimant recovers what has been paid for the benefit of the defendant.[187]

Where the claimant seeks reimbursement or contribution from the defendant, the claimant will usually sue the defendant directly. But the claimant may be able to seek restitution using another route, namely the remedy of subrogation.[188] Subrogation enables the claimant to rely on the rights of the third party against the defendant, even though the defendant's liability to the third party has been discharged by the claimant's payment.[189] The main advantage of this is that it enables the claimant to take advantage of any security which the creditor had in respect of his or her claim against the defendant,[190] or it may be relied on where a direct restitutionary claim against the defendant is not available. Although subrogation raises more complex questions, it will only be available once the claimant has established that the defendant has been unjustly enriched at the claimant's expense.[191]

---

[185] Birks, *An Introduction to the Law of Restitution*, 185.

[186] For discussion of when the debt will be discharged, see p 235, below.

[187] As regards recoupment, see *Owen v Tate* [1976] QB 402, 409 (Scarman LJ). As regards contribution, see *Deering v The Earl of Winchelsea* (1787) 2 Bos and Pul 270, 272; 126 ER 1276, 1277 (Eyre CB).

[188] See p 20, above.

[189] *Esso Petroleum Ltd v Hall Russell and Co Ltd* [1989] AC 643.

[190] Although this proprietary response is preferably treated as only available where the claimant can establish a claim to vindicate property rights rather than to reverse unjust enrichment. See further p 636, below.

[191] *Banque Financière de la Cité v Parc (Battersea) Ltd* [1999] 1 AC 221; *Menelaou v Bank of Cyprus plc* [2013] EWCA Civ 1960, [2014] 1 WLR 854.

(B) DETERMINING WHETHER A DEBT HAS BEEN DISCHARGED

If the claimant is to establish a restitutionary claim against the defendant where the claimant has paid money to the defendant's creditor purportedly to discharge a debt owed by the defendant to that creditor, it must first be shown that the defendant has been enriched by the payment. Although the discharge of an existing liability will usually constitute an enrichment, since it usually amounts to an incontrovertible benefit,[192] it is necessary to consider when a debt will be discharged by the claimant's payment.[193]

(i) Request by the Defendant

Where the defendant debtor requested the claimant to discharge the debt by paying the creditor, this will be effective to discharge the debt if the creditor accepted payment.[194]

(ii) Acceptance by the Defendant

Where the claimant paid the creditor purporting to discharge the debt but without any request by the defendant to make the payment, this will discharge the debt if both the creditor and the defendant accepted that the payment discharged the debt.[195] Such acceptance of the payment will only be effective to perfect the discharge of the debt where the claimant intended the payment to have this effect.[196]

(iii) Performance of an Act Which the Defendant Was Liable to Perform

Where the claimant performs an act which the defendant was liable to perform, this will discharge the defendant's liability, at least where the act is irrevocable.[197] So, for example, if the defendant is under a legal liability to keep a road in a good state of repair and the claimant mended the road, the claimant will clearly have discharged the defendant's liability, because the person to whom the liability was owed cannot restore the benefit which has been received.[198]

(iv) Automatic Discharge by an Unrequested Payment

The controversial question is whether the claimant's payment to the creditor, which was unrequested by the defendant and which has not been subsequently ratified by him or her, ever operates to discharge the debt automatically. The case law on this question is contradictory. One line of cases suggests, either expressly or implicitly, that the claimant's payment discharges the defendant's liability only where the defendant has accepted the discharge, so there is no doctrine of automatic discharge by mere payment to the creditor.[199] There are, however, a number of other cases where it has been accepted, again either explicitly or implicitly, that the claimant's payment will automatically discharge the

---

[192] See p 78, above.

[193] Although this is essentially a question of enrichment which could have been considered in Chapter 4, it is more appropriate to consider it here since the question of whether a debt has been discharged will typically be relevant in the context of a restitutionary claim founded on the ground of legal compulsion.

[194] *Simpson v Eggington* (1855) 10 Ex 845, 156 ER 683.

[195] *Customs and Excise Commissioners v National Westminster Bank plc* [2002] EWHC 2204 (Ch), [2003] 1 All ER (Comm) 327.

[196] *Re Rowe* [1904] 2 KB 483.   [197] See *Gebhardt v Saunders* [1892] 2 QB 452.

[198] D Friedmann, 'Payment of Another's Debt' (1983) 99 LQR 534, 541.

[199] See, for example, *Belshaw v Bush* (1851) 11 CB 190, 138 ER 444; *Simpson v Eggington* (1855) 10 Ex 845, 156 ER 683; *City Bank of Sydney v McLaughlin* (1909) 9 CLR 615; *Barclays Bank Ltd v WJ Simms, Son and Cooke (Southern) Ltd* [1980] QB 677; *Esso Petroleum Co Ltd v Hall Russell and Co Ltd* [1989] AC 643, 663 (Lord Goff); *Guardian Ocean Cargoes Ltd v Banco de Brasil SA* [1991] 2 Lloyd's Rep 68, 87 (Hirst J); *Crantrave Ltd v Lloyds Bank plc* [2000] QB 917.

debt and it is irrelevant that the defendant has not accepted the payment.[200] All that is needed is for the creditor to accept the payment. The debt will be discharged even where the creditor accepts a lesser amount from the claimant.[201] Other cases recognize, again either expressly[202] or implicitly,[203] that this automatic discharge without authorization by the debtor will only occur where the claimant was legally compelled to pay the creditor. Significantly, in *Ibrahim v Barclays Bank plc*[204] the Court of Appeal held that payment by a third party to a creditor under legal compulsion on account of a debt owed by a debtor will automatically discharge the debt, and this will be the case even if the legal compulsion arose from a contractual obligation which the third party had voluntarily assumed. Sutton identified another group of cases which recognize the principle of automatic discharge of liability where a part-owner of property discharged a debt which was charged on the property.[205]

The views of commentators are also contradictory. For example, Goff and Jones,[206] in an attempt to reconcile as many of these cases as possible, argue that the debt will be discharged automatically by an unrequested payment only when it was paid under legal compulsion or where the claimant's intention to pay was vitiated.[207] Birks and Beatson[208] have tentatively suggested that a payment does not automatically discharge the debt, save where the claimant is not a volunteer and has no immediate right of recovery against the creditor. Friedmann,[209] Stoljar,[210] and Burrows[211] on the other hand have argued that, so long as the claimant's payment was accepted by the creditor, it should automatically discharge the debt, regardless of the particular ground of restitution on which the claimant relies, and Birks subsequently regarded this approach as providing 'a much more stable basis from which to begin the enquiry'.[212]

The approach of the Court of Appeal in *Ibrahim v Barclays Bank*, is to be preferred as being consistent with basic principles of the law of unjust enrichment, but, even if the claimant was not legally compelled to pay the creditor, and did so voluntarily, this should discharge the debt owed by the defendant if payment was accepted by the creditor, although the voluntariness of the claimant's payment may defeat a claim for restitution against the defendant on the ground that the claimant was a risk-taker.[213] Whether payment by the claimant to the defendant's creditor should discharge the defendant's debt should depend on whether the defendant can be considered to be enriched by the

---

[200] *Welby v Drake* (1821) 1 C and P 557, 171 ER 1315; *Re Barnes* (1861) 4 LTNS 60; *Cook v Lister* (1863) 13 CB (NS) 543, 594–5; 143 ER 215, 235 (Willes J); *Hirachand Punamchand v Temple* [1911] 2 KB 330; *Liggett (Liverpool) Ltd v Barclays Bank Ltd* [1928] 1 KB 48.

[201] *Hirachand Punamchand v Temple* [1911] 2 KB 330.

[202] *City Electrical Supply Nominees Ltd v Thorn EMI Retail Ltd* (1991) 63 P and CR 143, 148 (Fox LJ).

[203] See, for example, *Exall v Partridge* (1799) 8 Term Rep 308, 101 ER 1405; *Edmunds v Wallingford* (1885) 14 QBD 811; *Moule v Garrett* (1872) LR 7 Exch 101; *Brook's Wharf and Bull Wharf v Goodman* [1937] 1 KB 534; *Owen v Tate* [1976] QB 402.

[204] [2012] EWCA Civ 640, [2013] Ch 400, [49] (Lewison LJ).

[205] RJ Sutton, 'Payments of Debts Charged Upon Property' in AS Burrows (ed), *Essays on the Law of Restitution* (Oxford: Clarendon Press, 1991), 71.

[206] C Mitchell, P Mitchell, and S Watterson (eds), *Goff and Jones: The Law of Unjust Enrichment* (8th edn, London: Sweet and Maxwell, 2010), 133, citing *City Electrical Supply Nominees Ltd v Thorn EMI Retail Ltd* (1991) 63 P and CR 143, 148 (Fox LJ).

[207] *Kleinwort Benson plc v Vaughan* [1996] CLC 620.

[208] PBH Birks and J Beatson, 'Unrequested Payment of Another's Debt' (1976) 92 LQR 188, 211.

[209] Friedmann, 'Payment of Another's Debt', 556.

[210] SJ Stoljar, *The Law of Quasi-Contract* (2nd edn, Sydney: The Law Book Co, 1989), 166.

[211] Burrows, *The Law of Restitution* (3rd edn), 463.

[212] Birks, *An Introduction to the Law of Restitution*, 191.   [213] See p 243, below.

receipt of the money by the creditor, because, once the debt has been discharged, the defendant will have received an incontrovertible benefit. Since the basic test for identifying an enrichment depends on whether the defendant has received an objective benefit, we are not at this stage concerned with the defendant's reaction to the payment by the claimant. Rather than focusing on the relationship between the claimant and the debtor, the focus should be on the relationship between the claimant and the creditor. If the claimant pays the creditor who accepts the payment, then, as a general rule, the debt should be considered to have been discharged.[214] This will constitute an objective benefit to the defendant, since the discharge of a debt clearly has an objective value. The next question is whether the defendant can argue that he or she did not value this benefit, the so-called principle of 'subjective devaluation'.[215] But surely, subject to one qualification, no reasonable person would accept an argument that the defendant did not value the discharge of a debt, simply because any reasonable person would regard the discharge as a real benefit. Therefore, the defendant should be considered to be enriched by the discharge of the debt, by virtue of the principle of incontrovertible benefit in the sense that the defendant has been saved necessary expense.[216] There is no need to resort to request or free acceptance to defeat the defendant's reliance on subjective devaluation, since it is sufficient that the discharge was incontrovertibly beneficial.

The only qualification to the application of the principle of incontrovertible benefit in this context occurs where the defendant has a defence to the creditor's claim or has a counterclaim.[217] In either case the objective value of the benefit is reduced or eliminated depending on the nature of the defence or counterclaim. If the defendant has a complete defence to the creditor's claim, the claimant's payment to the creditor will not have discharged a debt, since there will have been no debt to discharge. Consequently, the claimant would have to bring a restitutionary claim against the creditor, on the ground of mistake or failure of basis,[218] since the claimant expected the payment to discharge the debt and this did not occur. If the defendant's defence only reduces his or her liability to the creditor, or where the defendant has a counterclaim against the creditor, the claimant's payment to the creditor will still have discharged the defendant's liability. If the claimant then seeks restitution from the defendant, who argues that the effect of the defence or counterclaim is that the claimant's payment is of less or no value to him or her, this should reduce or eliminate the amount which the defendant should pay to the claimant. What should the claimant do then? By overpaying the creditor, it is the creditor who will have been enriched. Can the claimant secure restitution from the creditor? Since the debt will have been discharged there has been no failure of basis. But since the overpayment was not lawfully due to the creditor, it would be appropriate for the claimant to rely on the ground of legal compulsion or even mistake to recover this amount from the creditor and, being an overpayment, there will have been no legally effective basis for the creditor's receipt of this amount.[219]

This analysis depends on the debt being treated as discharged between the claimant and the creditor, for then this will be treated as enriching the defendant. But this is only the case if the creditor is entitled to keep the payment.[220] The creditor will not be entitled to

---

[214] Or, as Birks and Beatson analyse it, the acceptance of the payment by the creditor means that a benefit has already been executed: Birks and Beatson, 'Unrequested Payment of Another's Debt', 197. See also Friedmann, 'Payment of Another's Debt', 537.

[215] See p 69, above.   [216] Birks, *An Introduction to the Law of Restitution*, 186.

[217] See J Beatson, *The Use and Abuse of Unjust Enrichment* (Oxford: Clarendon Press, 1991), 203.

[218] See Chapter 13.   [219] *Fairfield Sentry Ltd v Migani* [2014] UKPC 9, [18] (Lord Sumption).

[220] Friedmann, 'Payment of Another's Debt', 537. See also Birks and Beatson, 'Unrequested Payment of Another's Debt', 201.

keep it if it can be shown that the claimant's intention that the creditor should receive the payment has been vitiated in some way, as will occur where the payment was made as the result of an operative mistake or the creditor had used unlawful threats to secure payment of money which was not due. Where, however, the claimant has been legally compelled to pay the creditor then, as between the claimant and the creditor, the debt will be treated as discharged because legal compulsion cannot operate as a ground of restitution as against the person to whom the money is lawfully due. In other words, the claimant's intention to pay the creditor cannot be treated as vitiated by reason of legal compulsion where the creditor is entitled to the payment. On the other hand, where the claimant purports to discharge the defendant's debt for reasons of necessity, this should not be regarded as sufficient automatically to discharge the debt, since the effect of the necessity is to vitiate the claimant's intention that the creditor should receive the payment.[221] Consequently, the circumstances of the payment need to be analysed carefully to determine whether the claimant has a claim against the creditor to recover the money.

If it is recognized that the debt is automatically discharged by the claimant's payment once it has been accepted by the creditor and there are no grounds for the claimant to secure restitution from him or her, it is still possible for the claimant and the creditor together to agree that the contract of discharge should be set aside. This would have the effect of reviving the debt so that the defendant would no longer be considered to have been enriched by the claimant's payment. This was recognized in *Walter v James*.[222] However, once the defendant debtor has accepted the payment as discharging the debt, this should prevent the claimant and the creditor from agreeing to revive the debt.[223] Beatson regarded the notion that the debt may be revived by the claimant and the creditor as 'enabling parties to impose a burden on a non-consenting third party'.[224] But what burden has been imposed? All that the parties have done is to restore their position to what it was before the claimant paid the creditor. No burden is being placed on the defendant beyond that which already existed. The only qualification to this should arise where the defendant has relied on the discharge of the debt in some way, so then the claimant and creditor should be estopped from arguing that the debt has been revived.

There is one potential difficulty with the argument that the payment of the defendant's debt by the claimant will automatically discharge the debt because the discharge is incontrovertibly beneficial to the debtor, namely that the claimant might be a volunteer whose motive in discharging the debt was to harass the defendant.[225] But this does not make the discharge of the debt itself of less value, it just means that the claimant is placed in a position in which he or she might exploit the defendant. It is for this reason that the fact that the claimant was a volunteer should be an irrelevant consideration when determining whether the claimant's payment discharged the defendant's debt. Rather, this is a separate consideration which needs to be examined in the context of identifying a relevant ground of restitution.[226]

The preferable interpretation of the law on discharge of debts can be summarized as follows. Where the claimant pays money to the creditor purporting to discharge a debt which is owed by the defendant this will automatically discharge the debt once the payment has been accepted by the creditor, regardless of the fact that the claimant was a volunteer, except where the claimant's intention that the creditor should receive the

---

[221] See p 298, below. But it will be virtually impossible for the claimant to establish that money was paid for reasons of necessity.

[222] (1871) LR 6 Exch 124.   [223] Friedmann, 'Payment of Another's Debt', 542.

[224] Beatson, *Use and Abuse of Unjust Enrichment*, 202.

[225] See the American case of *Norton v Haggett* (1952) 85 A 2d. 571.   [226] See p 243, below.

payment can be treated as vitiated by virtue of a recognized ground of restitution, such as mistake or duress. Crucially, for purposes of this chapter, following the decision in *Ibrahim v Barclays Bank plc*[227] it is absolutely clear that, where the claimant's payment is induced by legal compulsion, the debt owed by the defendant will be automatically discharged.

(C) RESTITUTION FROM THE DEBTOR

Where the claimant has discharged the defendant's liability to the creditor the claimant will wish to obtain restitution from the defendant, which will require the claimant to establish that the claim falls within one of the recognized grounds of restitution. In many cases this will be legal compulsion, though another potential ground of restitution might be necessity.[228] To establish legal compulsion it is necessary to show that the claimant was 'compellable by law' to make the payment.[229] Usually this takes the form of the creditor expressly threatening the claimant with the legal process if he or she does not pay the money as demanded. But legal compulsion may also be established where the threats derive implicitly from the circumstances in which the claimant finds him or herself. Whether the claimant can be considered to have been legally compelled to pay the creditor ultimately depends on whether the claimant exercised a free choice in discharging the liability.

Where the claimant can be regarded as having been legally compelled to pay the money, the claimant might seek either to be reimbursed by the defendant, where the defendant was wholly or primarily liable for the debt,[230] or to recover a contribution, where the parties were jointly liable to the creditor.

(i) Reimbursement

Where the claimant has been compelled by law to discharge the defendant's liability, the general principle is that the defendant will be required to reimburse the claimant for this expenditure if the defendant bears the ultimate liability for it.[231] The defendant will bear the ultimate liability either where the defendant bears the whole of the liability and the claimant bears none of it, or where the claimant's liability is subordinate to that of the defendant. Generally, the defendant's liability will be characterized as ultimate where any benefit which was derived from the existence of the liability has been enjoyed by the defendant.[232] For example, since a borrower has the use of the borrowed money rather than the guarantor, it is the borrower who will bear the ultimate liability for the debt.

(1) The Defendant Bears the Whole of the Liability

Where the defendant bears the whole liability and this liability has been discharged by the claimant, it is clearly appropriate that the defendant should make restitution to the claimant. This is illustrated by *Exall v Partridge*[233] where the claimant had left his carriage on land, which was leased by the defendant, for the defendant to repair. The defendant

---

[227] [2012] EWCA Civ 640, [2013] Ch 400.   [228] See Chapter 12.

[229] *Moule v Garrett* (1872) LR 7 Ex 101, 104 (Cockburn CJ).

[230] Reimbursement is not available where the claimant and defendant are joint debtors and guarantors, since one party does not bear the primary liability: *Berghoff Trading Ltd v Swinbrook Developments Ltd* [2008] EWHC 1785 (Comm), [29] (Teare J).

[231] *Re Downer Enterprises Ltd* [1974] 1 WLR 1460, 1468 (Pennycuick V-C).

[232] Birks, *An Introduction to the Law of Restitution*, 192.

[233] (1799) 8 Term Rep 308, 101 ER 1405. See also *Johnson v Royal Mail Steam Packet Co* [1867] LR 3 CP 38; *Edmunds v Wallingford* (1885) 14 QBD 811; and *Whitham v Bullock* [1939] 2 KB 81.

had not paid his rent to his landlord who consequently entered the land and lawfully seized the claimant's carriage in distress of rent. Since the claimant wanted to recover his carriage he was compelled to pay the rent to the landlord. The claimant then sought to recover the money he had paid to the landlord from the defendant. It was assumed that the claimant's payment had discharged the defendant's liability to the landlord, so clearly the defendant had been benefited. But it was still necessary to identify a ground of restitution. Duress of goods could not be established, both because the landlord had not acted unlawfully in seizing the carriage and because the money demanded was lawfully due to him. But it was held that the claimant could recover from the defendant what he had paid to the landlord on the ground that he had not paid the money voluntarily but had been compelled to do so by the landlord seizing his property.[234] Le Blanc J even described this as 'compulsion of law'.[235] This compulsion derived from the fact that the landlord had seized the claimant's goods by legitimate application of the legal process and, if the claimant wished to recover his carriage, he had no choice but to pay the money which the landlord sought. Although the landlord never said to the claimant that he must pay the debt, this was implicit since the landlord's actions clearly indicated that if the debt was not paid by someone he would retain the claimant's carriage. Since the defendant was not going to pay the rent, the claimant had no choice but to do so. Presumably, for reasons of consistency at least with economic duress and much of the rest of the law relating to unjust enrichment, the 'but for' test of causation is applicable in this type of case. If so, it follows that, where the claimant would have paid off the defendant's debts even if his or her goods had not been seized by the third party, restitution will be denied, simply because there is insufficient evidence that the compulsion of law had deprived the claimant of a free choice as to how to spend his or her money.

In *Exall v Partridge* the claimant's property had actually been seized by the third party. Exactly the same analysis should be possible where the third party has only threatened to seize the claimant's goods if the money is not paid. In the context of duress of property no distinction is drawn between threats to seize goods and actual seizure, so there is no reason why such a distinction should be drawn in respect of legal compulsion.[236] Also, it makes no difference whether the claimant has paid money to the third party to recover his or her goods or the claimant's goods have been sold by the third party to pay off the debt, for in each case the defendant's liability will have been discharged and the claimant will have been deprived of a free choice as to whether he or she should discharge the liability.[237]

In *Exall v Partridge* it was relatively straightforward to establish that the claimant was compelled to discharge the defendant's liability, since the fact that the claimant's property was taken by the third party was clearly outside the claimant's control, because the carriage was under the control of the defendant. Crucially, there was no question of the claimant acting voluntarily in leaving the carriage on the defendant's premises, because the defendant had requested the claimant to do this so that he could repair it. But what about a case where the claimant has left his property on the defendant's premises without being requested to do so? In *England v Marsden*[238] this was held to be sufficient to distinguish *Exall v Partridge*. The claimant had legitimately seized the defendant's goods but left them on the defendant's premises without being requested to do so and without any benefit to the defendant. The defendant's landlord then seized the goods as distress for rent which was owed to him by the defendant. The claimant paid the rent to recover the goods and then sought to recover this from the defendant, but his claim failed because he

---

[234] See, in particular, Grose J in *Exall v Partridge* (1799) 8 Term Rep 308, 311; 101 ER 1405, 1406.
[235] Ibid, 311; 1407.   [236] See *Maskell v Horner* [1915] 3 KB 106.
[237] *Edmunds v Wallingford* (1885) 14 QBD 811.   [238] (1866) LR 1 CP 529.

had acted voluntarily in leaving the goods on the defendant's premises. But this distinction, which depends on whether the defendant had requested the goods to be left on the premises or had benefited from the goods being left there, was later doubted in *Edmunds v Wallingford*.[239] Any such distinction should be rejected because it does not follow from the fact that the claimant has left his or her property on the defendant's premises without being requested to do so that the claimant was necessarily acting voluntarily when discharging the defendant's liability. Rather, given that the claimant's property has been seized, regardless of the reason why it was on the defendant's property, the significant question is whether the claimant had any real choice but to discharge the liability to recover his or her property and, since usually the claimant had no reasonable alternative but to discharge the liability, the defendant should reimburse the claimant. The only possible qualification to this might arise where the claimant left property on the defendant's premises knowing that there was a possibility that it might be seized by a landlord. Only in such a case might it be concluded that the claimant had taken the risk of the property being seized.[240]

(2) The Claimant's Liability is Ancillary to that of the Defendant

The alternative situation where the claimant will seek to be reimbursed by the defendant is where, although the claimant was liable to the third party, that liability is ancillary to that of the defendant. Typically this will arise where the claimant is acting as surety for the defendant's debt and the creditor threatens to sue the claimant unless the debt is discharged. The claimant will be liable to the third party to discharge the defendant's debt by virtue of the guarantee but, because the defendant bears the primary liability in respect of the debt, the defendant will be required to reimburse the claimant.[241]

This form of liability also arises in respect of the assignment of leases. This is illustrated by *Moule v Garrett*[242] where the claimant was a tenant who had covenanted with his landlord that he would keep the leased property in repair. The claimant assigned the lease to an assignee who subsequently assigned it to the defendant. The defendant failed to keep the property in repair. The landlord sued the claimant for breach of covenant, since this liability to keep the property in repair continued despite the assignment. The claimant then brought an action against the defendant to recover what he had paid to the landlord. Since the claimant had not assigned the lease directly to the defendant he could not sue on an implied covenant to indemnify him, simply because there was no privity of contract between the claimant and the defendant. Despite this, the defendant was required to reimburse the claimant because his payment had discharged the defendant's liability to the landlord. The defendant bore the primary liability since he had the immediate obligation to keep the property in repair and it was his default which resulted in the landlord suing the claimant for breach of the covenant. Cockburn CJ specifically justified the reimbursement by reference to the fact that the claimant had been compelled to pay the landlord.[243]

The principle in *Moule v Garrett* is only applicable where the claimant's payment to the landlord has discharged a liability owed by the defendant, for otherwise the defendant will not have been enriched. It is for this reason that *Moule v Garrett* was distinguished in

---

[239] (1885) 14 QBD 811. Although it was suggested that restitution would be denied if the claimant left the goods on the defendant's premises without the defendant's express consent.

[240] By analogy with *Esso Petroleum Ltd v Hall Russell and Co Ltd* [1989] AC 643.

[241] *Anson v Anson* [1953] 1 QB 636. See also *Re a Debtor* [1937] Ch 156, 163 (Greene LJ).

[242] (1872) LR 7 Exch 101. See also *Selous Street Properties Ltd v Oronel Fabrics Ltd* (1984) 270 EG 643, 749 and *Beckton Dickinson UK Ltd v Zwebner* [1989] QB 208.

[243] *Moule v Garrett* (1872) LR 7 Exch 101, 104.

Bonner v Tottenham and Edmonton Permanent Investment Building Society,[244] where the claimant tenant had assigned his lease to Price who had then mortgaged it to the defendant. When Price went bankrupt the defendant took possession, but failed to pay rent to the landlord. The landlord then sued the claimant for breach of his covenant to pay rent. The claimant was compelled to pay the landlord and then sought to recover this sum from the defendant. The claim failed because it was held that he had not discharged any liability of the defendant. This was because, unlike the defendant in *Moule v Garrett* who was an assignee, the defendant in *Bonner* was a sub-lessee and consequently was not liable to the landlord to pay the rent. Since the claimant had not discharged any liability of the defendant it could not be shown that the defendant had received any benefit from the claimant.[245]

Although the principle involving the discharge of the defendant's primary liability is particularly important in respect of sureties and assignments of leases, it is applicable in a wide variety of situations. For example, in *Brook's Wharf and Bull Wharf Ltd v Goodman Bros*[246] the defendant stored a number of packages of squirrel skins, which had been imported from Russia, in the claimant's bonded warehouse, from where they were stolen without negligence on the part of the claimant. The defendant remained liable to pay customs duties on the skins, but refused to pay. As a result the claimant was compelled under statute to pay the duties and then sought to recover this amount from the defendant. The claimant's action succeeded because, although it was legally obliged to pay the custom duties, this liability was ancillary to that of the defendant who remained primarily liable for the duties. Lord Wright MR recognized that, if the claimant was not reimbursed by the defendant, the result would be that the defendant would be 'unjustly benefited at the cost of the plaintiffs'.[247] In *McCarthy v McCarthy and Stone plc*[248] an employer had paid tax on behalf of an employee as it was required to do by virtue of a statutory scheme. Normally the employer would have been able to deduct this tax from the employee's salary but this was not possible because the employee had left the firm. It was held that the amount paid by the employer could be recovered from the former employee on the ground of legal compulsion because the former employee bore the primary liability for the tax.

Whilst the vast majority of the cases which are concerned with the discharge of the defendant's primary liability involve discharge simply by payment of money to the creditor, there are some examples of cases where the discharge of liability occurs by the claimant expending money on work. So, for example, in *Gebhardt v Saunders*[249] the claimant, who was the tenant of the defendant's house, had received a notice from the sanitary authority which required either the owner or the occupier to abate a nuisance arising from water and sewage collecting in the cellar of the house, with a financial penalty if the nuisance was not abated. The notice was directed at both the owner and the occupier because it was unclear what the cause of the problem was. If it was due to blocked drains, the claimant as occupier would have been liable to abate the nuisance, but if it arose from structural problems, the defendant as owner would have been liable. Since the problem needed to be resolved urgently, the claimant did the necessary work in the course of which it was discovered that the problem arose from a structural defect in the drains, so the defendant was liable. The claimant successfully recovered the costs and expenses in abating the nuisance from the defendant. The exact ground of restitution in this case is

---

[244] [1899] 1 QB 161. See also *Re Nott and Cardiff Corp* [1918] 2 KB 146; *Receiver for the Metropolitan Police District v Croydon Corp* [1957] 2 QB 154; and *Esso Petroleum Co Ltd v Hall Russell and Co Ltd* [1989] AC 643.

[245] See particularly Vaughan Williams LJ in *Bonner v Tottenham and Edmonton Permanent Investment Building Society* [1899] 1 QB 161, 177.

[246] [1937] 1 KB 534.   [247] Ibid, 545.   [248] [2007] EWCA Civ 664.   [249] [1892] 2 QB 452.

somewhat uncertain. It could have been a mistaken belief that there was an existing liability to do the work,[250] or even necessity,[251] but the judges appeared to assume that it was legal compulsion.[252] This was particularly because, since the notice from the sanitary authority was directed to the claimant as well as the defendant, if the claimant had failed to do anything he would have been liable to pay a penalty. To avoid paying the penalty, the claimant incurred expenditure on the work.[253] Since it eventually turned out that the claimant bore no liability at all, this case could be treated as falling within the first category of cases, where the defendant bears the whole liability. Whichever category the case falls within is of no legal importance, because it is clear that it was the defendant who bore the ultimate liability, and this is sufficient justification for the award of restitution on the ground of legal compulsion.

The cause of action arising from the discharge of another's obligation by operation of law is sometimes described as 'recoupment'. There is, however, a danger in using this term in that it can hide the fact that liability is founded on unjust enrichment. This danger is especially well illustrated by the decision of the Court of Appeal in *Niru Battery Manufacturing Co v Milestone Trading Ltd (No 2)*.[254] Two parties, A and B, had previously been found to be jointly and severally liable to another party, C. A was liable for the tort of negligence and B was liable to make restitution of a mistaken payment by virtue of the unjust enrichment principle. A discharged B's liability by paying C and then sought restitution from B.[255] The Court held that B was liable to make recoupment to A, which was considered to be both cause of action and remedy, because B's liability had been discharged completely. But this is only relevant where B bears the whole liability or is primarily liable. That was not the case here, where the liability was joint, and so the recoupment claim should have been rejected.

(3) Voluntary Payments

One problem which has arisen particularly in respect of the claimant discharging the defendant's liability to a creditor concerns the role of voluntariness or risk-taking.[256] It is obvious that a claimant who voluntarily discharges the defendant's liability in circumstances where the claimant would not suffer in any way if the liability was not discharged, is unable to establish a restitutionary claim based on legal compulsion, simply because of the absence of any compulsion.[257] But a difficult question arises where, for example, the claimant has voluntarily become surety for the defendant's liability without being requested to do so by the defendant, and is then compelled by the creditor to discharge the liability. Can the claimant rely on legal compulsion to obtain restitution from the defendant in these circumstances? It is obvious that the claimant was compellable by law to pay the creditor, but does it, and should it, make any difference that the claimant voluntarily became the surety?

---

[250] This was Birks's preferred explanation of the case. See Birks, *An Introduction to the Law of Restitution*, 191.

[251] See Chapter 12.

[252] See also *Andrew v St Olave's Board of Works* [1898] 1 QB 775.

[253] It might be doubted whether the threat of the penalty was a sufficient cause of the claimant incurring the expenditure. It is just as likely that he incurred the expenditure out of necessity, to stop sewage leaking into the cellar. But, where two grounds of restitution are operating, the claimant should be able to rely on both of them to show that they jointly caused him or her to benefit the defendant.

[254] [2004] EWCA Civ 487, [2004] 2 All ER (Comm) 289.

[255] The case also concerned claims for contribution and subrogation. See p 249, below.

[256] See p 36, above.

[257] There may, depending on the circumstances, be a claim grounded on mistake.

This question arose in *Owen v Tate*[258] where the claimant, without consulting the defendant, deposited a sum of money with the defendant's creditor as security for a loan. The reason for this was that the defendant's previous surety wished to recover the title deeds of her property which had been surrendered to the creditor and, as a favour to her, the claimant agreed to become surety in her place. When the defendant discovered that the claimant had become the surety it protested, but when it was pressed for payment by the creditor, it asked the creditor to have recourse to the money which the claimant had deposited. The claimant then sought to be reimbursed by the defendant. The Court of Appeal assumed that the claimant's payment had discharged the defendant's debt and, whether or not the principle of automatic discharge is accepted, this must have been correct, if only because the defendant had requested the creditor to resort to the claimant's payment to discharge the debt.[259] The only question remaining for the court concerned the relevance of the fact that the claimant had voluntarily become the surety in the first place. Scarman LJ identified two relevant principles. First, where the claimant is compelled to pay money which the defendant is liable to pay, the claimant has a right to be reimbursed by the defendant. Secondly, this is subject to the principle that the claimant will not be reimbursed where the claimant voluntarily paid the money or voluntarily assumed the obligation to pay.[260] The claimant will have acted voluntarily where he or she paid money or incurred liability in circumstances where there was 'no antecedent request, no consideration or consensual basis' to do so.[261] Since this second principle qualifies the first, and because the claimant had voluntarily guaranteed the defendants' liability, it followed that he had no right to be reimbursed by the defendant.[262] The only exception to this was recognized as arising where the claimant voluntarily incurred the liability in circumstances where it was reasonably necessary in the interests of the claimant or the defendant or both of them to do so.[263] The effect of this decision is that, where a claimant has incurred liability as a surety, he or she will be able to seek reimbursement from the defendant only where the defendant has expressly or impliedly requested the claimant to act as surety or where it was necessary for the claimant to become surety.

A similar approach was adopted in *Esso Petroleum Ltd v Hall Russell and Co Ltd*,[264] where restitution was denied because the claimant was compelled to discharge the defendant's liability pursuant to an agreement with the creditor which the claimant had voluntarily made. Since the claimant had voluntarily incurred the liability in the first place it was not possible for it then to claim that it had been legally compelled to pay the third party.[265] In *Ibrahim v Barclays Bank plc*[266] the Court of Appeal, in recognizing that a debt might be discharged automatically where the claimant had voluntarily incurred liability by contract, cited *Owen v Tate* without criticism as an example of a case where recoupment might be denied even though the debt had been discharged, presumably because the liability was voluntarily incurred. In other words, voluntariness does not prevent automatic discharge of the debt, at least where payment was legally compelled, but voluntariness will defeat recoupment.

---

[258] [1976] QB 402. See also *Esso Petroleum Co Ltd v Hall Russell and Co Ltd* [1989] AC 643.

[259] See p 235, above.

[260] *Re National Motor Mail-Coach Co Ltd* [1908] 2 Ch 515, 520 (Swinfen Eady J).

[261] *Owen v Tate* [1976] QB 402, 408 (Scarman LJ).

[262] See also *Re National Motor Mail-Coach Co Ltd* [1908] 2 Ch 515.

[263] *Owen v Tate* [1976] QB 402, 409–10 (Scarman LJ).   [264] [1989] AC 643.

[265] The claimant's claim also failed because it could not be established that it had discharged any liability of the defendant.

[266] [2012] EWCA Civ 640, [2013] Ch 400, [49] (Lewison LJ).

Owen v Tate has generally been considered to be wrongly decided.[267] The result appears unjust since the claimant had conferred a benefit on the defendant by discharging the debt, but the defendant was still not required to reimburse the claimant. If the case is analysed simply in terms of causation it is difficult to defend, since, at the time the claimant's money was taken to discharge the debt, legal compulsion was operating. Ultimately, the validity of the decision is a matter of policy. Should we regard somebody who has voluntarily assumed a liability as acting in such a way that restitution should be denied? The particular difficulty with *Owen v Tate* is that there is nothing to suggest that the claimant had done anything which was detrimental to the interests of the defendant. Even though, as Scarman LJ found,[268] the claimant had acted behind the back of the defendant in the interests of another party, the claimant had not harmed the defendant in any way. Despite this, Ormrod LJ[269] did suggest that the defendant's position was worsened by the intrusion of the claimant. If this really was shown to be the case, it would have been possible to conclude that the defendant had not in fact benefited from the discharge of the liability, so the defendant could plead subjective devaluation to negate the enrichment element of the unjust enrichment claim.

Voluntariness, as defined in *Owen v Tate*, does not defeat restitutionary claims in other areas where the ground of restitution is legal compulsion. So, for example, in *Edmunds v Wallingford*[270] the fact that the claimant's goods which were seized had been voluntarily left on the defendant's premises was held to be irrelevant. It is also inconsistent with the law of contribution, whereby a surety is entitled to contribution from a co-surety regardless of whether or not the claimant had been requested by the defendant to become a surety.[271] The emphasis in *Owen v Tate* on whether the defendant had requested the claimant to act as surety, whether expressly or impliedly, appears to arise from an unfortunate misunderstanding of the earlier cases on discharge of liability. In these cases[272] the claimant's action was typically founded on the count for money paid, which required the claimant to plead that the defendant had requested the payment. In many of these cases this request was implied in highly artificial circumstances. Rather than rejecting the need for a request, *Owen v Tate* has affirmed it as a requirement. This is unacceptable and should be rejected. It is an example of the forms of action continuing to rule us from their graves.[273]

The validity of *Owen v Tate* is therefore in doubt. The preferable view is that, where the claimant has been legally compelled to discharge the defendant's liability, the fact that the claimant has not been requested to do so should be irrelevant both to whether the debt was discharged and to whether the claim can be established. In those rare cases where the reason for the claimant voluntarily discharging the liability is so that the claimant can harass the defendant, it should be possible to deny restitution by means of subjective devaluation or by barring the claim on the ground that the claimant had been acting officiously.[274]

(4) Damages Paid to Two Claimants for Wrongful Interference with the Same Goods

A final category of reimbursement grounded on legal compulsion arises where a tortfeasor has been compelled to pay damages to two claimants for wrongful interference with the same goods. By virtue of section 7(4) of the Torts (Interference with Goods) Act 1977 any

---

[267] See Birks, *An Introduction to the Law of Restitution*, 311.   [268] *Owen v Tate* [1976] QB 402, 412.
[269] Ibid, 413.   [270] (1885) 14 QBD 811.   [271] See p 247, below.
[272] See, in particular, *Exall v Partridge* (1799) 8 Term Rep 308, 101 ER 1405.
[273] See further p 46, above.   [274] See p 36, above.

claimant who is unjustly enriched as the result of double enforcement of liability is liable to reimburse the wrongdoer to the extent of that enrichment. So, for example, if A has converted goods which are owned by B but had been found by C, both B and C might sue A for the tort of conversion. If A pays damages to both of them, C will be required by statute to pay the damages to B, who will then be unjustly enriched and so will be required to make restitution to A. This is a somewhat convoluted statutory attempt to avoid double liability. What is particularly significant for this book is that the liability to reimburse is specifically tied to unjust enrichment.

(ii) Contribution

Where both the claimant and the defendant are under a common and equal liability to the creditor (known as 'joint and several liability'), so that neither of them bears the ultimate liability, and the creditor compels the claimant to discharge the liability, the claimant will have a restitutionary claim against the defendant in the form of a claim for contribution.[275] If there was no doctrine of contribution in English law it would follow that which of the debtors was ultimately liable to discharge the debt would simply be a matter of chance depending on which debtor the creditor decided to sue, a result which is inequitable in the light of the fact that the debtors were equally liable to the creditor. There are two restitutionary routes for contribution, one at Common Law and the other by statute, both of which remain relevant. Contribution, rather than reimbursement, is relevant where the parties are under a common liability simply because, where the claimant has discharged his or her liability as well as that of the defendant, it would be inappropriate for the defendant to reimburse the claimant the whole amount spent, since the claimant also benefited from the payment by the discharge of his or her own liability. The rationale of contribution is that it provides a mechanism whereby the burden of liability can be shared between the parties.

Contribution can be analysed as embodying a restitutionary claim which is founded on the reversal of the defendant's unjust enrichment.[276] This is because the consequence of the claimant discharging the defendant's liability is that the defendant has been enriched by the receipt of a negative benefit and, since the claimant was compellable by law to discharge the liability, it follows that the ground of restitution is legal compulsion.[277] That contribution involves restitution grounded on legal compulsion is exemplified by *Spiers and Son Ltd v Troup*[278] where the claimant and the defendant both received a notice to pull down a party wall because it was in a dangerous condition. The claimant pulled down the wall and built a new wall which was taller and thicker than the old one and then sought a contribution from the defendant in respect of both the cost of demolition and rebuilding. It was held that, since the claimant had not been legally compelled to *rebuild* the wall, he could not obtain contribution from the defendant in respect of that expenditure. However, since both parties were equally liable to *demolish* the wall, it followed that the claimant could obtain contribution in respect of the cost of demolition, simply because the claimant had been legally compelled to incur this expenditure.

---

[275] For more detailed analysis of contribution see C Mitchell, *The Law of Contribution and Reimbursement* (Oxford: Oxford University Press, 2003).   [276] *Lavin v Toppi* [2015] HCA 4.

[277] Cf Mitchell, *The Law of Contribution and Reimbursement* who analyses cases involving contribution as grounded on unjust enrichment but with the ground of restitution founded on policy rather than legal compulsion.

[278] (1915) 84 LJKB 1986. See also *Legal and General Assurance Society Ltd v Drake Insurance Co Ltd* [1992] QB 887.

(1) Contribution at Common Law and Equity

The right to contribution at Common Law and Equity arises where the claimant and defendant are under a common liability to the same creditor in respect of the same debt,[279] regardless of whether they are jointly liable in the same instrument or severally liable in different instruments,[280] and the claimant pays a sum of money to the creditor in respect of that debt. Where the claimant discharges the liability completely, the defendant is required to make contribution in respect of his or her own share of the liability. So, if the claimant and defendant were jointly liable to pay the creditor £1,000 and the claimant discharged this liability completely, the defendant's contribution would be £500. The right to contribution is not confined, however, to where the claimant has discharged the common liability completely, but applies in all cases where the claimant has paid a sum which is more than his or her proportionate share of the common debt.

Although the right to contribution was first established in respect of co-sureties,[281] it now extends to all types of case where there is a common liability for the same debt. So the right to contribution is also applicable in respect of co-insurers,[282] co-partners,[283] co-mortgagors,[284] co-trustees,[285] and joint contractors.[286] But, in addition to these recognized categories, the right to contribution may arise from the particular facts of a case. This was recognized by Lord Kenyon CJ in *Child v Morley*:[287]

> I remember a case in Rolle's Abridgement, where a party met to dine at a tavern, and after dinner all but one of them went away without paying their quota of the reckoning, and that one paid for all the rest; and it was holden that he might recover from the others their aliquot proportions.

The general principle that where the parties are equally liable they must make an equal contribution can be modified by contract, so the parties may agree that they would be liable to contribute different sums. It is even possible to exclude the right to contribution by contract.[288] The High Court of Australia has, however, recognized that the right to contribution remains available as between co-sureties even though the creditor had covenanted not to sue the surety whose liability was discharged by the other surety.[289] This is because such a covenant does not discharge the surety's liability and such a ruling prevents the creditor from defeating a co-surety's right to contribution.

The right to contribution is also qualified where any of the people who are potentially liable to the creditor are insolvent[290] or cease to be liable for the debt. Such people are not liable to make contribution and so, where the liability has been discharged by the claimant, the remaining solvent parties must contribute equally to the common debt.[291] So, for example, where A, B, and C are sureties for a debt of £1,000 and the debtor and C both

---

[279] *Cooper v Twynam* (1823) Turn and R 424, 37 ER 1164.

[280] *Deering v The Earl of Winchelsea* (1787) 2 Bos and Pul 270, 126 ER 1276. As regards apportionment of liability in respect of liability insurance, see *Commercial Union Assurance Co Ltd v Hayden* [1977] QB 804.

[281] *Deering v The Earl of Winchelsea* (1787) 2 Bos and Pul 270, 126 ER 1276.

[282] *North British and Mercantile Insurance Co v London, Liverpool and Globe Insurance Co* (1876) 5 Ch D 569.

[283] *Re The Royal Bank of Australia, Robinson's Executors* (1856) 6 De G M and G 572, 43 ER 1356.

[284] *Re Mainwaring* [1937] Ch 96.   [285] *Chillingworth v Chambers* [1898] 1 Ch 685.

[286] *Boulter v Peplow* (1850) 9 CB 493, 137 ER 984.

[287] (1800) 8 TR 610, 614; 101 ER 1574, 1576.

[288] *Pendlebury v Walker* (1841) 4 Y and C Ex 424, 160 ER 1072.   [289] *Lavin v Toppi* [2015] HCA 4.

[290] *Deering v The Earl of Winchelsea* (1787) 2 Bos and Pul 270, 126 ER 1276.

[291] *Goff and Jones: The Law of Unjust Enrichment* (8th edn), 391.

become insolvent then, if A pays the whole debt, he can recover £500 from B, though this is subject to any contractual modification of the general principle of equal contribution. If the claimant pays only his or her share of the common debt which the creditor accepts in full settlement of the debt, the claimant can claim only a rateable contribution from the other people who are liable.[292] So, if A, B, and C are sureties for a debt of £900 and the creditor accepts payment of £300 from A in full settlement, A can only recover one third of £300 from B and from C.

(2) Civil Liability (Contribution) Act 1978

The effect of the Civil Liability (Contribution) Act 1978 is to extend the ambit of contribution beyond those cases where the claimant and the defendant are jointly liable in respect of the same debt, where contribution is still governed by the Common Law and Equity, to where they are jointly or otherwise liable in respect of the same damage which has been suffered by another person.[293] This means that, where the claimant and the defendant are liable to pay 'compensation' in respect of the 'same damage' to a third party, whether it arises from tort, breach of contract, breach of trust, unjust enrichment,[294] or any other form of liability,[295] and the claimant discharges the defendant's liability, the claimant is able to recover such contribution from the defendant as the court considers to be 'just and equitable having regard to the extent of [the defendant's] responsibility for the damage in question'.[296] When determining the defendant's responsibility for the damage, the court should consider the relative culpability of the claimant and the defendant and the causative potency of their conduct.[297] The court may determine that equal division of the liability is equitable or that the defendant is not liable to make any contribution or even that the defendant should be required to indemnify the claimant completely.[298] It has been recognized that the rationale of the Act is to ensure that the party whose liability has been discharged is not unjustly enriched.[299] This is significant, since it follows that the requirements for a claim in unjust enrichment need to be established, and the bars and defences to such a claim will be applicable, most significantly the defence of change of position.

The 1978 Act has a potentially wide ambit, since it relates to any person who has caused damage to another person. So, apart from the obvious cases of tortfeasors, joint contractors who are in breach of contract and breach of trust by trustees, the Act is also applicable, for example, to directors who have caused damage to their company. Where a contribution is claimed the fact that the claimant participated in an illegal activity does not, at least as a matter of principle, defeat the defendant's right to contribution.[300] But the relative blameworthiness of the parties will be a relevant consideration when the court is assessing

---

[292] *Ex parte Snowden* (1881) 17 Ch D 44, 47 (James LJ).

[293] Civil Liability (Contribution) Act 1978, s 1(1). The parties must be liable to the same person: *Birse Construction Ltd v Haiste Ltd* [1996] 1 WLR 675.

[294] *Friends' Provident Life Office v Hillier Parker May and Rowden (a firm)* [1997] QB 85.

[295] Civil Liability (Contribution) Act 1978, s 6(1). This is to be interpreted widely, but it does not include exemplary damages. See *K v P* [1993] Ch 140, 148 (Ferris J). In *BRB (Residuary) Ltd v Connex South Eastern Ltd* [2008] EWHC 1172 (QB), [2008] 1 WLR 2867 it was recognized that a claim for contribution lay under the Act even where the party seeking contribution had mistakenly admitted liability.

[296] Civil Liability (Contribution) Act 1978, s 2(1).

[297] *Madden v Quirk* [1989] 1 WLR 702.

[298] Civil Liability (Contribution) Act 1978, s 2(2). See further *City Index Ltd v Gawler* [2007] EWCA Civ 1382, [2008] Ch 313, p 250, below.

[299] *Dubai Aluminium Co Ltd v Salaam* [2002] UKHL 48, [2003] 2 AC 366, 388 (Lord Hobhouse).

[300] *K v P* [1993] Ch 140.

what a just and equitable award should be. Consequently, if the effect of the contribution would be to enable the claimant to retain the proceeds of fraud, then, at least where the defendant was not party to the fraud, it is unlikely that it would be just and equitable to require the defendant to make any contribution to the claimant.[301]

Although the 1978 Act will generally be applicable only where the claimant was legally compellable to pay the third party, there is an important exception to this where the claimant has *bona fide* settled or compromised the claim against him or her, since such a person can claim contribution from the defendant even though it was not clear on the facts, rather than as a matter of law, whether he or she was personally liable to the third party.[302]

The relationship between unjust enrichment claims and contribution under the 1978 Act was examined by the Court of Appeal in *Friends' Provident Life Office v Hillier Parker May and Rowden (a firm)*.[303] In this case the claimant had appointed the defendant chartered surveyors to check and authorize payment in respect of the developer's claims for the claimant's share of the costs arising from the development of a shopping centre. The defendant had recommended that the claimant pay the developer's claims which included sums for 'notional interest'. In fact, it was not necessary for the claimant to pay anything for notional interest under the development agreement and so it sought to recover this sum from the developer. This litigation settled and the claimant then sued the defendant for damages for negligence and breach of contract arising from the defendant's failure to advise the claimant that the notional interest was not payable. The defendant claimed a contribution from the developer under the 1978 Act on the basis that the developer was liable to repay the money it had received to the claimant on the ground of mistake or absence of basis. The question for the Court of Appeal was whether a restitutionary claim by the claimant against the developer could be treated as a claim in respect of the same damage as that alleged by the claimant against the defendant. This turned on whether the restitutionary remedy could be characterized as 'compensatory' within section 6(1) of the 1978 Act. The Court of Appeal held that both a claim for restitution and a claim for damages could be characterized as a claim for compensation for damage, so that contribution could be awarded under the 1978 Act. This would also be the case if the claimant's restitutionary claim against the developer was founded on the vindication of proprietary rights. As Auld LJ said:[304] '[The Act] clearly spans a variety of causes of action, forms of damage in the sense of loss of some sort, and remedies, the last of which are gathered together under the umbrella of "compensation".'

It did not matter that the liability of the defendant and the developer derived from different causes of action, namely tort and breach of contract on the one hand and one relating to unjust enrichment on the other, since it was sufficient that the liabilities arose from the same event, namely the claimant's payment for notional interest.

This conclusion was doubted by Lord Steyn in *Royal Brompton Hospital NHS Trust v Hammond*[305] on the ground that liability in unjust enrichment does not involve 'damage'. However, in *Niru Battery Manufacturing Co v Milestone Trading Ltd (No 2)*[306] the Court

---

[301] Ibid, 149 (Ferris J).

[302] Civil Liability (Contribution) Act 1978, s 1(4). In addition, s 1(2) enables the claimant to seek contribution even though he or she has ceased to be liable in respect of the damage in question since it occurred, but only if the claimant was so liable immediately before making or agreeing to make the payment in respect of which the contribution is sought. By s 1(3) the defendant remains liable to make contribution to the claimant even though he or she has ceased to be liable in respect of the damage in question, save where this extinction of liability occurred by virtue of the expiry of a limitation period.

[303] [1997] QB 85.   [304] Ibid, 103.   [305] [2002] UKHL 14, [2002] 1 WLR 1397.

[306] [2004] EWCA Civ 487, [2004] 2 All ER (Comm) 289.

of Appeal suggested that, if it had been necessary to decide the point, the dictum of Lord Steyn in *Royal Brompton Hospital Trust* would be treated as *obiter* and that it was bound by the earlier decision of the Court of Appeal in *Friends' Provident*.

The approach in *Friends' Provident* was confirmed and applied by the Court of Appeal in *City Index Ltd v Gawler*.[307] An employee of a company had stolen £9 million in breach of fiduciary duty. The money had been received by City Index, which knew of the breach of fiduciary duty, and was liable for unconscionable receipt[308] of the money transferred in breach of fiduciary duty. This claim was settled for £5.5 million. City Index then sought contribution from some of the company's directors and its auditor, on the ground that they had negligently failed to detect the theft. The liabilities of City Index and the directors and auditor did not appear on the face of it to involve the same damage, since liability in the tort of negligence is loss-based, whereas that for unconscionable receipt is gain-based, which is assessed by reference to the value of the money received. Nevertheless, the Court of Appeal held that the claims were deemed to involve the same damage, since even liability for unconscionable receipt can be analysed as loss-based and compensatory.[309] This is because, the defendant having received property in which the claimant had a proprietary interest, the remedy of accounting for the value of the property received involves returning value to the claimant, so essentially the claimant is compensated for the loss suffered from the misapplication of property.

At a doctrinal level this is incorrect, since the remedy for unconscionable receipt cannot be equated with that for the tort of negligence; it is assessed with reference to the value of the property at the time of the receipt,[310] which may be different to the loss suffered by the claimant at the time of transfer. This difference between the function of the remedies is even more marked if the defendant is liable to account for profits that he or she received subsequently from the use of the property which had been transferred in breach of duty. Nonetheless, the result of the decision can be defended on policy grounds, since it is surely only fair that one defendant, who has discharged his or her own liability as well as that of another defendant, should be able to obtain contribution from the other defendant where that liability relates to the same series of events. But such a liability to make contribution should operate only to the extent that the value of the claimant's loss corresponds to the value of the defendant's gain,[311] for only then can they be considered to be liable for the same damage.

This is yet another example of a problem concerning the application of a statute to restitutionary claims where the terms of the statute do not clearly cover such claims.[312] The problem would have been avoided had the 1978 Act made specific reference to restitutionary liability falling within its ambit. But, in the absence of such specific restitutionary language, the Court of Appeal's interpretation of the 1978 Act in *Friends' Provident*, *Niru Battery*, and *City Index* is acceptable, albeit somewhat artificial, since all these cases involved literal restitutionary liability, in that the defendant who was liable for unjust enrichment or unconscionable receipt had obtained a gain which reflected a corresponding loss suffered by the claimant, so the restitutionary relief has compensatory connotations in transferring the value of the defendant's gain back to the claimant who

---

[307] [2007] EWCA Civ 1382, [2008] Ch 313.   [308] See p 645, below.

[309] Consistent with *Friends' Provident Life Office v Hillier Parker May and Rowden* [1997] QB 85.

[310] See p 651, below.

[311] A Goymour, 'A Contribution to Knowing Receipt Liability?' [2008] RLR 113, 118.

[312] See also the interpretation of the Limitation Act 1980, discussed in Chapter 29, and the application of the Civil Jurisdiction and Judgments Act 1982 to restitutionary claims as examined by the House of Lords in *Kleinwort Benson Ltd v Glasgow City Council* [1999] 1 AC 153.

had suffered the loss. But it is possible for a claimant to bring a restitutionary claim even though it has not suffered a loss, as will be the case where a fiduciary has made a profit from his or her position as fiduciary and is required to disgorge that gain to the principal to whom the fiduciary duties are owed.[313] It is not possible to conclude that the disgorgement remedy in such circumstances is necessarily compensatory, because usually the claimant is not seeking to recover the value of something which he or she has lost. Consequently, if a third party was liable for assisting the fiduciary to breach his or her duty to the claimant, and was sued by the principal, that third party would not be able to seek contribution from the fiduciary because they would not be liable to pay compensation in respect of the same damage. There is no convincing policy reason for this and so it is an unacceptable lacuna in the law of contribution.

City Index Ltd v Gawler is also significant as regards the determination of the extent of the contribution available under the 1978 Act. According to that statute, the court can order contribution as appears just and equitable, having regard to the extent of the parties' responsibility for the damage. The Court of Appeal held that where the defendant who seeks contribution has received property in breach of trust or fiduciary duty, then, to the extent that the defendant has retained the value of that benefit, he or she should not be able to obtain contribution from the other defendant, simply because it would not be fair that another party should make contribution where the recipient was still benefiting from the receipt of the benefit. So, for example, A is jointly liable with B to C, with A being liable for unconscionably receiving £10,000 which was transferred in breach of fiduciary duty and B for the tort of negligence in not stopping this. A discharged the joint liability by entering into a final settlement with C for £5,000. If A had retained £3,000 of the money that she had received, it will be possible for her to seek only a maximum contribution from B of £2,000. In exercising its discretion as to the award of contribution, the court should have regard to the circumstances in which the money was dissipated and the relative fault of the party. In this example the fact that A had acted unconscionably and B had acted only negligently, might be a reason to reduce, or even eliminate, B's liability to make contribution, although this will turn on careful assessment of the facts. In *City Index* itself, the question of contribution between the parties as regards the value of the benefit which had not been retained by the party who was liable for unconscionable receipt was left for decision at trial.

(D) RESTITUTION FROM THE CREDITOR

The claimant's payment to a creditor will automatically discharge a debt owed by the defendant to the creditor once the creditor has accepted payment, at least where the payment was induced by legal compulsion, save where the claimant's intention to pay the creditor can be treated as vitiated.[314] This will be the case, for example, where the claimant paid the creditor as a result of a mistake. Since the debt owed by the defendant will not be discharged in such circumstances, the claimant is unable to obtain restitution from the defendant, simply because the defendant will not have been enriched. Rather, it is the creditor who will have been enriched, since the creditor has received the claimant's money and can still sue the defendant for payment. The claimant must then establish a ground of restitution to secure restitution. Usually, the reason why the claimant's payment did not discharge the debt will also constitute the ground of restitution. So, for example, if the claimant paid the money to the creditor due to the

---

[313] See Chapter 19.   [314] See p 235, above.

effect of an operative mistake, that mistake will prevent the debt from being discharged and will also ground the claimant's restitutionary claim against the creditor. This was what happened in *Barclays Bank v Simms*,[315] where the claimant bank had mistakenly paid the creditor of its customer once the customer had revoked the authority to do so. Robert Goff J assumed that the payment had not discharged the customer's liability to the creditor and so the customer was not considered to have received any benefit from the payment. But the claimant successfully secured restitution from the creditor who had received the payment. This case must have been correctly decided. The customer's debt could not be regarded as discharged by the claimant since its intention that the customer receive the payment was vitiated by the mistake, and this mistake also provided the ground for restitution from the creditor.

Alternatively, where the claimant pays money to the creditor purporting to discharge the defendant's debt and the debt is not discharged, the claimant may found restitution on the ground of failure of basis,[316] since the expected effect of the payment, namely the discharge of the liability, has not occurred.[317] Whether the basis for the payment has failed will depend on whether the payment was effective in any way, which will turn on what the claimant expected the payment to achieve. If, as will usually be the case, the claimant simply intended the payment to discharge the debt, and the debt has not been discharged, there will have been a total failure of basis and it should be irrelevant that the creditor treated the debt as being discharged and had refrained from suing the defendant.[318]

(E) IS LEGAL COMPULSION A GROUND OF RESTITUTION?

It has been suggested by Hilliard that legal compulsion should not be treated as a ground of restitution, because the cases considered in this section have nothing to do with the unjust enrichment principle.[319] The essence of this argument is that the cases which appear to involve legal compulsion are not actually concerned with whether the claimant's intention to benefit the defendant has been vitiated by compulsion, but rather focus on whether it is appropriate to award a remedy to distribute fairly the burden of discharging the obligation. So, for example, Hilliard says that where a surety has discharged a debt owed by the defendant it is not appropriate to analyse the surety's claim in terms of legal compulsion, because the surety voluntarily assumed the obligation. Hilliard prefers to describe the liability as involving the equitable distribution of liability.

It may, indeed, be more appropriate to describe the contribution cases in these terms, even though the statutory contribution scheme has been recognized as being founded on the unjust enrichment principle, particularly because of the judicial discretion to determine the extent of contribution with reference to what is just and equitable. But it is most definitely not a satisfactory explanation of the cases involving reimbursement, which were not considered by Hilliard. In such cases the claimant benefits the defendant as a result of pressure being imposed, which is most certainly on a par with the pressure imposed in cases involving duress of property or economic duress.[320] But that ground of restitution is not available to the claimant because the threat is lawful. It is for that reason that a distinct ground of legal compulsion must be recognized in its own right, at least for the recoupment cases. As regards the contribution cases, it remains useful to analyse the claims in

---

[315] [1980] QB 677. Cf *B Liggett (Liverpool) Ltd v Barclays Bank Ltd* [1928] 1 KB 48.
[316] See Chapter 13.   [317] *Walter v James* (1871) LR 6 Ex 124, 127 (Kelly CB).
[318] Beatson, *The Use and Abuse of Unjust Enrichment*, 202. Cf Friedmann, 'Payment of Another's Debt', 539.
[319] J Hilliard, 'A Case for Abolition of Legal Compulsion as a Ground of Restitution' (2002) 61 CLJ 551.
[320] See p 212, above.

terms of unjust enrichment, because this focuses attention on the fact that we are concerned with obtaining restitution rather than indemnity and it follows that defences, such as change of position, will be applicable.

5. THREATS TO SECURE THE PERFORMANCE OF A STATUTORY DUTY

A final ground of restitution which is founded on the principle of compulsion is of limited importance but it does have an independent existence, namely where the defendant demands payment to secure the performance of a statutory duty.[321] In the usual case in which a defendant receives payment from the claimant to perform a statutory duty where that payment has not itself been authorized by statute, restitution of the unauthorized payment will cause little difficulty, because the vast majority of such cases involve payments made to public authorities. The decision of the House of Lords in *Woolwich Equitable Building Society v IRC*[322] recognizes a right to restitution in such circumstances.[323] But this ground of restitution is confined to restitution from public authorities. In certain exceptional cases the defendant may be a private body which has received payments in excess of that which has been authorized by statute. This situation is most likely to arise where the defendant is in a monopolistic position,[324] such as a recently privatized company which imposes charges for the provision of essential services in excess of that which is authorized by statute or a regulator. In such circumstances it appears that the ground of restitution cannot be the fact that the company has received money which is not authorized by statute, which would be sufficient to ground the claim if the defendant was a public authority. Rather, restitution is triggered by the implied threats which might accompany the defendant's demand for payment. Since these threats accompany demands for a payment which is not due to the defendant, the threats should be considered to be illegitimate and restitution should follow if the threats caused the claimant to pay the defendant.

The leading case on this ground of restitution is *Great Western Railway v Sutton*[325] where the defendant was a railway company which had charged the claimant more for carrying goods than it was charging other customers. This was in contravention of a statute which required all similar customers to be charged on the same basis. The claimant was able to recover the excess payment in an action for money had and received on the ground that he had been compelled to make the payment, for if the claimant had not paid the excess amount he would not have been able to procure the defendant to perform its duty of carrying the claimant's goods.

This is in fact a highly artificial ground of restitution, primarily because, whilst the emphasis is placed upon the assumed compulsion derived from the defendant refusing to perform a statutory duty unless it is paid more than it can legitimately receive, the real reason for restitution is that the excess money received by the defendant was not due to it. The better approach is that adopted by the House of Lords in *Woolwich*, namely to justify

---

[321] See Burrows, *The Law of Restitution* (3rd edn), 266. This was recognized as a distinct ground of restitution founded on the principle of compulsion by Lord Goff in *Woolwich Equitable Building Society v IRC* [1993] AC 170, 165.   [322] [1993] AC 70.

[323] See Chapter 15.   [324] *Goff and Jones: The Law of Unjust Enrichment* (8th edn), 314.

[325] (1869) LR 4 HL 226. See also *South of Scotland Electricity Board v British Oxygen Co Ltd (No 2)* [1959] 1 WLR 587.

restitution by virtue of the *ultra vires* receipt of the defendant.[326] This principle should be developed to cover even private bodies where they receive more than is authorized by statute. Restitution would still lie in cases such as *Great Western Railway v Sutton*, but not because of artificially constructed compulsion, deduced from implied threats, but rather because of the defendant's unauthorized receipt. Alternatively, this type of case may be analysed with reference to the ground of absence of basis, at least where there was no liability for the claimant to pay anything to the defendant[327] or on the ground of a mistaken belief that the money was due, it now being irrelevant that the mistake was one of law.[328]

---

[326] See Chapter 15.   [327] See Chapter 13.   [328] See Chapter 9.

11

EXPLOITATION

1. GENERAL PRINCIPLES

(A) THE ESSENCE OF EXPLOITATION

It was seen in the last chapter that compulsion is not a ground of restitution in its own right but is a general principle on which a number of specific grounds of restitution are founded. The same is true of exploitation. Exploitation is a useful general principle to recognize, since it enables a number of disparate grounds of restitution to be treated together. These grounds have the common characteristic that the defendant has actually taken advantage of the claimant's weaker position in some way, or can at least be presumed to have taken advantage of the claimant. The essence of exploitation consequently involves the actual or potential abuse of power or influence by the defendant. The grounds of restitution which are founded on the principle of exploitation can be considered to be both claimant- and defendant-oriented. They are primarily claimant-oriented, in the sense that the effect of the actual or presumed exploitation means that the claimant's intent to transfer a benefit to the defendant can be treated as vitiated. But the grounds of restitution are also defendant-oriented, in the sense that it is the actual or presumed conduct of the defendant which constitutes the exploitation of the claimant's weaker position.[1]

(B) THE RELATIONSHIP BETWEEN EXPLOITATION AND OTHER PRINCIPLES

The boundary between exploitation and compulsion is particularly difficult to draw, primarily because the grounds of restitution which are founded on these two principles operate in a similar way, to vitiate the claimant's intention to benefit the defendant by virtue of the defendant's conduct. This is because the defendant's conduct in compelling the claimant to act or in exploiting his or her weakness deprives the claimant of the opportunity to exercise a sufficiently free choice as to whether to provide a benefit to the defendant.[2] Despite this apparent similarity between the two principles, they are crucially different. The essential feature of compulsion is that the claimant is not able to exercise a free choice to transfer a benefit because of pressure exerted by the defendant. The essential feature of exploitation, on the other hand, is that the claimant's lack of a free choice arises from the fact that the defendant occupied a superior position to that of the claimant, which the defendant either actually exploited or was in a position to exploit. To establish

---

[1] Sometimes, however, the exploitation might come from a third party. See p 269, below.
[2] See PBH Birks and NY Chin, 'On the Nature of Undue Influence' in J Beatson and D Friedmann (eds), *Good Faith and Fault in Contract Law* (Oxford: Clarendon Press, 1995), 58.

exploitation it is not necessary to show that the defendant has threatened or pressurized the claimant in any way; the ability to influence is sufficient.

There will, however, be cases where the defendant in threatening the claimant will also have exploited him or her so grounds of restitution founded both on compulsion and exploitation will be applicable. Usually, in such circumstances, it will be more appropriate for the claimant to emphasize the threats and so rely on grounds of restitution which are founded on the principle of compulsion. There will also be some cases where the defendant has exploited the claimant's weaker position by making a misrepresentation and so induced the claimant to make a mistake.[3] In such cases the claimant could rely on the mistake as an alternative ground of restitution. In most cases of exploitation, however, the claimant will be sufficiently aware of the circumstances such that it is not possible to conclude that he or she was mistaken, neither will the claimant lack the capacity to comprehend the nature of the transaction,[4] leaving only the grounds of restitution founded on exploitation as relevant to establish a claim in unjust enrichment.

(C) IDENTIFYING THE ENRICHMENT

Where the claimant wishes to seek restitution of a benefit which has been transferred to the defendant as a result of the defendant's exploitation of the claimant's weaker position, the enrichment will usually be in the form of money. But it is possible that, as a consequence of the defendant's exploitation, the defendant will have received non-monetary benefits from the claimant, such as goods or even services.[5] Restitution will be available by reason of the exploitation, regardless of the type of enrichment received by the defendant, although with goods and services the question of whether or not the defendant has actually been enriched may be more difficult to establish.[6]

(D) VITIATION OF TRANSACTIONS FOR EXPLOITATION

Usually the effect of the defendant's exploitation is that the claimant enters into a transaction with the defendant and transfers a benefit to him or her pursuant to it. If the claimant is to recover such benefits it is first necessary to establish that the transaction has been set aside by reason of the exploitation. This is because of the principle that restitutionary remedies will not be awarded to subvert transactions which provide a legitimate legal basis for the defendant's receipt of the enrichment.[7] These transactions will usually involve contracts, but they may also involve voluntary dispositions such as gifts.[8] The courts are more prepared to set aside gifts for exploitation than they are to set aside contracts.[9] This accords with the general policy of the law which is to uphold agreements wherever possible and only to set them aside exceptionally. Gifts are more readily set aside for another reason, namely that where the claimant has made a gift to the defendant without receiving anything in return this suggests that the claimant might have been exploited by the defendant.

---

[3] See Chapter 9. Similarly, the *non est factum* doctrine, p 196, above, could be justified by reference to the principle of exploitation.

[4] *Royal Bank of Scotland plc v Etridge (No 2)* [2002] 2 AC 773, 823 (Lord Hobhouse).

[5] See *O'Sullivan v Management Agency and Music Ltd* [1985] QB 428 where the claimant successfully brought an action for restitution in respect of services received by the defendant as a result of undue influence.

[6] See Chapter 4.   [7] See Chapter 7.

[8] See, for example, *Allcard v Skinner* (1887) 36 Ch D 145 and *Louth v Diprose* [1992] 75 CLR 621.

[9] *Wright v Carter* [1903] 1 Ch 27, 50 (Vaughan Williams LJ). See also the different tests for setting aside contracts and deeds for the disposition of gifts for mistake. See p 192, above.

Most of the cases which arise in the context of exploitation are concerned with the vitiation of contracts. The effect of exploitation of the claimant by the defendant is to render the contract voidable,[10] so if the claimant wishes to set it aside he or she must rescind it through the operation of the equitable jurisdiction.[11] As a consequence of rescission the defendant must make restitution to the claimant of any benefits which he or she had received pursuant to the transaction and the claimant will be required to make counter-restitution to the defendant of the value of any benefit which the claimant had received.[12] These restitutionary consequences of rescission can be explained by reference to the unjust enrichment principle, for without restitution the defendant would become unjustly enriched at the claimant's expense as a result of the contract being rescinded.[13]

(E) THE RELATIONSHIP BETWEEN EXPLOITATION AND WRONGDOING

In some situations where the defendant has obtained a benefit as a result of the exploitation of the claimant, the restitutionary claim may be founded on two alternative restitutionary principles. First, the claimant may be able to establish that one of the recognized grounds of restitution are applicable, so that restitution will be founded on the principle of reversing the defendant's unjust enrichment. Alternatively, the claim may be founded explicitly on the defendant's wrongdoing. This is particularly true where the defendant is a fiduciary and exploits his or her position at the expense of the claimant. This will constitute a breach of fiduciary duty for which a number of remedies are available, including restitution.[14] In such circumstances the claimant may bring alternative claims founded on unjust enrichment and wrongdoing, although the claimant will need to elect between them once judgment has been given.[15]

2. UNDUE INFLUENCE

(A) THE ESSENCE OF UNDUE INFLUENCE AS A GROUND OF RESTITUTION

(i) Establishing Undue Influence

Undue influence is an equitable ground of restitution which applies where the defendant is in a relationship of trust and confidence or a relationship of ascendancy and dependency with the claimant,[16] and the defendant abuses that relationship to induce the claimant to transfer a benefit to him or her, or the defendant is presumed to have abused that relationship to induce the transfer of a benefit. It follows that there are two ways of establishing undue influence, by actual abuse of a relationship of influence or by presumed

---

[10] Save where the contract is already void, for example by virtue of illegality. See p 286, below.

[11] On rescission generally see p 21, above. Rescission is subject to the usual bars of affirmation, lapse of time, intervention of third parties, and counter-restitution being impossible.

[12] *O'Sullivan v Management Agency and Music Ltd* [1985] QB 428. See also *Cheese v Thomas* [1994] 1 WLR 129 and *Mahoney v Purnell* [1996] 3 All ER 61.

[13] See p 24, above.   [14] See p 275, below and Chapter 19.   [15] See p 438, below.

[16] *Royal Bank of Scotland plc v Etridge (No 2)* [2002] 2 AC 773, 795 (Lord Nicholls); *National Commercial Bank (Jamaica) Ltd v Hew* [2003] UKPC 51. Where there is exploitation but no relationship of influence between the parties, a transaction may be set aside on the alternative ground of the defendant's unconscionable conduct. See p 278, below.

abuse of such a relationship.[17] Lewison has argued, extra-judicially, that there is only one type of undue influence, actual undue influence, which must be proved by the claimant with or without the aid of evidential presumptions.[18] That is correct but, if only for ease of exposition, it is helpful to distinguish between two different ways of establishing undue influence, all the time bearing in mind that there is only one single ground, namely that there is a relationship which is capable of giving rise to the necessary influence and that this influence had been unduly exerted by the defendant.[19] In *Daniel v Drew*[20] Ward LJ described the 'undue' component of undue influence as involving something being done to twist the claimant's mind. Where undue influence is presumed, the claimant's burden of proving that the influence exerted by the defendant was undue is assisted by reference to an evidential presumption of abuse, which will operate unless the defendant can adduce evidence to rebut it, usually by showing that the claimant had obtained independent advice.[21] The essence of establishing undue influence was helpfully summarized by Morgan J in *Annulment Funding Co Ltd v Cowey*:[22]

> an issue as to whether there was undue influence involves an issue of fact. The party asserting that there has been undue influence can call direct evidence which supports such a finding. Alternatively, that party can call evidence of other matters which justify the inference that undue influence was used. Either way, the party is attempting to prove the fact of undue influence.

(ii) The Rationale of Undue Influence as a Ground of Restitution

Undue influence constitutes a ground of restitution because the effect of the abuse of the defendant's relationship of influence with the claimant is that the claimant's decision to transact with the defendant cannot be regarded as freely exercised.[23] This was well expressed by Eldon LC in *Huguenin v Baseley*,[24] who said that the 'question is not whether [the claimant] knew what she was doing, had done, or proposed to do, but how the intention was produced'. Consequently, where the claimant has been induced to transact with the defendant by undue influence, the claimant's intention to enter into the transaction can be regarded as vitiated. The policy behind undue influence as a ground of restitution is to protect the vulnerable from exploitation by those who are in a stronger position than themselves,[25] rather than a policy to set aside transactions on the ground of the claimant's folly, imprudence or lack of foresight.[26] The essence of undue influence was elegantly summarized by Ward LJ in *Daniel v Drew*:[27]

> in all cases of undue influence the critical question is whether or not the persuasion or the advice, in other words the influence, has invaded the free volition of the donor to accept or

---

[17] *Allcard v Skinner* (1887) 36 Ch D 145, 171 (Cotton LJ).

[18] K Lewison, 'Under the Influence' [2011] RLR 1.

[19] *Royal Bank of Scotland plc v Etridge (No 2)* [2002] 2 AC 773, 795 (Lord Nicholls); *National Commercial Bank (Jamaica) Ltd v Hew* [2003] UKPC 51.

[20] [2005] EWCA Civ 507, [2005] WTLR 808, [31].   [21] Ibid. See p 263, below.

[22] [2010] EWCA Civ 711, [50].

[23] *National Westminster Bank plc v Morgan* [1985] AC 686, 705 (Lord Scarman), relying on a dictum of Lindley LJ in *Allcard v Skinner* (1887) 36 Ch D 145, 182. See also *Royal Bank of Scotland plc v Etridge (No 2)* [2002] 2 AC 773, 795 (Lord Nicholls); *Hammond v Osborn* [2002] EWCA Civ 885, [2002] WTLR 1125, [60] (Ward LJ); *Hurley v Darjan Estate Co plc* [2012] EWHC 189 (Ch), [2012] 1 WLR 1782, [40] (Miss Geraldine Andrews QC).   [24] (1807) 14 Ves Jun 273, 300; 33 ER 526, 536.

[25] *Royal Bank of Scotland plc v Etridge (No 2)* [2002] 2 AC 773, 795 (Lord Nicholls).

[26] *Allcard v Skinner* (1887) 36 Ch D 145, 183 (Lindley LJ).

[27] [2005] EWCA Civ 507, [2005] WTLR 807, [36].

reject the persuasion or advice or withstand the influence. The donor may be led but she must not be driven and her will must be the offspring of her own volition, not a record of someone else's. There is no undue influence unless the donor if she were free and informed could say 'This is not my wish but I must do it'.

(iii) Is Undue Influence Claimant- or Defendant-Oriented?

There has been much discussion as to whether undue influence is preferably treated as a ground of restitution which is claimant- or defendant-oriented. If it is claimant-oriented, the justification for its existence is that the effect of the undue influence is to impair the claimant's capacity to make decisions, so that his or her intention to transfer a benefit to the defendant can be regarded as vitiated.[28] If undue influence is defendant-oriented, it is justified as a ground of restitution by virtue of the defendant's conduct which can variously be described as 'wicked' or simply 'unconscionable'.[29] This was recognized by Lord Millett in *National Commercial Bank (Jamaica) Ltd v Hew*, in delivering the opinion of the Privy Council, who said that undue influence[30] 'arises whenever one party has acted unconscionably by exploiting the influence to direct the conduct of another which he has obtained from the relationship between them'.

But whether undue influence is a claimant- or defendant-oriented ground of restitution is ultimately a sterile debate, because it can be characterized as both. Undue influence should principally be treated as impairing the claimant's ability to exercise a free choice to enter into the transaction, since this is consistent with other grounds of restitution such as mistake and duress which similarly result in a vitiated intent to participate in the transaction. But it is dangerous to conclude from this that undue influence is entirely claimant-oriented, since this implies that the nature of the defendant's conduct is not relevant to the identification of undue influence. That is incorrect. To establish undue influence the claimant must prove, with or without the benefit of presumptions, some degree of responsibility for the undue influence on the part of the defendant. Consequently, undue influence can be considered to be both defendant- and claimant-oriented and nothing can usefully be gained from treating them as being either one or the other.

(iv) Is Undue Influence a Form of Wrongdoing?

It has sometimes been suggested that, where the claimant transferred a benefit to the defendant as a result of undue influence, the defendant can be considered to have committed a wrong. If this is correct, it follows that the restitutionary claim could be founded on the wrong rather than on the defendant's unjust enrichment. There is not, however, any justification for treating undue influence as a wrong, since it does not require proof of fault on the part of the defendant, neither does it involve any breach of duty.[31] But, despite this, there are cases which have characterized the person who unduly influenced the claimant as a wrongdoer.[32] Further, the emphasis in *National Commercial Bank (Jamaica) Ltd v Hew*[33] on unconscionable exploitation suggests that undue influence

---

[28] Birks and Chin, 'On the Nature of Undue Influence', 57.

[29] See R Bigwood, 'Undue Influence: "Impaired Consent" or "Wicked Exploitation"?' (1996) 16 OJLS 503.

[30] *National Commercial Bank (Jamaica) Ltd v Hew* [2003] UKPC 51.

[31] PBH Birks, 'Rights, Wrongs and Remedies' (2000) OJLS 1. See *Pesticcio v Niersmans* [2004] EWCA Civ 372, [20] (Mummery LJ).

[32] *Barclays Bank plc v O'Brien* [1994] AC 180, 196 (Lord Browne-Wilkinson) and *Royal Bank of Scotland plc v Etridge (No 2)* [2001] UKHL 44, [2002] 2 AC 773, 796 (Lord Nicholls of Birkenhead), 820 (Lord Hobhouse). See also *Allcard v Skinner* (1887) 36 Ch D 145, 171 (Cotton LJ).

[33] [2002] UKPC 65.

is being treated as a wrong involving fault.[34] This is even more apparent in the decision of the Court of Appeal in *Yorkshire Bank plc v Tinsley*,[35] where Peter Gibson LJ described undue influence as an 'equitable wrong'. In many cases it will not matter whether the claim is treated as being founded on a wrong or unjust enrichment, save that the emphasis on the wrong may influence what needs to be proved to establish the claim, by focusing on notions of fault, and it may also affect the determination of the remedy which is available, such that the defendant may be required to disgorge all profits made or to compensate the claimant for loss suffered. But, even if undue influence is eventually treated as a form of wrongdoing, there should continue to be a strict liability form of undue influence which triggers a restitutionary claim in unjust enrichment.

(B) ACTUAL UNDUE INFLUENCE

A crucial distinction needs to be drawn between two grounds of restitution which are recognized in Equity, although they are often both called undue influence. The first ground arises where the defendant compels the claimant to pay a sum of money or to enter into a contract as a result of lawful threats. This ground is founded upon the principle of compulsion, rather than exploitation, and for this reason it is analysed in Chapter 10. Since the essential feature of this ground is that the defendant has pressurized the claimant, it should properly be called 'undue pressure'[36] to distinguish it from undue influence. The other ground of restitution, which is called actual undue influence, is concerned with those cases where the defendant is shown to have unfairly exploited a position of influence over the claimant. This ground of restitution is properly treated as founded on the exploitation principle.[37] That actual undue influence is not founded on the principle of compulsion was recognized by Millett LJ in *Dunbar Bank plc v Nadeem*,[38] who stated that 'neither coercion, nor pressure, nor deliberate concealment is a necessary element in a case of actual undue influence'.

(i) Establishing Actual Undue Influence

To establish actual undue influence the claimant must show that a number of conditions have been satisfied. These conditions were identified by the Court of Appeal in *Bank of Credit and Commerce International SA v Aboody*.[39]

> (1) The defendant[40] must have had the ability to influence the claimant. This will require evidence that the relationship between the parties was such that the claimant trusted and had confidence in the defendant. This is illustrated by *Morley v Laughnan*,[41] where it was held that the deceased had become completely dependent on the defendant, who had converted the deceased to become a member

---

[34] See PBH Birks, 'Undue Influence as Wrongful Exploitation' (2004) 120 LQR 34.

[35] [2004] EWCA Civ 816, [2004] 1 WLR 2380, 2389. See also *Chater v Mortgage Agency Services Number Two Ltd* [2003] EWCA Civ 490, [2004] 1 P and CR 4, [20] (Scott-Baker LJ).

[36] *Lloyd's Bank Ltd v Bundy* [1975] QB 326, 338 (Lord Denning MR).

[37] *R v Attorney-General for England and Wales* [2002] UKPC 22.

[38] [1998] 3 All ER 876, 883.

[39] [1990] 1 QB 923, 967. The Court of Appeal characterized actual undue influence as 'Class 1', to distinguish it from presumed undue influence, which was characterized as 'Class 2'. The House of Lords in *Royal Bank of Scotland plc v Etridge (No 2)* [2001] UKHL 44, [2002] 2 AC 773 made no reference to this numerical characterization and the preferable view now that there is only one ground of undue influence, albeit that elements of the ground may be established with reference to presumptions. See p 257, above.

[40] Or, where relevant, a third party who induced the claimant to transact with the defendant. See p 269, below.   [41] [1893] 1 Ch 736.

of an exclusive and secluded religious sect, known as 'The Exclusive Brethren'. The deceased was found to have been particularly susceptible to influence, being impressionable, physically weak, highly strung, and morbidly religious. The ability of the defendant to influence the deceased was so extreme that he became the deceased's temporal and spiritual adviser and even regulated his diet and medicine.

(2) The defendant must have exercised this influence over the claimant. This will require evidence that the defendant had actually dominated the claimant. This was described by Sir Eric Sachs in *Lloyd's Bank Ltd v Bundy*[42] as arising 'when the will of one person has become so dominated by that of another that... "the person was the mere puppet of the dominator"'. It was, however, emphasized in *Aboody* that undue influence did not necessarily depend on proof of some positive act of coercion or pressure being exercised over the claimant; the influence can be more subtle.

(3) The influence must have been exercised unduly,[43] as will be the case where the defendant has victimized the claimant in some way, for example by forcing, tricking, or misleading the claimant into parting with assets or agreeing to part with assets,[44] such as through the deliberate non-disclosure of relevant information.[45] It is not necessary to prove that the defendant intended to injure the claimant. A wide variety of facts can be taken into account to determine whether influence has been exerted unduly, including the vulnerability of the claimant and the forcefulness of the defendant's personality.[46] In *BCCI v Aboody*[47] it was recognized that the exploitation of another's trust to procure them to enter transactions without proper consideration or explanation would involve the exercise of undue influence, because the influenced party's mind was 'a mere channel through which the will of [the other] operates'. The exertion of influence will also be undue where the defendant deliberately exploited his position of influence to gain an advantage at the expense of the claimant,[48] such as the making of an excessive profit.

(4) The undue influence must have caused the claimant to enter into the relevant transaction, and therefore it must have been operating at the time the transaction was entered into.[49] Although it was once suggested that the test of causation is that the influence was a 'but for' cause of the claimant entering the transaction,[50] it has since been recognized that it is sufficient that the undue influence was an operative cause of the claimant's action, by analogy with the test of causation for fraudulent misrepresentation[51] since undue influence can be considered to be a form of fraud.[52] Consequently, a transaction can be avoided for undue influence even if

---

[42] [1975] QB 326, 342.   [43] *Dunbar Bank plc v Nadeem* [1998] 3 All ER 876, 883 (Millett LJ).

[44] See *Allcard v Skinner* (1887) 36 Ch D 145, 181 (Lindley LJ).

[45] *Hewett v First Plus Financial plc* [2010] EWCA Civ 312, [2010] 2 FLR 177 (non-disclosure of affair to wife).

[46] *Daniel v Drew* [2005] EWCA Civ 507; [2005] WTLR 807, [32] (Ward LJ).

[47] [1990] 1 QB 923, 969.

[48] *Royal Bank of Scotland v Etridge (No 2)* [2001] UKHL 44, [2002] 2 AC 773, [9], (Lord Nicholls).

[49] *Thompson v Foy* [2009] EWHC 1076 (Ch), [2010] 1 P and CR 16, [100] (Lewison J).

[50] *BCCI v Aboody* [1990] 1 QB 923, 971 (Slade LJ).   [51] See p 187, above.

[52] *CIBC Mortgages plc v Pitt* [1994] 1 AC 200, 209 (Lord Browne-Wilkinson); *UCB Corporate Services Ltd v Williams* [2002] EWCA Civ 555, [2003] 1 P and CR 12, [86] and [91] (Jonathan Parker LJ); *UCB Group Ltd v Hedworth* [2003] EWCA Civ 1717, [77] (Jonathan Parker LJ); *Hewett v First Plus Financial Group plc* [2010] EWCA Civ 312, [2010] 2 FLR 177, [34] (Briggs J).

the claimant would have entered into the contract had the undue influence not been exercised. It is not necessary to show that the defendant was aware that he or she had exerted undue influence on the claimant.[53]

(ii) The Identification of Undue Influence

The facts of *Aboody* itself illustrate how the requirements for establishing undue influence are applied. In that case the defendant's husband had induced her to execute three charges on the matrimonial home as security for loans to a company in which they both owned shares. The house was registered in the wife's name only. The husband had induced his wife's consent to the execution of the charges by deliberately concealing crucial matters from her. The wife wanted the charges to be set aside on the ground of undue influence. The Court of Appeal accepted that the husband had the capacity to influence his wife since, as she trusted her husband, she habitually signed documents relating to the company without considering their contents. The husband had exercised this influence by inviting his wife to enter into the relevant transactions. This influence was found to have been unduly exercised because the husband had deliberately concealed from his wife the risks involved in the transactions. Finally, the exercise of this undue influence was a sufficient cause of the wife signing the relevant documents, since it was accepted that, if the husband had not unduly influenced his wife, she would not have signed them. Therefore, the four requirements for establishing undue influence were satisfied. But the Court of Appeal went on to hold that there was a fifth requirement, namely that the particular transaction was manifestly and unfairly disadvantageous to the claimant, and since this had not been established on the facts the charges were not set aside.

(iii) The Question of Manifest and Unfair Disadvantage

A requirement that the transaction was manifestly and unfairly disadvantageous to the claimant, as recognized in *Aboody*, involves consideration of whether the transaction itself was unfair, so-called substantive unfairness or contractual imbalance, rather than that the means by which the transaction was procured were unfair, so-called procedural unfairness.[54] This requirement of manifest disadvantage was subsequently rejected by the House of Lords in *CIBC Mortgages plc v Pitt*.[55] It might be thought that a requirement of manifest disadvantage is necessary before undue influence can be established since, without it, there is insufficient evidence of unacceptable exploitation of the claimant by the defendant. It is true that the fact that the transaction itself was manifestly disadvantageous may be of some evidential significance in establishing undue influence, since the terms of the transaction might assist the court in determining whether there was procedural unfairness. For example, the more unreasonable the terms of the agreement the less likely it is that the claimant would have freely agreed to them.[56] But there could still be cases where the terms of the particular transaction are perfectly reasonable but the defendant will still have unacceptably taken advantage of the claimant's weaker position. This is illustrated by the facts of *CIBC Mortgages plc v Pitt* itself, where a husband obtained his wife's consent to using their home, which was registered in their joint names, as security for a loan from a mortgage company. The House of Lords accepted that the husband had actually used undue influence to procure his wife's consent and so, as against him, the transaction was

---

[53] *Papous v Gibson-West* [2004] EWHC 396.   [54] See *Hart v O'Connor* [1985] AC 1000, 1018, PC.
[55] [1994] 1 AC 200.
[56] See *Royal Bank of Scotland plc v Etridge (No 2)* [2001] UKHL 44, [2002] 2 AC 773, 796 (Lord Nicholls of Birkenhead).

invalid.[57] It made no difference that the terms of the transaction itself were perfectly fair. The transaction was in principle invalid simply because of the methods to which the husband had resorted to procure the consent of his wife. The House of Lords was therefore correct to reject a requirement that the claimant must show that the transaction itself was manifestly disadvantageous before it is possible to conclude that there had been undue influence.

This rejection of manifest disadvantage as a distinct requirement of undue influence means that the true nature of this ground of restitution becomes apparent. This ground is invoked, not because the terms of the transaction are unfair, but rather because the means by which the defendant procured the claimant's consent to the transaction is regarded as unfair. Consequently, undue influence is concerned with the procedure by which the claimant consented to the transaction and not with the substance of the transaction itself. The essence of actual undue influence was encapsulated in an important dictum of Lord Browne-Wilkinson in the *Pitt* case:

> Actual undue influence is a species of fraud. Like any other victim of fraud, a person who has been induced by undue influence to carry out a transaction which he did not freely and knowingly enter into is entitled to have that transaction set aside as of right ... The effect of the wrongdoer's conduct is to prevent the wronged party from bringing a free will and properly informed mind to bear on the proposed transaction which accordingly must be set aside in equity as a matter of justice.[58]

Drawing an analogy with fraud also supports the argument that it should be sufficient that the undue influence was a contributory cause of the claimant transferring a benefit to the defendant, since that is the test of causation which applies when the defendant fraudulently induced the claimant to transfer a benefit by mistake.[59]

(C) USE OF PRESUMPTIONS TO ESTABLISH UNDUE INFLUENCE

(i) The Essential Features of the Evidential Presumption

Sometimes it will not be possible for the claimant to show that he or she was actually unduly influenced to enter into a transaction with the defendant or to transfer a benefit to the defendant. Instead, the circumstances of the case may be such that it will be possible to infer by means of a presumption that the defendant's influence was abused and this caused the claimant to enter into a contract with the defendant or to transfer a benefit. Restitution is justified in these circumstances, not because the defendant has been proved to have exploited the claimant, but because he or she is presumed to have done so.[60] Once undue influence is presumed the defendant must seek to rebut the presumption by adducing evidence that undue influence was not the cause of the claimant's actions.[61] If the presumption is rebutted, the claimant will not have established undue influence and so restitution will not be awarded.

The presumption of undue influence will only operate when two conditions are satisfied.[62] First, the claimant must have placed trust and confidence in the defendant in

---

[57] Whether the husband's undue influence affected the mortgage company was a separate question. See p 269, below.

[58] *CIBC Mortgages plc v Pitt* [1994] 1 AC 200, 209.   [59] See p 187, above.

[60] *National Westminster Bank plc v Morgan* [1985] AC 686, 704 (Lord Scarman).

[61] *Allcard v Skinner* (1887) 36 Ch D 145, 170 (Cotton LJ).

[62] *Royal Bank of Scotland plc v Etridge (No 2)* [2001] UKHL 44, [2002] 2 AC 773, 796 (Lord Nicholls of Birkenhead); *Turkey v Awadh* [2005] EWCA Civ 382, [2005] 2 P and CR 29, [38]–[39] (Chadwick LJ).

respect of matters such as the management of the claimant's financial affairs.[63] Secondly, the transaction must be such that it calls for an explanation. Since the satisfaction of both tests means that the claimant is presumed to have been induced by undue influence to have entered into a transaction or transferred a benefit to the defendant, there is no separate question of causation to be examined. Indeed, it is because it will sometimes be difficult or impossible for the claimant to prove that he or she had been induced to enter into the transaction as a result of undue influence that there is a role for an evidential presumption of undue influence.

(ii) Relationships of Influence

A relationship of influence is one where the claimant has placed his or her trust and confidence in the defendant so that the defendant is in a position which enables him or her to influence the claimant to enter into the particular transaction without necessarily dominating the claimant.[64] There are two methods for ascertaining which relationships will trigger the presumption.[65] The first requires the relationship to fall within a recognized group of relationships which are always presumed to be relationships where the claimant is under the defendant's influence;[66] the second method requires a relationship of trust and confidence to be established with reference to the particular facts of the case.

(1) Recognized Relationships of Influence

Where the relationship between the parties is recognized by law as being a relationship of influence, it is sufficient that the claimant establishes that his or her relationship with the defendant falls within one of these established categories without any need to prove that he or she placed trust and confidence in the defendant. So, for example, it will always be presumed that a parent has influence over his or her minor child,[67] that a guardian has influence over his or her ward,[68] and that a doctor has influence over his or her patient.[69] Other relationships have been treated as presumed relationships of influence, notably that a solicitor has influence over his or her client,[70] and that a trustee has influence over his or her beneficiary,[71] but such cases are better treated as involving an abuse of a fiduciary relationship of confidence, with restitution founded on wrongdoing rather than unjust enrichment.[72] Crucially, the relationship between a husband and wife is not a relationship which falls within these established categories of influence,[73] although a relationship of

---

[63] The presumption is not limited to where the defendant manages the claimant's financial affairs: *Thompson v Foy* [2009] EWHC 1076 (Ch), [2010] 1 P and CR 16, [114] (Lewison J).

[64] *Goldsworthy v Brickell* [1987] Ch 338, 401 (Nourse LJ).

[65] *National Commercial Bank (Jamaica) Ltd v Hew* [2003] UKPC 51.

[66] For the valid criticism of the recognition of these irrebuttable presumptions of influence as the product of a very different social context, see Lewison [2011] RLR 1, 9.

[67] *Lancashire Loans Ltd v Black* [1934] 1 KB 380. Where the child has passed the age of majority it seems that there will be an automatic presumption of influence for a short time afterwards and thereafter a relationship of influence will need to be established on the particular facts of the case: ibid, 419 (Greer LJ). See also *Bainbrigge v Browne* (1880) 18 Ch D 188.

[68] *Hatch v Hatch* (1804) 9 Ves 292, 32 ER 615.

[69] *Mitchell v Homfray* (1881) 8 QBD 587; *Radcliffe v Price* (1902) 18 TLR 466.

[70] *Wright v Carter* [1903] 1 Ch 27.   [71] *Ellis v Barker* (1870) LR 7 Ch App 104.

[72] See p 275, below, and Chapter 19.

[73] *National Westminster Bank plc v Morgan* [1985] AC 686, 703 (Lord Scarman). See also *Barclays Bank plc v O'Brien* [1994] 1 AC 180, 190 (Lord Browne-Wilkinson) and *Royal Bank of Scotland plc v Etridge (No 2)* [2001] UKHL 44, [2002] 2 AC 773, 797 (Lord Nicholls of Birkenhead).

influence might be identified from the particular facts of the case.[74] Somewhat surprisingly, however, in *Leeder v Stevens*[75] it was held that the relationship between fiancé and fiancée was a recognized relationship of influence and, even more controversially, so was an adulterous relationship between a man and his mistress who were in a long relationship and who contemplated marriage to each other in the future. This is a particularly controversial decision bearing in mind that the relationship between husband and wife is treated as factual relationship of influence. The same should be the case for an engaged couple and others who are in a sexual relationship.[76]

Where the relationship is one of the recognized relationships of influence there is an irrebuttable presumption of influence, but it must still be established that this influence is undue by the claimant establishing that the transaction requires explanation.[77]

(2) Factual Relationship of Influence

If the relationship between the claimant and the defendant does not fall within one of the recognized relationships of influence, the claimant must prove that his or her relationship with the defendant was such that the claimant placed such a degree of trust and confidence in the defendant that the claimant was under the defendant's influence, so that the defendant could take advantage of the claimant.[78] The relationship of influence might even arise during the transaction which the claimant is seeking to set aside.[79] Such factual relationships of influence have been identified in a wide variety of different contexts. For example, such a relationship has been found to exist between a housekeeper and her elderly employer,[80] between a junior employee and her employer's agent,[81] between a farm manager and the elderly owner of the farm,[82] between a mother superior and a nun in her convent,[83] and between a soldier and his commanding officer.[84] Such a relationship has even been recognized between a bank and a potential guarantor of debts owed to the bank, where the assistant bank manager had gone beyond the normal commercial role of the bank and had advised on general matters relating to the wisdom of a particular transaction.[85] But it does not follow from the fact that relationships of influence have previously been recognized in these situations that all similar relationships can be treated as relationships of influence; everything turns on the facts of the particular case. For example, in *National Westminster Bank plc v Morgan*[86] the House of Lords held that

---

[74] Similarly the relationship between aunt and nephew is not a recognized relationship of influence: *Randall v Randall* [2004] EWHC 2258 (Ch).

[75] [2005] EWCA Civ 50.

[76] See N Enonchong, 'The Irrebuttable Presumption of Influence and the Relationship Between Fiancé and Fiancée' (2005) 121 LQR 567.

[77] *Attorney-General v R* [2003] UKPC 22, [22] (Lord Hoffmann). See p 266, below.

[78] *Re Brocklehurst* [1978] Ch 14.

[79] *Turkey v Awadh* [2005] EWCA Civ 382, [2005] P and CR 29, [10] (Buxton LJ).

[80] *Re Craig* [1971] Ch 95.

[81] *Crédit Lyonnais Bank Nederland NV v Burch* [1997] 1 All ER 144.

[82] *Goldsworthy v Brickell* [1987] Ch 378. See also *O'Sullivan v Management Agency and Music Ltd* [1985] QB 428 where a relationship of influence was identified between a manager and a young singer-songwriter. Since the relationship was also characterized as a fiduciary relationship the case is better regarded as one involving abuse of a fiduciary relationship rather than undue influence. See Chapter 19.

[83] *Allcard v Skinner* (1887) 36 Ch D 145.

[84] *R v Attorney-General of England and Wales* [2003] UKPC 22. See J O'Sullivan, 'Who Dares Whinges: Duress, Undue Influence and the SAS' (2003) 62 CLJ 554.

[85] *Lloyd's Bank Ltd v Bundy* [1975] QB 326. See also *Harry v Tate and Lyle Refineries Ltd* [1982] 2 Lloyd's Rep 416, where a so-called 'fiduciary relationship' was identified between an employee and his employer's insurers.   [86] [1985] AC 686.

undue influence could not be presumed between a bank manager and the wife of one of his customers. The court stressed that the relationship between a banker and customer will only trigger the presumption of undue influence in the exceptional case where there is evidence that the relationship between the parties went beyond the normal business relationship of banker and customer.[87]

The most important relationship in practice which may be shown to involve trust and confidence is the relationship between a wife and her husband.[88] As regards such relationships it can never be assumed that, for example, a wife does repose trust and confidence in her husband as regards the management of their mutual financial affairs; this is something which needs to be established on the facts of each case. However, in *Barclays Bank plc v O'Brien*[89] Lord Browne-Wilkinson did suggest that 'the risk of undue influence affecting a voluntary disposition by a wife in favour of a husband is greater than in the ordinary run of cases where no sexual or emotional ties affect the free exercise of the individual's will'.[90] Although it is usually the wife who will be seeking to establish that her husband unduly influenced her, it will sometimes be the husband who seeks to establish that his wife unduly influenced him. This is illustrated by *Simpson v Simpson*[91] where the transfer of property by a husband to his wife was set aside because the husband was increasingly dependent on his wife by virtue of a terminal illness, such that there was a particular relationship of trust and confidence between them.

In determining whether there was a relationship of trust and confidence between the claimant and the defendant, the burden of proof is borne by the claimant, but he or she can adduce evidence of all the circumstances of the case to identify such a relationship. Whilst the terms of the transaction will never be sufficient evidence by itself to establish the necessary relationship, where the relationship between the parties is of a type which might involve trust and confidence, the terms of the transaction will be of particular significance in reaching the conclusion that such a relationship did indeed exist.[92]

(iii) Transaction Requires Explanation

It is not sufficient that the relationship between the parties is such that the claimant can be presumed or proved to have been under the influence of the defendant. The claimant must also show that this influence might have been abused.[93] This requires the claimant to adduce evidence that the transaction between the parties is such that it cannot reasonably be explained by the relationship.[94]

The old test to establish this required proof that the transaction was manifestly and unfairly disadvantageous to the claimant.[95] The new test involves a similar element of disadvantage, but this is judged with regard to any disadvantage arising from the transaction.

---

[87] As occurred in *Lloyd's Bank Ltd v Bundy* [1975] QB 326.

[88] *Royal Bank of Scotland plc v Etridge (No 2)* [2001] UKHL 44, [2002] 2 AC 773. See also relationships with an elderly person: *Hammond v Osborn* [2002] EWCA Civ 885. See generally F Burns, 'The Elderly and Undue Influence *Inter Vivos*' (2003) 23 LS 251 and B Sloan, 'Due Rewards of Undue Influence?—Property Transfers Benefiting Informal Carers' [2011] RLR 37.

[89] [1994] 1 AC 180, 191.

[90] Cf *Crédit Lyonnais Bank Nederland NV v Burch* [1997] 1 All ER 144, 155 (Millet LJ).

[91] [1992] 1 FLR 601.

[92] *Crédit Lyonnais Bank Nederland NV v Burch* [1997] 1 All ER 144, 154–5 (Millet LJ).

[93] *National Commercial Bank (Jamaica) Ltd v Hew* [2003] UKPC 51.

[94] *Royal Bank of Scotland plc v Etridge (No 2)* [2001] UKHL 44, [2002] 2 AC 773, 796 (Lord Nicholls); *Chater v Mortgage Agency Services Number Two Ltd* [2003] EWCA Civ 490, [30] (Scott Baker LJ).

[95] *National Westminster Bank plc v Morgan* [1985] AC 686.

This is an objective test,[96] which is applied by considering whether an ordinary person would not have entered into the transaction unless he or she had been unduly influenced to do so,[97] having regard to such matters as the nature of the relationship between the parties, their respective circumstances and the nature of the transaction.

The operation of the transaction requiring explanation test is illustrated by *Royal Bank of Scotland v Etridge (No 2)* itself, where the House of Lords recognized that, in the usual case where a wife becomes a surety for her husband's debts and accepts a charge on her interest in the matrimonial home, this is not necessarily to her disadvantage so as to be explicable only on the basis that the transaction was procured by undue influence. This is because the fortunes of the husband and wife are ordinarily bound up together, so the scheme is for their mutual benefit. Otherwise there is a danger that a wife would become a surety where the scheme is for her benefit, and then, once the couple's fortunes have changed, she might wish to have the charge set aside to preserve the matrimonial home for the benefit of the family. Something in addition to the transaction being a surety transaction must therefore be established before the transaction can be considered to be disadvantageous, such as the particular terms of the transaction.

Evidence that the transaction requires explanation can take many forms. For example, the claimant may have entered into an agreement with the defendant which was inequitable, irrational or unconscionable, such as a sale at an undervalue.[98] A gift is more likely to be regarded as requiring explanation than a contract, simply because the claimant will not have received any consideration in return. As Lord Scarman recognized in *National Westminster Bank plc v Morgan*,[99] 'gifts are transactions in which the donor by parting with his property accepts a disadvantage or a sacrifice'. This will usually be a matter of degree, since the greater the size of the gift the easier it will be to conclude that there was no good motive for the gift being made.[100] Whether the transaction requires explanation is to be judged by reference to the circumstances which existed at the time it was entered into, without reference to subsequent events.[101] A transaction will not be considered to require explanation if it is beneficial to the claimant, even though part of the transaction was not for the claimant's benefit.[102] Failure to obtain independent legal advice by the claimant before entering into the transaction might be relevant evidence in favour of the conclusion that an explanation is required.[103]

The facts of *Cheese v Thomas*[104] illustrate how this requirement of a transaction requiring explanation can be analysed. In this case the claimant's contribution of £43,000 to the purchase of a house, which was registered in the name of someone else, was characterized as disadvantageous by the Court of Appeal, even though the claimant had the right to live rent-free in the house for the rest of his life. The disadvantage arose because there were a number of drawbacks to the transaction, including that the claimant had put all his capital into the house, he could not compel the owner to sell the house if he

---

[96] *Vale v Armstrong* [2004] EWHC 1160; [2004] WTLR 1471, [44] (Evans-Lombe J).

[97] *Turkey v Awadh* [2005] EWCA Civ 382, [2005] 2 P and CR 29, [39] (Chadwick LJ).

[98] *National Westminster Bank plc v Morgan* [1985] AC 686, 704 (Lord Scarman); *Leeder v Stevens* [2005] EWCA Civ 50.

[99] *National Westminster Bank plc v Morgan* [1985] AC 686, 704 (Lord Scarman).

[100] *BCCI v Aboody* [1990] 1 QB 923, 961 (Slade LJ). See also *Allcard v Skinner* (1887) 36 Ch D 145, 185 (Lindley LJ); *Royal Bank of Scotland plc v Etridge (No 2)* [2001] UKHL 44, [2002] 2 AC 773, 798 (Lord Nicholls); *Hammond v Osborn* [2002] EWCA Civ 885 and *Goodchild v Bradley* [2006] EWCA Civ 1868.

[101] *BCCI v Aboody* [1990] 1 QB 923, 964 (Slade LJ).

[102] *Dunbar Bank plc v Nadeem* [1998] 3 All ER 876.

[103] *R v Attorney General for England and Wales* [2002] UKPC 22.

[104] [1994] 1 WLR 129. See also *Bank of Scotland v Bennett* [1997] 1 FLR 801.

wished to recover his contribution and move elsewhere and he was at risk of losing possession if the owner of the house failed to keep up with mortgage payments to the building society. This case illustrates that all the facts need to be examined and the advantages of the transaction need to be carefully balanced against the disadvantages.

A particularly extreme example of a transaction requiring explanation occurred in *Crédit Lyonnais Bank Nederland NV v Burch*,[105] where an employee agreed to give a charge over her flat and an unlimited guarantee for all of her employer's debts. This meant that she had committed herself to a liability which was well beyond her means and she risked the loss of her home and personal bankruptcy for the company which employed her, even though she had no interest in the company either as shareholder or director. Such a transaction was so disadvantageous to the employee that it was characterized as an unconscionable bargain.[106]

With the rejection of manifest disadvantage as a requirement to establish undue influence,[107] it might be considered that there is no longer a role for an equivalent requirement when seeking to establish a presumption of undue influence, but this is not correct. The requirement of a transaction requiring explanation is justifiable in this context simply because of the true function of presumed undue influence. Where the defendant has been shown to have actually unduly influenced the claimant, this is sufficient evidence that the claimant was unable to exercise a free choice to enter into a transaction with the defendant or to transfer a benefit. But, to presume undue influence, the fact that the nature of the relationship between the parties is such that the defendant had influence over the claimant is insufficient evidence to justify the inference that the claimant was unable to exercise a free choice by abuse of that influence. Something else needs to be shown before it is appropriate to make such an inference, and that extra element is evidence that the transaction requires explanation. It is this requirement which makes it possible to presume that the influence was unduly asserted.[108] For, if the claimant has entered into a transaction which requires explanation, this surely suggests that he or she might not have had a free choice to enter into the transaction.

(iv) Rebutting the Presumption of Undue Influence

Once the claimant has established that he or she was under the influence of the defendant and that the transaction requires explanation, undue influence will be presumed so that the ground of restitution will be established, unless the defendant can rebut the presumption. To do this the defendant must show that the transaction 'was the spontaneous act of the [claimant] acting under circumstances which enabled him to exercise an independent will and which justified the Court in holding that [the transaction] was the result of a free exercise of the [claimant's] will'.[109] This raises an issue of causation, since the defendant must show that the claimant entered into the transaction voluntarily and was not induced to do so by the defendant's influence.

---

[105] [1997] 1 All ER 144. See also *Steeples v Lea* [1998] 1 FLR 138.

[106] *Crédit Lyonnais Bank Nederland NV v Burch* [1997] 1 All ER 144, 151 (Nourse LJ). Cf Millett LJ, ibid, 152. On the equitable jurisdiction to relieve against unconscionable bargains, see p 278, below. This jurisdiction could have been relied on in *Burch* without any need to rely on undue influence, but since this had not been pleaded the Court of Appeal was not prepared to base its decision on this basis.

[107] *CIBC Mortgages plc v Pitt* [1994] AC 200. See p 262, above.

[108] *BCCI v Aboody* [1990] 1 QB 923, 957 (Slade LJ).

[109] *Allcard v Skinner* (1887) 36 Ch D 145, 171 (Cotton LJ). In *Zamet v Hyman* [1961] 1 WLR 1442, 1446 Lord Evershed MR said the presumption will only be rebutted if the defendant establishes that the claimant entered into the transaction 'after full, free and informed thought about it'.

Whether the defendant can rebut the presumption of undue influence depends upon all the facts of the case. By far the most common method of rebuttal is by showing that the claimant had received independent advice about the transaction, since if the claimant entered into the transaction even after having received such advice this suggests that the claimant had freely exercised his or her will. The adviser need not be a lawyer,[110] but the adviser must be independent of any influence from the defendant.[111] The advice must be fully informed and competent.[112] This means that the adviser should be qualified to give the advice and must be fully aware of the facts of the case. The function of the adviser is not simply to ensure that the claimant understands the transaction, since the adviser must also be satisfied that the transaction is one which the claimant could sensibly enter into if not improperly influenced. If the adviser is not satisfied of this, he or she should advise the claimant not to enter into the transaction.[113] The presumption will not be rebutted if the claimant had the opportunity to obtain legal advice but failed to avail him or herself of that opportunity. The defendant must show that the claimant did obtain the advice and acted on it, for as Millett LJ has recognized, if it was simply sufficient that the claimant obtained the advice, the influence which produced the claimant's desire to enter into the transaction in the first place would cause the claimant to disregard any advice that he or she should not enter into the transaction.[114] It follows that, if the presumption of undue influence is to be rebutted, it must be shown that the claimant was free from such influence,[115] and simply obtaining independent advice does not show this; the advice must actually be that the transaction is a sensible one for the claimant to enter into. Further, the circumstances in which the advice was given must also be taken into account to determine whether it was adequate to bring home to the claimant the nature and effect of the transaction.[116] Ultimately it is a question of fact whether the advice had the effect of emancipating the claimant from the effect of the influence.[117]

But showing that the claimant has received and acted on independent advice is not the only method of rebutting the presumption of undue influence.[118] The defendant can rely on any available evidence to show that the claimant had acted voluntarily and as a free agent and so rebut the presumption. For example, in *Re Brocklehurst*[119] a majority of the Court of Appeal held that the defendant could rebut the presumption of undue influence by showing that the deceased's gift to him of valuable shooting rights arose from the free and independent exercise of the deceased's will, motivated by the close friendship between the parties. The fact that the defendant's own conduct is unimpeachable is not sufficient to rebut the presumption of undue influence.[120]

(D) UNDUE INFLUENCE AND THIRD PARTIES

It has been assumed so far that the claimant has entered into a transaction or transferred a valuable benefit as a result of the defendant's undue influence, but this is not always the

---

[110] *Inche Noriah v Shaik Allie Bin Omar* [1929] AC 127, 135 (Lord Hailsham LC). [111] Ibid.

[112] *Wright v Carter* [1903] 1 Ch 27.

[113] *Crédit Lyonnais Bank Nederland NV v Burch* [1997] 1 All ER 144, 156 (Millett LJ).

[114] Ibid. Cf *Inche Noriah v Shaik Allie Bin Omar* [1929] AC 127, 135 (Lord Hailsham LC).

[115] *Vale v Armstrong* [2004] EWHC 1160, [2004] WTLR 1471, [55] (Evans-Lombe J).

[116] *Royal Bank of Scotland plc v Etridge (No 2)* [2002] 2 AC 773, 798 (Lord Nicholls).

[117] *Randall v Randall* [2004] EWHC 2258 (Ch), [39] (Judge Bartlett Jones QC). See *Pesticcio v Niersmans* [2004] EWCA Civ 372, [2004] WTLR 699 for a case where the advice from a solicitor was not considered to have emancipated the claimant from the effect of the undue influence.

[118] *Inche Noriah v Shaik Allie Bin Omar* [1929] AC 127. [119] [1978] Ch 14.

[120] *Hammond v Osborn* [2002] EWCA Civ 885, [2002] WTLR 1125, [32] (Nourse LJ); *Jennings v Cairns* [2003] EWCA Civ 1935, [2004] WTLR 361, [40] (Arden LJ).

case. The claimant may, instead, have entered into a transaction with the defendant or transferred a benefit to the defendant as a result of the undue influence of a third party.[121] In such circumstances the claimant's weakness is exploited by the third party and it is necessary to determine which of two innocent parties, the claimant or the defendant, should suffer from this exploitation.[122] Typically this problem has arisen where a husband has induced his wife to act as surety for his debts, or those of his business, by unduly influencing her to execute a charge over the matrimonial home in which she has a proprietary interest and, when the creditor wishes to enforce the charge, the wife argues that it was not valid because of undue influence. Although the third-party problem could arise in all cases where undue influence has been established, regardless of the nature of the relationship between the parties, the case of the husband unduly influencing the wife to enter into a transaction with a bank will be used as the typical model to analyse the law. These were essentially the facts of one of the leading cases in this area, the decision of the House of Lords in *Barclays Bank plc v O'Brien*,[123] save that the wife had been induced to consent to a second mortgage on the family home not because of undue influence, but by reason of the husband's misrepresentation as to the extent and duration of the charge.[124] The fact that the case was concerned with an induced mistake does not make any difference to its application to cases of undue influence. This is because misrepresentation, like undue influence, constitutes behaviour which can vitiate the claimant's intention to transfer a benefit and consequently the effect of both grounds of restitution is the same.

The main difficulty for the analysis of the *O'Brien* principle in a book on the law of restitution is whether the principle has anything to do with the law of restitution generally, and the law of unjust enrichment specifically. The key problem concerns the identification of an enrichment. It is the essence of the law of unjust enrichment that the defendant must have obtained a benefit which has to be restored to the claimant. Where a bank has acquired a security interest in the matrimonial home, or the wife has simply provided a personal guarantee to the bank, as a result of the husband's undue influence, it is possible to conclude that the bank has been enriched by the security interest or the right to sue the wife on the guarantee. But, if the transaction is rescinded for undue influence, the consequence of the rescission is that the bank's rights are eliminated and no tangible benefit is restored to the wife. It has consequently been assumed that the effect of rescission in such circumstances cannot be characterized as restitutionary.[125] Despite this, Lodder[126] has argued that the bank's rights are a legal enrichment and, following the rescission of the transaction for undue influence, restitution occurs, since the bank is deprived of its rights against the matrimonial home and the wife benefits because the matrimonial home is restored to her without the burden of the charge. This is a persuasive analysis.

But, if the wife's claim against the bank is analysed with reference to the law of restitution, it follows that the bank should be able to plead change of position as a defence.

---

[121] See J O'Sullivan, 'Undue Influence and Misrepresentation after *O'Brien*: Making Security Secure' in F Rose (ed), *Restitution and Banking Law* (Oxford: Mansfield Press, 1998), ch 3.

[122] *Barclays Bank plc v O'Brien* [1994] 1 AC 180, 195 (Lord Browne-Wilkinson).

[123] [1994] 1 AC 180.   [124] See p 199, above.

[125] See *National Commercial Bank (Jamaica) Ltd v Hew* [2003] UKPC 51.

[126] AVM Lodder, *Enrichment in the Law of Unjust Enrichment and Restitution* (Oxford: Hart Publishing, 2012), 60. See p 6, above. See also NY Nahan, 'Rescission: A Case for Rejecting the Classical Model?' (1997) Univ WALR 66, 72–3; R Chambers, 'Two Kinds of Enrichment' in R Chambers, C Mitchell, and J Penner (eds), *Philosophical Foundations of the Law of Unjust Enrichment* (Oxford: Oxford University Press, 2009), 259. Cf J O'Sullivan, 'Rescission as a Self-help Remedy: A Critical Analysis' (2000) 59 CLJ 509.

The fact that the bank has lent money to the husband as a result of the wife agreeing to the charge over the matrimonial home certainly looks like a change of position. But none of the cases which have examined this scenario have considered the change of position defence. Instead, whether the bank is able to enforce the charge against the wife depends on whether it has notice of the wife's equity[127] to set the transaction aside and had taken reasonable steps to ensure that the wife fully appreciated the consequences of the particular transaction.[128] If the bank does have such notice and has not acted reasonably to check that the wife is free of undue influence or an induced mistake, the bank cannot be considered to have acted reasonably and so the defence of change of position will not be available to it.[129] If the bank had no notice of the wife's equity, it is able to enforce the transaction despite the undue influence or induced mistake, and this can be rationalized with reference to the fact that, in lending money to the husband, the bank has changed its position so restitution of the right to the wife should be denied.

(E) THE NATURE OF THE RELIEF

(i) Restitution

Once undue influence has been established, and any transaction been set aside, the claimant will recover any benefit which has been transferred to the defendant as a result of the undue influence, but counter-restitution must be made to the defendant as well. In *Smith v Cooper*,[130] where the parties had cohabited in a property which had been purchased in their joint names, it was held that Cooper had contributed to the purchase price of the property as a result of undue influence by Smith. As a consequence, the value of the property was to be divided between the parties proportionate to their contribution to its purchase, with credit being given to Smith for his payments to the cost of renovation of the property and mortgage payments he had made.

(ii) Rescission is Absolute

Where a transaction is rescinded for undue influence it can only be set aside in its entirety and not so that part of the transaction remains valid.[131] Also, the transaction cannot be set aside on terms, for example by setting aside the whole transaction and substituting a new one for it. In *Zamet v Hyman*[132] it was held that the relief for undue influence is confined to setting aside the particular transaction and that the court could not substitute some other, fairer, transaction for it. This approach was endorsed by the Court of Appeal in *TSB Bank plc v Camfield*,[133] where it was held that a mortgage would be set aside completely as a result of a husband's misrepresentation and it would not be treated as valid to the extent

---

[127] Where the relationship between the person who has been unduly influenced and the third party is a standard contractual relationship rather than a suretyship, actual knowledge of the undue influence on the part of the third party is required to deprive that party of their contractual rights: *Darjan Estate Co plc v Huxley (No 2)* [2012] EWHC 189 (Ch), [2012] 1 WLR 1782.

[128] *Royal Bank of Scotland plc v Etridge (No 2)* [2002] 2 AC 773; *Padden v Bevan Ashford (a firm)* [2012] 1 WLR 1759, [2011] EWCA Civ 1616.

[129] See E Bant, *The Change of Position Defence* (Oxford: Hart Publishing, 2009), 155.

[130] [2010] EWCA Civ 722, [2010] 2 FLR 1521.

[131] *National Commercial Bank (Jamaica) Ltd v Huw* [2003] UKPC 51.   [132] [1961] 1 WLR 1442.

[133] [1995] 1 WLR 430. See also *Bank Melli Iran v Samadi-Rad* [1995] 2 FLR 367; *De Molestina v Ponton* [2002] 1 All ER (Comm) 587. In Australia partial rescission is accepted: *Vadasz v Pioneer Concrete (SA) Pty Ltd* (1995) 184 CLR 102 (rescission of guarantee relating to past but not future indebtedness). See L Proksch, 'Rescission on Terms' [1996] RLR 71; J Poole and A Keyser, 'Justifying Partial Rescission in English Law' (2005) 121 LQR 273.

of the maximum liability which the wife had accepted.[134] This general principle against partial rescission and rescission on terms is, however, subject to an apparent exception where rescission is conditional on the defendant making restitution to the claimant and the claimant making counter-restitution to the defendant of any benefits received under the transaction.[135] But this is consistent with rescission operating to set the transaction aside completely and so restore both parties to the position they occupied before entering into the transaction, by ensuring that they return any benefits received, or the value of any benefits received, to the other party.

The apparent reason for the courts' refusal to allow partial rescission or rescission on terms stems from the nature of rescission itself. Rescission is traditionally considered to be a form of self-help. The claimant rescinds the transaction and the only role for the courts is to determine whether the claimant has actually rescinded it or is entitled to do so.[136] There is consequently no scope for any halfway house; either the claimant is or is not entitled to rescind the transaction in question. But this is highly dubious reasoning. The better view is that rescission in Equity does indeed depend on the intervention of the court,[137] and it is the equitable jurisdiction which is engaged where rescission is sought on the ground of undue influence. In the exercise of that jurisdiction the court may be required to value a benefit received so as to secure restitution or counter-restitution, or otherwise rescission will be barred, so why should it not be possible for the court to intervene in other ways through the imposition of terms?[138]

In fact some cases show that rescission on terms is available.[139] The most important of these is *Cheese v Thomas*,[140] where the Court of Appeal set aside a transaction on terms where the transaction had been entered into through the exercise of undue influence. In that case the defendant, who was the claimant's great-nephew, was presumed to have unduly influenced the claimant into entering into a transaction to buy a house, whereby the claimant had contributed all of his capital, amounting to £43,000. The parties had agreed that the claimant would occupy the house for the rest of his life and it would then pass to the defendant, in whose name the house was registered. The balance of the purchase price and expenses, amounting to £40,000 in total, was funded by a building society loan made to the defendant and secured by a mortgage over the property. The defendant was to pay off this loan but he failed to keep up with the mortgage payments and the claimant then sought to set the transaction aside. It was conceded that there was a relationship of trust and confidence between the parties and the court held that the

---

[134] In *Yorkshire Bank plc v Tinsley* [2004] EWCA Civ 816, [2004] 1 WLR 2380, where a replacement mortgage was taken out as a condition of discharging an earlier mortgage which was voidable for undue influence, the replacement mortgage was also voidable, at least where the two mortgages were taken out with the same lender.

[135] See *TSB Bank plc v Camfield* [1995] 1 WLR 430, 434–5 (Nourse LJ). For an example of such conditional rescission see *Midland Bank plc v Greene* [1994] 2 FLR 82 and *Smith v Cooper* [2010] EWCA Civ 722, [2010] 2 FLR 1521.

[136] See *TSB Bank plc v Camfield* [1995] 1 WLR 430, 438 (Roch LJ).

[137] J O'Sullivan, 'Rescission as a Self-Help Remedy: A Critical Analysis'. See p 23, above.

[138] See J Poole and A Keyser, 'Justifying Partial Rescission in English Law', who argue that partial rescission is distinct from the equitable jurisdiction to secure restitution and counter-restitution, since partial rescission is concerned with fulfilling the parties' expectations, where those expectations were not affected by the vitiating factor for which rescission is sought.

[139] In some of the old cases on rescission for mistake the claimant was permitted to rescind the transaction but only on condition that a new contract was offered: *Solle v Butcher* [1950] 1 KB 671 and *Grist v Bailey* [1967] Ch 532. Today, rescission in Equity would not be allowed for mistake in such cases: *Great Peace Shipping Ltd v Tsalviris Salvage (International) Ltd* [2002] EWCA Civ 1407, [2003] AC 679. See p 193, above.

[140] [1994] 1 WLR 129.

transaction was manifestly disadvantageous to the claimant, so it was presumed that the claimant had entered into the transaction as a result of the defendant's undue influence. The court then needed to consider what remedy was appropriate. Since the value of the house had fallen by over £27,500, the real issue for the court was which party should bear this loss. If the orthodox approach to rescission was adopted, the transaction would be set aside in its entirety, so the claimant would recover his contribution to the purchase price plus interest and the defendant would suffer the loss. But the court imposed a condition on rescission, namely that the loss should be apportioned between the parties in proportion to their respective contributions to the purchase price. In reaching this conclusion the court emphasized the importance of characterizing the transaction involved.[141] In this case the transaction did not simply involve a payment by the claimant for the right to occupy the house. Rather, it was a joint venture between the claimant and the defendant, since the parties had agreed to contribute money to buy a house in which they would both have an interest. Since it is a feature of a joint venture that both parties participate equally in the transaction, it was held that the loss arising from the transaction would be apportioned between both of them.

But this identification of a joint venture is difficult to defend. The court emphasized that the parties should be treated as equal participants in the venture, particularly because the defendant was exonerated of any reprehensible behaviour in inducing the claimant to participate. But such a conclusion was not open to the court, simply because it had been presumed that the defendant had unduly influenced the claimant to enter into the transaction and this presumption had not been rebutted. Consequently, the parties should have been treated as unequal participants in the transaction, with the result that the transaction should have been set aside in its entirety. The Court did acknowledge that, had there not been a joint venture, the transaction would have been set aside completely, so that the claimant would have recovered what he had contributed and the defendant would have suffered the loss in value of the property.[142]

A further difficulty with the analysis of rescission in this case arises from the principle that rescission is barred where the claimant has received benefits under a transaction which he or she is unable to restore to the defendant.[143] This was in fact the situation in *Cheese v Thomas* since the claimant had received benefits under the transaction, namely rent-free occupation of the house. This benefit was received at the defendant's expense, since the defendant was the registered owner of the house and the claimant was merely a contractual licensee. Nevertheless, the fact that the claimant received this benefit should not have barred rescission, since courts are prepared to award the defendant an allowance which is assessed by reference to the reasonable value of the benefit received by the claimant, especially in Equity.[144] Since this benefit was the use of the house, it could have been valued and a sum of money equivalent to rent been paid to the defendant. In fact, the Court of Appeal procured this counter-restitution by simply off-setting the rent which the claimant should have paid for occupation against the interest which the defendant should have paid to the claimant on the money which he had received once the house had been sold. This is a highly inaccurate method of securing counter-restitution. The court should simply have valued the rent which the claimant

---

[141] Ibid, 136 (Sir Donald Nichols V-C).

[142] For an alternative analysis of the case as involving an implicit application of the defence of change of position, see M Chen-Wishart, 'Loss-Sharing, Undue Influence and Manifest Disadvantage' (1994) 110 LQR 173. See p 685, below.

[143] See further p 25, above.

[144] See, for example, *O'Sullivan v Management Agency and Music Ltd* [1985] QB 428.

owed and deducted this from the £43,000 plus interest which the defendant owed to the claimant.

In most cases of rescission for undue influence the only term which it is appropriate to impose as a condition for rescission is that the claimant must make counter-restitution to the defendant for any benefits obtained under the transaction. One exceptional circumstance has, however, been recognized where rescission on other terms is possible. This is where part of a complex transaction which was formed in stages was obtained by undue influence, then this part can be severed from the rest, which was not obtained by undue influence, without adding to or modifying the rights and obligations in that remaining part.[145] In most other cases the undue influence will generally taint the whole transaction so there is little scope for imposing terms as a condition for rescinding the transaction, save where this is necessary to achieve counter-restitution.[146]

(iii) Monetary Remedies in Lieu of Rescission

Even though rescission of a contract is the usual remedy following undue influence, and this remedy may often involve payment of money to effect or to complement rescission, it has sometimes been suggested that it is possible to award monetary remedies in lieu of rescission.[147] The key authority which appears to support such an approach is the difficult decision in *Mahoney v Purnell*.[148] In this case a transaction involving the sale of shares by a father-in-law to his son-in-law was liable to be set aside by reason of undue influence, but it was not possible to restore the parties to their original position because the relevant transaction had involved the sale of shares in a company which had subsequently been wound up. It was held that rescission was barred, but the court had a power to award the claimant 'equitable compensation'. Whilst the result of the case is defensible, the reasoning and the terms used are open to criticism. The case has been analysed as one where the court awarded the monetary equivalent of rescission simply because precise restitution was not possible.[149] Whether this is the correct interpretation depends on careful analysis of the underlying cause of action. There are two possibilities.

(1) Abuse of a Fiduciary Relationship

Although the judge focused on the defendant's presumed undue influence of the claimant, it appears that he was treating undue influence as a form of wrongdoing which justified

---

[145] *Barclays Bank plc v Caplan* [1998] 1 FLR 532.

[146] Cf where the claimant entered into a transaction as a result of misrepresentation, where the claimant thought, for example, that he or she had entered into a surety transaction for £5,000 but in fact the transaction was for £50,000. In such circumstances the actual surety transaction should be rescinded but terms could be imposed that a £5,000 surety transaction should be substituted since this is the amount which the claimant actually consented to guarantee. See p 28, above. See further GJ Virgo, 'Undue Influence and Misrepresentation after *O'Brien*: Making Security Secure: A Commentary' in F Rose (ed), *Restitution and Banking Law* (Oxford: Mansfield Press, 1998), 77.

[147] In the same way that damages can be awarded in lieu of rescission for misrepresentation by the Misrepresentation Act 1967, s 2(2) where a contract was induced by innocent or negligent misrepresentation. Although the basis for the assessment of these damages remains unclear (*William Sindall plc v Cambs CC* [1994] 1 WLR 1016), the better view is that these 'damages' are not restitutionary (cf PBH Birks, 'Unjust Factors and Wrongs: Pecuniary Rescission for Undue Influence' [1997] RLR 72, 75), but are a special measure designed to compensate the representee for the loss resulting from his or her inability to obtain rescission: H Beale (ed), *Chitty on Contracts* (31st edn, London: Sweet and Maxwell, 2012), para 6-104. It follows that the effect of s 2(2) is to create a limited statutory wrong of innocent misrepresentation which may be available if the justice of the case so requires.

[148] [1996] 3 All ER 61.

[149] O'Sullivan, 'Rescission as a Self-help Remedy: A Critical Analysis', 510.

the award of a compensatory remedy. The better view, however, is that undue influence can be established without any need to prove the commission of a wrong.[150] In fact, even though the case was treated as involving undue influence, the judge characterized the relationship of the parties as a fiduciary relationship[151] creating fiduciary duties which had been breached. If the claim was founded on the commission of such an equitable wrong, the award of an equitable compensatory remedy is justifiable since the defendant fiduciary is liable to account to the principal for the value of property which he or she no longer holds but which he or she is obliged to return to the claimant. On this reading of the case there was no need to rescind the transaction at all; the case was only concerned with compensation for loss suffered.

(2) Restitution for Undue Influence

Alternatively, the remedy of so-called 'equitable compensation' can be analysed as a restitutionary response to the defendant's unjust enrichment, where the ground of restitution is the undue influence itself. Consequently, the monetary award is not damages at all, since it is not giving effect to rights which arise from the commission of a wrong, but is simply operating to deprive the defendant of a benefit obtained from the undue influence. What the judge was in fact authorizing was restitutionary relief, since the 'equitable compensation' took the form of the claimant recovering from the defendant the value of the shares he had surrendered minus what he had received from the defendant.[152] But on this interpretation there is nothing peculiar about *Mahoney v Purnell* at all. As has been seen, where specific restitution is not possible, Equity will value the benefit received by the defendant and then effect restitution by means of transfer of the value. In other words, the monetary award was not made in lieu of rescission but was a condition of rescission to ensure that the parties were returned to the position they occupied before entering into the transaction.

3. ABUSE OF FIDUCIARY RELATIONSHIPS OF CONFIDENCE

Sometimes the relationship between the claimant and the defendant is such that it is possible to identify a duty of confidence owed by one of the parties to the other. The relationships which are relevant for these purposes are those which can be characterized as fiduciary, such as the relationship between solicitor and client,[153] trustee and beneficiary and agent and principal and other similar relationships.[154] Where there is a transaction between the fiduciary and the principal, it is presumed that the fiduciary exploited the other party and so the burden is on him or her to establish that the transaction was fair[155] and that there has been full disclosure of everything which is or may be material to the

---

[150] See p 257, above.

[151] This is doubtful because the requisite element of dependence was lacking. See p 276, below.

[152] The judge apparently assumed that compensation was the only remedy where the defendant no longer retained the shares which he had acquired from the claimant: *Mahoney v Purnell* [1996] 3 All ER 61, 90. But the remedy which was awarded was assessed by reference to the value of the shares received by the defendant and so can clearly be characterized as restitutionary.   [153] See *Wright v Carter* [1903] 1 Ch 27.

[154] *BCCI v Aboody* [1990] QB 923, 964. See *Financial Institutions Services Ltd v Negril Holdings Ltd* [2004] UKPC 40 where it was recognized that, exceptionally, the relationship between a banker and his or her customer might be characterized as fiduciary, but equitable relief is only available if the relationship has been abused.   [155] *Moody v Cox and Hatt* [1917] 2 Ch 71.

other party's decision to enter into the transaction.[156] Whether the principal was advised to obtain independent and competent advice will be a particularly important consideration in determining whether the transaction was fair. In *Tate v Williamson*[157] Lord Chelmsford LC identified the essential features of this principle:

> Wherever two persons stand in such a [fiduciary] relation that, while it continues, confidence is necessarily reposed by one, and the influence which necessarily grows out of that confidence is possessed by the other, and this confidence is abused, or the influence is exerted to obtain an advantage at the expense of the confiding party, the person so availing himself of his position will not be permitted to retain the advantage, although the transaction could not have been impeached if no such confidential relation had existed.[158]

(A) THE IDENTIFICATION OF FIDUCIARY RELATIONSHIPS OF CONFIDENCE

The terms 'fiduciary relationship' and 'relationships of confidence' have been used indiscriminately in some cases which should properly have been treated as involving undue influence,[159] whereas in other cases the courts have relied on undue influence when the doctrine of abuse of fiduciary relationships of confidence was more appropriate. Although the line between undue influence and abuse of a fiduciary relationship of confidence is a fine one, essentially a distinction needs to be drawn between those relationships where the defendant can influence the claimant and those where the claimant is totally dependent on the defendant. The doctrine of abuse of fiduciary relationships of confidence will only apply as regards the latter group of relationships.

(B) THE RELATIONSHIP BETWEEN UNDUE INFLUENCE AND ABUSE OF FIDUCIARY RELATIONSHIPS OF CONFIDENCE

The boundary between the doctrine of abuse of fiduciary relationships of confidence and undue influence is uncertain,[160] particularly because where there is a relationship of confidence there will also be the potential for undue influence. So, typically both may be pleaded on the same set of facts. But although the two principles overlap, they do not coincide.[161] The doctrine of abuse of fiduciary relationships of confidence has two important advantages over undue influence. First, it is not necessary to show that the claimant was, or might be, under the influence of the defendant. Thus, in *Moody v Cox and Hatt*[162] a transaction between a solicitor and his client was set aside by reason of the solicitor's non-disclosure of material details about the transaction, and it was irrelevant that the claimant was an independent man of business who would not have looked to the defendant for advice. All that needed to be established was that there was a fiduciary relationship between the parties and that the fiduciary had breached his duties by non-disclosure. The second advantage which the doctrine of abuse of a fiduciary relationship of

---

[156] *Demerara Bauxite Co Ltd v Hubbard* [1923] AC 673.

[157] (1866) LR 2 Ch App 55.   [158] Ibid, 61.

[159] *National Westminster Bank plc v Morgan* [1985] AC 686, 703 (Lord Scarman). For an example of indiscriminate use of these terms see *Lloyds Bank Ltd v Bundy* [1975] QB 326, 341 (Sir Eric Sachs) and *Roche v Sherrington* [1982] 1 WLR 599.

[160] *CICB Mortgages plc v Pitt* [1994] 1 AC 200, 209 (Lord Browne-Wilkinson).

[161] *BCCI v Aboody* [1990] QB 923, 962. In *Moody v Cox and Hatt* [1917] 2 Ch 71, 79 Lord Cozens-Hardy MR specifically held that equitable relief was awarded by reason of a breach of a relationship of confidence and not for undue influence.   [162] [1917] 2 Ch 71.

confidence has, at least where the claimant seeks to rely on the presumption of undue influence, is that there is no need to show that the transaction requires explanation. Once the relationship of confidence has been identified, the need for an explanation is assumed and the burden is on the fiduciary to show that the transaction was not unfair to the claimant. The heavy burden of proving that the transaction is fair is shifted where there is a relationship of confidence simply because of the potential for abuse of such relationships by the fiduciary.[163]

The different roles of undue influence and breach of a fiduciary relationship of confidence is illustrated by an example which was suggested by the Court of Appeal in *BCCI v Aboody*,[164] involving an 'old lady who was induced by her solicitor under strong pressure to sell him a large and inconvenient family home at full market value'. Although it might be possible to establish that the old lady had actually been unduly influenced by the solicitor to sell him her house, it would be much easier for her to base her claim on abuse of a fiduciary relationship of confidence, since then she would only need to establish that the solicitor owed her fiduciary duties, which is obvious, which he had breached by transacting with her. There would be no need to show that she was unduly influenced by her solicitor. The burden is then on the solicitor to establish that the transaction was perfectly fair and that he or she had made full disclosure to the old lady.

(C) ABUSE OF FIDUCIARY RELATIONSHIPS OF CONFIDENCE WITHIN THE LAW OF RESTITUTION

The place of the doctrine of abuse of fiduciary relationships of confidence within the law of restitution itself remains unclear. The better view is that, where the fiduciary has abused his or her relationship of confidence, this constitutes an equitable wrong on the part of the defendant, so the restitutionary claim will be founded on the wrong rather than the unjust enrichment principle. Therefore, this principle is fully considered in the context of restitution for equitable wrongs.[165] Whether a particular restitutionary claim is founded on unjust enrichment or wrongdoing will be important, since where the claim is based on wrongdoing the remedies are not necessarily restitutionary[166] and the operation of the defences may differ.

That the doctrine of abuse of fiduciary relationships of confidence is better treated as founded on wrongdoing rather than the reversal of the defendant's unjust enrichment is illustrated by *O'Sullivan v Management Agency and Music Ltd*,[167] where the claimant had entered into an exclusive management agreement with the defendant. Although the defendant had conceded that the agreement was voidable because the relationship between the parties was such that undue influence was presumed, the approach adopted by the Court of Appeal suggests that the case is better regarded as one where the restitutionary action was founded on the defendant's wrongdoing, namely breach of fiduciary duty. The Court recognized that the relationship between the parties was a fiduciary relationship and, if the defendant had not conceded that undue influence could be presumed, the existence of this fiduciary relationship would have meant that the transaction could have been presumed to be unfair. The burden would then have been on the defendant to prove that the agreement was fair and reasonable.[168] The defendant would not have been able to show this, because the terms of the agreement were such that

---

[163] Ibid, p 963. See also *CIBC Mortgages plc v Pitt* [1994] 1 AC 200, 209 (Lord Browne-Wilkinson).
[164] [1990] QB 923, 962.   [165] See p 502, below.   [166] See *Mahoney v Purnell* [1996] 3 All ER 61.
[167] [1985] QB 428.   [168] This was in fact recognized by Dunn LJ, ibid, 463.

the defendant was not in fact obliged to do any work for the claimant and because the defendant had not advised the claimant to obtain independent advice.

4. UNCONSCIONABLE CONDUCT

The recognition of undue influence as a ground of restitution has sometimes been justified on the ground that it involves unconscionable conduct on the part of the defendant.[169] Whilst unconscionable conduct may be presumed where a relationship of trust and confidence has been abused, it is incorrect to assume that restitution is justified for this reason where the claimant relies on undue influence. This is because undue influence is principally, but not completely, a claimant-oriented ground of restitution, in the sense that restitution is justified because the effect of the undue influence is that the claimant was unable to exercise a free choice as to whether or not to transact with the defendant, and there is no need specifically to prove that the defendant had acted unconscionably. There is, however, evidence of another equitable ground of restitution which, whilst founded on the principle of exploitation, is primarily defendant-oriented, in the sense that it will only be established where the defendant is considered to have been at fault.[170] This is the ground of unconscionable conduct. There is a further difference between this ground of restitution and undue influence in that unconscionable conduct does not depend on the identification of an existing relationship of influence or dependency between the claimant and the defendant.[171]

The essential features of unconscionable conduct was identified by Lord Hardwicke in *Earl of Chesterfield v Janssen*[172] as involving:

> fraud presumed or inferred from the circumstances or conditions of the parties contracting: weakness on one side, usury on the other, or extortion or advantage taken of that weakness. There has always been the appearance of fraud from the nature of the bargain.

So a transaction[173] will be voidable in Equity for reasons of unconscionable conduct, or a benefit transferred can be recovered, where the defendant has unconscionably exploited his or her superior bargaining position to the detriment of the claimant who is in a much weaker position.

(A) THE GENERAL PRINCIPLE OF UNCONSCIONABLE CONDUCT

In *Lloyd's Bank Ltd v Bundy*[174] Lord Denning MR recognized a general principle of inequality of bargaining power, which he said arose where the claimant:

> without independent advice, enters into a contract upon terms which are very unfair or transfers property for a consideration which is grossly inadequate, when his bargaining

---

[169] See N Bamforth, 'Unconscionability as a Vitiating Factor' [1995] LMCLQ 538; D Capper, 'Unconscionable Bargains' (2010) LQR 403.

[170] See *Commercial Bank of Australia Ltd v Amadio* (1983) 151 CLR 447, 474 (Deane J). See also *Morrison v Coast Finance Ltd* (1965) 55 DLR (2d) 710, 713 (Davey JA).

[171] Capper has argued that undue influence should be subsumed within the broader ground of unconscionability: D Capper, 'Undue Influence and Unconscionability: A Rationalisation' (1998) 114 LQR 479, but this would only result in a loss of certainty in the definition and application of the law.

[172] (1751) 2 Ves Sen 125, 157; 28 ER 82, 10.

[173] Which might be a bargain or a gift: *Evans v Lloyd* [2013] EWHC 1725 (Ch).

[174] [1975] QB 326.

power is grievously impaired by reasons of his own needs or desires, or by his own ignorance or infirmity, coupled with undue influences or pressures brought to bear on him by or for the benefit of the other.[175]

This principle of inequality of bargaining power has subsequently been doubted,[176] but, to the extent that this principle forms part of the general equitable jurisdiction to relieve against transactions induced by unconscionable conduct, it has a useful function. In *National Westminster Bank plc v Morgan*[177] Lord Scarman considered that the principle of undue influence is now sufficiently well developed to remove the need for any doctrine of inequality of bargaining power. But this is unconvincing, since undue influence will only operate where there is an actual or presumed relationship of influence between the parties, and this will often not be the case where two parties have entered into a bargain and one has the potential to exploit the other. The principle which underlies undue influence, namely that of exploitation, should be applicable even where there is no existing relationship of influence between the parties. Although Lord Denning in *Lloyds Bank Ltd v Bundy* said that this justified the recognition of a general principle of inequality of bargaining power, which encompassed all cases of duress, *colore officii*,[178] unconscionable transactions, undue pressure and undue influence, this is apt to mislead, since these specific grounds of restitution are so different from each other that nothing can usefully be gained from treating them together. But Lord Denning did identify a gap in the recognized grounds of restitution where 'an unfair advantage has been gained by an unconscientious use of power by a stronger party against a weaker'.[179] Consequently, there is a need to recognize a ground of restitution, which can usefully be called 'unconscionable conduct'. Although the name of this ground of restitution is new, the principles underlying it are not, for they have been recognized by Equity for a very long time and have been confirmed by the Court of Appeal[180] and the Privy Council.[181]

The biggest drawback with a principle of unconscionability is that its vagueness will make it unworkable. Bamforth in particular has warned against the danger of using pejorative terms such as 'unconscionability', and has called for precision and clarity when identifying criteria for assessing whether a transaction is unconscionable.[182] But it is possible to identify certain key principles which define the application of the principle of unconscionable conduct with some certainty. Crucially, it is clear that Equity will not set aside a transaction simply because it is harsh. As Sir Raymond Evershed MR said in *Tufton v Sperni*,[183] 'extravagant liberality and immoderate folly do not of themselves provide a passport to equitable relief'. To secure the intervention of Equity[184] by reason of the defendant's unconscionable conduct, the claimant needs to prove that three conditions have been satisfied. Whilst the unconscionable conduct doctrine is well developed in Australia, it does operate in English law too, and indeed many of the Australian cases have developed the doctrine with explicit reliance on English authorities.

(i) Inequality Between the Parties

The first requirement is that the claimant was suffering from a special disability or was placed in a special situation of disadvantage as against the defendant, so that there is a

---

[175] Ibid, 339.   [176] See *National Westminster Bank plc v Morgan* [1985] AC 686, 708 (Lord Scarman).
[177] Ibid.   [178] See p 395, below.   [179] *Lloyd's Bank Ltd v Bundy* [1975] QB 326, 337.
[180] *Crédit Lyonnais Bank Nederland NV v Burch* [1997] 1 All ER 144, 151 (Nourse LJ).
[181] *Hart v O'Connor* [1985] AC 1000.
[182] Bamforth, 'Unconscionability as a Vitiating Factor', 544.   [183] (1952) 2 TLR 516, 519.
[184] It is clear that there is no Common Law doctrine of inequality of bargaining power or anything equivalent to such a doctrine. See *CTN Cash and Carry Ltd v Gallaher Ltd* [1994] 4 All ER 714, 717 (Steyn LJ).

reasonable degree of inequality between the parties. The function of this requirement is to identify those cases where, because of the special disadvantage, claimants are unable to exercise an independent and worthwhile judgment as to what is in their interests.[185] It is not possible to draw up a complete list of all situations where there will be a sufficient degree of inequality, since ultimately this is a question of fact. In *Blomley v Ryan*[186] Fullagar J usefully described the type of disability or disadvantage which is involved:

> Among [these situations] are poverty or need of any kind, sickness, age, sex, infirmity of body or mind, drunkenness, illiteracy or lack of education, lack of assistance or explanation where assistance or explanation is necessary. The common characteristic seems to be that they have the effect of placing one party at a serious disadvantage vis-a-vis the other.

To this list may be added those cases where the claimant does not understand English very well,[187] where the claimant is in an emotional state following marriage breakdown,[188] and even where the claimant is infatuated with the defendant.[189]

(ii) Unconscionability

The second requirement is that the defendant's conduct must have been unconscionable, which is assessed by reference to whether the particular defendant was at fault in some way. The leading case on unconscionability is the decision of the Privy Council in *Hart v O'Connor*,[190] which concerned whether a transaction for the sale of land could be set aside where the vendor of the property was suffering from senile dementia but the purchaser was unaware of this disability. The decision of the Privy Council concerned two separate grounds for setting the transaction aside, namely the Common Law ground of contractual incapacity[191] and the alternative equitable ground that the defendant's conduct was unconscionable. It was held that to establish either ground it was not sufficient for the claimant to show that the terms of the transaction were unfair; rather it was necessary to establish that the defendant had committed equitable, or constructive, fraud. This is now the test of unconscionable conduct. But the decision of the Privy Council does not provide much assistance as to what this actually means. Lord Brightman, who delivered the Board's advice, said that equitable fraud 'is victimization, which can consist either of the active extortion of a benefit or the passive acceptance of a benefit in unconscionable circumstances'.[192] He went on to suggest that the defendant must have been in bad faith or had taken advantage of the claimant in some way.[193]

The preferable interpretation of *Hart v O'Connor* is that what must be shown is that the defendant acted in a morally reprehensible manner,[194] either because the defendant knew of the claimant's special disability or disadvantage, or should have known of it since the defendant was aware of particular facts which would have put the reasonable person on notice that the claimant had a special disability or disadvantage.[195]

---

[185] *Australian Competition and Consumer Commission v CG Berbatis* (2003) 214 CLR 51, [12] (Gleeson CJ), [55]–[56] (Gummow and Hayne JJ), [184] (Callinan J).

[186] (1956) 99 CLR 362, 405. For analysis of some of these situations, see p 283, below.

[187] *The Commercial Bank of Australia Ltd v Amadio* (1983) 151 CLR 447.

[188] *Backhouse v Backhouse* [1978] 1 WLR 243.   [189] *Louth v Diprose* [1992] 75 CLR 621.

[190] [1985] AC 1000.   [191] See Chapter 14.   [192] *Hart v O'Connor* [1985] AC 1000, 1028.

[193] Ibid. See also *Boustany v Piggott* (1993) 69 P and CR 298 (PC).

[194] *Portman Building Society v Dusangh* [2000] EWCA Civ 142, [2000] 2 All ER (Comm) 221; *Jones v Morgan* [2001] EWCA Civ 995, [35] (Chadwick LJ); *Yorkshire Bank plc v Tinsley* [2004] EWCA Civ 816, [2004] 1 WLR 2380.

[195] *Owen and Gutch v Homan* (1853) 4 HLC 997, 1035; 10 ER 752, 767 (Lord Cranworth LC); *The Commercial Bank of Australia Ltd v Amadio* (1983) 151 CLR 447, 467 (Mason J); *Nichols v Jessup* [1986] 1

(iii) Significant Imbalance in the Substance of the Transaction

Fault of the defendant is not sufficient to characterize the transaction as unconscionable; it must also be overreaching and oppressive in that there is a significant imbalance in the substance of the transaction to the disadvantage of the weaker party,[196] such as where the transaction is at a gross undervalue. A transaction will not be oppressive simply because it turns out to a party's disadvantage,[197] or that, in the eyes of the court, it was unreasonable.[198] Whether the transaction was oppressive is to be determined on the facts at the time the transaction was entered into and from the perspective of the disadvantaged party.[199]

(iv) Whether the Transaction Was Fair, Just, and Reasonable

Once the claimant has shown that he or she was suffering from a special disability or disadvantage, that the defendant's conduct was unconscionable, and that that there was a significant imbalance in the substance of the transaction, the transaction will be set aside, unless the defendant can show that the transaction was fair, just, and reasonable.[200] The defendant will be able to establish this by showing, for example, that the claimant had obtained independent legal advice, since this would place the parties on equal terms.[201] But the obtaining of such advice will only be relevant if its effect really is to place the parties on equal terms. So, for example, in *Boustany v Piggott*[202] a renegotiated lease was set aside by reason of the defendant's unconscionable conduct, even though the disadvantages of the transaction had been forcibly pointed out to the claimant by a barrister, because the defendant was present and was taking advantage of the claimant when the advice was given.[203]

(B) IDENTIFYING UNCONSCIONABLE CONDUCT

The application of this ground of restitution is illustrated by *Hart v O'Connor*[204] itself, where it was held that unconscionable conduct had not been established on the facts because the defendant, who had bought land from the claimant, was not aware of the claimant's dementia and there was nothing to put him on notice of this, since it appeared

---

NZLR 226, 236 (Somers J). Cf *Louth v Diprose* (1992) 175 CLR 621 and *Kakavas v Crown Melbourne Ltd* [2013] HCA 25 where the High Court of Australia adopted a subjective test of fault. On the general question of whether a subjective or an objective test of fault should be adopted see Bamforth, 'Unconscionability as a Vitiating Factor', 550, who argues that a subjective test of fault should be adopted since this ground of restitution is defendant-oriented and so should depend on clear proof of fault: ibid, 557. An objective test of unconscionability, albeit assessed with reference to the defendant's knowledge, is consistent with the usual interpretation of unconscionability in Equity. See GJ Virgo, 'Whose Conscience? Unconscionability in the Common Law of Obligations' in A Robertson and M Tilbury (eds), *The Common Law of Obligations: Divergence and Unity* (Oxford: Hart Publishing, 2015).

[196] *Alec Lobb (Garages) Ltd v Total Oil GB Ltd* [1983] 1 WLR 87, 95 (Peter Millett QC); *Crédit Lyonnais Bank Nederland NV v Burch* [1997] 1 All ER 144; *Portman Building Society v Dusangh* [2000] 2 All ER 221; *Mitchell v James* [2001] 1 All ER 116; *Jones v Morgan* [2001] EWCA Civ 995; *Singlar v Bashir* [2002] EWHC 883 (Ch); *Strydom v Vendside Ltd* [2009] EWHC 2130 (QB), [39] (Blair J).

[197] *Irvani v Irvani* [2000] 1 Lloyd's Rep 412, 425.

[198] *Multiservice Bookbinding Ltd v Marden* [1979] Ch 84, 110 (Browne-Wilkinson J).

[199] *Strydom v Vendside Ltd* [2009] EWHC 2130 (QB), [39] (Blair J).

[200] *Earl of Aylesford v Morris* (1873) LR 8 Ch App 484, 491 (Lord Selborne LC); *Portman Building Society v Dusangh* [2000] EWCA Civ 142, [2000] 2 All ER (Comm) 221.

[201] *Fry v Lane* (1888) 40 Ch D 312.   [202] (1993) 69 P and CR 298.

[203] For a similar approach to the role of independent advice for the purposes of establishing undue influence, see p 269, above.   [204] [1985] AC 1000.

that the vendor was acting in accordance with the most full and careful legal advice. Neither was there any evidence of objective unfairness since the terms of the bargain had been proposed by the claimant's solicitor and the land had been independently valued. As Lord Brightman concluded: 'There was no equitable fraud, no victimization, no taking advantage, no overreaching or other description of unconscionable doings which might have justified the intervention of equity...'[205]

The decision in *Hart v O'Connor* may usefully be contrasted with the later decision of the New Zealand Court of Appeal in *Nichols v Jessup*,[206] where the claimant had agreed to grant the defendant a right of way over her land, the effect of which would be to increase the value of the defendant's land by $45,000 and to decrease the value of the claimant's land by $3,000. The trial judge found that the consideration which the claimant had received for the transaction had been grossly inadequate, that she had not received legal advice, and that she was unintelligent and muddle-headed. The Court of Appeal held that, where the defendant knew or should have known that the claimant was at a significant disadvantage in appreciating the relative consequences of the transaction, the marked imbalance of benefit arising from it was evidence that the defendant had acted unconscionably. When the case was returned to the trial judge for reconsideration he concluded that the defendant had indeed acted unconscionably, because:

> although [the transaction was] not originally extorted by an unconscientious exercise of power [it] should be set aside in exercise of the Court's equitable jurisdiction on the ground that in all the circumstances it is not consistent with equity and good conscience that the [defendant] should enforce or retain the benefit of the transaction.[207]

The trial judge's decision is open to two main criticisms. First, it was based on the fact that the transaction was 'on any objective view...so manifestly one-sided', even though he had actually found that there was no moral fraud on the part of the defendant.[208] This is surely contrary to the decision of the Privy Council in *Hart v O'Connor*, where emphasis was specifically placed on the need to establish that the defendant had been at fault. Secondly, the question of unconscionable conduct should be judged at the time when the defendant entered into the transaction with the claimant.[209] The judge's conclusion that the agreement had not been extorted by unconscientious use of power should have meant that the transaction would not be set aside.

(C) UNCONSCIONABLE CONDUCT AND THIRD PARTIES

Where the claimant is induced to enter into a transaction with the defendant as a result of the unconscionable conduct of a third party, and the defendant's conduct cannot be characterized as unconscionable, the defendant will be able to enforce the transaction unless he or she had notice, whether actual or constructive, of the claimant's equity to set the transaction aside.[210] This reflects precisely the situation where a third party wishes to enforce a transaction which a party had been induced to enter as a result of undue influence.[211] So, for example, if an employer induces an employee to provide security for

---

[205] Ibid, 1024.   [206] [1986] 1 NZLR 226.
[207] *Nichols v Jessup (No 2)* [1986] 1 NZLR 237, 240 (Prichard J).   [208] Ibid, 239.
[209] As is the case where the claimant relies on undue influence. See *Allcard v Skinner* (1887) 36 Ch D 145, 191 (Bowen LJ).
[210] See *Yorkshire Bank plc v Tinsley* [2004] EWCA Civ 816, [2004] 1 WLR 2380.
[211] See p 269, above.

the employer's debts in favour of a bank and this can be characterized as unconscionable by virtue of the employer's conduct, the bank will still be able to enforce the security unless it has notice of the employer's impropriety.[212]

(D) EXAMPLES OF INEQUALITY

There are a number of well recognized categories of special disability or disadvantage. The potential for abuse in the first two categories, involving transactions with the poor and ignorant and with expectant heirs, might be so great that unconscionability on the part of the defendant might even be presumed after it has been shown that there is significant inequality in the substance of the transaction.[213] If so, once the claimant has established the special disability or disadvantage, the burden will be on the defendant to show that the transaction was fair, just, and reasonable.

(i) Transactions with the Poor and Ignorant

Equity is willing to set aside certain transactions if they are made with somebody who is both poor and ignorant, because such people are assumed to be particularly vulnerable to exploitation. So, for example, in *Fry v Lane*[214] a contract for sale at an undervalue was set aside where the vendor was characterized as poor and ignorant, because the temptation of receiving a sum of money immediately might mean that such a person did not consider the consequences of transacting with the defendant. This category of special disability continues to be relevant today, although the notions of poverty and ignorance were reinterpreted in *Cresswell v Potter*[215] so that poor meant 'a member of the lower income group' and ignorant was to be interpreted as meaning 'less highly educated'. In *Cresswell* the claimant, who was a telephonist, had released her interest in the matrimonial home to her husband on her divorce from him. This release was set aside because she was characterized as being poor and ignorant, it being sufficient that she was ignorant as to the operation of property transactions. It was also of crucial significance that the transaction had been at a significant undervalue and that she had not received any independent legal advice, something which was considered to be of particular importance in a conveyancing transaction.

In neither of these cases was the defendant's conduct specifically characterized as unconscionable. Indeed, in *Fry v Lane* it was held that there was no evidence of moral fraud or misconduct on the part of the defendant. This suggests that, where the defendant has transacted with somebody who is poor and ignorant, then, at least where the transaction is at a considerable undervalue, it will be presumed that the defendant had acted unconscionably and he or she will bear the burden of proving that the transaction was fair, just and reasonable. This is because the fact that a transaction with somebody who was poor and ignorant was at a gross undervalue is itself evidence of equitable fraud.[216] But much will turn on careful analysis of the facts. For example, in *Horry v Tate and Lyle Refineries Ltd*,[217] an employee who had settled a personal injuries claim with his

---

[212] See *Crédit Lyonnais Bank Nederland NV v Burch* [1997] 1 All ER 144, 153 (Millett LJ).

[213] See *Alec Lobb (Garages) Ltd v Total Oil Great Britain Ltd* [1985] 1 WLR 173, 182 (Dillon LJ).

[214] (1888) 40 Ch D 312. See also *Evans v Llewllin* (1787) 1 Cox 333, 29 Ex 1191.

[215] [1978] 1 WLR 255n. See also *Crédit Lyonnais Bank Nederland NV v Burch* [1997] 1 All ER 144; *Portman Building Society v Dusangh* [2000] EWCA Civ 142, [2000] 2 All ER (Comm.) 221, where being old, illiterate, and with a low income was characterized as the modern equivalent of 'poor and ignorant'; *Chagos Islanders v Attorney-General* [2003] EWHC 2222, [580] (Ouseley J).

[216] *Fry v Lane* (1888) 40 Ch D 312, 321 (Kay J).   [217] [1982] 2 Lloyd's Rep 416.

employer at an undervalue and without legal advice, was held not have been under a special disadvantage to justify relief on the ground of the settlement being unconscionable. Although there was inequality between the employee and the employer's insurers through whom the claim was settled, it was held that no special disadvantage arose from this inequality, because the employee was not under any economic pressure at the time the settlement was made and was not so grossly ignorant as to be unable to deal with the negotiations.

(ii) Transactions with Expectant Heirs

Where someone is expecting to receive an inheritance at some point in the future, their desire to receive money as soon as possible may make them peculiarly susceptible to moneylenders who may seek to lend money at extortionate rates of interest or purchase the inheritance at a gross undervalue. Such expectant heirs are characterized as being disadvantaged by a special disability; what Lord Selborne LC called 'the follies and vices of unprotected youth, inexperience, and moral imbecility'.[218] If the defendant's conduct in transacting with such people can be characterized as unconscionable, the transaction is liable to be set aside. The operation of this principle is illustrated by *Earl of Aylesford v Morris*[219] where the claimant stood to inherit his father's estate and took out a loan from the defendant to pay off his debts at an interest rate of 60 per cent. This was set aside because the nature of the relationship between the parties and the terms of the transaction was such that the defendant was presumed to have acted fraudulently. As a condition of setting the transaction aside, the claimant was required to repay the principal sum and a reasonable interest rate of 5 per cent. One of the crucial factors which influenced the court in characterizing this transaction as unconscionable was the fact that the claimant was inexperienced and immature. It was accepted that the presumption of unconscionability could have been rebutted if the defendant could prove that the claimant had obtained independent legal advice.

(iii) Salvage Agreements

Where a ship is in danger of sinking and urgently needs help, the rescuer is in a strong position to exploit the situation. If the salvage agreement which is entered into is manifestly unfair and unjust the court will set it aside.[220] For example, in *The Port Caledonia and The Anna*[221] a rescuer refused to provide a rope to assist with the rescue unless he was paid £1,000. The agreement to pay this sum was set aside on the ground that it was manifestly unfair and unjust.

(iv) Gross Inequality of Bargaining Power

In addition to these specific types of disability or disadvantage, the courts are sometimes prepared to identify a special disadvantage where on the exceptional facts of the case there is a gross inequality of bargaining power between the parties. Where the difference in the relative bargaining power of the parties is such that the defendant is at a great advantage and the defendant's conduct is characterized as unconscionable, the transaction is liable to be set aside. For example, where a husband and wife divorce and are suffering from emotional strain, if the husband retains the matrimonial home he is in a position of particular advantage, so if the wife agrees to transfer her interest in the house to her

---

[218] *Earl of Aylesford v Morris* (1873) LR 8 Ch App 484, 491.
[219] Ibid. See also *O'Rorke v Bolingbroke* (1877) 2 App Cas 814.
[220] See Lord Denning MR in *Lloyds Bank Ltd v Bundy* [1975] QB 326, 339.   [221] [1903] P 184.

husband for little or no consideration, the transaction is liable to be set aside if she is not encouraged to obtain independent legal advice.[222]

This is further illustrated by *The Commercial Bank of Australia v Amadio*,[223] where the defendants were induced to provide a guarantee so that the bank would be prepared to increase the approved overdraft limit of their son's company. This type of transaction might be set aside on the basis of the son's undue influence, if the son acted as the bank's agent or the bank had notice of the son's conduct. However, in the *Amadio* case the guarantee was set aside specifically because of the bank's unconscionable conduct. Although the High Court of Australia recognized that the bank's duty to make disclosure to its intending surety was very limited, it found that, on the exceptional facts of this case, there was a gross inequality of bargaining power between the bank and the parents, so that the parents stood in a position of special disadvantage vis-à-vis the bank. This gross inequality of bargaining power arose from a number of different factors, including the defendants' reliance on their son, their age (71 and 76 respectively), their limited command of written English, and their relative inexperience of business in which the son was engaged. The bank's conduct was regarded as unconscionable primarily because the bank manager, who had visited the defendants to obtain their signatures for the guarantee, knew of the circumstances which amounted to a special disadvantage, particularly that the defendants clearly did not understand the nature of the document which they were signing. Also, because the bank manager knew that the transaction was improvident from the viewpoint of the defendants it was 'inconceivable that the possibility did not occur to [him] that the [parents'] entry into the transaction was due to their inability to make a judgment as to what was in their best interests'.[224] But another feature which enabled the court to conclude that the bank's conduct was unconscionable was the fact that the relationship between the bank and the son was more than an ordinary business relationship. This was because the son's company was a major client of the bank and, crucially, the bank's wholly-owned subsidiary. So it was in the bank's best interests that the company was able to continue trading.

It is even possible that gross inequality of bargaining power may arise in a purely commercial context, as was recognized in *Multiservice Bookbinding Ltd v Marden*,[225] where Browne-Wilkinson J accepted that there might be gross inequality of bargaining power between a borrower and a lender, so that, if the borrowing transaction was unfair and unconscionable, it could be set aside. The transaction was not set aside because the claimant borrower in that case had obtained independent legal advice, there was no evidence of sharp practice and, crucially, the claimant was only seeking the loan in order to expand, so that if it did not like the lender's terms it could have refused to enter the transaction without the risk of becoming insolvent. Where the solvency of the borrower is dependent upon the obtaining of the loan, it might be possible to identify gross inequality of bargaining power, but unconscionability will still need to be identified and this will be difficult to establish. In *Strydom v Vendside Ltd*[226] the trial judge had held that the claimant had established a special disadvantage because there was inequality of bargaining power between the claimant, a former miner looking for advice and trusting a trade union to look after his interests, and the defendant trade union which was offering to pursue the miner's claims on its own terms and for its own interests. On appeal Blair J held[227] that this decision turned on the special facts of the case, because there was normally no inequality of bargaining power between a union and its members.

---

[222] *Backhouse v Backhouse* [1978] 1 WLR 243.   [223] (1983) 151 CLR 447.
[224] Ibid, 466–7 (Mason J).   [225] [1979] Ch 84.   [226] [2009] EWHC 2130 (QB).
[227] Ibid, [37].

The operation of the doctrine of unconscionable conduct in the commercial sphere has proved to be particularly significant in Australia and Canada. Even there the inequality or imbalance must be 'overwhelming'[228] such that there is a gross inequality of bargaining power between the parties.[229] This will be difficult to establish. There must be 'something more than commercial vulnerability to elevate disadvantage into special disadvantage'.[230] For example, in *Australian Competition and Consumer Commission v CG Berbatis Holdings Pty Ltd*,[231] tenants, who had no legal entitlement to the renewal of their lease, needed to renew it in order to sell their business for a substantial price. The tenants had claims against the landlord, who insisted that, as a condition of renewing the lease, they should discontinue their legal action. The tenants took legal advice and agreed to the condition. This was held not to be an unconscionable bargain because the tenants were not at a special disadvantage. They suffered no lack of ability to judge or protect their financial interests and, crucially, they had the benefit of legal advice.

There may, however, be other features which enable the court to identify a special disability or disadvantage in a commercial context. In Canada, for example, special disadvantage has been held to include ignorance of business.[232] In England, in *Jones v Morgan*[233] the trial judge had recognized that the weaker party was at a special disadvantage because he was 'naïve, trusting and unbusiness-like and not a match for an astute business man' like the stronger party. Although the judgment was reversed on appeal, this was because the defendant's conduct was not considered to be unconscionable, rather than because the special disadvantage could not be identified.[234] Significantly the UNIDROIT *Principles of International Commercial Contracts*[235] states that relevant disabilities include dependence, economic distress or urgent needs, improvidence, ignorance, inexperience, and lack of bargaining skill.

(E) STATUTORY REGIMES

The most important statutory provision relating to unconscionable transactions is the Consumer Credit Act 1974 which gives the court extensive powers to deal with credit agreements where the relationship between the creditor and the debtor arising from the agreement is unfair to the debtor because of the terms of the agreement, the way in which the creditor has enforced his rights under the agreement or anything else which the creditor has done or failed to do.[236] The powers of the court include the power to require the creditor to repay the whole or part of any sum paid under the agreement.[237] Significantly, if the debtor alleges that the relationship between the debtor and creditor is unfair, the burden is placed on the creditor to prove otherwise.[238]

5. THE PARTIES ARE NOT *PAR DELICTUM*

It is a fundamental principle of the law of restitution that restitutionary claims will fail where the claimant has participated in an illegal transaction.[239] This was recognized by

---

228 *Cain v Clarica Life Insurance Co* (2005) 263 DLR (4th) 368.
229 *The Bell Group Ltd v Westpac Banking Corporation (No 9)* [2008] WASC 239, [89] (Owen J).
230 *Australian Competition and Consumer Commission v Samton Holdings Pty Ltd* [2002] 117 FCR 301, [64].
231 [2003] HCA 18.   232 *Cain v Clarica Life Insurance Co* (2005) 263 DLR (4th) 368, [32].
233 [2001] EWCA Civ 995, [40].   234 See also *Liddle v Cree* [2011] EWHC 3294 (Ch).
235 UNIDROIT *Principles of International Commercial Contracts* (2010), art 3.2.7.(1)(a).
236 Consumer Credit Act 1974, s 140A, inserted by the Consumer Credit Act 2006.
237 Ibid, s 140B(1)(a).   238 Ibid, s 140(b)(2)(9).   239 See Chapter 27.

Lord Mansfield in *Holman v Johnson*[240] in the form of the illegality defence, whereby if the parties are equally at fault in participating in the illegal transaction the loss will lie where it falls. But, if a defence to restitutionary claims is founded on the principle of equal fault, it should follow that if the claimant is less at fault than the defendant the restitutionary claim should not be defeated by the taint of illegality. That this is implicit within the illegality defence was recognized by Lord Mansfield in *Smith v Bromley*.[241]

There are three recognized categories where the defendant will be considered to be more responsible than the claimant for the illegality by operation of law and so restitution will be available despite the illegality. These categories exist for the protection of the claimant. They were recognized by Lord Mansfield in *Smith v Bromley*,[242] who said: 'But there are other laws, which are calculated for the protection of the subject against oppression, extortion, deceit etc. If such laws are violated and the defendant takes advantage of the claimant's condition or situation, then the plaintiff shall recover ...'

Of these, the fact that the claimant was induced to transfer a benefit to the defendant as a result of the defendant's deceit is properly treated as involving restitution for an induced mistake.[243] The other two categories, however, of oppression and extortion, should be analysed as falling under the principle of exploitation, whether actual or potential, by the defendant of the claimant. That these cases are properly analysed as a ground of restitution in its own right was recognized by Lord Denning in *Kiriri Cotton Co Ltd v Dewani*,[244] where he treated it on a par with restitution for mistake or failure of basis.

(A) OPPRESSION

Where the defendant has exploited the claimant's weakness oppressively restitution will be awarded to the claimant by reason of the oppression, even though the claimant participated in an illegal transaction. This is particularly well illustrated by a line of cases involving creditors who refused to enter into settlement agreements unless they received preferential treatment from the debtor, such preferential treatment being illegal. This occurred in *Smith v Cuff*[245] where the claimant was allowed to recover money paid to the defendant creditor in an action for money had and received. As Lord Ellenborough CJ said, the parties are not '*par delictum* where one holds the rod and the other bows to it'.[246]

What the judges are looking for in such cases is sufficient evidence of inequality between the parties to enable them to ignore the claimant's turpitude in entering into the illegal transaction in the first place. If the claimant's conduct is regarded as voluntary because there was insufficient oppression, the restitutionary claim will fail.[247] Oppression arising from the particular circumstances of the case rather than from the defendant's actions is not sufficient to show that the parties are not *in pari delicto*. So, for example, in *Bigos v Bousted*[248] the claimant was forced to enter into a loan agreement which contravened the exchange control regulations because he was desperate for money to be able to send to his daughter abroad to improve her health. Despite the difficult circumstances in which the claimant found himself, the court still held that the parties were *in pari delicto* and the claimant was not able to recover the security he had provided for the loan.

---

[240] (1775) 1 Cowp 341, 343; 98 ER 1120, 1121.   [241] (1760) 2 Doug 696n, 697; 99 ER 441, 442.
[242] Ibid, 697; 443.   [243] See p 187, above.   [244] [1960] AC 102, 205.
[245] (1817) 6 M and S 160, 105 ER 1203.   [246] Ibid, 165; 1205.
[247] *Wilson v Ray* (1839) 10 Ad and E 82, 113 ER 32.   [248] [1951] 1 All ER 92.

(B) EXPLOITATION

Sometimes a statutory provision which makes a transaction illegal is regarded as existing for the purposes of protecting from exploitation a particular group of people to which the claimant belongs. In such a case the claimant is regarded as not being *in pari delicto* with the defendant and so restitution will be allowed. This is illustrated by *Kiriri Cotton Co Ltd v Dewani*[249] where the claimant tenant paid a premium to his landlord in circumstances where both parties were unaware that such a payment was illegal by virtue of a statute. The claimant was allowed to recover the premium because it was held that the statute existed to protect tenants like him and so the parties were not *in pari delicto*. In other words, the responsibility for ensuring compliance with the law was placed on the landlord rather than the tenant. Although this was not a case where the landlord had set out to exploit the claimant in contravention of the statute, it is at least a case where there was a potential for exploitation, as reflected by the fact that a statute was enacted to protect tenants.

For restitution to be awarded on this ground it is necessary to determine whether the policy of the statute is to protect people like the claimant.[250] So, for example, in *Green v Portsmouth Stadium Ltd*[251] it was held that money paid by a bookmaker to the owner of a racecourse in excess of the amount authorized by statute was an illegal payment, but that it could not be recovered because the relevant statutory provision had not been enacted for the purpose of protecting bookmakers from exploitation, but sought simply to regulate racecourses.

---

[249] [1960] AC 192.   [250] See further p 721, below.   [251] [1953] 2 QB 190.

12

NECESSITY

1. GENERAL PRINCIPLES

(A) THE PRINCIPLE OF NECESSITY

In the same way that there are general principles of compulsion and exploitation on which a number of specific grounds of restitution are based, there is also a general principle of necessity by reference to which a number of specific grounds of restitution can be identified. Although the existence of a general principle of necessity is beyond doubt in English law,[1] the principle is not well developed in Common Law legal systems, unlike civil law systems which have a well developed doctrine of *negotiorum gestio* which is applicable where the claimant has provided a benefit to the defendant in circumstances of necessity.[2] Consequently, in English law the ambit and rationale of necessity within the law of restitution is a matter of some uncertainty. But it is clear that restitution by reference to necessity exists. This has been recognized by the Supreme Court in *The Kos*,[3] where, whilst a general rule against restitution on the ground of necessity was acknowledged,[4] the exceptions to it were considered to be more important.

(B) THE PRINCIPLE OF VOLUNTARINESS

The predominant reason for the underdeveloped nature of the necessity principle in English law is because of the importance of the principle of voluntariness which operates to bar restitutionary claims.[5] The success of restitutionary claims grounded on necessity will depend on how the principle of voluntariness is defined. In *Falcke v Scottish Imperial Insurance Co*[6] Bowen LJ identified the essence of the principle of voluntariness when he stated that:

> The general principle is, beyond all question, that work or labour done or money expended by one man to preserve or benefit the property of another do not according to English law create any lien upon the property saved or benefited, nor even, if standing alone, create any

---

[1] It was recognized by the House of Lords in *Re F (Mental Patient: Sterilisation)* [1990] 2 AC 1.

[2] See JP Dawson, 'Negotiorum Gestio: The Altruistic Intermeddler' (1961) 74 Harv LR 817; J Kortmann, *Altruism in Private Law: Liability for Nonfeasance and Negotiorum Gestio* (Oxford: Oxford University Press, 2005).

[3] *ENE Kos 1 Ltd v Petroleo Brasileiro SA (No 2)* [2012] UKSC 17, [2012] 2 AC 164, [20] (Lord Sumption).

[4] Citing *Falcke v Scottish Imperial Insurance Co* (1886) 34 Ch D 234, 248 (Bowen LJ).

[5] See p 36, above. This is sometimes called 'officiousness': *ENE Kos 1 Ltd v Petroleo Brasileiro SA (No 2)* [2012] UKSC 17, [2012] 2 AC 164, [19] (Lord Sumption). For discussion of this principle see in particular EW Hope, 'Officiousness' (1929) 15 Cornell LQ 5 and PBH Birks, 'Negotiorum Gestio and the Common Law' (1971) 24 CLP 110.　　　　　　　　　　　　　　　　　　　　　　　　[6] (1886) 34 Ch D 234.

obligation to repay the expenditure. Liabilities are not to be forced on people behind their backs any more than you can confer a benefit upon a man against his will.[7]

It follows that the claimant will have acted voluntarily where he or she acted without the consent or knowledge of the defendant. Restitution will be denied because the claimant will be deemed to have taken the risk that he or she would not be reimbursed by the defendant for the work done or the money which had been expended, without a prior request from the defendant to do so. If this is the correct interpretation of the voluntariness principle it follows that it will be virtually impossible to obtain restitution in the context of claims grounded on necessity, because typically the defendant will be unaware that the claimant had intervened. The definition of the voluntariness principle can, however, be clarified further, to make it compatible with allowing restitution for some cases of necessitous intervention, although the authorities are not consistent as to what this clarified definition should be. Two distinct interpretations of the principle are viable.

(i) The Claimant Acted Selfishly Rather Than Benevolently

The first interpretation, as exemplified by *Falcke* itself, suggests that the claimant will be considered to have acted voluntarily if he or she acted selfishly rather than benevolently for the defendant. In *Falcke* the claimant was the mortgagor of a life insurance policy, who had paid a large annual premium to ensure that the policy did not lapse. Although it might be argued that it was necessary for the claimant to act to preserve the insurance policy, it was held that he was not able to recover the amount he had paid from the defendant, who was the executrix of the mortgagee of the policy, because the claimant had been acting as an officious volunteer, motivated by a desire to protect his own proprietary interest in the policy rather than that of the defendant. Consequently, the claimant had acted from motives of self-interest rather than benevolence.

(ii) The Claimant Intervened When Not Legally Obliged to Do So

The alternative interpretation of voluntariness in the context of necessity limits the ambit of the restitutionary claim much more dramatically. Under this interpretation the claimant will only be able to rely on necessity where he or she was legally obliged to intervene. The recognition and application of this interpretation of voluntariness is illustrated by *Macclesfield Corporation v Great Central Railway*,[8] where the defendant railway company was obliged by statute to keep a bridge in good repair. The claimant highway authority had requested the defendant to repair the bridge, but the defendant refused to do so. Since the bridge was in a dangerous state of disrepair, the claimant undertook the necessary repairs and then sought restitution of its expenses from the defendant. The claim failed. The Court of Appeal did not examine whether the claimant had acted in circumstances of necessity, but concluded that the claim should fail simply because the claimant had acted voluntarily since it was not under any legal liability to carry out the work.[9] This interpretation of the voluntariness principle had earlier been recognized by Eyre CJ in *Nicholson v Chapman*,[10] who suggested that 'perhaps it is better for the public that these voluntary acts of benevolence from one man to another,

---

[7] Ibid, 248. Bowen LJ went on to recognize an exception to this principle in the context of maritime salvage. See p 305, below.

[8] [1911] 2 KB 528. See also *Binstead v Buck* (1777) 2 Black W 1117, 96 ER 660.

[9] Ibid, 539 (Farwell LJ), 540 (Kennedy LJ).   [10] (1793) 2 Hy Bl 254, 259; 126 ER 536, 539.

which are charities and moral duties, but not legal duties, should depend altogether for their reward upon the moral duty of gratitude'.[11]

(iii) The Preferable Interpretation of Voluntariness

Of these two interpretations of voluntariness the former is preferable since there is no obvious reason why a claimant who has acted in the interests of the defendant, who has been enriched as a result, should be denied restitutionary relief simply because the claimant was not legally obliged to act. Where, however, the claimant has acted for his or her own selfish reasons, he or she should be considered to have acted voluntarily and the claim for restitution grounded on necessity should be defeated.

(C) THE RATIONALE OF THE NECESSITY PRINCIPLE

Even where a claimant who has transferred a benefit to the defendant can be considered not to have been acting voluntarily for him or herself, it is still important to determine whether the claimant was indeed acting in circumstances of necessity, which requires careful consideration as to why grounds of restitution founded on necessity should be recognized. Two possible justifications can be identified.

(i) Public Policy

The first justification for recognizing grounds of restitution founded on necessity is for reasons of public policy to encourage the claimant to intervene to assist others who are in need of help.[12] This seems to be the reason why a doctrine of maritime salvage exists,[13] as Eyre CJ accepted in *Nicholson v Chapman*[14] when he said that: 'Principles of public policy dictate to civilised and commercial countries, not only the propriety, but even the absolute necessity, of establishing a liberal recompense for the encouragement of those who engage in so dangerous a service.'

But the doctrine of maritime salvage has usually been treated as *sui generis* and probably has little if anything to do with the law of restitution at all.[15] More generally, whilst public policy can be used to explain why grounds of restitution founded on necessity ought to be recognized, the notion of public policy is not sufficiently certain to predict when the claimant was acting in circumstances of necessity. Reliance on public policy by itself lays the law of restitution open to the charge of palm-tree justice.

(ii) Interference with the Claimant's Free Choice

The preferable explanation of why necessity should constitute a principle by reference to which grounds of restitution can be recognized is that the effect of the necessity is to vitiate the claimant's intention to provide a gratuitous benefit to the defendant. The crucial question when determining whether the claimant had indeed acted in circumstances of necessity is whether he or she had a free choice in providing a benefit for the defendant. Where, for example, there is an emergency which requires immediate action on the part of the claimant, whether it be to rescue the defendant or his or her property or to perform an act which the defendant has a duty to perform, the circumstances which create the emergency may operate to constrain the claimant's freedom of choice to intervene, so that it is possible to conclude that the claimant did not intend to provide a gratuitous benefit to the defendant. This justification was specifically recognized in *The Great*

---

[11] But see p 300, below.

[12] See AS Burrows, *The Law of Restitution* (3rd edn, Oxford: Oxford University Press, 2011), 480.

[13] See p 305, below.   [14] (1793) 2 Hy Bl 254, 257; 126 ER 536, 538.   [15] See p 306, below.

Northern Railway Company v Swaffield,[16] where it was held to be reasonable for a railway company to incur expenditure in stabling a horse which it had transported but which had not been collected by the defendant. Kelly CB justified the claimant's conduct in the following terms:[17]

> I think we need do no more than ask ourselves, as a question of common sense and common understanding, had they any choice? They must either have allowed the horse to stand at the station—a place where it would have been extremely improper and dangerous to let it remain; or they must have put it in safe custody, which was in fact what they did . . .

It has sometimes even been suggested that where the claimant acts in circumstances of necessity he or she has no choice but to act.[18] Although this may sometimes be true, for example where the claimant reacts instinctively to save the defendant, in most cases, particularly those in which the claimant brings a restitutionary claim, he or she will have had the opportunity to decide whether or not to intervene. So, rather than confining necessity to those very rare cases where the claimant had no choice but to intervene, it is more accurate to define necessity as arising where the claimant's freedom of choice was constrained by the circumstances facing the defendant so that there was no real choice open to the claimant but to intervene. This was recognized by Sir Montague Smith in *Australasian Steam Navigation Co v Morse*[19] who said that:

> the word 'necessity' when applied to mercantile affairs . . . cannot of course mean an irresistible compelling power—what is meant by it in such cases is, the force of circumstances which determines the course a man ought to take.

This justification for the recognition of the necessity principle has the added advantage that it reconciles the principle of denying restitution where the claimant is a volunteer with allowing restitution in circumstances of necessity. This is because it will only be the most exceptional cases in which the circumstances are such that the claimant had no real choice but to intervene and, where this is so, it will not be possible to show that the claimant was acting voluntarily simply because he or she would be acting benevolently.

(iii) Distinguishing Between Necessity and Compulsion

This justification for the existence of necessity as a ground of restitution is virtually identical to the justification for those grounds of restitution which are founded on compulsion, so much so that it is sometimes difficult to distinguish clearly between compulsion and necessity since both involve pressure affecting the voluntariness of the claimant's actions. But there is a key difference between the two principles which justifies their separate treatment. Compulsion involves threats being made against the claimant, whether explicitly or implicitly, by the words or actions of the defendant, or sometimes a third party. Such threats can be classified as being of the 'do this, or else . . .' variety. In other words, the threat takes the form that some detriment will be suffered by somebody if the claimant does not do what the defendant or a third party demands. Necessity, on the other hand, does not involve threats or pressure of the 'do this, or else . . .' variety. Rather, the circumstances of the case require the claimant to act to prevent harm being suffered. Typically, the pressure will derive from some form of disaster, whether natural or man-made. So, to take a mundane example, if the defendant's house was burgled whilst she was on holiday, the defendant's neighbour may have incurred expenditure to ensure that a

---

[16] (1874) LR 9 Ex 132.   [17] Ibid, 135.
[18] This was the view of Lord Simon of Glaisdale in *DPP for Northern Ireland v Lynch* [1975] AC 653, 690.
[19] (1872) LR 4 PC 222, 230.

window which was broken in the course of the burglary was repaired, so that no-one else would break in. The pressure on the neighbour in these circumstances was not of the kind that, if he did not repair the window, some detrimental consequence would inevitably result at the hands of a person who had made threats. Consequently, this is a case of necessity rather than compulsion. This is a subtle, but legitimate, distinction which needs to be drawn because the policy issues concerning the existence and ambit of the principle of necessity are different from those which relate to compulsion.

(D) DETERMINING WHETHER THE CLAIMANT ACTED IN CIRCUMSTANCES OF NECESSITY

Although necessity is defined subjectively, in the sense that we are concerned with whether the claimant had no real choice but to assist the defendant, this is a matter which is particularly difficult to prove. Consequently, the courts often refer to an objective test, namely whether a reasonable person would have acted in the same way had that person been in the same situation as the claimant.[20] A number of principles can be identified which will assist in the determination of whether the claimant's intervention really was reasonable.[21] Whilst many of these principles have been recognized as relevant in those cases where necessity has been examined in the context of restitutionary claims, it is not necessary to establish all of them before restitutionary relief will be awarded.[22] Rather, they should be treated as characteristics of what constitutes reasonable conduct on the part of the claimant so that he or she can be considered to have acted in circumstances of necessity. Consideration of these principles will also assist the court in determining whether the claimant had acted voluntarily.

(1) The claimant's intervention will invariably be reasonable where the circumstances were such that intervention was urgently required to protect life, health, or property. Generally this means that there must have been an emergency which required immediate action, otherwise the person or property would be lost or at least suffer serious injury or damage. Whether there was an emergency is to be determined at the time when the emergency becomes apparent.[23] But it is possible in exceptional cases for the claimant's intervention to be justified by reason of necessity even though an immediate response may not be required. This will be the case where there is no immediate danger, 'but there was a possible contingency that serious consequences might have ensued',[24] such as where the defendant is in a permanent or semi-permanent condition whereby he or she is unable to consent to necessary, but not urgent, medical treatment.[25] It is for this reason that the underlying

[20] See *The Australasian Steam Navigation Co v Morse* (1872) LR 4 PC 222, 230 (Sir Montague Smith) and *Re F (Mental Patient: Sterilisation)* [1990] 2 AC 1, 75 (Lord Goff).

[21] See FD Rose, 'Restitution for the Rescuer' (1989) 9 OJLS 167, especially 182–199 and G Jones, *Restitution in Public and Private Law* (London: Sweet and Maxwell, 1991), 128.

[22] Rose, 'Restitution for the Rescuer', 182.

[23] *The Winson* [1982] AC 939, 965 (Lord Simon of Glaisdale).

[24] *The Ella Constance* (1864) 33 LJ Adm 189, 193 (Dr Lushington). Jones, in *Restitution in Public and Private Law*, 145, suggests that, where the claimant intervenes to preserve the defendant's property 'the contingency of serious consequences should be *probable* rather than *possible*', whereas if the claimant intervenes to preserve life or health, it should be sufficient that there was a possible risk of serious consequences, ibid, 159. Jones justifies this distinction on the ground that life is more precious than property.

[25] See *Re F (Mental Patient: Sterilisation)* [1990] 2 AC 1 where the court allowed a sexually-active mental patient to be sterilized on the ground that this was necessary for her own well-being.

principle for the purposes of restitution is necessity rather than emergency. As Lord Goff has said:

> the relevance of an emergency is that it may give rise to a necessity to act in the interests of the assisted person without first obtaining his consent. Emergency is, however, not the criterion or even a prerequisite; it is simply a frequent origin of the necessity which impels intervention.[26]

(2) A key factor in the identification of circumstances of necessity is that it was impracticable, but not necessarily impossible, for the claimant to communicate with the defendant and obtain the defendant's consent or instructions before intervening.[27] Where it is possible for the claimant to communicate with the defendant, the claimant can still be considered to have acted in circumstances of necessity if he or she asked the defendant for instructions and none were forthcoming.[28] If the claimant could have communicated with the defendant before intervening but failed to do so, the claimant is likely to be considered to have acted voluntarily.

(3) The claimant should be an appropriate person to intervene, otherwise his or her action will appear to be voluntary.[29] Whether the claimant was an appropriate person to intervene will depend upon the particular facts of the case, but the claimant is more likely to have been such a person if there was a pre-existing relationship between the claimant and the defendant, such as where the claimant was a friend or relative of the defendant, or the claimant possessed particular skills which were relevant to the intervention. If the claimant was aware that there was a more appropriate person who was ready and willing to intervene, this strongly suggests that the restitutionary claim should fail.

(4) Even though it was reasonable for the claimant to have intervened, it should also be shown that the claimant's actions were reasonable since they were in the defendant's best interests.[30] Relevant factors which should be considered when determining whether the claimant's conduct was reasonable, include the potential consequences if the claimant had not intervened and the cost of the intervention relative to the benefit to the defendant.

(5) Restitution for reasons of necessity should be denied in all cases where the claimant was aware that the defendant did not wish him or her to intervene. In particular, where the defendant has asked the claimant not to provide the benefit, restitution should be denied, since this suggests that the claimant was acting voluntarily.[31]

(6) Restitution should be denied where the claimant intended to act gratuitously, because, if the claimant never expected to be remunerated for the benefit provided, he or she should be considered to have acted as a volunteer. Consequently, it is highly significant to the determination of whether a restitutionary remedy should be awarded that the claimant always intended to charge the defendant for the benefit which the defendant had received.[32] Where the claimant has provided services in a professional capacity, the intention to charge the defendant for the services should be presumed.

---

[26] Ibid, 75.   [27] Ibid.   [28] *The Winson* [1982] AC 939, 961 (Lord Diplock).
[29] *Re F (Mental Patient: Sterilisation)* [1990] 2 AC 1, 76 (Lord Goff).   [30] Ibid, 75 (Lord Goff).
[31] Ibid, 76 (Lord Goff).
[32] See *Re Rhodes* (1890) 44 Ch D 94; *Aster Healthcare Ltd v Shefi* [2014] EWCA Civ 1350.

(7) Restitution should be denied if the predominant reason for the claimant's intervention is to protect his or her own personal interests, for this means that the
claimant was a volunteer.[33] Similarly, restitution should be denied where the
claimant's misconduct contributed to the emergency arising in the first place. So,
for example, if the claimant intentionally created the risk of harm, so that he or she
could intervene and then claim remuneration from the defendant, the claim should
fail on the ground that the claimant had been acting voluntarily.

(E) THE DEFENDANT MUST HAVE BEEN ENRICHED AT THE CLAIMANT'S EXPENSE

(i) Identifying the Enrichment

Restitution should be awarded by virtue of necessity regardless of the type of enrichment
which has been received by the defendant. Even where the alleged enrichment takes the
form of goods or services, it will be relatively easy to establish that the defendant has been
enriched because necessity will only be established where a reasonable person would have
intervened, so it will usually be the case that the defendant will have been incontrovertibly
benefited by the intervention, since the defendant will have been saved an inevitable
expense.[34]

(ii) Valuing the Enrichment

When assessing the value of an enrichment, [35] if the enrichment involves a service, a
distinction needs to be drawn between three different measures, namely reward, reimbursement, and remuneration. Where the claimant has acted in circumstances of necessity
it is not appropriate to reward him or her for doing so within the law of restitution, simply
because a reward does not reverse an unjust enrichment.[36] But it will be appropriate to
reimburse the claimant's expenditure incurred in intervening, and it may be appropriate
to remunerate the claimant for the provision of his or her services, at least where the
claimant is a professional, because these sums will reflect the extent of the defendant's
enrichment.[37] So, for example, if the claimant is a vet who saves the life of the defendant's
valuable racehorse in circumstances of necessity after the horse has been injured in an
accident, the defendant's enrichment can legitimately be regarded as including the value of
any drugs or materials used by the vet as well as the reasonable value of the vet's services,
since the defendant would have had to pay these sums if the claimant had not intervened.
It would not be appropriate, however, to award an additional sum to reward the vet for
intervening, at least in a claim grounded on unjust enrichment, since such a sum would
not reverse the defendant's enrichment.

(iii) Determining Whether the Enrichment Was Received at the Expense of the Claimant

Although it will often be easy to establish that the defendant had been enriched by the
claimant's necessitous intervention, it may be more difficult to establish that this enrichment had been received at the expense of the claimant. This can be illustrated by reference
to the example of the claimant who intervenes to save the life of the defendant's racehorse.
Can the defendant be considered to be enriched at the claimant's expense if the claimant

---

[33] *Falcke v Scottish Imperial Insurance Co* (1886) 34 Ch D 234.   [34] See p 80, above.
[35] See generally p 95, above.   [36] See the discussion of maritime salvage at p 305, below.
[37] This was recognized by Ralph Gibson LJ in *The Goring* [1987] QB 687, 708.

was not a professional vet? Clearly such a claimant should be entitled to recover the expenditure which he or she had reasonably incurred, since this is expenditure which the defendant had saved and this benefit was received at the claimant's expense, since the claimant had suffered a loss in providing the benefit. But should such a claimant be entitled to receive any remuneration for his or her services? The defendant will have been saved this amount by not needing to employ a professional vet, so it constitutes an enrichment. If the claimant was a professional vet the defendant's benefit in remuneration saved corresponds with an identifiable loss suffered by the claimant,[38] namely the remuneration the claimant would have been able to charge had it been possible to bargain with the defendant. If, however, the claimant was not a professional vet, he or she would presumably not have entered into a contract to provide the service and so it will not be possible to conclude that he or she had suffered any loss of remuneration in providing the service to the defendant, so the defendant's gain does not correspond with the claimant's loss.

(iv) Limiting the Restitutionary Remedy

Where the claimant has intervened to preserve the defendant's property, it would be unacceptable if the restitutionary award exceeded the value of the property, simply because the effect would be to cause the defendant to suffer a loss rather than simply to reverse the defendant's enrichment. Consequently, the 'value of the property preserved should be the ceiling of any restitutionary award'.[39]

2. NECESSITOUS INTERVENTION
BY A STRANGER

There are two grounds of restitution which can be considered to be founded on the principle of necessity, relating to where there is a pre-existing legal relationship between the claimant and the defendant and where there is no such relationship. This latter ground of restitution will be considered first.

In certain recognized categories the claimant will be able to obtain restitution from the defendant by virtue of necessitous intervention, even though there is no pre-existing legal relationship between the parties. The claimant in these circumstances is conveniently characterized as a 'stranger' even though he or she may have been known to the defendant, simply because there is no legal relationship between the parties, such as an agency relationship.

(A) DISCHARGE OF THE DEFENDANT'S LEGAL LIABILITY

Restitution has been awarded in a number of cases where the consequence of the claimant's necessitous intervention is the discharge of a legal liability which was owed by the defendant to a third party.

(i) Burial

If the person who is ultimately responsible for arranging the burial of the deceased[40] is not able to do so, it will be necessary for somebody to intervene and make the necessary

---

[38] See p 116, above, for analysis of the correspondence principle.

[39] Jones, *Restitution in Public and Private Law*, 154.

[40] Today this is the personal representative of the deceased (*Rees v Hughes* [1946] KB 517), but the husband used to be responsible for the burial of his wife (*Jenkins v Tucker* (1788) 1 H Bl 91, 126 ER 55). Where a child dies a parent is probably responsible for arranging the burial.

arrangements. The reason why the necessity principle applies in such circumstances was identified in *Rogers v Price*[41] as arising from '[the] common principles of decency and humanity, the common impulses of our nature...and to do that which is immediately necessary upon the subject in order to avoid what, if not provided against, may become an inconvenience to the public'. In such circumstances the person who incurred the expenditure or provided professional services is entitled to be reimbursed or remunerated by the defendant who was under a duty to arrange the burial. This is illustrated by *Jenkins v Tucker*[42] where the deceased had died whilst her husband was in Jamaica. The deceased's father arranged for his daughter's funeral and was able to recover the expenditure incurred from her husband because he had 'acted in discharge of a duty which the defendant was under a strict legal necessity of himself performing, and which common decency required at his hands...'.[43] Although today there is a statutory right of restitution which is applicable where a local authority is obliged to bury or cremate a person, whereby the authority can recover the expenditure incurred from the deceased person's estate,[44] the old cases at common law continue to be a very good illustration of the recognition and application of the doctrine of necessity in a restitutionary context.

Where the claimant has arranged for the burial of the deceased, restitution of expenditure will only be allowed if two conditions are satisfied.

(1) The claimant who made the arrangements for the burial must have been a proper person to respond to the necessity. This may be a parent,[45] a sibling,[46] or even a professional undertaker, so long as he or she was engaged by an appropriate person.[47]

(2) The benefit which the claimant provided must have been reasonable. So, for example, the claimant would only be able to recover expenditure which he or she had incurred in arranging for the funeral if it was reasonably incurred. An important factor which indicates what might be reasonable expenditure is to consider what the defendant would have paid for the funeral, considering his or her rank and fortune.[48]

(ii) Provision of Medical Treatment

In the same way that the burial cases recognize that the claimant may be able to obtain restitutionary relief based on the fact that it was necessary to arrange for the funeral, there is another group of cases which recognized that if the claimant provides medical treatment to the victim of an accident who is in immediate need of such treatment, the claimant may obtain restitution from the defendant who was under a legal duty to arrange for the services to be provided. This group of cases concerned the provision of urgent medical treatment to paupers where the parish officer of the parish where the pauper was at the time of the illness or injury was under a legal obligation to care for the pauper. In these cases the claimant, in providing necessary medical treatment for the pauper, had discharged the parish officers' legal duty and this was regarded as a sufficient basis to enable

---

[41] (1829) 3 Y and J 28, 34; 148 ER 1080, 1082 (Garrow B).   [42] (1788) 1 H Bl 91, 126 ER 55.
[43] Ibid, 93; 57 (Lord Loughborough).   [44] Public Health (Control of Disease) Act 1984, s 46(5).
[45] *Jenkins v Tucker* (1788) 1 H Bl 91, 126 ER 55.
[46] *Bradshaw v Beard* (1862) 12 CB (NS) 344, 142 ER 1175.
[47] *Rogers v Price* (1829) 3 Y and J 28, 148 ER 1080 where the undertaker was appropriately engaged by the defendant's brother.   [48] *Jenkins v Tucker* (1788) 1 H Bl 91, 126 ER 55.

the claimant to be reimbursed for the expenses incurred.[49] The fact that the claimant had discharged the defendant's legal liability meant that the defendant had been enriched by the claimant's intervention. The ground of restitution in these cases was clearly founded on necessity, because the pauper had to be in urgent need of medical attention.

(iii) Discharge of a Debt

Where the claimant discharges the defendant's debt in circumstances of necessity, the claimant can obtain restitution from the defendant, with the ground of restitution being founded on the principle of necessity. This was recognized in *Owen v Tate*,[50] where Scarman LJ suggested that where there was some necessity for the claimant to assume an obligation, such as a guarantee of the defendant's liability, and the claimant was required to pay money under the guarantee to discharge the defendant's liability, the defendant would be required to make restitution to the claimant 'if it is just and reasonable to do so'.[51] This dictum was applied in *The Zuhal K and Selin*,[52] where the claimant had entered into a guarantee of the defendant's liability to a third party, since this was the only practicable way that it could secure the release of the defendant's ship, which had been arrested by the owners of cargo. If the ship had not been released the consequent delay would have been very costly for the claimant. After the claimant had been compelled to pay on the guarantee it was able to recover the amount paid from the defendant. Even though the restitutionary claim succeeded, no ground of restitution was identified. Although it could have been concluded that the ground of restitution was founded on necessity, the case is better analysed as an example of legal compulsion, since the claimant had been compelled to pay money to the defendant's creditor by virtue of the guarantee.[53] Even if legal compulsion had been relied on to secure restitution, there would still have been a role for the necessity principle in that the need for the claimant to release the ship would have defeated any argument that the claimant had entered into the guarantee voluntarily.[54]

There are other cases where the claimant's conduct in discharging the defendant's liability can be regarded as arising in circumstances of necessity, so that this could constitute a ground of restitution. For example, in *Gebhardt v Saunders*[55] the claimant's restitutionary claim succeeded where it had repaired a sewer, even though the obligation to repair was placed on the defendant. Again, the ground of restitution was not identified but the result is clearly consistent with the application of the principle of necessity.

(B) PRESERVATION OF LIFE, HEALTH, AND PROPERTY

There are a number of cases where restitutionary relief has been awarded by reason of necessity where the effect of the claimant's intervention is to preserve the defendant's life, health, or property, even though the claimant has not discharged any liability of the defendant.

---

[49] *Lamb v Bunce* (1815) 4 M and S 273, 105 ER 836. See also *Simmons v Wilmot* (1800) 3 Esp 91, 170 ER 549 and *Tomlinson v Bentall* (1826) 5 B and C 737, 108 ER 738.

[50] [1976] QB 402, 409.

[51] There is no reason why the court should have a discretion to award restitutionary relief where it is considered to be just and reasonable to do so. Such a discretion is not recognized in respect of any other claims founded on the reversal of the defendant's unjust enrichment.

[52] [1987] 1 Lloyd's Rep 151.   [53] See p 241, above.

[54] Which would have defeated the claim following the decision in *Owen v Tate* [1976] QB 402. See p 244, above.   [55] [1892] 2 QB 452.

(i) Preservation of Life or Health

Although there is little authority on the point, in principle a claimant who has intervened to save the defendant's life or the life of somebody for whom the defendant is legally responsible, such as the defendant's child, or to preserve the health of such a person, should be entitled to restitution. But, restitution will only be awarded in such circumstances if the claimant has intervened in circumstances of necessity[56] and to the extent that the defendant has been enriched at the expense of the claimant. This will depend on whether the claimant has incurred reasonable expenditure or has rendered professional services for which he or she is entitled to reasonable remuneration. In a Canadian case,[57] a surgeon who intended to charge for his services was held entitled to recover remuneration for his professional services in his reasonable, but unsuccessful, attempt to revive a person who committed suicide. Whether this should properly be analysed as falling within the law of restitution would turn on whether the deceased's estate can be considered to be enriched by the service if it was unsuccessful and whether the claim might be defeated by subjective devaluation.

(ii) Supply of Necessaries

Where the claimant has supplied necessaries to somebody affected by some form of incapacity, such as mental disorder or infancy, the supplier will be able to recover the value of the necessaries from the person who was incapacitated, by means of a restitutionary action,[58] at least where the supplier intended to charge for the necessaries.[59] What constitutes necessaries is a question of fact, with relevant considerations being the reasonable requirements of the incapacitated person, their 'station in life' and their means.[60] The definition of necessaries is not confined to necessities which the defendant requires to keep alive. It includes the provision of both goods and beneficial services. In *Re Rhodes*[61] it was accepted that the provision of a room in a private lunatic asylum for a woman of unsound mind did constitute the provision of necessaries, whereas in *Nash v Inman*[62] the supply of a large number of waistcoats of 'extravagant and ridiculous style' to an undergraduate were not necessaries.[63]

The difficulty with this ground of restitution at common law relates to why there might be a requirement that the claimant must have intended to charge for the supply of the necessaries, when the fact that the claimant did not intend to charge the defendant for the benefit is not an explicit requirement for restitution in other contexts, such as where the claimant arranges for the burial of the deceased. Perhaps the reason is simply that, in the context of the burial cases there is less scope for voluntary intervention and taking advantage of the defendant,[64] whereas there is much more scope for this in respect of the provision of necessaries for those who are incapacitated. Consequently, to dispel any notion that the claimant was a volunteer it must be shown that the claimant intended to charge for the benefit provided. This will usually be the case where the claimant is a

---

[56] *Shallcross v Wright* (1850) 12 Beav 558, 50 ER 1174.

[57] *Matheson v Smiley* [1932] 2 DLR 787. Affirmed in *Skibinski v Community Living British Columbia* [2010] BCSC 1500, (2010) BCLR (5th) 271, albeit in a public service context.

[58] *Nash v Inman* [1908] 2 KB 1.   [59] *Re Rhodes* (1890) 44 Ch D 94.

[60] Ibid, 107 (Lopes LJ). For purposes of the Sale of Goods Act 1979 'necessaries', according to s 3(3), are goods suitable to the recipient's condition in life and his actual requirements at the time. See also Mental Capacity Act 2005, s 7(2); *Aster Healthcare Ltd v Shafi* [2014] EWCA Civ 1350.

[61] (1890) 44 Ch D 94.   [62] [1908] 2 KB 1.

[63] Even though the student was studying at Trinity College, Cambridge.

[64] See SJ Stoljar, *The Law of Quasi-Contract* (2nd edn, Sydney: The Law Book Co, 1989), 202.

professional who is supplying the necessaries in the course of that profession. Such a person is less likely to be a volunteer than is a relative who is presumed, as was the case in *Re Rhodes*, to have supplied the benefit gratuitously. This presumption was particularly appropriate in that case simply because the annual cost of keeping the woman in the asylum was £140, whereas her annual income was only £96. Since the benefit which was provided was beyond the woman's means it was assumed that it was provided gratuitously by her relatives and so the restitutionary claim failed.

In fact, today, most cases of the supply of necessaries to incapacitated people are governed by statute, and there is no requirement that the supplier intended to charge for the supply; this is assumed. Where the necessaries take the form of goods sold to a minor or to a person who was incapacitated from making a contract due to intoxication, there is a statutory right for the supplier to recover the reasonable price of the goods.[65] Where necessary goods or services are supplied to a person who lacks capacity to contract for them, that person must pay a reasonable price to the person who supplied them.[66]

(iii) Preservation of Property

Even though restitution was denied in *Falcke v Scottish Imperial Insurance Co*,[67] where the claimant had paid premiums to preserve an insurance policy which would otherwise have lapsed, this was only because the claimant was acting to protect his own interest in the property rather than that of the defendant.[68] It could therefore be concluded that the claimant had been acting as a volunteer. It does not follow that restitution will automatically be denied where the claimant has intervened to protect the defendant's property, as long as the claimant was not acting voluntarily, even though some cases assume that there is a blanket rule denying restitution in such circumstances. An example of a case where restitution was denied is *Binstead v Buck*[69] where the claimant looked after the defendant's stray dog for 20 weeks.

There are, however, a number of other cases in which it has been recognized that restitution should be, or could have been, awarded where the claimant intervened in circumstances of necessity to protect the defendant's property. For example, in *Nicholson v Chapman*[70] timber which had been left on the bank of the River Thames was carried away by the tide and was left on a tow path, where it was found by the defendant, who moved it to safety beyond the reach of the tide. The defendant's claim that he had a lien over the timber as security for the expenditure incurred in rescuing it was rejected. But Eyre CJ did suggest that the defendant should be entitled to recover from the owner his reasonable expenditure in rescuing the timber and that a court would 'go as far as it could go towards enforcing' such payment.[71] In *Jenkins v Tucker*[72] Lord Loughborough suggested that, where the defendant's goods had been seized for payment of tax and the claimant had redeemed the goods by paying the tax for the defendant, the claimant could recover the money paid from the owner. This action nicely mirrors an equivalent restitutionary action where the *claimant's* goods have been seized by a third party in respect of a liability owed by the defendant and the claimant discharged the defendant's debt to

---

[65] Sale of Goods Act 1979, s 3(2).   [66] Mental Capacity Act 2005, s 7.
[67] (1886) 34 Ch D 234.   [68] Ibid, 251 (Bowen LJ). See p 290, above.
[69] (1777) 2 Black W 1117, 96 ER 660. See also *Sorrell v Paget* [1950] 1 KB 252. But see *Guildford Borough Council v Hein* [2005] EWCA Civ 979 where it was recognized that there might be an agency of necessity where a local authority retained the possession of the defendant's dogs which she had been disqualified from keeping for reasons of neglect. See p 303, below.
[70] (1793) 2 H Bl 254, 126 ER 536.   [71] Ibid, 257; 538.   [72] (1788) 1 H Bl 91, 126 ER 55.

recover the goods. Here the ground of restitution would be legal compulsion.[73] Where the *defendant's* goods have been seized and the claimant intervenes to discharge the liability, the ground of restitution would presumably be characterized as founded on the necessity principle.

These cases therefore suggest that, where the claimant intervenes to protect the defendant's property in circumstances of necessity, it may be possible to establish a restitutionary claim. It must follow that this claim will be a personal one and the claimant will not be awarded a proprietary remedy, such as a lien over the property which has been protected,[74] since there is no obvious reason why the claimant should be considered to have a proprietary interest in the defendant's property simply by virtue of the claimant's necessitous intervention. The personal remedy will only lie to the extent that the claimant has intervened to protect and preserve property and will not lie to the extent that the claimant has improved the property, because the improvement cannot be justified by the need to act urgently. As Stoljar has said, '[m]any, probably most, common law instances of officious conduct are in fact those of a volunteer merely improving property, his acts going well beyond what urgent preservation would demand'.[75] It is for this reason that restitution was denied in such cases as *Taylor v Laird*,[76] where the claimant had improved property in which the defendant had an interest as a tenant in common and the claimant then sought restitution from the defendant.

(C) A GENERAL PRINCIPLE OF NECESSITOUS INTERVENTION

There is no reason why restitutionary claims founded on the circumstances of necessity should be confined to these established categories. Whilst the facts of a number of these cases will not occur again, particularly with the introduction of the welfare state and a national health service, the principles which are embodied in them will continue to be of general relevance. So long as the claimant's conduct in assisting the defendant can be regarded as reasonable, as assessed by reference to the established principles, restitution should lie even though the facts do not fall within one of the established categories of necessity.

3. AGENCY AND OTHER PRE-EXISTING LEGAL RELATIONSHIPS

The only substantive difference between this ground of restitution and that of necessitous intervention by a stranger is that this second ground depends on there being some form of pre-existing legal relationship between the parties.[77] The importance of this difference is simply that, where there is such a relationship, when the claimant intervenes in circumstances of necessity he or she will generally be considered to have been an appropriate person to intervene, with the consequence that it will be much more difficult to characterize the claimant as a volunteer.[78] Nevertheless, even though there is a pre-existing legal relationship between the parties, it will still be vital for the claimant to show that his or her

---

[73] *Exall v Partridge* (1799) 8 Term Rep 308, 101 ER 1405. See p 239, above.

[74] *Nicholson v Chapman* (1793) 2 H Bl 254, 126 ER 536. See also *Falcke v Scottish Imperial Insurance Co* (1886) 34 Ch D 234, 248 (Bowen LJ).

[75] Stoljar, *The Law of Quasi-Contract* (2nd edn), 208.   [76] (1856) 25 LJ Ex 329.

[77] *Jebara v Ottoman Bank* [1927] 2 KB 254, 271 (Scrutton LJ).

[78] *The Winson* [1982] AC 939, 961 (Lord Diplock).

conduct was reasonable before restitution can be awarded and the general principles as to what constitutes reasonable conduct are relevant here, as in the case where a stranger has intervened.[79] Whether, however, this ground of restitution has any remaining significance to the law of unjust enrichment turns on whether the defendant's liability arises by virtue of the pre-existing relationship or by reference to the law of unjust enrichment.[80]

(A) AGENCY OF NECESSITY

The origins of the doctrine of necessitous intervention by someone who is in a legal relationship with the defendant lie in the doctrine of agency of necessity, where an agent went beyond his or her authority by intervening on behalf of the principal in an emergency. Because of the circumstances of necessity, particularly the impracticability of the agent communicating with the principal, the courts were prepared to treat the agent as though he or she had the necessary authority to do what was reasonably necessary to save the principal's property, by implication.[81] If an agency of necessity was established, the agent would be reimbursed for the expense incurred in rescuing the principal's property, but by virtue of the law of agency rather than unjust enrichment.

The doctrine of agency of necessity was initially relevant only in respect of the carriage of goods by sea, where the master took action to save the ship or cargo in an emergency. It was then extended to those cases which concerned the carriage of goods by land. This is illustrated by *The Great Northern Railway Co v Swaffield*,[82] where the claimant railway company had transported a horse to a station on behalf of the defendant. When the horse arrived there was nobody to collect it, so the claimant sent it to a stable. A number of months later the claimant paid the stabling charges and then sought to recover what it had paid from the defendant. The claimant's restitutionary claim succeeded, even though this involved the extension of the doctrine of agency of necessity to include carriers of goods by land. There was an agency of necessity because the claimant was found to have had no choice but to arrange for the proper care of the horse.

The doctrine of agency of necessity was then extended beyond cases involving carriage of goods to other cases in which the claimant had been forced by an emergency to act beyond his or her existing authority. This extension of the principle was recognized in *Prager v Blatspiel, Stamp and Heacock Ltd*,[83] although the element of emergency was not established on the facts. In *Prager* the defendant, who was a fur merchant, bought and dressed skins on behalf of the claimant to be delivered to Romania. The outbreak of the First World War made it impossible either for the defendant to send the skins to Romania or to communicate with the claimant. The defendant then sold the skins. When the claimant eventually asked the defendant to transport the skins to him, the defendant argued that it had been forced to sell the skins because they were deteriorating, making it necessary that they were sold forthwith. On the facts of the case it was held that the defendant was not an agent of necessity, simply because, as the skins were dressed, they were in no danger of deteriorating. But it was accepted that, if the skins had been deteriorating rapidly, the defendant would have been authorized to sell them by virtue of an agency of necessity.

---

[79] See p 293, above.   [80] See further p 304, below.   [81] *Gaudet v Brown* (1873) LR 5 PC 134.
[82] (1874) LR 9 Ex 132. This is now properly analysed as a case where the defendant's liability to the claimant arose from bailment rather than unjust enrichment. See *ENE Kos 1 Ltd v Petroleo Brasileiro SA (No 2)* [2012] UKSC 17, [2012] 2 AC 164, [24] (Lord Sumption). See further p 305, below.
[83] [1924] 1 KB 566.

The principle underlying the doctrine of agency of necessity was extended beyond those cases where there was a pre-existing relationship of principal and agent to where there was a pre-existing relationship of bailor and bailee. This was recognized in *The Winson*[84] where the claimant, who was a professional salvor, had entered into an agreement to salvage the defendant's cargo of wheat after its ship had been stranded on a reef. The cargo was salvaged and taken to Manila where it was stored under cover to ensure that it did not deteriorate. The claimant informed the defendant that it was going to put the wheat into storage and the defendant did not object. The claimant then sought to recover the storage expenses from the defendant. Since the storage was not covered by the salvage agreement, the claimant could not sue under the contract. However, once the wheat had arrived in the Philippines, the relationship between the parties was one which was founded on a gratuitous bailment. Consequently, the claimant argued that, in storing the wheat, it was acting as an agent of necessity. The claimant's claim for restitution of the storage expenses which had been incurred succeeded before the House of Lords, because the claimant's conduct was considered to have been reasonable. But Lord Diplock, who gave the leading judgment, stressed that the claimant should not be characterized as an agent of necessity, since he considered that the notion of agency should be confined to where the agent was deemed to have authority to create contractual rights and obligations between the principal and a third party. He did not regard the term as being appropriate where the claim was for reimbursement, as it was here, where the pre-existing relationship was founded on bailment rather than agency. Lord Diplock did suggest that the conditions which need to be satisfied before an agency of necessity is established will not necessarily have to be satisfied before the bailor obtains reimbursement from the bailee. Consequently, for example, restitution will not be denied simply because the claimant was in fact able to communicate with the defendant, it being sufficient, as occurred in *The Winson* itself, that, despite the communication with the defendant by the claimant, the defendant had failed to give any instructions to the claimant as to what to do with the wheat.

(B) FACTORS FOR THE IDENTIFICATION OF NECESSITY

Where there is a pre-existing legal relationship between the parties, restitution may be awarded by reason of necessity if certain conditions are satisfied, as was recognized in *The Choko Star*.[85] However, as Lord Diplock recognized in *The Winson*,[86] the key issue for the courts to determine is whether the claimant's conduct was reasonable, so the fact that one of these conditions is not satisfied does not mean that the claimant's conduct must automatically be considered to have been unreasonable.

(1) There must be an actual and definite commercial necessity for the claimant to intervene, having regard to the particular circumstances of the case.[87] It was for this reason that an agency of necessity was not established in *Sachs v Miklos*,[88] where the defendant had agreed to store the claimant's furniture free of charge. After a considerable time the claimant had not reclaimed the furniture and, since the defendant wished to rent out the room where it was stored, he attempted to contact the claimant. Despite numerous attempts to make contact, the defendant could not

---

[84] *China Pacific SA v Food Corporation of India, The Winson* [1982] AC 939. See also *Guildford Borough Council v Hein* [2005] EWCA Civ 979, [33] (Clarke LJ), [80] (Waller LJ).
[85] [1990] 1 Lloyd's Rep 516.   [86] [1982] AC 939, 961.
[87] *Prager v Blatspeil, Stamp and Heacock Ltd* [1924] 1 KB 566, 572 (McCardie J).
[88] [1948] 2 KB 23.

find the claimant and so he sold the furniture. The claimant then returned to claim his furniture and, when he discovered that it had been sold, sued the defendant in conversion. Although the defendant argued that he was an agent of necessity, the Court of Appeal held that this had not been established, simply because there was no emergency which required the furniture to be sold at that time. Similarly, in *Munro v Willmott*[89] where the defendant had sold the claimant's car which had been left on his premises for a number of years. Again, the defendant was not characterized as an agent of necessity because the sale of the car was not required as a matter of real emergency but was done simply for the defendant's convenience. It would have been different in both cases if the claimant's property had been perishable, such as fruit or vegetables,[90] so that there was a commercial necessity for the property to be disposed of, otherwise it would have perished.

(2) It must have been practically impossible to obtain the defendant's instructions as to what should be done in time.[91] Restitutionary relief may, however, still be awarded where the claimant asked the defendant for instructions and the defendant failed to respond.[92]

(3) The burden is on the claimant to show that he or she was acting in good faith in the best interests of the defendant.[93] It follows that the claimant's action must have been reasonable and prudent in the particular circumstances of the case and must have been taken to protect the interests of the defendant, otherwise it will appear to be voluntary.[94]

(C) PLACE WITHIN THE LAW OF UNJUST ENRICHMENT

The problem with the action for reimbursement in circumstances of necessity where there is a pre-existing legal relationship between the parties is whether it really forms part of the law of unjust enrichment. The difficulty arises from the requirement that there must be a pre-existing relationship, whether it be agency or bailment or whatever. The effect of the doctrine is that the claimant's authority under this relationship is extended to include the reaction to the emergency.[95] This suggests that this doctrine is part of the law governing the pre-existing relationship, such as contract, rather than the law of unjust enrichment, with the consequence that, if the claimant has a remedy, it will be contractual rather than restitutionary. Whilst this may be true in most cases, there is still a role for the doctrine to apply within the law of unjust enrichment, as was recognized by the Supreme Court in *The Kos*,[96] although this role is likely to be very limited, if it actually exists at all. In that case the claimant, the owner of a ship, brought proceedings against the defendant charterers for expenses incurred in caring for the defendant's cargo whilst it was on board the claimant's ship. The cargo had been bailed to the claimant under a contract which had come to an end whilst the cargo was still in their possession. On the facts of the case a contractual

---

[89] [1949] 1 KB 295.

[90] Now see the Torts (Interference with Goods) Act 1977, ss 12, 13, and Sch 1 which enables a bailee to sell uncollected goods provided the bailor has been notified or the bailee has been unable to trace the bailor.

[91] *Sims and Co v Midland Railway Co* [1913] 1 KB 103, 112 (Scrutton LJ). See *Springer v Great Western Railway Company* [1921] 1 KB 257.

[92] *The Winson* [1982] AC 939, 961 (Lord Diplock).

[93] *Prager v Blatspeil, Stamp and Heacock Ltd* [1924] 1 KB 566, 572 (McCardie J).

[94] See *Springer v Great Western Railway Company* [1921] 1 KB 257.

[95] *De Bussche v Alt* (1878) 8 Ch D 286, 310.

[96] *ENE Kos 1 Ltd v Petroleo Brasileiro SA (No 2)* [2012] UKSC 17, [2012] 2 AC 164.

claim for reimbursement succeeded, but the Supreme Court also considered that the claimant could recover as a non-contractual bailee. This was because, since the bailment was originally under a contract which had terminated, the claimant had no choice but to remain in possession of the cargo. It had a continuing duty as a non-contractual bailee to take reasonable care of the cargo and this duty provided the basis for imposing an obligation on the charterers to pay for the cost of that care. The decisions in *Great Northern Railway v Swaffield*[97] and *The Winson*[98] were analysed in the same way. It follows that the liability arises from the law of bailment, which is an independent source of rights and obligations,[99] rather than the distinct doctrine of agency of necessity and also the law of unjust enrichment. But it does not follow that there is no scope for an unjust enrichment claim in such cases, since this was expressly acknowledged by Lord Sumption,[100] who considered that the measure of recovery might be different, although he did not explain how. Lord Mance considered that the bailee could recover for their time and expense in looking after the cargo.[101] He also considered that the bailor might be subject to a restitutionary liability 'in respect of any benefit they could be said to have had through the storage on board the vessel of the cargo'. But since this benefit must have been obtained at the expense of the claimant bailor, it is difficult to see how this would be different from the bailor's time and expense in looking after the cargo.

This suggestion that the bailor would have an alternative claim in unjust enrichment, albeit with the same measure of recovery as under the law of bailment, does cause significant doctrinal difficulties since, where the duty arises under bailment, this is a legally effective basis for liability,[102] which should mean that there is no scope for an independent claim in unjust enrichment. Similarly, where there is agency of necessity, the principal will be liable to pay the claimant under the law of agency, which again constitutes a legally effective basis, thus excluding a claim in unjust enrichment. It is only where there is no genuine agency relationship and no bailment that there can be any legitimate scope for a claim in unjust enrichment where there is a pre-existing relationship between the parties. Since agency and bailment are likely to cover most, if not all, of the cases where there is a pre-existing relationship between the parties, it follows there is likely to be little scope for an unjust enrichment claim in such circumstances.

4. NECESSITY IN THE CONTEXT OF MARITIME ADVENTURES

(A) SALVAGE

The law on salvage[103] is highly complex but, to the extent that it involves restitution, it can be considered to be founded on the principle of necessity. Although the doctrine of maritime salvage can be analysed, at least to some extent, by reference to the unjust enrichment principle, it is not possible to justify the award of restitutionary remedies in terms of an absence of a freely exercised choice to intervene on the part of the salvors, unlike the other grounds of restitution which are founded on the principle of necessity.

---

[97] See p 302, above.   [98] See p 303, above.

[99] *Yearworth v North Bristol NHS Trust* [2009] EWCA Civ 37, [2010] QB 1, 22 (Lord Judge CJ).

[100] *ENE Kos 1 Ltd v Petroleo Brasileiro SA (No 2)* [2012] UKSC 17, [2012] 2 AC 164, [31].

[101] Ibid, [55].   [102] See p 133, above.

[103] For detailed examination of salvage see FD Rose (ed), *Kennedy and Rose on The Law of Salvage* (8th edn, London: Sweet and Maxwell, 2013).

This is particularly because most salvors today are professionals who do not find themselves in circumstances of necessity but actually seek out such emergencies, and so would be characterized as volunteers who are acting officiously from motives of self-interest. Indeed, in *Falcke v Scottish Imperial Insurance Co*[104] Bowen LJ specifically excluded maritime salvage from the principle that liabilities are not to be forced upon people behind their backs. The salvage award which such salvors receive is primarily justified by public policy[105] to encourage salvage services to be provided.

(i) Establishing Maritime Salvage

The essential features of maritime salvage are that when a ship or cargo is in danger those people who reasonably incur expenditure in successfully rescuing the ship or cargo are entitled to remuneration from the owners.[106] It is crucial that the salvage is successful; there is no reward for failure.[107] So a salvage award will only be made if and to the extent that property has been saved by the salvor. The salvor must be acting voluntarily, which means that he or she must not be under a pre-existing duty to carry out the salvage. So, for example, the crew of a ship will generally not be able to claim salvage from its owners, since their terms of employment will require them to salvage the vessel or its cargo.

(ii) Characterizing the Salvage Award

Whilst maritime salvage is often dependent on contract,[108] this is not essential, and, to the extent that salvage work is effected outside contract, aspects of the salvage award may be considered to be restitutionary to reverse the defendant's unjust enrichment. This is supported by the fact that the owner of cargo or a ship will only be liable to pay for salvage if he or she had actually received a benefit. Crucially, however, the remedy which the salvor is awarded is not necessarily restitutionary, since it can also include an element of reward. The rationale behind the salvage award is to compensate the salvor for the services provided but also 'in the interests of public policy, encourage other mariners in like circumstances to perform like services'.[109] It is because of the element of reward which is included in the salvage award that maritime salvage cannot be regarded as falling completely within the law of restitution, simply because the remedy which is awarded does not seek only to reverse the defendant's unjust enrichment. That the salvage award is not completely restitutionary is illustrated by the types of factors which the courts take into account when fixing the award. For example, the court is to consider such matters as the value of the property saved, the degree of danger involved and the particular skill of the salvor. In fact, professional salvors are entitled to a more generous award than those salvors who act on the spur of the moment, because the law seeks to encourage professional salvors as a matter of public policy. Similarly, the salvage award may include an additional sum for saving life. Even though the salvage award may be made up in part of a restitutionary remedy to enable the salvor to recover the reasonable value of the services provided, even this amount lies in the discretion of the court.

Maritime salvage is better treated as being *sui generis*. Whilst it involves elements which are clearly restitutionary, particularly because the doctrine will only be triggered where the

---

[104] (1886) 34 Ch D 234, 249.   [105] *Nicholson v Chapman* (1793) 2 Hy Bl 254, 126 ER 536.

[106] The doctrine of maritime salvage does not extend to non-tidal waters (*The Goring* [1988] AC 831) nor to the rescue of property on land: *Sorrell v Paget* [1950] 1 KB 252, 260 (Bucknill LJ). Salvage has been extended to include the salvage of lives and aircraft. Provision is made by statute to reimburse expenses incurred in bringing shipwrecked seamen ashore and for burial expenses: Merchant Shipping Act 1995, s 73(2).

[107] *Semco Salvage and Marine Pte Ltd v Lancer Navigation Co Ltd* [1997] AC 455, 459 (Lord Mustill).

[108] For an example, see *Semco Salvage*, ibid.   [109] *The Telemachus* [1957] P 47, 49 (Willmer J).

defendant has received a benefit, it must not be artificially squeezed into the law of restitution. There are different considerations of policy at play in respect of salvage, which do not apply in other cases of necessitous intervention.

(B) GENERAL AVERAGE

The doctrine of general average also arises in the context of maritime emergencies. An act of general average[110] is committed where an extraordinary sacrifice or expenditure is incurred in the course of a maritime adventure for the benefit of the adventure. The doctrine of general average can be analysed in restitutionary terms since it can be considered to be founded on the reversal of unjust enrichment. This is because a defendant will be liable to those claimants who suffered loss or incurred expenditure if the defendant was a party to the maritime adventure and benefited from the claimant's acts.[111] Crucially, the defendant is only liable if the consequence of the claimant's intervention is that the defendant's property has been preserved.[112] It follows that the ground of restitution will be founded on the principle of necessity and that the doctrine of general average can be considered to fall within the law of restitution, although in practice provision is typically made for it by contract.

[110] See FD Rose, 'General Average as Restitution' (1997) 113 LQR 569.

[111] See *Birkley v Presgrave* (1801) 1 East 220, 228; 102 ER 86, 89 (Lawrence J) and the Marine Insurance Act 1906, s 66(1), (2).

[112] See *Chellew v Royal Commission on the Sugar Supply* [1921] 2 KB 627.

13

FAILURE OF BASIS

1. GENERAL PRINCIPLES

(A) THE PRINCIPLE OF FAILURE OF BASIS

Where the claimant transfers a benefit to the defendant pursuant to a transaction which is subject to a condition, known as a basis, and this condition has not been satisfied, there has been a failure of the basis for the transfer of the benefit which may enable the claimant to bring a claim for restitution. Traditionally, this principle was called failure of consideration. This is, however, potentially confusing[1] because consideration has a particular meaning in the law of contract, where it refers to the advantage conferred or the detriment suffered which makes a promise binding.[2] Consideration for the purposes of the law of restitution is not concerned with the existence of the promises under a contract, but with the performance of promises and other non-promissory conditions as well. Consequently, even though the language of 'failure of consideration' will be found in many of the cases and commentaries, the language of failure of basis is used in this book.[3] Indeed, this term has now found favour in the Supreme Court.[4]

Failure of basis is not a ground of restitution in its own right, but is a general principle which underlies the existence of a number of particular grounds of restitution. They operate in broadly the same way as the other recognized grounds of restitution, namely that restitution should be awarded because the claimant's intention that the defendant should receive the benefit has been vitiated. This was recognized by Lord Wright in *Fibrosa Spolka Akcyjna v Fairbairn Lawson Combe Barbour Ltd*:[5] 'There was no intent to enrich [the defendant] in the events which happened.... The payment was originally conditional. The condition of retaining it is eventual performance. Accordingly, when that condition fails, the right to retain the money must simultaneously fail.'

But, whereas for grounds of restitution such as mistake and duress, the claimant's intention is vitiated at the point when the claimant transfers the benefit to the defendant, this is not generally the case where the claimant relies on grounds of restitution which are founded on the principle of failure of basis. This is because in such cases the claimant does validly intend the defendant to receive the benefit at the time of the transfer. This intention is vitiated only because of subsequent events. Consequently, the effect of the

---

[1] J Goodwin, 'Failure of Basis in the Contractual Context' [2013] RLR 24.

[2] *Midland Bank Trust Co Ltd v Green* [1981] AC 513, 531 (Lord Wilberforce).

[3] It will be used to explain the analysis of the cases even where those cases used the language of failure of consideration.

[4] *Barnes v Eastenders Cash and Carry plc* [2014] UKSC 26, [2015] AC 1, [105] (Lord Toulson). See also *Spaul v Spaul* [2014] EWCA Civ 679, [50] (Rimer LJ). Sometimes 'failure of condition' has been used. See *Fibrosa Spolka Akcyjna v Fairbairn Lawson Combe Barbour Ltd* [1943] AC 32, 64–5 (Lord Wright); *Anderson v McPherson (No 2)* [2012] WASC 19, [235] (Edelman J).

[5] [1943] AC 32, 64–5.

basis for the transfer failing is retrospectively to vitiate the claimant's intention that the defendant should receive the benefit.[6] It is therefore preferable to treat the claimant's intention as qualified by means of the condition, so that if the condition is not satisfied the basis will have failed and the claimant's intent that the defendant should retain the benefit will no longer be effective.

The grounds of restitution which are founded on failure of basis are most likely to operate in a contractual context, where the usual basis for the transfer of a benefit to the defendant is that he or she promises to do something in return for the benefit received. Consequently, the fundamental principle that restitution is not available whilst the contract subsists is especially significant.[7]

(B) THE GROUNDS OF RESTITUTION FOUNDED ON THE PRINCIPLE OF FAILURE OF BASIS

There are three grounds of restitution which are founded on the principle of failure of basis: where the basis has totally failed, where the basis has partially failed, and where the basis failed as a matter of law, often known as absence of basis. Whilst the ground of total failure of basis has long been recognized,[8] the role of partial failure of basis as a ground of restitution is much less secure. Although it is clear that partial failure of basis is the recognized ground of restitution where a contract has been discharged by frustration,[9] there is increasing evidence that the ground of total failure of basis is itself being watered down, through a growing manipulation of the notion of when the basis can be considered to have failed totally, with the consequence that we are moving ever closer to the recognition of partial failure of basis as a general ground of restitution in its own right. The existence of a third ground of restitution which arises where there is an absence of basis is controversial, although this ground has received some judicial recognition.[10] It is important to emphasize at the outset that, whilst this ground appears to equate with Birks's absence of basis thesis,[11] it is different since it operates as a ground of restitution and it is defined restrictively.

(C) THE DEFINITION OF BASIS

Basis for these purposes refers to the condition which constituted the ground for the claimant transferring a benefit to the defendant. The basis is to be determined objectively rather than by reference to the subjective motives of the claimant.[12] Any particular purpose or motive of the claimant in transferring the enrichment can, however, be taken into account in identifying the basis, but only if such a purpose or motive had been communicated to the defendant before the enrichment was transferred or any contract was made,[13] so that the defendant had an opportunity to object to it,[14] so that

---

[6] The only exception to this analysis of failure of basis is where there never was any possibility of the condition for the transfer of the benefit being satisfied. See further p 371, below.

[7] See p 134, above.

[8] See *Moses v Macferlan* (1760) 2 Burrows 1005, 1012; 97 ER 676, 681 (Lord Mansfield).

[9] See p 355, below.   [10] See p 373, below.   [11] See p 127, above.

[12] *Giedo van der Garde BV v Force India Formula One Team Ltd* [2010] EWHC 2373 (QB), [286] (Stadlen J). See also *Lissack v Manhattan Loft Corporation Ltd* [2013] EWHC 128 (Ch), [87] (Roth J).

[13] *Lissack v Manhattan Loft Corporation Ltd* [2013] EWHC 128 (Ch).

[14] *Giedo van der Garde BV v Force India Formula One Team Ltd* [2010] EWHC 2373 (QB), [286] (Stadlen J).

the basis can be considered to be shared.[15] So, for example, a basis will not be identified where the claimant cleaned the defendant's car without the defendant's knowledge or prior request, but in the expectation that the defendant would pay for the work. The claimant cannot establish that there has been a failure of basis if the defendant refuses to pay, since there was no understanding between the parties that it was a condition of the claimant doing the work that the defendant would pay. Denial of restitution in such circumstances is consistent with the general principle that no claimant can obtain restitution where he or she is a volunteer who has taken the risk of not being paid for doing the work.[16]

The basis for the transfer of an enrichment can be interpreted in two different ways, depending on the nature of the condition.

(i) Failure of the Defendant to Perform His or Her Part of the Bargain

The usual interpretation of basis relates to where the condition on which the transfer of the benefit is contingent is the promised performance by the defendant for which the claimant had bargained.[17] So, for example, if the claimant and the defendant entered into a contract whereby the defendant agreed to sell a car to the claimant for £10,000, the claimant paid the full price in advance but the defendant failed to supply the car, the basis for the claimant's payment will have failed because the claimant did not receive from the defendant what she had promised to provide. In such a situation the claimant would usually sue for compensatory damages for breach of contract, but a restitutionary remedy would be more attractive if the value of the car was less than £10,000, since damages for breach of contract would be assessed by reference to the value of the car which the claimant should have received, which would be less than the money received by the defendant.

The defendant's expected performance need not, however, arise in a contractual context for the claimant to establish that the basis has failed. In *Spaul v Spaul*[18] Romer LJ recognized that there could be a failure of basis where there was a failure of an informal arrangement which fell short of a binding contract, but there still had to be some form of joint endeavour between the parties. So, for example, if the claimant provided a benefit to the defendant on the understanding that it would be paid for under a contract which the parties were negotiating, but the negotiations failed due to the withdrawal of the defendant, the claimant should be able to recover the value of the benefit on the ground of total failure of basis,[19] even though the defendant was not obliged by contract to pay for the benefit, because of the mutual expectation that a contract would be made.[20]

(ii) Failure of a Contingent Condition

The alternative meaning of basis relates to where the transfer of the benefit to the defendant is subject to a condition involving the existence of an identified state of affairs

---

[15] See *Burgess v Rawnsley* [1975] Ch 429, 442 (Browne LJ). In *Lissack v Manhattan Loft Corporation Ltd* [2013] EWHC 128 (Ch), [87] Roth J considered it sufficient that the defendant ought reasonably to have known that the claimant expected to be paid for the benefit transferred.

[16] See p 36, above.

[17] *Fibrosa Spolka Akcyjna v Fairbairn Lawson Combe Barbour Ltd* [1943] AC 32, 48 (Viscount Simon LC); *Stocznia Gdanska SA v Latvian Shipping Co* [1998] 1 WLR 574, 588 (Lord Goff); *Barnes v Eastenders Cash and Carry plc* [2014] UKSC 26, [2015] AC 1, [106] (Lord Toulson).

[18] [2014] EWCA Civ 679, [46].   [19] See p 343, below.

[20] Although this could equally be analysed as the failure of a contingent condition that a contract would be made, see below.

or occurrence of an event which involves no promised performance by the defendant.[21] Restitution is justified in such a case because the basis for the transfer of the benefit will have failed if the condition is not satisfied.

An example of a contingent condition operating as a basis is *Chillingworth v Esche*,[22] where the claimant agreed, subject to contract, to buy land from the defendant and paid a deposit to the defendant. A contract was drawn up by the defendant, but the claimant refused to sign it and claimed repayment of the deposit. The claim for restitution succeeded because the money had been paid on the condition that a binding contract would be made and, since no contract had been signed, the contingency failed. Consequently the basis for the defendant receiving the money disappeared, it being irrelevant that the failure of the condition was due to the failure of the claimant, rather than the defendant, to sign the contract. Another example is *Barnes v Eastenders Cash and Carry plc*[23] where a receiver had provided services in managing a company's property on behalf of the Crown Prosecution Service (CPS) for which it had been agreed that the receiver would be remunerated from the assets he was managing, enforced by means of a lien over those assets. The lien was found to be invalid, so the receiver was unable to be paid as originally agreed. It was held that the CPS was liable to make restitution to the receiver in respect of the services provided, with the ground of restitution being failure of basis, namely that he would be remunerated from the company's assets.

This second interpretation of basis means that a claimant who, for example, gives money to the defendant on condition that he or she marries a particular person, will be able to recover the gift if the defendant does not marry that person.[24] This is also illustrated by *Re Ames' Settlement*,[25] where a marriage settlement was established whereby the settlor covenanted to pay £10,000 within one year of the parties' marriage. Although the marriage did take place it was held to be void *ab initio* since the husband was incapable of consummating it. Consequently, the basis for the payment had failed totally since the marriage, on which the settlement was conditional, was deemed never to have been made.

(D) THE NATURE OF THE ENRICHMENT

Traditionally, those grounds of restitution which are founded on the principle of failure of basis have only been invoked to obtain restitution of money from the defendant. This is because the ground of total failure of basis originated in the action for money had and received.[26] But, with the abolition of the forms of action, there is no longer any reason why this ground of restitution should be inapplicable where the enrichment received by the defendant takes the form of goods or services. Recognition of the principle of symmetry[27] in particular would suggest that restitutionary remedies should be available regardless of the type of benefit received by the defendant.[28] A number of cases have implicitly recognized that restitutionary remedies are available where the basis has failed even

---

[21] *Barnes v Eastenders Cash and Carry plc* [2014] UKSC 26, [2015] AC 1, [109] (Lord Toulson).

[22] [1924] 1 Ch 97. See also *Guardian Ocean Cargoes Ltd v Banco de Brazil SA* [1991] 2 Lloyd's LR 68.

[23] [2014] UKSC 26, [2015] AC 1.

[24] See also the Law Reform (Miscellaneous Provisions) Act 1970, s 3(2) by virtue of which the gift of an engagement ring is presumed to be an absolute gift, but this presumption may be rebutted by proving that the ring was given on condition, whether express or implied, that it shall be returned if the marriage does not take place.

[25] [1946] Ch 217. See also *P v P* [1916] 2 IR 400.

[26] The distinction was affirmed in *Taylor v Motability Finance Ltd* [2004] EWHC 2619 (Comm). See p 136, above.   [27] See p 125, above.

[28] See PBH Birks, 'Failure of Consideration' in F Rose (ed), *Consensus ad Idem—Essays in the Law of Contract in Honour of Guenter Treitel* (London: Sweet and Maxwell, 1996), 185–6.

where the enrichment is goods or services.[29] That the grounds of restitution based on failure of basis are available generally regardless of the nature of the enrichment, was recognized explicitly by the House of Lords in *Cobbe v Yeoman's Row Management Ltd*,[30] where a claim succeeded on the ground of total failure of basis where the claimant had provided services to the defendant on the basis that a written contract would be made between them, but no such contract was made. Despite this, a number of cases have now recognized that, where the claimant has provided services to the defendant pursuant to a contract which the defendant has breached, the claimant will be confined to a contractual claim.[31] Since there is no such restriction where the claimant has paid money to the defendant pursuant to a contract which the defendant then breaches, the principle of symmetry between types of enrichment has itself been breached. This is indefensible.

(E) THE RELATIONSHIP BETWEEN DAMAGES FOR BREACH OF CONTRACT AND RESTITUTION TO REVERSE UNJUST ENRICHMENT

Where the claimant has paid money in advance to the defendant in respect of a contract which the defendant then breaches, the claimant has two remedial options. First, the claimant might sue the defendant for breach of contract and recover damages. These damages will usually be compensatory, although it is possible for a disgorgement remedy to be awarded to deprive the defendant of any gain made as a result of breaching the contract.[32] The award of such a gain-based remedy has nothing, however, to do with the reversal of the defendant's unjust enrichment, since the restitutionary claim is founded on the wrong of the breach of contract.[33] Alternatively, the claimant might seek to recover the advance payment by virtue of the failure of basis. Such a claim would be founded on the reversal of the defendant's unjust enrichment.

In *Baltic Shipping v Dillon*[34] the High Court of Australia held that the award of compensatory damages for breach of contract and restitutionary remedies to reverse the defendant's unjust enrichment are incompatible, so that they can only be awarded as alternatives. In principle this must be correct. The usual function of compensatory damages for breach of contract is to fulfil the claimant's expectations by placing the claimant in the position which he or she would have occupied had the contract not been breached. The function of restitutionary remedies, on the other hand, is to return the claimant to the position which he or she occupied before the contract was breached by restoring to the claimant any gain made by the defendant at the claimant's expense. If the claimant was awarded expectation damages to carry him or her forward it would generally be absurd and contradictory also to award the claimant a restitutionary remedy to take the claimant back to the position before the benefit was transferred. In part this is because if, by awarding compensatory damages, the claimant is deemed to be placed in the position which he or she would have occupied had the contract not been breached, it will not be possible to show that the basis for the enrichment has failed, since the claimant will be considered to have received what he or she expected to receive under the contract.

---

[29] See, in particular *Pulbrook v Lawes* (1876) 1 QBD 284, discussed at p 351, below. Where a contract is frustrated restitution will lie in respect of money and non-money benefits. See p 357, below.

[30] *Cobbe v Yeoman's Row Management Ltd* [2008] UKHL 55, [2008] 1 WLR 1752.

[31] See p 136, above.   [32] *Attorney-General v Blake* [2001] 1 AC 268. See p 473, below.

[33] See Chapter 18.

[34] (1993) 176 CLR 344. See also *Walstab v Spottiswode* (1846) 15 M and W 501, 514; 153 ER 952, 953 (Pollock CB).

Similarly, if the claimant has recovered the benefit which he or she had transferred to the defendant under the contract in a restitutionary claim, the basis for the claimant requiring the defendant to perform the contract will have been removed, since that performance will have been conditional on receipt of the benefit from the claimant.[35] If the defendant is not required to perform his or her side of the bargain, there is no ground for holding the defendant liable for breach of contract.

But this incompatibility between awarding damages for breach and restitution for failure of basis is not as clear-cut as the High Court of Australia suggest. Rather than saying that compensatory damages and restitutionary remedies are incompatible, it is preferable to assert that both types of remedy may be awarded in the same action so long as there is no double recovery.[36] If the claimant is awarded a restitutionary remedy it should still be possible in principle to award him or a compensatory remedy as well, but in assessing the loss suffered by the claimant it is vital to take into account the effect of the restitutionary remedy which has been awarded.[37] So, for example, if the claimant is able to recover the value of any benefit transferred under the contract to the defendant by virtue of failure of basis, it should still be possible for the claimant to claim damages to compensate for a distinct loss, such as personal injury.[38]

In most cases, however, the claimant will wish either to claim compensatory damages or restitution and will not be seeking to recover both. The decision as to which remedy to pursue will depend on which remedy is more lucrative, by reference to whether or not the defendant's gain is greater than the claimant's loss arising from the breach of contract,[39] which will be determined by the operation of rules on remoteness, mitigation of loss and the type of loss which is recoverable under the law of damages. Further, a claim for restitution might trigger a proprietary restitutionary claim, at least if the defendant knew that there had been a failure of basis for his or her receipt of the enrichment.[40]

2. ESTABLISHING TOTAL FAILURE OF BASIS

By far the most significant ground of restitution which is founded on the principle of failure of basis arises where the basis has failed totally. Restitution can be awarded where no part of the condition on which the transfer of a benefit to the defendant is contingent has been fulfilled. So, for example, if the claimant pays the defendant in advance the purchase price of a car which the defendant fails to deliver, the basis for the payment will have failed totally since the claimant failed to receive any benefit, and the defendant will be required to repay the advance payment. The reason that total failure of basis is recognized as a ground of restitution is because, where the transfer is qualified by virtue of a condition which fails, the transfer can be considered to be non-voluntary.[41]

---

[35] *Baltic Shipping Co v Dillon* (1993) 176 CLR 344, 359 (Mason CJ).

[36] See K Barker, 'Restitution of Passenger Fare' [1993] LMCLQ 291. Compensatory damages and restitutionary remedies may both be awarded where the claim is grounded on the wrong of breach of contract if there is no double recovery. See p 438, below.

[37] See *Giedo van der Garde BNV v Force India Formula One Team Ltd* [2010] EWHC 2373 (QB), [291] (Stadlen J). In *DO Ferguson and Associates v Sohl* (1992) 62 Build LR 92 the claimant was awarded both restitution on the ground of total failure of basis and nominal damages of £1 for breach of contract.

[38] This had been recognized by Lord Denning MR in *Heywood v Wellers (a firm)* [1976] QB 446, 458. See also *Millar's Machinery Co Ltd v David Way and Son* (1935) 40 Com Cas 204.

[39] See p 326, below.   [40] *Re Farepak Food and Gifts Ltd* [2006] EWHC 3272. See p 600, below.

[41] *Gribbon v Lutton* [2001] EWCA Civ 1956, [2002] QB 902, [60] (Robert Walker LJ).

(A) THE REQUIREMENTS FOR ESTABLISHING TOTAL FAILURE OF BASIS

Where a claimant wishes to obtain restitution on the ground of total failure of basis certain requirements must be satisfied. Whether a particular requirement applies depends on the nature of the restitutionary claim.

(i) The Contract Must Cease to Be Operative

Where the claimant has transferred a benefit to the defendant pursuant to a contract it is first necessary to show that the contract has ceased to be operative.[42] The contract may no longer be operative for a number of reasons, the most important being that it was discharged for breach or was frustrated, but it may also have been terminated by rescission or been declared void. It is not possible, however, to discharge a contract for breach once the claimant has affirmed it; so affirmation will bar the claimant from bringing a restitutionary claim.[43] The requirement that the contract must cease to be operative before a restitutionary remedy can be awarded is an important safeguard against the abuse of the law of restitution by undermining the law of contract.[44] For, until the contract has been discharged, the contractual regime still operates to determine what remedies can be awarded.

But it does not necessarily follow from the fact that a contract has been discharged for breach that the contractual regime is inapplicable to the restitutionary claim. This is illustrated by the decision of the House of Lords in *The Trident Beauty*.[45] The claimant had chartered a vessel from a ship owner, who then assigned to the defendant its right to receive payments for hiring the vessel from the claimant. The claimant was informed of this assignment and paid an instalment to the defendant. The owner breached the contract and the claimant accepted the repudiation as discharging the contract. The claimant then sought to obtain restitution of the payment it had made to the defendant on the ground of total failure of basis, since the ship had been out of action for the whole period in respect of which the instalment was paid. The claim failed because there was a clause in the contract between the claimant and the owner to the effect that any overpaid hire had to be repaid at once. Since this contractual provision had come into operation before the contract was discharged, it still applied despite the discharge. This meant that the owner was obliged to repay the hire to the claimant by virtue of the contract, even though the hire had been paid to the defendant. As Lord Goff emphasized:

> as between shipowner and charterer, there is a contractual regime which legislates for the recovery of overpaid hire. It follows that, as a general rule, the law of restitution has no part to play in the matter; the existence of the agreed regime renders the imposition by the law of a remedy in restitution both unnecessary and inappropriate.[46]

---

[42] *Guinness plc v Saunders* [1990] 2 AC 663, 697–8 (Lord Goff); *Taylor v Motability Finance Ltd* [2004] EWHC 2619 (Comm), [23] (Cooke J); *Mowlem plc v Stena Line Ports Ltd* [2004] EWHC 2206; *S and W Process Engineering Ltd v Cauldron Foods Ltd* [2005] EWHC 153 (TCC). See Chapter 7 for detailed exposition of this requirement.

[43] *Kwei Tek Chao v British Traders and Shippers Ltd* [1954] 2 QB 459. See also *Goodman v Pocock* (1850) 15 QB 576, 117 ER 577.

[44] S Smith, 'Concurrent Liability in Contract and Unjust Enrichment: The Fundamental Breach Requirement' (1999) 115 LQR 245.

[45] *Pan Ocean Shipping Co Ltd v Creditcorp Ltd* [1994] 1 WLR 161. See also the analysis of entire contracts at p 340, below.

[46] *Pan Ocean Shipping Co Ltd v Creditcorp Ltd* [1994] 1 WLR 161, 164. Other reasons were given for the failure of the claim, including that a claimant should not be given a choice as to which party to sue, whether the

The denial of restitution in these circumstances may seem unjust, because the defendant was allowed to retain the instalment even though the claimant had received no benefit in respect of that payment.[47] Although the claimant did have a cause of action against the owner in contract, this was worthless because the owner was not considered to be worth suing. Nevertheless, the decision of the House of Lords is correct, since it implicitly acknowledges that the law of restitution is subservient to the law of contract. The claimant had agreed to the inclusion of the clause which required the owner to repay overpaid hire payments, and so the claimant bore the risk that the owner would not be able to repay this money. This risk had been allocated by the contract and it was not for the law of restitution to reallocate such risks.

(ii) The Defendant is No Longer Ready, Willing, and Able to Perform

It has sometimes been suggested that there is a general requirement which must be satisfied before restitution can be awarded on the ground of total failure of basis, namely that the defendant is no longer ready, able, and willing to perform his or her part of the bargain. The leading case where this requirement was recognized is *Thomas v Brown*,[48] where the claimant contracted to buy a shop from the defendant and paid him a deposit. This contract was unenforceable since the vendor's name had not been disclosed on the contract as was required by the Statute of Frauds. Before the shop was conveyed to the claimant he sought to recover the deposit on the ground of total failure of basis, but he was unable to do so. Two reasons were given for this: first, because the claimant had voluntarily paid the deposit with full knowledge that the vendor's name was not disclosed in the contract. It was not considered to be acceptable for the claimant in such circumstances subsequently to object to the non-disclosure. Secondly, the defendant always remained ready, willing, and able to execute the conveyance, so there was nothing unconscionable in the defendant retaining the deposit.

The difficulty with the requirement that the defendant must no longer be ready, willing, and able to perform is whether it is additional to the requirement that the contract must no longer be operative or whether it is a separate requirement which only arises in certain circumstances. The latter is the better view. Where a contract has been discharged, for breach for example, it is clear that the defendant is no longer able to perform his or her contractual promise because that obligation is terminated on discharge of the contract. Consequently, it follows automatically from the discharge that the defendant is unable to perform his or her side of the bargain and so it is not necessary to consider in addition whether the defendant is ready and willing to perform. Where, however, the contract is unenforceable, as in *Thomas v Brown*, the policy of the law which makes the contract unenforceable makes it unnecessary to show that the contract has been discharged,[49] but the claimant must instead show that the defendant is no longer ready, able and willing to perform the contract.

owner in contract or the defendant in restitution. See Lord Woolf, ibid, 171. But if the claimant can establish a claim in restitution, the fact that there is an alternative claim against another party, or even the same party, in contract is irrelevant, so long as the remedies which are awarded are compatible and do not result in double recovery.

[47] See G Tolhurst, 'Assignment, Equities, *The Trident Beauty* and Restitution' (1999) 58 CLJ 546 who argues that it was unconscionable of the defendant to deny the claimant's expectation that the right to repayment would be respected by the defendant. But it is unclear on what basis the defendant can be considered to have acted unconscionably, since it had not made any representations to induce any expectation on the part of the claimant.

[48] (1876) 1 QBD 714. See also *Monnickendam v Leanse* (1923) 39 TLR 445.

[49] As was recognized by Deane J in *Pavey and Matthews Pty Ltd v Paul* (1986) CLR 221, 256.

In those circumstances where there is no contract between the claimant and the defendant, but the transfer of a benefit by the defendant is contingent on there being a particular state of affairs or event, neither requirement needs to be considered, because there is no contract to be set aside and the basis for the transfer is not conditional on the defendant's performance, so readiness, ability, and willingness to perform is irrelevant. This is illustrated by *Chillingworth v Esche*[50] where the claimant recovered a deposit which he had paid to the defendant pursuant to an agreement which was 'subject to contract'. Although it was the claimant who refused to sign the contract and the defendant remained ready, able, and willing to sell his land, the claimant recovered the deposit simply because the condition on which the deposit was contingent, namely the signing of the contract, had not been satisfied. Since the defendant had never promised that he would sign the contract, his continued willingness to sign it did not prevent the basis from failing totally.

It follows from this analysis that there are three different types of basis which might fail and the requirements to establish total failure will vary depending on the nature of the basis which is involved.

(1) Where the basis involves the performance of a contractual obligation or the satisfaction of a contractual condition restitutionary relief will only be available where the contract has been discharged.

(2) Where the basis arises under a contract which is unenforceable or involves non-contractual performance by the defendant it is not necessary to show that the contract ceases to operate but it is necessary to show that the defendant is no longer ready, able or willing to perform.

(3) Where the basis involves the satisfaction of a non-contractual condition which does not require performance on the part of the defendant there are no requirements which need to be satisfied other than to show that the basis has failed totally.

(iii) The Basis Must Have Failed Totally

Regardless of the nature of the basis which forms the condition for the transfer of a benefit to the defendant, restitution of the benefit will depend on whether the basis has failed totally, save where one of the other recognized grounds of restitution is applicable.

(1) Determining Whether the Basis Has Failed

The proper test for determining whether the basis has failed was authoritatively determined by the House of Lords in *Stocznia Gdanska SA v Latvian Shipping Co*,[51] where Lord Goff recognized that: 'the test is not whether the promisee has received a specific benefit, but rather whether the promisor has performed any part of the contractual duties in respect of which the payment is due.'[52]

Although this dictum related to a case involving performance of a contractual obligation, it is of relevance to all types of basis. The key point is that the basis will not have failed totally if any part of the condition by reference to which the claimant has transferred a

---

[50] [1924] 1 Ch 97.   [51] [1998] 1 WLR 574.

[52] Ibid, 588. Cf *Taylor v Motability Finance Ltd* [2004] EWHC (Comm) where Cooke J, [25], assumed that where the claim arises from the supply of goods or services by the claimant, a restitutionary claim grounded on total failure of basis will fail if the claimant has substantially performed the contract. This is inconsistent with the essence of failure of basis, which is concerned with satisfaction of the basis by reference to which the claimant's performance is conditional, which will typically, but not invariably, involve performance by the defendant.

benefit to the defendant has been satisfied.[53] There is no *de minimis* exception to this bar.[54] Typically the condition will be satisfied by the receipt of any benefit by the claimant, but, as Lord Goff acknowledged, this will not always be the case.[55] If the basis was only fulfilled where the claimant had received a benefit, there would be many cases where the basis for the transfer of the enrichment could never be satisfied. For example, if the claimant paid the defendant to paint the house of the claimant's daughter, the claimant would never receive a benefit personally. The importance of Lord Goff's dictum is that, in the contractual context at least, whether the basis has failed totally will depend on the terms of the contract, objectively construed.[56]

But Lord Goff's dictum cannot be regarded as an exclusive definition of the notion of basis for the purposes of determining whether it has totally failed. This is because the basis need not involve the performance of a promise by the defendant, but may simply involve the occurrence of an event or the existence of a state of affairs.[57] Consequently, although Lord Goff's dictum expands the notion of basis for the purposes of the law of restitution, it cannot be treated as a complete definition of that concept. The definition of basis which is appropriate in each case will ultimately depend on what it is that the claimant had bargained for under the transaction[58] or what condition had been accepted and, in a contractual context at least, whether the basis has failed will depend on whether the defendant had performed any part of his or her 'essential obligation' under the contract.[59] Consequently, the nature of the bargain between the parties is of decisive importance when determining whether or not the basis has failed totally.

The significance of the transaction to the interpretation of total failure of basis is illustrated by those contracts consisting of obligations which are characterized as entire. These are contracts where the obligation of one party to perform does not arise until the other party has fully performed their contractual obligations. So, for example, if the claimant paid the defendant in advance under a contract where the defendant's obligation is entire, if that defendant has not fully performed the obligation as promised the basis for the payment will have failed completely, because the condition for the defendant's retention of the money paid is full performance of the obligation under the contract, regardless of the fact that the claimant may have received some benefit from the defendant under the contract.[60] Although this might appear unjust, it is consistent with the funda-mental principle that, where the contract has allocated the risk of non-performance to one party, here the defendant, it is not for the law of restitution to subvert that allocation. In the context of an entire contract the notion of basis is therefore defined to mean only full performance of the defendant's contractual obligation.

---

[53] *Giedo van der Garde BV v Force India Formula One Team Ltd* [2010] EWHC 2373 (QB), [288] (Stadlen J).

[54] Ibid, save if the benefit received can be characterized as collateral or incidental. See p 319, below.

[55] *Stocznia Gdanska SA v Latvian Shipping Co* [1998] 1 WLR 574, 588. In *Giedo van der Garde BV v Force India Formula One Team Ltd* [2010] EWHC 2373 (QB), [264], Stadlen J said that it would be sufficient that the defendant's performance is 'advantageous' to the claimant in some way.

[56] *Giedo van der Garde BV v Force India Formula One Team Ltd* [2010] EWHC 2373 (QB), [268] (Stadlen J). See p 310, above. Goodwin, 'Failure of Basis in the Contractual Context', 28, has argued that the total failure requirement is unnecessary because the court identifies the objective basis for which a benefit was transferred, and, in the light of this construction, the basis will either fail or it will not. This does not reflect the analysis in the cases, but it does emphasize how many of the difficulties in this area can be resolved through careful construction of the bargain between the parties. [57] See p 310, above.

[58] *Rover International Ltd v Cannon Film Sales Ltd (No 3)* [1989] 1 WLR 912, 923 (Kerr LJ).

[59] *Guinness Mahon Co Ltd v Chelsea and Kensington LBC* [1999] QB 215, 240 (Robert Walker LJ).

[60] *Giles v Edwards* (1797) 7 Term Rep 181, 101 ER 920.

(2) Distinguishing Between Contracts to Sell and Contracts to Build and Sell

Since the effect of Lord Goff's dictum in *Stocznia* is that the determination of whether the basis has failed totally depends on the terms of the contract, some difficult questions of contractual construction can arise. This has been particularly significant in the context of contracts in which the defendant agrees to sell goods to the claimant which the defendant has made. It was recognized in *Stocznia* that, if the contract is construed simply as an agreement where the defendant promises to sell goods to the claimant, the claimant will be able to rely on the ground of total failure of basis only if he or she has not received any goods from the defendant, since the defendant had only promised to supply goods. Where, however, the contract is construed as one where the defendant agrees both to manufacture and supply the goods, the claimant will not be able to rely on the ground of total failure of basis once the defendant has started to manufacture the goods, because this is part of what the defendant had promised to do. It is irrelevant in this type of case that the claimant has not actually received a specific benefit from the defendant.[61] Lord Lloyd in *Stocznia* did recognize that the distinction between these two types of contracts is fine, but it is decisive to the success or failure of the restitutionary claim.[62] This distinction between contracts of sale and contracts of service and sale can be illustrated by analysing two decisions of the House of Lords.

In *Fibrosa Spolka Akcyjna v Fairbairn Lawson Combe Barbour Ltd*[63] the claimant had entered into a contract with the defendant to purchase machinery, which the defendant manufactured. The claimant made an advance payment to the defendant. The contract was frustrated by the outbreak of the Second World War before the defendant was able to deliver the machines to the claimant, but after the defendant had incurred expenditure in manufacturing them. The House of Lords held that the claimant could recover the advance payments on the ground of total failure of basis, because it had not received any of the machinery which had been promised by the defendant. It was irrelevant that the defendant had incurred expenditure under the contract, simply because it was construed as an ordinary contract for the sale of goods. The manufacture of the machinery was not considered to form part of the basis for the claimant's payment.[64]

This case can be compared with *Hyundai Heavy Industries Co Ltd v Papadopoulos*.[65] The claimant had contracted to build and sell a ship to the purchaser, who agreed to pay for the ship in instalments, with these payments being guaranteed by the defendant. The purchaser paid the first instalment, but defaulted on the second and consequently the claimant treated the contract as discharged. The claimant then sued the defendant on the guarantee for payment of the second instalment. It was unanimously held that the defendant was liable under the terms of the guarantee, but three of the judges recognized that the defendant's liability as surety could also be founded on the fact that, despite the discharge of the contract, the purchaser remained liable to pay the second instalment because this liability had already accrued before the contract was discharged. In reaching this decision the judges assumed that the purchaser could not have claimed repayment of the instalments on the ground of total failure of basis. This was relevant because, if the purchaser had a right to obtain restitution of the payments had the instalments been paid,

---

[61] *Stocznia Gdanska SA v Latvian Shipping Co* [1998] 1 WLR 574, 589 (Lord Goff), 600 (Lord Lloyd).

[62] See also Kerr LJ in *Rover International Ltd v Cannon Film Sales Ltd (No 3)* [1989] 1 WLR 912, 931.

[63] [1943] AC 32. Today, the defendant's loss could be apportioned under the Law Reform (Frustrated Contracts) Act 1943. See p 358, below.

[64] Ibid, 56 (Lord Russell), 64 (Lord Wright), and 83 (Lord Porter).

[65] [1980] 1 WLR 1129. This case was affirmed in *Stocznia Gdanska SA v Latvian Shipping Co* [1998] 1 WLR 574 which also concerned a contract to build and sell ships.

it would not have been liable to pay the instalments once the contract had been discharged. Whilst the majority recognized that, had this simply been a contract of sale rather
than a contract to build and sell, the purchaser could have obtained restitution of the
instalments which had already been paid on the ground of total failure of basis, it was
accepted that, because this was a contract to build and sell, the basis would not have failed
totally once the claimant had incurred expenditure in building the ship before the contract
was discharged, even though the purchaser had not received any benefit from this
expenditure. The result of this case can be justified on the ground that, since the purchaser
was required to pay instalments to the claimant before receiving any specific benefit, this
effectively meant that the purchaser was expected to bear the risk of any default, so that if
the contract was discharged he or she should suffer the loss. If the contract allocates the
risks in this way, it is not for the law of restitution to reallocate the risks.

(3) Contracts to Provide Services

Where the contract involves the provision of a service by the defendant the claimant will
not be able to rely on the ground of total failure of basis if the claimant has benefited from
this service in any way. The application of this principle is illustrated by the decision of the
High Court of Australia in *Baltic Shipping Co v Dillon*,[66] where the claimant had paid in
advance for a 14-day cruise. On the eighth day the ship capsized and, although the
defendant had repaid the fare in respect of the remaining six-day period, the claimant
sought restitution of the whole fare which she had paid on the ground of total failure of
basis. Her claim failed because the basis had not failed totally, since she had received the
benefit of the cruise for eight days.

(B) MANIPULATING THE NOTION OF TOTAL FAILURE OF BASIS

Although this ground of restitution depends on the basis failing totally, the courts have
manipulated the notion of *total* failure. There are, in particular, two judicial techniques by
virtue of which certain benefits received by the claimant can be discounted so that they
will not prevent the basis from failing totally. The first technique involves ignoring the
receipt of collateral benefits and the second involves the apportionment of benefits
received.

(i) Receipt of Collateral Benefit

Where the claimant has received a benefit from the defendant this will only be considered
to be a relevant benefit for the purposes of establishing whether or not the basis has failed
totally where it was an essential benefit for which the claimant had bargained. If the benefit
did not form part of the main benefit bargained for under the contract,[67] it will be
considered to be collateral and can be discounted, so that its receipt will not prevent the
basis from failing totally. This should be determined from the perspective of the claimant
and by reference to his or her purpose in contracting with the defendant, albeit that this
purpose is to be determined objectively.

The application of this collateral benefit principle is illustrated by *Rowland v Divall*[68]
where the claimant had bought a car from the defendant and, having used it for over four
months, discovered that it had been stolen and was compelled to return it to its true

---

[66] (1993) 176 CLR 344.

[67] *Giedo van der Garde BV v Force India Formula One Team Ltd* [2010] EWHC 2373 (QB), [285] (Stadlen J).

[68] [1923] 2 KB 500. See also *Warman v Southern Counties Car Finance Co Ltd* [1949] 2 KB 576 and *Barber v NWS Bank plc* [1996] 1 WLR 641.

owner. He then sought to recover the purchase price from the defendant on the ground of total failure of basis and succeeded, even though he had used the car for a substantial period of time. This period of use was characterized as a collateral benefit, since the real benefit for which the claimant had bargained was lawful possession of the car with good title and he had not obtained this at all. This is a somewhat strange conclusion, since anybody who purchases a car presumably expects to be able to use it, but the decision illustrates a desire to prevent the rigours of the total failure of basis doctrine from barring restitution where the award of a restitutionary remedy appears appropriate.[69]

Rowland v Divall can be contrasted with *Yeoman Credit Ltd v Apps*,[70] where the defendant had entered into a hire purchase agreement with the claimant by virtue of which he obtained possession of a car in an unroadworthy condition. Despite this, he used the car for six months. The defendant failed to keep up with the hire payments and the claimant recovered the car. The claimant then sued the defendant for arrears and the defendant counterclaimed for recovery of the hire payments he had made on the ground of total failure of basis. The defendant's counterclaim failed because he had obtained some benefit from the use of the car. *Rowland v Divall* was distinguished because, in that case, the contract was one of purchase and so the claimant had not obtained that for which he had bargained, namely good title, whereas in *Yeoman Credit Ltd v Apps*, the contract was one of hire purchase, so the claimant was assumed simply to have bargained for the use of the car, and this he had obtained, albeit the quality of the use was not what he had expected.

Rowland v Divall was followed by the Court of Appeal in *Rover International Ltd v Cannon Film Sales Ltd (No 3)*,[71] where the claimant was able to recover money which it had paid to the defendant in respect of a contract for the distribution of films in Italy. One ground for restitution of this sum was that the basis for the payment had totally failed, even though the claimant had received films from the defendant under the contract. This was because the receipt of the films was not considered to constitute the receipt of a benefit under the contract, since 'delivery and possession [of the films] were not what [the claimant] had bargained for'.[72] Rather, the claimant was deemed to have bargained for the opportunity to earn a substantial share of the gross receipts from the distribution contract and it had not been able to earn anything because the contract, being a pre-incorporation contract, was void. Consequently, since the claimant got nothing of what it had bargained for, the court was able to order restitution of the money it had paid to the defendant.

The interpretation of total failure of basis in both *Rowland v Divall* and *Rover International* is open to criticism, since the benefit which was received in both cases surely formed a necessary part of the bargain. In *Rowland v Divall*, for example, the use of the car was a crucial benefit which the claimant expected to obtain as an essential part of the contract to purchase the car. Similarly, in *Rover International* the claimant could not make any profit from the distribution of the films if it had not received them in the first place. The cynical interpretation of these cases is that the court considered that restitution should be awarded and did not wish to be defeated in this objective by the fact that the basis must fail totally if it is to constitute a ground of restitution. This covert manipulation of the concept of basis by characterizing the receipt of certain benefits as collateral is unsatisfactory, leading as it does to great uncertainty. It would have been so much easier in

---

[69] *Rowland v Divall* was followed in *Butterworth v Kingsway Motors Ltd* [1954] 1 WLR 1286 where the claimant recovered the purchase price of the car on the ground of total failure of basis even though he had used the car for 11 months.

[70] [1962] 2 QB 508.   [71] [1989] 1 WLR 912.   [72] Ibid, 925 (Kerr LJ).

these cases if it was acknowledged that partial failure of basis is a satisfactory ground of restitution in its own right. For that is the effect of these decisions, namely that restitution is being awarded on the ground of failure of basis even though the claimant had received some benefit by virtue of the defendant's performance of his or her side of the bargain.

The complexity and significance of characterizing benefits received as collateral is especially well illustrated by the difficult and important case of *Giedo van der Garde BNV v Force India Formula One Team Ltd.*[73] Van der Garde is a racing driver with an ambition to become a Formula One driver.[74] He entered into a contract with the defendant whereby he agreed to pay $3 million to the defendant in return for being permitted to drive a Formula One racing car in testing, practice, or racing for a minimum of 6,000 kilometres during the 2007 racing season. The aim of this was to enable him to gain sufficient experience to progress to become a Formula One driver. The claimant paid the defendant the money but, in breach of contract, the defendant only permitted the claimant to drive just over 2,000 kilometres. The claimant sought restitution of the money paid. One obstacle to his claim was that he had received certain benefits under the contract, including the provision of sponsorship spaces on his car and a race suit and paddock passes. It was held that these benefits were not essential to the contract, which was concerned with giving the claimant sufficient driving experience, so that they could be treated as collateral benefits. He had, however, received some driving experience which could not be characterized as a collateral benefit, since it formed the essential part of the bargain. Whether this barred a restitutionary claim grounded on total failure of basis required consideration of the second technique for manipulating the total failure requirement.

(ii) Apportionment of the Basis

The second mechanism for avoiding the strict rigours of the total failure requirement is through the apportionment of the basis where the benefits to be provided under a contract can be considered to be divisible. What this means is that where, for example, the claimant has purchased a number of different items from the defendant and paid for them in advance, if the defendant fails to supply one of these items and the claimant accepts those which have been delivered, the claimant might be able claim repayment of the price of the item which was not delivered on the ground that, as regards that item, the basis has totally failed.[75] In other words, it might be possible to apportion the basis for the payment of the goods between the goods received and the goods which the claimant had not received, so the receipt of the former does not preclude restitution on the ground of total failure of basis in respect of the payment for the latter.

Traditionally apportionment was only considered to be available where the contract provided for apportionment either expressly or impliedly, such as where provision is made for delivery of goods in instalments. In *Goss v Chilcott*[76] the Privy Council expanded the situations where apportionment is available to include those cases where it could be carried out without difficulty. In that case a finance company had lent money to the defendants on the security of a mortgage over their property. In a separate

---

[73] [2010] EWHC 2372 (QB).

[74] He is presently a reserve driver for a Formula One racing team.

[75] As was recognized by Bovill CJ in *Whincup v Hughes* (1871) LR 6 CP 78, 81. See also *Devaux v Connolly* (1849) 8 CB 640, 137 ER 658.

[76] [1996] AC 788. Apportionment has also been recognized by the High Court of Australia in *David Securities Pty Ltd v Commonwealth Bank of Australia* (1992) 175 CLR 353, 383; *Roxborough v Rothmans of Pall Mall Australia Ltd* (2001) 76 ALJR 203. See also *Fibrosa Spolka Akcyjna v Fairbairn Lawson Combe Barbour Ltd* [1943] AC 32, 77 (Lord Porter).

transaction the defendants had lent this money to a director of the finance company. The purpose of this transaction was effectively to enable the director to borrow money from the company of which he was director, which he was prohibited from doing. The director, in his capacity as agent of the finance company, altered the mortgage instrument without the consent of the defendants. This meant that the security was unenforceable as against the defendants, so their contractual liability to repay the money to the finance company was automatically discharged. The finance company having gone into liquidation, the claimant liquidator sought to recover the amount of the loan from the defendants in a restitutionary claim founded on the ground of total failure of basis. The difficulty for the claimant was that the defendants had already made two payments to the finance company in respect of interest, so they argued that the basis for the transaction had not totally failed. Lord Goff delivered the opinion of the Privy Council and held that the basis for the transaction had failed totally. This was because the restitutionary claim related to repayment of capital and no part of the capital had been repaid, rather the defendants had simply been repaying interest. This is a perfectly acceptable conclusion since, although the defendant's obligation to pay interest and capital arose under the same transaction, the obligations arose for different reasons, interest payments being payments for the use of the capital rather than the return of the capital. To the extent that it is possible to say, as it was in this case, that the money paid by the defendants related either to interest or to capital and that only interest had been repaid, the decision is correct.

However, Lord Goff also said:

> even if part of the capital sum had been repaid, the law would not hesitate to hold that the balance of the loan outstanding would be recoverable on the ground of failure of consideration; for at least in those cases in which apportionment can be carried out without difficulty, the law will allow partial recovery on this ground ...[77]

This is more difficult to justify. Where, for example, the claimant lends £1,000 to the defendant who repays £400, can it really be said that, as regards the outstanding amount, the basis had failed totally? What is being apportioned in this case? Surely it should only be possible to apportion the basis in this way if, for example, the contract of loan itself provided for repayment by instalments. As the High Court of Australia said in *David Securities Pty Ltd v Commonwealth Bank of Australia*,[78] it is only where the parties have impliedly acknowledged that the basis may be apportioned by the structure of the transaction that apportionment will be possible. In such circumstances, if two of five instalments have been paid it could still be argued that the basis has failed totally in respect of the final three instalments, which would then be recoverable. But in *Goss v Chilcott* the whole loan was repayable three months after it was made; it was only the interest payments which were payable in instalments. There is therefore no justification for saying that, if the defendants had repaid part of the loan, the basis would have failed totally in respect of the outstanding sum, simply because there was nothing in the loan transaction to suggest that the payments could be apportioned in this way.

Although the dictum of Lord Goff was *obiter* and was from a decision of the Privy Council, this broad approach to apportionment was adopted in *Giedo van der Garde BNV v Force India Formula One Team Ltd*,[79] where Stadlen J identified the appropriate test as being whether, as a matter of common sense, the court considers that it is able to make an apportionment of the benefits to be provided under the contract by an objective analysis of

---

[77] *Goss v Chilcott* [1996] AC 788, 798.   [78] (1992) 175 CLR 353, 383.
[79] [2010] EWHC 2372 (QB), [297]. See D Winterton and F Wilmot-Smith, 'Steering a Course on Contract Damages and Failure of Consideration' (2012) 128 LQR 23.

the nature of the contract and the circumstances in which the benefit is to be delivered or performed by the defendant. He justified the apportionment principle on the ground that restitution will not be barred where the benefit which the claimant has received is 'part or all of the consideration for another part of the money paid by the claimant pursuant to a different part of or obligation under the contract...'[80] In *Barnes v Eastenders Cash and Carry plc*[81] Lord Toulson acknowledged that the courts would be willing to sever the basis 'where it reflects commercial reality'.

In *Giedo van der Garde* Stadlen J emphasized that the court should adopt a flexible and robust approach to apportionment. It follows that apportionment is possible even where the contract has provided for payment by the defendant as a lump sum for goods or services which have been provided by the claimant. Whether apportionment is possible will require careful examination of the nature of the contract and the identity of the performance which the claimant can be considered to expect in return for the benefit which has been transferred.[82] For example, in *Whincup v Hughes*[83] the claimant paid a watchmaker a lump sum for his son to be the watchmaker's apprentice for six years. After one year the watchmaker died and the claimant sought to recover part of the money he had paid. This claim failed on the ground that the basis for the payment had not failed totally. In *Giedo van der Garde* Stadlen J said that apportionment of the basis was not possible in *Whincup v Hughes* because of the particular context of the contract of service. This was because the benefits and burdens of the watchmaker's services to the apprentice varied over time, since the benefit and burden of the service would have been much greater in the first year than in the fifth.[84] In *Marks and Spencer plc v BNP Paribas Securities Services Trust Co (Jersey) Ltd*,[85] it was recognized that, where rent had been paid quarterly in advance and the lease ended through the exercise of a break clause on a specified date in the middle of the quarter, the excess rent could not be recovered since there was not a total failure of basis. Morgan J held that it was not appropriate to apportion the rent between the period when the tenant occupied the premises and when it did not. In the light of *Goss v Chilcott* and *Guido van der Grade*, this is difficult to justify, because the quality of the benefit from occupying the premises would not have varied during the period of occupation. Indeed, as Morgan J acknowledged, restitution will be awarded of the surplus amount paid in respect of the hire of a ship,[86] so there is no reason why rent of a property should be treated differently.[87]

In *Giedo van der Garde* Stadlen J considered carefully whether apportionment was available on the facts of the case itself. Having already held that some of the benefits which the claimant had received were collateral,[88] the key question was whether the claimant could recover part of the $3 million he had paid to test drive at least 6,000 kilometres, when he had only driven just over 2,000 kilometres. Stadlen J accepted that, in principle, it would be possible to apportion the lump sum payment and express it as $500 per kilometre. It would follow that, for each kilometre that he had not been able to drive, there was a total failure of basis.[89] However, on the peculiar facts of this case, Stadlen

---

[80] *Giedo van der Garde BNV v Force India Formula One Team Ltd* [2010] EWHC 2372 (QB), [360].

[81] [2014] UKSC 26, [2015] AC 1, [114].

[82] See also F Wilmot-Smith, 'Reconsidering "Total" Failure' (2013) CLJ 414, 435.

[83] (1871) LR 6 CP 78.

[84] *Giedo van der Garde BNV v Force India Formula One Team Ltd* [2010] EWHC 2372 (QB), [305].

[85] [2013] EWHC 1279 (Ch), [42] (Morgan J).

[86] *Wehner v Dene Steam Shipping Co* [1905] 2 KB 92; *The Mihalios Xilas* [1979] 1 WLR 1018.

[87] On the facts of the case a term was implied to provide for recovery of the surplus.

[88] See p 321, above.

[89] *Giedo van der Garde BNV v Force India Formula One Team Ltd* [2010] EWHC 2372 (QB), [362].

J concluded that he was unable to apportion the basis in this way, because the driving options included practice driving before Grand Prix races, which would have been much more beneficial to the claimant in his desire to become a Formula One racing driver. Since the question of apportionment was to be determined at the time the contract was made, and not in the light of subsequent events, it followed that the value of the benefit which the claimant expected to receive from the defendant would vary depending on the type of driving which was available to him, similar to the benefit of the watchmaker's services in *Whincup v Hughes* which varied over time. Essentially, therefore, apportionment was not possible because the value of each kilometre driven would vary depending on whether it was test or practice driving. It followed that the restitutionary claim failed. The claimant was, however, able to recover substantial damages for breach of contract.

Although apportionment was unavailable in *Giedo van der Garde*, the broad interpretation of that principle, following the approach of Lord Goff in *Goss v Chilcott*, whereby apportionment is available even where the claimant has made a lump sum payment, constitutes a significant way of avoiding the total failure bar, and makes the continued existence of that bar vulnerable. This had been recognized by the High Court of Australia in *David Securities Pty Ltd v Commonwealth Bank of Australia*,[90] where the plurality acknowledged that, once it is accepted that the basis can be apportioned, 'any rationale for adhering to the traditional rule requiring *total* failure of consideration disappears'.[91] Although it is not yet possible to conclude that partial failure of basis is an independent ground of restitution in its own right, particularly because the Privy Council in *Goss v Chilcott* affirmed that the basis must fail totally,[92] and this rule was subsequently affirmed in *Stocznia* and by Stadlen J in *Giedo van der Garde*, the wide interpretation of apportionment significantly restricts the application of the total failure requirement.

The fact that this wide interpretation of apportionment provides a significant mechanism for manipulation of the total failure of basis requirement is illustrated by the bizarre decision of the Court of Appeal in *DO Ferguson v Sohl*,[93] a decision which was commended by Stadlen J in *Giedo van der Garde*.[94] In *Ferguson v Sohl* the claimant had paid £6,268 to the defendant, of which £4,673 constituted an overpayment. It was held that the claimant could recover the overpayment on the ground of total failure of basis. Hirst LJ specifically stated[95] that the money was recoverable even though it formed part of a larger payment. But it is an abuse of language to say that the money was recoverable on the ground of total failure of basis since the basis had not failed totally. The result might be explained on the ground of apportionment of basis, but there was nothing in the contract which enabled such an apportionment to be made. Consequently, the case is better analysed as one where restitution was awarded on the ground of partial failure of basis. The importance of the case is that the Court of Appeal clearly considered that restitution should follow as a matter of common sense because the claimant had paid money to the defendant for work which had never been done. Indeed, in commending the decision in *Giedo van der Garde*, Stadlen J said[96] '[it is] a good example of the willingness of the court to adopt a flexible and robust approach so as to avoid, if consistent with existing principle, leaving a victim of unjust enrichment without an effective remedy'.

---

[90] Ibid.   [91] Ibid, emphasis in the original.
[92] *Goss v Chilcott* [1996] AC 788, 797.   [93] (1992) 62 BLR 95.
[94] *Giedo van der Garde BNV v Force India Formula One Team Ltd* [2010] EWHC 2372 (QB), [323].
[95] *DO Ferguson v Sohl* (1992) 62 BLR 95, 105. Surprisingly, no reference was made to mistake as a possible ground of restitution.
[96] *Giedo van der Garde BNV v Force India Formula One Team Ltd* [2010] EWHC 2372 (QB), [323].

The real problem with the notion of apportionment of basis is how principled it can be considered to be, or whether it is really just a smoke-screen behind which the judge can avoid the total failure of basis requirement.

(C) IS THE REQUIREMENT THAT THE BASIS MUST TOTALLY FAIL DEFENSIBLE?

The reliance of the courts on mechanisms such as characterization of benefits as collateral and apportionment of basis, appears to stem from a desire to award restitutionary remedies, even where the basis for a particular transaction has only failed partially. In *Giedo van der Garde BNV v Force India Formula One Team Ltd*[97] Stadlen J described the total failure requirement as 'unsatisfactory and liable in certain cases to work injustice'. But, as the law stands, restitution on the ground of partial failure of basis will only be awarded in certain limited categories.[98] It would surely make the law of restitution more just if partial failure of basis was recognized as a ground of restitution in its own right.[99]

(i) Arguments in Favour of Recognizing Partial Failure of Basis

A number of reasons can be identified why partial failure of basis should be recognized as a general ground of restitution.

(1) Where the claimant has transferred a benefit to the defendant and has obtained part of the expected basis in return, restitution can still be justified since the claimant's intention that the defendant should retain the benefit, which is contingent on the fulfilment of a condition, has still been vitiated to the extent that the condition has not been completely fulfilled.

(2) Recognizing partial failure of basis would also mean that there would no longer be any need for the courts to manipulate the concept of basis to enable it to conclude that the basis had totally failed where it was felt that restitution was justified. It would still, of course, be necessary to identify what the anticipated basis was, in order to determine whether the benefits the claimant had received had been bargained-for, since if they were the claimant could not obtain restitution of money paid in advance in respect of those benefits.

(3) Partial failure of basis is already recognized as a ground of restitution where a contract has been frustrated.[100] There is no reason why the ground of restitution following the termination of a contract should differ depending on whether the contract has been discharged for frustration or for breach. Indeed, the fact that Parliament in the Law Reform (Frustrated Contracts) Act 1943 accepted the legitimacy of partial failure of basis as a ground of restitution should mean that there is no reason why the Common Law should not extend this ground of restitution to other areas where the contract has ceased to operate.

(4) Stoljar[101] analysed in detail the history of the doctrine of total failure of basis and concluded that the total failure requirement is an historical myth, although some of the older cases can be interpreted as suggesting that the failure must be material. The total failure requirement appears to have developed in the nineteenth century

---

[97] Ibid, [367].   [98] See p 355, below.

[99] See Birks, 'Failure of Consideration', 179; P Mitchell, 'Artificiality of Failure of Consideration' (2010) 29 UQLJ 191.

[100] Law Reform (Frustrated Contracts) Act 1943, s 1(2), (3). See p 357, below.

[101] SJ Stoljar, 'The Doctrine of Failure of Consideration' (1959) 75 LQR 53.

by virtue of the rules on pleading and proof. But those rules no longer exist, so the total failure requirement should no longer be necessary either.[102]

(ii) Arguments Against Recognizing Partial Failure of Basis

The requirement that the basis must fail totally has traditionally been justified for two main reasons. First, because of a concern about unsettling the parties' contractual bargain.[103] Where, for example, the claimant has entered into a contract to buy 1,000 oranges from the defendant at £1 each, and has paid £1,000 in advance, if the defendant delivers 500 oranges but fails to deliver the rest, the claimant can either sue for damages for breach of contract or for restitution, with the ground being total failure of basis through apportionment of that basis. If the market value of the oranges is £1, it makes no difference whether the claimant seeks damages for breach, namely what the defendant must pay the claimant to enable her to buy 500 oranges, or restitution of the defendant's gain, since it will be £500 in each case. If, however, the market value of oranges has risen so that they now cost £2 each, it would be preferable for the claimant to seek damages for breach of contract, which would be assessed at £1,000, rather than restitution of the £500. It is where the market has fallen, for example where oranges now cost 50p each, that the claimant would prefer to bring a claim for restitution. The key question then is whether it should be possible for the claimant to opt out of the contractual regime where she has entered a bad bargain such as this, where the contractual price of oranges is higher than the market value, and pursue a claim in unjust enrichment instead. But the requirement that the basis must have failed totally cannot be justified by the need to ensure that claimants remain bound by bad bargains. A claimant can recover money paid on the ground of total failure, regardless of whether the bargain was good or bad. So, if the defendant fails to supply any oranges the claimant could recover the advance payment, even if the market value of oranges has slumped. The fact that the defendant has supplied some oranges, or some service where the basis is not apportionable, should make no difference to the restitutionary claim. The contractual bargain is always respected in that, if it is still operating, restitution will be denied. But, once the contract has been set aside, the nature of the bargain should generally be irrelevant, save exceptionally where the structure of the bargain continues to apply, such as where an obligation is characterized as entire[104] or where the contract can be construed so that the claimant can be considered to have taken the risk that, should the basis fail, he or she should be confined to the remedies for breach of contract rather than seeking restitution for the defendant's unjust enrichment.[105]

The second justification which has been suggested for maintaining the total failure requirement relates to the ability of the court to require the claimant to make counter-restitution to the defendant. In most cases where the basis has only failed partially this is because the claimant had received a benefit from the defendant. It would be unjust to require the defendant to make restitution to the claimant in such circumstances without requiring the claimant to make counter-restitution to the defendant of the value of the benefit received. Unfortunately, the ability of the courts to require counter-restitution has developed very slowly. The attitude of the Common Law courts was that, if the claimant

---

[102] See also R Goff, 'Reform of the Law of Restitution' (1961) 24 MLR 85, 90.

[103] J Taylor, 'Total Failure of Consideration and *Roxborough v Rothmans*' (2004) 120 LQR 30.

[104] See further p 335, below.

[105] Goodwin, 'Failure of Basis in the Contractual Context', considers that a claimant should be considered to take this risk in all cases, which would mean that there would be no scope for restitution on the ground of failure of basis in the contractual context. That does not represent the law and such artificial deemed risk-taking should not be recognized.

had received a benefit from the defendant, this could only be restored to the defendant *in specie* and only then, apparently, where the transaction was voidable for a fraudulent misrepresentation. It followed that, if the claimant had received a benefit which had been dissipated or by its nature could not be restored, such as a service, counter-restitution was not possible and so the claim for restitution would fail. The attitude of Equity became much more generous in such circumstances, because Equity was willing to require the claimant to restore the value of the benefit which had been received if the benefit itself could not be restored.[106] There is some evidence that this approach would also be adopted at Common Law as well.[107] If so, it would follow that, in every case where the claimant had not received everything which he or she had expected to receive under a contract which was no longer operating, the claimant could recover the benefits which had been transferred to the defendant but the claimant would need to make counter-restitution of the value of all benefits which the defendant had provided. It will only be in the most exceptional circumstances that it would not be possible to value the benefit received from the defendant; but where this is the case it should follow that the claimant's restitutionary claim would be barred.[108]

Wilmot-Smith[109] has sought to defend the essence of the total failure requirement through a radical reinterpretation of what that requirement actually entails, namely that it requires only for there to be a substantial failure of the basis before restitution is justified. This means that restitution will lie if a substantial part of the basis is not satisfied. His interpretation is consistent with the collateral benefit cases, where the language of collaterality indicates that the failure was not substantial; with the entire contract cases, where any failure of performance by a party whose obligation is entire is characterized as substantial; and with cases involving the transfer of goods or the supply of services, where part payment by the defendant is normally treated as insubstantial performance. He defends the substantial performance requirement on the basis that the law of unjust enrichment should not undermine the law of contract and should ensure that restitution is only available where damages are inadequate. Whilst this analysis of the law seeks to rationalize and reinvent the total failure requirement, it cannot be considered to be a satisfactory explanation of the modern law where the courts certainly recognize that there is a total failure rather than substantial failure requirement. The fact that Wilmot-Smith seeks to reinterpret what is meant by total failure, reflects the real concern about the injustices caused by that requirement. Wilmot-Smith would wish to moderate restitution on the ground of failure of basis by limiting it to where the basis failed substantially. How 'substantial' is to be interpreted will raise new problems. This test does not represent the law and nor should it do so.

(iii) The Consequences of Recognizing Partial Failure of Basis

If partial failure of basis was recognized as a general ground of restitution in its own right the key consequence would be that, to the extent that any part of the anticipated basis for a transfer of an enrichment had failed, restitution should be available. Where the claimant

---

[106] See *Erlanger v New Sombrero Phosphate Co* (1878) 3 App Cas 1218; *O'Sullivan v Management Agency and Music Ltd* [1985] QB 428. See p 25, above.

[107] *Smith New Court Securities Ltd v Scrimgeour Vickers (Asset Management) Ltd* [1997] AC 254, 262 (Lord Browne-Wilkinson).

[108] For analysis of the issues concerning the relationship between 'counter-restitution' and total failure of basis see E McKendrick, 'Total Failure of Consideration and Counter-restitution: Two Issues or One?' in PBH Birks (ed), *Laundering and Tracing* (Oxford: Clarendon Press, 1995), and Birks, 'Failure of Consideration', 193–8.   [109] Wilmot-Smith, 'Reconsidering "Total" Failure'.

had received some benefit from the defendant this would need to be valued and the claimant would be required to make counter-restitution of that value to the defendant. There would still be an advantage for the claimant to show that the basis had failed totally, for then there would be no obligation to make counter-restitution.

If partial failure of basis was recognized as a general ground of restitution its operation could potentially cause difficulties in those cases where the basis had not failed totally but the claimant had received no specific benefit from the defendant, as illustrated by the cases where the defendant had agreed to build and deliver a ship which he had started to build before the contract was discharged.[110] Although the claimant should be able to obtain restitution of the benefit which had been transferred to the defendant on the ground of partial failure of basis, how should the work done by the defendant be taken into account? Should this work be valued and this amount be deducted from what the defendant is required to restore to the claimant? This would mean that the claimant is required to make counter-restitution to the defendant in respect of a benefit which the claimant had not actually received. Consequently, since the claimant had not received any benefit, it might be concluded that the claimant is not required to make counter-restitution to the defendant because the claimant had not been unjustly enriched. The better view, however, is that the solution should depend on the appropriate construction of the contract. If the defendant's promised performance includes work as well as sale, the claimant should be considered to have freely accepted the work done by the defendant, and so should be estopped from denying that he or she had not actually received a specific benefit from the defendant.[111] Such a result would at least be consistent with the rationale of the build and sale cases, where the building of the ship is considered to constitute part of the basis for the advance payment.

(iv) Will the Courts Recognize Partial Failure of Basis?

There was some indication in the decision of the House of Lords in *Westdeutsche Landesbank Girozentrale v Islington LBC*[112] of a greater willingness to accept partial failure of basis as a ground of restitution. As Lord Goff said:[113]

> There has long been a desire among restitution lawyers to escape from the unfortunate effects of the so-called rule that money is only recoverable at common law on the ground of failure of consideration where the failure is total, by reformulating the rule upon a more principled basis; and signs that this will in due course be done are appearing in judgments throughout the common law world.

Although it is likely that the Supreme Court[114] will at some point recognize that partial failure of basis is a ground of restitution in its own right, we have not yet reached that position. Indeed, soon after delivering the opinion of the Privy Council in *Goss v Chilcott* Lord Goff sounded a note of caution in *Stocznia* when he said of the ground of total failure of basis:[115]

> This rule has been subject to considerable criticism in the past; but it has to be said that in a comparatively recent Report (Law Com. No. 121(1983) concerned with Pecuniary

---

[110] See *Stocznia Gdanska SA v Latvian Shipping Co* [1998] 1 WLR 574.   [111] See p 85, above.
[112] [1996] AC 669.   [113] Ibid, 682.
[114] In *Barnes v Eastenders Cash and Carry plc* [2014] UKSC 26, [2015] AC 1, [114], Lord Toulson acknowledged 'the lively academic debate' as to whether the failure of basis had to be total, but the issue was not fully argued and did not need to be determined in that case.
[115] *Stocznia Gdanska SA v Latvian Shipping Co* [1998] 1 WLR 574, 590. See also *Taylor v Motability Finance Ltd* [2004] EWHC (Comm), [25] (Cooke J).

Restitution on Breach of Contract) the Law Commission has declined to recommend a change in the rule, though it was there considering recovery by the innocent party rather than by the party in breach.

The House of Lords had the opportunity in that case to reject the requirement that the basis must fail totally, but it declined to do so. Consequently, although a very strong case can be made for the recognition of partial failure of basis as a general ground of restitution, that recognition is still some way off.[116]

(D) TWO PROBLEMS IN THE APPLICATION OF TOTAL FAILURE OF BASIS

The application of the ground of total failure of basis faces two particular difficulties which require careful analysis, namely whether restitution is available from third parties on this ground and whether a claimant who has participated in an illegal transaction can rely on it.

(i) Restitution from Third Parties

In *The Trident Beauty*[117] it was seen that the claimant, who had paid money to the defendant, was unable to recover that money by claiming that there had been a total failure of basis, because a term in the contract between the claimant and the ship owner excluded the right to restitution. But would the claimant's restitutionary claim have succeeded had there been no such provision in the contract? The defendant was clearly enriched at the claimant's expense and there was total failure of basis, since the claimant had not received the benefit for which he had bargained, namely the use of the ship. The problem was that the claimant was seeking to obtain restitution from a party who was never intended to provide the basis for the payment, since the ship did not belong to the defendant. Lord Woolf considered this to be a reason to deny restitution,[118] whereas Lord Goff accepted that the matter was open for debate.[119] The matter should be beyond debating now and restitution should be awarded even though the defendant who was enriched was not a party to the contract between the claimant and the party who was expected to provide the benefit. Restitution on the ground of mistake is not barred where the benefit is mistakenly transferred to the defendant rather than a third party,[120] so why should restitution for total failure of basis be treated any differently? Burrows has argued that restitution should be denied in such circumstances because the contract of assignment between the ship owner and the defendant did not contemplate an obligation on the part of the defendant to repay the instalment.[121] But why should this bar the restitutionary claim? The defendant was not a party to the contract between the claimant and ship owner so, as long as the contract which the claimant had made did not bar the restitutionary claim, the contract of assignment should have no effect on the claimant's restitutionary claim against the defendant. In principle restitution should lie on the ground of total failure of basis even against a party who was not expected to provide the benefit for which the claimant had bargained, simply because the consequence of the failure of basis is that

---

[116] Total failure of basis was recognized in *Marks and Spencer Plc v BNP Paribas Securities Services Trust Co (Jersey) Ltd* [2013] EWHC 1279 (Ch), [42] (Morgan J) and *Barnes v Eastenders Cash and Carry plc* [2014] UKSC 26, [2015] AC 1, [114] (Lord Toulson).

[117] *Pan Ocean Shipping Co Ltd v Creditcorp Ltd ('The Trident Beauty')* [1994] 1 WLR 161. See p 314, above.

[118] *Pan Ocean Shipping Co Ltd v Creditcorp Ltd ('The Trident Beauty')* [1994] 1 WLR 161, 171.

[119] Ibid, 166.

[120] *Barclays Bank Ltd v WJ Simms, Son and Cooke (Southern) Ltd* [1980] QB 677. See p 171, above.

[121] AS Burrows, 'Restitution from Assignees' [1994] RLR 52, 55.

the claimant's intention that the defendant should be enriched is vitiated. The fact that the basis failed due to the failure of a third party rather than the defendant who actually received the benefit is of no significance to whether the claimant's intention can be treated as vitiated.

Whether the principle that restitution can lie on the ground of total failure of basis against a defendant who has been paid, even though he or she was not expected to provide the benefit to the claimant, is of any practical significance depends on the nature of the relationship between the claimant and the third party. Where, for example, C contracted with B to build a house and B entered into a sub-contract with A to install windows, if B has become insolvent before paying A, A will be unable to sue C for restitution of the value of the services provided, because the continued existence of the contract between A and B will bar such a claim.[122] Usually, therefore, any claim against a third party on the ground of total failure of basis will be barred by virtue of a subsisting contract between the claimant and another party.

(ii) Denial of Restitution Where the Claimant Has Participated in an Illegal Transaction

Even though a claimant has participated in an illegal transaction it may be possible for him or her to obtain a restitutionary remedy by relying on one of the established grounds of restitution, such as mistake or duress.[123] This is not, however, possible where the claimant relies on the ground of total failure of basis, despite dicta in certain cases to the contrary.[124] So, for example, in *Parkinson v College of Ambulance*[125] the claimant had paid a sum of money to a charity on the understanding that the charity would be able to arrange for him to receive a knighthood. This was an illegal transaction. The knighthood was not forthcoming and the claimant sought to recover the money. Clearly the basis for the payment had totally failed, but, because the claimant had participated in an illegal transaction, he was unable to recover his money by virtue of the illegality defence.[126]

That restitution will be denied in such cases has been confirmed by the Court of Appeal in *Taylor v Bhail*.[127] The claimant builder had entered into a building contract with the defendant. At the defendant's request the claimant's estimate for the work was inflated by £1,000 to enable the defendant to perpetrate a fraud on his insurance company. The claimant completed the work and, after the defendant had refused to pay for all the work he had done, the claimant sued for breach of contract. His action failed on the ground that he had been tainted by illegality since he was a party to a conspiracy to defraud. Millett LJ also considered whether he could have brought a restitutionary claim for the reasonable value of his services and concluded that he could not because of the taint of illegality. Millett LJ identified two reasons for this conclusion.[128]

(1) The illegality rendered unenforceable any implied promise by the defendant to pay the reasonable value of the services, in the same way that the express promise to pay is unenforceable. But this is outdated reasoning founded on notions of quasi-contract which no longer have any part to play in the modern law of unjust

---

[122] *MacDonald Dickens and Macklin v Costello* [2011] EWCA Civ 930, [2012] QB 244. See also *Lumbers v W Cook Builders Pty Ltd* [2008] HCA 27. See p 142, above.

[123] See pp 186 and 205, above,

[124] See, for example, *Bloxsome v Williams* (1824) 3 B and C 232, 235; 107 ER 720, 721 (Bayley J) and *Shaw v Shaw* [1965] 1 WLR 537, 539 (Lord Denning MR).

[125] [1923] 2 KB 1. See also *Berg v Sadler and Moore* [1937] 2 KB 158; *Wacker* [2003] QB 1207, [32] (Kay LJ).

[126] See Chapter 27.   [127] [1996] CLC 377.   [128] Ibid, 383.

enrichment.[129] The obligation to make restitution is imposed by operation of law and does not depend upon the implication of any promise to pay. It does not follow, therefore, that because the claimant could not sue on the illegal contract he was necessarily prevented from bringing a restitutionary claim.

(2) Where the transaction is illegal any enrichment received by the defendant is not unjust, since the denial of restitution 'is the price which the claimant must pay for having entered into an illegal transaction in the first place'.[130] But this begs the question. Where the claimant has paid the defendant in the expectation that he or she would receive a benefit in return, and none is forthcoming, the defendant appears to be unjustly enriched at the claimant's expense. The question then is whether the total failure of basis is sufficient to negate the taint of illegality. The implication of *Taylor v Bhail* and *Parkinson* is that it is not.

In *Patel v Mirza*[131] another reason was given as to why participation in an illegal transaction should defeat a claim grounded on total failure of basis. In that case the claimant sought restitution of money which he had paid to the defendant pursuant to a contract which was illegal because it constituted the crime of insider dealing,[132] involving the intended use of inside information to profit from the purchase and sale of shares. The illegal purpose was not carried out because the expected inside information was not obtained. It appears, therefore, that there was a total failure of basis. It was recognized, however, that illegality will defeat a claim for restitution for reasons of public policy if the claimant needs to rely on the illegality to establish that the basis for the payment had failed totally.[133] This is a significant restriction on restitution in the context of claims for total failure of basis, because such claims often arise in a contractual context and the claimant will only be able to seek restitution after establishing that the contract is no longer operating. Although an illegal contract is void, it will only be possible for the claimant to establish such invalidity by relying on the illegality, which he or she will be prevented from doing by the rule in *Patel v Mirza*, save if the claimant can rely on another reason why the contract is no longer operating.

The Court of Appeal in *Patel v Mirza* did, however, confirm that the claimant will be able to rely on illegality once the claimant can establish that he or she is no longer tainted by it, by establishing that he or she has withdrawn from the illegal transaction before any part of the illegal purpose has been executed. But, as will be seen below,[134] the modern interpretation of this withdrawal principle means that it is virtually indistinguishable from the ground of total failure of basis.

The claimant will also be able to rely on the illegality and obtain restitution on the ground of total failure of basis where the claimant is not considered to be as blameworthy as the defendant for participating in the transaction. This is illustrated by *Mohamed v Alaga and Co*,[135] where the claimant sued the defendant firm of solicitors for work done in preparing and presenting asylum claims. A contract between the claimant and the defendant concerning payment to the claimant for the introduction of clients to the defendant was illegal, but the restitutionary claim succeeded in respect of the services provided. The services could be severed from the illegal fee-sharing part of the contract

---

[129] See *United Australia Ltd v Barclays Bank Ltd* [1941] AC 1, discussed at p 46, above.
[130] *Taylor v Bhail* [1996] CLC 377, 383.   [131] [2014] EWCA Civ 1047, [2015] 2 WLR 405.
[132] Contrary to the Criminal Justice Act 1993, Part V.
[133] See *Tinsley v Milligan* [1994] 1 AC 340. See p 718, below.   [134] See p 353, below.
[135] [2001] 1 WLR 1815.

because the claimant was less blameworthy than the defendant firm of solicitors, which was assumed to know the rules of the profession.[136]

In *Benedetti v Sawiris*[137] Lord Neuberger acknowledged, obiter, that failure of basis might lie where a contract was ineffective due to illegality. The general rule which defeats a restitutionary claim founded on total failure of basis where the claimant participated in an illegal transaction is difficult to defend. It would be preferable to allow restitution on this ground even if the claimant has been tainted by illegality, so long as it is not of a particularly serious kind[138] or where allowing restitution would stultify the policy of the law which rendered the contract illegal in the first place, which is the approach adopted in Australia.[139]

3. THE OPERATION OF TOTAL FAILURE OF BASIS

Total failure of basis is the relevant ground of restitution in a number of different contexts, which raise particular problems which will be examined in turn.

(A) CONTRACTS WHICH ARE DISCHARGED FOR BREACH

Where a contract has been discharged for breach[140] there are two remedial options available. First, the claimant may seek a remedy for the breach itself. Normally this will be compensatory damages assessed with reference to the claimant's loss, but in certain exceptional circumstances it is possible to award a gain-based remedy, which is assessed with reference to the benefits obtained by the defendant as a result of breaching the contract.[141] This remedy is not founded on the reversal of the defendant's unjust enrichment, but instead on the wrong of the breach of contract, hence this remedial option is considered in Part III.

Alternatively, once the contract has been discharged for breach, the claimant may seek to obtain a restitutionary remedy which is not founded on the breach but is based on total failure of basis, in the sense that the condition for the transfer of benefits to the defendant has not been and will not be satisfied as a result of the breach of contract. Here restitution is founded on the reversal of the defendant's unjust enrichment. The relevance of the breach of contract is simply that, if it is a repudiatory breach (which is a breach of a condition or a term the breach of which is sufficiently serious) or renunciation[142] which has been accepted by the claimant as discharging the contract, the contract ceases to be operative, so opening the way for the restitutionary claim. But the breach itself does not constitute the underlying cause of action for the claim.

Where the claimant's restitutionary claim is founded on total failure of basis it should make no difference that it was the claimant who breached the contract. This is because the fact that the claimant committed a wrong by breaching the contract should not affect a claim founded on the reversal of the defendant's unjust enrichment. Unfortunately, the

---

[136] Cf *Awwad v Geraght and Co* [2001] QB 570 where the claimant was a partner in the firm of solicitors.

[137] [2013] UKSC 50, [2014] AC 938, [175].

[138] See p 723, below and GJ Virgo, 'The Effects of Illegality on Claims for Restitution in English Law' in WJ Swadling (ed), *The Limits of Restitutionary Claims: A Comparative Analysis* (London: UKNCCL, 1997), 181–2.

[139] *Equuscorp Pty Ltd v Haxton* [2012] HCA 7, (2012) 86 ALJR 296.

[140] For examination of when a contract may be discharged for breach, see H Beale (ed), *Chitty on Contracts* (31st edn, London: Sweet and Maxwell, 2012), ch 24.

[141] *Attorney-General v Blake* [2001] 1 AC 268. See Chapter 18.

[142] See Beale (ed), *Chitty on Contracts* (31st edn), ch 24.

courts have not always recognized this, so it is necessary to analyse separately the cases where the defendant breached the contract and where the claimant did so.

(i) Breach of Contract by the Defendant

(1) Restitution of Money Paid

Where the contract is breached by the defendant, the innocent claimant who has accepted the breach as repudiating the contract will be able to obtain restitution of money paid on the ground of total failure of basis. This is illustrated by *Giles v Edwards*,[143] where the defendant contracted to sell all of his cordwood to the claimant and agreed that the wood would be cut and corded before the claimant collected it. The claimant paid for the wood in advance but, when he went to collect it, the defendant had only corded part of the wood. Since the defendant had not done what he had promised to do, it was held that the claimant could repudiate the contract because of the defendant's breach and recover the advance payment. Although no ground of restitution was specifically recognized, the result of the case is consistent with the ground being that of total failure of basis. This was because the defendant's obligation was entire, so the claimant's contractual obligation to pay for the wood did not arise until the defendant had performed his side of the bargain. Consequently, the defendant's part performance of the contract did not mean that the basis had only failed partially; the basis was simply delivery of all the corded wood.[144]

Similarly, where the claimant has paid a deposit to the defendant who then fails to perform, the claimant will be able to recover the deposit, as well as any other advance payments, on the ground of total failure of basis.[145] This is because the deposit is paid as security for the claimant's performance; the claimant does not take the risk that the defendant will breach the contract.[146] Even so, a deposit cannot be recovered despite the defendant's breach if some basis for the deposit has been achieved. In *Sharma v Simposh Ltd*[147] the claimant was unable to recover a deposit because he had obtained the benefit for which the payment was made, namely that the defendant had taken the property it was selling to the claimant off the market. Consequently, there had not been a total failure of basis.

(2) Restitution of Non-Money Benefits

Since restitution for the value of services on the ground of failure of basis has been recognized where the services were provided in anticipation of a contract being made,[148] there is no reason why such a claim should not be available where the services have been provided pursuant to a contract which has been discharged for breach. Similarly, a restitutionary claim should lie for the value of goods which have been transferred to the defendant subject to a condition which fails.

The legitimacy of such a claim is illustrated by *De Bernardy v Harding*,[149] where the defendant was in charge of letting seats to see the funeral of the Duke of Wellington. The defendant entered into an agreement with the claimant whereby the claimant would sell

---

[143] (1797) 7 Term Rep 181, 101 ER 920.

[144] Cf *Stocznia Gdanska SA v Latvian Shipping Co* [1998] 1 WLR 574. See p 316, above.

[145] *Barber v NWS Bank plc* [1996] 1 WLR 641. See also *Gribbon v Lutton* [2001] EWCA Civ 1956, [2002] QB 902, [60] (Walker LJ). Provision for recovery of the deposit in that case was, however, considered to be made by contract.

[146] Cf where the claimant fails to perform. See p 338, below.

[147] [2011] EWCA Civ 1383, [2013] Ch 23, [55] (Toulson LJ).

[148] *Cobbe v Yeoman's Row Management Ltd* [2008] UKHL 55, [2008] 1 WLR 1752. See p 345, below.

[149] (1853) 8 Exch 821, 155 ER 1586. See also *Chandler Bros Ltd v Harding* [1936] 3 All ER 179.

tickets for the funeral abroad. After the claimant had incurred expense in making the necessary arrangements, the defendant informed him that he would sell all of the tickets himself. The claimant then forwarded the names of applicants for tickets to the defendant and sought payment from the defendant in respect of the expenditure he had incurred and the services he had provided. The defendant reimbursed the claimant for his expenditure but refused to pay him for his services. It was held that the claimant had a choice to sue either for breach of contract or to accept the discharge of the contract and sue for the work he had done. If the claimant had brought a restitutionary claim for the work done, the claim would presumably have succeeded. The claimant's services were incontrovertibly beneficial to the defendant, since he had been saved expense which he would inevitably have incurred had the claimant not advertized the sale of tickets abroad. It could also be shown that there had been a total failure of basis, since the claimant had not been paid for his services. Although the defendant did reimburse the claimant for the expenditure incurred, it would have been possible to apportion the basis for the claimant's work between expenditure incurred and the value of the claimant's service.

Whether a restitutionary claim grounded on total failure of basis will be available where a non-money benefit has been provided pursuant to a contract which is discharged for breach remains a controversial matter. In *Taylor v Motability Finance Ltd*[150] a distinction was drawn between non-money benefits and money claims, it being assumed that the ground of total failure of basis only applied in respect of the latter. In that case the defendant had terminated a contract of employment with the claimant. The claimant brought a claim for restitution for the value of the services provided, grounded on failure of basis. This claim was rejected because, as the claimant had fully performed his contractual obligations, the contractual regime continued to govern as regards the remedies available even though the contract had been discharged for breach,[151] so the claimant was confined to compensatory damages. But this would not have been the case had the claimant paid money to the defendant pursuant to the contract. The consequent distinction between claims for money and non-money benefits is illogical. The distinction was reluctantly rejected by the Victorian Court of Appeal in *Sopov v Kane Constructions Ltd*,[152] but only because the court considered itself bound by authority to reject the distinction.

In *Elek v Bar-Tur*[153] the significance of the distinction between money and non-money benefits was recognized and clarified. In that case it was held that a claimant, who had provided services pursuant to a contract which had been repudiated following breach by the defendant, could bring a restitutionary claim to recover the value of the services. But this was only because the claimant had been unable to complete his contractual performance and, as a consequence, the defendant's counter-performance had not yet become due. Where, however, the claimant had fully performed and was entitled to payment under the contract, as in *Taylor v Motability Finance*, the claimant could not bring a claim for unjust enrichment. In *Howes Percival LLP v Page*[154] the qualification of the approach in *Taylor v Motability Finance* was not considered, but the court affirmed and applied the fundamental distinction between money and non-money benefits. Consequently it was held, in a case where a solicitor had a conditional right to receive payment for services only if the litigation was successful, that, where the defendant had committed a repudiatory breach of the contract, the solicitor had no right to obtain restitution of the value of the services provided but could only seek damages for breach of contract. Denying the

---

[150] [2004] EWHC 2619 (Comm).   [151] See p 136, above.   [152] [2009] VSCA 141.
[153] [2013] EWHC 207 (Ch), [2013] 2 EGLR 159.   [154] [2013] EWHC 4104 (Ch).

solicitor a restitutionary claim in this case might be considered to be acceptable, since a conditional fee arrangement means that the solicitor bore the risk, but surely that is only a risk of losing the case and not that the client would breach the contract.[155]

It follows that the distinction between claims for restitution of money and non-money benefits exists in English law. It is a distinction which is unjustifiable and should be rejected.

(3) Losing Contracts

Where the defendant has breached a contract the claimant will be able to obtain restitution on the ground of total failure of basis even where the contract was, from the claimant's perspective, a bad bargain.[156] Where such a losing contract is breached, the restitutionary claim will not be defeated by the fact that, had the claimant sued the defendant for breach, compensatory damages would be lower than the restitutionary award. The fact that the contract was a losing contract is irrelevant to the restitutionary claim since restitutionary remedies are assessed by reference to the defendant's gain rather than the claimant's loss. This is illustrated by *Wilkinson v Lloyd*,[157] where the claimant had agreed to buy shares from the defendant, the transfer being conditional on the defendant obtaining the consent of the directors of the relevant company to the transfer. The claimant paid the defendant for the shares without realizing that the defendant had not been able to obtain the directors' consent. After he had discovered this, the claimant accepted that the contract had been discharged for breach. The claimant then sued the defendant for repayment of the purchase price on the ground of total failure of basis, since he had not received any of the shares. The claimant's action succeeded, even though the value of the shares had fallen below the purchase price he had paid.

Similarly, where the enrichment is a non-money benefit, and assuming that restitutionary claims are available in respect of such benefits, the fact that the benefit was transferred pursuant to a losing contract has been assumed to be an irrelevant consideration when determining whether the claimant can bring a restitutionary claim.[158] This matter was considered explicitly for the first time in England in *Taylor v Motability Finance Ltd*.[159] Cooke J stated that there is no justification for the award of a restitutionary remedy which is in excess of the contract price, since the award of such a remedy would put the claimant in a better position than he or she would have been in had the contract not been breached, which would be unjust. He emphasized that, when determining the *quantum meruit*, regard should be had to the contract both as a guide to the value which the parties put on the service and to ensure justice between the parties. It is unclear whether this approach would extend to claims for restitution of money paid pursuant to a losing contract, to ensure that the claimant cannot recover more in restitution than he or she could recover in a claim for breach of contract, although the implicit assumption of Cooke J was that claims for money are treated differently. The better view, however, is that regardless of the nature of the enrichment, the fact that the claimant suffered a loss under the contract should be of no relevance to the restitutionary claim because, by definition,

---

[155] See further p 137, above.   [156] See further p 326, above.

[157] (1845) 7 QB 25, 115 ER 398. See also the American case of *Bush v Canfield* (1818) 2 Conn 485.

[158] *Lodder v Slowey* [1904] AC 442 (PC); *Renard Constructions (ME) Pty Ltd v Minister of Public Works* (1992) 26 NSWLR 234. See also the American case of *Boomer v Muir* (1933) 24 P 2d 570 where $258,000 was awarded as the value of the work done, although only $20,000 was still due under the contract. The Law Commission has recommended that *quantum meruit* should not be based on the contract price: *Pecuniary Restitution on Breach of Contract* (Law Com No 121, 1983), para 2.52. See further p 99, above.

[159] [2004] EWHC 2619 (Comm), [26].

the contract is no longer subsisting. Cooke J's approach in *Taylor v Motability Finance* depends on his assumption that, where a *quantm meruit* claim is brought, the contractual regime remains operative.[160] This is unnecessarily complicated and the preferable view is that, once the contract is no longer operating, an unjust enrichment claim can be made regardless of the nature of the enrichment and unaffected by the contractual regime, save that the contract price may be reliable evidence of the value of the non-money benefit.[161]

It has sometimes been suggested that awarding restitution to a claimant who has entered into a losing contract might subvert the allocation of risks under the contract where the risk of the contract being a bad bargain has been allocated to the claimant. So, for example, if the claimant agrees to buy goods from the defendant and pays in advance, it might be assumed that the claimant is expected to take the risk that the goods could fall in value.[162] This is a difficult question. The better view is that, where it is clear that the contract has allocated the risk of loss to the claimant, the law of restitution should not be used to subvert this allocation of risk, even though the contract has been discharged by the claimant for breach.[163] In such a case the claim to restitution would be defeated by the contract. But such a conclusion should only be drawn where the risk has clearly been allocated to the claimant by the contract. The fact that the claimant has paid the defendant in advance should not be sufficient to presume that the risk of loss has been allocated to the claimant. If the parties really do intend to allocate the risk of loss in this way they should do so explicitly by including a particular term to this effect in the contract itself or the court might imply such a term but only if it is consistent with the objective construction of the contract.

(4) Compensatory Damages for Wasted Expenditure

The total failure of basis requirement cannot be avoided by construing the claim as one for damages for loss suffered instead. It has been recognized that a claimant, who paid money under a contract which was subsequently terminated for breach, cannot claim all the money paid as compensatory damages for wasted expenditure if there was no total failure of basis, because awarding such a remedy would undermine the requirement of the law of restitution that the basis must fail totally.[164] Consequently, if the claimant paid money to the defendant who provided some of the anticipated benefit in return, so there is only a partial failure of basis, the claimant cannot recover all of the money paid as compensatory damages for wasted expenditure.[165]

(ii) Breach of Contract by the Claimant

Restitution should also be awarded on the ground of total failure of basis where the contract has been discharged for a repudiatory breach committed by the claimant. The fact that the restitutionary claim was effectively self-induced, in the sense that had the claimant not breached the contract it would not have been discharged and so restitution would not have been available, should not be sufficient to deny the restitutionary claim. The fact that the breach was self-induced could only be relevant if English law regarded breach of contract as so wrong that it should be discouraged by denying restitution to the claimant on the ground of public policy. But English law does not characterize breach of

---

[160] See p 136, above.   [161] See p 102, above.

[162] See Goodwin, 'Failure of Basis in the Contractual Context'.

[163] This is consistent with the approach of the House of Lords in *Pan Ocean Shipping Co Ltd v Creditcorp Ltd* [1994] 1 WLR 161. See p 314, above.

[164] *Khan v Malik* [2011] EWHC 1319 (Ch), [130] (Christopher Nugee QC).   [165] Ibid, [132].

contract in this way,[166] for, if it did, the usual remedy for breach of contract would be specific performance rather than compensatory damages. So long as the contract-breaker compensates the victim for any loss suffered as a result of the breach, there is no reason of principle or policy why he or she should not claim restitution.

That English law does not prevent the contract-breaker from obtaining restitution is illustrated by the fact that, where the innocent party brings a restitutionary claim founded on total failure of basis as a result of the breach, the contract-breaker is allowed to bring a counterclaim for restitution on the same ground. If the contract-breaker is allowed to bring a counterclaim, it should follow that he or she can bring a direct claim for restitution once the contract has been discharged for breach. This has in fact been recognized, although there has been some uncertainty as to whether the ground of restitution is total failure of basis and the law is more complicated where the enrichment takes the form of a non-money benefit.

(1) Restitution of Money Paid

Where the claimant has paid money to the defendant and then breaches the contract, the preferable view is that the claimant is able to recover this money on the ground of total failure of basis. This is illustrated by *Dies v British and International Mining and Finance Co Ltd*.[167] The claimant entered into a contract with the defendant for the purchase of rifles and ammunition and paid part of the purchase price in advance. The claimant did not take delivery of the rifles and ammunition and so the defendant discharged the contract for breach. The claimant then successfully recovered the advance payment from the defendant, subject to the defendant's claim for damages in respect of loss suffered as a result of the breach. Unfortunately, the judge specifically rejected total failure of basis as the ground of restitution and concluded that the claimant's right to recover the money derived from the terms of the contract itself.[168] This reasoning is unsatisfactory today, but it was understandable at the time the case was decided, since restitutionary remedies were awarded by reference to the implied contract theory. Two years later that theory was rejected by the House of Lords in *United Australia Ltd v Barclays Bank*.[169] The real significance of *Dies* lies in the fact that the claimant was able to obtain restitution even though he had breached the contract. Despite the rejection of total failure of basis as the reason for the restitutionary claim succeeding, total failure of basis should be treated as the best explanation of the result now that the implied contract theory has itself been rejected.[170] This is because the claimant had paid the money to the defendant without receiving anything which he had originally expected in return. This is an archetypal case of total failure of basis.

That the contract-breaker is able to recover money from the defendant on the ground of total failure of basis is further supported by the decision of the Court of Appeal in *Rover International Ltd v Cannon Film Sales (No 3)*,[171] where the defendant had granted the claimant a licence to exhibit nine films on Italian television. The fee for the licence was to be paid in three instalments. The claimant paid the first two instalments and then the

---

[166] See p 481, below.

[167] [1939] 1 KB 724. See also *Newland Shipping and Forwarding Ltd v Toba Trading FZC* [2014] EWHC 661 (Comm), [75] (Leggatt J).

[168] *Dies v British and International Mining and Finance Co Ltd* [1939] 1 KB 724, 744.

[169] [1941] AC 1.

[170] See *Cadogan Petroleum Holdings Ltd v Global Process Systems* [2013] EWHC 214 (Comm).

[171] [1989] 1 WLR 912. This aspect of the case did not involve Rover International Ltd which had entered into a pre-incorporation contract. See p 369, below.

defendant purported to terminate the contract for breach by the claimant and counter-claimed for payment of the final instalment. It was held that, if the claimant had paid this instalment, it would have been able to recover it on the ground of total failure of basis, the basis having failed because the claimant had not received any films from the defendant. Consequently, the defendant could not sue for payment of the instalment from the claimant. Logically, therefore, the contract-breaker would have been able to recover the first two instalments which it had paid if it had brought a claim for repayment.

The contract-breaker's restitutionary claim founded on total failure of basis is subject to an important qualification, namely that restitution will be denied to the extent that it is excluded by terms in the contract. In such circumstances the law of restitution cannot be used to subvert the law of contract. This is particularly important in respect of the recovery of advance payments by the contract-breaker, because there may be a number of different reasons why the contract-breaker made these payments. In particular, a crucial distinction needs to be made between an advance payment, on the one hand, and a non-refundable deposit or payment of a sum which is forfeit if the claimant breaches the contract. Where the payment constitutes an advance payment of the purchase price it can be recovered on the ground of total failure of basis, if the claimant did not receive any benefit pursuant to the contract.[172] If, however, the payment is characterized as a deposit it cannot be recovered on the ground of total failure of basis, simply because the purpose of such a payment is to operate as security for the claimant performing the contract.[173] In other words, the deposit operates by allocating to the claimant the risk of the contract not being performed and, if the contract is not performed because of the claimant's breach, then, at least as a general rule, he or she cannot resort to the law of restitution to subvert this contractual allocation of risk.[174]

This distinction between advance payments and deposits was recognized in *Howe v Smith*,[175] where the claimant had paid a sum of money to the defendant and, the claimant having breached the contract, it was held that he was unable to recover the payment because it was a deposit. Fry LJ defined a deposit as an 'earnest to bind the bargain so entered into [which] creates by the fear of its forfeiture a motive in the payer to perform the rest of the contract'.[176] Whether a particular payment is a deposit or simply a part payment depends on the construction of the contract.[177] Although the claimant in *Chillingworth v Esche*[178] recovered a deposit from the defendant, this was because the payment was made 'subject to contract' and, since no contract was ever signed, the claimant who sought repayment was not in breach of any contract. Consequently, the advance payment was not a true deposit since it was 'an anticipatory payment intended only to fulfil the ordinary purpose of a deposit if and when the contemplated agreement should be arrived at'.[179]

---

[172] *Palmer v Temple* (1839) 9 Ad and E 508, 112 ER 1304. See also *Mayson v Clouet* [1924] AC 980; *McDonald v Dennys Lascelles* (1933) 48 CLR 457 and *Dies v British and International Mining and Finance Co Ltd* [1939] 1 KB 724.

[173] *Howe v Smith* (1884) 27 Ch D 89; *Monnickendam v Leanse* (1923) 39 TLR 445.

[174] The deposit is recoverable if the contract is not performed because of the defendant's breach, because the claimant does not bear the risk of the defendant's non-performance. See p 333, above.

[175] (1884) 27 Ch D 89.   [176] Ibid, 101.

[177] *Palmer v Temple* (1839) 9 Ad and E 508, 112 ER 1304. In *Sharma v Simposh* [2011] EWCA Civ 1383, [2012] Ch 23, [51] Toulson LJ recognized that whether a pre-contract deposit is returnable will depend on careful construction of any agreement between the parties. See also *Robinson v Lane* [2010] EWCA Civ 385, [15] (Sir Richard Buxton).

[178] [1924] 1 Ch 97. See p 316, above.   [179] *Chillingworth v Esche* [1924] 1 Ch 97, 115 (Sargant LJ).

The only exception to the general rule that deposits are not recoverable by the contract-breaker arises where the deposit is of such an excessive amount that it is deemed to be a penalty. Equity will intervene to relieve the defendant against the consequences of forfeiture of a penalty, at least where it can be shown that the defendant acted unconscionably.[180] Although Birks argued that the equitable rules relating to relief against forfeiture fall within the law of restitution,[181] the better view is that it is a contractual doctrine which simply operates to strike out particular clauses in the contract and so it does not constitute a ground of restitution in its own right.[182] The effect of this is that, even where a forfeiture clause has been struck out as penal, if the claimant wishes to recover the payment he or she must still base the restitutionary claim on one of the recognized grounds of restitution, such as total failure of basis. This is consistent with the rule that, where a deposit is paid in respect of a contract which is void, the deposit can only be recovered where the failure of basis is total.[183]

(2) Restitution of Non-Money Benefits

Where the contract-breaker wishes to bring a restitutionary claim in respect of non-money benefits which have been received by the defendant, total failure of basis should again be available as a ground of restitution. The courts have, however, been reluctant to allow restitution in such circumstances and, if such restitutionary claims are unavailable where the defendant breached the contract, it might be thought to be even more likely that such claims will be unavailable where the claimant has breached the contract. But, where the claimant breached the contract he or she will not have an alternative claim for breach, so the concern to confine the claimant to a contractual claim cannot arise. Further, again for reasons of symmetry, the recognized grounds of restitution should be applicable regardless of the type of enrichment which has been received by the defendant.[184]

That the contract-breaker may have a restitutionary claim against the innocent party in respect of non-money benefits was recognized *obiter* by some members of the House of Lords in *Miles v Wakefield Metropolitan District Council*.[185] In that case the claimant registrar refused to conduct marriage ceremonies on Saturday mornings in breach of contract, pursuant to an industrial dispute. The House of Lords decided that the claimant's employer was entitled to deduct salary in respect of the period when the claimant refused to work. Lords Brightman and Templeman went on to consider what the position would have been if the industrial action had taken the form of a 'go slow'. Because the claimant would then have been working in a manner which was designed to harm the employer it would not have been obliged to pay the claimant under the contract. But the judges suggested that the claimant would have been entitled to a *quantum meruit* in respect of the work which had been accepted by the employer.[186] Whilst the recognition of a *quantum meruit* claim in favour of the contract-breaker is to be welcomed, it is in fact misguided in the circumstances of an industrial dispute which takes the form of a 'go slow', simply because the contract will not have been terminated and fundamental principles of the law of unjust enrichment deny restitutionary claims where the contract still operates.[187] Despite this, the

---

[180] *Stockloser v Johnson* [1954] 1 QB 476; *Galbraith v Mildenhall Estates* [1965] 2 QB 478.

[181] PBH Birks, *An Introduction to the Law of Restitution* (rev edn, Oxford: Clarendon Press, 1989), 214, suggested that the ground of restitution might be inequality.

[182] See AS Burrows, *The Law of Restitution* (3rd edn, Oxford: Oxford University Press, 2011), 353.

[183] *Sharma v Simposh Ltd* [2011] EWCA Civ 1383, [2012] Ch 23.   [184] See p 125, above.

[185] [1987] AC 539.   [186] Ibid, 553 (Lord Brightman), 661 (Lord Templeman).

[187] See Lord Bridge, ibid, 552. Cf J Beatson, 'Restitution and Contract: Non-Cumul?' (2001) 1 Theoretical Inquiries in Law 83, 96 who considers this to be an example of a situation where there was a gap in the contractual allocation of risk. See further p 138, above.

case remains important because two members of the House of Lords were prepared to accept that a contract-breaker could bring a restitutionary claim in respect of non-money benefits. Although the judges did not identify the relevant ground of restitution, it is clear that total failure of basis would have been available if the claimant had not been paid anything for the work which he had done.

The restitutionary claim in respect of non-money benefits may be modified or excluded by contract. This is illustrated by *Sumpter v Hedges*[188] where the claimant had contracted to construct a number of buildings on the defendant's land for the payment of a lump sum. The claimant completed over half of the work which he had agreed to do,[189] but he was unable to finish because he ran out of money. The defendant accepted the claimant's repudiatory breach and the contract was discharged. The defendant completed the building himself, using the materials which the claimant had left behind. The claimant then sought to recover the value of the work he had done and the value of the materials he had left behind. The claim succeeded in respect of the materials which had been used by the defendant, but the claimant failed to recover the value of his services. There were two reasons for this decision, one contractual and one restitutionary. The contractual reason was that, because the parties had agreed that the payment would be a lump sum, the claimant's obligation was entire, so the defendant was not liable to pay the claimant for his work under the contract until the work had been completed. The other reason was that the law of restitution could not assist the claimant because it was held that, for the claimant to bring a *quantum meruit* claim, it was necessary to identify a fresh contract to pay and the defendant had not done anything from which a fresh contract could be implied. This decision might therefore be treated as explicable because of the court's reliance on the implied contract theory. Now that theory has been rejected it might be thought that there should be no bar to allowing a restitutionary claim to succeed in such circumstances. *Sumpter v Hedges* was, however, followed in *Bolton v Mahadeva*,[190] which was decided after the rejection of the implied contract theory. In *Bolton v Mahadeva* the claimant agreed to install a central heating system into the defendant's home but, in breach of contract, he installed a system which did not heat adequately and gave out fumes. It was held that the claimant was not entitled to recover any part of the contract price in respect of the goods supplied and the work done, even though the cost of remedying the defect was much less than the original contract price, being £174, whereas the contract price was £560. But again the claimant's obligation was characterized as entire.

It might be concluded that in both of these cases the defendant was unjustly enriched at the claimant's expense, since each defendant had received part of the benefit which had been requested, namely the building and installation of the central heating system respectively, and there had been a total failure of basis since neither claimant had been paid for the work which he had done.[191] But more careful analysis of the cases suggest that the basis had not failed, because of the particular nature of the contracts in each case.[192] The

---

[188] [1898] 1 QB 673. See B McFarlane and R Stevens, 'In Defence of *Sumpter v Hedges*' (2002) 118 LQR 569. See also *Munro v Butt* (1858) 8 E and B 738, 120 ER 275 and *Boston Deep Sea Fishing and Ice Co v Ansell* (1888) 39 Ch D 339.

[189] The contract price was £565 and the claimant had done work which was valued at £333.

[190] [1972] 1 WLR 1009.

[191] Though it seems that the claimant in *Sumpter v Hedges* had received some money from the defendant. If so, it would not be possible to conclude that the basis had totally failed, unless the payment could be apportioned, because, for example, it related to the supply of certain materials rather than the provision of the claimant's services. See p 321, above.

[192] This interpretation of *Sumpter v Hedges* was affirmed by the Court of Appeal in *Cleveland Bridge UK Ltd v Multiplex Construction (UK) Ltd* [2010] EWCA Civ 139, [135] (Sir Anthony May).

contracts in both *Sumpter v Hedges* and *Bolton v Mahadeva* involved entire obligations, whereby the defendant is not liable to pay the claimant until the work has been completed. Consequently, it was not possible to conclude that there had been a total failure of basis because no payment became due until the performance had been completed.[193]

The effect of this analysis of entire contracts is that the risk of the claimant failing to complete the contract is placed squarely on him or her. Where the risk of failure has been allocated to the claimant by the contract it is not for the law of restitution to subvert it. Consequently, whenever a contract is construed as imposing an entire obligation on the claimant it should be presumed that the claimant bears the risk of non-completion. This presumption will, however, be rebutted in three situations where it is not appropriate for the defendant to rely on the entire contract rule to prevent the claimant from being paid for the work which he or she has done. There is a fourth statutory situation which creates a presumption against an obligation being treated as entire in certain circumstances.

(a) The Contract Has Been Substantially Performed

Where the contract has been substantially performed it would be inequitable for the defendant to argue that the contract has not been completely performed so that he or she is not obliged to pay for the work which was done. In such circumstances the contract-breaker can sue on the contract and the innocent party will be able to bring a counterclaim for damages to the extent that the contract-breaker's actual performance fails to comply with the performance which he or she had contracted to provide. This is illustrated by *Hoenig v Isaacs*[194] where the claimant agreed to decorate and furnish the defendant's flat for the payment of a lump sum of £750. However, when the defendant inspected the claimant's work he discovered a number of defects which would have cost just over £55 to remedy. It was held that the claimant had substantially performed the contract[195] and so the defendant was liable to pay the claimant the contract price subject to a deduction in respect of the cost of making good the defects.

Usually, where the contract-breaker has substantially, but not completely, performed the contract, the breach will not be sufficiently serious to constitute a repudiatory breach, so he or she will be able to sue on the contract rather than bring a claim in restitution. However, in certain circumstances, such as where the contract-breaker is a ship owner who breached a contract by deviating from the agreed route, the very fact of deviation will be treated as a sufficiently serious breach to enable the innocent party to accept the repudiation. In such a case the contract-breaker should be able to bring a restitutionary claim in respect of carrying the cargo for the defendant if the contract was substantially performed. That such a claimant would have a restitutionary claim in such circumstances was tentatively accepted by some members of the House of Lords in *Hain SS Co Ltd v Tate and Lyle Ltd*.[196]

(b) Part Performance of a Contract Containing an Entire Obligation

The defendant may be considered to have benefited from the claimant's part performance, despite the fact that the work had been provided under a contract containing an entire

---

[193] McFarlane and Stevens, 'In Defence of *Sumpter v Hedges*'.

[194] [1952] 2 All ER 176. See also *H Dakin and Co Ltd v Lea* [1916] 1 KB 566.

[195] Although Somervell LJ did say, ibid, 179, that the case was close to the border-line as to what constitutes substantial performance.

[196] [1936] 3 All ER 597, 603 (Lord Atkin), 612 (Lord Wright MR), 616 (Lord Maugham). The ship owner's restitutionary claim did not arise on the facts of the case because it was held that the cargo owner had waived the breach arising from the deviation from the agreed route.

obligation, if the defendant had accepted what the claimant had done once the contract had been discharged.[197] The effect of such acceptance is either that the defendant waives the requirement that the contract must be substantially performed before he or she is obliged to pay the claimant, or that the defendant is estopped from arguing that the claimant's obligation was entire.[198] That the defendant is liable to the claimant where he or she accepted the part performance is illustrated by *Hoenig v Isaacs*,[199] where it was held that, since the defendant could have rejected the defective furniture which had been supplied by the claimant rather than use it, he was prevented from arguing that he was not liable to pay for it on the ground that it was defective.[200] Similarly, by virtue of section 30(1) of the Sale of Goods Act 1979, where the seller of goods has not delivered all the goods which he or she had agreed to supply, the purchaser has an option to reject what has been delivered, but if the purchaser accepts the goods he or she must pay for them at the contract rate.

But, if acceptance of the claimant's part performance prevents the defendant from relying on the fact that the claimant's obligation was entire, why did this not enable the claimant to obtain restitution in *Sumpter v Hedges* and *Bolton v Mahadeva*? This was because the defendant will only be considered to have accepted a benefit if he or she had a free choice as to whether or not to accept what the claimant had provided. In *Hoenig v Isaacs* the defendant did not have to accept the furniture which was supplied by the claimant, but in *Sumpter v Hedges*, where the claimant had commenced work on the defendant's land, the defendant had no choice but to complete the building, since if the building was left in an uncompleted state it would be a nuisance to the land.[201] Similarly, in *Bolton v Mahadeva* the claimant had installed the central heating system into the defendant's house and the defendant had no choice but to accept the system, which constituted a fixture and could not have been removed easily.

(c) The Defendant Prevented the Claimant from Performing the Obligation in Breach of Contract

The defendant will also be unable to rely on the fact that the claimant's obligation was entire where the defendant prevented the claimant from performing the obligation in breach of contract.[202]

(d) The Apportionment Act 1870

The consequences of an obligation being entire can also be avoided by means of the Apportionment Act 1870, which has been described as effectively raising a presumption against treating an obligation as entire.[203] Section 2 of the Act provides that all periodical payments in the nature of income, including rents, annuities and dividends, shall be considered to accrue from day to day 'and shall be apportionable in respect of time accordingly'. This provision has a potentially important role as regards the operation of the ground of total failure of basis where non-money benefits have been provided pursuant to an entire obligation. This is illustrated by *Item Software (UK) Ltd v Fassihi*,[204]

---

[197] See, for example, *Steele v Tardiani* (1946) 72 CLR 386, 405 (Dixon J).

[198] See *Miles v Wakefield Metropolitan District Council* [1987] AC 539, 553 (Lord Brightman).

[199] [1952] 2 All ER 176.   [200] See Somervell LJ, ibid, 179–80.

[201] *Sumpter v Hedges* [1898] 1 QB 673, 676 (Collins LJ). See also *Munro v Butt* (1858) 8 E and B 738, 120 ER 275.

[202] *Munro v Butt*, ibid; *Hoenig v Isaacs* [1952] 2 All ER 176, 181 (Denning LJ). See also *Appleby v Myers* (1867) LR 2 CP 651.

[203] *Item Software (UK) Ltd v Fassihi* [2004] EWCA Civ 1244, [2005] ICR 450, [72] (Arden LJ).

[204] [2004] EWCA Civ 1244, [2005] ICR 450.

where the Apportionment Act 1870 was applied to enable an employee, who had been dismissed, to recover a proportionate part of his monthly salary for the period he had actually worked, despite his breach of the contract of employment. The claimant's contract stated that his salary would be paid at the end of each month in arrears. He was sacked on 26 June and claimed payment for the work he had done since 1 June. This claim was successful since, by virtue of the Act, his salary was deemed to have accrued each day rather than each month, so he was able to recover a proportionate part of his salary in respect of the work which he had actually done and regardless of the reason why his employment was terminated. This provision effectively operates as a literal form of apportionment of the basis, so that payment accrues in respect of work done each day and regardless of the fact that the defendant's contractual obligation to pay does not accrue until later.

Even though the entire obligations rule is subject to a number of exceptions, it is still capable of producing unjust results. The denial of restitution in cases such as *Bolton v Mahadeva* means that the defendant obtains the benefit of the claimant's part performance without being obliged to pay anything for it. Although this may simply be the effect of the parties' agreeing that the relevant obligation be entire, in many cases the presumption that the claimant should bear the risk of non-completion of performance may be unrealistic, particularly because the parties may be unaware of the consequences of the obligation being made entire. Where the parties did not intend to allocate the risk in this way there is no reason why the claimant should be prevented from obtaining restitution in respect of goods or services which have been received by the defendant under the contract, even though the contract has not been fully performed. It is for this reason that a recommendation of the Law Commission[205] should be adopted, namely that the contract-breaker who partly performed a contract should be entitled to recover the value of the work provided, even if the contract was entire. The Law Commission proposed that the valuation of the work should be subject both to a *pro rata* contract price ceiling and to the innocent party's right to a set off or to counterclaim for damages in respect of the claimant failing to complete the contract. Also, consistent with the general principles relating to the restitutionary action founded on total failure of basis, the contract-breaker would not be able to obtain restitution unless the contract had first been discharged. Finally, the Law Commission recommended that the parties should be able to exclude the right to restitution in the contract itself. The effect of this reform would be that a contract-breaker could obtain a restitutionary remedy regardless of the fact that the claimant was subject to an entire obligation which had not been fully performed. This would not involve the law of restitution subverting the law of contract since it would be possible to exclude the restitutionary claim in the contract itself. What this really means is that the imposition of risk of failure could only be placed on the claimant expressly and not by presumption. This would be a highly desirable reform.

(B) ANTICIPATED AND INCOMPLETE CONTRACTS

Where the claimant and the defendant are negotiating a contract and, in the expectation that the contract will be made, the claimant incurs expenditure then, if no contract is made either expressly or impliedly, clearly the claimant has no contractual remedy against the

---

[205] *Pecuniary Restitution on Breach of Contract* (Law Com No 121, 1983). See AS Burrows, 'Law Commission Report on Pecuniary Restitution on Breach of Contract' (1984) 47 MLR 76.

defendant, but he or she may be able to bring a restitutionary claim grounded on failure of basis.[206]

Similarly, where the claimant transfers a benefit to the defendant pursuant to a contract which turns out to be incomplete. That such a restitutionary claim is available in this type of case was recognized by the Supreme Court in *Benedetti v Sawiris*.[207] In that case the claimant had provided services for the benefit of the defendant anticipating that he would be paid under a contract which was not concluded. Although the decision of the Supreme Court was that the claimant could not recover from the defendant, because the defendant's liability was considered to have been discharged by previous payments,[208] that the defendant was liable in unjust enrichment was accepted and Lord Reed specifically recognized that the ground of restitution was founded on failure of basis in order to correct 'the injustice arising from the defendant's receipt of the claimant's services on a basis which was not fulfilled'.[209]

Even with the endorsement of the Supreme Court, restitution in respect of anticipated contracts remains a controversial and difficult area of the law of restitution, primarily because of the care which must be taken in determining the boundaries between contractual and restitutionary claims. It is vital to ensure that the law of restitution does not subvert the law of contract. Consequently, if it is possible to identify an express contract or to imply a contract between the parties, the claimant should sue on the contract and not in restitution.[210] So, for example, if there is a contract for the claimant to do specified work for the defendant and the defendant has requested the claimant to do work outside the contract, the claimant may be entitled to be paid a reasonable sum for the work done outside the contract by virtue of an implied contract. The danger, however, is that a contract is implied too readily in these anticipated and incomplete contract cases. This makes a mockery of the law through the introduction of fictional contracts. Consequently, where it is not possible to imply a contract between the parties in respect of the claimant's performance,[211] simply because the state of the negotiations between the parties is such that it is not possible to determine what the terms of any such contract were intended to be, there will be scope to establish a claim in unjust enrichment instead, grounded on total failure of basis. Indeed, in *Benedetti v Sawiris* there had been no attempt argue that there was an implied contract between the parties governing the provision of the services by the claimant. But, even where a claim is brought in unjust enrichment, it is vital to ensure that a claimant who is considered to have taken the risk that no contract would be made should not be able to recover restitution. This is an area of the law where the principle that restitution is not available to the volunteer is of crucial importance.[212]

---

[206] For an extensive survey of the law and the issues arising see E McKendrick, 'Work Done in Anticipation of a Contract which Does Not Materialise' in W Cornish, R Nolan, J O'Sullivan, and G Virgo (eds), *Restitution: Past, Present and Future* (Oxford: Hart Publishing, 1998), ch 11. See also J Edelman, 'Liability in Unjust Enrichment when a Contract Fails to Materialise' in AF Burrows and E Peel (eds), *Contract Formation and Parties* (Oxford: Oxford University Press, 2010), ch 9; R Havelock, 'Anticipated Contracts that do not Materialise' [2011] RLR 72.

[207] [2013] UKSC 50, [2014] AC 938.   [208] See p 134, above.

[209] *Benedetti v Sawiris* [2013] UKSC 50, [2014] AC 938, [99].

[210] *RTS Flexible Systems Ltd v Molkerai Alois Müller Gmbh* [2010] UKSC 14, [2010] 1 WLR 753. See also *Benourad v Compass Group plc* [2010] EWHC 1882 (QB), [106] (Beatson J). S Hedley, 'Work Done in Anticipation of a Contract Which does not Materialise: A Response' in W Cornish, R Nolan, J O'Sullivan, and G Virgo (eds), *Restitution: Past, Present and Future* (Oxford: Hart Publishing, 1998), ch 12, considers that liability in these cases should simply turn on whether or not there was an agreement to pay for the work done. See also S Hedley, *Restitution: Its Division and Ordering* (London: Sweet and Maxwell, 2001), 62; P Davies, 'Contract and Unjust Enrichment: A Blurry Divide' (2010) LQR 175.

[211] *Whittle Movers Ltd v Hollywood Express Ltd* [2009] EWCA Civ 1189.   [212] See p 36, above.

(i) Establishing Unjust Enrichment

One of the difficulties in establishing a restitutionary claim where the claimant has acted in respect of a contract which is anticipated or incomplete, relates to proving that the defendant had obtained an enrichment, as has previously been examined.[213] Typically, it will be possible to show that the defendant had been enriched, either because the defendant had received an objective benefit and was prevented from relying on the subjective devaluation principle because of request or free acceptance,[214] or, in those cases where an objective benefit has not been received, where the defendant was estopped from denying this.[215] In some cases the restitutionary claim will fail simply because it cannot be shown that the claimant had been enriched.[216]

Once the question of the defendant's enrichment has been established, it is then necessary to identify the relevant ground of restitution, this will typically be total failure of basis as recognized by the Supreme Court in *Benedetti v Sawiris*,[217] but crucially, and somewhat confusingly, also in *Yeoman's Row Management Ltd v Cobbe*.[218] In that case the claimant had entered into an oral agreement in principle with the defendant to buy the defendant's land. No written contract was made. The claimant successfully made an application for planning permission to develop the land. Negotiations broke down and the claimant sought restitution from the defendant in respect of his services in obtaining planning permission. Lord Scott, with whom the other Lordships agreed, recognized three claims, namely unjust enrichment, *quantum meruit* and total failure of basis. In fact, the claim was founded on unjust enrichment with the remedy being the reasonable value of the claimant's services, but, crucially, the ground of restitution was total failure of basis, because the claimant's work in obtaining the planning permission was conditional on the land being conveyed to the claimant. Since this condition failed it followed that there was a total failure of basis.

This ground of restitution can be used to explain the result in earlier cases, even though it was not specifically identified. For example, in *William Lacey (Hounslow) Ltd v Davis*[219] the claimant submitted to the defendant an estimate for the work in rebuilding the defendant's property and, although the parties did not enter into a binding contract, the defendant led the claimant to believe that a contract would be made. The defendant asked the claimant to incur expenditure for a purpose which did not relate to the performance of the anticipated contract, and the claimant agreed to do this in the belief that it would be recompensed from the profit which it would make under the contract once it was made. When no contract was made the claimant successfully brought a *quantum meruit* claim to recover the reasonable value of the services which had clearly benefited the defendant.[220] Although the ground of restitution was not clearly identified in the case, the trial judge appeared to suggest that it was mistake. But that is an unsatisfactory explanation. The

---

[213] See p 92, above.

[214] See, for example, *William Lacey (Hounslow) Ltd v Davis* [1957] 1 WLR 932; *British Steel Corporation v Cleveland Bridge and Engineering Co* [1984] 1 All ER 504; and *Tahar Benourad v Compass Group plc* [2010] EWHC 1882 (QB), [106] (Beatson J).

[215] See, for example, *Brewer Street Investments Ltd v Barclays Woollen Co Ltd* [1954] 1 QB 428.

[216] See, for example, *Jennings and Chapman Ltd v Woodman Matthews and Co* [1952] 2 TLR 409. See also *Regalian Properties plc v London Dockland Development Corporation* [1995] 1 WLR 212, discussed at p 346, below.

[217] [2013] UKSC 50, [2014] AC 938, [86] (Lord Reed), [175] (Lord Neuberger). See also *Valencina v Llupar* [2012] EWCA Civ 396, [51] (Mummery LJ).   [218] [2008] UKHL 55, [2008] 1 WLR 1752.

[219] [1957] 1 All ER 932.

[220] As was recognized by Rattee J in *Regalian Properties plc v London Dockland Development Corporation* [1995] 1 WLR 212, 225.

claimant had not made any mistake as to any existing facts, rather it had made a misprediction as to what would happen in the future, and this is not a ground of restitution.[221] Surely the preferable explanation for the success of the restitutionary claim was that the basis for the provision of the claimant's services had failed totally, since the condition by reference to which the claimant's expenditure was subject was that the claimant would be reimbursed under the contract and, when no contract was made, the basis for the work failed totally.

Similarly, in *British Steel Corporation v Cleveland Bridge and Engineering Co Ltd*[222] the defendant wanted the claimant to supply steel nodes and, after obtaining an estimated price from the claimant, sent it a letter to the effect that the defendant intended to enter into a contract with the claimant on the defendant's standard terms and requested that the claimant commence work on the nodes pending the issue of the contract. No such contract was ever made because the parties failed to agree terms. The claimant delivered to the defendant all but one of the steel nodes which the defendant wanted. The defendant refused to pay for them on the ground that they had been delivered late and out of sequence. The claimant then sued for the reasonable value of the nodes and succeeded. It was clear that the defendant had received a valuable benefit.[223] Even though the trial judge, Robert Goff J, did not identify a specific ground of restitution in this case, surely it was total failure of basis since the claimant had not received anything for the nodes it had supplied.

(ii) Risk-taking

Whilst it is clear that, if the claimant bore the risk that the anticipated contract might not be made, restitution will be denied,[224] the identification of whether the claimant did indeed bear the risk of the contract not being made is, however, fraught with uncertainty.[225] This has proved to be especially significant in cases where the parties have made an agreement which is 'subject to contract', in other words the agreement is subject to a formal written contract being made. Just because an agreement was 'subject to contract' does not automatically exclude a restitutionary claim,[226] but it is important to consider whether the claimant should be considered to have borne the risk of no contract being made.

In *Regalian Properties plc v London Docklands Development Corporation*[227] restitution was denied to a claimant who had incurred expenditure after entering into an agreement which was subject to contract. The claimant had entered into the agreement with the defendant for the development of the defendant's land. This agreement was expressly made subject to contract. The defendant requested the claimant to obtain designs from architects and encouraged it to incur other preliminary expenditure amounting to almost £3 million, so that the claimant was in a position to obtain the building lease from the defendant and so that it could perform the contract once the lease was obtained. Because

---

[221] See p 162, above.   [222] [1984] 1 All ER 504.

[223] The fact that the nodes had been delivered out of sequence related to the question of valuation rather than whether or not the delivery of the nodes constituted a valuable benefit. See p 102, above.

[224] *MSM Consulting Ltd v United Republic of Tanzania* [2009] EWHC 121 (QB), [171] (Clarke J).

[225] F Wilmot-Smith, 'Replacing Risk-Taking Reasoning' (2011) 127 LQR 610 considers that the question whether the claimant is a risk-taker does not involve the operation of a distinct bar but is determined through proper construction of the relevant basis for the work which the claimant has undertaken. In the context of anticipated contracts at least this appears to be correct. Sometimes the allocation of risk will be express: *Eugena Ltd v Gelda Corp Ltd* [2004] EWHC 3273 (QB), [123] (Judge Hegarty QC).

[226] See *Valencina v Llupar* [2012] EWCA Civ 396, where the allocation of risk by an agreement being made subject to contract was not considered.   [227] [1995] 1 WLR 212.

of a fall in property values no contract was ever made, but the claimant sought restitution from the defendant. The trial judge held that the claim failed because, as the agreement was subject to contract, the parties were free to withdraw at any time, so the expenditure which was incurred in anticipation of the contract had been incurred at the claimant's risk. Whilst the judge was correct to reject the restitutionary claim, the reasons given for his conclusion are not satisfactory, particularly because of the apparent inconsistency with *Chillingworth v Esche*,[228] which was not cited, where the claimant did obtain restitution even though the agreement was 'subject to contract'. In fact, *Regalian* is easily distinguishable from *Chillingworth v Esche*, for in that case the claimant had paid money to the defendant, so there was an obvious enrichment. In *Regalian*, although the claimant had incurred expenditure in preparation for the performance of the contract, this did not benefit the defendant in any way, as was recognized by the trial judge,[229] because the expenditure was incurred to place the claimant in a position to obtain and perform the expected contract. If the question of enrichment is put to one side, it was possible to conclude that there had been a total failure of basis, since the condition on which the claimant's expenditure was contingent was the making of a contract and, since the agreement was expressly made subject to contract, this was a condition of which the defendant was aware. But without any enrichment, the fact that the basis had failed totally was irrelevant.

Presumably, therefore, if the defendant in *Regalian* had received an enrichment the restitutionary claim would have succeeded, because the case would then appear to be indistinguishable from *Chillingworth v Esche*. But the trial judge in *Regalian* emphasized that the restitutionary claim failed specifically because the agreement was subject to contract such that the claimant had incurred the expenditure at its own risk. If this is correct, why was the fact that the agreement was 'subject to contract' in *Chillingworth* considered to be irrelevant, when it was treated as barring the claim in *Regalian*? The only satisfactory explanation for this is that in *Regalian* the fact that the agreement was 'subject to contract' was interpreted as allocating the risk that no contract would ever be made to the claimant.[230] This was indeed recognized by the trial judge:

> Each party to such negotiations must be taken to know (as in my judgment Regalian did in the present case) that pending the conclusion of a binding contract any cost incurred by him in preparation for the intended contract will be incurred at his own risk, in the sense that he will have no recompense for those costs if no contract results.[231]

The fact that the negotiations were made 'subject to contract' should only be considered to be relevant, however, if it really can be said that the clause is intended to allocate the risk of no contract being made. This would be a way of distinguishing *Regalian* from *Chillingworth v Esche*, if it is possible to conclude that making the agreement subject to contract in the latter case was not intended to allocate the risk of no contract being made to the claimant. The different contexts of the two cases suggest that such a distinction could be drawn. *Chillingworth v Esche* involved the sale of land, where agreements are automatically made subject to contract, so it is not possible to assume that the parties have deliberately allocated the risk of no contract being made. In *Regalian*, however, there was no practice of making such agreements subject to contract, so the fact that this is what occurred suggests that there was a deliberate decision to allocate the risk of no contract being made. If this explanation is correct it means that the particular context of the agreement will

---

[228] [1924] 1 Ch 97. See p 316, above.   [229] Ibid, 225.

[230] That pre-contract deposits are usually recoverable save if there is a precise, clear, and express agreement to the contrary was recognized in *Robinson v Lane* [2010] EWCA Civ 385, [15] (Sir Richard Buxton); *Sharma v Simposh* [2011] EWCA Civ 1383, [2012] Ch 23, [51] Toulson LJ.   [231] [1995] 1 WLR 212, 231.

always need to be considered carefully when determining the consequences of the agreement being made subject to contract.

In *Yeoman's Row Management Ltd v Cobbe*[232] the restitutionary claim succeeded even though the agreement made between the parties was an oral agreement in principle which, whilst not expressly made subject to contract, was dependent on a written contract for the sale of land being made. Even though the claimant, who had obtained planning permission to develop the land, was considered to be a risk-taker in doing so, and this barred the claims that the property was held on constructive trust or that proprietary estoppel could be established, risk-taking was not even considered as regards the restitutionary claim. This might be explained by analogy with *Chillingworth v Esche*, as another case involving sale of land where agreements are automatically made subject to contract, but the parties in *Yeoman's Row* had not yet reached that point in their negotiations. That the claimant could be considered to be a risk-taker for one claim but not for another is incomprehensible. Surely, if the claimant was considered to have taken the risk that a written contract might not be made, then the restitutionary claim should also have failed.

Wilmot-Smith[233] has identified certain canons of construction to assist in the determination of whether the claimant can be considered to have borne the risk of no contract being made. These include that the claimant is less likely to bear the risk where the work the claimant has done is anticipatory rather than preparatory and where the work is more likely to benefit the defendant. But ultimately determination of risk allocation requires careful examination of all the facts of the case.

(iii) Introducing a Fault Requirement

Some of the cases which involve benefits transferred pursuant to anticipated contracts which fail to materialize suggest that the award of a restitutionary remedy depends on the relative fault of the parties. This was recognized in *Brewer Street Investments Ltd v Barclays Woollen Co Ltd*,[234] where the claimant and the defendant had entered into negotiations for the lease of the claimant's premises by the defendant. After an agreement had been made, which was subject to contract, the defendant requested the claimant to make certain alterations to the premises, which the claimant did. No final agreement was made and the claimant sought to recover the costs of the work from the defendant. It was held that, since no final agreement had been made due to the fault of the defendant, the claimant's restitutionary claim succeeded.[235]

This principle of fault was also relied on by Sheppard J in the Australian case of *Sabemo Pty Ltd v North Sydney Municipal Council*,[236] where he held that the defendant was liable to make restitution to the claimant for work done in respect of a contract which was anticipated but did not materialize, because the defendant had deliberately decided not to enter into the agreement.[237] Presumably, if the defendant had failed to enter into the agreement in circumstances in which he or she was acting in good faith, such as where the defendant reasonably disagreed with the terms of the proposed agreement, he or she would not have been considered to be at fault. Sheppard J contemplated that, if neither

---

[232] [2008] UKHL 55, [2008] 1 WLR 1752. See p 345, above.

[233] Wilmot-Smith, 'Replacing Risk-Taking Reasoning'.

[234] [1954] 1 QB 428. See also *Jennings and Chapman Ltd v Woodman Matthews and Co* [1952] 2 TLR 409.

[235] *Jennings and Chapman Ltd v Woodman Matthews and Co* [1952] 2 TLR 409, 438 (Romer LJ). Somervell LJ suggested, ibid, 434, that if the failure to make a final agreement was not due to the fault of either party the claim would still have succeeded, but he also acknowledged that if the claimant had been at fault the claim would have failed. Denning LJ did not consider either party to have been at fault.

[236] [1977] 2 NSWLR 880.   [237] Ibid, 900.

party was at fault, each party would have borne the risk that no agreement might be made so that the expenditure could not be recovered.

English law does not generally recognize a doctrine of good faith and fair dealing in pre-contractual negotiations,[238] despite the decision of the Court of Appeal in *Brewer Street Investments*, for the orthodox position of English law is that the parties are free to make contracts or not. Nevertheless, there are signs of the recognition of a principle of good faith generally into English contract law,[239] which might be used as an additional consideration in determining whether the restitutionary claim should succeed. Such an approach would, of course, be inconsistent with the general principle that claims founded on unjust enrichment are claims of strict liability. It was, however, seen previously that questions of fault are often relevant to the interpretation of grounds of restitution and defences.[240] Fault in respect of anticipated contracts might constitute another example.

(iv) Unconscionability

In *Countrywide Communications Ltd v ICL Pathway Ltd*[241] the claimant had provided public relations and communication services in respect of a bid by the defendant to introduce a card system for the provision of benefits by the Post Office. There was no binding agreement, either express or implied, to appoint the claimant to provide these services, but the claimant anticipated that, if it assisted with the bid, it would get the formal contract if the bid was successful. It was accepted that the work done by the claimant was for the benefit of the defendant. The defendant's bid was successful but the claimant's services were eventually dispensed with and no contract was made. The claimant brought a claim for *quantum meruit*[242] in respect of the work which it had done. The trial judge considered a wide range of cases on anticipated contracts and found it impossible to formulate a general principle which governs all the different situations. He emphasized that much of the problem was caused by trying to categorize these claims as involving unjust enrichment when the real issue was whether the claimant should be compensated for a loss which was unfairly sustained. Consequently, he preferred to analyse the claim in respect of anticipated contracts as being founded on justice and unconscionability. In determining whether there was an obligation to pay for the benefits provided, the judge identified a number of relevant factors.[243] These included: whether the benefit would normally be provided free of charge; whether the claimant bore the risk of no contract being made; whether the defendant had obtained a real benefit; whether the defendant was at fault in preventing the contract from being made. The judge particularly emphasized the significance of the defendant being enriched and recognized the relevance of the claim being analysed as restitutionary. The application of these principles led the judge to conclude that the claimant should be recompensed for the work it had done. It was particularly significant that the defendant had been benefited and had assured the claimant that a contract would be made if the bid succeeded.

---

[238] *Walford v Miles* [1992] AC 128.

[239] See, for example, *Yam Seng Pte Ltd v International Trade Corporation Ltd* [2013] EWHC 111 (QB). See generally LE Trakman and K Sharma, 'The Binding Force of Agreements to Negotiate in Good Faith' (2014) CLJ 598.

[240] See p 34, above.   [241] [2000] CLC 324.

[242] An alternative claim based on breach of contract was rejected since no contract had made, either express or implied.

[243] These were commended by Clarke J in *MSM Consulting Ltd v United Republic of Tanzania* [2009] EWHC 121 (QB), [171]. See also *Benourad v Compass Group plc* [2010] EWHC 1882 (QB), [106] (Beatson J).

This analysis is a real cause for concern. The uncertainty of founding the claim on the justice of the case and unconscionability is unacceptable, despite the attempt of the judge to identify some factors which could assist the court in determining this. The real irony of the decision is that the claim could easily have been analysed as a claim founded in unjust enrichment. The defendant had been benefited by services provided by the claimant. The claimant expected to be paid for the work under a contract. That contract was not forthcoming and so the basis had totally failed. Whilst the claimant had taken a risk that the contract might not be made if the bid was not successful, it was not considered to have taken the risk that a contract would not be made if the bid was successful. Analysing liability with reference to an apparent cause of action founded on unconscionability can only serve to confuse; the underlying cause of action should instead have been treated as one involving the defendant's enrichment at the claimant's expense grounded on total failure of basis.

(v) Alternative Claims

In some cases where the claimant has incurred expenditure pursuant to an anticipated or incomplete contract the remedy will not lie within the law of restitution at all, because it is not possible to show that the defendant had been enriched. In such circumstances it may be possible for the claimant to identify a collateral contract whereby the defendant agrees to reimburse the claimant for the expenditure which had been incurred.[244] It might even be possible for the claimant to sue the defendant in tort if, for example, the defendant had said that he or she would make a contract but never intended to do so, for the defendant could then be liable to the claimant for misrepresentation.

Alternatively, the claimant might in the future be able to establish a claim founded on promissory estoppel, even though the orthodox approach in English law is that this operates as a shield rather than a sword so that it does not constitute a cause of action.[245] Whilst the Privy Council in *Attorney-General of Hong Kong v Humphreys Estate*[246] held that, on the facts of that case where the claimant had incurred expenditure in respect of an agreement which was 'subject to contract', the claimant could not found an action for reimbursement on estoppel, it was accepted that in certain circumstances the defendant's conduct would mean that he or she would be estopped from denying that the parties had entered into a contract, even where the agreement was 'subject to contract', so a contractual claim would succeed.

(C) UNENFORCEABLE CONTRACTS

Where the claimant transfers a benefit to the defendant under a contract which is unenforceable, he or she cannot recover the value of the benefit under the contract, since this would involve the enforcement of what is unenforceable. It may, however, be possible to bring a restitutionary claim since, being an independent legal obligation, liability in unjust enrichment does not involve enforcement of the contract.[247] A contract may be unenforceable for a number of reasons, but often unenforceability arises as a result of failure to comply with statutory formalities relating to the contract.

---

[244] *Turriff Construction Ltd v Regalia Knitting Mills Ltd* [1972] EGD 257.

[245] Unlike proprietary estoppel: see *Salvation Army Trustee Co Ltd v West Yorkshire Metropolitan County Council* (1981) 41 P and CR 179. In Australia promissory estoppel is a cause of action: *Walton Stores (Interstate) Ltd v Maher* (1988) 164 CLR 387.   [246] [1987] AC 114.

[247] As was recognized by the House of Lords in *Westdeutsche Landesbank Girozentrale v Islington LBC* [1996] AC 669.

There used to be a number of statutory formalities in English law, particularly by virtue of the Statute of Frauds 1677. Today, most of these formalities have been removed, but formalities remain particularly important for contracts involving sale of land.[248] Section 2 of the Law of Property (Miscellaneous Provisions) Act 1989 requires contracts for the sale and other dispositions of land to be in writing and to be accompanied by a signature of, or on behalf of, each party to the contract. Failure to comply with these formalities means that the contract is unenforceable, but not invalid.

Where the claimant wishes to obtain restitution of a benefit which has been transferred pursuant to an unenforceable contract, the ground of restitution will typically be total failure of basis. Although such a restitutionary claim will succeed even though the contract has not been set aside,[249] it must be shown that the defendant is no longer ready, able, and willing to perform his or her part of the bargain.[250] This is well illustrated by *Monnickendam v Leanse*,[251] where the claimant had contracted to buy the defendant's house. The claimant paid the defendant a deposit but, because the contract was unenforceable for lack of writing, the claimant repudiated the contract and sought to recover the deposit. It was held that, because the defendant remained ready and willing to perform the contract, the claimant could not recover the deposit. But it was accepted that, if the contract had been repudiated by the defendant, the claimant would have been able to recover the deposit, since this would have meant that the defendant was no longer willing to perform.[252]

Restitution of benefits which have been transferred pursuant to an unenforceable contract may be awarded regardless of whether the enrichment is money[253] or a non-money benefit.[254] This is particularly well illustrated by *Pulbrook v Lawes*,[255] where the claimant had entered into an oral agreement with the defendant for the lease of a house, on condition that certain alterations were made to it. The claimant paid to have the drawing room of the house painted and to have gas pipes installed. After the alterations had been done, the defendant defaulted and no lease was executed. The claimant sought to recover the amount he had spent in altering the house, but was unable to sue the defendant on the contract because it was unenforceable due to lack of writing. The claimant did successfully bring a claim to recover the reasonable value of the work done. The ground of restitution was specifically held to be akin to that of total failure of basis, which was established because the claimant had incurred the expenditure in the expectation that he would take a lease of the house and no lease had been executed. But the difficulty in analysing this case as involving the reversal of the defendant's unjust enrichment relates to the identification of the benefit, particularly because Blackburn J described the work as 'fanciful painting of no benefit to the house'. Since, however, some of the work had been requested by the defendant, and it was assumed that some of the work was

---

[248] Note also contracts made with minors which are unenforceable against the minor under the Minors' Contracts Act 1987. Where a minor has transferred a benefit to the defendant under such a contract there is a statutory right to restitution, but this is properly characterized as being grounded on the minor's incapacity rather than total failure of basis. See p 385, below.

[249] *Pavey and Matthews Pty Ltd v Paul* (1986) CLR 221, 256 (Deane J).

[250] See the discussion of *Thomas v Brown* (1876) 1 QBD 714 at p 315, above.

[251] (1923) 39 TLR 445.   [252] Ibid, 447 (Horridge J).   [253] See *Monnickendam v Leanse*, ibid.

[254] See *Scarisbrick v Parkinson* (1869) 20 LT 175 and the decision of the Supreme Court of Canada in *Deglman v Guaranty Trust Co of Canada and Constantineau* [1954] 3 DLR 785. *Scott v Pattison* [1923] 2 KB 723 has sometimes been treated as a further example, but in that case the claimant recovered remuneration in respect of work he would have done had he not been sick. Since he had not actually done this work it is not possible to treat this aspect of the case as restitutionary, since there was no evidence that the defendant had been enriched.   [255] (1876) 1 QBD 284.

beneficial to the house, the defendant could be considered to have been enriched, at least to some extent.

The most complex issue relating to whether restitution can be awarded where a benefit has been transferred pursuant to an unenforceable contract concerns whether the policy which made the contract unenforceable should prevent the restitutionary claim from succeeding as well. In principle, because the obligation to make restitution is an independent obligation imposed by law and does not arise from any agreement between the parties, the restitutionary obligation should not be affected by the policy of the statute which makes the contract unenforceable. This was recognized by the High Court of Australia in *Pavey and Matthews Pty Ltd v Paul*,[256] where the claimant renovated the defendant's cottage, having made an oral contract to do so. The defendant regarded the price for the work as excessive and, having paid part of it, refused to pay the balance.[257] The claimant was not able to sue the defendant on the contract to recover the balance because, being an oral contract, it was unenforceable as a result of a statutory provision which required such an agreement to be in writing. The claimant therefore brought a restitutionary claim for the reasonable value of its services and succeeded. The High Court specifically recognized that, by allowing the claim to succeed, it was not contravening the policy of the statute. The statute sought to ensure that the terms of building contracts were in writing and clear so that builders could not make spurious claims against customers. But this policy did not affect the restitutionary claim, because the court was not enforcing the defendant's contractual promise to pay the claimant but was enforcing an independent obligation to make restitution, an obligation which was triggered by the fact that the defendant had been unjustly enriched at the claimant's expense, and this obligation did not depend in any way on proving the terms of the contract.

Although in cases such as *Pavey and Matthews* the statutory policy which made the contract unenforceable did not affect the claimant's right to restitution, great care must always be taken to ensure that the policy of the statute is not undermined by awarding restitution. It is therefore vital to identify the policy of the statute carefully in an attempt to determine why the contract was made unenforceable. For example, in *Dimond v Lovell*[258] a car hire agreement, which was characterized as a consumer credit agreement, was held to be unenforceable under the Consumer Credit Act 1974. It was further held that the hirer could not bring a restitutionary claim for the defendant's use of the vehicle, since this would be inconsistent with the policy of the Act, because Parliament intended that if a consumer credit agreement was improperly executed the debtor would not have to pay.[259] It follows that the defendant's enrichment would not be characterized as unjust because allowing restitution would undermine the policy of the statute.[260]

---

[256] (1986) 162 CLR 221.

[257] This means that it is difficult to identify the ground of restitution which was relied on in this case. Since the claimant had been partly paid the ground of restitution could not be total failure of basis, unless the money received could be apportioned. The relevant ground might have been partial failure of basis, although this was not acknowledged, and some dicta suggests that the defendant was required to make restitution because she had freely accepted the benefit: (1986) 162 CLR 221, 228 (Mason and Wilson JJ). See also *Proactive Sports Management Ltd v Rooney* [2010] EWHC 1807 (QB) where a contract with the footballer Wayne Rooney was unenforceable on grounds of unreasonable restraint of trade, but a claim for *quantum meruit* succeeded because he had freely accepted the services provided. Whether free acceptance constitutes a ground of restitution is considered, at p 122, above.

[258] [2002] 1 AC 384. See also *Wilson v First County Trust Ltd (No 2)* [2003] UKHL 40, [2004] 1 AC 816 (no restitution of money lent pursuant to unenforceable money lending agreement with pawnbroker).

[259] *Dimond v Lovell* [2002] 1 AC 384, 398 (Lord Hoffmann).

[260] See further p 377, below.

Even though it was decided in *Pavey and Matthews* that the obligation to make restitution was independent of and unaffected by the unenforceable contract, this will not always be the case, since there may be circumstances where the terms of the contract will be highly relevant to the restitutionary claim. For example, the fact that a contract was made shows that the benefit which was provided by the claimant was not intended as a gift and the contract may also assist the court in valuing the benefit which was received by the defendant.[261] Similarly, the contract may need to be referred to where the ground of restitution is total failure of basis, since it will assist in identifying what was the anticipated basis for the transfer of the benefit to the claimant.[262] It should be possible to refer to the contract in any of these circumstances as evidence of the parties' intention even though it is unenforceable, save where the contract is considered to be particularly unreliable. This is most likely to be the case where the contract was made unenforceable because of a policy to prevent abuse of a weak party by a stronger party. Where the contract is unreliable for this reason it should not be taken into account for the purposes of establishing any elements of the restitutionary claim.

(D) WITHDRAWAL FROM AN ILLEGAL TRANSACTION

Although the general rule is that a claimant who has transferred a benefit to the defendant in respect of an illegal transaction cannot bring a restitutionary claim on the ground of total failure of basis, because he or she continues to be tainted by the illegality,[263] restitution will be available where the claimant can establish that he or she is no longer tainted. The easiest way to establish this is by showing that the claimant has withdrawn from the illegal transaction.[264]

This withdrawal principle, otherwise known as the *locus poenitentiae*, has long been recognized as a ground of restitution in its own right,[265] but careful analysis of the principle suggests that it is closely related to the ground of total failure of basis and should, at the very least, be considered to be founded on the failure of basis principle.

The policy behind the withdrawal principle is to deter the claimant from performing the illegal transaction by allowing restitution to be awarded before the claimant has become tainted by the illegality. Originally the principle was only applicable if two conditions were satisfied. First, the claimant must have withdrawn from the illegal transaction before it had been wholly or substantially executed.[266] Secondly, the claimant must have repented of the illegality.[267] The principle was radically reinterpreted by the Court of Appeal in *Tribe v Tribe*.[268] In that case the claimant feared that he would be forced to sell his shares in the family business to meet potential liabilities to creditors. Consequently, he transferred the shares to his son. The son never paid for the shares and was never intended to do so. This transfer of shares was an illegal transaction because the claimant's purpose was to defraud his creditors. No creditors were deceived, however, because alternative arrangements were made which prevented the liabilities from arising. Once the risk that the assets would be taken had passed, the claimant requested his son to return the shares

---

[261] *Pavey and Matthews Pty Ltd v Paul* (1986) 162 CLR 221, 257 (Deane J). See also *Scarisbrick v Parkinson* (1869) 20 LT 175. See p 99, above.

[262] *Pavey and Matthews Pty Ltd v Paul* (1986) 162 CLR 221, 227 (Mason and Wilson JJ), 257 (Deane J).

[263] See Virgo, 'The Effects of Illegality on Claims for Restitution in English Law', 163–7. See p 330, above.

[264] See p 719, below.

[265] See R Merkin, 'Restitution by Withdrawal from Illegal Contracts' (1981) 97 LQR 420.

[266] *Taylor v Bowers* (1876) 1 QBD 291; *Kearley v Thompson* (1890) 24 QBD 742.

[267] *Bigos v Bousted* [1951] 1 All ER 92. See also *Alexander v Rayson* [1946] 1 KB 169, 190.

[268] [1996] Ch 107.

to him, but he refused to do so. Since the equitable presumption of advancement applies in respect of transfers of property from a father to his son,[269] it was presumed that the claimant had given the shares to his son. To rebut this presumption the claimant needed to show that his purpose was not to transfer the shares to his son absolutely, but that the son would hold the shares until the threat from his creditors had passed. But this was an illegal purpose and, for reasons of public policy, such purposes cannot rebut the presumption of advancement. Despite this, the Court of Appeal held that the father had withdrawn from the illegal transaction. Consequently, he ceased to be tainted by the illegality and so was able to plead his true intention in transferring the shares to his son to show that he had never intended to give the shares to him absolutely.[270]

In accepting that the claimant could rely on the withdrawal principle, the Court of Appeal held that there were two conditions which needed to be satisfied.

(1) *No part of the illegal purpose must have been carried into effect.* This did not bar restitution on the facts because it was assumed that the claimant's purpose was to deceive creditors and, since no creditors had been deceived, no part of the father's purpose had been carried into effect. Whether this is correct depends on the identification of what the claimant's purpose actually was in transferring the shares to his son. It could just as easily, and perhaps more accurately, have been concluded that his purpose was simply to make it appear that he did not own shares and that purpose had been achieved. But clearly the identification of the claimant's purpose can be manipulated to secure what is perceived to be a just result, in the same way that the notion of total failure of basis can be manipulated to secure restitution.[271] Where, however, the illegal purpose has been carried into effect, if only partly, restitution will not be available.[272]

(2) *The claimant must have withdrawn from the illegal transaction.* It is no longer necessary to show that the claimant has repented of the illegality,[273] so it was irrelevant that the father had only sought restitution once it was clear that the purpose of the transaction would never be fulfilled and even though there was no evidence of contrition on his part. The conclusion that the father had withdrawn on the facts of this case means that the test of withdrawal appears to be easily satisfied. Withdrawal does not require a voluntary decision on the part of the claimant to have nothing more to do with the illegal transaction, for if this was the test of withdrawal it was clear that the claimant had not satisfied it. Rather, all the claimant had done was to make a claim for restitution of the shares once he had realized that the danger of creditors seizing his assets had passed. This was confirmed in *Patel v Mirza*,[274] where the claimant obtained restitution by virtue of the withdrawal principle even though he had not repented of the illegality, it being sufficient that the claimant had sought restitution before any part of the illegal agreement had been carried into effect to any extent. In that case the claimant had paid money to the defendant pursuant to a contract which was illegal because it constituted the crime of insider dealing, involving the intended use of inside information to profit

---

[269] See p 589, below.

[270] The withdrawal principle was consequently relied on to enable the father to bring a proprietary restitutionary claim. This aspect of the case is discussed at p 591, below. Despite this, the case remains good authority on the ambit of the withdrawal principle generally.

[271] See p 319, above.   [272] *Collier v Collier* [2002] EWCA Civ 1095.

[273] See also *Patel v Mirza* [2014] EWCA Civ 1047, [2015] 2 WLR 405.   [274] Ibid.

from the purchase and sale of shares. The claimant was found to have withdrawn from the agreement even though the only reason for the withdrawal was because the illegal purpose was frustrated for reasons outside the control of the claimant, namely that the expected inside information was not obtained. Consequently, withdrawal does not require any change of mind on the part of the claimant, it is simply sufficient that the illegal purpose was frustrated.[275]

The reinterpretation of the withdrawal principle in *Tribe v Tribe*, expanded in *Patel v Mirza*, as requiring no part of the illegal purpose to have been fulfilled and liberating it from the requirement of repentance and even a change of mind on the part of the claimant, means that now when a restitutionary claim is founded on this principle it is in fact being founded on the ground of total failure of basis, where the condition on which the benefit is transferred is a non-promissory contingency. In the same way that the basis will not have failed totally if any part of the contingency is satisfied, so too restitution will not be available by reference to the withdrawal principle if any part of the illegal purpose is fulfilled.

The next stage in the development of the law in this area is that the courts should recognize that restitutionary claims will succeed in all cases of total failure of basis, despite the fact that the claimant had participated in an illegal transaction. The only qualification should be that restitution will be denied in those cases where the illegality involves the commission of a serious criminal offence, such as murder, such that no court would wish to assist the claimant on the grounds of public policy.[276] If partial failure of basis is ever recognized as a general ground of restitution in its own right, it too should be available even where the claimant has participated in an illegal transaction, save where restitution is denied for distinct reasons of public policy.

4. PARTIAL FAILURE OF BASIS

Although the most common ground of restitution which is founded on the principle of failure of basis is that of total failure of basis, and even though that ground of restitution has been interpreted in such a way that effectively restitution is being awarded on the ground of partial failure of basis, in one particular situation the applicable ground of restitution is specifically partial failure of basis, namely where the contract has been frustrated.

Where benefits have been transferred in respect of a contract which is later frustrated, the restitutionary regime is, for the most part, governed by the Law Reform (Frustrated Contracts) Act 1943. This statute was enacted in the light of the unsatisfactory nature of the common law regime concerning the consequences of a contract being frustrated. Unfortunately the common law regime still applies to certain contracts, including contracts for the carriage of goods by sea, contracts of insurance and contracts for the

---

[275] Cf *Bigos v Bousted* [1951] 1 All ER 92 where the withdrawal principle did not apply where the frustration of the illegal purpose resulted from the refusal of the other party to participate in the transaction. This decision was described as 'dubious' by Millett LJ in *Tribe v Tribe* [1996] Ch 107, 135, although Rimer LJ in *Patel v Mirza* [2014] EWCA Civ 1047, [2015] 2 WLR 405, [41], considered it to be sound because there had been no 'voluntary withdrawal'. But there was no 'voluntary withdrawal' in *Patel* either, save that, once the agreement was frustrated, the claimant then sought restitution. Distinguishing between *Bigos v Bousted* and *Patel* with reference to the voluntariness of the withdrawal is unconvincing. See *Patel v Mirza*, [96] (Gloster LJ).

[276] See *Patel v Mirza* [2014] EWCA Civ 1047, [2015] 2 WLR 405, [117] (Vos LJ). For further discussion of this limitation see p 723, below.

sale of goods where the goods have perished.[277] Where the common law applies, the ground of restitution continues to be that of total failure of basis, whereas under the Law Reform (Frustrated Contracts) Act 1943 the ground of restitution is effectively partial failure of basis, although this phrase is not used in the statute itself.

(A) THE DEFINITION OF FRUSTRATION

Whenever a contract is frustrated it is discharged automatically.[278] The law relating to when a contract is frustrated is complex,[279] but the essence of frustration was identified by Lord Radcliffe in *Davis Contractors Ltd v Fareham Urban District Council*:[280] '[F]rustration occurs whenever the law recognizes that without default of either party a contractual obligation has become incapable of being performed because the circumstances in which the performance is called for would render it a thing radically different from that which was undertaken by the contract.'

A contract will therefore only be frustrated where its performance would be radically different as a result of some extraneous event or change of circumstances which took place without the fault of either party.[281] Consequently, frustration cannot be self-induced.

(B) RESTITUTION OF BENEFITS TRANSFERRED BEFORE A CONTRACT IS FRUSTRATED

Before the different restitutionary regimes are examined, there is one matter of great practical importance which must be emphasized, namely that the question of restitutionary relief following the frustration of a contract rarely reaches the courts. This is illustrated by the fact that, since the enactment of the Law Reform (Frustrated Contracts) Act 1943, only two cases have been reported concerning its interpretation. This may be because the interpretation of the Act is clear, so there is no need to resort to the courts, but, as will be seen, the interpretation of the Act is certainly not free from difficulty. The better explanation for the scarcity of cases is that parties tend to provide for the consequences of frustration in their contracts by a *force majeure* clause or because disputes arising from frustration tend to be settled by arbitration.[282]

(i) The Common Law

At one stage the attitude of the common law to restitutionary claims following the frustration of a contract was to reject such claims and to let the loss lie where it fell.[283] However, in *Fibrosa Spolka Akcyjna v Fairbairn Lawson Combe Barbour Ltd*[284] the House of Lords recognized that money, which had been paid pursuant to a contract which was subsequently frustrated, could be recovered, but only if the basis for the payment had totally failed. In that case the claimants had entered into a contract with the defendants for the purchase of machinery. The claimant paid one third of the purchase price in advance

---

[277] Law Reform (Frustrated Contracts) Act 1943, s 2(5).

[278] *J Lauritzen AS v Wijsmuller BV (The Super Servant Two)* [1990] 1 Lloyd's LR 1.

[279] For detailed examination of this question see GH Treitel, *Frustration and Force Majeure* (3rd edn, London: Sweet and Maxwell, 2014).

[280] [1956] AC 696, 729. See also *National Carriers Ltd v Panalpina (Northern) Ltd* [1981] AC 675, 700 (Lord Simon).

[281] *J Lauritzen AS v Wijsmuller BV (The Super Servant Two)* [1990] 1 Lloyd's LR 1, 10 (Bingham LJ).

[282] See A Stewart and JW Carter, 'Frustrated Contracts and Statutory Adjustment: The Case for a Reappraisal' (1992) CLJ 66, 108.

[283] *Chandler v Webster* [1904] 1 KB 493.   [284] [1943] AC 32.

but the contract was frustrated by the outbreak of the Second World War before any of the machinery had been delivered. It was held that the claimant could recover the advance payment because the basis for that payment had failed totally and also that the defendant was not able to set off the expenditure which it had incurred in preparing the machines for delivery under the contract.

That restitution will not lie where the basis had partially failed is illustrated by *Whincup v Hughes*[285] where a father had paid a sum of money to have his son apprenticed to a watchmaker for six years. The watchmaker died after one year, frustrating the contract. It was held that the father could not recover the money paid in respect of the remaining five years because the basis for the payment had only failed partially, since the benefit of one year's service had been received.

(ii) The Law Reform (Frustrated Contracts) Act 1943

The main purpose of the Law Reform (Frustrated Contracts) Act 1943 was to remove the perceived injustice of the common law, particularly the denial of restitution where the basis had only partially failed. A further injustice of the common law was that, although it was possible for the claimant to bring a restitutionary claim following frustration where the basis had failed totally, it was not possible to take into account any expenditure which had been incurred by the defendant.[286] Although the 1943 Act provides a solution to both of these difficulties, it is complicated and uncertain in scope. One reason for this complexity results from the difficulty in identifying the Act's rationale. Whilst it seems tolerably clear that the Act creates a statutory regime which is founded on the reversal of the defendant's unjust enrichment,[287] although no reference to restitution or unjust enrichment is included in the Act,[288] it is equally clear that the Act does not simply operate to ensure that the value of any benefit obtained by the defendant under a contract which is subsequently frustrated is restored to the claimant. This is because the Act also seeks to apportion losses arising from the frustrating event between the parties. The real difficulty in analysing the statutory regime relates to the reconciliation of these two different policies of reversing unjust enrichment and loss apportionment.

There are two key provisions in the Act. The first, section 1(2), applies where the defendant has been enriched by the receipt of money, and the second, section 1(3), applies where the enrichment is a non-money benefit. Before either provision can be applied it must be shown that the contract has been discharged for frustration and that the contract was governed by English law.[289]

(1) Restitution of Money

Where the claimant has paid money to another party to the contract before it was frustrated the claimant is able to recover such sums 'as money received by [the other party] for the use of' the claimant.[290] The effect of this provision is that the claimant is given a statutory right to obtain restitution from the defendant. Although the claimant

---

[285] (1871) LR 6 CP 78. See further p 323, above.

[286] As was recognized by Viscount Simon LC in the *Fibrosa* case [1943] AC 32, 49.

[287] *BP Exploration Co (Libya) Ltd v Hunt (No 2)* [1979] 1 WLR 783, 799 (Robert Goff J). Cf AM Haycroft and DM Waksman, 'Restitution and Frustration' [1984] JBL 207, 225 who argue that the function of the Act is to apportion losses rather than to reverse unjust enrichment.

[288] Lawton LJ in *BP Exploration Co (Libya) Ltd v Hunt (No 2)* [1981] 1 WLR 232, 243 emphasized that the court was not assisted in its interpretation of the Act by words which did not appear in it.

[289] Law Reform (Frustrated Contracts) Act 1943, s 1(1).

[290] Ibid, s 1(2). The provision also states that the claimant will cease to be liable to pay money to the defendant under the discharged contract.

does not need to identify specifically the elements of an unjust enrichment action, the statutory right of recovery is consistent with a restitutionary claim to reverse the defendant's unjust enrichment. It is crucial to the statutory claim that the defendant has received money, an incontrovertible benefit, from the claimant, so the defendant must have been enriched at the claimant's expense. The ground of restitution can be said to be partial failure of basis, since the right to recovery exists even though the claimant has received some benefit under the contract. This means that if *Whincup v Hughes*[291] was decided today, the father would be able to recover part of the advance payment, even though his son had only been apprenticed for a year.

The claimant is able to recover the payment from the defendant under section 1(2) even though this means that the claimant will be escaping from a bad bargain, in that had the contract not been frustrated the claimant would have suffered a loss.[292] The fact that the contract was a bad bargain ceases to be relevant, because the effect of frustration is to discharge the contract so it no longer affects the restitutionary claim.[293]

Although section 1(2) appears to create a wide right of recovery it is subject to some significant limitations.

(1) The claimant will only be able to recover money which was paid before the contract was discharged for frustration. If, however, the claimant had paid the defendant after discharge, he or she would be able to obtain restitution on the ground of mistake.[294]

(2) The claimant will only be able to rely on section 1(2) where he or she had paid money to somebody who is party to the contract which was frustrated.

(3) It is possible for the parties to contract out of the statutory regime,[295] although the courts will carefully construe the contract to ensure that the parties really did intend to exclude the statutory scheme following the frustration of the contract.[296]

The claimant's right to restitution is qualified by the proviso to section 1(2). The effect of this is that, if the defendant had incurred expenses in or for the purpose of the performance of the contract[297] before the contract was discharged, the court has a discretion to allow the defendant to retain all or part of the money he or she had received from the claimant, if it considers it to be just to do so having considered all the circumstances of the case. Similarly, if the claimant was liable to pay the defendant before the contract was frustrated, the defendant may recover all or some of this amount in respect of the expenditure which he or she had incurred. The burden of proving that the proviso is applicable is borne by the defendant.[298] The amount which the defendant is allowed to retain or to recover from the claimant is limited in two ways. First, it must not exceed the expenses which the defendant actually incurred. Secondly, it is limited to the amount which the defendant received from the claimant or which the claimant was liable to pay to the defendant. So, for example, if the claimant paid £10,000 to the defendant and was liable to pay a further £5,000 to the defendant before the contract was frustrated, and

---

[291] (1871) LR 6 CP 78.

[292] *BP Exploration Co (Libya) Ltd v Hunt (No 2)* [1979] 1 WLR 783, 800 (Robert Goff J).

[293] A similar rule applies where a contract is discharged for breach. See p 332, above.

[294] See *Oom v Bruce* (1810) 12 East 225, 104 ER 87.

[295] Law Reform (Frustrated Contracts) Act 1943, s 2(3).

[296] *BP Exploration Co (Libya) Ltd v Hunt (No 2)* [1979] 1 WLR 783, 829 (Robert Goff J).

[297] This expenditure is also deemed to include reasonable sums in respect of overhead expenses or work or services personally performed by the defendant: s 1(4).

[298] *Gamerco SA v ICM/Fair Warning (Agency) Ltd* [1995] 1 WLR 1226, 1235 (Garland J).

the defendant incurred expenditure of £18,000 in performance of the contract, the defendant will, subject to the exercise of the court's discretion, be able to retain the £10,000 and recover the £5,000 but will be out of pocket in respect of the remaining £3,000.

The proviso is a very important limitation on the claimant's right to obtain restitution, but it is a limitation which does not appear to be consistent with the analysis of section 1(2) as a provision which creates a statutory right of restitution to reverse the defendant's unjust enrichment. In *BP v Hunt*[299] Robert Goff J tried to rationalize the proviso in restitutionary terms by concluding that it embodied a statutory form of the defence of change of position.[300] Whilst the proviso certainly shares some characteristics of that defence, it does not embody all its features, particularly the requirement that the change of position must be extraordinary and that the change of position was caused by the receipt of the benefit.[301]

The proviso is, in fact, subject to a qualification which provides an important clue to its purpose. According to the proviso, expenditure incurred by the defendant will only be relevant if it was incurred in or for the purpose of the performance of the contract. It follows that the purpose of the proviso is simply to enable the defendant to retain or recover those expenses which were incurred in the expectation that the contract would be performed. This is perfectly justifiable. If the claimant is able to recover the payment which he or she had made to the defendant under the contract, it is surely only fair that the defendant can reclaim his or her expenditure which had been incurred with reference to the contract. So the real function of the proviso is to enable the courts to allocate losses which have arisen as a result of the contract being frustrated.

That the proviso should be interpreted in this way was acknowledged by Garland J in the only case to have considered the application of section 1(2). In *Gamerco SA v ICM/ Fair Warning (Agency) Ltd*[302] the claimant had agreed to promote a concert in Madrid involving the band 'Guns N'Roses'. Four days before the concert was due to be held, the local authority banned the use of the stadium which had been booked because of fears that it was not safe. The claimant was unable to find an alternative venue and so the concert was cancelled, frustrating the contract. The claimant had paid the defendant $412,500 pursuant to the contract and wished to recover this sum under section 1(2). The defendant had, however, incurred expenditure in relation to the performance of the contract of about $50,000 and wanted to retain this amount. Garland J accepted that the court was obliged 'to do justice in a situation which the parties had neither contemplated nor provided for, and to mitigate the possible harshness of allowing all loss to lie where it has fallen'.[303] This did not, however, mean that the court was obliged to apportion the losses equally between the parties or that the defendant could recoup all of its expenditure. The court sought instead to apportion the losses having regard to all of the circumstances of the case. One of the circumstances which the judge considered to be relevant was that the claimant had incurred expenditure of $450,000.[304] Consequently, its loss was much greater than that of the defendant and so the judge decided not to allow the defendant to retain any amount in respect of the expenditure which it had incurred.

---

[299] [1979] 1 WLR 783, 800.

[300] See also E Bant, *The Change of Position Defence* (Oxford: Hart Publishing, 2009), 245.

[301] See p 682, below.

[302] [1995] 1 WLR 1226. See P Clark, 'Frustration, Restitution and the Law Reform (Frustrated Contracts) Act 1943' [1996] LMCLQ 170.

[303] *Gamerco SA v ICM/Fair Warning (Agency) Ltd* [1995] 1 WLR 1226, 1237.

[304] Presumably the claimant could not recover this expenditure from the defendant under s 1(3) because there was no evidence that the defendant had received a valuable benefit as a consequence.

Although the effect of section 1(2) and its proviso is to enable losses to be apportioned between the parties, it is only partially effective in this regard. For example, the defendant will only be able to recover expenditure to the extent that the claimant has paid money, or is liable to pay money, to the defendant before the contract was frustrated. Also, if the claimant incurred expenditure in or for the performance of the contract, and this did not involve the payment of money to the defendant or the defendant receiving a valuable benefit, the claimant is unable to recoup this money specifically from the defendant. Whether section 1(2) should be replaced by a provision which enables the court to apportion all the losses between the parties, as occurs in other countries,[305] will be examined after the operation of section 1(3) is considered.

(2) Restitution of Non-Money Benefits

The restitution of non-money benefits which have been obtained by the defendant before the contract was frustrated is governed by section 1(3) of the 1943 Act. This is a complex provision but essentially it applies whenever the defendant, who was a party to the contract with the claimant, has received a valuable benefit other than money by reason of anything which was done by the claimant in, or for the purpose of, the performance of the contract. A defendant who has received such a benefit before the contract was frustrated is liable to pay the claimant such sum as the court considers to be just having regard to all the circumstances of the case. This sum must not exceed the value of the benefit to the defendant who obtained it. Section 1(3) requires the examination of three separate matters. First, the identification of the valuable benefit. Secondly, the valuation of this benefit. Thirdly, the assessment of the sum which it would be just for the defendant to pay to the claimant. These three matters will be considered in turn and then their application will be examined with reference to the difficult case of BP Exploration Co (Libya) Ltd v Hunt (No 2).[306] But it is first necessary to consider the rationale of section 1(3).

In BP Exploration Co (Libya) Ltd v Hunt (No 2)[307] Robert Goff J assumed that the rationale of section 1(3) was to ensure that the defendant was not unjustly enriched as a result of the contract being frustrated. Others have argued that section 1(3) should be interpreted simply as a mechanism to allocate losses between the parties.[308] The better view is that section 1(3), like section 1(2), exists both to reverse the defendant's unjust enrichment and to allocate losses suffered as a result of the frustration. This is because section 1(3) involves two distinct elements. The first concerns the identification of the valuable benefit, which constitutes the ceiling on the claimant's award. This element is concerned with the reversal of the defendant's unjust enrichment, since it must be shown that the defendant had received a valuable benefit at the claimant's expense. As with section 1(2), the ground of restitution can be considered to be partial failure of basis. Once this valuable enrichment has been identified it is necessary to identify the just sum which should be awarded. This cannot be greater than the value of the benefit received by the defendant, but it could be less. This second aspect of section 1(3) is concerned with the allocation of losses arising from the frustration of the contract. Failure to identify this composite approach to section 1(3) has made its interpretation unnecessarily complex.

To establish a claim under section 1(3) the claimant must first show that the defendant had received a valuable non-money benefit under the contract. The statute does not define

---

[305] Such as the British Columbian Frustrated Contracts Act 1974, the New South Wales Frustrated Contracts Act 1978, and the South Australian Frustrated Contracts Act 1988.

[306] [1979] 1 WLR 783.   [307] Ibid, 799.

[308] See, for example, E McKendrick, 'Frustration, Restitution and Loss Apportionment' in AS Burrows (ed), Essays on the Law of Restitution (Oxford: Clarendon Press, 1991), 147.

benefit for these purposes, so the common law definition is presumably applicable. This means that we are only concerned with those benefits which have been received by the defendant and that an objective test of benefit should be adopted.[309] However, as section 1(3) specifically recognizes, whether this benefit can be considered to be valuable should be determined with reference to whether the recipient valued it. This constitutes a recognition of the principle of subjective devaluation. So, if the defendant received an objective benefit but did not value it at all, he or she should not be considered to have received a valuable benefit. But if this principle of subjective devaluation is applicable under the Act, it should be possible to defeat the defendant's reliance on that principle by showing that the benefit was incontrovertibly beneficial or that the defendant had freely accepted or requested it.[310] Unlike the general analysis of enrichment for purposes of unjust enrichment, for the purposes of section 1(3) if the defendant had received something to which he or she attaches a value, but which the reasonable person would not regard as valuable, the defendant should still be regarded as having received a benefit.[311]

Where the defendant has received goods, the identification of the valuable benefit will not usually cause any difficulty. Where the alleged benefit takes the form of services, the identification of the benefit is more complex. In *BP v Hunt* Robert Goff J accepted that pure services, namely services which do not produce an end product, could constitute a valuable benefit,[312] though obviously such services should only be treated as beneficial where they have been received by the defendant.[313] He also held that where the service results in a valuable end product the relevant benefit for the purposes of the Act is the end product and not the provision of the service. Consequently, it will be the end product which must be valued and which will provide the ceiling on the award of the just sum, even though the value of the service may be greater than the value of the end product. This interpretation of the Act is inconsistent with the common law of enrichment,[314] and Robert Goff J himself objected to it, but felt bound by the terms of the statute to interpret the phrase 'valuable benefit' in this way.[315]

Although the claimant's expenditure in providing the service may exceed the value of the benefit received by the defendant, this is an irrelevant consideration at this stage of the analysis, since we are simply concerned to identify the defendant's enrichment. The claimant's expenditure will be a relevant consideration when determining the award of the just sum. However, and this is the real drawback of section 1(3), the award of the just sum is limited by the value of the defendant's valuable benefit, so if the claimant's expenditure exceeds the value of this benefit the claimant will not be able to recover all of his or her expenditure. This may be considered to be unjust, but it follows logically from the treatment of section 1(3) as operating to reverse the defendant's unjust enrichment. If we are concerned, as well we may be, that the claimant's expenditure in providing the service is not being taken into account when identifying the valuable benefit, that is an argument to the effect that the restitutionary response which underlies section 1(3) is inappropriate where a contract has been frustrated. Instead, we should adopt a scheme which is more concerned with the allocation of losses.

---

[309] See p 65, above.   [310] See p 78, above.

[311] As recognized by Robert Goff J in *BP Exploration Co (Libya) Ltd v Hunt (No 2)* [1979] 1 WLR 783, 802.

[312] Ibid.

[313] This notion that the benefit must have been received by the defendant before it can constitute a valuable benefit was recognized in *Parsons Bros Ltd v Shea* (1968) 53 DLR (2d) 86 concerning the interpretation of the Newfoundland Frustrated Contracts Act 1956, which is similar to the 1943 Act.

[314] See p 76, above.   [315] *BP Exploration Co (Libya) Ltd v Hunt (No 2)* [1979] 1 WLR 783, 802.

Once the benefit has been identified it must then be valued and this value will constitute the ceiling on the award of the just sum. Presumably, the objective value of the benefit will be used but, since the principle of subjective devaluation is incorporated into section 1(3), it follows that if the defendant would not have valued the benefit so highly, this lower valuation should be adopted unless it was incontrovertibly beneficial or the defendant had freely accepted it.[316] The pro rata contract price will presumably be an important evidential factor in determining the value the defendant placed on the benefit.

In *BP v Hunt*[317] Robert Goff J complicated the question of valuing the benefit received by the defendant by considering section 1(3)(a) and (b) at this stage, when those subsections are properly treated as relevant to determining the award of the just sum.

By section 1(3)(a) the court is to have regard to the expenditure incurred by the defendant in connection with the performance of the contract before it was frustrated. The consequence of Robert Goff J's conclusion that section 1(3)(a) is relevant to the valuation of the defendant's benefit is that any such expenditure which was incurred by the defendant can be deducted from the valuable benefit. But this is inconsistent with the clear words of section 1(3) which treats the defendant's expenditure relating to the contract as relevant to the assessment of the just sum and not the valuable benefit. Also, to treat the defendant's expenditure as relating to the determination of the valuable benefit, is inconsistent with Robert Goff J's conclusion that section 1(3)(a) embodies a defence of change of position. If this was correct then section 1(3)(a) should only apply once the benefit has been identified, for the defence of change of position at common law only applies after the claimant has established that the defendant had been enriched. Consequently, the defendant's expenditure which was incurred in connection with the performance of the contract should only be taken into account when the court is determining the award of the just sum.

By section 1(3)(b) the court is to have regard to the effect of the frustrating event on the benefit which was received by the defendant. The consequence of Robert Goff J's assumption that section 1(3)(b) is relevant to the valuation of the defendant's benefit is that, if the benefit which was received by the defendant was destroyed by the frustrating event, the inevitable conclusion must be that the defendant had not received a valuable benefit for the purposes of the 1943 Act. If this is correct, it would mean that *Appleby v Myers*[318] would still be decided in the same way today. In that case the claimant had installed machinery which was destroyed in a fire. It was held that the claim for the value of the machinery supplied and the work done failed completely. According to Robert Goff J the effect of section 1(3)(b) in this type of case is that, since any benefit which the defendant had received was destroyed, the defendant cannot be considered to have received a valuable benefit. Consequently, if the ceiling to the award of the just sum is zero, the award of the just sum can only be zero. But this is a highly dubious interpretation of section 1(3)(b) for two reasons. First, because the structure of section 1(3) makes it clear that section 1(3)(b) is only relevant to the determination of the just sum and not the identification of the valuable benefit. Secondly, in the law of restitution the defendant is enriched once a benefit has been received. Subsequent events are only relevant when considering whether the defendant has a defence to the claim, such as the defence of change of position. That this principle is incorporated within section 1(3) is made clear by the requirement that the valuable benefit must have been received before the contract was frustrated. Since we are considering whether the defendant had received a benefit before

---

[316] See Stewart and Carter, 'Frustrated Contracts and Statutory Adjustments', 92.
[317] *BP Exploration Co (Libya) Ltd v Hunt (No 2)* [1979] 1 WLR 783, 802–5.
[318] (1867) LR 2 CP 651.

the contract was frustrated and what its value was, it is not appropriate to consider the events which happened after the benefit was received; subsequent events, such as the effect of the frustrating event on the benefit, should only be considered when the award of the just sum is determined.

Once the court has determined that the defendant has received a valuable benefit, it must then determine the just sum which should be awarded to the claimant, a sum which cannot exceed the value of the defendant's benefit. The better interpretation of this aspect of section 1(3) is that it is not concerned with the reversal of the defendant's unjust enrichment, but is simply concerned with the allocation of losses between the parties. This is because section 1(3) specifies that the court must have regard to all the circumstances of the case to determine the just sum. It is at this stage of the claim under section 1(3) that the particular circumstances in subsections (a) and (b) should be taken into account. Consequently, under section 1(3)(a), the court should consider the expenditure which was incurred by the defendant in connection with the contract. Although Robert Goff J assumed in *BP v Hunt*[319] that section 1(3)(a), like the proviso to section 1(2), incorporated a defence of change of position, there is again no warrant for such a conclusion. The defence of change of position requires a change in the defendant's circumstances which was causally linked to the receipt of a benefit from the claimant,[320] but this requirement is not incorporated into section 1(3)(a). The real function of section 1(3)(a) is simply to enable the court to take into account any relevant loss which was suffered by the defendant as a result of the contract being frustrated.

The effect of the frustrating event on the valuable benefit should also be taken into account when determining the just sum as a result of the proper interpretation of section 1(3)(b), whether that effect was to destroy the benefit or simply to reduce its value. Again, the true function of section 1(3)(b) is to enable the court to apportion the losses between the parties. So, for example, if the valuable benefit was worth £50,000 when it was received but it was destroyed by the frustrating event so that the defendant was left with nothing, the justice of the case may require the court to reduce the amount which is awarded to the claimant to take into account the loss suffered by the defendant. Whether the effect of this destruction is that the defendant should not be required to pay the claimant anything or, perhaps more fairly, that the defendant must pay the claimant half the value of the benefit, is something which lies in the discretion of the court.

This analysis of the just sum is simple, although perhaps it leaves too much to the discretion of the court.[321] But it is at least clear that the purpose of the just sum is to allocate losses between the parties, albeit that this is constrained by the value of the benefit which was received by the defendant. It is most unfortunate therefore that Robert Goff J adopted a very different interpretation of the just sum in *BP v Hunt*, where he assumed that this was to be determined by the principle of unjust enrichment. In other words, the just sum would be assessed by reference to the value of the benefit which was transferred under the contract.[322] But, since it is clear that Parliament intended the just sum to be, at least potentially, different from the valuable benefit which constitutes the ceiling to an

---

[319] [1979] 1 WLR 783, 806. See also Bant, *The Change of Position Defence*, 248.   [320] See p 682, below.

[321] The Court of Appeal in *BP Exploration Co (Libya) Ltd v Hunt (No 2)* [1981] 1 WLR 232, 238 held that the determination of the just sum lies in the discretion of the trial judge and an appellate court would only intervene with the trial judge's decision if it was plainly wrong or unjust.

[322] The Court of Appeal was not prepared to interfere with this method for assessing the just sum, although the Court emphasized that it gained no help in interpreting the statute from the use of words which were not included in it, presumably such as 'unjust enrichment': *BP Exploration Co (Libya) Ltd v Hunt (No 2)* [1981] 1 WLR 232, 243.

award, Robert Goff J adopted a different meaning of benefit for the purposes of assessing the just sum, namely the value of the benefit which had been *provided* by the claimant, rather than the value of the benefit *received* by the defendant. This is highly artificial and confusing. This artifice stems from a desire to squeeze the square peg of section 1(3) into the round hole of the law of restitution founded on the reversal of the defendant's unjust enrichment. It would have been so much easier if Robert Goff J had recognized that the function of the just sum is simply to apportion losses between the parties.

When assessing the just sum there are two factors not mentioned in the statute which may be of particular relevance. The first, which was recognized by Robert Goff J, was the terms of the contract. Because of his assumption that the just sum was assessed with reference to the reasonable value of the claimant's services, it is obvious that Robert Goff J would treat the contract as 'by far the most useful evidence of a fair remuneration to be awarded in respect of the services rendered'.[323] But, even if the assessment of the just sum is not restricted to the value of the claimant's services, the terms of the contract remain a key factor in the equation, but not as important as was envisaged by the judge. For he thought that in most cases the just sum would be limited to a rateable proportion of the contract price so that the claimant would not be able to escape the consequences of a bad bargain.[324] Whilst the fact that the claimant had entered into a bad bargain should be a relevant consideration, it should not be the prime determinant of the just sum, since the court must have regard to all the circumstances of the case. The second factor which should be considered, a factor which was specifically rejected by Robert Goff J, is the conduct of both parties, particularly whether they had breached the contract before it was frustrated. In *BP v Hunt* itself the defendant alleged that the claimant had committed certain breaches of the contract and a deduction should be made from the just sum to reflect this. But the trial judge held that, even if it could be shown that the claimant had acted unreasonably, this was of no relevance to the assessment of the just sum.[325] But surely, if the claimant had the opportunity to minimize his or her loss before the frustrating event occurred and failed to do so, this is a factor which should be relevant to the assessment of the just sum.[326] The conduct of the defendant should similarly be taken into account when determining the sum which it is just to award.

The application of section 1(3) may be excluded by the contract, but the court will only consider the statutory scheme to have been excluded where the parties, being aware of the risks of frustration, had clearly intended such exclusion, as was recognized by the House of Lords in *BP v Hunt*.[327] Also, as with section 1(2), there is no scope under section 1(3) for including an interest element in respect of the period during which the defendant had received the benefit of the claimant's services. The question of the award of interest can only be considered once the just sum has been assessed.[328]

The application of the principles which underlie section 1(3) can be illustrated by analysing the decision of Robert Goff J in *BP v Hunt* itself. The facts of the case were complicated, but essentially the dispute related to an oil concession which had been granted to Hunt by the Libyan government. Hunt was unable to develop the concession himself and so he entered into a joint venture with BP, whereby he agreed to grant BP half

---

[323] *BP Exploration Co (Libya) Ltd v Hunt (No 2)* [1979] 1 WLR 783, 822.   [324] Ibid, 806.

[325] Though if the impossibility of performance of the contract was self-induced the claimant will not be able to argue that it had been frustrated. See p 356, above.

[326] See B Dickson, 'An Action for Unjust Enrichment' (1983) 34 NILQ 106, 122 and Haycroft and Waksman, 'Restitution and Frustration', 222.

[327] *BP Exploration Co (Libya) v Hunt (No 2)* [1983] 2 AC 352 (HL).

[328] *BP Exploration Co (Libya) v Hunt (No 2)* [1981] 1 WLR 232, 244 (CA).

of the concession and to allow it to explore for oil and to develop the concession if oil was found. BP was to pay for the cost of exploration and development but, once the oil came on stream, it was to receive half of the oil and additional 'reimbursement oil' to reimburse it for its contributions to the exploration and development of the concession. BP spent millions of pounds exploring for oil, and it eventually found a large oilfield and began to extract oil. The contract was frustrated when the Libyan government expropriated BP's share of the concession and two years later Hunt's share was also expropriated. When the contract was frustrated BP had only been reimbursed one third of the oil which was due to it. Consequently, BP sued Hunt under section 1(3) in respect of the valuable benefit which Hunt had received. This was the first case to consider the 1943 Act and, whilst the case went on to be heard by the Court of Appeal[329] and the House of Lords,[330] these appeals related to specific matters and did not concern the general principles underlying the Act. Hence Robert Goff J's judgment continues to be the most important analysis of the operation of section 1(3).

Robert Goff J approached the case in the following way. First, he identified the valuable benefit obtained by Hunt before the contract was frustrated as the end product of BP's services, namely the enhancement in the value of Hunt's oil concession rather than the value of BP's work in finding and extracting the oil. This is dubious as a matter of the law of enrichment, since Hunt already had the oil concession so the only benefit which was obtained at BP's expense was its service. That service unlocked the concession but did not create it.[331] Secondly, in determining the value of this benefit, the judge considered the effect of the frustrating event, by virtue of section 1(3)(b). Since the expropriation of BP's interest had dramatically reduced the value of Hunt's interest, the judge considered that this had reduced the value of the benefit which Hunt had received to half the oil he had obtained from the oilfield plus the compensation he had obtained from the Libyan government. But this confuses what factors it is appropriate to take into account at this stage. All the judge should have been concerned with was the identification and valuation of the benefit which had been received; subsequent events should only have been relevant to the assessment of the just sum. The judge valued the benefit at $85 million, so this constituted the ceiling on the award. Finally, the judge assessed the just sum by reference to restitutionary principles. Since he assumed that the benefit for these purposes was the services provided by the claimant rather than the end product received by the defendant, he valued the just sum at $35 million and, since this was less than the value of the valuable benefit, this was the amount which he ordered Hunt to pay to BP. This just sum was effectively made up of the expenses incurred by BP on behalf of Hunt, as evidenced by the terms of the contract, plus the amount of money and oil which had been paid by BP to Hunt with a deduction for the amount which Hunt had reimbursed BP before the contract was frustrated. Perhaps the award of $35 million was entirely appropriate, but it is clear that the basis for assessing this sum was not. The judge should have considered all of the circumstances of the case, not just the value of the services provided.

(C) THE NEED FOR PRINCIPLED REFORM

Subsections 1(2) and 1(3) of the 1943 Act are somewhat schizophrenic provisions, embodying as they do both principles of restitution founded on the reversal of the defendant's unjust enrichment and the allocation of losses between the parties. But this

---

[329] Ibid.   [330] *BP Exploration Co (Libya) v Hunt (No 2)* [1983] 2 AC 352 (HL).
[331] See p 76, above.

attempt to allocate losses is half-hearted. There are a number of situations where a party will have incurred expenditure but he or she will not be able to recover it, even if the court considers this to be just. For example, the defendant's expenditure incurred in connection with performance of the contract before it was frustrated can only be recouped if the claimant had paid or was liable to pay money to the defendant or the defendant had received a valuable benefit from the claimant. Would it not be better to replace the 1943 Act with a new scheme whereby all the losses of the parties which arise from the contract being frustrated may be apportioned between them?

(i) Arguments Against Loss Apportionment

Burrows is not convinced that there is a need for a statutory regime which involves the apportionment of losses.[332] This is for a number of reasons. For example, the traditional approach of the law of contract is that each party should take the risk of loss arising from frustration rather than having that loss apportioned between them. Also loss apportionment can result in uncertainty, and if we really want to apportion losses it will be necessary to take into account the relative fault of the parties, adding to the complexity of the analysis. His conclusion is that the case for loss apportionment is unproven and that the award of restitutionary relief achieves sufficient justice following frustration. Stewart and Carter also reject a scheme of loss apportionment on the ground that there is no reason why one party to a contract should act as an insurer for the loss suffered by the other party, by having to bear some or all of the other's loss.[333] They consider that a common law scheme which is simply founded on the principle of reversing unjust enrichment is perfectly adequate. But the refusal of the English courts so far to recognize partial failure of basis as a ground of restitution surely makes reliance on the common law of restitution inadequate in this context.

(ii) Arguments in Favour of Loss Apportionment

McKendrick, on the other hand, has argued that we should adopt a scheme of full apportionment of losses.[334] He accepts that, whilst the need to restore benefits to the claimant must remain an important part of the relief which is available when a contract is frustrated, this restitution interest is not the only interest which needs to be protected, since it is also necessary to consider the reliance interest. This interest is in particular need of protection in the context of frustrated contracts simply because both parties are equally innocent of the contract being frustrated, so it is unfair simply to let the loss lie where it fell. This is not necessarily the case in the other situations where a contract is not operating, such as for breach or failure or when the contract was null and void. However, it does not follow that, in the context of frustrated contracts, losses should be apportioned equally between the parties, simply because one party may have suffered greater losses than the other. Consequently, McKendrick concludes that there is a need to take into account the particular circumstances of the case when allocating losses between the parties. In particular, loss apportionment should be excluded if the risk of frustration has been allocated by the parties in the contract itself.

---

[332] Burrows, *The Law of Restitution* (3rd edn), 366.

[333] Stewart and Carter, 'Frustrated Contracts and Statutory Adjustments', 109.

[334] McKendrick, 'Frustration, Restitution and Loss Apportionment', 169. See also Haycroft and Waksman, 'Restitution and Frustration', who consider the 1943 Act to be sufficiently flexible to allow for the adjustment of losses without the need for reform.

(iii) A Middle Way

What is needed is a statutory mechanism which adequately protects both the restitutionary and the reliance interests but without recourse to an unrestrained judicial discretion. The preferable solution is to adopt the model of the British Columbian Frustrated Contracts Act 1974. The general scheme of that Act is that each party must make restitution in respect of anything done by way of contractual performance by the other.[335] For the purposes of this Act a broad definition of benefit is adopted encompassing 'something done in the fulfilment of contractual obligations whether or not the person for whose benefit it was done received the benefit'.[336] Consequently, the defendant should be deemed to have been benefited either where he or she had obtained a benefit from the claimant or where the claimant had incurred expenditure in relation to the performance of the contract. Whilst such a broad notion of 'benefit' may be somewhat misleading, this simple technique of expanding what is meant by benefit will ensure that the defendant is not allowed to retain any unjust enrichment, and also that the expenditure which the claimant incurred may be recovered. If the defendant had also incurred expenditure he or she would either be able to set this off against the claimant's claim or bring a claim him or herself for restitution from the claimant. Whilst this statutory regime cannot be considered to be completely restitutionary, since the defendant's liability is not confined to the benefit which he or she had received, it would at least operate within the framework of the law of restitution. In addition, the British Columbian Act provides that, where the effect of the frustrating event is to diminish the value of the contractual performance, the losses should be shared equally between the parties.[337] This is less convincing, since it is more just for losses to be apportioned according to the particular circumstances of the case.

(D) ANOTHER EXAMPLE OF PARTIAL FAILURE OF BASIS: REJECTION OF GOODS

When the Consumer Rights Act 2015 comes into force, another statutory example of partial failure of basis will effectively be recognized. One effect of the Act is that, if a consumer has exercised the statutory right to reject goods, so that the contract of sale is treated as terminated, the consumer has a statutory right to recover money which has been paid under the contract,[338] or anything else which had been transferred under the contract.[339] This statutory right to restitution will apply even though the consumer has received some benefit under the contract, so that the basis will not have failed totally. This is even more clear in section 21 which enables the consumer to recover money paid in respect of some of the goods, where the consumer has only exercised the right to reject partially. This Act, which only applies to protect consumers,[340] will provide a significant restriction on the total failure of basis requirement.

5. VOID TRANSACTIONS

(A) UNCERTAINTY AS TO THE GROUND OF RESTITUTION

Where the claimant has transferred a benefit to the defendant pursuant to a contract which is void it should be relatively easy for the claimant to establish that the defendant

---

[335] British Columbian Frustrated Contracts Act 1974, s 5(1).   [336] Ibid, s 5(4).
[337] Ibid, s 5(3).   [338] Consumer Rights Act 2015, s 20(10).   [339] Ibid, s 20(11).
[340] Meaning an individual who is acting for purposes which are wholly or mainly outside his or her trade, business, craft, or profession: ibid, s 2(3).

has been unjustly enriched at the claimant's expense. The most appropriate ground of restitution would appear to be total failure of basis. This should be easier to establish where a contract is void than where, for example, the contract has been discharged for breach, since the fact that a contract is void means that, as a matter of law, there was no contract, so nothing needs to be set aside before the restitutionary claim can be brought. The claimant then only needs to show that the basis for the benefit which was transferred to the defendant had failed totally.[341] But what of the case in which the contract is void but the basis has not failed totally? Is it possible to establish a ground of restitution then? There is some evidence that there is indeed a separate ground of restitution which may be available in such circumstances, a ground which is dependent on the fact that the contract is void: the ground of absence of basis. Where the claimant claims that there has been a total failure of basis, the essence of the claim is that the basis has failed as a matter of fact. In other words, if the claimant transferred a benefit to the defendant, usually on condition that the defendant would do something in return which the defendant had failed to do, the claimant's intention that the defendant should receive the benefit can be treated as vitiated. Where, however, the claimant has transferred a benefit to the defendant pursuant to a contract which void, the expected basis can never be satisfied as a *matter of law*.[342] This is because, if the contract is void, the law assumes that there never was a contract. As a result, the claimant's intention that the defendant should receive the benefit can be treated as vitiated from the outset, because the defendant was never under a valid obligation to provide a benefit in return. It follows that there can never be a valid basis for the defendant's receipt of an enrichment as a matter of law in respect of a void contract, even if the defendant did actually perform as the claimant had anticipated. This ground of absence of basis therefore avoids the total failure of basis requirement. In *Haugesund Kommune v Depfa ACS Bank*[343] Aikens LJ said that the distinction between total failure and absence of basis was simply a matter of choosing the most apt terminology and had no legal implications. But the preferable view is that it does matter whether the ground of restitution is analysed as total failure or absence of basis, since the latter ground will be applicable even where the claimant has received part or all of the anticipated benefit from the defendant.

Determining the appropriate ground of restitution as regards those benefits which are transferred in respect of void contracts is controversial. It is clear that total failure of basis may be a relevant ground of restitution in such circumstances, and this will be examined first. The potential application of absence of basis as a ground of restitution will then be considered.

(B) TOTAL FAILURE OF BASIS

In many cases where the claimant has transferred a benefit to the defendant under a contract which is void the ground of restitution has either been expressly recognized as total failure of basis or the fact that the basis had failed totally adequately explains why the

---

[341] See PBH Birks, *Unjust Enrichment* (2nd edn, Oxford: Oxford University Press, 2005) who used the example of the void contract as the main justification for his preference for the absence of basis thesis rather than the recognition of particular grounds of restitution. See p 127, above. This is a different conception of absence of basis as it is used in this chapter, where it signifies a ground of restitution within the orthodox analysis of the unjust enrichment principle.

[342] See also Goodwin, 'Failure of Basis in the Contractual Context', 41 who identifies the relevant failure of basis as the defendant's liability to perform his or her contractual obligation.

[343] [2010] EWCA Civ 579, [2012] QB 549, [62].

restitutionary claim succeeded. Although a contract may be void for a number of different reasons, the question of restitution of benefits transferred in respect of such contracts has arisen in three particular contexts.

(i) Pre-Incorporation Contracts

Where one of the parties to a contract is a company which was not incorporated when the contract was made then, as between these parties,[344] the contract is void. That a restitutionary claim may be brought in respect of any benefits which were transferred in respect of such a contact was recognized by the Court of Appeal in *Rover International Ltd v Cannon Film Sales Ltd (No 3)*.[345] Whilst all of the judges accepted that the claimant company, which had paid money to the defendant under a pre-incorporation contract, could recover that money on the ground of mistake,[346] it was only Kerr LJ who specifically recognized that the claim could also be founded on total failure of basis,[347] though Nicholls LJ agreed with his reasoning, so it presumably represents part of the ratio of the case. The defendant had also benefited from services provided by the claimant under the contract and conceded that the claimant was entitled to a *quantum meruit*. Although no ground of restitution was identified in respect of this claim, again the ground of restitution should also be considered to be either mistake or total failure of basis.

(ii) Infancy

Before the enactment of the Minors' Contracts Act 1987, contracts which were made with infants were void unless they involved the supply of necessities.[348] Money which had been paid under a contract which was void for infancy could be recovered if the basis had totally failed.[349] Similarly, other benefits which had been transferred under a contract made with an infant were recoverable on the ground of total failure of basis as well. This is illustrated by *Pearce v Brain*,[350] where the claimant who was an infant contracted with the defendant to exchange his motor bike for the defendant's car. The contract was void but it was accepted that the claimant could recover the bike if the basis for the transaction had failed totally. But since the claimant had used the car the basis had not totally failed.

(iii) Absence of Authority

A contract may also be void where one of the parties lacked authority to make it.[351] A number of cases recognize that a restitutionary claim may succeed in respect of benefits which were transferred under such a contract, although the ground of restitution has never been specifically identified. In principle, a claimant who transfers benefits to the defendant under a contract which is void for want of authority should be able to obtain

---

[344] By the Companies Act 2006, s 51(1) a pre-incorporation contract has effect as though it was made with the person who purported to act for the company or as agent for it, who is consequently personally liable on the contract.

[345] [1989] 1 WLR 912. See also *Cotronic (UK) Ltd v Dezonie* [1991] BCLC 721 where a restitutionary claim succeeded in respect of building services which had been provided under a pre-incorporation contract. Although the ground of restitution was not identified, it could have been total failure of basis.

[346] Although the mistake appears to have been a mistake of law which was not a ground of restitution at the time.

[347] *Rover International Ltd v Cannon Film Sales Ltd (No 3)* [1989] 1 WLR 912, 924.

[348] See p 299, above.

[349] As was effectively recognized in *Valentini v Canali* (1889) 24 QBD 166, although on the facts the basis had not failed totally.

[350] [1929] 2 KB 310.   [351] *Guinness plc v Saunders* [1990] 2 AC 663.

restitution on the ground of total failure of basis, but the two leading cases where restitutionary relief was awarded in respect of a contract which was void for want of authority cannot easily be explained with reference to this ground.

In *Craven-Ellis v Canons Ltd*[352] the claimant purported to enter into a contract with the defendant company whereby it was agreed that the claimant would act as managing director for the defendant which would pay the claimant for his services. After the claimant had done some work for the defendant he claimed his remuneration, but the defendant refused to pay him. The claimant was unable to sue the defendant on the contract because it was void for want of authority, since neither the claimant nor the other directors who made the agreement on behalf of the defendant possessed the requisite qualification shares which authorized them to make the agreement, as was required by the company's articles of association. The claimant consequently sought to recover reasonable remuneration for the work he had done and his claim succeeded. Although the ground of restitution was never identified, it appears that for Greer LJ the relevant ground was mistake,[353] namely a mistaken belief that a valid contract had been made. This is dubious, however, because the mistake was surely one of law, which was not a recognized ground of restitution at the time. It might be considered that the ground of restitution could alternatively have been total failure of basis. Whether it would have been possible to establish this ground is a matter of some difficulty since the directors were not authorized to act for the defendant, so the defendant company was unaware of the basis which the claimant expected to receive for the provision of his services, save if the defendant's contemplation of the claimant's expectation could be assumed though an objective interpretation of the facts.[354]

The second case where restitution was awarded in the context of a contract which was void for want of authority is the decision of the House of Lords in *Guinness plc v Saunders*,[355] which causes even more difficulties in identifying a relevant ground of restitution. In *Guinness* the claimant company had paid the defendant £5.2 million for his assistance in a successful takeover bid. This contract was void for want of authority under the company's articles of association, and the claimant successfully recovered the money it had paid to the defendant. The ground of restitution was not specifically identified by the court, but it could not have been total failure of basis because the defendant had provided some beneficial services to the claimant. This would not have been an obstacle if absence of basis is recognized as a ground of restitution, since, as a matter of law, the services would not have been validly received because the defendant was not authorized to provide them. The ground of restitution could not have been mistake as to the existence of a valid contract, because the mistake was one of law which was not a recognized ground of restitution at the time,[356] although this would have been a relevant ground today. The preferable explanation of the case is actually that restitution was awarded by virtue of the defendant having breached his fiduciary duty as a director of the company. Consequently, restitution was not awarded to reverse the defendant's unjust enrichment, but was simply a remedy arising from the commission of a wrong by the defendant.[357]

---

[352] [1936] 2 KB 403.

[353] Ibid, 413, where Greer LJ accepted that the contract was void because of the claimant's mistake and so presumably accepted that this constituted the ground of restitution.

[354] See p 309, above.   [355] [1990] 2 AC 663.

[356] PBH Birks, 'Restitution Without Counter-Restitution' [1990] LMCLQ 330, 332.

[357] See p 507, below.

(C) ABSENCE OF BASIS

Although in some of the cases where restitution has been awarded in respect of benefits transferred under a void contract the ground of restitution is clearly total failure of basis, the majority of cases where restitution has been awarded are simply consistent with this as the ground of restitution. In cases where the claimant has received a benefit from the defendant it will not be possible to establish that the failure of basis was total. There is consequently scope for arguing that the ground of restitution in some of these cases should be absence of basis; if the contract is void the anticipated basis could never legally occur. Whether absence of basis is a recognized ground of restitution remains controversial, although there are three strands of cases which suggest that such a ground of restitution is recognized in English law. These are the annuity cases, cases where payments have been made to discharge a liability which does not exist, and the swaps litigation.

(i) The Annuity Cases

In a number of cases in the late eighteenth and early nineteenth centuries restitutionary claims were brought in respect of annuities. The grant of an annuity was a common method of borrowing money whereby the borrower, in return for a sum of money from the lender, agreed to pay an annuity to the lender during the lender's lifetime in lieu of interest and the return of the loan. The Annuity Acts of 1777 and 1813 were passed to regulate the granting of annuities and required compliance with certain formalities, such as registration of the annuity. Failure to comply with these formalities resulted in the contract being treated as null and void. The importance of this in the present context is that it was recognized in a number of cases that restitution of the money under the void annuity contracts was possible even though payments had been made by both parties.[358]

   Some commentators have explained these cases on the ground of total failure of basis or mistake.[359] But this is not convincing. If there was a failure of basis it was partial, since payments had been received by the lender, and if there was a mistake it was one of law, and English law was clear that, subject to exceptions none of which were applicable in these annuity cases, neither partial failure of basis nor mistake of law were grounds of restitution at the time. So some other explanation for restitution needs to be identified. The most appropriate explanation is that of absence of basis. Since the annuities were null and void the basis for the lender's payment never could be obtained, as a matter of law.[360]

(ii) Payments to Discharge a Liability Which Does Not Exist

In *Woolwich Equitable Building Society v IRC*[361] a majority of the House of Lords recognized that the payment of tax to the Revenue, after a tax demand which the Revenue was not authorized to make, was recoverable. Although the actual ground of restitution was the fact that the tax had been paid to a public authority which was not entitled to receive it,[362] both Lords Goff and Browne-Wilkinson referred to the fact that the claimant would not have received any consideration for the payment.[363] This was because the claimant had paid the money to the Revenue in the expectation that this would discharge its tax liability. But since there was no liability to discharge, there could no legal basis for the payment.

---

[358] See, for example, *Hicks v Hicks* (1802) 3 East 16, 102 ER 502.

[359] PBH Birks, 'No Consideration: Restitution after Void Contracts' (1993) 23 Univ WALR 195, 214; AS Burrows, 'Swaps and the Friction Between Common Law and Equity' [1995] RLR 15, 18.

[360] See *Westdeutsche Landesbank Girozentrale v Islington LBC* [1994] 4 All ER 890, 930 (Hobhouse J).

[361] [1993] AC 70.   [362] See p 398, below.

[363] *Woolwich Equitable Building Society v IRC* [1993] AC 70, 166 (Lord Goff), 197–8 (Lord Browne-Wilkinson).

(iii) The Swaps Litigation

The most important example of the ground of absence of basis in operation arises from the cases which formed the so-called 'swaps litigation'. In these cases the claimants had entered into interest rate swap transactions with the defendants in circumstances where such transactions were null and void. Essentially an interest rate swap transaction is a speculative contract whereby two parties gamble on how interest rates will change. The simplest form of transaction involves an agreement between two parties whereby each one agrees to pay a sum of money to the other over a stated number of years, which is divided into accounting periods. This money is calculated by reference to the interest which would have accrued during each accounting period on a notional capital sum. The rate of interest of one party will be fixed, whereas that of the other party will be floating, meaning that it will be assessed by reference to a variable market rate. At the end of each accounting period one party will be liable to pay the other. Whether it is the fixed or the floating rate payer who will be liable depends on the movements of the interest rates. Often in the course of a swaps transaction the floating rate of interest would vary above and below the fixed rate of interest, meaning that at some stage in the course of the transaction each party would be liable to pay the other. Essentially, such swaps transactions involve the parties gambling on the fluctuation of interest rates.

From the early 1980s local authorities began to enter into such interest rate swap transactions with a number of different financial institutions. In 1990, however, the House of Lords held that such transactions were beyond the statutory powers of the local authorities and so were void.[364] This was because participation of local authorities in such transactions could not be considered to be incidental to their power to lend and borrow money, simply because these transactions did not involve the lending or borrowing of money. Consequently, the party who had paid the most under such transactions, either the local authority or the financial institution depending on the particular circumstances of the case, brought restitutionary claims to recover the balance of the money paid. A large number of such actions were instigated and certain characteristic actions were identified and were pursued as test cases. The most important of these was *Westdeutsche Landesbank Girozentrale v Islington LBC*,[365] which was heard with *Kleinwort Benson Ltd v Sandwell Borough Council* before Hobhouse J, although his decision in respect of the latter case was not the subject of an appeal. In both of these cases it was the banks which sought restitution of the balance of the money from the local authorities at common law. There were two obstacles in the way of the claim.

> (1) *Sinclair v Brougham*. In *Sinclair v Brougham*[366] the House of Lords held that an action for money had and received could not succeed if the award of restitution would involve the indirect enforcement of an invalid transaction. Consequently, restitutionary relief would be unavailable, as it was in that case, where the claimant sought restitution of an *ultra vires* loan, because the value of the restitutionary remedy would be the same as the amount of the loan, so the effect of restitution would be to repay and so enforce the loan. In *Westdeutsche Landesbank* both Hobhouse J and the Court of Appeal held that this principle was inapplicable to

---

[364] *Hazell v Hammersmith and Fulham LBC* [1992] 2 AC 1.

[365] [1994] 4 All ER 890 (Hobhouse J); [1994] 1 WLR 938 (Court of Appeal); [1996] AC 669 (House of Lords). The decisions of Hobhouse J and the Court of Appeal are the most important in respect of the identification and definition of absence of basis as a ground of restitution. The House of Lords was more concerned with proprietary restitutionary claims in Equity: see Chapter 21.

[366] *Sinclair v Brougham* [1914] AC 398.

the facts of the case simply because the interest rate swaps transaction was not a borrowing transaction, but was a futures contract which does not, by its very nature, involve the lending of any money. Consequently, if the defendant local authority was required to make restitution to the bank this would not involve the indirect enforcement of the transaction, since the effect of restitution would simply be to restore the parties to the position they occupied before the transaction was entered into. Even where the transaction involves a loan it now appears that restitution of the money lent could be awarded, simply because it is now recognized that the obligation to make restitution is imposed by law and is independent of the contractual obligation to repay the loan.[367] Consequently, the rule in *Sinclair v Brougham* is no longer applicable.

(2) *Identifying the ground of restitution.* The second obstacle to the claim concerned the identification of a relevant ground of restitution. The claimants could not rely on mistake since the only mistake made was one of law, concerning the legal validity of the payment and, since the mistake of law bar still applied, there was nothing to suggest that any of the exceptions to it were applicable. Equally, the claimants could not rely on total failure of basis since, save for two transactions, the claimants had been paid some money in the course of the transaction. However, Hobhouse J recognized that the claim could succeed by virtue of the ground of absence of basis for the claimants' payment to the defendant. This analysis was endorsed by the Court of Appeal.[368]

This recognition of absence of basis as a ground of restitution is not free from difficulty. Despite the explicit recognition of the ground in *Westdeutsche Landesbank* whether it does exist remains uncertain and, even if it does exist, its ambit and relevance[369] is unclear. Five particular problems can be identified.

(1) The Effect of Subsequent Decisions

Although absence of basis was clearly recognized by Hobhouse J and the Court of Appeal in *Westdeutsche Landesbank*, its status must be reconsidered in the light of the House of Lords decision in that case. Unfortunately, the decision of that court is of little assistance, since it was much more concerned with the nature of the equitable proprietary claim than with the claim for money had and received. Nevertheless, the judgments of Lords Goff and Browne-Wilkinson do provide some clues as to whether absence of basis is a valid ground of restitution. Although Lord Goff declined to express any concluded view, he did say that there was considerable force in the criticisms which had been expressed concerning the validity of absence of basis as a ground of restitution, and he would have preferred that the ground of restitution was failure of basis.[370] Although this does not constitute a clear rejection of absence of basis, it seems that, in the light of Lord Goff's earlier description of the requirement of total failure of basis as being unprincipled and producing unfortunate effects, he was assuming that restitution should have been awarded on the ground of partial failure of basis. But he did not at any stage explicitly state this, and anyway his

---

[367] As recognized in *Haugesund Kommune v Depfa ACS Bank* [2010] EWCA Civ 579, [2012] QB 549.

[368] *Westdeutsche Landesbank Girozentrale v Islington LBC* [1994] 1 WLR 938. See also *Kleinwort Benson Ltd v Birmingham City Council* [1996] QB 380, 393 (Evans LJ) and 394 (Saville LJ).

[369] See *Haugesund Kommune v Depfa ACS Bank* [2010] EWCA Civ 579, [2012] QB 549, [62] (Aikens LJ). See p 375, below.

[370] *Westdeutsche Landesbank Girozentrale v Islington LBC* [1996] AC 669, 683.

comments were *obiter* since the question of the ground of restitution for the purposes of a common law restitutionary action was not the subject of an appeal.

Lord Browne-Wilkinson, on the other hand, did appear to recognize the validity of absence of basis as a ground of restitution, although he too used the language of total failure of basis. In his analysis of *Sinclair v Brougham*[371] he suggested that the claimants in that case should have succeeded in their common law claim for recovery of money, which had been lent to a building society pursuant to a transaction which was *ultra vires* the building society. He specifically recognized that the ground of restitution in that case should have been total failure of basis.[372] Crucially, he concluded that the basis had failed totally, even though the building society had done what it had promised to do, because the claimants had paid money to the building society 'in consideration of a promise to repay. That promise was ultra vires and void; therefore the consideration for the payment of the money wholly failed.'[373]

In the light of this reasoning he went on to endorse the decision of the Court of Appeal in *Westdeutsche Landesbank*, that money had been paid to the defendant on a basis which had wholly failed. But, even though Lord Browne-Wilkinson used the language of failure of basis, his emphasis on the fact that the transaction was *ultra vires* and void means that his analysis is actually indistinguishable from that of Hobhouse J. At the very least Lord Browne-Wilkinson could not be referring to the notion of total failure of basis as it is normally used, because the claimants in *Sinclair v Brougham* had received a factual benefit in that their money was deposited with the defendant. The only way that this basis could fail totally is if it failed as a matter of law, since the defendant lacked the capacity to receive the claimants' money. It is this notion of legal failure of basis, arising from the fact that the contract was void, which is identical to the approach of Hobhouse J, which is, if anything, clearer and more honest because he is prepared to call it absence of basis rather than total failure of basis.

The clear division of opinion between Lords Goff and Browne-Wilkinson, and the failure of the other judges to address this issue, means that it is not possible to conclude that absence of basis has no role as a ground of restitution in English law. Consequently, the judgments of Hobhouse J and the Court of Appeal continue to be of vital importance to the recognition of absence of basis as a ground of restitution.

Since the decision of the House of Lords in *Westdeutsche Landesbank* the Court of Appeal reconsidered the nature of the restitutionary claim arising from payments made under an interest rate swap transaction in *Guinness Mahon and Co Ltd v Kensington and Chelsea Royal LBC*.[374] The claimant bank's restitutionary claim against a local authority succeeded, although the actual ground of restitution is difficult to identify with certainty. Morritt LJ considered that the ground of restitution was total failure of basis and that this was the ground which was relied on in *Westdeutsche Landesbank* itself, even though he accepted that the defendant had performed its part of the transaction.[375] But he also recognized that the reason why there was a total failure of basis was simply because the contract was *ultra vires*.[376] This is a virtually identical approach to that adopted by Lord Browne-Wilkinson in *Westdeutsche Landesbank*. Waller LJ doubted whether absence of

---

[371] [1914] AC 398.   [372] *Westdeutsche Landesbank Girozentrale v Islington LBC* [1996] AC 669, 710.
[373] Ibid.
[374] [1999] QB 215. This decision was commended by Lord Hope in *Kleinwort Benson Ltd v Lincoln CC* [1999] 2 AC 349, 415.
[375] *Guinness Mahon and Co Ltd v Kensington and Chelsea Royal LBC* [1999] QB 215, 224.
[376] Ibid, 227.

basis was an appropriate ground of restitution.[377] For Robert Walker LJ the choice between total failure of basis and absence of basis was simply a matter of terminology.[378] Although the approaches of the three judges suggest a tendency to prefer total failure to absence of basis, it is clear that they all treated the notion of failure of basis differently in the context of void contracts, essentially because the basis had failed as a matter of law rather than fact.

The Court of Appeal had a further opportunity to consider absence of basis in *Haugesund Kommune v Depfa ACS Bank*.[379] A bank had lent money to Norwegian public authorities in circumstances where the authorities lacked the capacity to borrow the money. It followed that the bank was unable to sue on the contract of loan, which was void. The question then was whether the bank could obtain a restitutionary remedy to recover the value of the loan. Aiken LJ indicated[380] that whether the ground of restitution was analysed as total failure or absence of basis was simply a matter of choosing the most apt terminology, but it was without legal significance. But the distinction is not simply a matter of semantics. Where money has been paid by the claimant to the defendant and the claimant has received some benefit in return it will generally not be possible to conclude that the basis has failed totally. That is what occurred in *Haugesund Kommune*, since the bank, having lent money to the public authorities, had received quarterly payments of interest and other payments so that the basis had factually not failed totally, save if the payments could be apportioned.[381] But, since the payments were made pursuant to a void contract, they were never validly received by the claimant as a matter of law and could legitimately be ignored: the basis had not failed but was absent. Legal analysis is much clearer if total failure and absence of basis remain distinct.

The cases subsequent to the decisions of the trial judge and the Court of Appeal in *Westdeutsche Landesbank* are not necessarily inconsistent with the recognition of a ground of absence of basis. On some occasions that ground has even been specifically identified, most notably in *Primlake Ltd (In Liquidation) v Matthews Associates*[382] where Lawrence Collins J recognized the ground of 'absence of consideration in the sense of no legal basis for the payments'.

(2) The Relationship Between Absence of Basis and Total Failure of Basis

Even though absence of basis was specifically relied on to enable restitution of money to be awarded, it is odd that Hobhouse J in *Westdeutsche Landesbank* awarded restitution both on the ground of total failure of basis, in respect of those transactions where only the claimant had paid money to the defendant without receiving anything in return, and absence of basis, in respect of those transactions where the claimant and the defendant had both paid money to the other party and the claimant was simply seeking to recover the net payment from the defendant. If absence of basis is recognized it should be applicable in all cases where money has been paid under a transaction which is void, and the question of whether or not the claimant received any benefit under the transaction should be irrelevant, save that the claimant should be required to make counter-restitution to the defendant.

---

[377] Ibid, 231.

[378] Ibid, 239. See also *Haugesund Kommune v Depfa ACS Bank* [2010] EWCA Civ 579, [2012] QB 549, [62] (Aikens LJ).   [379] [2010] EWCA Civ 579, [2012] QB 549.

[380] Ibid, [62].   [381] *Goss v Chilcott* [1996] AC 788. See p 321, above.

[382] [2006] EWHC 1227 (Ch), [2007] 1 BCLC 666, [335] (Lawrence Collins J). See also *Dorchester upon Medway CC v Kent CC, The Times*, 5 March 1998.

(3) Fully Executed Transactions

One of the interest rate swap transactions in *Kleinwort Benson Ltd v Sandwell Borough Council*[383] was fully executed, in that the agreed period of the transaction had expired before the House of Lords declared that it was *ultra vires*. But, despite this, the restitutionary claim still succeeded on the ground of absence of basis, because of the assumption that any benefit which the claimant had received under the transaction was not validly received since the transaction was void from the outset. But should restitutionary relief be available to re-open a transaction once it is complete?

Birks argued that a distinction should be drawn between those transactions which are closed, meaning that they are fully executed, and those which remain open.[384] He asserted that where a transaction is fully executed it is not possible to conclude that the claimant's intention that the defendant should retain the money paid has been vitiated in any way, so there is consequently no reason why restitution should be awarded in such circumstances. In other words, the claimant has received exactly that for which he or she had bargained. Birks's rejection of the argument that restitution should be awarded even where the transaction has been executed is weakened by his recognition that, where there is a relevant mistake, the claimant can obtain restitution by reason of mistake even where the transaction has been fully executed.[385] He was forced to accept that restitution will be awarded in such circumstances because, for mistake to operate as a ground of restitution, it is sufficient that the mistake was operative at the time the benefit was received by the defendant. Subsequent events are irrelevant to establish the mistake, although they may enable the defendant to plead a defence of change of position.

In fact, there is no difficulty in allowing restitution in respect of a fully executed swaps transaction even where the ground of restitution is absence of basis. This was recognized by the Court of Appeal in *Guinness Mahon and Co Ltd v Kensington and Chelsea Royal London BC*.[386] The claimant bank had entered into an interest rate swap transaction with the defendant local authority which the parties agreed would last for five years, until 1987. By the end of the agreement the defendant had received over £380,000 more than it had paid. Subsequently, this type of agreement was declared void and so the claimant sought restitution of the net amount which the defendant had received, even though the agreement was fully executed. The Court of Appeal held that the claim should succeed because there was no basis for distinguishing between open and closed transactions. This must be right if the basis for restitution is absence of basis arising from the fact that the transaction was null and void. If there never was any transaction, the question of whether the apparent transaction had been completely performed or not is totally irrelevant. The court particularly stressed that, if the transaction had been completely performed, the defendant had no better right to the money than if it had only been partly performed. This conclusion also avoids the unjust situation which would arise if the claimant was able to recover every payment made to the defendant until the penultimate payment, but would not be able to recover a penny once the final payment had been made.

(4) Nullity of Purpose

Whilst it is clear that absence of basis should be an appropriate ground of restitution where a benefit has been transferred under a contract which is a nullity, is it possible for

---

[383] [1994] 4 All ER 890.   [384] Birks, 'No Consideration: Restitution after Void Contracts', 206.
[385] Ibid, 229.   [386] [1999] QB 215.

the claimant to rely on absence of basis where no contract has been made, but the benefit was transferred for a particular purpose which was a nullity? For example, if the claimant has entered into an agreement with the defendant which is subject to contract, it has already been seen that if the claimant pays money to the defendant in the expectation that a contract will be made and no contract is forthcoming, the claimant might be able to recover the money on the ground of total failure of basis, even though the defendant never promised that a contract would be made.[387] If, however, the claimant received some benefit from the defendant in return for the payment, it would not be possible for the claimant to rely on the ground of total failure of basis.[388] But, if the contract could never be made as a matter of law, would the claimant be able to recover the money on the ground of absence of basis? This question was identified but was not answered in *Friends' Provident Life Office v Hillier Parker May and Rowland*.[389] The better view is that if, as a matter of law, no contract could validly be made the expected basis could never be obtained and so the claimant should be able to obtain restitution on the ground of absence of basis in exactly the same way as occurred in *Westdeutsche Landesbank* itself.

(5) Policy of Invalidity

When considering whether restitution is available where a benefit has been transferred to the defendant pursuant to a void transaction, it is important to consider whether the policy which makes the transaction void would be undermined by awarding restitution.[390] This is because it would be inconsistent for the law to invalidate the transaction on one hand but to allow restitution on the other if it has the effect of actually enforcing the transaction. Typically, this issue will arise where a transaction has been rendered void by statute. The relevance of the policy of invalidity was specifically considered by the Court of Appeal in *Haugesund Kommune v Depfa ACS Bank*,[391] where the policy of the Norwegian statute which rendered the loan transaction void was examined and it was held that it would not be undermined by allowing the lender to recover the loan from the borrower by means of a claim in restitution rather than by suing on the void contract, even though the effect was the same. In reaching this conclusion it was considered to be significant that the lender had not taken the risk that the contract with the public authority might be void because of the public authority's lack of capacity. If the borrower had been a private citizen who lacked capacity for reasons of social protection of people who are vulnerable to exploitation, the policy in favour of protecting such a person would be undermined if they were found liable to make restitution of what they had borrowed. Consequently, in such a case, the policy behind the invalidity of the loan transaction should also bar the restitutionary claim. Similarly, at a time when gambling contracts were void,[392] it was held that money paid to the winner by the loser could not be recovered by the loser on the ground that the transaction was void, because this would undermine the policy of the statute rendering such contracts void.[393]

---

[387] See, for example, *Chillingworth v Esche* [1924] 1 Ch 97, discussed at p 316, above.
[388] See *Sharma v Simposh Ltd* [2011] EWCA Civ 1383, [2013] Ch 23.
[389] [1997] QB 85, 99 (Auld LJ).
[390] See the decision of the High Court of Australia in *Equuscorp Pty Ltd v Haxton* [2012] HCA 7.
[391] [2010] EWCA Civ 579, [2012] QB 549.
[392] Under the Gaming Act 1845. This Act was repealed by the Gambling Act 2005.
[393] *Morgan v Ashcroft* [1938] 1 KB 49.

(D) SHOULD ABSENCE OF BASIS BE RECOGNIZED AS A GROUND OF RESTITUTION?

The identification of the most appropriate ground of restitution where the claimant has transferred a benefit to the defendant pursuant to a void transaction remains controversial. Analysis of the case law suggests that three grounds of restitution are potentially applicable, namely total failure of basis, absence of basis, and mistake. With the recognition by the House of Lords in *Kleinwort Benson v Lincoln CC*[394] that mistake of law can ground a restitutionary claim, it will be much easier to establish that the defendant has been unjustly enriched in respect of contracts which have been held to be void. Consequently, there is now less need for a ground of absence of basis. But such a ground may sometimes still be of some significance where a causative mistake cannot be established, for example because the transaction was declared void by statute[395] or the claimant suspected that there was no liability to pay the money,[396] and so it is still necessary to consider whether such a ground can be justified.

The chief criticism of absence of basis is that it is not appropriate to treat the claimant's intention to benefit the defendant as vitiated simply because the underlying contract is void. In the swaps cases the claimant paid money to the defendant on condition that, if the defendant became liable to pay the claimant under the agreement, this money would be paid to the claimant. If the claimant received no payment from the defendant restitution would be available on the ground of total failure of basis. But, where the claimant did receive payment from the defendant, can the claimant's intention to pay the defendant really be treated as vitiated? The answer has to be 'yes', because the essence of the ground of absence of basis is that the basis has failed as a matter of law. Where the claimant pays money to the defendant in respect of a contract which later turns out to have been void, the claimant paid the defendant on the basis that the defendant would be legally liable to transfer a benefit to the defendant in return. If that liability does not exist, the basis for the payment is absent and restitution should lie. This is clear where the claimant has not received anything from the defendant. But this reasoning applies even if the claimant did receive a benefit from the defendant under the contract, because the basis for that receipt is not legally valid and so should not operate to bar the claim for restitution. The claimant must return to the defendant any benefit which had been received, but likewise the defendant must return any benefit to the claimant. This is a logical and defensible consequence of the underlying transaction being null and void from the start.

It does not result from this analysis that, as Birks thought, English law made a dramatic move to the recognition of a theory of absence of basis to establish the unjust component of the unjust enrichment formula, rather than orthodox grounds of restitution.[397] Absence of basis is an orthodox ground of restitution which applies where the claimant transferred a benefit to the defendant on condition that the defendant was liable to perform an obligation in return, typically because the claimant assumed that there was a valid contract. If that contract is void, so that there is no liability on the defendant, the condition for the transfer has failed and so failure of basis can be established, simply because there never was a basis in the first place. Consequently, the claimant's intention to benefit the defendant is vitiated and restitution should follow. This analysis is consistent with the theory underlying the recognition of grounds of restitution.

---

[394] [1999] 2 AC 349. See p 162, above.

[395] The House of Lords in *Kleinwort Benson* held that such a mistake of law would not ground a restitutionary claim. For criticism of this conclusion see p 184, above.

[396] Though restitution of payments made in such circumstances may be defeated by the bar of voluntary submission to an honest claim. See p 149, above.   [397] See p 127, above.

14

INCAPACITY

1. GENERAL PRINCIPLES

(A) INCAPACITY OF THE CLAIMANT

Where the claimant lacks capacity to enter into a transaction this in itself should constitute a ground of restitution to enable the claimant to recover any benefits transferred to the defendant pursuant to the transaction. Two reasons can be identified to justify the recognition of incapacity as a ground of restitution in its own right.

(i) Absence or Vitiation of Intent

The effect of the claimant's incapacity will be that he or she cannot be considered to have intended that the defendant should receive a benefit. This will either occur because the claimant is incapable of forming the necessary intent at all, or because the effect of the incapacity is to impair the claimant's capacity such that he or she appears to have formed an intent but cannot be considered to have exercised a free will in transferring the benefit to the defendant.[1] As Fullagar J said in the Australian case of *Blomley v Ryan*,[2] 'the primary question [is] as to the reality of the assent' of the incapacitated person. The distinction between absence of consent and impaired consent is a matter of degree which depends on the extent of the impairment on the claimant's awareness and understanding of what he or she was doing. Where capacity is absent any transaction entered into by the incapacitated person will be void and restitution should follow automatically. Where capacity is merely impaired, whether restitution should follow will depend on the extent of the impairment and the defendant's awareness of the impairment.

(ii) Policy Demands Restitution

The recognition of incapacity as a ground of restitution can also be justified on policy grounds. This is because the rules which state that the claimant lacked capacity to transact with the defendant can be interpreted as incorporating a requirement that the incapacitated person should be restored to the position which he or she occupied before the benefit was transferred to the defendant. This interpretation of the incapacity rules is justified because these rules are founded on a policy of protecting people from the consequences of the incapacitated person's actions. This policy of protection clearly operates where the claimant is mentally incapacitated or is an infant, where the incapacitated person is in particular need of protection.[3] Where the claimant is a company or a public authority, the policy of protection is still relevant, but here it is the shareholders or the taxpayers

---

[1] *Johnson v Clark* [1908] 1 Ch 303, 316 (Parker J).   [2] (1956) 99 CLR 362, 401.
[3] See, for example, Lord Denning MR in *Chaplin v Leslie Frewin (Publishers) Ltd* [1966] Ch 71, 90: 'For the protection of the young and foolish...'

respectively who are in particular need of protection from the consequences of the company's or public authority's actions.

(B) INCAPACITY OF THE DEFENDANT

Where it is the defendant who is incapacitated this may be relevant to restitutionary claims in two different ways.

(i) Defendant's Incapacity as a Defence

The incapacity of the defendant has sometimes been considered to operate as a defence to the claim for restitution. Whether incapacity does indeed operate as a general defence to restitutionary claims is considered in Chapter 28.

(ii) Defendant's Incapacity as a Ground of Restitution

The defendant's incapacity may exceptionally itself constitute a ground of restitution to enable the claimant to obtain restitution from the defendant,[4] but it seems that this will only occur where policy demands that the incapacitated defendant should not retain the benefit. This will be the case where, for example, the defendant is a public authority which lacked capacity to receive money from the claimant.[5] In other cases, such as where the defendant was suffering from a mental disorder or was a minor, the defendant's incapacity should not constitute a ground of restitution.[6] This is because the claimant's intention to benefit the defendant cannot be considered to have been vitiated simply because the defendant was mentally disordered or a minor and the policy of protecting such people does not require them to make restitution to the claimant. Similarly, where the claimant sought restitution from a company in respect of goods delivered or services rendered pursuant to a contract which was *ultra vires* the company, the fact that the defendant lacked capacity could not constitute a ground of restitution for the restitutionary claim.[7] In such cases where policy does not demand restitution, the claimant can still obtain restitution from the incapacitated defendant, but only if one of the other grounds of restitution is applicable. For example, the claimant may have transferred a benefit to the defendant who was a minor and who has refused to pay for the benefit. Since the contract is unenforceable, the claimant cannot sue the defendant on it, but the claimant might be able to obtain restitution on the ground of total failure of basis.[8]

---

[4] See E O'Dell, 'Incapacity' in PBH Birks and FD Rose (eds), *Lessons of the Swaps Litigation* (Oxford: Mansfield Press, 2000), ch 5. See also *National Bank of Egypt International Ltd v Oman Housing Bank SAOC* [2002] EWHC 1760 (Comm), [2003] 1 All ER (Comm) 246, where the claimant lent money to a bank in circumstances where the bank lacked the capacity to borrow the money, and it was recognized that the claimant could recover it.

[5] As was recognized by the House of Lords in *Woolwich Equitable Building Society v IRC* [1993] AC 70, examined in Chapter 15.

[6] Though where the claimant transfers property to a minor, the court has a discretion to enable the claimant to recover that property or its substitute if it considers it to be just to do so. See the Minors' Contracts Act 1987, s 3(1), examined at p 730, below.

[7] *Re Jon Beauforte (London) Ltd* [1953] Ch 131. Today the claimant would be able to sue the defendant company on the contract even though it was *ultra vires*: Companies Act 2006, s 40.

[8] See Chapter 13.

2. THE CATEGORIES OF INCAPACITY

If the claimant's incapacity can constitute a ground of restitution it is vital to determine what constitutes incapacity for these purposes. A number of different types of incapacity can be identified which need to be analysed with some care since there is a great deal of uncertainty, both as to the requirements for establishing each type of incapacity and as to the effect of each type on the restitutionary claim.

(A) MENTAL INCAPACITY

Mental incapacity is defined as where a person is unable to make a decision[9] for him or herself because of an 'impairment of, or a disturbance in the functioning of, the mind or brain',[10] which may be permanent or temporary.[11] It covers a wide variety of conditions including people whose mental development has been slow, whose brains have been damaged or who suffer from some type of recognized physical illness, such as the effects of a brain tumour,[12] or psychological condition, such as schizophrenia or senile demen-tia.[13] Whatever the type of mental incapacity, whether the claimant can be considered to be incapacitated is a question of degree. The fact that a claimant suffers a mental condition may be relevant to restitutionary claims in four different circumstances.

(i) Powers of the Court of Protection

Sometimes, where the mental condition is such that a person is incapable of managing his or her own property and affairs, the Court of Protection may make an order or appoint a deputy to make decisions on behalf of that person.[14] Any gift made by the mentally incapacitated person once a deputy has been appointed will be void,[15] whereas any contract which disposes of the person's property and which was made without the authority of the court, does not bind the mentally incapacitated person, though it may be ratified by the court.[16] Save where the transaction has been ratified, any property which was transferred or gift made may be recovered by the court or the deputy on behalf of the mentally incapacitated person.

(ii) *Non Est Factum*

In an extreme case where the claimant purports to sign a contract and the mental incapacity is such that he or she does not realize the nature of the document which he or she signing, the contract will be void on the ground of *non est factum*.[17] Consequently, the claimant will be able to obtain restitution of benefits transferred to the defendant on the grounds of mistake or total failure of basis.

(iii) Exploitation

Where a mentally incapacitated claimant has transferred a benefit to the defendant, the claimant may be able to obtain restitution of the benefit without relying on incapacity specifically, but by establishing that one of the grounds of restitution which are founded

---

[9] Meaning that the person is unable to understand, retain, or weigh information relating to a decision or to communicate a decision: Mental Capacity Act 2005, s 3(1).

[10] Ibid, s 2(1).   [11] Ibid, s 2(2).   [12] *Simpson v Simpson* [1989] Fam Law 20.

[13] *Re Beaney* [1978] 1 WLR 770.   [14] Mental Capacity Act 2005, s 16(2).

[15] *Re Walker* [1905] 1 Ch 160.   [16] *Baldwyn v Smith* [1900] 1 Ch 588.

[17] See p 196, above.

on the exploitation principle can be established.[18] For example, the claimant may be able to show that the defendant had unduly influenced the claimant or that the defendant had acted unconscionably in exploiting the claimant's weakness.

(iv) Incapacity

In all other cases the transaction which the claimant entered into will be treated as valid unless two conditions are satisfied.[19]

(1) Failure to Understand the Nature and Effect of the Transaction

It must first be established that the claimant did not understand the nature and effect of the transaction at the time he or she entered into it.[20] The extent to which the claimant must fail to understand the nature and effect of the transaction depends on the type of transaction and its potential effect on the claimant's circumstances. A particularly import-ant consideration concerns the type and value of any property which the claimant transferred to the defendant. So, for example, in *Re Beaney*[21] the deceased, who was suffering from advanced senile dementia, transferred her house, which was her only valuable asset, to her eldest daughter. The transfer was set aside because the deceased had not understood that the consequence of the transaction was to make an absolute gift of the house to her daughter and the effect of this transfer on the claims of her other children had not been explained to her. As Martin Nourse QC said:[22]

> [I]f the subject matter and value of a gift are trivial in relation to the donor's other assets a low degree of understanding will suffice. But, at the other extreme, if its effect is to dispose of the donor's only asset of value and thus for practical purposes to pre-empt the devolution of his estate under his will or on his intestacy, then the degree of understanding required is as high as that required for a will and the donor must understand the claims of all potential donees and the extent of the property to be disposed of.

(2) Defendant's Knowledge of the Incapacity

The second condition is that the defendant must have known that the claimant lacked the capacity to understand what he or she was doing.[23] Knowledge refers to actual or constructive notice, so it is sufficient that the defendant had sufficient awareness of the facts which would indicate to the honest and reasonable person that the other party to the contract was suffering from mental infirmity.[24] But why should this be relevant, particu-larly because such a requirement does not apply where the claimant is a minor?[25] The only possible explanation for this requirement is that, where the claimant is suffering from a mental disorder, there may be nothing to indicate to the defendant that the claimant might be suffering from mental infirmity, whereas it is easier to establish that the defendant has been put on notice that the claimant is an infant and is required to investigate what the claimant's age is.

---

[18] See Chapter 11.

[19] The ground of mental incapacity is distinct from that of unconscionable conduct, see p 278, above, because for the latter it is also necessary to prove that the relevant transaction was fair, just and reasonable. That is not a requirement for the mental incapacity doctrine.

[20] *Re Beaney* [1978] 1 WLR 770.

[21] Ibid. See also *Simpson v Simpson* [1989] Fam Law 20 and the decision of the High Court of Australia in *Gibbons v Wright* (1954) 91 CLR 423.   [22] *Re Beaney* [1978] 1 WLR 770, 774.

[23] *Imperial Loan Co v Stone* [1892] 1 QB 599, 601 (Lord Esher MR). This was affirmed by the Privy Council in *Hart v O'Connor* [1985] AC 1000.

[24] *Hassard v Smith* (1872) IR 6 Eq 429.   [25] See p 385, below.

(3) Consequences of the Conditions Being Satisfied

Where the mentally incapacitated claimant has transferred a benefit to the defendant in circumstances where both these conditions have been satisfied, the claimant will be able to recover the benefit. Where, however, the claimant has entered into a contract with the defendant in circumstances where both conditions have been satisfied it is first necessary to show that the contract has ceased to operate before restitutionary relief can be awarded. It is unclear whether the claimant's incapacity makes the contract void[26] or voidable.[27] The preferable view is that the incapacity renders the contract voidable, save where the claimant's incapacity is so severe that he or she could not be considered to know that he or she was entering into a transaction at all, for then the doctrine of *non est factum* will apply. If the claimant was aware of what he or she was doing but fails to understand the nature and effect of the contract and the defendant knew this, the claimant can rescind the contract, although this will be subject to the usual bars on rescission, including that the claimant must be in a position to make counter-restitution to the defendant.[28] Once the contract has been rescinded, the claimant will be able to recover all the benefits which he or she had transferred to the defendant. Where, however, the mentally incapacitated person is supplied with necessaries, he or she must pay a reasonable price for them.[29]

(B) INTOXICATION

Intoxication is treated as a ground of restitution in the same way as mental incapacity. So where, for example, the claimant was so intoxicated at the time of signing a contract that he or she did not realize that the nature of the contract was different from that which he or she intended to sign, the doctrine of *non est factum* will be applicable and the contract will be void. In every other case in which the claimant was intoxicated at the time of entering into a transaction with the defendant, this will make the transaction voidable so long as the claimant was so intoxicated that he or she did not understand the nature and effect of the transaction and the defendant knew that the claimant was intoxicated at the time.[30] This means that the claimant must have been really drunk, rather than merely tipsy, before he or she can be regarded as incapacitated. Where, however, the intoxicated person is supplied with necessaries he or she must pay a reasonable price for them.[31]

(C) SOMNAMBULISM

It has sometimes been suggested that, if the claimant entered into a transaction with the defendant whilst sleepwalking, the transaction can be set aside.[32] Sleepwalking is to be treated as a form of temporary mental incapacity. Whilst it is highly unlikely that such a case would ever arise, transactions entered into whilst sleepwalking should be treated in the same way as acts performed whilst intoxicated. Consequently, any transaction entered into whilst sleepwalking should only be rescinded if the claimant lacked understanding of

---

[26] See, for example, *Daily Telegraph Newspaper Co Ltd v McLaughlin* [1904] AC 776 and *Simpson v Simpson* [1989] Fam Law 20.

[27] *Imperial Loan Co Ltd v Stone* [1892] 1 QB 599, 602 (Lopes LJ) and *Gibbons v Wright* (1954) 91 CLR 423.

[28] *Molton v Camroux* (1849) 4 Ex 17, 154 ER 117. For analysis of the bars to rescission, see p 25, above.

[29] Mental Capacity Act 2005, s 7.

[30] *Gore v Gibson* (1845) 13 M and W 623, 153 ER 260. See also *Molton v Camroux* (1849) 4 Ex 17, 154 ER 1107 and *Matthews v Baxter* (1873) LR 8 Exch 132.

[31] Sale of Goods Act 1979, s 3(2).

[32] *Gore v Gibson* (1843) 13 M and W 623, 627; 153 ER 260, 262 (Alderson B).

what he or she was doing and the other party knew that the claimant was sleepwalking. If the claimant signed a contract whilst sleepwalking this could be set aside on the ground of *non est factum*, since the claimant would not have been aware of the nature of the document which he or she was signing.[33]

(D) MINORITY

(i) The Problems Raised by Minority

The role of minority as a ground of restitution raises issues of some complexity. This is largely due to changes in the law concerning the effect of minority on the validity of transactions. The common law on the effect of minority was replaced by a statutory regime in 1874,[34] the main effect of which was to treat contracts made with minors as void, subject to certain exceptions. This statutory regime was abolished by the Minors' Contracts Act 1987,[35] with the effect that the common law rules on the validity of contracts made with minors have been resurrected. This means that contracts made with minors are no longer void. It also means that those cases which were decided between 1874 and 1987 need to be analysed with some care. To make matters even more confusing, the definition of what constitutes a minor has also changed. Today a minor is defined as a child under 18,[36] whereas the previous age of majority was 21. It follows that there is now less opportunity for contracts to be made with minors, though the issue continues to be of some practical importance.

(ii) The Effect of Minority on the Validity of Contracts

Where a minor has transferred benefits to the defendant pursuant to a contract between them and the minor wishes to recover these benefits, the first question which needs to be considered is whether the contract continues to be operative. This is because of the fundamental principle that restitutionary relief is only available where the contract has ceased to operate.[37] Between 1874 and 1987 contracts made with minors were void, so there was nothing to bar the minor's restitutionary claim. Today, the effect of the contract on the minor depends on the nature of the contract. The contract may fall into one of two categories.[38]

(1) Contracts in which the minor acquired an interest of a permanent or continuous nature, such as contracts for the acquisition of interests in land or shares in a company.[39] These contracts are valid and binding until the minor disclaims the contract whilst still a minor or within a reasonable time of having attained the age of majority.[40]

(2) Other contracts which are not continuous do not bind the minor unless they are ratified within a reasonable time after he or she has attained the age of majority.

The distinction between these types of contracts makes legal analysis of the effect of the claimant's minority on the contract somewhat difficult. Where the contract can be characterized as continuous in its operation, it is acceptable to conclude that the contract operates until it is rescinded. Where the contract is not continuous it is not strictly true to

---

[33] *Gibbons v Wright* (1954) 91 CLR 423. [34] The Infants' Relief Act 1874.
[35] Section 4(2). [36] Family Law Reform Act 1969, s 1. [37] See p 134, above.
[38] See H Beale (ed), *Chitty on Contracts* (31st edn, London: Sweet and Maxwell, 2012), paras 8-002 *et seq.*
[39] See *Steinberg v Scala (Leeds) Ltd* [1923] 2 Ch 452.
[40] *Lovell and Christmas v Beauchamp* [1894] AC 607.

say that the contract needs to be rescinded, since it does not bind the minor during his or her minority and will only bind once the age of majority has been attained and the contract is ratified. Since these contracts cannot affect the claimant whilst he or she is a minor there is no need to rescind them. These types of contract cannot therefore constitute an obstacle to the minor's restitutionary claim if he or she transferred benefits to the defendant under the contract.

(iii) The Effect of Minority on Other Transactions

Where a minor makes a gift to a person of full capacity, the disposition should be regarded as valid until the minor wishes to set it aside.[41]

(iv) The Role of Minority in Restitutionary Claims

(1) There Must Be a Total Failure of Basis

Where a minor is not bound by a transaction by reason of his or incapacity, it follows that the minor will be able to obtain restitution of benefits transferred under the transaction as long as one of the recognized grounds of restitution is applicable. Whether the fact that the claimant was a minor can operate as a ground of restitution in its own right is a matter of some controversy. The general approach in English law is that restitution will not lie simply on the ground of minority, since it must also be shown that the basis for the transfer of the benefit has totally failed.[42] This is illustrated by *Steinberg v Scala (Leeds) Ltd*,[43] where the claimant had repudiated a contract for the purchase of shares whilst she was still a minor and then sought to recover the purchase price from the company. Her restitutionary action failed on the ground that there had not been a total failure of basis, because she had obtained the very thing for which she had bargained, namely a shareholding in the company. This was a valuable benefit, which entitled her to receive a dividend and to attend general meetings of the shareholders. Similarly, in *Pearce v Brain*[44] the claimant, who was a minor, exchanged his motorbike for the defendant's car. After the claimant had driven the car for 70 miles it broke down. The claimant then sought to recover the bike or its value, but his action failed on the ground that there had not been a total failure of basis since he had obtained some benefit from the transaction, namely the use of the car for a few days.

(2) The Relevance of Minority

Where the conditions for establishing total failure of basis have been satisfied this will constitute the ground of restitution on which the claimant bases his or her restitutionary claim. It would seem, therefore, that the fact that the claimant was a minor would be irrelevant. This is not, however, the case, since pleading minority in conjunction with total failure of basis does have one important advantage to the claimant. This is because, where the claimant is an adult who entered into a contract of a continuous nature and who wishes to obtain restitution on the ground of total failure of basis, it is first necessary for the claimant to repudiate the contract, for example by showing that the defendant had breached it. This is likely only to be possible where the defendant's breach was repudiatory, which it might not be possible to establish.[45] Where, however, the claimant is a minor who entered into a contract of a continuous nature, he or she can rescind the contract simply by virtue of the fact that he or she was a minor and without needing to

---

[41] *Zouch de Abbott v Parsons* (1765) 3 Burr 1794, 1806; 97 ER 1103, 1110.
[42] See Chapter 13 for analysis of total failure of basis as a ground of restitution.
[43] [1923] 2 Ch 452. See also *Corpe v Overton* (1833) 10 Bing 252, 131 ER 901.
[44] [1929] 2 KB 310.   [45] See p 314, above.

establish a repudiatory breach. It is then only necessary to show that there has been a total failure of basis before the claimant can obtain restitution.

(3) Should it Be Necessary to Establish that the Basis Has Totally Failed?

Is it really appropriate to ground restitution on total failure of basis in those cases where the claimant was a minor at the time of contracting with the defendant? Careful analysis of the cases which recognize the requirement that there must have been a total failure of basis suggests that they are concerned with the distinct, but apparently similar, principle that restitution should be denied to the claimant if he or she is unable to make full counter-restitution to the defendant. If this is correct, it follows that the appropriate ground of restitution in these cases should be that the claimant lacked capacity to enter into the contract with the defendant, but restitution should be denied to the claimant if he or she is unable to restore all the benefits which were received from the defendant.[46] This is a much more satisfactory position.

That the claimant's minority should operate as a ground of restitution in its own right is perfectly acceptable. The reason why contracts made with minors are usually unenforceable against them presumably derives from a desire to protect minors from the consequences of entering into foolish transactions and such protection will only be partial if restitution is denied.[47] There is no reason why the policy which makes the contract unenforceable against the minor should not be followed through to its logical conclusion to ensure that the benefits which were transferred under the contract should be restored to the minor, subject to the minor paying for any benefits which he or she had obtained under the contract. But, despite this, the law considers that the position of the defendant should not be ignored and, if the claimant is unable to restore benefits which had been received from the defendant, it is only just that restitution should be denied. Support for this approach can be found in the decision of the Divisional Court in *Valentini v Canali*,[48] where the claimant, who was a minor, leased a house from the defendant. The claimant agreed to pay £102 for the use of the defendant's furniture and paid £68 on account. After using the house and the furniture for a few months the claimant sought to recover the £68. His action failed because, as Lord Coleridge CJ said:[49]

> When an infant has paid for something and has consumed or used it, it is contrary to natural justice that he should recover back the money which he has paid. Here the infant plaintiff who claimed to recover back the money which he had paid to the defendant had the use of a quantity of furniture for some months. He could not give back his benefit or replace the defendant in the position in which he was before the contract.

Lord Coleridge did not suggest that restitution should be denied because there had been no total failure of basis. Rather, restitution was denied because, as he thought, the claimant could not make counter-restitution to the defendant.

It is much more consistent with the fundamental principles of the law of restitution that the restitutionary claim should be defeated because the claimant cannot make counter-restitution to the defendant, than it is to say that the claim should fail because the claimant cannot rely on the ground of total failure of basis. Similarly, where the claimant needs to

---

[46] C Mitchell, P Mitchell, and S Watterson (eds), *Goff and Jones: The Law of Unjust Enrichment* (8th edn, London: Sweet and Maxwell, 2010), 645. See also AS Burrows, *The Law of Restitution* (3rd edn, Oxford: Oxford University Press, 2011), 313 and GH Treitel, 'The Infants' Relief Act 1874' (1957) 73 LQR 194.

[47] As Lord Denning MR said in *Chaplin v Leslie Frewin (Publishers) Ltd* [1966] Ch 71: 'If the infant is to be protected, the law must be able to intervene as well after as before the disposition is made.'

[48] (1889) 24 QBD 166.   [49] Ibid, 167.

rescind a contract it has long been accepted that rescission will be barred if the claimant cannot make counter-restitution to the defendant. The importance of this analysis is that the more liberal interpretation of the bar that counter-restitution is impossible should be applicable to restitutionary claims founded on the claimant's minority.[50] It follows that the restitutionary claim should not be barred simply because the claimant cannot make exact counter-restitution to the defendant. It should be sufficient that the claimant can restore the *value* of any benefit received to the defendant without necessarily having to restore the actual benefit received. This means that in a case such as *Valentini v Canali*, the claimant would have been able to rescind the contract and recover the money paid to the defendant, if he had made counter-restitution by paying the defendant the reasonable price for hiring the furniture.

(4) Exploitation

Where a minor has transferred a benefit to the defendant he or she may be able to obtain restitution of the benefit without relying on incapacity, but instead by establishing that one of the grounds of restitution which are founded on the principle of exploitation can be established.[51] For example, the minor might be able to show that the defendant had unduly influenced him or her or that the defendant had acted unconscionably in entering into the transaction with him or her.

(E) INCAPACITY OF PUBLIC AUTHORITIES

Where a public authority transfers a benefit to the defendant in circumstances where the authority lacked the capacity to do so, the incapacity may operate as a ground of restitution to enable the benefit to be recovered.[52] This is illustrated by *Auckland Harbour Board v R*[53] where the Privy Council held that money which had been paid out of the consolidated fund[54] by the Minister of Railways was recoverable since he was only authorized to make the payment if the recipient of the money had granted a lease, and the money had been paid even though no lease had been granted. Consequently the payment was unauthorized by Parliament and so it was *ultra vires*. Restitution is justified on the ground of the public authority's incapacity for reasons of policy, namely that it protects the public from the consequences of public authorities misusing public funds.[55]

Whilst the ground of restitution is clear and the award of restitution is justifiable, the judgment of Viscount Haldane in *Auckland Harbour Board* has caused some confusion. He said that payment 'from the consolidated fund made without Parliamentary authority is simply illegal and *ultra vires*, and may be recovered by the Government if it can, as here, be traced'.[56] Does this reference to tracing mean that the State's restitutionary claim is founded on the vindication of the public authority's proprietary rights, with the consequence that restitution will only be obtained if, and to the extent that, the public authority can identify property in the hands of the defendant in which the claimant has retained a proprietary interest? This would be unnecessarily restrictive and the better view is that

---

[50] See p 26, above.   [51] See Chapter 11.

[52] The question of whether restitutionary relief is available against a public authority which lacked the capacity to receive a benefit is considered in Chapter 15.

[53] [1924] AC 318. See also *Commonwealth of Australia v Burns* [1971] VR 825 and *Sandvik Australia Pty Ltd v Commonwealth of Australia* (1989) 89 ALR 213.

[54] This is the central fund into which taxes are paid: *Auckland Harbour Board v R* [1924] AC 318, 326.

[55] See *Commonwealth of Australia v Burns* [1971] VR 825, 827 (Newton J).

[56] *Auckland Harbour Board v R* [1924] AC 318, 327.

Viscount Haldane was not using 'traced' in any technical sense. Rather, what he appears to have meant is simply that it is possible to show that money from the consolidated fund had been received by the defendant. In other words, 'traced' is simply being used in the sense of the money being received 'at the expense of' the State.[57]

That a public authority's incapacity may constitute a ground of restitution in its own right has been something which has received little judicial attention. In a number of cases the public authority has based its claim on other grounds of restitution, such as mistake, when incapacity would have served just as well and might even have been easier to establish.[58] This is particularly true of some of the interest rate swap cases, where a local authority sought to obtain restitution of money paid to financial institutions under transactions which the authority did not have capacity to enter into.[59] In these cases the local authority appears to have relied on the ground of absence of basis, as recognized by Hobhouse J in *Westdeutsche Landesbank Girozentrale v Islington LBC*,[60] when it could have simply relied on the ground that the claimant lacked capacity to enter into the transaction. At the very least, by basing the restitutionary claim on the claimant's incapacity, it is easier to justify the award of restitutionary relief because of the policy of ensuring that the interests of those who provided the funds in the first place are protected against the misuse of the funds.

Statutory provision may be made for restitution of money unlawfully paid by a public authority. If so, that provision will typically exclude the common law claim. So, for example, in *R (on the application of Child Poverty Action Group) v Secretary of State for Work and Pensions*[61] the statutory scheme for the recovery of overpaid social security benefits[62] excluded the common law claim to restitution. This statutory scheme only applies where a payment of such a benefit had been made as the result of an erroneous award arising from misrepresentation or non-disclosure by the recipient and does not extend to the recovery of payments made as a result of a mistake in assessing the award which would be covered the common law claim, presumably grounded on mistake.

---

[57] This was the interpretation which Newton J preferred in *Commonwealth of Australia v Burns* [1971] VR 825, 828.

[58] Recognition of the ground of mistake of law provides another route for public authorities to obtain restitution. See p 162, above.

[59] See, in particular, *South Tyneside Metropolitan Borough Council v Svenska International plc* [1995] 1 All ER 545.

[60] [1994] 4 All ER 890. See p 373, above.   [61] [2010] UKSC 54, [2011] 2 AC 15.

[62] Social Security Administration Act 1992, s 71.

15

RESTITUTION FROM PUBLIC AUTHORITIES

1. GENERAL ISSUES

(A) PRAGMATISM AND POLICY

Restitutionary claims against[1] public authorities raise distinct issues of policy and principle in the law of restitution. The viability of such claims is a matter of great public importance, since some of these claims can involve very large sums of money, especially those which involve overpaid taxes. For example, in one case[2] the claim was to recover £205 million of overpaid tax plus interest payments of £1.25 billion, and in another the amount due to claimants amounted to over £5 billion.[3] It is, consequently, a matter of importance to the public, either as the beneficiaries of public authority services or the victims of overpayments to public authorities, to determine when and why such overpayments can be recovered.

There are two contradictory questions of public policy which need to be taken into account when determining the ambit of restitutionary claims against public authorities.

(i) Constitutional Considerations

(1) Domestic Considerations

There is a constitutional dimension to restitutionary claims brought against public authorities which derives from the principle that, where a public authority is not entitled to the money which it has received, that money should be repaid to the citizen from whom it was unlawfully taken. The justification for this principle is that, since the power of the public authority to demand payment from the citizen can only exist under the law, if the demand was made unlawfully the public authority has no right to retain what it received and must make restitution. That public authorities can only demand payment where they are lawfully authorized to do so is a fundamental principle of English law which is enshrined in Article 4 of the Bill of Rights 1689. This states that 'levying money for or to the use of the Crown, by pretence of prerogative, without grant of Parliament, for longer time, or in other manner than the same is or shall be granted is illegal'.

This principle continues to be of profound importance today. The effect of it is that public authorities can only demand payment where they have statutory authority to do so. This was recognized in *Attorney-General v Wilts United Dairies Ltd*,[4] where it was held to be illegal for the Food Controller, a public authority, to require payment of a sum of

---

[1] Restitutionary claims brought *by* public authorities are considered at p 387, above.
[2] *Littlewoods Retail Ltd v HMRC* [2015] EWCA 515.
[3] *Test claimants in the FII Group Litigation v HMRC* [2012] UKSC 19, [2012] AC 337.
[4] (1921) 37 TLR 884 (CA), (1922) 127 LT 822 (HL).

money as a condition for the grant of a licence to purchase milk. This was because there was no express authority from Parliament to demand the money, which was consequently held to be contrary to the Bill of Rights. As Atkin LJ said:[5] 'If an officer of the Executive seeks to justify a charge upon the subject made for the use of the Crown (which includes all the purposes of the public revenue), he must show, in clear terms, that Parliament has authorised the particular charge.'

The logical consequence of this constitutional principle is that, where the public authority receives payment as a result of an unlawful demand, it should make restitution to the payer.[6] That the payer should be entitled to restitution as of right seems even more obvious in the light of the fact that, where the Crown pays money out of the consolidated fund without statutory authority, it is able to recover it by virtue of its incapacity to make the payment in the first place.[7]

(2) EU Considerations

Many of the recent cases concerning restitutionary claims from public authorities involve claims against the Revenue for overpaid taxes, where the payments of the taxes had been held by the Court of Justice of the European Union (CJEU; previously ECJ) to be unlawfully received. As a consequence, the CJEU requires the national courts to ensure that an appropriate remedy is awarded. Crucially, EU law recognizes the fundamental principle that a public authority which has received tax unlawfully is liable to the taxpayer, whose rights against the public authority crystallize once payment has been made and the charge has been declared illegal.

Whilst the existence of this fundamental principle of EU law is clear, the way the claim and remedy is formulated is a matter for the national court to determine. But this formulation must be compatible with principles of EU law as well. Two principles are particularly significant.[8] The first is the principle of effectiveness, which means that the national law's claims and remedies are effective to reverse the economic consequences of breaching EU law. The other is the principle of equivalence, which means that the rights of the taxpayer to recover taxes which are unlawfully received by virtue of EU law must be equivalent to the rights of a taxpayer to recover payments from public authorities which are unlawful by national law. These dual principles have proved to be highly significant in the judicial assessment of claims for restitution of overpaid tax.

The CJEU is only concerned that the claims and remedies relating to taxes overpaid in breach of EU law are effective and equivalent. It is not concerned with how the claims and remedies are characterized. It follows that the remedy awarded need not be restitutionary. It could be a compensatory remedy, for the loss suffered by the taxpayer in paying tax which is not due, with the claim grounded on the tort of breach of statutory duty.[9] Such claims have not been pursued, however, as regards recovery of overpaid tax, presumably because, in order to establish such a claim, it is necessary to show that the breach of EU law involves a 'grave and manifest' disregard of the limits of the State's discretion,[10] and this will be difficult to establish in respect of claims for restitution of overpaid tax.[11]

---

[5] Ibid, 886.   [6] *Woolwich Equitable Building Society v IRC* [1993] AC 70, 172 (Lord Goff).

[7] *Auckland Harbour Board v R* [1924] AC 318. See p 387, above.

[8] See M Schlote, 'The Principle of Effectiveness and Restitution of Overpaid Tax' in S Elliott, B Häcker, and C Mitchell (eds), *Restitution of Overpaid Tax* (Oxford: Hart Publishing, 2013), ch 10. The principles of legal certainty and legitimate expectation have proved significant as well. See p 409, below.

[9] As recognized in *R v Secretary of State for Transport, ex parte Factortame* [2000] 1 AC 524.

[10] Joined Cases C-46/93 and C-48/93 *Brasserie du Pêcheur SA v Federal Republic of Germany* [1996] QB 404.

[11] This condition was held not to be satisfied by the trial judge and the Court of Appeal in the *FII* litigation. See *Test claimants in the FII Group Litigation v HMRC* [2012] UKSC 19, [2012] AC 337, [206] (Lord Sumption).

Consequently, the focus in the English courts has been on establishing a claim for a restitutionary remedy founded on the public authority's unjust enrichment. This is typically called a *San Giorgio* claim,[12] regardless of what the relevant ground of restitution is, although it is not called this in European jurisprudence. How such a claim and consequent remedies should be formulated compatibly with the principles of effectiveness and equivalence has proved to be a matter of particular controversy. Crucially, if the unjust enrichment principle as interpreted in national law does not provide an effective or equivalent remedy the claim and the remedy need to be changed to ensure that they are effective and equivalent.

In an important decision in *Test Claimants in the FII Group Litigation v HMRC (No 2)*,[13] Henderson J characterized the *San Giorgio* claim as being hybrid, as he considered it to embrace restitutionary and compensatory responses such that he wished to call it 'restitutionary compensation'. He acknowledged that it was primarily restitutionary in effect,[14] but that it might have compensatory implications since relief might be measured with respect to the loss occasioned by the claimant as a result of paying tax which was not due, most notably when awarding interest which should indemnify the claimant for his or her loss of use of the money paid to the Revenue. Whilst the language of 'restitutionary compensation' appears inappropriate to the English lawyer's sense of elegant classification, it is at least accurate in its description of the functions of the relief required by EU law.[15]

(ii) Implications for the General Community

Even though the claimant who has paid money to a public authority which was not lawfully due to it, appears to have an absolute right to restitution by virtue of national and EU constitutional considerations, this is complicated by a different consideration of public policy, deriving from the fact that such claims are likely to involve large sums of money, whether because one or two claimants seek to recover large sums or because there are numerous claims for relatively minor sums. Where a public authority has received such sums in circumstances where it can be shown to be unjustly enriched, awarding restitutionary remedies may seriously jeopardize the availability of public funds with consequent deleterious effects on the community.[16] It follows, according to this second public policy argument, that restitutionary claims against public authorities should be deterred for the benefit of the public generally.

(iii) Balancing Principle and Pragmatism

Consequently, the question of whether a restitutionary claim can successfully be brought against a public authority involves a clash of principle and pragmatism. For constitutional principle demands that a public authority which has unlawfully received money should return it, but pragmatism suggests caution, to preserve the security of the public authority's receipts for the greater public good. These arguments are essentially incompatible but, as will be seen, some form of compromise can be reached by accepting the right of the payer to bring a restitutionary claim but ensuring that the public authority has a number of special defences, or differently interpreted general defences, to ensure that there is no

---

[12] Following *Amministrazione delle Finanze dello Stato v SpA San Giorgio* [1983] ECR 3595.
[13] [2014] EWHC 4302 (Ch).   [14] Ibid, [261].
[15] The hybrid nature of the relief is analogous to that awarded by reference to the hypothetical bargain measure as a response to wrongdoing. See Chapter 16.
[16] *Glasgow Corporation v Lord Advocate* 1959 SC 203, 230 (Lord Clyde).

unnecessary disruption of public finances which could have profoundly detrimental effects on the effectiveness of the public authority.[17]

(B) DEFINING PUBLIC AUTHORITIES

'Public authorities' may be defined widely to include the emanations of the State in whatever form. Consequently, a 'public authority' can include central and local authorities, Universities, 'Non-Departmental Public Bodies',[18] and even nationalized industries. Some of the issues raised in this chapter will also be applicable to privatized public utilities. Although these utilities are in form no different from any other company which is motivated by the need to make profit, so that notions of jeopardizing their finances should only be of a secondary concern, public utility companies maintain a powerful, sometimes near monopolistic, position so that they can be considered to straddle the public and private law divide. This raises important questions as to whether any different considerations should apply in respect of restitutionary claims brought against such companies.

Most of the cases concerning restitution from public authorities involve payment of tax to the Revenue, known as Her Majesty's Revenue and Customs (HMRC). The defendants in these cases are the Commissioners for Her Majesty's Revenue and Customs. This is a non-ministerial department linked to the Treasury, which is part of the executive arm of government.[19] Consequently, although the Commissioners are nominally the defendants in the restitution claims, since they are embedded within the executive arm of the Government, and the tax monies raised are paid into the Consolidated Fund and spent by the Government, it is appropriate to treat the defendant as effectively being the Government. Consequently, in this chapter 'the Revenue' and 'the Government' will be used interchangeably to identify the defendant.

(C) ESTABLISHING UNJUST ENRICHMENT

The claim for recovery of payments made to public authorities which were not lawfully due is formulated in English law as falling within the law of restitution grounded on the unjust enrichment principle.[20] The restitutionary claim need not have been formulated in that way, however. In Canada, for example, the claim for restitution is treated as part of public law and not the private law of restitution.[21] Even in England, however, the unjust enrichment claim has significant public law connotations, which affect its interpretation, although the claim clearly falls within the private law structure of the unjust enrichment claim.[22] It follows that the elements of the unjust enrichment formula need to be established.[23]

---

[17] See p 408, below.

[18] *Bloomsbury International Ltd v Sea Fish Industry Authority* [2009] EWHC 1721 (QB), [2010] 1 CMLR 12.

[19] *Test Claimants in the FII Group Litigation v HMRC* [2014] EWHC 4302 (Ch), [351] (Henderson J).

[20] *Deutsche Morgan Grenfell v IRC* [2006] UKHL 49, [2007] 1 AC 558.

[21] *Kingstreet Investment Ltd v New Brunswick (Department of Finance)* 2007 SCC 1, [33] and [40] (Bastarache J). Private law claims against public authorities founded on unjust enrichment are recognized in Canada where the claim is for restitution of payments other than tax: *Alberta v Elder Advocates of Alberta Society* [2011] 2 SCR 261.

[22] See R Williams, *Unjust Enrichment and Public Law: A Comparative Study of England, France and the EU* (Oxford: Hart Publishing, 2010). See further p 400, below.   [23] See p 9, above.

Invariably the restitutionary claim will be brought against a public authority where the authority has received money which it was not authorized to receive.[24] These are called *ultra vires* payments. Where the public authority has received money directly from the claimant, there is no doubt that the authority has been enriched and this was at the claimant's expense. There have been cases, however, where the defendant received the enrichment from a third party, in which case it may still be possible to establish that the enrichment was received at the claimant's expense, but only in circumstances where in economic or commercial reality the expense was so received.[25]

The key question, therefore, will be whether a ground of restitution can be identified. In considering this it is important to remember that a claim in unjust enrichment will fail if there was a legitimate legal basis for the defendant's receipt of an enrichment.[26] That is why it is an essential feature of a claim for restitution against a public authority that the payment received by the public authority was *ultra vires*, for then there will be no legitimate legal basis for the public authority's receipt. A payment may be regarded as *ultra vires* the public authority for three reasons.

(i) Invalid Statutory Provisions

Where money is paid to a public authority pursuant to an invalid statutory provision it follows that the money is not lawfully due to the public authority and so it will be characterized as *ultra vires*.[27]

(ii) Unauthorized Transactions

Payment to a public authority will also be characterized as *ultra vires* if it is made pursuant to a transaction in which the public authority was not authorized to participate. The best illustration of this type of *ultra vires* payment arises from the interest rate swaps litigation, where financial institutions paid money to local authorities pursuant to interest rate swaps transactions which the House of Lords held they lacked the capacity to enter.[28] In these cases, however, the fact that the defendant was a public authority did not prove significant to the claim for restitution, even though the reason why the transactions were void was because the financial institutions had made the contracts with public authorities, who lacked the capacity to speculate with taxpayers' money by entering into such transactions.

(iii) Mistake

The final reason why the receipt of a payment might be considered to be *ultra vires* the public authority is because of a mistake which meant that, even though the public authority was authorized to demand payment of money in principle, the claimant was not liable to pay the money, either at all or at least not the full amount which was received. The mistake might be factual as regards the assessment of the sum which was due or a mistake of law arising from the misinterpretation of a particular regulation which was valid but was never intended to apply to such a payer.

In all of these situations, even though the initial payment to the public authority may have been *ultra vires*, it is possible for Parliament to pass retrospective legislation to

---

[24] The claim could involve non-money benefits, but then the test of enrichment will need to be considered carefully. See Chapter 4.

[25] *Investment Trust Companies (in liquidation) v HMRC* [2015] EWCA Civ 82. See p 107, above. See generally C Mitchell, 'Restitutionary Claims by Indirect Taxpayers' in S Elliott, B Häcker, and C Mitchell (eds), *Restitution of Overpaid Tax* (Oxford: Hart Publishing, 2013), ch 6.

[26] See Chapter 7.   [27] *Woolwich Equitable Building Society v IRC* [1993] AC 70.

[28] *Hazell v Hammersmith and Fulham LBC* [1992] 2 AC 1.

validate the payment. Such legislation does not contravene the European Convention on Human Rights,[29] but, at least if the receipt is *ultra vires* because of infringement of EU law, the legislation must comply with the principles of effectiveness and equivalence.[30]

The key question which needs to be considered in this chapter is whether the person who made an *ultra vires* payment to the public authority can sue the authority for restitution and, if so, what the relevant ground of restitution is. Whilst this analysis will concentrate on restitutionary claims at common law, it will also be necessary to examine certain specific statutory provisions which recognize significant rights to obtain restitution of *ultra vires* payments from public authorities, which will prevail over a claim at common law.

2. THE GROUNDS OF RESTITUTION

There are a variety of grounds of restitution which are available to recover *ultra vires* receipts from public authorities. Following the decision of the House of Lords in *Deutsche Morgan Grenfell v IRC*[31] none of these grounds of restitution are exclusive, so the claimant can choose to base his or her claim on the most relevant ground.

(A) MISTAKE

With the abolition of the mistake of law bar by the House of Lords in *Kleinwort Benson Ltd v Lincoln CC*,[32] there is much greater scope for the claimant who has made an *ultra vires* payment to a public authority to obtain restitution by reference to mistake. This is because many cases involving *ultra vires* payments, but certainly not all,[33] arise because the claimant was mistaken as to the law, since typically the claimant incorrectly believed that he or she was liable to pay the money to the public authority.[34]

The key advantage of founding a claim on mistake is that this will extend the limitation period. Section 32(1)(c) of the Limitation Act 1980[35] states that, where an action involves relief from the consequences of a mistake, time does not begin to run until the claimant discovered the mistake or could with reasonable diligence have discovered it. Although the application of this extended limitation period has been significantly curtailed by legislation,[36] where it applies it constitutes a very strong reason for a claimant to frame the claim as grounded on mistake, although this does leave the defendant with the option to plead the defence of change of position.[37]

(B) DURESS

Where a defendant obtains a benefit as a result of an unlawful demand the ground of duress might be engaged.[38] Since the restitutionary claim in respect of *ultra vires* payments to a public authority is by definition unlawful, the claimant will be able to obtain restitution on the ground of duress of the person if the payment was caused by the public

---

[29] *National Provincial Building Society v UK* [1997] STC 1466.   [30] See p 390, above.
[31] [2006] UKHL 49, [2007] 1 AC 558.   [32] [1999] 2 AC 349. See Chapter 9.
[33] See *Woolwich Equitable Building Society v IRC* [1993] AC 70 where the claimant had not been made a mistake, either of fact or of law. See p 398, below.
[34] See *Deutsche Morgan Grenfell v IRC* [2006] UKHL 49, [2007] 1 AC 558.
[35] See further p 737, below.   [36] See p 409, below.   [37] See p 409, below.
[38] See Chapter 10. See generally N Enonchong, 'Restitution from Public Authorities: Any Room for Duress?' in S Elliott, B Häcker, and C Mitchell (eds), *Restitution of Overpaid Tax* (Oxford: Hart Publishing, 2013), ch 4.

authority threatening to restrain, or actually restraining, the claimant, or duress of goods if the claimant threatened to seize, or actually seized, the claimant's property. Alternatively, restitution could be grounded on economic duress if the defendant threatened to breach a contract, commit a tort, or do some other unlawful act. So, for example, the claimant might be able to recover money from the defendant on the ground of economic duress if the claimant paid the money as the result of an unlawful threat by the defendant to withdraw a licence if the money was not paid.[39] But the most likely form of duress to be applicable in respect of restitutionary claims against public authorities is duress of goods, since often the authority will have the sanction to seize the claimant's goods if the money demanded is not paid.[40] Such a threat is unlawful because the authority is not authorized to seize goods in respect of a debt which is not lawfully due. Where, however, the authority threatens to institute legal proceedings to recover the money if it is not paid, this does not constitute duress[41] because the claimant was given an opportunity to dispute the legality of the demand in legal proceedings. Consequently, payment in response to such a threat is characterized as voluntary and is not recoverable on the ground of duress.

(C) EXTORTION BY COLOUR OF OFFICE (*COLORE OFFICII*)

(i) Defining Extortion by Colour of Office

Extortion by colour of office, also known as *colore officii*,[42] is a ground of restitution which is founded on the general principle of compulsion, like duress.[43] Extortion by colour of office is confined in its operation to restitution from public authorities or public officials. It arises where 'a public officer demands and is paid money he is not entitled to, or more than he is entitled to, for the performance of his public duty'.[44]

It is unclear to what extent this ground of restitution is different from that of duress. The preferable view is that duress will only be established where the claimant can show that the public authority had obtained payment as the result of an unlawful threat. For the purposes of extortion by colour of office it is not necessary for the claimant to prove that the public authority had actually threatened the claimant in any way. The necessary compulsion can be implied where a public authority or official has demanded payment from the claimant, because of the peculiar powers of enforcement, and even punishment, which are available to such bodies or people if the payment is not made. For example, if the authority demands excessive payment for a licence, the claimant may have no choice but to pay the money since the licence is vital to his or her business. The public authority does not need to threaten that it will not issue the licence if the money is not paid, because it is implicit in the demand that if the money is not forthcoming the claimant will not get the licence. The refusal of the authority to issue the licence would in fact be unlawful because the money demanded was not lawfully due to the public authority. This was recognized by Lord Denning in *Lloyds Bank Ltd v Bundy*,[45] who said that these cases arise

[39] This would also be covered by the ground of restitution known as 'extortion by colour of office'. See below.

[40] See *Maskell v Horner* [1915] 3 KB 106. Enonchong suggests in 'Restitution from Public Authorities', 90, that this may also be relevant to claims for restitution of payments made to utilities which have been privatized.

[41] *William Whiteley Ltd v R* (1910) 101 LT 741.

[42] '*Colore officii*' was described by Glidewell LJ in *Woolwich Equitable Building Society v IRC* [1993] AC 70, 80 as an 'archaic phrase [which] is at best vague and at worst almost meaningless at the present day'.

[43] See Chapter 10.   [44] *Mason v New South Wales* (1959) 102 CLR 108, 140.

[45] [1975] QB 326, 337.

where the public official is 'in a strong bargaining position by virtue of his official position or public profession'. It follows that this ground of restitution can be considered to be founded on both the principles of compulsion and exploitation. But the best explanation of extortion by colour of office is that it is founded on compulsion. This was recognized by Isaacs J in *Sargood Brothers v The Commonwealth*:[46]

> The right to recovery after a demand *colore officii* rests upon the assumption that the position occupied by the defendant creates virtual compulsion, where it conveys to the person paying the knowledge or belief that he has no means of escape from payments strictly so called if he wishes to avert injury to or deprivation of some right to which he is entitled without such payment.

(ii) Identifying Extortion by Colour of Office

One of the best illustrations of the application of this ground of restitution is *Morgan v Palmer*,[47] where publicans in a town who needed licences to sell liquor were required to pay four shillings to the mayor. This continued for over 65 years. It was held that such payments were *ultra vires* and the claimant was allowed to recover what he had paid because the parties were not on equal terms. This suggests that the court presumed compulsion simply because the mayor was in a stronger bargaining position.

But this ground of restitution and the principle of implicit compulsion have not always been recognized. For example, in *Twyford v Manchester Corporation*[48] a monumental mason was charged fees in respect of the work he had done in a cemetery owned by the Manchester Corporation when the Corporation had no right to make such charges. The restitutionary claim failed because the defendant had never threatened that the claimant would be excluded if he did not pay the sums demanded. This means that the claimant could not have established duress, but there was surely scope for identifying an implied threat to exclude the claimant arising from the fact that the defendant was in a much stronger position, possessing as it did powers to exclude the claimant if the money was not paid.

(iii) Is Extortion by Colour of Office Still a Significant Ground of Restitution?

Although the ground of extortion by colour of office has proved to be of some significance in respect of restitutionary claims brought against public authorities, it is probably a ground of restitution which no longer matters following the recognition by the House of Lords in *Woolwich Equitable Building Society v IRC*[49] of a new ground of restitution of relevance to restitutionary claims against public authorities, which does all of the work of extortion by colour of office and more.[50] The better view, therefore, is that, whilst extortion by colour of office is of historical interest and laid important foundations for the recognition of the new ground of restitution in *Woolwich*, it is a ground which is no longer of any significance to the modern law of restitution.

---

[46] (1910) 11 CLR 258, 277.

[47] (1824) 2 B and C 729, 107 ER 584. See also *Dew v Parsons* (1819) 2 B and Ald 562, 106 ER 471 and *Brocklebank Ltd v R* [1925] 1 KB 52.

[48] [1946] Ch 236. See also *Slater v Burnley Corporation* (1888) 59 LT 636.

[49] [1993] AC 70. See p 398, below.

[50] Cf Enonchong, 'Restitution from Public Authorities', 85, who considers that there is still a role for *colore officii* where payments other than tax are made to a public authority. If *Woolwich* is only applicable to restitution of overpaid taxes, then there is a continued role for *colore officii* in respect of other *ultra vires* payments, but there is no reason why the *Woolwich* principle should be so confined.

(D) TOTAL FAILURE OF BASIS

Usually failure of basis will only be applicable as a ground of restitution where the basis for the claimant's payment has totally failed.[51] This ground will consequently generally be of no relevance in the context of recovery of *ultra vires* payments, since often the basis on which the claimant made the payment will not have failed totally. This is illustrated by *Westdeutsche Landesbank Girozentrale v Islington LBC*[52] where the claimant bank had paid the defendant local authority pursuant to a number of *ultra vires* interest rate swaps transactions. As regards most of these transactions the claimant could not show that the basis for its payments had totally failed because it had also received money from the defendant. Restitutionary relief was, however, awarded in respect of two of the transactions on the ground of total failure of basis, since the claimant had not received any money from the defendant in respect of these transactions. Depending on how the apportionment principle is applied, there might be scope to apportion the benefits which the claimant has received in return.[53]

(E) ABSENCE OF BASIS

Absence of basis has been the ground of restitution which has been of particular importance in the context of restitution from public authorities, most notably the interest rate swaps cases. Indeed, it was this ground which was relied on by both the trial judge and the Court of Appeal to justify the award of restitution at common law in *Westdeutsche Landesbank Girozentrale v Islington LBC*.[54] It was held that there was no basis for the claimant's payments to the defendant because the swaps transactions were null and void. Since *ultra vires* payments to public authorities are void payments, it follows that absence of basis is a potentially important ground of restitution in respect of the recovery of such payments from public authorities.[55] It might be considered that absence of basis should only be applicable where the claimant has paid money to a public authority pursuant to a contract, where the claimant expects to receive a benefit in return for the payment, and not where the claimant pays tax or duty to the public authority. But there is no reason why absence of basis cannot be applicable to the recovery of such *ultra vires* payments. This is because the claimant will have paid the authority in the belief that the payment will have discharged his or her liability to the authority. This is the anticipated basis for the payment. But if the money was not due, it follows that there is no liability which can be discharged and so the basis for the payment will have failed by operation of law. Such an argument was recognized by Lord Mansfield in *Campbell v Hall*,[56] where the claimant recovered duties which he had paid on sugar exported from Grenada on the ground that the duty had been unlawfully demanded because it had never been authorized by Parliament. The duty was recoverable specifically because it had been paid without consideration being provided.[57]

---

[51] See Chapter 13.   [52] [1994] 4 All ER 890 (Hobhouse J); [1994] 1 WLR 938 (CA).

[53] See p 321, above.

[54] [1994] 4 All ER 890 (Hobhouse J); [1994] 1 WLR 938 (CA). See Chapter 13.

[55] C Webb, 'Reasons for Restitution' in S Elliott, B Häcker, and C Mitchell (eds), *Restitution of Overpaid Tax* (Oxford: Hart Publishing, 2013), 108, considers this to be a preferable explanation of why restitution should be granted against public authorities, because it is a private law ground of restitution.

[56] (1774) 1 Cowp 204, 98 ER 1245.

[57] See also *Dew v Parsons* (1819) B and Ald 562, 106 ER 471 and *Queens of the River Steamship Co Ltd v The Conservators of the River Thames* (1899) 15 TLR 474.

(F) ULTRA VIRES RECEIPT

(i) The Background

Restitutionary claims against public authorities have succeeded in other cases where none of the established grounds of restitution appear to have been applicable. The success of the restitutionary claim in these cases can only be justified by virtue of an independent ground of restitution which is peculiar to restitutionary claims against public authorities.[58] Other cases have rejected a general right of restitution founded on the receipt of an *ultra vires* payment, primarily because of the fear that allowing restitution for this reason would unsettle public finances.[59] Most importantly, such a general ground of restitution was rejected by the Supreme Court of Canada in *Air Canada v British Columbia*,[60] where a majority of the court rejected the taxpayer's claim to recover *ultra vires* payments for three main reasons:

(1) if the restitutionary claim was allowed to succeed the State would need to recover the money from a new generation of taxpayers who had not benefited from the provision of State services funded by the tax;

(2) arranging for the repayment to the original taxpayers and issuing new tax demands would be economically inefficient; and

(3) repaying tax to the original taxpayers would disrupt public finances.

Whilst all of these factors are possible dangers arising from restitutionary claims being brought against public authorities, they should not prevent the acceptance of a general right of recovery and should be dealt with by developing specific defences for the protection of public authorities where the greater public good requires such protection. This was the approach which was advocated by Wilson J in a powerful dissenting judgment, where she argued that there should be a general right of recovery where money is paid to public authorities which is not lawfully due.[61]

(ii) The *Woolwich* Ground

A new ground of restitution, available against public authorities for the recovery of payments made pursuant to an *ultra vires* demand, was recognized by the House of Lords in *Woolwich Equitable Building Society v IRC*.[62] The Inland Revenue had assessed the tax liability of the Woolwich Building Society by reference to regulations made under the Finance Act 1985; regulations which were subsequently held by the House of Lords to be *ultra vires* and so rendered the tax demand invalid.[63] The effect of this was that the claimant paid nearly £57 million more tax to the Revenue than was actually due. The Revenue repaid this money to the claimant with interest, but it refused to pay interest in respect of the period when it first received the payment until the decision of the trial judge

---

[58] See, for example, *Steele v Williams* (1853) 8 Exch 625, 155 ER 1502; *South of Scotland Electricity Board v British Oxygen Co Ltd* [1959] 1 WLR 587.

[59] See, for example, *National Pari-Mutuel Association Ltd v R* (1930) 47 TLR 110.

[60] (1989) 58 DLR 161.

[61] See also WR Cornish, 'Colour of Office: Restitutionary Redress against Public Authority' [1987] JMCL 41 and PBH Birks, 'Restitution from the Executive: A Tercentenary Footnote to the Bill of Rights' in P Finn (ed), *Essays on Restitution* (Sydney: The Law Book Co, 1990), ch 6.

[62] [1993] AC 70. For commentary see E McKendrick, 'Restitution of Unlawfully Demanded Taxes' [1993] LMCLQ 88; J Beatson, 'Restitution of Taxes, Levies and Other Imposts: Defining the Extent of the *Woolwich* Principle' (1993) 109 LQR 401; GJ Virgo, 'The Law of Taxation is Not an Island—Overpaid Taxes and the Law of Restitution' [1993] BTR 442.

[63] *R v IRC, ex p Woolwich Equitable Building Society* [1990] 1 WLR 1400.

that the regulations were void. Consequently, the claimant sought to recover this interest, amounting to £6.73 million. The success of this claim depended on whether the Revenue was liable to repay the claimant from the moment it had received the money or later, when the regulations were held to be void. If the Revenue's liability arose by virtue of its unjust enrichment, it would have existed from the moment it received the money. Clearly the Revenue had been enriched at the claimant's expense. The key question, therefore, was whether the claim fell within one of the recognized grounds of restitution.

In determining which grounds of restitution were applicable, a number of features concerning the payment by the claimant to the Revenue need to be emphasized. The claimant paid the sums demanded by the Revenue, even though it disputed the legality of the demand, because it felt that it had no choice but to pay. This was because on its face the demand was lawful. If the claimant had refused to pay the money it would have been the only financial institution to do so. Consequently, any proceedings brought by the Revenue to recover the tax would have been gravely embarrassing to the claimant and would have resulted in adverse publicity. If the claimant had failed to pay but the Revenue's demand was eventually vindicated, the claimant had feared that it would incur heavy penalties, and the interest owing to the Revenue would have far outweighed any return that could have been obtained by investment of the disputed sum. Finally, at the time when the payments were made, it was not possible to identify the amount which was in dispute. Therefore, the claimant decided to pay but lodged a protest with the Revenue when it did so.

The judges in the House of Lords considered whether various grounds of restitution were applicable.

(1) Mistake
The claimant had not paid the tax as the result of a mistake because the claimant had disputed its liability to pay the tax from the start. Further, if there had been a mistake it would have been one of law, which was not a ground of restitution at the time.

(2) Duress
Although the Revenue possessed statutory powers to distrain against a taxpayer's goods, without needing a court order, if a taxpayer did not pay the tax, the Revenue had not actually threatened the claimant with distraint. Nevertheless, Lords Browne-Wilkinson and Slynn, whilst accepting that the traditional definition of duress was not satisfied on the facts, considered that the claimant was under such pressure to pay the tax that it was compelled to do so with the result that the payment was not voluntary and so was recoverable.[64] Lord Goff recognized the existence of such pressure but, because the possibility of distraint by the Revenue was very remote, concluded that compulsion could not be established on the facts.[65]

(3) Absence of basis
Lord Browne-Wilkinson also referred to the fact that the claimant had paid the money for no basis,[66] in that there was no tax liability to discharge, as a further reason why the restitutionary claim should succeed.

(4) Receipt of an ultra vires payment
The references to duress and absence of basis were merely supplementary arguments in favour of the claimant's right to obtain restitution. The true ground of restitution in the

---

[64] *Woolwich Equitable Building Society v IRC* [1993] AC 70, 198 (Lord Browne-Wilkinson) and 204 (Lord Slynn).

[65] Ibid, 172–3.			[66] Ibid, 198.

case was that 'money paid by a citizen to a public authority in the form of taxes or other levies paid pursuant to an *ultra vires* demand by the authority is *prima facie* recoverable by the citizen as of right'.[67]

The essential feature of this ground of restitution, which was identified by Lord Goff and endorsed by Lords Slynn and Browne-Wilkinson,[68] is that restitution should be awarded simply because the tax was unlawfully demanded under an *ultra vires* statute. This exists as a ground of restitution not because the claimant's intention that the defendant should receive the payment can be regarded as vitiated, though this is possible, but because of fundamental constitutional principles arising from the Bill of Rights, that no public authority can retain money which it had no authority to receive.[69] This is therefore a policy-oriented ground of restitution.[70] Although the validity of the tax was solely a matter for national law, a key factor in the recognition of this new ground of restitution was that EU law recognizes an equivalent right in respect of charges levied by Member States contrary to Community law.[71] As Lord Goff recognized, 'at a time when Community law is becoming increasingly important, it would be strange if the right of the citizen to recover overpaid charges were to be more restricted under domestic law than it is under European law'.[72]

Since this is a ground of restitution which exists for reasons of policy rather than as a means for establishing that the claimant's intention to benefit the defendant has been vitiated, Williams has convincingly argued that a claim for restitution founded on this ground of restitution is properly analysed as a hybrid claim, consisting of both public and private law components.[73] Public law provides the reason for restitution by establishing the ground of restitution and the private law creates the entitlement for the return of the money. This analysis is significant, both theoretically in justifying restitutionary claims against public authorities, but also practically in determining the limits of the claim, especially when formulating defences.[74]

(iii) Determining the Ambit of the Ground of Ultra Vires Receipt

There are a number of consequential questions and issues about the ambit and effect of this new ground of restitution.

(1) Is a Demand for Payment Necessary?

It was recognized by the Supreme Court in *Test Claimants in the FII Group Litigation v HMRC*[75] that the *Woolwich* ground is not limited to where the public authority has demanded payment, it being sufficient that the payment has been 'unlawfully exacted'.[76] Indeed, there had been no demand for payment of the tax in *Woolwich* itself and restitution was awarded. The fact that a demand is not required was justified by the Supreme Court in *FII* on the basis that the *Woolwich* ground is founded on the constitutional principle that there should be no taxation without Parliamentary authority, and so it should be available whatever procedure is used for levying and paying a particular tax.

---

[67] Ibid, 177 (Lord Goff).   [68] Ibid, 196 (Lord Browne-Wilkinson) and 201 (Lord Slynn).
[69] Ibid, 172 (Lord Goff).   [70] See p 124, above.
[71] *Amministrazione delle Finanze dello Stato v SpA San Giorgio* [1983] ECR 3595. See p 391, above.
[72] *Woolwich Equitable Building Society v IRC* [1993] AC 70, 177.
[73] Williams, *Unjust Enrichment and Public Law: A Comparative Study of England, France and the EU.*
[74] See further p 408, below.
[75] [2012] UKSC 19, [2012] AC 337. See also *Investment Trust Companies (in liquidation) v HMRC (No 2)* [2013] EWHC 665 (Ch), [51] (Henderson J).
[76] *Test Claimants in the FII Group Litigation v HMRC* [2012] UKSC 19, [2012] AC 337, [186] (Lord Sumption). See also Lord Walker, ibid, [79].

It follows that the ground will be available where taxpayers have self-assessed their tax liability or where tax has been deducted from an employee's salary by an employer who has accounted for it to the Revenue.

In concluding that the *Woolwich* ground applies even if the tax has not been demanded, Lord Walker in *FII* reformulated the ground in the following way:[77] 'We should restate the *Woolwich* principle so as to cover all sums paid to a public authority in response to (and sufficiently causally connected with) an apparent statutory requirement to pay tax which (in fact and in law) is not lawfully due.'

(2) Is the Woolwich Ground Limited to Payments Which Are Ultra Vires by Virtue of an Invalid Statute?

The House of Lords in *Woolwich*[78] left open whether this new ground of restitution is confined to cases where payments were *ultra vires* only because they have been paid pursuant to an invalid statute, as occurred on the facts of *Woolwich* itself. The ambit of the *Woolwich* principle was subsequently clarified by the Supreme Court in *Test Claimants in the FII Group Litigation v HMRC*,[79] which held that it applied to *ultra vires* payments which arose either from unlawful legislation or lawful legislation which had been mistakenly interpreted by the Revenue.

It remains unclear, however, whether the *Woolwich* ground also applies where a tax overpayment is caused by the claimant's spontaneous mistake. Although a claimant in such a case would have a claim for restitution grounded on mistake, this would be subject to the defence of change of position, whereas a claim based on the *Woolwich* ground would not be subject to such a defence.[80] It might therefore be significant whether the *Woolwich* ground is available where the claimant had made a mistake. Lord Sumption in the *FII* case[81] considered that the *Woolwich* ground would not be available where the claimant had made a spontaneous mistake, such as miscalculating the tax due or forgetting that the tax had already been paid. He considered this to follow from the decision that the *Woolwich* ground depended on there being some unlawful exaction by the Revenue,[82] which he assumed required the Revenue to have taken some positive steps to mislead the taxpayer into believing that the tax was due. But this comes close to treating the ground of restitution as requiring proof of some form of wrongdoing, which is artificial and inconsistent with its public law foundations that the receipt of the money is *ultra vires* simply because it is unauthorized.[83] Consequently, the better view is that of Lord Walker who said that the *Woolwich* ground requires a 'perceived obligation to pay',[84] which could encompass a spontaneous mistake on the part of the claimant that he or she was liable to pay money to the public authority which was not due to it.

(3) Is the Woolwich Ground Confined to the Recovery of Overpaid Taxes?

Although *Woolwich, Deutsche Morgan Grenfell*, and *FII* were all concerned with the recovery of overpaid taxes, the *Woolwich* ground of restitution should be applicable to the recovery of any overpaid levy from a public authority, as was recognized by *Test*

---

[77] Ibid.

[78] *Woolwich Equitable Building Society v IRC* [1993] AC 70, 177 (Lord Goff), 205 (Lord Slynn).

[79] [2012] UKSC 19, [2012] AC 337.   [80] See p 409, below.

[81] *Test Claimants in the FII Group Litigation v HMRC* [2012] UKSC 19, [2012] AC 337, [186].

[82] See further p 400, above.

[83] See now *Test Claimants in the FII Group Litigation v HMRC* [2014] EWHC 4302 (Ch), p 410, below.

[84] *Test Claimants in the FII Group Litigation v HMRC* [2012] UKSC 19, [2012] AC 337, [79].

Claimants in the FII Group Litigation v HMRC.[85] Although Lord Walker defined the claim with reference to restitution of taxes, he accepted that 'tax' should be generously construed, so that it might cover a charge such as the congestion charge payable to drive into Central London. In *Waikato Regional Airport Ltd v A-G*[86] the Privy Council recognized that the *Woolwich* principle extended to the recovery of governmental levies and in *Hemming v Westminster CC*[87] it was applied to that part of the licence fees paid to run sex shops which was unlawfully demanded. A major limitation on the application of the *Woolwich* principle is that, as characterized in *FII*,[88] it presumably does not apply to commercial receipts which lack the attributes of a tax, such as the payments received from a bank pursuant to a void interest rate swap transaction.[89] It is consequently important to distinguish between those payments which are received by a public authority in a public and in a private capacity. This is a difficult distinction to draw, although presumably payments made to a public authority in return for services supplied by it as a public authority will be covered by the *Woolwich* principle if the charges for the services are *ultra vires*.

(4) Must the Claimant Have Protested About the Lawfulness of the Demand?

Although in *Woolwich* the claimant had protested to the Revenue when it made its payment that the money was not lawfully due, the success of the restitutionary claim should not be conditional on the claimant protesting against the validity of the demand, for in many cases the claimant will be unaware that the demand was unlawful. Also, a requirement of a protest accompanying the payment would largely confine recovery to those claimants who have the resources to examine the validity of the demand. But the fact that the claimant did protest about the validity of the payment is of evidential importance, since it suggests that the payment was not made voluntarily.

(5) Is the Woolwich Ground Exclusive?

It is a part of Williams's thesis that, having concluded that a restitutionary claim founded on the *Woolwich* ground is a hybrid claim of public and private law components, a claimant who seeks restitution from a public authority in circumstances where a number of grounds of restitution are available should be confined to the *Woolwich* ground, which should prevail over all others.[90] It follows that there is a hierarchy of reasons why a public authority should make restitution and the *Woolwich* ground should prevail because of its public law component that the public authority's receipt was unlawful. But, just because the *Woolwich* claim is justified by public law, there is no reason of logic why a claimant should rely on that ground rather than any other. Certainly, it may well be easier to establish the *Woolwich* ground, because it is only necessary to show that the receipt of the money was beyond the powers of the public authority, but there will be some circumstances where it is more advantageous to the claimant to rely on another ground, particularly mistake. This is primarily[91] because of the effect of limitation periods. If a claimant brings a claim grounded on the *Woolwich* principle, the usual limitation period

---

[85] Ibid, [80] (Lord Walker).   [86] [2003] UKPC 50, [2004] 3 NZLR 1.

[87] [2013] EWCA Civ 591. The Supreme Court subsequently held that the fee had not been unlawfully demanded: [2015] UKSC 25, [2015] 2 WLR 1271.

[88] *Test Claimants in the FII Group Litigation v HMRC* [2012] UKSC 19, [2012] AC 337, [80] (Lord Walker).

[89] See p 372, above.

[90] R Williams, 'Overpaid Taxes: A Hybrid Public and Private Approach' in S Elliott, B Häcker, and C Mitchell (eds), *Restitution of Overpaid Tax* (Oxford: Hart Publishing, 2013), 30.

[91] The choice of the ground of restitution may also affect the operation of defences such as change of position, but that defence will be available to a mistake claim and not to one grounded on the *Woolwich* principle. See p 409, below.

of six years applies.[92] Where, however, the claim is grounded on mistake, time does not begin to run until the claimant discovered the mistake or could reasonably have done so.[93] This might enable the claimant to bring a claim for restitution from a public authority many years after the payment was made.

Whether the claimant can choose to found a claim for restitution from a public authority on the ground of mistake in order to gain the benefit of the extended limitation period was considered by the House of Lords in *Deutsche Morgan Grenfell v IRC*.[94] It was held that the claimant is free to formulate the claim in mistake even though a claim grounded on *ultra vires* receipt is available. It follows that there is no hierarchy of grounds of restitution.

In *Deutsche Morgan Grenfell* the claimant sought a restitutionary remedy in respect of taxes which it had paid prematurely[95] because it had not been able to elect to delay payment in breach of EU law, because the election to delay payment was available where a subsidiary company had paid dividends to a parent company resident in the UK, but not if the parent company was resident in another Member State of the EU. The ECJ held that this was discriminatory and unlawful,[96] with the consequence that the UK was required to provide a remedy. The claimant had made three payments of tax without the benefit of electing to delay payment, the first of which was made over six years before the claim was brought and so was time barred, save if the claimant could establish a claim grounded on mistake of law, in which case time would not start to run until the decision of the ECJ that the discrimination was unlawful. The House of Lords affirmed that a claimant who wishes to recover overpaid taxes, in circumstances where statutory provisions for recovery do not apply, can do so either by reference to the *Woolwich* principle or by virtue of a mistake of law. It was emphasized that concurrent claims are recognized in contract and tort and should also be recognized within the law of unjust enrichment. It is simply a matter for the claimant to choose which ground of restitution is better; a decision which may legitimately be influenced by different rules as to the limitation period. It was further held that the claimant had made a mistake in paying the tax prematurely, since the ruling of the ECJ was considered to have operated retrospectively to enable the claimant to assert that its payment of tax was mistaken.[97] There was disagreement as to whether the mistake related to the failure to elect to delay payment of the tax[98] or to the liability to pay the tax,[99] but ultimately nothing turned on this difference of opinion, although the former view is preferable and consistent with the view that the existence of the tax liability did not constitute a lawful basis for the Revenue's receipt which would bar the claim.[100]

The approach of the House of Lords in *Deutsche Morgan Grenfell* was confirmed by the Supreme Court in *Test Claimants in the FII Group Litigation v HMRC*.[101] In that case a number of taxpayers had paid excessive taxation of over £5 billion on dividends, in breach of EU law,[102] for which English law was required to provide a remedy. Since a claim

---

[92] See p 735, below.   [93] Limitation Act 1980, s 32(1)(c). See further p 737, below.

[94] [2006] UKHL 49, [2007] 1 AC 558. See GJ Virgo, '*Deutsche Morgan Grenfell*: The Right to Restitution of Tax: Back to Basics' [2007] BTR 27.

[95] See M Chowdry and C Mitchell, 'Tax Legislation as a Justifying Factor' [2005] 13 RLR 1, 17, who argue that the restitutionary claim should have failed simply because the obligation to pay tax was valid. But the claim was not for restitution of the tax paid, but was instead for the defendant's benefit in unlawfully receiving the payment earlier than it would otherwise have done. See further p 146, above.

[96] Cases C-397/98 and C-410/98 *Metallgesellschaft Ltd v IRC* [2001] Ch 620.   [97] See p 186, above.

[98] *Deutsche Morgan Grenfell v IRC* [2006] UKHL 49, [2007] 1 AC 558, [62] (Lord Hope) and [88] (Lord Scott).

[99] Ibid, [32] (Lord Hoffmann).   [100] See Chapter 7.

[101] [2012] UKSC 19, [2012] AC 337. See also See *Investment Trust Companies (in liquidation) v HMRC (No 2)* [2013] EWHC 665 (Ch), [51] (Henderson J).

[102] Case C-446/04 *Test Claimants in the FII Group Litigation v IRC* (Note) [2012] 2 AC 436.

grounded on *Woolwich* was time barred, the taxpayers sought to found their claim on mistake. The Supreme Court held that, to gain the benefit of the extended limitation period, the mistake had to constitute an essential element of the cause of action and not simply form the context of the claim. It follows that the extended limitation period is only available where mistake is pleaded as the ground of restitution in the unjust enrichment claim and not where the *Woolwich* ground is pleaded. In addition, the Supreme Court confirmed that, where the *Woolwich* ground and mistake ground are both available where a public authority has received an *ultra vires* payment, they should also be available by virtue of the principles of effectiveness and equivalence, to enforce analogous rights under EU law.[103]

It is clear from these cases that a significant reason for bringing a restitutionary claim against a public authority grounded on mistake is to benefit from extended limitation periods. Another possible advantage, as recognized by Henderson J in *Investment Trust Companies v HMRC (No 2)*,[104] is that the *Woolwich* claim is only available where the public authority is directly enriched at the expense of the claimant, whereas a mistake claim is available even where the public authority is indirectly enriched, such as where a third party has paid tax to the Revenue but the burden of that tax is actually borne by the claimant.[105] This is because it is only taxpayers who are directly liable for the payment of overpaid tax who are subject to the coercive powers of the State and so fall within the *Woolwich* principle. The claimants in *Investment Trust Companies v HMRC*, who were contractually liable to third parties for the amount of tax which the third parties had been liable to pay the Revenue, could bring a claim grounded on mistake instead. Henderson J considered that allowing the person who had borne the economic burden of the tax, when they were not under a statutory obligation to pay the tax, to rely on the *Woolwich* ground would undermine the constitutional significance of that ground.[106] Whilst a logical conclusion, it does confuse the different aspects of the unjust enrichment formula. Whether the Revenue is enriched directly or indirectly at the expense of the claimant is surely a question of construction of the private law component of the unjust enrichment claim, which has nothing to do with the public law component of the ground of restitution. It should follow that the developments in the law concerning the interpretation of the at the expense of the claimant requirement,[107] should apply regardless of the ground of restitution which is engaged.

(6) Procedure for Seeking Restitution

In the light of the fact that an unjust enrichment claim founded on the *Woolwich* ground is properly characterized as hybrid claim, involving public law and private law components, it is important to consider whether the public law component affects the procedure for establishing that the receipt of the payment was *ultra vires*. Originally restitution of an *ultra vires* payment required a dual stage procedure, as occurred in the *Woolwich* litigation itself.[108] The first public law stage involved an application by judicial review for a declaration that the demand was unlawful. The limitation period

---

[103] *Test Claimants in the FII Group Litigation v HMRC* [2012] UKSC 19, [2012] AC 337, [21] (Lord Hope), [130] (Lord Clarke), [235] (Lord Reed). Lords Hope and Clarke referred to different remedies, whereas the preferable analysis is that of Lord Reed who referred to different causes of action involving the *Woolwich* claim and a mistake claim. See also *Prudential Assurance Co Ltd v HMRC* [2013] EWHC 3249 (Ch), [2014] 2 CMLR 10, [182] (Henderson J).

[104] [2013] EWHC 665 (Ch), [2013] STC 1129, [44].   [105] See p 108, above.

[106] This point was not considered by the Court of Appeal: *Investment Trust Companies v HMRC* [2015] EWCA Civ 82.

[107] See p 107, above.   [108] *R v IRC, Ex p Woolwich Equitable Building Society* [1990] 1 WLR 1400.

for making such an application was three months from the date when the ground of challenge arose.[109] Once the receipt was declared *ultra vires*, it was then necessary to commence private law proceedings to recover the money. The reason for this convoluted procedure was because it was not possible to award restitutionary remedies in judicial review proceedings. It is now possible to make such an award,[110] which means that a claimant can challenge the validity of the public authority's receipt and recover payment in the same proceedings. But this would still be subject to the strict three-month limitation period.

In fact the courts have recognized that, where the claimant wishes to obtain restitution on the ground of *ultra vires* receipt, it is not necessary first to bring judicial review proceedings.[111] The claimant can bring a restitutionary claim at common law to show that the money was not due and, once this has been established, recover the payment from the public authority in the same proceedings. This is a perfectly acceptable approach,[112] since the dominant issue for the claimant relates to the existence of a private law right,[113] namely the right to restitution because the defendant was unjustly enriched at the claimant's expense, even though the existence of this right is dependent on the consideration of a public law issue, concerning whether the public authority is authorized to receive the particular payment. This avoids the cumbersome procedure involving both judicial review and a separate claim for restitution, and avoids the very short limitation period which is inherent in an application for judicial review.[114]

(7) Restricting the Right to Restitution

Where the claimant seeks to obtain restitution from the defendant on the ground of *ultra vires* receipt, the right to restitution at common law may be restricted in two ways. First, it may be removed by statute so that the claimant will have to rely on the statutory mechanism for restitution.[115] It follows that the common law defences to restitution will not apply and the defendant will be confined to the defences under the statute. Secondly, the parties may have made express provision for restitution of overpayments by contract, or such an agreement can be implied.[116] Again, the consequence of this will be that the common law restitutionary mechanism, including the general defences to restitutionary claims, will be excluded since claims in unjust enrichment cannot subvert contractual mechanisms for recovery.[117]

---

[109] Civil Procedure Rules, r 54.5(3).   [110] Ibid, r 54(3)(2).

[111] *British Steel v Commissioners of Customs and Excise* [1997] 2 All ER 366. See also *Autologic Holdings plc v IRC* [2005] UKHL 54, [2006] 1 AC 118.

[112] Although it was criticized as an abuse of process by Sedley LJ in *NEC Semi-Conductors v IRC* [2006] EWCA Civ 25, [2006] STC 606, [97]. See also *Jones v Powys Local Health Board* [2008] EWHC 2562 (Admin) where a claim for restitution of care fees had to be pursued as a claim for judicial review rather than as a private law claim, because it required determination as to whether it was reasonable for a public authority to conclude that the person receiving care was liable to pay for it. Restitution of overpaid taxes was distinguished on the basis that there was never a liability to pay the unlawful tax. The issue for decision in *Jones* was eminently suitable to be dealt with in judicial review proceedings.

[113] See *Roy v Kensington and Chelsea and Westminster Family Practitioner Committee* [1992] 1 AC 624 where the House of Lords recognized the importance of the private law right being dominant when determining whether the claim should be characterized as a public law or private law claim.

[114] *Hemming v Westminster CC* [2013] EWCA Civ 591, [138] (Beatson LJ).

[115] *Autologic Holdings plc v IRC* [2005] UKHL 54, [2006] 1 AC 118. [20] (Lord Nicholls), [62] (Lord Millett). See p 406, below, for the statutory mechanisms for restitution.

[116] *Sebel Products Ltd v Commissioners of Customs and Excise* [1949] 1 Ch 409.

[117] See p 141, above.

(8) Interest

It was recognized in *Prudential Assurance Co Ltd v HMRC*[118] that, regardless of whether the receipt of the tax is *ultra vires* by virtue of national law or EU law,[119] the claimant has a right to compound interest.[120] Such interest is available regardless of whether the tax is not due at all or is due but has been paid prematurely,[121] and is to be assessed until the date when the Revenue repays the tax since it remains enriched until that point. This is consistent with the treatment of interest generally in the law of restitution.[122]

3. PARTICULAR STATUTORY PROVISIONS

In addition to restitution of *ultra vires* payments at common law, there are certain statutory provisions which provide for the recovery of overpaid taxes and duties.[123] Unfortunately, these provisions are not consistent as to when the claimant will be able to recover such overpayments. These differences involve such matters as the conditions which must be satisfied before the money can be recovered, whether there is a right to relief or whether it is subject to an administrative discretion, the types of defences which are available and whether or not interest should be awarded. The nature of these differences is illustrated by comparing two particular provisions.

(A) TAXES MANAGEMENT ACT 1970

Schedule 1AB of the Taxes Management Act 1970[124] provides for the recovery of overpaid income tax or capital gains tax which is not due, regardless of whether or not the money was paid by mistake. The Commissioners are not liable to give effect to a claim for restitution of such tax in various situations,[125] including where the tax liability was mistakenly assessed in accordance with a practice generally prevailing at the time, except where the tax was charged contrary to EU law. The limitation period for making a claim under this provision is usually four years,[126] save where it would be unconscionable for the Commissioners to retain the money. Where this provision is applicable it excludes the common law ground of restitution of overpaid tax contrary to domestic law,[127] but not tax which has been overpaid contrary to EU law.[128] Since, particularly after the 2009 reform of the provision, it is of very wide application in respect of recovery of income and capital gains tax, it follows that the common law claim grounded on *Woolwich* has been reduced significantly.

(B) VALUE ADDED TAX ACT 1994, SECTION 80

Section 80 of the Value Added Tax Act 1994 makes provision for the recovery of overpaid VAT.[129] The effect of this statute is that where VAT has been paid in circumstances in

---

[118] [2013] EWHC 3249 (Ch), [2014] 2 CMLR 10.   [119] Ibid, [206] (Henderson J).

[120] Ibid, [210] (Henderson J).   [121] Ibid, [207] (Henderson J).   [122] See p 29, above.

[123] These provisions include s 241 of the Inheritance Tax Act 1984 (which provides for the repayment of overpaid inheritance tax) and s 29 of the Finance Act 1989 (which provides for the repayment of overpaid excise duty and car tax).

[124] Substituted by Finance Act 2009, Sch 52(1).   [125] Taxes Management Act 1970, Sch 1AB 2.

[126] Ibid, Sch 1 AB 3(1).   [127] *Monro v HMRC* [2008] EWCA Civ 306, [2009] Ch 69.

[128] *Test Claimants in the FII Group Litigation v HMRC* [2012] UKSC 19, [2012] AC 337, [10] (Lord Hope), [117]–[119] (Lord Walker), [127] (Lord Clarke), and [204]–[205] (Lord Sumption).

[129] As amended by the Finance (No 2) Act 2005, s 3(11).

which the money was not due to the Commissioners, they are liable to repay that amount to the payer, as long as the amount was not paid more than three years before the claim was made.[130] Consequently, there is a general right to repayment, regardless of the circumstances of payment, so that recovery is not confined to cases of mistaken payment. Overpaid VAT can only be recovered under this section by the party who was directly accountable for the tax to the Commissioners, so, as regards such claims, the common law restitutionary regime is excluded.[131] Where, however, the unlawful VAT was paid by a third party but the burden was borne by the claimants, it has been held that, although the claimants could not recover the payment under the statute because they were not accountable for the tax as end consumers of services provided by the third party, the statutory scheme was inapplicable and a claim at common law grounded on *Woolwich* was held to be available.[132]

There are two issues of particular significance relating to the operation of the statutory regime. The first concerns the award of interest on any VAT which is overpaid,[133] particularly whether simple or compound interest should be awarded.[134] The matter was referred to the CJEU in respect of a claim to repay overpaid VAT which had been charged in contravention of EU law.[135] It was held that there was an obligation to pay interest, but it was for each Member State to determine the rate and method of assessment, but with regard to the principles of equivalence and effectiveness. When the matter was then reconsidered in the English court, the Court of Appeal held that compound interest could be awarded.[136]

The second issue relates to a particular defence recognized by the Value Added Tax Act 1994. By section 80(3) recovery of overpaid VAT is denied if repayment would unjustly enrich the payer. The proper interpretation of this defence is a matter of some controversy. The defence was considered by the Inner House of the Court of Session in *Customs and Excise Commissioners v McMaster Stores (Scotland) Ltd.*[137] Lord President Hope identified a number of principles to assist in the determination of what constituted unjust enrichment for these purposes, particularly that, since the defence is statutory, the common law principle of unjust enrichment is not relevant to its interpretation.[138] To establish the defence it must be shown both that the claimant would be enriched by the recovery of the overpaid VAT and that this recovery would be unjust. The receipt would be unjust if the taxpayer was placed in a better position than it would have been in had the tax not been paid, as will occur where the taxpayer has passed on the burden of the tax to its customers. So, for example, if the taxpayer overpaid £5,000 VAT and then recouped this amount from customers by increasing the price of goods, the burden of paying the extra VAT will be borne by the customers rather than the taxpayer, so the effect of making restitution to the taxpayer would be that it would be in a better financial position than it occupied before the VAT had been paid. It will, however, be difficult to prove that the taxpayer will have passed on its loss by increasing prices, since the volume of sales might have fallen as a result.

---

[130] Value Added Tax Act 1994, s 80(4).

[131] Ibid, s 80(7). See *Investment Trust Companies v HMRC* [2015] EWCA Civ 82.

[132] *Investment Trust Companies v HMRC* [2015] EWCA Civ 82. See also *Littlewoods Retail Ltd v HMRC* [2014] EWHC 868 (Ch), [450] (Henderson J).

[133] Value Added Tax Act 1994, s 78.   [134] See p 29, above.

[135] Case C-591/10 *Littlewoods Retail Ltd v HMRC* [2012] STC 1714.

[136] *Littlewoods Retail Ltd v HMRC* [2015] EWCA Civ 515.   [137] [1995] STC 846.

[138] See also *Restitution: Mistakes of Law and Ultra Vires Public Authority Receipts and Payments* (Law Com No 227, 1994), 121.

The application of the defence was also considered in *Baines and Ernst Ltd v Commissioners of Customs and Excise*.[139] The claimant had been founded as a debt collection agency and was liable to pay VAT at the standard rate. It then changed to providing debt management services and was informed that it was liable to pay VAT at the same rate, when in fact it was exempt from paying the tax. The claimant had invoiced clients for services at a rate of 15% plus VAT, amounting to 17.625%. When the claimant was informed that its services were VAT exempt it increased its charge to 17.625%. The claimant said that, if its claim for restitution was successful, it would not repay any money to its clients. The key issue was whether allowing recovery of the overpaid VAT would unjustly enrich the claimant within section 80(3). A number of principles were identified as regards the application of the defence: the burden of proving unjust enrichment is on the Commissioners; there is no presumption of passing on simply because the price is stated to be inclusive of VAT; even where there has been passing on of the burden of VAT it does not necessarily follow that restitution to the claimant will involve unjust enrichment,[140] because, for example, the effect of an increase in prices may be to reduce the claimant's profits as a result of a fall in sales; crucially, therefore, whether the claimant was unjustly enriched requires an 'economic analysis in which all the relevant circumstances are taken into account'.[141] The trial judge concluded that, in the light of these principles, the claimant had in fact passed on the burden of the VAT to its clients and so it would be unjustly enriched if restitution was awarded.

Although the unjust enrichment defence has been criticized, its legitimacy has been affirmed by the ECJ,[142] where it was recognized that the application of the defence requires full economic analysis of the facts of the case, which is a matter for the national court.

4. DEFENCES

Although general defences to restitutionary claims are considered in Part V of this book, it is appropriate to consider particular issues relating to the application of defences to claims for restitution from public authorities, simply because the application of these defences has proved to be highly significant to the formulation of restitutionary claims and to the choice of which cause of action should be pursued.

(A) LIMITATION PERIODS

It is clear from the earlier analysis in this chapter that the operation of different limitation periods has proved to be the prime trigger for choosing to found a claim on mistake or on the *Woolwich* ground, since, where mistake constitutes the ground of restitution[143] the limitation period does not start to run until the claimant did discover or could reasonably have discovered[144] that it had a

---

[139] [2004] UKVAT V18769.   [140] Ibid, [98].   [141] Ibid, [100].

[142] Case 309/06 *Marks and Spencer plc v Commissioners of Customs and Excise*; Case C- 398/09 *Lady and Kid v Skatteministeriet* [2012] STC 854.

[143] As recognized in *Test Claimants in the FII Group Litigation v HMRC* [2012] UKSC 19, [2012] AC 337.

[144] Where the unlawfulness of the tax has been determined by the CJEU it has been held that time will begin to run once that court declared the payment of the tax to be unlawful: *Test Claimants in the FII Group Litigation v HMRC* [2014] EWHC 4302 (Ch), [465] (Henderson J). Where, however, the unlawfulness of the tax has been resolved by the domestic courts, if the matter has been determined by the House of Lords or Supreme Court, time will only begin to run from that point, even if the unlawfulness of the tax has been

claim,[145] whereas for claims grounded on *Woolwich* the normal six-year limitation period applies.[146] Limitation periods are legitimate as regards the *San Giorgio* claim for restitution of tax paid in breach of EU law by virtue of the need for certainty, as long as the period is reasonable.[147]

The significance of this extended limitation period for mistake based claims is now much reduced in significance. The key statutory provisions for restitution, relating to overpaid income tax, capital gains tax, and VAT,[148] constitute an exclusive regime for restitution of those taxes where they apply, for which the limitation period is four years. Further, the application of the extended limitation period for claims grounded on mistake was retrospectively abrogated by statute,[149] although the retrospective nature of these provisions have been held to infringe EU law in respect of their application to restitution of taxes paid in breach of EU law,[150] by infringing principles of legitimate expectation, efficacy and effectiveness in not providing transitional provisions.

(B) CHANGE OF POSITION

The application of the defence of change of position[151] means that, where a public authority can show that it has so changed its position in reliance on the receipt of money that it would be inequitable to require it to make restitution, it should have a defence to the extent of that change of position. The application of the defence to claims against public authorities is restricted for the following reasons. First, where the claim for restitution is a *San Giorgio* claim, involving restitution of taxes the receipt of which is unlawful by EU law, the defence of change of position does not apply regardless of whether the claim is formulated with reference to the *Woolwich* ground or mistake,[152] because the defence is considered to be incompatible with the principle of effectiveness.[153]

Secondly, in *Test Claimants in the FII Group Litigation v HMRC (No 1)*[154] Henderson J had recognized that the defence of change of position is not available for a claim based on the *Woolwich* ground, but is available for claims founded on mistake. This was because the *Woolwich* ground is founded on the unlawful levying of tax, which he considered to be a legal wrong so that the Revenue is a wrongdoer in receiving the tax, and the defence of change of position is unavailable to such a defendant.[155] This is, however, a controversial conclusion, since unlawful receipt of tax does not obviously involve the commission of any wrong. This is even more dubious after the decision of the Supreme Court in *FII* that the *Woolwich* ground does not even require proof of a demand for payment, so the Revenue

---

established at first instance, since finality would only be achieved with the decision of the final court of appeal, and even though the claimant had brought proceedings for restitution earlier: ibid, [461].

[145] Limitation Act 1980, s 32(1)(c).   [146] See further p 737, below.

[147] Case C-362/12 *Test Claimants in the FII Group Litigation v HMRC* [2014] 2 CMLR 33, [33]. A limitation period of three years is considered reasonable: ibid, [34].   [148] See p 406, above.

[149] Finance Act 2004, s 320 for payments made before 8 September 2003 but where the claim was commenced after that date; Finance Act 2007, s 107 where the claim was commenced before that date.

[150] As recognized in *Test Claimants in the FII Group Litigation v HMRC* [2012] UKSC 19, [2012] AC 337 concerning Finance Act 2007, s 107; *Test Claimants in the FII Group Litigation v IRC and another* (Case C-362/12) [2014] 2 CMLR 33 concerning Finance Act 2004, s 320.

[151] See Chapter 25 for detailed exposition of this defence.

[152] *Test Claimants in the FII Group Litigation v HMRC (No 2)* [2014] EWHC 4302 (Ch), [406] (Henderson J).

[153] *Prudential Assurance Co Ltd v HMRC* [2013] EWHC 3249 (Ch), [2014] 2 CMLR 10, [188] (Henderson J);

[154] [2008] EWHC 2893 (Ch), [2009] STC 254, [339]. This was not considered by the Court of Appeal or the Supreme Court. See also *Littlewoods Retail Ltd v HMRC* [2010] EWHC 1071 (Ch), [2010] STC 2072, [105] (Vos J).

[155] *Lipkin Gorman (a firm) v Karpnale Ltd* [1991] AC 546. See p 692, below.

may simply have passively received the unlawful payment rather than actively sought it. Subsequently, in *Test Claimants in the FII Group Litigation v HMRC (No 2)*,[156] although Henderson J affirmed that the Revenue in that case had been a wrongdoer in receiving tax in breach of EU law, he acknowledged that the reason why the change of position defence is not available to a claim founded on the *Woolwich* ground is not because the defendant had committed a wrong, because no wrong may have been committed by the Revenue, but because the defence would stultify or undermine the high constitutional policy which underpins the recognition of the *Woolwich* ground.[157]

Thirdly, in *Test Claimants in the FII Group Litigation v HMRC (No 2)*[158] Henderson J left open whether the change of position defence is available where the restitutionary claim is grounded on mistake, although he had previously held that the defence was available in such circumstances.[159] Allowing the defence where the ground of restitution is mistake, even where the defendant is a public authority, but denying it where the *Woolwich* ground is engaged, would reflect the difference between a purely private law ground of restitution and a hybrid ground which is justified by its essentially public law nature.

Fourthly, the change of position defence requires proof of an extraordinary change of position which would not have been incurred had the payment not been received by the defendant. In *Test Claimants in the FII Group Litigation v HMRC (No 2)*[160] Henderson J recognized that the essential test is whether the award of restitution would make the Revenue worse off than if the tax had not been paid in the first place. The Revenue does not bear any greater burden than the ordinary defendant in establishing the defence, so it is sufficient that, but for the receipt of the tax, the Revenue's position would not have changed. This will, however, be very difficult for the Revenue to establish. It is highly unlikely that the receipt of the tax payment from the claimant would have affected the Government's budgetary process or its expenditure.[161] Consequently, as regards claims grounded on mistake, it will be difficult for the Government to establish the defence, and, in *FII*, Henderson J held that the Revenue had not been able to show that its position had changed as a result of the receipt of tax payments. It has, however, been recognized that, in respect of Government expenditure, it is not necessary to show a precise link between particular receipt and particular items of expenditure.[162] Rather, it is possible

> to infer that planned expenditure would not have taken place at the level which it did but for the availability of the tax receipts which were taken into account in fixing departmental budgets. In such circumstances it would be inequitable to require restitution to be made for tax which was paid by mistake when the money has long ago been spent in the public interest and everybody assumed in good faith that it had been validly levied.[163]

But it is unclear why the application of the defence should be weighted in favour of the public authority in this way. Indeed, Cleary[164] has argued that the defence should not be

---

[156] [2014] EWHC 4302 (Ch).

[157] Ibid, [315]. Relying on the analysis of E Bant, 'Restitution from the Revenue and Change of Position' [2009] LMCLQ 166, 172.   [158] [2014] EWHC 4302 (Ch).

[159] In *Test Claimants in the FII Group Litigation v HMRC (No 1)* [2008] EWHC 2893 (Ch), [2009] STC 254. See also *Bloomsbury International Ltd v Sea Fish Industry Authority* [2009] EWHC 1721, [133]–[144] (Hamblen J).

[160] [2014] EWCH 4302 (Ch), [347].

[161] *Littlewoods Retail Ltd v HMRC* [2010] EWHC 1071 (Ch), [2010] STC 2072, [111] (Vos J).

[162] *Bloomsbury International Ltd v Sea Fish Industry Authority* [2009] EWHC 1721 (QB), [2010] 1 CMLR 12, [137] (Hamblen J); *Test Claimants in the FII Group Litigation v HMRC* [2014] EWHC 4302 (Ch), [356] (Henderson J).

[163] *Test Claimants in the FII Group Litigation v HMRC* [2014] EWHC 4302 (Ch), [356] (Henderson J).

[164] N Cleary, 'Property, Proportionality and the Change of Position Defence' in S Elliott, B Häcker, and C Mitchell (eds), *Restitution of Overpaid Tax* (Oxford: Hart Publishing, 2013), ch 5.

available in principle to public authorities, by virtue of the need to protect the proprietary rights of the taxpayer. This follows from Article 1 of the First Protocol to the European Convention on Human Rights, by virtue of which the State can only justify the expropriation of assets where it is proportionate to an objectively identifiable aim. Generally a public authority will not be able to establish this because, as Cleary argues, the cost to the public should not be regarded as a sufficient justification for expropriation of assets, save perhaps in cases where there would be serious adverse consequences for public finances if restitution was awarded and no other revenue raising measure would be reasonably effective to achieve the same result.[165]

(C) PASSING ON

Although the defence of passing on is not generally available in the law of unjust enrichment,[166] it is recognized as applying to claims for restitution of overpaid VAT, in the form of the unjust enrichment defence,[167] and it is the only defence recognized by EU law[168] as regards *San Giorgio* claims to ensure that the taxpayer is not unjustly enriched by restitution.[169] This is considered to be a justifiable defence because restitution should not be awarded where the claimant has not borne the burden of the unlawful tax. The defence will only apply to *San Giorgio* claims to the extent that the taxpayer directly passed on the loss and even then it is necessary to consider carefully whether the loss has actually been passed on. There may, for example, have been a fall in sales by increasing prices which consequently reduced the loss which was passed on.[170] Outside of such claims and the restitution of overpaid VAT, it is unclear whether the passing on defence is applicable. In *Woolwich* Lord Goff left open the question of whether a taxpayer who has 'passed on' the burden of the tax to another should be precluded from seeking restitution.[171] Since the passing on defence is not available for claims in unjust enrichment generally, the preferable view is that it should not be available for claims founded on the *Woolwich* ground either, since the constitutional principle should prevail so that, as between the public authority and the taxpayer, the latter should obtain restitution.

(D) SETTLEMENT

Restitution will not be awarded where the payment was made pursuant to a contractual settlement.[172] The Law Commission has recommended[173] that restitution should also be denied where the relevant payment was made in response to litigation which had been commenced by the public authority, but not where the litigation was merely threatened.

---

[165] Cf Y Hu, 'Change of Position and the Revenue' [2011] RLR 112 who argues that there should be a presumption in favour of restitution which would be rebutted if the public authority established that the award would result in fiscal chaos.

[166] See p 118, above.　　　[167] Value Added Tax Act 1994, s 80(3). See p 406, above.

[168] *Amministrazione delle Finanze dello Stato v SpA San Giorgio* (1982) [1983] ECR 3595.

[169] Case C-398/09 *Lady and Kid v Skatteministeriet* [2012] STC 854, [20] and [25].

[170] Case C-310/09 *Ministre du Budget, des Comptes Publics et de la Fonction Publique v Accor SA* [2012] STC 438, [74].

[171] *Woolwich Equitable Building Society v IRC* [1993] AC 70, 177–8.

[172] *Woolwich Equitable Building Society v IRC* [1993] AC 70; *Test Claimants in the FII Group Litigation v HMRC* [2012] UKSC 19, [2012] AC 337, [79] (Lord Walker).

[173] *Restitution: Mistakes of Law and Ultra Vires Public Authority Receipts and Payments* (Law Com No 227, 1994).

Such a defence of compromise is consistent with the general bar to restitutionary claims at common law founded on the claimant's voluntary submission to an honest claim.[174]

(E) CHANGE IN A SETTLED VIEW OF THE LAW

Where the claim to restitution is founded on a mistake of law the Law Commission[175] has recommended that restitution should be denied where the payment was made in accordance with a settled view of the law that the money was due and that view was subsequently changed by a decision of a court or tribunal.[176] This defence was not recommended to be applicable where the claim for restitution is founded on *Woolwich* since, in such circumstances, the rationale for restitution is based on the impropriety of the public authority retaining funds without statutory authority. The very fact of the change in a settled view of the law will confirm such impropriety.

In *Deutsche Morgan Grenfell Group plc v IRC*[177] the House of Lords rejected any defence that the money was paid when there was a settled view as to the state of the law, and it was correct to do so. Even if the money was paid on the basis of a settled view of the law which is later proved to be mistaken, restitution should follow simply because it is subsequently acknowledged that the money was not due to the public authority. The argument of constitutional impropriety in the public authority retaining money which was not due to it should prevail over that founded on the disruption to public finances arising from a mistake as to a settled view of the law.

(F) DISRUPTION OF PUBLIC FINANCES

Lord Goff in *Woolwich* doubted the advisability of imposing special limits upon recovery in the case of ultra vires levies to deal with the problem that a right of recovery might lead to serious disruption of public finances.[178] The Law Commission,[179] whilst acknowledging that protection of public finances was a legitimate policy aim,[180] rejected a general defence of serious disruption to public finances on the ground that such a defence was too uncertain.

---

[174] See p 149, above.

[175] *Restitution: Mistakes of Law and Ultra Vires Public Authority Receipts and Payments* (Law Com No 227, 1994).

[176] Support for such a defence can be found in the judgment of Lord Goff in *Kleinwort Benson Ltd v Lincoln CC* [1999] 2 AC 349, 382.

[177] [2006] UKHL 49, [2007] 1 AC 559, [18] (Lord Hoffmann), [145] (Lord Walker).

[178] *Woolwich Equitable Building Society v IRC* [1993] AC 70, 175–6.

[179] *Restitution: Mistakes of Law and Ultra Vires Public Authority Receipts and Payments* (Law Com No 227, 1994).   [180] Ibid, paras 10.5–10.8.

PART III

RESTITUTION FOR WRONGS

16

GENERAL PRINCIPLES

1. THE ESSENCE OF RESTITUTION FOR WRONGS

In Part II those restitutionary claims which are founded on the reversal of the defendant's unjust enrichment were examined. In this Part the emphasis shifts to those restitutionary claims which are founded on the commission of a wrong by the defendant. There are four types of wrongdoing which may trigger the award of gain-based remedies, namely tort, breach of contract, equitable wrongdoing, and the commission of a criminal offence. For the purposes of this book the detailed rules which determine whether or not a wrong has been committed will not be examined, since this is adequately dealt with in the specialized works on each of these subjects. What this Part is concerned with is whether, once the claimant has established that the defendant has committed a wrong, the claimant can obtain a gain-based remedy from the defendant. This is a difficult matter to resolve, since there is great uncertainty as to which wrongs can and should trigger the award of gain-based remedies. A further difficulty is that, unlike restitution founded on the reversal of the defendant's unjust enrichment where the only remedy available is restitutionary, in those cases where restitution is founded on the commission of a wrong the claimant may be able to obtain other remedies in the alternative, particularly remedies to compensate the claimant for loss suffered rather than to deprive the defendant of gains obtained through the commission of the wrong.

(A) THE RELATIONSHIP BETWEEN RESTITUTION FOR WRONGS AND THE REVERSAL OF UNJUST ENRICHMENT

For those commentators[1] and judges[2] who have argued that the law of restitution is only concerned with the reversal of the defendant's unjust enrichment, it is necessary to show how a defendant who has obtained benefits through the commission of a wrong can be considered to be unjustly enriched at the claimant's expense. Clearly such a defendant can be shown to have been enriched and, because this arose from the commission of a wrong, it is possible to conclude that the enrichment was unjustly obtained, albeit that a distinct cause of action relating to the wrongdoing needs to be established to identify a separate cause of action in unjust enrichment. But the real difficulty arises in establishing that this enrichment was obtained at the claimant's expense, because the defendant's enrichment will not necessarily have been subtracted from the claimant. For this reason, if restitution

---

[1] PBH Birks originally treated restitution for wrongs as founded on the reversal of unjust enrichment (*An Introduction to the Law of Restitution* (rev edn, Oxford: Clarendon Press, 1989), 313), but he subsequently changed his mind: PBH Birks, 'Misnomer' in W Cornish, R Nolan, J O'Sullivan, and G Virgo (eds), *Restitution: Past, Present and Future* (Oxford: Hart Publishing, 1998), ch 1.

[2] See, in particular, Peter Gibson LJ in *Halifax Building Society v Thomas* [1996] Ch 217, 224.

for wrongs is to be explained by reference to the reversal of unjust enrichment principle, it is necessary to re-define the notion of 'at the claimant's expense' where the claim is founded on the commission of a wrong, so that, rather than showing that the defendant's benefit was subtracted from the claimant, it is sufficient that the benefit derived from the commission of a wrong which involved the breach of a duty owed to the claimant.[3] It would follow that gain-based remedies are available to the claimant so long as the defendant's benefit can be shown to have resulted from the commission of the wrong, even though the benefit was not subtracted from the claimant. This is consistent with the definition of the law of restitution which is adopted in this book, namely that body of law which is concerned with the award of gain-based remedies.[4] It is, however, highly artificial to regard restitution for wrongdoing as founded on the principle of reversing unjust enrichment by reinterpretation of the 'at the expense of' requirement.[5] It is easier and more accurate simply to analyse restitution for wrongdoing in the following way.

(i) Proof of a Cause of Action Involving Wrongdoing

The claimant must be the victim of a wrong which was committed by the defendant. It is not necessary to show that any enrichment was obtained by the defendant at the claimant's expense or that the claimant can found his or her claim on a recognized ground of restitution. It is sufficient that the claimant can sue the defendant for the commission of a wrong.

(ii) The Wrong Triggers Gain-Based Remedies

The wrong must have been of a type which has been recognized as triggering gain-based remedies. Questions of policy need to be examined carefully to determine whether the award of a gain-based remedy is appropriate as a response to the commission of that type of wrong.

(iii) The Defendant Obtained a Benefit

The defendant must have obtained a benefit as a result of the commission of the wrong, for without proof of such a benefit it will not be possible to award the claimant any gain-based remedy.[6] To determine whether the defendant has been benefited for the purposes of a restitutionary claim founded on wrongdoing, the definition of enrichment which is applicable to an action founded on the reversal of unjust enrichment should apply.[7] This means that the defendant must have received an objective benefit which it is not possible to devalue subjectively, for example because the enrichment is incontrovertibly beneficial, requested or freely accepted. That the principle of subjective devaluation is applicable where a restitutionary claim is founded on the commission of a wrong was recognized by the Court of Appeal in *Ministry of Defence v Ashman*.[8] Usually, however, where the defendant has committed a wrong the defendant will have obtained money, which is incontrovertibly beneficial. One issue of particular controversy concerns whether gain-based remedies for wrongs are confined to where the defendant obtains a positive

---

[3] See Birks, *An Introduction to the Law of Restitution*, 42.

[4] Compare the view that restitution is to be interpreted literally to restore to the claimant what has been subtracted from him or her, with disgorgement being used to describe those remedies where a gain derived from another party is transferred to the claimant. See p 4, above and p 418, below.

[5] See p 11, above and *Morris v Tarrant* [1971] 2 QB 143, 162 (Lane J). That restitution for wrongs is not founded on the unjust enrichment principle was recognized by Millett J in *Macmillan Inc v Bishopsgate Investment Trust plc (No 3)* [1995] 1 WLR 978, 988.

[6] *Hambly v Trott* (1776) 1 Cowp 371, 376; 98 ER 1136, 1139 (Lord Mansfield).

[7] See Chapter 4 above.   [8] [1993] 2 EGLR 102.

benefit from the commission of a wrong or whether it can encompass a negative benefit, such as money saved. The House of Lords in *Attorney-General v Blake*[9] appeared to assume that gain-based remedies are confined to depriving the defendant of benefits actually received, by focusing on the recovery of profits. But there is no reason why the defendant should not be required to make restitution of money saved by the commission of a wrong,[10] and a number of cases have awarded a gain-based remedy in such circumstances.[11]

It follows from this analysis that the underlying cause of action for a claim of restitution for wrongs is the wrong itself and is not founded on the unjust enrichment of the defendant. In other words, the defendant's liability to make restitution to the claimant is a secondary liability which is parasitic on the primary obligation not to commit the wrong.[12]

(B) ADVANTAGES OF TREATING RESTITUTION FOR WRONGS AS NOT FOUNDED ON UNJUST ENRICHMENT

There are a number of advantages which follow from the recognition that the relevant cause of action is the wrong rather than the defendant's unjust enrichment. First, it reflects the approach which is generally adopted in practice, whereby gain-based remedies are awarded for wrongdoing without any attempt to analyse the case in terms of unjust enrichment. There is particularly no need to show that the claim falls within any of the established grounds of restitution, it being sufficient that the claim is founded on a recognized form of wrongdoing.

Secondly, the rejection of an unjust enrichment analysis emphasizes that the key questions of principle and policy which are of concern to the law of restitution in this context relate to the determination of the appropriate remedy for the wrong rather than the definition of the wrong.

Thirdly, it has consequences for pleading and proof, for the application of defences and for the application of the rules of private international law to restitutionary claims.[13] As regards pleading and proof, the claimant must establish the elements of the wrong rather than unjust enrichment. As regards defences, the fact that the claim is founded on the commission of a wrong rather than unjust enrichment will affect the operation of defences, such as limitation periods, which are dependent on the nature of the cause of action.[14] As regards private international law, the fact that the claim is characterized as being founded on wrongdoing will determine the rules of jurisdiction and choice of law which are applicable.

(C) ALTERNATIVE ANALYSIS

Since the underlying cause of action for restitution for wrongdoing and restitution for unjust enrichment are different, it may be possible for the claimant to establish both types of claim on the same set of facts. This has been called 'alternative analysis'.[15] So, for

---

[9] [2001] 1 AC 268, 284 (Lord Nicholls).

[10] See further pp 448 and 480, below, concerning restitution for torts and restitution for breach of contract respectively.

[11] See, in particular, *Experience Hendrix LLC v PPX Enterprises Inc* [2003] EWCA Civ 323, [2003] 1 All ER (Comm) 830, 840 (Mance LJ). See p 478, below.

[12] D Friedmann, 'Restitution for Wrongs: The Basis of Liability' in W Cornish, R Nolan, J O'Sullivan, and G Virgo (eds), *Restitution: Past, Present and Future* (Oxford: Hart Publishing, 1998), 133.

[13] See GJ Virgo, 'What is the Law of Restitution About?' in W Cornish, R Nolan, J O'Sullivan, and G Virgo (eds), *Restitution: Past, Present and Future* (Oxford: Hart Publishing, 1998), 318–28.

[14] See Chapter 29.   [15] Birks, *An Introduction to the Law of Restitution*, 44.

example, if the claimant is induced to pay £100 to the defendant as a result of a fraudulent misrepresentation, the claimant may base the restitutionary claim on the fact that the defendant has been unjustly enriched at the claimant's expense, with the ground of restitution being the induced mistake.[16] Alternatively, the claimant may wish to base the claim on the tort of deceit.[17] Usually the result of the claim will be the same regardless of the cause of action which is chosen, but sometimes it will be a matter of importance to the claimant whether the claim is founded on the commission of a wrong or the reversal of the defendant's unjust enrichment. One of the most significant factors affecting how the action is framed relates to what the claimant needs to prove to establish the cause of action. It may, for example, be easier to prove that the defendant has been unjustly enriched than that the defendant has committed a wrong, primarily because liability for unjust enrichment is strict whereas liability for a number of wrongs requires proof of fault.

The fact that alternative analysis is possible means that some of the old cases in particular need to be treated with care because, although they may appear to have decided that a restitutionary remedy could be awarded for the type of wrong which was committed, the cause of action might today be interpreted as having been founded on unjust enrichment.

(D) DOES RESTITUTION FOR WRONGS PROPERLY FORM PART OF THE LAW OF RESTITUTION?

Regardless of whether restitution for wrongs is considered to be based on the principle of unjust enrichment or the fact that the defendant has committed a wrong, it is clear that the claimant can obtain remedies which are assessed by reference to the benefit obtained by the defendant as a result of the commission of the wrong. But should these remedies necessarily be characterized as restitutionary? Sometimes where a gain-based remedy is awarded to the claimant, the benefit which was obtained by the defendant did not derive from the claimant, so how can the benefit be *restored* to the claimant? It is more accurate to say that, rather than the defendant being liable to restore a benefit to the claimant, he or she must disgorge the value of the benefit to the claimant.[18] It follows that there is a distinction between those gain-based remedies which are literally restitutionary and those which involve disgorgement. The former category of remedy is relevant where the defendant's gain is subtracted from the claimant as a result of the commission of a wrong. The award of such remedies can be justified by reference to the corrective justice principle,[19] by the defendant giving back to the claimant what the claimant had lost as a result of the commission of the wrong. This clearly falls within the law of restitution. Disgorgement remedies operate where the defendant is required to give up a gain made from the commission of the wrong, even though that gain was not obtained directly from the claimant. The award of such remedies might be justified by reference to the principle of distributive justice.[20] Despite the difference in justification for their award, turning on the difference between giving back and giving up, both categories of remedy are

---

[16] See p 187, above.

[17] As to whether gain-based remedies are available for this tort, see p 462, below.

[18] See FA Farnsworth, 'Your Loss or My Gain? The Dilemma of the Disgorgement Principle in Breach of Contract' (1985) 94 Yale LJ 1339, 1342; LD Smith, 'The Province of the Law of Restitution' (1992) 71 CBR 672, 696; J Edelman, *Gain-Based Damages: Contract, Tort, Equity and Intellectual Property* (Oxford: Hart Publishing, 2002), 72.

[19] See p 5, above.   [20] See p 6, above.

gain-based since they focus on depriving the defendant of a gain made as a result of committing the wrong. Consequently, it is perfectly legitimate to treat disgorgement remedies as falling within the law of restitution broadly defined, since they are assessed by reference to the value of the benefit which was obtained by the defendant from the commission of the wrong, rather than by reference to the loss suffered by the claimant.

Even if it is accepted that all gain-based remedies can be characterized as restitutionary, it might still be appropriate to distinguish clearly between claims which are founded on restoring to the claimant what he or she has lost as a result of the commission of the wrong and claims which require the defendant to disgorge what has been obtained from another party as a result of the wrong, for different policies may underpin each type of claim. This is the basic thesis of Edelman in his book on the award of gain-based remedies for the commission of wrongs.[21] He asserts that the award of gain-based remedies which seek to restore to the claimant what he or she has lost are easier to justify than disgorgement remedies, which should only be awarded where the defendant has acted cynically, although he does not make clear what 'cynically' means for these purposes. As will be seen in Chapter 18, the basic dichotomy suggested by Edelman appears to have been adopted when awarding gain-based remedies for breach of contract.

Great care must be taken when using the word 'restitution' in the context of wrongs since it can sometimes have a compensatory meaning. This is illustrated by the decision of the House of Lords in *Target Holdings Ltd v Redferns (a firm)*,[22] where Lord Browne-Wilkinson[23] described the remedy of ordering the reconstitution of a trust as 'restitution'.[24] Whilst this may be accurate in a descriptive sense, since reconstituting a trust involves restoring it to its state before the trust property was misappropriated, the use of 'restitution' is unfortunate in this context since reconstitution of a trust is a compensatory remedy, involving assessment by reference to what the trust lost rather than what the defendant gained.[25] Similarly, in *Swindle v Harrison*[26] the Court of Appeal described the remedy of equitable compensation for breach of fiduciary duty as 'restitutionary'. Such a description is incorrect because equitable compensation is assessed by reference to the claimant's loss rather than the defendant's gain.[27]

There is an unfortunate tendency for the courts to use the language of 'compensation' to include gain-based remedies. For example, in *FHR European Ventures Ltd v Cedar Capital Partners LLC*,[28] in the context of a claim relating to a bribe received by a fiduciary, the Supreme Court described the personal remedy available as 'equitable compensation',[29] which is assessed as a sum equal to the value of the bribe. But, since the bribe will have been received from a third party, it is inappropriate to describe the remedy which is assessed by reference to the value of the bribe as compensatory, even with the prefix 'equitable'. It is a disgorgement remedy which operates to deprive the defendant of the gain rather than to compensate the claimant for loss suffered.

---

[21] Edelman, *Gain-Based Damages*.   [22] [1996] AC 421.   [23] Ibid, 434.

[24] See too *AIB Group (UK) plc v Redler* [2014] UKSC 58, [2014] 3 WLR 1367, [65] (Lord Toulson) and [109] (Lord Reed).

[25] C Rickett, 'Equitable Compensation: The Giant Stirs' (1996) 112 LQR 27, 28; J Edelman and SB Elliott, 'Money Remedies Against Trustees' (2004) 18 TLI 116.

[26] [1997] 4 All ER 705.   [27] See SB Elliott, 'Restitutionary Compensatory Damages' [1998] RLR 135.

[28] [2014] UKSC 45, [2015] AC 250.   [29] Ibid, [1] (Lord Neuberger).

(E) THE RELATIONSHIP BETWEEN RESTITUTION FOR WRONGS AND PROPRIETARY RESTITUTIONARY CLAIMS

Where the defendant has wrongly taken the claimant's property the claimant may have two alternative restitutionary claims, one for a personal remedy founded on wrongdoing and the other founded on the vindication of property rights. For example, if the defendant takes the claimant's car without permission and then sells it, the tort of conversion will have been committed. The claimant may seek a personal restitutionary remedy founded on the tort or, alternatively, may bring a proprietary restitutionary claim to recover the proceeds of the sale of the car, such a claim being founded on the claimant's continuing title in the car and its traceable product.[30]

This distinction between proprietary claims and claims founded on wrongs is not, however, as neat as first appears, because a number of forms of wrongdoing require proof that the defendant has interfered with the claimant's proprietary rights, which in turn requires proof that the claimant has a continuing interest in the particular property. This is illustrated by the tort of conversion. But where the claimant sues for this tort, even though he or she must be shown to have an interest in the property converted, the cause of action is still founded on the tort and not on the vindication of property rights. Consequently, the award of restitutionary remedies following the commission of the tort of conversion are properly considered in this Part, rather than in Part IV where proprietary restitutionary claims are examined. It should be emphasized, however, that this is merely a matter of convenience for the exposition of the subject and because of the legacy of history as to how causes of action are characterized. It does not mean that the commission of the tort of conversion has nothing to do with proprietary restitutionary claims.

The overlap between restitution for wrongs and proprietary restitutionary claims may arise in another context. Sometimes, where the defendant commits an equitable wrong, the court may recognize that the defendant holds the benefit obtained from the wrong on constructive trust for the claimant.[31] The consequence of this is that the claimant will have an equitable proprietary interest in the property held by the defendant, so the claimant will be able to bring a restitutionary proprietary claim to vindicate this property right.[32]

2. THE PRINCIPLES UNDERLYING THE AWARD OF RESTITUTIONARY REMEDIES FOR WRONGS

In *Devenish Nutrition Ltd v Sanofi-Aventis SA (France)*[33] Arden LJ recognized that recent decisions of the courts had produced 'a cultural change in the law in favour of the classification of remedies on a coherent basis rather than on the basis of some formulaic division between different wrongs'. It follows that, whilst subsequent chapters do consider the operation of the law of restitution with reference to particular types of wrongdoing, it is important to focus on the remedies and seek coherence in their interpretation and operation regardless of the nature of the wrong which has been committed. That is what this chapter seeks to achieve.

---

[30] See Chapter 21.   [31] See p 509, below.   [32] See Chapter 22.
[33] [2008] EWCA Civ 1086, [2009] Ch 390, [67].

(A) THE FUNDAMENTAL PRINCIPLES

·There are two conflicting principles which relate to the award of a restitutionary remedy for the defendant's wrongdoing.[34] The first is that the defendant should not profit from his or her wrong.[35] If this principle is accepted and is taken to its logical conclusion it follows that, whenever the defendant obtains a benefit as a result of committing a wrong, he or she should be liable to pay the claimant the value of that benefit regardless of the type of wrong committed. The second principle contradicts the first, since it denies gain-based relief to the claimant where the effect of holding the defendant liable to pay the value of the benefit to the defendant would be that the claimant profits from the defendant's commission of the wrong.[36] This is much more likely to be the case where a disgorgement remedy rather than a literal restitutionary remedy in available, since the latter simply returns to the claimant what the claimant lost, where as the former requires the defendant to give up to the claimant what the defendant had gained from the commission of the wrong, even if this was not gained from the claimant. If this second principle prevailed it would mean that gain-based relief would be unavailable in any case where the claimant had suffered no loss as a result of the defendant's wrongdoing.[37] This would result in a significant restriction in the scope for the award of gain-based relief for wrongdoing, since often the defendant will have obtained a benefit from the commission of a wrong in circumstances where the claimant will have suffered little or no loss.

One method of reconciling these two principles is by concluding that any benefit obtained by the defendant should be paid to the State rather than to the claimant. This can already occur where the defendant has committed a criminal offence and he or she is deprived of any benefit obtained through the confiscation of the proceeds of the crime.[38] But this is because it is the function of the State to enforce the criminal law. Also State intervention is preserved for particularly culpable or harmful conduct which deserves criminalization for the benefit of the public. This is not the case with most forms of wrongdoing which involve the infringement of private rights. Sometimes, however, judges have stated that they would prefer to leave the matter to the State, so that, if no statutory provision has been made for disgorgement, the law of restitution should not be used to provide a remedy.[39] But, as Birks recognized:

> If the courts continue to subscribe to that view they will acquiesce in a trend towards the disempowerment of the individual and the alienation of the citizen from the legal system. Faith in the law and in individual action within the law will give way to helpless grumbling against the bureaucracy.[40]

In fact, the law of restitution itself has been able to reach a compromise between the two conflicting principles, by recognizing that a gain-based response is appropriate only in

---

[34] See *Halifax Building Society v Thomas* [1996] Ch 217, 229 (Glidewell LJ); *Attorney-General v Blake* [2001] 1 AC 268, 278 (Lord Nicholls).

[35] *Attorney-General v Guardian Newspapers Ltd (No 2)* [1990] 1 AC 109, 286 (Lord Goff); *Attorney-General v Blake* [2001] 1 AC 268, 278.

[36] *Fyffes Group Ltd v Templeman* [2000] 2 Lloyd's Rep 643, 672 (Toulson J).

[37] Although note Stevens's analysis of substitutive damages which are available as a substitute for the right infringed and which encompass gains made as a result of the infringement of the right: R Stevens, *Torts and Rights* (Oxford: Oxford University Press, 2007), 60.   [38] See p 535, below.

[39] See, in particular, *Halifax Building Society v Thomas* [1996] Ch 217, 229 (Peter Gibson LJ) and 230 (Glidewell LJ). See also *Chief Constable of Leicestershire v M* [1989] 1 WLR 20, 23 (Hoffmann J).

[40] PBH Birks, 'The Proceeds of Mortgage Fraud' (1996) 10 TLI 2, 5.

respect of certain types of wrong. Where the defendant has committed one of these wrongs, the law of restitution considers that it is sometimes preferable that the claimant should obtain the benefit of the wrong rather than allow the defendant to profit from its commission, even though the result may be that the claimant profits from the wrong since he or she had suffered little or no financial loss as a consequence.[41] Consequently, it is necessary to determine which types of wrong will trigger a gain-based response. A number of factors can be identified which will assist in the determination of this.[42]

(B) DETERMINING WHICH WRONGS WILL TRIGGER A GAIN-BASED RESPONSE

(i) Interference with Property Rights

Where the wrong involves the defendant obtaining a benefit by using or interfering with the claimant's asset, gain-based relief is likely to be available. The award of restitution in such circumstances is consistent with the two principles which underlie restitution for wrongs. First, the defendant will have obtained a benefit as a result of the commission of a wrong which involves interference with somebody else's property rights, and it is not appropriate that the defendant should retain that benefit. Secondly, since the profits derived from the use of the claimant's asset, it is appropriate that the defendant makes restitution of the value of that benefit to the claimant. So, for example, where the defendant takes the claimant's car and hires it out without permission, it is appropriate that the money received by the defendant should be paid to the claimant since it constitutes the fruits of the claimant's asset.

The award of gain-based remedies where the defendant obtains a benefit as the result of wrongful interference with the claimant's asset is justified by the fact that English law considers property rights to be deserving of particular protection from interference; the so-called right to exclusive enjoyment of an asset. This was recognized by Lord Shaw in *Watson, Laidlaw and Co Ltd v Pott, Cassels and Williamson*[43] who said that 'wherever an abstraction or invasion of property has occurred, then, unless such abstraction or invasion were to be sanctioned by law, the law ought to yield a recompense under the category or principle . . . either of price or of hire'.

In a very important analysis of the principles which underlie restitution for wrongs, Jackman[44] has also identified the principle of interference with property rights as being of prime importance in explaining many of the cases where a gain-based remedy has been awarded for wrongs. He justifies the award of gain-based remedies for such wrongdoing as a means of protecting what he calls 'facilitative institutions'. He considers property to be an institution which needs to be protected by the law and the award of gain-based remedies ensures proper respect for the institution since it is a mechanism for deterring harm to it, by ensuring that all benefits which the defendant derives from the property should be disgorged to the claimant.

The problem with this proprietary principle relates to the determination of what constitutes property rights. This is the weakness of Friedmann's analysis of the award of

---

[41] See especially *Crown Dilmun v Sutton* [2004] EWHC 52, [212] (Peter Smith J). Stevens explains these awards as a substitute for the right which has been infringed: *Torts and Rights*, 61.

[42] See IM Jackman, 'Restitution for Wrongs' (1989) 48 CLJ 302; IM Jackman, *The Varieties of Restitution* (Sydney: The Federation Press, 1998). See generally Edelman, *Gain-Based Damages*.

[43] (1914) 31 RPC 104, 119. See also *Surrey CC v Bredero Homes Ltd* [1993] 1 WLR 1361, 1369 (Steyn LJ).

[44] Jackman, 'Restitution for Wrongs', 305–11.

gain-based remedies for wrongs.[45] He accepts that such remedies are particularly appropriate where the effect of the wrong is interference with the claimant's property rights. But, to explain many of the cases where gain-based relief has been awarded, he adopts a very wide interpretation of property to include 'quasi-property', a phrase which covers 'interests in ideas, information, trade secrets and opportunity'.[46] But, if the notion of property is extended in this artificial way, it is unclear when this extension should end. Whilst interference with property rights is a useful principle for determining when gain-based relief is available, it is not the only principle and the notion of property rights must not be extended artificially.[47]

(ii) Deterrence and Ethical Standards

In some situations gain-based remedies can be justified on the grounds that they are necessary to deter wrongdoing and to maintain ethical standards.[48]

(1) Abuse of a Relationship of Trust and Confidence

Where the defendant abuses a relationship of trust and confidence with the claimant, the award of gain-based relief will be available in Equity.[49] It is not every relationship between the parties which deserves such protection, but, where there is a relationship of trust and confidence, this is, to use Jackman's terminology, a facilitative institution which deserves particular protection from the law.[50] This is because the key characteristic of such relationships is that the claimant is dependent on the defendant for advice and management, so the defendant is placed in a particularly powerful position where there is a constant temptation to exploit the claimant. It is to deter the defendant from succumbing to this temptation that restitution of any benefits obtained by breach of trust or confidence will be awarded to the claimant.[51] This is why a gain-based remedy may be awarded even though there is no evidence that the defendant did actually abuse the relationship of trust and confidence.

(2) Illegal Conduct

Where the wrong committed by the defendant involves the commission of an illegal act it is entirely appropriate for the defendant to disgorge benefits acquired from the commission of that wrong to the claimant. The award of gain-based relief in such circumstances is justified by the need to deter defendants from committing such wrongs. It is for this reason that such relief is appropriate where the defendant has obtained a benefit by committing a crime.[52]

(3) The Defendant's Culpability

Although it has sometimes been suggested that gain-based remedies should be available where the defendant's conduct in committing the wrong is particularly blameworthy, the nature of the defendant's culpability cannot operate as a principle to identify those wrongs

---

[45] D Friedmann, 'Restitution of Benefits Obtained Through the Appropriation of Property or the Commission of a Wrong' (1980) 80 Columbia Law Review 504.

[46] Ibid, 512.   [47] Friedmann, 'Restitution for Wrongs: The Basis of Liability'.

[48] Friedmann, 'Restitution of Benefits Obtained Through the Appropriation of Property or the Commission of a Wrong'.   [49] See Chapter 19.

[50] Jackman, 'Restitution for Wrongs', 311–17. See also S Worthington, 'Reconsidering Disgorgement for Wrongs' (1999) MLR 218.

[51] *Murad v Al-Saraj* [2005] EWCA Civ 959, [2005] WTLR 1573, [74] (Arden LJ). See generally M Conaglen, *Fiduciary Loyalty: Protecting the Due Performance of Non-Fiduciary Duties* (Oxford: Hart Publishing, 2010), especially ch 4.   [52] See Chapter 20.

for which gain-based relief is available, simply because the defendant's culpability will vary from case to case. The House of Lords recognized in *Attorney-General v Blake*[53] that the fact that the defendant has deliberately committed a wrong is not a reason in its own right to award restitution. But, once it has been determined by reference to other principles that gain-based relief is appropriate for a particular type of wrongdoing, the defendant's culpability may be taken into account to determine the type of relief which is appropriate on the particular facts of the case. So, for example, the fact that the defendant deliberately committed a wrong may be a reason why the defendant should be required to disgorge all benefits received as a result of the wrongdoing.[54]

(iii) Inadequacy of Compensatory Remedies

In those cases where the typical remedy awarded for the commission of a wrong is damages to compensate the claimant for loss suffered as a result of the wrong, gain-based remedies are appropriate where such compensatory remedies are inadequate. This is a particularly significant reason why gain-based remedies may exceptionally be available where the defendant has obtained a benefit as a result of breaching a contract.[55]

3. THE TYPES OF GAIN-BASED REMEDY FOR WRONGDOING

Once it has been accepted that the wrong committed by the defendant was of a type for which gain-based relief is available, it is then necessary to determine what type of remedy should be awarded.

(A) MONEY HAD AND RECEIVED

Where the defendant has obtained money as a result of the wrong he or she may be required to pay this amount to the claimant by means of the remedy of money had and received. This is a Common Law[56] restitutionary remedy, even though it is sometimes still described as an 'action'. It is a prerequisite for this remedy to be awarded that the money which the defendant obtained as a result of the commission of the wrong was subtracted from the claimant. So, for example, if the defendant wrongly obtained the claimant's money by deceit, the defendant may be required to repay the money to the claimant by means of the action for money had and received.[57]

(B) ACCOUNT OF PROFITS

Account of profits is a mechanism to require the taking of a literal account, to determine the profits made after deducting expenses incurred, after which the defendant is required to disgorge the net profit made from the wrong. An account of profits is a discretionary

---

[53] [2001] 1 AC 268, 286 (Lord Nicholls).

[54] The deliberate nature of the breach of contract was influential in both *Attorney-General v Blake* [2001] 1 AC 268 and *Experience Hendrix LLC v PPX Enterprises Inc* [2003] EWCA Civ 323, [2003] 1 All ER (Comm) 830. See p 476, below. See also *Jegon v Vivian* (1871) LR 6 Ch App 742, 761 (Lord Hatherley LC). See generally Edelman, *Gain-Based Damages*, who argues that disgorgement damages should be awarded where the defendant acted cynically in committing the wrong.   [55] See Chapter 18. See generally p 440, below.

[56] It is, therefore, not available where the defendant commits an equitable wrong.

[57] Alternatively, the claimant may bring a restitutionary claim founded on unjust enrichment, the ground of restitution being an induced mistake. See p 187, above.

equitable remedy[58] and consequently it may be defeated by equitable defences such as laches.[59] It may also be unavailable if the claimant's conduct can be regarded as unconscionable, as will be the case where the claimant stood by whilst the defendant made the profit and then claimed to be entitled to those profits.[60] Although the remedy of an account of profits is equitable, it is not confined in its operation to equitable wrongs, since it is clearly available[61] in respect of some torts[62] and for breach of contract.[63] It is often difficult to ascertain exactly what profits the defendant made as a result of the wrongdoing, since usually the profits will have been increased by the contribution of the defendant's own ideas, property and money. Consequently, the courts do not require absolute accuracy in the determination of the profits which derived from the commission of the wrong.[64] As Lord Nicholls recognized in *Attorney-General v Blake*:[65] 'Despite the niceties and formalities once associated with taking an account, the amount payable under an account of profits need not be any more elaborately or precisely calculated than damages.'

This remedy is clearly gain-based, since it requires the defendant's gain to be ascertained and transferred to the victim of the wrong,[66] but it straddles both the literal restitutionary and disgorgement function of gain-based remedies. For, where the claimant has paid money to the defendant as the result of the commission of a wrong, the appropriate remedy may be an account of the profits. Equally, where the defendant has obtained a profit from a third party, he or she may be liable to account for this profit too. Indeed, in *Murad v Al-Saraj*,[67] a case involving breach of fiduciary duty, Arden LJ described the remedy as a 'procedure to ensure the restitution of profits which ought to have been made for the beneficiary'. Jonathan Parker LJ in the same case,[68] however, described the remedy as being neither restitutionary nor compensatory but designed to strip the fiduciary of profits. But a remedy which is focused on the stripping of the defendant's profits is properly analysed as restitutionary in the sense of its being a gain-based remedy, albeit a remedy which may sometimes operate to disgorge profit rather than being literally restitutionary. The remedy cannot be characterized as compensatory[69] because it has long been recognized that it is irrelevant that the claimant could not have obtained the profit him or herself.[70]

---

[58] *Seager v Copydex Ltd* [1967] 1 WLR 923, 932 (Lord Denning MR).   [59] See p 741, below.

[60] *Re Jarvis (deceased)* [1958] 1 WLR 815, 820 (Upjohn J).

[61] Through the operation of Equity's auxiliary jurisdiction, in the same way that the equitable remedy of an injunction is available to restrain tortious conduct and specific performance to enforce contractual obligations. See K Barnett, *Accounting for Profit for Breach of Contract* (Oxford: Hart Publishing, 2012), 85.

[62] See, in particular, the torts which involve interference with intellectual property rights, discussed at p 460, below.

[63] *Attorney-General v Blake* [2001] 1 AC 268. See p 473, below.

[64] *Watson, Laidlaw and Co Ltd v Pott, Cassels and Williamson* (1914) RPC 104, 114 (Lord Atkinson). See also *My Kinda Town Ltd v Soll* [1982] FSR 147, 159 (Slade J).

[65] [2001] 1 AC 268, 288.

[66] See *My Kinda Town Ltd v Soll and Grunts Investments* [1982] FSR 147, 156 where Slade J said that the purpose of ordering an account of profits is 'to prevent an unjust enrichment of the defendant'. This can only be correct if 'unjust enrichment' is used in a purely descriptive sense rather than as a substantive principle. See p 8, above.

[67] [2005] EWCA Civ 959, [2005] WTLR 1573, [85].   [68] Ibid, [108].

[69] Cf *WWF—World Wide Fund for Nature v World Wrestling Federation Entertainment Inc* [2007] EWCA Civ 286, [2008] 1 WLR 445, [59] (Chadwick LJ).

[70] See, for example, *IDC v Cooley* [1972] 1 WLR 443; *Murad v Al-Saraj* [2005] EWCA Civ 959, [2005] WTLR 1573, [59] (Arden LJ).

A problem with ordering an account of profits is that requiring the defendant to give up all profits made might unfairly benefit the claimant,[71] especially where all the profit made cannot be attributed to the commission of the wrong. Two mechanisms have been identified which can assist in the assessment of the profits for which the defendant should account to the claimant.

(1) *Limiting the period for which the account must be taken.* Where the nature of the wrong is such that the defendant earns a profit over a period of time, and is still earning the profit at the time of the trial, a difficult question arises as to whether the defendant should be required to account both for all the profits which have already been made and also those which may be made in the future. This was a matter which was examined in *Warman International Ltd v Dwyer*[72] where the High Court of Australia recognized that, where it is equitable to do so, the defendant may only be required to account for the profits generated over a specified period of time. This was the type of account which was ordered in *Warman International Ltd v Dwyer* itself. The defendant in that case was an employee who had breached his fiduciary duty by taking a business opportunity for himself. It was held that the defendant was only required to account for those profits which he would not have incurred but for the breach of fiduciary duty,[73] which was found to be two years' profits made from the exploitation of the business opportunity.

(2) *The equitable allowance.* Alternatively, the defendant may be awarded an allowance in respect of those profits which were earned by virtue of the defendant's own efforts and this sum will be deducted from the amount for which the defendant has to account to the claimant.[74] The preferable explanation of this allowance is that, where the defendant has made a profit as a result of the exercise of his or her time and skill, it is not possible to say that all of the defendant's profits derived from the commission of the wrong. It follows that the equitable allowance seeks to apportion profits so that the claimant only recovers those profits which derive from the wrong and the defendant is allowed to retain those profits which can be considered to derive from his or her own contribution. It will, of course, be very difficult to apportion the profits exactly, but at least the existence of the allowance gives the court the opportunity to determine in general terms how much of the profits derived from the defendant's input, so that the defendant is not required to account for those profits because they did not derive from the commission of the wrong.[75] But the award of the allowance is not automatic, since the decision to award it, and the amount awarded, depends on the operation of judicial discretion which will be influenced by a variety of factors, including the good faith of the defendant.[76] But, despite this, the existence of the allowance is still preferably analysed as being grounded on principles of causation, albeit that the award will be tempered by judicial discretion.

---

[71] See *Fyffes Group Ltd v Templeman* [2000] 2 Lloyd's Rep 643, 672 (Toulson J).

[72] (1995) 182 CLR 544. See also *Murad v Al-Saraj* [2005] EWCA Civ 959, [2005] WTLR 1573, [115] (Jonathan Parker LJ).

[73] The High Court also suggested that the profits might be split between the claimant and the defendant, but this would normally be appropriate only where there was an antecedent profit-sharing arrangement.

[74] See *Re Jarvis, deceased* [1958] 1 WLR 815, *Boardman v Phipps* [1967] 2 AC 46 and *Warman International Ltd v Dwyer* (1995) 182 CLR 544, [33]. See also *Docker v Somes* (1834) 2 My and K 655, 39 ER 1095.

[75] *Warman International Ltd v Dwyer* (1995) 182 CLR 544, [33].

[76] *Boardman v Phipps* [1967] 2 AC 46; *Guinness v Saunders* [1990] 2 AC 663; *Warman International Ltd v Dwyer* (1995) 182 CLR 544.

(C) RESTITUTIONARY DAMAGES

(i) The Nature of Restitutionary Damages

The term 'restitutionary damages' is apt to mislead, since 'damages' suggests the award of a compensatory remedy which is assessed by reference to the claimant's loss, but the addition of the word 'restitutionary' immediately contradicts this. The use of the phrase 'restitutionary damages' has been criticized, most notably by Lord Nicholls in *Attorney-General v Blake*,[77] where he described the expression as 'unhappy' and rejected it. The Court of Appeal in that case[78] had no hesitation in calling the gain-based remedy awarded for breach of contract 'restitutionary damages'[79] and Lord Steyn used this expression in the House of Lords.[80] This accords with the recommendation of the Law Commission that the judiciary should use this term to describe the gain-based remedy awarded for wrongdoing.[81] If 'damages' is interpreted simply to mean a pecuniary remedy, the addition of the word 'restitutionary' simply clarifies that this is a remedy which is assessed by reference to what the defendant obtained from the claimant as a result of committing a wrong,[82] whereas compensatory damages are assessed with reference to the loss suffered by the claimant.

Even if the notion of restitutionary damages is recognized it is clear that it not a term of art. Typically, those judges and commentators who recognize the notion of restitutionary damages consider it to be wide enough to encompass all pecuniary restitutionary remedies which are awarded in respect of wrongdoing.[83] If this is correct it means that the notion of restitutionary damages encompasses money had and received and the remedy of an account of profits. But, since these remedies have a distinct meaning, it is preferable to confine the notion of restitutionary damages to a particular form of financial remedy which is different from those other two remedies, namely where the defendant has not obtained a positive benefit from the commission of the wrong but has simply saved money as a result of committing a wrong. Such a defendant may be ordered to pay the equivalent of the amount saved to the claimant and this should properly be characterized as restitutionary damages. Even Lord Nicholls may have changed his mind about the use of the term restitutionary damages. In *Commercial Remedies: Current Issues and Policies*[84] it is reported that he pronounced, extra-judicially at a conference, that 'the measure of recovery could extend from expense saved through to stripping a proportion of the profits made through to stripping all of the profits made from the breach'. Once it is accepted that a remedy should be available where expense has been saved, that remedy needs to be described in some way. It cannot be called an account of profits because there was no profit obtained. Consequently, 'restitutionary damages' is an appropriate term.[85]

---

[77] [2001] 1 AC 268, 284.   [78] *Attorney-General v Blake* [1998] Ch 439, 459.

[79] See also *Ministry of Defence v Ashman* [1993] 2 EGLR 102.

[80] *Attorney-General v Blake* [2001] 1 AC 268, 291.

[81] *Aggravated, Exemplary and Restitutionary Damages* (Law Com No 247, 1997), 51–2. Barnett in *Accounting for Profit for Breach of Contract*, 146, prefers the expression 'disgorgement damages'.

[82] PBH Birks, 'Restitutionary Damages for Breach of Contract: *Snepp* and the Fusion of Law and Equity' [1987] LMCLQ 421.

[83] See in particular PBH Birks, 'Civil Wrongs: A New World' in PBH Birks, *Butterworths Lectures 1990–1991* (London: Butterworths, 1992), 71.

[84] A Burrows and E Peel (eds), *Commercial Remedies: Current Issues and Policies* (Oxford: Oxford University Press, 2003), 129. Cf Barnett, *Accounting for Profit for Breach of Contract*, 146, who prefers to call all gain-based remedies for breach of contract 'disgorgement damages', whether they involve full or partial disgorgement.

[85] In *Attorney-General v Blake* [2001] 1 AC 268, 284 Lord Nicholls did use the language of 'benefit' as well as 'profit'. See also *Warman International Ltd v Dwyer* (1995) 182 CLR 544, 558.

(ii) Are 'Restitutionary Damages' Really Restitutionary?

Whether the award of damages in circumstances where the defendant has saved money is necessarily a restitutionary remedy is a particularly controversial matter, since in many cases it is possible to characterize the remedy as both compensatory, by reference to the amount lost by the claimant, and restitutionary, by reference to the amount saved by the defendant. This is primarily because the method which is adopted to determine the amount which the defendant saved through the commission of the wrong is what the defendant would have had to pay the claimant to obtain that which was actually obtained by committing the wrong. So, for example, if the defendant had taken the claimant's car without the claimant's permission and so saved the cost of hire the measure of damages will be the amount the defendant would have had to pay to the claimant to hire the car. It has been argued by Sharpe and Waddams[86] that the damages which the claimant receives in such circumstances are compensatory rather than restitutionary. This is because such damages seek to compensate the claimant for the loss of the opportunity to bargain with the defendant for an appropriate fee for the use of the claimant's property. The authors argue that the damages should be assessed as equal to the full profits made by the defendant, because the defendant in breaching the contract 'has prevented anyone from knowing how much in fact would have been paid for the right taken'.[87]

Such a compensatory analysis might sometimes be appropriate, at least where the claimant would have been willing to hire the property to the defendant or somebody else, but a principle of lost opportunity to bargain cannot be used to explain the function of the remedy which has been awarded in every case where the defendant has saved money by interfering with the claimant's property. This is because damages have been awarded in a number of cases where the defendant has interfered with the claimant's property even though there was no evidence that the claimant would have bargained with the defendant or even that the claimant would have used the property itself,[88] and sometimes it is clear that the claimant would definitely not have bargained with the defendant.[89] If the damages which were awarded in these cases are to be treated as compensatory rather than restitutionary it is necessary to introduce a fiction that the claimant would have been prepared to bargain with the defendant, even though this might be contradicted by the evidence. Such artificiality can be avoided simply by concluding that the claimant may be awarded a remedy which is assessed by reference to the amount saved by the defendant as a result of the wrongdoing.

A further danger in analysing these remedies as operating only to compensate the claimant for loss suffered, is that such an analysis increasingly depends on a strange and artificial notion of loss to ensure that the claimant obtains a remedy. Where the defendant has been enriched as a result of the commission of a wrong, but the claimant suffered no real financial loss, it is appropriate to consider the award of a restitutionary remedy which explicitly focuses on the defendant's benefit, rather than create a constructive loss.[90]

---

[86] RS Sharpe and SM Waddams, 'Damages for Lost Opportunity to Bargain' (1982) 2 OJLS 290. See *Inverugie Investments Ltd v Hackett* [1995] 1 WLR 713.

[87] Sharpe and Waddams, 'Damages for Lost Opportunity to Bargain', 296. See *Severn Trent Water Ltd v Barnes* [2004] EWCA Civ 570, p 449, below.

[88] See, the analysis in *The Mediana* [1900] AC 113, 177 (Earl of Halsbury LC); *Watson, Laidlaw and Co Ltd v Pott, Cassels and Williamson* (1914) 31 RPC 104, 119 (Lord Shaw).

[89] See, in particular, *Strand Electric and Engineering Co Ltd v Brisford Entertainments Ltd* [1952] 2 QB 246, *Penarth Dock Engineering Co Ltd v Pounds* [1963] 1 Lloyd's Rep 359 and *Gondall v Dillon Newspapers Ltd* [2001] RLR 221.

[90] See *Attorney-General v Blake* [2001] AC 268, 279 (Lord Nicholls). Cf ibid, 299 (Lord Hobhouse).

(D) NEGOTIATION DAMAGES

Despite the argument in the last section that the remedy which is awarded where the defendant has obtained a negative benefit in not negotiating with the claimant is properly analysed as restitutionary damages, the courts have gradually recognized a new type of remedy, relevant to particular torts, breach of contract and some equitable wrongs, which has regularly been characterized as compensatory.[91] This pecuniary remedy has sometimes been described as user damages or the hypothetical bargain measure, but it is more elegantly called 'negotiation damages',[92] which describes what the damages are providing for, namely what the claimant has lost and the defendant has gained by not negotiating with each other to release the claimant's right. This is a court imposed hypothetical bargain which seeks to determine the price which the parties would reasonably have agreed for the claimant to allow the defendant to interfere with the claimant's right.

The leading case on the award of this type of remedy is *Wrotham Park Estate Co Ltd v Parkside Homes Ltd*.[93] The defendant had built houses in breach of a restrictive covenant and it was held that the appropriate remedy was damages in lieu of an injunction to demolish the houses. The claimant had suffered no obvious financial loss as a result of the breach, because the value of its land was unaffected by the development. The remedy which was awarded was assessed by reference to the price which the claimant would reasonably have demanded of the defendant to agree to a waiver of the covenant. This bargain was most definitely hypothetical because it was acknowledged that the claimant would not have agreed to relax the covenant on any terms.[94] The price was assessed as five per cent of the defendant's profit from building the houses. But it is unclear how this figure was determined. Further, it is unclear whether this hypothetical bargain measure should be characterized as compensatory, by reference to what the claimant had lost in not being able to bargain with the defendant,[95] or restitutionary,[96] by reference to what the defendant had saved in not having entered an agreement with the claimant.

A further crucial question concerns why the defendant in *Wrotham Park* was not liable to account for all of the profits which it had made as a result of the breach of the covenant. This was presumably because it could not be established that all of these profits derived from the breach, since most of the profits arose from the defendant's contribution to the building of the houses. Consequently, the defendant could only have been liable to disgorge those profits which would not have been made but for the breach, but in a case such as this it is virtually impossible to determine which profits derived from the breach.

---

[91] *WWF—World Wide Fund for Nature v World Wrestling Federation Entertainment Inc* [2007] EWCA Civ 286, [2008] 1 WLR 445, [59] (Chadwick LJ); *Force India Formula One Team Ltd v 1 Malaysia Racing Team Sdn Bhd* [2012] EWHC 616 (Ch), [381] (Arnold J). Cf *Giedo van der Garde BV v Force India Formula One Team Ltd* [2010] EWHC 2373 (QB), [528] (Stadlen J). See further p 448, below.

[92] *Primary Group (UK) Ltd v Royal Bank of Scotland plc* [2014] EWHC 1082 (Ch). See also *Lunn Poly Ltd v Liverpool and Lancashire Properties Ltd* [2006] EWCA Civ 430, [2006] 2 EGLR 29, [14] (Neuberger LJ); *Force India Formula One Team Ltd v 1 Malaysia Racing Team Sdn Bhd* [2012] EWHC 616 (Ch), [383] (Arnold J).

[93] [1974] 1 WLR 798.   [94] This was recognized by Brightman J, ibid, 815.

[95] This was how Megarry V-C explained the case in *Tito v Waddell (No 2)* [1977] Ch 106, 335, as did Millett LJ in *Jaggard v Sawyer* [1995] 1 WLR 269, 291 and Lord Hobhouse in *Attorney-General v Blake* [2001] 1 AC 268, 298. See also *Lunn Poly Ltd v Liverpool and Lancashire Properties Ltd* [2006] EWCA Civ 430, [2006] 2 EGLR 29, [29] (Neuberger LJ); *Pell Frischmann Engineering Ltd v Bow Valley Iran Ltd* [2009] UKPC 45, [2011] 1 WLR 2370, 50; *Force India Formula One Team Ltd v 1 Malaysia Racing Team Sdn Bhd* [2012] EWHC 616 (Ch), [381] (Arnold J); *One Step (Support) Ltd v Morris-Garner* [2014] EWHC 2213 (QB), [104] (Phillips J).

[96] *Attorney-General v Blake* [2001] AC 268, 283–4 (Lord Nicholls of Birkenhead); *Experience Hendrix LLC v PPX Enterprises Inc* [2003] EWCA Civ 323, [2003] 1 All ER (Comm) 830, 839 (Mance LJ); *Giedo van der Garde BV v Force India Formula One Team Ltd* [2010] EWHC 2373 (QB), [508] (Stadlen J).

The formula which was adopted, namely five per cent of the profits, is artificial but it is at least realistic since it represents a reasonable sum which would have been demanded by somebody in the position of the claimant before agreeing to relax the covenant.

Subsequent cases have clarified how this reasonable sum should be assessed. In *Pell Frischmann Engineering Ltd v Bow Valley Iran Ltd*[97] the Privy Council recognized that, when determining the reasonable sum to be paid by reference to a hypothetical bargain between the parties, it is to be assumed that both parties would have acted reasonably in the negotiations and the focus should be on how those negotiations would have progressed in the light of the information known to the parties at the time and the particular commercial context. In *Vercoe v Rutland Fund Management Ltd*[98] Sales J emphasized that the award of this measure of damages requires the court to assess a fair price for the release or relaxation of the claimant's right, having regard to the likely parameters arising from ordinary commercial considerations, any additional factors which affect the just balance to be struck between the competing interests of the parties and the need to ensure that the relief awarded is not disproportionate to the claimant's interest in proper performance of the obligation. In assessing the award it may be relevant to take expert evidence into account, especially where the hypothetical agreement is closely analogous to normal commercial bargains in an established market.[99] In *Force India Formula One Team Ltd v 1 Malaysia Racing Team Sdn Bhd*[100] Arnold J identified the following principles for the assessment of the negotiation measure:

(1) They are to be assessed by considering what sum would have been arrived at in negotiations by the parties, had they been making reasonable use of their respective bargaining positions, having regard to the information available to them and the commercial context when the notional negotiation would have taken place.

(2) It is irrelevant that one or both of the parties would not have agreed to the deal.

(3) If there has not been any negotiation between the parties it is reasonable for the court to look at the eventual outcome and to consider whether this is a useful guide to what the parties would have thought at the time of their hypothetical bargain.

(4) The court can take into account other factors, including delay on the part of the claimant in asserting his or her rights.

Whilst assistance has consequently been provided in determining the negotiation measure, by identifying relevant principles, a fundamental controversy remains as to whether they are properly considered to be compensatory or restitutionary. Whilst the dominant analysis now is that they are compensatory,[101] that is not the universal view. In determining the appropriate characterization of this remedy, it is useful to consider the decision of the Privy Council in *Horsford v Bird*,[102] where the claimant had sued the defendant for the tort of trespass to his land in Antigua. The defendant had built a boundary wall purportedly between his property and that of the claimant, but in fact the defendant had encroached on the claimant's land and added 455 square feet to his property. The Privy

---

[97] [2009] UKPC 45, [2011] 1 WLR 2370, [49].   [98] [2010] EWHC 424 (Ch), [292].
[99] Ibid, [298].   [100] [2012] EWHC 616 (Ch), [386].
[101] *One Step (Support) Ltd v Morris-Garner* [2014] EWHC 2213 (QB), [104] (Phillips J). In *Lunn Poly Ltd v Liverpool and Lancashire Properties Ltd* [2006] EWCA Civ 430, [2006] 2 EGLR 29, [29], although Neuberger LJ considered the damages to be compensatory, he also described them as 'quasi-equitable' and concluded that, whilst they were normally to be assessed at the date of breach of the contract, the judge may select a different valuation date or take into account events after the breach when determining the award.
[102] [2006] UKPC 3. See further GJ Virgo, 'Hypothetical Bargains: Compensation or Restitution?' (2006) 65 CLJ 272.

Council concluded that two types of pecuniary remedy should be awarded. First, mesne profits specifically to compensate the claimant for the defendant's use of the claimant's land until the point when the trial judge determined that damages should be awarded in lieu of an injunction to remove the wall. Secondly, damages in lieu of an injunction representing the price which the claimant would reasonably have demanded for the defendant to purchase part of the claimant's property. This price was initially assessed by reference to the value of the land which the defendant had appropriated, but this amount was then doubled because the appropriation of the land had enhanced the amenity value of the defendant's own property by providing vehicular access and a garden, plus the defendant had saved money in not having to demolish the wall and rebuild it along the proper boundary. This analysis is significant because there was explicit reliance on the benefit obtained by the defendant in committing the tort; this is consistent with a gain-based characterization of the remedy. But it is unclear what the justification was for doubling of the value of the land appropriated. This is unprincipled and close to a punitive award.

Analysing negotiation damages as a compensatory measure seems misplaced, and liable to mislead, where it is clear that the claimant would not have entered into the hypothetical bargain. For, where no bargain would have been made, how can the claimant have suffered loss from the failure to bargain? Surely in such circumstances it is more sensible to focus on the benefit which was actually obtained by the defendant in not paying the claimant to alter the settlement. The preferable approach is to treat negotiation damages as having both compensatory and restitutionary characteristics, since any bargain would take into account losses suffered by the claimant and gains made by the defendant. In many situations the appropriate characterization is of no significance since the loss suffered by the claimant is the same as the benefit obtained by the defendant in not making the bargain. But sometimes, as *Horsford v Bird* shows, the proper characterization will affect the amount awarded and it is therefore unhelpful to treat the negotiation measure as absolutely compensatory. In fact, this hybrid characterization of remedies has been previously recognized by the Privy Council in *Inverugie Investments Ltd v Hackett*[103] in the context of assessing damages for the tort of trespass. In that case the defendant had excluded the claimant for 15 years from apartments which the claimant had leased from the defendant. During this period the defendant leased out the apartments itself, but only achieved an occupancy of about 40 per cent. It was held that damages should be assessed by reference to a reasonable rental value of all the apartments which the claimant had leased whilst the defendant was committing the trespass, after deduction of what the claimant had saved in not having to pay rent as a result of the defendant's trespass. It was irrelevant that the premises had not been fully occupied. Crucially, the court said that the damages 'need not be characterized as exclusively compensatory, or exclusively restitutionary; it combines elements of both'.[104] This was not a case involving the negotiation measure, but does support a more sophisticated approach to the characterization of remedies. For in *Inverugie* the award could not be considered solely compensatory, because the claimant's actual loss was confined to the income which it did not receive from the apartments. Since the defendant's occupancy throughout the 15-year period was only about 40 per cent, which would presumably have been the same for the claimant, awarding the claimant the full rental value of the apartments would have over-compensated him. Similarly, the remedy could not be characterized as purely gain-based because, as the Privy Council recognized, the defendant had not derived a benefit

---

[103] [1995] 1 WLR 713. See further p 456, below.
[104] *Inverugie Investments Ltd v Hackett* [1995] 1 WLR 713, 718.

from all of the apartments all of the time, but it was still expected to pay a reasonable rent for the use of the apartments throughout the period during which the tort had been committed.

Consequently, rather than a polarized debate about whether the negotiation measure is either compensatory or restitutionary, a holistic approach to the remedy should be adopted.[105] The negotiation measure has restitutionary characteristics, but is not limited by them.

(E) EXEMPLARY DAMAGES

Where the defendant has committed a tort,[106] such as assault, false imprisonment and even negligence,[107] but not a breach of contract[108] or breach of fiduciary duty,[109] the court may award the claimant exemplary damages[110] in addition to any damages which are awarded to compensate the claimant for any loss suffered. Exemplary damages will only be awarded in very special circumstances, but for present purposes the most important of these is where the defendant committed the tort calculating that he or she would make a profit which might well exceed any compensation which was payable to the claimant.[111] Whilst exemplary damages cannot be regarded as a completely restitutionary remedy, since the measure of such damages is not necessarily confined to the profit which the defendant made from the commission of the tort, they have been characterized as 'a blunt instrument to prevent unjust enrichment by unlawful acts'.[112] Despite this, the unsatisfactory nature of exemplary damages as a weapon in the restitutionary armoury is reflected in the rationale behind the award of such damages, which is not simply to deprive the defendant of any benefit made from the wrongdoing but is primarily to punish the defendant for such cynical wrongdoing and to deter the defendant from engaging in such unacceptable conduct in future.[113] Consequently, such damages are an inaccurate way of ensuring that the defendant does not profit from the wrong.[114]

(F) CONSTRUCTIVE TRUST

In certain circumstances where the defendant has obtained profits through the commission of an equitable wrong he or she will be required to hold the profits on constructive

---

[105] SM Waddams, 'Gains Derived from Breach of Contract: Historical and Conceptual Perspectives' in D Saidov and R Cunnington (eds), *Contract Damages: Domestic and International Perspectives* (Oxford: Hart Publishing, 2008), 192. Cf R Cunnington, 'The Border Between Compensation, Restitution and Punishment' (2006) 122 LQR 382, 386.

[106] The previous limitation, of awarding exemplary damages only for torts which had previously recognized that such damages were available, has been removed: *Kuddus v Chief Constable of Leicestershire* [2001] UKHL 29, [2002] 2 AC 122.

[107] *A v Bottrill* [2002] UKPC 44, [2003] 1 AC 449.

[108] H Beale (ed), *Chitty on Contracts* (31st edn, London: Sweet and Maxwell, 2012), para 26-043.

[109] *Vyse v Foster* (1872) 8 Ch App 309, 333 (James LJ). See also *Harris v Digital Pulse Pty Ltd* (2003) 56 NSWLR 298.

[110] For analysis of the law relating to the award of exemplary damages and recommendations as to reform see *Aggravated, Exemplary and Restitutionary Damages* (Law Com No 247, 1997), 53–184.

[111] See *Rookes v Barnard* [1964] AC 1129, 1226 (Lord Devlin).

[112] *Broome v Cassell and Co Ltd* [1972] AC 1027, 1130 (Lord Diplock).

[113] *Rookes v Barnard* [1964] AC 1129, 1221 (Lord Devlin).

[114] See A Beever, 'The Structure of Aggravated and Exemplary Damages' (2003) 23 OJLS 87 who advocates the abolition of exemplary damages since punishment is not an appropriate function of private law. This would be desirable.

trust for the claimant.[115] Although the recognition that the defendant holds property on constructive trust is not a remedy as such,[116] the recognition of the constructive trust does have remedial consequences, because the claimant will have an equitable proprietary interest which can be vindicated by means of a proprietary restitutionary claim. Where the defendant holds property on constructive trust this has three proprietary advantages for the claimant. First, since the claimant will have an equitable proprietary interest in the profits, it follows that he or she will have priority over the defendant's unsecured creditors if the defendant becomes insolvent before the profits are transferred to the claimant. Secondly, the claimant will be able to claim the fruits of the profits from the defendant. So, for example, if the profits which are held on constructive trust are invested in shares, the claimant will be able to claim the shares and any dividends which have been paid in respect of them. Thirdly, the claimant can assert proprietary rights against innocent third parties who have received and retained the asset or its traceable substitute,[117] as well as recipients who received but have not retained the asset or its traceable substitute in circumstances where their initial receipt is unconscionable.[118]

In English law the constructive trust is characterized as institutional, since it arises by operation of law rather than judicial discretion.[119] The preferable analysis of the trust, however, is that whilst it arises by operation of law where the defendant's receipt of the profits can be characterized as unconscionable, the three proprietary advantages of the trust can be modified through the exercise of judicial discretion for certain defined reasons.[120]

(G) RESTORATION OF PROPERTY

Another restitutionary remedy which arises where the defendant has committed a wrong is for the court to order that any property which the defendant obtained through the commission of the wrong should be restored to the claimant. This is illustrated by section 3(3)(a) of the Torts (Interference with Goods) Act 1977 which applies where the defendant has tortiously obtained and retained goods belonging to the claimant. This provision enables the court to order the defendant to restore the goods to the claimant, although this remedy is only available to the extent that damages are an inadequate remedy, and it creates no right to restitution, since the making of the order lies in the discretion of the court.

(H) INJUNCTIONS

In some circumstances the court may be willing to grant an injunction to prevent the defendant from profiting from the commission of a wrong.[121] Clearly this does not operate as a restitutionary remedy, but it is a pre-emptive remedy to prevent the situation from arising where the defendant has obtained a benefit which must be given up to the claimant.

---

[115] See p 509, below.

[116] See p 595, below for examination of the notion of the remedial constructive trust.

[117] See p 632, below.   [118] See p 645, below.

[119] *FHR European Ventures Ltd v Cedar Capital Partners LLC* [2014] UKSC 45, [2015] AC 250, [47].

[120] See further p 567, below.

[121] Such a remedy was awarded by the Court of Appeal in *Attorney-General v Blake* [1998] Ch 439 to prevent a defendant from profiting from a breach of contract. The House of Lords awarded the remedy of an account of profits instead: [2001] 1 AC 268.

4. CAUSATION AND REMOTENESS

Regardless of the nature of the gain-based remedy which is sought following the commission of a wrong, the claimant must show that the receipt of a benefit by the defendant was caused by the commission of the wrong.

(A) THE GENERAL PRINCIPLE OF CAUSATION

In *CMS Dolphin Ltd v Simonet*[122] Lawrence Collins J recognized that there must be 'some reasonable connection' between the wrong and the benefit which was obtained as a result of it. Traditionally, the test of causation which has been used in respect of restitutionary claims founded on wrongdoing is the 'but for' test. Consequently, the defendant will only be liable to make restitution where the claimant can show that the defendant would not have obtained the particular benefit but for the commission of the wrong.[123] This test of causation will be established by showing that the relevant wrong was the principal cause of the benefit being obtained, but it need not be the sole cause. Further, it appears that the burden of proving causation is placed on the claimant, although there are certainly exceptions to this where, for policy reasons, the burden is placed on the defendant.[124]

How easy it is to satisfy the 'but for' test of causation will depend on the nature of the restitutionary claim. Where the claimant seeks literal restitution of the benefit which the claimant argues the defendant obtained from the claimant as a result of wrongdoing, causation will be easily established since, but for the commission of the wrong, the benefit would not have been obtained. Where, however, the benefit was obtained from a third party, and so the claimant seeks disgorgement, it will be more difficult to establish that the receipt of the benefit was caused by the commission of the wrong. This is illustrated by *My Kinda Town Ltd v Soll*,[125] where the defendant had committed the tort of passing off by using as a name for a restaurant a name which was similar to that used by the claimant. It was held that the defendant was liable to account for the profits it had made from customers who had confused the defendant's restaurant with those of the claimant. This was simply because, but for the commission of the tort, these profits would not have been obtained. Clearly in cases such as this it will be particularly difficult to determine which benefits obtained by the defendant are attributable to the commission of the wrong.

Where the defendant is alleged to have profited from breach of fiduciary duty the test of causation is interpreted much more liberally. In *Murad v Al-Saraj*[126] it was held that, where the defendant was alleged to have profited from breach of fiduciary duty, the court was not concerned with what would have happened but for the breach but only whether the profits fell within the scope of the fiduciary duty. Consequently, a defendant fiduciary will be liable to account to the claimant for profits made from the breach of fiduciary duty even if the profit would have been made had the defendant not committed the wrong. So here the test of causation is not one of 'but for' cause, but simply one of contributory cause. This more liberal approach to causation for breach of fiduciary duty is due to the need to

---

[122] [2001] 2 BCLC 704, [97].

[123] See Farnsworth, 'Your Loss or My Gain?', 1343. See also *Murad v Al-Saraj* [2005] EWCA Civ 959, [2005] WTLR 1573, [62] (Arden LJ).

[124] See, for example, breach of fiduciary duty. See below.

[125] [1982] FSR 147, reversed as to liability in the Court of Appeal: [1983] RPC 407.

[126] [2005] EWCA Civ 959, [2005] WTLR 1573.

deter defendants from the temptation of abusing a relationship of trust and confidence.[127] Where, however, the defendant is liable for dishonestly assisting a breach of fiduciary duty,[128] a defendant who has profited from the assistance will be liable to account for those profits which were causally connected to the assistance, but here the test of causation is not 'but for', but rather whether the assistance was a real and effective cause of the profits being made.[129] Arguably, this distinct test of causation is justified because the defendant accessory is not a fiduciary, so a test of direct causation is required, but because the defendant must have acted dishonestly to be liable, the strict 'but for' test is inappropriate. This is similar to the law of mistake, where the test of causation for a spontaneous mistake is that of 'but for' causation, whereas the test of causation where the mistake was induced by fraud is simply that the mistake was an operative cause of the claimant transferring a benefit to the defendant.[130]

(B) ASSESSING THE DEFENDANT'S CONTRIBUTION

In those cases where the benefits obtained by the defendant resulted from both the commission of the wrong and the defendant's own contribution, that contribution should be reflected in the remedy which the claimant is awarded. This may occur by apportioning the profits which arose from the wrong, to reflect the fact that some of the profits were made by virtue of the defendant's contribution.[131] Alternatively, the defendant might be liable to account for all of the profits made as a result of the commission of the wrong, but is awarded a personal allowance to reflect the reasonable value of the defendant's contribution, at least where the defendant's conduct is not reprehensible.[132] A further option is to conclude that the claimant is only entitled to receive the profits made by the defendant for a certain period, thereafter the profits are deemed not to have derived from the commission of the wrong.[133]

(C) THE PRINCIPLE OF REMOTENESS OF GAIN

In the same way that remedies which seek to compensate the claimant for loss suffered are subject to a principle of remoteness of loss, the award of gain-based remedies are limited by a principle of remoteness of gain. Without such a limiting principle, all gains which accrue to the defendant as a result of the wrongdoing would be liable to be transferred to the claimant. This could constitute over-protection of the claimant from the effects of the defendant's wrongdoing by emphasizing the principle that no wrongdoer should gain from the commission of the wrong, without sufficient consideration of whether the value of all of this gain should properly be transferred to the claimant. It is for this reason that a principle of remoteness of gain is needed, the effect of which is that the defendant will only be liable to give up benefits to the claimant if they were obtained in circumstances which were not too remote from the commission of the wrong.

The nature of the problem is illustrated by the following example. If the defendant takes £10,000 from the claimant without consent, it is obvious that the benefit which was obtained by the defendant as a result of the conversion was £10,000. But what if the

---

[127] See p 423, above.   [128] See p 521, below.
[129] *Novoship (UK) Ltd v Mikhaylyuk* [2014] EWCA Civ 908, [2015] 2 WLR 526. See p 524, below.
[130] See p 187, above.
[131] See *Attorney-General v Guardian Newspapers (No 2)* [1990] 1 AC 109, 266 (Lord Brightman).
[132] See p 426, above.
[133] See *Warman International Ltd v Dwyer* (1995) 128 ALR 201. See p 426, above.

defendant used part of the money to buy shares and the value of the shares increased? Can the claimant successfully argue that this increase in value arose from the wrong or should this profit be regarded as too remote from the commission of the wrong? This depends on how the notion of remoteness is defined.

The preferable test of remoteness is that a gain is not too remote from the commission of the wrong where it arises directly from the commission of that wrong.[134] Gains which arise indirectly from the commission of the wrong should be considered to be too remote and so do not need to be disgorged.[135] So, where the defendant wrongfully takes the claimant's car, all the benefits which the defendant gains from the use of that car should be considered to arise directly from the wrongdoing. So, if the defendant hires the car to third parties, any money obtained from such hiring should be disgorged to the claimant. Similarly, if the defendant used the car and saved the cost of hire, the value of this negative benefit should be paid to the claimant in the form of restitutionary damages. If, however, the defendant obtained £500 from the use of the car and bought shares with this money, any dividends paid to the defendant in respect of the shares need not be disgorged to the claimant, since they did not arise directly from the wrongful use of the claimant's car. A possible qualification to this will arise if the claimant could establish a proprietary claim to the profits obtained by the defendant, as would occur if the profits are found to be held on constructive trust, for then the claimant would be able to claim all the profits made from the use of the car, regardless of whether they arose directly or indirectly.[136]

Some support for this principle that indirect benefits are too remote can be found in the decision of the Court of Appeal in *Halifax Building Society v Thomas*.[137] One of the issues in that case concerned whether a restitutionary claim could be made in respect of the proceeds of sale of a flat which had been purchased by the defendant with a loan from the claimant. This loan had been made as a result of the defendant's fraudulent misrepresentation as to his identity. When the flat was sold by the claimant there was a surplus after the loan had been discharged. It was held that the defendant could claim this surplus because it had not been made at the expense of the claimant.[138] Whilst this reasoning should be criticized since, had the defendant received the proceeds of sale, the restitutionary claim would have been founded on tort rather than unjust enrichment, so there was no need to show that the benefit was received at the claimant's expense, the intuitive response of the court was correct. This is because the surplus proceeds of sale were not obtained directly from the commission of the wrong, but were gained indirectly once the defendant had used the loan to purchase the flat, by virtue of the fact that the value of the flat had increased.[139] Similarly, in *Chief Constable of Leicestershire v M*[140] the defendant

---

[134] This test of remoteness was endorsed by the Court of Appeal in *Attorney-General v Blake* [1998] Ch 439, 459. The matter was not considered by the House of Lords.

[135] Birks called this the principle of the first non-subtractive receipt: Birks, *An Introduction to the Law of Restitution*, 352. The distinction between direct and indirect gains is a more elegant way of describing the same idea.

[136] See, for example, *Attorney-General of Hong Kong v Reid* [1994] 1 AC 324. See further p 511, below.

[137] [1996] Ch 217. See also *Boyter v Dodsworth* (1796) 6 TR 681, 101 ER 770; *Ex p Vaughan* (1884) 14 QBD 25 and *Chief Constable of Leicestershire v M* [1989] 1 WLR 20.

[138] *Halifax Building Society v Thomas* [1996] Ch 217, 227 (Peter Gibson LJ).

[139] See P Watts, 'The Limits of Profit-Stripping for Wrongs' (1996) 112 LQR 219, 220. If, however, the court had recognized that, had the defendant received the proceeds of sale, they had been received in circumstances where the defendant had been acting unconscionably, it would follow that the proceeds would have been held on constructive trust and so the defendant would have been liable to disgorge all the proceeds to the claimant regardless of whether they arose directly or indirectly from the commission of the wrong. See p 509, below.

[140] [1989] 1 WLR 20.

had made profits from the sale of properties he had purchased with the assistance of a mortgage advance which he had obtained by deception. Hoffmann J did not accept that these profits derived from the deception but concluded that they arose from the loan which was obtained by deception. In other words, the profit was too remote from the wrong and did not have to be disgorged.

Whilst the analysis of Peter Gibson LJ in *Halifax Building Society v Thomas* using the language of 'at the expense of the claimant' can be criticized as confusing restitutionary claims for wrongs with claims for unjust enrichment, might the language of 'at the expense of the claimant' be preferable to the language of remoteness? The better view is that it would not. It is certainly inapplicable where the benefit was obtained from a third party rather than from the claimant. Even where the defendant's gain has resulted in some loss to the claimant it is better to focus on whether the defendant's gain derived directly from the wrong rather than to focus on whether it came directly from the claimant, and this can be expressed most clearly with reference to the language of remoteness of gain.

(D) MORE THAN ONE VICTIM

There is one particular problem of causation which arises where there are a number of potential claimants.[141] In such circumstances it will sometimes be very difficult, if not impossible, to show that the benefit obtained by the defendant derived from the commission of a wrong against a particular claimant. For example, if the defendant owns a factory which discharges pollutants into the air, causing a nuisance to nearby residents, but no loss to them, and the defendant saved £100,000 as a result of failing to install the necessary devices which would have drastically reduced pollution, what should be the measure of the claimants' remedy? This will depend on who sues the defendant. If only one resident sues, but ten have been affected, should the one person who sues recover the full amount which the defendant saved, or only a proportion? If the claimant is awarded only a proportion, how should this be ascertained?

Where it is possible to apportion the defendant's gain amongst all potential claimants, this is the proper course to take. So, for example, in *Jaggard v Sawyer*[142] the defendant had breached a covenant which had been made with nine other people. Only one of these sued the defendant and the remedy which was awarded was ascertained by identifying the full amount which the defendant would have been liable to pay if all the victims had sued and then one ninth of this amount was allocated to the claimant. But this was an easy case, since the number of potential claimants was readily ascertained. In other cases it might be very difficult to predict how many people had been affected by the defendant's wrong, so it would not be possible to ascertain how the benefit obtained by the defendant as a result of the commission of the wrong should be allocated to any particular claimant who sued the defendant. In such circumstances there are only two possible solutions. The first is that the claimant should be denied gain-based remedies completely. For this reason, the Court of Appeal has held that exemplary damages will not be awarded where there are a large number of claimants.[143] Alternatively, the defendant should be required to disgorge all benefits to the claimant who successfully sues first. Such an approach has been recommended by the Law Commission as appropriate where the defendant is liable to pay

---

[141] *Aggravated, Exemplary and Restitutionary Damages* (Law Com No 247, 1997), 50–1. There is no problem where there is more than one defendant, since each defendant will simply be liable to disgorge the benefit which he or she had obtained as a result of the commission of the wrong. See ibid, 49.

[142] [1995] 1 WLR 269.   [143] *AB v South West Water Services Ltd* [1993] QB 507.

exemplary damages.[144] Since the fundamental principle of the law of restitution for wrongs is that the defendant should not profit from the commission of the wrong, this approach would also be appropriate in the context of restitutionary remedies, where it is not possible to apportion the defendant's gain between different claimants.

5. THE RELATIONSHIP BETWEEN GAIN-BASED AND COMPENSATORY REMEDIES FOR WRONGDOING

(A) ELECTION BETWEEN INCONSISTENT REMEDIES

Sometimes the claimant will be able to claim a compensatory remedy as well as a gain-based remedy for the same wrong. In such cases it is a fundamental principle of the law of remedies that the claimant is not able to recover both types of remedy to the extent that they are inconsistent.[145] Where the remedies are inconsistent with each other the claimant must elect between them. Once the claimant has made this election, any claim to the other remedy which was not chosen is lost forever.[146] Although the cases use the language of inconsistency of remedy, in reality the real concern is to ensure that the claimant does not accumulate remedies excessively.[147]

(B) WHEN MUST THE ELECTION BE MADE?

Although the normal time for election is by the time the judgment is given in the claimant's favour and is being entered against the defendant,[148] this rule only applies where the claimant was in possession of all the necessary information to be able to make the election. As Lightman J recognized in *Island Records Ltd v Tring International plc*:[149]

> a party should in general not be required to elect or be found to have elected between remedies unless and until he is able to make an informed choice. A right of election, if it is to be meaningful and not a mere gamble, must embrace the right to readily available information as to his likely entitlement in case of both the two alternative remedies.

A delay in making the election is more likely to be countenanced where the judgment is a default or summary judgment,[150] where the claimant may not have had sufficient information as to the profits made by the defendant when the judgment was given. But a delay will also be countenanced where, as occurred in *Island Records*, a split trial procedure is

---

[144] *Aggravated, Exemplary and Restitutionary Damages* (Law Com No 247, 1997), 189.

[145] *Sutherland v Caxton* [1936] Ch 323, 336 (Farwell J); *Mahesan s/o Thambiah v Malaysia Government Officers' Co-operative Housing Society Ltd* [1979] AC 374; *Island Records Ltd v Tring International plc* [1996] 1 WLR 1256, 1258 (Lightman J); *Tang Man Sit v Capacious Investments Ltd* [1996] AC 514, 521.

[146] *United Australia Ltd v Barclays Bank Ltd* [1941] AC 1. See also *Island Records Ltd v Tring International plc* [1996] 1 WLR 1256, 1258 (Lightman J).

[147] See S Watterson, 'Alternative and Cumulative Remedies: What is the Difference?' [2003] RLR 7, who concludes that there should be no need for election between remedies; it being sufficient that the claimant is prohibited from accumulating remedies which exceed the minimum necessary to realize the aim of each remedy. See also S Watterson, 'An Account of Profits or Damages? The History of Orthodoxy' (2004) OJLS 471.

[148] See *United Australia Ltd v Barclays Bank Ltd* [1941] AC 1, 19 (Viscount Simon LC).

[149] [1996] 1 WLR 1256, 1258. See also *Warman International Ltd v Dwyer* (1995) 182 CLR 544, 570.

[150] *Tang Man Sit v Capacious Investments Ltd* [1996] AC 514.

adopted, whereby the issues of liability and assessment of remedies are separated, with the second hearing only being held if the decision on liability is favourable to the claimant. Delay in exercising the right of election will not be countenanced, however, if the delay is unreasonable by prejudicing the defendant.[151] But, where the delay is reasonable, the court will be prepared to defer entry of judgment for a reasonable time to allow the claimant to obtain the necessary information to make an informed election. The court will even be prepared to make discovery and other orders to provide the claimant with the necessary information.[152]

(C) *TANG MAN SIT V CAPACIOUS INVESTMENTS LTD*

The unusual facts of *Tang Man Sit v Capacious Investments Ltd*[153] provided the Privy Council with the opportunity to consider when the claimant can be considered to have elected between inconsistent remedies. In *Tang Man Sit* a landowner had agreed to assign some houses to the claimant, but the deed of assignment was never executed. The landowner then let the houses without the claimant's approval. After the landowner's death the claimant sued the landowner's personal representatives for breach of trust and sought an account of the profits which the landowner had made from letting the houses in breach of trust. But the claimant also claimed compensation for the lost market rental on the houses, for the fall in the value of the properties resulting from the houses being encumbered by tenancies and for damage arising from their occupation. The trial judge found for the claimant and ordered the defendant both to account for the profits made and to compensate the claimant for the loss suffered, this loss to be assessed subsequently. The claimant recovered part of the profits and also proceeded with the assessment of the loss suffered. It discovered that the compensation for loss would be much greater than the profits which the defendant had made and so the claimant sought to recover the damages from the defendant, giving credit for the profits which it had already received. The issue for the Privy Council was whether the claimant had elected to receive the profits with the consequence that it was unable to recover damages for loss.

The Privy Council first recognized that the remedies of compensation and account of profits were inconsistent. This was because the account of profits represented the money which the defendant had received from the use of the properties in breach of trust, whereas compensation represented the financial return the claimant would have received for the same period had it been able to use the properties; the wrong which enabled the defendant to gain the profit also caused loss to the claimant. Because of the inconsistency between the remedies, the claimant was required to elect between them. The question then was at what point the claimant is required to make an election. Even though the trial judge had already entered judgment for the claimant, the Privy Council held that the claimant had not exercised the right of election until it claimed compensation rather than restitution. The delay in making the election was not considered to be unreasonable because the form of the trial judge's order was for both an account of profits and compensation. This meant that the claimant's acceptance of the profits from the defendant did not constitute an election, particularly because the claimant was proceeding with the necessary steps for the assessment of damages and the defendant had not paid the profits to the claimant under the misapprehension that the claimant had accepted profits rather than compensatory damages.

---

[151] *Island Records Ltd v Tring International plc* [1996] 1 WLR 1256, 1259 (Lightman J).
[152] Ibid.   [153] [1996] AC 514.

(D) DETERMINING WHEN COMPENSATORY AND GAIN-BASED REMEDIES ARE INCONSISTENT

It does not follow from the decision of the Privy Council in *Tang Man Sit* that gain-based and compensatory remedies are necessarily inconsistent,[154] although great care must be taken to ensure that the two remedies are compatible. For example, in *Tang Man Sit* itself if the claimant had elected to take the profits it is clear that it could not also have claimed compensation for the income it had lost from being unable to lease the properties, since the defendant's profits arose from the same event which caused the claimant's loss, namely that the defendant rather than the claimant had leased the properties. But there would have been nothing to stop the claimant seeking, in addition to the remedy of an account of profits, compensation in respect of the capital loss to the properties arising from the breach of trust, namely that the tenancies had resulted in wear and tear to the properties and that the value of the properties had decreased by reason of their being leased.

The crucial question in determining the compatibility of the remedies is whether the award of a gain-based remedy reduces the claimant's loss. If it does, it follows that compensatory and gain-based remedies are inconsistent and the claimant must elect between them. This is illustrated by *Mahesan s/o Thambiah v Malaysia Government Officers' Co-operative Housing Society Ltd*,[155] where the defendant, in return for a bribe, had caused the claimant to buy land at an overvalue. The claimant sued the defendant both for the amount of the bribe and for damages for fraud for the loss caused by the purchase. It was held by the Privy Council that the two remedies were incompatible because, if the claimant recovered the amount of the bribe, this would have reduced its loss in buying the land at an overvalue. Consequently the claimant had to elect between the two remedies.

(E) INADEQUACY OF COMPENSATORY DAMAGES

In *Attorney-General v Blake*[156] the House of Lords recognized that, where the normal remedies for breach of contract (namely compensatory damages, specific performance and injunctions) are inadequate, the court could, if justice demanded, grant a gain-based award of an account of profits. This derives from a general principle that gain-based remedies will not be granted if compensatory damages are deemed to provide an adequate remedy. The principle of inadequacy of compensatory damages was relied on by the Court of Appeal in *Devenish Nutrition Ltd v Sanofi-Aventis SA (France)*,[157] to deny an account of profits as a remedy for the tort of breach of statutory duty because, amongst other reasons,[158] compensatory damages remained an adequate remedy. In that case the claimant had purchased vitamins from the defendant at an unlawfully inflated price. The claimant had sold the vitamins to third parties at a profit, the effect of which was that the claimant had passed on its loss to the third parties. Consequently, the claimant could not have recovered compensatory damages from the defendant. The Court of Appeal held that the claimant could not recover a gain-based remedy either, because compensatory damages remained an adequate remedy. It was recognized that, where the claimant had

---

[154] That an account of profits and compensation are not always inconsistent was accepted by the Privy Council at [1996] AC 514, 522. See also *Springform Inc v Toy Brokers* [2002] FSR 776; L Bentley and C Mitchell, 'Combining Money Awards for Patent Infringement' [2003] 11 RLR 79. Cf Lightman J in *Island Records Ltd v Tring International plc* [1995] 1 WLR 1256, 1258.

[155] [1979] AC 374. See also *Petrotrade Inc v Smith* [2000] 1 Lloyd's Rep 486; *Fyffes Group Ltd v Templeman* [2000] 2 Lloyd's Rep 643.

[156] [2001] AC 268, 285 (Lord Nicholls).   [157] [2008] EWCA Civ 1086, [2009] Ch 390.

[158] See further p 448, below.

suffered no loss, compensatory damages might be inadequate,[159] but this would not necessarily be the case where the loss had been passed on because, allowing the claimant to obtain a gain-based remedy in such circumstances, would result in a windfall which was considered to be unacceptable because the law should not transfer monetary gains from one underserving recipient to another.[160] But this confuses two separate issues, namely whether it is appropriate to restrict the claimant to a compensatory award and whether a gain-based remedy should be denied because the claimant had passed the loss on. It would have been preferable to recognize that, where the loss has been passed on, compensatory damages are not an adequate remedy, but a gain-based remedy might be denied for a distinct reason, namely that the loss has been passed on. Passing on of loss is not a defence to a claim grounded on unjust enrichment,[161] so it is difficult to see why it should be relevant in the context of a claim grounded on wrongdoing where the defendant has benefited from the commission of the wrong.

The requirement of inadequacy of compensatory damages is not recognized where account of profits is regarded as the normal remedy in Equity, for example for breach of fiduciary duty,[162] whereas the requirement exists for the award of other equitable remedies such as injunctions and specific performance.[163] That is presumably because the effect of injunctions and specific performance was to enforce Common Law rights, whereas the relevant right involving breach of fiduciary duty arose from within Equity and did not involve any extra-jurisdictional enforcement. This explains the true function of the inadequacy of compensatory damages principle, namely that such a remedy, where available in principle, should have priority over any other remedy, which are consequently only available exceptionally. But, if compensatory damages are inadequate, it is appropriate to award other remedies, including gain-based remedies. It follows that the decision in *Devenish* is suspect because compensatory damages were plainly inadequate, since the claimant had suffered no loss, rendering the award of a gain-based remedy appropriate. That compensatory damages should be considered to be an inadequate remedy when the claimant had suffered no significant loss, such that only nominal damages would otherwise be awarded, is consistent with the approach adopted when determining whether specific performance should be ordered.[164] It is also consistent with the approach of the House of Lords in *Attorney-General v Blake* where a gain-based remedy for breach of contract was justified precisely because the claimant had suffered no loss as a result of the breach.[165]

6. THE AVAILABLE DEFENCES FOR RESTITUTION FOR WRONGS

Where the claimant seeks restitution from the defendant in circumstances in which the defendant has committed a wrong, the question of which defences are available to the defendant is a matter of some complexity, depending on the nature of the restitutionary claim. There are three fundamental principles which need to be borne in mind when determining what defences are available to the defendant.

---

[159] *Devenish Nutrition Ltd v Sanofi-Aventis SA (France)* [2008] EWCA Civ 1086, [2009] Ch 390, [105] (Arden LJ).

[160] Ibid, [157] (Tuckey LJ).   [161] See p 118, above.   [162] See p 488, below.

[163] See, for example, *American Cyanamid Co v Ethicon Ltd (No 1)* [1975] AC 396, 408 (Lord Diplock); *Co-operative Insurance Society v Argyll Stores (Holdings) Ltd* [1998] AC 1, 11 (Lord Hoffmann).

[164] *Beswick v Beswick* [1968] AC 58. See also R Austen-Baker, 'Difficulties with Damages as a Ground for Specific Performance' (1999) KCLJ 1.

[165] See p 475, below.

(A) RESTITUTIONARY CLAIM FOUNDED ON THE DEFENDANT'S WRONGDOING

Where the restitutionary claim is founded on the commission of a wrong by the defendant, any defence which applies to the wrong should also apply to the restitutionary claim. If the effect of the defence is to extinguish the cause of action then there can be no wrong on which the claim can be based. For example, as regards limitation periods, the relevant limitation period should be that which relates to the particular wrong rather than to a cause of action founded on unjust enrichment.[166] Similarly, when tortious causes of action were defeated by the *actio personalis* bar, by virtue of which the personal representatives of a deceased wrongdoer could not be liable for a wrong committed by the deceased, this bar would defeat the claim even where the claimant sought restitutionary relief.[167]

(B) APPLICATION OF THE GENERAL DEFENCES TO RESTITUTIONARY CLAIMS

In addition, where the restitutionary claim is founded on the defendant's wrong then, because the claimant seeks restitutionary relief, the general defences to restitutionary claims should also be applicable.[168] The most important of these is the defence of change of position.[169] The effect of this defence is that, if the defendant has changed his or her position in reliance on the receipt of a benefit, restitution should be barred to the extent the defendant's position has changed. But this is subject to a very important qualification, namely that the defence will not be available to a defendant who was a wrongdoer.[170] The preferable view is that, rather than deny the defence to any wrongdoer, it is appropriate to distinguish between degrees of wrongdoing, so that the defence should generally be available to an innocent wrongdoer.[171]

(C) RESTITUTIONARY CLAIM FOUNDED ON THE REVERSAL OF THE DEFENDANT'S UNJUST ENRICHMENT

Where the restitutionary claim is founded on the reversal of the defendant's unjust enrichment even though the defendant has also committed a wrong, then, by virtue of the principle of alternative analysis, any defence which applies to an action founded on the wrong should not be applicable to the claim founded on unjust enrichment. This is because the claimant does not need to establish the wrong in order to show that the defendant has been unjustly enriched. It follows that the claimant could avoid the application of defences which relate to the wrong by founding the claim on unjust enrichment instead. But, before the court allows this to happen, it should carefully consider whether the policy which underlies the defence should be extended to a claim founded on unjust enrichment. This is exactly what the House of Lords did in *The Universe Sentinel*,[172] where the claimant sought to recover money which had been paid

---

[166] *Beaman v ARTS Ltd* [1948] 2 All ER 89 (Denning J). *Chesworth v Farrar* [1967] 1 QB 407, where the claimant was allowed to bring a restitutionary claim despite the fact that the tortious limitation period had passed, is better regarded as a case where the cause of action was the vindication of a proprietary right rather than wrongdoing.

[167] *Hambly v Trott* (1776) 1 Cowp 371, 375; 98 ER 1136, 1139 (Lord Mansfield).   [168] See Part V.

[169] See Chapter 25.   [170] *Lipkin Gorman (a firm) v Karpnale Ltd* [1991] 2 AC 548, 580 (Lord Goff).

[171] See p 696, below.

[172] *Universe Tankships Inc of Monrovia v International Transport Workers Federation* [1983] AC 366. See also *Dimskal Shipping Co SA v International Transport Workers Federation, The Evia Luck* [1992] 2 AC 152, 167 (Lord Diplock).

to the defendant trade union as a result of its threats that, unless the money was paid, it would prevent the claimant's ship from sailing. The restitutionary claim was founded on the reversal of the defendant's unjust enrichment, the ground of restitution being economic duress. The claimant could also have sued the defendant for the tort of interfering with contract, but it had not done so because there was a statutory immunity in favour of the defendant in respect of torts which were committed in the furtherance of a trade dispute. The question for the House of Lords was whether the policy underlying this statutory provision should be extended to the action founded on unjust enrichment. It was held that the immunity should be extended to the restitutionary claim.[173] This was an appropriate decision because the statutory immunity was not dependent on the nature of the cause of action on which the claim was based, but was concerned with whether the defendant should be held liable for any remedy in respect of conduct which related to a trade dispute.

7. RECOMMENDATIONS FOR REFORM

The Law Commission, in reviewing the law of restitution for wrongs,[174] considered that it is preferable to leave the development of the law to the common law. It was surely right to reach this conclusion, since the law concerning the award of gain-based remedies for wrongs is at an early stage of development, so that it would be inappropriate to curtail development by the judges. But the Law Commission did conclude that, since it recommended that the award of exemplary damages should be placed on a statutory footing, it should follow that restitutionary damages should be available wherever exemplary damages could be awarded. Consequently, the Law Commission recommended that legislation should provide that restitutionary damages may be awarded where the defendant has committed a tort, an equitable wrong or a statutory wrong and the defendant's conduct showed a deliberate and outrageous disregard of the claimant's rights.[175] The Law Commission also recommended that the award of such damages should be a matter for the judge and that this statutory power should not infringe any other power to award restitutionary damages.

If the development of the law of restitution for wrongs is left to the common law, how should that law be developed? The answer is that it should continue to develop gradually with continuous regard to the principles which underlie the award of gain-based remedies for wrongdoing. Although it might be considered that such remedies should be available regardless of the type of wrong which is committed, this is a dangerous approach, simply because each type of wrongdoing raises very different issues of policy as to the remedy which is appropriate. For example, the award of restitutionary remedies for breach of contract and the commission of a criminal offence raise very different questions which need to be examined in respect of the particular wrong itself. Nevertheless, the analysis of the Law Commission and the identification of the fundamental principles in this chapter should mean that judges can be more confident in awarding gain-based remedies for wrongs in the future.

---

[173] In fact the money was recoverable simply because it was paid in respect of matters which did not relate to a trade dispute.

[174] *Aggravated, Exemplary and Restitutionary Damages* (Law Com No 247, 1997).   [175] Ibid, 43.

17
RESTITUTION FOR TORTS

1. GENERAL PRINCIPLES

Where the claimant is the victim of a tort the most common remedy is damages to compensate him or her for loss suffered. But this is not the only remedy which is available. Exemplary damages may be awarded to punish the defendant for cynically committing a tort,[1] and other remedies are available which are purely restitutionary in effect, notably restitutionary damages and money had and received. The most important question relating to the award of restitutionary remedies for torts is whether they are available regardless of the tort which is committed or whether they are only available in respect of certain torts. If the latter is the case, it is then necessary to identify the criteria which are used to identify those torts for which restitutionary relief is available. The focus for this discussion is the so-called doctrine of 'waiver of tort' which has been particularly influential in the development of the law in this area.

(A) THE DOCTRINE OF WAIVER OF TORT

The doctrine of waiver of tort has had a malign influence on the rational development of the law of restitution for wrongs by virtue of its ambiguity and tendency to mislead. In *United Australia Ltd v Barclays Bank Ltd*[2] Lord Romer described the phrase 'waiver of tort' as picturesque but inaccurate. The doctrine can be interpreted in three different ways.

(i) Waiver of a Compensatory Remedy

The usual interpretation of the doctrine is that the claimant can elect not to claim compensation for the tort and can choose instead to recover a restitutionary remedy.[3] It is, however, misleading to say that a claimant who elects a restitutionary remedy is waiving the tort. In fact, it is vital that the claimant does not waive the tort because the tort constitutes the cause of action on which the restitutionary claim is founded.[4] All the claimant is doing is waiving the right to obtain remedies assessed by reference to the loss suffered, and instead elects remedies which are assessed by reference to the benefit gained by the defendant as a result of committing the tort.

That this is the proper analysis of this interpretation of the waiver of tort doctrine is supported by its history. The need to waive the tort originated as a device to enable the claimant to obtain a restitutionary remedy from the defendant where the cause of action was the defendant's wrongdoing. Such a waiver was required because, if the claimant wished to obtain restitution from the defendant, it used to be necessary to identify a promise by the defendant to repay the claimant. But if the defendant had committed a tort

---

[1] See *Rookes v Barnard* [1964] AC 1129. [2] [1941] AC 1, 34.
[3] Cf S Hedley, 'The Myth of "Waiver of Tort"' (1984) 100 LQR 653.
[4] *Chesworth v Farrar* [1967] 1 QB 407, 417 (Edmund Davies J).

against the claimant such a promise to repay would be incongruous, save where the claimant had ratified the wrong first. Such ratification was therefore required if the claimant wished to bring a restitutionary claim. Eventually the ratification of the wrong became a fiction, but at least it provided a route to imply a contract and so obtain restitutionary remedies.

With the rejection of the implied contract theory by the House of Lords in *United Australia Ltd v Barclays Bank Ltd*,[5] the demise of the doctrine of waiver of tort should have followed automatically. If it was no longer necessary to imply a promise to make restitution, it should have followed that it was no longer necessary to show that the claimant had ratified the wrong before he or she could obtain restitutionary relief for the defendant's tort. But, unfortunately, the House of Lords in that case did not appreciate the logical consequence of the rejection of the implied contract theory, since the court affirmed the continued existence of the waiver of tort doctrine.

In *United Australia* the claimant had received a cheque which had been fraudulently endorsed by its secretary, who did not have authority to do so, in favour of M Ltd, a company with which the secretary was associated. M Ltd paid the cheque into its account with the defendant bank. The defendant collected the proceeds of the cheque and placed them to the credit of M Ltd's account. The claimant then sought to recover the value of the cheque from M Ltd by suing both for money had and received and money lent. Before the claimant had obtained final judgment, the action against M Ltd was automatically stayed after the claimant entered into compulsory liquidation. The claimant then sued the defendant for damages for negligence and for conversion of the cheque. The defendant pleaded that it could not be sued by the claimant because, by initially commencing proceedings against M Ltd, the claimant had elected to waive the tort. This argument was rejected by the House of Lords, so the claimant was able to sue the defendant and obtain compensatory damages for the tort of conversion. On the facts of the case it was particularly easy to conclude that the commencement of proceedings against M Ltd had not involved waiver of the tort by the claimant, since the tort of conversion committed by M Ltd was separate from that committed by the defendant. In other words, the remedies which the claimant sought were cumulative rather than alternative, being founded on different acts of conversion.[6] The claimant would only have been prevented from seeking compensation for its loss against the defendant if the claimant had fully recouped all of its loss in the earlier proceedings against M Ltd.[7] But the court specifically recognized that its decision would have been the same if the claimant had initially sued the defendant for money had and received and then, before final judgment was given, had commenced proceedings against the same defendant for compensation. This is because the commencement of proceedings does not involve an election between restitutionary and compensatory remedies.[8] Compensation would only have been denied to the claimant if it had elected to take the restitutionary remedy, for it would then have been bound by that election. The implication of this decision, therefore, is that the claimant would only have irrevocably waived the tort once it had elected to take a restitutionary remedy. It follows from this that the court implicitly recognized that the waiver of tort doctrine is concerned with waiving the usual compensatory remedy for the tort, rather than waiving the underlying cause of action.

---

[5] [1941] AC 1.

[6] See Lord Wright, '*United Australia Ltd v Barclays Bank Ltd*' (1941) 57 LQR 184, 190.

[7] *United Australia Ltd v Barclays Bank Ltd* [1941] AC 1, 20 (Viscount Simon LC). See also *Tang Man Sit v Capacious Investments Ltd* [1996] AC 514, 523.

[8] See *Tang Man Sit v Capacious Investments Ltd* [1996] AC 514, discussed at p 438, above.

That the doctrine of waiver of tort relates to choosing between alternative remedies has been accepted in subsequent cases, most notably by Edmund Davies J who said in *Chesworth v Farrar*[9] that:

> A person upon whom a tort has been committed has at times a choice of alternative remedies, even though it is a *sine qua non* regarding each that he must establish a tort has been committed. He may sue to recover damages for the tort, or he may waive the tort and sue in quasi-contract to recover the benefit received by the wrongdoer.

Even if the doctrine is interpreted in this way it is misleading to speak of 'waiver of tort'. It is clear that the claimant does not need to waive anything, since he or she simply needs to elect between restitutionary and compensatory remedies. Crucially, claimants must ensure that they do not waive the tort itself for that is the underlying cause of action regardless of the remedy which the claimant seeks. As Birks said, '[waiver of tort] has become a loose and anachronistic description of the decision by the victim of such a tort to seek restitution'.[10]

(ii) Waiver of the Cause of Action

The doctrine of waiver of tort can be interpreted in another way, as recognized by Peter Gibson LJ in *Halifax Building Society v Thomas*,[11] who defined the doctrine 'as meaning that the [claimant] chooses not to sue in tort for damages but sues instead in restitution for the recovery of the benefit taken by the wrongdoer'. Although the phrase 'sues instead in restitution' is ambiguous, what the judge appears to have meant was that the claimant could waive a cause of action in tort in favour of a cause of action 'in restitution'. In other words, where the claimant is the victim of a tort then, rather than found the restitutionary claim on the defendant's wrongdoing, he or she may be able to bring a cause of action which is founded on the reversal of unjust enrichment. This sense of waiver of tort therefore involves alternative analysis.[12] So, for example, if the defendant induced the claimant to pay money to him or her by virtue of a fraudulent misrepresentation, the claimant might sue the defendant for the tort of deceit or might instead bring a claim founded on the defendant's unjust enrichment, with the ground of restitution being induced mistake. Similarly, if the defendant has falsely imprisoned the claimant and made it a condition of release that the claimant should pay a sum of money to the defendant, the claimant can base a restitutionary claim either on the tort of false imprisonment or, by a claim founded on the unjust enrichment principle, with the ground of restitution being duress of the person.[13]

Although the claimant's election to bring a claim grounded on the unjust enrichment principle rather than tort makes it appear that he or she has waived the tort, this is only true in a purely descriptive sense. It is not technically true because simply by basing the claim on unjust enrichment does not extinguish the tort. As was recognized by the House of Lords in *United Australia Ltd v Barclays Bank Ltd*,[14] the claim in tort will only be extinguished once final judgment has been obtained against the defendant. Until that point the claimant is able to discontinue the proceedings based on unjust enrichment and commence proceedings founded on the tort. Where the claimant founds the claim in restitution on the defendant's unjust enrichment the claimant is not waiving the tort but is simply ignoring it.[15]

---

[9] [1967] 1 QB 407.
[10] PBH Birks, *An Introduction to the Law of Restitution* (rev edn, Oxford: Clarendon Press, 1989), 317.
[11] [1996] Ch 217, 227.   [12] See p 417, above.
[13] *Duke de Cadaval v Collins* (1836) 4 A and E 858, 111 ER 1006.   [14] [1941] AC 1.
[15] PBH Birks, 'Restitution and Wrongs' (1982) 35 CLP 53, 55.

(iii) Ratification of the Defendant's Wrongdoing

The only true case of waiver of tort occurs where the claimant has actually ratified the defendant's wrongdoing.[16] This notion of waiver of tort will only be applicable where the defendant purported to act as the claimant's agent but lacked the authority to do so. For example, if the defendant sold the claimant's car, purporting to act as the claimant's agent but without authority to do so, there are two options available to the claimant. The claimant could sue the defendant for the tort of conversion and obtain compensatory or restitutionary remedies. Alternatively, the claimant could ratify the sale and so retrospectively authorize the defendant's actions. Consequently, the defendant would be subject to the usual obligations of an agent, including the obligation to account to the claimant for the purchase price which had been received from the purchaser. Since the effect of the ratification by the claimant is to extinguish the tort,[17] it follows that, once the claimant has ratified the wrong, he or she is unable to sue the defendant on the tort. It is for this reason that such ratification is properly called waiver of tort and the doctrine should properly be confined to this specific context.

(B) IS THERE A ROLE FOR THE DOCTRINE OF WAIVER OF TORT IN THE MODERN LAW OF RESTITUTION?

Apart from the exceptional case where the claimant has truly ratified the defendant's wrongdoing, the doctrine of waiver of tort should be rejected. Where the claimant chooses to base the restitutionary claim on the unjust enrichment principle rather than the tort, references to the doctrine of waiver can only cause confusion. The alternative analysis principle is a perfectly acceptable way of explaining what has happened. Where the claimant chooses to claim a restitutionary remedy rather than compensation for the tort, any reference to waiver of tort is misleading, since it suggests that the claimant's cause of action is not founded on the tort where he or she seeks a restitutionary remedy. This is patently untrue. The doctrine should be confined to the agency context and it should otherwise be removed from the law of restitution.

(C) RESTITUTIONARY REMEDIES FOR TORTS

(i) General Principles

Once it is accepted that restitutionary remedies are potentially available for the victim of a tort, it is still necessary to determine in what circumstances the commission of a tort may trigger the award of such remedies. When considering this question a number of key principles can be identified.

(1) The Compensation Principle

The general principle underlying the award of remedies for the commission of a tort is that the claimant who establishes that a tort has been committed will recover damages which are equivalent to the loss which he or she has suffered.[18] This is the compensation principle. It is a principle of fundamental importance to the law of restitution for torts

---

[16] This was called 'extinctive ratification' by Birks, *An Introduction to the Law of Restitution*, 315.

[17] *Verschures Creameries Ltd v Hull and Netherlands Steamship Co Ltd* [1921] 2 KB 608. See *United Australia Ltd v Barclays Bank Ltd* [1941] AC 1, 28 (Lord Atkin).

[18] *Stoke-on-Trent City Council v W and J Wass Ltd* [1988] 1 WLR 1406, 1410 (Nourse LJ). See also *Ministry of Defence v Ashman* [1993] 2 EGLR 102, 105 (Hoffmann LJ).

since, if compensatory damages are considered to be an adequate remedy, the claimant will not be able to seek a gain-based-remedy for the tort.[19]

The notion of adequacy of compensatory damages is open to manipulation. It has even been held that, if the claimant has suffered no loss, gain-based remedies might not be available because compensatory damages remain an adequate remedy. This was recognized by the Court of Appeal in *Devenish Nutrition Ltd v Sanofi-Aventis SA (France)*.[20] The dispute in *Devenish* arose from cartel agreements amongst competing suppliers of vitamins to increase their prices, which contravened EU competition law and constituted the tort of breach of statutory duty. The claimant had purchased vitamins from one of the suppliers to the prohibited agreements and then resold them for a profit. The claimant then sued the defendant for the tort of breach of statutory duty and sought an account of the defendant's profits rather than compensatory damages, because it had mitigated its loss by passing the overcharge on to its customers. The Court of Appeal held that a gain-based remedy was precluded where compensatory damages were an adequate remedy. In determining whether compensatory damages are adequate, the court identified two principles:

(i) Difficulties in proving loss do not automatically render damages inadequate,[21] save where the evidential difficulties are not the responsibility of the claimant.[22]

(ii) Where no loss is suffered, as distinct from not being proven, compensatory damages may be regarded as an inadequate remedy,[23] but where loss was not suffered because it had been passed on to customers, compensatory damages are not necessarily rendered inadequate,[24] since allowing the claimant to obtain an account of profits in such circumstances would result in a windfall,[25] which is unacceptable because the law should not transfer monetary gains from one underserving recipient to another.[26]

As a result of this second principle it was held that an account of profits was not available. This was described as embodying the 'passing-on defence'. But whether the fact of passing-on really can negate loss suffered is a matter of significant evidential difficulty, which was ignored by the court. The claimant had argued at a late stage that the effect of the cartel agreements was to squeeze its margin so that it did suffer a loss despite the fact that the increase in prices had been passed on to customers. The fact that it is virtually impossible to prove that loss really had been passed on is a significant reason why a passing-on defence has not been recognized in the law of unjust enrichment.[27] A more serious problem with the decision in *Devenish* relates to confining the claimant to nominal damages rather than awarding a gain-based remedy. Surely, if the claimant has not suffered loss, because it has been passed on, compensatory damages are no longer an adequate remedy and a gain-based remedy should have been available.

(2) Negotiation Damages

Sometimes damages will be awarded for tortious interference by the defendant with the claimant's property or proprietary right even though the claimant has not suffered any pecuniary loss as a result of the interference. In these circumstances the damages which are awarded to the claimant are assessed by reference to what the defendant would have

---

[19] *Devenish Nutrition Ltd v Sanofi-Aventis SA (France)* [2008] EWCA Civ 1086, [2009] Ch 390.
[20] Ibid.   [21] Ibid, [146] (Longmore LJ); [157] (Tuckey LJ).   [22] Ibid, [105] (Arden LJ).
[23] Ibid.   [24] Ibid, [110] (Arden LJ).   [25] Ibid, [146] (Longmore LJ).
[26] Ibid, [157] (Tuckey LJ).   [27] See p 118, below.

paid for the use of the property if he or she had negotiated with the claimant for its use. This is the so-called 'user principle',[28] which is increasingly being called 'negotiation damages'.[29] It is a matter of some controversy whether the damages which are awarded by reference to this principle should be characterized as compensatory or restitutionary.[30] In a number of cases in which such a remedy has been awarded the remedy could be characterized either as compensating the claimant for the loss arising from the defendant's use of the property without paying for it, or as depriving the defendant of a benefit, namely what the defendant saved by not paying the claimant for the use of the property. Indeed, in *Inverugie Investments Ltd v Hackett*[31] the Privy Council said that this remedy 'need not be characterised as exclusively compensatory, or exclusively restitutionary: it combines elements of both'. Despite this, there is a tendency in the cases to characterize negotiation damages as essentially compensatory.[32]

This is well illustrated by the decision of the Court of Appeal in *Strand Electric and Engineering Co Ltd v Brisford Entertainments Ltd*,[33] where the defendant had hired switchboards from the claimant for use in the defendant's theatre. After the contract of hire had come to an end the defendant retained the equipment and the claimant sued for the tort of detinue.[34] It was accepted that the defendant was liable and the court held that the measure of damages should be assessed by reference to what the defendant would have had to pay to hire the equipment for the period during which the tort was being committed. For Somervell and Romer LJJ these damages were intended to compensate the claimant for the loss it had suffered by virtue of the fact that the defendant's detention of the equipment had meant that the claimant was unable to make a profit from hiring the equipment to somebody else. But this identification of loss was highly artificial since it appeared that the claimant would not have been willing to hire out the equipment for the period during which the defendant had possession of it.[35] Consequently, Denning LJ said that the damages were restitutionary[36] and were assessed by reference to the benefit which the defendant had received by detaining the property without having to pay for its hire. But it is more appropriate to characterize the remedy as hybrid, since it embodies elements of compensation for the loss suffered by the claimant had it negotiated with the defendant, since the court is to assume that the claimant would have done so,[37] and the gain made by the defendant in not having to pay for the use of the property.

(3) Identification of Loss to Establish the Tort

Sometimes, whether the claimant has suffered loss as a result of the defendant's actions will be of crucial importance in determining whether the claimant can sue the defendant for a tort, since the identification of loss suffered by the claimant is a crucial element in establishing the cause of action. In such situations the question of loss suffered is an issue of substance rather than remedy. This was recognized by the Court of Appeal in *Stoke-on-*

---

[28] *Stoke-on-Trent City Council v W and J Wass Ltd* [1988] 1 WLR 1406, 1416 (Nicholls LJ).

[29] See p 429, above.   [30] See further p 430, above.

[31] [1995] 1 WLR 713, 718.

[32] See *Severn Trent Water Ltd v Barnes* [2004] EWCA Civ 570, where damages for trespass to land were awarded to compensate the claimant for the loss of the opportunity to bargain with the defendant for the price of interfering with the claimant's land rather than to deprive the defendant of any gain made by committing the tort. See also *Harris v Williams-Wynne* [2006] EWCA Civ 104, [2006] P and CR 27.

[33] [1952] 2 QB 246.   [34] Today, this would be the tort of conversion.

[35] It is for this reason that Sharpe and Waddam's analysis of such cases as involving the award of compensatory damages for the lost opportunity to bargain cannot be defended: RS Sharpe and SM Waddam, 'Damages for Lost Opportunity to Bargain' (1982) 2 OJLS 290. See p 428, above.

[36] See also *ACES System Development Pte Ltd v Yenty Lily* [2013] SGCA 53.   [37] See p 431, above.

Trent City Council v W and J Wass Ltd,[38] concerning the tort of nuisance which the claimant local authority alleged the defendant had committed by holding a market in close proximity to a market held by the claimant. Whereas the claimant had statutory authority to hold a market, the defendant lacked any authority to do so. Since the markets were held on the same day the defendant was held to be liable even though it could not be shown that the claimant had suffered any loss; such loss was presumed. But it was accepted that, if the markets had not been held on the same day, the defendant would only be liable to the claimant if it could be shown that the claimant had suffered loss as a result. If no loss had been suffered then 'there is no cause of action'[39] and without a cause of action there can be no question of remedies being awarded, whether compensatory or restitutionary, since no tort could be established.

(ii) The Obstacle of *Phillips v Homfray*

Care must be taken when analysing old cases which are consistent with restitutionary remedies being awarded for torts, both because a number of these cases are ambiguous as to whether the remedy awarded was intended to be compensatory or restitutionary, and also because it is sometimes unclear whether the underlying cause of action is tort or the reversal of the defendant's unjust enrichment. In addition, there are some cases which appear to suggest that gain-based remedies cannot be available where the defendant has committed a tort. The most influential of these have been the cases which arose from the litigation in *Phillips v Homfray*.[40] The complex litigation in *Phillips v Homfray*, which lasted for over 20 years in the late nineteenth century, has been one of the major obstacles to the recognition of gain-based remedies for torts. In fact, careful analysis of the various decisions which made up this litigation shows that they do not prevent gain-based remedies being awarded for torts.

(1) The Course of the Litigation

In *Phillips v Homfray* the deceased had committed the tort of trespass by drawing coal from the claimant's land and using passages under that land to transport this coal and also coal which had been mined from his own land. The Court of Appeal[41] held that the claimant was entitled to recover the value of the coal which the deceased had mined from the claimant's land and was also entitled to a remedy in respect of the use of the passages under the land for the transfer of the coal. The Court ordered that an inquiry should be held to ascertain the amount and value of coal which had been mined from the claimant's land and what the cost for the use of the passages should be. The deceased died before this inquiry was held. As the law stood at the time, the deceased's personal representatives could not be liable for any tort committed by the deceased,[42] so the case returned to the Court of Appeal to determine whether the deceased's personal representatives were entitled to have the inquiry discharged.[43] The Court of Appeal was only required to consider whether the deceased's estate remained liable to the claimant in respect of the deceased's use of the passages under the claimant's land. This effectively turned on a

---

[38] [1988] 1 WLR 1406.   [39] Ibid, 1419 (Nicholls LJ).

[40] See WMC Gummow, 'Unjust Enrichment, Restitution and Proprietary Remedies' in P Finn (ed), *Essays on Restitution* (Sydney: The Law Book Co, 1990), 60–7. See also PBH Birks, 'Civil Wrongs: A New World' in PBH Birks, *Butterworth Lectures 1990–1991* (London: Butterworths, 1992), 65–7; WJ Swadling, 'The Myth of *Phillips v. Homfray*' in GH Jones and WH Swadling (eds), *The Search for Principle* (Oxford: Oxford University Press, 1999), 277.

[41] *Phillips v Homfray* (1871) LR 6 Ch App R 770.

[42] This bar is called *actio personalis moritur cum persona*. It was abolished by the Law Reform (Miscellaneous Provisions) Act 1934.   [43] *Phillips v Homfray* (1883) 24 Ch D 439.

question of alternative analysis, namely whether the claim was dependent on the tort of trespass, which would not have survived the deceased's death, or whether it could be founded on the defendant's unjust enrichment, an action which would have survived the death of the deceased. The court held that the action was founded on the tort of trespass and so it did not survive the death of the deceased. The court relied on two additional reasons for its decision that the claimant did not have a restitutionary claim which survived the deceased's death.[44]

(a) The court first concluded that the deceased had not received a benefit by using the passages under the claimant's land. The court assumed that the deceased would have benefited from the trespass only if he had acquired property or the proceeds of property from the claimant as a result of the trespass. It did not consider that the negative benefit, which arose from the fact that the deceased had saved money by not paying the claimant for the use of the passages, was a real benefit for these purposes.[45] It followed that a restitutionary claim was unavailable because there was nothing for the deceased's estate to disgorge to the claimant.

(b) The court also held that the claimant could not waive the trespass, primarily because it was not possible to imply a contract that the deceased would pay for the use of the passages where the deceased had never intended to pay for such use.

(2) Analysis of the Case

If this decision is taken at face value it appears to constitute a major restriction on the ability to award gain-based remedies for torts, both because of the restrictive interpretation of what constitutes an enrichment and because of the suggestion that restitutionary relief is only available where it is possible to imply a contract to pay the claimant for the use of his or her property. The conclusion that such a contract cannot be implied if the defendant never intended to pay for the use of the claimant's property constitutes a fundamental obstacle to the success of restitutionary claims arising from the commission of a tort, simply because in most cases the defendant does not intend to pay for the unauthorized use of the claimant's property, and hence the defendant's conduct is characterized as wrongful. Careful analysis of the Court of Appeal's decision, however, shows that it was wrongly decided for two reasons, such that it should not be interpreted as barring restitutionary claims founded on torts.

(1) It is clear that if the claim was founded on tort it should have been barred by the *actio personalis* bar, since this bar related to the underlying cause of action. It is for this reason impossible to defend the assertion of the Court of Appeal that, if the deceased had obtained property or proceeds from the claimant as a result of the trespass, a restitutionary claim would lie against the estate. This assertion is indefensible because, even where the deceased had obtained a positive benefit from the tort, the underlying cause of action is still the tort and any claim on the tort must be barred by the *actio personalis* bar. Whether the benefit which the defendant obtained was positive or negative is totally irrelevant. The question is simply whether a tort could be established and, on the facts of the case, it was not possible to establish this. But it does not follow that all restitutionary claims founded on tort are barred, at least where the defendant has obtained a negative

---

[44] Ibid, 466 (Bowen and Cotton LJJ).

[45] Cf Baggallay LJ, ibid, 471–2. This is consistent with the approach of the House of Lords in *Attorney-General v Blake* [2001] 1 AC 268. See p 427, above.

benefit. *Phillips v Homfray* turned on the application of a bar which was peculiar to certain tort claims and, anyway, that bar has since been abolished.

(2) Even though the claimant could not rely on the commission of a tort to establish a restitutionary claim, it does not follow that the claimant could not bring any restitutionary claim, because he may have brought a claim founded on the defendant's unjust enrichment. Although the Court of Appeal held that such a claim could not be established because it was not possible to imply a contract, such reasoning has since been rejected.[46] Could the claimant have established that the deceased had been unjustly enriched at his expense? As regards the identification of an enrichment, the suggestion of the Court of Appeal that the saving of expenditure cannot constitute an enrichment is inconsistent with the modern approach to the definition of enrichment.[47] If the court's suggestion was correct it would mean that restitution would never lie for pure services or where the claimant had discharged the defendant's debt by paying a third party. Surely the deceased had been incontrovertibly benefited by the saving of a factually necessary expense, since the only way of getting the coal out of the mine was by paying the claimant for the use of the passages under his land.[48] Clearly this benefit had been obtained at the claimant's expense and the relevant ground of restitution could have been that of ignorance, because the claimant was unaware that the defendant was trespassing under his land.[49] It therefore seems that the defendant had been unjustly enriched at the claimant's expense.

But it is also necessary to consider whether the policy of the *actio personalis* bar should have been applicable to such a restitutionary action. It seems that this bar only applied to claims which were founded on tort and had no application to a claim founded on reversing the defendant's unjust enrichment. This is supported by the final case in the *Phillips v Homfray* saga, which concerned whether the claimant could recover the value of the coal which the deceased had extracted from the claimant's land.[50] The Court of Appeal accepted that, if this claim had been founded on the tort of trespass, it would have been barred by the *actio personalis* bar, but, since the action was characterized by the judges as an equitable action to recover the benefits which the defendant had received by wrongfully taking the claimant's coal, the underlying cause of action was not tort. In fact, this aspect of the claim could be analysed as founded on the claimant's continuing proprietary interest in the coal which had been taken without his knowledge,[51] so the restitutionary claim was founded on the vindication of property rights rather than tort and so would not have been affected by the *actio personalis* bar.

(3) Conclusion: Phillips v Homfray *is a Red Herring*

The implication of this analysis is that the controversial decision in the *Phillips v Homfray* saga, namely the case which was decided in 1882, is wrongly decided, both because it was wrong to suggest that the claimant had not been enriched and because the claim was not necessarily founded on the commission of a tort by the deceased. Careful analysis of the series of cases which formed the *Phillips v Homfray* litigation suggest that there is nothing in any of the decisions which prevents the award of gain-based remedies for tort.

---

[46] *United Australia Ltd v Barclays Bank Ltd* [1941] AC 1.   [47] See Chapter 4.
[48] This was recognized by Baggallay LJ in (1883) 24 Ch D 439, 471.   [49] See Chapter 8.
[50] *Phillips v Homfray* [1892] 1 Ch 465.   [51] See p 572, below.

2. TORTS FOR WHICH GAIN-BASED REMEDIES ARE AVAILABLE

Once it is accepted that gain-based remedies are available in principle where the defendant commits a tort, it is necessary to determine which torts will trigger a restitutionary response. Those torts which are committed when the defendant interferes with the claimant's property rights are most likely to trigger gain-based remedies,[52] but there is some evidence that other torts which are not proprietary may trigger a similar response.

(A) TRESPASS TO LAND

The tort of trespass to land[53] can be committed in a variety of ways, including the temporary use of the claimant's land without permission or the unlawful expropriation of the land. The nature of the trespass will have an effect on the nature of the remedy which is awarded. Whilst the typical remedy which is awarded is undoubtedly compensatory with reference to the loss suffered by the claimant, the award of literal restitutionary and even disgorgement remedies has been recognized. In *Stadium Capital Holdings v St Marylebone Properties Co plc*[54] Peter Smith J said:

> there has been a development over a series of cases of awarding damages not on the basis of the land to be used by the plaintiff but the basis upon which the defendant has used the land, and this starts basically with the decision in *Penarth Dock Engineering Co Ltd v Pounds* ... where Lord Denning MR says precisely that. The test of the measure of damages is not what the plaintiff had lost but what benefit the defendant obtained by having the use of the berth. This introduces a flexible basis for assessment because it requires the court to look at the use that was made. It is fair to say, in the case that we have been taken through, that the vast majority of those resolve it by charging a reasonable fee for the occupation of the land by the trespasser; but, in the light of these authorities, which end up in *Attorney General v Blake* ... my view is that this area is flexible, and in an appropriate case it is possibly arguable that the measure of damages can represent 100%. It is equally possible that the measure of damages could be debated [sic] by the amount of expenditure the wrongdoer incurs in obtaining the benefit, and in between it is possible that damages could be assessed by a license fee that would be artificially negotiated by the parties in the lines of *Wrotham Park* above and succeeding authorities.

This is a very significant dictum since it indicates that there are a range of remedial options open to the court which can most certainly be restitutionary and may even involve depriving the defendant of all gains made from the commission of the trespass,[55] although the latter remedy, in the form of account of profits, is only available in the most serious cases, particularly where the commission of the tort is considered to be especially cynical.[56]

In determining how remedies for trespass to land are assessed, it is important to distinguish between trespass involving the temporary deprivation of land and the permanent expropriation of land. In the former case, the remedy is sometimes called 'mesne profits' and relates to the use of the land. In the latter case, the court may order the

---

[52] See *Devenish Nutrition Ltd v Sanofi-Aventis SA (France)* [2008] EWCA Civ 1086, [2009] Ch 390, [39] (Arden LJ).

[53] See E Cooke, 'Trespass, Mesne Profits and Restitution' (1994) 110 LQR 420.

[54] [2010] EWCA Civ 952.   [55] Ibid, [14].

[56] *Ramzan v Brookwide Ltd* [2010] EWHC 2453 (Ch), [2011] 2 All ER 38. See p 454, below.

defendant to restore the land to the clamant, in which case an additional pecuniary remedy will be awarded relating to the use value of the land until it is restored to the claimant. The court may, however, decline to restore the land to the claimant, but will make an order for payment of the capital value of the land, as well as require the defendant to pay for the use of the land up until the order for payment of the capital value has been made, at which point the land will lawfully belong to the defendant. Whether the tortious claim arises from temporary deprivation of use or permanent exclusion from use of the land, the most common form of the remedy awarded is negotiation damages, assessed by reference to the fee which the parties would have negotiated for the defendant to interfere with the claimant's proprietary right.[57] Such a remedy may be characterized as compensatory,[58] but it has been characterized as restitutionary.[59] In fact, analysis of the leading authorities reveals that the remedy is properly characterized as hybrid, embodying loss and gain-based considerations.[60]

(i) Capital Value of Land

Where the court declines to restore the land which has been expropriated by the defendant to the claimant, the court will assess the capital value of the land. This may be determined simply by reference to the market value of the land, which reflects the value of the claimant's loss and the defendant's gain. In some circumstances, however, the court will consider more carefully what the parties would reasonably have negotiated for the claimant to sell the land to the defendant, which may be higher than the market value of the land if the defendant would have paid more for the land than the market value. This is illustrated by *Ramzan v Brookwide Ltd*,[61] where a store room[62] of an Indian restaurant had been unlawfully incorporated by the defendant into its neighbouring property to form a residential flat which was then leased. It was recognized that, in lieu of an order reinstating the store room to the claimant, the defendant was required to pay for its capital value. In assessing this value, the court had regard to the particular value of the store room to the defendant, who possessed the flat into which the store room was incorporated.[63] This reflects a restitutionary analysis. It cannot be considered to reflect a loss to the claimant, because it was found that the claimant would never have been willing to negotiate with the defendant for the sale of the store room. Increasing the capital value of the property to reflect the particular advantage to the defendant in having the store room is consistent with the general approach to the identification and valuation of an enrichment for purposes of a claim in unjust enrichment. That approach involves two tests to determine the value of a benefit, namely the market value and the objective value where the market would have taken into account particular circumstances of the defendant in valuing the enrichment.[64] If a person in the position of the defendant would gain

---

[57] See *Horsford v Bird* [2006] UKPC 3, p 430, above; *Field Common Ltd v Elmbridge BC* [2008] EWHC 2079 (Ch); *Stadium Capital Holdings v St Marylebone Properties Co plc* [2010] EWCA Civ 952; *Ramzan v Brookwide Ltd* [2010] EWHC 2453 (Ch), [2011] 2 All ER 38; *Jones v Ruth* [2011] EWCA Civ 804.

[58] *Severn Trent Water Ltd v Barnes* [2004] EWCA Civ 570; *Ramzan v Brookwide Ltd* [2010] EWHC 2453 (Ch), [2011] 2 All ER 38.

[59] *Field Common Ltd v Elmbridge BC* [2008] EWHC 2079 (Ch).   [60] See p 431, above.

[61] [2010] EWHC 2453 (Ch), [2011] 2 All ER 38.

[62] This was a 'flying freehold': the store room was physically located in the defendant's property but it belonged to the claimant who had access to it from his own property.

[63] See also *Horsford v Bird* [2006] UKPC 3, p 430, above, where the capital value of the land which had been expropriated by the defendant was also assessed with reference to the particular value of the land to the defendant, so that its value was considered to be higher than the market value.

[64] *Benedetti v Sawiris* [2013] UKSC 50, [2014] AC 938. See p 65, above.

particular advantages from the land, this should be taken into account when valuing the defendant's benefit. So, if a store room in the claimant's property is worth more to the defendant because it increases the size of the flat which the defendant leased, it is appropriate for this to be taken into account when assessing the value of the defendant's benefit in unlawfully expropriating the store room.

(ii) Use of Land

(1) Negotiation Damages

In assessing the value of the use of land, often the benefit to the defendant from using the land without permission will reflect the claimant's loss in not being able to use it. So, for example, if the defendant has leased the land to a tenant at market rent, and the claimant would otherwise have rented the land at market rent, the defendant's gain will correspond with the claimant's loss. But often evidence of the value of the use of land will not be so readily available. Consequently, the court will typically resort to the negotiation measure. Sometimes this has explicitly been characterized as a compensatory measure. For example, in *Ramzan v Brookwide Ltd*[65] the defendant was required to pay for its use of the claimant's store room until the point when the court ordered that the defendant was required to pay for its capital value, at which point the property was lawfully possessed by the defendant. Geraldine Andrews QC recognized that, at least in cases of permanent expropriation of the property, the use value should be assessed with reference to a percentage of the capital value of the property.[66] This is because, had the defendant purchased the land rather than unlawfully expropriated it, the defendant would have paid the claimant the capital value of the land before occupying it, and the claimant would have received income in respect of that capital payment.[67] Consequently, this was considered to be a compensatory measure. The use value of the store room assessed with reference to its annual market rent was £190 per annum. But this was not considered to be an appropriate measure of the claimant's loss, since the store room was used by the defendant as part of the residential flat which was rented out for profit. Consequently, the reasonable payment for the use of the store room had to reflect the particular value of that room to the defendant. This was assessed as 4.5 per cent of the capital value of the land. This was explicitly analysed as damages to compensate the claimant for loss suffered, which was found to be higher than the gross profits which the defendant had made from renting the flat. But it is difficult to see why the measure is exclusively compensatory, especially because the judge emphasized that the claimant would not have been willing to enter into an agreement for the defendant to use the store room,[68] so there was no loss of an opportunity to bargain, and because the judge had explicit regard to the benefit to the defendant from the use of the store room. Surely this reflects the proper analysis of negotiation damages as having both compensatory and restitutionary considerations, with regard to losses and gains.

The significance of the restitutionary component of negotiation damages is also reflected in the decision of the Court of Appeal in *Jones v Ruth*,[69] a case involving exploitation rather than expropriation of land. In that case the defendant had trespassed on the claimant's land in a variety of ways over a four-year period whilst the defendant was rebuilding his neighbouring property. Negotiation damages were awarded in lieu of an injunction for the defendant's use of the claimant's land, which was assessed as one

---

[65] [2010] EWHC 2453 (Ch), [2011] 2 All ER 38.   [66] As in *Horsford v Bird* [2006] UKPC 3.
[67] *Ramzan v Brookwide Ltd* [2010] EWHC 2453 (Ch), [2011] 2 All ER 38, [30].
[68] Ibid, [35].   [69] [2011] EWCA Civ 804, [2012] 1 WLR 1495.

third of the increase in the net value of the defendant's land as a result of the trespass. This assessment has a clear restitutionary focus on the value of the defendant's gain as a result of the trespass. In assessing this amount Patten LJ emphasized that the parties would be assumed to have negotiated reasonably, so the defendant would not have agreed to give up all of the profit which was attributable to the building works and the claimant would be assumed to have been willing to allow interference with her proprietary rights. This again reflects the hybrid nature of the negotiation measure.

This hybrid measure, with compensatory and restitutionary components, has previously been recognized explicitly in respect of trespass to land. In *Inverugie Investments Ltd v Hackett*[70] the claimant, who leased apartments within a Bahamian hotel complex, was ejected from the complex by the defendant who owned it. The defendant then used the apartments which had been leased by the claimant over the next 15 years for hotel guests. The average occupancy of the apartments over this period was only about 40 per cent. The claimant sued the defendant for trespass to land and sought damages which were to be assessed by reference to a reasonable rent for the apartments. The defendant conceded that the claimant was entitled to a reasonable rent, so the only question for the Privy Council was how this rent should be assessed. The Privy Council affirmed that, when assessing damages for trespass, it is irrelevant that the claimant could not have let the property to anybody else or could not have used it for him or herself.[71] It was sufficient that the defendant's tort had deprived the claimant of the use of the property. Consequently, the defendant was required to pay for its use of the claimant's apartments and this was to be assessed by reference to the reasonable rental value of all of the apartments which the claimant had leased throughout the whole period the defendant was committing the trespass, after deduction of what the claimant had saved in not having to pay rent as a result of the defendant's trespass. It was irrelevant that the premises had not been fully occupied. Crucially, the court said of the 'user principle', which provided the basis for the award of the damages in this case, that it combined compensatory and restitutionary elements.[72] But was this hybrid characterization accurate? It might be considered that the damages which were awarded sought to compensate the claimant for loss suffered from the tort. But the claimant's actual loss was confined to the amount of income which it had not received from the apartments and, since the occupancy throughout the 15-year period was only about 40 per cent, awarding the claimant the full rental value of the apartments would have over-compensated him. It might be argued that the claimant had lost the opportunity to bargain with the defendant, but if he had bargained with the defendant for the use of the apartments, the fact that the apartments would not have been used throughout the year would have been taken into account in reaching the bargain. Should the damages be characterized as restitutionary instead? The difficulty with a restitutionary analysis is that the Privy Council found that the defendant had not derived a benefit from all of the apartments all of the time, but it was still expected to pay a reasonable rent for the use of the apartments throughout the period during which the tort had been committed. This can be justified with reference to restitutionary principles since, by having the use of the claimant's apartments throughout the year, the defendant could be regarded as having received an objective benefit, namely the opportunity to obtain income from the use of the apartments. Since the defendant had not received a financial benefit in respect of all the apartments throughout the period of the trespass, it could seek subjectively to devalue this objective benefit by 60 per cent, representing the period for which it did not receive any income from the apartments. But subjective devaluation may be defeated by the principles

---

[70] [1995] 1 WLR 713.   [71] Ibid, 717.   [72] Ibid, 718.

of request, incontrovertible benefit, and free acceptance.[73] Clearly the defendant had not been incontrovertibly benefited but, by virtue of its actions in ejecting the claimant, it could be considered to have freely accepted the benefit, because, in ejecting the claimant, the defendant should be considered to have taken the risk that the apartments would not be occupied throughout the year. Although such reasoning was not relied on in *Inverugie Investments*, it is consistent with fundamental principles of the law of restitution and does enable a result to be reached which is intuitively correct. Crucially, this is a case where the restitutionary component of the negotiation measure is of essential significance to justify the damages which were awarded.

(2) Restitutionary Damages

Sometimes the remedy which has been awarded has been entirely restitutionary focused as regards the assessment of the defendant's gain as a result of the trespass to land, such that the remedy is properly characterized as restitutionary rather than negotiation damages. This is illustrated by the decision of the Court of Appeal in *Ministry of Defence v Ashman*,[74] which was unanimously affirmed by the Court of Appeal in *Ministry of Defence v Thompson*.[75] In *Ashman* the defendant and her husband, who was a member of the Royal Air Force, had occupied premises which were owned by the claimant. The defendant's husband moved out of the property but the defendant continued to occupy the premises with her two children. The claimant asked the defendant to vacate the property, but she refused to do so because she had nowhere else to go. The claimant then claimed possession of the premises and damages for trespass. The issue for the Court of Appeal was whether these damages should be assessed by reference to the market rent for such premises, by the subsidized rent which a serviceman would actually pay for the premises or by some other measure. Hoffmann LJ recognized that, although the usual measure of damages for tort is to compensate the claimant for loss suffered, it is possible for the claimant to elect to recover restitutionary damages measured by reference to the value of the benefit obtained by the defendant as a result of committing the tort.[76]

Where the claimant has elected to claim a restitutionary remedy for the defendant's trespass to his or her land, as the claimant had done in *Ministry of Defence v Ashman*,[77] it is then only necessary to value the benefit which the defendant had received; there is no need to consider the claimant's loss or what the claimant would have done had the defendant vacated the property when requested. Hoffmann LJ recognized that, when the defendant's benefit is valued, it is usually the objective value of the benefit which is relevant.[78] In that case this would be the rent payable on the open market, which was the amount the defendant saved by continuing to occupy the claimant's premises. But this objective value could be subjectively devalued by the defendant where the particular benefit might not have been worth so much to the defendant as it would to anyone else.[79] In *Ashman* it was considered that the defendant could subjectively devalue the value of the benefit because she had no choice but to stay in the premises until the local authority was willing to re-house her, so she could not be considered to have freely accepted the benefit.

---

[73] See p 78, above.   [74] [1993] 2 EGLR 102.   [75] [1993] 2 EGLR 107.

[76] *Ministry of Defence v Ashman* [1993] 2 EGLR 102, 105. Kennedy LJ, ibid, 104, described this approach as 'somewhat analogous to quasi-contractual restitution'. But there is no analogy; this is restitution.

[77] [1993] 2 EGLR 102.

[78] This is consistent with the general approach to the determination of enrichment for the purposes of the action founded on the reversal of the defendant's unjust enrichment. See p 97, above.

[79] *Ministry of Defence v Ashman* [1993] 2 EGLR 102, 105 (Hoffmann LJ).

Although the Court of Appeal did not specifically consider whether the benefit to the defendant in occupying the premises was incontrovertibly beneficial to her, the Court did in effect find that she had been incontrovertibly benefited by remaining in the premises, since she was getting accommodation for herself and her children which otherwise she would necessarily have had to pay for. It follows that the defendant could not have subjectively devalued the benefit which she had received completely. But it is not enough simply to identify an incontrovertible benefit; such a benefit must also be valued. It could not be valued at the market rate since, even if the defendant had been able to find somewhere else to live, she would not necessarily have spent that much money on the rent. Since she was willing to pay for local authority housing, this was considered to be the reasonable value of the benefit she had received and this constituted the measure of the restitutionary damages which were awarded. Consequently, the defendant was considered to have received a benefit which was valued by reference to the amount which she would have been prepared to pay for other accommodation; this was her incontrovertible benefit. If the defendant had been seeking private rented accommodation the market rate would have been the appropriate value of the benefit.[80] Logically, if the defendant had been looking for free accommodation with a friend she could not be considered to have received any valuable benefit at all, so the claimant would be confined to compensatory damages.

The question of valuation of the benefit was considered further in *Ministry of Defence v Thompson*, the facts of which were virtually identical to those of *Ashman*, where it was held that the actual value to the defendant of the benefit of continuing to occupy the claimant's premises was the higher of the rent which the defendant had previously paid for the premises and what she would have had to pay for local authority accommodation which was suitable to her needs.[81] These two measures were relevant because it was clear that the defendant was willing to pay both these sums. The previous rent was what the defendant had 'voluntarily been willing to pay for that house and, therefore, must have been the minimum value of the benefit of occupation'[82] and the cost of local authority accommodation was what the defendant intended to pay once such accommodation had been found, and so this cost constituted what the defendant had saved by committing the trespass on the claimant's land.

Usually, the value to the defendant of the use of the claimant's premises will be equivalent to its ordinary letting value.[83] The facts of *Ashman* and *Thompson* were unusual, primarily because the actual rent of the premises was well below its market value. But, despite the unusual facts, the decisions are of crucial importance because, as Hoffmann LJ recognized, it is now time to 'call a spade a spade' and recognize the existence of restitutionary remedies for torts.[84] Such recognition of restitutionary damages will not cause any injustice to the claimant, because, if his or her loss is greater than the defendant's actual benefit, the claimant can simply elect to claim compensatory rather than restitutionary damages. But, with the growing dominance of the negotiation measure, is there any scope for restitutionary damages, or will this simply be incorporated into the negotiation measure, as one component to assist in the determination of the agreement between the parties? That certainly

---

[80] Cooke, 'Trespass, Mesne Profits and Restitution', 428.

[81] *Ministry of Defence v Thompson* [1993] 2 EGLR 107 (Hoffmann LJ). In *Ashman* the damages were assessed by reference to the rent for local authority housing because this would have been slightly higher than what the defendant had been paying for the occupation of the claimant's premises.

[82] *Ministry of Defence v Thompson* [1993] 2 EGLR 107, 108 (Hoffmann LJ).

[83] As occurred in *Swordheath Properties Ltd v Tabet* [1979] 1 WLR 285.

[84] *Ministry of Defence v Ashman* [1993] 2 EGLR 102, 105.

appears to be how damages are now assessed in most cases. It must not be forgotten either that there may well be cases where the negotiation measure is likely to be higher than the pure restitution measure, so the claimant should be free to seek the negotiation measure if he or she wishes.[85] But if the restitutionary measure is likely to give the claimant more damages, there is no reason why the claimant should not be allowed to elect that remedy. That is consistent with the dictum of Peter Smith J in *Stadium Capital Holdings v St Marylebone Properties Co plc*.[86]

(3) Account of Profits

There will be certain exceptional circumstances where the defendant will be liable to account for profits made as a result of the trespass to land. Such a remedy will not, however, be available simply because the claimant pleads it. Rather, an account of profits will only be available where the commission of the tort is considered to be particularly serious. This is illustrated by *Ramzan v Brookwide Ltd*,[87] where an account of profits would have been awarded, had not the negotiation measure been more lucrative for the claimant. The trespass to land in that case was characterized as particularly serious because it involved outright and cynical expropriation of the claimant's property, which was amalgamated with the defendant's property to make a profit which could not have been made but for the expropriation. This was considered to be more serious than the trespass to land in *Horsford v Bird*,[88] because in that case the expropriation of land was for the personal benefit of the defendant and not for commercial reasons to make a profit. It is notable that an account of profits is limited to the most serious cases of trespass to land, involving significant culpability and motivated by a desire to deter such wrongdoing.[89] This is similar to the preferred justification for the remedy of an account of profits for breach of contract.[90]

(B) CONVERSION

Where the defendant has converted the claimant's goods, for example by selling them, the remedy for the commission of such a tort is restitutionary because the defendant must pay the value of the proceeds of sale to the claimant without any inquiry being undertaken as to what the market value of the goods was at the time of sale, which would be the measure of the claimant's loss.[91] In other words, the remedy for conversion can be assessed by reference to the defendant's gain rather than the claimant's loss where the value of that gain is greater than the loss suffered by the claimant. It is irrelevant that the claimant suffered no loss because he or she would not have used the property during the period of use by the defendant or could not have hired it out.[92]

---

[85] In *Ramzan v Brookwide Ltd* [2010] EWHC 2453 (Ch), [2011] 2 All ER 38 the negotiation measure was considered to be higher than the defendant's gain from the tort. See below.

[86] [2010] EWCA Civ 952. [87] [2010] EWHC 2453 (Ch), [2011] 2 All ER 38.

[88] [2006] UKPC 3. See p 430, above.

[89] Also reflected by the fact that exemplary damages were awarded of £60,000, three times the profit made by the defendant. [90] See p 480, below.

[91] Cooke, 'Trespass, Mesne Profits and Restitution', 421. Usually, the market value and the proceeds of sale will be the same, but this is not necessarily the case. The claimant will elect restitutionary relief where the proceeds of sale are greater than the market value of the goods.

[92] *Strand Electric & Engineering Co Ltd v Brisford Entertainments Ltd* [1952] 2 QB 246; *Penarth Dock Engineering Co v Pounds* [1963] 1 Lloyd's Rep 359; *Swordheath Properties Ltd v Tabet* [1979] 1 WLR 285.

The award of a gain-based remedy for conversion is illustrated by *Lamine v Dorrell*[93] where the defendant had committed the tort by selling the claimant's debentures without permission. It was held that the claimant could recover the sale price in an action for money had and received, without any attempt to ascertain what the market value of the debentures was. Similarly, in *Chesworth v Farrar*[94] the claimant's landlord converted the claimant's property and the claimant recovered the sale price of the goods without any attempt to ascertain what the market value of the goods was at the time of the sale. This remedy was acknowledged to be restitutionary because it was held that the limitation period for tort did not apply to the claim.[95] Where the defendant has converted the claimant's property by simply using it without selling it, the claimant's remedy should be characterized as restitutionary damages which are assessed by reference to what the defendant saved by not having to pay the claimant for the use of the property.[96]

(C) INTERFERENCE WITH INTELLECTUAL PROPERTY RIGHTS

Where the defendant interferes with the claimant's intellectual property rights the defendant's liability will be tortious. Originally, however, the liability was equitable and this equitable legacy continues to have an influence upon the remedies which are available. Today, the defendant's liability for interference with intellectual property rights may either arise by statute or the common law. Statutory relief exists for breaches of copyright[97] and patents,[98] whereas the remedies for infringement of trademarks[99] and passing off[100] continue to be governed by the common law.

It is generally accepted that, where the defendant interferes with any type of intellectual property right, a restitutionary remedy is available, whether it is measured by reference to the profits which the defendant made from infringing the right or by reference to what the defendant would have had to pay to obtain the claimant's consent to interfere with the right. The awarding of gain-based remedies in this context is consistent with the principles relating to the award of gain-based remedies for wrongdoing generally, on the basis that restitution is justified by virtue of the policy of protecting property rights. There is, however, no consistency between the different regimes governing intellectual property rights as to which type of remedy is available and what the conditions are for awarding such remedies. Because of this inconsistency, each type of intellectual property right will be considered in turn.

(i) Breach of Copyright

Where the defendant has profited from the breach of copyright he or she will be liable to account to the claimant for the profits obtained, regardless of the fault of the defendant in breaching the copyright,[101] but the profits will not be held on constructive trust for the

---

[93] (1701) 2 Ld Raym 1216, 92 ER 303. See also *United Australia Ltd v Barclays Bank Ltd* [1941] AC 1.

[94] [1967] 1 QB 407.   [95] This aspect of the decision is criticized at p 442, above.

[96] See the decision of Denning LJ in *Strand Electric and Engineering Co Ltd v Brisford Entertainments Ltd* [1952] QB 246. See also *Hillesden Securities Ltd v Ryjak Ltd* [1983] 2 All ER 184; *Kuwait Airways Corp v Iraqi Airways Co (No 6)* [2004] EWHC 2603 (Comm), [234] (Cresswell J).

[97] Copyright, Designs and Patents Act 1988, s 96(2). See also s 229(2) of the Act which allows an account of profits to be awarded where the defendant has infringed a design right.

[98] Patents Act 1977, s 61(1)(d).   [99] *Edelsten v Edelsten* (1863) 1 De GJ and Sm 185, 46 ER 72.

[100] *Lever v Goodwin* (1887) 36 Ch D 1.

[101] Copyright, Designs and Patents Act 1988, s 96(2). A similar provision applies to an infringement of a design right: ibid, s 229(2).

copyright holder.[102] Damages are also available as a remedy for breach of copyright, but not if the defendant's infringement of the copyright was innocent, in the sense that the defendant did not know and had no reason to know of the existence of the copyright.[103] It is unclear whether this means that restitutionary damages are unavailable for such innocent breaches of copyright. In addition, where the infringement is innocent but the defendant profited from it then, although the defendant is liable to account, the court may make an allowance for the defendant's skill and effort in making the profit.[104]

(ii) Infringement of Patents

Where the defendant has knowingly or negligently infringed a patent an account of profits or an award of damages is available.[105] But where the patent was innocently infringed the claimant is unable to obtain either remedy.[106]

(iii) Passing Off

An account of profits will only be awarded if the defendant deliberately passed off the claimant's goods.[107]

(iv) Infringement of Trademarks

An account of profits will only be awarded if the defendant deliberately interfered with the claimant's trademark.[108] Where the defendant innocently infringed the claimant's trademark the claimant will still be able to obtain a compensatory remedy.[109]

Whilst there is an unacceptable inconsistency in the award of gain-based relief for those torts which are concerned with interference with intellectual property rights, it is clear that the culpability of the defendant is generally a relevant consideration when determining the type of remedy which should be awarded.

(D) PRIVATE NUISANCE

Whether restitutionary remedies are available where the defendant commits the tort of private nuisance is a particularly controversial matter. In *Carr-Saunders v Dick McNeil Associates Ltd*[110] the defendant committed a nuisance by erecting extra storeys to its property which reduced the amount of natural light to the claimant's property. The claimant was awarded damages in lieu of an injunction and these damages appear to have been assessed by reference to the amount necessary to compensate the claimant for loss of use and amenity. Millett J did, however, say that, if there had been evidence of the profit which the defendant had gained by committing the tort, this would have been taken into account in assessing the award of damages. This suggests that a remedy assessed by reference to the defendant's benefit arising from the tort may be available where a nuisance is committed, at least where the tort involves interference with the claimant's property rights.

The decision of the Court of Appeal in *Stoke-on-Trent City Council v W and J Wass Ltd*[111] suggests, however, that gain-based remedies are not available where the defendant

---

[102] *Twentieth Century Fox Film Corporation v Harris* [2013] EWHC 159 (Ch).

[103] Copyright, Designs and Patents Act 1988, s 97(1). Similar provision is made for innocent infringement of a design rights: ibid, s 233(1).

[104] *Redwood Music Ltd v Chappell and Co Ltd* [1982] RPC 109.   [105] Patents Act 1977, s 61(1).

[106] Ibid, s 62(1).   [107] *My Kinda Town Ltd v Soll* [1982] FSR 147.

[108] *Edelsten v Edelsten* (1863) 1 De GJ and S 185, 46 ER 72.

[109] *Gillette UK Ltd v Edenwest Ltd* [1994] RPC 279.   [110] [1986] 2 All ER 888.

[111] [1988] 1 WLR 1466.

has committed a nuisance. In that case the defendant had deliberately committed a nuisance by operating a market in close proximity to the claimant's market which infringed the claimant's right to hold a market in a particular area. The claimant was granted an injunction to restrain further infringement of this proprietary right. Although the claimant had not been shown to have suffered any loss of custom by virtue of the tort, the trial judge awarded the claimant damages which were assessed by reference to a licence fee which the claimant would have charged the defendant to operate its market. This remedy could be characterized as either compensatory, by virtue of the licence fee which the claimant had not been able to charge, or restitutionary, by reference to the amount saved by the defendant in not having to pay a licence fee to the claimant. But the Court of Appeal overruled the trial judge's decision and awarded nominal damages, on the basis that generally damages for tort could only compensate the claimant for actual loss suffered. Similarly, in *Forsyth-Grant v Allen*[112] the remedy of an account of profits was held not to be available for the tort of nuisance arising from interference with the claimant's right to light because this was not considered to involve any misappropriation of the claimant's rights but only infringement of the reasonable enjoyment of property.[113] Negotiation damages were recognized as being available in principle, although not on the facts because the claimant had been unwilling to negotiate with the defendant. That is incorrect, however, since negotiation damages are to be assessed on the basis that the parties would have willingly negotiated with each other.[114]

In the light of the general principles which have been identified in this chapter, nuisance should be considered to be a proprietary tort for which gain-based relief is available, even though it does not involve misappropriation of property but only interference with enjoyment. But, similarly, conversion need not involve misappropriation of a chattel but just interference with its use, and so too the tort of trespass of land. The Supreme Court in *Coventry v Lawrence*,[115] whilst not formally recognizing that gain-based remedies are available for the tort of nuisance, did at least leave open the possibility of such remedies being awarded.[116] Some of the Justices also recognized that negotiation damages could be awarded in lieu of an injunction and that it was appropriate in assessing these damages to take into account the benefit to the defendant in not suffering from an injunction being awarded.[117] Whether an account of profits or negotiation damages is appropriate should depend on the circumstances in which the tort was committed, as has been recognized for the tort of trespass to land, with account of profits confined to the more serious cases, such as where the tort was committed deliberately and in order to make a profit, since it is appropriate to use the remedy of an account of profits to deter the commission of the tort in such circumstances.[118]

(E) DECEIT

Some cases are consistent with gain-based remedies being awarded in respect of the tort of deceit. For example, in *Hill v Perrott*[119] the defendant had fraudulently induced the claimant to sell goods to a third party who was insolvent and so was unable to pay for them. The defendant then obtained the goods from the third party. It was held that a contract would be implied to prevent the defendant from profiting from the fraud, and so

---

[112] [2008] EWCA Civ 505.   [113] Ibid, [32] (Patten J).   [114] See p 430, above.
[115] [2014] UKSC 13, [2014] AC 822.
[116] Ibid, [131] (Lord Neuberger), [173] (Lord Clarke), [239] (Lord Carnwath).
[117] Ibid, [131] (Lord Neuberger), [173] (Lord Clarke).   [118] See p 459, above.
[119] (1810) 3 Taunt 274, 128 ER 109.

the defendant was required to pay the claimant for the goods.[120] This remedy is clearly consistent with the general principle relating to gain-based remedies being awarded where the tort committed by the defendant has interfered with the claimant's proprietary rights, since, but for the defendant's lie, the claimant would not have been induced to sell the goods to the third party.[121]

A more recent decision of the Court of Appeal, however, appears at first sight to cast doubt on the proposition that gain-based remedies are available where the defendant has deceived the claimant.[122] In *Halifax Building Society v Thomas*[123] the defendant had obtained a mortgage advance from the claimant by means of a fraudulent misrepresentation that he was somebody else with a better credit rating. This was a criminal offence. The defendant used the mortgage advance to purchase a flat. After the defendant had defaulted on his interest payments and the claimant had discovered the misrepresentation, the claimant sold the flat. The claimant used the proceeds of sale to discharge the loan and was left with a surplus. The claimant argued that it was entitled to retain the surplus on the ground that, if the defendant had received the proceeds of sale, it would have been liable to account to the claimant for all of the proceeds because they had been obtained by wrongdoing.[124] The Court of Appeal rejected this argument on the ground that the claimant had relied on its contractual rights in selling the flat and so had affirmed the mortgage. Probably what the court meant by this was that, by electing to affirm the mortgage when it knew that the defendant had obtained the mortgage by fraud, the claimant had literally waived the tort of deceit with the consequence that the tort was extinguished and so there was no wrong on which the restitutionary claim could be based.[125] But whether this is correct depends on what is required for waiver of the tort. Could it really be said that the claimant's failure to rescind the transaction meant that it had ratified the wrongdoing? This cannot be the case since, if the flat had been sold at a loss so the proceeds of sale would not have discharged the loan completely, the claimant would still have been able to sue the defendant in tort. In other words, the failure to rescind the transaction did not constitute a waiver of the tort and so the Court's decision must be considered to be incorrect.[126]

The Court of Appeal in *Halifax Building Society v Thomas* said nothing to suggest that gain-based remedies are unavailable in principle where the defendant has committed the

---

[120] Restitution might be justified in this case by reference to the unjust enrichment principle, with the ground of restitution being induced mistake, although it would be difficult to establish that the defendant's benefit had been obtained at the claimant's expense since it was actually obtained from the third party. Nevertheless, it might be possible to satisfy the 'at the expense of' requirement by having regard to the economic reality of the transfer. See p 107, above. It is, however, far easier to explain the case as one involving restitution for the tort of deceit.

[121] See also *Abbotts v Barry* (1820) 2 Brad and B 369, 129 ER 1009 where, on similar facts, the defendant was held liable to account to the claimant for the proceeds of sale of the goods which he had received from the third party and then sold. Here the justification for restitution was the fact that the sale which had been induced by fraud did not involve transfer of title, so the restitutionary remedy was awarded to vindicate the claimant's continuing proprietary interest in the goods.

[122] Note also the dictum of Lord Steyn in *Smith New Court Securities Ltd v Citibank NA* [1997] AC 254, 283 that the only method of assessing damages for the tort of deceit is by reference to the claimant's financial loss.

[123] [1996] Ch 217.

[124] In fact, the defendant had been convicted of a criminal offence and a confiscation order was made for the proceeds of the crime. One reason for the failure of the claimant to retain the surplus proceeds of sale was because the effect of the confiscation order was that the defendant would not profit from the crime. See p 529, below for discussion of this aspect of the case.   [125] See p 447, above.

[126] See C Mitchell, 'No Account of Profits for a Victim of Deceit' [1996] LMCLQ 314, 316. See also PBH Birks, 'The Proceeds of Mortgage Fraud' (1996) 10 TLI 2, 3.

tort of deceit. It follows, therefore, that if the defendant had sold the flat and was left with a surplus after the mortgage advance had been repaid, the claimant should have been able to recover this profit from the defendant. Allowing gain-based relief in such a case is consistent with the notion that such relief is available where a proprietary tort is committed, because the effect of the defendant's deceit was that the claimant was induced to lend its money to the defendant. There is, however, one particular difficulty in allowing the claimant to recover the surplus proceeds of sale in such circumstances, namely whether the surplus arose directly from the commission of the wrong. Peter Gibson LJ suggested that the profit could not be said to arise directly from the wrong because the profit was not obtained at the claimant's expense.[127] Whilst a notion of 'at the claimant's expense' is inappropriate in such a case, because the cause of action is the wrong and not unjust enrichment, the judge's conclusion was correct; the making of the profit would have been too remote from the commission of the wrong. The loan was received from the building society as a direct result of the wrongdoing, but the surplus proceeds of sale could only be considered to be an indirect result of the wrong once the house had been sold.[128] Consequently, the Court of Appeal's decision that the claimant was not entitled to retain the surplus proceeds of sale was the right result but for the wrong reason. Where, however, the defendant obtains a benefit as a direct result of the deceit, he or she should be required to disgorge this benefit to the claimant, although usually where the defendant has obtained a benefit from the claimant by deceit, the claimant will be able to bring a restitutionary claim founded on the reversal of the defendant's unjust enrichment, where the ground of restitution is the induced mistake.[129]

(F) RECEIPT OF PRIVATE INFORMATION

English law does not yet recognize a tort of invasion of privacy.[130] Equity has, however, protected confidential relationships for many years in the form of the action for breach of confidence.[131] Recently this action has been characterized as a tort,[132] although its equitable foundations[133] remain significant in determining the nature of the claim and the remedies which are awarded, so it is considered in Chapter 19 with the other equitable wrongs.[134] Account of profits is available for breach of the duty of confidence, even though the action does not involve interference with property rights, but rather is a claim founded on unconscionability.[135]

It appears that a distinct tort has emerged, however, which is derived from the action of breach of confidence but does not depend on the identification of an obligation of confidence.[136] This arises where information has been acquired or received and the

---

[127] *Halifax Building Society v Thomas* [1996] Ch 217, 227.

[128] Whether it should make any difference that the surplus was the proceeds of crime is discussed at p 529, below. The Court of Appeal also rejected an argument that the defendant should be considered to hold the proceeds of sale on a constructive trust. This aspect of the case is also discussed at p 531, below.

[129] IM Jackman, 'Restitution for Wrongs' (1989) 48 CLJ 302, 310.

[130] *Campbell v Mirror Group Newspapers Ltd* [2004] UKHL 22, [2004] 2 AC 457.

[131] See p 514, below.   [132] *Walsh v Shanahan* [2013] EWCA Civ 411, [55] (Rimer LJ).

[133] *Moorgate Tobacco Co Ltd v Philip Morris Ltd (No 2)* (1984) 156 CLR 414, 438 (Deane J); *Stephens v Avery* [1988] Ch 449, 455 (Sir Nicolas Browne-Wilkinson V-C).

[134] See p 516, below.

[135] See *Moorgate Tobacco Co Ltd v Philip Morris Ltd (No 2)* (1984) 156 CLR 414, 438 (Deane J). See also *Vestergaard Fradsen A/S v Bestnet Europe Ltd* [2013] UKSC 31, [2013] 1 WLR 1556, [22] (Lord Neuberger).

[136] *A v B plc* [2003] QB 195; *Campbell v Mirror Group Newspapers Ltd* [2004] UKHL 22, [2004] AC 457.

acquirer or recipient knows or ought to know that there is an expectation of privacy.[137] This is appropriately called the tort of misuse of private information,[138] for which the remedy of account of profits might be available in the exercise of the court's discretion.

(G) BREACH OF STATUTORY DUTY

In *Devenish Nutrition Ltd v Sanofi-Aventis SA*[139] the Court of Appeal recognized that a gain-based remedy was not available for the tort of breach of statutory duty, in that case arising from infringement of competition law whereby the claimant had purchased vitamins from the defendants at inflated prices as a result of an unlawful cartel agreement between the suppliers. The rejection of gain-based remedies in such circumstances was for two reasons. First, the Court considered itself to be bound by its earlier decision in *Stoke-on-Trent CC v W and J Wass Ltd*,[140] which was interpreted as recognizing that gain-based awards are not available for non-proprietary torts. Secondly, because compensatory damages remained an adequate remedy, even though the claimant had passed on its loss to customers and so would not have been able to claim compensatory damages.[141] Neither reason is convincing. *Wass* did not decide that gain-based remedies were unavailable to non-proprietary torts. Even if it did, surely the tort committed in *Devenish* was sufficiently proprietary, for the effect of the breach of statutory duty was that the claimant paid its money to the defendants who had consequently interfered with the claimant's enjoyment of its property. Further, *Wass* was decided before the House of Lords in *Blake* set the law on gain-based remedies on a new course and so, even if it did restrict gain-based remedies to torts involving the misappropriation of property, this should be reconsidered after *Blake*.

As regards the adequacy of compensatory damages reason, if the claimant has not suffered any loss, for example because the burden of the claimant's overpayment to the defendants had been passed on to the claimant's customers, compensatory damages are surely inadequate. It is then necessary to consider whether the case falls within the 'exceptional' category for the award of gain-based remedies, as recognized in *Blake*. In that case Lord Nicholls recognized that: 'A useful general guide, although not exhaustive, is whether the plaintiff had a legitimate interest in preventing the defendant's profit-making activity and hence in depriving him of this profit.'[142] In fact, there was no such legitimate interest in *Devenish* because there had already been a public action brought by the European Commission to identify an infringement of the competition rules and substantial fines had been imposed as a result. But a legitimate interest might be identified where there has been no prior public action, in order to encourage private parties to deploy additional resources to the task of identifying anti-competitive conduct which is of benefit to the community.

In fact, the claimant in *Devenish* might have pursued an alternative claim in unjust enrichment against the defendants who had been enriched at its expense as the result of a causative mistake as to the money which was lawfully due. The fact that the claimant had passed on its loss to its customers does not defeat such a claim,[143] although the fact that the money had been paid pursuant to a valid contract would be a more significant obstacle

---

[137] *Primary Group (UK) Ltd v Royal Bank of Scotland plc* [2014] EWHC Ch 1082, [223] (Arnold J).

[138] *Walsh v Shanahan* [2013] EWCA Civ 411. See C Hunt, 'Rethinking Surreptitious Takings in the Law of Confidence' (2012) IPQ 66.

[139] [2008] EWCA Civ 1086, [2009] Ch 390. See p 448, above.

[140] [1988] 1 WLR 1406. See p 461, above.   [141] See p 440, above.   [142] [2001] 1 AC 268, 284–5.

[143] *Kleinwort Benson Ltd v Birmingham CC* [1977] QB 380.

to an unjust enrichment claim, save if the additional payment could be severed from the amount which was properly due.[144] It might alternatively have been possible to bring a claim for statutory restitution of the unlawful payment, by virtue of sections 47A and 58A of the Competition Act 1998, which provides for a pecuniary remedy to be awarded where there has been a breach of competition law, which includes the award of a gain-based remedy.[145]

3. IS THERE A GENERAL PRINCIPLE IN FAVOUR OF THE AWARD OF GAIN-BASED REMEDIES FOR TORTS?

Analysis of the cases show that the possibility of a gain-based remedy being awarded for tort will generally only be seriously considered where the defendant's wrongdoing involves interference with the claimant's property in some way. Whilst it has sometimes been assumed that this is limited to misappropriation of property, it should certainly include interference with property rights, including the enjoyment of property. But if the focus is on wrongful proprietary interference, gain-based remedies will not be available where, for example, the defendant commits the torts of assault, battery, false imprisonment, malicious prosecution or defamation.[146] In such circumstances the claimant will be confined to compensatory or perhaps exemplary damages, rather than a gain-based remedy. Usually where these torts have been committed the defendant will not have obtained a benefit, so the question of the availability of gain-based remedies does not arise.[147] But for some other non-proprietary torts the defendant may have obtained a benefit from the commission of the tort and so it might be appropriate to require the defendant to transfer this benefit to the claimant. This may sometimes be the case with the tort of negligence,[148] where, for example, the defendant negligently causes injury to the claimant as a result of economizing on safety precautions. It is also possible that the defendant might benefit from the commission of the tort of defamation where, for example, it can be shown that a newspaper's circulation rose dramatically as a result of the publication of defamatory remarks about the claimant. Similarly, where the defendant commits the tort of inducing a breach of contract, he or she may have obtained a benefit as a result of the wrongdoing, but this cannot usually be considered to involve interference with proprietary rights.[149]

It is consequently necessary to consider whether it is possible to justify confining gain-based relief to the proprietary torts. Is there a case for extending the law so that a gain-based remedy is potentially available for all torts? Although it is clear that this view does not yet represent English law,[150] it is a view which should be recognized by the courts.

---

[144] Similar to the success of the restitutionary claim in *Roxborough v Rothmans of Pall Mall Australia Ltd* (2001) 76 ALJR 203. See p 138, above.

[145] *BCL Old Co Ltd v Aventis SA* [2005] CAT 2, [28].

[146] In *United Australia Ltd v Barclays Bank Ltd* [1941] AC 1, 12, Viscount Simon LC suggested that the torts of defamation and assault could not be 'waived'.

[147] *Hambly v Trott* (1776) 1 Cowp 371, 376; 98 ER 1136, 1139 (Lord Mansfield).

[148] Cf Jackman, 'Restitution for Wrongs', 311.

[149] That restitutionary remedies are available where the defendant has induced a breach of contract was recognized in the American case of *Federal Sugar Refining Co v US Sugar Equalisation Board Inc* (1920) 268 F 575.

[150] *Stoke-on-Trent CC v W and J Wass Ltd* [1988] 1 WLR 1406, 1415 (Nourse LJ); *Devenish Nutrition Ltd v Sanofi-Aventis SA (France)* [2008] EWCA Civ 1086, [2009] Ch 390, [39] (Arden LJ).

Wherever the defendant has obtained a benefit as the result of the commission of a tort the claimant should be able to elect a gain-based remedy whereby the defendant is required to transfer to the claimant the value of any benefit obtained by the commission of the tort, although a full account of the defendant's profits should be confined to the most serious forms of wrongdoing, which will typically be assessed with reference to the defendant's culpability in seeking to profit from the commission of the wrong. Restitution is justified simply because no wrongdoer should be allowed to benefit from the commission of a wrong and the claimant is an appropriate recipient of the benefit because he or she is the victim of the wrong. This principle should be of general application regardless of the type of tort which the defendant has committed, since there is no policy reason why gain-based remedies should not be available in such circumstances.

The potential importance of recognizing that restitutionary relief should be available regardless of the tort committed by the defendant is illustrated by the remedies which are available for the tort of defamation. As the law stands, because defamation is concerned with hurt to feelings and injury to reputation[151] rather than injury to property, gain-based remedies are not available. Although exemplary damages can be awarded, they are a very blunt tool to deprive the defendant of benefits obtained from the tort, since their rationale is punishment rather than to ensure that the defendant does not profit from the commission of the tort,[152] and, as the Law Commission has recognized, such damages should only be awarded in exceptional circumstances.[153] It would be much more appropriate to recognize that a gain-based remedy is available, simply to ensure that the defendant is not allowed to profit from the commission of the tort.[154]

[151] See *Cairns v Modi* [2012] EWCA Civ 1382, [2013] 1 WLR 1015, [28] (Lord Judge CJ).

[152] *Rookes v Barnard* [1964] AC 1129, 1221 (Lord Devlin).

[153] *Aggravated, Exemplary and Restitutionary Damages* (Law Com No 247, 1997), 197.

[154] KH York, 'The Extension of Restitutional Remedies in the Tort Field' (1957) 4 UCLA Rev 499. A gain-based remedy for defamation was awarded in the American case of *Ventura v Kyle* 2014 WL 6687499 (Minnesota).

18

RESTITUTION FOR BREACH OF CONTRACT

1. GENERAL PRINCIPLES

Where the defendant has breached a contract the orthodox remedial response is that the claimant can obtain damages which are assessed by reference to any loss or injury which he or she has suffered as a consequence.[1] Usually the purpose of such damages is to place the claimant in the position he or she would have been in had the contract not been breached.[2] This involves the protection of what has been called the 'expectation interest'.[3] Sometimes, where it is not possible to ascertain what position the claimant would have occupied had the contract not been breached, the purpose of the award of damages is to place the claimant in the position which he or she would have occupied had the contract not been entered into. In such cases the claimant will be reimbursed for the expenditure which he or she had incurred before the contract was breached.[4] This involves the protection of the so-called 'reliance interest'.[5]

What we need to consider in this chapter is whether there is a third interest which should be protected by the award of damages where the defendant has breached a contract, namely the 'restitution interest'.[6] In other words, in those cases where the claimant did not suffer any loss as a result of the breach of contract but the defendant obtained a benefit, or where the value of the defendant's benefit arising from the breach exceeds any loss suffered by the claimant, should it be possible for the remedy which is awarded for the breach of contract to be ascertained by reference to the value of the benefit which had been obtained by the defendant?

(A) THE GENERAL PRINCIPLE DENYING RESTITUTION FOR BREACH OF CONTRACT

A number of cases have recognized that gain-based remedies are not available where the defendant has breached a contract.[7] This was acknowledged most clearly by Megarry V-C

---

[1] *Attorney-General v Blake* [2001] 1 AC 268, 278 (Lord Nicholls).

[2] *Robinson v Harman* (1848) 1 Ex 850, 855; 154 ER 363 (Parke B).

[3] It is more accurately described as the 'performance interest': D Friedmann, 'The Performance Interest in Contract Damages' (1995) 111 LQR 628.

[4] *Anglia Television Ltd v Reed* [1972] 1 QB 60.

[5] See LL Fuller and WR Perdue, 'The Reliance Interest in Contract Damages' (1936–37) 46 Yale LJ 52.

[6] This was recognized by Steyn LJ in *Surrey CC v Bredero Homes Ltd* [1993] 1 WLR 1361, 1369. See also Fuller and Perdue, 'The Reliance Interest in Contract Damages', 54.

[7] See, for example, *Teacher v Calder* [1899] AC 451, 467 (Lord Davey); *The Siboen and the Sibotre* [1976] 1 Lloyd's Rep 293, 337 (Kerr J); and *Surrey CC v Bredero Homes Ltd* [1993] 1 WLR 1361, 1364 (Dillon LJ).

in *Tito v Waddell (No 2)*,[8] where the defendant mining company had contracted with the claimants, the inhabitants of Ocean Island, to replant the island once the defendant had completed its mining operations there. The defendant failed to replant the island and the claimants sued for breach of contract. They were awarded only nominal damages since they had not suffered any loss as a result of the breach. This was because the claimants were no longer living on the island, and did not intend to return to it, so they would not have incurred expenditure themselves in replanting the island. Also, the difference between the value of the island with and without replanting was trivial. The claimants had claimed that the measure of damages should be the amount of money which the defendant had saved in failing to replant the island as it had promised, but Megarry V-C rejected this gain-based measure. He said:[9] 'If the defendant has saved himself money, as by not doing what he has contracted to do, that does not of itself entitle the plaintiff to recover the saving as damages: for it by no means necessarily follows that what the defendant has saved the plaintiff has lost.'

The judge assumed that damages for breach of contract could only be measured by reference to the claimant's loss and he considered this to be an absolute rule without exceptions.

(B) METHODS FOR AWARDING GAIN-BASED REMEDIES FOR BREACH OF CONTRACT

Despite the general rule against the award of gain-based remedies for breach of contract, such remedies have been awarded in a variety of circumstances. The House of Lords in *Attorney-General v Blake*[10] radically developed the law in this area, so much so that in *Experience Hendrix LLC v PPX Enterprises Inc*,[11] Mance LJ described the decision as marking a new start in this area of the law. He considered that earlier cases might be relevant to the future development of the law but that *Blake* freed the courts from some of the constraints imposed by earlier authorities. Before *Blake* is examined it is useful to consider the earlier authorities and methods adopted whereby gain-based remedies were awarded in respect of breaches of contract, but it is important to recognize that the decision of the House of Lords in *Blake* has liberalized the law in a number of crucial respects.

(i) Alternative Analysis

A fundamental distinction needs to be drawn between restitution *following* breach of contract and restitution *for* breach of contract. Where the claim is for restitution following termination of the contract for breach, the cause of action is not the breach of contract but the reversal of the defendant's unjust enrichment. Consequently, the claimant must establish that the defendant has obtained a benefit at the claimant's expense and in circumstances which fall within one of the established grounds of restitution, which will typically be total failure of basis.[12] So, for example, if the claimant contracted to buy a car from the defendant for £10,000, which the claimant paid in advance, but the defendant failed to deliver the car, the claimant can repudiate the contract for breach and recover the £10,000 on the ground of total failure of basis. Where the claim is founded on unjust enrichment the only relevance of the breach of contract is that, if it is sufficiently serious, it will enable the claimant to set the contract aside and then pursue a claim for restitution.

---

[8] [1977] Ch 106.   [9] Ibid, 332.   [10] [2001] 1 AC 268.
[11] [2003] EWCA Civ 323, [2003] 1 All ER (Comm) 830, 836.   [12] See Chapter 13.

The cause of action is not founded on the breach of contract itself but is founded instead on the defendant's unjust enrichment.

(ii) Contractual Term Specifying a Restitutionary Remedy

The parties may insert a clause into the contract which stipulates that damages for breach of contract should be assessed by reference to the benefit gained by the defendant as a result of the breach rather than the claimant's loss.[13] That such a clause is effective to justify the award of restitutionary remedies for breach of contract was recognized by the Privy Council in *Reid-Newfoundland Co v Anglo-American Telegraph Co*.[14] The defendant had entered into a contract with the claimant to use a telegraph wire for the transmission of messages which related to the defendant's railway business. To ensure that the wire was not used to transmit messages which related to other aspects of the defendant's business, a term was included in the contract to the effect that the defendant could not use the wire to transmit commercial messages 'except for the benefit and account' of the claimant. The defendant used the wire for the transmission of messages which were unrelated to its railway business and was held liable to account to the claimant for the profits which accrued to it from the use of the wire. Such a remedy was appropriate because of the clause which had been inserted into the contract, the effect of which was that any profit which was made by the defendant in breach of the agreement was deemed to have been received for the benefit of the claimant. The right to restitutionary remedies in such cases derives from the contract itself, rather than by operation of law, and so falls within the law of contract rather than the law of restitution.[15]

(iii) Identification of a Fiduciary Relationship

In certain cases it is possible to identify a fiduciary relationship between two contracting parties.[16] Where such a relationship can be found, the underlying cause of action will be breach of fiduciary duty rather than breach of contract. Since the usual remedy for breach of fiduciary duty is gain-based and because the identification of a fiduciary relationship is open to manipulation, this is a potentially important mechanism for obtaining gain-based relief arising from a breach of contract, although the courts are reluctant to identify a fiduciary relationship in a purely commercial context.[17] The relevance of identifying a fiduciary relationship between two contracting parties is illustrated by *Reading v Attorney-General*,[18] where the claimant, a sergeant in the British army stationed in Egypt, sought to recover money which had been seized from him by his employer, the Crown. The Crown had seized the money because it constituted bribes which the claimant had received for assisting in the smuggling of liquor. The House of Lords held that the Crown could retain this money because it constituted profits which the claimant had obtained in breach of his contract of employment, and to support this conclusion the Court concluded that the claimant owed fiduciary duties to his employer. It follows from this that, had the sergeant retained the bribes, the Crown could have sued him for breach of fiduciary duty and recovered the bribes which he had obtained.[19]

---

[13] See S Rowan, 'For the Recognition of Remedial Terms Agreed *Inter Partes*' (2010) LQR 448, 457.

[14] [1912] AC 555. See also *Surrey CC v Bredero Homes Ltd* [1993] 1 WLR 1361, 1364 (Dillon LJ).

[15] See p 141, above.   [16] For examination of the notion of a fiduciary relationship, see p 488, below.

[17] See *Hospital Products Ltd v US Surgical Corporation* (1984) 156 CLR 41 (High Court of Australia). See further p 490, below.   [18] [1951] AC 507.

[19] The bribes would, in fact, now be held on constructive trust for the claimant. See *FHR European Ventures Ltd v Cedar Capital Partners LLC* [2014] UKSC 45, [2015] AC 250. See p 512, below.

(iv) Tortious Wrongdoing

Sometimes, where the defendant has breached a contract with the claimant, the defendant will also have committed a proprietary tort[20] so that the claimant will be able to obtain a restitutionary remedy founded on the tort rather than the breach of contract. For example, in *Penarth Dock Engineering Co Ltd v Pounds*[21] the claimant sued the defendant for both breach of contract and the tort of trespass to property by virtue of the defendant's failure to remove a pontoon from the claimant's dock. The claimant was awarded damages which were measured by reference to the amount which the defendant had saved in not having to pay rent for the dock. Although it seems that the claimant's primary claim was for breach of contract, it is clear that Lord Denning MR felt able to award a restitutionary remedy because the defendant had also committed the tort of trespass, for which restitutionary relief was clearly available.

(v) Price Payable for Interference with Property Rights

Where the consequence of the breach of contract is that the defendant interferes with one of the claimant's proprietary rights, gain-based remedies may be available because of the general policy of the law which seeks to protect such rights from wrongdoing, by requiring the defendant to give up those benefits which were obtained by interfering with the claimant's property.[22] This is particularly well illustrated by *Wrotham Park Estate Co Ltd v Parkside Homes Ltd*.[23] The defendant had built houses on a piece of land without obtaining the prior consent of the claimant, a neighbouring landowner, as was required by a restrictive covenant which had been registered as a land charge. As a result of this breach of covenant the claimant sought an injunction requiring the houses which had been built to be demolished. This was refused on the ground that it would constitute an unacceptable waste of much needed houses, but damages were awarded in lieu of the injunction. These damages were assessed by reference to the amount of money which the claimant could reasonably have demanded from the defendant to relax the covenant. This was calculated to be five per cent of the profits which it was reasonably anticipated that the defendant would make from building the houses.

This decision has proved to be controversial and in assessing it three key questions need to be considered.

(1) Can the damages which were awarded to the claimant be regarded as restitutionary rather than compensatory? Although the claimant had not suffered any financial loss from the breach of the covenant, because the value of its land was unaffected by the development, the damages could still be characterized as compensating the claimant for the loss of the opportunity to bargain with the defendant to relax the covenant.[24] But this would be highly artificial because it was clear that the claimant would never have agreed to relax the covenant on any terms.[25] The damages could be regarded, therefore, as restitutionary, since they represent the value of the benefit to the defendant from the breach, namely the amount saved by the defendant in not paying for the relaxation of the covenant. This conclusion is strengthened by the

---

[20] See Chapter 17.   [21] [1963] 1 Lloyd's Rep 359. See also *Bracewell v Appleby* [1975] Ch 408.

[22] See p 422, above.

[23] [1974] 1 WLR 798. See also *Gafford v Graham* [1999] 7 P and CR 73; *Amec Developments v Jury's Hotel Management* [2001] EGLR 81; *Lane v O'Brien Homes Ltd* [2004] EWHC 303 (QB).

[24] This was how Megarry V-C explained the case in *Tito v Waddell (No 2)* [1977] Ch 106, 335, as did Millett LJ in *Jaggard v Sawyer* [1995] 1 WLR 269, 291. See also RS Sharpe and SM Waddams, 'Damages for Lost Opportunity to Bargain' (1982) 2 OJLS 290 and SJ Stoljar, 'Restitutionary Relief for Breach of Contract' (1989) 2 JCL 1.   [25] This was recognized by Brightman J at [1974] 1 WLR 798, 815.

fact that the trial judge specifically relied on a number of tort cases where the remedy awarded can only be characterized as restitutionary. In the light of subsequent developments in the law relating to the assessment of negotiation damages, the remedy in *Wrotham Park* is best analysed as hybrid, consisting of compensatory and restitutionary components, with regard to what the claimant lost in not negotiating with the defendant and what the defendant gained from not negotiating with the claimant.[26]

(2) Assuming that the award does have at least a restitutionary component, why was the court prepared to assess the remedy as being 5 per cent of the total profits, rather than a full account of all the profits made by building the houses in breach of the restrictive covenant? This was presumably because of the principle of causation, the effect of which is that the defendant could only have been liable to account for those profits which would not have been made but for the breach of the contract. In *Wrotham Park* the defendant's breach of covenant only related to the failure to obtain the claimant's consent to relax the covenant. It could never be proved that all of the defendant's profits arose from this breach, since most of the profits arose from the defendant's input in building the houses, so the defendant could only have been liable to disgorge those profits which derived from the breach. But in a case such as this it is virtually impossible to determine which profits derived from the breach. The formula which was adopted is artificial, but it does at least represent a reasonable sum which would have been demanded by somebody in the position of the claimant before agreeing to relax the covenant. The decision of David Clarke J in *O'Brien Homes Ltd v Lane*[27] is consistent with this, since he emphasized that the defendant's expected profit from the breach of covenant should be the starting point for the assessment of what the parties would have agreed to release the defendant from the relevant prohibition, in that case a restriction to the building of three houses. Further, he emphasized that this should be assessed when the defendant sought to be released from the contract, rather than when the contract was made. This was significant because, when the contract was made it was not clear whether planning permission for a fourth house would be granted, whereas by the time the defendant would have wished to be released from the restriction planning permission had been granted so the defendant would have been willing to pay more for the release. The judge also recognized that these damages need not necessarily be limited to a relatively small percentage of the defendant's profit. In that case the claimant was awarded £150,000 in a case where the defendant's profit from breaching the contract was £280,000.

(3) The final and most important question about the *Wrotham Park* case is why damages, with at the very least a restitutionary component, were awarded in this particular case? The preferable explanation is that the defendant's breach of covenant constituted interference with the claimant's proprietary rights. The relevant proprietary right was the restrictive covenant itself, as reflected by the fact that the covenant was registered as a land charge and created a right for the benefit of the claimant as the owner of the neighbouring land. By awarding a remedy with a restitutionary component, the trial judge was protecting this particular proprietary right, which is consistent with the fundamental principles which underlie the award of gain-based remedies for wrongdoing where the protection of property rights is a fundamental objective.

---

[26] See p 431, above. See further p 479, below.   [27] [2004] EWHC 303 (QB).

Some subsequent cases adopted a very restrictive interpretation of the *Wrotham Park* case. For example, in *Surrey CC v Bredero Homes Ltd*,[28] another case concerning the building of houses in breach of a covenant, the Court of Appeal held that, since the claimants had suffered no loss, they were not able to recover substantial damages for the defendant's breach and a restitutionary remedy was not awarded. Dillon LJ distinguished *Wrotham Park* on the basis that the damages in that case were awarded in Equity in lieu of an injunction, whereas in the *Surrey* case the claimants had never sought an injunction and were simply seeking damages for breach of contract at Common Law.[29] But he did not explain why this should make any difference. Steyn LJ, on the other hand, acknowledged that restitutionary damages could be awarded where the defendant had breached a contract and he accepted that the damages in *Wrotham Park* were restitutionary and were justified because the defendant had invaded the claimant's property rights,[30] whereas in the *Surrey* case the defendant's conduct did not 'involve any invasion of the claimant's interests even in the broadest sense of that word'.[31] In the light of the general principles which underlie the award of restitutionary remedies for wrongdoing, this approach is preferable. In the *Surrey* case it is clear that the defendant had not interfered with any of the claimant's proprietary rights,[32] since the covenant in that case was simply a contractual promise not to build save in accordance with the planning permission which had already been obtained, whereas the right in *Wrotham Park* was a restrictive covenant, which is a proprietary right which attaches to land.

In *Jaggard v Sawyer*,[33] however, the Court of Appeal rejected a claim for a restitutionary remedy where the defendant had built a drive on land in breach of a covenant that the land would only be used as a private garden. The Court awarded damages in lieu of an injunction which were assessed by reference to what the defendant would have had to pay all the parties to the covenant to secure their consent to relax it. Millett LJ was adamant that the damages were compensatory and not restitutionary,[34] even though the breach of covenant involved an interference in the claimant's proprietary right.

This confusing body of law has now been clarified by the decision of the House of Lords in *Attorney-General v Blake*.[35] Lord Nicholls approved of the approach in *Wrotham Park* whereby remedies can be awarded where the defendant has interfered with the claimant's property right. He considered that such remedies are explicitly restitutionary, since they are assessed by reference to the value of the defendant's benefit from the breach, namely what the defendant would have had to pay the claimant to interfere with the property right.[36] Lord Nicholls justified the award of such remedies on the basis that property rights are superior to contractual rights because they may survive against an indefinite class of person.

(C) *ATTORNEY-GENERAL V BLAKE*: THE NEW APPROACH

Despite the general principle against the award of gain-based remedies for breach of contract, the House of Lords in *Attorney-General v Blake*[37] recognized that restitutionary

---

[28] [1993] 1 WLR 1361.   [29] Ibid, 1367.   [30] Ibid, 1369.   [31] Ibid.

[32] As both Dillon and Steyn LJJ expressly recognized, ibid, 1365 and 1371 respectively.

[33] [1995] 1 WLR 269.   [34] Ibid, 291. See also Sir Thomas Bingham MR, 281.

[35] [2001] 1 AC 268.

[36] Ibid, 283–4. See also *Experience Hendrix LLC v PPX Enterprises Inc* [2003] EWCA Civ 323, [2003] 1 All ER (Comm) 830, 839 (Mance LJ). Cf *Attorney-General v Blake* [2001] 1 AC 268, 298, where Lord Hobhouse explicitly characterized such damages as compensatory.   [37] [2001] 1 AC 268.

remedies can be available where the defendant has breached a contract, but only in the most exceptional circumstances. *Attorney-General v Blake* involved a claim by the British government to the royalties made by Blake in respect of his autobiography which was published in breach of contract. George Blake had been a member of the British Secret Intelligence Service, but he was also an agent of the Soviet Union. He was consequently convicted of unlawfully communicating information to the Soviets, but he escaped from prison to Moscow where he wrote his autobiography, *No Other Choice*. In this book he disclosed information about the Secret Service. This constituted a breach of section 1 of the Official Secrets Acts 1911 and 1920, because Blake had disclosed official information without lawful authority. It also constituted a breach of the contract which he had signed on joining the Service, by virtue of which he had agreed not to divulge any official information he obtained as a result of his employment. The book was published in the United Kingdom without the permission of the Crown. The Attorney-General sued, on behalf of the Crown, to recover all the sums which had been received or were receivable by the publisher. Since the breach of contract did not involve interference with the Crown's property rights, the *Wrotham Park* principle was not applicable. The issue then was whether it was appropriate to develop another principle to require Blake to account for all profits made as a result of the breach of contract.

(i) The Approach of the Court of Appeal

The Court of Appeal recognized that the remedy of an account of profits could be awarded for a breach of contract in two particular contexts.

(1) Skimped Performance

A gain-based remedy is justified where the defendant agreed to provide a particular service for the claimant but, after the claimant had paid the full price for it, the defendant provided a less extensive service.[38] In such circumstances the defendant should be required to disgorge to the claimant the amount saved by breaching the contract. This is because in such a case compensatory damages are an inadequate remedy, since by requesting the particular performance the claimant has shown that he or she has an interest in it being performed, and the benefit obtained by the defendant, namely the amount saved, arises directly from the breach of the contract.

(2) Doing What the Defendant Contracted Not to Do

Where the defendant promised not to do something and then obtained a benefit as a result of doing this, the defendant should disgorge any benefits obtained as a result of the breach. This occurred in *Blake* itself, since the defendant had disclosed information in his autobiography which he had previously agreed he would not disclose, and obtained benefits, in the form of royalties, as a direct result of this breach of contract. The award of a gain-based remedy in such a case can be justified because the benefit derived directly from the breach of contract, and because the claimant had suffered no loss, so compensatory damages would not adequately protect its interest in the performance of the contract.

---

[38] See the facts of *City of New Orleans v Fireman's Charitable Association* (1891) 9 Sol 486: failure to provide the stipulated fire-fighting service.

(ii) Principles Underpinning the Decision of the Majority in the House of Lords

The approach of the House of Lords to the award of restitutionary remedies was summarized by Lord Nicholls as follows:

> My conclusion is that there seems to be no reason, *in principle*, why the court must in all circumstances rule out an account of profits as a remedy for breach of contract... When, exceptionally, a just response to a breach of contract so requires, the court should be able to grant the discretionary remedy of requiring a defendant to account to the plaintiff for the benefits he has received from his breach of contract. In the same way as a plaintiff's interest in performance of a contract may render it just and equitable for the court to make an order for specific performance or grant an injunction, so the plaintiff's interest in performance may make it just and equitable that the defendant should retain no benefit from his breach of contract.[39]

It was held that the facts of the *Blake* case were exceptional and justified the award of the remedy of an account of profits. The majority identified a variety of principles which are relevant when identifying whether an account of profits is an appropriate remedy for breach of contract.

(1) The award of an account of profits in respect of a breach of contract is an exceptional remedy.[40] It follows that the normal remedy for breach of contract is the award of compensatory damages.

(2) No fixed rules can be prescribed as to when an account of profits should be awarded. Rather, the court must have regard to all the circumstances of the case, including the subject matter of the contract, the purpose of the contractual provision which had been breached, the circumstances in which the breach occurred, the consequences of the breach and the circumstances in which the relief is being sought.[41]

(3) A gain-based remedy will only be awarded following a breach of contract where other remedies are inadequate. So, for example, if a compensatory remedy or a specific remedy to enforce performance of the contract are adequate, these will trump the award of an account of profits. Whether the award of compensatory damages is inadequate should be considered in the light of what the claimant wanted the contract to achieve. If the claimant has a particular interest in the performance of the contract, which is not readily measurable in money if the contract is not performed, it is appropriate that the claimant's remedy is assessed by reference to what the defendant had gained by failing to perform it. Although the determination of whether compensatory damages are adequate is a matter of some uncertainty,[42] the recognition of this principle is significant since it ensures that the award of gain-based remedies does not undermine the fundamental principle that the usual remedy for breach of contract should be damages which seek to compensate the claimant for loss suffered. Compensatory damages will be considered to be inadequate when, for example, the contract relates to unique goods which may be impossible to value. In *Blake*, compensatory damages were not adequate because the release of information about the Secret Intelligence Service had no market value. Clearly, where the claimant has suffered no financial loss and specific remedies are unavailable, a restitutionary remedy is a possibility.[43]

---

[39] *Attorney-General v Blake* [2001] 1 AC 268, 284.   [40] Ibid, 285.

[41] Ibid.   [42] See p 440, above.

[43] Although compare with *Devenish Nutrition Ltd v Sanofi-Aventis SA (France)* [2008] EWCA Civ 1086, [2009] Ch 390, p 448, above, where compensatory damages were held to be an adequate remedy even where the

(4) A key consideration is whether the claimant has a legitimate interest in preventing the defendant's profit-making activities and so in depriving the defendant of his or her profit.[44] The Crown was held to have such an interest in preventing a former member of the intelligence services from profiting from breaches of an undertaking not to divulge any official information gained as a result of his employment. Blake was therefore not entitled to receive the royalties which had been received by his publishers from the publication of the autobiography. Further, the Crown had a continuing interest in deterring other servants of the State from disclosing information in breach of contract.

(5) The approach of the Court of Appeal was rejected. First, the fact that the defendant skimped on the promised performance was not considered to be relevant, primarily because this would involve the defendant saving money rather than obtaining a positive benefit and so an account of profits would not be available. Where the defendant has provided cheaper and inferior goods or services the appropriate remedy is to refund the difference in price as compensatory damages for the breach of contract.[45] This occurs by virtue of the so-called performance interest for which compensatory damages will be awarded where it is reasonable[46] for the claimant to insist on performance of the contract or the claimant has a legitimate interest in performance.[47] In such a case the compensatory award provides the claimant with an adequate substitute for the skimped performance. Secondly, the test that the defendant had done what he or she had promised not to do was considered to be defined too widely because it embraced all express negative obligations,[48] and, if such a principle was recognized, it would follow that gain-based remedies would be potentially available in a wide variety of circumstances.

(6) Further, the House of Lords confirmed that the following factors were not sufficient in their own right to justify the award of a gain-based remedy for breach of contract: the breach was cynical and deliberate; the breach enabled the defendant to enter into a more profitable contract elsewhere; and, by entering into a new and more profitable contract, the defendant put it out of his or her power to perform the contract with the claimant.[49]

(7) The award of an account of profits was justified on the facts because the defendant had deliberately and repeatedly breached his contract in publishing his autobiography, the contractual obligations owed by the spy were considered to be closely akin to those of a fiduciary,[50] and because he had compromised national security and had committed a serious criminal offence.[51] A full account of profits was considered to be a just response to the breach.[52]

---

claimant had passed its loss on to a third party and so compensatory damages were unavailable since there was no loss to be compensated.

[44] *Attorney-General v Blake* [2001] 1 AC 268, 285.

[45] Ibid, 285 (Lord Nicholls), 291 (Lord Steyn).

[46] *Ruxley Electronics and Construction Ltd v Forsyth* [1996] AC 344, 372 (Lord Lloyd).

[47] *Alfred McAlpine Construction Ltd v Panatown* [2001] 1 AC 518, 592 (Lord Millett).

[48] *Attorney-General v Blake* [2001] 1 AC 268, 286 (Lord Nicholls), 291 (Lord Steyn).

[49] Ibid, 286 (Lord Nicholls), 291 (Lord Steyn).

[50] Ibid, 287 (Lord Nicholls), 292 (Lord Steyn). In *CMS Dolphin Ltd v Simonet* [2001] 2 BCLC 704, [142], Lawrence Collins J held that breach of a director's contractual duty of fidelity would have justified a gain-based remedy, because he was willing to characterize the contractual obligation as fiduciary.

[51] *Attorney-General v Blake* [2001] 1 AC 268, 292 (Lord Steyn).   [52] Ibid.

(iii) Lord Hobhouse's Dissent

Lord Hobhouse rejected the approach of the majority for three reasons.[53] First, he considered the remedy of an account of profits, albeit a just response, to be motivated by a desire to punish Blake and to deprive him of the fruits of his earlier crime in circumstances where the profits were not obtained directly from the Crown. This is certainly true, but it is a consequence of recognizing a remedy which seeks to deprive the defendant of profits made as a result of committing the wrong. That is a fundamental principle of English law, the significance of which was down-played by Lord Hobhouse. Secondly, he could not see that there was a gap in the law which needed to be filled by the creation of a new remedy. But account of profits is not a new remedy, although its expansion to a non-proprietary Common Law claim founded on a breach of contract was certainly novel. Finally, he concluded that the remedy of an account of profits was based on protection of property rights and should not be awarded in a case such as *Blake* where no property rights had been affected by the breach of contract. Again, whilst it is clear that gain-based remedies are available where the profit has arisen from interference with property rights,[54] there is no reason why the remedies should be confined to such a context.

(iv) Subsequent Developments

Despite the revolutionary significance of the decision of the House of Lords in *Blake* in recognizing the award of gain-based remedies for breach of contract, the policies and principles underpinning the award of these remedies was unclear. Subsequent judicial developments have sought to put some flesh on the bare bones of *Blake*. As will be seen, the effect of these authorities over time has been to restrict significantly the award of a full account of the defendant's profits made from breach of contract, such that it will only be in cases with such exceptional facts as *Blake* itself that an account of profits will be awarded. Much of the focus has been on the award of *Wrotham Park* damages or the hypothetical bargain measure, which have now coalesced into the single measure of negotiation damages, which may involve the award of a partial account of the defendant's profits, although the actual sum awarded may be influenced by other considerations, particularly the claimant's loss.

One of the first cases to consider the application of *Blake* was *Esso Petroleum Co Ltd v Niad Ltd*.[55] This was a commercial case which arose from a pricing agreement, called 'Pricewatch', which was made by Esso with dealers who sold their petrol. The effect of the agreement was that dealers agreed regularly to report to Esso the price of petrol sold by local competitors and to abide by the prices set daily by Esso, which were intended to match the competition. The dealers received financial support from Esso in recompense. On four occasions this agreement was deliberately breached by Niad, which charged higher prices than had been agreed but still received the financial support from Esso. Esso sought an account of the profits which had been made by Niad in breach of the Pricewatch agreement. This remedy was awarded for a variety of reasons which the trial judge considered were sufficient to treat the case as exceptional, following *Blake*. These reasons included that the defendant's breach of contract was deliberate and repeated; compensatory damages was not an adequate remedy, because it was not possible to ascertain Esso's loss arising from lost sales following breach; the obligation to abide by

---

[53] Ibid, 298.   [54] See p 422, above.

[55] [2001] All ER (D) 324. See J Beatson, 'Courts, Arbitrators and Restitutionary Liability for Breach of Contract' (2002) 118 LQR 377.

the prices set by Esso was considered to be fundamental to the agreement; Niad's conduct had undermined the scheme and the company's advertising campaign relating to it; and Esso had a legitimate interest in preventing Niad from profiting from the breach of contract.

In no other case has a full account of profits been awarded for breach of contract. So, for example, in *The Sine Nomine*,[56] which involved a commercial arbitration, the owners of a ship had wrongfully withdrawn the vessel from charter after the market had risen, which had made the contract less profitable. It was accepted that no account of profits was available. This was surely right because compensatory damages were an adequate remedy in the circumstances. Similarly, in *WWF World Wide Fund for Nature v World Wrestling Federation Entertainment Inc*[57] no account of profits was awarded where the World Wrestling Federation had used the initials WWF in breach of an agreement, since the breach was not considered to be exceptional within the *Blake* principle. In *One Step (Support) Ltd v Morris-Garner*[58] an account of profits was not awarded for breach of a non-competition and non-solicitation covenant, even though the breach was deliberate since the defendants had planned to compete even before the covenant was made, because the breaches were characterized as being relatively straightforward and unremarkable, and so did not satisfy the *Blake* test of being exceptional.

Other cases since *Blake* have adopted a restitutionary analysis of the remedy available for breach of contract, but without requiring the defendant to make a full disgorgement of profits. One of the most significant cases is *Experience Hendrix LLC v PPX Enterprises Inc*,[59] where the Court of Appeal awarded a remedy for breach of contract which was explicitly characterized as restitutionary. The defendant had repeatedly breached a settlement agreement made in 1973 relating to the use of master recordings made by Jimi Hendrix without paying royalties. A gain-based remedy was justified in principle because there was no evidence of financial loss suffered by the claimant as a result of the breach,[60] so compensatory damages were inadequate and, since the claim related to past profits, the remedies of specific performance and injunction were inapplicable. Further, as in *Blake*, the defendant did what it had promised not to do; it had deliberately and flagrantly[61] breached the contract and the claimant was considered to have a legitimate interest in preventing the defendant from profiting from the breach.[62] The court did not, however, order the defendant to account for all the profits which derived from the breach, since the case was not considered to be exceptional within the *Blake* formula. This was because the dispute did not concern a sensitive subject such as national security, the defendant was not in a fiduciary or quasi-fiduciary relationship with the claimant[63] and the breaches

---

[56] [2002] 1 Lloyd's Rep 805. See also *University of Nottingham v Fishel* [2001] RPV 367.

[57] [2002] FSR 32. The Court of Appeal dismissed an appeal but without needing to consider the application of the *Blake* principle. In subsequent proceedings before the Court of Appeal the claimant was held to be unable to seek negotiation damages because it had already unsuccessfully sought an account of profits and both remedies were compensatory and so juridically similar: [2007] EWCA Civ 286, [2008] 1 WLR 445, [59] (Chadwick LJ). Whilst negotiation damages can be analysed as having a compensatory component, it is a nonsense to describe an account of profits as compensatory; they are categorically a disgorgement remedy. See p 424, above.   [58] [2014] EWHC 2213 (QB).

[59] [2003] EWCA Civ 323, [2003] 1 All ER (Comm) 830. See ID Campbell and OP Wylie, 'Ain't No Telling (Which Circumstances are Exceptional)' (2003) CLJ 605.

[60] *Experience Hendrix LLC v PPX Enterprises Inc* [2003] EWCA Civ 323, [2003] 1 All ER (Comm) 830, 845 (Mance LJ).   [61] Ibid, 848 (Peter Gibson LJ).

[62] For these reasons Barnett considers that full disgorgement of profits should have been awarded: K Barnett, 'Deterrence and Disgorging Profits for Breach of Contract' [2009] RLR 79, 90.

[63] *Experience Hendrix LLC v PPX Enterprises Inc* [2003] EWCA Civ 323, [2003] 1 All ER (Comm) 830, 848 (Peter Gibson LJ).

occurred in a commercial context. The remedy which was awarded was a reasonable sum assessed with reference to what the claimant would reasonably have demanded for the defendant's use of the recordings in breach of the agreement, by analogy with the approach adopted in *Wrotham Park*. The court was, however, unable to reach a final conclusion on the evidence before it as to what the appropriate sum should be.

Experience Hendrix is also significant for another reason, because the court recognized that the award of gain-based remedies for breach of contract is not tied specifically to the assessment of damages in lieu of an injunction.[64] So this measure will be available even if the claimant has not applied for an injunction or could not do so. To use an example suggested by Mance LJ, if the defendant has used land for a concert in breach of a restrictive covenant when the claimant was out of the country, the fact that the claimant had not been able to apply for an injunction to stop the infringement of the property right should not prevent the claimant from obtaining a gain-based remedy assessed by reference to what the defendant would have had to pay to the claimant to agree to waive the covenant.

The remedy awarded in *Experience Hendrix* appears to be a halfway house between the award of no gain-based remedy and a full account of the profits made from the breach, since the remedy was to be assessed with reference to the defendant's profits made from the breach of contract without requiring the defendant to disgorge all those profits. Some commentators have suggested that there is now a sliding-scale of remedies available for breach of contract ranging from a full account of profits through to the negotiation measure, which can deprive the defendant of some of the profits made, and on to a full compensatory award.[65] Analysing negotiation damages as a hybrid remedy,[66] which has compensatory and restitutionary components, might support this sliding-scale approach, since such damages straddle both the restitutionary and the compensatory function. But this sliding-scale characterization is still misleading, because it ignores the fact that gain-based remedies, in the context of breach of contract at least, are subsidiary to compensatory remedies. This has been recognized in all the cases on the award of gain-based remedies for breach of contract, which emphasize that they should only be available if compensatory damages are inadequate. The availability of compensatory remedies needs to be considered first and then the hybrid and pure restitutionary remedies can be considered, with account of profits only being available in particularly exceptional circumstances.

In fact, the remedy recognized in *Experience Hendrix* is better treated as a distinct form of remedy for a breach of contract, which relies on the user principle as recognized in *Wrotham Park Estate Co Ltd v Parkside Homes Ltd*,[67] and has become negotiation damages.[68] It follows that, where compensatory damages and specific performance are inadequate remedies for a breach of contract, there are two remedies which are available: account of profits and negotiation damages, the former of which ensures disgorgement of profit and the latter being a hybrid remedy, with compensatory and restitutionary

---

[64] Ibid, 842 (Mance LJ), 848 (Peter Gibson LJ). See also *World Wide Fund for Nature v World Wrestling Federation Inc* [2007] EWCA Civ 286, [2008] 1 WLR 445, [54] (Chadwick LJ); *Giedo van der Garde BV v Force India Formula One Team Ltd* [2010] EWHC 2373 (QB), [528] (Stadlen J).

[65] See the report of Lord Nicholls' comments, 'Breach of Contract, Restitution for Wrongs and Punishment: Review of Discussion' in AS Burrows and E Peel (eds), *Commercial Remedies: Current Issues and Problems* (Oxford: Oxford University Press, 2003), 129. See also AS Burrows, *Remedies for Torts and Breach of Contract* (3rd edn, Oxford University Press, 2004), 401–4; M Graham, 'Restitutionary Damages: The Anvil Struck' (2004) 120 LQR 26.

[66] See p 431, above. [67] [1974] 1 WLR 798. [68] See p 429, above.

components.[69] But, however the remedies are analysed, the most important practical question concerns when one remedy rather than the other will be available. In a very significant judgment in *Vercoe v Rutland Fund Management Ltd*,[70] Sales J identified a number of principles to determine when the remedy of account of profits should be available. The key aim concerns the identification of the just response to the particular wrong, so that the remedy awarded is not disproportionate to the wrong done to the claimant. This is to be determined by assessing whether the claimant's objective interest in performance of the relevant obligation makes it just and equitable that the defendant should retain no benefit from the breach. Where the claimant has a particularly strong interest in full performance, he or she should be entitled to choose between compensatory or negotiation damages and account of profits. The claimant might have a particularly strong interest in full performance of the contract where, for example, the breach of contract involves infringement of property rights, including intellectual property rights, or where it would not be reasonable to expect the contractual right to be released for a reasonable fee, such as the right to have state secrets maintained, as in *Blake*, or where the contractual right arises under a fiduciary relationship.[71] If the claimant does not have a strong interest in performance, as will be the case in a more commercial context, account of profits should not be available and the claimant should be confined to the negotiation measure; such a claimant will not be able to elect for an account of profits.

Particular guidance has been provided for the assessment of the negotiation measure as a remedy for breach of contract.[72] The aim is to determine a reasonable sum which would have been agreed by the parties for the claimant to waive his or her contractual right. It is to be assumed that both parties would have acted reasonably in these negotiations, and it is important for the court to have regard to the commercial context and the information which was known by the parties at the time of the negotiation.[73] It may be appropriate to have regard to the defendant's anticipated profits arising from the breach of contract,[74] if this would have reasonably been taken into account by the parties in conducting their negotiations. The negotiation measure has been considered to be more appropriate than an account of profits where the breach of contract involves interference with property rights in respect of property which is regularly bought and sold in a market.[75] Crucially, it has been recognized that the negotiation measure is available even though the breach of contract does not involve interference with property rights.[76]

(v) Summary of the Key Principles

Since the decision of the House of Lords in *Blake* various principles have been identified to determine when gain-based remedies can be awarded for breach of contract. It is clearly recognized that such remedies are subsidiary to compensatory remedies, so that they are only available where compensatory remedies are inadequate. This will typically be because the claimant has not suffered any provable loss. The remedy of a full account of profits will only be available in the most exceptional of circumstances. The only clear example of what

---

[69] *Giedo van der Garde BV v Force India Formula One Team Ltd* [2010] EWHC 2373 (QB), [508] (Stadlen J).

[70] [2010] EWHC 424 (Ch), [339]–[343].

[71] See *Jones v Ricoh Ltd* [2010] EWHC 1743 (Ch), [89] (Roth J); *Luxe Holding Ltd v Midland Resources Holding Ltd* [2010] EWHC 1908 (Ch), [55] (Roth J).   [72] See further p 430, above.

[73] *Frischmann Engineering Ltd v Bow Valley Iran Ltd* [2009] UKPC 45, [2011] 1 WLR 2370, [49] (Lord Walker). See also *Vercoe v Rutland Fund Management Ltd* [2010] EWHC 424 (Ch), [292] (Sales J); *Force India Formula One Team Ltd v 1 Malaysia Racing Team Sdn Bhd* [2012] EWHC 616 (Ch), [384] (Arnold J).

[74] *Giedo van der Garde BV v Force India Formula One Team Ltd* [2010] EWHC 2373 (QB), [508] (Stadlen J).

[75] *Vercoe v Rutland Fund Management Ltd* [2010] EWHC 424 (Ch), [340] (Sales J).

[76] *Giedo van der Garde BV v Force India Formula One Team Ltd* [2010] EWHC 2373 (QB), [533] (Stadlen J).

constitutes such circumstances is the *Blake* case itself. Whilst it is clear that these circumstances do not require proof of interference with property rights, it appears that the most significant factor is that the defendant is in a relationship with the claimant which can be considered to be very close to a fiduciary relationship, which suggests that the award of an account of profits will be especially rare in respect of the breach of a commercial contract.[77] Where the case is not exceptional,[78] but orthodox compensatory damages are unavailable, the negotiation measure can be awarded, which is properly characterized as a hybrid remedy, since it has regard both to the claimant's loss and to the defendant's gain.

2. SHOULD GAIN-BASED REMEDIES GENERALLY BE AVAILABLE FOR BREACH OF CONTRACT?

Whilst the principles underpinning the award of gain-based remedies are gradually emerging, it is still necessary to consider as a matter of policy whether this limited approach to the award of such remedies for breach of contract is satisfactory or whether such remedies should be available more generally or at all. Indeed, in Australia gain-based remedies for breach of contract have been rejected.[79] Should they be rejected in England as well?

(A) HOW WRONGFUL IS A BREACH OF CONTRACT?

To determine whether gain-based remedies should generally be available for breach of contract in English law, it is necessary to reconsider some of the basic principles which relate to the award of gain-based remedies for wrongdoing. The key principle which justifies the award of such remedies for wrongs is that the wrongdoer should not be allowed to benefit from the wrong.[80] What needs to be considered is whether the nature of breach of contract is such that any defendant who benefits from the breach should not be allowed to retain that benefit. Although breach of contract cannot be considered to be of the same magnitude of wrongfulness as committing a tort or crime or even a breach of fiduciary duty, the fact that it is wrongful has been recognized for the purposes of economic duress.[81] In many cases, however, a breach of contract is only technically wrongful and sometimes a breach of contract may even be economically efficient and so can be considered to be justified, so long as the claimant is adequately compensated for any loss suffered.[82] A breach of contract will be efficient where, for example, a vendor

---

[77] *Jones v Ricoh Ltd* [2010] EWHC 1743 (Ch), [89] (Roth J).

[78] *One Step (Support) Ltd v Morris-Garner* [2014] EWHC 2213 (QB), [104] (Phillips J).

[79] *Hospitality Group Pty Ltd v Australian Rugby Football Union Ltd* [2001] FCA 1040.

[80] See p 421, above.

[81] See p 207, above. See also *Ahmed Angullia bin Hadjee Mohamed Sallah Angullia v Estate and Trust Agencies (1927) Ltd* [1938] AC 624, 640 (Lord Romer).

[82] See R Posner, *Economic Analysis of Law* (7th edn, Boston, MA: Little Brown & Co, 2007); D Campbell and D Harris, 'In Defence of Breach: A Critique of Restitution and the Performance Interest' (2002) LS 208. For criticism of the theory of efficient breach see D Friedmann, 'The Efficient Breach Fallacy' (1989) 18 JLS 1; LD Smith, 'Disgorgement of the Profits of Breach of Contract: Property, Contract and "Efficient Breach"' (1992) 24 Canadian Business Law Journal 121; and R O'Dair, 'Restitutionary Damages for Breach of Contract and the Theory of Efficient Breach: Some Reflections' (1993) 46(2) CLP 113; P Jaffey, 'Efficiency, Disgorgement and Reliance in Contract: A Comment on Campbell and Harris' (2002) LS 570; K Barnett, *Accounting for Profit for Breach of Contract* (Oxford: Hart Publishing, 2012), 115.

contracted to sell goods to the claimant but sold them instead to a third party who valued them more than the claimant and so was prepared to pay more for them. In such circumstances it would appear that the breach of contract should not be deterred by awarding gain-based remedies to deprive the defendant of any benefit obtained from the breach, since the breach can serve a useful economic function.

The problem with this argument concerns the identification of those cases where a breach of contract can be considered to be economically efficient, since in the vast majority of cases the costs which arise from the breach will exceed any benefits derived it.[83] This includes costs arising from contracts which the claimant may have made with other parties and which the claimant is forced to repudiate or renegotiate as a result of the defendant's breach.[84]

(B) IDENTIFYING SITUATIONS WHERE THE BREACH OF CONTRACT IS SUFFICIENTLY WRONGFUL

There are, in fact, three different situations where the nature of the defendant's breach of contract may be considered to be sufficiently wrongful to justify the award of gain-based remedies.

(i) Cynical Breach of Contract

Sometimes the defendant's conduct in breaching the contract may be considered to be so cynical or opportunistic[85] that the defendant should not be allowed to profit from the breach.[86] Whilst this argument is superficially attractive, it is virtually impossible to apply in practice, because of the uncertainty in determining what constitutes a cynical breach. Is this merely a deliberate breach of contract or one where the defendant calculates that, after compensating the claimant for any loss suffered, he or she would still make a profit from the breach? But in either case what is really wrong with breaching the contract in such circumstances? A cynical breach can still be an efficient breach and reference to the motive of the defendant in breaching the contract is 'contrary to the general approach of [the English] law of contract'.[87] It would also result in greater uncertainty in the assessment of damages, something which should be avoided if at all possible in the context of commercial contracts. Consequently, no exception to the general rule against the award of gain-based remedies for breach of contract should be founded simply on the fact that the defendant's breach can be characterized as cynical. This conclusion was accepted by the House of Lords in *Attorney-General v Blake*.[88]

---

[83] See Friedmann, 'The Efficient Breach Fallacy', 7.   [84] Ibid, 13.

[85] *Restatement Third: Restitution and Unjust Enrichment* (ALI, 2011), para 39, comment c.

[86] This principle was recognized in Ireland in *Hickey v Roche*, reported [1993] RLR 196. It has been advocated by PBH Birks, 'Restitutionary Damages for Breach of Contract: *Snepp* and the Fusion of Law and Equity' [1987] LMCLQ 421. See also J Edelman, *Gain-Based Damages: Contract, Tort, Equity and Intellectual Property* (Oxford: Hart Publishing, 2002), who argues that a cynical breach of contract should justify the award of disgorgement damages, namely where the breach is deliberate or reckless with a view to gain: 86. See also Barnett, *Accounting for Profit from Breach of Contract*, 44, who justifies accounting for profits where the breach of contract is advertent in that the defendant consciously or advertently disregarded the rights of the claimant; such a defendant deserves to be punished.

[87] *Surrey CC v Bredero Homes Ltd* [1993] 1 WLR 1361, 1370 (Steyn LJ).

[88] [2001] 1 AC 268, 286 (Lord Nicholls).

(ii) Defendant Entered into a More Profitable Contract

It has sometimes been suggested that gain-based remedies are appropriate where the defendant has breached the contract with the claimant in order to enter into a more profitable contract with someone else.[89] Those who support this view tend to regard the decision of the Israeli Supreme Court in *Adras Building Material Ltd v Harlow and Jones GmbH*[90] as representing the ideal solution to the problem. In *Adras* the claimant agreed to buy 7,000 tons of steel from the defendant. The defendant supplied some of this steel to the claimant, but it then received an offer from a third party to buy the remaining steel for a higher price. Consequently the defendant agreed to supply the remaining steel to the third party. The claimant sued the defendant for breach of contract and claimed that it should obtain restitution of the difference between the original contract price and the price obtained by the defendant from the resale to the third party. A majority of the Supreme Court found for the claimant and recognized a general right to the award of restitutionary damages whenever the defendant obtained a benefit as a result of a breach of contract. But great care must be taken before the restitutionary principles recognized in *Adras* are transplanted into English law, primarily because the approach of Israeli law to breach of contract is fundamentally different from that of English law. For Israeli law expects contractual promises to be performed and it is for this reason that, as was recognized in *Adras* itself, the general remedy for breach of contract is specific performance. On the other hand, the attitude of English law to the binding nature of promises is much more ambivalent. In England when the defendant breaches a contract the usual remedial response is to award damages and only certain types of contract are specifically enforceable.[91] This fundamentally different attitude means that, although the unrestricted award of restitutionary damages might be entirely appropriate in Israel, this is not necessarily the case in England, particularly because it does not necessarily follow that compensatory damages are an inadequate remedy.

(iii) Specifically Enforceable Contracts

A third circumstance where gain-based relief may be an appropriate remedy for a breach of contract is where the contract which is breached is specifically enforceable. This is consistent with the principles recognized by the House of Lords in *Blake* because contracts are only specifically enforceable where compensatory damages are an inadequate remedy. That gain-based remedies should be available whenever the defendant has breached a specifically enforceable contract has been advocated by a number of commentators.[92] This is because, where a contract is considered to be specifically enforceable, the policy of the law favours the performance of the contract. If the defendant fails to perform the contract, in circumstances in which the contract can no longer be specifically enforced, it is entirely appropriate that the defendant should make restitution to the claimant, both because

---

[89] See especially Barnett, *Accounting for Profit for Breach of Contract*, ch 4, who advocates an account of profits in such circumstances only where specific relief is no longer available and the promisor has made a profit: ibid, 117.   [90] (1988) 42 (1) PD. See [1995] RLR 235.

[91] *Co-operative Insurance Society Ltd v Argyll Stores (Holdings) Ltd* [1998] AC 1, 11 (Lord Hoffmann).

[92] See J Beatson, *The Use and Abuse of Unjust Enrichment* (Oxford: Clarendon Press, 1991), 17; Birks 'Restitutionary Damages for Breach of Contract', 442; SM Waddams, 'Restitution as Part of Contract Law' in AS Burrows (ed), *Essays on the Law of Restitution* (Oxford: Clarendon Press, 1991), 208–12; O'Dair, 'Restitutionary Damages for Breach of Contract and the Theory of Efficient Breach'; RC Nolan, 'Remedies for Breach of Contract: Specific Enforcement and Restitution' in F Rose (ed), *Failure of Contracts: Contractual, Restitutionary and Proprietary Consequences* (Oxford: Hart Publishing, 1997). See also Barnett, *Accounting for Profit for Breach of Contract*, ch 5.

breach of specifically enforceable contracts should be deterred, and because, if the defendant does breach such a contract, he or she should not be allowed to profit from the clear wrong of doing so. In fact, where restitutionary remedies are awarded for breach of contract this should be considered to be simply a monetized form of specific perform-ance, assuming that if the contract had been performed the claimant would have obtained the benefit which the defendant had obtained.[93]

It follows that it is important to determine in what circumstances a contract will be specifically enforceable. There are four particular characteristics of such contracts.[94] First, compensatory damages must be an inadequate way of protecting the claimant's interests. Secondly, the claimant must have a legitimate interest in the performance of the contract. Thirdly, the claimant's interest must not be capable of protection by reasonable mitigating action by the claimant. Finally, the specific performance must not require constant supervision by the courts, as will be the case where the defendant is required to perform a contract over a period of time rather than where he or she is simply required to achieve a particular result.[95] Specific performance will not be ordered where the claimant's conduct is such that equitable relief is not merited or where the making of such an order would conflict with fundamental social and economic policies which are opposed to the com-pulsion of performance, such as the policy against compelling a defendant to employ the claimant.

The importance of the distinction between contracts which are and which are not specifically enforceable was recognized by Purchas LJ in *Williams v Roffey Bros and Nicholls (Contractors) Ltd*,[96] who stated that, save for contracts which are specifically enforceable, it is perfectly acceptable for a party to a contract deliberately to breach that contract if he or she is able to cut losses as a result. The decision of the Israeli Supreme Court in *Adras* also reflects the significance of the distinction, since in that case restitu-tionary damages were awarded only because of the assumption of Israeli law that all contractual promises should be performed, hence the fact that in Israel specific perform-ance is the primary contractual remedy. The special treatment of specifically enforceable contracts is also supported by some of the English cases which have examined the question of the award of gain-based remedies for breach of contract and which have emphasized that gain-based remedies are appropriate in lieu of a specific order to compel performance.[97]

But this link between the award of gain-based remedies to contracts which are specif-ically enforceable is coincidental, because of the tendency for a number of these earlier cases to involve a breach of contract which involves interference with property rights. *Blake* has now released these awards from the strait-jacket of specific enforceability of the obligation which has been breached.[98] Nevertheless, Barnett has usefully extrapolated from the cases and from *Blake* itself what she calls the 'agency problem',[99] for which the

---

[93] Cf *Surrey CC v Bredero Homes Ltd* [1993] 1 WLR 1361, 1371.

[94] See Beatson, *The Use and Abuse of Unjust Enrichment*, 17.

[95] *Co-operative Insurance Society Ltd v Argyll Stores (Holdings) Ltd* [1998] AC 1, 12 (Lord Hoffmann). Lord Hoffmann also recognized that a contractual obligation would not be specifically enforced if the terms of the order could not be precisely drawn: ibid, 13–14.   [96] [1991] 1 QB 1.

[97] See *Wrotham Park Estate Co Ltd v Parkside Homes Ltd* [1974] 1 WLR 798; *Pell Frischmann Engineering Ltd v Bow Valley Iran Ltd* [2009] UKPC 45, [2011] 1 WLR 2370, [46] (Lord Walker).

[98] *Experience Hendrix LLC v PPX Enterprises Inc* [2003] EWCA Civ 323, [2003] 1 All ER (Comm) 830, 842 (Mance LJ), 848 (Peter Gibson LJ); *World Wide Fund for Nature v World Wrestling Federation Inc* [2007] EWCA Civ 286, [2008] 1 WLR 445, [54] (Chadwick LJ); *Giedo van der Garde BV v Force India Formula One Team Ltd* [2010] EWHC 2373 (QB), [528] (Stadlen J).

[99] Barnett, *Accounting for Profit for Breach of Contract*, ch 5.

award of an account of profits can provide an appropriate solution. This problem arises where the defendant has promised not to act in a particular way and there is no adequate incentive for the defendant to keep to this promise. In such circumstances compensatory damages are typically inadequate because these contracts often involve non-financial interests, and specific relief will be unavailable because the obligation will already have been breached. Consequently, account of profits can be justified to deter the defendant from breaching such a contract and so to provide an incentive to negotiate with the promisee for the release of the promise not to perform. She justifies this deterrence objective because of the analogy with cases which involve fiduciaries profiting from breach of fiduciary duty.[100] This is the most convincing justification for the recognition of gain-based remedies for breach of contract, even though it does not necessarily justify the award of a full account of profits, since typically the defendant will only be required to disgorge the amount which the parties would reasonably have agreed to waive the obligation, which involves the negotiation measure.

(C) CONCLUSIONS

It follows from this analysis that, whilst breach of contract can be considered to be a wrong which engages the principle that no defendant should profit from their wrong, the typically commercial context of the breach of contract, and the legitimacy of the notion of efficient breach, means that this is a wrong which should not necessarily be deterred by the law of restitution depriving the defendant of any benefit obtained from the breach of contract. None of the three justifications for the award of gain-based remedies for breach of contract are so convincing as to provide a rational justification for the award of gain-based remedies for breach, save, perhaps where the breach involves the defendant doing the very thing which he or she had promised not to do, in circumstances where compensatory damages are not an adequate remedy. That is what happened in *Attorney-General v Blake*. But even then something else is needed to justify a full account of profits. That additional element is that the relationship between the claimant and the defendant can be characterized as one which is almost a fiduciary relationship. It follows that in the future it will only be those cases the facts of which are identical or very close to *Blake* that a full account of profits arising from the breach of contract can be justified. In all other cases where compensatory damages are inadequate, the negotiation measure of damages will be available instead.

---

[100] See further Chapter 19.

19

RESTITUTION FOR EQUITABLE WRONGDOING

1. GENERAL PRINCIPLES

(A) THE RATIONALE BEHIND THE AWARD OF GAIN-BASED REMEDIES FOR EQUITABLE WRONGDOING

Where the defendant has committed a tort or breached a contract, gain-based remedies tend to be available only in exceptional circumstances. Where, however, the defendant has breached an equitable duty which he or she owed to the claimant, such relief is much more common. There are two reasons for this. First, the Equitable jurisdiction relating to the award of remedies tends to be more adaptable than the equivalent Common Law jurisdiction. Secondly, the policies which justify the award of gain-based remedies for wrongdoing are much more likely to come into play where the defendant commits an equitable wrong.[1] This is because the typical equitable duty which the defendant owes to the claimant arises from a relationship of trust and confidence. As Jackman has recognized,[2] the nature of such relationships gives the defendant an opportunity to abuse and exploit the claimant, so that the relationship is in particular need of protection. Consequently, it is necessary to deter the defendant from exploiting the relationship and this is done by ensuring that, at the very least, the value of any benefit which the defendant obtained from the breach of duty should be paid to the claimant to whom the duty was owed. It is irrelevant that the claimant did not suffer any loss by reason of the breach of duty, since the function of the award of gain-based remedies is to ensure that the defendant does not benefit from the commission of the equitable wrong.

There is one other principle which underlies the award of gain-based remedies for wrongs which is particularly important in the context of equitable wrongdoing, and this relates to the moral nature of the defendant's breach of duty. Analysis of the cases in Equity suggests that, where the defendant can be considered to be more culpable in breaching his or her equitable duty, a more extensive form of gain-based remedy may be available. Also, where the defendant is not considered to be culpable in breaching his or her duty, an equitable allowance will be awarded to reflect the value of the defendant's contribution to the benefit which he or she obtained.[3] Culpability in Equity is assessed by reference to the old equitable language of conscience and unconscionability. Whilst these words have been interpreted in various ways, in the particular context of determining liability for equitable wrongs and the award of gain-based remedies the defendant will be

---

[1] See p 422, above.   [2] IM Jackman, 'Restitution for Wrongs' (1989) 48 CLJ 302, 311.
[3] Compare *Boardman v Phipps* [1967] 2 AC 46 and *O'Sullivan v Management Agency and Music Ltd* [1985] QB 428 with *Guinness plc v Saunders* [1990] 2 AC 663.

considered to have acted unconscionably when, in the light of his or her knowledge of the facts, a reasonable person in the position of the defendant would have acted differently.[4]

(B) TYPES OF REMEDY WHICH ARE AVAILABLE FOR EQUITABLE WRONGDOING

Where the defendant has committed an equitable wrong the following remedies may be available.

(i) Account of Profits

Usually, where the defendant obtains a profit as a result of committing an equitable wrong, the remedy which is awarded will be an account of profits. This is a personal remedy so that the defendant is simply liable to pay to the claimant the value of the benefit which he or she obtained from the wrong. This is clearly a gain-based remedy, even though the Supreme Court has described it as constituting 'equitable compensation'.[5] But compensation focuses on remedying the claimant's loss, whereas account of profits focuses on the defendant's gain, so using the language of compensation to describe account of profits can only cause categorical confusion.

(ii) Proprietary Remedies

The courts have acknowledged that a proprietary remedy will be available following the commission of an equitable wrong where the nature of the wrong is such that any benefit gained by the defendant is held on constructive trust for the claimant.[6] Where property is held on constructive trust it follows that the claimant has an equitable proprietary interest in the property, which he or she can vindicate by means of restitutionary proprietary claim.[7] One of the most controversial matters concerning the award of gain-based remedies for equitable wrongdoing relates to the determination of when and why proprietary relief should be available.[8]

(iii) Equitable Compensation

Although the normal remedy for equitable wrongdoing is restitutionary, it does not follow that other forms of remedy are excluded. Most importantly, the notion of equitable compensation is recognized by English law.[9] Although this remedy has sometimes been called restitutionary,[10] since the effect of it is to restore the claimant to the position which he or she occupied had the wrong not been committed, the remedy has nothing to do with the law of, restitution because it is not assessed by reference to the gain made by the defendant but is instead assessed by reference to the loss suffered by the claimant. It is

---

[4] See p 650, below.

[5] *FHR European Ventures Ltd v Cedar Capital Partners LLC* [2014] UKSC 45, [2015] AC 250, [6] (Lord Neuberger).

[6] See especially *FHR European Ventures Ltd v Cedar Capital Partners LLC*, ibid. The nature of the constructive trust is examined at p 512, below.

[7] See Chapter 21.   [8] This is considered at p 513, below.

[9] See, in particular, *Nocton v Lord Ashburton* [1914] AC 932, 956–7 (Viscount Haldane LC); *Bishopsgate Investment Management Ltd v Maxwell (No 2)* [1994] 1 All ER 261; *Target Holdings Ltd v Redferns (a firm)* [1996] AC 421; *Mahoney v Purnell* [1996] 3 All ER 61; *Bristol and West Building Society v Mothew* [1998] Ch 1, 17 (Millett LJ); and *Swindle v Harrison* [1997] 4 All ER 705. See also the decision of the High Court of Australia in *Warman International Ltd v Dwyer* (1995) 128 ALR 201.

[10] See *Swindle v Harrison* [1997] 4 All ER 705, 714 where Evans LJ described the equitable remedy for restoring the claimant to the position he or she occupied before the defendant committed a fraudulent wrong as 'restitution'.

nonetheless important to be aware of the existence of equitable compensatory remedies, because their presence in Equity's armoury will no doubt circumscribe the importance of gain-based remedies,[11] although crucially the award of gain-based remedies in Equity is not dependent on compensatory damages being inadequate.[12]

2. THE CATEGORIES OF EQUITABLE WRONGDOING

Although a wide variety of equitable wrongdoing can be identified, there are three key categories of such wrongs which can trigger gain-based remedies:[13] breach of fiduciary duty, breach of confidence, and accessorial liability. Rather than concentrating on the nature of the equitable wrongs themselves, the analysis which follows will seek to determine when gain-based remedies will be awarded for such wrongdoing and the type of gain-based remedies which are awarded.

(A) BREACH OF FIDUCIARY DUTY

Where the defendant is in a fiduciary relationship with the principal he or she is in a position to exploit the principal and so, by virtue of the policy of protecting such relationships against abuse, gain-based remedies are available where the defendant has breached his or her fiduciary duty. Before examining the types of duty that fiduciaries owe to their principals, it is first necessary to examine when a fiduciary relationship can be identified.[14]

(i) The Identification of Fiduciary Relationships

Traditionally, a person is treated as a fiduciary because he or she is subject to fiduciary obligations,[15] and so it is vital to determine what those duties are and when they might be recognized as arising. A fiduciary has been described by Birks as 'one who has discretion, and therefore, power, in the management of another's affairs, in circumstances in which that one cannot reasonably be expected to monitor him or take other precautions to protect his own interests'.[16]

There is no absolute definition of when the defendant can be considered to be a fiduciary. There are, however, certain types of relationship which are always treated as fiduciary. So, for example, trustees, company directors, solicitors, agents, and partners will always be treated as owing fiduciary duties to their principal. But the classes of fiduciary relationships are not closed,[17] and so if the relationship between the parties does not fall

---

[11] J Edelman and SB Elliott, 'Monetary Remedies Against Trustees' (2004) 18 TLI 116, reject the language of equitable compensation and prefer the more sophisticated distinction between substitutive and reparative compensation. The former involves monetary substitution for property which a fiduciary no longer holds and the latter damages to make good losses suffered.   [12] See p 440, above.

[13] See D Davies, 'Restitution and Equitable Wrongs: An Australian Analogue' in F Rose (ed), *Consensus ad Idem—Essays in the Law of Contract in Honour of Guenter Treitel* (London: Sweet and Maxwell, 1996), 163.

[14] D Hayton, 'Fiduciaries in Context: An Overview' in PBH Birks (eds), *Privacy and Loyalty* (Oxford: Clarendon Press, 1997), 292.

[15] *Bristol and West Building Society v Mothew* [1998] Ch 1, 18 (Millett LJ). See PD Finn, *Fiduciary Obligations* (Sydney: Law Book Co, 1977), 2.

[16] PBH Birks, 'Equity in the Modern Law: An Exercise in Taxonomy' (1996) 26 Univ WALR 1, 18.

[17] *English v Dedham Vale Properties Ltd* [1978] 1 WLR 93.

within any of the recognized classes, the particular nature of the relationship needs to be carefully examined to determine whether there are sufficient hallmarks of a fiduciary relationship to enable the court to conclude that the relationship is indeed fiduciary. In *Bristol and West Building Society v Mothew*[18] Millett LJ identified the essential characteristics of fiduciary relationships as follows: 'A fiduciary is someone who has undertaken to act for or on behalf of another in a particular matter in circumstances which give rise to a relationship of trust and confidence. The distinguishing obligation of a fiduciary is the obligation of loyalty.'[19] This is the touchstone against which the defendant's relationship with his or her principal should be assessed to determine whether the defendant owes fiduciary obligations.

Edelman has suggested a radical reappraisal of when fiduciary duties are recognized.[20] He considers that fiduciary obligations are express or implied duties that arise where one party voluntarily undertakes to act in the interests of the other. He considers that the test for implying such duties is the same as that for the implication of terms in a contract, namely whether a party, by his or her words or conduct, gave rise to an understanding or expectation in a reasonable person that he or she would behave in a particular way.[21] But, whilst fiduciary duties clearly can be expressly agreed or implied as a matter of fact, this cannot explain all cases, since sometimes such duties will be imposed by law without regard to express or implied manifestations of consent. The better view is that, once the hallmarks of a fiduciary relationship have been identified, either because the relationship falls within one of the recognized categories or is a *de facto* fiduciary relationship, fiduciary duties will be imposed by operation of law but may be modified or excluded by the parties.[22]

Whilst it is clear that an express trustee is always a fiduciary, whether resulting and constructive trustees should be characterized as owing fiduciary duties is a controversial matter. The preferable view is that a trustee should be considered to be subject to distinct fiduciary duties only if he or she voluntarily assumed the position of trustee.[23] It follows that a constructive trustee should not be considered to be a fiduciary, because such a trustee will not have knowingly subjected him or herself to fiduciary obligations.[24] Whether a resulting trustee is a fiduciary would depend on the category of resulting trust that is involved. If the resulting trust arises automatically from the failure of an express trust,[25] it would be appropriate to treat the resulting trustee as a fiduciary,[26] since the trustee already owed fiduciary duties under the express trust that would have been voluntarily assumed. Where, however, the resulting trust is presumed,[27] there is no reason to impose fiduciary duties on the trustee because the trustee has not voluntarily assumed such a position.

One of the most important questions relating to the identification of a fiduciary relationship is the extent to which parties to a commercial transaction can be considered to owe fiduciary duties to other parties to the transaction. This was examined by the Privy Council in *Re Goldcorp Exchange plc*,[28] where a restrictive interpretation of fiduciary

---

[18] [1998] Ch 1, 18. [19] See also *Alberta v Elder Advocates of Alberta Society* 2011 SCA 23.

[20] J Edelman, 'When Do Fiduciary Duties Arise?' (2010) 126 LQR 302. [21] Ibid, 317.

[22] See M Conaglen, 'Fiduciary Duties and Voluntary Undertakings' (2013) 7 Journal of Equity 105.

[23] See Edelman, 'When Do Fiduciary Duties Arise?'.

[24] P Millett, 'Restitution and Constructive Trusts' (1998) 114 LQR 399, 405. See also LD Smith, 'Constructive Fiduciaries' in PB Birks (ed), *Privacy and Loyalty* (Oxford: Clarendon Press, 1997), 263.

[25] See p 592, below. [26] See R Chambers, *Resulting Trusts* (Oxford: Clarendon Press, 1997), 196–200.

[27] See p 588, below. [28] [1995] 1 AC 74.

duties was adopted.[29] In that case the claimants had bought bullion from the defendant company. The bullion had not been allocated to the claimants, who consequently argued that the defendant had breached its fiduciary duty to them. This argument was easily rejected because the court was unable to identify duties which could be characterized as fiduciary rather than merely contractual. The identification of fiduciary duties, especially in a commercial context, can have profound consequences on the risks inherent in such relationships and the recognition in this case that fiduciary duties are fundamentally different from merely contractual obligations should prevent the concept from being abused purely from a desire to secure a just result. As Lord Mustill memorably said, 'high expectations do not necessarily lead to equitable remedies'.[30] Millett LJ emphasized extra-judicially that: 'It is the first importance not to impose fiduciary obligations on parties to a purely commercial relationship who deal with each other at arms' length and can be expected to look after their own interests.'[31]

But the restrictive approach to the recognition of fiduciary relationships in the *Goldcorp* case has not always been adopted. Sometimes the inherent uncertainty as to what constitutes a fiduciary relationship appears to have been manipulated to ensure that the defendant is liable to make restitution to the claimant. This is illustrated by *English v Dedham Vale Properties Ltd.*[32] The defendant was a property development company which wanted to purchase the claimant's land. The purchase price which was agreed reflected the fact that planning permission for development of the site was unlikely. But, before the contracts were exchanged, the defendant applied for planning permission and obtained it, although it failed to inform the claimant of this. Once the claimant had discovered that the defendant had obtained planning permission, it successfully claimed the profit which the defendant had made as a result of the development, on the ground that the defendant owed the claimant fiduciary duties. It was held that the defendant was a fiduciary because it was deemed to have been acting as an agent on behalf of the claimant when it obtained planning permission. But this is a highly artificial finding of such a relationship, since there was nothing on the facts to suggest that either party had ever contemplated that the defendant was acting as the claimant's agent. As Birks suggested, the finding of a fiduciary relationship seems to have been a convenient method of ensuring that the defendant was liable to make restitution to the claimant.[33] A commercial relationship should be converted into a fiduciary one only in limited circumstances and the key test should be whether the defendant has voluntarily undertaken to act for another.[34] This has been acknowledged by the Supreme Court of Canada in *Galambos v Perez*,[35] which held that an ad hoc fiduciary relationship should be recognized if two conditions are satisfied:

(1) there is an express or implied undertaking by one party that he or she will act in the best interests of the other; and

(2) that person has a discretionary power to affect the principal's legal or practical interests.

---

[29] See also *Hospital Products International v United States Surgical Corporation* (1984) 156 CLR 41 (High Court of Australia).

[30] *Re Goldcorp Exchange plc* [1995] 1 AC 74, 98.

[31] P Millett, 'Equity's Place in the Law of Commerce' (1998) 114 LQR 214, 217–18. Cf A Mason, 'The Place of Equity and Equitable Remedies in the Contemporary Common Law World' (1994) 110 LQR 238, 245–6.

[32] [1978] 1 WLR 93.

[33] PBH Birks, *An Introduction to the Law of Restitution* (rev edn, Oxford: Clarendon Press, 1989), 331.

[34] Edelman, 'When Do Fiduciary Duties Arise?'.   [35] 2009 SCR 48, [2009] 3 SCR 247.

Consequently, in that case, where an office manager of a law firm had lent money to the firm to stave off its insolvency, it was held that the lawyer was not in a fiduciary relationship with the office manager because he was unaware that the advances had been made, so there was no undertaking that he would act in her best interests and he had no discretionary power that would affect her interests. For similar reasons a fiduciary relationship should not have been identified in *English v Dedham Vale Properties*.

(ii) The Nature and Ambit of Fiduciary Duties

A number of different principles can be identified relating to the nature and ambit of fiduciary duties.[36]

(1) In an important dictum from an American case Frankfurter J said:

> To say that a man is a fiduciary only begins the analysis: it gives direction to further inquiry. To whom is he a fiduciary? What obligation does he owe as a fiduciary? In what respects has he failed to discharge these obligations? And what are the consequences of his deviation from duty?[37]

In other words, it is not enough to decide that the defendant is a fiduciary: this is simply the initial question. This has been recognized explicitly in English law. In *Bristol and West Building Society v Mothew*[38] the Court of Appeal acknowledged that there is more than one category of fiduciary relationship and that different categories of relationship possess different characteristics and attract different kinds of fiduciary obligation.[39] Crucially, it is dangerous to assume that all fiduciaries are subject to the same duties in all circumstances.[40]

(2) A particular relationship may fall within more than one category of fiduciary relationship. Also, the different categories of relationship may last for varying periods and the duties owed by the fiduciary will differ depending on the category of relationship which is being considered.

(3) In *Bristol and West Building Society v Mothew*[41] Millett LJ recognized that not every breach of duty by a fiduciary is a breach of fiduciary duty. Rather, fiduciary duties are 'those duties which are peculiar to fiduciaries and the breach of which attracts legal consequences differing from those consequent upon the breach of other duties'.[42] So, for example, although all fiduciaries are under an obligation to use proper skill and care in the discharge of their duties, the breach of this obligation is not a breach of a fiduciary duty because it is not a duty which is peculiar to fiduciaries.[43] Whether the duty that has been breached is fiduciary or non-fiduciary will sometimes have substantive consequences,[44] both as regards the rules of causation and remoteness which apply, and also as regards the determination of the appropriate remedy, with full disgorgement of profits being the typical remedy for breaches of fiduciary duty and compensatory damages for breach of non-fiduciary duties.

---

[36] For detailed examination of the nature and ambit of fiduciary duties see Finn, *Fiduciary Obligations*.

[37] *Securities and Exchange Commission v Chenery Corporation* (1943) 318 US 80, 85–6.

[38] [1998] Ch 1. For more general analysis of the nature of fiduciary obligations see Millett, 'Equity's Place in the Law of Commerce', 218–23. [39] See p 492, below.

[40] *Henderson v Merrett Syndicates Ltd* [1995] 2 AC 145, 206 (Lord Browne-Wilkinson).

[41] [1998] Ch 1, 16. See also *Hilton v Barker, Booth and Eastwood* [2005] UKHL 8, [2005] 1 WLR 567, 575 (Lord Walker). [42] *Bristol and West Building Society v Mothew* [1998] Ch 1, 16.

[43] *Henderson v Merrett Syndicates Ltd* [1995] 2 AC 145, 180 (Lord Goff) and 205 (Lord Browne-Wilkinson); *White v Jones* [1995] 2 AC 207, 274 (Lord Browne-Wilkinson).

[44] *Bristol and West Building Society v Mothew* [1998] Ch 1, 16 (Millett LJ).

(4) Fiduciary duties are considered to be proscriptive in effect. This means that the duties do not identify what fiduciaries *must* do, but identify what they *should not* do.

(5) For a fiduciary to be liable for breach of fiduciary duty he or she must have breached the duty by an intentional act; unconscious omission is not sufficient.[45] But, crucially, a fiduciary will be held liable even if he or she did not act fraudulently or in bad faith and even if the fiduciary honestly thought that he or she was acting in good faith.[46]

(6) A fiduciary obligation does not continue after the termination of the relationship which gave rise to the duty,[47] save where the fiduciary has resigned specifically to exploit an opportunity acquired as a fiduciary.[48] Whilst this exception might be analysed as continuation of the fiduciary obligation after resignation, and so an exception to the general rule that fiduciary duties terminate on resignation, it is better analysed as a breach of duty whilst still in a fiduciary relationship, by virtue of the disloyalty in resigning in order to exploit the opportunity.[49] Indeed, if the fiduciary resigns for legitimate reasons and then exploits the opportunity, this will not constitute a breach of fiduciary duty. There are other potential exceptions to the rule that fiduciary duties end on the termination of the relationship. The first is where information is imparted to the fiduciary in confidence whilst the fiduciary relationship subsists. The obligation to maintain confidence is unrelated to the fiduciary continuing to be employed and so the obligation continues even after the relationship has been terminated.[50] The second exception is where the principal remains dependent on the fiduciary despite the formal termination of the relationship, so that the former fiduciary continues to be able to exert influence over the principal.

(iii) The Categories of Fiduciary Relationship

There are three distinct categories of fiduciary relationship. Each one possesses different characteristics and attracts different kinds of fiduciary obligation.[51]

(1) The Relationship of Trust and Confidence

The most important category of fiduciary relationship is the relationship of trust and confidence. The essence of this relationship is that the fiduciary has undertaken to act for or on behalf of somebody else in circumstances that give rise to a relationship of trust and confidence.[52] In other words, the principal is entitled to the single-minded loyalty of the fiduciary.[53]

The identification of this relationship of trust and confidence is illustrated by the decision of the Court of Appeal in *Attorney-General v Blake*.[54] Blake, who had been a member of the British Secret Intelligence Service and also an agent of the Soviet Union, published his autobiography which disclosed information about the secret service. This

---

[45] Ibid, 19 (Millett LJ).

[46] *Murad v Al-Saraj* [2005] EWCA Civ 969, [2005] WTLR 1573, [67] (Arden LJ).

[47] *CMS Dolphin Ltd v Simonet* [2001] EWHC 415 (Ch), [2001] 2 BCLC 704, [95] (Collins J); *In Plus Group Ltd v Pyke* [2002] EWCA Civ 370, [2002] 2 BCLC 201, [71] (Brooke LJ).

[48] *Foster Bryant Surveying Ltd v Bryant* [2007] EWCA Civ 200, [2007] 2 BCLC 239.

[49] Ibid, [69] (Rix LJ).

[50] *Attorney-General v Blake* [1998] Ch 439 (CA); *Attorney-General v Guardian Newspapers Ltd (No 3)* [1990] 1 AC 109.   [51] Millett, 'Equity's Place in the Law of Commerce', 219.

[52] *Bristol and West Building Society v Mothew* [1998] Ch 1, 18 (Millett LJ).

[53] See S Worthington, 'Fiduciaries: When is Self-Denial Obligatory?' (1999) 58 CLJ 500; M Conaglen, 'The Nature and Function of Fiduciary Loyalty' (2005) 121 LQR 452.

[54] [1998] Ch 439. This aspect of the decision was not considered by the House of Lords on appeal.

breached an agreement not to disclose information gained as a result of his employment by the Crown and it also constituted a breach of the Official Secrets Acts. The book was published in the United Kingdom without the permission of the Crown. The Attorney-General sued, on behalf of the Crown, to recover all the sums which had been received or were receivable by the publisher. One argument made by the Attorney-General was that, if Blake had received these profits, he would have been liable to account for them to the Crown because they were made in breach of fiduciary duty. The Court of Appeal accepted that there was a fiduciary relationship of trust and confidence between Blake and the Crown, because Blake was employed to act in the best interests of the Crown. But it also recognized that this duty only lasted as long as the relationship of trust and confidence continued and that such a relationship ended once the employee had ceased to be employed. Consequently, once Blake ceased to be employed by the Crown, he no longer owed a duty of loyalty to the Crown as a fiduciary. A duty of loyalty will subsist despite the termination of employment, if the employee has entered into a contractual undertaking not to damage the employer's interests once the employee had left that employment. But, if such an agreement was breached, liability would be founded on breach of contract rather than breach of fiduciary duty. It was the breach of this agreement which founded the basis for the claim before the House of Lords.[55]

Beneath the umbrella of the fiduciary's obligation of loyalty are two basic duties, as recognized by Lord Herschell in *Bray v Ford*:[56] 'it is an inflexible rule of a court of equity that a person in a fiduciary position ... is not, unless otherwise expressly provided, entitled to make a profit; he is not allowed to put himself in a position where his interest and duty conflict'.

These are the so-called 'no profit' and 'no conflict' duties. These duties are peculiar to fiduciaries[57] and are preferably treated as distinct.[58]

(a) The No-Conflict Duty

The no-conflict duty is engaged where a fiduciary finds him or herself in a position where the fiduciary's personal interest conflicts with his or her duty to the principal, or may conflict in a real and sensible manner;[59] the fiduciary must then prefer the duty to the principal to his or her personal interest,[60] save where the principal has given free and fully informed consent to enable the fiduciary to prefer his or her interest. So, for example, a fiduciary is prohibited from competing with the principal's business, for then the personal interests of the fiduciary will, or might, conflict with the interests of the principal that the fiduciary is bound to protect.[61] The fiduciary is not permitted to adduce evidence to show that there was no actual conflict of personal interest and duty; liability is founded on the existence of potential, rather than actual, conflict.

Nolan[62] has argued that, where the claimant seeks a restitutionary remedy from the fiduciary in respect of a benefit which was obtained in contravention of the 'no-conflict' duty, this restitutionary claim should be treated as founded on unjust enrichment rather

---

[55] See p 473, above.   [56] [1896] AC 44, 50.

[57] *Bristol and West Building Society v Mothew* [1998] Ch 1, 16 (Millett LJ).

[58] *Ultraframe (UK) Ltd v Fielding* [2005] EWHC 1638 (Ch), [2006] FSR 16, [1305] (Lewison J).

[59] *Boardman v Phipps* [1967] 2 AC 46, 124 (Lord Upjohn).

[60] *Aberdeen Railway Company v Blaikie Bros* (1854) 1 Macq 461, 471 (Lord Cranworth). As regards fiduciary duties owed by directors to companies the no-conflict rule is enacted in the Companies Act 2006, s 175 (1).   [61] *Re Thomson* [1930] 1 Ch 203.

[62] RC Nolan, 'Conflicts of Interest, Unjust Enrichment and Wrongdoing' in W Cornish, R Nolan, J O'Sullivan, and G Virgo (eds), *Restitution: Past, Present and Future* (Oxford: Hart Publishing, 1998), 99. See *Tito v Waddell (No 2)* [1977] Ch 106, 248 (Megarry V-C).

than restitution for wrongs. So, for example, if the fiduciary purchases property from the principal at an undervalue, the defendant's liability to make restitution will be founded on his or her unjust enrichment, since the defendant will have obtained a benefit at the claimant's expense, as the benefit was subtracted from the claimant. Nolan failed to identify a recognized ground of restitution which would be applicable in such circumstances, but suggested that a ground should be recognized because the claimant's consent to benefit the defendant can be considered to be impaired.[63] Whilst this is a persuasive argument, particularly because it is consistent with a number of cases, its success depends on how the liability of a fiduciary is analysed, namely whether a fiduciary who infringes the no-conflict rule should be characterized as a wrongdoer? Since the liability of the defendant depends on the fact that he or she was a fiduciary, and failed to reach the high standards which are expected of a fiduciary, it is preferable to treat infringement of the no-conflict duty as a form of wrongdoing, for which restitutionary relief is available. This is not, however, inconsistent with Nolan's thesis, since the principal could still base a claim on the unjust enrichment principle by means of alternative analysis if a relevant ground of restitution could be identified.

(b) The No-Profit Duty

The no-profit duty prohibits fiduciaries from obtaining an advantage by virtue of their position as fiduciary, either for themselves or for a third party, save where the principal has given fully informed consent to the fiduciary obtaining the advantage following full and frank disclosure by the fiduciary,[64] or the profit is otherwise authorized. So, for example, fiduciaries are prohibited from making a profit by using an opportunity or knowledge which they are able to use because of their position as a fiduciary. It is no defence that the fiduciary would have made the profit even if he or she had acted properly,[65] nor that the fiduciary had acted honestly and in the principal's best interests, nor that the principal actually benefited, nor that the principal could not have obtained the benefit for him or herself. The rationale behind this strict interpretation of the no-profit rule is that the fiduciary is precluded from using his or her position to advantage anybody's interests other than those of the principal, this being a vital component of the fundamental obligation of loyalty. It does not follow that the fiduciary is prevented from obtaining any benefit at all whilst he or she acted as a fiduciary.[66] Many fiduciaries are professionals who are legitimately paid for their work, including professional trustees. The real concern is to ensure that fiduciaries do not make an unauthorized or secret profit from their position.

Both the no-conflict and the no-profit duties are interpreted very strictly, so that fiduciaries are liable even though they were acting honestly and to the best of their ability, without fraud or bad faith.[67] It follows that the highest standards of behaviour are expected from fiduciaries to avoid the imposition of liability. Various reasons have been suggested to justify such high standards including the need to control the exercise of discretionary powers;[68] to ensure that the fiduciary resists the temptation to serve him or

---

[63] Nolan, 'Conflicts of Interest, Unjust Enrichment and Wrongdoing', 93.

[64] *Gwembe Valley Development Co Ltd v Koshy (No 3)* [2003] EWCA Civ 6048, [2004] 1 BCLC 131; *Murad v Al-Saraj* [2005] EWCA Civ 959, [2005] WTLR 1573.

[65] *Murad v Al-Saraj* [2005] EWCA Civ 959, [2005] WTLR 1573.

[66] C Harpum, 'Fiduciary Obligations and Fiduciary Powers—Where Are We Going?' in PBH Birks (eds), *Privacy and Loyalty* (Oxford: Clarendon Press, 1997), 154.

[67] *Regal (Hastings) Ltd v Gulliver* [1967] AC 134n, 386 (Lord Russell).

[68] E Weinrib, 'The Fiduciary Obligation' (1975) 24 UTLJ 1, 9; I Samet, 'Guarding the Fiduciary's Conscience: A Justification of a Stringent Profit-Stripping Rule' (2008) OJLS 763.

herself rather than the principal;[69] to deter other fiduciaries from failing to comply with high standards of behaviour;[70] or to ensure the proper performance of non-fiduciary duties,[71] such as failing to comply with the reasonable standard of skill and care. It follows that fiduciary duties are prophylactic, which means that they exist to prevent a particular state of affairs from occurring. That state of affairs is that the fiduciary acts in such a way as to be disloyal to the principal and Equity seeks to prevent such disloyalty by imposing the most severe duty of loyalty.[72] This might be criticized as being too strict, especially when the fiduciary's actions benefit the principal, but it must not be forgotten that these duties are not absolute. Fiduciaries can immunize themselves against liability for breach of fiduciary duty by seeking the fully informed consent of the principal in advance of taking the action, or even by seeking the approval of the court. If such consent is not forthcoming, the fiduciary should not take the action.

A number of specific rules can be identified which are derived from the no-conflict and the no-profit duties.

(c) The Self-Dealing Rule

The self-dealing rule provides that a fiduciary is barred from dealing on behalf of him or herself and the principal in the same transaction.[73] So, for example, trustees cannot sell trust property to themselves;[74] neither can trustees sell their own property to the trust.[75] Breach of this rule renders the transaction voidable,[76] so that the principal can rescind it without needing to prove that the transaction is unfair.[77] Once the transaction has been rescinded, the fiduciary is liable to account to the principal for any profits that were made from the transaction. The self-dealing rule can be excluded by the relevant instrument that governs the fiduciary relationship,[78] and the transaction will not be voidable where the fiduciary had obtained the fully informed consent of the principal to the transaction.[79] The reason why self-dealing transactions are voidable is because where, for example, a trustee is seeking to sell his or her own property to the trust, there is a real danger of conflict between the fiduciary's personal interest in getting the highest price and his or her duty to the beneficiary of the trust to obtain the lowest price. This risk exists regardless of the fairness of the transaction.

(d) The Fair-Dealing Rule

The fair-dealing rule will be breached where a fiduciary enters into a transaction in a personal capacity with the principal. This will render the contract voidable, save where the fiduciary can show that he or she took no advantage of the fiduciary position, made full disclosure to the principal of all material facts, the transaction was fair[80] and there had been full disclosure of everything which might be material to the principal's decision to

---

[69] Worthington, 'Fiduciaries: When is Self-Denial Obligatory?', 506. See also R Flannigan, 'The Adulteration of Fiduciary Doctrine in Corporate Law' (2006) 122 LQR 449.

[70] *Murad v Al-Saraj* [2005] EWCA Civ 959, [2005] WTLR 1573, [74] (Arden LJ).

[71] Conaglen, 'The Nature and Function of Fiduciary Loyalty', 453.

[72] G Jones, 'Unjust Enrichment and the Fiduciary's Duty of Loyalty' (1968) 84 LQR 472, 474.

[73] *Tito v Waddell (No 2)* [1977] Ch 106, 241 (Sir Robert Megarry V-C).

[74] *Ex p Lacey* (1802) 6 Ves 625, 626 (Lord Eldon LC); *ex p James* (1803) 8 Ves 337, 345 (Lord Eldon LC).

[75] *Armstrong v Jackson* [1917] 2 KB 822, 824 (McCardie J).

[76] *Holder v Holder* [1968] 1 Ch 353, 398.

[77] *Tito v Waddell (No 2)* [1977] Ch 106, 241 (Sir Robert Megarry V-C).

[78] *Sargeant v National Westminster Bank plc* (1990) 61 P & CR 518.

[79] *Ex p James* (1803) 8 Ves 337, 353 (Lord Eldon LC).

[80] *Moody v Cox and Hatt* [1917] 2 Ch 71; *Tito v Waddell (No 2)* [1977] Ch 106, 241 (Megarry V-C).

enter into the transaction.[81] So, for example, if a trustee purchases a beneficiary's interest in trust property, the contract can be set aside by the beneficiary unless the trustee can establish the fairness of the transaction and that he or she had not taken advantage of the principal.[82] The rationale behind the rule is that any contract between the principal and fiduciary is suspect because of the conflict between the fiduciary's personal interest and his or her duty to the principal.

(e) Acting for More Than One Principal

A fiduciary may also be liable for breaching the no-conflict duty even though there is no conflict between the fiduciary's personal interest and duty, but instead, where the fiduciary acts for more than one principal, there is a conflict between the duty owed to both principals.[83] A fiduciary is not prevented from acting for more than one principal, and professional fiduciaries such as solicitors and agents will often do so. Where, however, the interests of the two principals come into conflict, any transaction entered into by the fiduciary on behalf of one or both of the principals will be voidable and the fiduciary will be liable to account for any profit made as a result, save where the principals have given their fully informed consent to the fiduciary acting for the other. This consent may be express or it may be implied where the principal was aware that the fiduciary was acting for another principal. So, for example, where the fiduciary is a solicitor who was acting for both the mortgagor and the mortgagee, and both of the clients knew that the solicitor was acting for the other party, there will be no breach of the no-conflict rule.[84]

The rationale behind this rule is that the conflict of duty and duty means that the fiduciary is unable to provide undivided loyalty to each principal. It is no defence that making full disclosure to one principal will involve breach of the duty owed to the other,[85] since the fiduciary should not put him or herself in a position where the duties conflict.[86] Liability for a conflict of duties owed to different principals can be avoided by an express or implied term in the contract of appointment which allows the fiduciary to act for other principals.[87]

(f) Interference with the Principal's Property

Probably the clearest case where gain-based remedies are available for breach of a fiduciary duty is where the fiduciary appropriates the principal's property or obtains a benefit from its use without permission to do so.[88] This is illustrated by *Brown v IRC*[89] where the defendant solicitor received clients' money which he deposited in a bank account. The defendant then used the interest on this account for his own purposes. This constituted a breach of the no-profit duty because the defendant had used income

---

[81] *Demerara Bauxite Co Ltd v Hubbard* [1923] AC 673.

[82] *Thomson v Eastwood* (1877) 2 App Cas 215, 236 (Lord Cairns LC). Conaglen has argued that fairness should simply be an evidential factor taken into account by the court in determining whether the principal gave his or her fully informed consent to the transaction: M Conaglen, 'A Re-appraisal of the Fiduciary Self-dealing and Fair-dealing Rules' (2006) CLJ 366, 368.

[83] *Clarke Boyce v Mouat* [1994] 1 AC 428; *Marks and Spencer plc v Freshfields Bruckhaus Deringer (a firm)* [2004] EWHC 1337 (Ch), [2004] 1 WLR 2331. Conaglen considers this to be a fiduciary principle that is distinct from where there is a conflict between personal interest and duty, but which has the same prophylactic objectives: 'Fiduciary Regulation of Conflicts Between Duties' (2009) LQR 111, 119.

[84] *Bristol and West Building Society v Mothew* [1998] Ch 1, 19 (Millett LJ).

[85] *Moody v Cox and Hatt* [1917] 2 Ch 71.

[86] *Hilton v Barker, Booth and Eastwood* [2005] UKHL 8, [2005] 1 WLR 567, [44] (Lord Walker).

[87] *Kelly v Cooper* [1993] AC 205.   [88] For directors see Companies Act 2006, s 175 (2).

[89] [1965] AC 244.

which belonged to the clients for himself and without their authority. Although information has sometimes been characterized as property that can be misappropriated,[90] the better view is that information lacks the key hallmarks of property and so cannot be misappropriated,[91] and so the fiduciary will consequently not be liable to account for profit obtained from the exploitation of such information.

A particularly good example of profiting from appropriation of property is *Keech v Sandford*,[92] which concerned a lease of the profits of Romford market in Essex. The lessee had devised his estate, including the lease, to a trustee to be held on trust for an infant. Before the lease was due to expire, the trustee applied to the lessor for its renewal for the benefit of the infant. The lessor refused because, being a lease of profits only, the remedy for recovery of rent could be enforced only under the covenant to pay, but this would not have bound the infant. The lessor was, however, willing to renew the lease for the trustee personally. The trustee took the renewed lease of the profits from the market and the infant then sought the lease to be assigned to him. He succeeded in doing so and also recovered the profits obtained by the trustee before the lease was assigned. Although the case is poorly reported, it is clear that the trustee's liability was founded on his breach of duty since he obtained the opportunity to profit from the renewal of the lease in his capacity as trustee. King LC recognized that he should have let the lease expire rather than obtain it himself. In fact this is better analysed as a case in which the trustee appropriated trust property because the practice at the time was that the opportunity to renew a tenancy was recognized as a legal right, so that the trustee had acquired a trust asset by seizing for his own benefit an opportunity that was effectively owned by the trust.[93]

(g) Exploitation of Opportunities

Where fiduciaries have obtained a benefit by exploiting an opportunity which arose from their position as fiduciary, this also constitutes the breach of a fiduciary duty because they profited from their position as fiduciary.[94] It has been suggested that, where the opportunity which has been exploited is a 'maturing business opportunity', in the sense of it being an opportunity which the principal was seeking to exploit, the exploitation by the fiduciary of the opportunity is like the appropriation of property from the claimant.[95] It is, however, doubtful whether such an opportunity can really be characterized as proprietary, since it lacks many of the characteristics of property. Further, liability can arise even if the principal was not actively pursuing the opportunity.

Typically, where a fiduciary has obtained a profit through the exploitation of an opportunity it will have been available by virtue of the fiduciary's position. Controversially, liability for exploitation of an opportunity has also been imposed even where the opportunity came to the fiduciary in a different capacity. In *Bhullar v Bhullar*[96] a director of a company was held liable to the company for the profits he obtained from the acquisition of property which was located next to that of the company, even though the director discovered the property as a passer-by rather than as director. The director's

---

[90] *Quarter Master UK Ltd v Pyke* [2005] 1 BCLC 245, [71] (Paul Morgan QC).

[91] *Boardman v Phipps* [1967] 2 AC 45.

[92] (1726) Sel Cas 61, 25 ER 223. See A Hicks, 'The Remedial Principle of *Keech v Sandford* Reconsidered' (2010) CLJ 287; J Getzler, 'Rumford Market and the Genesis of Fiduciary Obligations' in AS Burrows and Lord Rodger (eds), *Mapping the Law* (Oxford: Oxford University Press, 2006), ch 31.

[93] *Sinclair Investments (UK) Ltd v Versailles Trade Finance Ltd* [2011] EWCA Civ 347, [2012] 1 AC 776, [58] (Lord Neuberger MR).

[94] *Regal (Hastings) Ltd v Gulliver* [1967] 2 AC 134n. For directors, see Companies Act 2006, s 175(2).

[95] *CMS Dolphin Ltd v Simonet* [2001] 2 BCLC 704, [96] (Lawrence Collins J).

[96] [2003] EWCA Civ 424, [2003] 2 BCLC 241.

liability was founded on his failure to inform the company of the opportunity and his subsequent exploitation of it. The liability is, however, better justified as involving breach of the no-conflict duty on the ground that, since the property was physically proximate to that of the company, it would have been in the company's best interests to purchase the property. Since the director was interested in purchasing the property for himself, it followed that his own interest conflicted with that of the company, so that there was a breach of fiduciary duty at the point at which he discovered the opportunity, regardless of the fact that he had profited from purchasing the property. If the case is analysed in this way, it follows that the crucial feature of the no-profit rule remains valid, namely that the opportunity that was exploited was available to the fiduciary only by virtue of his or her fiduciary position.

The application of this exploitation of opportunity principle is more complicated where the defendant has exploited an opportunity after having resigned from his or her fiduciary position. The courts adopt a pragmatic and flexible approach to liability in such circumstances that is based on common sense and the merits of the case.[97] It is clear that if the defendant resigns in order to exploit the opportunity he or she will be liable for breach of fiduciary duty;[98] there must be a connection between the resignation and the exploitation of the opportunity.[99] Where, however, the fiduciary resigns for legitimate reasons, for example because of dissatisfaction with the principal, and subsequently obtains the opportunity to compete with the principal, which he or she exploits, there will be no breach of fiduciary duty, because there is no evidence of any disloyalty.[100] Similarly, where the fiduciary relationship has broken down, but the fiduciary has not resigned, the fiduciary will be able to exploit any opportunity and engage in competing business because he or she is no longer in a fiduciary relationship.[101]

The defendant will be liable to disgorge to the claimant any profits obtained by exploitation of the opportunity in breach of duty, regardless of the fact that the defendant acted reasonably and in good faith. It is also irrelevant that the principal would not have been able to exploit the opportunity him or herself.[102] The strictness of this rule is based on public policy.[103] This is particularly well illustrated by the decision of the House of Lords in *Boardman v Phipps*.[104] One of the defendants, a solicitor to a trust, realized that a company in which the trust held a minority of the shares was badly managed. Since the trust did not have sufficient capital to take over the company and reconstruct it, as two of the three trustees had confirmed (the third being senile and lacking capacity to agree[105]), the solicitor used his own money to buy shares himself. One of the beneficiaries of the trust also contributed his own money to buy shares. Through the exercise of his own skill, but also by means of information which he had obtained in his capacity as a fiduciary, the solicitor turned the company into a highly profitable organization. It was held by a majority that both the solicitor and the beneficiary had breached their fiduciary duty to

---

[97] *Foster Bryant Surveying Ltd v Bryant* [2007] EWCA Civ 200, [2007] 2 BCLC 239.

[98] *Industrial Development Consultants Ltd v Cooley* [1972] 1 WLR 443; *Canadian Aero Services Ltd v O'Malley* (1973) 40 DLR (4th) 371; *CMS Dolphin Ltd v Simonet* [2001] 2 BCLC 704.

[99] *CMS Dolphin Ltd v Simonet* [2001] 2 BCLC 704, [91].

[100] *Island Export Finance Ltd v Umunna* [1986] BCLC 460; *Ultraframe (UK) Ltd v Fielding* [2005] EWHC 1638 (Ch), [2006] FSR 16.

[101] *In Plus Group Ltd v Pyke* [2002] EWCA Civ 370, [2002] 2 BCLC 201.

[102] *Keech v Sandford* (1726) Sel Cas t King 61, 25 ER 223; *Regal (Hastings) Ltd v Gulliver* [1967] 2 AC 134n.

[103] *Quarter Master UK Ltd v Pyke* [2005] 1 BCLC 245.

[104] [1967] 2 AC 46. See also *Cook v Deeks* [1916] 1 AC 554; *Regal (Hastings) Ltd v Gulliver* [1967] 2 AC 134n; *Crown Dilmun v Sutton* [2004] EWHC 52, [2004] 1 BCLC 468.

[105] She died before the shares were purchased by the defendants.

the trust, the former as solicitor and the latter because he had been acting as though he was a trustee. They had breached their fiduciary duty because their personal interests conflicted with their duty to the trust and they had profited from their position as fiduciaries by exploiting information that they had obtained whilst acting as fiduciaries, without gaining the fully informed consent of the trustees for their plans. Consequently they were held liable to account to the trust for the profits they had made, this profit being held on constructive trust, although the solicitor was awarded an allowance which was assessed by reference to the value of his services to the trust.

Boardman v Phipps is a difficult case to justify. It was accepted by the majority that the defendants had not interfered with the claimant's property, since the information which they had obtained in their capacity as fiduciaries could not be treated as trust property.[106] Neither were the defendants acting in bad faith, as was reflected by the fact that the solicitor was awarded an allowance for the work which he had done.[107] Consequently, the imposition of a liability to disgorge their profits can only be justified by the policy of deterring fiduciaries from making a profit from their position as fiduciaries. It is important to remember that a fiduciary will not have breached the no-conflict and no-profit duties if they have obtained the fully informed consent of their principal. In *Boardman v Phipps* it appears that the relevant consent was that of the beneficiaries of the trust to whom the fiduciaries owed their duties. The consent of the beneficiaries was not considered to be fully informed.[108] The strictness of the result in *Boardman v Phipps* was further mitigated by the fact that the solicitor was awarded an equitable allowance to reflect the value of his services in managing the company to make it profitable.[109]

But, despite this, was there really anything wrong with what the defendants did? There was nothing to suggest that they had abused their relationship of trust and confidence. They had acted honestly and reasonably and took the risk with their own money that they would be able to improve the company's fortunes, but were still liable to account to the trust for the profit that they had obtained and even thought the trust had not been in a position to buy more shares, because this was not authorized by the investment clause in the will and there was no trust money available to buy shares, so there was no possibility of the fiduciaries competing with the trust. The imposition of liability hardly seems fair. Whether the decision should be considered to be correct depends on the message we think we should be giving to fiduciaries. If we wish to make it clear that fiduciaries should be expected to give their full attention to the person to whom they owe their duties, and that they should never place themselves in a position where they might be tempted to act disloyally, the decision in *Boardman v Phipps* must be correct. Alternatively, where there is no hint of fraud in the conduct of the defendant, surely it is much more realistic and just to commend the defendant for what he or she had done, rather than to hold the defendant liable to make restitution to the claimant. This was the view of the minority in the case, who held that the defendants should not be liable to account for the profits they had made because they had been acting in good faith and because the beneficiaries had made it clear that they were not interested in a scheme to obtain the majority of the company's shares.

The strict interpretation of liability for exploiting an opportunity in breach of fiduciary duty was, however, affirmed by the Court of Appeal in *Murad v Al-Saraj*,[110] for two reasons.[111] First, in the interests of efficiency, because the principal might not be able to monitor easily the fiduciary's actions on a daily basis. Secondly, to provide an incentive to

---

[106] See also *Crown Dilmun v Sutton* [2004] EWHC 52, [2004] 1 BCLC 468, [202] (Peter Smith J).
[107] See further p 507, below.   [108] *Boardman v Phipps* [1967] 2 AC 46, 104 (Lord Cohen).
[109] See p 507, below.   [110] [2005] EWCA Civ 959, [2005] WTLR 1573.
[111] Ibid, [74] (Arden LJ).

all fiduciaries to resist temptation to conduct themselves improperly; the policy of deterrence underlies the strictness of this form of liability. In *Murad* the defendant was held liable for breach of the no-profit duty when he had profited from participation in a joint venture by failing to disclose that his contribution to the purchase of a hotel was made by offsetting unenforceable obligations that were owed to him by the vendor, including commission for his introduction of the claimants to the vendor. Arden LJ acknowledged[112] that the application of the no-profit rule was strict, so that the defendant was liable for breach of fiduciary duty even though, if he had made full disclosure of the nature of his financial contribution, the claimants would still have proceeded with the joint venture, although they would have demanded a greater share of the profit. The Court acknowledged that the time may have come to revisit the inflexibility of these fiduciary duties, especially where the fiduciary has acted in good faith and the principal would not have wanted to exploit the opportunity him or herself,[113] however such a review could now only be undertaken by the Supreme Court.

This flexible approach to the finding of liability has been recognized by the Supreme Court of Canada[114] and by the Privy Council[115] where, in the context of directors exploiting corporate opportunities which had been declined by their companies and where there had been full and frank disclosure of their desire to take the opportunity, directors were not held liable to account for their profits. There is no reason why such a flexible rule should not be recognized in English law. Indeed, it has been recognized that a profit can be retained where the consent of the principal has been obtained following full and frank disclosure of all relevant matters.[116] Where this has occurred and the principal has declined the opportunity there is no legitimate reason why the fiduciary should be prevented from retaining the profit made from the exploitation of the opportunity. It follows that the restrictions imposed on fiduciaries by virtue of the no-profit duty, and the no-conflict duty as well,[117] can be mitigated if fiduciaries obtain prior authorization for what they wish to do. This is consistent with the fundamental obligation of loyalty, since loyal fiduciaries will reveal their intentions about the exploitation of opportunities to the principal.

(h) Receipt of a Bribe or Secret Commission

Where a fiduciary has received a bribe or secret commission to induce him or her to act against the interests of the principal, this is one of the clearest cases where the fiduciary should be considered to have broken his or her fiduciary duty, by contravening both the no-conflict and the no-profit duties. Gain-based relief in such cases is justified simply on the ground that fiduciaries should be deterred from accepting bribes which will influence them to act against the best interests of their principal. One of the best ways of deterring such conduct is by depriving the defendant of the bribe which he or she received. This is illustrated by *Reading v Attorney-General*[118] where the defendant was a sergeant in the British army serving in Egypt. He was bribed to sit on lorries whilst wearing military uniform so that alcohol could be illegally transported without being stopped by the police.

---

[112] Ibid, [82]. See also Jonathan Parker LJ [121] and Clarke LJ [158].

[113] Ibid, [82] (Arden LJ), [121] (Jonathan Parker LJ).

[114] *Peso-Silver Mines Ltd v Cropper* (1966) 58 DLR (2d) 1.

[115] *Queensland Mines Ltd v Hudson* [1978] 52 ALJR 379 (PC).

[116] *Ultraframe (UK) Ltd v Fielding* [2005] EWHC 1638 (Ch), [2006] FSR 16, [1318] (Lewison J). See M Conaglen, 'The Extent of Fiduciary Accounting and the Importance of Authorisation Mechanisms' (2011) CLJ 548.

[117] As recognized in *Bray v Ford* [1896] AC 44, 51 (Lord Herschell).

[118] [1951] AC 507. See also *Attorney-General v Goddard* (1929) 98 LJKB 743; *Petrotrade Inc v Smith* [2000] 1 Lloyd's Rep 486.

The defendant was convicted of a crime. Most of the bribes which he had received were seized by the Crown and he sought to recover them. His action failed because he had been acting in breach of his fiduciary duty and so he would have been liable to account for the bribes to the Crown.[119]

This liability has been extended to include the receipt of a secret commission. In *Daraydan Holdings Ltd v Solland International Ltd*[120] the defendant agent received a secret commission of 10 per cent of the contract price in return for him exerting his influence to obtain contracts between a third party and his principal. This secret commission was held to be a secret profit which could be recovered by the principal. It was held to be irrelevant whether the agent had solicited the secret commission or had been offered it by the third party.[121]

Where a principal is induced to enter into a contract with a third party as a result of the fiduciary being bribed by the third party, the contract is voidable.[122] In such circumstances the contract could be rescinded at Common Law for fraud,[123] or in Equity by virtue of breach of the no-conflict duty,[124] there being an irrebuttable presumption that the agent was influenced by the bribe.[125] Where the principal rescinds the transaction tainted by a bribe, he or she does not have to give credit for the amount of the bribe as part of the obligation to make restitution of benefits received under the contract, even where the principal has already recovered the bribe from the fiduciary.[126]

(2) The Relationship of Confidentiality

The fiduciary relationship of confidentiality will arise where information is imparted by the principal to a fiduciary in confidence.[127] Although such a relationship of confidentiality may arise when one person is employed by another, the relationship does not depend on employment. Consequently, this fiduciary relationship will continue even where the employee is no longer employed by the employer. This was recognized by the Court of Appeal in *Attorney-General v Blake*[128] where the Court of Appeal, relying on an earlier decision of the House of Lords,[129] recognized that members of the Secret Intelligence Service, such as Blake, owe a life-long duty of confidence to the Crown. This means that if the fiduciary breaks the confidence he or she will be considered to have breached a fiduciary duty.

The essential obligation arising from the relationship of confidentiality is that the fiduciary must maintain the confidentiality of the information which he or she possesses. But this obligation only lasts as long as the information itself remains confidential. This was recognized by the Court of Appeal in *Blake*. Since the information which Blake had published in his autobiography was no longer confidential, it followed that he had not breached his fiduciary duty of confidence by disclosing this information.

Liability for abusing a fiduciary relationship of confidentiality is different from liability for the action for breach of confidence,[130] as was recognized by the Court of Appeal in

---

[119] The controversial question of the nature of the remedy which should be awarded where the fiduciary has received a bribe is examined at p 510, below.

[120] [2004] EWHC 622 (Ch), [2005] Ch 119.   [121] Ibid, [60].

[122] *Logicrose Ltd v Southend United Football Club Ltd* [1988] 1 WLR 1256.

[123] *Mahesan v Malaysia Government Officers' Co-operative Housing Society Ltd* [1979] AC 374, 383; *Petrotrade Inc v Smith* [2000] 1 Lloyd's Rep 486, 490. See p 23, above.

[124] *Logicrose Ltd v Southend United Football Club Ltd* [1988] 1 WLR 1256.

[125] *Hovenden and Sons v Millhof* (1900) 83 LT 41, 43.

[126] *Logicrose Ltd v Southend United Football Club Ltd* [1988] 1 WLR 1256.

[127] *Attorney-General v Blake* [1998] Ch 439, 454 (Lord Woolf MR).   [128] Ibid.

[129] *Attorney-General v Guardian Newspapers Ltd (No 3)* [1990] 1 AC 109.   [130] See p 514, below.

Blake.[131] The crucial distinction between these two forms of liability is that the former depends on there being a relationship between the parties which can be characterized as fiduciary in nature, whereas the action for breach of confidence simply depends on the defendant having confidential information in circumstances where there was a duty to protect the confidentiality. Also, whereas liability for abusing a fiduciary relationship of confidence is strict,[132] liability in the action for breach of confidence depends on the defendant being at fault in some way.[133]

(3) The Relationship of Influence

Another type of fiduciary relationship is that of influence.[134] This will arise where the nature of the relationship between the parties is such that one party is so dependent on the other that the other party is in a position to exploit the former, who is peculiarly vulnerable to the exploitation. Any relationship can potentially be characterized as one of influence.[135] Relationships which might particularly be characterized in this way include the relationship of solicitor and client,[136] trustee and beneficiary, and agent and principal.

The crucial characteristic of a relationship of influence is that the principal is utterly dependent on the defendant. This is illustrated by *Tate v Williamson*[137] where the deceased, who was in financial difficulties having 'contracted habits of extravagance at University',[138] sought the advice and assistance of his great-uncle, who deputed his nephew, the defendant, to help the deceased. The deceased offered to sell his reversionary interest to the defendant, who agreed to buy it for £7,000. Before the agreement for purchase was signed the defendant received notification that the interest was valued at £20,000, but he did not disclose this information to the deceased. It was held that the relationship between the parties was such that the defendant was under a duty to communicate to the deceased all the information he had which related to the value of the property. The defendant's failure to inform the deceased of the valuation meant that the transaction was set aside. The relationship between the parties was characterized as fiduciary, because the defendant had placed himself in such a position of influence by undertaking to arrange the deceased's debts, that he was under fiduciary duties which prevented him from purchasing the deceased's property without making full disclosure. In a very important dictum Lord Chelmsford LC identified the essential features of this fiduciary relationship:

> Wherever two persons stand in such a [fiduciary] relation that, while it continues, confidence is necessarily reposed by one, and the influence which necessarily grows out of that confidence is possessed by the other, and this confidence is abused, or the influence is exerted to obtain an advantage at the expense of the confiding party, the person so availing himself of his position will not be permitted to retain the advantage, although the transaction could not have been impeached if no such confidential relation had existed.[139]

Where the principal enters into a transaction either with the fiduciary or a third party in circumstances where the fiduciary might have influenced the principal to enter into the

---

[131] [1998] Ch 439, 453.

[132] See, for example, *Warman International Ltd v Dwyer* (1995) 128 ALR 201. [133] See p 516, below.

[134] This has sometimes been described as a relationship of confidence, but such a description fails to distinguish this relationship from the other two types of fiduciary relationship.

[135] *BCCI v Aboody* [1990] QB 923, 964. [136] See *Wright v Carter* [1903] 1 Ch 27.

[137] (1866) LR 2 Ch App 55.

[138] The deceased died, at the age of 24, from his addiction to drink.

[139] *Tate v Williamson* (1866) LR 2 Ch App 55, 61.

transaction, it is presumed that the fiduciary exploited the principal, and so the burden is on the party who wishes to enforce the transaction to show that it was fair.[140] This is illustrated by *Demerara Bauxite Co Ltd v Hubbard*[141] where a solicitor purchased property from his former client, in circumstances where the antecedent relationship of influence between the parties continued. Lord Parmoor identified the crucial feature of this type of fiduciary relationship as follows:

> in the absence of competent independent advice a transaction...between persons in the relationship of solicitor and client, or in a confidential relationship of a similar character, cannot be upheld, unless the person claiming to enforce the contract can prove, affirmatively, that the person standing in such a confidential position has disclosed, without reservation, all the information in his possession, and can further show that the transaction was, in itself, a fair one, having regard to all the circumstances.[142]

The transaction will only be treated as valid, therefore, where there has been full disclosure of everything which is or may be material to the principal's decision to enter into the transaction and where the other party can show that the transaction itself was fair, particularly that the transaction was not at an undervalue.[143] Since the determination of whether the transaction was fair requires consideration of all the circumstances of the case, it follows that the question of fairness depends on whether the transaction was substantively fair, namely that the terms were fair, and procedurally fair, namely that the means which were used to induce the principal to enter into the transaction were fair. Consequently, whether the principal was advised to obtain independent and competent advice will be a particularly important consideration in determining whether the transaction was fair.

There is an obvious similarity between liability for undue influence[144] and liability for abusing a fiduciary relationship of influence, since in both cases the defendant's liability is founded on the actual or potential exploitation of the claimant. The boundary between the two forms of liability is uncertain,[145] particularly because where there is a relationship of influence there will also be the potential for undue influence. It has, however, been recognized that whilst the two forms of liability overlap, they do not coincide.[146] The crucial distinction between the two forms of liability is that a fiduciary relationship of influence will only be recognized where the principal is utterly dependent on the fiduciary.

It follows from the fact that, although liability for breach of a fiduciary relationship of influence is more restrictive than liability for undue influence, where the relevant fiduciary relationship can be identified the claimant who seeks restitution has two possible restitutionary claims. First, the claimant could bring a claim founded on the reversal of the defendant's unjust enrichment, with the ground of restitution being undue influence.[147] Alternatively, the claimant could bring a claim against the fiduciary founded on the breach of fiduciary duty. Although the claimant has a choice as to which restitutionary route to adopt, a claim founded on abuse of a relationship of influence does have certain advantages over the doctrine of undue influence, namely that it is neither necessary to show that the principal was actually influenced by the defendant or that the transaction requires explanation before the presumption of influence is established. Once the relationship of

---

[140] *Moody v Cox and Hatt* [1917] 2 Ch 71.   [141] [1923] AC 673.   [142] Ibid, 681.

[143] *Wright v Carter* [1903] 1 Ch 27.   [144] See Chapter 11.

[145] *CICB Mortgages plc v Pitt* [1994] 1 AC 200, 209 (Lord Browne-Wilkinson).

[146] See *Moody v Cox and Hatt* [1917] 2 Ch 71, 79 (Lord Cozens-Hardy MR) and *BCCI v Aboody* [1990] QB 923, 962.   [147] See p 257, above.

influence has been identified, it is assumed that the transaction requires explanation and the burden is on the defendant to show that the transaction was not unfair to the claimant. The heavy burden of proving that the transaction is fair is shifted where there is a relationship of influence simply because of the potential for abuse of such relationships by the fiduciary.[148]

(iv) Gain-Based Remedies Which Are Available for Breaches of Fiduciary Duty

Although it is now possible to award compensatory remedies for breach of fiduciary duty,[149] the usual remedy is still gain-based.

(1) Rescission

Where a transaction has been entered into as a result of a breach of fiduciary duty, it will be voidable and can be rescinded by the principal, regardless of whether the transaction is made with the fiduciary or a third party.[150] Rescission will be barred, however, (i) if it is not possible to return the parties to their original position; (ii) if property has been transferred under the transaction to a *bona fide* purchaser for value; (iii) if the principal has affirmed the transaction; or (iv) if too much time has elapsed before the principal has sought to rescind it. Where the fiduciary breaches the conflict of duty and duty rules by acting for more than one principal, it is possible for a transaction entered into as a result to be rescinded, although this may be available only if the principal with whom the transaction was made was aware of the inconsistent duties.[151]

(2) Account of Profits

The typical remedy for breach of fiduciary duty is to require the defendant to account to the claimant for all the profits obtained from the breach.[152] The remedy is most definitely gain-based rather than compensatory because it does not depend on whether the principal could have made the profit.[153] When taking the account it is not necessary to show that the profits were a 'but for' cause of the breach. Rather, it is sufficient that the profits fall within the scope of the fiduciary's duty of loyalty to the principal.[154] This is justified because the special position of the fiduciary means that the breach of fiduciary duty is not the fact that the fiduciary had made a profit, but that the fiduciary seeks to keep this profit for him or herself.[155] For policy reasons the courts refuse to speculate about what would have happened had the breach of duty not occurred,[156] so it is irrelevant that the profit would have been made even had there been no breach of duty. Further, this strict approach to causation in the context of breach of fiduciary duty is justified by the very high standards of loyalty we expect of fiduciaries and from a desire to deter disloyal behaviour.[157] It is appropriate, however, to deduct expenses incurred by the defendant

---

[148] *BCCI v Aboody* [1990] QB 923, 963 and *CICB Mortgages plc v Pitt* [1994] 1 AC 200, 209 (Lord Browne-Wilkinson). See p 277, above.   [149] *Swindle v Harrison* [1997] 4 All ER 705.

[150] See Chapter 1 for analysis of rescission generally.

[151] *Transvaal Land Co v New Belgium (Transvaal) Land and Development Co* [1914] 2 Ch 488.

[152] *Nocton v Lord Ashburton* [1914] AC 932, 956–7 (Viscount Haldane VC); *Murad v Al-Saraj* [2005] EWCA Civ 959, [2005] WTLR 1573, [56] (Arden LJ).

[153] *Murad v Al-Saraj* [2005] EWCA Civ 959, [2005] WTLR 1573, [59] (Arden LJ).

[154] *Novoship (UK) Ltd v Mikhaylyuk* [2014] EWCA Civ 908, [2015] 2 WLR 526, [96].

[155] Cf where a non-fiduciary is liable as an accessory for assisting a breach of trust, where the liability to account for profits is dependent on the profits being caused by the assistance. See p 521, below.

[156] *Murad v Al-Saraj* [2005] EWCA Civ 959, [2005] WTLR 1573, [76] (Arden LJ).

[157] See T Etherton, 'The Legitimacy of Proprietary Relief' (2014) 2 Birkbeck LR 59, 74.

in making the profit, as well as a sum to represent reasonable overheads.[158] The burden is placed on the defendant to show that a particular profit did not derive from the breach of duty.[159] This shift in the burden of proof is presumably justified by the stringent policy that fiduciaries should not profit in any way from their breach of duty. Consequently, it is presumed that all profits were derived from the breach, and it is for the defendant to show that this was not the case. If the defendant is unable to distinguish the profits made from the breach with the profits made legitimately from other sources, he or she will be liable to disgorge all the profits, because of the policy, reflected in the law of tracing as well,[160] that everything is presumed against a fiduciary in breach of duty.[161]

This strict approach to causation is particularly well illustrated by *Murad v Al-Saraj*[162] where a majority of the Court of Appeal recognized that the fiduciary, who had failed to disclose a material fact to his principals in breach of fiduciary duty, was liable to account for the whole profit he made as a result of the principals entering into a joint venture with him, even though some profit might still have been made had the fiduciary made the relevant disclosure. The fiduciary would only not have been liable to account for other profits which had arisen from a different transaction. The claimants and the defendant had entered into a joint venture to buy a hotel. The defendant fraudulently told the claimants that the purchase price was £4.1 million, when it was actually £3.6 million, and that he would contribute £500,000 in cash. This contribution took the form, in part, of a secret commission for introducing the claimants to the vendor, and a set off of certain non-enforceable obligations. The trial judge found that, had the actual purchase price and the set off been disclosed to the claimants, they would still have agreed to the joint venture but with a higher profit share for themselves. The majority held that this was irrelevant and the defendant was liable to disgorge all the profits, both revenue and capital, which he had made from the joint venture following the sale of the hotel, even though some profit would still have been made had the defendant not breached his fiduciary duty.[163] The majority appears to have assumed that, since but for causation is relevant to establishing loss for the purposes of equitable compensation[164] and because loss is not relevant to the account of profits, it must follow that but for causation is not relevant either. But this conclusion does not follow. Nevertheless, the conclusion is consistent with the earlier decision of the Court of Appeal in *United Pan-Europe Communications NV v Deutsche Bank AG*[165] where Morritt LJ[166] said: 'I see no justification for any further requirement that the profit shall have been obtained by the fiduciary 'by virtue of his position'. Such a condition suggests an element of causation which neither principle not the authorities require.' But this is inconsistent with the decision of the House of Lords in *Regal v Gulliver* where this 'further requirement' was recognized.[167] To confuse matters further this requirement was even recognized by Jonathan Parker LJ in *Murad v Al-Saraj*[168] itself.

Clarke LJ dissented from the majority's approach on the basis that the question of whether the defendant would have made the profit even had there not been a breach of fiduciary duty is relevant to the extent of the account of profits, although he accepted that

[158] *Murad v Al-Saraj* [2005] EWCA Civ 959, [2005] WTLR 1573, [107] (Jonathan Parker LJ).
[159] Ibid, [77] (Arden LJ).   [160] See p 619, below.
[161] *Warman International Ltd v Dwyer* (1995) 182 CLR 544.
[162] [2005] EWCA Civ 959, [2005] WTLR 1573.   [163] Ibid, [62] (Arden LJ).
[164] See *Swindle v Harrison* [1997] 4 All ER 705.   [165] [2000] 2 BCLC 461.   [166] Ibid, [47].
[167] As it was in *Warman International Ltd v Dwyer* (1995) 182 CLR 544, 559.
[168] [2005] EWCA Civ 959, [2005] WTLR 1573, [116] (Jonathan Parker LJ).

it was not relevant to whether there was any liability to account at all.[169] Clarke LJ preferred to treat the assessment of the profits as being dependent on what was an equitable result. But that way confusion and uncertainty lies.

The decision of the majority in *Murad v Al-Saraj* creates significant difficulties when determining the extent of the account of profits. It is clear that the fiduciary who has breached his or her duty need not account for all profits made from whatever source;[170] some link to the breach of duty must be established. For it would be absurd to say, for example, that a defendant who has breached his or her fiduciary duty and who at the same time won a large sum in a lottery would have to account for that lottery win. So, if causation is relevant and, as the Court of Appeal in *Murad v Al-Saraj* recognized, the profit must arise 'within the scope and ambit of the relevant fiduciary duty',[171] what profit derived from the breach of fiduciary duty? Surely, if the defendant would have made a profit anyway had there not been a breach of duty, the only profit which was caused by the breach must be the difference between the profit which was made and what would otherwise have been made. Consequently, there is no justification for the rejection of the but for test of causation when accounting for profits following a breach of fiduciary duty. It should be shown that, but for the breach,[172] the profit would not have been made. This does not involve the watering down of the policy of deterring breaches of fiduciary duty. It is simply a matter of ensuring that the profit which must be disgorged derives from the breach of duty.

The principle of remoteness of benefits, whereby the defendant is only liable to account for profits which derive directly from the commission of the wrong,[173] is interpreted differently where the defendant has profited from a breach of fiduciary duty, so that the fiduciary is also liable to account for profits which arise indirectly from the commission of the wrong. So, for example, in *Gwembe Valley Development Co Ltd v Koshy (No 3)*,[174] the defendant fiduciary was held liable to account for all the profits he had made from unauthorized loan transactions. The account included those profits which derived directly from the commission of the wrong, in the form of payments made to him, and also indirect benefits arising from the increase in the value of his shareholding in the company. It follows from this, for example, that if a fiduciary has received a bribe, he or she should be liable to account for the value of the bribe and any income obtained from its investment.[175] This relaxation of the rules on remoteness is presumably justified by the policy to deter breaches of fiduciary duty by ensuring that the fiduciary is deprived of all benefits which derive from the commission of the wrong. It was recognized by the Court of Appeal in *Sinclair Investments (UK) Ltd v Versailles Trade Finance Ltd*[176] that the effect of the defendant being required to account for benefits indirectly obtained from the commission of the wrong meant that, if the defendant had received a bribe in breach of fiduciary duty and had invested the bribe in land which had increased in value, the defendant would be liable to account to the principal for the value of that land.[177]

---

[169] Ibid, [141].   [170] Ibid, [62] (Arden LJ).   [171] Ibid, [116] (Jonathan Parker LJ).

[172] The language of but for causation was used by Clarke LJ in his dissenting judgment in *Murad v Al-Saraj*, ibid, [160].

[173] See p 435, above.   [174] [2003] EWCA Civ 1048, [2004] 1 BCLC 131.

[175] *Murad v Al-Saraj* [2005] EWCA Civ 959, [2005] WTLR 1537, [85] (Arden LJ).

[176] [2011] EWCA Civ 347, [2012] 1 AC 776.

[177] Ibid, [90] (Lord Neuberger MR). Today all the profit, whether obtained directly or indirectly, could be held on constructive trust. See p 512, below.

A problem with ordering that an account of profits be taken is that there is a danger that requiring the defendant to give up all profits made from the breach of duty might unfairly benefit the claimant.[178] Two mechanisms are available to limit the account.

(1) *Limiting the period for which the account must be taken.* Where the nature of the breach of fiduciary duty is that the defendant earns a profit over a period of time, and might still be earning the profit at the time of the trial, a difficult question arises as to whether the defendant is required to account for all of the profits which have been made and also those which may be made in the future. This was a matter which was examined in *Warman International Ltd v Dwyer*[179] where the High Court of Australia recognized that, where it is equitable to do so, the defendant may only be required to account for the profits generated over a specified period of time. In that case the account was limited to two years of profits to reflect the policy that the defendant should only account for the profits 'made within the scope and ambit of his duty'.[180]

(2) *The equitable allowance.* The defendant may be awarded an equitable allowance in respect of those profits that were earned by virtue of the defendant's own efforts and this sum will be deducted from the amount for which the defendant has to account to the claimant.[181] The assessment of the allowance is not necessarily limited to the value of the fiduciary's work, but can also include part of the profit made from the venture if it is considered to be just to award this.[182] The award of the allowance is not automatic and will be awarded only where it is equitable to do so. The decision to award the allowance, and the amount awarded, depends on the operation of judicial discretion, which will be influenced by a variety of factors, including the good faith of the defendant.[183] So where there is an abuse of the fiduciary relationship by the fiduciary, the allowance might be reduced[184] or not awarded at all.

Although the award of the equitable allowance to a fiduciary who has breached his or her fiduciary duty was recognized by the House of Lords in *Boardman v Phipps*,[185] a subsequent decision of the same court, *Guinness plc v Saunders*,[186] casts doubt on the legitimacy of the award of an allowance to the fiduciary in such circumstances. In *Guinness plc v Saunders*, £5.2 million had been paid to a director of Guinness for the advice and services that he had given in respect of the takeover of another company by Guinness. It was accepted that this money had been received by the director in breach of his fiduciary duty and consequently he was liable to repay it to Guinness. But the director argued that he was entitled to an equitable allowance for the services that he had supplied to the company. The House of Lords rejected this claim on two grounds. First, because Equity had no power to grant an allowance to a director who had breached his or her

---

[178] See *Fyffes Group Ltd v Templeman* [2000] 2 Lloyd's Rep 643, 672 (Toulson J). See further p 426, above.

[179] [1994] 182 CLR 546. See also *Murad v Al-Saraj* [2005] EWCA Civ 959, [2005] WTLR 1573, [115] (Jonathan Parker LJ).

[180] *Warman International Ltd v Dwyer* [1994] 182 CLR 546, 559.

[181] *Boardman v Phipps* [1967] 2 AC 46; *Warman International Ltd v Dwyer* (1995) 182 CLR 544, [33].

[182] *O'Sullivan and Management Agency and Music Ltd* [1985] QB 428, 468 (Fox LJ).

[183] *Boardman v Phipps* [1967] 2 AC 46; *Guinness v Saunders* [1990] 2 AC 663; *Warman International Ltd v Dwyer* (1995) 182 CLR 544.

[184] *O'Sullivan and Management Agency and Music Ltd* [1985] QB 428, 468 (Fox LJ); *Nottingham University v Fishel* [2000] ILRL 471, 485 (Elias J).

[185] [1967] 2 AC 46.   [186] [1990] 2 AC 663.

fiduciary duty if the company's articles made no provision for such a payment.[187] The reason for this is that the court is reluctant to interfere with the affairs of the company, and so the decision to award an allowance should be a matter for the company and not for the court. Secondly, because of the fundamental principle that trustees are not entitled to be remunerated for their services except where such remuneration is provided for in the trust deed, it was considered to follow that a fiduciary should not be awarded an equitable allowance save in the most exceptional circumstances under which the award of the allowance would not encourage the fiduciary to put him or herself in a position in which his or her personal interest conflicted with the duty that was owed to the principal.[188] Since the nature of the director's breach of duty was to place him in a position in which his personal interest conflicted with his duty to the company, it followed that the equitable allowance was denied to him.

But neither of these reasons is convincing. First, why should the allowance be unavailable where the fiduciary is a director? If the defendant has incurred expense and provided services, particularly where the expense and services have benefited the claimant company, why should this not be taken into account when determining the extent of the defendant's liability to the claimant? Secondly, the award of the equitable allowance should not be considered to be encouraging the fiduciary to place him or herself in a position in which personal interest and duty to the principal conflict. This is because the equitable allowance should not enable the fiduciary to profit from his or her breach of duty; rather it should simply ensure that the fiduciary is remunerated for expense incurred and services provided. There can surely be no objection to a fiduciary being remunerated, since this would not encourage the fiduciary to breach his or her fiduciary duty. It has, in fact, been recognized that there is nothing wrong with the court granting an allowance to remunerate a fiduciary for services provided to the principal.[189] The real objection arises where the fiduciary is allowed to profit from the breach of duty.[190] Despite this, *Guinness v Saunders* was followed in *Quarter Master UK Ltd v Pyke*[191] where an equitable allowance was not awarded to two directors who had exploited a business opportunity for themselves, on the ground that directors should not profit from their breach of fiduciary duty and that the directors concerned had not demonstrated special skills or taken unusual risks.

The major difficulty with the award of an equitable allowance arises from the uncertainty as to the reason for awarding the allowance. Two justifications can be identified.[192] First, the award of an equitable allowance might constitute a mechanism to ensure that the claimant is not unjustly enriched at the fiduciary's expense. This unjust enrichment would otherwise arise because, if the effect of the defendant's work is that the claimant obtains a benefit, the claimant will have been enriched at the defendant's expense. The ground of restitution would be total failure of basis, in that the defendant would have expected to be remunerated for his or her services by retaining the profit, but the defendant would receive nothing if he or she were liable to disgorge all of the profit to the claimant. Although this unjust enrichment explanation of the equitable allowance can be used to justify why the

---

[187] Ibid, 692 (Lord Templeman).   [188] Ibid, 701 (Lord Goff).

[189] *Dale v IRC* [1954] AC 11, 27 (Lord Normand).

[190] But note *O'Sullivan v Management Agency and Music Ltd* [1985] QB 428, in which the Court of Appeal contemplated that the allowance might include a profit element, but only where it is considered to be just to include this.   [191] [2004] EWHC 1815 (Ch); [2005] 1 BCLC 245.

[192] See M Harding, 'Justifying Fiduciary Allowances' in A Robertson and HW Tang (eds), *The Goals of Private Law* (Oxford: Hart Publishing, 2009), ch 14, who prefers to justify the allowance on the basis of desert, in that the fiduciary's deserving conduct outweighs the application of policies of deterrence to the fiduciary.

allowance was awarded in certain cases in which the principal was benefited by what the fiduciary had done,[193] this explanation has never been recognized by the courts and, crucially, the nature of the allowance that is awarded does not appear to be assessed by reference to the value of the benefit obtained by the principal. Rather, the allowance seeks only to remunerate the fiduciary for his or her work and skill.[194] Also this explanation of the equitable allowance would be inapplicable in any case in which the principal had not obtained a benefit from the fiduciary simply because the principal would not have been enriched at the fiduciary's expense.

The alternative, and preferable, explanation of the equitable allowance is that, where the defendant has made a profit as a result of the exercise of his or her time and skill, it is not possible to say that all of the defendant's profits derived from the commission of the wrong. Since the defendant should be required to disgorge only those profits that did arise from the wrongdoing, it follows that the equitable allowance seeks to apportion profits so that the claimant recovers only those profits that derive from the breach of trust or fiduciary duty, and the defendant is allowed to retain those profits that can be considered to derive from his or her work and skill. It will, of course, be very difficult to apportion the profits exactly, but at least the existence of the allowance gives the court the opportunity to determine in general terms how much of the profits derived from the defendant's contribution. This explanation of the award of the allowance was expressly recognized by the High Court of Australia in *Warman International Ltd v Dwyer*, which noted that the allowance was available:[195]

> when it appears that a significant proportion of an increase in profits has been generated by the skill, efforts, property and resources of the fiduciary, the capital which he has introduced and the risks he has taken, so long as they are not risks to which the principal's property has been exposed. Then it may be said that the relevant proportion of the increased profits is not the product or consequence of the plaintiff's property but the product of the fiduciary's skill, efforts, property and resources.

If the equitable allowance seeks to apportion the profits between those profits that derive from the breach and those deriving from the defendant's personal contribution, it should have followed that the director in *Guinness plc v Saunders* was awarded an allowance, because he had provided valuable services for the remuneration that he had received. But the denial of the allowance in that case might be justified on another ground, although it was a ground that was not specifically recognized by the court. Although the House of Lords assumed throughout that the director had been acting in good faith, there was clearly a suspicion of bad faith, since criminal charges had been brought as a result of the acquisition of the company by Guinness and an application had been made to extradite the director to the United States. If the House of Lords had been satisfied on the balance of probabilities that the director had been acting in bad faith, it would have been appropriate, in the exercise of the equitable jurisdiction, to decline to award an equitable allowance.

(3) Proprietary Remedies Following the Recognition of a Constructive Trust

The most controversial question relating to the award of gain-based remedies for breach of fiduciary duty is whether profits made from the breach of duty should be held on

---

[193] Most notably *Boardman v Phipps* [1967] 2 AC 46. But if the equitable allowance does seek to ensure that the claimant is not unjustly enriched, it should also have been awarded in *Guinness plc v Saunders* [1990] 2 AC 663, in which the company had also been benefited by the defendant's services.

[194] See *Boardman v Phipps* [1967] 2 AC 46, 102 (Lord Cohen) and 112 (Lord Hodson).

[195] *Warman International Ltd v Dwyer* (1995) 128 ALR 201, 212.

constructive trust for the principal, so that the principal will have an equitable proprietary interest in the profits which he or she can vindicate by virtue of proprietary restitutionary remedies.[196] This gives the principal priority over the fiduciary's unsecured creditors if the fiduciary became insolvent. The principal is entitled not just to the value of the profits obtained by the fiduciary but also the fruits of those profits. Further, the principal can assert proprietary rights against innocent third parties who have received the profits or its traceable substitute.

Where the fiduciary has profited by interfering with the principal's proprietary rights, it is clear that the fiduciary will hold this property on constructive trust for the principal.[197] This includes where the fiduciary has obtained a bribe or a secret commission and it can be shown that this was derived from money paid by the principal to the fiduciary.[198] The recognition of a constructive trust in such circumstances is defensible because the profits made by the defendant can be considered to represent the fruits of the claimant's property. Consequently, it is entirely appropriate that the claimant should have an equitable proprietary interest in the profits. In addition, it is justifiable that the fiduciary should hold property on constructive trust where the consequence of the breach of duty is that the fiduciary obtains property which the principal would have obtained had the defendant not breached his or her duty. Goode has described the property which the defendant obtains in such circumstances as a 'deemed agency gain',[199] which should be held on constructive trust for the principal simply because the demands of the fiduciary relationship are such that it should be assumed that the defendant obtained the property for his or her principal rather than for him or herself. This is illustrated by *Cook v Deeks*[200] where the directors of the claimant company were negotiating a contract with a third party on behalf of the company. Rather than signing the contract on behalf of the company, some of the directors signed it on behalf of themselves. It was held that the directors were liable for a breach of fiduciary duty and held the profits they had made on constructive trust for the company. This can be justified because, had the defendants not breached their duty, the company would have obtained the contract, so the defendants' gain could be presumed to have been made on behalf of the company.[201]

The most controversial issue arises where the fiduciary has obtained a benefit from a third party rather than depriving the claimant of property or the opportunity to make a profit. This has proved to be particularly controversial where the fiduciary has received a bribe or a secret commission from a third party. In such circumstances the profit cannot be considered to have derived from the principal. Consequently, the orthodox view was that only the personal remedy of an account of profits was available, and not a proprietary constructive trust. The leading case was *Lister and Co v Stubbs*[202] where it was held that the defendant, a foreman who bought supplies for the claimant and who had accepted

---

[196] See Chapter 22.

[197] See *Primlake Ltd v Matthews Associates* [2006] EWHC 1227 (Ch), [2007] 1 BCLC 666, [334] (Lawrence Collins J).

[198] *Daraydan Holdings Ltd v Solland International Ltd* [2004] EWHC 622 (Ch), [2005] Ch 119.

[199] See RM Goode, 'Property and Unjust Enrichment' in AS Burrows (ed), *Essays on the Law of Restitution* (Oxford: Clarendon Press, 1991), 230.

[200] [1916] 1 AC 554. See also *Keech v Sandford* (1726) Sel Cas t King 61, 25 ER 223, p 497, above.

[201] In *CMS Dolphin Ltd v Simonet* [2001] 2 BCLC 704, [96], Lawrence Collins J characterized the exploitation of a maturing business opportunity as appropriation of property belonging to the principal, with the result that the defendant fiduciary would hold the profits of the exploitation on constructive trust for the principal. It is unprincipled however, to treat a maturing business opportunity as the principal's property.

[202] (1890) 45 Ch D 1. See also *Metropolitan Bank v Heiron* (1880) LR 5 Ex D 319.

secret commissions from one of the suppliers in return for placing orders with that supplier, was liable to account to the claimant for the value of the commission. The defendant had invested some of the money in land, but it was held that the claimant did not have an equitable proprietary interest in the land. It followed that the relationship between the parties was not one of trustee and beneficiary but was simply one of debtor and creditor.

However, in *Attorney-General for Hong Kong v Reid*[203] the Privy Council recognized that a defendant fiduciary who had received a bribe held that bribe on constructive trust for the principal. The defendant fiduciary in this case held a number of public offices in Hong Kong, including that of Director of Public Prosecutions. He had accepted bribes to induce him to frustrate the prosecution of some criminals. He purchased land with this money and the claimant claimed that the land was held on constructive trust for it. The Privy Council agreed and specifically rejected *Lister and Co v Stubbs* for the following reason. Where a defendant receives a bribe in breach of fiduciary duty it is clear that the defendant is liable to account to the principal for the value of the bribe immediately it is received, simply because it is the receipt of the bribe which constitutes the breach of duty. There is consequently a personal liability to account to the principal. However, by virtue of the equitable maxim that Equity looks on as done what ought to be done, Equity presumes that the fiduciary has accounted for the value of the bribe when it is received. It follows, therefore, that Equity considers the principal to have an equitable proprietary interest in the bribe immediately it is received, with the result that the defendant holds the bribe on constructive trust for the principal.

The Privy Council in *Reid* considered that it was appropriate to recognize that the principal had an equitable proprietary interest in the bribe as a matter of policy, even though this would mean that the unsecured creditors of the fiduciary would be deprived of their right to share in the money if the fiduciary were to become insolvent, because it was considered that the unsecured creditors could not be in a better position than their debtor. Also, it would not be appropriate for the fiduciary to retain any increase in the value of the bribe because of the principle that wrongdoers should not profit from their wrong. So, on the facts of *Reid*, although it was clear that the defendant was liable to account for the value of the bribe received, it was also inappropriate for him to retain the increase in the value of the land.

Reid was, however, a decision of the Privy Council which conflicted with earlier decision of the House of Lords[204] and decisions of the Court of Appeal.[205] Despite this, *Reid* was followed in some cases[206] and can be considered to be consistent with earlier decisions, notably *Boardman v Phipps*,[207] where the shares which were purchased in breach of fiduciary duty were held on constructive trust even though there had been no interference with the claimant's property rights. The decision in *Reid* was, however, rejected by the Court of Appeal in *Sinclair Investments (UK) Ltd v Versailles Trade Finance Ltd*.[208] In that case the claimant had advanced money to a company to be used to purchase goods. The money was used fraudulently for other purposes. The defendant had sold shares in the company that he already owned for a profit. These shares had not

---

[203] [1994] 1 AC 324.   [204] *Tyrrell v Bank of London* (1862) 10 HL Cas 26.

[205] Including *Metropolitan Bank v Heiron* (1880) 5 Ex D 319 and *Lister and Co v Stubbs* (1890) LR 45 Ch D 1.

[206] *Ocular Sciences Ltd v Aspect Vision Care Ltd* [1997] RPC 289, 412–13 (Laddie J); *Fyffes Group Ltd v Templeman* [2002] 2 Lloyd's Rep 643; *Daraydan Holdings Ltd v Solland International Ltd* [2004] EWHC 622 (Ch), [2005] Ch 119.

[207] [1967] 2 AC 46. See p 498, above.   [208] [2011] EWCA Civ 347, [2012] 1 AC 776.

been acquired with money in which the claimant had a proprietary interest, but the profit that he had obtained on their sale was attributable to his dishonest conduct in creating the appearance of trading which had not taken place, which had inflated the apparent turnover and profits of the company, so increasing its market value. It was held that the defendant had breached his fiduciary duty but he was only personally liable to account for the profits, which were not held on constructive trust for the claimant.

Although the profit in this case was not a bribe or a secret commission, the Court of Appeal considered that it should be analysed in the same way, because the profit made by the director was an unauthorized secret profit that had resulted from his breach of fiduciary duty.[209] The Court of Appeal held that the fact that a breach of fiduciary duty enabled the defendant to make a profit was not sufficient to give the claimant a proprietary interest in that profit. The rationale behind the recognition of the constructive trust in *Reid* was considered and was rejected as a matter of authority, as a matter of principle, and as a matter of policy. The key principle was that profits should only be held on constructive trust where they derived directly or indirectly from the principal's property or from the exploitation of an opportunity which had been available to the principal,[210] since the defendant will then have profited from interference with the principal's property rights, although this is difficult to justify where the defendant has only exploited an opportunity which should have been procured for the principal. The key policy was that the claims of the unsecured creditors of the fiduciary should not be defeated by recognizing that the fiduciary's property was held on constructive trust for the principal.

The decision of the Court of Appeal in *Sinclair Investments* was, however, overruled by the Supreme Court in *FHR European Ventures LLP v Cedar Capital Partners LLC*.[211] It was held that, wherever a fiduciary is liable to account for profits made as a result of a breach of fiduciary duty, those profits will be held on constructive trust for the principal, even though they did not derive from interference with the principal's property or from the exploitation of an opportunity which should have been exploited for the principal. Consequently, wherever a fiduciary receives a bribe or secret commission in breach of fiduciary duty, that bribe or secret commission will be held on constructive trust. The decision in *Lister v Stubbs* was also overruled. The constructive trust recognized by the Supreme Court is an institutional constructive trust which arises by operation of law and is justified because the fiduciary is treated as though he or she had acquired the bribe or secret commission on behalf of the principal, who therefore has an equitable proprietary interest in it. This assumption that the bribe has been acquired for the principal has been defended by virtue of the need to ensure fiduciary fidelity.[212]

The decision of the Supreme Court in *FHR European Ventures* does at least resolve a long-standing controversy as to the role of the constructive trust where the fiduciary has profited from breach of their fiduciary duty. The Supreme Court cut through authorities to the contrary and rejected the principles and policies identified by the Court of Appeal in *Sinclair*.[213] The real difficulty with *FHR European Ventures* relates to the Supreme Court's

---

[209] The decision was applied to a case involving bribes and secret commissions in *Cadogan Petroleum plc v Tolley* [2011] EWHC 2286 (Ch).

[210] *Sinclair Investments (UK) Ltd v Versailles Trade Finance Ltd* [2011] EWCA Civ 347, [2012] 1 AC 776, [88] (Lord Neuberger MR).   [211] [2014] UKSC 45, [2015] AC 250.

[212] P Millett, 'Bribes and Secret Commissions Again' (2012) CLJ 583. See also LD Smith, 'Constructive Trusts and the No-Profit Rule' (2013) CLJ 260.

[213] The judgment of the court being delivered by Neuberger LJ, who, as Lord Neuberger, delivered the unanimous judgment in the Supreme Court in *FHR European Ventures*. See WMC Gummow, 'Bribes and Constructive Trusts' (2015) 131 LQR 21.

emphasis that the constructive trust was institutional, arising by operation of law, rather than remedial,[214] which enables the operation of the trust to be modified through the exercise of judicial discretion.[215] Whether an institutional constructive trust is appropriate in this context depends on whether the three proprietary advantages of the constructive trust[216] can necessarily be justified where the fiduciary has profited from breach of duty. If any of these advantages cannot be justified it would be appropriate to modify the institutional constructive trust through the operation of judicial discretion, such that the trust operates as a remedial constructive trust.

First, where the defendant has profited from the investment of the profit made in breach of fiduciary duty, he or she should not benefit from this indirect profit, so that the institutional constructive trust should not be modified to exclude such profits, because of the strict nature of fiduciary duties. So, for example, it was not appropriate for the defendant in *Attorney-General for Hong Kong v Reid*[217] to have benefited from the investment of the bribes in land.

The second advantage of the constructive trust is that the principal has priority over the fiduciary's unsecured creditors if the fiduciary became insolvent. Lord Millett[218] has argued that such an advantage is justifiable, because the fiduciary's creditors claim through the fiduciary and should have no claim to property to which they are not entitled. In *Grimaldi v Chameleon Mining NZ (No 2)*[219] Justice Finn, in recognizing that normally a bribe should be held on constructive trust, added that, if the fiduciary was bankrupt, a lien should suffice to ensure practical justice. This was *obiter* and would not protect the interests of the unsecured creditors since even where there is a lien the principal would have priority,[220] but would only be unable to claim the fruits of the profits made from the breach of duty. But even though the approach of the English courts in recognizing an institutional constructive trust appears to militate against flexibility in the operation of the constructive trust, in a very significant dictum in *FHR European Ventures*[221] the Supreme Court recognized that concern about the position of unsecured creditors of the defendant fiduciary has considerable force in some contexts, although it has limited force in the context of bribes and secret commissions. The Court did not elaborate beyond this and it is unclear why the position of unsecured creditors might matter more in some contexts, although it is unclear which, and why not where the profit took the form of bribes or secret commissions. But, acknowledging that the position of the unsecured creditors of the fiduciary might need to be considered in some cases, is highly significant. It might suggest a willingness of the English court to recognize the constructive trust in principle, but then its effect might be modified to ensure that, whilst the fiduciary does not benefit from the profit, the relative positions of the principal and unsecured creditors are treated equally. In fact, this modification of the constructive trust is more justifiable in cases where the fiduciary's profit is derived from a third party than from the principal. For where the profit is taken from the principal, so that the principal has suffered a loss which needs to be reversed, the principle of corrective justice might justify the principal's claim ranking

---

[214] The Supreme Court specifically rejected the recognition of the remedial constructive trust. See further p 595, below.

[215] As is the case in Australia: *Grimaldi v Chameleon Mining NZ (No 2)* [2012] FCAFC 6, [569]–[584] (Finn J). See L Ho, 'Bribes and the Constructive Trust as a Chameleon' (2012) 128 LQR 486.

[216] See p 510, above.   [217] [1994] 1 AC 324.

[218] Millett, 'Bribes and Secret Commissions Again'.   [219] [2012] FCAFC 6, [583].

[220] See p 635, below.

[221] *FHR European Ventures LLP v Cedar Capital Partners LLC* [2014] UKSC 45, [2015] AC 250, [43].

above that of the fiduciary's unsecured creditors. Where, however, the gain is made from a third party, without the principal suffering a loss, the principal of corrective justice is not necessarily engaged, since there is no loss to reverse.[222] Rather, the relevant principle is that of distributive justice,[223] whereby the gain made by the fiduciary needs to be distributed from the fiduciary to the principal, but the principal should not be considered to have a stronger claim than that of the fiduciary's unsecured creditors. Consequently, usually[224] where the fiduciary has received a bribe or a secret commission, this should be held on constructive trust for the principal, but this should be modified to ensure that the principal's claim to the profits ranks equally with that of the fiduciary's unsecured creditors.

The third advantage of the institutional constructive trust is that the principal is able to assert a proprietary restitutionary claim against a third-party recipient of the property which was held on trust.[225] This result is much more difficult to justify where the third-party recipient is innocent of any wrongdoing,[226] for why should the claim of the principal, to profits which have not been taken from the principal, prevail over that of an innocent volunteer? In such circumstances it would be appropriate to modify the institutional constructive trust so that the principal and third-party volunteer share the property equally. Where, however, the third party's receipt can be considered to be unconscionable, because they knew or suspected that the fiduciary had obtained the profit in breach of fiduciary duty, it is appropriate to enable the principal to assert their equitable proprietary rights against the third party, whose conscience has been tainted. So, for example, in *Attorney-General for Hong Kong v Reid* assets were transferred to the fiduciary's wife and his solicitor who appear to have been aware that they had been purchased with bribe money. In such circumstances it is appropriate that the proprietary claim of the principal should prevail over such recipients whose consciences have been tainted by their knowledge of the breach of duty. However, as English law stands, the principal has a proprietary claim against the third-party recipient who has received and retained the property or its substitute which was held on constructive trust, regardless of the recipient's ignorance of the breach of fiduciary duty. This is an unfortunate consequence of the recognition of the institutional constructive trust, which could be avoided if there was greater willingness to modify the proprietary impact of such a trust.

(B) BREACH OF CONFIDENCE

Where the defendant breaches an obligation of confidence by disclosing confidential information, the claimant can bring an action for breach of confidence, the remedy for which may be gain-based. Holding the defendant liable for breaking a confidence is justified as a means of maintaining the integrity of relationships of confidence.[227] This was recognized by Lord Keith of Kinkel in *Attorney-General v Guardian Newspapers Ltd (No 3)*:[228]

> [As] a general rule, it is in the public interest that confidence should be respected, and the encouragement of such respect may in itself constitute a sufficient ground for recognising

---

[222] See p 5, above.

[223] K Barnett, 'Distributive Justice and Proprietary Remedies over Bribes' (2015) LS 302. See also M Harding, 'Constructive Trusts and Distributive Justice' in E Bant and M Bryan (eds), *Principles of Proprietary Remedies* (Sydney: Thomson Reuters, 2013), ch 2.

[224] Where the secret commission has been obtained from the principal the corrective justice principle will be engaged. See p 510, above.   [225] See p 632, below.

[226] Where the third-party recipient has provided value and has acted in good faith the principal's proprietary claim will be defeated. See Chapter 23.

[227] See Jackman, 'Restitution for Wrongs', 315.   [228] [1990] 1 AC 109, 256.

and enforcing the obligation of confidence even where the confider can point to no specific detriment to himself.

A distinction needs to be drawn between liability for breaching the fiduciary duty of confidence[229] and the action for breach of confidence. Whilst many defendants who owe an equitable duty of confidence will also owe fiduciary duties, such that breach of their duty of confidence might trigger liability for breach of fiduciary duty, fiduciary duties and duties of confidence do not necessarily exist at the same time.[230] Further, receipt of confidential information does not necessarily create a fiduciary relationship.[231] If a fiduciary breaches the duty of confidence his or her liability for breach of fiduciary duty will be strict.[232] Where, however, the defendant owes a duty of confidence but is not a fiduciary, liability will be founded on the action for breach of confidence and the defendant must be shown to be at fault in some way.[233]

(i) The Doctrinal Basis of Breach of Confidence

A duty of confidence may be imposed expressly or impliedly by contract.[234] So, for example, where the defendant is an employee or agent of the claimant, he or she may be under a contractual duty not to use confidential information obtained from the claimant without the claimant's consent. In such cases liability for breach of confidence will be founded on an action for breach of contract.[235]

As regards the equitable action of breach of confidence, there have been many different views expressed as to its doctrinal basis, with it variously being considered to be founded on vindicating property rights or being *sui generis*. Recently it has been explicitly recognized as a tort.[236] This emphasizes that the action is grounded on wrongdoing, but the use of tortious language must not hide its equitable nature. The action is founded on the obligation of conscience[237] and responds to wrongdoing in the form of unconscionable conduct. The essence of the action was correctly identified by Deane J in *Moorgate Tobacco Co Ltd v Philip Morris Ltd (No 2)*:[238] 'its rational basis does not lie in proprietary right. It lies in the notion of an obligation of conscience arising from the circumstances in or through which the information was communicated or obtained.'

(ii) The Identification of the Duty of Confidence

The essence of the claim for breach of confidence[239] was identified by Megarry J in *Coco v A N Clark (Engineers) Ltd*:[240]

First, the information itself...must 'have the necessary quality of confidence about it'. Secondly, that information must have been communicated in circumstances importing an

---

[229] See p 501, above.   [230] *Bolkiah v KPMG* [1999] 2 AC 222, 235 (Lord Millett).

[231] *Indata Equipment Supplies Ltd v ACL Ltd* [1998] FSR 248, 262.

[232] See, for example, *Warman International Ltd v Dwyer* (1995) 128 ALR 201.

[233] *Vestergaard Frandsen A/S v Bestnet Europe Ltd* [2013] UKSC 31, [2013] 1 WLR 1556, [24] (Lord Neuberger). See further p 516, below.

[234] *Faccenda Chicken v Fowler* [1987] Ch 117.

[235] *Vercoe v Rutland Fund Managers Ltd* [2010] EWHC 424 (Ch), [329] (Sales J).

[236] *Walsh v Shanahan* [2013] EWCA Civ 411, [55] (Rimer LJ).

[237] *Stephens v Avery* [1988] Ch 449, 455 (Sir Nicolas Browne-Wilkinson V-C).

[238] (1984) 156 CLR 414, 438. See also *Vestergaard Frandsen A/S v Bestnet Europe Ltd* [2013] UKSC 31, [2013] 1 WLR 1556, [22] (Lord Neuberger).

[239] See T Aplin, L Bentley, P Johnson, and S Malynicz (eds), *Gurry on Breach of Confidence: The Protection of Confidential Information* (2nd edn, Oxford: Oxford University Press, 2012).

[240] [1969] FSR 415, 419. See also *Attorney-General v Guardian Newspapers Ltd (No 2)* [1990] 1 AC 109, 268 (Lord Griffiths); *Campbell v MGN Ltd* [2004] UKHL 22, [2004] 2 AC 457, [13] (Lord Nicholls); *OBG Ltd v Allan* [2007] UKHL 21, [2008] 1 AC 1, [111] (Lord Hoffmann).

obligation of confidence. Thirdly, there must have been an unauthorised use of the information to the detriment of the party communicating it.[241]

Subsequent developments mean that there is no need for a prior relationship of confidence to be violated.[242] The duty of confidence will arise automatically if it is plain that the information is confidential because it is personal and private,[243] but in such circumstances the defendant must know or ought to have known that the information was confidential. This was recognized by Arnold J in *Primary Group (UK) Ltd v Royal Bank of Scotland plc*[244] where he described the 'equitable obligation of confidence' as arising:

> not only where confidential information is disclosed in breach of an obligation of confidence (which may itself be contractual or equitable) and the recipient knows, or has notice, that that is the case, but also where confidential information is acquired or received without having been disclosed in breach of confidence and the acquirer or recipient knows, or has notice, that the information is confidential.

The latter situation arises either where the information has been acquired improperly or where it has been received adventitiously. Aspects of Arnold J's analysis are controversial, especially whether the acquisition of information without breach of an obligation of confidence involves an equitable claim or what might be characterized as a distinct tort of misuse of private information where there is an expectation of privacy.[245] This relates to the emergence of what might be characterized as a new tort of privacy, influenced by the European Convention on Human Rights, which has resulted in the action eschewing the language of equitable confidence and relationship-centred notions of loyalty, trust and good faith.[246] But if a distinct tort of privacy has emerged, gain-based remedies are still available for the tortious wrongdoing,[247] and there still remains a distinct equitable claim grounded on breach of confidence.

(iii) Gain-Based Remedies for Breach of Confidence

Gain-based remedies for breach of confidence typically take two forms, namely an account of profits and negotiation damages, which are preferably characterized as having compensatory and restitutionary components.[248] But, whilst gain-based remedies are common for this type of action, they are not the only remedies which are available. Sometimes compensatory damages may be awarded,[249] as may an injunction to stop a confidential relationship from being abused or damages in lieu of the grant of an injunction.[250]

(1) Account of Profits

Where the defendant has made a profit from the breach of confidence he or she may be liable to account for this profit to the claimant. Such a remedy is more likely to be available

---

[241] In *Primary Group (UK) Ltd v Royal Bank of Scotland plc* [2014] EWHC Ch 1082, Arnold J, [208], also recognized that the unauthorized use must be without lawful excuse.

[242] *Attorney-General v Guardian Newspapers Ltd (No 2)* [1990] 1 AC 109, 281 (Lord Goff); *A v B plc* [2003] QB 195, 207 (Lord Woolf CJ).

[243] *Douglas v Hello! Ltd (No 3)* [2005] EWCA Civ 595, [2006] QB 125, [83].

[244] [2014] EWHC Ch 1082, [223]. Cf *Vestergaard Frandsen A/S v Bestnet Europe Ltd* [2013] UKSC 31, [2013] 1 WLR 1556, [25], where Lord Neuberger assumed that the mental state to trigger the duty of confidence is subjective, suggesting that constructive notice will not suffice. The approach of Arnold J is to be preferred as being consistent with equitable notions of unconscionability which encompasses objective fault.

[245] C Hunt, 'Rethinking Surreptitious Takings in the Law of Confidence' (2012) IPQ 66.

[246] Ibid, 73.   [247] See p 464, above.   [248] See p 431, above.

[249] *Dowson and Mason Ltd v Potter* [1986] 2 All ER 418.

[250] *Attorney-General v Guardian Newspapers Ltd (No 2)* [1990] AC 109, 286 (Lord Goff).

where the defendant has knowingly breached the confidence. This is illustrated by *Peter Pan Manufacturing Corporation v Corsets Silhouette Ltd*,[251] where the defendant had manufactured and sold bras knowingly using confidential information which it had obtained from the claimant. The defendant was held liable to account to the claimant for the profits which it had made as a result of breaking the confidence.

Where the defendant is liable for breach of fiduciary duty it is not necessary to show that but for the breach of duty the defendant would not have made a profit.[252] Since the action for breach of confidence does not depend on maintaining the highest standards of loyalty, the but for test of causation should be adopted.

(2) Negotiation Damages

An alternative remedy, where the defendant has inadvertently breached the duty of confidence, is for the claimant to be awarded damages assessed by reference to a notional reasonable price to buy the defendant's release from the obligation of confidence,[253] known as 'negotiation damages'.[254] Whilst this method for assessing damages is preferably treated as hybrid, embodying both compensatory and restitutionary elements,[255] in the context of breach of confidence the remedy is typically characterized as compensatory.[256] The award of this remedy is illustrated by *Seager v Copydex Ltd*[257] where the defendant inadvertently used confidential information in manufacturing a carpet-grip. The basis for assessing the damages was held to depend on the nature of the information which was confidential.[258] If the information which the defendant had used was of a type which could be provided by any competent consultant, it was held that damages should be assessed by reference to the fee which the defendant saved by not employing such a consultant. Such damages can easily be characterized as gain-based since they are assessed by reference to the defendant's benefit, namely what he or she had saved in not paying a consultant. Alternatively, if the information can be characterized as special in that it could not have been obtained by employing a consultant, the damages should be assessed by reference to the market price for the information. To determine the market price it is necessary to consider what a willing purchaser would have paid a willing seller for the information.[259] This too could be characterized as having a gain-based component, since the defendant will have benefited from not having to pay the market value for the information.

(3) Choice of Remedy

The claimant cannot elect between the negotiation measure of damages or an account of profits as a matter of right,[260] in contrast to a claim for breach of fiduciary duty for which the principal does have a right to claim an account of profits. Rather, the choice of the

---

[251] [1964] 1 WLR 96.   [252] See p 504, above.

[253] *Vercoe v Rutland Fund Management Ltd* [2010] EWHC 424 (Ch), [292] (Sales J).

[254] *Primary Group (UK) Ltd v Royal Bank of Scotland plc* [2014] EWHC Ch 1082. See also *Force India Formula One Team Ltd v 1 Malaysia Racing Team Sdn Bhd* [2012] EWHC 616 (Ch), [383] (Arnold J). See generally p 429, above.   [255] See p 431, above.

[256] See *Force India Formula One Team Ltd v 1 Malaysia Racing Team Sdn Bhd* [2012] EWHC 616 (Ch), [381] (Arnold J); *CF Partners (UK) LLP v Barclays Bank plc and another* [2014] EWHC 3049 (Ch), [1203], (Hildyard J). See W Day, 'An Application of *Wrotham Park Damages*' (2015) 131 LQR 218.

[257] *(No 1)* [1967] 1 WLR 923; *(No 2)* [1969] 1 WLR 809.

[258] *Seager v Copydex Ltd (No 1)* [1967] 1 WLR 923, 932 (Lord Denning MR).

[259] *Seager v Copydex Ltd (No 2)* [1969] 1 WLR 809, 813 (Salmon and Winn LJJ).

[260] *Attorney-General v Blake* [2001] 1 AC 268, 279 (Lord Nicholls); *Vercoe v Rutland Fund Management Ltd* [2010] EWHC 424 (Ch), [334] (Sales J).

appropriate remedy for breach of confidence is a matter for judicial discretion.[261] In *Vercoe v Rutland Fund Managers Ltd*[262] Sales J sought to identify a principled approach to the award of pecuniary remedies for breach of confidence. He said:

> the test is whether the claimant's interest in performance of the obligation in question (whether regarded as an equitable obligation or a contractual obligation) makes it just and equitable that the defendant should retain no benefit from his breach of that obligation . . . The law will control the choice between these remedies, having regard to the need to strike a fair balance between the interests of the parties at the remedial stage, rather than leaving it to the discretion of the claimant.

Sales J acknowledged that, even in those cases where the breach involves the use of confidential information which is closely akin to a patent, as in *Seager v Copydex*, it does not necessarily follow that an account of profits will be awarded. Key factors to take into account in determining the remedy include:

(1) Where the confidential information does not resemble classic intellectual property rights then it is much more likely that the claim will be treated as one simply involving a personal obligation, as in contract or tort, such that orthodox compensatory remedies are more likely, encompassing the negotiation measure.

(2) The fact that the breach of confidence arises in the commercial context militates against the award of an account of profits, because a degree of self-seeking and ruthless behaviour is accepted in that context.[263]

(3) Where the confidential information is transmitted in breach of a confidential relationship which can be characterized as being similar to a fiduciary relationship, an account of profits is more likely.[264] This is because the self-seeking behaviour of a fiduciary should be restrained by virtue of the obligations of trust and loyalty, such that abusive behaviour should be deterred.

On the particular facts of the *Vercoe* case it was held that the award of an account of profits was not appropriate. This was because there was no fiduciary or similar relationship between the parties; the relationship between the parties was contractual as regards the development of a business opportunity; the confidential information was not akin to intellectual property; and the negative covenant not to use confidential information was broadly equivalent to the restrictive covenant in the *Wrotham Park* case,[265] where the negotiation measure was awarded. Consequently, in *Vercoe* the remedy for breach of confidence was the award of a sum which would have reasonably been negotiated to enable the defendant to exploit the information.

An additional consideration when determining which pecuniary remedy should be awarded arises from the equitable nature of the action for breach of confidence, which is founded on the defendant's unconscionable conduct. It appears that the more unconscionable the defendant's conduct, the more likely that account of profits rather than negotiation damages will be awarded. Consequently, if the defendant deliberately or recklessly breached the duty of confidence, this subjective unconscionability should be a significant factor in justifying the award of the typically more extensive remedy of an

---

[261] *Walsh v Shanahan* [2013] EWCA Civ 411, [63] (Rimer LJ).

[262] [2010] EWHC 424 (Ch), [339].

[263] See also *Experience Hendrix LLC v PPX Enterprises Inc* [2003] EWCA Civ 323, [2003] 1 All ER (Comm) 830. See p 478, above.

[264] *Vercoe v Rutland Fund Managers Ltd* [2010] EWHC 424 (Ch), [344].

[265] *Wrotham Park Estate Co Ltd v Parkside Homes Ltd* [1974] 1 WLR 798. See p 471, above.

account of profits. That is why the award of an account of profits could be justified in *Peter Pan Manufacturing Corp v Corsets Silhouette Ltd*.[266] If, however, the defendant inadvertently breached the duty of confidence, the negotiation measure is more appropriate. That is why an account of profits could not be justified in *Seager v Copydex*.[267]

(4) Proprietary Remedies Following the Recognition of a Constructive Trust

In principle, where the defendant makes a profit by misusing confidential information, that profit should not be held on constructive trust for the claimant, because there is no reason why the claimant should be considered to have an equitable proprietary interest in the profits. Confidential information is not property,[268] so the defendant has not made a profit by interfering with the claimant's property.

Various cases have concluded that the profits arising from breach of confidence cannot be held on constructive trust.[269] But others have recognized that profits or property obtained as a result of the breach might be held on constructive trust.[270] In *LAC Minerals Ltd v International Corona Resources Ltd*[271] the Supreme Court of Canada held that a constructive trust would be imposed as a remedy for a breach of confidence, so that the claimant had a proprietary interest in the defendant's profits. But the imposition of a constructive trust in such circumstances is explicable simply by the fact that this was a Canadian decision, where the remedial constructive trust is recognized. In England, the constructive trust is considered to be a substantive institution rather than a remedy, so that it will only be invoked where the claimant has an equitable proprietary interest in property held by the defendant by operation of law in recognized circumstances, and obtaining profits from breaching the equitable duty of confidence does not fall within any of these recognized categories.[272] Even following the decision of the Supreme Court in *FHR European Ventures LLP v Cedar Capital Partners LLC*[273] there is no reason to conclude that profits made from breach of confidence should be held on constructive trust for the claimant, save if the obligation to respect confidence is regarded as equivalent to the obligation of loyalty expected of a fiduciary. But the fact that breach of the duty of confidence does not involve breach of any fiduciary duty is vital here. The principles and policies relating to the imposition of a constructive trust on property held by a fiduciary, grounded on loyalty, do not obviously arise in the context of breach of the duty of confidence, even though the defendant may have breached the duty deliberately. This follows from the fact that the duty of confidence is not dependent on there being a relationship of trust and confidence between the claimant and the defendant.

---

[266] [1964] 1 WLR 96.

[267] [1967] 1 WLR 923. 931 (Lord Denning MR), 935–6 (Salmon LJ), 939 (Winn LJ). See also *Vestergaard Frandsen A/S v Bestnet Europe Ltd* [2013] UKSC 31, [2013] 1 WLR 1556, [24] (Lord Neuberger).

[268] *Boardman v Phipps* [1967] 2 AC 46, 127 (Lord Upjohn); *OBG Ltd v Allen* [2007] UKHL 21, [2008] AC 1, [275] (Lord Walker).

[269] *Ocular Sciences v Aspects* Vision [1997] RPC 289; *Satnam Investments Ltd v Dunlop Heywood and Co Ltd* [1999] 3 All ER 652.

[270] *Attorney-General v Guardian Newspapers Ltd (No 2)* [1990] 1 AC 109; *United Pan-Europe Communications NV v Deutsche Bank AG* [2000] 2 BCLC 461, [43] (Morritt LJ).

[271] (1989) 61 DLR (4th) 14.

[272] HW Tang, 'Confidence and the Constructive Trust' (2003) LS 135; P Stanley, *The Law of Confidentiality: A Restatement* (Oxford: Hart Publishing, 2008), 152; M Conaglen, 'Thinking about Proprietary Remedies for Breach of Confidence' [2008] IPQ 82. Cf D Sheehan, 'Information, Tracing Remedies and the Remedial Constructive Trust' [2005] 13 RLR 82.

[273] [2014] UKSC 45, [2015] AC 250. See p 512, above.

(C) EQUITABLE ESTOPPEL

Although the orthodox attitude of English law is that estoppel operates as a defensive shield and not as a sword, meaning that the claimant can only rely on the estoppel to prevent the defendant from pleading a defence and not to found a cause of action,[274] there is an exceptional type of estoppel which constitutes a cause of action.[275] This form of estoppel has variously been called proprietary estoppel, estoppel by acquiescence and estoppel by encouragement, though it appears that these terms are simply describing the same principle.[276] Although the expression 'proprietary estoppel' is most often used to describe this form of estoppel, this is misleading, since the estoppel is not confined to claims to property. Consequently, the expression 'equitable estoppel' is to be preferred.

Liability for this form of estoppel will arise where the defendant has made a representation relating to a right or benefit on which the claimant relies to his or her detriment. In such circumstances the defendant will be bound by this representation because, where the claimant has acted to his or her detriment in reliance on the representation, 'it would be unconscionable and unjust to allow the defendants to set up their undoubted rights against the claim being made by the plaintiff'.[277]

Since this form of liability is founded on the unconscionable nature of the defendant's conduct,[278] it follows that equitable estoppel is properly characterized as constituting a form of equitable wrongdoing.

(i) Establishing the Estoppel

To establish liability for equitable estoppel a number of conditions need to be satisfied. The defendant must have created or encouraged a belief or expectation on the part of the claimant that he or she would receive some benefit and the claimant must have relied on this to his or her detriment and to the knowledge of the defendant.[279] Sometimes it has been recognized that, rather than the defendant encouraging the claimant's mistaken expectation, it is sufficient that the defendant has acquiesced in this mistake.[280] Finally, the defendant must have done something or refrained from doing something which prevented the claimant's expectation from being fulfilled.[281]

(ii) Identifying the Appropriate Relief

Once liability for equitable estoppel has been established the court will determine what is the minimum equity to do justice to the claimant. The range of remedial relief for equitable estoppel was identified by Brennan J in *Waltons Stores (Interstate) Ltd v Maher*:[282]

---

[274] Such as the doctrine of promissory estoppel: *Central London Property Trust v High Trees House* [1947] KB 130.

[275] See *Attorney-General of Hong Kong v Humphreys Estate* [1987] AC 114, 127 (Lord Templeman) and *Salvation Army Trustee Co Ltd v West Yorkshire Metropolitan CC* (1980) 41 P and CR 179. That even promissory estoppel may operate as a cause of action was recognized by the High Court of Australia in *Walton Stores (Interstate) Ltd v Maher* (1988) 164 CLR 387.

[276] *Crabb v Arun DC* [1976] Ch 179, 194 (Scarman LJ).

[277] Ibid. See also *Taylor Fashions Ltd v Liverpool Victoria Trustees Co Ltd* [1982] QB 133, 151 (Oliver J); *Gillett v Holt* [2001] Ch 210, 225 (Robert Walker LJ); *Blue Haven Enterprises Ltd v Tully* [2006] UKPC 17, [24] (Lord Scott). See generally B McFarlane, *The Law of Proprietary Estoppel* (Oxford: Oxford University Press, 2013), ch 5.

[278] M Halliwell, 'Estoppel: Unconscionability as a Cause of Action' (1994) LS 15.

[279] *Gillett v Holt* [2001] Ch 210.

[280] *Ramsden v Dyson* (1866) LR 1 HL 129, 140–1 (Lord Cranworth).

[281] *Attorney-General of Hong Kong v Humphreys Estate (Queen's Garden) Ltd* [1987] 1 AC 114.

[282] (1988) 164 CLR 387, 419.

Sometimes it is necessary to decree that a party's expectations be specifically fulfilled by the party bound by the equity; sometimes it is necessary to grant an injunction to restrain the exercise of legal rights either absolutely or on condition; sometimes it is necessary to give an equitable lien on property for the expenditure which a party has made on it.

In identifying the minimum equity the court will consider all the circumstances of the case, but particularly the nature of the defendant's conduct[283] and the competing interests of the parties. The relief must not be disproportionate to the claimant's detriment.[284]

Normally the relief which is awarded to satisfy the claimant's equity cannot be characterized as gain-based, since the response is tailored simply to satisfy the claimant's expectations which were induced by the defendant.[285] For example, in *Dillwyn v Llewelyn*[286] the defendant purported to give land to the claimant and approved of the claimant's construction of a building on the land. The gift was invalid and so the defendant remained owner of the land. But, since the claimant had spent money constructing the building in reliance on his expectation of title, and the defendant knew this, it was considered to be unconscionable for the defendant not to satisfy the claimant's belief that he owned the land. Consequently, the defendant was required to transfer the land to the claimant. This was not a restitutionary remedy, since it was not assessed by reference to the defendant's gain as a result of his wrongdoing, but it was a remedy which existed simply to fulfil the claimant's expectations.[287]

But exceptionally the relief which is awarded can be characterized as gain-based. For example, in *Chalmers v Pardoe*[288] the defendant, who had leased land from the Native Land Trust Board of Fiji, agreed that the claimant could build a house on part of the land. The defendant also agreed that he would ensure that the claimant became tenant of the land on which the house was built. The claimant consequently built the house but the defendant declined to take the necessary steps to enable the claimant to become the tenant. The Privy Council would have been prepared to grant an equitable charge on the land for the benefit of the claimant but, because the prior consent of the Native Land Trust Board had not been obtained, the transaction was consequently illegal. The Privy Council did, however, recognize that, because it was unconscionable that the defendant should retain the benefit of the building, he would be required to repay to the claimant the sums expended upon the construction of the house. Clearly this remedy can be characterized as restitutionary since, rather than fulfilling the claimant's expectations, it simply sought to restore the benefit which had been received by the defendant.

(D) DISHONESTLY INDUCING OR ASSISTING IN A BREACH OF TRUST OR FIDUCIARY DUTY

Where the defendant has dishonestly assisted a trustee or fiduciary to breach their duty, or has induced such a breach of duty, the defendant will be liable to the claimant to whom the

---

[283] *Pascoe v Turner* [1979] 1 WLR 431, 436 (Cumming-Bruce LJ).

[284] *Sledmore v Dalby* (1996) 72 P & CR 196, 204 (Roch LJ).

[285] E Cooke, 'Estoppel and the Protection of Expectations' (1997) 17 LS 258.

[286] (1862) 4 De GF and J 517, 45 ER 1285.

[287] See also *Inwards v Baker* [1965] 2 QB 29; *Crabb v Arun RDC* [1976] Ch 179; *Salvation Army Trustee Company v West Yorkshire Metropolitan County Council* (1981) 41 P & CR 179.

[288] [1963] 1 WLR 677. See also *The Unity Joint Stock Mutual Banking Association v King* (1858) 25 Beav 72, 53 ER 563 and *Lee-Parker v Izzett (No 2)* [1972] 1 WLR 775. *Hussey v Palmer* [1972] 1 WLR 1286 is another case where the relief can be characterized as restitutionary since the claimant was content to recover her expenditure rather than to receive an interest in the property to which she had contributed.

duty was owed.[289] The defendant's liability for dishonest assistance is a form of accessorial liability,[290] since the defendant is a secondary party to the wrong committed by the trustee or fiduciary who breaches his or her duty. It follows that the accessory is tainted by this wrongdoing and so his or her liability is also a form of equitable wrongdoing.

(i) Establishing Liability for Dishonest Assistance

To establish liability for dishonest assistance the following conditions must be met:

(1) There must have been a breach of trust or fiduciary duty,[291] but this need not have been a dishonest and fraudulent breach on the part of the trustee or fiduciary.[292]

(2) The defendant must have procured, induced or assisted the breach.[293]

(3) The defendant must have been at fault in some way. The appropriate test of fault for this claim has been a matter of controversy. In *Williams v Central Bank of Nigeria*[294] Lord Sumption described this claim as 'knowing assistance'[295] and considered it to be based on fraud, but also added that the 'liability of a knowing assister has always depended on the unconscionability of *his* conduct'.[296] In the space of one paragraph the whole gamut of equitable fault is encompassed without any apparent awareness that these terms might bear different meanings.

In fact, the accepted test of fault is that of dishonesty, as was recognized by the Privy Council in *Royal Brunei Airlines Sdn Bhd v Tan*.[297] In *Tan* a number of important principles were identified concerning the nature of this cause of action: first, its existence was justified by analogy with the tort of procuring a breach of contract. In the same way that it is possible to be liable in tort for interference with the proper performance of the institution of a contract, so too there should be liability for interference with the proper performance of the institution of the trust or fiduciary relationship. Secondly, liability should not be strict because it is not based on the receipt of property, but instead on the defendant's assistance in the breach. In other words, liability is obligation-based and not property-based and it was not considered to be appropriate to hold a defendant personally liable as an accessory without proof of fault. Thirdly, dishonesty was interpreted as an objective test, so the defendant is considered to have acted dishonestly if he or she failed to act as an honest person would have acted in the circumstances.[298] This was interpreted as involving a two-stage test: first, what did the defendant know about the circumstances at the time relating to the proposed transaction and his or her participation in it? Secondly, in the light of that knowledge, would the reasonable person have considered the defendant's conduct to be dishonest? In assessing this, the court will have regard to personal attributes of the defendant, such as experience and intelligence, and the reason why the defendant acted as he or she did. So, if the defendant is a professional, such as a solicitor, the objective standard of honesty will be higher. The significance of this test of dishonesty is that the defendant is not the arbiter as to what is or is not dishonest. The defendant

---

[289] *Royal Brunei Airlines Sdn Bhd v Tan* [1995] 2 AC 378.

[290] *Ultraframe (UK) Ltd v Fielding* [2005] EWHC 1638 (Ch), [2006] FSR 16, [1600] (Lewison J). SB Elliott and C Mitchell, 'Remedies for Dishonest Assistance' (2004) 67 MLR 16.

[291] *Barlow Clowes International Ltd v Eurotrust International Ltd* [2005] UKPC 37, [2006] 1 WLR 1476, [28].

[292] *Royal Brunei Airlines Sdn Bhd v Tan* [1995] 2 AC 378.   [293] Ibid.

[294] [2014] UKSC 10, [2014] AC 1189, [35].

[295] See also *Vestergaard Frandsen v Bestnet Europe Ltd* [2013] UKSC 31, [2013] 1 WLR 1556, [26] (Lord Neuberger).   [296] Ibid (emphasis in original).

[297] [1995] AC 378. See also *Twinsectra Ltd v Yardley* [2002] UKHL 12, [2002] 2 AC 164.

[298] *Royal Brunei Airlines Sdn Bhd v Tan* [1995] 2 AC 378, 389.

might consider his or her conduct to be honest, but, in the light of the defendant's knowledge of the circumstances, the reasonable person might disagree.

The meaning of dishonesty was considered further in *Twinsectra v Yardley*[299] where Lord Hutton concluded that the test of dishonesty recognized in *Tan* was a hybrid test, which would be satisfied where the defendant's conduct was dishonest by the standard of reasonable people and the defendant realized that the conduct was dishonest by those standards. This mirrors the test adopted by the criminal law for purposes of property offences.[300] But this was not the interpretation adopted by Lord Nicholls in *Tan*. His reference to subjectivity was only a reference to the need first to consider what the defendant knew and then, in effect, to give that knowledge to the reasonable person and determine how the reasonable person would have characterized the defendant's conduct in the light of that knowledge.[301] This interpretation was subsequently recognized by the Privy Council in *Barlow Clowes International Ltd v Eurotrust International Ltd*,[302] where Lord Hoffmann, delivering the judgment of the Privy Council, interpreted Lord Hutton's judgment in *Twinsectra*, as well as his own, as being consistent with the objective test of dishonesty as recognized in *Tan*. Although not binding on the English courts, this is clearly a highly persuasive decision.

In *Abou-Rahmah v Abacha*,[303] Arden LJ in the Court of Appeal was willing to apply the definition of dishonesty as recognized by the Privy Council. She recognized that *Barlow Clowes* had clarified that *Twinsectra* had not recognized a hybrid test of dishonesty, so that the defendant was not required to be conscious of his or her wrongdoing.[304] She recognized that, exceptionally, the High Court or Court of Appeal might follow a decision of the Privy Council rather than a decision of the House of Lords. *Abou-Rahmah* was such an exceptional case, because *Barlow Clowes* did not depart from *Twinsectra*, but simply gave guidance as to its proper interpretation, the members of the Privy Council were all members of the House of Lords and two members of the majority in *Twinsectra* were also in *Barlow Clowes*.[305] She also considered that, as a matter of policy, there was no reason, when considering civil liability, why the law should have regard to the defendant's views as to the morality of his or her actions. But, even applying the objective test of dishonesty, on the facts of the case she did not consider that the defendant's general, rather than specific, suspicions, about fraudulent activities were sufficient to render him dishonest. The other two judges agreed that the defendant was not dishonest, but did not consider that it was necessary to consider the conflict between *Twinsectra* and *Barlow Clowes*, since the defendant's conduct was not even objectively dishonest, because he was not suspicious about the legitimacy of particular payments, although Pill LJ did acknowledge the value of *Barlow Clowes* in interpreting *Twinsectra*,[306] and Rix LJ referred to dishonesty 'in the *Twinsectra* sense . . . as clarified in *Barlow Clowes*'.[307] In *Starglade Properties Ltd v Nash*[308] Morritt LJ recognized that '[t]here is a single standard of honesty objectively determined

---

[299] [2002] UKHL 12, [2002] 2 AC 164.   [300] *Ghosh* [1982] QB 1053.

[301] See the judgment of Lord Millett in *Twinsectra Ltd v Yardley* [2002] UKHL 12, [2002] 2 AC 164.

[302] [2005] UKPC 37, [2006] 1 WLR 1476.   [303] [2006] EWCA Civ 1492, [2007] 1 All ER (Comm) 827.

[304] Ibid, [65].

[305] In *Sinclair Investments (UK) Ltd v Versailles Trade Finance Ltd* [2011] EWCA Civ 347, [2012] 1 AC 776 the Court of Appeal approved the approach adopted in *Abou-Rahmah* because it was a forgone conclusion that, had the case gone to the House of Lords, the decision of the Privy Council would have been followed: [74] (Neuberger LJ). See also *Starglade Properties Ltd v Nash* [2010] EWCA Civ 1314 and *Fiona Trust & Holding Corp v Privalov* [2010] EWHC 3199 (Comm), [1437] (Andrew Smith J).

[306] *Abou-Rahmah v Abacha* [2006] EWCA Civ 1492, [2007] 1 All ER (Comm) 827, [94].

[307] Ibid, [40].   [308] [2010] EWCA Civ 1314.

by the court. That standard is applied to specific conduct of a specific individual possessing the knowledge and qualities he actually enjoyed'.[309]

This objective test of dishonesty can be justified for policy reasons. It is appropriate to require defendants to comply with objectively determined standards of honesty. Although this test of dishonesty differs from that which is adopted in the criminal law, this is entirely appropriate.[310] The criminal law is concerned to ensure that the defendant is aware of his or her moral wrongdoing, since that establishes culpability and justifies punishment; the focus is on a dishonest state of mind. The civil law is not concerned with establishing culpability, since the aim is not to punish the defendant, but simply to provide a remedy. Consequently, the focus is placed on the dishonesty of the defendant's conduct rather than his or her state of mind, and this can be determined objectively, albeit with regard to the defendant's knowledge and suspicions of the circumstances.

(ii) Determining the Remedy Which is Awarded

Once the defendant has been found liable for dishonestly assisting or inducing a breach of trust or fiduciary duty it is then necessary to determine the appropriate remedy which should be awarded.[311] Traditionally the accessory is said to be liable to account as a constructive trustee. But this recognition of a constructive trust is not consistent with the normal notion of a constructive trust which only applies where the defendant is in receipt of identifiable property in which the claimant has an equitable proprietary interest.[312] Where the defendant has simply been an accessory to the breach of trust or breach of fiduciary duty he or she will not necessarily have received any property which can be the subject of a constructive trust.[313]

This formula of liability as a constructive trustee has now been convincingly rejected as fictional and unnecessary.[314] The use of the constructive trust and constructive trusteeship is of no significance in these claims. As Millett LJ said in *Paragon Finance plc v DB Thakerar and Co*:[315] '[T]he expressions "constructive trust" and "constructive trustee" are misleading for there is no trust and usually no possibility of a proprietary remedy; they are nothing more than a formula for equitable relief.' Where the defendant accessory is held liable, the appropriate remedy is personal; there are no proprietary connotations at all.

Although the typical remedy will be to compensate the claimant for loss suffered as a result of the breach of trust or fiduciary duty,[316] in *Novoship (UK) Ltd v Mikhaylyuk*[317] the Court of Appeal recognized that it was possible to award the remedy of an account of profits where the defendant had profited from dishonestly assisting a breach of fiduciary duty. This remedy was justified on the ground that the dishonest assister is liable to account as if he was a trustee, so is liable to account for any profits made as a result of the

---

[309] Ibid, [26].

[310] *Twinsectra v Yardley* [2002] UKHL 12, [2002] 2 AC 164, 197 (Lord Millett).

[311] Elliott and Mitchell, 'Remedies for Dishonest Assistance'.

[312] *Westdeutsche Landesbank Girozentrale v Islington LBC* [1996] AC 669, 705 (Lord Browne-Wilkinson).

[313] If the defendant has received property he or she may be liable for unconscionable receipt. See p 645, below.

[314] *Paragon Finance plc v DB Thakerar and Co* [1999] 1 All ER 400, 408 (Millett LJ). See also *Williams v Central Bank of Nigeria* [2014] UKSC 10, [2014] AC 1189.

[315] [1999] 1 All ER 400, 408; *Dubai Aluminium Co Ltd v Salaam* [2002] UKHL 4448, [2003] 2 AC 366, 404 (Lord Millett).

[316] *Twinsectra Ltd v Yardley* [2002] UKHL 12, [2002] 2 AC 164, [107] (Lord Millett).

[317] [2014] EWCA Civ 908, [2015] 2 WLR 526. See P Davies, 'Gain-Based Remedies for Dishonest Assistance' (2015) 131 LQR 173.

assistance. But the court also emphasized that the dishonest assister is not a fiduciary, and this has implications for the assessment of the remedy. In particular, unlike where a fiduciary is liable to account for all profits made which fall within the scope of the duty of loyalty,[318] the dishonest assister is only liable to account for those profits which were directly causally connected to the assistance. The appropriate test of causation is not that of 'but for' cause, but rather whether the cause was a real or effective cause of the profits. On the facts of the case, the defendant had assisted the fiduciary in breaching his fiduciary duty by negotiating shipping charters when he knew that the fiduciary had paid bribes. The assister had profited from these shipping charters but, since these profits had arisen from an unexpected change in the market, this was held to be insufficiently connected to the assistance to be caused by it. Further, the court held that, even where the profits were directly caused by the assistance, the award of an account of profits was not automatic, and the remedy would be withheld if it was considered to be disproportionate in the light of the form and extent of the wrongdoing.[319] These are two significant restrictions on the award of a gain-based remedy for dishonest assistance.

The recognition that gain-based remedies are available where the defendant has assisted a breach of trust or fiduciary duty is consistent with the assister being treated as a wrongdoer who should not profit from their wrong. It follows, for example, that the briber who has paid a bribe to the fiduciary may be liable for dishonestly assisting a breach of fiduciary duty, although double recovery is not permitted and the principal can only recover the amount of the bribe and any additional loss he or she can prove, however he or she chooses to frame the action and even if he or she sues both the fiduciary and the briber.[320] Even though the accessory's liability depends on the commission of a wrong committed by the fiduciary, it does not follow that the accessory is liable to account for the profits made by the fiduciary; rather, the accessory is only liable to account for those profits which he or she made from the dishonest assistance, in other words from the accessory's own wrongdoing. This was recognized by Lewison J in *Ultraframe (UK) Ltd v Fielding*[321] on the basis that the liability of the accessory is personal and is not punitive. So, for example, in *Fyffes Group Ltd v Templeman*,[322] the defendant who had bribed an employee to breach his fiduciary duty might have been liable for the profits that had been made as a result of the principal entering into a transaction with the defendant. On the facts, however, a disgorgement remedy was not awarded because the claimant would still have entered the contract had the defendant not bribed the employee, so that the profits that the defendant made were not caused by the bribery, but were simply ordinary profits that would have been earned regardless of the dishonest assistance.

---

[318] See p 504, above.

[319] *Novoship (UK) Ltd v Mikhaylyuk* [2014] EWCA Civ 908, [2015] 2 WLR 526, [119] (Longmore LJ).

[320] *Mahesan v Malaysia Government Officers' Co-operative Housing Society Ltd* [1979] AC 374, 382–3; *Arab Monetary Fund v Hashim (No 9)* [1993] 1 Lloyd's Rep 543; *Petrotrade Inc v Smith* [2000] 1 Lloyd's Rep 486; *Fyffes Group Ltd v Templeman* [2000] 2 Lloyd's Rep 643.

[321] [2005] EWHC 1638 (Ch), [2006] FSR 16, [1600].   [322] [2000] 2 Lloyd's Rep 643.

20

CRIMINAL OFFENCES

1. GENERAL PRINCIPLES AND POLICIES

When an offender has committed a criminal offence the law of restitution may be relevant in two ways.[1] First, the offender may have received a benefit as a result of the commission of the crime, so the question for the law of restitution is whether there is a cause of action which will enable the victim or the State to recover the proceeds of the crime. Secondly, a consequence of the offender committing the crime may be that he or she is entitled to obtain a benefit, under a life assurance policy for example. Here, the question for the law of restitution is whether the offender can be prevented from obtaining this benefit. Whether the victim or the State can claim the proceeds of crime or the offender can obtain a benefit arising from the commission of the crime will depend upon the application of the same fundamental principle, namely that no wrongdoer should be allowed to profit from the commission of a wrong.[2] Since there is no clearer wrong than the commission of a criminal offence, the application of the 'no profit principle' means that, as a general rule, the victim of the crime or the State should recover the proceeds of the crime from the offender, and the offender should not be entitled to obtain a benefit which he or she would otherwise be able to claim as a result of the commission of the crime.

2. RESTITUTIONARY CLAIMS BROUGHT BY THE VICTIM

(A) THE GENERAL PRINCIPLE

It is a fundamental principle of the law of restitution that no criminal can retain a benefit which accrues to him or her as a result of the commission of a crime.[3] Similarly, anybody who obtains the proceeds of crime from the criminal will be liable to make restitution, as was recognized by Lord Commissioner Wilmot in *Bridgeman v Green*:[4] 'Let the hand receiving it be ever so chaste, yet if it comes through a corrupt polluted channel, the obligation of restitution will follow it . . .'

But, despite the clear recognition of this fundamental principle, it does not follow automatically that the victim of the crime is necessarily entitled to recover the benefit

---

[1] See generally GJ Virgo, 'The Law of Restitution and the Proceeds of Crime—A Survey of English Law' [1998] RLR 34.

[2] This principle was recognized by Lord Hardwicke LC in *Bridgeman v Green* (1755) 2 Ves Sen 627, 628; 28 ER 399, 400. See p 421, above.

[3] *St John Shipping Corp v Joseph Rank Ltd* [1957] 1 QB 267, 292 (Devlin J). See also *Attorney-General v Guardian Newspapers Ltd (No 2)* [1990] 1 AC 109, 286 (Lord Goff).

[4] *Bridgeman v Green* (1757) Wilm 58, 65; 97 ER 22, 25.

which the defendant had obtained, since the victim must base his or her restitutionary claim on one of the principles which underlie the law of restitution.

(B) CLAIMS FOUNDED ON UNJUST ENRICHMENT

The victim may be able to bring a restitutionary claim on the basis that the criminal was unjustly enriched at the victim's expense. This is because the commission of a criminal offence may enable the victim to establish one of the recognized grounds of restitution. So, for example, if the defendant falsely imprisoned the claimant and demanded the payment of money from him or her as a condition of release, the defendant will have committed the crimes of false imprisonment[5] and blackmail,[6] but the claimant will be able to recover the money paid on the ground of duress of the person.[7]

(C) CLAIMS FOUNDED ON THE VINDICATION OF PROPERTY RIGHTS

Alternatively, the victim may be able to establish a restitutionary claim against the criminal on the basis that the victim seeks to vindicate his or her continuing proprietary rights. This will often be the case where the defendant steals the claimant's property or handles stolen property. This is illustrated by *Lipkin Gorman (a firm) v Karpnale Ltd,*[8] where money was stolen from the claimant, a firm of solicitors, by one of its partners, who gambled with the money at the defendant's casino. The claimant recovered some of the money which had been stolen, and this is preferably analysed on the basis that the defendant had received money which belonged to the claimant.[9] It was irrelevant that the defendant in this case was not the criminal, it being sufficient that the defendant had received the proceeds of crime from the criminal.[10]

(D) CLAIMS FOUNDED ON WRONGDOING

(i) Torts and Breaches of Fiduciary Duty

Finally, the victim of the crime may found his or her restitutionary claim on the commission of a wrong. Where the crime also constitutes the commission of a restitution-yielding tort, it is clear that the claimant may sue the criminal in tort and seek a gain-based remedy. So, for example, where the defendant commits a crime involving fraud[11] as a result of which property is taken from the victim, this may also constitute the tort of deceit and so the claimant can obtain a restitutionary remedy from the criminal in respect of that tort.[12] Alternatively, the crime committed by the criminal might involve breach of fiduciary duty,

---

[5] This is a common law offence. See D Ormerod (ed), *Smith and Hogan, Criminal Law* (13th edn, Oxford: Oxford University Press, 2011), 678.   [6] Theft Act 1968, s 21.

[7] See, for example, *Duke de Cadaval v Collins* (1836) 4 Ad and El 858, 111 ER 1006. See p 211, above.

[8] [1991] 2 AC 548. See p 560, below.   [9] See further p 560, below.

[10] Where the claimant wishes to recover stolen property from a thief the court may require the thief to return the property, its substitute or its value to the victim: Theft Act 1968, s 28.

[11] Contrary to the Fraud Act 2006.

[12] See *Halifax Building Society v Thomas* [1996] Ch 217 where the defendant was convicted of conspiring to obtain a mortgage advance by deception. On the facts, the restitutionary claim to recover the proceeds of the crime failed because the claimant had elected to affirm the mortgage despite the defendant's fraud. But if the mortgage had not been affirmed, and it could have been shown that the defendant had obtained a benefit as a result of the crime, the claim should have succeeded.

so the victim will be able to bring a restitutionary claim against the defendant based upon that breach.[13]

(ii) Founding a Claim on the Crime Itself

(1) Objections to Restitutionary Claims Founded on the Commission of Crimes

Where the victim of the crime is unable to sue the criminal for the commission of a tort or breach of fiduciary duty is it possible to found a restitutionary claim on the crime itself? In principle the answer should be 'yes', because the commission of a crime may often be an even more heinous form of wrongdoing. There are no cases, however, where a claimant has brought a restitutionary claim founded on the commission of a crime. The main reason for this is that the crime will typically also constitute a tort so that the victim of the crime will have a claim for compensation from the defendant. Where the victim's loss is equivalent to the defendant's gain and it is clear that the victim can recover compensation for loss suffered as a result of the crime, whether at common law or by virtue of particular statutory provisions,[14] there is no need to bring a somewhat speculative claim for restitution.

Sometimes, however, the victim may not have suffered any loss or the defendant's gain might exceed the victim's loss and so a restitutionary claim would be attractive.[15] That such a restitutionary claim might be brought was, however, doubted by Glidewell LJ in *Halifax Building Society v Thomas*:[16] 'The proposition that a wrongdoer should not be allowed to profit from his wrongs has an obvious attraction. The further proposition, that the victim or intended victim of the wrongdoing, who has in the event suffered no loss, is entitled to retain or recover the amount of the profit is less obviously persuasive.' Two reasons can be suggested for this reluctance to allow the victim to recover the proceeds of the crime.

First, the award of gain-based remedies is easier to justify where the defendant has committed a tort or broken a fiduciary duty than where a crime has been committed. This is because in those cases where the defendant committed a tort or broke a fiduciary duty it will be clear that the defendant has breached a duty which was owed to the victim. Where, however, the defendant has committed a crime the law treats this as involving the breach of a duty which is owed to the State, hence the power of the State to punish the criminal. But, despite this, in those cases where the victim has been harmed by the commission of a crime it is appropriate to conclude that this involves a breach of duty which was owed to the victim. The fact that the defendant has harmed the victim, either physically or by interfering with his or her property, and has obtained a benefit as a result, should be sufficient to enable the victim to claim the defendant's benefit. Although, in fact, in many cases where the criminal's profit derives from interference with the victim's property, the

---

[13] See, for example, *Reading v Attorney-General* [1951] AC 507 and *Attorney-General for Hong Kong v Reid* [1994] 1 AC 324. Receipt of bribes by a fiduciary in the course of business will typically constitute a crime under the Bribery Act 2010, s 2.

[14] Such as the power of a criminal court to order the offender to pay compensation to the victim in respect of personal injury, loss or damage resulting from the offence: Powers of Criminal Courts (Sentencing) Act 2000, s 130.

[15] A criminal court has the power to make a restitution order on conviction: Powers of Criminal Courts (Sentencing) Act 2000, s 148. See *R v Ferguson* [1970] 1 WLR 1246; *R v Church* (1970) 55 Cr App R 65; *R v Parker* [1970] 2 All ER 458. Magistrates' courts may also make orders for the delivery of property in the possession of the police to the person who appears to be the owner: Police (Property) Act 1897. See M Dyson and S Greene, 'The Properties of the Law: Restoring Personal Property Through Crime and Tort' in M Dyson (ed), *Unravelling Tort and Crime* (Cambridge: Cambridge University Press, 2014), ch 14.

[16] [1996] Ch 217, 229.

victim will have a tortious claim for conversion for which a gain-based remedy will be available.[17] But this will not always be the case, such as where the defendant has stolen choses in action which are capable of being property for the purposes of theft[18] but not for the tort of conversion,[19] because such rights cannot be possessed.

Another reason for the judicial reluctance to recognize that the victim of a crime can recover the profits from the criminal is that the policy of preventing the criminal from profiting from the crime is a matter for Parliament, using the statutory mechanism of confiscation. It is often asserted that it is not for the courts to interfere with this policy by extending the law to deprive the criminal of the proceeds of the crime. This was recognized by Peter Gibson LJ in *Halifax Building Society v Thomas*:[20]

> In considering whether to extend the law of constructive trusts in order to prevent a fraudster benefiting from his wrong, it is also appropriate to bear in mind that Parliament has acted in recent years ... on the footing that without statutory intervention the criminal might keep the benefit of his crime. Moreover, Parliament has given the courts the power in specific circumstances to confiscate the benefit rather than reward the person against whom the crime has been committed.[21]

But, whilst it is clear that the State has the prime interest in ensuring that criminals do not profit from their crimes, it does not follow that the judges lack a subsidiary power to deprive criminals of the proceeds of their crimes for the benefit of the victim where the statutory powers are inadequate to deprive the criminal of all the proceeds. The inadequacy of the statutory powers is exemplified by the fact that the statutory powers of confiscation are limited to where the crime committed by the defendant was sufficiently serious and cannot be invoked unless the defendant has been convicted of a crime.[22] Further, where the victim has instituted civil proceedings or might do in respect of loss, injury or damage arising from criminal conduct, the court has a power rather than a duty to make a confiscation order.[23]

There is surely a role for the law of restitution as developed by the judiciary to serve an interstitial function to ensure that the criminal does not retain the proceeds of crime.[24]

(2) The Case for Recognizing Restitutionary Claims Founded on Crimes

There is consequently no obvious objection to the law of restitution recognizing that the victim of a crime should have a right to obtain the proceeds of the crime from the criminal, although this right should be subsidiary to the power of the State to obtain such proceeds. This restitutionary right of the victim is justified for two main reasons.

First, it is a fundamental policy of English law that no defendant should profit from his or her crime. Where the State has not deprived the criminal of these profits it is entirely

---

[17] See p 459, above.   [18] Theft Act 1968, s 4(1).

[19] *OBG v Allan* [2007] UKHL 21, [2008] 1 AC 1, [102]–[106] (Lord Hoffmann); *Armstrong GmbH v Winnington Networks* [2012] EWHC 10 (Ch) [2013] Ch 156, [45] (Stephen Morris QC).

[20] [1996] Ch 217, 229. See also Glidewell LJ, ibid, 230.

[21] See also Hoffmann J in *Chief Constable of Leicestershire v M* [1989] 1 WLR 20, 23.

[22] Although note the powers of civil recovery by state officials which do not depend on the defendant being convicted of a crime: Proceeds of Crime Act 2002, Part V. See p 542, below.

[23] Proceeds of Crime Act 2002, s 6(6).

[24] See Glidewell LJ in *Halifax Building Society v Thomas* [1996] Ch 217, 230: 'The enactment of this legislation does not, of course, lead inevitably to the conclusion that neither common law nor equity provides a means by which [the criminal] could be prevented from enjoying the profit of the crime.' Though he did add that 'the readiness of Parliament to address the problem by legislation weakens the case for providing a solution by judicial creativity'.

appropriate that the victim should be allowed to instigate such an action as 'the instrument of a social purpose'.[25]

The second justification is just as important. In some cases where the claimant is the victim of a crime he or she will have suffered harm for which compensation is not available in the normal way. Enabling the claimant to obtain the proceeds of the crime will therefore act as some sort of recompense for the harm which has been suffered. So, for example, if a third party paid the defendant £1,000 to assault the claimant, it is surely entirely appropriate that the claimant recovers £1,000 from the defendant, both because the defendant should not be allowed to profit from the crime and because this operates as some form of recompense for the injury and trauma suffered by the victim. As Birks said, in such circumstances the recovery of the proceeds of crime which exceeds the claimant's loss 'is not an undeserved windfall but … a remedy for an individual wrong'.[26]

(3) The Nature of the Gain-Based Relief

If the defendant is held liable to make restitution to the victim as a result of the commission of a crime the remedy which should be awarded will typically be an account of the profits obtained as a result of the crime. It is, however, possible that the court will conclude that the defendant holds the proceeds of crime on constructive trust for the victim, so it follows that the victim could bring a proprietary restitutionary claim to recover the property which is held on trust. The potential importance of the constructive trust in the context of restitutionary claims founded on the commission of a crime arises from the judgment of Lord Browne-Wilkinson in *Westdeutsche Landesbank Girozentrale v Islington LBC*.[27] The judge recognized that 'when property is obtained by fraud equity imposes a constructive trust on the fraudulent recipient: the property is recoverable and traceable in equity'.[28] It follows that the constructive trust will be particularly important where the defendant has committed any crime which can be considered to involve fraudulent conduct[29] on the part of the defendant, because such conduct is unconscionable. Indeed, Lord Browne-Wilkinson specifically recognized that a thief who stole a bag of coins would hold those coins on constructive trust for the victim.[30]

(iii) Obstacles to Restitutionary Claims Founded on Crimes

If the victim does bring a claim to obtain the proceeds of the crime there are three main obstacles which must first be surmounted, which will dramatically limit the scope of any claim.

(1) Causation and Remoteness

The general rule of causation in respect of wrongs is the 'but for' test.[31] The application of this test to a claim for restitution of the proceeds of crime means that the victim must show that, but for the commission of the crime, the benefit would not have been obtained by the defendant. For reasons of consistency with most other claims for restitution for wrongs, this test of causation should apply to claims to the proceeds of crime. Similarly, the general principle of remoteness should apply to claims for restitution of the proceeds of crime, namely that the benefit must have arisen directly from the commission of the wrong. This was recognized in *Halifax Building Society v Thomas*,[32] where the defendant

---

[25] PBH Birks, 'The Proceeds of Mortgage Fraud' (1996) 10 TLI 1, 5.   [26] Ibid.
[27] [1996] AC 669.   [28] Ibid, 716.
[29] Such as theft or the offences contrary to the Fraud Act 2006.
[30] *Westdeutsche Landesbank Girozentrale v Islington LBC* [1996] AC 669, 716.   [31] See p 434, above.
[32] [1996] Ch 217.

had obtained a mortgage advance by deception and had used this to purchase a flat which had subsequently increased in value. Peter Gibson LJ said:[33]

> Further I am not satisfied that in the circumstances of the present case it would be right to treat the unjust enrichment of [the criminal] as having been gained 'at the expense of' [the claimant], even allowing for the possibility of an extended meaning for those words to apply to cases of non-subtractive restitution for a wrong... I do not overlook the fact that the policy of law is to view with disfavour a wrongdoer benefiting from his wrong, the more so when the wrong amounts to fraud, but it cannot be suggested that there is a universally applicable principle that in every case there will be restitution of benefit from a wrong... On the facts of the present case... the fraud is not in itself a sufficient factor to allow [the plaintiff] to require [the criminal] to account for it.

This was therefore a case in which the claimant could not simply rely on the fact that it was the victim of a fraud to obtain the proceeds of the crime. The explanation for this can be found in the earlier decision in *Chief Constable of Leicestershire v M*,[34] the facts of which were almost identical to those of *Halifax Building Society v Thomas*, in that the offender had made profits from the sale of properties he had purchased with the assistance of a mortgage advance which he had obtained by deception. Hoffmann J did not accept that these profits constituted the proceeds of crime, because they were not obtained by deception but rather arose from the loan which was obtained by deception. In other words, the profit was too remote from the crime.

It follows that if the victim is to recover the proceeds of crime from the criminal it must be shown that they were obtained directly from the crime, rather than indirectly, as will occur where the criminal has profited from investing the proceeds of the crime. This strict approach to the question of remoteness of benefit is at least consistent with the approach which is adopted where the claimant's restitutionary action is founded on tort.[35] If the victim of a crime can recover only those benefits which the defendant obtained directly from the commission of the offence, it follows that the victim should recover all those benefits which the criminal obtained directly from the victim, and presumably also those benefits which the criminal was promised as an inducement to commit the crime, such as a payment to commit a battery, simply because the bribe was only paid to the criminal to ensure that the crime was committed.

If, however, the court concludes that, by virtue of the defendant's fraudulent conduct, he or she holds the proceeds of crime on constructive trust for the claimant, the question of remoteness of benefit will be much less important. This is because all profits obtained as a result of the crime will be subject to the constructive trust, regardless of whether they arose directly or indirectly. This is illustrated by the decision of the Privy Council in *Attorney-General for Hong Kong v Reid*[36] where the court concluded that the defendant held the bribe he had received on constructive trust for the claimant. This meant that the claimant had an equitable proprietary interest in the bribe and subsequently the property which had been purchased with the bribe. In fact, the recognition of a constructive trust would have avoided the problem of remoteness in *Halifax Building Society v Thomas*,[37] because it could have been concluded that the property which the defendant purchased using the mortgage advance was held on constructive trust for the claimant building

---

[33] Ibid, 227.   [34] [1989] 1 WLR 20.

[35] It also accords with the test of remoteness which is adopted for the purposes of the forfeiture rule, examined at p 547, below.

[36] [1994] 1 AC 324. Confirmed by the Supreme Court in *FHR European Ventures LLP v Cedar Capital Partners LLC* [2014] UKSC 45, [2015] AC 250. See p 512, above.   [37] [1996] Ch 217.

society, since the defendant had obtained the mortgage advance by fraud. If the property was held on constructive trust it would follow that the proceeds of the sale of the house would also be held on the constructive trust, regardless of the fact that the property had increased in value.

(2) The Operation of the Illegality Defence

It is an accepted principle of the law of restitution that no court will allow a restitutionary claim to be brought which is founded on an illegal act.[38] This is known as the illegality defence. In principle this means that the victim would not be able to rely on the commission of a crime to obtain restitution from the criminal. This will not, however, usually be the case, because there is an accepted exception to this defence where the parties are not equally responsible for the illegal act.[39] Usually the victim will not have participated in the commission of the crime and so will not have been tainted by the illegality.[40]

(3) The Human Rights Act 1998

Would the imposition of civil liability on the defendant to make restitution of the proceeds of crime to the victim infringe the European Convention on Human Rights (ECHR), which was incorporated into English law by the Human Rights Act 1998? It might be concluded that such civil liability does infringe the European Convention because the defendant is being treated as a criminal, even though he or she had not been convicted of a crime.[41] This imposition of civil liability lacks the safeguards of criminal procedure, most notably the different standards of proof; the civil standard of proof being on the balance of probabilities, whereas the criminal standard is proof beyond reasonable doubt. Whether such civil restitutionary liability will be considered to infringe the criminal's human rights is a matter of some uncertainty. The preferable view is that, because restitutionary liability is a civil liability which does not involve the defendant being convicted of an offence and because the restitutionary remedy does not seek to punish the defendant, the imposition of such liability should not be considered to infringe the rights of the criminal which are protected by the ECHR.

(iv) The Potential Implications of Recognizing Restitutionary Claims Founded on Crimes

The potential operation of a claim to recover the proceeds of crime where the cause of action is the crime itself can be illustrated by reference to two situations where a benefit will have been obtained as a result of the commission of a crime.

(1) Rosenfeldt v Olson

The first example is the decision of the British Columbia Court of Appeal in *Rosenfeldt v Olson*.[42] In this case the accused was suspected of murdering 11 children. In order to secure his agreement to plead guilty to murder and to disclose the location of the bodies, the police agreed to pay $100,000 to be held on trust for the benefit of the accused's wife and their child. The parents of seven of the accused's victims claimed that this money was impressed with a constructive trust for their benefit. Their claim failed on the ground that the accused's wife and child had not been unjustly enriched at the expense of the parents. This was because the money which had been paid had not been subtracted from the

---

[38] *Holman v Johnson* (1775) 1 Cowp 341, 343; 98 ER 1120, 1121 (Lord Mansfield). See Chapter 27.
[39] See p 720, below.   [40] See *Kiriri Cotton Co Ltd v Dewani* [1960] AC 192.
[41] See, in particular, Article 6(2) of the ECHR: 'Everyone charged with a criminal offence shall be presumed innocent until proved guilty according to law.'   [42] (1986) 25 DLR (4th) 472.

victims. But this decision shows the dangers of assuming that the only claim within the law of restitution is that founded on unjust enrichment. It is obvious that the recipients of the money had not been unjustly enriched at the expense of the parents, but it could still have been argued that the parents of the victims should have founded their restitutionary claim on the commission of the accused's crimes. It should make no difference that the actual victims were the children and not the parents, since the crucial consideration is that the accused should not be allowed to profit from his crime, and neither should those who obtain a benefit as a direct result of that crime. But, even if a claim founded on the crime was recognized in principle, it was clear that the benefit received by the wife and her child had not been obtained as a direct result of the accused committing the crime, and so, in accordance with general principles of remoteness, it was correct that the restitutionary claim failed.[43]

(2) Recovering the Literary Proceeds of Crime

If a restitutionary claim founded on the commission of a crime is recognized, it would be particularly important where a criminal, usually a killer, obtains money by selling the story to a newspaper or television company or publishes a book about the crime.[44] Should the victim, or where relevant the victim's personal representatives, be allowed to recover this money? A number of States in the United States and in Australia have enacted laws to prevent convicted criminals from retaining profits by marketing their stories, with the profits usually being made available for the benefit of the victims of the crime and their families.[45] In England, statutory provision has been made for this problem whereby the literary proceeds of crime can be confiscated by the State,[46] but could the victim or his or her estate claim such proceeds from the defendant? Clearly, but for the commission of the crime the defendant would not have had a story to sell and so would not have obtained the money, so the 'but for' test of causation is satisfied. But there are two potential objections to the defendant having to make restitution to the victim.

First, the defendant might argue that the money which he or she received for selling the story was only obtained indirectly from the crime, since the money derived from the story rather than from the commission of the crime itself. The benefit would therefore be too remote. One response to this argument is to assert that, as a matter of public policy, a criminal who has obtained any benefit as a result of the commission of heinous crimes, such as murder, should not be allowed to argue that the benefit was too remote from the crime. Alternatively, it could be argued that, since the commission of the crime was a vital element of the criminal having a story to sell in the first place,[47] the profits flowed directly from the crime. Secondly, the defendant might also argue that he or she had assisted in the writing of the story and so may claim that, even if part of the benefit which he or she obtained was to be disgorged to the claimant, there should be an apportionment to reflect his or her personal contribution. Whilst such an argument would succeed where the claim

---

[43] Even though the accused had committed particularly heinous crimes and so perhaps a more liberal test of remoteness of benefit might be adopted, as discussed below, there is no reason why a different test of remoteness should be adopted where the claimant seeks to recover the proceeds of crime from a third party, such as the accused's spouse and child.

[44] A Freiberg, 'Confiscating the Literary Proceeds of Crime' [1992] Crim LR 96, who gives the example of Pottle and Randle who obtained £30,000 in respect of the publication of their book, *The Blake Escape: How We Freed George Blake and Why*.

[45] See S Okuda, 'Criminal Antiprofit Laws: Some Thoughts in Favor of Their Constitutionality' (1985) 76 Cal LR 1353 and Freiberg, 'Confiscating the Literary Proceeds of Crime', 97.

[46] Coroners and Justice Act 2009, Part 7. See p 541, below.

[47] Okuda, 'Criminal Antiprofit Laws', 1360.

was founded on the defendant's breach of fiduciary duty,[48] it should be defeated where the claim is founded on a crime committed by the defendant, again for reasons of public policy that a defendant who has committed a serious crime should not be allowed to benefit in any way from its commission.

(v) Restitution from Third Parties

Whilst the claimant might be able to establish a restitutionary claim to recover the proceeds of the crime from the criminal, it will be even more difficult to establish such a claim against anybody else who assisted the criminal in obtaining the proceeds without being party to the offence.[49] For example, a ghost writer or publisher who assists in the writing and publication of the defendant's story should not be liable to disgorge the benefits they obtained from the publication of the story.[50] This is because any benefit which the ghost writer or the publisher obtained was surely too remote from the commission of the crime in the first place. The reach of restitution will be too wide if it embraces claims against both the criminal and anybody who assisted the criminal in obtaining an indirect benefit from the crime without themselves being guilty of a crime in their own right.

Where, however, the third party receives property from the criminal which is held on constructive trust for the victim, the victim will be able to bring a restitutionary claim to vindicate his or her proprietary rights.[51] Where the third party receives property from the criminal in which the victim does not have a continuing proprietary interest, but the third party is aware that the property represents the proceeds of crime, the third party may be considered to have acted unconscionably so that he or she will hold the property on constructive trust for the victim.

3. RESTITUTIONARY CLAIMS BROUGHT BY THE STATE

Benefits obtained by an offender as a result of committing a crime may be confiscated by the State by virtue of statutory powers, primarily under the Proceeds of Crime Act 2002.[52] This statutory confiscation scheme does not fall within the private law of restitution since the proceeds of crime are paid to the State and not the victim, so cannot be regarded as involving literal restitution, since nothing is being returned to anyone.[53] Since, however, the law of restitution is preferably defined as involving the law of gain-based responses,[54]

---

[48] See, for example, *Boardman v Phipps* [1967] 2 AC 46 and *O'Sullivan v Management Agency and Music Ltd* [1985] QB 428.

[49] The victim will have a restitutionary claim against an accessory who obtained a benefit as a result of assisting or encouraging the commission of a crime, because the accessory is guilty of a crime in his or her own right.

[50] Invariably those States in the United States which have statutes prohibiting the criminal from profiting from the commission of the crime do not prohibit the publisher, ghost writer, or producer from retaining profits derived from the criminal's story: Okuda, 'Criminal Antiprofit Laws'.

[51] See Chapter 22. This will be subject to the defence of *bona fide* purchase: see Chapter 23. The third party could also be liable for knowingly receiving the proceeds of crime which are subject to a constructive trust (see p 645, below) or dishonestly assisting the criminal in breaching the trust (see p 521, above).

[52] See generally GJ Virgo, 'Crime and Restitution Revisited' [2009] RLR 29.

[53] Although it has sometimes been suggested that the confiscation regime does involve the restoration of the status quo existing before a crime was committed. See *May* [2008] UKHL 28, [2008] 1 AC 1028 [7], referring to the objective of the Hodson Committee (1984) which proposed the enactment of a statutory confiscation regime.　　　　[54] See p 3, above.

the confiscation regime properly falls within the law of restitution. For the fundamental feature of the statutory confiscation regime is that the defendant is required to give up benefits which can be regarded as having been obtained through the commission of a crime. Consequently, it is only to the extent that the defendant can be regarded as having benefited from the commission of crime that confiscation operates. It is for this reason that confiscation does not involve the imposition of a fine, since that involves the defendant being deprived of something which he or she had not obtained from the crime.[55] Confiscation is not, however, confined to the disgorgement of identifiable criminally-acquired assets,[56] but is concerned with the disgorgement of value.[57] If the defendant no longer has those assets he or she can still be deprived of other assets of equivalent value. So liability is dependent on receipt and not retention of a benefit.[58] Confiscation liability may, therefore, be analysed as either proprietary or personal.

The statutory confiscation regime falls within the law of restitution for wrongs. Where the defendant has been convicted of a crime, the State can ensure that the defendant is deprived of any benefit arising from the commission of that crime and this is motivated by the same principle which underpins the private law of restitution for wrongs, namely that no wrongdoer should be allowed to benefit from the commission of a wrong.[59] As regards the confiscation regime, the offender can be considered to have committed a wrong against the State by breaching the duty to abide by the criminal law of the land. Since detailed analysis of these provisions concerning disgorgement to the State is adequately dealt with in specialized works on the subject,[60] it will be sufficient here simply to identify the key provisions relating to confiscation of the proceeds of crime.

(A) THE STATUTORY CONFISCATION REGIME FOLLOWING CRIMINAL CONVICTION

The statutory confiscation regime was consolidated in the Proceeds of Crime Act 2002[61] by virtue of which the Crown Court can make confiscation orders as part of the sentencing process.[62] The essence of such orders is to remove from criminals the proceeds of their crimes,[63] by valuing the proceeds and imposing a personal liability on the defendant to pay value to the State. This has been called 'value confiscation'.[64] The Assets Recovery Agency was established by the Act to enforce confiscation orders made by the court. In 2012/13 6,392 orders were made, resulting in the confiscation of £133 million, although this only amounts to 26 pence in every £100 of estimated proceeds of crime.[65] Confiscation orders will be considered where the defendant has been convicted of a crime and the Director of the Assets Recovery Agency requests a confiscation order or the court believes that such an order is appropriate.[66]

---

[55] *May* [2008] UKHL 28, [2008] 1 AC 1028, [48(1)]; *CPS v Jennings* [2008] UKHL 29, [2008] 1 AC 1046, [13].

[56] Cf civil recovery orders, p 542, below.

[57] In *Waya* [2012] UKSC 51, [2013] 1 AC 294, [2], Lord Walker and Hughes LJ, described 'confiscation' as a misnomer.

[58] *Currey* (1994) 16 Cr App R (S) 421; *Patel* [1999] EWCA Crim 2268, [2000] 2 Cr App R (S)10.

[59] See p 421, above.

[60] See, in particular, AR Mitchell, SME Taylor, and KV Talbot, *Mitchell, Taylor and Talbot on Confiscation and the Proceeds of Crime* (3rd edn, London: Sweet and Maxwell).

[61] J Ulph, 'Confiscation Orders, Human Rights and Penal Measures' (2010) 126 LQR 251.

[62] *Zinga* [2014] EWCA Crim 52, [2014] 1 WLR 2228.

[63] *Waya* [2012] UKSC 51, [2013] 1 AC 294, [20] (Lord Walker and Hughes LJ).

[64] *Serious Organised Crime Agency v Perry* [2012] UKSC 35, [2013] 1 AC 182, [31] (Lord Phillips).

[65] National Audit Office, *Confiscation Orders* (2013).   [66] Proceeds of Crime Act 2002, s 6.

When determining whether a confiscation order can be made against the defendant three separate questions need to be considered:[67]

(1) Has the defendant benefited from general criminal conduct if he or she has a criminal lifestyle or, if he or she does not have a criminal lifestyle, has the defendant benefited from particular criminal conduct?[68] A defendant will have such a lifestyle if he or she has been convicted of a specified offence, such as money laundering or drug trafficking, or the offence forms part of a course of criminal activity involving the commission of a minimum number of other crimes or was committed over at least six months.[69] The consequence of living a criminal lifestyle is that the court will presume certain things about the defendant's property, such as that any property transferred to the defendant within six years of the proceedings being commenced is the proceeds of crime.[70] It is open to the defendant then to rebut these presumptions.[71] The benefit must be obtained 'as a result of or in connection with' the commission of a crime.[72] Where the defendant has been convicted of one offence and the court considers that the defendant has obtained benefits from a course of criminal conduct, the court may order that all of these benefits should be confiscated, even though some of the benefits arise from crimes in respect of which the defendant has not been convicted and which have never been formally taken into consideration in criminal proceedings.

(2) If the defendant has benefited from criminal conduct, what was the value of the benefit which the defendant obtained?[73] An objective test of market valuation is adopted.[74] So, for example, where a thief steals property, the value of the benefit will be what it would have cost the thief to acquire the property lawfully on the open market.[75] There is no scope for subjective devaluation.[76] The value of the benefit is the greater of the value of the property when it was obtained, adjusted for inflation, or its current value.[77] The benefit includes property which has been substituted directly or indirectly for the original property.[78]

(3) What sum can be recovered from the defendant? It is assumed that the amount to be confiscated from the defendant is the value of the benefit which the defendant has obtained.[79] The recoverable amount may be less, however, if the defendant shows that the amount he or she has available[80] is less than the value of the benefit.[81] In such circumstances the recoverable amount will be limited to the financial resources of the defendant at the date of the determination of the confiscation award or, if the available amount is nil, the recoverable amount will be a nominal sum.[82] The reason why the recoverable sum is allowed to be less than the value of the benefits received arises from the fact that the consequence of the defendant defaulting on the confiscation award is a liability to be imprisoned, and so the defendant 'cannot be ordered

---

[67] *May* [2008] UKHL 28, [2008] 1 AC 1028, [8].   [68] Proceeds of Crime Act 2002, s 6(4)(b) and (c).
[69] Ibid, s 75.   [70] Ibid, s 10.
[71] This does not infringe the European Convention on Human Rights: *Grayson v United Kingdom* (2008) 48 EHRR 722.   [72] Proceeds of Crime Act 2002, s 76(4).
[73] Ibid, s 76(7). Detailed rules as to valuation of benefits are included in ss 79–80.   [74] Ibid, s 79(2).
[75] *CPS Nottinghamshire v Rose* [2008] EWCA Crim 239; *Allpress* [2009] EWCA Crim 8; *Nelson* [2009] EWCA Crim 1573, [2010] QB 678.
[76] See p 69, above.   [77] Proceeds of Crime Act 2002, s 80(2).
[78] Ibid, s 80(3).   [79] Ibid, s 7(1).
[80] This is the total value of all the defendant's free property and all tainted gifts minus the amount payable in pursuance of obligations which have priority: ibid, s 9(1).
[81] Ibid, s 7(2).   [82] Ibid.

to pay a sum which it is beyond his or her means to pay'.[83] In determining the recoverable amount the court cannot take account of the effect of a confiscation order on the defendant's creditors.[84] Having determined the recoverable amount the court will make a confiscation order requiring the defendant to pay that amount, save where it would be so disproportionate so as to constitute a violation of the defendant's rights under Article 1 of the First Protocol to the ECHR, relating to the protection of property.[85]

This tripartite structure to the confiscation scheme bears striking similarities to the statutory scheme under the Law Reform (Frustrated Contracts) Act 1943, especially section 1(3) concerning claims for the value of non-money benefits provided before a contract was frustrated, where these benefits are to be identified and valued and the claimant may be awarded a just sum which does not exceed the value of the benefit received by the defendant.[86]

(i) Definition of Benefit

Under the Proceeds of Crime Act 2002 the defendant can be considered to have obtained a benefit in two ways. First, if the defendant 'obtains property as a result of or in connection with'[87] the criminal conduct, regardless of whether the defendant intended to obtain a benefit.[88] Property includes money, real and personal property, things in action and other intangible or incorporeal property[89] and it may be acquired anywhere in the world.[90] Alternatively, the defendant will be benefited if he or she has obtained a pecuniary advantage 'as a result of or in connection with the conduct'.[91] This encompasses a negative enrichment, such as the evasion of the defendant's own tax liability.[92] The nature of benefit for these purposes is illustrated by *Davey*,[93] where the defendant had cut down a tree on his neighbour's property, which increased the value of the defendant's property by £50,000 because it gave him a view of the harbour. A confiscation order was made to remove this financial benefit which was valued at the increase in the value of the house plus the amenity value, amounting in total to £75,000.

(ii) Obtaining a Benefit

A defendant will be considered to have benefited from his or her criminal conduct if the defendant 'obtains property as a result of or in connection with the conduct'.[94] Whilst property will be obtained where the defendant owns it, obtaining is interpreted more broadly and in a non-technical way in this context,[95] primarily because criminals do not usually obtain legal title to property obtained through crime. Rather, the essence of

---

[83] *May* [2008] UKHL 28, [2008] 1 AC 1028, [41].

[84] *Serious Fraud Office v Lexi Holdings plc* [2008] EWCA Crim 1443, [2009] QB 376. In the same way that the recognition of an institutional constructive trust over the profits derived from breach of fiduciary duty appears to disregard the interests of the defendant's creditors. See also p 513, above.

[85] *Waya* [2012] UKSC 51, [2013] 1 AC 294; *Barnes v Eastenders Cash & Carry plc* [2014] UKSC 26, [2015] AC 1.

[86] See *BP v Hunt (No 2)* [1979] 1 WLR 783. See p 357, above.

[87] Proceeds of Crime Act 2002, s 76(4).

[88] *Morgan* [2013] EWCA Crim 1307, [2014] 1 WLR 3450.

[89] Proceeds of Crime Act 2002, s 84(1).

[90] *Serious Organised Crime Agency v Perry* [2012] UKSC 35, [2013] 1 AC 182, [37].

[91] Proceeds of Crime Act 2002, s 76(5).

[92] *Sivaraman* [2008] EWCA Crim 1736, [2009] 1 Cr App R (S) 469; *Morgan* [2013] EWCA Crim 1307, [2014] 1 WLR 3450 (evading landfill tax).

[93] [2013] EWCA Crim 1662.   [94] Proceeds of Crime Act 2002, s 76(4).

[95] *Ahmad; Fields* [2014] UKSC 36, [2015] AC 299, [45].

obtaining property for these purposes is that the defendant has assumed the rights of the owner of the property, and will be satisfied where the defendant has possession of the property or directs what should happen to it. Joint defendants can acquire possession in common of property, such that they all 'obtain' the whole of the property,[96] although this will require careful consideration of the facts, turning on the respective roles of the defendants in the crime. Where a benefit has been obtained by a company of which the defendant was the sole controller, who used the company to conceal the benefit, the corporate veil may be pierced so that the benefit will be treated as the defendant's.[97]

(iii) Total Value or Profit?

In *May*[98] the House of Lords held that the relevant benefit for the confiscation regime is the total value of the property or advantage obtained and is not limited to the defendant's net profits after deduction of expenses or deduction of amounts paid to co-conspirators. So, for example, where the defendant sells drugs, the relevant benefit is not the defendant's profit but the sale price,[99] and the defendant cannot deduct any amount received which had been paid to an accomplice, such as a bribe.[100]

Determining the value of the benefit is moderated by the need to ensure that the confiscation order is not disproportionate, so that it does not become an additional punitive sanction like a fine.[101] So, for example, if the defendant has already restored the proceeds of crime to the victim, a confiscation order should not be made.[102] The question of proportionality proved to be significant in *Waya*[103] where the defendant had bought a flat for £775,000, with £465,000 provided by a mortgage lender fully secured, but to obtain this loan the defendant had made false representations. The defendant later repaid the mortgage in full. The defendant was convicted of fraud and a confiscation order was sought, at which point the flat was worth £1.85 million. The Court of Appeal had made a confiscation order of £1.1 million, representing 60 per cent of the present value of the flat, since the original mortgage loan represented 60 per cent of the original purchase price. This was reduced by a majority of the Supreme Court, which sought to determine the benefit which the defendant had derived from the use of the loan, namely the extent to which the flat had increased in value over its acquisition price as a result of the original mortgage, which was assessed at £392,400. The minority[104] adopted a more simple approach, which they considered to be consistent with the language of the Proceeds of Crime Act. They considered that the defendant had obtained the flat as a result of or in connection with the fraud, but to require the value of the flat to be confiscated would be disproportionate, because the defendant had also contributed his own money to its purchase. Consequently, the true benefit obtained by the defendant was considered to be much more modest, and involved the obtaining of the mortgage loan on more generous

---

[96] Ibid, [46].   [97] *Sale* [2013] EWCA Crim 1306, [2014] 1 WLR 663.

[98] [2008] UKHL 28, [2008] 1 AC 1028, [48(1)].

[99] *Simons* (1993) 98 Cr App R 100; *Green* [2008] UKHL 30, [2008] 1 AC 1053; *Islam* [2009] UKHL 30, [2009] AC 1076, [25] (Baroness Hale), [35] (Lord Mance). In *Elsayed* [2014] EWCA Crim 333, [2014] 1 WLR 3916 it was held that the value of drugs was to be assessed on a retail rather than a wholesale basis, which has regard to the circumstances in which they were obtained and what the defendant planned to do with the drugs. This mirrors precisely the approach adopted for the identification of an enrichment whereby the market value of an enrichment may be modified with regard to the objective value of the benefit to the defendant: *Benedetti v Sawiris* [2013] UKSC 50, [2014] AC 938. See p 65, above.

[100] *Patel* [1999] EWCA Crim 2268, [2000] 2 Cr App R (S) 10.

[101] *Sale* [2013] EWCA Crim 1306, [2014] 1 WLR 663, [45] (Treacy LJ).

[102] *Waya* [2012] UKSC 51, [2013] 1 AC 294, [28] (Lord Walker and Hughes LJ).

[103] Ibid.   [104] Lords Phillips and Reed, ibid.

terms than he would have done had he told the truth, this being causatively linked to the commission of his crime, rather than the increase in the value of the flat. Since this was likely to be a very small amount, the minority would simply have quashed the confiscation order. Whilst the restrictive approach of the minority appears fairer, its weakness relates to the identification of the benefit which the defendant obtained as a result of the crime, which turns on whether he would have been able to procure a mortgage loan had he told the truth. If he would, then the approach of the minority makes sense. But, if the only way that he could obtain the advance was by his fraud, it follows that the benefit of the increase in the value of the flat could not have been obtained but for his fraud. It does not follow that the full increase in value should be attributed to the fraud, since that would be disproportionate, but, as the majority recognized, the increase in the value of the flat which could be attributed to the mortgage loan.

(iv) Joint Receipt

Property may be considered to be jointly received by more than one party[105] and in such circumstances will not be apportioned between them,[106] but will be valued for each of them as the market value of the property, regardless of the interest of the other parties to the joint enterprise. So, for example, if the proceeds of crime are transferred into a joint bank account, each signatory of that account can be regarded as having obtained the whole benefit. This is illustrated by *Chrastny (No 2)*[107] where the proceeds of crime were jointly received by a husband and wife. He absconded from the jurisdiction and she was liable for the whole amount.

The significance of joint receipt was considered by the House of Lords in *May*.[108] Sixteen conspirators were involved in a conspiracy to cheat the Revenue of £4.5 million of VAT which was wrongly reclaimed. Companies were used to perpetrate the fraud, which were controlled by the defendants. The House of Lords held that the nature of the fraud enabled the corporate veils to be pierced and that the wrongly reclaimed VAT was to be treated as the joint property of those who controlled the companies. There was no requirement to apportion the benefit between the controllers. It followed that each controller of the company was liable for the full amount received, so that the same sum could be recovered 16 times and the State would recover more than HM Customs and Excise could have lost. This result proves that the statutory regime has nothing to do with literal restitution; since the amount confiscated does not necessarily reflect what the victim had lost. The regime is concerned with disgorging a gain and that gain can be amplified depending on the nature of the circumstances of receipt. But this result raises some difficult issues of principle. The House of Lords affirmed in *May* that the function of confiscation was not to impose a fine but to deprive a defendant of a benefit. But, if the benefit can be amplified by virtue of joint receipt so that each receiver is liable to disgorge what they are deemed to have received, this can only be characterized as penal and akin to a fine. The Supreme Court in *Ahmad; Fields*[109] recognized it would be disproportionate for the State to take the same proceeds twice over, so it was held that the confiscation order would not be enforced once the sum had been recovered by way of satisfaction of another confiscation order made in relation to the same joint benefit. It follows that the liability of joint defendants is joint and several, in that they are each individually liable, but if one party discharges the full liability, their liability to the State is extinguished. Presumably, the one who discharged the liability of them all can then seek contribution from the others,

---

[105] *May* [2008] UKHL 28, [2008] 1 AC 1028, [16].
[106] *Ahmad; Fields* [2014] UKSC 36, [2015] AC 299. [107] [1991] 1 WLR 1385.
[108] [2008] UKHL 28, [2008] 1 AC 1028. [109] [2014] UKSC 36, [2015] AC 299.

subject to the exercise of the court's discretion as to whether it is appropriate to provide restitutionary relief as between criminals.[110]

(v) Couriers or Custodians

Couriers or custodians of property or other minor contributors to a crime, who are rewarded by payment of a specific fee and who have no interest in the property or the proceeds of sale, are unlikely to be found to have obtained that property, so the relevant benefit will be the fee paid rather than the value of the property.[111] In other words, *de facto* possession of property does not involve the recipient obtaining an interest in that property.[112] This is consistent with the law on bailment. It has been recognized that where a bailor delivers goods to a bailee to keep for the bailor, the latter retains possession of the goods,[113] although this will turn on the particular terms of the bailment. The crucial distinction is between manual possession and the right to possession.[114] So, for example, a drugs courier does not have the right to possess the drugs and so the drugs will not be the relevant benefit for purposes of the statutory confiscation regime. Whether the defendant is regarded as a receiver of the drugs or a mere courier will depend on the facts as regards the nature of the defendant's responsibility relating to the disposition of the drugs.

(vi) Money Launderers

In *Allpress*[115] the Court of Appeal held that money launderers can be liable to a confiscation order, but only to the extent that they had obtained a benefit from the crime, so they should be treated in the same way as custodians or couriers. In reaching this decision the Court carefully considered the nature of money. Although money is treated differently from tangible property,[116] this is not significant for the purposes of the confiscation regime, since the question is the same whether the property is money or tangible property, namely whether the recipient has a power of disposition or control over the property.

The application of this principle to the confiscation regime is illustrated by the situation where a shopper in a supermarket pays money to a till operator at the checkout. The till operator does not benefit from the receipt of the money or from the money being under their power of disposition or control. They do have some degree of power of disposition or control but their powers are limited by virtue of their employment contract. Physical possession is not a benefit for the purposes of the confiscation regime. The same result would be reached even if the till operator knew or suspected that the money was tainted by crime and so would be liable for the money laundering offence.[117] So, for example, if the defendant is asked to collect an envelope which contains the proceeds of crime and transfers that money to a third party, the defendant will not have an interest in that money for the purposes of the confiscation scheme.

These principles were applied to a number of the appeals which were considered in *Allpress*. So, for example, one defendant was a cash courier, who took the proceeds of drug

---

[110] See p 251, above.   [111] *Ahmad; Fields* [2014] UKSC 36, [2015] AC 299.

[112] *Allpress* [2009] EWCA Crim 8, [2009] 2 Cr App R (S) 399, [70]. Although the Proceeds of Crime Act 2002, s 84(2)(h) does state that the right to possession of property other than land constitutes an interest in property.

[113] *Ancona v Rogers* (1876) 1 Ex D 285, 292 (Mellish LJ).

[114] *Allpress* [2009] EWCA Crim 8, [2009] 2 Cr App R (S) 399, [75]. Approved in *Mackle* [2014] UKSC 5, [2014] AC 678.

[115] [2009] EWCA Crim 8, [2009] 2 Cr App R (S) 399.

[116] So, for example, Lord Haldane in *Sinclair v Brougham* [1914] AC recognized that title to money passes when it is paid over as currency.   [117] Proceeds of Crime Act 2002, s 327.

trafficking to various countries. It was held that the relevant benefit was the £800 she was paid for doing so and not the money she was laundering. However, a partner in a firm of solicitors was held to be a trustee of money obtained pursuant to a VAT fraud which had been transferred into a client account and this was therefore considered to be his property. It was accepted that there might be exceptional cases where money is paid into the defendant's bank account and it will not constitute property which the defendant had obtained for purposes of the confiscation regime. So, for example, if the proceeds of crime are credited to a wife's bank account which is controlled by her husband, she will be a nominee and so will not obtain any property herself for the purposes of the confiscation regime.

(vii) Tainted Gifts

Where the defendant has given assets away which derive or are presumed to derive from the proceeds of crime, they are still to be taken into account when determining the recoverable amount,[118] even if the defendant is unable to recover the gift from the donee.[119] This consequently provides a mechanism to prevent the defendant from in effect pleading change of position.

(B) CRIMINAL MEMOIRS

The statutory confiscation regime has been expanded by Part 7 of the Coroners and Justice Act 2009 to confiscate proceeds following a criminal conviction[120] which arises from the exploitation of material relating to a relevant offence, by means of so-called 'exploitation proceeds orders'.[121] Such orders can be made where the defendant has derived a benefit from the exploitation of any material which pertains to a relevant offence or from steps taken or to be taken with a view to making such exploitation.[122] Exploitation can occur by any means, such as by publication of written or electronic materials, the production of visual images, words or sounds, or live entertainment, representation or interview.[123] The defendant will be regarded as having derived a benefit if the benefit is secured for another person, such as a payment for an interview which is to be paid to the defendant's child.[124] In determining whether to make an exploitation proceeds order the court must have regard to a variety of factors, including the nature and purpose of the exploitation, whether the activity or product is in the public interest, its social, cultural or educational value, the seriousness of the relevant offence and the offensiveness of exploitation to the victim of the offence, the family of the victim, and the general public.[125]

The amount which can be recovered must not exceed the lesser of the total value of the benefits obtained and the available amount.[126] When assessing the total value of the benefits, where the benefit is in kind, such as goods or services, the objective open market value is to be adopted less the value of any consideration provided for the benefit.[127]

This regime will clearly be relevant where a defendant writes memoirs about his or her criminal exploits, but it will extend beyond that to encompass potentially any criminal who profits from the exploitation of their crimes in whatever media, including film and journalism. This regime builds on the confiscation regime in the Proceeds of Crime Act 2002 by expanding the net of those profits which derive from the crime, to include indirect

---

[118] Proceeds of Crime Act 2002, s 9(1)(b).

[119] *Smith* [2013] EWCA Crim 502, [2014] 1 WLR 898.

[120] Coroners and Justice Act 2009, s 156(2), or where the defendant is found to be not guilty by reason of insanity or to have committed the criminal act under a disability.

[121] Ibid, s 155.   [122] Ibid, s 155(2).   [123] Ibid, s 160(2).   [124] Ibid, s 160(3).

[125] Ibid, s 162(3).   [126] Ibid, s 163(1).   [127] Ibid, s 163(4).

profits. It mirrors developments in the law relating to breach of fiduciary duty where expansive notions of causation and remoteness have been adopted.[128]

(C) CIVIL RECOVERY ORDER

Part V of the Proceeds of Crime Act 2002 also enables certain state officials, such as constables, customs officers and the director of the Asset Recovery Agency, to apply to the High Court for a civil recovery order to recover property obtained through the commission of criminal conduct, even though the defendant may not been convicted of a crime in respect of that property and may simply be the recipient of property which is the product of a crime.[129] It is not necessary for anybody to have been convicted of a crime for this civil process to be engaged.[130] The process is concerned with confiscation of property rather than the value of property. It is not possible to make a civil recovery order against property which is not located in the United Kingdom.[131] Significantly, it is possible for the victim of a crime, such as theft or fraud, to apply to the court for a declaration that property which might otherwise be recovered by the State as the proceeds of crime, was property or represents property of which the victim was deprived by unlawful conduct.[132] This constitutes an important mechanism for the victims of crime to obtain restitution of property obtained by the defendant as a result of the commission of crime.[133]

(D) COMMON LAW CLAIMS FOR RESTITUTION

It was recognized by the Court of Appeal in *Attorney-General v Blake*[134] that the Attorney-General, as the guardian of the public interest, could bring a public law civil claim to ensure that criminals were prevented from receiving the proceeds of the crime.[135] The House of Lords rejected this public law ground of recovery. Lord Nicholls recognized that an order depriving the claimant of the proceeds of crime and transferring it to the State involved the confiscation of property without compensation,[136] and the courts have no power to make such an order at common law.[137]

4. DENIAL OF BENEFITS ARISING FROM THE COMMISSION OF CRIMES

(A) DOES THE DENIAL OF BENEFITS TO A CRIMINAL FORM PART OF THE LAW OF RESTITUTION?

Where one consequence of an offender committing a crime is that he or she is entitled to receive a benefit, the general principle that no offender should profit from wrongdoing

---

[128] See p 504, above.

[129] See *Serious Organised Crime Agency v Perry* [2012] UKSC 35, [2013] 1 AC 182, [39].

[130] For the due process implications of this procedure see C King, 'Civil Forfeiture and Article 6 of the ECHR: Due Process Implications for England and Wales and Ireland' (2014) LS 371.

[131] *Serious Organised Crime Agency v Perry* [2012] UKSC 35, [2013] 1 AC 182, [39].

[132] Proceeds of Crime Act 2002, s 281.

[133] See *The National Crime Agency v Robb* [2014] EWHC 4384 (Ch) for an illustration of the victims of fraud obtaining restitution of the property of which they had been defrauded by virtue of s 281.

[134] [1998] Ch 439.   [135] See p 543, below.   [136] *Attorney-General v Blake* [2001] 1 AC 268, 289.

[137] See *Malone v Commissioner of Police of the Metropolis* [1980] QB 49; *Webb v Chief Constable of Merseyside Police* [2000] All ER 209.

means that the benefit should be denied to him or her. But does the analysis of this application of the no-profit principle properly fall within a work on the law of restitution? Burrows suggests that it does not, simply because the law of restitution is concerned with the transfer of benefits to the claimant, whereas the question which is being considered here is whether the conduct of the offender is such as to prevent the benefit from being received by the criminal in the first place.[138] But this is an unnecessarily restrictive interpretation of the ambit of the law of restitution. Although the denial of benefits to a criminal is not restitutionary in the sense that it does not involve the application of gain-based remedies, it is appropriate to examine the rules relating to the denial of benefits to a criminal in a book on restitution.[139] This is because both preventing the defendant from receiving the proceeds of the crime and transferring the proceeds of crime to the victim or to the State are motivated by the same policy consideration, namely that no criminal should be allowed to profit from the crime. The same question of public policy arises regardless of whether it is considered before or after the defendant has obtained the proceeds of the crime.

In *Attorney-General v Blake*[140] the House of Lords recognized that the State has no specific power at common law to prevent a criminal from obtaining the proceeds of a crime; such a power can only exist by virtue of legislation.[141] Instead, a private law power was developed which had the effect of preventing Blake from profiting from his crime, by means of the remedy of an account of profits which lay only because Blake had committed a breach of contract. But where there is no contract to be breached, the common law recognizes another private law doctrine to prevent a criminal from profiting from his or her crime, in the form of the forfeiture principle.

(B) THE FORFEITURE PRINCIPLE

(i) The Ambit of the Forfeiture Principle

It is a fundamental principle of English law that a criminal is not able to enforce rights or recover benefits which accrue to him or her as a result of the commission of certain types of criminal offence.[142] This is a rule of public policy. As Fry LJ said in *Cleaver v Mutual Reserve Fund Life Association*:[143] 'The principle of public policy invoked is in my opinion rightly asserted. It appears to me that no system of jurisprudence can with reason include amongst the rights which it enforces rights directly resulting to the person asserting them from the crime of that person.'

Where the defendant is entitled to benefits as a result of an unlawful killing, the rule which precludes him or her from obtaining those benefits is called the forfeiture rule.[144] But the principle which underlies the forfeiture rule is not confined to where the crime which has been committed is an unlawful killing. Fry LJ recognized in *Cleaver* that the general principle may also be invoked where the criminal has committed a crime involving fraud.[145] The forfeiture principle is in fact potentially applicable in respect of

---

[138] AS Burrows, *The Law of Restitution* (3rd edn, Oxford: Oxford University Press, 2011), 641.

[139] It is consistent with the expansive interpretation of restitution encompassing the giving up of rights: see p 6, above. Depriving the defendant of benefits from crime is included within the American Law Institute's *Restatement Third on Restitution and Unjust Enrichment* (St Paul, MN: American Law Institute Publishing, 2011).

[140] *Attorney-General v Blake* [2001] 1 AC 268. See p 473, above.

[141] Following the enactment of Part 7 of the Coroners and Justice Act 2009 an exploitation proceeds order could be made against a defendant such as Blake. See p 541, above.

[142] *Cleaver v Mutual Reserve Fund Life Association* [1892] 1 QB 147, 156 (Fry LJ); *Beresford v Royal Insurance Co* [1938] AC 586, 598 (Lord Atkin).

[143] [1892] 1 QB 147, 156.   [144] *Re K (deceased)* [1986] Ch 180, 185 (Vinelott LJ).

[145] *Cleaver v Mutual Reserve Fund Life Association* [1892] 1 QB 147, 156.

all crimes, but the courts have accepted that it is only the commission of certain types of criminal conduct which will trigger its operation.[146] The test which the courts have adopted is whether the offender intentionally committed the crime. This was recognized by Lord Denning MR in *Hardy v Motor Insurers' Bureau*,[147] where he said that 'no person can claim reparation or indemnity for the consequences of a criminal offence where his own wicked and deliberate intent is an essential ingredient in it'.

Whilst the application of the forfeiture principle prevents the criminal from obtaining all benefits which accrue as a result of the commission of the crime, most cases are concerned with whether the criminal can obtain an indemnity under an insurance policy. Consistent with the forfeiture principle, such an indemnity will be denied where the criminal intentionally committed the crime,[148] but not where it was committed negligently or innocently.[149] So, for example, it has long been recognized that a criminal who deliberately sets fire to his or her own property to claim on an insurance policy for damage to that property will not be able to recover the money from the insurance company.[150] The forfeiture principle also prevents those who claim through the criminal from recovering benefits which arise from the commission of a crime.[151]

(ii) The Relationship Between the Forfeiture Principle and the Illegality Defence

The principle that criminals, or those claiming through criminals, are not able to obtain benefits arising from a crime, is closely related to the principle that a court will not enable a party to obtain restitution of benefits transferred pursuant to an illegal transaction.[152] Indeed, both of these principles are founded on the same general principle of *ex turpi causa non oritur actio*, namely that the courts will not assist criminals and similar wrongdoers.[153] Also both principles are principles of public policy rather than principles of justice.[154]

Nevertheless, the forfeiture principle and the illegality defence remain distinct, there being a number of important differences between them. For example, a transaction may be illegal without necessarily involving the commission of a crime. Also the illegality defence is only applicable once a benefit has been transferred, whereas the forfeiture principle applies before any benefit has been received. Most importantly, it is much easier to defend the strict application of the forfeiture principle because the criminal is clearly a wrongdoer, whereas the claimant who seeks to recover a benefit which has been obtained by the defendant under an illegal transaction may have been an innocent party or less tainted by the illegality than the defendant. The effect of these differences is that, whilst it is necessary to acknowledge the common policy behind the forfeiture principle and the principle denying restitution on the ground of illegality, the two principles should be kept separate because they apply in different circumstances.

---

[146] See Lord Wright in *Beresford v Royal Insurance Co Ltd* [1937] 2 KB 197, 220.

[147] [1964] 2 QB 745, 760.

[148] *Haseldine v Hoskin* [1933] 1 KB 822. See also *Geismar v Sun Alliance and London Insurance Ltd* [1978] QB 383, 395 (Talbot J).

[149] *Tinline v White Cross Insurance Association Ltd* [1921] 3 KB 327; *James v British General Insurance Co Ltd* [1927] 2 KB 311. See also *Euro-Diam Ltd v Bathurst* [1990] QB 1, 40 (Kerr LJ).

[150] *Beresford v Royal Insurance Co Ltd* [1938] AC 586, 595 (Lord Atkin).

[151] *The Amicable Society for a Perpetual Life Assurance Office v Bolland* (1830) 4 Bligh (NS) 194, 5 ER 70.

[152] *Holman v Johnson* (1775) 1 Cowp 341, 343; 98 ER 1120, 1121 (Lord Mansfield). See p 709, below.

[153] See *Euro-Diam Ltd v Bathurst* [1990] QB 1, 35 (Kerr LJ).

[154] *Dunbar v Plant* [1998] Ch 412, 422 (Mummery LJ).

(iii) The Rationale of the Forfeiture Principle

A number of explanations have been given for the existence of the forfeiture principle.[155] One explanation is that it exists to deter potential criminals from committing crimes in order to obtain benefits.[156] This may explain why the application of the forfeiture principle is confined to where the criminal has intentionally committed the crime, since it is only in this situation that the threat of forfeiture of benefits is likely to have any deterrent effect at all. But it is most unlikely that this principle of private law would constitute any greater deterrent than that already provided by the criminal law. Another explanation of the principle is that it stems from a desire to punish the criminal for committing the crime, but it is surely inappropriate for private law to punish the criminal, this being a function for which only the criminal courts are suited. If the civil courts seek to punish the criminal in addition to the punishment which is imposed by the criminal courts, there is an obvious danger of excessive punishment.[157] A final explanation for the forfeiture principle is that it is justified on the ground simply that no criminal should be able to resort to the law to recover benefits to which they have become entitled as a result of their crimes.[158] This is probably the main reason for the existence of the rule, namely a general distaste that the law should be used to assist criminals in any way.[159]

(C) THE FORFEITURE RULE

It is in connection with the commission of unlawful killings where the forfeiture principle has proved to be most important. Here the principle is called the forfeiture rule,[160] as has been recognized by the Forfeiture Act 1982. Section 1 states that: 'the "forfeiture rule" means the rule of public policy which in certain circumstances precludes a person who has unlawfully killed another from acquiring a benefit in consequence of the killing.'

Originally, any benefits which accrued to an offender as a result of the commission of murder and other felonies were forfeited to the Crown, but this rule was abolished by the Forfeiture Act 1870. Consequently, the effect of the forfeiture rule today is that the benefits which accrue to the criminal as a result of an unlawful killing are forfeited to the person who is entitled to them once the claims of the criminal, or those claiming through the criminal, are discounted. The uncompromising rigidity of this forfeiture rule has often been criticized[161] and its application has now been qualified by the Forfeiture Act 1982.[162]

(i) The Types of Unlawful Killing Which Trigger the Forfeiture Rule

It is clear that the forfeiture rule applies in respect of benefits which accrue as the result of the defendant committing the crime of murder,[163] in other words where the defendant has

---

[155] See J Shand, 'Unblinkering the Unruly Horse: Public Policy in the Law of Contract' (1972) 30 CLJ 144.

[156] *Beresford v Royal Insurance Co Ltd* [1938] AC 586, 598 (Lord Atkin); *Gray v Barr* [1971] 2 QB 554, 581 (Salmon LJ); *Re H (deceased)* [1990] 1 FLR 441, 446 (Peter Gibson J).

[157] As recognized by Devlin J in *St John Shipping Corp v Joseph Rank Ltd* [1957] 1 QB 267, 292.

[158] *Gray v Barr* [1970] 2 QB 626, 640 (Geoffrey Lane J). See also *Euro-Diam Ltd v Bathurst* [1990] QB 1, 35 (Kerr LJ).

[159] As Wilmot CJ said in *Collins v Blantern* (1767) 2 Wils 347, 350; 95 ER 859, 852: 'no polluted hand shall touch the pure fountains of justice'.

[160] For general discussion of this rule see TK Earnshaw and PJ Pace, 'Let the Hand Receiving It Be Ever So Chaste' (1972) 37 MLR 481.

[161] See, for example, J Chadwick, 'A Testator's Bounty to His Slayer' (1914) 30 LQR 211.

[162] But the rule continues to be applied strictly in other jurisdictions which have no equivalent statutory provision. See, for example, *Re Edwards* [2014] VSC 392 (Victoria, Australia).

[163] See, for example, *Cleaver v Mutual Reserve Fund Life Association* [1892] 1 QB 147.

caused the death of a person intending either to kill or to cause serious injury to the victim.[164] It is irrelevant that the murderer was not motivated by a desire to profit from the killing; the very fact of committing murder is sufficient to preclude the killer from obtaining any benefits as a result.[165]

Whether the forfeiture rule is applicable to all forms of manslaughter has been a controversial matter. In *Dunbar v Plant*[166] the Court of Appeal accepted by a majority that the forfeiture rule should apply to all cases of manslaughter, since there was no logical basis for distinguishing between different types of unlawful killing. If this is correct, it follows that the forfeiture rule is potentially applicable where the defendant commits voluntary manslaughter, whether by loss of control,[167] diminished responsibility,[168] or pursuant to a suicide pact,[169] and also where the killer commits involuntary manslaughter, whether reckless, constructive or gross negligent.

It is not, however, correct to say that there is no logical basis for distinguishing between different types of unlawful killing, for it has been recognized on a number of occasions that a distinction can be drawn on the basis of the killer's culpability.[170] Consequently, it has been suggested that the forfeiture rule should only be applicable where the killer committed a crime intentionally or deliberately and it is irrelevant that the actual killing was unintentional or that the crime did not involve violence or threats of violence.[171] This test covers all cases of murder and voluntary manslaughter, which is simply murder committed in certain extenuating circumstances. So, for example, if the defendant is convicted of manslaughter by reason of diminished responsibility, the forfeiture rule will prevent him or her from obtaining any property under the victim's will.[172] Constructive manslaughter would also be caught by the rule, since that crime requires the defendant to have committed an unlawful act intentionally.[173] It would also cover the case where the defendant was guilty of assisting or encouraging the victim to commit suicide, since the defendant would have been committing the crime intentionally.[174] The test will not, however, cover the crime of gross negligence manslaughter, since that crime does not require proof of any intentional conduct.

Even though a distinction can be drawn between different types of unlawful killing on the basis of culpability, the better view is that of the majority in *Dunbar v Plant* that the forfeiture rule should apply to all types of unlawful killing. This is appropriate because the enactment of the Forfeiture Act in 1982 has meant that the forfeiture rule can be modified where justice demands.[175] If such an Act did not exist it would be appropriate to interpret the forfeiture rule restrictively to minimize unjust results. Since, however, the judges have

---

[164] The forfeiture rule will not be applicable to a person who committed murder or any other unlawful killing but was found to be insane, simply because such a person is acquitted of the crime by virtue of insanity: Criminal Procedure (Insanity) Act 1964, s 1. See *Re Houghton* [1915] 2 Ch 173; *Re Pitts* [1931] 1 Ch 546.

[165] *Cleaver v Mutual Reserve Fund Life Association* [1892] 1 QB 147.

[166] [1998] Ch 412. That the forfeiture rule should apply to all cases of manslaughter had been recognized previously. See, for example, *In the Estate of Hall* [1914] P 1, 7 (Hamilton LJ) and *Re Giles (deceased)* [1972] Ch 544.

[167] Coroners and Justice Act 2009, ss 54–56.   [168] Homicide Act 1957, s 2.   [169] Ibid, s 4.

[170] *Gray v Barr* [1970] 2 QB 626, 640 (Geoffrey Lane J). See also *Gray v Barr* [1971] 2 QB 554, 569 (Lord Denning MR); *R v Chief National Insurance Commissioner, ex parte Connor* [1981] 1 QB 758, 766 (Lord Lane CJ); *Re K (deceased)* [1985] Ch 85, 98 (Vinelott J); *Re H (deceased)* [1990] 1 FLR 441 (Peter Gibson J).

[171] See *Dunbar v Plant* [1998] Ch 412, 425 (Mummery LJ).

[172] *Re Giles* [1972] Ch 544; *Re Royse* [1985] Ch 22.   [173] *Church* [1966] 1 QB 59.

[174] *Dunbar v Plant* [1998] Ch 412, 425 (Mummery LJ). At least where the suicide occurred, as in that case. The modern offence of assisting or encouraging a suicide, contrary to the Coroners and Justice Act 2009, s 59, can be committed even where a suicide has not been committed, but it is unlikely that the defendant would acquire any rights which need to be forfeited in such circumstances.

[175] See p 552, below.

a power to modify the application of the rule where appropriate, it is not necessary to interpret the rule itself restrictively.

If the forfeiture rule is to apply to all forms of manslaughter it should also apply to other forms of unlawful killing, such as causing death by dangerous driving,[176] even though this does not require proof of intent to commit the crime. The forfeiture rule should also apply to other forms of liability relating to unlawful killing, such as where the defendant is an accessory to an unlawful killing.

(ii) Proving the Killer's Guilt

For the forfeiture rule to apply it must be shown that the killer was guilty of an unlawful killing. As a general rule, if the killer has been convicted of an unlawful killing in criminal proceedings, this conviction is admissible evidence in civil proceedings and will be sufficient proof of guilt for the purposes of those proceedings, though it is still possible for the killer to show in the civil proceedings that he or she was not guilty of the unlawful killing.[177] But if the defendant is acquitted in criminal proceedings, all this means is that the defendant's guilt was not proved beyond all reasonable doubt. It is still possible for the defendant to be deprived of benefits arising from the crime in civil proceedings where the standard of proof is the more easily satisfied test of the balance of probabilities.[178] So, in *Gray v Barr*,[179] although the killer had been acquitted of homicide, he was still denied an indemnity from his insurers by virtue of the forfeiture rule. This rule will even be applicable if the killer had never been tried for the particular offence which he or she is alleged to have committed.[180]

(iii) Application of the Forfeiture Rule

(1) Entitlement to the Benefit Must Be Caused by the Killing

For the forfeiture rule to be applicable to prevent the criminal from obtaining benefits it must be shown that the unlawful killing directly caused the criminal to become entitled to the benefits.[181] The usual 'but for' test of causation is applicable for these purposes. So it must be shown that the consequence of the killing is that the killer became entitled to benefits to which he or she would not otherwise have been entitled or that the killer had become entitled to benefits sooner than he or she would otherwise have done.[182] The forfeiture rule should be applicable where the killer has simply accelerated the acquisition of the benefit because, by killing the victim, the killer has deprived the victim of the opportunity to change his or her mind as to the destination of the benefit and has removed the possibility that the killer might have predeceased the victim. This is illustrated by *Re Edwards*,[183] a decision of the court of Victoria in Australia. The deceased had acted violently towards his wife. During a fight she stabbed and killed him. She was convicted of defensive homicide,[184] as she had no reasonable ground for believing that the conduct

---

[176] Contrary to the Road Traffic Act 1988, s 1 (as substituted by the Road Traffic Act 1991, s 1).

[177] Civil Evidence Act 1968, s 11.

[178] *Dunbar v Plant* [1998] Ch 412. The Court of Appeal affirmed that the standard for proving in civil proceedings that the killer was guilty of murder is the civil standard on the balance of probabilities: *Francisco v Diedrick*, The Times, 3 April 1998.

[179] [1971] QB 554.   [180] *Dunbar v Plant* [1998] Ch 412.

[181] *Cleaver v Mutual Reserve Fund Life Association* [1892] 1 QB 147, 156 (Fry LJ); *St John Shipping Corp v Joseph Rank Ltd* [1957] 1 QB 267, 292 (Devlin J). Cf *Re H (deceased)* [1990] 1 FLR 441, 442 where Peter Gibson J said that the forfeiture rule prevented the killer from benefiting directly or indirectly from the crime.

[182] TG Youdan, 'Acquisition of Property by Killing' (1973) 89 LQR 235.

[183] [2014] VSC 392.   [184] Crimes Act 1958, s 9AD.

was necessary to defend herself from serious injury or death. The deceased had left all his estate to his wife. If she did not survive him, it went to his mother-in-law and to a charity. The effect of the forfeiture rule was that the wife lost the estate and, because the gift overs failed because the wife had survived the deceased, the estate went to the deceased's daughter from his first marriage from whom he was estranged. McMillan J justified the forfeiture rule as an instantiation of a wider principle of public policy that a person should not be allowed to profit from their crime. She added that neither hardship on the defendant nor low moral culpability of the killer was a basis for disapplying the rule.[185]

In certain circumstances it will be difficult to show that the killer became entitled to benefits because of the unlawful killing. For example, if the killer unlawfully wounded the victim who, before he or she died, made a will in favour of the killer, it is not possible to say that the killer had become entitled to the benefits as a result of the killing, since the benefits accrued as a result of the victim's acts after the fatal injury had been caused. Similarly, if before death the victim had the opportunity to alter the devolution of his or her estate but failed to do so, it could be argued that the killer became entitled to benefits as a result of the victim's omission rather than the killing. But it would only be possible to conclude that the victim's omission had broken the chain of causation where the victim knew that he or she had the opportunity to alter the devolution of property and consciously failed to do so. In the absence of clear evidence to this effect, this will be a very difficult to prove.

There will be a point at which the killing is too remote a cause of the benefits accruing to the killer and in such circumstances the forfeiture rule will not operate to deprive the killer of such benefits. This is illustrated by a South African case[186] where a father killed his parents who had bequeathed property to his child, and the child died shortly after the parents had been killed. It was held that the father could inherit the property which the child had been bequeathed by its grandparents. Although it could be argued that, but for the father killing his parents, the child would not have received the property and so the father would not have been able to inherit, the killing had ceased to be an operative cause, since the father did not receive the property from his parents directly. Consequently, the forfeiture rule was held to be inapplicable.

(2) The Types of Benefits to Which the Forfeiture Rule May Apply

Where the forfeiture rule is applicable it may prevent the killer from obtaining a number of different benefits. For example, a killer is not entitled to benefit under the will[187] or intestacy[188] of the deceased. Similarly, a killer is not entitled to benefit from a life insurance policy on the victim's life.[189] The forfeiture rule has even been applied to deprive a killer of social welfare payments, such as a widow's pension, to which he or she would otherwise have been entitled.[190]

(3) Application of the Forfeiture Rule to Cases Where There is a Joint Tenancy

A particular problem arises in respect of the application of the forfeiture rule where there is a joint tenancy. For example, where a husband and wife are joint owners of the

---

[185] In England the rule would be modified under the Forfeiture Act. See p 552, below. No similar statute has been enacted in Victoria.

[186] *Ex p Steenkamp* (1952) (1) SA 744 (T).

[187] *Re Giles (deceased)* [1972] Ch 544.

[188] *Re Sigsworth* [1935] 1 Ch 89.

[189] *Cleaver v Mutual Reserve Fund Life Association* [1892] 1 QB 147. In *Gray v Barr* [1971] 2 QB 554 the forfeiture rule prevented the killer from claiming an indemnity from his insurers in respect of his liability for the unlawful death of the victim.

[190] *Chief National Insurance Commissioner, ex p Connor* [1981] 1 QB 758.

matrimonial home and the wife kills her husband, what happens to their respective interests in the property? The effect of a joint tenancy is that each joint tenant is assumed to own the whole of the legal interest over the relevant property, subject to the co-existing and co-extensive rights of the other joint tenants. This means that, if there are two joint tenants and one of them dies, the other is automatically entitled to the property absolutely. But, if one of the joint tenants dies as a result of being unlawfully killed by the other joint tenant, should the forfeiture rule come into operation and so prevent the killer from obtaining the property? This problem does not arise where there is a tenancy in common, since in such a case the property is owned equally by the tenants in common, so that if one tenant kills the other, the killer will not be deprived of the interest which he or she already possesses, but the forfeiture rule will prevent the killer from obtaining the interest of the deceased to which he or she might otherwise have been entitled.[191] But the application of the forfeiture rule is more complicated where there is a joint tenancy, essentially because the effect of killing the other joint tenant is that the killer's rights are enlarged rather than created as a result of the commission of the crime. There are two possible solutions to this problem.

First, the killer should be allowed to retain his or her beneficial interest in half of the property for life, but on his or her death the interest should revert to the beneficiaries of the victim's estate. This has the advantage that the killer's estate is eventually deprived of the beneficial interest in his or her half of the property and this is justified because, by killing the victim, the killer has deprived the victim of the chance of surviving the killer and so of becoming entitled to the whole of the property.[192] Consequently, it should be assumed that the victim would have survived the killer and so would have taken the property absolutely by virtue of survivorship. But this smacks of double punishment since, in addition to the punishment of the killer for the unlawful killing, the killer's estate will also be deprived of property to which the killer was already entitled before the crime was committed. There is no warrant for extending the operation of the forfeiture rule in this way. To make matters worse, the effect of this punishment of depriving the killer's estate of the property is that the killer's beneficiaries are effectively being punished for the killer's crime, whereas the killer was allowed to enjoy the benefit of half of the property.

The second, and preferable, solution to the problem is that the killer should be entitled to retain half of the beneficial interest in the property, but the other half should pass to the deceased's next of kin.[193] The best way of achieving this solution is as follows. By the usual rule of survivorship the entire legal interest in the property will be vested in the killer. The killing should, however, be treated as a severance of the joint tenancy so that the beneficial interest vests in the victim and the killer as tenants in common.[194] The doctrine of survivorship would apply so that the killer would hold the asset in which she already had a proprietary interest on constructive trust for the person who would otherwise be entitled to the estate of the deceased.[195] Where there are three joint tenants, one of whom kills the other, again the killer should not be deprived of an existing proprietary interest, but the principle of survivorship should still operate in favour of the other joint tenant, who would consequently obtain the victim's interest in the property.[196]

[191] *Davitt v Titcumb* [1990] Ch 110.
[192] G Jones, *Restitution in Public and Private Law* (London: Sweet and Maxwell, 1991), 69.
[193] *Re K (deceased)* [1985] Ch 85, 100 (Vinelott J).
[194] This solution was approved in *Dunbar v Plant* [1998] Ch 412, 418 (Mummery LJ).
[195] The solution adopted in the Irish case of *Cawley v Lillis* [2011] IEHC 515.
[196] See Street J in *Rasmanis v Jurewitsch* [1968] 2 NSWLR 166, 168.

The advantage of this solution to the problem of joint tenants who kill is that the forfeiture rule prevents the killer from benefiting from the commission of the crime without depriving the killer, or those claiming through him or her, of an existing proprietary right. Consequently, in the case of a wife who has killed her husband, the forfeiture rule should not be used to deprive her of her own interest in the matrimonial home, since this right did not arise as a result of the killing. Rather, she should be prevented from acquiring her deceased husband's share of the matrimonial home. The effect of this solution is still that the killer is deprived of an existing right, namely the right of a joint tenant to gain the entire estate should the other joint tenant predecease him or her, but this is entirely appropriate since, by virtue of the killing, any chance that the other joint tenant would have naturally predeceased the killer has been removed.

(4) Application of the Forfeiture Rule Where the Victim is a Life Tenant

A similar problem to that of killings by joint tenants arises where property has been settled on one person for life with remainder to another person, and that person unlawfully kills the life tenant. The effect of the death is that the killer is entitled to the estate immediately, but this would mean that the killer would profit from the crime, which is contrary to public policy.[197] But, if the forfeiture rule is invoked to prevent the killer from obtaining the property, he or she would be deprived of a proprietary interest which already existed before the killing. To reconcile these conflicting policies it is necessary to identify the true benefit which the killer obtains by unlawfully killing the life tenant. This benefit is that the killer accelerates the enjoyment of the life interest. The best method for preventing the killer from enjoying this benefit is by determining what the life tenant's life expectancy was and preventing the killer from enjoying the property until it was likely that the victim would have died naturally.[198] Consequently, the killer should hold the property on a constructive trust in favour of the victim's estate until the victim was expected to have died naturally.

(5) Claims of Third Parties

Whether third parties are able to claim benefits which accrue as a result of the commission of an unlawful killing turns on whether the third parties' claim relates to a benefit which accrued to the killer as a result of the crime. If the claim is so related it will be defeated by the forfeiture rule, because the effect of the rule is that the killer cannot obtain the benefit, and, if the killer does not have the benefit, the third party cannot claim it either.[199] Such benefits are tainted by the crime and so are caught by the forfeiture rule. If, however, the third party has an independent claim to the benefit, he or she will not be affected by the forfeiture rule because the claim is untainted by the crime.

The typical example of a case where the third party's claim is tainted by the crime is where personal representatives of the killer wish to claim benefits to which the killer would have been entitled had the forfeiture rule not been applicable. If the effect of the forfeiture rule is that the killer could not have obtained the benefits, neither should the personal representatives. This is illustrated by *Beresford v Royal Insurance Co*[200] where the personal representatives of the deceased who had committed suicide were unable to recover policy moneys from an insurance company, with which the deceased had obtained a life insurance policy. This was because at the time suicide was a crime and it was contrary to public policy that the

---

[197] *Cleaver v Mutual Reserve Fund Life Association* [1892] 1 QB 147, 157 (Fry LJ).

[198] Youdan, 'Acquisition of Property by Killing', 250.

[199] *Cleaver v Mutual Reserve Fund Life Association* [1892] 1 QB 147, 155 (Lord Esher MR); *In the Estate of Cunigunda (otherwise Cora) Crippen (deceased)* [1911] P 108, 112.

[200] [1938] AC 586.

personal representatives should recover the fruits of the crime, namely the money which was due as a result of the death of the suicide victim.

An example of a case where a third party was able to claim benefits because the claim was untainted by the commission of the crime is the decision of the Court of Appeal in *Cleaver v Mutual Reserve Fund Life Association*,[201] where a wife killed her husband who had a policy of life insurance with the defendants. The executors of the deceased claimed the sum insured from the defendants. Whilst it was admitted that the wife could not benefit from this money because of the forfeiture rule, this rule could not be relied on to prevent the defendants from paying the money to the deceased's executors. It was only once the executors had received this money that they would have been prohibited from paying it to the wife by virtue of the forfeiture rule.

(6) Allocation of Benefits Which Are Caught by the Forfeiture Rule

If the killer and those claiming through the killer are unable to obtain benefits by virtue of the forfeiture rule, such benefits should be considered to be retained by the victim's estate and so should be transferred to those people who are beneficiaries of that estate, except for the killer. Normally benefits, such as property, will pass to the victim's residuary legatee[202] or to those who are entitled to the property if the victim died intestate.[203] If the killer was the sole residuary legatee, the property should be distributed as though the victim had died intestate.[204] If the property was left to a class of beneficiaries, one of whom was the killer, the killer's share should be divided equally between the other members of the class.[205]

It has sometimes been suggested that, rather than the victim's estate passing to the next person in succession after the criminal, it should pass as *bona vacantia* to the Crown.[206] But there is no reason why the forfeiture rule should be used to deprive the successor of his or her rights to the estate, since these rights were not created by the commission of the crime, but rather arose from the law of intestacy or by virtue of the terms of the victim's will. In other words, the successor's rights are not tainted by the commission of the crime.

(7) Proprietary Implications of the Forfeiture Rule

A consequence of the principle that no criminal should profit from his or her crime is that title to property which would otherwise accrue to the criminal, or to those claiming through him or her, cannot pass. But this result is not free from difficulty. This is because in many cases, whether by virtue of statute or the common law, legal title should indeed pass to the criminal, and there is no provision in statute or the common law to the effect that an exception should be made where the passing of property is triggered by the criminal's own act. For the forfeiture rule to work it must be assumed that, for reasons of public policy, every legal rule contains an implied term to the effect that no criminal who, by the commission of the crime, has triggered the passing of property should be allowed to benefit from the crime.[207] It would be a much more honest response to apply the relevant statutory and judicial laws literally, without artificial interpretation. This would mean that legal title to property would pass to the criminal. But, because of the principle that no criminal should profit from his or her crime, Equity should ensure that, because of the killer's unconscionable conduct, an equitable interest in the property is

---

[201] [1892] 1 QB 147.   [202] As occurred in *Re Peacock* [1957] Ch 310.

[203] *Re Sigsworth* [1935] Ch 89.   [204] *Re Pollock* [1941] 1 Ch 219; *Re Callaway* [1956] Ch 559.

[205] *Re Peacock* [1957] Ch 310.   [206] See *Re Callaway* [1956] Ch 559.

[207] See, for example, *Re Royse* [1985] Ch 22 where it was assumed that the application of the Inheritance (Provision for Family and Dependants) Act 1975 was subject to the forfeiture rule, even though the Act makes no provision for this rule.

created in favour of the victim, with the result that the criminal should hold the property on a constructive trust for the victim's estate.[208] This would have the advantage that the operation of the forfeiture rule would not conflict with the clear words of statute and judicial precedent but would continue to fulfil the policy that no criminal should profit from his or her crime. This is the approach adopted in the United States, where Equity intervenes to prevent the killer from profiting from his or her unconscionable conduct by imposing a constructive trust.[209]

A consequence of this would be that, if the property which had been acquired by or through the criminal had been received by a third party, the beneficiaries of the victim of the crime would be able to recover the property from that third party, who would be bound by the beneficiaries' equitable proprietary interests. But this is subject to the qualification that the property could not be recovered from a third party who was a *bona fide* purchaser for value.[210]

The significance of the proprietary response is illustrated by *Re DWS*.[211] In this case a son murdered his parents, who died intestate. Their grandchild claimed that he was entitled to his grandparents' estate because his father was not entitled to his parents' estate by virtue of the forfeiture rule. However, the Administration of Estates Act 1925 prevents a person from succeeding to the estate of an intestate person if his or her parent is still alive. Consequently, the Court of Appeal held by a majority[212] that the grandson could not succeed to his grandparents' estate, which consequently went to collateral relations. This is a particularly unfair result which could have been avoided by concluding that, rather than the forfeiture rule operating to prevent the father from succeeding to the estate at all, it should only have prevented him from succeeding to the estate beneficially, so that he should have held the estate on constructive trust for his son. This solution would be consistent with the legal realities of the case and the words of the statute: legal title to the parents' estate passed to the murderer, but because he had acquired those rights unconscionably, he should have held the property on constructive trust for his son. An alternative solution has now been adopted by Parliament. By the Estates of Deceased Persons (Forfeiture Rule and Law of Succession) Act 2011, the Administration of Estates Act 1925 and the Wills Act 1837 are amended, so that a murderer who has, for example, killed a parent will be deemed to have died immediately before the death of the parent. It follows that the victims' estate in a case such as *Re DWS* would pass to the person next entitled either under the will or on an intestacy, namely, in that case, the murderer's own child, bypassing the murderer.

(iv) The Forfeiture Act 1982

The inflexible common law forfeiture rule was modified by the Forfeiture Act 1982. Although this Act does not apply where the defendant has committed murder,[213] in every other case where the forfeiture rule has precluded a person who has unlawfully killed another person from acquiring any interest in property, the application of that rule may be

---

[208] Youdan, 'Acquisition of Property by Killing', 253. This would be consistent with Lord Browne-Wilkinson's interpretation of the constructive trust in *Westdeutsche Landesbank Girozentrale v Islington LBC* [1996] AC 669, 716. See p 595, below.

[209] *Restatement Third on Restitution and Unjust Enrichment*, para 45: the so-called 'slayer rule', but not where a statute prevents the killer from acquiring legal title, in which case the property passes to the person with the paramount equitable claim.

[210] See Chapter 23.   [211] [2001] Ch 568.

[212] Sedley LJ held that the estate should pass to the Crown as *bona vacantia* in the hope that the Crown would transfer all or some of it to the grandson.   [213] Forfeiture Act 1982, s 5.

modified by order of the court.[214] Obviously this power to modify the forfeiture rule will be relevant only where the forfeiture rule is applicable in the first place, so it remains necessary to consider the application of the forfeiture rule at common law. But the Forfeiture Act is not automatically applicable simply because the forfeiture rule applies. The Act will only apply where the killer has committed an unlawful killing either as principal or accessory,[215] but it does not apply to inchoate offences which relate to unlawful killing, such as attempts to kill the victim. The Act only applies where somebody is prevented by the forfeiture rule from acquiring an interest in property. The notion of 'interest in property' includes any beneficial interest in property which the offender would have acquired under the will of the deceased or on his or her intestacy,[216] and property which was held on trust for any person and which the offender would have acquired as a result of the death of the deceased.[217] This would cover the case where one joint tenant kills the other and, subject to the operation of the forfeiture rule, would have obtained the property absolutely by virtue of the principle of survivorship. The definition of 'interest in property' means that the Act does not apply to benefits which would have been obtained under an insurance policy had not the forfeiture rule been applicable, save where the proceeds of the policy are held on trust for the killer.[218]

The court will modify the forfeiture rule only if it is satisfied that, having regard to the conduct of the killer and of the deceased and of any other circumstances of the case which appear to be material, the justice of the case requires the rule to be modified.[219] The forfeiture rule may be disapplied completely[220] or it may be modified in part.[221] In exercising their discretion as to whether or not the forfeiture rule should be modified judges must not seek to do justice between the parties to the dispute but should rather consider whether the culpability of the defendant justifies the strict application of the rule.[222] In *Dunbar v Plant*[223] Mummery LJ said that:

> The court is entitled to take into account a whole range of circumstances relevant to the discretion, quite apart from the conduct of the offender and the deceased: the relationship between them; the degree of moral culpability for what has happened; the nature and gravity of the offence; the intentions of the deceased; the size of the estate and the value of the property in dispute; the financial position of the offender; and the moral claims and wishes of those who would be entitled to take the property on the application of the forfeiture rule.

The application of the Forfeiture Act is well illustrated by the decision of the Court of Appeal in *Re K (deceased)*,[224] in which a wife, having killed her husband, was convicted of manslaughter for which she received a sentence of two years' probation. This lenient sentence was justified because of the particular circumstances of the killing. The wife had been abused by her husband for a number of years. On the day of the killing her husband had beaten her again and, intending to frighten him away, she picked up a loaded shotgun, released the safety catch and aimed it at him. The gun accidentally went off and killed him. The wife claimed that she was entitled to an interest under her husband's will and was also entitled to the matrimonial home. The Court, having accepted that the forfeiture rule was applicable, held that the wife should be granted complete relief from the forfeiture of all

---

[214] Ibid, s 2(1). The Act applies regardless of when the unlawful killing occurred: s 7(4). It applies even though the killer has not been convicted of an offence: *Dunbar v Plant* [1998] Ch 412.

[215] Forfeiture Act 1982, s 1(2).　　[216] Ibid, s 2(4)(a).　　[217] Ibid, s 2(4)(b).

[218] *Dunbar v Plant* [1998] Ch 412.　　[219] Forfeiture Act 1982, s 2(2).

[220] Ibid, s 2(1). See, for example, *Dunbar v Plant* [1998] Ch 412.

[221] Forfeiture Act 1982, s 2(5). See *Re K (deceased)* [1986] Ch 180.　　[222] *Dunbar v Plant* [1998] Ch 412.

[223] Ibid, 427–8.　　[224] [1986] Ch 180.

the benefits which had accrued to her on the death of her husband. A number of factors were considered to be relevant to the exercise of the court's discretion.

(1)   The most important factor was the degree of moral culpability of the wife in committing the crime; her offence was considered to be at the least serious end of the spectrum of manslaughter offences. This was because she had been provoked to kill her husband and this had been reflected in the sentence of probation which she had received.

(2)   The moral culpability of the wife and of her husband were compared. Whilst the wife had been loyal to her husband, it was considered to be relevant that he had abused her for a number of years.

(3)   The relative financial position of the wife as compared with the other people who were entitled under the husband's will was taken into account. The court stressed that the husband had made appropriate provision for his wife and was under no moral duty to make provision for anybody else.

(4)   The conduct of the other beneficiaries under the husband's will was also considered, particularly since a number of them had confirmed, after the death of the husband, that the terms of the husband's will should be respected, despite the potential application of the forfeiture rule.[225]

Further, in *Dunbar v Plant*[226] the Court of Appeal exercised its discretion to disapply the forfeiture rule completely in a case where the defendant had assisted and encouraged the suicide of her fiancée, where he had killed himself pursuant to a suicide pact. It was held that the forfeiture rule should not be applied to prevent the defendant from obtaining benefits from the deceased's estate for a number of reasons. The most important was that the nature of the defendant's crime was such that she had not received any penal sanction for it, consequently her culpability did not justify the application of the rule. Also the deceased had intended that the relevant benefits, namely the proceeds of an insurance policy and his interest in their house, should be received by the defendant on his death.[227]

By virtue of the enactment of the Forfeiture Act 1982 the injustice which arose from the strict adherence to the principle that no criminal could benefit from the commission of a criminal offence has been alleviated to some extent. But that Act is not totally satisfactory. In particular, it should be extended to cases of murder, since there are some cases of murder where the killer's true culpability does not warrant the strict application of the forfeiture rule. For example, in certain cases of mercy killing, where one spouse kills the other to alleviate suffering, there is no reason why the killer should be prevented from obtaining benefits which would otherwise have accrued to him or her on the death of the victim. Different murders can involve different degrees of culpability and this should be reflected in the way the forfeiture rule is applied in such cases. It is also most unfortunate that the Act does not apply to relieve the forfeiture of benefits which would have been received under an insurance policy had not the forfeiture rule been applicable. Most importantly, the Forfeiture Act places the judiciary in a particularly difficult position, since it provides no assistance as to how the judges' discretion should be exercised. In fact, in all reported cases concerning the application of the Act the judges have disapplied the forfeiture rule completely rather than modify the application of the rule.[228]

---

[225]   See also *Re H (deceased)* [1990] 1 FLR 441.   [226]   [1998] Ch 412.

[227]   Mummery LJ dissented on the ground that weight should be given to the moral claims and wishes of the deceased's family.

[228]   The only case where the forfeiture rule was modified rather than disapplied was the decision of the trial judge in *Dunbar v Plant*, but the Court of Appeal overruled this decision. Other cases where the rule was disapplied completely include *Re K* [1986] Ch 180 and *Re S* [1996] 1 WLR 235.

PART IV

PROPRIETARY RESTITUTIONARY CLAIMS

21

ESTABLISHING PROPRIETARY RESTITUTIONARY CLAIMS

1. THE NATURE OF PROPRIETARY RESTITUTIONARY CLAIMS

The examination of the law of restitution so far has concentrated on two different principles on which restitutionary claims can be founded: unjust enrichment and wrong-doing. This Part will examine the third and final principle on which such claims may be based, namely the vindication of the claimant's property rights, a principle which was recognized by the House of Lords in *Foskett v McKeown*.[1]

(A) QUESTIONS OF TERMINOLOGY

A fundamental distinction should be drawn between proprietary claims and proprietary remedies.[2] All restitutionary claims which are founded on the vindication of the claimant's proprietary rights[3] are properly classified as proprietary claims, since they are dependent solely upon the identification and protection of proprietary rights. But the restitutionary remedies by virtue of which these property rights are vindicated are not necessarily proprietary remedies, since, depending on the particular circumstances of the case, the appropriate remedy may either be proprietary or personal. [4] If a proprietary remedy is awarded the claimant may recover particular property,[5] whereas if a personal restitutionary remedy is awarded the claimant will recover only the value of particular property.[6] Personal remedies operate against one person, the defendant, who received the claimant's property, whereas proprietary remedies operate against the property which the defendant has and in which the claimant has a proprietary interest. The key distinction between the two types of remedy, as recognized by Goode, is that personal remedies are founded on the *obligation* to pay, whereas proprietary remedies are founded on the continuing *ownership* of the relevant asset.[7]

---

[1] [2001] 1 AC 102.

[2] This distinction was recognized by Millett LJ in *Trustee of the Property of FC Jones and Sons (a firm) v Jones* [1997] Ch 159, 168.

[3] Such a description of the underlying principle does have some judicial support. See, for example, *Tinsley v Milligan* [1994] 1 AC 340, 368 (Lord Lowry); *Foskett v McKeown* [2001] 1 AC 102, 129 (Lord Millett).

[4] See *Boscawen v Bajwa* [1996] 1 WLR 328, 334 (Millett LJ).

[5] For discussion of this and other proprietary restitutionary remedies, see p 632, below.

[6] See p 641, below.

[7] RM Goode, 'Ownership and Obligation in Commercial Transactions' (1987) 103 LQR 433.

(B) THE NATURE OF THE RESTITUTIONARY REMEDY

The remedies which are available to claimants to enable them to vindicate proprietary rights may either be personal or proprietary, though in each case the remedy is restitutionary since it enables the claimant either to recover the value of the property or to assert a proprietary interest in the property received or its product or substitute.[8]

(i) Personal Restitutionary Remedies

The personal restitutionary remedies[9] which are available where the claimant seeks to vindicate a proprietary right include recovery of the value of money received by the defendant under the Common Law action of money had and received[10] and the equitable remedy of account of profits.[11] Where the claimant seeks a personal remedy he or she only needs to show that, when the defendant received the relevant property, the claimant had a proprietary interest in it. The fact that the defendant has dissipated the property after its receipt without acquiring a substitute does not defeat the claim, though dissipation of the property may enable the defendant to plead the defence of change of position.[12]

(ii) Proprietary Restitutionary Remedies

The proprietary restitutionary remedies,[13] sometimes known as remedies *in rem*, enable the claimant to assert property rights over property which is held by the defendant. There are two types of proprietary restitutionary remedy: first, remedies by virtue of which the claimant can recover the property which is held by the defendant; secondly, remedies which recognize that the claimant has a security interest in property which is held by the defendant. Proprietary restitutionary remedies can only be awarded if the claimant continues to have a proprietary interest in property which is held by the defendant at the time the claimant commences the restitutionary claim. Proprietary remedies are not concerned with returning the value of what the defendant has received to the claimant, but they are concerned simply with the assertion of proprietary rights against particular property. It follows that, if the defendant dissipated the property which he or she had received before the claimant brought his or her claim, the claimant will often be forced to rely on personal remedies. Proprietary restitutionary remedies may, however, still be awarded even though the specific property has been dissipated, so long as the defendant retains a product of the property or a substitute for it.[14]

Proprietary restitutionary remedies have three main advantages over personal restitutionary remedies.

(1) Where the defendant has become bankrupt or insolvent a personal remedy may be useless. This is because the effect of a personal remedy is to create a debt owed by the defendant to the claimant. Until the debt has been paid the claimant is a creditor of the defendant, but he or she will not have any security interest in the defendant's property. Consequently, the claimant's claim for payment will not be distinguished from those claims of the other general creditors of the defendant as regards the distribution of the defendant's assets. This will not be a hardship if the defendant has sufficient assets to pay off all the creditors. But, if the defendant has insufficient assets to pay off all the creditors, the claimant may not receive the full

---

[8] See *Boscawen v Bajwa* [1996] 1 WLR 328, 334 (Millett LJ).   [9] See p 641, below.

[10] As occurred in *Lipkin Gorman (a firm) v Karpnale Ltd* [1991] 2 AC 548.

[11] See p 424, above.   [12] See Chapter 25.   [13] See p 632, below.

[14] Whether the claimant can assert a proprietary right against a product of or substitute for the claimant's original property depends upon the application of the tracing rules. See p 607, below.

amount which is due, and may not receive anything at all. This is because, when assets are distributed upon the debtor's insolvency or bankruptcy, they are distributed according to a list of priorities. Unsecured creditors will not receive anything until the claims of creditors with proprietary rights and preferential creditors have been satisfied and the expenses of the insolvency proceedings paid. Consequently, if the claimant can show that he or she has a proprietary interest in some of the assets in the defendant's possession, the claimant will rank above the general unsecured creditors in the distribution of the defendant's assets and, subject to the nature of the proprietary interest, the claimant's claim is more likely to be satisfied.[15] In particular, in those cases where it is clear that the defendant never received title to the relevant property, that property should not form part of the general pool of assets which are available for distribution amongst the defendant's general creditors. For, where the defendant has never enjoyed beneficial ownership of the property in question, there is no reason why his or her creditors should benefit from the defendant's receipt of the property in which the claimant had retained a proprietary interest.

(2) A second advantage of some proprietary remedies arises where the property which has been obtained by the defendant has increased in value. In such circumstances, the claimant would clearly prefer to assert his or her rights against the property itself and so gain the benefit of the increased value. Where, however, the property has fallen in value, the claimant will wish to claim a personal restitutionary remedy which would be assessed by reference to the value of the property at the time it was received by the defendant.

(3) A third advantage of proprietary remedies is that they relate to the property received rather than the person who receives them. Consequently, a proprietary remedy is available even where the relevant property has been transferred to a third party who may have no reason to think that the party who transferred the property had no legal or equitable title to the property.[16]

(C) THE NATURE OF THE CLAIM

When the claimant wishes to vindicate his or her proprietary rights, he or she simply needs to establish that, when the defendant received the property in question, the claimant had an interest in it, either legal or equitable. The claimant may have such a proprietary interest either because the nature of the transfer to the defendant means that title to the property did not pass to the defendant or because the circumstances existing at the time of the transfer is such that a proprietary interest is created by operation of law.

(i) Distinguishing Between Vindication of Property Rights and Reversal of Unjust Enrichment

The most important feature of the action to vindicate property rights is that it forms part of the law of property and has nothing to do with the principle of reversing the defendant's unjust enrichment.[17] Consequently, it is not necessary to show that the defendant has

---

[15] The extent of the priority which the claimant will gain over other creditors will depend upon the type of proprietary remedy which is awarded. See p 632, below.

[16] Save where the recipient provided value for this receipt. See Chapter 23.

[17] *Foskett v McKeown* [2001] 1 AC 102, 109 (Lord Browne-Wilkinson), 115 (Lord Hoffmann), 118 (Lord Hope), and 129 (Lord Millett).

been unjustly enriched at the claimant's expense. Once the claimant has shown that the defendant has property, whether it be chattels, land, intellectual property rights or, most importantly, money, in which the claimant had a proprietary interest at the time of receipt, nothing else needs to be proved to establish the claimant's cause of action. If the defendant has the claimant's property, he or she should return it, or its value, to the claimant.

A key example of the significance of this analysis is the decision of the House of Lords in *Lipkin Gorman (a firm) v Karpnale*,[18] where Cass, one of the partners of the claimant firm of solicitors, stole money from the claimant's client account and gambled with it at the defendant's casino. The claimant brought a restitutionary claim for money had and received against the defendant. Although the House of Lords acknowledged that the claim succeeded by virtue of the defendant's unjust enrichment,[19] the elements of the unjust enrichment formula were not considered. The reason why the House of Lords considered that the casino should make restitution was because the money which had been stolen from the client account belonged to the claimant firm of solicitors. So Lord Templeman recognized that[20] 'in a claim for money had and received by a thief, the plaintiff victim must show that money belonging to him was paid by the thief to the defendant and that the defendant was unjustly enriched and remained unjustly enriched'.

The claim should properly be analysed as being based on the vindication of the firm's property rights in the money and was effectively analysed in this way by both Lords Templeman and Goff. Lord Templeman's analysis was rather unsophisticated. He asserted that the claim depended on the defendant's retention of the money, whereas Lord Goff emphasized that the claim was a personal claim which turned on whether the club had received money in which the firm had a continuing proprietary interest at the time of receipt. But Lord Goff acknowledged that the claimant needed to establish a basis on which it was entitled to the money and it could do so by showing that the money was its legal property. Particular reliance was placed on the decision of Lord Mansfield in *Clarke v Shee and Johnson*,[21] where the claimant recovered money which had been stolen by his servant, who had used it to buy lottery tickets. The claimant successfully sued the defendants, who ran the lottery. Crucially, Lord Mansfield specifically recognized that the claimant sued 'for his identified property'.[22] The significance of this to Lord Goff was that the claim was 'founded simply on the fact that, as Lord Mansfield said, the third party cannot in conscience retain the money—or, as we say nowadays, for the third party to retain the money would result in his unjust enrichment at the expense of the owner of the money'.[23]

Now it is true that Lord Goff used the unjust enrichment principle to justify restitution in that case, but he did not need to do so, because the claim turned on the vindication of a property right. That is why in *Lipkin Gorman* itself, rather than searching for a ground of restitution, Lord Goff focused on showing that the defendant had received money which belonged to the firm. But establishing the claimant's proprietary right to the money received by the defendant was not straightforward. Lord Goff recognized that the firm did not have any proprietary rights in the money which had been taken from the client bank account because Cass as partner had authority to draw money from the account. However, he concluded that, since the bank owed the money to the claimant, the claimant owned a chose in action at law which it could identify in the cash drawn from the bank account by the solicitor and into the money which had been received by the defendant.

---

[18] [1991] 2 AC 548.   [19] See p 48, above.
[20] *Lipkin Gorman (a firm) v Karpnale* [1991] 2 AC 548, 559–60.   [21] (1774) 1 Cowp 197, 98 ER 1041.
[22] Ibid, 200–1; 1043.   [23] *Lipkin Gorman (a firm) v Karpnale* [1991] 2 AC 548, 572.

But this does not satisfactorily deal with the fact that the money drawn by Cass belonged to him because he had authority to draw on the account. Whilst his act of drawing the money constituted theft, because he had interfered with another's property rights dishonestly, this did not render the withdrawal unauthorized. Lord Goff's analysis is unconvincing and he seemed almost too ready to reach the desired result of allowing restitution but without providing convincing reasons, especially as to how it was possible to identify a continuing proprietary interest in money which clearly belonged to the thief.[24]

There was a further difficulty in establishing a proprietary claim, since the money drawn from the client account might have been mixed with Cass's own money when he gambled at the club, so that it would have lost its identity. This is because tracing at Law is defeated by mixing in a fund.[25] But counsel for the defendant had conceded that title to the money would not have been lost had it been mixed. This is a very odd concession. Had it not been made it is likely that the claim for restitution would have failed or, perhaps more likely, the House of Lords would have taken the opportunity to rule that it was possible to trace at Law even through a mixture.[26]

There was, in fact, an alternative proprietary claim available to the firm, but this had not been pursued. Although the effect of Cass having authority to draw money meant that legal title to the money passed to him, his reason for doing so was such that he would have been acting in breach of fiduciary duty,[27] so the money would have been held on constructive trust for the claimant, which would have been able to trace it in Equity to the defendant, since equitable tracing is not defeated by mixing.[28] But counsel for the firm did not make such a claim, presumably because the personal claim would have been for what is now known as unconscionable receipt,[29] which would have required proof of fault on the part of the defendant at the time of receipt and would have been difficult to establish on the facts.[30]

There was, consequently, no need to establish a claim founded on the reversal of the defendant's unjust enrichment, since the claim was founded on the vindication of the claimant's property rights and had nothing to do with unjust enrichment.[31] It is for this reason that no ground of restitution was identified by the House of Lords, even though a number of commentators have sought to identify one from the facts of the case.[32] In the light of this conclusion that *Lipkin Gorman* has nothing to do with unjust enrichment and everything to do with vindication of proprietary rights, it is ironic that the case has become the leading case on the recognition of unjust enrichment in English law.

That vindication of proprietary rights is distinct from the unjust enrichment principle was recognized by the House of Lords in *Foskett v McKeown*,[33] which is the seminal case

---

[24] That a thief can be guilty of a crime whilst still obtaining property rights has been explicitly recognized by the House of Lords: *R v Hinks* [2001] AC 241.

[25] *Trustee of the Property of FC Jones v Jones* [1997] Ch 159, 168 (Millett LJ). See further p 615, below.

[26] See p 629, below.

[27] As Lord Goff acknowledged: [1991] 2 AC 548, 572. See p 488, above.

[28] See further p 618, below.   [29] See p 645, below.

[30] Note also LD Smith, 'Simplifying Claims to Traceable Proceeds' (2009) 125 LQR 338, who argues that Common Law actions for money had and received in respect of the proceeds of an unauthorized disposition could be analysed as a Common Law claim for money held on trust. This might mean that the solicitor held the money on trust for the firm, which would explain how the firm could trace to the property received by the club, but it would still depend on the solicitor's withdrawal of the money being unauthorized.

[31] See also *Macmillan Inc v Bishopsgate Investment Trust plc (No 3)* [1996] 1 WLR 387. See GJ Virgo, 'Reconstructing the Law of Restitution' (1996) 10 TLI 36.

[32] See PBH Birks, 'The English Recognition of Unjust Enrichment' [1991] LMCLQ 473, 483 and E McKendrick, 'Restitution, Misdirected Funds and Change of Position' (1992) 55 MLR 377.

[33] [2001] 1 AC 102. See further p 568, below.

of proprietary restitutionary claims. In *Foskett* the claimants claimed an equitable proprietary interest in the death benefit paid under a life insurance policy, which had been
taken out by the claimants' trustee on his own life. The trustee had stolen over £20,000
from the trust, which he used to pay two of the five annual premiums for the policy. The
trustee committed suicide and his children received a lump sum payment of £1 million.
The claimants recovered £400,000 of this, on the basis that they had contributed two-fifths
of the premiums. The real significance of this case is that it was held that the claim did not
depend on establishing unjust enrichment. As Lord Millett said:[34]

> The transmission of a claimant's property rights from one asset to its traceable proceeds is
> part of our law of property, not of the law of unjust enrichment. There is no 'unjust factor'
> to justify restitution (unless 'want of title' be one, which makes the point). The claimant
> succeeds if at all by virtue of his own title, not to reverse unjust enrichment.

In other words, it was not necessary to show that the defendant had received money at the
claimant's expense and that the case fell within one of the recognized grounds of
restitution. It was sufficient that the defendant had received property in which the
claimant had an equitable proprietary interest, even though this interest related to
different money from that which had been stolen from the claimant. The approach of
the House of Lords was rigorously principled. As Lord Browne-Wilkinson said:[35]

> The crucial factor in this case is to appreciate that the [claimants] are claiming a proprietary
> interest in the policy moneys and that such proprietary interest is not dependent on any
> discretion vested in the court. Nor is the purchaser's claim based on unjust enrichment. It is
> based on the assertion by the purchasers of their equitable proprietary interest in identified
> property.

A number of commentators have rejected this analysis of proprietary restitutionary
claims, most notably Birks.[36] He did accept that, where the claimant wishes to recover an
asset which belonged to him or her from the start, the claim falls within the law of
property and has nothing to do with unjust enrichment. Where, however, the claimant
wishes to recover an asset which is different from that which initially belonged to the
claimant, it is necessary to show that the claimant has a right to such substitute property
and, Birks asserted, the claimant could only establish that by means of the unjust
enrichment principle and not simply by the assertion of property rights. Crucial to Birks's
argument is the need to distinguish clearly between events and responses and to identify
an event before the appropriate response can be considered. The law, he asserted,
recognizes four events, namely consent, wrongs, unjust enrichment, and other events.
He argued that the vindication of property rights is not an event and concluded that
restitution could not be a response to it. Rather, unjust enrichment is an event to which
restitution is the only response, so, to obtain a right to the substitute property, the
claimant must show that the defendant had been unjustly enriched at the claimant's
expense. At the heart of the debate about the legitimacy of the vindication of property
rights principle is a basic question: how can a claimant bring a proprietary claim against
substitute property when the claimant has never had an interest in that property originally? Is it sufficient to conclude that the substitute property represents the original
property by virtue of principles of property law, as the House of Lords concluded in
Foskett v McKeown, or must the unjust enrichment principle be used?

---

[34] *Foskett v McKeown* [2001] 1 AC 102, 127.   [35] Ibid, 108.

[36] PBH Birks, *Unjust Enrichment* (2nd edn, Oxford: Oxford University Press, 2005), 36. See also PBH Birks,
'Property, Unjust Enrichment and Tracing' [2001] CLP 231; AS Burrows, *The Law of Restitution* (3rd edn, Oxford:
Oxford University Press, 2011), ch 16; LD Smith, *The Law of Tracing* (Oxford: Clarendon Press, 1997), 300.

There is a further question: why does this matter? In practice, the method of analysis is often irrelevant because the same result will be achieved. But there may be substantive consequences depending on the analysis adopted, especially as regards the application of the defence of change of position, which might only be relevant if the unjust enrichment analysis was adopted.[37] Further, what needs to be proved to establish the claim will vary depending on the analysis which is adopted. Finally, the debate about the validity of the vindication of property rights principle reveals a great deal about the nature of the law of restitution, property law, and the appropriate method for classifying claims, particularly the relevance of distinguishing between events and responses.

Despite the rigorous arguments of those who prefer to use the unjust enrichment analysis to explain how rights can be asserted in substitute property, that principle is in fact irrelevant and misleading. The approach of the House of Lords in *Foskett v McKeown* was correct for the following reasons:

(1) Much of the recent debate about the legitimacy of the principle of vindication of property rights has got stuck on the question of language. Birks was obviously right to state that 'vindication of property rights' is not an 'event'.[38] It is a principle which is simply not framed in those terms. But the principle could be rebranded into an event if it is necessary to do so. For example, the event could be that the defendant has interfered with the claimant's property rights in some way. There are then a number of responses to that event, including compensation, but the most important involves the award of gain-based remedies, either personal or proprietary.[39]

(2) There is no case which explicitly recognizes that property rights can derive from the defendant's unjust enrichment.[40] Birks[41] considered that *Foskett v McKeown* was such a case, even though the majority judgments clearly contradict this, and that there are other cases which are consistent with this approach, including *Sinclair v Brougham*,[42] but this has been overruled,[43] and *Chase Manhattan Bank v Israel-British Bank*,[44] but this case has been reinterpreted by the House of Lords.[45] Further, neither of these cases explicitly recognizes that property rights can derive from unjust enrichment. There is simply no empirical evidence to support the assertion that property rights can derive from the defendant's unjust enrichment.

(3) Birks[46] and others[47] have wished to draw a distinction between so-called 'pure property rights', which are subsisting and usually arise by the consent of the parties through a contract or declaration of trust, and restitutionary property rights, which

---

[37] See p 696, below.

[38] Birks, 'Property, Unjust Enrichment and Tracing', 239; Birks, *Unjust Enrichment* (2nd edn), 35.

[39] See RB Grantham and CEF Rickett, 'Trust Money as an Unjust Enrichment: A Misconception' [1998] LMCLQ 514, 519.

[40] The decision of the House of Lords in *Banque Financière de la Cité v Parc (Battersea) Ltd* [1999] 1 AC 221 perhaps comes closest to recognizing this, since the remedy of subrogation was justified on the ground that it reversed the defendant's unjust enrichment arising from mistake, although the remedy is properly characterized as personal rather than proprietary. See p 636, below. Further, this decision was delivered before that of the same court in *Foskett v McKeown* [2001] 1 AC 102.

[41] Birks, *Unjust Enrichment* (2nd edn), 34–6.   [42] [1914] AC 398.

[43] *Westdeutsche Landesbank Girozentrale v Islington LBC* [1996] AC 669.   [44] [1981] Ch 105.

[45] *Westdeutsche Landesbank Girozentrale v Islington LBC* [1996] AC 669. See p 598, below.

[46] See especially Birks, *Unjust Enrichment* (2nd edn), ch 8.

[47] See D Fox, 'Legal Title as a Ground of Restitutionary Liability' [2000] RLR 465; AS Burrows, 'Proprietary Restitution: Unmasking Unjust Enrichment' (2001) 117 LQR 412, 417; R Chambers, 'Two Kinds of Enrichment' in R Chambers, C Mitchell, and J Penner (eds), *Philosophical Foundations of the Law of Unjust Enrichment* (Oxford: Oxford University Press, 2009), ch 9.

arise by operation of law in substitute property. The effect of this distinction is that, if the claimant wishes to recover the property in which he or she has a subsisting proprietary interest, then restitution is a matter for the law of property, whereas, if the claimant wishes to recover substitute property, this will depend on the claimant establishing that the defendant has been unjustly enriched. But no convincing reason is given as to why we should divide up proprietary rights in this way. Such a division is highly artificial because, regardless of the reason for the existence of the right, all these rights are proprietary and may trigger restitutionary remedies.[48] Whether or not the claimant has a proprietary right is a matter for the law of property and it is only once such rights have been recognized that the question of restitutionary relief becomes relevant. If we create artificial distinctions between pure proprietary rights and restitutionary proprietary rights the danger is that we ignore the fundamental policy of the law which is to protect property rights, regardless of how the right arose.

(4) If the unjust enrichment principle is to be used to enable claims to be made against substitute property, the elements[49] of that principle would need to be established in the usual way. The enrichment element will be relatively easy to satisfy, since property is a benefit which generally cannot be subjectively devalued, save where the defendant has given full value for receipt of the property.[50] But the establishment of the other two elements causes real problems, which can be avoided if the vindication of property rights principle is used instead.

First, where the claimant wishes to recover substitute property from the defendant it will necessarily follow that the enrichment received by the defendant cannot have been received directly at the claimant's expense, since substitute property can only have been received indirectly from the claimant. Although it has been recognized that the 'at the expense' requirement can be satisfied by indirect receipt,[51] this is exceptional and only where there is a close causal connection between the transfer from the claimant and the defendant's receipt, such that the defendant can be considered to have received the enrichment from the claimant as a matter of economic reality.[52] Whilst this test might be considered to be satisfied where the defendant has received substitute property, or has received property transferred via a third party,[53] this will not necessarily be the case and, anyway, adds a further level of complexity in determining what economic reality means in this context.

Secondly, although some commentators have suggested that the applicable grounds of restitution are the same as those which were discussed in Part II,[54] if the established grounds of restitution for unjust enrichment are to be used to show that the receipt of the enrichment was unjust, this causes problems both of interpretation and as regards the reach of proprietary claims. For example, if the claimant transferred property by mistake, should the usual test of a causative mistake be adopted? If it is, proprietary relief will tend to give the claimant excessive protection, because the consequences of such relief include giving the claimant priority over the defendant's other creditors and enabling the claimant to claim increases in the value of property. Why should a claimant who made a simple spontaneous mistake be allowed such proprietary protection? If a more restrictive test of

---

[48] See RB Grantham, 'Doctrinal Bases for the Recognition of Proprietary Rights' (1996) 16 OJLS 561, 574.

[49] See p 9, above.　　　[50] See *Foskett v McKeown* [2001] 1 AC 102, 129 (Lord Millett).

[51] See p 107, above.

[52] *Investment Trust Companies v Commissioner of Her Majesty's Revenue and Customs* [2015] EWCA Civ 82.

[53] As in *Relfo Ltd v Varsani* [2014] EWCA Civ 360, [2015] 1 BCLC 14. See p 625, below.

[54] To the extent that he recognized different grounds of restitution within the super-ground of absence of basis, this was the approach of Birks: *Unjust Enrichment* (2nd edn).

mistake is to be adopted, a reason would need to be identified to distinguish between different types of mistake to determine which ones will trigger proprietary relief, and it is surely far better to do this explicitly within the established principles of the law of property. But, in many cases where a claimant wishes to recover substitute property, the established grounds of restitution will not be applicable. Where, for example, property has been misappropriated, it will not have been transferred as the result of a mistake, duress or exploitation because the claimant will be unaware of the misappropriation. So what ground of restitution would be applicable? Birks has suggested that absence of consent should be the ground,[55] Burrows talks about powerlessness or ignorance,[56] and Goff and Jones refer to lack of consent and want of authority,[57] but no case has recognized such grounds of restitution in the proprietary context. This absence of recognition of grounds of restitution relevant to restitutionary proprietary claims is not surprising, because it is not necessary to rely on the unjust enrichment principle at all.[58] It is sufficient that the defendant has received property in which the claimant has a proprietary interest at the time of its receipt, where the claimant seeks a personal restitutionary remedy, or continues to have a proprietary interest in it, where the claimant seeks a proprietary restitutionary remedy.

(ii) The Relationship Between Proprietary Restitutionary Claims and Restitution for Wrongs

There are certain wrongs which are dependent on proof that the defendant has interfered with the claimant's proprietary rights, particularly the torts of conversion and trespass. Should restitutionary claims relating to such torts be treated as founded on the wrong or as involving the vindication of proprietary rights? This is a difficult question, but the preferable view is that such claims are best treated as founded on the wrong.[59] This is for two reasons: first, because the wrong itself must be specifically pleaded, and secondly, because the remedy which is available is not necessarily restitutionary, but may involve the award of compensatory damages. This is a characteristic of a claim founded on wrongdoing rather than vindication of proprietary rights, for which the remedy must be restitutionary.

Where the claimant seeks a restitutionary remedy in respect of a wrong committed by the defendant the remedy will usually be personal. There are, however, cases where the defendant has been awarded a proprietary restitutionary remedy and the event which triggered this was a wrong.[60] In such cases there is clearly an overlap between restitution for wrongs and the vindication of property rights. It is preferable, however, to treat such claims as ultimately founded on the wrong, since it is the wrong which triggers the recognition of the claimant's proprietary right.[61]

---

[55] Birks, 'Property, Unjust Enrichment and Tracing', 246.

[56] Burrows, 'Proprietary Restitution', 418. See also ibid, 423.

[57] C Mitchell, P Mitchell, and S Watterson (eds), *Goff and Jones: The Law of Unjust Enrichment* (8th edn, London: Sweet and Maxwell, 2011), ch 8. Cf *Handayo v Tjong Very Sumito* [2013] SGA 44, [111] (VK Rajah JA).

[58] *Foskett v McKeown* [2001] 1 AC 102, 127 (Lord Millett).   [59] See p 420, above.

[60] See, for example, *FHR European Ventures Ltd v Cedar Capital Partners LLC* [2014] UKSC 45, [2015] AC 250 where the Supreme Court awarded the claimant a proprietary restitutionary remedy for the defendant's breach of fiduciary duty.   [61] See ibid.

(D) THE ROLE OF DISCRETION

One of the key policy questions which underpins proprietary restitutionary claims concerns whether a normative approach can be adopted when considering such claims, by virtue of which the identification and vindication of proprietary rights would depend on the discretion of the court by reference to notions of justice and Equity. Such a discretionary approach has been advocated by a number of judges[62] and commentators,[63] especially those who consider that property rights in substitute property should be recognized by virtue of the unjust enrichment principle. But such a discretionary approach was clearly rejected by the House of Lords in *Foskett v McKeown*,[64] most notably by Lord Millett who said:[65] 'Property rights are determined by fixed rules and settled principles. They are not discretionary. They do not depend upon ideas of what is "fair, just and reasonable". Such concepts, which in reality mask decisions of legal policy, have no place in the law of property.'[66]

Lord Browne-Wilkinson also recognized that proprietary claims do not depend on any discretion vested in the court; such cases involve 'hard-nosed property rights'.[67] But he did accept that a proprietary interest might not be recognized if such recognition would be 'unfair'.[68] This notion of fairness is sometimes encountered in the context of the tracing rules,[69] but it clearly contradicts the fundamental principle that the recognition of proprietary rights is rule-based. It would be better to rationalize the decision not to recognize a proprietary interest by reference to principled defences rather than rely on the uncertainty of concepts such as fairness and equity. This is an area where certainty is paramount for a number of reasons, particularly because a consequence of recognizing proprietary rights may be that the claimant gains priority over the defendant's unsecured creditors if the defendant becomes bankrupt or insolvent, so the award of such a remedy will be to the prejudice of these other creditors, and also has a proprietary claim against the innocent recipients of the property if they have not provided value for their receipt. Therefore, the court must always be vigilant against affording the claimant excessive protection at the expense of third parties. This has been recognized in a number of cases. For example, in *Re Stapylton Fletcher Ltd*[70] Judge Paul Baker QC said: 'The court must be very cautious in devising...interests and remedies which erode the statutory scheme for distribution on insolvency. It cannot do so because of some perceived injustice arising as a consequence only of the insolvency.'[71]

Ultimately, the court must simply strive to balance the interests of two innocent parties, namely the claimant and the defendant's creditors, by reference to clear principles. In doing so one of the most important considerations relates to whether or not the claimant can be considered to have taken the risk of the defendant's insolvency or bankruptcy.[72] For, if the claimant did take the risk, or can be deemed to have taken it, there is no reason why the claimant's claim should be preferred to that of the defendant's other creditors and

---

[62] For example, Sir R Walker, '*Foskett v McKeown*' [2000] RLR 573, 575.

[63] Burrows, 'Proprietary Restitution', 423–8; C Rotherham, 'Tracing Misconceptions in *Foskett v McKeown*' [2003] 11 RLR 57. See generally C Rotherham, *Proprietary Remedies in Context* (Oxford: Hart Publishing, 2002); F Finch and S Worthington, 'The *Pari Passu* Principle and Ranking Restitutionary Rights' in FD Rose (ed), *Restitution and Insolvency* (Oxford: Mansfield Press, 2000), 1.

[64] [2001] 1 AC 102.   [65] Ibid, 127.

[66] Cf Lord Hope who said, ibid 120, that, since there was no principle or authority to assist with the division of the property in that case, it should be divided in such proportions as were equitable, having regard to the equities affecting each party.

[67] Ibid, 109.   [68] Ibid.   [69] *Re Diplock* [1948] Ch 465, 548.   [70] [1994] 1 WLR 1181, 1203

[71] See also *Re Polly Peck International plc (No 2)* [1998] 3 All ER 892, 827 (Mummery LJ).

[72] Burrows, 'Proprietary Restitution', 423–8.

so the claimant should rank equally with those creditors.[73] The principal situation where it is acceptable to prefer the claimant's claim over those of the defendant's other creditors is where the claimant was completely unaware that property had been taken from him or her, for example where a thief has stolen some of the claimant's property. In such a case it is perfectly acceptable that the claimant be afforded proprietary protection since he or she was not given the opportunity to arrange for the restitutionary claim to be secured. Equally, if the claimant made arrangements to obtain a security interest but for some reason this security is invalid, it should be acceptable that the claimant be afforded a degree of proprietary protection to fulfil his or her legitimate expectations that any claim against the defendant would be secured.[74]

It does not follow from this emphasis on principle that there is no role for discretion in the recognition of proprietary rights. In fact, judicial discretion properly defined inevitably involves discretion exercised with reference to principle. This was recognized by Hart[75] who argued that discretion is fundamentally different from arbitrary choice: discretion by its nature is guided by rational principles, so that a decision which is not susceptible to principled justification is not an exercise of discretion at all but involves an arbitrary choice. It follows that there is no reason why the recognition and enforcement of proprietary rights should not be modified by the exercise of judicial discretion, as long as this is done on a principled basis. This will prove to be significant later when equitable proprietary rights are considered with reference to the so-called remedial constructive trust.[76]

(E) A FRAMEWORK FOR ANALYSING A TYPICAL PROPRIETARY RESTITUTIONARY CLAIM

When the claimant seeks a restitutionary remedy to vindicate a proprietary right there are a number of different questions which need to be considered in a specific order. The preferable mode of analysis is as follows.

(1) Does the claimant have a legal or equitable proprietary interest in an asset, whether an existing interest or one which has been created by operation of law? This is known as the 'proprietary base'.[77]

(2) Can the claimant follow or trace this proprietary interest from his or her own hands to those of the defendant, even though other property has been substituted for the claimant's property or it has become mixed with property belonging to somebody else?

(3) What is the nature of the claim to this property and what is the appropriate remedy to vindicate the claimant's proprietary rights?[78] If the claimant seeks a proprietary restitutionary remedy it will be necessary to show that the defendant has retained property in which the claimant can identify his or her proprietary interest; whereas if a personal restitutionary remedy is sought it is enough that the defendant received the property, without needing to show that it was retained.

(4) Does the defendant have a defence to defeat or restrict the claim?

---

[73] This may be the case, for example, where the claimant entered into a transaction with the defendant which was void. See Lord Goff in *Westdeutsche Landesbank Girozentrale v Islington LBC* [1996] AC 669, 684.

[74] See p 640, below.

[75] HLA Hart, 'Discretion', written in 1956 and published in (2013) Harvard Law Review 652.

[76] See p 595, below.

[77] See the analysis in *Smalley v Bracken Partners* [2003] EWCA Civ 1875, [2004] WTLR 599.

[78] This will be affected by whether the claim is brought in Equity or at Common Law.

The application of this framework for analysing equitable proprietary claims is particularly well illustrated by *Foskett v McKeown*,[79] which is now the leading case on such claims. The correctness of the decision will be considered subsequently, but what is important for now is to understand this logical approach that needs to be adopted when analysing proprietary claims.

In *Foskett* a group of investors wished to invest in property on the Algarve in Portugal to develop as a golf course. A sum of £2.6 million was deposited by them and was settled on trust for them until the land was purchased; this was called the development trust. A few years earlier, one of the trustees had set up a life insurance policy on his life. The terms of the policy were such that, if he died, the sum of £1 million would be paid to him. He settled the policy on trust for his three children. He was required to pay an annual insurance premium of £10,220. On the receipt of a premium, a notional allocation of units would take place and the insurers would cancel units to meet the cost of life cover for the next year. If the premiums were to cease to be paid, the units would continue to be cancelled until there were no units left. Once there were no units left, the policy would lapse.

The trustee paid the first three premiums from his own money. He then stole £10,220 from the trust to pay for the fourth premium and did the same the following year. He then committed suicide. The fact that he died at his own hand did not invalidate the policy. It followed that his children were eligible to receive a lump sum payment of £1 million from the insurance company.

The beneficiaries of the development trust discovered that the trustee had misappropriated £20,440 from the trust fund. They argued that, since their money had been used to pay two of the five premiums that had contributed to the payment of £1 million, it followed that they should have two-fifths of that sum, amounting to £400,000. The children contested this on the basis that the money belonged to them in Equity and either they should keep the whole £1 million or they should simply reimburse the beneficiaries for what their father had misappropriated from the trust fund, namely £20,440.

There were essentially four possible solutions to this dispute.

(1) As the beneficiaries argued, since the money that had been used to pay the fourth and the fifth premiums belonged to them in Equity and this had been used to pay two of the five premiums, they should get a two-fifths share of the £1 million.

(2) The children should be required only to repay the £20,440 that had been stolen from the trust fund.[80]

(3) The beneficiaries should recover nothing. This argument, which was also made by the children, was dependent on the peculiar nature of the insurance policy. The premiums that were paid were not automatically used to maintain the insurance policy; rather, the premiums were used to purchase units. The first three premiums had purchased sufficient units such that, even if the fourth and the fifth premiums had not been paid, the insurance policy would not have lapsed and the £1 million would still have been paid. Consequently, it was argued that the beneficiaries' money had not contributed to the receipt of the £1 million in any way.

(4) The fourth solution, which was not argued in the case, was that, because the fourth and the fifth premium had been stolen from the trust, which was a criminal offence, it followed that the £1 million was the proceeds of crime. Since English law recognizes that recipients of the proceeds of crime should be required to give up

---

[79] [2001] AC 102.   [80] This was the solution adopted by the Court of Appeal: [1998] Ch 265.

those proceeds to the victim and cannot be seen to benefit from them,[81] it might have been argued that, even though the children were innocent of the crime themselves, they could not be seen to benefit from their father's crime in anyway, so the beneficiaries should recover the whole of the £1 million.

The House of Lords, by a bare majority, adopted the first solution, so that the beneficiaries recovered £400,000. In reaching this decision, it is possible to identify a number of distinct stages in the analysis of the majority.

(i)   The claim was concerned with the vindication of the claimants' property rights and had nothing to do with whether the defendant was unjustly enriched.[82]

(ii) The beneficiaries had an equitable proprietary base. This was easily established because the trustee held the money that the investors had deposited on an express trust,[83] so they clearly had an equitable proprietary interest in the money that had been misappropriated from the trust fund.

(iii) It was not possible to follow the money that was misappropriated into the £1 million death benefit. This was because the money that had been stolen had inevitably become mixed with other money, so that it had lost its identity. Consequently, it was necessary to trace[84] the value of this money into substitute property, namely the death benefit. The process of tracing in this case was complex and controversial,[85] but the majority accepted that it was possible to trace the trust funds into the premiums that were paid to the insurance company, then into the life insurance policy, and then into the death benefit.

(iv) The choice of remedy in this case was controversial,[86] but the majority held that the most appropriate way of vindicating the beneficiaries' property rights was by recognizing that the beneficiaries had a share of the death benefit in proportion to their contribution to the payment of the premiums, namely £400,000.

(v)   The House of Lords also considered whether the children had any defences to the proprietary claims and concluded that they did not, primarily because they were volunteers who had received a gift.

The proper method of analysis of proprietary restitutionary claims should take place with reference to these five different stages, with particular focus on stages (ii) to (v). This is how such claims will be analysed in this Part.

2. IDENTIFICATION OF THE PROPRIETARY INTEREST

The first question which must be considered to establish a proprietary restitutionary claim is whether the claimant has a proprietary interest in the property which was received by the defendant. This notion of a subsisting proprietary interest was usefully described by

---

[81] See p 526, above.

[82] *Foskett v McKeown* [2001] 1 AC 102, 109 (Lord Browne-Wilkinson), 115 (Lord Hoffmann), 118 (Lord Hope), and 129 (Lord Millett). Lord Steyn concluded that the children were not unjustly enriched because the payment of the premiums did not constitute an enrichment: ibid, 112.

[83] Ibid, 126 (Lord Millett).   [84] See p 607, below.   [85] See p 609, below.

[86] See further p 633, below.

Birks as the proprietary base,[87] which indicates that it is the necessary foundation upon which the proprietary claim will be built. The proprietary base may be established in two different ways. First, the claimant may have a continuing proprietary interest where the nature of the transfer was such that title to the property did not pass to the defendant. In this type of case the claimant's proprietary interest will have been retained.[88] Secondly, even though the legal title may have passed to the defendant, the claimant will have a proprietary interest in the property received by the defendant where the circumstances surrounding the transfer were such that it is possible to recognize that the claimant has an equitable interest in the particular property. In this type of case the claimant's proprietary interest will have been created.[89]

(A) RETENTION OF A PROPRIETARY INTEREST

In determining whether the claimant has retained title in the property which was received by the defendant it is necessary to examine the rules of property law concerning the transfer of title.[90]

(i) The General Rules for the Passing of Title

The fundamental principle relating to the passing of title, regardless of whether the transaction is one of sale or gift, is that title will only pass where the parties intend it to do so.[91] Usually the parties will intend title to pass where the property is delivered to the purchaser or donee, either actually or constructively. Constructive delivery includes where title deeds are delivered or goods are set aside for storage.[92] Where there is no evidence of the parties' actual intent they will be presumed to intend that title will pass on delivery.

Title can only pass, however, where the property was in existence at the time of the transfer and was ascertainable, even though it had not been ascertained.[93] It is for this reason that the claim of the main group of claimants in *Re Goldcorp Exchange Ltd*[94] failed. In *Goldcorp* some of the claimants had entered into a contract to purchase bullion from a company which had gone into insolvent liquidation. It was essential to these claims to the bullion that the claimants had a proprietary interest in it. This was because a bank had lent money to the company and it had obtained a security interest in the bullion by means of a floating charge. Since the company had insufficient assets to satisfy the claims of both the claimants and the bank, the claimants needed to show that they had a proprietary interest which ranked above that of the bank. The difficulty which faced the claimants was that, although they had paid the purchase price for the bullion and had agreed with the

---

[87] PBH Birks, *An Introduction to the Law of Restitution* (rev edn, Oxford: Clarendon Press, 1989), 378–85. This phrase was adopted by Millett J in *Macmillan Inc v Bishopsgate Investment Trust plc (No 3)* [1995] 1 WLR 978, 989. See also *Smalley v Bracken Partners* [2003] EWCA Civ 1875, [2004] WTLR 599.

[88] Sometimes legal title will pass to the defendant but it will be revested in the claimant, for example by rescission. See p 480, below.

[89] See Grantham, 'Doctrinal Bases for the Recognition of Proprietary Rights' who characterizes these two approaches in terms of the 'property approach' and the 'duty approach'.

[90] For analysis of the rules relating to the passing of title in money see D Fox, *Property Rights in Money* (Oxford: Oxford University Press, 2008).

[91] *Middleton* (1873) LR 2 CCR 38, 43. See the Sale of Goods Act 1979, s 17.

[92] *Re Stapylton Fletcher Ltd* [1994] 1 WLR 1181.

[93] See the Sale of Goods Act 1979, s 16. Ascertainment may occur by exhaustion: Sale of Good (Amendment) Act 1995, s 1(2), amending the Sale of Goods Act 1979.

[94] [1995] 1 AC 74. See also *Re London Wine Co (Shippers) Ltd* (1986) PCC 121.

company that it would store the bullion on their behalf, the bullion had not specifically been allocated to them. It was for this reason that the Privy Council held that the property in the bullion had not passed to the claimants. Since the claimants' bullion could not be ascertained it was not possible to conclude that the claimants had a proprietary interest in any particular property.[95]

Alternatively, the claimants in *Re Goldcorp Exchange Ltd* argued that they had a proprietary interest in the bullion by virtue of estoppel. Their argument was that, since the company had promised to allocate the bullion to each claimant, it was estopped from denying that it had done so and consequently it could be assumed that the claimants did have a proprietary interest in the bullion. This argument was summarily dismissed by the Privy Council, because estoppel could only give the claimants the pretence of a title where no title exists and such a fictional title could not give the claimants priority over the bank's real proprietary interest in the bullion. Estoppel is essentially a rule of evidence and cannot be used to conjure a title. This is surely right. It is one thing to estop the defendant by virtue of the representations which it has made and which have been relied upon by the claimant to his or her detriment. It is a completely different thing to bind a third party by virtue of the defendant's representations. In other words, estoppel can be used as a defence but cannot be used to establish a cause of action.[96]

A second group of claimants in *Re Goldcorp Exchange Ltd* were in a somewhat different position, because they had bought bullion from a different company which had since been taken over by Goldcorp Exchange Ltd. Before this takeover occurred their bullion had been ascertained and appropriated and it was conceded, rightly, that this was sufficient to pass title to the claimants. Consequently, they had a proprietary base on which their proprietary claim could be founded.[97]

The law relating to the passing of title where a purchaser has bought part of an identified bulk has been amended by the Sale of Goods Amendment Act 1995. By virtue of this Act it will be presumed that the parties intended that title should pass where the purchaser has bought part of an identified bulk and has paid part of the price in advance.[98] This presumption of intention can be rebutted by evidence that title was to pass at a later date.

Even where the claimant has initially retained legal title, that title will automatically pass as soon as the claimant's property, or its product or substitute, ceases to be identifiable.[99] This will be determined by reference to the tracing rules.[100]

(ii) Circumstances in Which Title Will Not Pass

In addition to the general rules as to when title in property will pass, there are certain recognized situations in which title will not pass to the defendant. Sometimes the claimant will make it clear that he or she has no intention that title in the particular property should pass to the defendant. This is illustrated by those transactions in which the claimant agrees

---

[95] Cf *Re Stapylton Fletcher Ltd* [1994] 1 WLR 1181 where the property in identical bottles of wine was held to have passed to the purchasers of wine, even though the bottles had not been appropriated to each customer, it being sufficient that the purchasers' bottles were kept separate from the vendor's trading stock. The effect of this was that the purchasers held the wine as tenants in common. See also *Hunter v Moss* [1994] 1 WLR 452, p 581, below.

[96] *Re Stapylton Fletcher Ltd* [1994] 1 WLR 1181, 1203 (Judge Paul Baker QC). Cf the doctrine of proprietary estoppel which can be used to create proprietary rights and so ground a proprietary claim. See p 581, below.

[97] In fact, the proprietary claim of this group of claimants failed because they were unable to identify the bullion in which they had a proprietary interest.

[98] Sale of Goods (Amendment) Act 1995, s 1(3).

[99] *Westdeutsche Landesbank Girozentrale v Islington LBC* [1996] AC 669, 703 (Lord Browne-Wilkinson).

[100] See p 610, below.

to sell property to the purchaser but includes a reservation of title clause to ensure that legal title to the property does not pass to the purchaser until he or she has paid for it.[101] Similarly the claimant will not intend title to pass to the defendant where the transaction is a bailment.

Also, title will not pass to the defendant either where the claimant lacks an intention that title should pass or where the claimant's intention can be treated as vitiated. Such vitiation of intention will only arise in certain exceptional cases. Analysis of the categories of cases in which the claimant's intention is vitiated suggest that they mirror the recognized grounds of restitution within the action founded on the reversal of unjust enrichment. But it must be emphasized that these categories have a different function in the context of proprietary restitutionary claims and are consequently defined in a different way from the recognized grounds of restitution. For, in this context, we are not concerned with whether the claimant actually intended to benefit the defendant. Rather, we are concerned to determine whether the claimant actually intended that title in the property should pass to the defendant.

(1) Ignorance

Where the claimant is unaware that his or her property has been taken by the defendant, or that it was taken by a third party and has subsequently been received by the defendant, the claimant clearly does not intend that title to the property should pass to the defendant and so he or she retains a proprietary interest in it. So, for example, where the claimant's property is stolen, title will not pass to the thief.[102] In a number of cases the claimant, who was ignorant that his or her property had been taken, was able to bring a restitutionary claim against the defendant who was either the direct or the indirect recipient of the property. In each of these cases the courts emphasized that the effect of the claimant's ignorance was that it prevented title from passing to the defendant.

(a) Direct recipients

In *Neate v Harding*[103] the defendants went into the house of the claimant's mother and took the claimant's money. It was held that the claimant could recover the amount of money which had been taken in an action for money had and received. Pollock CB emphasized that the money belonged to the claimant and continued to belong to him even though it had been taken by the defendants. As he said, '[t]he owner of property wrongfully taken has a right to follow it ... treat it as his own, and adopt any act done to it'.[104] In *Merry v Green*[105] the court specifically relied on the claimant's ignorance to explain why his property had not passed to the defendant. In this case the claimant had sold a bureau in a public auction to the defendant, who later discovered that a purse containing money was hidden in a secret drawer inside the bureau. It was held that the claimant could recover the value of the money since he had never intended it to be delivered to the defendant.

(b) Indirect recipients

In a number of cases the claimant has been able to bring a restitutionary claim against a defendant who has received property belonging to the claimant via a third party, in

---

[101] This is called a *Romalpa* clause after the case which first recognized the validity of such clauses: *Aluminium Industrie Vassen BV v Romalpa Aluminium Ltd* [1976] 1 WLR 676.

[102] *Ilich* (1987) 69 ALR 231, 244 (Wilson and Deane JJ). This is also implicit in the decision of the House of Lords in *Lipkin Gorman (a firm) v Karpnale Ltd* [1991] 2 AC 548.

[103] (1851) 6 Exch 349, 155 ER 577. See also *Holiday v Sigil* (1826) 2 Car and P 177, 172 ER 81 and *Moffat v Kazana* [1968] 3 All ER 271.

[104] *Neate v Harding* (1851) 6 Exch 349, 350, 155 ER 577, 578.   [105] (1841) 7 M and W 623, 151 ER 916.

circumstances where the claimant was unaware that the third party had taken the property. In each case the success of the claim depended on proof that, when the defendant received the property, the claimant continued to have a proprietary interest in it. Consequently, the award of restitutionary relief could be justified because the defendant had interfered with the claimant's continuing ownership of the property. This is illustrated by *Clarke v Shee and Johnson*[106] where the claimant's clerk had received payments from the claimant's customers which he used to buy lottery tickets from the defendants, without the knowledge of the claimant. The claimant successfully recovered this money from the defendants in an action for money had and received. Lord Mansfield specifically recognized that the claimant's action succeeded because he was able to identify his money in the hands of the defendants.[107]

Another important decision in this context is that of Denning J in *Nelson v Larholt*.[108] In this case the claimant beneficiaries of the deceased brought an action to recover money which had been paid to the defendants without their knowledge by the deceased's executors. Denning J held that the claimants' action succeeded both in Equity and in an action for money had and received. In an important dictum he identified the essential principle relating to the recovery of money which has been taken from the claimant without his or her knowledge:[109]

> If [money] is taken from the rightful owner, or indeed, from the beneficial owner, without his authority, he can recover the amount from any person into whose hands it can be traced, unless and until it reaches one who receives it in good faith and for value and without notice of the want of authority... This principle has been evolved by the courts of law and equity side by side... It is no longer appropriate, however, to draw a distinction between law and equity... The right here is not peculiar to equity or contract or tort, but falls naturally within the important category of cases where the court orders restitution, if the justice of the case so requires.

This suggestion that the approaches of Law and Equity have fused is unduly optimistic, but this remains an important dictum since it recognizes that the claimant has a proprietary restitutionary claim where his or her money has been taken without authority.

The best example of this principle in operation is the decision of the House of Lords in *Lipkin Gorman (a firm) v Karpnale Ltd*,[110] where it was accepted that the claimant retained a proprietary interest in the money which had been stolen from it by one of its partners and which had been received by the defendant. Consequently, the claimant was able to recover the value of the money in an action for money had and received by virtue of its proprietary rights. Clearly the claimant did not intend title in the money to pass because it was unaware that the money had been taken. Similarly, in *Foskett v McKeown*[111] the claimants were able to establish an equitable proprietary claim where property which was held on trust for them was stolen by the trustee.

---

[106] (1774) 1 Cowp 197, 98 ER 1041. This case was specifically affirmed by the House of Lords in *Lipkin Gorman (a firm) v Karpnale Ltd* [1991] 2 AC 548.

[107] See also *Marsh v Keating* (1834) 1 Bing NC 198, 131 ER 1094; *Calland v Loyd* (1840) 6 M and W 26, 151 ER 307.

[108] [1948] 1 KB 339.   [109] Ibid, 342–3.

[110] *Lipkin Gorman (a firm) v Karpnale Ltd* [1991] 2 AC 548.

[111] [2001] 1 AC 102. See p 568, above. See also *Macmillan Inc v Bishopsgate Investment Trust plc (No 3)* [1996] 1 WLR 387.

(2) Mistake

Where the claimant has made a mistake[112] this will only prevent title in property from passing to the defendant where the mistake is fundamental, since it is only such mistakes which can be regarded as sufficiently serious to vitiate the claimant's intention that title should pass to the defendant.[113] The notion of a fundamental mistake is notoriously uncertain, but it is possible to define the principle to some extent. The question whether title passes to the defendant when the claimant is affected by a mistake is a question which has been rigorously examined in the context of the crime of theft, when it is necessary to determine whether the property mistakenly transferred by the victim can be considered to belong to the victim or to the defendant.[114] A number of criminal cases have recognized that a mistake will be fundamental in three situations,[115] with the consequence that the claimant's intention to transfer the property to the defendant will have been vitiated so that title to the property will not pass. These cases should be regarded as applicable to the law of restitution as well, because the question for both the criminal law and the law of restitution is the same: when does a mistake prevent title from passing?

(a) Mistake as to the identity of the recipient

That a mistake as to the identity of the recipient of the property will constitute a fundamental mistake is illustrated by *Middleton*,[116] a criminal case in which the defendant, who wished to withdraw money from his post office saving's account, was handed a sum of money by the post office clerk. This sum was more than was standing to the defendant's credit at the time. The clerk paid this amount of money because he had referred to a letter which authorized the payment, but the letter referred to another depositor. It was held that in these circumstances the mistake of the clerk was such that it prevented the title in the money from passing to the defendant. The clerk's mistake was fundamental since he was mistaken as to the identity of the defendant and this mistake vitiated his intent to pay the defendant.[117] The claimant's mistake as to identity will, however, only vitiate his or her intention where the identity of the recipient is a matter of fundamental importance.[118]

(b) Mistake as to the identity of the property

That a mistake as to the identity of the property will constitute a fundamental mistake was recognized in *Ashwell*[119] where the defendant was convicted of stealing a sovereign. The defendant had asked the victim to lend him a shilling but the victim handed over a much

---

[112] Presumably, after the decision of the House of Lords in *Kleinwort Benson Ltd v Lincoln City Council* [1999] 2 AC 349, this encompasses both mistakes of law and fact.

[113] *Barclays Bank Ltd v Simms* [1980] QB 677, 689 (Robert Goff J). See also *Chambers v Miller* (1862) 13 CBNS 125, 143 ER 50.

[114] The offence is now defined by the Theft Act 1968, s 1. The question of whether the victim has retained title for the purposes of theft is less important today because, by virtue of s 5(4) of the Theft Act 1968, if the defendant is under an obligation to restore property received by mistake, that property is deemed to belong to the person who is entitled to restitution.

[115] See the decision of the High Court of Australia in *Ilich* (1987) 69 ALR 231, 243 (Wilson and Dawson JJ). See also G Williams, 'Mistake in the Law of Theft' (1977) 36 CLJ 62, 64.

[116] (1873) LR 2 CCR 38. See also *Cundy v Lindsay* (1878) 3 App Cas 459 and *R E Jones Ltd v Waring and Gillow Ltd* [1926] AC 670, 696 (Lord Sumner).

[117] *Middleton* (1873) LR 2 CCR 38, 42.

[118] *Citibank NA v Brown Shipley and Co Ltd* [1991] 2 All ER 690, 699 (Waller J).

[119] (1885) 16 QBD 190. See also *Middleton* (1873) LR 2 CCR 38, 45.

more valuable sovereign, thinking that it was a shilling. Cave J held that 'as there was a mistake as to the identity of the coin no property passed'.[120]

(c) Mistake as to the quantity of the property

Whether a mistake as to the quantity of the property which is transferred should be regarded as a fundamental mistake is a matter of some controversy, but where the claimant transfers more property to the defendant than he or she intended this must be a fundamental mistake because the claimant did not intend to transfer the excess property to the defendant. Birks described such a mistake as one 'which all men would agree that it decisively vitiated the intention to give'.[121] This view has also been endorsed in a number of judicial pronouncements.[122] There are, however, other cases which suggest that a mistake as to quantity does not prevent title from passing.[123]

That a mistake as to the quantity of the property transferred can constitute a fundamental mistake was recognized by the High Court of Australia in *Ilich*,[124] where the defendant was charged with stealing money from the victim. The defendant assumed that money, which had been left on a table by the victim, constituted payment by the victim for the work the defendant had done as a locum in a veterinary practice, and so the defendant took the money. The High Court accepted that the victim had made a fundamental mistake in overpaying the defendant and so in principle title to the money did not pass.[125]

Whether a similar result would be reached in this country must be considered in the light of the difficult case of *Chase Manhattan Bank NA v Israel-British Bank (London) Ltd.*[126] In this case the claimant bank mistakenly paid $2 million to the defendant bank, thinking that it was liable to pay the money but forgetting that it had already been paid. The claimant sought to recover the money. Since the defendant had gone into liquidation and did not have sufficient assets to pay off all of its unsecured creditors, it was crucial for the claimant to establish that it had a proprietary interest in the money so that it could claim a proprietary restitutionary remedy, and so achieve priority over the general creditors. The trial judge held that the claimant had an equitable proprietary interest in the money which had been paid to the defendant, with the result that the money was held on constructive trust for the claimant.[127] It is implicit in this decision that legal title to the money had passed to the defendant. But why did title pass when the claimant's mistake related to the amount of money paid and so could be considered to have been fundamental? In fact, a finding of fundamental mistake should have been easier to reach in *Chase Manhattan* than it was in *Ilich* because, when determining whether there is a fundamental mistake as to quantity, the nature of the transaction between the parties is significant. A distinction should be drawn between those cases where the claimant intends the defendant to have some money but simply overpays the defendant, and those cases

---

[120] *Ashwell* (1885) 16 QBD 190, 201. This was doubted in *Potisk* (1973) 6 SASR 389 on the basis that the mistake did not relate to the identity of the metal disc which was handed over but to its value, and so the mistake should not have been treated as a fundamental mistake. But surely the identity of a coin depends on the value which is ascribed to it, so that a mistake as to the type of coin handed over is properly characterized as a fundamental mistake.

[121] Birks, *An Introduction to the Law of Restitution*, 158. See also G Williams, 'Mistake in the Law of Theft' (1977) 36 CLJ 62, 64.

[122] See *Eldan Services Ltd v Chandag Motors Ltd* [1990] 4 All ER 459, 462 (Millett J) and *Friends' Provident Life Office v Hillier Parker May and Rowden* [1995] 4 All ER 260, 275 (Auld J). See also *Russell v Smith* [1958] 1 QB 27.

[123] See, for example, *Moynes v Cooper* [1956] 1 QB 439.   [124] (1987) 69 ALR 231.

[125] On the facts of the case title did pass because the defendant was considered to be a *bona fide* purchaser for value. See Chapter 23.

[126] [1981] Ch 105.   [127] On this aspect of the decision see p 598, below.

where the claimant pays the defendant twice in two separate transactions. The best example of a simple case of overpayment is *Ilich* itself, where arguably the mistake was not sufficiently fundamental after all. This was because the victim only intended to give the defendant part of the money, but it was not possible to identify which money was intended to pass and which was paid by mistake.[128] Consequently, the victim's intention that title to the money should pass should not have been treated as vitiated. But the facts of *Chase Manhattan* were very different, because in that case it was possible to identify which money the claimant did not intend the defendant to have, namely the whole of the second payment. As regards the payment of this money, the claimant's mistake should have been treated as fundamental so that the claimant retained legal title to the money.[129] Despite this identification of a fundamental mistake, the reason why legal title was considered to have passed to the defendant in this case was presumably not because of the nature of the mistake but simply because the claimant's money had been paid into the defendant's bank account and so it was not possible to identify it at Law.[130]

The preferable view therefore is that, whenever the claimant makes a fundamental mistake as to the identity of the recipient or the identity or quantity of the property which has been transferred, title to that property will not pass because the claimant's intention to transfer title will have been vitiated by a fundamental mistake. All other mistakes are mistakes as to motive only and will not prevent property from passing. So, for example, a mistake as to a liability to pay money to the defendant will not prevent title from passing, because it is not sufficiently fundamental to vitiate the claimant's intention that title to the money should pass to the defendant. The mistake will, instead, have a lesser consequence, namely to vitiate the claimant's intention to benefit the defendant so that the claimant will be able to recover the amount of money paid by mistake by reference to the unjust enrichment principle.[131]

(3) Misrepresentation

Where the defendant has induced a mistake to be made by the claimant so that he or she transfers property to the defendant, generally title will pass to the defendant,[132] save where the mistake which has been induced can be characterized as fundamental.[133] This is defined in the same way as for spontaneous mistakes. Where the induced mistake was not fundamental but was induced by a fraudulent misrepresentation it will be possible to rescind at Law any transaction entered into as a result of the misrepresentation and revest title in the claimant.[134]

(4) Powerlessness

Although powerlessness has never been specifically recognized as a reason why the claimant did not intend title to be transferred to the defendant, it is obvious that, in the same way that the claimant lacks such an intention where he or she is ignorant of the

---

[128] This was recognized by Brennan J in *Ilich* (1987) 69 ALR 231, 254.

[129] This analysis is supported by a number of theft cases where it was held that title passed to the defendant where money had simply been overpaid. See, for example, *Moynes v Cooper* [1956] 1 QB 439 and *Attorney-General's Reference (No 1 of 1983)* [1985] QB 182. Cf *Shadrokh-Cigari* [1988] Crim LR 465, a case of overpayment where it was held that property did not pass because of the supposed application of *Chase Manhattan*. But *Chase Manhattan* was distinguishable because it involved a double payment rather than a simple overpayment.

[130] See p 615, below.   [131] See Chapter 9.

[132] *Clough v North Westers Rly Co* (1871) LR 7 Exch 26 and *Moynes v Coopper* [1956] 1 QB 439, 445 (Lord Goddard CJ).

[133] *Cundy v Lindsay* (1878) 3 App Cas 459. See p 574, above.   [134] See p 580, below.

transfer, similarly the claimant will lack such an intention where he or she is powerless to resist the transfer. So, for example, if the defendant enters the claimant's house, ties him up and then takes his property, title in that property will not pass to the defendant because clearly the claimant did not intend title to pass.

(5) Compulsion

Compulsion will not operate to vitiate the claimant's intention that title should pass save in the most exceptional case where the pressure is so extreme that the claimant had no choice but to do as the defendant demanded.[135] For example, if the defendant threatened to kill the claimant if he or she failed to pay a sum of money to the defendant, since the pressure was so extreme the claimant had no choice but to do as the defendant demanded, and so any apparent intention of the claimant that the defendant should obtain title to the money should be treated as vitiated.

An example of such a case is *Duke de Cadaval v Collins*,[136] where the claimant was arrested by the defendant, on the false ground that he owed the defendant £10,000. To secure his release, the claimant paid the defendant £500. It was held that the claimant could recover this money in an action for money had and received. Lord Denman CJ held that 'the property in the money... never passed from the plaintiff, who parted with it only to relieve himself from the hardship and inconvenience of a fraudulent arrest'.[137] The restitutionary claim was therefore brought to vindicate the claimant's continuing proprietary interest. Since a threat to continue to deprive the claimant of his liberty is a particularly serious threat, Lord Denman's analysis is perfectly acceptable, since the claimant could be treated as having no choice at all but to pay the defendant. Where the threat is less extreme, such as a threat to meddle with the claimant's property or reputation, title to money paid as a result of the threat will presumably pass to the defendant and so the claimant's restitutionary claim can only be founded upon the reversal of unjust enrichment.[138] Consequently, it is highly unlikely that duress of goods or economic duress could ever be considered to be so serious as to vitiate the claimant's intention that title in the property should pass to the defendant.

(iii) Particular Circumstances in Which Title Will Pass

Although in most cases where the claimant transfers property to the defendant title will pass to the defendant, it is worth emphasizing three situations where title will pass because it might be thought that the nature of the transfer would prevent this.

(1) Failure of Basis

(a) Total failure of basis

Where the claimant has transferred property to the defendant in the expectation that a benefit would be received in return and this benefit is not forthcoming, this failure of basis will not revest title in the claimant.[139] This was recognized by the Privy Council in *Re Goldcorp Exchange Ltd*,[140] where the claimants had paid money for bullion which was never allocated to them. Even though the basis for their payment had failed totally it was held that title to the money had passed to the defendant company and could not be revested. Consequently, the claimants were confined to a restitutionary claim founded on

---

[135] D Fox, 'The Transfer of Legal Title to Money' [1996] RLR 60, 68. Usually, where compulsion operates, the claimant does have a choice as to whether or not to submit, albeit not a free choice. See p 206, above.

[136] (1836) 4 Ad and E 858, 111 ER 1006.   [137] Ibid, 864; 1009.   [138] See Chapter 10.

[139] Though failure of basis may operate to create an equitable proprietary interest in the claimant. See p 593, below.   [140] [1995] 1 AC 74.

the reversal of the defendant's unjust enrichment, with the ground of restitution being total failure of basis.[141] This is surely right. The claimants initially intended title to pass in the expectation that a benefit would be received. The failure to receive a benefit subsequently is not a sufficient reason to revest title in the claimants.

(b) Absence of basis[142]

Sometimes there may appear to be greater scope for a proprietary restitutionary claim to be made where the basis for a transaction has failed, such as where the claimant transfers property to the defendant pursuant to a transaction which turns out to be null and void. Whether it is possible in such a case to treat the claimant's intention that title should be transferred to the defendant as vitiated was an issue which arose in the interest rate swaps litigation, where money was paid by banks and local authorities pursuant to interest rate swap transactions which were held to be null and void because they were *ultra vires* the local authorities. Even though the transactions were void the House of Lords in *Westdeutsche Landesbank Girozentrale v Islington LBC*[143] recognized that title to the money did pass under the transactions, so the claimant was unable to bring a proprietary claim to recover it.[144]

Whether *Westdeutsche Landesbank* is correct depends on whether the claimant's intention to transfer title should be considered to have been vitiated when as a matter of law the transaction was void from the start. In *Westdeutsche Landesbank* Lord Goff considered the proper analogy to be with a case of breach of contract where there has been a total failure of basis.[145] This is not convincing because, where a contract has been set aside for breach, it is obvious that title to property will already have passed. Where, however, the contract is void the situation is different because there never was an underlying transaction. Despite this difference, the decision of the House of Lords is surely correct. The question with which we are concerned is whether the claimant's intention to transfer title can be regarded as vitiated. At the time *Westdeutsche Landesbank* was decided a claimant could not rely on mistake of law to establish a restitutionary claim. Consequently, the claimant relied on failure of basis, specifically absence of basis. But, just because the expected basis for the claimant's transfer of property can never be received as a matter of law, this is not a reason to vitiate the claimant's intention that title should pass.[146] The House of Lords has, however, subsequently recognized that a mistake of law may ground a restitutionary claim.[147] It follows that, where a claimant transfers a benefit to the defendant in the belief that the underlying transaction was valid when it was in fact void, the claimant was mistaken at the time the benefit was transferred. If this could be considered to be a fundamental mistake it would be sufficient to vitiate the claimant's intention that title to property should pass to the defendant. It is unlikely, however, that such a mistake will be fundamental since it is not a mistake as to the identity of the defendant or the property or even as to the quantity of the property transferred. It is simply a mistake as to the liability to pay the defendant and this is not fundamental since it is a mistake only as to motive.[148]

---

[141] See Chapter 13. This claim was worthless because the defendant was insolvent.

[142] See p 371, above.   [143] [1996] AC 669.

[144] That title passes under an *ultra vires* transaction was accepted in *Ayers v South Australian Banking Corp* (1871) LR 3 PC 548. See also *Challinor v Bellis* [2015] EWCA Civ 59, [108] (Briggs LJ).

[145] *Westdeutsche Landesbank Girozentrale v Islington LBC* [1996] AC 669, 689 (Lord Goff).

[146] Save, perhaps, where the court considers that, since public policy demands that the transaction should be void, public policy should also demand that title to the property should be revested in the claimant. But this is a difficult argument because of the inherent uncertainty in determining what public policy demands.

[147] *Kleinwort Benson Ltd v Lincoln CC* [1999] 2 AC 349.   [148] See p 574, above.

(2) Illegality

If the claimant has paid money to the defendant pursuant to an illegal transaction, the fact of illegality will not prevent title in the property from passing to the defendant. This was recognized in *Singh v Ali*.[149] This is presumably because, even though the transaction itself is void for reasons of public policy, the claimant intended that property should pass and the law recognizes this intention. But such a conclusion contradicts the basic policy of the law relating to illegal transactions which is simply that such transactions should have no effect.[150]

(3) Incapacity

(a) Minority

Where the claimant transfers property to the defendant the fact that the claimant is a minor will not prevent title from being transferred.[151] Similarly, where the claimant transfers property to the defendant, the fact that the defendant is a minor will not prevent title from being transferred. As regards this latter situation, however, the effect of section 3 (1) of the Minors' Contracts Act 1987 is that a minor may be required to transfer to the other party to the contract any property which was acquired by the minor under the contract or any property which represents the original property, as long as the court considers it to be just and equitable that such a transfer is made. No case has yet considered the meaning of this statutory provision, so it remains unclear when it will be just and equitable to make such a transfer of property. If the provision is interpreted literally, however, it seems that it is confined to proprietary restitutionary claims. Consequently, if the minor has disposed of the property which has been obtained, and there is no other property which represents it, restitution under the statute will be denied. The statute will also only be applicable where property has been transferred pursuant to a contract and will not extend to the recovery of gifts.

(b) Institutional incapacity

Where the claimant transfers property to the defendant and one of the parties to the transaction is an institution which lacks capacity to participate in it, this should not prevent title from passing. It has, however, been suggested that where a public authority makes a payment which it lacks capacity to make it will have a proprietary claim to recover what it has paid.[152] But this is inconsistent with *Westdeutsche Landesbank* which suggests that title will pass even though it is transferred pursuant to an *ultra vires* transaction. The only possible justification for concluding that title should not pass where a public authority lacks capacity to transfer the property, is by reference to public policy. Consequently, it may be concluded that the policy which makes the transaction *ultra vires* in the first place, namely to protect taxpayers, should be followed through to its logical conclusion to ensure that the public authority cannot lose its proprietary rights.

---

[149] *Singh v Ali* [1960] AC 167. See also *Belvoir Finance v Stapleton* [1971] QB 210. Cf MJ Higgins, 'The Transfer of Property Under Illegal Transactions' (1962) 25 MLR 149 who argues that property should not pass under illegal transactions. Restitution of property which has been transferred pursuant to an illegal transaction is examined at p 589, below.

[150] See Chapter 27.   [151] *Chaplin v Leslie (Frewin) Publishers Ltd* [1966] Ch 71.

[152] See Lord Goff in *Woolwich Equitable Building Society v IRC* [1993] AC 70, 177, commenting on *Auckland Harbour Board v The King* [1924] AC 318.

(4) Exploitation

Since the grounds of restitution which are founded on exploitation are equitable it follows that the defendant's exploitation of the claimant will not prevent legal title from passing to the defendant.[153]

(iv) Particular Circumstances in Which Title Will Be Revested in the Claimant

Sometimes, where title has passed to the defendant, it may subsequently be revested in the claimant. The most important example of this is where the claimant has transferred property to the defendant pursuant to a contract which he or she is able to rescind at Law, by virtue of fraudulent misrepresentation, duress, or non-disclosure.[154] Where one party has transferred an asset to the other party pursuant to a contract which is voidable, title to the asset will be transferred to the other party.[155] Rescission at Common Law is a self-help mechanism which automatically revests legal title in the claimant.[156] It follows that, after rescinding the transaction, the claimant will be able to bring a proprietary restitutionary claim to vindicate his or her proprietary right. If the property has been dissipated, rescission of the transaction cannot have any proprietary consequences, since there will not be any title which can be revested in the claimant.[157]

Where property has been transferred under a contract which has been breached or frustrated then, once the contract has been repudiated by the other party, it is terminated only from the moment of repudiation and does not operate to revest title in the claimant. The difference between rescission and repudiation is that rescission operates to undo the transaction, whereas repudiation terminates the transaction for the future.

This analysis of rescission at Law has been convincingly challenged by Swadling who has concluded, following careful consideration of nineteenth century cases,[158] that rescission at Common Law should not have any proprietary consequences.[159] This is a persuasive argument. If a void or illegal contract can be effective to transfer legal title, then why should a contract which has been rescinded revest legal title?

(v) Retention of Equitable Title

Where the claimant has an existing equitable interest in property that is mixed with other property or is transferred to a third party, it is necessary to show that the claimant has retained that equitable interest in the original or substitute property. Normally, the interest will be retained even if the property is transferred to a third party who is unaware of that interest. So, for example, in *Foskett v McKeown*,[160] the claimants were able to establish that they had retained an equitable proprietary interest in money that was stolen by the trustee. Also, in *Re Diplock*,[161] the executors of the deceased's estate mistakenly paid part of the money from the estate to third parties. The deceased's next of kin, who should have received the property, were able to bring a proprietary claim to recover it on behalf of the estate, since they had retained an equitable proprietary interest in the property, despite the executors' mistaken transfer.

---

[153] *Allcard v Skinner* (1887) 36 Ch D 145, 190 (Bowen LJ).

[154] See p 21, above.   [155] *Load v Green* (1846) 15 M and W 216, 221; 153 ER 828, 830 (Parke B).

[156] See, in particular, *Car and Universal Finance v Caldwell* [1965] 1 QB 524.

[157] Although the defendant will be liable to make restitution of the value of any benefit received under the transaction. See p 24, above.

[158] Especially *Load v Green* (1846) 15 M and W 216, 153 ER 828.

[159] WJ Swadling, 'Rescission, Property and the Common Law' (2005) 121 LQR 123.

[160] [2001] 1 AC 102.   [161] [1948] Ch 465. See also *Nelson v Larholt* [1948] 1 KB 339.

(B) CREATION OF A PROPRIETARY INTEREST

Even where legal title to the property has passed to the defendant it may still be possible for the courts to recognize that the claimant has a proprietary interest in the property because the circumstances of the transfer may be such that an equitable proprietary interest will be created. The essential nature of equitable proprietary rights was identified by Lord Browne-Wilkinson in *Westdeutsche Landesbank Girozentrale v Islington LBC*:[162]

> A person solely entitled to the full beneficial ownership of money or property, both at law and in equity, does not enjoy an equitable interest in that property. The legal title carries with it all rights. Unless and until there is a separation of the legal and equitable estates, there is no separate equitable interest.

In other words, an equitable proprietary interest will not exist until there has been an event which enables the equitable title to be created. This will occur when the circumstances of the transfer of the property to the defendant enables the court to conclude that the property is held on trust by the defendant for the claimant.

The determination of when equitable proprietary interests will be created is a highly controversial matter, but a number of mechanisms can be identified.[163]

(i) The Express Trust

The usual mechanism for the creation of an equitable proprietary interest is the express trust. Whether an express trust has been validly created will depend on whether it has satisfied the three certainties, namely certainty of intent,[164] certainty of subject matter, and certainty of object,[165] and whether it has been properly constituted by means of the effective transfer of legal title to the trustee. It follows from this, for example, that an express trust will only be recognized if the property which is alleged to be subject to the trust is ascertainable.[166] It is for this reason that in *Re Goldcorp Exchange Ltd*,[167] where the claimants had purchased bullion which had not been specifically allocated to them, the Privy Council held that the property was not held on an express trust. For, in such circumstances, where the actual identity of the bullion which had been purchased remained uncertain, it was not possible to say which part of the bulk was subject to the trust. This principle was qualified by the Court of Appeal in *Hunter v Moss*.[168] In this case the defendant, who owned 950 of the 1,000 issued shares of a company, made an oral declaration that he would hold 5 per cent of the company's issued shares on trust for the claimant. Subsequently, the defendant argued that the trust had not been properly constituted because there was no certainty as to its subject matter. But the Court held that the trust was completely constituted because the shares were indistinguishable and so it was sufficient that the defendant owned enough shares to constitute the trust without needing to identify which ones were subject to the trust.

---

[162] [1996] AC 669, 706.

[163] Property rights can also be created by virtue of the doctrine of proprietary estoppel, but only where this is necessary to protect the claimant's reasonable reliance on the defendant's representation: *Thorner v Major* [2009] UKHL 18, [2009] 1 WLR 776. See S Bright and B McFarlane, 'Proprietary Estoppel and Property Rights' (2005) 64 CLJ 449.

[164] See, for example, *Duggan v Governor of Full Sutton Prison* [2004] EWCA Civ 78, [2004] 1 WLR 1010.

[165] GJ Virgo, *Principles of Equity and Trusts* (Oxford: Oxford University Press, 2012), 80–114.

[166] *Westdeutsche Landesbank Girozentrale v Islington LBC* [1996] AC 669, 705 (Lord Browne-Wilkinson).

[167] [1995] 1 AC 74.

[168] [1994] 1 WLR 452. See also *White v Shortall* [2006] NSWC 1379 and *Pearson v Lehman Brothers Finance SA* [2010] EWHC 2914 (Ch), [244] (Briggs J).

Where property is held on trust and that property is sold by the trustee to a third party where the trustee is authorized by the trust instrument to do so, the beneficiary will no longer have an interest in that property by virtue of the doctrine of overreaching.[169] It follows that the third-party recipient will not hold that property on trust for the beneficiary. The purchase price for the asset received by the trustee will be held on trust for the beneficiary. Where, however, the property has been misapplied the beneficiary will have a continuing equitable interest in that property, save where the third party is a *bona fide* purchaser for value.[170]

(ii) The Resulting Trust

(1) The Essence of the Resulting Trust

The resulting trust[171] is a potentially important mechanism for recognizing equitable proprietary interests, which can be vindicated by an equitable proprietary claim. One of the most controversial questions concerning proprietary restitutionary claims relates to the determination of when the defendant will hold property on a resulting trust. A resulting trust arises where property has been transferred to the defendant and a recognized trigger for the trust occurs, which might arise at the time of transfer or subsequently, so that the property is then held by the defendant on trust for the claimant. The trust is called 'resulting' since the equitable proprietary interest in the property returns, or 'results', back in Equity to the person who transferred the property in the first place.

There are two categories of resulting trust. The first is the presumed resulting trust, which arises where the claimant gratuitously transferred property to the defendant or provided consideration for the transfer of property to the defendant.[172] Secondly, a resulting trust will arise automatically where the claimant transferred property to the defendant to be held on an express trust that fails, either initially or subsequently. In both cases the equitable proprietary interest in the property can be considered to result back to the claimant, so that the defendant holds the property on trust for the claimant.

(2) Theoretical Foundations for Recognizing the Resulting Trust

Although the courts have distinguished between automatic and presumed resulting trusts, in *Westdeutsche Landesbank Girozentrale v Islington LBC*[173] Lord Browne-Wilkinson suggested, *obiter*, that all resulting trusts should be considered to be presumed trusts. He said: 'Both types of resulting trust are traditionally regarded as examples of trusts giving effect to the common intention of the parties. A resulting trust is not imposed by law against the intentions of the trustee (as is a constructive trust) but gives effect to his presumed intention.'

This has proved to be a significant dictum that might provide a coherent explanation of all resulting trusts. The dictum itself is, however, rather confused. First, the reference to the common intention of the parties cannot be correct. Such a common intention has proved significant to the common intention constructive trust, which is largely concerned with determining the beneficial interests of cohabiting couples in the family home, but not to the resulting trust. Secondly, if intention is relevant to explain when a resulting trust is recognized, it cannot be the intention of the trustee that is relevant, but only that of the

---

[169] RC Nolan, 'Property in a Fund' (2004) 120 LQR 108; D Fox, 'Overreaching' in PBH Birks and A Pretto (eds), *Breach of Trust* (Oxford: Hart Publishing, 2002), 95.

[170] See Chapter 23.

[171] For a general examination of the resulting trust see R Chambers, *Resulting Trusts* (Oxford: Clarendon Press, 1997).

[172] *Tinsley v Milligan* [1994] 1 AC 340, 371 (Lord Browne-Wilkinson).   [173] [1996] AC 669, 708.

transferor. Thirdly, if an intention is presumed, it is not clear what the transferor is being presumed to have intended.

Rather than focusing on a positive intent that property should be held on trust for the transferor, some commentators[174] have argued that it should be sufficient to show that the transferor did not intend the recipient to benefit from the receipt of the property. This approach was specifically recognized by Lord Millett in *Air Jamaica v Charlton*,[175] albeit in giving the advice of the Privy Council. He also recognized it in *Twinsectra Ltd v Yardley*,[176] but none of the other judges considered it. In *Air Jamaica*, he said:[177]

> Like a constructive trust, a resulting trust arises by operation of law, though unlike a constructive trust it gives effect to intention. But it arises whether or not the transferor intended to retain a beneficial interest—he almost always does not—since it responds to the absence of any intention on his part to pass a beneficial interest to the recipient.

This theory is consistent with a number of cases where a resulting trust was recognized even though the intention of the transferor to create a trust could not be established, because, for example, it was clear that the transferor did not want a resulting trust[178] or the intention was unenforceable.[179] Despite this, it is inconsistent with a number of other cases, most notably *Westdeutsche Landesbank*,[180] by virtue of which the intention of the transferor is significant to the proper analysis of all resulting trusts. According to this approach a resulting trust will only arise where the transferor of property can be considered to have intended that the property would be held on trust for him or her on the occurrence of certain events.[181] The crucial question relates to how this intention is established, for which it is necessary to distinguish between presumed and automatic resulting trusts.

(a) Presumed Resulting Trust

Whilst the so-called 'presumed resulting trust' is clearly recognized, it is important to be clear as to what it is that is being presumed. It is not a presumption of a resulting trust, because legal presumptions involve presumptions of fact and a presumption that a resulting trust exists would be a presumption of a legal response.[182] It has, anyway, been recognized that the presumption of resulting trust is not a rule of law, but a presumption of intention.[183] The presumption is preferably analysed as being that, where the claimant has voluntarily transferred property to the defendant or paid the purchase price for property held by the defendant, the claimant intended the property to be held on trust for him or herself. This is what Swadling has described as being a presumed intention to

---

[174] Notably, PBH Birks, 'Trusts Raised to Reverse Unjust Enrichment: The *Westdeutsche* Case' [1996] 4 RLR 3 and Chambers, *Resulting Trusts*, 8.

[175] [1999] 1 WLR 1399, 1412. See also *Chan Yuen Lan v See Fong Mun* [2014] SGCA 36, [44] (Rajah JA). See R Leow and T Liau, 'Resulting Trusts: A Victory for Unjust Enrichment?' (2014) CLJ 500.

[176] [2002] UKHL 12, [2002] 2 AC 164, 190.

[177] *Air Jamaica v Charlton* [1999] 1 WLR 1399, 1412.

[178] *Vandervell v IRC* [1967] 2 AC 291 where the consequence of recognizing that property which had been transferred was subject to a resulting trust was to defeat a tax avoidance scheme.

[179] *Hodgson v Marks* [1971] Ch 892.

[180] *Westdeutsche Landesbank Girozentrale v Islington LBC* [1996] AC 669, 689 (Lord Goff), 708 (Lord Browne-Wilkinson).

[181] *Tinsley v Milligan* [1994] 1 AC 340, 371 (Lord Browne-Wilkinson) and *Westdeutsche Landesbank Girozentrale v Islington LBC* [1996] AC 669, 708 (Lord Browne-Wilkinson). See WJ Swadling, 'A New Role for Resulting Trusts?' (1996) 16 LS 110.

[182] WJ Swadling, 'Explaining Resulting Trusts' (2008) 124 LQR 72, 79.

[183] *Stack v Dowden* [2007] UKHL 17, [2007] 2 AC 432, [60] (Baroness Hale).

declare a trust.[184] This is a presumption that can be rebutted by the recipient of the property adducing evidence that the transferor did not intend the property to be held on trust, for example by showing that the transferor intended to make a gift.[185]

(b) Automatic Resulting Trust

Whilst Swadling provided a sensible explanation of the presumed resulting trust, he was unable to identify a similar rationale for the recognition of automatic resulting trusts where an express trust had failed, and so concluded that such trusts defy legal analysis.[186] He concluded that this category of resulting trust cannot be explained by relying on a presumption of an intention to declare a trust, because this category of resulting trust simply arises by operation of law where an express trust has failed, and no additional facts are required to be proved.[187]

Those commentators who have propounded the absence of intent to benefit explanation of the resulting trust, explain the automatic resulting trust simply on the basis that the claimant will not have intended the defendant to benefit from the receipt of the trust property where the trust has failed. Swadling[188] has rightly criticized this, since the theory does not explain why property should be held on a resulting trust rather than there simply being a personal liability to restore the value of property to the claimant.

It is possible, however, to explain the recognition of automatic resulting trusts without referring either to presumed intent or absence of intent. Rather, the automatic resulting trust should be considered to arise by operation of the law imputing an intention that, in the circumstances which happened, a trust would be declared for the claimant. This imputed intention does not purport to reflect what the claimant did intend, but rather what the claimant would objectively be considered to have intended if thought had been given to the possibility of the express trust failing. In other words, where there is an initial or subsequent failure of an express trust, it is appropriate for Equity to recognize that the recipient of the property was intended to be a trustee rather than to receive the property beneficially; had the settlor considered the possibility of the trust failing, he or she would have intended to have a beneficial interest in the property. That the automatic resulting trust responds to an imputed intention was effectively recognized by Harman J in *Re Gillingham Bus Disaster Fund*,[189] where the surplus of a fund was held on resulting trust for those who had made donations to it. It was held that the recognition of an automatic resulting trust did not rest on the state of mind of the transferor, since in most cases the transferor would not expect the money to be returned, but the trust arises where the expectation of the transferor that the trust will absorb the fund completely is 'for some unforeseen reason cheated of fruition, and is an inference of law based on after-knowledge of the event'.

(c) Other Categories of Resulting Trust

Birks and Chambers,[190] in particular, sought to expand the role of the resulting trust dramatically by reference to their thesis that this trust responds to the claimant's absence of intention that the defendant should receive property beneficially. This thesis is of

---

[184] Swadling, 'Explaining Resulting Trusts', 79.

[185] See also J Mee, 'Presumed Resulting Trusts, Intention and Declaration' (2014) CLJ 86.

[186] Swadling, 'Explaining Resulting Trusts', 102.

[187] Ibid, 95.   [188] Ibid, 99.   [189] [1958] Ch 300, 310.

[190] See R Chambers, 'Resulting Trusts' in AH Burrows and Lord Rodger (eds), *Mapping the Law* (Oxford: Oxford University Press, 2006), ch 13.

potential significance both where the defendant is unjustly enriched at the claimant's expense and where a transaction is rescinded.

(i) Unjust Enrichment Most of the grounds of restitution for purposes of a claim founded on the defendant's unjust enrichment establish that the claimant's intention to transfer an enrichment to the defendant can be regarded as absent or defective in some way.[191] Birks and Chambers reasoned from this vitiation of intention to conclude that, in many cases of unjust enrichment, the enrichment received by the defendant should be held on resulting trust for the claimant.[192] Where an intention to transfer an enrichment has been vitiated, they conclude that the enrichment received must be held on resulting trust for the claimant who did not intend to benefit the defendant in the circumstances. If this is correct it has significant implications by converting a personal liability to restore value to the claimant into a proprietary claim. This would be especially significant where the defendant is insolvent, for then the claimant's claim will rank above the defendant's unsecured creditors. But why should the claimant be given such priority? The biggest weakness with the 'absence-of-intent' theory of the resulting trust concerns whether the recognition of such a potentially wide doctrine of resulting trust will give claimants excessive proprietary protection.[193] If the defendant is to be considered to hold property on resulting trust whenever the claimant's intention to benefit the defendant is vitiated, it follows that the defendant will hold property on resulting trust in most cases in which the defendant will have been unjustly enriched, since much of the law of unjust enrichment turns on the claimant's intention to benefit the defendant being vitiated, for example by mistake or duress.

Consequently, Chambers sought to restrict the recognition of the resulting trust to those cases where the defendant was not free to use the property that had been transferred for his or her own benefit.[194] So, in most cases in which there has been a total failure of basis, a resulting trust would not be recognized because the defendant would have been free to use the property for his or her own benefit when it was transferred, with the vitiation of the claimant's intention to benefit the defendant arising only subsequently when the basis for the transfer had failed. If, however, the basis for the defendant's receipt of an enrichment failed because it was transferred pursuant to a contract which was void, then, since such a transaction was never legally valid, it might be concluded that the defendant never received the property beneficially, and so should be held on resulting trust for the claimant. The decision of the House of Lords in *Sinclair v Brougham*[195] is consistent with this argument, since it was recognized that property which was transferred pursuant to a void transaction was held on resulting trust for the transferor. In that case the claimants had deposited money with a building society, which did not have capacity to borrow the money. It was held that, because this transaction was *ultra vires* and so void, the building society held the money on trust for the depositors. This decision was, however, overruled by the House of Lords in *Westdeutsche Landesbank Girozentrale v Islington LBC*,[196] which held that no resulting trust arises when property is transferred to

---

[191] See p 121, above.

[192] Alternatively, note B Häcker, 'Proprietary Restitution After Impaired Consent Transfers: A Generalized Power Model' (2009) 68 CLJ 324, who argues that the transferor of property whose consent to the transfer of property has been impaired, such as where the transfer was induced by fraud or by duress, has a power to bring a trust into existence, although the power cannot be exercised once the property had been obtained by a *bona fide* purchaser for value.

[193] *Westdeutsche Landesbank Girozentrale v Islington LBC* [1996] AC 669, 716 (Lord Browne-Wilkinson).

[194] Chambers, *Resulting Trusts*, 145.   [195] [1914] AC 398.

[196] [1996] AC 669, 713 (Lord Browne-Wilkinson, with whom Lords Slynn, ibid, 718, and Lloyd, ibid, 738, concurred). Lord Goff was simply prepared to distinguish the case: ibid, 688.

the defendant under a void contract. The claimant in that case was a bank that had paid the defendant local authority a sum of money in respect of a transaction which was held to be void because the defendant lacked capacity to enter into it. The defendant conceded that it was liable to repay this money to the claimant, so the only question before the House of Lords was whether the claimant could claim compound interest from the defendant in respect of the amount that was due to it. Compound interest was then available only in respect of equitable claims, so the claimant needed to establish that it had an equitable proprietary interest in the money which the defendant had received. The claimant sought to show this by arguing that, since the transaction was void, the purpose of the transaction had failed and so the money was held on resulting trust for the claimant. This was rejected by the House of Lords for a number of reasons:

(1) because if a resulting trust was recognized, it would give unacceptable priority to the claimant if the defendant were to become insolvent—priority that would not be available if the transaction were merely voidable;

(2) because of a reluctance to import equitable principles into commercial dealings;[197] and

(3) because the claimant, having entered into a commercial transaction, took the risk of the defendant's insolvency.[198]

This must be correct. Where the claimant intends to transfer a benefit to the defendant for a particular purpose and that purpose can never be satisfied, there is no obvious reason why the property should be held on resulting trust for the claimant.

This is a significant decision in undermining the absence-of-intent analysis of the resulting trust. Chambers reconciled the decision with his absence-of-intent thesis by concluding that the defendant was free to use the money transferred for its own benefit.[199] But that was not true as a matter of law since, because the transaction was void from the start, the defendant could never have used the money for its own purposes. Further, the reasons suggested by the House of Lords for refusing to recognize a resulting trust in that case are of wider significance in supporting a restrictive interpretation of the role of the resulting trust.

Another problem with the attempt by Birks and Chambers to expand the role of the resulting trust by reference to proof of an absence of intent to benefit the defendant is that they assume that an intention to transfer property is either vitiated or it is not. In fact, vitiation of intention is a matter of degree. This is especially well illustrated by claims for recovery of mistaken payments. In the law of unjust enrichment, it is sufficient to show that the claimant's mistake caused him or her to pay money to the defendant.[200] But different, and more stringent, tests of mistake are required to set aside a contract,[201] or to show that legal title to property has not been transferred to the defendant.[202] In each case it can be concluded that the claimant's intention to contract with or transfer property to the defendant has been vitiated, but different tests of mistake are required. Similarly, even if the resulting trust can be justified by reference to the absence of intent to benefit the defendant, it does not follow from the fact that the claimant transferred property to the defendant by mistake that the property will necessarily be held on resulting trust. That

---

[197] Ibid, 704 (Lord Browne-Wilkinson).
[198] Ibid, 684 (Lord Goff). [199] Chambers, *Resulting Trusts*, 162.
[200] *Kleinwort Benson Ltd v Lincoln City Council* [1999] 2 AC 349. See p 170, above.
[201] See p 193, above. [202] See p 574, above.

vitiation of intention must be a matter of degree is, in fact, a crucial part of the Birks' and Chambers' theory of the resulting trust. For there to be a resulting trust where property is transferred to the defendant by mistake, for example, legal title to that property must be vested in the defendant to be characterized as a trustee. So the absence of intent theory assumes that the claimant's intention to transfer legal title has not been vitiated but it is the claimant's intention to benefit the defendant which has been vitiated, whatever that means.

In any case, the preferable view of the resulting trust is that it does not respond to an absence of intent, but to a presumed or imputed intention that the property should be held on resulting trust for the claimant, and there is no reason why such an intention should be imputed or presumed simply because the defendant has been unjustly enriched at the expense of the claimant. In most cases in which the claimant has a claim in unjust enrichment the recognized categories of resulting trust will not be engaged. So, for example, where property has been transferred to the defendant in circumstances where there has been a total failure of basis, there will be no presumption of resulting trust because the claimant's expectation of receiving something in return for the transfer will not make it a voluntary transfer, so the presumption of resulting trust will not be engaged.[203] Where the claimant has transferred property to the defendant by mistake, such as where the claimant believes that he or she is discharging a liability owed to the defendant that does not exist, the transfer will not appear to be voluntary and so the presumption of resulting trust will not be engaged. If, however, the transfer was intended to be a gift, but the claimant was mistaken, for example, as to the identity of the donee, the presumption of resulting trust would appear to be engaged because the transfer was intended to be voluntary,[204] but the fact that the donor intended to make a gift, albeit that it was to the wrong person, can be relied on by the donee to rebut the presumption, simply because an intention to make a gift is inconsistent with the presumed intent that the property be held on trust for the donor.[205] Consequently, the donor would only have a claim in unjust enrichment against the donee for the value of the gift; there would be no proprietary claim.

(ii) Rescission Where property has been transferred to the defendant pursuant to a contract that is voidable, because, for example, the claimant was induced to enter into it as a result of misrepresentation or undue influence, the claimant can rescind the contract in Equity. The effect of rescission will be that the property will be held on trust by the defendant for the claimant. This has sometimes been analysed as a resulting trust. For example, *El Ajou v Dollar Land Holdings plc*[206] recognized this as an 'old-fashioned institutional resulting trust'. But what sort of resulting trust would it be? It could not be an automatic resulting trust, because property had not been previously been transferred to the defendant on an express trust. But neither could it be a presumed resulting trust, because the transfer had not been voluntary, being transferred pursuant to a contractual obligation rather than purportedly as a gift. This might, instead, be regarded as a resulting trust triggered either by the defendant's unjust enrichment, since the defendant would be unjustly enriched once the contract has been rescinded, or simply a resulting trust established by showing that the claimant did not intend the defendant to enjoy the benefit of the property once the contract had been rescinded. But neither explanation is consistent

---

[203] See p 588, below.

[204] S Worthington, 'Proprietary Restitution—Void, Voidable and Uncompleted Contracts' (1995) 9 TLI 113, 114.

[205] See Swadling, 'A New Role for Resulting Trusts?', 116, who considers that the fact that the intention of the donor to make a gift is known to the court will mean that the presumption of resulting trust will not even be engaged.   [206] [1993] 3 All ER 717, 734.

with the preferable analysis of the resulting trust being founded on presumed intent. The preferable explanation of the trust that arises on rescission of a contract is consequently that it is a constructive trust which follows from the defendant's unconscionable conduct in inducing the contract.[207] Indeed, Millett J recognized in *Lonrho plc v Fayed (No 2)*[208] that where a contract has been rescinded for fraudulent misrepresentation, any property transferred would be held on constructive trust.

(d) Conclusions

It follows that there is no need to expand the resulting trust to encompass unjust enrichment and rescission. In addition, the absence-of-intent theory to explain the resulting trust should be rejected as being unprincipled, inconsistent with much authority, and unacceptable for policy reasons in expanding potential proprietary claims. Instead, the resulting trust can arise only where the circumstances of the transfer of property falls within one of the recognized cases in which a resulting trust is presumed or where an express trust has failed. In both situations the underlying trigger for the resulting trust is most appropriately considered to be the transferor's presumed or imputed intention that the property should be held on trust for him or her.

A significant consequence of recognizing the presumed and imputed intent analysis of the resulting trust is that the operation of the trust is interpreted restrictively. As a result of this the third mechanism for recognizing equitable proprietary interests, the constructive trust, is interpreted much more broadly.[209] Nevertheless, as far as the claimant is concerned, whether the defendant is characterized as a resulting or constructive trustee is irrelevant, since the crucial question is whether the claimant can be considered to have an equitable proprietary interest in property held by the defendant, and it does not matter to the claimant how this proprietary interest arises.

(3) The Recognized Categories of Resulting Trust

(a) Presumption of Resulting Trust

Where the claimant has transferred property to the defendant or purchased property which is vested in the defendant's name alone or in their joint names, or directly contributed in some way to the purchase of the property,[210] and the claimant does not receive any consideration for this transaction, it will be presumed that the claimant intended the defendant to hold the property on trust for the claimant.[211] The justification for this presumption is that Equity assumes that people do not act altruistically, but rather with some degree of self-interest and an expectation of some return, so that they would wish to obtain a beneficial interest in the property received by the defendant.[212] But this presumption of an intention to declare a trust can be easily[213] rebutted by the transferee showing that the transferor did intend the transferee to take the property beneficially, for example by proving that the transferee was intended to receive the property absolutely as a gift.[214] Such an intention will itself be assumed, in the form of the presumption of

---

[207] See p 207, below.   [208] [1992] 1 WLR 1, 12. See also *The National Crime Agency v Robb* [2014] EWHC 4384 (Ch), [51] (Etherton C).

[209] *Westdeutsche Landesbank Girozentrale v Islington LBC* [1996] AC 669, 715–16 (Lord Browne-Wilkinson). See p 595, below.

[210] *Laskar v Laskar* [2008] EWCA Civ 347, [2008] 1 WLR 2695.

[211] See *Tinsley v Milligan* [1994] 1 AC 340, 371 (Lord Browne-Wilkinson); Chambers, *Resulting Trusts*, ch 1.

[212] See *Stack v Dowden* [2007] UKHL 17, [2007] 2 AC 432, [60] (Baroness Hale).

[213] *Aroso v Couuts and Co* [2001] 1 WTLR 797, 806 (Lawrence Collins J).

[214] *Westdeutsche Landesbank Girozentrale v Islington LBC* [1996] AC 669, 708 (Lord Browne-Wilkinson).

advancement,[215] where the relationship between the transferor and the transferee is such that the transferor bears some responsibility for the transferee, such as where the claimant transfers property to his wife[216] or child,[217] so that a gift is likely to have been intended. But this presumption of advancement can also be rebutted by the transferor proving that no gift was intended.

Where, however, a couple are joint legal owners of the family home, the presumptions of resulting trust and advancement are not used to determine their beneficial interests in the property.[218] This has subsequently been extended to where the property has been registered in the name of one party only.[219] Where the property has been purchased for investment rather than as a family home, however, the presumption of resulting trust or, if applicable, the presumption of advancement will be engaged.[220]

The distinction between presumptions of resulting trust and advancement has proved to be especially significant where property has been transferred pursuant to an illegal transaction. Illegality encompasses a wide variety of conduct encompassing criminal activity and conduct that is otherwise considered to be unlawful or immoral.[221] As regards the operation of the presumptions of resulting trust and advancement, the most relevant form of illegality concerns the transfer of property to the defendant in order to hide it from creditors or others, such as an ex-spouse. But the illegality may also involve tax evasion and benefit fraud. For reasons of public policy, it is not possible to plead an illegal purpose.[222] This will not prevent the presumption of resulting trust or advancement from being engaged, but it will mean that the party against whom the presumption applies will not be able to assert his or her illegal purpose to rebut the presumption. So, for example, where a husband transfers property to his wife to hide it from his creditors, it will be presumed that he had intended to make a gift of the property to her, by virtue of the application of the presumption of advancement. The husband will not be able to rebut this presumption by adducing evidence that his purpose was to hide his assets from his creditors rather than to benefit his wife, because that would involve pleading an illegal purpose.[223] If, however, the wife had transferred property to her husband to hide it from her creditors, the presumption of resulting trust rather than advancement will apply. Her husband might wish to rebut the presumption by showing that the transaction was intended to effect an illegal purpose, but he will not be able to plead such a purpose.

This inability to plead an illegal purpose has been extended to express trusts.[224] In *Collier v Collier*[225] the claimant had leased two properties to his daughter to hide them from his creditors. The daughter had provided consideration for the transfers, so neither the presumptions of resulting trust nor advancement were engaged. The father sought to adduce evidence of his purpose to establish that the properties were intended to be held on an express trust for him, but he was unable to do so because this would involve him revealing that his purpose was illegal.

---

[215] J Glister, 'The Presumption of Advancement' in C Mitchell (ed), *Constructive and Resulting Trusts* (Oxford: Hart Publishing, 2010), ch 10. The presumption of advancement was abolished by the Equality Act 2010, s 199, but this provision has not yet been brought into force.

[216] *Tinker v Tinker* [1970] P 136.   [217] *Tribe v Tribe* [1996] Ch 107.

[218] *Stack v Dowden* [2007] UKHL 17, [2007] 2 AC 432.   [219] *Abbott v Abbott* [2007] UKPC 53.

[220] *Laskar v Laskar* [2008] EWCA Civ 347, [2008] 1 WLR 2695.   [221] See further p 716, below.

[222] *Tinsley v Milligan* [1994] 1 AC 340. This principle derives from *Holman v Johnson* (1775) 1 Cowp 341, 343; 31 ER 934, 932 (Lord Mansfield). See further p 718, below.

[223] *Gascoigne v Gascoigne* [1918] 1 KB 223; *Re Emery's Investment Trusts* [1959] Ch 410; *Palaniappa Chettiar v Amnasalam Chettiar* [1962] AC 294; *Tinker v Tinker* [1970] P 136.

[224] And also to constructive trusts: *Barrett v Barrett* [2008] EWHC 1061 (Ch), [2008] 2 P & CR 17.

[225] [2002] EWCA Civ 1095, [2002] BPIR 1057.

That the presumption of resulting trust will apply despite the claimant's involvement in an illegal transaction was recognized by the House of Lords in *Tinsley v Milligan*.[226] Tinsley and Milligan had been in a lesbian relationship. They had both contributed to the purchase of a house, but it was registered in the sole name of Tinsley on the understanding that they would have joint beneficial interests in it. This arrangement was to make it appear that Milligan was a lodger, so that she could make fraudulent claims for housing benefit to which she was not entitled. Both parties had participated in the fraud and benefited from it. Subsequently their relationship ended and Tinsley brought an action for possession of the house, asserting that she had sole ownership of it. Milligan counter-claimed that she had a beneficial interest in the property because the nature of their relationship was such that a resulting trust could be presumed. Tinsley argued that Milligan could not ask the court to enforce the trust in her favour because of her illegal conduct in perpetrating benefit fraud. By a majority, it was held that Milligan's counter-claim should succeed, because she did not need to rely on her illegal conduct to assert her beneficial interest: to trigger the presumption of resulting trust she simply had to show that she had contributed to the purchase price and she did not need to refer to the illegal purpose to show this.[227] The only way in which Tinsley could have sought to rebut this presumption was by showing that Milligan had intended Tinsley to have sole title to the property to enable her to perpetrate the fraud. But Tinsley could not establish this because it would have involved her pleading that the transaction was intended to effect an illegal purpose.

It follows that there is a crucial difference between referring to a transaction that happens to be tainted by illegality and relying explicitly to an illegal purpose. It does not follow, however, that a party is always prevented from relying on an illegal purpose. In *Silverwood v Silverwood*[228] money was given by a grandmother to two of her grandchildren. It was presumed that this was held on resulting trust for the grandmother. The grandchildren sought to rebut this presumption by pleading that the grandmother had intended the transfer of the money to be a gift. It was held that the executor of the grandmother's will could plead that the purpose behind the transfer of the money was actually to perpetrate a fraud on the Department of Social Security, since it had enabled the grandmother to obtain income support. Here, the illegal purpose was being pleaded to defeat an attempt to rebut a presumption rather than to rebut a presumption of resulting trust. This involves a very fine distinction being drawn and one that is difficult to defend. If it is legitimate to rely on the illegal purpose to prevent a presumption being rebutted, as in *Silverwood v Silverwood*, why in cases such as *Tinsley v Milligan* cannot the illegal purpose be used to rebut the presumption of resulting trust? But the two cases can be reconciled by reference to why the illegal purpose is being pleaded. In *Tinsley v Milligan* Tinsley sought to rely on Milligan's illegal purpose to show that, through her illegal behaviour, she did not deserve to receive the assistance of the court. But Milligan's illegal purpose was not being pleaded specifically to rebut the presumption of resulting trust by showing that she actually intended the transfer of property to Tinsley to be a gift. She did not. They had both intended to have joint beneficial interests in the property and the illegality of Milligan's purpose did not indicate any contrary

---

[226] [1994] 1 AC 340. See also *Lowson v Coombes* [1999] Ch 373.

[227] Lord Goff dissented on the ground that to obtain relief in equity the applicant must come with clean hands. In fact, the clean hands maxim is a principle of justice which is designed to prevent those guilty of serious misconduct from securing a discretionary equitable remedy, such as an injunction or specific performance: *Dunbar v Plant* [1998] Ch 412, 422 (Mummery LJ). It follows that the maxim should not be relevant where a party seeks to vindicate an equitable proprietary right.

[228] (1997) 74 P & CR 453.

intention. In fact, it confirmed that a gift was not intended by explaining why they had agreed that the property should be registered in Tinsley's name alone. In *Silverwood v Silverwood*, on the other hand, the grandmother's illegal purpose was of real evidential significance in suggesting that the grandmother had not intended the money to be a gift to the children outright. The illegal purpose actually confirmed the presumed intention that the money should be held on resulting trust for the grandmother. It follows that an illegal purpose can be pleaded, but only to establish what the transferor of property or the contributor of the purchase price actually intended to achieve.

Despite this conclusion, it has been clearly accepted that, at least as regards the presumption of advancement, it is not possible to rely on an illegal purpose to rebut the presumption of an intention to make a gift.[229] The analysis of *Tinsley v Milligan* and *Silverwood v Silverwood* might mean that this conclusion can no longer be justified, and that it should be possible for the transferor of property or the payer of money to plead an illegal purpose to rebut the presumption by using that purpose to prove that a gift was not intended. But there is another route to obtaining a beneficial interest in property despite the operation of the presumption of advancement. In *Tribe v Tribe*[230] it was held that the claimant is entitled to plead an illegal purpose to rebut the presumption of advancement where he or she has withdrawn from the illegal transaction before any part of the illegal purpose has been fulfilled. In that case, a father had illegally transferred shares to his son to conceal them from his creditors. Once the threat from his creditors had passed, the father asked his son to return the shares to him. The son refused to do so. The son argued that the presumption of advancement applied and the father was unable to rebut this by pleading his illegal purpose to establish that a gift had not been intended. It was held that, since none of the creditors had been aware of the transfer of shares, none of them had been deceived and so no part of the illegal purpose had been carried into effect.[231] Consequently, the father could be considered to have withdrawn from the illegal transaction and could rely on his actual purpose to rebut the presumption of advancement. It was irrelevant that the father had sought to recover the shares only once the threat from the creditors had passed. The principle recognized in *Tribe v Tribe* was developed from the principle known as *locus poenitentaie*, which required the claimant to repent of the illegality before relying on their illegal purpose to rebut a presumption. Millett LJ in *Tribe v Tribe* confirmed that repentance is no longer required, it being sufficient that the claimant has voluntarily withdrawn from the transaction before any part of the illegal purpose has been satisfied.[232] But a forced withdrawal from the illegal scheme will not suffice[233] and the withdrawal principle will not apply once considerable steps have been taken towards the accomplishment of the illegal purpose, such as presenting a false picture to creditors or the Revenue, which goes beyond merely preparatory steps, such as drafting authentic-looking documents.[234] Withdrawal will, however, be established even though the only reason for withdrawal is that it is impossible to carry out the agreement as originally envisaged for reasons outside the control of the claimant.[235]

---

[229] *Tinker v Tinker* [1970] P 136.   [230] [1996] Ch 107. See p 353, above.

[231] See *Collier v Collier* [2002] EWCA Civ 1095, [2002] BPIR 1057, in which the purpose of deceiving creditors by transferring property to the claimant's daughter had been fulfilled and so the transferor of the property could not be considered to have withdrawn from the illegal transaction.

[232] See also *Patel v Mirza* [2014] EWCA Civ 1047, [2015] 2 WLR 405. See I Samet, 'Locus Poenitentiae: Repentance, Withdrawal and Luck' in C Mitchell (ed), *Constructive and Resulting Trusts* (Oxford: Hart Publishing, 2010), ch 12, for a critique of the move from repentance to withdrawal.

[233] *Tribe v Tribe* [1996] Ch 107, 135 (Millett LJ).

[234] *Q v Q* [2008] EWHC 1874 (Fam), [2009] 1 FLR 935.

[235] *Patel v Mirza* [2014] EWCA Civ 1047, [2015] 2 WLR 405. See p 720, below.

The law on the effect of illegality on the operation of the presumptions of resulting trust and advancement has been much criticized, with widespread calls for reform. The result turns on which presumption applies, which is arbitrary and simply turns on where the burden of proof lies. Where a resulting trust is presumed, the claimant will be able to establish a beneficial interest that the defendant will not be able to rebut, despite the claimant's illegal purpose. Where the presumption of advancement applies, the property will be presumed to have been an outright gift to the defendant and the claimant will not be able to rebut this presumption by pleading his or her true intent. This distinction will disappear if the abolition of the presumption of advancement is brought into force, when the presumption of resulting trust will apply in all cases. The position will then be that the presumption of resulting trust will be engaged despite the claimant's illegal purpose and the defendant recipient will not be able to plead the illegal purpose of the transaction, unless the defendant can be considered to have withdrawn from the transaction before any part of the illegal purpose had been satisfied.

The Law Commission has reviewed the law of illegality generally and in particular as regards the law of trusts.[236] It concluded that the principle that a party cannot plead an illegal purpose 'was deeply embedded' and 'produces complex and arbitrary results, depending on the detailed intricacies of trust law'.[237] The effect of *Tinsley v Milligan* is that a beneficial interest can be enforced under a resulting trust even though the claimant has been involved in very serious criminality, such as where property has been transferred by a terrorist. Whilst some of the unfortunate consequences of the law will be removed if the presumption of advancement is ever abolished, the law will still be unsatisfactory. Consequently, the Law Commission has recommended statutory reform of the law to introduce a statutory discretion as to the appropriate result where a trust has been created to conceal the beneficiary's interest in connection with a criminal purpose. This would include both express and presumed resulting trusts, and would apply where property has been transferred to hide it from creditors or an ex-spouse, since this would constitute the crime of fraud.[238] In such circumstances, the court would have a discretion to determine whether the claimant's beneficial interest in the property should be enforced. This discretion would be exercised only exceptionally. The Law Commission identified various factors to assist the court in the exercise of this discretion, such as the conduct and intention of the parties, the value of the beneficial interest, whether enforcing the beneficial interest would further the criminal purpose, and whether refusing to enforce the interest would have any deterrent value. Where the intended beneficiary is not allowed to enforce the beneficial interest, the court should have a power to determine who should be entitled to it, whether it be the settlor, trustee, or another beneficiary, but the property should not be declared to be ownerless and transferred to the State.

The proposals of the Law Commission are to be commended. The discretion of the court would be structured and would balance the need for predictability of result with the need to ensure that the law of trusts is not used as a mechanism with which to perpetrate criminal offences.

(b) Automatic Resulting Trusts

Where the claimant transfers property to the defendant on an express trust and that trust fails initially or subsequently, the property will be held on resulting trust for the claimant.[239]

---

[236] *The Illegality Defence* (Law Com No 320, 2010).   [237] Ibid, 2.
[238] Fraud Act 2006, ss 2 (fraud by false representation) and 3 (fraud by failing to disclose information).
[239] *Re Vandervell's Trusts (No 2)* [1974] Ch 269, 294 (Megarry J). See Chambers, *Resulting Trusts*, ch 2.

This is illustrated by *Re Ames' Settlement*[240] where, pursuant to a pre-nuptial marriage settlement, property was transferred after the marriage had been performed. The marriage was retrospectively annulled for non-consummation and the trust failed, so the property was held on resulting trust for the covenantor because the money had been transferred on the basis that there was a valid marriage. Similarly, in *Air Jamaica v Charlton*,[241] an express trust of surplus funds that should have arisen following the discontinuance of a pension scheme was void for infringing the perpetuity rule. It was held that the surplus of the fund should be held on resulting trust for the employer and the employees who had contributed to the fund, in proportion to their contributions and regardless of any benefit that they had received from the fund. Also, where a trust has been properly constituted and the purpose of the trust has been fulfilled, any trust property remaining will be held on resulting trust for the person who constituted the trust in the first place.[242] Where it is impossible or impractical to effect restitution to the claimant the property which has been received by the defendant will pass to the State by way of *bona vacantia*. So, for example, where money is raised by anonymous street collections for a particular purpose and that purpose fails, it is impossible to identify the donor of the money so the money will pass to the State.[243]

(c) The *Quistclose* Trust

Where property has been transferred for a specific purpose,[244] such as where money has been lent to a borrower to be used in a particular way, the recipient of that property must use it for that purpose and may hold it on trust for the transferor if the purpose fails. This trust is of real commercial significance, since where, for example, money has been lent, the recognition of the trust will mean that the debt owed by the borrower will be converted into a trust that will give the lender a proprietary interest in the money and so priority over the borrower's creditors if the borrower becomes insolvent. This trust has become known as the *Quistclose* trust, after the name of the case in which the House of Lords first recognized it.[245] Quistclose had lent money to Rolls Razor Ltd specifically to enable Rolls Razor to pay a dividend that it had previously declared, but which it could not afford to pay. This money was paid into a bank account which was specially opened for the purpose. Rolls Razor went into liquidation, so the dividends could not be paid. The bank wished to use the money in the account to discharge debts owed by Rolls Razor to the bank. Quistclose said that the bank could not do this because Quistclose had an equitable interest in the money. The House of Lords accepted this argument. It held that, when money is lent for a particular purpose,[246] the lender has an equitable right to see that the money is applied for that purpose. If the purpose fails, and the parties have agreed expressly or impliedly that in such circumstances the money should be repaid to the lender, the money will be held on trust for the lender.[247] It was found that the mutual intention of the parties was that the money lent should not become part of Rolls Razor's assets, but was to be used exclusively to pay those creditors who were entitled to the

---

[240] [1946] 1 Ch 217.   [241] [1999] 1 WLR 1399.

[242] See, for example, *Re Abbott* [1900] 2 Ch 326.

[243] *Re West Sussex Constabulary's Widows, Children and Benevolent Fund* [1971] Ch 1.

[244] See *Challinor v Bellis* [2015] EWCA Civ 59, where a *Quistclose* trust was not recognized because the terms of the transfer left the money transferred at the free disposal of the recipient with no restriction on its use for a particular purpose.

[245] *Barclays Bank Ltd v Quistclose Investments Ltd* [1970] AC 567.

[246] The principle is not confined in its operation to where money has been lent to enable a borrower to pay other creditors. See Chambers, *Resulting Trusts*, 85; *Box v Barclays Bank* [1998] Lloyd's LR Bank 185.

[247] *Barclays Bank Ltd v Quistclose Investments Ltd* [1970] AC 567, 581–2 (Lord Wilberforce).

dividend. If the dividend could not be paid, the money was then to be returned to *Quistclose*.

The nature of this trust and the ambit of this *Quistclose* principle are matters of particular controversy.[248] One of the most controversial questions concerns the proper characterization of the trust. The decision of the House of Lords in *Quistclose* is consistent with this as being a primary express trust for the creditors which, once it fails, is replaced by a secondary resulting trust for the lender.[249] This secondary trust might even be analysed as an express trust itself, contingent on the failure of the primary trust, since it was intended that, if the primary trust failed, then the money lent would be held on trust for the lender.[250] In *Twinsectra Ltd v Yardley*, however, Lord Millett recognized that the primary trust is properly characterized as a resulting trust.[251] In that case a solicitor, Sims, received money from a lender, Twinsectra, on behalf of Yardley, who had made arrangements to borrow the money. Sims undertook to Twinsectra to retain the money until it was used to acquire property. In breach of this undertaking, the money was paid to another solicitor, Leach, who paid some of it out on Yardley's instructions for other purposes. Sims became bankrupt and Twinsectra sued Leach for dishonestly assisting a breach of trust committed by Sims,[252] but this liability depended on whether Sims had held the money on trust. All of the judges in the House of Lords recognized that the money had been held on trust for Twinsectra. The majority recognized that this was an express trust. Lord Millett held that the money was held on a *Quistclose* trust, which he characterized as being a resulting trust from the outset because the lender has not disposed of the whole of the beneficial interest in the property transferred.[253] He recognized that such a trust did not arise simply because money is paid for a particular purpose, since many loans are made for particular purposes. What is required is that the money was not intended to be at the free disposal of the borrower, but was to be used exclusively for the specific purpose and for no other. Since the money had been lent for the exclusive purpose of buying property and had been applied for a different purpose, it followed that the money was held by Sims on resulting trust for Twinsectra, but subject to a power for the money to be used by Yardley in accordance with the undertaking.

The proper characterization of the *Quistclose* trust as either express or resulting is not especially useful. What is significant is that this is a genuine trust which creates an equitable proprietary interest for the claimant if the money is not applied in accordance with the power. There is no single trust template that applies where property has been transferred for a particular purpose.[254] There will be different responses depending on the particular circumstances of the case.[255] Sometimes the *Quistclose* trust will be an express trust for the lender.[256] On other occasions the trust will be characterized an express trust for a purpose. Such trusts are generally void and, consequently, an automatic resulting

---

[248] See WJ Swadling (ed), *The Quistclose Trust: Critical Essays* (Oxford: Hart Publishing, 2004). See also P Millett, 'The *Quistclose* Trust: Who Can Enforce It?' (1985) 101 LQR 269.

[249] *Barclays Bank Ltd v Quistclose Investments Ltd* [1970] AC 567, 580.

[250] See *Re Australian Elizabeth Theatre Trust* (1991) 102 ALR 681, 691 (Gummow J).

[251] *Twinsectra Ltd v Yardley* [2002] UKHL 12, [2002] 2 AC 164, [100] (Lord Millett). See also ibid, [7] (Lord Steyn), [13] (Lord Hoffmann), and [25] (Lord Hutton); *Latimer v IRC* [2004] UKPC 14, [2004] 1 WLR 1466, 1478 (Lord Millett).   [252] See p 521, above.

[253] *Twinsectra Ltd v Yardley* [2002] UKHL 12, [2002] 2 AC 164, [100]. See also Lord Millett, '*Quistclose* Trusts: *Twinsectra v Yardley* Explained' (2011) 1 T&T 7.

[254] J Glister, 'The Nature of *Quistclose* Trusts: Classification and Reconciliation' (2004) 63 CLJ 632, 633.

[255] Lord Millett, 'Foreword' in WJ Swadling (ed), *The Quistclose Trust: Critical Essays* (Oxford: Hart Publishing, 2004).

[256] *Latimer v IRC* [2004] UKPC 14, [2004] 1 WLR 1466, [41] (Lord Millett).

trust will be triggered for the lender. The resulting trustee will still have a power to apply the money for that agreed purpose, but, once the purpose can no longer be fulfilled, the power will be revoked, as in *Quistclose*, or, where the money has been applied for a different purpose, that will constitute a breach of the resulting trust, as in *Twinsectra v Yardley*. It follows that the so-called *Quistclose* trust is not a peculiar trust, but simply involves the application of the law relating to automatic result trusts.

(iii) The Constructive Trust

(1) The Nature of the Constructive Trust

A further mechanism by which the claimant can obtain an equitable interest in property held by the defendant is the constructive trust. A constructive trust is a true trust like any other, where the constructive trustee has legal title to identifiable property that is held for the benefit of the beneficiaries. But the distinctive feature of a constructive trust is that it arises by operation of law, without regard to the intentions of the parties.[257] The constructive trust clearly differs, therefore, from an express trust, which is created by the settlor's intent, and the resulting trust, which is triggered by a presumed or imputed intent on the part of the transferor that property is to be held on trust for him or her. Further, according to Lord Browne-Wilkinson, the constructive trust responds to unconscionable conduct on the part of the recipient.[258]

Much of the complexity of the law in this area derives from fundamental confusion as to what is meant by the constructive trust. In fact, five different meanings of the constructive trust can be identified.[259]

(a) Institutional Constructive Trust

The institutional constructive trust is the orthodox model for analysing these trusts, which are treated as arising by operation of law on the occurrence of a certain event where a constructive trust has previously been recognized.[260] These events have the common characteristic that the defendant's conscience can be considered to have been affected by the circumstances surrounding the transfer of property.[261] Under this category of the constructive trust, the court simply recognizes that the trust has already arisen, without having any discretion as to whether or not to do so.

(b) Remedial Constructive Trust

This is recognized where a judge, in the exercise of his of her discretion, considers it to be appropriate that proprietary relief is available to the claimant. Unlike the institutional constructive trust, the remedial version involves the judicial creation of equitable proprietary interest.

The essential distinction between institutional and remedial constructive trusts was summarized by Lord Browne-Wilkinson in *Westdeutsche Landesbank Girozentrale v Islington LBC*:[262]

> Under an institutional constructive trust the trust arises by operation of law as from the date of the circumstances which give rise to it: the function of the court is merely to declare

---

[257] *Air Jamaica v Charlton* [1999] 1 WLR 1399, 1412 (Lord Millett).
[258] *Westdeutsche Landesbank Girozentrale v Islington LBC* [1996] AC 669, 705 (Lord Browne-Wilkinson).
[259] Ibid, 714.
[260] *Halifax Building Society v Thomas* [1996] Ch 217, 229 (Peter Gibson LJ).
[261] See P Millett, 'Restitution and Constructive Trusts' (1998) 114 LQR 399, 400.
[262] [1996] AC 669, 714.

that such trust has arisen in the past. The consequences that flow from such a trust having arisen (including the potentially unfair consequences to third parties who in the interim have received the trust property) are also determined by rules of law, not under a discretion. A remedial constructive trust, as I understand it, is different. It is a judicial remedy giving rise to an enforceable obligation: the extent to which it operate retrospectively to the prejudice of third parties lies in the discretion of the court.

This type of trust has been recognized in Australia, Canada, and New Zealand, but not in England.[263]

(c) Constructive Trust as Remedy

Where the claimant has an existing equitable interest in property that has been misappropriated and that property, or substitute property which can be regarded as representing the original property,[264] has been received by a third-party defendant, the claimant will wish to recover the property from the defendant.[265] A mechanism for doing so is the constructive trust. The court can order that the defendant holds the property on constructive trust for the claimant and the claimant can then call for the property to be transferred to him or her. Here, the constructive trust operates simply as a remedial mechanism to enable the transfer of the property to the claimant in Equity. It is different from the remedial constructive trust, because that involves the creation of an equitable proprietary interest that had not previously existed. Where the constructive trust as remedy is used, there is already an equitable proprietary interest in existence, which will typically have been created by an express trust; the constructive trust simply operates as a conduit for the transfer of property from the defendant to the claimant. Whether it is appropriate to use the language of the constructive trust as remedy in this context is, however, a matter of some controversy. It has been suggested that, if the claimant's original equitable interest arises under an express trust, the defendant who has received the property, or its substitute, should hold that property on the same trust.[266] But this argument is unconvincing. The defendant who has received the property will not be under the same trust obligations as the original express trustee, such as being subject to an obligation to invest the trust property. The better view, therefore, is that the recipient does indeed hold the property under a distinct trust, which, because it arises by operation of law, should be characterized as a constructive trust.

(d) Liability as a Constructive Trustee

English law recognizes certain causes of action arising from the defendant's interference with trust property or involvement with a breach of fiduciary duty. These actions are known as unconscionable receipt[267] and dishonest assistance.[268] The liability of the defendant in these claims has traditionally been described as a liability to account as a constructive trustee. But such language is inappropriate. The defendant's liability is only a

---

[263] *FHR European Ventures LLP v Cedar Capital Partners LLC* [2014] UKSC 45, [2015] AC 250. See also *Re Polly Peck International (No 2)* [1998] 3 All ER 812, 823 (Mummery LJ) and 830 (Nourse LJ); *Metall und Rohstoff AG v Donaldson, Lufkin and Jenrette Inc* [1990] 1 QB 391, 478–80; and *Halifax Building Society v Thomas* [1996] Ch 217, 229 (Peter Gibson LJ). Whether such a trust should be recognized in England is considered at p 603, below.   [264] By virtue of the tracing rules, see p 616, below.

[265] As occurred in *Foskett v McKeown* [2001] 1 AC 102. See p 633, below.

[266] Lord Millett, 'Proprietary Restitution' in S Degeling and J Edelman (eds), *Equity in Commercial Law* (Sydney: Lawbook Co, 2005), 315–16. See also *Foskett v McKeown* [2001] 1 AC 102, 108 (Lord Browne-Wilkinson).

[267] See p 645, below.   [268] See p 521, above.

personal liability, either to restore the value of any property received in breach of trust or fiduciary duty or to compensate the claimant for loss suffered as a result of the defendant's assistance with a breach of trust or fiduciary duty or exceptionally to award a gain-based personal remedy. The remedy is not proprietary because it involves only a personal liability to account or to compensate and so has nothing to do with the constructive trust. This was recognized by Lord Millett in *Dubai Aluminium Co Ltd v Salaam*.[269]

(e) Common Intention Constructive Trust

Although the constructive trust traditionally arises without regard to the intention of the parties, there is a distinct form of constructive trust that is triggered with reference to the express, implied, or imputed intention of the parties, and which is known as the common intention constructive trust. This is a trust that arises from an agreement or understanding of the parties as to whether they have a beneficial interest in property and, if so, what the extent of that interest might be. This is especially significant where a couple have cohabited and their home is registered either in the name of them both[270] or in the name of one of them only.[271] Although the language of the constructive trust is used in these cases, this is very different from the ordinary constructive trust, because it responds to the intention of the parties, although equitable proprietary rights are recognized as a consequence. [272]

(f) Summary

The orthodox view in English law is that the constructive trust is a substantive institution which will be recognized in certain circumstances;[273] this is a real trust. But Birks[274] suggested that all constructive trusts are fictions, like the fictional implied contract which was at the core of the law of restitution for many years,[275] because the declaration of trust only exists in the eye of the law. But is this trust really fictional? Surely it simply involves a different method of declaring a trust, but it does involve a real trust with real proprietary interests. The deemed declaration of a constructive trust is a deliberate attempt by Equity to recognize a real trust in certain well-defined circumstances. There is no fiction. If the trust was not real then it would indeed be fictional, which is why the so-called constructive trust which is recognized where the defendant is held liable for unconscionable receipt or dishonest assistance should not be called a trust at all, since it is only a cipher for a personal remedy. Since the constructive trust is a real trust it follows that, from the date of creation of the trust, the beneficiary has an equitable proprietary interest in the trust property which can be vindicated as appropriate.

(2) Circumstances When an Institutional Constructive Trust Will Be Recognized

Lord Scott[276] recognized that it is not possible to prescribe exhaustively the circumstances under which a constructive trust will be created, so the focus should instead be placed on

---

[269] [2002] UKHL 48, [2003] 2 AC 366, 404. See also *Paragon Finance plc v DB Thakerar and Co* [1999] 1 All ER 400, 408 (Millett LJ) and *Williams v Central Bank of Nigeria* [2014] UKSC 10, [2014] AC 1189.

[270] *Stack v Dowden* [2007] UKHL 17, [2007] 2 AC 432 and *Jones v Kernott* [2011] UKSC 53, [2012] 1 AC 776.   [271] *Oxley v Hiscock* [2004] EWCA Civ 546, [2005] QB 211.

[272] This has been extended to commercial arrangements: *Yaxley v Gotts* [2000] Ch 162; *Banner Homes Group Plc v Luff Developments Ltd* [2000] Ch 372; *Crossco No 4 Unlimited v Jolan Ltd* [2011] EWCA Civ 1619. See also *Yeoman's Row Management Ltd v Cobbe* [2008] UKHL 55, [2008] 1 WLR 1752.

[273] See, for example, *Metall und Rohstoff AG v Donaldson, Lufkin and Jenrette Inc* [1990] 1 QB 391, 478–80 and *Halifax Building Society v Thomas* [1996] Ch 217, 229 (Peter Gibson LJ).

[274] Birks, 'Property, Unjust Enrichment and Tracing', 242. See also WJ Swadling, 'The Fiction of the Constructive Trust' (2011) CLP 1.   [275] See p 45, above.

[276] In *Cobbe v Yeoman's Row Management Ltd* [2008] UKHL 55, [2008] 1 WLR 1752, [30].

recognizing particular factual circumstances under which the constructive trust will, and will not, be relevant. The constructive trust has been recognized in a variety of different circumstances.

(a) Breach of Fiduciary Duties

Where the defendant owes a fiduciary duty to the claimant and receives property in breach of that duty[277] the defendant may be required to hold that property on constructive trust for the claimant. This does not involve the operation of the constructive trust as a remedy, because the principal did not have an equitable proprietary interest in the property prior to the breach of duty. Rather, this proprietary interest arises by operation of law. This was recognized by the Supreme Court in *FHR European Ventures LLP v Cedar Capital Partners LLC*[278] where it was held that a bribe received by a fiduciary in breach of fiduciary duty was held on constructive trust for the principal, and this was specifically characterized as an institutional rather than a remedial constructive trust.

(b) Unconscionable Retention

Constructive trusts will also be recognized more generally in circumstances where the defendant's conduct can be considered to be unconscionable, even though the defendant did not owe fiduciary duties to the claimant. Although unconscionability is at the heart of this category, as it is with all categories of constructive trust, it is a distinct category because unconscionability is determined with specific regard to the fault of the defendant. This is the effect of an important dictum of Lord Browne-Wilkinson in *Westdeutsche Landesbank Girozentrale v Islington LBC*[279] relating to the appropriate interpretation of *Chase Manhattan Bank NA v Israel-British Bank (London) Ltd.*[280] In *Chase Manhattan Bank* it was held that, where the claimant had mistakenly paid the defendant the same amount of money twice, although legal title in the money which had been mistakenly paid had passed to the defendant, it was still possible for the court to recognize that the claimant had an equitable proprietary interest in the money. As Goulding J said:[281] 'a person who pays money to another under a factual mistake retains an equitable property in it and the conscience of the other is subjected to a fiduciary duty to respect his proprietary rights.'

Even though the claimant's mistake might have been characterized as fundamental,[282] presumably legal title to the money had passed to the defendant because it was no longer possible to identify the claimant's money at Law as it had been mixed in the defendant's bank account.[283] It is unclear, however, how Goulding J could conclude that the claimant had an equitable proprietary interest in the money that had been received by the defendant. One explanation is that the claimant's intention to benefit the defendant had been vitiated by its fundamental mistake so that the money was held on resulting trust for the claimant.[284] Lord Browne-Wilkinson in *Westdeutsche Landesbank Girozentrale v Islington LBC*[285] stated, however, that Goulding J was wrong to conclude that the claimant had an equitable proprietary interest in the money from the moment it had been received by the defendant simply because it had been paid by mistake, because there needed to be an identifiable event to create the equitable interest, and the fact that the claimant has paid money to the defendant by mistake is not a sufficient event to create such an interest.

---

[277] See p 488, above.   [278] [2014] UKSC 45, [2015] AC 250. See p 512, above.
[279] [1996] AC 669, 714–15. See also Lord Browne-Wilkinson, ibid, 705, and *Hussey v Palmer* [1972] 1 WLR 1286, 1290 (Lord Denning MR).   [280] [1981] Ch 105.
[281] Ibid, 119.   [282] See p 574, above.   [283] See further p 615, below.
[284] See p 585, above.   [285] [1996] AC 669, 715.

Although Lord Browne-Wilkinson did not express his conclusion in these terms, the effect of his analysis of *Chase Manhattan Bank* is that the defendant's unjust enrichment by receipt of a mistaken payment is not a sufficient reason to trigger a constructive trust. But he did recognize that the money paid by mistake was subsequently held on constructive trust for the claimant, so that the claimant did indeed have an equitable proprietary interest in the money. This constructive trust arose because the defendant became aware that the claimant had paid the money to it by mistake within two days of its receipt of the money. As Lord Browne-Wilkinson said: 'Although the mere receipt of the moneys, in ignorance of the mistake, gives rise to no trust, the retention of the moneys after the recipient bank learned of the mistake may well have given rise to a constructive trust...'[286] In other words, the justification for the recognition of the claimant's equitable proprietary interest in the money paid by mistake was that the defendant's conscience had been affected by its knowledge of the mistake whilst it was in possession of the money. Once the defendant was aware of the mistake it should have repaid the money to the claimant, and its failure to do so constituted the unconscionable conduct that justified the recognition of the constructive trust. Lord Browne-Wilkinson went on to recognize that a thief who stole a bag of coins would similarly hold that property on a constructive trust, because of the thief's unconscionable conduct in committing theft and retaining the stolen property.[287] Constructive trusts will be triggered by this principle of unconscionable retention in other circumstances as well, such as where the defendant has obtained property by fraud.[288]

If a constructive trust can be recognized once the defendant becomes aware that the claimant has paid money by mistake, presumably a constructive trust will arise whenever the defendant is aware that he or she has received a benefit that should not have been received and so should be returned. So, for example, if the defendant realizes that the claimant has paid money to him or her under a contract that is void, there is no reason why the defendant cannot be considered to have acted unconscionably in not repaying the money to the claimant. Consequently, on the facts of *Westdeutsche Landesbank* itself, where money had been paid by a bank in respect of a contract with a public authority that was void, the defendant public authority would presumably have held the money on constructive trust for the claimant bank had the money not ceased to be identifiable before the defendant discovered that the transaction was void. It follows that, once a defendant has discovered that a contract in respect of which money has been paid is void, the defendant's continued retention of that money is unconscionable. But the constructive trust will be effective only if the defendant continues to have the money that can be the subject matter of the trust. If the defendant no longer has the money, there is no property on which the trust can bite and so there can be no effective trust. If a constructive trust can

---

[286] Ibid. See also *Bank of America v Arnell* [1999] Lloyd's Rep 399; *Papamichael v National Westminster Bank plc* [2003] 1 Lloyd's Rep 341, 372 (Judge Chambers QC); *Commerzbank AG v IMB Morgan plc* [2004] EWHC 2771 (Ch), [2005] 1 Lloyd's Rep 298, [36] (Lawrence Collins J); *Re Farepak Food and Gifts Ltd* [2006] EWHC 3272 (Ch), [40] (Mann J); *Armstrong DLW GmbH v Winnington Networks Ltd* [2012] EWHC 10 (Ch), [2013] Ch 156. In Singapore see *Wee Chiaw Sek Anne v Ng Li* [2013] SCCA 36 [169]–[184]; in Australia see *Wambo Coal Co Pty Ltd v Ariff* [2007] NSWSC 589.

[287] *Westdeutsche Landesbank Girozentrale v Islington LBC* [1996] AC 669, 716. See also *Bankers Trust Co v Shapira* [1980] 1 WLR 1274; *Armstrong DLW GmbH v Winnington Networks Ltd* [2012] EWHC 10 (Ch) [2013] Ch 156, [276] (Stephen Morris QC).

[288] *Stocks v Wilson* [1913] 2 KB 235, 244 (Lush J); *Halley v The Law Society* [2003] EWCA Civ 97, [48] (Carnwath LJ); *Papamichael v National Westminster Bank plc* [2003] 1 Lloyd's Rep 341, 374 (Judge Chambers QC); *Commerzbank AG v IMB Morgan plc* [2004] EWHC 2771 (Ch), [2005] 1 Lloyd's Rep 298), [36] (Lawrence Collins J); *Sinclair Investment Holdings SA v Versailles Trade Finance Ltd* [2005] EWCA Civ 722; *Campden Hill Ltd v Chakrani* [2005] EWHC 911 (Ch).

be recognized where the defendant knew that the transaction was void, what of the case where the defendant knows that the basis for the transaction has failed totally? There seems no obvious reason why a constructive trust could not exist in such circumstances also. Consequently, if *Re Goldcorp Exchange*[289] were decided today it might be possible to conclude that the defendant held a quantity of bullion on constructive trust for the purchasers because it had been 'behaving in a systematically unconscientious way. It had not the least intention of honouring its contracts in the manner which it made them'.[290] Indeed, in *Re Farepak Food and Gifts Ltd*[291] it was recognized that claimants, who had paid in advance for goods or services, could in principle claim that the money was held on constructive trust for them where the defendant, at the time of receiving payment, had already decided that the goods and services would not be provided because it would cease trading so that there would be a total failure of basis, although this could not be established on the facts.

There are three particular problems relating to the unconscionable retention head of constructive trusts.

(i) What Has Happened to the Legal Title?   In all cases in which a constructive trust has been recognized the trustee must have legal title to the property. But this causes serious problems where, for example, property has been stolen, since, in such circumstances, the claimant's legal title to the property will not have passed to the defendant until it ceases to be identifiable at Law[292] because, for example, it has become mixed with the defendant's own property. But, if the legal title has not passed, how can the defendant thief hold the stolen property on constructive trust for the victim? Since the property will still belong to the victim, it would appear that the thief cannot also hold the property on constructive trust for the victim.[293] This was specifically recognized as a problem in *Shalson v Russo*.[294] Despite this, Lord Browne-Wilkinson in *Westdeutsche Landesbank*[295] and the High Court of Australia[296] have recognized that a thief will indeed hold property on constructive trust for the victim. An explanation for this result has been suggested by Tarrant, who has argued that the thief holds his or her rights to possess the stolen property on trust for the victim.[297] It has been recognized that a thief does indeed have a possessory title to the stolen property, so, for example, if that property is unlawfully taken from a thief by a third party, the thief can assert his or her possessory rights against that third party.[298] It has further been recognized that the thief, or the person who obtains the stolen property from the thief, has a good title to the stolen property against anybody in the world except for the victim of the theft.[299] It follows that the victim of theft has both a residuary legal title in the

---

[289] [1995] 1 AC 72. See p 77, above.

[290] Birks, 'Trusts Raised to Reverse Unjust Enrichment', 21.

[291] [2006] EWHC 3272 (Ch). See also *Neste Oy v Lloyd's Bank plc* [1983] 2 Lloyd's Rep 658 and *Armstrong DLW GmbH v Winnington Networks Ltd* [2012] EWHC 10 (Ch), [2013] Ch 156, [129] (Stephen Morris QC).

[292] This is the effect of *Lipkin Gorman (a firm) v Karpnale Ltd* [1991] 2 AC 548.

[293] S Barkehall Thomas, 'Thieves as Trustees: The Enduring Legacy of *Black v S Freedman and Co*' (2009) 3 J Eq 52. Also R Chambers, 'Trust and Theft' in E Bant and M Harding (eds), *Exploring Private Law* (Cambridge: Cambridge University Press, 2010), ch 10, who adopts an unjust enrichment analysis of the proprietary right that arises in such cases, as a consequence of his unacceptable assumption that unjust enrichment liability can create proprietary rights. See p 585, above.

[294] [2003] EWHC 1637 (Ch), [2005] Ch 281, [110] (Rimer J).

[295] [1996] AC 696, 716.   [296] *Black v F S Freedman and Co* (1910) 12 CLR 105.

[297] J Tarrant, 'Property Rights to Stolen Money' (2005) 32 UWALR 234, 245; J Tarrant, 'Thieves as Trustees: In Defence of the Theft Principle' (2009) 3 J Eq 170, 172.

[298] *Costello v Chief Constable of Derbyshire* [2001] EWCA Civ 387, [2001] WLR 1437.

[299] *Islamic Republic of Iran v Barakat Galleries Ltd* [2009] QB 22, [15] (Lord Phillips).

stolen property and also an equitable proprietary interest in the thief's possessory title by virtue of the thief's unconscionable retention of that property. The victim then has a choice as to whether rely on his or her legal property right to assert a claim against the thief or the subsequent possessor of the stolen property, or instead to assert a claim founded on his or her equitable rights to the property against the thief or subsequent possessor of it. The advantage of relying on the equitable property right is that the remedies in Equity to vindicate property rights are much more extensive than at Law,[300] and the claimant is able to make a claim to recover the stolen property or its proceeds even though it has become mixed with other property.[301]

(ii) The Degree of Fault   What degree of fault is required on the part of the defendant before his or her conduct in retaining the property can be considered to be unconscionable? If the claimant paid money by mistake or if the transaction was invalid, it is clear that the defendant's knowledge of the mistake or the invalidity of the transaction will be sufficient to characterize the defendant as acting unconscionably in not repaying the money to the claimant. Presumably, it will also be sufficient that the defendant believes or suspects that the claimant was mistaken or that the transaction was invalid.[302] But should it be sufficient that the defendant ought to have known of the mistake or the invalidity of the transaction? If unconscionability were to encompass an objective test of what the defendant ought to have known, it would dramatically widen the circumstances in which a constructive trust will be recognized. But, due to the policy of the law to restrict claims to recover property, particularly because of the adverse effect that they have on the defendant's creditors where the defendant is insolvent, the better view is that the rules for the imposition of constructive trusts should be interpreted restrictively with regard to the defendant's conscience. Consequently, the defendant's conscience should only be considered to be affected where he or she was actually aware of the claimant's mistake or the invalidity of the transaction[303] and, in the light of that knowledge or suspicion, he or she should have returned the benefit received.[304]

(iii) Timing   At what point must the defendant's conscience be affected? Clearly, if the defendant knew of the mistake or the invalidity of the transaction when the property was received, it would be appropriate to recognize that the property was held on constructive trust for the claimant from that moment. Lord Browne-Wilkinson's interpretation of *Chase Manhattan Bank* suggests that acquiring knowledge of the mistake two days after receipt of the money would have been sufficient to characterize the defendant's conduct in retaining the money as unconscionable. But what if the defendant discovers the mistake months or even years later? The natural limit to the period during which we should consider whether the defendant's conscience has been affected is once the defendant has lost the property received from the claimant, or the proceeds of or substitute for that property.[305] In other words, the question of recognizing a constructive trust is bound up with the question of following and tracing of property:[306] if the claimant's property ceases to be identifiable according to the following and tracing rules, a constructive trust cannot

---

[300] See p 632, below.   [301] See p 618, below.

[302] Although in *Papamichael v National Westminster Bank plc* [2003] 1 Lloyd's Rep 341, 373, Judge Chambers QC said that actual knowledge is required.

[303] In *Westdeutsche Landesbank Girozentrale v Islington LBC* [1996] AC 669, 705 Lord Browne-Wilkinson emphasized that the defendant's conscience will only be affected where he or she knew 'of the factors which are alleged to affect' his or her conscience.

[304] *Fitzalan-Howard (Norfolk) v Hibbert* [2009] EWHC 2855 (QB), [49] (Tomlinson J).

[305] *Westdeutsche Landesbank Girozentrale v Islington LBC* [1996] AC 669, 707 (Lord Browne-Wilkinson); *Re Goldcorp Exchange Ltd* [1995] 1 AC 74.   [306] See p 607, below.

be imposed, simply because there will be no identifiable fund to which the trust can attach.[307] This is the reason why a constructive trust was not recognized on the facts of *Westdeutsche Landesbank* because, when the defendant learned that the transaction was void, the claimant's money had ceased to be identifiable.[308]

But if this analysis is right it might mean that the recognition of an equitable proprietary interest in *Sinclair v Brougham*[309] was correct after all.[310] For, in that case when the defendant discovered that it lacked capacity to receive deposits, the money it had received from the depositors was still traceable. This method of resurrecting *Sinclair v Brougham* was not intended by the House of Lords in *Westdeutsche Landesbank*. The only way that this result can be avoided, with the added benefit of dramatically restricting the recognition of equitable proprietary interests through constructive trusts, is by saying that the question of whether or not the defendant's conscience has been affected should be judged only at the time the relevant property was received by the defendant. This would mean that both *Sinclair v Brougham* and *Chase Manhattan* should be rejected. This is inevitable; either they are both right or they are both wrong. This restrictive approach to the recognition of equitable proprietary interests also avoids the artifice of saying that the defendant own a piece of property absolutely and only subsequently will an equitable proprietary interest be carved from it for the benefit of the claimant. Whether such an interest can be recognized should be judged only at the time of receipt.

(c) Rescission

A further situation where the courts have recognized that property is held on constructive trust for the claimant is where the claimant has rescinded in Equity a contract made with the defendant.[311] In *The National Crime Agency v Robb*[312] Etherton C recognized that, when a transaction induced by fraudulent misrepresentation is rescinded, the property which was transferred pursuant to the transaction will be held on constructive trust for the transferor, assuming that it is possible to identify the transferred property or its traceable proceeds in the hands of the defendant.[313]

Since rescission in Equity only takes effect on the order of the court,[314] it follows that the claimant has no equitable proprietary interest in the property until the court order is made which will have the effect of vesting equitable title in the claimant, who can then recover the property.[315] Before the court order is made the claimant only has a mere Equity to rescind the contract, which is not sufficient to establish a proprietary restitutionary claim.[316] It is for this reason that the claimant will be barred from rescinding the transaction if a third party acquires an equitable interest in the property for value and without notice of the claimant's right to rescind.[317] It has, however, been recognized that,

---

[307] *Papamichael v National Westminster Bank plc* [2003] 1 Lloyd's Rep 341, 372 (Judge Chambers QC).

[308] *Westdeutsche Landesbank Girozentrale v Islington LBC* [1996] AC 669, 689 (Lord Goff) and 707 (Lord Browne-Wilkinson).   [309] [1914] AC 348. See p 585, above.

[310] See Birks, 'Trusts Raised to Reverse Unjust Enrichment', 22.

[311] See p 23, above. For rescission at law see p 580, above.

[312] [2014] EWHC 4384 (Ch), [49]. See also *Lonrho plc v Fayed (No 2)* [1992] 1 WLR 1, 12 (Milett J); *Daly v Sydney Stock Exchange* (1986) 65 ALR 193, 204 (Brennan J).

[313] *The National Crime Agency v Robb* [2014] EWHC 4384 (Ch), [51] (Etherton C).

[314] See p 23, above.

[315] *Bristol and West Building Society v Mothew* [1998] 1 Ch 1, 23 (Millett LJ).

[316] *Phillips v Phillips* (1862) 4 De GF and J 208, 45 ER 1164; *Shalson v Russo* [2003] EWHC 1637 (Ch), [2005] Ch 281, [111] (Rimer J); *The National Crime Agency v Robb* [2014] EWHC 4384 (Ch), [80] (Etherton C).

[317] *Westminster Bank Ltd v Lee* [1956] Ch 7.

where the contract was induced by fraud, the claimant will obtain an equitable proprietary interest in the property transferred from the point at which he or she makes the election to rescind,[318] and that this operates retrospectively to the date when the Equity to rescind arose.[319] Whether the equitable proprietary right arises on making the election to rescind or when the court makes its order matters, since the Equity to rescind will be defeated where the property has been obtained by a *bona fide* purchaser for value.

(d) Miscellaneous Cases Where Constructive Trusts Will Be Recognized

The defendant will hold property on constructive trust in a number of other circumstances. For example, where property has been transferred to the defendant on the understanding that the defendant would respect another party's rights, it is unconscionable for the defendant subsequently to deny that other party's rights, so the property will be held on constructive trust for that person.[320] Similarly, a constructive trust has been recognized where an executor sought to obtain a benefit through the abuse of his position.[321] Where a criminal obtains property as the result of the commission of a criminal offence, this property might be held on constructive trust for the victim of the crime, by virtue of the forfeiture principle.[322] Where one party leaves property in their will to another, such as their spouse, with a prior understanding that that person will leave the property in their will to an identified person,[323] the property will be held on constructive trust by that other person for the benefit of the identified person. [324]

(3) The Remedial Constructive Trust

Whereas an institutional constructive trust arises by operation of law from the date of the event which gives rise to it, the remedial constructive trust arises through the exercise of the judge's discretion when it is considered to be just to recognize that the claimant has an equitable proprietary interest in property received by the defendant.[325] The recognition of such a remedy would have a profound effect on the law of restitution, since it would apparently enable judges to create equitable proprietary interests where it was felt that the justice of the case demanded it. This would enable the court to transfer an asset which belongs to the defendant, and in which the claimant did not have a pre-existing legal or equitable interest, to the claimant.[326] The key difference between the institutional and the remedial constructive trust is that, to recognize a remedial constructive trust, it is not necessary to establish that the claimant has a pre-existing proprietary right; the purpose of the remedial constructive trust is to create such a proprietary right.[327]

---

[318] *Banque Belge pour l'Etranger v Hambrouck* [1921] 1 KB 321, 332 (Atkin LJ); *Lonrho plc v Fayed (No 2)* [1992] 1 WLR 1, 12 (Millett J); *El Ajou v Dollar Land Holdings plc* [1993] 3 All ER 717, 734 (Millett J); *Shalson v Russo* [2003] EWHC 1637 (Ch), [2005] Ch 281, 316, [122] (Rimer J).

[319] *The National Crime Agency v Robb* [2014] EWHC 4384 (Ch), [80] (Etherton C).

[320] *Binions v Evans* [1972] Ch 359; *Ashburn Anstalt v Arnold* [1989] Ch 1. See B McFarlane, 'Constructive Trusts Arising on a Receipt of Property *Sub Conditione*' (2004) 120 LQR 667; N Hopkins, 'Conscience, Discretion and the Creation of Property Rights' (2006) 4 LS 475.

[321] *James v Williams* [2000] Ch 1.   [322] See p 549, above.

[323] This is called a 'mutual wills contract'.

[324] *Ollins v Walters* [2008] EWCA Civ 782, [2009] Ch 212.

[325] *Westdeutsche Landesbank Girozentrale v Islington LBC* [1996] AC 669, 714 (Lord Browne-Wilkinson). See also *Metall Und Rohstoff AG v Donaldson Lufkin & Jenrette Inc* [1990] 1 QB 391, 479 (Slade LJ); *Re Goldcorp Exchange Ltd* [1995] 1 AC 74, 104 (Lord Mustill); *London Allied Holdings v Lee* [2007] EWHC 2061 (Ch).

[326] Birks, 'Trusts Raised to Reverse Unjust Enrichment', 14.

[327] *Re Polly Peck International plc (No 2)* [1998] 3 All ER 812, 830 (Nourse LJ).

In England the constructive trust is characterized as an institutional trust which arises by operation of law by virtue of clearly defined principle. In some other jurisdictions such as Australia,[328] Canada,[329] and New Zealand,[330] the constructive trust is a remedial trust which arises by operation of judicial discretion. England is notoriously suspicious of the judge exercising such discretion: judges are not trusted. So, for example, Lord Camden in *Doe v Kersey*[331] said:

> The discretion of a Judge is the law of tyrants; it is always unknown; it is different in different men; it is casual, and depends upon constitution, in temper and passion. In the best it is often times caprice; in the worst it is every vice, folly and passion to which human nature is liable.

As a consequence of this scepticism about judicial discretion, in England the remedial constructive trust is not recognized, as recently confirmed by the Supreme Court.[332] Surprisingly, the Supreme Court cited the judgment of Lord Browne-Wilkinson in *Westdeutsche Landesbank Girozentrale v Islington LBC*[333] in support of this conclusion, but, whilst Lord Browne-Wilkinson certainly did not formally recognize the remedial constructive trust, he was clearly not adverse to the recognition of such a trust, just not at that point in time.

Lord Neuberger, who delivered the speech of the Supreme Court rejecting the remedial constructive trust in England, has expressed his concerns about the remedial constructive trust extra-judicially.[334] He noted that 'the notion of a remedial constructive trust displays equity at its flexible flabby worst'. He considered it to be 'unprincipled, incoherent and impractical'. He was opposed to its recognition in England for the following reasons:

(i)   it would render the law unpredictable;

(ii) it would be an affront to the Common Law view of property rights and interests;

(iii) it would involve the courts usurping the role of the legislature: the creation of new property rights should be left to Parliament.[335] This possibly reflects a concern about use of the remedial constructive trust to contravene priorities on insolvency as identified by statute.[336]

But the real concern about the recognition of the remedial constructive trust is simply that we need clear rules as to whether or not equitable proprietary rights have been created, and the remedial constructive trust is antithetical to such clarity and predictability.[337] Birks consequently described the remedial constructive trust as a remedy that is 'ugly,

---

[328] *Muschinski v Dodds* (1985) 160 CLR 583; *Grimaldi v Chameleon Mining NL (No 2)* (2012) 200 FCR 296, [569] (Justice Finn).

[329] *Pettkus v Becker* (1980) 117 DLR (3d) 257.   [330] *Powell v Thompson* [1991] 1 NZLR 597.

[331] (1795) (CP) quoted in Bower's *Law Dictionary* (1839).

[332] *FHR European Ventures Ltd v Cedar Capital Partners LLC* [2014] UKSC 45, [2015] AC 250, [47]. See also *Re Sharpe* [1980] 1 WLR 219; *Re Polly Peck International plc (No 2)* [1998] 3 All ER 812, 830 (Nourse LJ); *Cobbold v Bakewell Management Ltd* [2003] EWHC 2289 (Ch), [17] (Rimer J); *Shalson v Russo* [2005] Ch 281, [118] (Rimer J); *Re Farepak Food and Gifts Ltd* [2006] EWHC 3272 (Ch), [38] (Mann J).

[333] [1996] AC 669, 714–16.

[334] D Neuberger, 'The Remedial Constructive Trust—Fact or Fiction', delivered on 10 August 2014 to the Banking Services and Finance Law Association Conference, New Zealand.

[335] But the Supreme Court in *FHR European Ventures Ltd v Cedar Capital Partners LLC* [2014] UKSC 45, [2015] AC 250 surely did create a new property right in bribe money which had not existed previously. See p 512, above.

[336] See the decision of the Court of Appeal in *Re Polly Peck International plc (No 2)* [1998] 3 All ER 812.

[337] P Millett, 'Equity—The Road Ahead' (1995) 9 TLI 35, 42.

repugnant alike to legal certainty, the sanctity of property and the rule of law'.[338] He also recognized that:[339]

> The law of remedies is not exempt from the demands of certainty and predictability: nor is the law as a whole intellectually respectable if, even at the level of remedies, it takes refuge in an inscrutable case to case empiricism. Practising lawyers need to be able to advise their clients as to the likely results of litigation. The judges on whom these results depend need the insulation from personal criticism which only objectively ascertainable rules and principles can provide.

In fact, in those jurisdictions where the remedial constructive trust is recognized, it does not involve the exercise of an unprincipled judicial discretion. Equally, the English approach to the constructive trust involves more flexibility than is typically acknowledged.

In both England and Australia in particular a sterile debate has developed about the constructive trust where there are two camps, institutional versus remedial. It is preferable to ditch the intemperate language and the lazy characterization and acknowledge that there is just one constructive trust which is recognized by both jurisdictions. Indeed, as Deane J said in *Muschinski v Dodds*,[340] 'for the student of equity, there can be no true dichotomy between the two notions'. He added:[341]

> The fact that the constructive trust remains predominantly remedial does not, however, mean that it represents a medium for the indulgence of idiosyncratic notions of fairness and justice. As an equitable remedy, it is available only when warranted by established equitable principles or by the legitimate processes of legal reasoning, by analogy, induction and deduction, from the starting point of a proper understanding of the conceptual foundations of such principles ... proprietary rights fall to be governed by principles of law and not by some mix of judicial discretion, subjective views about which party 'ought to win' ... and 'the formless void' of individual moral opinion ...

In fact, *Muschinski v Dodds* might be considered to be one of the worst examples in Australian jurisprudence of remedial discretion. The case concerned a cohabiting couple who held the home they had purchased and developed in proportion to their contribution to it by means of a constructive trust, but this trust was only imposed at the time the reasons of the court were published. Justice Finn has described this as 'an astounding proposition'.[342] In some other Australian cases the remedial nature of the constructive trust is expressed with reference to the importance of only recognizing the trust if there are no other appropriate remedies available.[343] This itself is somewhat concerning, even though it purports to be principled, because it appears that there is no proprietary interest until the court creates one at the time of trial having considered what other remedies might be appropriate. It would be more appropriate to acknowledge that the constructive trust exists at the time of the relevant event, but the claimant might not be allowed to vindicate his or her equitable right because an alternative remedy would be more appropriate. Consequently, the constructive trust which already exists could be revoked if other judicial orders are capable of doing full justice.

In England the characterization of the constructive trust as institutional which cannot be modified by the exercise of judicial discretion, does not reflect the true operation of the

---

[338] PBH Birks, 'Property and Unjust Enrichment: Categorical Truths' [1997] NZ Law Rev 623, 641.

[339] PBH Birks, 'The Remedies for Abuse of Confidential Information' [1990] LMCLQ 460, 465.

[340] (1985) 160 CLR 583, 614.   [341] Ibid, 615.

[342] *Grimaldi v Chameleon Mining NL (No 2)* (2012) 200 FCR 296, [569].

[343] *Bathurst CC v PWC Properties Pty Ltd* (1998) 195 CLR 566, 585; *John Alexander's Clubs Pty Ltd v White City Tennis Club Ltd* [2010] HCA 19, (2010) 241 CLR 1, [37], [128].

constructive trust. For example, where the elements of proprietary estoppel have been established, the claimant's rights might be vindicated by recognizing a constructive trust through the exercise of judicial discretion.[344] In *Boardman v Phipps*[345] fiduciaries who profited from breaching their fiduciary duty were found to hold their profit on constructive trust for the principal. But this trust was modified in respect of one of them, who was awarded an equitable allowance to reflect the value of his work in making the profit.[346] Further, even in England there has been some judicial support for the recognition of the remedial constructive trust. For example, in *Westdeutsche Landesbank Girozentrale v Islington LBC*,[347] Lord Browne-Wilkinson suggested that it might be appropriate for this type of trust to be introduced into English law because it would enable proprietary relief to be tailored to the particular circumstances of the case, although he refused to decide the point since it was not directly in issue.

The appropriate model of the constructive trust consequently is one where the trust arises by operation of law where the defendant's receipt or retention of property is unconscionable, actual or deemed,[348] but this trust can be modified with reference to recognized principles, such that the trust might be defeasible. This characterization of the constructive trust would assuage some of Lord Neuberger's concerns. It does not subvert the statutory insolvency regime, for what Equity has created Equity can take away, as long as it is done on a principled basis. Indeed, the very creation of equitable proprietary rights by operation of judge-made law might be regarded as upsetting statutory insolvency regimes, but there are numerous examples of Equity doing that. Modification of the institutional constructive trust is much less controversial than, for example, the *Quistclose* trust.[349]

Once it is accepted that the constructive trust might be modified, it is important to consider when such modification might be justified. Three different scenarios can be identified which derive from the three distinct advantages of proprietary relief,[350] namely where the defendant is insolvent; where the property has increased in value and where the property has been received by an innocent third party. The relevance of these factors can be illustrated by considering potential modification of the constructive trust of stolen property and mistaken payments.[351]

Where a thief holds stolen property for the victim should this trust be modified for any of these reasons? First, if the thief has become insolvent, should the thief's creditors be able to assert a claim against the stolen assets? Since the stolen property never legitimately formed part of the thief's pool of assets, there is no reason why the thief's creditors should gain priority over the victim. Secondly, if the stolen asset has increased in value, there is no reason why the claimant should be deprived of the benefit of this increase, since the thief should not profit from his or her crime in any way.[352] Thirdly, should innocent third parties who have obtained possession of the asset have any better claim than the thief?[353] If the third party's conscience was not affected in any way at the time of receipt, since they neither knew nor suspected that the property had been stolen, surely their claim should be

---

[344] *Thorner v Major* [2009] UKHL 18, [2009] 1 WLR 776. See p 520, above.
[345] [1967] 2 AC 46. See p 498, above.   [346] See p 507, above.
[347] [1996] AC 669, 716. See also *Re Goldcorp Exchange Ltd* [1995] 1 AC 74, 104 (Lord Mustill); *London Allied Holdings v Lee* [2007] EWHC 2061 (Ch), [247] (Etherton J); *Thorner v Major* [2009] UKHL 18, [2009] 1 WLR 776, [20] (Lord Scott).
[348] See p 598, above.   [349] See p 593, above.   [350] See p 558, above.
[351] For similar analysis of the potential role of the remedial constructive trust where the defendant has profited from the breach of fiduciary duty, see p 513, above.   [352] See p 526, above.
[353] If the third-party recipient of the stolen property or its traceable substitute had provided value and acted in good faith, the victim's equitable proprietary claim would be defeated. See Chapter 23.

at least as good and possibly even better than that of the victim of the theft. It follows that the constructive trust of stolen property should not be modified to benefit creditors of the thief or the thief him or herself, but there might be a case to treat the constructive trust as revoked once the asset has been received by an innocent third party who has not provided value for the receipt.[354]

Where money paid by mistake is held on constructive trust because of the defendant's unconscionable retention, should this trust ever be modified? First, if the defendant has become insolvent, there is no reason why the defendant's creditors should have a better claim to the trust property than the claimant. Secondly, the defendant should not be allowed to gain from the retention of the asset, save where that gain cannot be causatively linked to the receipt. So, if the asset is invested and increases in value, the defendant should hold that increase on constructive trust. But, if the defendant used money paid by mistake to buy a lottery ticket which wins the jackpot, to determine whether that jackpot should be held on constructive trust should depend on whether it can be shown that, but for the receipt of the money paid by mistake, the defendant would not have bought the ticket. If the defendant would have bought the ticket anyway, and used the money paid by mistake by chance, this would be an appropriate reason to modify the constructive trust so that the jackpot is not held on trust. If the defendant did not rely on the receipt to buy the ticket, there is no reason why the claimant should have a proprietary claim to the jackpot. Thirdly, should the equitable proprietary right of the claimant be defeated by innocent receipt, not for value? Whilst the law assumes that the claimant should have a proprietary restitutionary claim against a third-party recipient who has not provided value,[355] this is difficult to defend. The claimant should be confined to a proprietary claim against the unconscionable recipient of the mistaken payment and not have a proprietary claim against an innocent third-party recipient, at least where the only reason why the equitable proprietary right was created was because of the initial recipient's unconscionable retention. If the third party's receipt cannot similarly be characterized as unconscionable, there is no reason why the claimant should have a proprietary claim against that recipient.

It is important to emphasize that much of this analysis of the 'remedial constructive trust' is speculative, especially because the institutional constructive trust appears so entrenched in England. But it is the failure to consider carefully what is meant by institutional versus remedial constructive trusts that has resulted in an unsophisticated analysis of the constructive trust. If it was recognized instead that the constructive trust arises by virtue of recognized principles but can be modified in a principled way, the constructive trust would cease to be the blunderbuss that it is today.

3. FOLLOWING AND TRACING

Once the claimant can establish that he or she has retained a legal interest in property or that an equitable interest can be recognized, it is then necessary for the claimant to identify a proprietary interest in the property which had been received by the defendant. To establish this the claimant will need to rely on the following and tracing rules.

---

[354] In *Relfo Ltd v Varsani* [2014] EWCA Civ 360, [2015] 1 BCLC 14, [1], Arden LJ, stated that money or its substitute can be recovered from a third party where the money was stolen by the fiduciary, if the money or its substitute was knowingly received by the third party. See also *FHR European Ventures LLP v Cedar Capital Partners LLC* [2014] UKSC 45, [2015] AC 250, [44] where Lord Neuberger indicated that bribe money held on constructive trust by a fiduciary could be claimed from a *knowing* recipient.

[355] *Re Diplock's Estate* [1948] Ch 465, 539.

(A) THE FUNCTION OF FOLLOWING AND TRACING

(i) The Essence of Following

The essence of following is that the claimant is able to show that the actual property in which he or she has a proprietary interest has been received by the defendant.[356] If the identity of the claimant's property has been lost or the property has been destroyed, the claimant will no longer be able to follow it. Where the claimant transfers the property directly to the defendant there is no difficulty in following the property. Where, however, the property is received indirectly by the defendant the question of following may be more difficult. It is for this reason that particular rules have been formulated which assist the claimant to follow his or her property into the defendant's hands.[357]

(ii) The Essence of Tracing

Where the original property cannot be followed (because, for example, it has been dissipated) it is necessary for the claimant to show that the value of the property in which he or she originally had a proprietary interest can be identified in property that has been received by the defendant.[358] In other words, the tracing rules enable the claimant to identify substitute property in the defendant's hands which the claimant had not previously owned but which can be considered to represent the claimant's original property. Only once the claimant has done this can he or she claim the property in the hands of the defendant or the value of that property.[359] So, for example, if the claimant paid £10,000 to a friend because of a fundamental mistake and the friend then used that money to buy a car, which she then sold for £15,000 and used the proceeds of sale to buy shares which she gave to her daughter, the claimant may wish to claim the shares from the daughter. To establish such a claim, the claimant will need to show both that he retained a proprietary interest in the original £10,000 which he paid by mistake and that this proprietary interest can be traced into the car, the proceeds of the car and ultimately into the shares, so that the value in the original £10,000 now subsists in the shares. Whether the claimant can establish this depends on the application of the tracing rules[360] which are evidential rules and presumptions that enable the claimant to prove that value in the original property is now represented in substitute property. The essence of tracing was identified by Lord Millett in *Foskett v McKeown*:[361]

> Tracing is thus neither a claim nor a remedy. It is merely the process by which the claimant demonstrates what has happened to his property, identifies its proceeds and the persons who have handled or received them, and justifies his claim that the proceeds can be regarded as representing his property. Tracing is also distinct from claiming. It identifies the traceable proceeds of the claimant's property. It enables the claimant to substitute the traceable proceeds for the original asset as the subject matter of his claim. But it does not affect or establish his claim.

Further, in *Shalson v Russo*[362] Rimer J described tracing as 'the process by which a claimant seeks to show that an interest he had in an asset has become represented by an interest in a different asset'.

In some cases it may be relatively easy for the claimant to show that value in one asset is now represented in another asset, such as where shares have been misappropriated from a

---

[356] *Foskett v McKeown* [2001] 1 AC 102, 127 (Lord Millett). See Smith, *The Law of Tracing*, 4.
[357] See p 613, below.   [358] *Foskett v McKeown* [2001] 1 AC 102, 128 (Lord Millett).
[359] Smith, *The Law of Tracing*, 3.   [360] See p 613, below.   [361] [2001] 1 AC 102, 127.
[362] [2003] EWHC 1637 (Ch), [2005] Ch 281, [102].

trust and are sold for cash, and the cash is then used to buy a car. In such a case, value is cleanly transferred from one asset to another via the cash. But there will be other cases that are much more factually complicated, such as where many different amounts are credited to a bank account, including the claimant's money, and many different amounts are paid from this bank account. In this situation it will not be obvious whether the value of the claimant's money that has been credited to the account remains in the account, so the tracing rules are needed to identify where the money contributed by the claimant can be considered to be located.

The operation of the tracing rules is illustrated particularly well by the facts of *Foskett v McKeown*.[363] In that case, the beneficiaries sought to recover a proportionate share of the payment of a death benefit from the children of the trustee, where the fourth and fifth annual premium had been paid from the beneficiaries' trust. The initial proprietary base was established by virtue of the money being held on an express trust for the beneficiaries. It was then necessary to establish by reference to the equitable tracing rules that the money from the trust fund could be traced from that fund, through various bank accounts, into the premiums which were paid to the insurance company and from there into the payment of the death benefit following the suicide of the trustee. The first part of the tracing exercise was straightforward, since it could be shown that the claimants' money had been used to pay two premiums.[364] The difficulty in the case concerned tracing from the premiums into the payment of the death benefit, via the insurance policy, which turned on the appropriate analysis of the function of the premiums in the light of the unusual nature of the insurance policy. This was a unit-linked life policy under which the premiums were used to pay for the cost of life cover through the allocation of units that were exhausted over time. Each premium bought a number of units and each unit kept the policy going for a bit longer. The policy would lapse only once all of the units had been used up. Paying a premium was rather like topping up a parking meter: each time a payment is made, the car can be parked for an additional period of time. Since the first three premiums, which were paid from the trustee's own money, had purchased a substantial number of units, it followed that even if the fourth and fifth premiums had not been paid, the policy would not have lapsed at the time of the trustee's death, because the units purchased from the first three premiums were still operating. So what was the effect of the fourth and fifth premiums?

For Lord Steyn, who dissented,[365] the fact that the policy would not have lapsed had the fourth and fifth premiums not been paid meant that there was no link between the payment of those premiums and the receipt of the death benefit, so tracing was not possible. This involved a simple causative approach to the tracing exercise: the fourth and fifth premiums had not contributed to the death benefit being paid. The majority disagreed and adopted a different approach to the tracing exercise. Although they acknowledged that, in the events that happened, the premiums paid from the trust fund were not required to prevent the insurance policy from lapsing, they also recognized that this need not have been the case.[366] If, for example, the trustee had lived longer, the premiums would have contributed to the maintenance of the policy. Consequently, Lord Browne-Wilkinson recognized that[367] 'the beneficial ownership of the policy, and therefore the policy moneys, cannot depend on how events turn out. The rights of the parties in

[363] [2001] 1 AC 102. See p 568, above.
[364] For tracing into and through bank accounts in Equity, see p 618, below.
[365] *Foskett v McKeown* [2001] 1 AC 102, 113.
[366] Ibid, 111 (Lord Browne-Wilkinson) and 138 (Lord Millett).   [367] Ibid, 111.

the policy, one way or another, were fixed when the relevant premiums were paid when the future was unknown'. It followed that it was possible to trace the two premiums into the insurance policy, which was property in its own right because it consisted of a bundle of rights to which the policy holder was entitled in return for payment of the premiums, and from that to the death benefit, which represented the traceable proceeds of the policy and indirectly of the premiums.

In reaching the conclusion that it was possible to trace into the death benefit, the majority identified two fundamental principles of tracing.

(1) Attribution Rather Than Causation

If the tracing rules were to depend on establishing a causal link between the receipt of the original asset and obtaining a substitute asset, in the sense that, but for the receipt of the original asset the substitute would not have been obtained, tracing into the death benefit could not have been possible in *Foskett v McKeown* because the fourth and fifth premiums did not cause the death benefit to be obtained. But, since the majority recognized that tracing was possible on the facts, it follows that tracing need not depend on identifying a causal link between the original and substitute asset. Rather, tracing depends on attribution.[368] In *Foskett v McKeown* it was sufficient that the death benefit could be attributed to the fourth and fifth premiums, and this could be shown because the death benefit was to be paid, according to the terms of the insurance policy, in consideration for all of the premiums paid, which therefore included the fourth and fifth premiums.[369] This shift away from causation to attribution is important to our understanding of tracing, especially when it is coupled with a second key conclusion about the nature of tracing.

(2) Tracing Value Rather Than Identifying Property

All of the judges in *Foskett v McKeown* recognized that tracing was not concerned with the identification of chains of property, but instead focused on the identification of value within property. It is this value that is the essence of the claimant's proprietary right and it is this value that is traced. This was expressly recognized by Lord Millett:[370]

> We speak of tracing one asset into another, but this too is inaccurate. The original asset still exists in the hands of the new owner, or it may have become untraceable. The claimant claims the new asset because it was acquired in whole or in part with the original asset. What he traces, therefore, is not the physical asset itself but the value inherent in it.

The recognition of these two principles in *Foskett v McKeown* means that the operation of the tracing rules should be easier. Tracing does not depend on causation in any meaningful sense. Rather, we are concerned only with logical progression: with the identification of value in various locations without regard to the effect of that value on particular property, in that it need not be shown that the property was acquired because of that value. In *Foskett v McKeown* the claimants' value could be traced from the trust fund, through bank accounts, into two premiums, then into the policy itself, and finally into the proceeds of that policy. In a telling phrase, Lord Millett talked of establishing 'transactional links';[371] this is now the essential feature of tracing.

---

[368] Ibid, 137 (Lord Millett). Compare Lord Hope who, dissenting, expressly stated that the death benefit was not attributable to the payment of the premiums: ibid, 122.

[369] Ibid, 116 (Lord Hoffmann), 119 (Lord Hope), and 133 (Lord Millett).

[370] Ibid, 128.   [371] Ibid.

Although the decision of the majority in *Foskett v McKeown* is very significant to the modern understanding of the function of the law of tracing, the conclusion that it was possible to trace into the death benefit was dubious for two reasons. First, the assertion that the court is not concerned with how events turned out, but rather with proprietary rights at the time at which the premiums were paid, is inconsistent with the key conclusion that tracing is simply a matter of evidence. Consequently, the court should have regard to all of the evidence, and so, if the premiums paid from the trust fund might have contributed to the payment of the death benefit but did not actually do so, this should have defeated the tracing exercise. Secondly, even though the majority relied on the fact that the terms of the insurance policy stated that the £1 million was paid in consideration of all of the premiums, it is not clear why this contractual term was sufficient to influence proprietary rights to the money. In particular, the fourth and fifth premiums were used to buy units that formed part of a mixed fund of units, since the first three premiums had also purchased units that had not all been used up. Until the trustee's suicide, these units were gradually used to prevent the policy from lapsing. But which units would have been used first? The logical answer is that the first in time would have been used first, which would mean that the units attributable to the fourth and fifth premiums remained outstanding, and this conclusion could not be changed by the inclusion of a contractual term that the premiums were paid in consideration of all premiums, unless that term stated explicitly that the most recently paid premiums were to be treated as used first. It follows that, for both of these reasons, the preferable view is that it should have been possible to trace the trust funds into the fourth and fifth premiums and into the purchase of units, but it should not have been possible to trace into the payment following the trustee's death.

(iii) Tracing into Substitute Assets

A matter of particular controversy as regards the application of the tracing rules concerns how a right in one piece of property can be asserted against a substitute asset. In particular, does this right in the substitute property arise automatically or as a result of the exercise of a power by the claimant? The law on this point is confused. There is authority which suggests that the claimant obtains an immediate interest in the substitute asset,[372] and Lord Millett in *Foskett v McKeown* adopted such an approach.[373] Alternatively, there is authority that suggests that the claimant has only a power to crystallize his or her proprietary interest in the substitute asset. This power analysis was recognized by Lord Goff as regards Common Law proprietary claims.[374] *Foskett v McKeown* itself provides some support for this power analysis. Lord Millett did recognize that the claimant has a power,[375] but this relates to the choice to pursue a claim either against the original asset or its substitute, as long as both can still be identified. The preferable view is that once the original asset cannot be identified, the equitable interest relating to that asset is extinguished and is automatically replaced by a proprietary interest in the substitute. Where, however, the original asset and the substitute can both be identified, the claimant can elect either to claim the original asset or its substitute.[376] If the claimant chooses to claim the substitute, this will extinguish the proprietary interest in the original

---

[372] *Cave v Cave* (1880) 15 Ch D 639 (Fry J). See also *Re Diplock's Estate* [1948] Ch 465; Smith, *The Law of Tracing*, 356–61.

[373] *Foskett v McKeown* [2001] 1 AC 102, 134.

[374] *Lipkin Gorman (a firm) v Karpnale Ltd* [1991] 2 AC 548, 573. See also *Re French's Estate* (1887) 21 LR Ir 283.   [375] *Foskett v McKeown* [2001] 1 AC 102, 127.

[376] See *Boscawen v Bajwa* [1996] 1 WLR 328, 342 (Millett LJ).

asset and transfer it to the substitute, unless that substitute has been obtained by a *bona fide* purchaser for value.

This election analysis has a number of advantages. In particular, it explains why the claimant cannot bring proprietary claims against both the original property and the substituted property. By assuming that the claimant has a power to shift the proprietary interest from the original property to its substitute and that this can occur only once the power of election has been exercised, it follows that the claimant is able to bring only one proprietary claim at a time. But this election analysis does cause problems of its own.[377] For example, if the effect of this analysis is that the claimant has no interest in the substitute until the power of election has been exercised, it should follow that, if the defendant who is in possession of the substitute becomes insolvent before the claimant has made the election, the claimant's right to the substitute ought to be extinguished.[378]

(iv) Distinguishing Between Tracing and Claiming

The decision in *Foskett v McKeown* is also important because of the clear distinction which was drawn between tracing and claiming. The purpose of tracing is to see whether a link can be established between the original asset and the substitute property. Sometimes tracing has been regarded as a remedy in its own right,[379] but that is patently incorrect. As Lord Steyn said, it is 'a process of identifying assets: it belongs to the law of evidence. It tells us nothing about legal or equitable rights to the assets traced'.[380] So, in *Foskett* the function of the tracing rules was only to identify a link to the death benefit, so that the claimant had a proprietary interest in it. It was then necessary to make a claim to that property and determine how the proprietary interest could be vindicated. This is the claiming exercise and it was this which proved to be the key issue in the case, namely whether a lien or a proportionate share was the most appropriate remedy for vindicating the claimant's proprietary interest.[381] In many cases the appropriate remedy will be a matter for the claimant to choose,[382] but this will depend on both remedies being available to the claimant as a matter of law.

(v) Distinguishing Between Tracing at Common Law and in Equity

The tracing rules are complex essentially because of the fundamental differences between tracing at Common Law and in Equity.[383] Tracing at Law is relevant where the claimant has a legal proprietary base; the equitable tracing rules apply where a claim is founded on an equitable proprietary base. Separate tracing rules developed depending on whether the claim relates to legal or equitable property rights, because the Common Law courts would not recognize equitable rights and the Court of Chancery was not bound to apply the Common Law tracing rules.[384] Consequently, that Court 'developed its own more sophisticated rules of identification and recognized a wider range of proprietary interests which

---

[377] See S Khurshid and M Matthews, 'Tracing Confusion' (1979) 95 LQR 78, and N Andrews and J Beatson, 'Common Law Tracing: Springboard or Swan-Song?' (1997) 113 LQR 21, 24.

[378] Grantham, 'Doctrinal Bases for the Recognition of Proprietary Rights', 570.

[379] See *Sinclair v Brougham* [1914] AC 398.

[380] *Foskett v McKeown* [2001] 1 AC 102, 113, citing PBH Birks, 'The Necessity of a Unitary Law of Tracing' in R Cranston (ed), *Making Commercial Law, Essays in Honour of Roy Goode* (Oxford: Oxford University Press, 1997), 239. See also *Foskett v McKeown*, 109 (Lord Browne-Wilkinson) and 128 and 139 (Lord Millett). Confusingly, despite earlier recognizing the distinction between tracing and claiming, Lord Millett considered the question of claiming under the heading of 'The tracing rules': ibid, 129–33.

[381] See p 632, below.   [382] *Foskett v McKeown* [2001] 1 AC 102, 130 (Lord Millett).

[383] *Re Diplock's Estate* [1948] Ch 465, 518–21.   [384] Ibid.

the plaintiff could claim in a substituted asset'.[385] In fact, this is historically inaccurate, and there is no evidence of distinct tracing rules at Common Law and in Equity until the twentieth century.[386]

In *FHR European Ventures LLP v Cedar Capital Partners LLC*[387] the Supreme Court asserted that Common Law tracing is possible without a proprietary interest. No authority was provided for this *obiter dictum*, which is inconsistent with fundamental principles underpinning the law of tracing.

As will be seen,[388] this distinction between tracing at Common Law and in Equity is indefensible. Although some commentators[389] and judges[390] have argued that there is no longer any distinction between tracing at Law and in Equity, it is not yet possible to reach such a conclusion, because the distinction has been clearly recognized in a number of authorities.[391] In *Foskett v McKeown*, some of the judges called for the unification of the tracing rules at Common Law and in Equity,[392] but this was clearly *obiter* since the basic requirements for tracing in Equity were clearly established in that case.

(B) FOLLOWING

The rules on following exist to enable the claimant to establish that the defendant has received the claimant's property. The rules themselves cause no great difficulty and are usefully described and analysed by Smith in his book, *The Law of Tracing*. The rules are particularly important when the claimant's property has been mixed with the defendant's, where it is necessary to determine whether the claimant's property has lost its identity and so cannot be followed.[393] It will not be possible to follow the claimant's property where it has been subsumed into another asset, has become a fixture or has been merged with another asset to form a new one.[394] Where it is no longer possible to follow the claimant's property it may be possible to trace the value of the property into a substitute asset.

(C) TRACING AT COMMON LAW

(i) Tracing into Pure Substitutes and Products

The Common Law tracing rules are logical but restrictive. The fundamental principle underlying these rules is that the claimant will be able to identify the value of his or her property in the substitutes for that property,[395] as long as the substitute has not become mixed with other property so that it loses its identity.[396] So, to take the simplest case, if the

---

[385] Ibid.

[386] The wrong turning appears to have been made by Viscount Haldane in *Sinclair v Brougham* [1914] AC 348, 419–21. See GJ Virgo, '*Re Hallett's Estate*' in C Mitchell and P Mitchell (eds), *Landmark Cases in Equity* (Oxford: Hart Publishing, 2012), 389.

[387] [2014] UKSC 45, [2015] AC 250, [44].   [388] See p 628, below.

[389] See especially Smith, *The Law of Tracing*, 5, and Khurshid and Matthews, 'Tracing Confusion'.

[390] *Bristol and West Building Society v Mothew* [1998] Ch 1, 23, 716 (Millett LJ).

[391] *Agip (Africa) Ltd v Jackson* [1990] Ch 265, 286 (Millett J); [1991] Ch 547, 566 (Fox LJ); *El Ajou v Dollar Land Holdings plc* [1993] 3 All ER 717, 733 (Millett J); *Boscawen v Bajwa* [1996] 1 WLR 328; *Shalson v Russo* [2005] Ch 281, 314 (Rimer J).

[392] *Foskett v McKeown* [2001] 1 AC 102, 113 (Lord Steyn) and 128–9 (Lord Millett). Lord Browne-Wilkinson expressly did not consider this: ibid, 109.

[393] Smith, *The Law of Tracing*, 70 et seq.   [394] Ibid, 104.

[395] *Banque Belge pour l'Etranger v Hambrouck* [1921] 1 KB 321; *Lipkin Gorman (a firm) v Karpnale Ltd* [1991] 2 AC 548.

[396] *Trustee of the Property of FC Jones v Jones* [1997] Ch 159, 169 (Millett LJ).

defendant stole the claimant's car and sold it, the claimant would be able to trace his or her continuing proprietary interest into the proceeds of sale, assuming that they still exist and have not been polluted by irretrievable mixing with any other money. If the defendant used the proceeds of sale to buy another car, without contributing any part of the purchase price him or herself, the claimant could trace into that car and then bring a proprietary restitutionary claim to it. The ability of the claimant to claim the substitute for the original property is called the exchange-product theory.

The logic behind these tracing rules is clear. To the extent that the substitute directly represents the original property there can be no objection to allowing tracing into the substitute. If the claimant's original property ceases to exist, there will be no choice but to trace the value of the original property into its substitute. For example, if the defendant took the claimant's car and sold it to a third party who drove the car and crashed it so that it was destroyed, the claimant cannot recover the car, but he or she can instead trace into the substitute, the proceeds of sale, in the hands of the defendant. Where, however, the original property and the proceeds of sale continue to exist, the claimant has a choice as to whether to claim the original property or the proceeds of sale.[397] This is simply a matter for the claimant to decide whether or not to claim the original property or the substitute and has nothing to do with adoption or ratification.[398] If the defendant has exercised skill and labour in effecting a profitable exchange, it is not possible to reflect this in a claim at Law because there is no scope for the award of an allowance. The defendant might, however, be able to bring a claim founded on unjust enrichment, with the ground of restitution being mistake as to the ownership of the property.

(ii) Tracing into Profits

Usually, where the claimant has traced property at Law he or she simply traces into the substitute for the property. It has been recognized by the Court of Appeal in *Trustee of the Property of FC Jones v Jones*[399] that the claimant can also trace at Law into the profits made from the use of his or her property. In that case, the partners in a firm of potato growers committed an act of bankruptcy. One of the partners drew cheques for £11,700 from a partnership bank account and paid them to his wife, who in turn paid the cheques into her account with a firm of commodity brokers. This money was applied on the potato futures market, and the wife made a large profit and deposited £50,760 into a deposit account at her bank. This money was never mixed with her own money. The trustee in bankruptcy of the partnership claimed this whole amount. The trustee was legally entitled to the money in the partnership bank account from the date of the bankruptcy,[400] but the key question was whether he could trace at Law into the profits that had been credited to the wife's bank account.[401] It was held that he could, because there was a chain of straight substitutions from the money in the partnership account to the chose in action representing the funds deposited at the wife's bank account. It did not matter that the original money paid from the partnership bank account had nearly quintrupled in value; the trustee in bankruptcy was entitled to claim this profit simply because it derived from the original money without being mixed with any other money of the wife.

---

[397] *Marsh v Keating* (1834) 1 Bing (NC) 198, 131 ER 1094.
[398] *Lipkin Gorman (a firm) v Karpnale Ltd* [1991] 2 AC 548, 573 (Lord Goff).
[399] [1997] Ch 159.
[400] This is no longer the law: Insolvency Act 1986, ss 278 and 306.
[401] An equitable proprietary claim could not be established because statute had passed the entire interest in the partnership money to the trustee in bankruptcy, so it could not have been held on trust by the wife.

(iii) Tracing into Mixed Products

The major limitation on the efficacy of tracing at Law is that it is not possible to trace into a mixed product,[402] save where it is possible to separate the components of the product. There are two reasons why tracing into a mixed fund at Law is not possible: first, because of the inadequacies of legal proprietary remedies, especially that it is not possible to create a security interest over a mixed fund at Law by means of charging the fund for the amount due.[403] Secondly, because the Law adopts a rigidly logical approach to tracing. Where there has been an irretrievable mixing it is simply not possible to say in what property the claimant has a proprietary interest. Consequently, where such mixing has occurred, the claimant's legal title to the property will be extinguished.

The key implication of this restriction on tracing at Law arises where the claimant's money becomes mixed in the defendant's bank account, so that it is not possible to say which money belongs to the claimant and which to the defendant. It has sometimes been suggested that the effect of the restriction on Common Law tracing into mixed products is that, if the claimant's money is paid into a bank account, tracing will automatically fail. But this is not the case. The Common Law is willing to trace into a bank account, even though the property in which the claimant has a proprietary interest has changed its identity from a sum of money to a debt owed by the bank to the account holder. But, since this debt represents completely the sum of money which originally existed, assuming that no other money had been credited to this account either before or after the claimant's money had been credited to it, the debt can simply be regarded as the substitute for the claimant's money. A good example of tracing in such circumstances is *Banque Belge Pour L'Etranger v Hambrouck*[404] where the first defendant forged a number of cheques so that £6,000 was debited from the account of his employer at the claimant bank and this sum was credited to his own bank account. The first defendant then drew sums from this account which he paid to his mistress and she paid these sums into her own bank account. The claimant bank sought to recover this money from the mistress. At the time of the bank's action the mistress's account was credited with £315. The Court of Appeal held that the claimant was able to trace into this credit because only the proceeds of the fraud had been paid into the account of the first defendant and his mistress, so that there had not been any mixing of money. It did not matter that the tracing process did not relate to sums of money throughout, since at various stages credits were substituted for actual money. This did not matter because the credits simply represented the money and neither the credits nor the money were ever tainted by any other money or credits which did not derive from the fraud.

Modern banking practice is such that it is increasingly difficult to trace into and through a bank account. This is especially because of electronic transfers, which mean that the claimant is unable to show that the money received by the defendant necessarily represents the claimant's money. This limitation on the efficacy of tracing at Law was recognized in *Trustee of the Property of FC Jones v Jones*,[405] in which Millett LJ affirmed that it was not possible to trace through inter-bank clearing and that tracing at Law would be defeated where value is passed by an electronic funds transfer. The practical

---

[402] *Taylor v Plumer* (1815) 3 M and S 562, 105 ER 721; *Agip (Africa) Ltd v Jackson* [1991] Ch 547; *El Ajou v Dollar Land Holdings* [1993] 3 All ER 717. LD Smith, 'Tracing in *Taylor v. Plumer*: Equity in the Court of King's Bench' [1995] LMCLQ 240 has argued that *Taylor v Plumer* actually turned on tracing in Equity. This was recognized by Millett LJ in *Trustee of the Property of FC Jones v Jones* [1997] Ch 159, 169 but he still affirmed the rule that tracing at Law is barred if the property has been mixed with other property.

[403] *Agip (Africa) Ltd v Jackson* [1991] Ch 547, 563 (Fox LJ).

[404] [1921] 1 KB 321.   [405] [1997] Ch 159, 168.

significance of this is illustrated by *Agip (Africa) Ltd v Jackson*,[406] where the claimant bank had been defrauded of substantial sums of money by its chief accountant. The case focused on a payment to a company that had a bank account in London. Before the payment was made, the company had nothing credited to this account. Once the payment had been made, the balance was transferred to the defendant firm of accountants, and then to another company, and finally overseas to the fraudsters. The claimant sought to recover the value of the money received by the defendant. It succeeded in Equity, but failed at Law because of mixing, since there had been a telegraphic transfer of the money between accounts, so nothing passed except for a stream of electrons.

The inability of the Common Law to trace through a mixed fund explains why tracing in Equity has proved so much more significant in practice, since Equity will trace through mixed funds. But, for the equitable tracing rules to be engaged, the claimant must first establish an equitable proprietary base; it is not yet possible to rely on the equitable tracing rules where the claimant has only a legal proprietary base. There are some signs, however, of greater flexibility being introduced into the Common Law tracing rules, albeit in jurisdictions other than England. For example, in *BMP Global Distribution Inc v Bank of Nova Scotia*,[407] the Supreme Court of Canada recognized that the transfer of money through the clearing system does not constitute a systematic break in the chain of possession of the funds, so that it would be possible to trace at Law into a mixed bank account if it is possible to identify the funds.[408] This cannot yet be regarded as representing English law, but it does provide further evidence for the gradual breakdown of the long-standing distinction between the tracing rules at Law and in Equity.

(D) TRACING IN EQUITY

The main advantage of tracing in Equity is that it will not be defeated by the irretrievable mixing of property.[409] This difference in approach between Law and Equity has been expressed in terms that the Common Law views property as physical assets, whereas Equity is able to view property metaphysically.[410] Consequently, where money in which the claimant has a proprietary interest is mixed in a bag with the defendant's money, so that it is not possible to say which coins or notes belong to which party, tracing at Law will fail because the Common Law cannot identify the actual coins or notes in which the claimant has a proprietary interest. But Equity is able to assume that the claimant's property continues to exist in the mixture, albeit that it is not possible to say which coins or notes belong to which party. The reason Equity can do this is because, when the claimant has traced an equitable proprietary interest into a mixed fund, an equitable charge will be placed on the whole fund as security for the claim.[411] Consequently, Equity does not specifically regard any particular part of the fund as actually belonging to the claimant, but is prepared to assume that the claimant has an equitable interest in the mixture by means of a charge on the fund.

---

[406] [1990] Ch 265, affirmed by the Court of Appeal: [1991] Ch 547.   [407] [2009] SCC 15.

[408] This was considered to be consistent with *Banque Belge pour l'Etranger v Hambrouck* [1921] 1 KB 321 and *Agip (Africa) Ltd v Jackson* [1991] Ch 547, although the latter case was specifically concerned with tracing in equity.

[409] *Re Hallett's Estate* (1880) 13 Ch D 696; *Sinclair v Brougham* [1914] AC 398; *Agip (Africa) Ltd v Jackson* [1991] Ch 417.   [410] *Re Diplock* [1948] Ch 465, 520.

[411] *Re Hallett's Estate* (1880) 13 Ch D 696, 708–10 (Jessel MR); *Sinclair v Brougham* [1914] AC 398, 420–2 (Viscount Haldane LC), 441–2 (Lord Parker of Waddington), and 459–60 (Lord Sumner); *El Ajou v Dollar Land Holding* [1993] 3 All ER 717, 735–6 (Millett J).

Since Equity is prepared to trace into and through a mixed fund, complex rules have been developed to determine how such tracing can occur. This will be examined after a further distinction between tracing at Law and Equity has been considered, namely that, to trace in Equity, it is first necessary to identify a fiduciary relationship.

(i) The Fiduciary Requirement

The orthodox requirement for tracing in Equity is that it is necessary to show that the property in which the claimant had an equitable proprietary interest passed to the defendant through the hands of a fiduciary in breach of duty.[412] In other words, there must have been an unauthorized disposition of property.[413] It is not, however, necessary to show that the defendant owed fiduciary duties to the claimant, since it suffices that the fiduciary through whose hands the property passed was an intermediary between the claimant and the defendant.[414] This is illustrated by *Re Diplock*[415] in which the executors of Diplock's will distributed £203,000 amongst 139 different charities. The validity of the will was successfully challenged by the next of kin,[416] who then sought to recover the money that had been paid to the charities. It was held that their equitable proprietary claim succeeded, even though their money had been mixed in some cases with the money already held by the charities in bank accounts. It did not matter that there was no fiduciary relationship between the next of kin and the charities, because it was sufficient that there was a prior fiduciary relationship between the next of kin and the executors, who had transferred the estate in breach of fiduciary duty.

Although the condition for tracing in Equity that the property has passed through the prism of a fiduciary relationship has been recognized in many cases, it is controversial. The requirement has been expressly rejected in New Zealand.[417] In *Agip (Africa) Ltd v Jackson*[418] Millett J affirmed that, in England, a fiduciary relationship is required to permit the assistance of Equity to be invoked, but he accepted that this requirement has been widely condemned[419] and depended on authority rather than principle. He recognized that it was not necessary to show that the fund had been the subject of fiduciary obligations before it got into the wrong hands; it was sufficient that the transfer to the defendant had created the fiduciary relationship. This is significant to our understanding of what the fiduciary relationship is being required to do. This can also be identified from *Re Diplock* itself, in which the actual requirement for tracing in Equity was that there was 'a fiduciary or quasi-fiduciary relationship or of a continuing right of property recognised in Equity'.[420] The key requirement for tracing in Equity today should consequently be that the claimant has a 'right of property recognised in equity', which is either a continuing

---

[412] *Re Hallett's Estate* (1880) 13 Ch D 696, 710 (Jessel MR); *Re Diplock's Estate* [1948] Ch 465; *Agip (Africa) Ltd v Jackson* [1991] Ch 547, 566 (Fox LJ); *El Ajou v Dollar Land Holdings plc* [1993] 3 All ER 717, 733 (Millett J); *Boscawen v Bajwa* [1996] 1 WLR 328, 335 (Millett LJ); *Bank of America v Arnell* [1999] Lloyd's Rep Bank 399. *Re Diplock's Estate* was specifically affirmed by Lord Browne-Wilkinson in *Westdeutsche Landesbank Girozentrale v Islington LBC* [1996] AC 669, 714.

[413] *Space Investments Ltd v Canadian Imperial Bank of Commerce Trust Co (Bahamas) Ltd* [1986] 1 WLR 1072. If the disposition is authorized, the claimant's proprietary interest will be overreached, so that the claimant no longer has an equitable proprietary interest in the asset.

[414] *Re Diplock's Estate* [1948] Ch 465. See also *Boscawen v Bajwa* [1996] 1 WLR 328.

[415] [1948] Ch 465.

[416] *Chichester Diocesan Fund and Board of Finance Inc v Simpson* [1944] AC 341.

[417] *Elders Pastoral Ltd v Bank of New Zealand* [1989] 2 NZLR 180.

[418] [1990] Ch 265, 290.

[419] Including subsequently by himself: P Millett, 'Tracing the Proceeds of Fraud' (1991) 107 LQR 71.

[420] *Re Diplock* [1948] Ch 465, 520.

right or one that is created as a result of a breach of a fiduciary or some other duty.[421]
Rather than focusing on a fiduciary relationship, the only condition for the equitable
tracing rules to apply should be that the claimant can establish an equitable proprietary
base.[422] This approach was implicitly recognized in *Campden Hill Ltd v Chakrani*,[423] in
which Hart J held that the fiduciary relationship can be established from the 'division of
the legal and beneficial ownership' of the property,[424] and, in *Re Diplock* itself, the Court
recognized the principle that:[425]

> equity may operate on the conscience not merely of those who acquire a legal title in
> breach of some trust, express or constructive, or of some other fiduciary obligation, but of
> volunteers provided that as a result of what has gone before some equitable proprietary
> interest has been created and attaches to the property in the hands of the volunteer.

This was actually highly significant on the facts of *Re Diplock* itself, because the next of kin,
being the potential beneficiaries under a will, had no initial equitable interest in the
undistributed property.[426] The only way in which such an equitable proprietary interest
could be created was by treating the executors as owing a fiduciary duty to the next of kin
that they had breached by mistakenly transferring the estate to the charities. As a result of
this breach of fiduciary duty, the charities should be treated as holding the money on
constructive trust for the next of kin, because the property should have been transferred to
them. The Court of Appeal in *Re Diplock's Estate* did not consider this aspect of the
decision, but the creation of an equitable proprietary interest was clearly essential before
the next of kin could trace in Equity and then bring an equitable proprietary claim.

(ii) Unmixed Funds

It is clearly possible to trace value at Equity into an unmixed fund. So, for example, if a
trustee misappropriates trust property, such as shares, which he or she sells and the
proceeds of sale are credited to a bank account that has no other money credited to it, the
beneficiary will be able to trace into that bank account. Similarly, if a trustee wrongly uses
trust money to pay the whole purchase price in respect of a particular asset, the beneficiary
can trace into that asset.[427]

(iii) Mixed Funds

A mixed fund will arise where money in which the claimant has an equitable proprietary interest has become mixed with somebody else's money. This mixing may be a
physical mixing, such as where £100 of the claimant's money is put into a bag that
already contains £100 of the defendant's money. Alternatively, this may be a notional
mixing, such as where the claimant's money is credited to the defendant's bank account
that already has money credited to it. Equity allows tracing into and through a mixed
fund, as was recognized by Millett J in *El Ajou v Dollar Land Holding*:[428]

---

[421] See AJ Oakley, 'The Prerequisites of an Equitable Tracing Claim' (1975) CLP 64; R Pearce, 'A Tracing
Paper' [1976] Conv 277, 288.
[422] See *Westdeutsche Landesbank Girozentrale v Islington LBC* [1994] 1 WLR 938, 947 (Dillon LJ) and 953
(Leggatt LJ). Although this decision was overruled by the House of Lords, nothing was said about this point.
See also Grantham, 'Doctrinal Bases for the Recognition of Proprietary Rights', 65 and Smith, *The Law of
Tracing*, 123–30.
[423] [2005] EWHC 911 (Ch).   [424] Ibid, [74].   [425] *Re Diplock* [1948] Ch 465, 530.
[426] *Commissioner of Stamp Duties (Qld) v Livingston* [1965] AC 694.
[427] *Re Hallett's Estate* (1880) 13 Ch D 696, 709 (Jessel MR).
[428] *El Ajou v Dollar Land Holding* [1993] BCLC 735, 753.

The victims of a fraud can follow[429] their money in equity through a bank account where it has been mixed with other moneys because equity treats the money in such accounts as charged with the repayment of their money. If the money in the account subject to the charge is afterwards paid out of the account and into a number of different accounts, the victims can claim a similar charge of each of the recipient accounts. They are not bound to choose between them...Equity's power to charge a mixed fund with the repayment of trust moneys...enables the claimant to follow the money not because it is theirs, but because it is derived from a fund which is treated as if it were subject to a charge in their favour.

Complex rules have developed to balance the interests of the different contributors to the mixed fund. Different rules and presumptions exist depending on whether the claimant's money has been mixed with that of a fiduciary or of an innocent third party.

(1) Mixing with the Fiduciary's Money

Where the fiduciary has mixed the claimant's money with his or her own, either physically or notionally, the onus is on the fiduciary to distinguish the separate assets; to the extent that he or she is unable to do so, they will belong to the claimant.[430] This is because, where a fiduciary wrongly mixes his or her own money with that of the claimant, the fiduciary has created an evidential difficulty as to what has happened to the claimant's money. In such a case the evidential difficulty will be resolved against the interests of the fiduciary, save where the fiduciary can show otherwise on the balance of probabilities.[431] Whether the fiduciary is able to show this will turn on the facts. An example of a case in which it was held that the trustee had not used the trust fund to purchase an asset was *Re Tilley's Will Trust*,[432] in which the trustee had mixed trust funds with her own funds in her bank account and then bought some properties for development. It was held that these properties were not purchased with the trust money that had been credited to her bank account, but from the use of overdraft facilities that were available to her.

A consequence of the general principle relating to the fiduciary's creation of an evidential difficulty by mixing property is that the claimant is able to rely on one of two alternative presumptions to assist with the tracing exercise. The claimant can rely on whichever presumption is most favourable to him or her.

(a) Fiduciary Spent Own Money First

The first presumption is that the fiduciary spent his or her own money first, so the claimant will be able to trace into the sum remaining in the fund.[433] The significance of this presumption is illustrated by *Re Hallett's Estate*,[434] in which Hallett, a solicitor, had settled money on trust for himself, his wife, and his children. The trustees of the settlement transferred some of the trust property to Hallett to invest. He did so, but then sold the investments and paid the proceeds to his personal bank account. He had also been given some bonds by a client to look after. He sold those bonds and the proceeds of sale were also credited to his bank account. He made various payments from and to this account. He died insolvent, and the trustees of the settlement and his client brought proprietary claims to the money that was still credited to his bank account. At the date of his death, there

---

[429] Despite using the language of following, Millett J is actually referring to tracing.

[430] *Lupton v White* (1808) 15 Ves Jun 432, 33 ER 817; *Re Tilley's Will Trust* [1967] 1 Ch 1179, 1183 (Ungoed-Thomas J).

[431] *Sinclair Investments (UK) Ltd v Versailles Trade Finance Ltd* [2011] EWCA Civ 347, [2012] Ch 453, [100] (Lord Neuberger MR). [432] [1967] 1 Ch 1179.

[433] *Re Hallett's Estate* (1880) 13 Ch D 696.   [434] Ibid.

were sufficient funds credited to that account to meet the claims of both the trustees and the client, but the crucial question for the Court of Appeal was whether they could both recover in priority to Hallett's general creditors. This turned on whether the payments that had been made from the account were made with Hallett's money or that of the claimants. It was held that Hallett, who was in a fiduciary relationship with both the trustees and the client, should be presumed to have drawn his own money out of the account first, so that the money that remained credited to the account could be distributed between the trustees and the client.

(b) Fiduciary Spent the Claimant's Money First

The alternative presumption is that the fiduciary spent the claimant's money first. The claimant will want to rely on this presumption where the fiduciary has used money from the mixed fund to purchase an asset and dissipated the remaining amount of the fund; the claimant can trace into the purchased asset by presuming that the fiduciary intended to purchase that asset using the claimant's money rather than his or her own money.[435] The operation of this presumption is illustrated by *Re Oatway*,[436] in which the facts were the opposite of those in *Re Hallett's Estate*. The trustee in *Re Oatway* had paid trust money into his bank account that was already credited with his own money. The trustee then withdrew money from the account, which he used to buy shares. The remaining money credited to the bank account was then dissipated. It was held that the beneficiary could trace into the shares, even though, when the shares were purchased, the balance to the credit of the bank account exceeded the value of the shares, so that there would still have been some money credited to the account that could meet the claimant's claim, before that amount was then dissipated. All of the money credited to the bank account was subject to a charge in favour of the trust, so that any asset purchased with value from the trust was also subject to a charge.

   The implication of these dual presumptions is to manipulate the tracing rules to ensure that the interests of the beneficiaries are protected whenever possible. The result is inconsistent with one of the principles recognized in *Foskett v McKeown*, namely that proprietary rights should be vested at once and should not depend on subsequent events.[437] But, in *Re Oatway*, whether the claimant could trace into the money that was still credited to the account after the shares were purchased or into the shares themselves depended on events after the share purchase, namely the dissipation of the money credited to the bank account. The approach in *Re Oatway* is more consistent with the essentially evidential function of the tracing rules, and the principle in *Foskett v McKeown* to the contrary should be rejected.

(2) Mixing With the Money of an Innocent Third Party

(a) General Rule

Where the mixed fund consists of money in which the claimant has an equitable interest and also money from an innocent third party, such as the beneficiary of another trust fund, the general rule is that the money in the mixed fund will be assumed to belong equally to both parties.[438] If the third party has mixed the claimant's money with his or her own, the third party is sometimes called an 'innocent volunteer', meaning someone

---

[435] *Re Oatway* [1903] 2 Ch 356; *Re Tilley's Will Trusts* [1967] Ch 1179.
[436] [1903] 2 Ch 356.   [437] See p 611, above.
[438] *Sinclair v Brougham* [1914] AC 398; *Re Diplock's Estate* [1948] 1 Ch 465, 524.

who had not given consideration for the claimant's property and who had no reason to suspect that somebody else had a proprietary interest in the money. If the third party did know, or had reason to suspect, that somebody else had a proprietary interest in the property, he or she will be treated as a wrongdoer[439] and the tracing rules relating to mixing by fiduciaries will apply.

The essential features of the tracing rules relating to an innocent volunteer were identified by the Court of Appeal in *Re Diplock*, as follows:[440]

> In the case, however, of a volunteer who takes without notice ... if there is no question of mixing, he holds the money on behalf of the true owner whose equitable right to the money still persists as against him. On the other hand, if the volunteer mixes the money with money of his own, or receives it mixed from the fiduciary ... he must admit the claim of the true owner, but is not precluded from setting up his own claim in respect of the moneys of his own which have been contributed to the mixed fund. The result is that they share *pari passu*.

Pari passu simply means that the claimant and the innocent volunteer share the fund in proportion to their contribution to it.[441] So, for example, if the fund consists of £1,000, with £250 derived from the claimant and £750 from the innocent volunteer, they will share the fund, and any increase or decrease in the value of that fund, in the proportion of one to three.[442]

The innocent volunteer may not have mixed the fund, but might receive the fund already mixed. For example, if a trustee of two trust funds, Trust A and Trust B, misappropriates £250 from Trust A and £750 from Trust B, and then gives the fund to his daughter, then, as between the beneficiaries of the two trusts, 'there is no basis upon which any of the claims can be subordinated to any of the others',[443] so the beneficiaries will share the fund in the proportion of one to three.

(b) The Rule in *Clayton's Case*

An exception to this general rule that the claimant and innocent third party rank equally in their claim to the fund arises where the mixing takes place in a current bank account, but not a deposit account, so that the rule in *Clayton's case*[444] applies, namely that the money that was first paid into the bank account is deemed to be the money that was first paid out of it. So, for example, if a trustee misappropriates £1,000 from trust fund B and deposits this in his current bank account, which is already credited with £1,000 that has been misappropriated from trust fund A, but no other money is credited to the account, and the trustee then withdraws and dissipates £1,000, it will be presumed that it was the money from trust fund A that was taken, because this was the money that was credited to the bank account first. So the beneficiaries of trust fund A will suffer the loss and the beneficiaries of trust fund B will have a restitutionary proprietary claim.

The reason why the rule applies only to current accounts and not deposit accounts is because current accounts are active, so that there may be a large number of transactions involving the account every day, which makes it difficult to establish whose money has been withdrawn from the account.

---

[439] *Boscawen v Bajwa* [1996] 1 WLR 328, 337 (Millett LJ).   [440] *Re Diplock* [1948] Ch 465, 539.
[441] *Sinclair v Brougham* [1914] AC 398, 442 (Lord Parker).
[442] K Hodkinson, 'Tracing and Mixed Funds' [1983] Conv 135, who also suggests that the innocent volunteer should be awarded an allowance for effort where he or she has enhanced the value of the mixed fund.
[443] *Foskett v McKeown* [2001] 1 AC 102, 132 (Lord Millett).   [444] (1817) 1 Mer 572.

But the rule in *Clayton's case* is only a presumption which and it can be rebutted, for example by proving that the defendant intended to withdraw the claimant's money from the bank account. The rule will not be applicable where the mixed fund is made up of contributions from the claimant and the fiduciary, simply because a different presumption operates in respect of such a mixed fund, namely the presumption that works best in favour of the claimant and against the fiduciary.[445] So the rule is applicable only where the mixed fund consists of contributions from different trusts or contributions from trust funds and innocent volunteers that have been wrongfully mixed.[446]

The rule in *Clayton's case* will also be inapplicable if it is impracticable or unjust to rely on it.[447] So, for example, in *Barlow Clowes International Ltd v Vaughan*[448] the rule was not applied because the large number of proprietary claims made the operation of the rule impracticable. A rateable basis of distribution of assets amongst the claimants was adopted instead, so that withdrawals were apportioned according to the amount that had been contributed to the fund. In fact, the 'rule' in *Clayton's case* is increasingly being treated as an exception to a rule that the money should distributed rateably between the innocent volunteers who contributed to the mixed fund.[449] In *Russell-Cooke Trust Co v Prentis*,[450] it was recognized that *Clayton's case* could be displaced very easily by reference to the counter-intentions of the parties, the justice of the case, or where it could be seen that payments credited to a bank account had not led to payments out chronologically.

The rule is consequently very weak and has been described as apportioning 'a common misfortune through a test which has no relation whatever to the justice of the case'.[451] It can produce unjust results where, for example, a relatively small number of claimants become entitled to the bulk of the available assets because value misappropriated from them was credited to the bank account more recently. An alternative to the rule is the 'rolling charge', which is adopted in the US, whereby each debit to the account containing the mixed fund is attributable to all of the claimants *pro rata*. But this has been rejected as too complicated, at least in a case in which there are a lot of claimants.[452] Where money is credited to a deposit account, losses following dissipation of money are borne proportionately in relation to the value of the contributions from the innocent volunteers. There is no reason why the same should not now apply to money deposited in current accounts. *Clayton's case* itself actually concerned the order of appropriation of payments from an account and was not about tracing, so there is no reason to apply it in respect of proprietary claims. As McConville has convincingly argued,[453] the rule provided a mode of accounting as between a creditor, such as a trustee, and his or her debtor, such as a banker, and is immaterial to the assessment of who is entitled to the value credited to a bank account. Consequently the rule in *Clayton's case* should be rejected,[454] and, where

---

[445] *Re Hallett's Estate* (1880) 13 Ch D 696; *Re Oatway* [1903] 2 Ch 356.

[446] *Barlow Clowes International Ltd v Vaughan* [1992] 4 All ER 22. See *Pennell v Deffell* (1853) 4 De GM & G 372, 43 ER 551.

[447] *Commerzbank AG v IMB Morgan plc* [2004] EWHC 2771 (Ch).

[448] [1992] 4 All ER 22. See also *The National Crime Agency v Robb* [2014] EWHC 4384 (Ch).

[449] *Russell-Cooke Trust Co v Prentis* [2002] EWHC 2227 (Ch), [2003] 2 All ER 478, [55] (Lindsay J); *Commerzbank AG v IMB Morgan plc* [2004] EWHC 2771 (Ch), [50] (Lawrence Collins J).

[450] [2002] EWHC 2227 (Ch), [2003] 2 All ER 478.

[451] *Re Walter J Schmidt & Co* 298 F 314, 316 (1923) (Judge Learned Hand).

[452] *Barlow Clowes International Ltd v Vaughan* [1992] 4 All ER 22, 28 (Dillon LJ).

[453] DA McConville, 'Tracing and the Rule in *Clayton's* Case' (1963) 79 LQR 388, 407–8.

[454] As has occurred in New Zealand: *Re Registered Securities Ltd* [1991] 1 NZLR 545.

the mixed fund is not sufficient to meet the claims of all claimants, the losses should be attributed to all of them in proportion to their contribution.

(c) Third-Party and Fiduciary Contributions

Where the mixed fund comprises, for example, value that is derived from the defaulting fiduciary and two innocent claimants, the claimants will be treated as one party and the value contributed by the fiduciary will be treated according to the usual presumptions relating to fiduciaries, to determine whether the fiduciary is deemed to have withdrawn his or her own money from the fund first. So, if money was withdrawn and was dissipated, this is deemed to have been the fiduciary's money, but if the money was withdrawn and used to buy an asset, this is deemed to have been the money of the two claimants. If the fiduciary is presumed to have dissipated his or her own money, any remaining value credited to the bank account will be apportioned between the claimants in proportion to their contribution to the mixed fund. Alternatively, if an asset has been purchased from the mixed fund and this is presumed to have been purchased with the claimants' contributions, they will have an interest in the asset that is proportionate to their contributions.[455] Consequently, any increase or decrease in the value of the asset will be borne rateably between them.

(iv) Restrictions on Equitable Tracing

Equitable tracing enables the claimant to trace value into a specific asset or fund only where it is possible to say that some or all of the value of the asset or fund represents the value of the property in which the claimant originally had an equitable interest. Consequently, equitable tracing will fail or will be restricted in the following circumstances.

(1) Dissipation of the Asset or Fund

Where the asset in which the claimant has an equitable interest has been destroyed, or where the fund has been dissipated and no specific asset can be identified that derives from it, tracing will fail. So, for example, where the defendant buys wine with the trust money and then drinks it, there is nothing into which the value can be traced.[456] Similarly, where the original asset is destroyed or undergoes a change in chemical composition so that it becomes a different asset.[457] Tracing will also be defeated where the claimant's money is used to discharge a debt, such as where it is paid into an overdrawn bank account, since there will be no asset that can be considered to represent the claimant's property.[458] Consequently, it is not possible to trace *through* an overdrawn account. But it does not follow that it is not possible to trace *into* an overdrawn account to the discharged debt, since, exceptionally, a proprietary remedy involving the revival of the debt might be available.[459]

---

[455] *Re Diplock's Estate* [1948] Ch 465, 539; *Lord Provost of Edinburgh v The Lord Advocate* (1879) 4 App Cas 823 (HL Sc).   [456] *Re Diplock's Estate* [1948] Ch 465, 521.

[457] *Borden (UK) Ltd v Scottish Timber Products Ltd* [1981] Ch 25.

[458] *Shalson v Russo* [2003] EWHC 1637 (Ch), [2005] Ch 281, [140] (Rimer J); *Serious Fraud Office v Lexi Holdings plc* [2009] EWCA Crim 1443, [2009] QB 376, [50] (Keene J); *Re BA Peters Ltd* [2008] EWCA Civ 1604, [2010] 1 BCLC 142, [15] (Lord Neuberger).

[459] See the remedy of subrogation, discussed p 636, below. See also the discussion of backward tracing, p 624, below.

(2) Lowest Intermediate Balance

If the claimant's money is mixed with other money, for example in a bank account, and subsequently the balance of that account is reduced to less than the amount of the claimant's money that had been deposited, the amount that the claimant can recover is necessarily limited to the maximum amount that can be regarded as representing his or her money.[460] So, for example, if the defendant trustee paid £1,000 of the trust money into his own bank account, which already had £1,000 credited to it, and the defendant then dissipated £1,500, the maximum value that the claimant can claim is £500. This is because the first £1,000 that was spent is deemed to have been the defendant's money, because of the presumptions relating to fiduciaries. But since another £500 was spent, this must have been the claimant's, leaving only £500 left to satisfy the claimant's claim. The lowest intermediate balance rule will apply even if the defendant trustee has subsequently paid in his or her own money to the fund so as to restore the original balance. This is because the trustee could not be considered to intend to clothe his or her own money with a trust in favour of the claimant. It would be different, however, if the subsequent payments were made to a separate trust bank account from which the trust funds had been dissipated, for then the payments could be considered to be a substitute for the trust money because there would then be a sufficient intention for the new money to be held on the old trust.[461]

The practical significance of the lowest intermediate balance rule is illustrated by *James Roscoe (Bolton) Ltd v Winder*,[462] in which over £455 of trust money was paid into a bank account by a trustee. The balance of that account then fell to £25, but, at the date of the trustee's death, it had increased to £358. It was held that the account could be charged only to £25 for the benefit of the trust, since this was the lowest intermediate balance in the account after the trust money had been paid in. What had clearly happened was that the trust money must have been spent except to the extent of £25. It was considered whether the amount that had subsequently been credited to the account could be regarded as being impressed with the trust. This was rejected because there was insufficient evidence that the trustee intended the subsequent payments to be subject to the trust. This aspect of the decision is difficult to defend and appears to be inconsistent with the general presumptions of intent relating to fiduciaries, as recognized in *Re Hallett's Estate*[463] in particular: the Court of Appeal accepted in that case that, where a trustee has acted, he or she should be regarded as acting in the best interests of the trust. It is for that reason that, when money is dissipated from a mixed fund, this is presumed to be the trustee's money. So surely this presumption should work in the same way when money is subsequently credited to a denuded bank account: the trustee should be presumed to be returning trust money to the account?

(3) Backward Tracing

The orthodox view of the law of equitable tracing is that a claimant is not able to trace into property that was already in the defendant's possession before the claimant's money was received, because in such circumstances the defendant's property cannot be regarded as representing the claimant's money, even if the claimant's money was

---

[460] *James Roscoe (Bolton) Ltd v Winder* [1915] 1 Ch 62; *Re Goldcorp Exchange Ltd* [1995] 1 AC 74; *Bishopsgate Investment Management Ltd v Homan* [1995] Ch 211; *Campden Hill Ltd v Chakrani* [2005] EWHC 911 (Ch).

[461] *James Roscoe (Bolton) Ltd v Winder* [1915] 1 Ch 62, 69 (Sargant J). See also *Re Diplock's Estate* [1948] Ch 465, 552 (unmixing of money by placing it in a separate bank account).

[462] [1915] 1 Ch 62.   [463] (1880) 13 Ch D 696.

used to pay for the property by discharging a debt that had been incurred in respect of it.[464] In other words, so-called 'backward tracing' is not available as part of the tracing exercise. So, for example, if the defendant purchases a car and incurs a debt to the vendor, the money that has been received from the claimant might be used by the defendant to discharge the debt. Although the claimant's money can be traced into the hands of the vendor of the car, to whom the debt was owed, it will not usually be possible to bring a proprietary claim against the vendor because he or she is likely to have a defence of being a good faith purchaser.[465] But it is also not possible to trace into the car because the defendant had already acquired it, even though the claimant's money has actually been used to pay for it. It follows that tracing appears to be concerned only with forward-looking exchanges of value and cannot be considered to have any retrospective operation. This has been defended by Conaglen[466] as being consistent with precedent, and with the principles and policies that underlie the law of tracing.

Nevertheless, in *Foskett v McKeown*[467] in the Court of Appeal, Sir Richard Scott V-C tentatively recognized the principle of backward tracing, although he declined to decide the point. He said that '[t]he availability of equitable remedies ought ... to depend upon the substance of the transaction in question and not upon the strict order in which associated events happen'. Hobhouse LJ[468] and Morritt LJ[469] explicitly rejected the proposition that tracing could be used to identify value in a previously acquired asset.

Although the House of Lords in *Foskett v McKeown*[470] did not expressly consider the backward tracing principle, the approach adopted by the majority as regards equitable tracing is certainly consistent with it: if tracing is not concerned with causation as such, in the sense that but for the receipt of the claimant's property the substitute asset would not have been obtained, but is concerned with attribution of value, it is surely possible to attribute value from the original asset to the substitute asset if the claimant's money has been used to discharge a debt incurred in respect of the substitute asset. Consequently, the backward tracing principle should be recognized in English law.[471] If backward tracing was recognized, it would enable the claimant to trace into a previously acquired asset both where the defendant used the claimant's money to discharge a debt that the defendant had incurred by borrowing money to acquire the asset, and where the claimant's money is paid into an overdrawn bank account where the overdraft resulted from the defendant purchasing the asset. This has been advocated by Smith on the ground that a payment that discharges a debt is 'just delayed payment, and the traceable proceeds are whatever was acquired in the past when the debt was incurred'.[472] In *Relfo Ltd v Varsani*[473] Arden LJ recognized that, in order to trace money into substitute property, it is not necessary that the payments should occur in any particular order. So, for example, where a third party pays money to the defendant in the expectation that the

---

[464] *Bishopsgate Investment Management Ltd v Homan* [1995] Ch. 211, 221 (Leggatt LJ). See also *Re Tilley's Will Trust* [1967] 1 Ch 1179, in which the trust fund was used to reduce an overdraft that had been incurred to purchase properties and it was not contemplated that the claimant could trace into those properties.

[465] See Chapter 23.   [466] M Conaglen, 'Difficulties with Tracing Backwards' (2011) LQR 432.

[467] [1998] Ch 265, 283–4. See also *Bishopsgate Investment Management Ltd v Homan* [1995] Ch 211, 217 (Dillon LJ); *Boscawen v Bajwa* [1996] 1 WLR 328, 341 (Millett LJ); *Jyske Bank (Gibraltar) Ltd v Spjeldnaes* (unreported) 23 July 1997; *Shalson v Russo* [2003] EWHC 1637 (Ch), [2005] Ch 285, [141] (Rimer J).

[468] *Foskett v McKeown* [1998] Ch 265, 289.   [469] Ibid, 296.   [470] [2001] 1 AC 102 (HL).

[471] See *Shalson v Russo* [2003] EWHC 1637 (Ch), [2005] Ch 285, [142] (Rimer J).

[472] LD Smith, 'Tracing into the Payment of a Debt' (1995) 54 CLJ 290, 292.

[473] [2014] EWCA Civ 360, [2015] 1 BCLC 14, [63].

third party would be reimbursed from money transferred from the trust of which the claimant is a beneficiary, the claimant could trace the value of his or her money to the defendant. This is a potentially significant expansion of the tracing rules, which does not limit tracing to direct substitutional transfers. Whilst not expressly recognizing backward tracing, Arden LJ's dictum is certainly consistent with the recognition of that principle.

There is, in fact, a decision of the Court of Appeal the result of which is consistent with the recognition of backward tracing. In *Re Diplock*[474] some of the money that should have been paid to the testator's next of kin by the executors had been paid by mistake to the Heritage Craft Schools, which had used the money to pay a debt that had been incurred to enable it to improve a building. It was held that, even though the money had actually been used to discharge the debt, it had effectively been used to pay for the improvements and so it was possible to trace the value of the money into the improvements. This is consistent with the courts examining the substance of the transaction rather than being confined to a consideration of events in the exact order in which they occurred. But the proprietary claim did not succeed in that case, apparently because it was not considered to be just to allow such a claim where the recipient charity had innocently used the money to improve its own property.[475] Further, in *Shalson v Russo*[476] it was recognized that the claimant could, in principle, trace through the payment of an overdraft debt into a yacht for which the defendant had partially paid through the overdraft borrowing, although it was necessary for the claimant to show that the overdraft could not have been paid off without the misappropriated money.

We cannot yet say that backward tracing is recognized in English law, but the recognition of such a principle is logical and is consistent with the fundamental principles of tracing, as recognized by the House of Lords in *Foskett v McKeown*, particularly where it can be shown that the purchase of an asset and the discharge of a consequent liability is part of the same transaction in which the asset is obtained first and then the debt to the vendor is discharged.[477] But where money has been borrowed from a third party to enable the defendant to purchase property from the vendor,[478] and the claimant's money is used to discharge this debt, it might be considered to be too great a jump to trace into the asset that the defendant purchased, because the contract of purchase and the contract of loan are distinct transactions. But if the loan were incurred to enable the defendant to purchase the property, it would be appropriate to conclude that the discharge of the loan could be attributed to the purchase of the property, so that the claimant could then trace into it, regardless of whether the loan was provided by the vendor or a third party. Consequently, the key justification for the recognition of backward tracing is that the purchase of the property and the discharge of the loan incurred to purchase that property can be considered to form part of the same series of events. The key question of policy then is whether it should make any difference whether the money was borrowed from a third party or the vendor, which will turn on how wide the notion of 'the same transaction' should be interpreted, which will be dependent on the question of policy as to whether the restitutionary claims of beneficiaries or principals should receive more protection than the interests of the insolvent defendant's unsecured creditors.[479]

---

[474] [1948] Ch 465, 548–9.   [475] See further p 627, below.
[476] [2003] EWHC 1637 (Ch), [2005] Ch 285, 328.
[477] See R Chambers, 'Tracing and Unjust Enrichment' in J Neyers, M McInnes, and S Pitel (eds), *Understanding Unjust Enrichment* (Oxford: Hart Publishing, 2004), 298–9.
[478] As in *Boscawen v Bajwa* [1996] 1 WLR 328.
[479] See Conaglen, 'Difficulties with Tracing Backwards', 455.

(4) Inequitable to Trace

In *Re Diplock*,[480] the Court of Appeal recognized that tracing would be defeated where it would be inequitable to allow the claimant to trace into property held by the defendant. This will occur, for example, where an innocent volunteer has used the money received to improve or alter his or her land.[481] So, for example, one of the charities that received the mistaken payment was Guy's Hospital, which spent £14,000 on reconstructing two children's wards. It was held that it was not equitable to enable the next of kin to trace into this property. A number of reasons were identified as to why tracing should be barred in such a case, including that the value of the property might not have increased by the improvement, it might be difficult to determine whether the charge should attach to the whole property or just the part improved, and, most significantly, it may simply be unfair to expect an innocent volunteer to sell the property to discharge the liability. Similarly, where one of the charities had used the money paid by mistake to pay off a secured bank loan, it was held to be inequitable to compel the hospital to sell the land to discharge the charge.[482]

This apparent bar to tracing should be rejected, or at least analysed more subtly. The better view is that this 'bar' does not defeat tracing. So, for example, the claimant should be able to trace into the defendant's improved property. Rather, the 'bar' operates at the subsequent claiming stage, when determining whether the claimant can assert a right against the traceable asset. Further, rather than being a simply matter of judicial discretion as to whether it is fair that a remedy should be awarded, the bar is better analysed as being a defence to the claim, specifically in the form of the defence of change of position,[483] although this raises a further issue as to whether it is appropriate for a proprietary claim to be defeated by the defendant's innocent change of position.[484]

(v) A Move to a More Pragmatic Approach?

Despite the orthodox approach of equitable tracing, which requires clear representation of the value of the claimant's property in the asset or fund that is in the defendant's possession or under his or her control, dicta in some cases suggest that it is possible to trace into the defendant's general assets even though no specific asset can be identified as representing the claimant's money.[485] This has been described as the 'swollen assets theory', since the defendant's assets will have been swollen by the receipt of property to which the claimant had a proprietary claim. Tracing into the defendant's general assets can be justified on the basis that, if the defendant has dissipated those assets in which the claimant had a proprietary interest, then, because the defendant could have dissipated other assets that he or she owned, it is right that the claimant should be able to make a claim against those other assets.[486] But such a flexible approach to tracing is not consistent with the orthodox tracing rules, which require value to be identified in particular assets, and the swollen assets theory has been confined to the specific situation in which an insolvent bank trustee wrongly deposits trust money with itself in a mixed fund and uses this money

---

[480] [1948] Ch 465, 546.   [481] Ibid, 548.
[482] Ibid, 550.   [483] See p 696, below. See *Boscawen v Bajwa* [1996] 1 WLR 328, 340 (Millett LJ).
[484] See p 697, below.
[485] See, in particular, *Space Investments Ltd v Canadian Imperial Bank of Commerce Trust Co (Bahamas) Ltd* [1986] 1 WLR 1072, 1074 (Lord Templeman).
[486] Ibid. For a defence of this theory see W Evans, 'Rethinking Tracing and the Law of Restitution' (1999) 115 LQR 469.

in its general business.[487] In such circumstances, a charge can be granted over the mixed fund. The reason for this exception involving an insolvent bank trustee can be justified by reference to general principles underpinning equitable tracing.[488] If a bank is a trustee and trust money has been deposited with it, the bank will be required to keep that money in a separate bank account. If the bank wrongly uses that money in its general banking business, it can be assumed that the trust money forms part of a mixed fund with all money deposited with the bank. The beneficiaries will be able to trace into this fund, as long as the value of that fund does not fall below the value of the claimant's contribution to it.

The courts have been right to reject the general incorporation of the swollen assets theory into the tracing rules, since such a theory confuses the fundamental distinction between proprietary claims in which the claimant seeks a personal remedy and those claims in which he or she seeks a proprietary remedy. Where the claimant seeks a personal remedy, it is sufficient for him or her to establish that the defendant received property in which the claimant had a proprietary interest; it is irrelevant that this property was dissipated subsequently. Where, however, the claimant seeks a proprietary remedy, he or she must establish that the defendant has particular assets that can be considered to represent the claimant's property.[489] It is only where particular assets can be identified that represent the claimant's original property that it is appropriate that the claimant should gain priority over the defendant's general creditors.

Nevertheless, recent cases do suggest a trend towards the development of a more pragmatic approach to the equitable tracing rules. For example, where the claimant's money is paid into different bank accounts, the courts have been prepared to place an equitable charge on each account even though the claimant was unable to identify which sums had been credited to which accounts.[490] In *Shalson v Russo*,[491] however, the claimant's money was deposited into the defendant's overdrawn bank account and tracing was defeated, even though the defendant had other accounts in credit at other financial institutions. Rimer J refused to treat all of the bank accounts as forming a single fund because it was possible to show that the claimant's money had been deposited in the bank account that was overdrawn.

Other examples of a greater willingness to use tracing rules to secure what is perceived to be a just result include recent suggestions that backward tracing should be recognized. Finally, the emphasis on attribution rather than causation in *Foskett v McKeown*[492] is further evidence of pragmatism in the interpretation and application of the tracing rules.

(E) THE FUTURE OF THE TRACING RULES

Although the orthodox approach to the law of tracing treats the tracing rules at Law and Equity as distinct,[493] there are growing calls for their assimilation.[494] Some commentators

---

[487] *Re Goldcorp Exchange Ltd* [1995] 1 AC 74, 105 (Lord Mustill); *Bishopsgate Investment Management Ltd v Homan* [1995] Ch 211, 218 (Dillon LJ).

[488] See L Gullefer, 'Recovery of Misappropriated Assets; Orthodoxy Re-Established?' [1995] LMCLQ 446, 447.

[489] *Re Diplock's Estate* [1948] Ch 465, 521.

[490] *El Ajou v Dollar Land Holdings plc* [1993] 3 All ER 717.

[491] [2003] EWHC 1637 (Ch), [2005] Ch 281, [140] (Rimer J).   [492] [2001] 1 AC 102.

[493] Confirmed by Rimer J in *Shalson v Russo* [2003] EWHC 1637 (Ch), [2005] Ch 281, [104].

[494] See FOB Babafemi, 'Tracing Assets: A Case for the Fusion of Common Law and Equity in English Law' (1971) 34 MLR 12; RM Goode, 'The Right to Trace and Its Impact in Commercial Transactions' (1976) 92 LQR 360, 396.

have asserted that the rules have always been assimilated[495] and there is some indication from the case law that this view is shared by some members of the judiciary.[496] Although the rules have not yet been formally assimilated, the artificial distinction between the rules at Common Law and Equity should be rejected. A unified approach to tracing is required that incorporates the acceptable features of both regimes.[497] As Lord Millett emphasized in *Foskett v McKeown*:[498]

> Given its nature, there is nothing inherently legal or equitable about the tracing exercise. There is thus no sense in maintaining different rules of tracing at law and in equity. One set of tracing rules is enough... There is certainly no logical justification for allowing any distinction between them to produce capricious results in cases of mixed substitutions by insisting on the existence of a fiduciary relationship as a precondition for applying equity's tracing rules. The existence of such a relationship may be relevant to the nature of the claim which the plaintiff can maintain, whether personal or proprietary, but that is a different matter.

If the rules were assimilated, it would follow that, regardless of whether the proprietary base is legal or equitable, the claimant would be able to trace through a mixed fund without needing to establish a fiduciary relationship to do so. But such assimilation of the rules would not collapse proprietary claims at Law and in Equity. It would still be highly relevant that a claim was founded on a legal or an equitable proprietary base, since this would affect the nature of the claim and the nature of the remedy that was available. Assimilation of the tracing rules would not result in the assimilation of the rules on claiming or remedies.[499] For example, if a thief steals your money and deposits it in his bank account, which is already credited with other money, you will have retained legal title to the money. If the tracing rules were not changed, the mixing in the bank account would defeat the claim at Law, since legal title to the mixture would have passed to the thief. If tracing into a mixture were possible at Law, you would still retain legal title to the money in the mixture and would be able to bring a proprietary claim at Law. But the Common Law remedies to vindicate property rights are essentially limited to personal remedies,[500] so you would be able to recover only the value of the money paid plus profits obtained from the investment of that money,[501] but, being a personal remedy, if the defendant became insolvent, you would not have priority over any of the other creditors of the defendant. This example shows that, even if the tracing rules were assimilated, in many cases this would be not be of any advantage to the claimant, who would prefer to obtain a proprietary remedy in Equity. There are two possible solutions to this problem. One is to recognize that the claimant who has retained legal title to property can elect to bring an equitable proprietary claim on the basis that the defendant who is in possession of the property holds the possessory title on trust for the claimant. This is artificial, but does at least give the claimant the option of obtaining more advantageous equitable remedies. The alternative solution is to assimilate the remedies that are available to vindicate property rights, so at the very least it would be possible to charge the defendant's property even though the claim was founded on a legal proprietary right, and maybe even to allow the

---

[495] Smith, *The Law of Tracing*, 5; Birks, 'The Necessity of a Unitary Law of Tracing', 239.

[496] See especially *Foskett v McKeown* [2001] 1 AC 102, 113 (Lord Steyn) and 129 (Lord Millett), both *obiter dicta*. See also *Chief Constable of Kent v V* [1983] 1 QB 34, 41 (Lord Denning MR).

[497] See *Nelson v Larholt* [1948] 1 KB 339, 342–3 (Denning J); *Bristol and West Building Society v Mothew* [1998] Ch 1, 23 (Millett LJ). [498] [2001] 1 AC 102, 129.

[499] See RH Maudsley, 'Proprietary Remedies for the Recovery of Money' (1959) 75 LQR 234.

[500] See p 632, below. [501] *Trustee of the Property of FC Jones v Jones* [1997] Ch 159.

claimant to recover stolen property or substitute property. This would be a radical reform that goes far beyond the relatively straightforward assimilation of the tracing rules. The assimilation of the claiming rules and the range of available remedies would drastically reduce the need to establish an equitable proprietary base outside of the express trust. But without such assimilation, of claiming, remedies, or even tracing, the equitable rules on proprietary claims remain incredibly important in the commercial world, as recognized by Briggs J in rejecting the view that these rules are old-fashioned, unduly restrictive, and 'inappropriate for the protection of investors in the modern world'.[502]

---

[502] *Re Lehman Brothers International (Europe) Ltd* [2009] EWHC 3228 (Ch), [2010] 2 BCLC 301, [198].

22

RESTITUTIONARY CLAIMS AND REMEDIES TO VINDICATE PROPERTY RIGHTS

1. GENERAL PRINCIPLES

(A) PROPRIETARY AND PERSONAL REMEDIES

Once a claimant has established that he or she has a legal or equitable proprietary interest which can be followed or traced into property which had been received by the defendant, the claimant can establish a restitutionary claim to vindicate his or her proprietary rights.[1] The questions which need to be examined in this chapter are: what is the nature of the claim to this property and what is the appropriate remedy to vindicate this proprietary right? These remedies can take two forms. The first are proprietary remedies where the claimant is able to recover the property itself or acquire a security interest in the property which is in the defendant's hands. The second are personal remedies where the defendant is only able to recover the value of the property received by the defendant. Typically, proprietary remedies are preferable, since they all give the claimant priority over the defendant's unsecured creditors if the defendant becomes insolvent and enable the claimant to assert property rights even against an innocent third-party recipient, save if that recipient has provided value for the receipt,[2] and some of them enable the claimant to recover the fruits of the property. But all proprietary remedies are worthless once the property in which the claimant has a proprietary interest has been dissipated. It in this situation that personal remedies become particularly attractive.

(B) DISTINGUISHING BETWEEN CLAIMS AND REMEDIES

A distinction needs to be drawn between the claim and the remedy which is available to vindicate that claim. It is assumed for the purposes of this chapter that the claimant is able to identify a proprietary base and so has a proprietary right and is able to follow or trace this proprietary right into property which is held by the defendant. The only remaining questions, therefore, relate to the nature of the claim which the claimant can bring to vindicate his or her proprietary right and then the most appropriate remedy which is available to achieve this objective.

---

[1] See Chapter 21.   [2] See Chapter 23.

2. PROPRIETARY CLAIMS AND REMEDIES

(A) COMMON LAW PROPRIETARY CLAIMS AND REMEDIES

As a general rule, the Common Law has no proprietary remedies.[3] Consequently, if the claimant has retained legal title in property which has been received by the defendant, the claimant can only claim the value of this property rather than the property itself.[4] The only true exception to this relates to land, where the claimant is able to recover land from the defendant.[5] There is also the remedy of delivery up of goods under section 3(3) of the Torts (Interference with Goods) Act 1977, which is a proprietary remedy which is available where the defendant has committed a tort involving interference with the claimant's property rights, such as conversion. But this remedy is discretionary and is only available where compensatory damages are an inadequate remedy.[6]

There are certain other exceptional circumstances where one party may be able to recover specific property from another party in legal proceedings. For example, in *Greenwood v Bennett*[7] it was recognized that the court could order that a car should be transferred to the original owner in interpleader proceedings, where the possessor of the car was requesting the court to determine who had the better claim to it.

(B) EQUITABLE PROPRIETARY CLAIMS AND REMEDIES

Equity has developed much more extensive proprietary remedies to enable the claimant to vindicate his or her equitable property rights. These remedies are only available where the claimant can establish an equitable proprietary base in the property retained by the defendant. Further, the award of these remedies is a matter of right rather than judicial discretion.[8]

(i) Constructive Trust

The court may recognize that the defendant holds the property in his or her possession on trust for the claimant. Where the defendant was an express trustee, then the substitute property will be held on the same trust.[9] But where the defendant is a third-party recipient of the trust property or substitute property, this property will be held on constructive trust, since it arises by operation of law, even though the original equitable proprietary interest arose under an express trust,[10] because the recipient of the property will not be subject to the same duties as the express trustee. The effect of recognizing that the property is held on constructive trust will be that the defendant becomes liable to transfer all, or a proportion, of the property to the claimant.

---

[3] *OBG Ltd v Allan* [2007] UKHL 21, [2008] AC 1, [308] (Baroness Hale).

[4] *Trustee of the Property of FC Jones and Sons (a firm) v Jones* [1997] Ch 159, 168 (Millett LJ).

[5] In an action for ejectment.

[6] See also the Minors' Contracts Act 1987, s 3. See p 579, above.

[7] [1973] QB 195. See p 82, above.

[8] *Foskett v McKeown* [2001] 1 AC 102, 109. Although note the analysis of the modified constructive trust, at p 605, above.   [9] As in *Foskett v McKeown*, ibid, itself.

[10] But see, to the contrary, Lord Millett, 'Proprietary Restitution', in S Degeling and J Edelman (eds), *Equity in Commercial Law* (Sydney: Lawbook Co, 2005), 315–16. See also *Foskett v McKeown* [2001] 1 AC 102, 108 (Lord Browne-Wilkinson).

(1) Transfer of Property

Where the claimant can show that he or she has an equitable proprietary interest in property that is in the possession of the defendant, the court may declare that the property is held on constructive trust for the claimant and it will order the defendant to transfer this property to the claimant.[11]

(2) Proportionate Share

A constructive trust may also be imposed where the claimant is considered to have an equitable proprietary interest in a proportionate share of the property that is in the defendant's possession. This remedy will be more attractive to the claimant than an equitable charge where the property has increased in value.

When determining whether the claimant is able to claim a proportionate share of a mixture, it has been necessary to distinguish between cases in which the defendant is a fiduciary or is an innocent volunteer.

(a) Fiduciary

In *Foskett v McKeown*[12] the House of Lords recognized that, by virtue of the principle that a fiduciary should not be allowed to profit from their position, it followed that where a trustee wrongly uses trust money to provide part of the cost of acquiring an asset, the balance coming from the trustee's own money, the beneficiary can elect between claiming a proportionate share of the asset and enforcing a charge against the asset to secure his or her personal claim. This election is available regardless of whether the trustee mixed the trust money with his or her own property and then paid for the asset from the mixture, or the trustee part-paid for the asset from his or her own funds and made a separate payment from the trust fund. The beneficiary will claim a proportionate share where the value of the asset has increased, so that the claimant will gain a proportionate share of the increased value. So, for example, if the asset were purchased for £1,000, and the trust fund contributed £750 and the trustee £250, the beneficiary would be able to claim three-quarters of the value of the asset. So, if the asset had increased in value to £2,000, the beneficiary would be able to claim a share worth £1,500. The claimant would be able to compel the trustee to sell the asset and transfer that amount to him or her.

This remedy of a proportionate share was awarded in *Foskett v McKeown*. Since the claimants were able to trace two of the five premiums into the death benefit, it was held by a majority that they were entitled to receive two-fifths of the death benefit. Whether it was appropriate to award the claimants such a remedy is a matter of some controversy. What is the just result in a case such as this, in which both claimants and defendants were innocent of any wrongdoing? The judges themselves expressed divergent views as to where the justice of the case lay on the facts.[13] It is certainly fair that the claimants should recover the amount that had been misappropriated from the trust and which was used to pay two of the premiums.[14] But should they get more than this? The claimants had been the victims of a criminal misappropriation of trust property, which had been used to make an involuntary contribution to the insurance policy. The children had made no such contribution and it was their father who committed the crime.[15] But should the sins of the father be visited upon the children? Is it of any use even to consider such matters? Lord

---

[11] *Boscawen v Bajwa* [1996] 1 WLR 328, 334 (Millett LJ).

[12] [2001] 1 AC 102, 131 (Lord Millett).

[13] Compare *Foskett v McKeown* [2001] 1 AC 102, 115 (Lord Steyn) with [1998] Ch 265, 303 (Morritt LJ) and [2001] 1 AC 102, 140 (Lord Millett).

[14] *Foskett v McKeown* [2001] 1 AC 102, 119 (Lord Hope).   [15] Ibid, 112 (Lord Steyn).

Hope[16] was willing to consider the terms of the insurance policy, the conduct of the parties, and the consequences to them of allowing and rejecting the claim, in order to determine whether it was fair, just, and reasonable for the claimant to be awarded a proportionate interest in the proceeds of the insurance policy. But how are such factors to be weighed against each other? If such an approach had been adopted by all of the judges in the case, it is not clear what the decision would have been. The introduction of a vague discretion that is not 'directed by principled analysis of the facts' is unworkable;[17] it is no way in which to determine how property rights should be recognized and vindicated.

The awarding of a proportionate share in *Foskett v McKeown* has been criticized, by Berg especially,[18] not because the remedy was excessive, but because it did not go far enough. He considers that the claimants should have received the whole of the death benefit, by virtue of the policy that there should not be any incentive for trustees wrongfully to mix trust funds with their own. So a trustee, or anybody who claims through a trustee such as the children in this case, should be required to disgorge the whole of the benefit that they had wrongfully obtained. But this argument fails to distinguish between claims grounded on the commission of the wrong of a breach of trust, in which disgorgement of all profits is the norm subject to the award of equitable allowances, and claims grounded on the vindication of property rights, in which the law is essentially concerned only with identifying value in property and other policies have no part to play.

(b) Innocent Volunteer

Where the claimant's money has been mixed with that of an innocent volunteer and the mixed fund has been used to purchase an asset, the claimant and the innocent volunteer will both have equitable interests in the asset in proportion to the value of their contribution.[19] In such circumstances, the claims of both parties are equal, so it is not appropriate for one to have priority over the other. The recognition that the parties share the asset proportionately means that any increase in the value of the property will be shared between them. Where the asset has fallen in value, this loss will be shared equally between the contributors in proportion to their contribution and the claimant will not be able to elect for a charge instead.[20]

(c) Fiduciary and Innocent Volunteer

Where a trustee, for example, has misappropriated trust money from two trusts, mixed this with his or her own money, and then used the mixture to purchase an asset, following the decision of the House of Lords in *Foskett v McKeown*, all of the contributors will share the property in proportion to their own respective contributions.

(d) Remedial Constructive Trust

If the remedial constructive trust[21] was recognized in English law, the proprietary consequences of recognizing the constructive trust might be modified, but in a principled way, so that the claimant might not be given priority over any of the other creditors of the

---

[16] Ibid, 120.

[17] See Sir R Walker, 'Tracing after *Foskett v McKeown*' [2000] 8 RLR 573, 575. See also *Foskett v McKeown* [2001] 1 AC 102, 115 (Lord Steyn).

[18] A Berg, 'Permitting a Trustee to Retain a Profit' (2001) 117 LQR 366.

[19] *Edinburgh Corporation v Lord Advocate* (1879) 4 App Cas 823, 841 (Lord Hatherley). See also *Re Hallett's Estate* (1880) 13 Ch D 696.

[20] *Re Diplock's Estate* [1948] Ch 465, 532; *Foskett v McKeown* [2001] 1 AC 102, 109 (Lord Browne-Wilkinson) and 132 (Lord Millett).   [21] See p 603, above.

defendant or be able assert a proprietary claim against the innocent volunteer recipient of property in which the claimant has an equitable proprietary interest. The remedial constructive trust has, however, not yet been recognized in England and was rejected by the Supreme Court in *FHR European Ventures LLP v Cedar Capital Partners LLC*.[22]

(ii) Equitable Charge

An alternative remedy to the recovery of particular property or the award of a proportionate share is to impose a charge on the property to secure repayment of the amount that the defendant owes to the claimant. This gives the claimant a power to sell the relevant asset to which the charge is attached and so recover the value received and retained by the defendant plus interest,[23] but no more. The claimant also has a security interest that gives the claimant priority over the defendant's other unsecured creditors should the defendant become insolvent.

Where the claimant's money has been used to acquire property, it is appropriate for the claimant to be able to recover that property where the claimant contributed all of the value to its acquisition, or to have a proportionate share in it where the claimant contributed some of the value. As has already been seen, even in cases involving acquisition of property the claimant may elect to have a charge over the property. Where, however, the claimant's contribution has been used only to improve or maintain property that is already in the defendant's possession rather than to acquire it, it will not be appropriate for the claimant to acquire a beneficial interest in the property so that he or she can benefit from any increase in its value. Consequently, where the value contributed by the claimant is used to improve or maintain the property, the court will treat the property as charged with a sum that represents the value of the claimant's contribution.[24] This applies whether the defendant is a fiduciary or an innocent volunteer, although in the latter case the charge will be imposed only where it would not be unfair to the defendant,[25] which is why no charge was awarded on the improved building of the Heritage Craft School in *Re Diplock's Estate*.[26]

The function of the equitable charge as a remedy to vindicate property rights was considered in *Foskett v McKeown*. The key issue in that case was whether the appropriate remedy should be a charge over the proceeds of the policy to enable the beneficiaries to recover the money that had been misappropriated, or whether they were entitled to a proportion of the proceeds calculated by reference to the amount of their money that was used to pay the premiums. The Court of Appeal[27] had concluded that a charge was the appropriate remedy, by analogy with cases in which trust money has been used to improve or maintain an asset. This is consistent with the nature of the life insurance policy in that case, since the death benefit would have been due even if the fourth and fifth premiums had not been paid; those premiums therefore did not contribute to the acquisition of the death benefit, but maintained the policy, so that additional units were purchased that would be available in future years. The majority in the House of Lords preferred the analogy with a trustee who has mixed trust money with his or her own money in a bank account, which has then been used to obtain another asset.[28] In such cases, awarding a proportionate share remedy is appropriate and so that remedy was awarded in this case.

---

[22] [2014] UKSC 45, [2015] AC 250.

[23] See *Kali and Burlay v Chawla* [2007] EWHC 2357 (Ch), [43] (Judge Hodge QC).

[24] *Boscawen v Bajwa* [1996] 1 WLR 328, 335 (Millett LJ).

[25] *Re Diplock's Estate* [1948] Ch 465, 547; *Foskett v McKeown* [2001] 1 AC 102, 109 (Lord Browne-Wilkinson).

[26] See p 626, above.   [27] *Foskett v McKeown* [1998] Ch 265.

[28] *Foskett v McKeown* [2001] 1 AC 102, 110 (Lord Browne-Wilkinson) and 115 (Lord Hoffmann). Lord Steyn did not consider this to be a useful analogy: ibid, 114.

This is consistent with the attribution approach to tracing, since the death benefit was analysed as being attributable in part to the fourth and fifth premiums that had therefore contributed to the death benefit being obtained.[29]

(iii) Subrogation

(1) The Function of Subrogation

Subrogation[30] is a remedy[31] which is designed to ensure 'a transfer of rights from one person to another ... by operation of law'.[32] Essentially, the function of the remedy is to enable the claimant to rely on the rights of a third party against a defendant. This is often described as the claimant being allowed to 'stand in the shoes' of the third party.

In the leading case of *Banque Financière de la Cité v Parc (Battersea) Ltd*[33] the House of Lords acknowledged that two forms of subrogation are recognized in English law, which have been said to be 'radically different'.[34] The first is that which arises by virtue of the express or implied agreement of the parties.[35] For example, an insurer who has paid a claim under an indemnity insurance policy in respect of a particular loss will have a right to be subrogated to, and to enforce the rights of, the insured person against any third person who caused the loss. Since this right to subrogation arises by virtue of contract, it has nothing to do with the law of restitution.[36] Secondly, the equitable remedy of subrogation may be awarded by operation of law as a restitutionary remedy.[37] The typical case where subrogation will be an appropriate remedy in the context of a proprietary restitutionary claim is where the claimant's money is used by the defendant to discharge a debt which the defendant owed to a secured creditor. In such circumstances the claimant can be subrogated to the secured creditor's charge and gain the benefit of that security as against other creditors of the borrower. In effect the benefit of the charge is treated as though it had been assigned to the claimant[38] so that the claimant will obtain the benefit of that charge.

The basis for awarding the remedy of subrogation has proved to be controversial. It has sometimes been suggested that it is a response to the defendant's unjust enrichment at the expense of the claimant.[39] Significantly, in *Menelaou v Bank of Cyprus plc*[40] the Court

---

[29] See p 610, above.

[30] For detailed analysis, see C Mitchell and S Watterson, *Subrogation: Law and Practice* (Oxford: Oxford University Press, 2007).

[31] *Sander v Pearson* [2013] EWCA Civ 1822, [15] (Arden LJ).

[32] *Orakpo v Manson Investments Ltd* [1978] AC 95, 104 (Lord Diplock); *Re TH Knitwear (Wholesale) Ltd* [1988] Ch 275, 284 (Slade LJ).   [33] [1999] 1 AC 221.

[34] *Banque Financière de la Cité v Parc (Battersea) Ltd* [1999] 1 AC 221, 231 (Lord Hoffmann). See also *Cheltenham and Gloucester Plc v Appleyard* [2004] EWCA Civ 291, [32] (Neuberger LJ).

[35] This has been described as 'subsisting rights subrogation': Mitchell and Waterson, *Subrogation: Law and Practice*, para 1.07. See *Alliance Bank JSC v Aquanta Corp* [2011] EWHC 3281 (Comm), [22] (Burton J); *Ibrahim v Barclays Bank Plc* [2011] EWHC 1897 (Ch), [2012] 1 BCLC 33, [7] (Vos J).

[36] *Hobbs v Marlowe* [1978] AC 16, 39 (Lord Diplock). See p 141, above.

[37] Mitchell and Watterson, *Subrogation: Law and Practice*, describe this as 'extinguished rights subrogation'. See *Syed Ibrhaim v Barclays Bank plc* [2011] EWHC 1897 (Ch), [7] (Vos J).

[38] *Banque Financière de la Cité v Parc (Battersea) Ltd* [1999] 1 AC 221, 236 (Lord Hoffmann). See also *Boscawen v Bajwa* [1996] 1 WLR 328, 333 (Millett LJ).

[39] *Boscawen v Bajwa* [1996] 1 WLR 328, 335 (Millett LJ); *Banque Financière de la Cité v Parc (Battersea) Ltd* [1999] 1 AC 221; *Liberty Mutual Insurance Co (UK) Ltd v HSBC Bank plc* [2002] EWCA Civ 691; *Cheltenham and Gloucester plc v Appleyard* [2004] EWCA Civ 291, [33] (Neuberger LJ); *Filby v Mortgage Express (No 2) Ltd* [2004] EWCA Civ 759, [62] (May LJ); *Lehman Commercial Mortgage Conduit Ltd v Gatedale Ltd* [2012] EWHC 848 (Ch); *Sandher v Pearson* [2013] EWCA Civ 1822. In *Anfield (UK) Ltd v Bank of Scotland* [2010] EWHC 2374 (Ch), [2011] 1 WLR 2414, [10], Proudman J proceeded, at [11], to emphasize that subrogation required proof of some unconscionable conduct or unjust factor.

[40] [2013] EWCA Civ 1960, [2014] 1 WLR 854.

of Appeal specifically recognized that the equitable remedy of subrogation operated to reverse unjust enrichment. If this is correct, it follows that it will be necessary to establish that the defendant was enriched at the expense of the claimant and that a ground of restitution can be identified, which might be difficult to establish. In that case unjust enrichment was easier to establish, since the claimant bank had mistakenly released charges on one property which enabled funds to become available to enable the defendant to purchase another property. The defendant was considered to have been indirectly enriched at the expense of the claimant,[41] with the ground of restitution being mistake. As a consequence the claimant was subrogated to the vendor's unpaid lien against the defendant.

But, in the light of the approach to equitable proprietary claims that is adopted in this book, the preferable view is that the equitable remedy of subrogation operates to vindicate the claimant's equitable property rights. Such a conclusion has been endorsed by the High Court of Australia.[42] Consequently, the normal conditions for proprietary claims need to be established, namely that the claimant has an equitable interest in property that can be traced into property received by the defendant. Then it will be appropriate to consider how best the claimant's property rights can be vindicated. The proprietary remedy of subrogation does, however, work differently from the other proprietary remedies that we have examined. Those remedies assume that the defendant has retained property in which the claimant has an equitable proprietary interest. The typical scenario in which subrogation will be relevant is where the claimant's value has been used to discharge a debt. As we have already seen,[43] the discharge of a debt will defeat the tracing exercise.[44] But it is still possible to trace into the discharged debt, and then, if the conditions for awarding subrogation are satisfied, the proprietary rights that have been destroyed through the discharge of the debt can be resurrected by allowing the claimant to stand in the shoes of another creditor of the defendant and obtain the benefit of any security that that creditor had against the defendant. In other words, subrogation provides a mechanism with which to obtain a charge over the defendant's property in circumstances under which the claimant has not been able to trace into property that remains in the defendant's possession, and so the claimant will gain priority over the defendant's general creditors if the defendant is insolvent. It is the defendant's insolvency that is usually the reason why the claimant seeks to be subrogated to the security of a third party against the defendant.

The reason why subrogation has been analysed as a remedy to reverse the defendant's unjust enrichment derives from the decision of the House of Lords in *Banque Financière de la Cité v Parc (Battersea) Ltd.*[45] But the facts of that case were highly unusual and actually the remedy itself was personal rather than proprietary, since the claimant only obtained priority over the defendant and not as regards any of the other creditors of the debtor company.[46] Usually, however, subrogation will operate as a proprietary remedy since the claimant will obtain the benefit of the third party's security completely. Consequently, to the extent that the third party had priority over other creditors of the defendant, the claimant will gain equal priority. Indeed, in *Cheltenham and Gloucester*

---

[41] See p 109, above.

[42] *Bofinger v Kingsway Group Ltd* [2009] HCA 44. See also *Halifax plc v Omar* [2002] EWCA Civ 21, [2002] 2 P & CR 377; *Eagle Star Insurance Co Ltd v Karasiewicz* [2002] EWCA Civ 940. See S Midwinter, 'Subrogation Finds Some "Well-settled Principles"' [2003] LMCLQ 6.   [43] See p 623, above.

[44] Unless the doctrine of backward tracing is recognized, so that the claimant will be able to trace into the previously acquired asset in respect of which the debt was incurred. See p 624, above.

[45] [1999] 1 AC 221, 231 (Lord Hoffmann). See also *Boscawen v Bajwa* [1996] 1 WLR 328, 335 (Millett LJ); *Investment Trust Companies (in liquidation) v HMRC* [2015] EWCA Civ 82, [53] (Patten LJ).

[46] *Banque Financière de la Cité v Parc (Battersea) Ltd* [1999] 1 AC 221, 228 (Lord Steyn) and 237 (Lord Clyde).

plc v Appleyard[47] Neuberger J considered that the classic form of the subrogation remedy is proprietary, in that it enables a lender who expects to obtain a security to claim subrogation to another security and that the reference to *Banque Financière* is unlikely to be of assistance in a conventional case.

Banque Financière remains an important case, however, to determine the correct operation of subrogation. In that case the claimant had lent a sum of money to the debtor company, which used the money to pay off part of a debt owed by it to a third party, this debt having been secured by a charge over property. The defendant company, which was in the same group as the debtor, had a second charge over the same property. When the claimant lent the money to the debtor company, the claimant received a letter of postponement which stated that the claimant's debt would be paid off in priority to any other company in the group. Clearly the intention behind this letter was to give the claimant priority over the defendant, but it was ineffective to give the claimant priority as a matter of law. The debtor company became insolvent and the question for the House of Lords to resolve was whether the debt which that company owed to the claimant should be discharged before that which was owed to the defendant. The court concluded that the defendant had been unjustly enriched at the expense of the claimant. The defendant was enriched at the claimant's expense because the claimant's money was used partially to discharge the liability of the third party, and this improved the chances of the defendant being repaid. This enrichment was unjust because the claimant had mistakenly believed that the effect of the letter of postponement was that it had priority over the defendant and, had it not made this mistake, it would not have lent the money in the first place.[48] The court concluded that the most appropriate remedy to reverse the defendant's unjust enrichment was to subrogate the claimant to the rights of the third party against the debtor company. This meant that, as between the claimant and the defendant, the claimant had the benefit of the third party's charge so that the claimant obtained priority over the defendant. The particularly important feature of the remedy of subrogation in this case was that it operated as a personal remedy, since the claimant only obtained priority over the defendant and not as regards any of the other creditors of the debtor company.[49] Generally, however, subrogation operates as a proprietary remedy which is good against the world, so it should be recognized that it is only applicable where the claimant has an equitable proprietary interest which can be traced into a discharged secured debt.

(2) The Principles Underlying the Remedy of Subrogation

(a) **Operation of Law**

The remedy of subrogation arises by operation of law and does not depend on the parties' intention that the remedy should be available.[50]

(b) **Resurrection of Discharged Security**

The claimant may still get the benefit of a creditor's security against the defendant by means of the subrogation remedy even though that security has been discharged.[51] This was recognized in *Boscawen v Bajwa* by Millett LJ,[52] who accepted that a discharged

---

[47] [2004] EWCA Civ 291.   [48] See Chapter 9 for examination of mistake as a ground of restitution.

[49] *Banque Financière de la Cité v Parc (Battersea) Ltd* [1999] 1 AC 221, 228 (Lord Steyn) and 237 (Lord Clyde). See also *Filby v Mortgage Express (No 2) Ltd* [2004] EWCA Civ 759.

[50] *Banque Financière de la Cité v Parc (Battersea) Ltd* [1999] 1 AC 221, 231 (Lord Hoffmann).

[51] That the claimant can obtain the benefit of a creditor's *undischarged* security was recognized by the House of Lords in *Banque Financière de la Cité v Parc (Battersea) Ltd* [1999] 1 AC 221.

[52] *Boscawen v Bajwa* [1996] 1 WLR 328, 341.

security can be resurrected. So, for example, if the claimant's money has been used by the defendant to discharge a secured debt owed by the defendant to a third party, it will be possible for the claimant to get the benefit of the security even though it has been discharged.

An aspect of the decision of the Court of Appeal in *Re Diplock's Estate*[53] appears, however, to suggest a contrary conclusion. The executors of the testator's estate had mistakenly paid some money to the Leaf Homeopathic Hospital, which it used to discharge a mortgage over the hospital's property. It was held that the claimants could not trace into the discharged debt and so be subrogated to the mortgage, because the mortgage had ceased to exist once the debt had been discharged. The denial of the remedy in this case could be justified on the basis that the hospital had innocently changed its position by using the money to discharge a liability.[54] But this explanation is dubious for two reasons. First, it has been recognized in the law of unjust enrichment that the defence of change of position is not available where the defendant has used money paid by mistake to discharge a debt, because the defendant will not have suffered any detriment by discharging the debt since he or she is simply substituting one creditor, the claimant, for another.[55] Secondly, the defence of change of position is probably not available to proprietary claims in which the claimant seeks a proprietary remedy.[56] The result in *Re Diplock's Estate* is better explained as turning on a question of evidence rather than law, namely that it simply could not be shown that the claimant's money had been used to discharge the mortgage. If the money could not be traced into the mortgage, it would not be possible to be subrogated to the discharged security.[57]

Subrogation will be available even where the chargee's original charge was void for illegality, at least where the chargee was not party to the illegality.[58]

(c) Intentional Transfer

Where the claimant has intentionally lent money that has been used to discharge a secured debt, the claimant will be subrogated to the discharged security only if the claimant had intended the loan to be secured, but for some reason the security was not valid.[59] The award of the subrogation remedy can be justified on the ground that it is unconscionable to frustrate the claimant's intention that he or she was to obtain the benefit of a security.

The application of this principle is illustrated by *Boscawen v Bajwa*,[60] in which the Abbey National lent money to the purchaser of a house, with the loan being secured by a legal charge. This money was paid to the purchaser's solicitors. In breach of trust, that firm of solicitors transferred the money to the vendor's solicitors before completion and the money was used to discharge the vendor's mortgage with the Halifax. The sale of the house fell through. The creditors of the vendor had obtained a charging order against the property that was sold, with the proceeds of sale paid into court. The creditors claimed the proceeds of sale, but the Abbey National claimed that it was entitled by subrogation to the security right of the Halifax, being the vendor's former mortgagee, and so it was entitled to a charge on the proceeds of sale that ranked above the vendor's creditors. The

[53] [1948] 1 Ch 465, 549–50.

[54] *Boscawen v Bajwa* [1996] 1 WLR 328, 341 (Millett LJ). See p 696, below.

[55] *Scottish Equitable plc v Derby* [2001] 3 All ER 818. See further p 684, below.

[56] See p 696, below.

[57] See LD Smith, 'Tracing Into The Payment of a Debt' (1995) 54 CLJ 290, 295.

[58] *Lehman Commercial Mortgage Conduit Ltd v Gatedale Ltd* [2012] EWHC 848 (Ch).

[59] *Banque Financière de la Cité v Parc (Battersea) Ltd* [1999] 1 AC 221. See also *Cheltenham and Gloucester plc v Appleyard* [2004] EWCA Civ 291, [40] (Neuberger LJ); *Butler v Rice* [1910] 2 Ch 277; *Ghana Commercial Bank v Chandiram* [1960] AC 732.   [60] [1996] 1 WLR 328.

Court of Appeal found for the Abbey National for the following reasons. An equitable proprietary base could be identified because the money was held on trust by the purchaser's solicitors for the Abbey National. It could trace its money in Equity into the payment that was used to discharge the mortgage by the vendor, despite mixing with other money in the vendor's solicitor's client account, including some of the vendor's money. Subrogation was awarded to enable the Abbey National to vindicate its property rights because it was held that the vendor's solicitor must have intended to keep the mortgage alive for the benefit of the Abbey National. The Court of Appeal emphasized that it focused on the vendor's solicitor's intention to keep the security alive rather than the intention of the Abbey National when lending the money in the first place, because the Abbey National's money had not been paid directly to discharge the vendor's mortgage, but had been transferred via the purchaser's and the vendor's solicitors. This seems unnecessarily complicated. The key question should simply have been what the Abbey National's intention was in paying the money in the first place, and since it had clearly intended to obtain the benefit of a security, it followed that a subrogation remedy was entirely appropriate.

(d) Unintentional Transfer

Where the claimant has not intentionally lent money, but the money has been misappropriated and has been used to discharge a secured debt, subrogation may be available even though the claimant was ignorant of the transfer and could not have intended to obtain any security. In this situation, the remedy will be triggered because it would be unconscionable for the defendant to deny the claimant's proprietary interest.[61] So, for example, if the defendant trustee misappropriates trust money and uses this to discharge a mortgage, the claimant beneficiaries can be subrogated to the mortgagee's security interest by virtue of the defendant's unconscionable conduct.

(e) No Better Position

The claimant cannot obtain subrogation to put him or her in a better position than that in which he or she would have been had the claimant obtained all of the rights for which he or she had bargained.[62]

(f) Exclusion of the Remedy

It is possible to exclude the remedy of subrogation expressly by contract. Similarly, the contract between the claimant and the defendant may impliedly exclude the remedy of subrogation. This is illustrated by *Capital Finance Co Ltd v Stokes*,[63] in which the claimant and the defendant had agreed that the claimant should obtain a security by way of a legal charge. This charge was unenforceable because it had not been registered, but it was held that, because a legal charge was a better interest than an equitable charge, the agreement between the parties prevented the claimant from being subrogated to a third party's equitable charge against the defendant. In other words, the intention that the claimant should have the benefit of a legal charge prevented the claimant from being subrogated to a lesser equitable charge.

---

[61] Ibid, 335.
[62] *Cheltenham and Gloucester plc v Appleyard* [2004] EWCA Civ 291, [41] (Neuberger LJ); *Filby v Mortgage Express (No 2) Ltd* [2004] EWCA Civ 759, [63] (May LJ).
[63] [1969] 1 Ch 261. See also *Liberty Mutual Insurance Co (UK) Ltd v HSBC Bank plc* [2002] EWCA Civ 691.

(g) Negligent Failure to Register Security

A lender of money could be subrogated to a charge that had been redeemed in circumstances under which the lender had intended the loan to be secured, but had negligently failed to register the charge. This was recognized in *Anfield (UK) Ltd v Bank of Scotland plc*.[64] Where, however, the borrower of the money had acted to its detriment in the reasonable, but false, belief that the loan was unsecured, as a consequence of the lender's negligence, subrogation might not be available. This was justified on the ground that the borrower's enrichment would not then be unjust, which was consistent with the unjust enrichment analysis of subrogation adopted in that case and the application of a defence of change of position. The preferable view, however, and one that is consistent with the analysis of subrogation as remedy to vindicate property rights, is that the justice of the case is not relevant to the operation of the law of subrogation and so the borrower's detrimental reliance on the assumed unsecured nature of the loan should be irrelevant.

(h) Public Policy

The claimant may not be awarded the remedy of subrogation for reasons of public policy. This is illustrated by *Orakpo v Manson Investments Ltd*[65] where the claimant was not subrogated to the rights of a third party because this would have been contrary to the policy of the Moneylenders Acts.

3. PERSONAL CLAIMS AND REMEDIES

This section is concerned with those cases where the claimant seeks to secure a personal restitutionary remedy in circumstances in which it is an essential element of the claim that he or she has a legal or equitable proprietary interest in the property which the defendant had received, and sometimes continues to retain.

(A) PERSONAL CLAIMS AND REMEDIES AT LAW

Where the claimant can establish that he or she had a legal interest in the property that was received by the defendant, the claimant may be able to recover the value of the property received by the defendant in three different situations.

(i) Conversion

Although the Common Law lacks any general proprietary remedy to enable the claimant to recover property from the defendant, restitutionary remedies may be available for the tort of conversion, which involves the wrongful taking, keeping or disposing of another's goods. Although nominally tortious this has been recognized as a remedy to protect the ownership of goods.[66] Interference with a possessory title is sufficient, even if possession had been obtained unlawfully.[67] It is not, however, possibly to convert intangible property,[68] because such property cannot be possessed. If the claimant wishes to recover

---

[64] [2010] EWHC 2374 (Ch), [2011] 1 WLR 2414.   [65] [1978] AC 95.

[66] *Kuwait Airways Corp v Iraqi Airways Co (Nos 4 and 5)* [2002] 2 AC 883, [77] (Lord Nicholls); *OBG Ltd v Allan* [2007] UKHL 21, [2008] AC 1, [308] (Baroness Hale).

[67] *Costello v Chief Constable of Derbyshire Constabulary* [2001] EWCA Civ 387, [2001] 1 WLR 1437. See D Fox, 'Enforcing a Possessory Title to a Stolen Car' (2002) 61 CLJ 27.

[68] *OBG Ltd v Allan* [2007] UKHL 21, [2008] 1 AC 1, [102]–[106] (Lord Hoffmann); *Armstrong GmbH v Winnington Networks* [2012] EWHC 10 (Ch), [2013] Ch 156, [45] (Stephen Morris QC). See generally S

damages for the tort of conversion it is necessary to show that he or she has a legal proprietary interest in property and that property, or its substitute, was converted by the defendant acting in some way which is inconsistent with the claimant's proprietary rights. Although the remedy which is awarded will typically be compensatory damages, the claimant may wish to waive the tort and bring a restitutionary claim to recover the value of the property which the defendant had converted.[69]

(ii) Action for Money Had and Received

Where the defendant has received money in which the claimant has retained a legal proprietary interest, the claimant can recover the value of the money received by means of a claim traditionally called the 'action for money had and received'. This will be the case where the claimant brings a restitutionary claim against the defendant who received the claimant's money via a third party. In such a case the claimant is usually unable to bring a claim founded on unjust enrichment because it will not be possible to show that the defendant has been unjustly enriched at the claimant's direct expense, save where this can be established as a matter of economic reality.[70] The claimant may instead seek to show that the defendant received property in which the claimant retained a proprietary interest.[71] It is sufficient that the defendant received the property in which the claimant has a legal proprietary interest; it is not necessary to show that the defendant has retained this property or anything representing this property.[72] It is also not necessary to show that the defendant was at fault in any way in receiving the property.

The key case that illustrates this type of claim is *Lipkin Gorman (a firm) v Karpnale Ltd*.[73] In that case, over £320,000 had been stolen from the client account of the claimant firm of solicitors by one of its partners, who had gambled with it at the defendant's casino. The House of Lords held that the defendant was liable to make restitution to the claimant by means of a personal action for money had and received. The nature of this claim has been a matter of particular controversy. The House of Lords recognized that it was founded on the reversal of the defendant's unjust enrichment, although the ground of restitution was not identified. Some commentators have suggested that the ground of restitution was that the claimant was ignorant that its money had been stolen.[74] An alternative view is that this claim was simply concerned with the vindication of the claimant's property rights in the money, those rights having been retained because the money had been stolen.[75] The latter is the preferable view and is supported by the

---

Watterson and A Goymour, 'Testing the Boundaries of Conversion: Account-Holders, Intangible Property and Economic Harm' [2012] LMCLQ 204, 215–18.

[69] See p 459, above. Alternatively, the court might order that the property is returned to the claimant. See the Torts (Interference with Goods) Act 1977, s 3(2), discussed at p 632, above.

[70] See p 107, above.

[71] *Clark v Shee and Johnson* (1774) 1 Cowp 197, 98 ER 1041; *Reid v Rigby* [1894] 2 QB 40; *Lipkin Gorman (a firm) v Karpnale Ltd* [1991] 2 AC 548; *Trustee of the Property of FC Jones & Sons v Jones* [1997] Ch 159; *Barros Mattos Jnr v MacDaniels Ltd* [2004] EWHC 1188 (Ch), [2005] 1 WLR 247; *OEM plc v Schneider* [2005] EWHC 1072 (Ch).

[72] See *Agip (Africa) Ltd v Jackson* [1990] Ch 265, 285 (Millett J).   [73] [1991] 2 AC 548.

[74] PBH Birks, 'The English Recognition of Unjust Enrichment' [1991] LMCLQ 473 and E McKendrick, 'Restitution, Misdirected Funds and Change of Position' (1992) 55 MLR 377. Criticized by WJ Swadling, 'Ignorance and Unjust Enrichment: The Problem of Title' (2008) OJLS 627.

[75] See GJ Virgo, 'What is the Law of Restitution About?' in W Cornish, R Nolan, J O'Sullivan, and G Virgo (eds), *Restitution: Past, Present and Future* (Oxford: Hart Publishing, 1998), 314–16.

recognition of the House of Lords in *Foskett v McKeown*[76] of the vindication of property rights principle.[77]

Another explanation for the result in *Lipkin Gorman* has been suggested by Smith,[78] namely that, although the claimant was bringing a claim for money had and received at Common Law, this could have been founded on the claimant's equitable proprietary interest in money. Smith has identified a number of old cases which recognized that money had and received is available as a remedy to vindicate equitable proprietary rights under a trust. This is not how the House of Lords decided *Lipkin Gorman*, since that decision was explicitly founded on a legal property right, but this does provide a useful way of justifying the result in the case. Lord Goff did acknowledge that, if legal title had vested in the solicitor, he would have held the money on trust for the firm.[79] As a thief and a solicitor, this would have been a constructive trust triggered by the defendant's unconscionable retention of the money.[80] The firm would then have been able to trace in Equity through the mixed fund into the money received by the defendant. If this approach of providing a Common Law claim where there is an equitable proprietary interest was developed, it would enable equitable property rights to be vindicated by the award of personal remedies without the proof of fault. That is inconsistent with the general tenor of personal claims against third parties in Equity, in which fault is usually required,[81] and this might be a significant policy reason against allowing a Common Law claim to be used to vindicate an equitable property right.

However it is analysed, *Lipkin Gorman* is a difficult case to explain and justify. But in line with the approach adopted by the judges in the case, it should simply be treated as involving the vindication of Common Law property rights by means of a personal claim for money had and received, without the need to prove fault. The defendant will then be liable to pay to the claimant the value of the property that has been received, judged at the time of receipt, but subject to the application of the defence of change of position.[82]

(iii) Action for Debt

It was recognized by the Court of Appeal in *Trustee of the Property of FC Jones and Sons (a firm) v Jones*[83] that, where the claimant could establish that the defendant had received property in which the claimant had legal title, the claimant could bring an action for debt against the defendant and obtain an order for payment of the money. This is a personal claim, which has the same practical consequences as the action for money had and received, namely that the claimant is able to recover the value of the money that was received by the defendant. The advantage of bringing a claim in debt is that, if the defendant has invested the money received and obtained income from that investment, then this income must also be paid to the claimant. This makes the action for debt look increasingly proprietary in its operation, save that if the defendant becomes insolvent, the claimant will not have priority over any of the defendant's other creditors, but will rank as a general unsecured creditor.

---

[76] [2001] 1 AC 102.

[77] *Armstrong DLW GmbH v Winnington Networks Ltd* [2012] EWHC 10 (Ch), [2013] Ch 156, [75] (Stephen Morris QC). See further p 560, above.

[78] LD Smith, 'Simplifying Claims to Traceable Proceeds' (2009) 125 LQR 338.

[79] *Lipkin Gorman (a firm) v Karpnale Ltd* [1991] 2 AC 548, 572.   [80] See p 598, above.

[81] See p 652, below.   [82] See p 698, below.   [83] [1997] Ch 159.

(B) PERSONAL CLAIMS AND REMEDIES IN EQUITY

Where the defendant has received property in which the claimant has an equitable proprietary interest there are a number of personal claims which enable the claimant to recover the value of his or her property.

(i) Administration of Estates

The House of Lords in *Ministry of Health v Simpson*[84] recognized an apparently limited personal restitutionary action in Equity, whereby beneficiaries of a deceased's estate were able to recover money which had been paid to the defendants by the personal representatives who were administering the estate and who mistakenly believed that the money was properly paid to the defendants. This equitable action has two unusual features. First, unlike many equitable claims which depend on the defendant's conscience having been affected in some way before equitable liability is imposed, the defendant's liability is strict. Secondly, the beneficiaries are only able to bring an action against the recipients of the estate once they have exhausted their remedies against the personal representatives. This limitation is difficult to defend, but it may simply exist because the personal representatives can be considered to have been at fault in making the mistake in the first place and, being an equitable claim, this form of liability should prevail over strict liability.

The proper analysis of this equitable action is a matter of some controversy. It might be analysed as a strict liability equitable proprietary claim, with the beneficiaries vindicating their equitable proprietary rights against the defendants who had received property from the estate by mistake. But this proprietary analysis will not work, since the beneficiaries of an unadministered estate have neither a legal nor an equitable interest in the estate until the personal representatives have discharged all of the deceased's debts.[85] Until this has occurred, the beneficiary has only an expectation of the property being distributed. Consequently, the beneficiaries have no equitable proprietary interest to vindicate. The preferable way of analysing *Ministry of Health v Simpson* is that the beneficiaries are bringing a claim on behalf of the estate rather than themselves to vindicate the distribution scheme of the administration of the estate.[86] The personal representatives are responsible for bringing the claim for recovery of property transferred by mistake. But, if they do not do so, the potential beneficiaries should sue the personal representatives to restore the value of the estate. If they are not able to do that successfully, Equity enables them to bring a claim against the recipient of the property. If they are successful, the value of the property received is not paid to the beneficiaries, but is returned to the estate, which still needs to be administered. Throughout this process, the beneficiaries cannot benefit directly, since they have only an expectation that they will receive something in the administration of the estate. This expectation will be defeated if the third-party recipient of the property was a *bona fide* purchaser for value.[87]

It follows that this strict liability personal claim arises in the very specific context of a defective transfer of property in the administration of an estate. Nevertheless, the strict liability claim has been recognized outside of that context. For example, in *GL Baker Ltd v Medway Building and Supplies Ltd*[88] the principle was applied to enable a beneficiary to recover money mistakenly transferred by a trustee in the administration of an *inter vivos*

---

[84] [1951] AC 251, on appeal from *Re Diplock's Estate* [1948] Ch 465.
[85] *Commissioner of Stamp Duties (Queensland) v Livingston* [1965] AC 694.
[86] See D Sheehan, 'Disentangling Equitable Personal Liability for Receipt and Assistance' [2008] RLR 41, 61.
[87] *Baker (GL) Ltd v Medway Building and Supplies Ltd* [1958] 1 WLR 1216, 1220 (Danckwerts J); *Re J Leslie Engineers Co Ltd* [1976] 1 WLR 292, 299 (Oliver J).   [88] [1958] 1 WLR 1216.

trust. This may be treated as an aberration or perhaps as a logical extension of the principle recognized in *Ministry of Health v Simpson*, under which the beneficiary has a right to sue the third-party recipient in Equity where the right to sue is derived from the trustee. But the beneficiary could not have benefited personally from this claim. If the claim was successful, the recipient would be liable to repay the money to the trust fund rather than to the beneficiary directly.

(ii) Action for Unconscionable Receipt

The equitable action for unconscionable receipt, sometimes known as 'knowing receipt',[89] can be considered to be the equitable equivalent of the Common Law claim for money had and received. Both claims are dependent on proof that the defendant had received property in which the claimant had a proprietary interest; either a legal interest for the action for money had and received, or an equitable interest for the action for unconscionable receipt. A further similarity between the two claims is that they will both succeed as long as it can be shown that the defendant received the property without it being necessary to show that the defendant had retained the property. Further, the remedy that is awarded for both types of claim is a personal restitutionary remedy, since it is assessed by reference to the value of the property that the defendant received at the time of its receipt. Despite these similarities between the two claims, there is one fundamental difference between them: whereas liability in the action for money had and received is strict, liability for the action for unconscionable receipt depends on proof that the defendant was at fault in some way. The degree of fault which must be proved is a matter of particular controversy, especially as to whether fault is to be assessed subjectively (with regard to the defendant's thought processes) or objectively (with regard to the standard of the reasonable person). But the reason why fault must be established is also a controversial matter which requires careful consideration.

Liability for unconscionable receipt is sometimes described as secondary liability,[90] since it is assumed that the defendant's liability depends on there having been a breach of trust or fiduciary duty. This is not correct. Secondary liability requires proof that the accessory has caused, assisted or encouraged the breach of trust or fiduciary duty. That does not need to be proved to establish liability for unconscionable receipt, especially because such liability arises after the relevant breach and sometimes after a number of transfers of property between different parties. Such a remote recipient cannot be considered to have assisted, encouraged or caused the breach of trust or fiduciary duty.

(1) Conditions of Liability

In order to establish liability for unconscionable receipt, the following conditions need to be met.

(a) Receipt of Property

The defendant must have received property in which the claimant has an equitable proprietary interest. This is established by applying the equitable following and tracing rules.[91] Property includes chattels and money but not contractual rights arising under

---

[89] This language is still used. See, for example, *Williams v Central Bank of Nigeria* [2014] UKSC 10, [2014] AC 1189, [35] (Lord Sumption).

[90] *Novoship (UK) Ltd v Mikhaylyuk* [2014] EWCA Civ 908, [2015] 2 WLR 526, [68].

[91] *Boscawen v Bajwa* [1996] 1 WLR 328, 334 (Millett LJ).

an executory contract.[92] Although it has sometimes been suggested that the receipt of confidential information might be regarded as the receipt of property,[93] the preferable view is that information cannot be characterized as property for these purposes.[94]

Whether the defendant has received property may sometimes raise difficult questions. So, for example, in *Trustor v AB Smallbone (No 2)*[95] it was held that, where property has been received by a company, its receipt cannot be attributed to an individual who controls the company because of the fundamental doctrine that a company has a separate corporate personality from its directors and shareholders. But receipt by a company may be attributed to the controller of it where the recipient company was acting as agent for the controller or where the veil of incorporation can be pierced, such as where the company has been used as an artificial device to conceal the true facts. Where the veil cannot be pierced then, although receipt-based liability cannot be imposed on the controller, the company can be liable for unconscionable receipt in its own right,[96] although it will be necessary to attribute the relevant fault to the company from the fault of the person who is the directing mind and will of the company.

(b) Breach of Trust or Fiduciary Duty

It is a condition of liability for unconscionable receipt that there has been a breach of trust[97] or fiduciary duty. Where property has been transferred in breach of trust, the claimant will have a prior equitable proprietary interest which can be vindicated. It has been recognized that the action is also available where property has been transferred in breach of fiduciary duty.[98] But, for such a claim to be treated as grounded on the vindication of property rights, it would be necessary to establish that the claimant had a proprietary interest in the property which was transferred in breach of fiduciary duty. Following the recognition by the Supreme Court that property received in breach of fiduciary duty by the fiduciary will be held on constructive trust for the principal,[99] it will be much easier to establish this equitable proprietary interest.

The nature of the breach of trust or fiduciary duty is irrelevant. In particular, it need not be a fraudulent breach.[100] The receipt of property by the defendant must have been a direct consequence of the relevant breach of trust or fiduciary duty. This was recognized in *Brown v Bennett*,[101] in which receivers of a company that had gone into administrative receivership sold the business to the defendant. Some of the former shareholders and directors of the company, to whom the receivers had assigned their causes of action, sued the defendant for unconscionable receipt of the company's assets knowing that the directors of the company had breached their fiduciary duty. It was held that the receipt of the company's assets was not a direct consequence of the breach of fiduciary duty, because the assets had been purchased from independent sellers, namely the receivers. The effect of this decision is that, if the receipt of property arises from a separate legitimate transaction, the defendant cannot be liable for the receipt, regardless of the state of his or

---

[92] *Criterion Properties Ltd v Stratford UK Properties Ltd* [2004] UKHL 28, [2004] 1 WLR 1846, [27] (Lord Scott).

[93] *Satnam Investments Ltd v Dunlop Heywood* [1999] 3 All ER 652.

[94] *Farah Constructions Pty Ltd v Say-Dee Pty Ltd* [2007] HCA 22, [118]–[119]. See also *OBG Ltd v Allan* [2007] UKHL 21, [2008] AC 1, [275] (Lord Walker).   [95] [2001] 1 WLR 1177.

[96] *Ultraframe (UK) Ltd v Fielding* [2005] EWHC 1638, [2006] FSR 16, [1576] (Lewison J).

[97] *Novoship (UK) Ltd v Mikhaylyuk* [2014] EWCA Civ 908, [2015] 2 WLR 526, [89].

[98] *Arthur v Attorney-General of the Turks and Caicos Islands* [2012] UKPC 30, [31].

[99] *FHR European Ventures LLP v Cedar Capital Partners LLC* [2014] UKSC 45, [2015] AC 250. See p 512, above.

[100] *Agip (Africa) Ltd v Jackson* [1990] Ch 265, 292 (Millett J).   [101] [1999] 1 BCLC 649.

her knowledge of the background to the transfer. This was illustrated by an example suggested by Morritt LJ in *Brown v Bennett*.[102] A mansion house is vested in trustees, who, in breach of trust, let it fall into disrepair over a number of years. The trustees are replaced and the new trustees decide to sell the property to a neighbour, who has seen the property fall into disrepair. The purchase of the property by the neighbour would not render him liable for unconscionable receipt, even though he was well aware of the trustees' breach of trust, because, assuming that the transaction was at a proper price, the breach of duty did not cause the neighbour to acquire the land; this arose from a separate, valid transaction which consequently broke the chain of causation.

But this emphasis on the receipt being a direct result of the breach appears inconsistent with the prime requirement of the claim that it is enough that the value of the claimant's property can be traced to the defendant's receipt, even if the property has passed through various hands and has been substituted on the way. A better explanation for the result in *Brown v Bennett*, and for Morritt LJ's hypothetical example, is that the defendant was a *bona fide* purchaser for value, which will defeat the claimant's equitable proprietary interest, or, alternatively, that the vendors of the property were not acting in breach of trust in selling the property. This is a preferable way of denying liability than by reference to unnecessary concepts of causation.

(c) Beneficial Receipt

The property must be received by the defendant for his or her own use and benefit,[103] rather than ministerially. This means that, if the property is received by the defendant merely as agent for another, the defendant cannot be liable for unconscionable receipt, unless the defendant subsequently misappropriates the property for his or her own use, since then the defendant will be benefiting from the property. Where the defendant has received the property ministerially, he or she might still be liable for dishonest assistance.[104]

The requirement of beneficial receipt for the receipt-based claim is significant. For example, where money is transferred to a bank in breach of trust, the bank cannot be liable for unconscionable receipt, even though its employees might know of the breach of trust, because it will not have received the money for itself, but ministerially for its customer. That, at least, is the orthodox view. An exception has been recognized where the money was paid into an overdrawn account, which has the effect of discharging a debt owed by the customer to the bank, so that then the bank will have received the money beneficially rather than ministerially.[105] But surely all money that is paid to a bank is received by it beneficially rather than ministerially, because the relationship between bank and customer is one of debtor and creditor, so the bank receives the money for itself and is liable only to pay to the customer the amount that has been received, rather than the actual money that has been transferred?[106] In other words, payment to a bank simply creates a debt owed to the customer and the bank is free to do what it wants with the money that was transferred to it. In *Uzinterimpex JSC v Standard Bank plc*[107] the Court of Appeal confirmed the general principle that receipt-based liability turns on the defendant receiving property for

---

[102] Ibid, 655.

[103] *Agip (Africa) Ltd v Jackson* [1990] Ch 265, affirmed [1991] Ch 547 (CA); *Trustor AB v Smallbone (No 2)* [2001] 1 WLR 1177.

[104] See p 521, above.   [105] *Agip (Africa) Ltd v Jackson* [1990] Ch 265, 292 (Millett J).

[106] S Gleeson, 'The Involuntary Launderer: The Banker's Liability for Deposits of the Proceeds of Crime' in PBH Birks (ed), *Laundering and Tracing* (Oxford: Oxford University Press, 1995), 126–7; M Bryan, 'Recovering Misdirected Money from Banks: Ministerial Receipt at Law and in Equity' in F Rose (ed), *Restitution and Banking Law* (Oxford: Mansfield Press, 1998), 182.   [107] [2008] EWCA Civ 819.

his or her own use and benefit, but Moore-Bick LJ did suggest *obiter* that, since a bank has the benefit of its customers' money until it is called upon to repay, it should follow that a bank could be liable for unconscionable receipt when money is credited to a customer's bank account. Consequently, the ambit of liability for unconscionable receipt would be much more significant, although it must not be forgotten that the defendant recipient cannot be liable for receiving property transferred in breach of trust or fiduciary duty unless it is at fault as regards the receipt.

(d) Fault

The defendant must have been at fault either when he or she received the property in breach of trust or fiduciary duty or, if the receipt was innocent, the defendant was at fault subsequently whilst still in receipt of the property.

It has been a matter of controversy for some time as to what should be the appropriate level of fault for equitable receipt-based liability. Many cases have held that an objective test of fault applies, sometimes described as 'constructive knowledge', so that it is sufficient that the defendant had failed to make such inquiries as a reasonable person would have made as to whether property had been transferred in breach of trust or breach of fiduciary duty.[108] Other cases have held that a subjective test applies, so it must be established that the defendant actually knew or suspected that the property had been received in breach of trust or fiduciary duty.[109]

The applicable level of fault was considered by the Court of Appeal in *Bank of Credit and Commerce International (Overseas) Ltd v Akindele*,[110] in which it was held that the appropriate test is one of unconscionability as regards the retention of the benefit of the property received.[111] In *Akindele* employees of a company breached their fiduciary duty by procuring the company to enter into an artificial investment agreement with the defendant, the effect of which was that the defendant invested US$10 million and subsequently received a payment of nearly US$17 million from the company. The claimants, who were the company's liquidators, sued the defendant for knowing receipt of the money on the ground that he had received the money knowing of the employees' breach of fiduciary duty. The Court of Appeal held that it was not necessary to show that the defendant had acted dishonestly to be liable for a receipt-based claim, because the receipt might be passive and dishonesty was considered only to relate to actions.[112] Rather, the key test was whether the defendant's knowledge of the circumstances relating to the breach of trust or fiduciary duty made it unconscionable for the defendant to retain the benefit of the property that had been received. This could be established if the defendant actually knew of the circumstances in which the money was transferred; constructive knowledge would not be sufficient. On the facts, there was insufficient evidence that the defendant knew enough to make retention of the value of the money received unconscionable. He was unaware of any facts that questioned the propriety of the loan transaction, despite the very high rate of interest (which he assumed was because he was

---

[108] See, for example, *Karak Rubber Co Ltd v Burden (No 2)* [1972] 1 WLR 602, 632 (Brightman J); *Belmont Finance Corp Ltd v Williams Furniture Ltd (No 2)* [1980] 1 All ER 393, 405 (Buckley LJ) and 412 (Goff LJ); *Rolled Steel Products (Holdings) Ltd v British Steel Corp* [1986] Ch 246, 306 (Browne-Wilkinson LJ); *Agip (Africa) Ltd v Jackson* [1990] Ch 265, 291 (Millett J); *Houghton v Fayers* [2000] 1 BCLC 511, 516 (Nourse LJ).

[109] *Re Montagu's Settlement Trust* [1987] Ch 264; *Eagle Trust plc v SBC Securities Ltd* [1993] 1 WLR 484, 503 (Vinelott J); *Cowan de Groot Property Ltd v Eagle Trust plc* [1992] 4 All ER 700; *Eagle Trust plc v SBC Securities Ltd (No 2)* [1996] 1 BCLC 121; *Hillsdown Holdings plc v Pensions Ombudsman* [1997] 1 All ER 862.

[110] [2001] Ch 437. See also *Arthur v Attorney-General of the Turks and Caicos Islands* [2012] UKPC 30.

[111] *Bank of Credit and Commerce International (Overseas) Ltd v Akindele* [2001] Ch 437, 455 (Nourse LJ). See R Havelock, 'The Transformation of Knowing Receipt' [2014] RLR 1.

[112] Unlike the action for dishonestly assisting a breach of trust or breach of fiduciary duty. See p 521, above.

considered to be a high-worth customer). Unconscionability could not be established from the defendant's suspicions about the general reputation of the company; any suspicion had to relate to the particular transaction. Consequently, he was not liable to account for the value of the profit that he had received.

The House of Lords was presented with the opportunity to clarify the appropriate test of fault in *Criterion Properties plc v Stratford UK Properties LLC*.[113] This case concerned a 'poison pill' agreement whereby the managing director and another director of Criterion signed an agreement, purportedly on behalf of Criterion, with the defendant Oaktree, which gave Oaktree the contractual right to be bought out of a partnership with Criterion on favourable terms if another party were to gain control of Criterion or if its chairman or managing director were to cease to be involved in the management of the company. The managing director of Criterion was dismissed and Oaktree sought to exercise its option to be bought out. However, Criterion sought to set the agreement aside on the ground that it was unauthorized. The Court of Appeal[114] held that, although the directors of Criterion might have lacked authority to make the agreement, whether Oaktree could enforce the agreement turned on whether it was unconscionable for Oaktree to hold Criterion to the agreement, a matter that needed to be considered at trial. A variety of factors and considerations were identified to determine such unconscionability, including the fault of both parties to the agreement, the defendant's knowledge of the circumstances constituting the breach of duty, whether the parties had obtained legal advice, and the actions and knowledge of the parties in the context of the commercial relationship as a whole. It appears from this that 'unconscionable' is given a subjective interpretation, but also that relative fault and factual context are significant.

The decision went on appeal to the House of Lords,[115] where the court was given the opportunity to clarify what 'unconscionability' means for these purposes. But the court concluded that the unconscionability test was not relevant to the case, since no property had been received by the defendant pursuant to the agreement. It was held that the only issue to resolve was whether there was a valid poison pill agreement, which turned on whether the directors of Criterion were authorized to sign the agreement on behalf of the company.[116] Since this matter had not yet been determined, it was directed to go to trial.

Crucially, the House of Lords rejected the approach adopted by the Court of Appeal in *Bank of Credit and Commerce International (Overseas) Ltd v Akindele*,[117] which was also considered to have turned on the question of authority to enter into the loan agreement rather than unconscionability. As Lord Nicholls said:[118]

> If a company (A) enters into an agreement with B under which B acquires benefits from A, A's ability to recover these benefits from B depends essentially on whether the agreement is binding on A. If the directors of A were acting for an improper purpose when they entered into the agreement, A's ability to have the agreement set aside depends upon the application of familiar principles of agency and company law. If, applying these principles, the agreement is found to be valid and is therefore not set aside, questions of 'knowing receipt' by B do not arise. So far as B is concerned there can be no question of A's assets having been misapplied. B acquired the assets from A, the legal and beneficial owner of the assets, under a valid agreement made between him and A.

---

[113] [2004] UKHL 28, [2004] 1 WLR 1846.

[114] *Criterion Properties plc v Stratford UK Properties LLC* [2002] EWCA Civ 1783, [2003] 1 WLR 2108.

[115] *Criterion Properties plc v Stratford UK Properties LLC* [2004] UKHL 28, [2004] 1 WLR 1846.

[116] Although it was acknowledged that the defendant's knowledge of the circumstances was relevant when considering whether there was apparent authority to sign: [2004] 1 WLR 1846, [30] (Lord Scott).

[117] [2001] Ch 437.

[118] *Criterion Properties plc v Stratford UK Properties LLC* [2004] UKHL 28, [2004] 1 WLR 1846, [4].

So the primary issue in cases such as *Criterion* and *Akindele* concerns the validity of the agreement, determined with reference to the principles of agency and corporate law. If the agreement is valid, then any property acquired by B would have been acquired legitimately and there would not have been any misapplication of A's assets. It is only if the underlying agreement is invalid that the receipt-based claim could arise.

Unconscionability has also proved significant in determining whether the defence of change of position to claims in unjust enrichment can be established.[119] That defence is not available if the defendant has acted in bad faith, which has been equated with unconscionability. In that context, unconscionability has been interpreted as including dishonesty, a failure to act in a commercially acceptable way,[120] and wilfully and recklessly failing to make such inquiries as an honest and reasonable person would make,[121] but not negligence.[122] That unconscionability for the receipt-based claim and for change of position should be interpreted in the same way was recognized by the Court of Appeal in *Abou-Rahmah v Abacha*,[123] in which it was held that general suspicions on the part of the defendant about the nature of the trustee's or fiduciary's conduct is not sufficient to constitute unconscionability; the defendant must be suspicious about the particular transaction involving the transfer of property.[124] In *Armstrong DLW GmbH v Winnington Networks Ltd*[125] Stephen Morris QC held that unconscionability for the purposes of a claim in unconscionable receipt encompassed both subjective awareness by the defendant of possible impropriety and also where, on the facts actually known to the defendant, a reasonable person would have appreciated that the transfer was in breach of trust or would have made such inquiries or sought advice which would have revealed the probability of breach of trust. In *Arthur v Attorney-General of the Turks and Caicos Islands*[126] Sir Terence Etherton described knowing receipt as 'involving unconscionable conduct amounting to equitable fraud. It is a classic example of lack of *bona fides*'. But this confirms the ambiguity of unconscionability, since equitable fraud and absence of good faith can incorporate objective notions of fault.

Lord Millett in *Dubai Aluminium Co Ltd v Salaam*[127] concluded that liability is founded on proof of dishonesty and described it as involving dishonest receipt. Lord Neuberger also emphasized in *Williams v Central Bank of Nigeria*[128] that the liability of the recipient is founded on dishonesty. In fact, despite the rejection of dishonesty in *Akindele*, this is the preferable way of analysing fault for this claim. The relevant fault should be considered to involve conduct which is objectively assessed in the light of the defendant's own knowledge or suspicion of the facts. It is the defendant's receipt of the property in such circumstances which should be considered to render that receipt unconscionable. This interpretation of fault for the receipt-based claim is consistent

---

[119] See Chapter 25.

[120] *Niru Battery Manufacturing Co v Milestone Trading Ltd* [2002] EWHC 1425 (Comm), [2002] 2 All ER (Comm) 705, 741. This was endorsed in the Court of Appeal: [2003] EWCA 1446 (Civ); *Abou-Rahmah v Abacha* [2006] EWCA Civ 1492, [2007] 1 All ER (Comm) 827.

[121] *Papamichael v National Westminster Bank* [2003] Lloyd's Rep 341, 369 (Judge Chambers QC).

[122] *Maersk Air Ltd v Expeditors International (UK) Ltd* [2003] 1 Lloyd's Rep 491, 499.

[123] [2006] EWCA Civ 1492, [2007] 1 All ER (Comm) 827.

[124] Criticized by J Lee, 'Changing Position on Change of Position' [2007] RLR 135, 139.

[125] [2012] EWHC 10 (Ch), [2013] Ch 156, [132].   [126] [2012] UKPC 30, [4].

[127] [2002] UKHL 48, [2003] 2 AC 366, 391.

[128] [2014] UKSC 10, [2014] AC 1189, [64]. See also *Vestergaard Frandsen v Bestnet Europe Ltd* [2013] UKSC 31, [2013] 1 WLR 1556, [42] (Lord Neuberger). Lord Sumption in *Williams* did, however, assert that liability does not require proof of dishonesty: [35]. Although he did not explain what he meant by dishonesty for these purposes, he appeared to relate it to fraudulent conduct in the sense of subjective awareness of the breach of trust or fiduciary duty.

therefore with the interpretation of dishonesty for purposes of the action for dishonest assistance, which is assessed by reference to an objective standard albeit in the light of the defendant's knowledge or suspicions of the facts.[129] It follows that, for the receipt-based claim, the defendant's behaviour is unconscionable (or dishonest) when he or she should have made restitution of the value of the property received in the light of the facts involving breach of trust or fiduciary duty which the defendant knew or suspected.

(2) The Remedies for Unconscionable Receipt

Once these conditions have been satisfied the defendant will be held liable to the claimant as a constructive trustee.[130] This form of liability has now been convincingly rejected as fictional and unnecessary.[131] As Millett LJ said in *Paragon Finance plc v DB Thakerar and Co*:[132] 'the expressions "constructive trust" and "constructive trustee" are misleading for there is no trust and usually no possibility of a proprietary remedy; they are nothing more than a formula for equitable relief'.

The liability of the defendant is a personal one to restore the value of the property received rather than to restore property itself.[133] This is a gain-based remedy.[134] The inappropriateness of the proprietary language of the constructive trust is emphasized by the fact that, if the defendant has received and retained property in which the claimant has an equitable proprietary interest, the claimant will be able to bring a proprietary claim to vindicate his or her property rights and recover the property which has been retained. The true function of the action for unconscionable receipt is that it provides for a remedy where there are no longer rights in specific property to be vindicated and, although that remedy uses the language of accounting as if the defendant was a constructive trustee, the defendant is simply liable to account for the value of the property received without needing to identify any trusteeship.

The analogy with constructive trusteeship might, however, have some lingering relevance when determining at what time the property should be valued. If the action for unconscionable receipt is considered to be the equitable counterpart of the Common Law action for money had and received,[135] the remedy should be assessed at the point of receipt. The traditional language of accountability as a constructive trustee might, however, suggest that the defendant recipient should be liable for all benefits received, so any increase in the value of the property should be taken into account and the remedy should be assessed at the time of judgment, which is consistent with the equitable practice relating to the taking of an account.[136] Indeed, in *Crown Dilmun v Sutton*[137] Peter Smith J held that a defendant who had unconscionably received property in breach of fiduciary duty was liable to account for all of the profits that it had received or would subsequently make. The only restriction was that the account would have to be taken before the end of the

---

[129] See p 523, above.

[130] See *Gwembe Valley Development Co Ltd v Koshy* [2003] EWCA Civ 1048, [2004] 1 BCLC 131, [88].

[131] *Paragon Finance plc v DB Thakerar and Co* [1999] 1 All ER 400, 408 (Millett LJ). See also *Williams v Central Bank of Nigeria* [2014] UKSC 10, [2014] AC 1189.

[132] *Paragon Finance plc v DB Thakerar and Co* [1999] 1 All ER 400; *Dubai Aluminium Co Ltd v Salaam* [2002] UKHL 48, [2003] 2 AC 366, 404 (Lord Millett).

[133] *Paragon Finance plc v DB Thakerar and Co* [1999] 1 All ER 400, 408 (Millett LJ); *Crown Dilmun v Sutton* [2004] EWHC 52, [2004] 1 BCLC 468, [204] (Peter Smith J).

[134] *Royal Brunei Airlines v Tan* [1995] 2 AC 378, 386; *Twinsectra v Yardley* [2002] UKHL 12, [2002] 2 AC 164, 194 (Lord Millett).

[135] See further p 652, below.   [136] See p 506, above.

[137] [2004] EWHC 52, [2004] 1 BCLC 468, [27]. See also *City Index Ltd v Gawler* [2007] EWCA Civ 1382, [2008] Ch 313, [64] (Arden LJ); *Ultraframe v Fielding* [2005] EWHC 1638, [2006] FSR 16, [1577] (Lewison J).

six-year limitation period after the claimant first became aware of its claim.[138] Further, the judge recognized that, in taking the account, the defendant might be awarded a personal allowance to reflect his or her own contribution to making the profit, although such an allowance might be denied by virtue of the defendant's conduct.[139] Since the defendant's receipt will already have been shown to have been unconscionable in order for the defendant to be held liable, this will probably prevent the defendant from obtaining the personal allowance.

Exceptionally, there may be circumstances under which the gain to the defendant is smaller than the value of the loss suffered by the claimant. In such a situation, the claimant can elect for the remedy of equitable compensation rather than the value of the defendant's gain.[140] It is possible for a defendant who has discharged liability for unconscionable receipt to seek contribution from any other party who was jointly liable for the same 'damage', including a defendant who is liable for the tort of negligence, on the basis that both claims can be construed as involving restoring to the claimant value lost.[141]

(3) The Future of the Action for Unconscionable Receipt

The real problem with the action for unconscionable receipt is that liability involves both restitution for wrongdoing, because of the need to establish that the defendant was at fault, and restitution founded on the vindication of proprietary rights, which depends on the defendant having received property in which the claimant had an equitable proprietary interest. The need to establish fault has been criticized, most notably by Lord Nicholls of Birkenhead writing extra-judicially.[142] According to Lord Nicholls it would be more appropriate to distinguish between two distinct forms of liability. The first would be grounded on the commission of a wrong, for which fault would be required in the form of dishonesty, in the objective sense that the defendant's conduct would be characterized by an honest person as dishonest, and for which the defence of change of position would not be applicable because a dishonest defendant would have acted in bad faith. The second would be receipt-based and would be founded on the vindication of equitable property rights; it would be the exact counterpart of the Common Law action for money had and received. Where the defendant had received, but no longer retains, property in which the claimant had an equitable proprietary right, then the fact that the defendant has interfered with the claimant's equitable proprietary rights means that it is appropriate that the defendant's liability should be strict, subject to the defences of change of position and *bona fide* purchase.

Such a strict liability personal claim is already recognized at Law in the form of the action for money had and received and also in Equity in the context of the administration of estates.[143] But, as a matter of policy and principle, should Equity develop such a strict liability personal claim where the defendant has received property in which the claimant had an equitable interest and which would be the mirror-image of the Common Law claim? The imposition of strict liability might be justified both at Law and in Equity because, where a defendant has received property in which the claimant has a proprietary

---

[138] *Crown Dilmun v Sutton* [2004] EWHC 52, [2004] 1 BCLC 468, [30].   [139] See p 507, above.

[140] See *City Index Ltd v Gawler* [2007] EWCA Civ 1382, [2008] Ch 313, [64] (Arden LJ).

[141] Ibid, See p 250, above.

[142] D Nicholls, 'Knowing Receipt: The Need for a New Landmark' in W Cornish, R Nolan, J O'Sullivan, and G Virgo (eds), *Restitution: Past, Present and Future* (Oxford: Hart Publishing, 1998), 231. See also *Twinsectra v Yardley* [2002] UKHL 12, [2002] 2 AC 164, 194 (Lord Millett) and *Dubai Aluminium Co Ltd v Salaam* [2002] UKHL 48, [2003] 2 AC 366, 391 (Lord Millett); Lord Millett, 'Proprietary Restitution', 311; Lord Walker, 'Dishonesty and Unconscionable Conduct in Commercial Life—Some Reflections on Accessory Liability and Knowing Receipt' (2005) 27 Sydney LR 187.   [143] See p 645, above.

interest, the strength of that proprietary interest requires the defendant to make restitution of its value regardless of the defendant's fault and even though the defendant has not retained the property. The *quid pro quo* for recognizing a strict liability claim should be that the defendant is able to rely on the defence of change of position. This is what happened in *Lipkin Gorman (a firm) v Karpnale Ltd*[144] at Common Law and there is no reason why the same should not be true in Equity. But is it appropriate to require Equity to develop a new cause of action simply to reflect what occurs at Law? Smith[145] has argued that this is not appropriate, because equitable proprietary rights are not protected in the same way as legal ones. For example, equitable proprietary rights are not defeated by the *bona fide* purchase defence[146] and beneficiaries with equitable proprietary rights do not have direct claims in the torts of conversion[147] or negligence.[148] Legal and equitable proprietary rights are different, and cannot be assimilated. Gardner[149] has defended the need to establish fault before personal liability is imposed in Equity on third-party recipients on the ground that receipt-based liability derives from the failure to preserve trust property and, for such liability to arise, the recipient must have been aware of the need to preserve the property, hence the need to prove unconscionability.

The distinct approach to personal liability in Equity can also be justified for policy reasons. It is simply not appropriate for third party recipients of property in which the claimant has an equitable proprietary interest to be held strictly liable for the value of the property received, because equitable interests tend to be hidden. It is only where the third-party recipient knew, or suspected, that there might be such interests in the property received that it is appropriate to hold the third party personally liable.[150] If such strict liability was recognized in Equity, it would place unacceptable burdens on third-party recipients, such as banks, which had no reason to suspect that the claimant might have a proprietary interest in the property received. Whilst it is true that the imposition of such liability would require there to be generous defences of *bona fide* purchase for value and change of position, this would still place an onerous burden on an innocent recipient to establish the defences.[151]

In Australia, the recognition of a strict liability receipt-based claim has been rejected as a 'grave error', primarily on the ground that it is unjust to impose such liability on the defendant who has no idea that he or she has received property in breach of trust or fiduciary duty.[152] As the law stands in England, the strict liability receipt-based claim is not recognized in Equity,[153] although certain senior members of the judiciary have contemplated the introduction of such a claim. For example, in *Dubai Aluminium Co Ltd v Salaam*[154] Lord Millett supported the recognition of a strict liability claim in Equity. He described the action for unconscionable receipt as involving concurrent liability. One claim was fault-based and required proof of the defendant's unconscionable conduct. For

---

[144] [1991] 2 AC 548.

[145] LD Smith, 'Unjust Enrichment, Property and the Structure of Trusts' (2000) 116 LQR 412.

[146] See p 657, below.

[147] *MCC Proceeds Inc v Lehman Brothers International (Europe) Ltd* [1998] 4 All ER 675.

[148] *Leigh and Sillivan Ltd v Aliakmon Shipping Co Ltd* [1986] AC 785, 812 (Lord Brandon).

[149] S Gardner, 'Moment of Truth for Knowing Receipt' (2009) 125 LQR 20, 23.

[150] See Sheehan, 'Disentangling Equitable Personal Liability for Receipt and Assistance'; K Low, 'Recipient Liability in Equity: Resisting the Siren's Lure' [2008] RLR 96.

[151] J Dietrich and P Ridge, 'The Receipt of What? Questions Concerning Third Party Recipient Liability in Equity and Unjust Enrichment' (2007) 31 MULR 47.

[152] *Farah Constructions Pty Ltd v Say-Dee Pty Ltd* [2007] HCA 292, [155].

[153] *Bank of Credit and Commerce International (Overseas) Ltd v Akindele* [2001] Ch 437.

[154] [2002] UKHL 48, [2003] 2 AC 366, 391. See also *Twinsectra v Yardley* [2002] UKHL 12, [2002] 2 AC 164, 194 (Lord Millett).

this type of claim, the receipt of property is incidental; it is the defendant's fault that grounds liability. Here, the claim is founded on the defendant's wrongdoing. The other claim is receipt-based and does not require proof of fault. Here, the claim is founded on the vindication of property rights. This is broadly consistent with the extra-judicial analysis of Lord Nicholls.[155]

Further, in a significant dictum in *Criterion Properties plc v Stratford UK Properties LLC*,[156] Lord Nicholls himself appeared to recognize a general strict liability claim in Equity founded on receipt-based liability. In considering the nature of the liability that would arise if an agreement under which party B acquired benefits from party A were set aside, he said:[157]

> If, however, the agreement *is* set aside, B will be accountable for any benefits he may have received from A under the agreement. A will have a proprietary claim, if B still has the assets. Additionally, and irrespective of whether B still has the assets in question, A will have a personal claim against B for unjust enrichment, subject always to a defence of change of position. B's personal accountability will not be dependent upon proof of fault or 'unconscionable' conduct on his part. B's accountability, in this regard, will be strict.

But this strict liability claim in unjust enrichment does not replace the claim in unconscionable receipt. Lord Nicholls was considering a simple case in which property is transferred by one party to another pursuant to a transaction that was void for want of authority. In such a case, the claimant can recover the value of the property transferred to the defendant by virtue of the defendant's unjust enrichment. The value of the property will be the enrichment. This will have been obtained directly at the expense of the claimant and one of the recognized grounds of restitution can be established, namely that there had been a total failure of basis by virtue of the invalidity of the underlying transaction. In fact, a claim in unjust enrichment succeeded in this way in *Westdeutsche Landesbank Girozentrale v Islington LBC*[158] as regards payments made to a bank under a contract that was void. There is nothing unusual about such a claim, but this is not the usual scenario of the claim in unconscionable receipt. That claim is relevant where property in which the claimant has an equitable proprietary interest is misappropriated by a trustee or fiduciary and it is then received by the defendant and dissipated. It is unlikely that the claimant will be able to sue the defendant in unjust enrichment, because the enrichment is not direct and the claimant will have been enriched at the expense of the trustee or the fiduciary.[159] Further, there may be difficulties in identifying a recognized ground of restitution to show that the third party's enrichment is unjust.[160] That is why the claimant needs to rely on his or her equitable proprietary interest to establish a claim against the defendant. Lord Nicholls' dictum in *Criterion Properties* is concerned with a two-party situation, in which a claim in unjust enrichment is available because the enrichment was direct and the ground of restitution is founded on failure of basis. Unconscionable receipt is available in a three-party situation, involving typically the beneficiary, the trustee, and a third party, and the law of unjust enrichment is not engaged.

We are left with a scenario in which Equity continues to recognize a receipt-based personal claim that requires proof of fault, regardless of the demands from senior members of the judiciary and many commentators that a strict liability claim should be

---

[155] Lord Nicholls, 'Knowing Receipt', 231.   [156] [2004] UKHL 28, [2004] 1 WLR 1846.
[157] Ibid, [4].   [158] [1996] AC 669. See p 372, above.
[159] See M Bryan, 'The Liability of the Recipient: Restitution at Common Law or Wrongdoing in Equity?' in S Degeling and J Edelman (eds), *Equity in Commercial Law* (Sydney: Lawbook Co, 2005), 339.
[160] Save if 'ignorance' is recognized as a ground of restitution. See Chapter 8.

recognized. The main reason for recognizing such a claim is because of the perceived need to assimilate the rules, in this context at least, between what happens at Common Law and what happens in Equity. But the equitable rules and their contexts are different. Recognition of a strict liability claim in Equity can be criticized for policy reasons as well. Further, even if a strict liability claim was introduced in Equity, it would not change the law dramatically. Any strict liability claim would be subject to the defence of change of position. That defence will be defeated if the defendant has acted in bad faith and recent cases on the defence of change of position have relied on the notion of unconscionability to determine whether or not the defendant can be considered to have acted in bad faith.[161] It follows that, even if the receipt-based claim becomes one of strict liability, the question of unconscionability cannot be avoided. The only difference between a strict liability claim and a fault-based claim would turn on who bears the burden of proof. As the law stands, the claimant must prove that the defendant's receipt was unconscionable. If a strict liability claim was introduced, the burden would shift to the defendant to prove that his or her receipt and subsequent conduct was not unconscionable. Since it is difficult to justify shifting the burden of disproof on to the defendant, the preferable view is that a strict liability receipt-based claim should not be recognized in Equity.

(iii) Subrogation

The House of Lords in *Banque Financière de la Cité v Parc (Battersea) Ltd*[162] recognized that subrogation may operate as a personal remedy.[163] Consequently, on the facts of that case, the claimant was able to rely on a third party's security rights against the defendant, but only as against the defendant and not as against any of the defendant's other creditors. More simply, the personal remedy of subrogation may operate to assign a third party's personal rights against the defendant to the claimant.[164] This will be a particularly useful remedy where the claimant's direct restitutionary claim against the defendant is barred and the claimant's money has been used by the defendant to discharge a debt owed to a third-party creditor. This is illustrated by *Re Wrexham, Mold and Connah's Quay Railway Co*[165] where the claimant could not sue the defendant directly because the borrowing transaction was *ultra vires*, but it was held that the claimant could rely on the rights of a third party to sue the defendant.

The role of subrogation as a personal restitutionary remedy is much less important today, however. When the law of restitution was founded on the notion of an implied contract, the remedy of subrogation provided a useful mechanism for enabling the claimant to secure restitution even though a contract could not be implied between the claimant and the defendant because, for example, the defendant lacked the capacity to enter into the transaction. But, with the rejection of the implied contract theory and the recognition that the obligation to make restitution is imposed by operation of law, the role of subrogation as a personal remedy is much less important. For today the claimant will be able to obtain restitution directly from the defendant by means of an action founded on unjust enrichment regardless of the fact that either party to the transaction lacked the capacity to enter into the transaction.[166]

---

[161] See p 650, above and, further, p 691, below.   [162] [1999] 1 AC 221.

[163] Although the remedy was awarded in that case to reverse the defendant's unjust enrichment, rather than to vindicate the claimant's proprietary rights. See p 637, above. See also *Cheltenham and Gloucester plc v Appleyard* [2004] EWCA Civ 291, [36] (Neuberger LJ); *Filby v Mortgage Express (No 2) Ltd* [2004] EWCA Civ 759.

[164] *Boscawen v Bajwa* [1996] 1 WLR 328, 333 (Millett LJ).   [165] [1899] 1 Ch 440.

[166] As was recognized by the House of Lords in *Westdeutsche Landesbank Girozentrale v Islington LBC* [1996] AC 669.

23

THE DEFENCE OF *BONA FIDE* PURCHASE

It might be thought that the proper place for analysis of the defence of *bona fide* purchase is in Part VI, where the general defences to restitutionary claims are considered. It is, however, more appropriate to examine the defence in this Part, because it is not available to all restitutionary claims. Rather, the defence is only available to defeat proprietary restitutionary claims.[1] The defence is not available where the claim is founded on the reversal of the defendant's unjust enrichment,[2] neither is it available where the claim is founded on the commission of a wrong, save where the wrong involves the claimant proving that the defendant had interfered with property in which the claimant has a proprietary interest.

1. THE FUNCTION OF THE DEFENCE

The function of the *bona fide* purchase defence is to make good defects in the defendant's title to property.[3] The defence constitutes an exception to the *nemo potest dare quod non habet* principle, by virtue of which the transferee cannot obtain rights to property which are better than those of the transferor. Consequently, where the transferor of property does not have good title to that property, the defendant can only be considered to have obtained good title if the conditions for the *bona fide* purchase defence have been satisfied. It is for this reason that the operation of the defence is confined to those restitutionary claims which involve the vindication of the claimant's property rights. Where the defence applies, the defendant cannot be considered to have interfered with the claimant's proprietary rights simply because, at the time when the defendant received the property, he or she is considered to have obtained good title to the property so that the claimant's property rights are extinguished. It follows that there are no longer any property rights of the claimant which can be vindicated so that the proprietary claim is defeated absolutely.

The operation of the *bona fide* purchase defence can be justified by the need to protect the security of commercial transactions. Where the defendant has obtained property in good faith and for value then, as between the owner of the property and the recipient, the

---

[1] WJ Swadling, 'Restitution and *Bona Fide* Purchase' in WJ Swadling (ed), *The Limits of Restitutionary Claims: A Comparative Analysis* (London: UKNCCL, 1997), 79. See also P Key, '*Bona Fide* Purchase as a Defence in the Law of Restitution' [1994] LMCLQ 421; RB Grantham and CEF Rickett, 'A Normative Account of Defences to Restitutionary Liability' (2008) CLJ 92, 113.

[2] *Foskett v McKeown* [2001] 1 AC 102, 129 (Lord Millett); *Papamichael v National Westminster Bank plc* [2003] 1 Lloyd's Rep 341, 377 (Judge Chambers QC).

[3] See *Boscawen v Bajwa* [1996] 1 WLR 328, 334 (Millett LJ). See also Swadling, 'Restitution and *Bona Fide* Purchase', 103.

latter should have the better claim to the property, since he or she should be secure in the validity of the receipt of the property if there is nothing to put him or her on notice that the transferor did not have a good title to transfer.[4]

2. AMBIT OF THE DEFENCE

The ambit of the *bona fide* purchase defence depends on whether the proprietary restitutionary claim is brought at Law or in Equity.

(A) COMMON LAW

(i) The Defence is Generally Inapplicable

The *bona fide* purchase defence has a very limited role at Common Law. In respect of most proprietary restitutionary claims the defence is inapplicable because of the operation of the *nemo dat* principle. So, for example, where a car is transferred to the defendant by a third party in circumstances where that third party does not have legal title to it, the defendant is not able to obtain any better title to the car, even if the defendant could be characterized as a *bona fide* purchaser for value because he or she had paid for the car and was not aware of the third party's lack of title.[5]

(ii) Proprietary Restitutionary Claims to Money

Where, however, the defendant receives money which has passed into circulation as currency,[6] the claimant's title is destroyed and the defendant obtains title to the money if he or she receives it in good faith and for value.[7] In other words, the *bona fide* purchase defence is applicable to extinguish the claimant's title to the money so that any proprietary restitutionary claim brought by the claimant in respect of the money will be defeated. The reason why the defence is recognized where the defendant has received money as a *bona fide* purchaser has been identified by Fox, who states that '[it] helps money to circulate readily in the economy in that it reduces the need for recipients to make detailed inquiries into the title of people who tender money in payment of debts or to buy goods'.[8]

(B) EQUITY

The *bona fide* purchase defence is generally applicable in respect of restitutionary proprietary claims which are brought in Equity, regardless of the nature of the property which the defendant received. Consequently, where the defendant has purchased a legal estate for value without notice of the claimant's equitable proprietary right, that right will be extinguished, regardless of the nature of the property which the defendant has purchased.[9] Where, however, the defendant has purchased an equitable proprietary interest for value the defence will not be available, because of the rule that the first equitable interest in time

---

[4] *Bishopsgate Motor Finance Corp v Transport Brakes Ltd* [1949] 1 KB 322, 336–7 (Denning J).

[5] See *Greenwood v Bennett* [1973] QB 195.

[6] D Fox, 'Bona Fide Purchase and the Currency of Money' (1996) 55 CLJ 547.

[7] *Miller v Race* (1758) 1 Burr 452, 457–8; 97 ER 398, 401 (Lord Mansfield). See also *Clarke v Shee and Johnson* (1774) 1 Cowp 197, 98 ER 10411; *Banque Belge pour l'Etranger v Hambrouck* [1921] 1 KB 321, 329 (Scrutton LJ) and *Ilich* (1987) 69 ALR 231.

[8] Fox, 'Bona Fide Purchase and the Currency of Money', 565.

[9] *Cave v Cave* (1880) 15 Ch D 639; *Re Diplock* [1948] Ch 465, 537.

takes priority.[10] Also the defence will not be available to a defendant who is sued for unconscionable receipt. This is because the claimant will already have had to prove that the defendant's receipt was unconscionable in order to establish the claim. Proof of such fault will negate the defendant's good faith, so that the defendant will not be able to plead the defence successfully.

3. CONDITIONS FOR ESTABLISHING THE DEFENCE

The burden of establishing the *bona fide* purchase defence is placed on the defendant[11] who must show on the balance of probabilities that two conditions have been satisfied. Once they have been established the defence operates absolutely, barring the claimant's proprietary restitutionary claim completely, although the claimant may still be able to found a restitutionary claim on the defendant's unjust enrichment or the commission of a wrong by the defendant.

(A) GOOD FAITH

The defendant must show that he or she acted in good faith in receiving the property from the transferor. What is meant by good faith depends on whether the restitutionary claim is brought at Law or in Equity.

(i) Common Law

At Common Law the notion of good faith is equated with honesty.[12] This is a subjective test which will not be satisfied if the defendant knew or suspected that the transferor had a defective title to the property which was transferred.

(ii) Equity

In Equity the notion of good faith is defined more widely than at Law to include an objective test of constructive notice. The recipient will not have acted in good faith if he or she knew of the claimant's equitable interest in the property, suspected it, or had constructive notice of it.[13] The defendant will have constructive notice of the claimant's equitable proprietary interest if the defendant failed to make enquiries that would have been made by a reasonable person in the defendant's position.[14] Notice will also be imputed to the defendant if his or her agent had actual or constructive notice of the defect in title, as long as the agent acquired notice in the course of the transaction that

---

[10] *Macmillan Inc v Bishopsgate Investment Trust plc* [1995] 1 WLR 978, 1000 (Millett J). But the defence will defeat an earlier mere equity, such as the equity to rescind a contract. See generally D O'Sullivan, 'The Rule in *Phillips v Phillips*' (2002) 118 LQR 296.

[11] *Re Nisbet and Pott's Contract* [1906] 1 Ch 386. Cf *Polly Peck International plc v Nadir (No 2)* [1992] 4 All ER 769.   [12] *Nelson v Larholt* [1948] 1 KB 339.

[13] *Barclays Bank v O'Brien* [1994] 1 AC 180, 195 (Lord Browne-Wilkinson).

[14] *Nelson v Larholt* [1948] 1 KB 339. See also *Macmillan Inc v Bishopsgate Investment Trust plc* [1995] 1 WLR 978, 1000 (Millett J); *Sinclair Investments (UK) Ltd v Versailles Trade Finance Ltd* [2011] EWCA Civ 347, [2012] Ch 453, [100] and [109] (Lord Neuberger MR). In *Armstrong DLW GmbH v Winnington Networks Ltd* [2012] EWHC 10 (Ch), [2013] Ch 156, [122], Stephen Morris QC equated notice for the *bona fide* purchase defence with the notion of bad faith in the defence of change of position (see p 691, below), so the defendant will only have constructive notice if, on the facts known to the defendant, the reasonable person would have been aware of the impropriety of the transaction or would have made inquiries about its propriety.

involved the transfer of property that the claimant wishes to recover. The defendant will not, however, be prevented from relying on the *bona fide* purchase defence simply because he or she had notice of a doubtful claim of the claimant to recover the property.[15] Further, where the defendant has received money in discharge of a debt, he or she will not usually be bound to inquire into the manner in which the payer acquired the money.[16]

(B) PURCHASE FOR VALUE

The defendant will only be able to rely on the defence if he or she provided value for the transfer of title to the property in which the claimant claims a proprietary interest. Value includes the giving of money or money's worth, including the discharge of a debt,[17] or, in Equity, marriage consideration.[18] It is not necessary for the courts to consider whether the value which was given for the property was adequate; it is sufficient that some value was given. This value requirement means that the defence cannot be relied on by the recipient of a gift, simply because such a recipient will not have provided any value for the transfer. The value which is provided by the defendant may be provided before or after the property was transferred to him or her, so long as when the property was transferred to the defendant or the value was provided by the defendant, whichever was the later, he or she was not fixed with notice of the claimant's proprietary interest.[19] The defendant cannot be considered to have provided value for the property if it was transferred pursuant to an illegal transaction.[20]

4. OPERATION OF THE DEFENCE

The defence has a number of peculiar characteristics.

(A) A COMPLETE DEFENCE

Where the conditions for establishing the defence have been satisfied the restitutionary claim is barred completely, rather than being barred merely to the extent that the defendant has provided value for the property.[21] It is consequently a different type of defence to that of change of position which only operates to the extent that the defendant's position has changed.[22]

(B) THE DEFENCE MAY BE APPLICABLE EVEN THOUGH THE DEFENDANT WAS NOT A *BONA FIDE* PURCHASER

Usually the *bona fide* purchase defence will be pleaded by the defendant who seeks to establish that he or she satisfied its conditions. But this need not be the case. It is possible that the claimant's property was transferred to a third party in circumstances where the

---

[15] *Carl-Zeiss Stiftung v Herbert Smith (No 2)* [1969] 2 Ch 276.
[16] *Thomson v Clydesdale Bank* [1893] AC 282, 287 (Lord Herschell).
[17] *Taylor v Blakelock* (1886) 32 Ch D 560.   [18] *Pullan v Koe* [1913] 1 Ch 9.
[19] *Ratcliffe v Barnard* (1871) LR 6 Ch App 652.
[20] *Lipkin Gorman (a firm) v Karpnale Ltd* [1991] 2 AC 548. See also *Clarke v Shee and Johnson* (1774) 1 Cowp 197, 98 ER 1041.
[21] *Ilich* (1987) 69 ALR 231, 245 (Wilson and Dawson JJ). See also *Lipkin Gorman v Karpnale Ltd* [1991] 2 AC 548.   [22] See Chapter 25.

claimant's intention to transfer title can be considered to be vitiated but the third-party recipient can be considered to be a *bona fide* purchaser of the property. Consequently, the third party will have obtained a good title to the property which he or she will be able to transfer to the defendant. The claim against the defendant to vindicate property rights cannot succeed in such circumstances simply because the claimant's title to the property has been defeated by reason of the third party being a *bona fide* purchaser for value. Once that interest has been defeated it cannot subsequently be resurrected against the defendant.

(C) THE DEFENCE APPLIES REGARDLESS OF WHETHER THE CLAIMANT SEEKS A PERSONAL OR PROPRIETARY RESTITUTIONARY REMEDY

The defence will apply regardless of whether the remedy which the claimant seeks is personal or proprietary. This is because the time at which the question of *bona fide* purchase is considered is when the defendant received the property or its proceeds. If at this point the defendant was in good faith and had provided value for the property, the claimant's title will be defeated and he or she will be unable to show that the defendant retained property in which the claimant had a proprietary interest or even that the defendant had received such property.

That the defence is available where the claimant seeks a personal restitutionary remedy was recognized by the House of Lords in *Lipkin Gorman (a firm) v Karpnale Ltd*,[23] where the claimant's action for money had and received was founded on its continuing proprietary interest. The House of Lords accepted that this action might have been defeated if the defendant had been a *bona fide* purchaser, although the defence could not be established on the facts since the money had been transferred pursuant to an unlawful gambling transaction, so the defendant could not be considered to have provided value. Similarly, it has been recognized that the equitable action for restitution arising from the mistaken payment of assets in the administration of an estate can be defeated if the recipient of property from the estate was a *bona fide* purchaser for value.[24]

(D) RESURRECTION OF THE PROPRIETARY INTEREST

A proprietary interest will not be defeated if the property is reacquired from the *bona fide* purchaser by a trustee[25] or where the transaction involving the transfer to the *bona fide* purchaser is rescinded, because the transaction will be a nullity and will operate retrospectively, converting the recipient into a volunteer.[26]

---

[23] [1991] 2 AC 548. See also *Clarke v Shee and Johnson* (1774) 1 Cowp 197, 98 ER 1041 and *Nelson v Larholt* [1948] 1 KB 339.

[24] *Ministry of Health v Simpson* [1951] AC 251 and *Re J Leslie Engineers Co Ltd* [1976] 1 WLR 292, 299 (Oliver J).   [25] *Wilkes v Spooner* [1911] 2 KB 473.

[26] *Independent Trustee Service Ltd v GP Noble Trustees Ltd* [2012] EWCA Civ 196, [2013] Ch 91. See B Häcker, 'The Effect of Rescission on *Bona Fide* Purchase' (2012) LQR 493.

PART V
GENERAL DEFENCES TO RESTITUTIONARY CLAIMS

24
FUNDAMENTAL PRINCIPLES

1. THE FUNCTION AND AMBIT
OF GENERAL DEFENCES

During the examination of the three different types of restitutionary claim in Parts II, III, and IV certain specific defences were considered.[1] These defences are, however, only of limited application. There are a number of other defences which are of general application to all, or almost all, restitutionary claims. These are called the general defences and they will be examined in this Part.

(A) THE DISTINCTION BETWEEN DEFENCES AND DENIALS

In determining the nature of restitutionary defences it is useful to distinguish between defences and denials.[2] A denial is an assertion by the defendant that an element of the cause of action is not established, whereas defences only arise once the cause of action has been established to indicate a reason why the defendant should not be liable or the liability should be reduced in some way. So, for example, in a claim grounded on unjust enrichment, if the defendant argues that there was a legal basis for the receipt of an enrichment, this is denial of the claim, because the claimant must prove that there was no legal basis for the enrichment.[3] If, however, the defendant argues that his or her position has changed after the enrichment has been received, this is a defence which the defendant bears the burden of proving, because the change of position is only considered to be relevant after the cause of action has been established.[4]

The line between defences and denials is not always clear. For example, when the definition of enrichment was considered[5] it was noted that the defendant could subjectively devalue an objective enrichment.[6] If the defendant relies on subjective devaluation, this appears to be construed by the courts as a denial of an element of the unjust enrichment claim. Subjective devaluation could, however, be formulated as a defence[7] such that it does not relate to the identification of the elements of the cause of action, but constitutes a particular reason why the defendant should not make restitution, from respect of his or her autonomy. Similarly, whilst the presence of a basis appears to be properly characterized as a denial, it could easily be formulated as a defence if the

---

[1] Such as the defence of good consideration in Chapter 9 (see p 189, above) and the defence of *bona fide* purchase in Chapter 23.

[2] A distinction recognized by C Mitchell and J Goudkamp, 'Denials and Defences in the Law of Unjust Enrichment' in C Mitchell and W Swadling (eds), *The Restatement Third: Restitution and Unjust Enrichment* (Oxford: Hart Publishing, 2013), ch 6. See p 60, above.

[3] See Chapter 7.   [4] See Chapter 25.   [5] See Chapter 4.   [6] See p 69, above.

[7] Lord Reed came close to construing it in this way in *Benedetti v Sawiris* [2013] UKSC 50, [2014] AC 938. See p 70, above.

existence of a lawful basis for receipt is not considered to constitute an element of the cause of action. Whether a particular rule is characterized as a denial or a defence is only of practical significance in determining who bears the burden of proof or disproof, with the burden allocated to the defendant if it is a defence and to the claimant if it is a denial. As a matter of principle, when determining the appropriate characterization it is necessary to consider whether the particular rule constitutes a component part of the cause of action. As a matter of policy it is important to consider who is in the best position to establish whether the rule does or does not apply. That might, for example, be a reason why subjective devaluation should properly be characterized as a defence, since the defendant is in the best position to establish that he or she did not value the enrichment which had been received.

(B) THE PRINCIPLES UNDERLYING THE GENERAL DEFENCES

Two fundamental principles can be identified to justify the recognition of the general defences.

(i) Justice Favours the Defendant Retaining the Benefit

The principle which justifies the recognition of the general defences in particular is that, because of the particular circumstances of the case, the justice of the defendant retaining a benefit outweighs the justice of the claimant recovering it.[8] This was recognized by Lord Mansfield in *Moses v Macferlan*[9] when he said that '[the defendant] may defend himself by every thing which shews that the plaintiff, *ex aequo et bono*, is not entitled to the whole of the demand, or to any part of it'. It is as a result of this principle, for example, that the restitutionary claim will be defeated to the extent that the defendant's position has changed in reliance on the validity of the receipt of the benefit.[10] Similarly, the claim may be defeated if the claimant had participated in an illegal transaction,[11] simply because such participation weakens the claimant's claim that the defendant ought to make restitution of any benefit.

This focus on justice can be related specifically to the principle of corrective justice.[12] As Grantham and Rickett[13] have recognized, '[t]o be consistent with the correlative structure of corrective justice, equal respect must be accorded to the defendant's interest in self-determination and his entitlement not to be deprived of his wealth except voluntarily'.

Consequently, the defences have an important function in protecting the autonomy of the defendant,[14] as a response to the imposition of liability to respect the claimant's autonomy.[15]

(ii) Security of Receipt

A second principle can also be identified which can be used to justify the recognition of the general defences, namely that the defendant's receipt of a benefit should be secure.[16] What this means is that, when a defendant receives a benefit, he or she should not be subjected to

---

[8] See *Baylis v Bishop of London* [1913] 1 Ch 127, 140 (Hamilton LJ).
[9] (1760) 2 Burr 1005, 1010; 97 ER 676, 679.   [10] See Chapter 25.
[11] See Chapter 27.   [12] See p 4, above.
[13] RB Grantham and CEF Rickett, 'A Normative Account of Defences to Restitutionary Liability' (2008) CLJ 92, 101.
[14] *Benedetti v Sawiris* [2013] UKSC 50, [2014] AC 938, [118] (Lord Reed).
[15] See further p 37, above.
[16] PBH Birks, 'The Fourth Part of the Principle' in PBH Birks, *Restitution—The Future* (Sydney: The Federation Press, 1992), 123.

any unnecessary insecurity when deciding what to do with it because he or she may have to make restitution to the claimant. One of the prime functions of the general defences is to identify those circumstances where it is reasonable for the defendant to treat the benefit as his or her own to do with as he or she wishes. So, for example, where the claimant has voluntarily transferred a benefit to the defendant, it is entirely appropriate that the defendant should be entitled to believe that the receipt of the benefit is secure so that he or she will not be obliged to make restitution to the claimant.[17]

(C) CLASSIFICATION OF DEFENCES AS 'ENRICHMENT-RELATED' AND 'UNJUST-RELATED'

The general defences have sometimes been classified as either 'enrichment-related' or 'unjust-related'.[18] The purpose of this classification is to show that the general defences have different functions. The so-called 'enrichment-related' defences operate where the defendant is not considered to be enriched as result of events occurring after the receipt of a benefit, whereas the 'unjust-related' defences operate where it is not considered to be just that the defendant should make restitution to the claimant. But nothing is to be gained from such artificial classification, particularly because restitutionary claims are not confined to the reversal of the defendant's unjust enrichment but are also founded on the commission of a wrong and the vindication of property rights for which the language of 'enrichment' and 'unjust' is inappropriate. A further objection is that such classification of the defences artificially restricts their analysis, principally because a number of them can be analysed as operating both to show that the defendant is no longer enriched and that it is not just for the defendant to make restitution to the claimant.[19] Ultimately, as Lord Mansfield recognized in *Moses v Macferlan*, all defences are related to the justice of the defendant making restitution and this should be the key issue with which we should be concerned.[20]

---

[17] See p 149, above.

[18] PBH Birks, *Unjust Enrichment* (2nd edn, Oxford: Oxford University Press, 2005), chs 9 and 10.

[19] See in particular the defence of change of position examined in Chapter 25.

[20] See Birks, *Unjust Enrichment* (2nd edn), 209. In that book Birks classified defences by reference to whether they were enrichment-related, which he called 'disenrichment' defences, or expense-related, which he called 'disimpoverishment' defences. This essentially equates to defences which are concerned with changes in the defendant's change of position, which are considered in Chapter 25, and changes in the claimant's circumstances, which are considered in Chapter 26.

25

DEFENCES ARISING FROM CHANGES IN THE DEFENDANT'S CIRCUMSTANCES

Sometimes the defendant's circumstances will change to such an extent after he or she has obtained a benefit that it is no longer just for the defendant to make full restitution of the benefit received. In such cases the defendant may be able to rely on one of three defences to defeat or circumscribe the restitutionary claim, namely estoppel, payment by an agent to his or her principal, and change of position. The availability of each defence will depend on the reason why the defendant's circumstances have changed.

1. ESTOPPEL BY REPRESENTATION

Estoppel is a defence which is not confined in its application to restitutionary claims, but it has had a particularly important role in this context. [1] In the light of the recognition of the defence of change of position, however, the role of estoppel as a general defence to restitutionary claims has become less important, although it cannot yet be considered to be irrelevant. Essentially the estoppel defence will be applicable where the defendant detrimentally changes his or her position in reliance on a representation made by the claimant that a benefit was validly received. Where estoppel is established the restitutionary claim will usually be barred completely. [2] This is because estoppel is a rule of evidence which determines the rights of the parties according to the facts as represented by them in order to protect the autonomy of the defendant who has relied on the representation. [3] The effect of the defence is to prevent the claimant from asserting the true situation where he or she has led the defendant to think that the situation is different, [4] and so respects the defendant's autonomy in detrimentally relying on the claimant's representation. [5]

---

[1] See generally E Bant, *The Change of Position Defence* (Oxford: Hart Publishing, 2009), ch 2.

[2] See *TRA Global Pty Ltd v Kebakoska* [2011] VSC 480 (Victoria).

[3] See J Hudson, 'Estoppel by Representation as a Defence to Unjust Enrichment—The Vine Has Not Withered Yet' [2014] RLR 19.

[4] Estoppel might, consequently, be characterized as a denial, since its effect is for the defendant to deny that an element of the cause of action has been established so that there is no liability. Since, however, the burden of proving estoppel is borne by the defendant, it is preferably characterized as a defence to the claim.

[5] RB Grantham and CEF Rickett, 'A Normative Account of Defences to Restitutionary Liability' (2008) CLJ 92, 109.

Although the defence of estoppel is potentially applicable to all three types of restitutionary claim, it is particularly relevant to claims founded on the reversal of the defendant's unjust enrichment and especially where the ground of restitution is mistake, simply because it is in this context that there is greater opportunity for the claimant to make a representation to the defendant that the enrichment was validly received. In fact, all of the reported cases concerning the application of estoppel to restitutionary claims relate to the recovery of mistaken payments. But there is no reason why the defence cannot apply where the claim is founded on other grounds of restitution and concerns other types of enrichment.

(A) THE CONDITIONS FOR ESTABLISHING THE DEFENCE OF ESTOPPEL

The leading case on the estoppel defence is *United Overseas Bank v Jiwani*,[6] where McKenna J identified three conditions which needed to be satisfied before the defence is applicable.[7] He also emphasized that the burden of proving these elements is, as with all defences, placed on the defendant.

(i) The Defendant is Led to Believe that He or She is Entitled to the Benefit

The claimant must either have made an unequivocal representation that the defendant was entitled to receive the particular benefit or have owed a duty of accuracy to the defendant which the claimant breached. McKenna J assumed that these were alternative conditions, so it is sufficient that either is established. It has, however, sometimes been assumed that these are not alternatives and so both a representation and a duty of accuracy must be identified in every case.[8] This would be unnecessarily limiting, particularly because the courts will only be able to find that a claimant owed a duty of accuracy to the defendant in the most exceptional of cases. Consequently, the view of McKenna J is to be preferred.

(1) Representation

Where the claimant is alleged to have represented that the defendant was entitled to receive the benefit, the representation must be collateral to the transfer in the sense that it cannot be implied from the mere fact that the claimant voluntarily transferred the benefit to the defendant.[9] So, for example, where a bank honours a cheque which is a forgery it does not represent that the cheque was genuine,[10] although an estoppel might be established if the bank was put on notice as to the validity of the cheque.

The representation may have been made expressly or might be implied from the circumstances surrounding the transfer, but in either case it must be clear and unequivocal and the claimant must have intended that the defendant act on it.[11] It has been recognized that the representation may relate either to the facts or to the law,[12] although where the representation relates to the state of the law it will often not be reasonable for the

---

[6] [1976] 1 WLR 964.   [7] Ibid, 968.

[8] See *RE Jones Ltd v Waring and Gillow Ltd* [1926] AC 670, 693 (Lord Sumner); *Weld-Blundell v Synott* [1940] 2 KB 107, 114 (Asquith J); *Lloyd's Bank Ltd v Brooks* (1950) 6 Legal Decisions Affecting Bankers 161, 168.

[9] *RE Jones Ltd v Waring and Gillow Ltd* [1926] AC 670.

[10] *National Westminster Bank Ltd v Barclays Bank International Ltd* [1975] QB 654.

[11] *Sidney Balson Investment Trust Ltd v E Karmios and Co (London) Ltd* [1956] 1 QB 529, 540 (Denning LJ).

[12] *Briggs v Gleeds* [2014] EWHC 1178 (Ch), [2014] 3 WLR 1469, [32] (Newey J), following the rejection of the mistake of law bar in *Kleinwort Benson Ltd v Lincoln City Council* [1999] 2 AC 349. See p 162, above.

defendant to rely on it, save where, for example, the representation was made by a lawyer to an unrepresented lay person.

The best example of an express representation is where, having transferred the benefit to the defendant, the claimant confirms that it was properly transferred to the defendant. This is illustrated by *Deutsche Bank (London Agency) v Beriro and Co*,[13] where the claimant mistakenly informed the defendant that a bill of exchange had been collected and consequently it paid a sum of money to the defendant. When the claimant discovered its mistake it sought to recover the money from the defendant, but it was estopped from asserting that the money had been paid by mistake because of its express representation that the bill had been collected.

The decision of the Court of Appeal in *Holt v Markham*[14] illustrates how a representation might be implied from the circumstances surrounding the payment. In this case the claimant paid the defendant air officer more money than he was entitled to receive. Two years later the claimant sought to recover the money on the ground that the defendant was retired and so was not entitled to receive all of the money. Whilst it was correct that the defendant was not entitled to receive the money, it was not because he was retired. The defendant informed the claimant of this, but he did not hear anything further for another two months. By the time the claimant eventually contacted the defendant to inform him that he was not entitled to receive the money for another reason, the defendant had lost the money which he had received by investing it in a failed business venture. Although the Court of Appeal held that the claimant's mistake was one of law and not fact so restitution was not available,[15] it also held that, even if the mistake had been one of fact, the claimant would have been estopped from relying on the mistake. Two different types of representation were identified by the judges. First, Scrutton LJ concluded that there was an implicit representation that the claimant would inform the defendant of any mistake it had made in paying the money to the defendant within a reasonable time of the money being paid.[16] This is highly artificial since it amounts to the implication of a representation from the mere fact that the claimant had paid the money to the defendant. Such an implied representation is only acceptable where the claimant owes a duty of accuracy to the defendant and there was nothing to suggest that such a duty existed in this case. More convincing was the reasoning of Bankes and Warrington LJJ, who identified an implied representation that the money had been properly paid to the defendant from the fact that the claimant had failed to respond to the defendant's letter.[17]

The representation on which the defendant relies must have been made by the claimant and not a third party. This is the effect of the decision of the House of Lords in *RE Jones Ltd v Waring and Gillow Ltd*,[18] where the claimant had been induced to pay money to the defendant as a result of a fraudulent misrepresentation made by a third party. It was held that the defence of estoppel was inapplicable, presumably because any representation as to the validity of the payment to the defendant came from the fraudster and not the claimant and the claimant was not responsible for the fraudster's representations.[19]

(2) Duty of Accuracy

In exceptional circumstances it will be possible to establish an estoppel even though the claimant did not make an actual representation of fact to the defendant, if the claimant owed a duty of accuracy to the defendant which he or she had breached. Although it is

---

[13] (1895) 73 LTR 669 (ns). See also *Avon County Council v Howlett* [1989] 1 WLR 605.
[14] [1923] 1 KB 504.   [15] Mistake of law does now ground a restitutionary claim. See p 162, above.
[16] *Holt v Markham* [1923] 1 KB 504, 514.   [17] Ibid, 511 (Bankes LJ) and 512 (Warrington LJ).
[18] [1926] AC 670.   [19] Ibid, 692 (Lord Sumner).

preferable to distinguish such a duty of accuracy from representations of fact, the effect of the claimant owing a duty of accuracy to the defendant is that, when the claimant transfers a benefit to the defendant, there is an inherent representation that the benefit was properly transferred.

Whether such a duty of accuracy exists will depend on the nature of the relationship between the claimant and the defendant. Such a duty is likely to arise where the claimant occupies a position of superiority over the defendant because he or she possesses all the information and expertise to assess the validity of the transfer of the benefit. The identification of such a duty of accuracy is illustrated by *Skyring v Greenwood*[20] where the defendant was an army paymaster who had credited a Major Skyring with certain allowances. Although the defendant was informed in 1816 that Skyring was not eligible to receive these allowances, the defendant continued to credit Skyring with them until Skyring died in 1821. When Skyring's executors sought to recover the sums which had been credited to him, the defendant refused to pay on the ground that the deceased had not been eligible to receive the allowances. The executors' action succeeded because the defendant had been under a duty to inform the deceased that he was not entitled to the allowance immediately the defendant had been informed that this was the case. Although the court specifically stated that it did not consider the defendant to have been estopped from denying that the money credited was actually due to the deceased, this was surely the effect of the decision. The defendant's breach of duty in failing to communicate with the deceased meant that he was estopped from arguing that the deceased was not eligible to receive the allowance. The existence of this duty of accuracy was also recognized in *Avon County Council v Howlett*[21] where it was suggested that a local government officer owed a duty of accuracy to an employee in respect of the overpayment of the employee's salary.

It is only in exceptional cases that the court will recognize that the claimant owes a duty of accuracy to the defendant. So, for example, in *National Westminster Bank Ltd v Barclays Bank International Ltd*[22] it was accepted that a bank does not owe a duty of accuracy when it honours a cheque, at least where there is nothing to suggest that the cheque was not genuine. Where, however, the claimant is aware of certain facts relating to the validity of the transfer of the payment to the defendant he or she may be under a duty to disclose these facts to the defendant. So, for example, in *Greenwood v Martins Bank Ltd*,[23] where the claimant's wife had withdrawn the claimant's money by forging his signature, it was held that he was estopped from relying on the forgery to recover his money from the defendant because, once he was aware of what his wife had done, he owed the defendant a duty to disclose the forgeries.

(ii) Reliance by the Defendant

The defendant must have relied on the claimant's representation, whether this be an express representation or a representation derived from a breach of the claimant's duty of accuracy. Reliance requires proof that the defendant made an assumption as to the state of affairs and this assumption caused the defendant to change his or her position.[24] The effect of this condition is that the defendant will not be able to rely on the estoppel defence if the defendant knew that he or she was not entitled to receive the benefit or was suspicious as to the validity of the transfer of the benefit but did not inform the claimant

---

[20] (1825) 4 B and C 281, 107 ER 1064.
[21] [1983] 1 WLR 605, 612 (Eveleigh LJ), 621 (Slade LJ). This was *obiter* because the claimant had conceded that it had made a representation to the defendant.
[22] [1975] QB 654, 662 (Kerr J).   [23] [1933] AC 51.   [24] Bant, *The Change of Position Defence*, 28.

of these suspicions,[25] or where the defendant simply did not believe the claimant's representation. In each of these circumstances it is not possible to conclude that the defendant relied on the claimant's representation. So, for example, if the claimant mistakenly paid the defendant twice and the defendant knew that the second payment was not due, the claimant cannot be estopped from claiming restitution of the mistaken payment, even if the claimant had represented to the defendant that the second payment was due. This is illustrated by *United Overseas Bank v Jiwani*[26] itself, where the court found that the defendant had not honestly believed that the money which had been credited to his account was actually due to him, so the estoppel defence failed.

The requirement that the defendant must have relied on the claimant's representation means that, for example, if the claimant mistakenly paid money to the defendant and this money was subsequently stolen from the defendant, there is no role for the defence of estoppel, simply because the defendant did not act in reliance on the validity of the receipt. But this is a situation where the defence of change of position would be available.[27]

(iii) Change of Circumstances

The defendant's circumstances must have changed in such a way as to make it inequitable to require him or her to make restitution to the claimant. This notion of change of circumstances involves two separate considerations.

(1) Causation

The defendant must establish that, but for the receipt of the benefit from the claimant, his or her circumstances would not have changed in the way they did.[28] This is illustrated by the facts of *United Overseas Bank v Jiwani*,[29] where the defendant, having been paid by the claimant by mistake, used this money to purchase a hotel. One reason the defence of estoppel failed was because the defendant could not show that his circumstances had changed as a result of his belief that the money was properly paid, since, even if the defendant had not received the money from the claimant, he would still have purchased the hotel, borrowing the money if necessary.

Similarly, if the defendant spends money on ordinary living expenses which he or she would have incurred anyway, the defence cannot be established. But the fact that the defendant spent the money on such expenses will not automatically prevent the defence from being established if it can be shown that the defendant would not have incurred this expenditure but for the receipt of the money from the claimant. This was recognized by the Court of Appeal in *Avon County Council v Howlett*[30] where the claimant had substantially overpaid sickness benefits to the defendant teacher as a result of a mistake. The defendant and his wife adjusted their expenditure in the light of this overpayment, for example by purchasing a second-hand car and a new suit, and they put some of the money away in savings. Thus, the overpayment was not spent on any extraordinary items, but was absorbed by small improvements in the defendant's daily quality of life. This was held to

---

[25] *Larner v LCC* [1949] 2 KB 683.   [26] [1976] 1 WLR 964.   [27] See p 683, below.

[28] Although in *Stenia v Hutchinson* [2006] EWCA Civ 1551, [2007] ICR 445, [117], it was held that the 'but for' cause test need not be satisfied, it being sufficient that the representation was a significant factor on which the defendant had relied. Bant has argued, in *The Change of Position Defence*, 35, that it should be sufficient that the representation was a cause of the defendant's change of position, by analogy with the test of causation for misrepresentation, see p 187, above, because the defendant's decision to change his or her position was induced by a mistaken belief. Cf the analysis of causation for the defence of change of position, p 682, below.

[29] [1976] 1 WLR 964.   [30] [1983] 1 WLR 605.

be a sufficient detrimental reliance to establish estoppel, in that the defendant had spent more money than he would otherwise have done had the overpayment not been received.

(2) Detriment

It must also be shown that the change of circumstances had been to the defendant's detriment. So, if the defendant received £1,000 from the claimant by mistake and, in reliance on the claimant's representation that the money was due, used it to buy shares which he or she would not have purchased but for the receipt of the money, and these shares increased in value, the defence of estoppel will not be open to the defendant, simply because he or she will not have suffered detriment as a result of the purchase. If, however, the defendant's investment was a bad one, this constitutes a detrimental change of circumstances. Consequently, in *Holt v Markham*[31] the defendant had detrimentally changed his position by investing money which he had received from the claimant in a company which went into liquidation. In *Deutsche Bank (London Agency) Ltd v Beriro and Co*[32] the defendant's position changed because he paid the money which had been received from the claimant to a third party. This constituted a detrimental change of circumstances because the defendant was unable to recover the money from the third party.

Whilst the defendant's detrimental change of circumstances will usually arise as a result of an act on the part of the defendant, the change may also arise by virtue of an omission. This is illustrated by *Avon CC v Howlett*[33] where, as a result of being overpaid sickness benefit, the defendant failed to claim social security benefit to which he would otherwise have been entitled. It was recognized that this constituted a detrimental change of circumstances.[34] Similarly, in *Greenwood v Martins Bank Ltd*[35] it was accepted that the defendant had detrimentally relied on the claimant's representation that his wife had not committed a forgery, by virtue of the defendant's failure to sue the wife in respect of the forgery when it had the opportunity to do so.

(iv) The Justice of the Case

Even where the defendant has detrimentally changed his or her position in reliance on the claimant's representation, the defence of estoppel may still fail if, as was acknowledged by McKenna J in *United Overseas Bank v Jiwani*,[36] it is not just to require the defendant to make restitution to the claimant. This will be the case where, for example, the defendant was under a duty to inform the claimant of his or her mistake and had failed to do so. This occurred in *Larner v LCC*,[37] where the defendant had failed to inform his employer of changes in his service pay which meant that the employer mistakenly paid him more money than he was entitled to receive. Similarly, the defence will fail if the defendant was a wrongdoer or he or she had made a misrepresentation to the claimant which contributed to the claimant mistakenly transferring the benefit to the defendant.[38]

(B) THE CONSEQUENCE OF THE CLAIMANT BEING ESTOPPED

The effect of successfully pleading estoppel is that usually the restitutionary claim is barred completely, even though the defendant may not have spent all of the money which was

---

[31] [1923] 1 KB 504.   [32] (1895) 73 LTR (ns) 669.   [33] [1983] 1 WLR 605.
[34] Ibid, 621 (Slade LJ).   [35] [1933] AC 51.   [36] [1976] 1 WLR 964, 968.
[37] [1949] 2 KB 683. This qualification was also recognized by Slade LJ in *Avon CC v Howlett* [1983] 1 WLR 605, 621.
[38] *George Whitechurch Ltd v Cavanagh* [1902] AC 117, 145 (Lord Brampton); *National Westminster Bank Ltd v Barclays Bank International Ltd* [1975] QB 654, 676 (Kerr J).

received. In other words the defence does not operate *pro tanto*,[39] unlike the defence of change of position.[40] The effect of this is illustrated by *Avon County Council v Howlett*[41] where the claim to recover £1,007, which the claimant had mistakenly paid to the defendant, was defeated even though the defendant had pleaded that he had only changed his position to the extent of £546. Estoppel is considered to operate as a complete defence to the restitutionary claim simply because it is an evidentiary rule which prevents the claimant from adducing facts which contradict the representation on which the defendant has detrimentally relied.[42] Whilst this obviously makes the defence more attractive to defendants, it is liable to produce unjust results, for if the defendant has been unjustly enriched by the receipt of £1,000 and, in reliance on the claimant's representation, parts with £200, he or she remains unjustly enriched to the extent of £800. The potential injustice arising from the operation of the defence was recognized by the judges in *Avon County Council v Howlett*,[43] particularly where the defendant's change of position is small in comparison with the value of the enrichment which he or she had received. There are a number of ways of avoiding this extreme result.

(i) *De Minimis*

If the defendant's position changed in only a very small way, this should not be sufficient to estop the claimant from denying the truth of the representation. Consequently, the defence should be subject to a *de minimis* qualification.

(ii) Apportionment of Payments

Burrows has suggested that a single representation of fact made by the claimant might be divided into a number of different representations which operate only to the extent that the defendant's position changed.[44] This suggestion is surely unworkable where the claimant has only made one payment to the defendant, as occurred in *Avon County Council v Howlett*, because it would be a fiction to assert that the claimant made more than one representation as to the validity of the single payment. But, where a number of payments have been made, it should be possible to consider each payment separately to determine to what extent the defendant's circumstances have changed in respect of each one.[45]

(iii) Imposition of Conditions

The court might be prepared to make the application of the defence conditional on the defendant accepting that he or she would return that part of the benefit to the claimant in respect of which his or her circumstances had not changed,[46] although Slade LJ left open whether the court had jurisdiction to obtain such an undertaking from the defendant.

---

[39] This was affirmed by Lord Goff in *Lipkin Gorman (a firm) v Karpnale Ltd* [1991] 2 AC 548, 579. See also *Avon County Council v Howlett* [1983] 1 WLR 605, 622 (Slade LJ) and *Greenwood v Martins Bank Ltd* [1932] 1 KB 371 (CA), affirmed [1933] AC 51 (HL).

[40] See p 678, below.   [41] [1983] 1 WLR 605.   [42] Ibid, 622 (Slade LJ).

[43] Ibid, 608 (Cumming-Bruce LJ) and 624 (Slade LJ).

[44] AS Burrows, *The Law of Restitution* (3rd edn, Oxford: Oxford University Press, 2011), 555.

[45] Note the similar approach in respect of the ground of restitution of total failure of basis where it is possible to apportion benefits received. See p 321, above.

[46] Such a solution was advocated by Viscount Cave LC and Lord Atkinson in *Jones Ltd v Waring and Gillow Ltd* [1926] AC 670, 688, but in that case such an undertaking was voluntarily proferred by the defendant.

(iv) Shifting the Burden of Proof

Cumming-Bruce LJ in *Avon CC v Howlett*[47] suggested that the burden of proof might be shifted, so that once the defendant has shown that he or she had suffered some detriment in reliance on the claimant's representation, the claimant must then prove that the defendant's circumstances changed only in respect of part of the benefit which he or she received. But such a recommendation is unlikely to work in practice, since the claimant is unlikely to know, let alone be able to prove, to what extent the defendant's circumstances had actually changed.

(v) Unconscionability

In *Avon CC v Howlett*[48] Eveleigh LJ suggested that in certain circumstances it might be unconscionable for the defendant to retain that part of the benefit in respect of which his or her position had not changed, but he did not identify what these circumstances might be. Cumming-Bruce LJ also recognized that restitution might still lie on the ground that it would be inequitable for the defendant to retain part of the benefit which he or she had received, but he declined to rule on when such an equity would be recognized.[49] Slade LJ was much less certain about the relevance of broad concepts of justice and equity, which he considered to be misleading and uncertain in application.[50]

The application of this test of unconscionability was considered further by the Court of Appeal in *National Westminster Bank plc v Somer International (UK) Ltd*.[51] In this case over £54,000 was mistakenly transferred by the claimant bank to the defendant company's bank account. The defendant had informed the claimant that it expected the receipt of a sum of about this amount. The claimant informed the defendant that the sum had been credited to its account. In reliance on this representation the defendant dispatched shipments of goods to a company to the value of over £13,000. Subsequently, this company ceased to trade. The claimant informed the defendant of the mistaken payment and sought repayment of the money. The trial judge recognized that the defendant could rely on the defence of estoppel, but only to the extent of its detrimental reliance. The Court of Appeal considered the operation of the defence of estoppel and concluded that there was scope for the operation of Equity[52] to ensure that the defence only applied to the extent of the detriment suffered.[53] Potter LJ held that the court would look at the matter broadly and would not require the defendant to demonstrate in detail the precise degree or value of the detriment suffered. On the facts of the case it was held that it was unconscionable for the defendant to retain the balance above the value of the goods which had been shipped. But this characterization of 'unconscionability' is interesting; the relative proportions are significant. The defendant had received £54,179 and had spent £13,180. This was effectively a ratio of 4:1 which was considered to be a sufficient disparity to prevent the estoppel defence from operating as a complete bar to the restitutionary claim. So how much must the defendant spend for there to be no disparity? Clarke LJ recognized[54] that the operation of the defence will depend on all the circumstances of the case, including the nature of the representation and the steps taken in reliance on it. He considered this to be an example of the principles of Equity being employed to mitigate

---

[47] [1983] 1 WLR 605, 609.   [48] Ibid, 612.   [49] Ibid, 608.   [50] Ibid, 621.

[51] [2001] EWCA Civ 970, [2002] 1 All ER 198.

[52] See *Jorden v Money* (1854) 5 HL Cas 185, 210 (Lord Cranworth).

[53] *National Westminster Bank plc v Somer International (UK) Ltd* [2001] EWCA Civ 970, [2002] 1 All ER 198, 215 (Potter LJ).

[54] Ibid, 217. Relying in particular on the judgment of Eveleigh LJ in *Avon CC v Howlett* [1983] 1 WLR 605, 611. See also *Johnson v Gore-Wood and Co* [2001] 2 WLR 72, 99 (Lord Goff).

the rigours of the Common Law. But he also emphasized that this reliance on unconscion-ability is principled and does not involve the exercise of discretion,[55] although he gave no indication as to why the defence should operate *pro tanto* on the facts of this case.

(C) IS THERE A CONTINUING ROLE FOR THE ESTOPPEL DEFENCE?

In the light of the recognition of the defence of change of position, a defence which operates only to the extent that the defendant's circumstances have in fact changed, there is a very strong argument for saying that there is no longer any role for estoppel as a defence to restitutionary claims. Indeed, in *RBC Dominion Securities Inc v Dawson*[56] the Newfoundland Court of Appeal held that the recognition of the defence of change of position meant that the defence of estoppel was no longer available in respect of restitu-tionary claims.

It is not possible, however, to conclude in England that the recognition of the change of position defence means that there is no longer a role for the defence of estoppel to restitutionary claims. Indeed, in recognizing the defence of change of position in *Lipkin Gorman (a firm) v Karpnale Ltd*[57] Lord Goff assumed that there was a continuing role for the defence of estoppel.[58] The two defences do operate in a different way, in that estoppel requires proof of a representation, whether collateral or implied, and arguably change of position requires a more extraordinary change of circumstances than is the case for estoppel. Also estoppel requires proof of reliance on the representation, whereas change of position typically requires proof of reliance on receipt of a benefit. But the crucial difference between the two defences is that estoppel can typically defeat the claim completely whereas change of position only defeats the claim to the extent that the defendant's position has changed. It follows that estoppel will continue to be the defence which the defendant will prefer to plead as long as he or she can establish the necessary representation.[59] But with the growing recognition that the estoppel defence should not bar the restitutionary claim completely, it is likely that the defence will cease to have any function in the law of restitution.[60]

2. TRANSFER OF A BENEFIT BY AN AGENT TO HIS OR HER PRINCIPAL

Where an agent has received a benefit from the claimant on behalf of his or her principal, the claimant can sue the agent for restitution of the benefit even where the principal

---

[55] *National Westminster Bank plc v Somer International (UK) Ltd* [2001] EWCA Civ 970, [2002] 1 All ER 198, 218.

[56] *RBC Dominion Securities Inc v Dawson* (1994) 111 DLR (4th) 230.

[57] [1991] 2 AC 548, 578 (Lord Goff). In *South Tyneside Metropolitan BC v Svenska International plc* [1995] 1 All ER 545 Clarke J assumed that the defence of estoppel continued to be applicable despite the recognition of the defence of change of position.

[58] Bant, *The Change of Position Defence*, 230, considers it to be premature to assume that estoppel has been subsumed within the change of position defence or has been rendered redundant.

[59] The Law Commission favoured the retention of the estoppel defence despite the recognition of the defence of change of position: *Restitution: Mistakes of Law and Ultra Vires Public Authority Receipts and Payments* (Law Com No 227, 1994), 48–9 and 141. See also Hudson, 'Estoppel by Representation as a Defence to Unjust Enrichment—the Vine Has Not Withered Yet', who defends the continued operation of estoppel as a complete defence as being true to its original function as an evidential rule which prevents the claimant from adducing evidence contrary to the represented facts.   [60] See p 698, below.

is disclosed.[61] The restitutionary action against the agent may be defeated, however, if the agent has transferred the benefit to his or her principal.[62] In such circumstances the claimant will be forced to bring a restitutionary claim against the principal instead. So, for example, the defence has been available to a bank which was contractually obliged to transfer money received to the account of a customer.[63]

(A) FEATURES OF THE AGENT'S DEFENCE

(i) The Defendant Must Have Received the Benefit as Agent

The agent's defence will not be available if the defendant received the benefit as principal, simply because in such circumstances the defendant will have received the benefit for his or her own use.[64] The defendant will not be considered to have received the benefit as agent in two particular circumstances:

(1) where the defendant did not have authority to receive the benefit on behalf of the supposed principal;[65]

(2) where the agent was acting on behalf of an undisclosed principal, so that the claimant was unaware that he or she was dealing with an agent.[66] Where, however, the agent is acting on behalf of an undisclosed principal, it may still be possible to defeat the restitutionary claim by reliance on the separate defence of change of position, which is not affected by such a limitation.

(ii) The Benefit Must Be Transferred to the Principal

The defence will only be available to the agent if he or she had transferred the benefit which he or she had received from the claimant to his or her principal. Usually it will be obvious that the benefit has been transferred. For example, where the agent received money from the claimant it is sufficient to show that the agent paid this money to the principal. But the agent can be considered to transfer a benefit to the principal in other ways. This was recognized by Lord Atkinson in *Kleinwort Sons and Co v Dunlop Rubber Co*[67] when he said that it is sufficient that the agent 'had paid over the money which he received to the principal, or settled such an account with the principal as amounts to

---

[61] See, for example, *Buller v Harrison* (1777) 2 Cowp 565, 98 ER 1243 and *Kleinwort Sons and Co v Dunlop Rubber Co* (1907) 97 LT 263. It has sometimes been suggested that the claimant can only sue the principal and not the agent to recover the benefit, because when the agent receives the benefit it is deemed to have been received by the principal: the so-called defence of ministerial receipt. See, for example, *The Duke of Norfolk v Worthy* (1808) 1 Camp 337, 170 ER 977 and *Ellis v Goulton* [1893] 1 QB 350. See also Bant, *The Change of Position Defence*, 233. But if this were correct there would not be any need to have a specific defence where an agent transfers a benefit to the principal. See generally R Stevens, 'Why do Agents "Drop Out"?' [2005] LMCLQ 101.

[62] *Jeremy D Stone Consultants Ltd v National Westminster Bank* [2013] EWHC 208 (Ch), [244] (Sales J).

[63] Ibid.

[64] *Newall v Tomlinson* (1871) LR 6 CP 405; *Baylis v Bishop of London* [1913] 1 Ch 127; *Kleinwort Sons and Co v Dunlop Rubber Co* (1907) 97 LT 263; *National Bank of Egypt International Ltd v Oman Housing Bank SAOC* [2002] EWHC 1760 (Comm), [2003] 1 All ER (Comm) 246.

[65] *Sorrell v Finch* [1977] AC 728.

[66] See *Sadler v Evans* (1766) 4 Burr 1984, 1986; 98 ER 34, 35; *Baylis v Bishop of London* [1913] 1 Ch 127, 133 (Cozens-Hardy MR); and *Agip (Africa) Ltd v Jackson* [1990] Ch 265, 288 (Millett J). Cf *Transvaal and Delagoa Bay Investment Co Ltd v Atkinson* [1944] 1 All ER 579 where the defence succeeded even though the agent was acting on behalf of an undisclosed principal, but the point was not argued.

[67] (1907) 97 LT 263, 265.

payment, or did something which so prejudiced his position that it would be inequitable to require him to refund'.

Essentially, the defence will only be available to the extent that the agent's circumstances have changed because the principal has effectively received the benefit from the agent.[68] So, for example, the agent can be deemed to have transferred money to the principal if the agent has expended the money on behalf of the principal and with the principal's authority, for example by paying it to a third party.[69] The defence will not, however, be available if the agent simply credited the principal with the payment,[70] because a credit entry can easily be reversed without the principal even knowing of its existence.

(iii) The Agent Must Not Have Notice of the Grounds for a Restitutionary Claim

The agent's defence will fail if the agent transferred the benefit received from the claimant to the principal once the agent had become aware of the claimant's restitutionary claim.[71]

(iv) The Agent Must Not Be Implicated in Wrongdoing

The agent will not be able to rely on the defence if he or she had received the benefit as a result of the commission of a wrong to which he or she was a party or where he or she was aware of the commission of the wrong.[72] So, for example, where the agent received money pursuant to an illegal transaction, he or she will not be able to rely on the defence if he or she paid this money to the principal.[73] Similarly the defence will not be available where the agent extracted money from the claimant by duress.[74] The defence is denied to the agent in such circumstances simply because it is inequitable for a wrongdoer, or somebody who has been tainted by the wrong, to rely on such a defence to defeat the restitutionary claim.

(v) No Need to Show Detriment

It has been a matter of some controversy whether the agent's defence will only be established if the agent suffered detriment as a result of transferring the benefit to the principal. In *Kleinwort Sons and Co v Dunlop Rubber Co*[75] Lord Loreburn LC emphasized that the defence would only be applicable if the agent's position could be considered to have been altered to his or her disadvantage. But, although usually the transfer of a benefit would indeed have been disadvantageous to the agent, this will not always be the case and, where there is no detriment, the defence should still be available.[76] So, for example, where the agent uses the money which has mistakenly been paid to him or her by the claimant to discharge a debt which the principal owed to the agent, this should be considered to involve a transfer of the benefit to the principal even though the agent has not suffered any loss as a result of it.[77]

---

[68] Ibid.

[69] *Holland v Russell* (1863) 4 B and S 14, 122 ER 365. See also *Transvaal and Delagoa Bay Investment Co Ltd v Atkinson* [1944] All ER 579.

[70] *Buller v Harrison* (1777) 2 Cowp 565, 98 ER 1243; *Cox v Prentice* (1815) 3 M and S 344, 105 ER 641.

[71] *Buller v Harrison* (1777) 2 Cowp 565, 98 ER 1243; *Niru Battery v Milestone Trading Ltd* [2002] EWHC 1425 (Comm), [2002] 2 All ER (Comm) 705, 741 (Moore-Bick J).

[72] *Snowdon v Davis* (1808) 1 Taunt 359, 127 ER 872.

[73] *Townson v Wilson* (1808) 1 Camp 396, 170 ER 997.

[74] *Snowdon v Davis* (1808) 1 Taunt 359, 127 ER 872.   [75] (1907) 97 LT 263, 264.

[76] *Australia and New Zealand Banking Group Ltd v Westpac Banking Corporation* (1988) 164 CLR 662.

[77] *Continental Caoutchouc and Gutta Percha Co v Kleinwort Sons* (1904) 90 LT 474.

(vi) The Defence Operates *Pro Tanto*

The defence will only be applicable to the extent that the benefit has been transferred to the principal. So, for example, if the agent receives £1,000 from the claimant by mistake and pays £750 of this to the principal, the agent will remain liable to repay the outstanding £250 to the claimant.

(vii) The Defence is Available to All Restitutionary Claims

The agent's defence is applicable regardless of the type of restitutionary claim brought by the claimant. So, for example, the defence has succeeded where the claim has been founded on the reversal of unjust enrichment, where the ground of restitution was spontaneous mistake,[78] induced mistake,[79] and duress of goods,[80] though in the latter two cases the defence only succeeded because the agent was unaware of the principal's wrongdoing. Millett J recognized in *Agip (Africa) Ltd v Jackson*[81] that the defence would also succeed where the claimant brought an action for money had and received founded on the vindication of proprietary rights. But in the same case Millett J held that there was no scope for the defence to operate where the claim was founded on the equitable action for unconscionable receipt.[82] This distinction between Common Law and equitable claims, which are founded on the same principle of the vindication of property rights, presumably arises from the fact that the agent in the action for unconscionable receipt is implicated in wrongdoing.

(B) THE RATIONALE OF THE AGENT'S DEFENCE

The rationale of the agent's defence is a matter of some uncertainty. A number of explanations of the defence can be identified.

(i) The Defendant is No Longer Enriched

In *Continental Caoutuc and Gutta Percha Co v Kleinwort Sons and Co*[83] Collins MR said that the reason for the defence is that the agent 'is a mere conduit-pipe [who] had not had the benefit of the windfall'. In other words, the defence operates because, as a result of events subsequent to the receipt of the enrichment by the agent, he or she is no longer enriched. Whilst this is certainly true of most cases where the agent's defence has succeeded, it cannot explain all of them, because there is no requirement that the agent suffered any detriment in transferring the benefit to the principal. Also, if the operation of the defence simply depended on whether or not the defendant had retained an enrichment, it would not be possible to justify the limitation on the operation of the defence that it only applies if the principal is disclosed. In addition, because of the recognition of the defence of change of position, if the rationale of the agent's defence was simply that the agent was no longer enriched, it would be very difficult to distinguish between the two defences, with the probable result that the agent's defence would be assimilated into the change of position defence.[84] There is no reason to think that this is the case.

---

[78] *Holland v Russell* (1863) 4 B and S 14, 122 ER 365.
[79] *Transvaal and Delagoa Bay Investment Co Ltd v Atkinson* [1944] 1 All ER 579.
[80] *Owen and Co v Cronk* [1895] 1 QB 265.   [81] [1990] Ch 265.
[82] Ibid, 289.   [83] (1904) 20 TLR 403, 405.   [84] See p 700, below.

(ii) The Justice of the Case

An alternative explanation of the defence, as suggested by Lord Atkinson in *Kleinwort Sons and Co v Dunlop Rubber Co*,[85] is that it is founded on equitable principles whereby it is unjust to require the agent to make restitution where he or she has transferred the benefit to the principal. But such a notion of justice is too vague a principle on which to found the defence, although it is clearly an influential factor in determining its ambit.

(iii) Determining the Proper Party to Sue

Another explanation of the defence is that it simply exists as a means of determining which is the better party to sue, either the agent or the principal.[86] This was recognized by the High Court of Australia in *Australia and New Zealand Banking Group Ltd v Westpac Banking Corporation*,[87] where it was held that the defence was applicable where the principal had 'effectively received the benefit of the payment with the consequence that prima facie liability to make restitution has become his'. In other words, where the benefit which was received by the agent has effectively been transferred to the principal, it is the principal who is the proper person against whom the restitutionary claim should be brought. But this explanation does not explain all the requirements of the defence, most notably the fact that it is limited to where the principal is disclosed.

(iv) Estoppel

The preferable explanation of the defence is that it is founded on estoppel. According to this explanation the agent will continue to be liable to the claimant unless the claimant can be estopped from bringing a restitutionary claim against the agent. Such an estoppel would be established if the claimant knows that he or she is dealing with an agent and so authorizes the transfer of the benefit to the principal.[88] This does at least explain why the defence only operates where the principal has been disclosed, but it does not explain why the defence operates even where there has been no detrimental reliance. Consequently, this must be a form of estoppel where it is sufficient that the agent has relied on the claimant's representation so that the agent transferred a benefit to the principal, it not being necessary to show that the agent suffered any detriment as a result.

3. CHANGE OF POSITION

(A) RECOGNITION OF THE DEFENCE

Although the notion of a defence of change of position[89] has existed in some limited embryonic form for some time,[90] its existence had been in doubt, since a number of cases

---

[85] (1907) 97 LT 263, 265.

[86] P Millett, 'Tracing the Proceeds of Fraud' (1991) 107 LQR 71, 76.

[87] (1988) 164 CLR 662, 674. See also *Portman Building Society v Hamlyn Taylor and Neck (a firm)* [1998] 4 All ER 202, 207 (Millett LJ); *Niru Battery v Milestone Trading Ltd* [2002] EWHC 1425 (Comm), [2002] 2 All ER (Comm) 705, 740 (Moore-Bick J).

[88] WJ Swadling, 'The Nature of Ministerial Receipt' in PBH Birks (ed), *Laundering and Tracing* (Oxford: Clarendon Press, 1995), 257–9; Grantham and Rickett, 'A Normative Account of Defences to Restitutionary Liability', 110.

[89] For general analysis of this defence see Bant, *The Change of Position Defence*.

[90] See, in particular, *Larner v LCC* [1949] 2 KB 683, 688 (Denning LJ); *Spiers and Pond Ltd v Finsbury MPC* (1956) 1 Ryde's Rating Cases 219; and *Barclays Bank Ltd v WJ Simms, Son and Cooke (Southern) Ltd* [1980] QB 677, 695 (Robert Goff J). In *BP Exploration Co (Libya) Ltd v Hunt (No 2)* [1979] 1 WLR 783, 800 and 804,

had specifically rejected such a defence in English law.[91] The defence was, however, expressly recognized by the House of Lords in *Lipkin Gorman*.[92] It was widely defined by Lord Goff as being 'available to a person whose position has so changed that it would be inequitable in all the circumstances to require him to make restitution, or alternatively to make restitution in full'.[93] This harks back to the principle expounded by Lord Mansfield in *Moses v Macferlan*[94] to justify the recognition of defences to a restitutionary claim, namely that the defendant 'may defend himself by everything which shows that the plaintiff *ex aequo et bono* is not entitled to the whole of the demand, or to any part of it'. Where the defendant's position has changed after receipt of a benefit it is only fair that this should be taken into account in determining whether and to what extent the defendant should make restitution to the claimant.

Despite this clear recognition of the defence its ambit was left uncertain because the House of Lords declined to elaborate on the details of the defence, preferring that this should be determined on a case by case basis.[95] A number of cases, decided since *Lipkin Gorman*, have elaborated on the ambit of the defence. The laws of certain Commonwealth countries where the defence has been recognized can also be considered to determine how the defence should be defined.[96] But there are still a number of fundamental questions which remain unresolved. One of the most important is whether the defence applies to all restitutionary claims. Lord Goff in *Lipkin Gorman* said that it was not appropriate in that case 'to identify all those actions in restitution to which change of position may be a defence'.[97] The rationale for and application of the defence has proved to be an important catalyst for the extensive debate amongst restitution scholars as to the function and structure of the law of restitution. This is an area where the often sterile debate about classification really matters.[98] A further vital question concerns the identification of the rationale of the defence, for until that is clearly recognized it will be impossible to determine its appropriate ambit.[99] It will also be necessary to examine how the change of position defence relates to the other restitutionary defences which are triggered by changes in the defendant's circumstances.[100]

The recognition of the defence is of vital importance to the development of the law of restitution. For, by recognizing that changes in the defendant's position after he or she has received a benefit is relevant to the success of the restitutionary claim, it is possible to adopt a wider interpretation of the underlying cause of action, particularly the grounds of restitution for purposes of the action founded on the reversal of the defendant's unjust

---

Robert Goff J explained the operation of the proviso to s 1 (2) and (3) of the Law Reform (Frustrated Contracts) Act 1943 as founded on the principle of change of position. See p 359, above.

[91] See, in particular, *Baylis v Bishop of London* [1913] 1 Ch 127, where it was held that, save for the agent's defence, which was anyway inapplicable on the facts because the principal was undisclosed, there was no general defence in English law where the defendant had transferred the benefit which had been received from the claimant. See also *Ministry of Health v Simpson* [1951] AC 251, 276 (Lord Simonds) and *Rover International Ltd v Cannon Film Sales Ltd (No 3)* [1989] 1 WLR 912, 935 (Dillon LJ).

[92] [1991] 2 AC 548, 558 (Lord Bridge), 568 (Lord Ackner), 578 (Lord Goff).

[93] Ibid, 580.   [94] (1760) 2 Burr 1005, 1010; 97 ER 676, 679.

[95] *Lipkin Gorman (a firm) v Karpnale Ltd* [1991] 2 AC 548, 558 (Lord Bridge) and 579 (Lord Goff).

[96] See, in particular, the decision of the Supreme Court of Canada in *Rural Municipality of Storthoaks v Mobil Oil Canada Ltd* (1975) 55 DLR (3d) 1, 13 and the decisions of the High Court of Australia in *David Securities Pty Ltd v Commonwealth Bank of Australia* (1992) 175 CLR 353, 385 and *Australia Financial Services Ltd and Leasing Pty Ltd v Hills Industries Ltd* [2014] HCA 14. The defence has also been recognized in New Zealand by the New Zealand (Judicature) Act 1908, s 94B, as inserted by s 2 of the Judicature Amendment Act 1958.

[97] *Lipkin Gorman (a firm) v Karpnale Ltd* [1991] 2 AC 548, 580. This is examined at p 695, below.

[98] See p 17, above.   [99] See p 680, below.   [100] See p 698, below.

enrichment.[101] The recognition of the defence will make it easier for the claimant to establish a restitutionary claim, because the interests of the defendant can be better protected by considering whether it is just for the defendant to make restitution in the light of any change in his or her position.

(B) THE RATIONALE OF THE CHANGE OF POSITION DEFENCE

In *Lipkin Gorman* Lord Goff identified the essence of the change of position defence as being that it is 'inequitable' for the defendant to make restitution.[102] This emphasis on equity as the foundation for the defence is significant for two reasons. First, it may indicate what the rationale of the defence is. The accepted view of many commentators is that the defence applies to claims founded on unjust enrichment and so its function is to negate or qualify at least one aspect of the unjust enrichment claim. But there is no definite conclusion as to which element of the claim should be negated or qualified. One interpretation is that the defence exists to negate the defendant's enrichment.[103] In other words, where the defendant has received an enrichment and has subsequently changed his or her position, the defendant's liability to make restitution should be curtailed because the enrichment has been reduced or negated. However, the emphasis on equity may mean that the defence should operate instead to determine whether the defendant's retention of the enrichment is unjust, since, if the defendant's position has changed then, to the extent of that change, it is not just for the defendant to make restitution.[104] Alternatively, the defence can be interpreted as operating both to determine the extent of the enrichment (the causation question) and the unjust requirement (the equity question).[105] This is, at least, consistent with the way the defence was identified by Lord Goff in *Lipkin Gorman* and is the preferable interpretation of its operation. The defence should be considered to have a dual function in that it exists to protect the defendant's reliance on the security of his or her receipt,[106] so that if the defendant changes his or her position as a result of the receipt of the enrichment it is not appropriate to make restitution, in order to protect the defendant's autonomy.[107] But the defence should also be interpreted as existing to counter-balance the principle of corrective justice which underpins the unjust enrichment principle itself.[108] For example, if the claimant is able to obtain restitution simply because of a spontaneous causative mistake without needing to prove any fault on the part of the defendant, it is only just that relevant changes in the defendant's circumstances should be taken into account in determining the restitutionary claim.[109] Consequently, the real function of the defence is to identify those cases where the justice of the defendant not

---

[101] See *Lipkin Gorman (a firm) v Karpnale Ltd* [1991] 2 AC 548, 581 (Lord Goff).

[102] Ibid, 580.

[103] PBH Birks, *Unjust Enrichment* (2nd edn, Oxford: Oxford University Press, 2005), 208–19; J Edelman, 'Change of Position: A Defence of Unjust Disenrichment' (2012) 92 Boston ULR 1009. See also Burrows, *The Law of Restitution* (3rd edn), 526 and RC Nolan, 'Change of Position' in PBH Birks (ed), *Laundering and Tracing* (Oxford: Clarendon Press, 1995), 136, who says that the defence is 'principally an enrichment related defence'.

[104] See Birks, *Unjust Enrichment* (2nd edn), 258–61.

[105] Further, see ibid, 207 and 209, who preferred to analyse the defence by dividing it into two types: one involving disenrichment and one involving a non-disenriching change of position. This is excessively complicated and can be avoided by insisting on disenrichment to establish the defence and then having regard to questions of justice, however defined, to determine whether the defendant is disabled from relying on it.

[106] But it can apply even where there is no reliance. See p 683, below.

[107] Grantham and Rickett, 'A Normative Account of Defences to Restitutionary Liability', 121. See also *Benedetti v Sawiris* [2013] UKSC 50, [2014] AC 938, [118] (Lord Reed).

[108] See p 4, above.   [109] Birks, *Unjust Enrichment* (2nd edn), 209.

making restitution outweighs the justice of the claimant obtaining restitution. In fact, it is not useful to relate the application of the defence to specific elements of the unjust enrichment principle at all. It is much more accurate to analyse it with reference to the remedial question of whether it is appropriate to require the defendant to make full restitution to the claimant in the light of subsequent events, having regard to the need to protect reliance on the security of receipt but ensuring that if the defendant remains enriched then it is appropriate for him or her to make restitution.[110]

Bant adopts a somewhat different approach to her analysis of the defence in *The Change of Position Defence*. She does not relate the defence to specific elements of the unjust enrichment claim, and indeed considers that it is available generally to qualify or defeat any claim for restitution.[111] In particular she does not consider that the defence responds to the defendant's disenrichment, but rather to the fact that the defendant's change of position is irreversible, for then it is not appropriate to require the defendant to make restitution.[112] Whilst this notion encompasses cases where the defendant is no longer enriched, she considers that the test of irreversibility better explains the characteristics of the defence, particularly the inclusion of non-pecuniary change of position.[113] She also considers that it is not necessary to consider as a separate requirement that the defendant changed his or her position in good faith, since she considers that the defendant's change of position must be reasonable.[114] Whilst this is a highly persuasive analysis of how the defence of change of position should be interpreted it cannot yet be considered to represent the state of English law.

The other significance of Lord Goff's emphasis on 'equity' when analysing the defence is that it may consequently be interpreted in a discretionary way, albeit grounded on principle, as reflected by a number of the recent decisions of the courts. For example, in *Dextra Bank and Trust Co Ltd v Bank of Jamaica*[115] the Privy Council emphasized that the House of Lords in *Lipkin Gorman* 'appears to have adopted a broad approach based on practical justice, and to have avoided technicality'.[116] Other cases have focused on considerations of unconscionability[117] and inequity.[118] Some members of the judiciary have sought to take a middle way between rule and discretion. For example, in *Commerzbank AG v Gareth Price-Jones*[119] Mummery LJ recognized that 'the decided cases steer a cautious course, aiming to avoid the dangers of a diffuse discretion and the restrictions of rigid rules'. Munby J, however, in the same case[120] asserted that the defence was 'intended to be a broadly stated concept of practical justice' and that 'technicality and black letter law are to be avoided'.

Placing the emphasis simply on what is equitable makes the defence potentially far too wide and uncertain. Indeed, the fear that the defence would be too vague and unpredictable was one of the main reasons why it had previously been rejected. As Hamilton LJ said in *Baylis v Bishop of London*,[121] 'we are not now free in the twentieth century to administer

---

[110] The decision of the Privy Council in *Dextra Bank and Trust Co v Bank of Jamaica* [2001] UKPC 50, [2002] 1 All ER (Comm) 193 is consistent with this approach. See also Birks, *Unjust Enrichment* (2nd edn), 209.

[111] Bant, *The Change of Position Defence*, 208.   [112] Ibid, 132.   [113] Ibid. See p 688, below.

[114] Ibid, 151. See further p 691, below.   [115] [2001] UKPC 50, [2002] 1 All ER (Comm) 193.

[116] Citing *Lipkin Gorman (a firm) v Karpnale Ltd* [1991] 2 AC 548, 581–93 (Lord Goff).

[117] *National Westminster Bank plc v Somer International* [2002] 1 All ER 198, 210 (Potter LJ); *Niru Battery Manufacturing Co v Milestone Trading Ltd* [2003] EWCA 1446 (Civ), [2004] QB 985.

[118] *Scottish Equitable plc v Derby* [2000] 3 All ER 793, 806 (Harrison J).

[119] [2003] EWCA Civ 1663, [2005] 1 Lloyd's Rep 298, [32].   [120] Ibid, [48].

[121] [1913] 1 Ch 127, 140. See also H Cohen, 'Change of Position in Quasi-Contracts' (1931–32) Harvard Law Review 1333, 1361.

that vague jurisprudence which is sometimes attractively styled "justice as between man and man"'. But in recognizing the defence in *Lipkin Gorman* Lord Goff emphasized that restitutionary defences should be formulated with reference to principle rather than arbitrary judicial decision, when he said:

> It does not, in my opinion, follow that the court has carte blanche to reject the [claimant's] claim simply because it thinks it unfair or unjust in the circumstances to grant recovery. The recovery of money in restitution is not, as a general rule, a matter of discretion for the court. A claim to recover money at common law is made as a matter of right; and, even though the underlying principle of recovery is the principle of unjust enrichment, never-theless, where recovery is denied, it is denied on the basis of legal principle.[122]

It follows that if the defence is to succeed it must be interpreted by reference to principles rather than through the exercise of arbitrary judicial decision.[123]

(C) THE CONDITIONS FOR ESTABLISHING THE CHANGE OF POSITION DEFENCE

The operation of the defence is founded on two fundamental principles.

(1) There must be a causative link between the receipt of the benefit by the defendant and his or her change of position, so that, but for the receipt of the benefit,[124] the defendant's position would not have changed.

(2) The defendant's position must have changed in circumstances which make it inequitable for him or her to make restitution to the claimant. Specific principles can be identified to assist in the determination of what is equitable for these purposes.

Both these principles underlie the defence because it is only where the defendant's position has changed by virtue of the receipt of the enrichment, and where it is just for the defendant to rely on the defence, that it is possible to conclude that the defendant's interest in the security of his or her receipt should prevail over the interest of the claimant in obtaining restitution.

(i) Causation

There must be a causal link between the receipt of the benefit by the defendant and his or her change of position, so that, but for its receipt, the defendant's position would not have changed. The leading case on the interpretation of causation for the purposes of the defence is *Scottish Equitable plc v Derby*.[125] In that case the defendant had invested money in a pension policy with the claimant life assurance company. The defendant took early retirement benefit, but this was not recorded in the claimant's records. The claimant sent the defendant a statement showing a fund of £201,000 and subsequently confirmed this. The statement should in fact have read £20,500. Consequently, the defendant received £11,000 more each year than he should have done and he used this money to reduce his mortgage and the rest was spent on making modest improvements to his lifestyle. The defendant also faced straitened financial circumstances by virtue of the fact that he was in the process of separating from his wife. The claimant sought restitution and the defendant

---

[122] *Lipkin Gorman (a firm) v Karpnale Ltd* [1991] 2 AC 548, 578.
[123] See *Phillip Collins Ltd v Davis* [2000] 3 All ER 808, 827 (Jonathan Parker J).
[124] *Test Claimants in the FII Group Litigation v HMRC (No 2)* [2014] EWHC 4302 (Ch), [343] (Henderson J).
[125] [2001] 3 All ER 818.

pleaded change of position. The Court of Appeal considered the appropriate test of causation and referred to the distinction between the wide and the narrow view of the defence as propounded by Burrows.[126] According to the narrow view, the defence will only arise where the defendant has relied to his or her detriment on the validity of the receipt of the enrichment.[127] According to the wide view, however, the defence will be available whenever the defendant's position has changed so that it is inequitable to make restitution, but a causal link is still needed between the receipt of the enrichment and the change of position. The Court of Appeal preferred this wide interpretation of the defence.[128] Consequently, it is not necessary to confine the defence to cases where the defendant relied on the validity of the receipt, although in many cases such detrimental reliance can be established. Rather, it is enough that the receipt of the enrichment caused the defendant to change his or her position. The Court further suggested that the appropriate test of causation was at least the 'but for' test.[129] In other words, but for the receipt of the enrichment the defendant's position would not have changed. It followed that, on the facts of the case, financial difficulties arising from the defendant's separation was not causally linked to the mistaken payment and so did not constitute a change of position.

According to this wider interpretation causation can be established in two ways: first, where it can be established that the defendant no longer retains the specific benefit which was received from the claimant, or, secondly, where the defendant's position has changed in other ways as a result of his or her reliance on the validity of the receipt of the benefit from the claimant.[130] The reason for distinguishing between the two tests of causation is simply because the second test depends on proof that the defendant detrimentally relied on the validity of the receipt to change his or her position, whereas the first test does not require any proof of reliance on the validity of the receipt.

In *Test Claimants in the FII Group Litigation v HMRC (No 2)*[131] Henderson J recognized that the defence is essentially concerned with disenrichment. A relevant consideration is how easy it would be for the defendant to reverse his or her enrichment but, unlike the approach adopted in Australia and advocated by Bant, the test is not simply one of irreversibility, since the change of position must also satisfy the but for test of causation.

(1) Loss of Benefit Test of Causation

According to the lost benefit test, the defence is open to the defendant if he or she no longer retains the actual benefit which had been received from the claimant. So, for example, if the claimant paid £1,000 to the defendant by mistake but this money was stolen from the defendant when walking home, the defence should in principle be available. Whether the defence will actually succeed would then depend on whether the circumstances are such that it would be inequitable to require the defendant to make restitution to the claimant, but the fact that the money was stolen will probably be sufficient for the defence to operate.[132] Similarly, if the enrichment is destroyed, for example by fire, the defence should in principle be available.

---

[126] Now see Burrows, *The Law of Restitution* (3rd edn), 528–31.

[127] This is the preferred view in Australia: *David Securities Commonwealth Bank of Australia* (1992) 175 CLR 353, 385; *State Bank of New South Wales Ltd v Swiss Bank Corp* (1995) 39 NSWLR 350, 356–7; *Citigroup v National* [2012] NSWCA 381, 82 NSWLR 391, [5–6] (Bathurst CJ, Allsop P, and Meagher JA) and [64–65] (Barrett JA); *Australian Financial Services and Leasing Pty Ltd v Hills Industries Ltd* [2014] HCA 14, [25] (French CJ), [81], [88] (Hayne, Crennan, Kiefel, Bell, and Keane JJ).

[128] See also *Philip Collins Ltd v Davis* [2000] 3 All ER 808, 827 (Jonathan Parker J).

[129] *Scottish Equitable plc v Derby*, 827 (Robert Walker LJ).

[130] See Bant, *The Change of Position Defence*, 144.

[131] [2014] EWHC 4302 (Ch), [354].   [132] See p 690, below.

(a) Establishing that the Benefit Was Lost

The essential feature of this test of causation is that the defendant no longer has the benefit which he or she received from the claimant. This satisfies the but for test of causation because, but for the receipt of the benefit, the defendant would not have lost it and, by losing it, he or she has suffered a detriment.[133] Although the test of causation is formulated in terms of whether the defendant has retained the benefit which was received from the claimant, it does not follow that this aspect of the defence is only relevant to proprietary restitutionary claims. Even where the claim is founded on the reversal of the defendant's unjust enrichment it may be defeated by the fact that the defendant no longer retains the enrichment which was received, simply because the fact that the defendant no longer has the enrichment may make it inequitable to require the defendant to make restitution.

(b) Retention of the Product of the Benefit

If the defendant has retained a product of the benefit, for example where he or she uses money received from the claimant to buy a car, it should not be possible to conclude that the defendant has lost the benefit, because he or she has retained the value of the original benefit, albeit in a different form.[134] In *RBC Dominion Securities Inc v Dawson*,[135] however, the Newfoundland Court of Appeal held that the defence of change of position could apply even where the defendant had substituted property for the original benefit received from the claimant. But this is surely inconsistent with the essential feature of the defence, namely that it is only inequitable for the defendant to make restitution to the claimant to the extent that the defendant's position has changed. Where the defendant has merely substituted one benefit for that received from the claimant it is not clear why the defence should succeed, since the defendant has retained the value of the benefit so that he or she has not necessarily suffered any detriment.[136] It is surely detriment suffered by the defendant which makes it inequitable for the defendant to make full or any restitution.[137] So, for example, where, as occurred in *Scottish Equitable plc v Derby*,[138] the defendant has used the money which he or she had received to discharge an existing debt which he or she would have had to pay anyway, the defence will usually not be available because the defendant has not suffered any detriment and remains enriched.[139] Similarly, where money has been used to purchase an item of value, the defendant remains enriched to the extent of the value of that item.[140]

(c) Fall in Value of the Benefit

If the defendant receives an asset from the claimant, or receives money which the defendant uses to purchase an asset, and the value of that asset falls, the defence should

---

[133] *Rose v AIB Group (UK) plc* [2003] EWHC (Ch) 1737, [2003] 1 WLR 2791, 2806 (Nicholas Warren QC); *MacDonald v Coys of Kensington (Sales) Ltd* [2004] EWCA Civ 47, [2004] 1 WLR 2775.

[134] See *Campden Hill Ltd v Chakrani* [2005] EWHC 911 (Ch), [87] (Hart J). The second test of causation, namely detrimental reliance on the validity of the receipt of the benefit, may be applicable instead. See p 686, below.   [135] (1994) 111 DLR (4th) 230.

[136] Bant, *The Change of Position Defence*, 134, considers this to be an example of an irreversible change of position because the defendant could not easily find equivalent secondhand furniture.

[137] See p 690, below.   [138] [2001] 3 All ER 818.

[139] See also *National Bank of Egypt International Ltd v Oman Housing Bank SAOC* [2002] EWHC 1760 (Comm), [2003] 1 All ER (Comm) 246; *Crédit Suisse (Monaco) SA v Attar* [2004] EWHC 374 (Comm). Although Robert Walker LJ did acknowledge in *Scottish Equitable plc v Derby* that paying off a debt might be detrimental if the loan which was discharged was on advantageous terms: [2001] 3 All ER 818, [35].

[140] *Barros Mattos Jnr v MacDaniels Ltd* [2004] EWHC 1188 (Ch), [2005] 1 WLR 247, [17]. See also *Crédit Suisse (Monaco) SA v Attar* [2004] EWHC 374 (Comm), [98].

be applicable to the extent that the value has fallen.[141] That the defence of change of position may operate in this way is probably illustrated by the decision of the Court of Appeal in *Cheese v Thomas*,[142] where the claimant and the defendant had jointly contributed to the purchase of a house. This transaction was set aside on the ground of undue influence, and the question before the court related to how the relief should be determined in the light of the fact that the value of the house had fallen. It was held that this loss in value should be borne by both parties in proportion to their respective contributions to the purchase of the house. Although the court justified this loss apportionment by reference to an inherent equitable discretion to do practical justice, Chen-Wishart[143] has argued that the result is consistent with the application of change of position, because, although the defendant was unjustly enriched by the receipt of money from the claimant, this was 'reduced by the subsequent loss to the value of the house in the recession'.[144] Consequently, the result of *Cheese v Thomas* suggests that the change of position defence may be applicable even where the value of the enrichment received from the defendant has fallen, but, as always, this will only be the case if it is equitable for the defendant to rely on the defence.

(d) The Change of Position Must Be Extraordinary

Although it appears that the causation test is easily established where the defendant no longer has the benefit which he or she received from the claimant, this is not the case. There is an additional requirement which also needs to be considered before causation is established, namely that the loss of the benefit did not occur in the ordinary course of events; the loss must be extraordinary. The reason for this requirement is illustrated by the following example. If the defendant received a sum of money by mistake from the claimant and the defendant used this money to defray ordinary living expenses, it is not possible to conclude that, but for the receipt of the money, the expense would not have been incurred, since if the money had not been received the defendant would have paid the expenses from his or her existing resources.[145] Consequently, in such circumstances the test of causation can only be satisfied where the expenditure is extraordinary. This requirement was specifically recognized by Lord Goff in *Lipkin Gorman*.[146] It follows that the defence will only be available in exceptional cases.[147]

In *Test Claimants in the FII Group Litigation v HMRC (No 2)*[148] Henderson J recognized that an extraordinary change of position does not require proof that the change of position was unusual, either intrinsically or for the particular defendant. It is sufficient that the change of position would not have been incurred but for the receipt of the enrichment. In other words, the language of extraordinariness simply embodies a test of but for causation. Consequently, increased expenditure of a routine nature can count, as long as it can be shown that the expenditure would not have been incurred but for the receipt of the enrichment.

The defendant's change of position will clearly be considered to be extraordinary where he or she no longer has the benefit for reasons outside his or her control. So, if the benefit

---

[141] See *Lipkin Gorman (a firm) v Karpnale Ltd* [1991] 2 AC 548, 560 (Lord Templeman).

[142] [1994] 1 WLR 129. See p 267, above.

[143] M Chen-Wishart, 'Loss Sharing, Undue Influence and Manifest Disadvantage' (1994) 110 LQR 173.

[144] Ibid, 178.

[145] *Barros Mattos Jnr v MacDaniels Ltd* [2004] EWHC 1188 (Ch), [2005] 1 WLR 247, [16] (Laddie J).

[146] [1991] 2 AC 548, 580. See also *Westminster Bank plc v Somer* [2002] 1 All ER 198, 213 (Potter LJ); *Barons Finance Ltd v Kensington Mortgage Co Ltd* [2011] EWCA Civ 1592, [28] (Tomlinson LJ).

[147] *Lipkin Gorman (a firm) v Karpnale Ltd* [1991] 2 AC 548, 580.

[148] [2014] EWHC 4302 (Ch), [353].

has been stolen or destroyed, the change of position should always be considered to be extraordinary. The test of extraordinary change of position will be most relevant where the benefit is money and the defendant has spent it. In such a situation the defendant's expenditure will be extraordinary where, for example, he or she engaged in a special project or undertook a special financial commitment as a result of the receipt of the benefit from the claimant.[149]

The test of extraordinary change of position is assessed by reference to changes in the defendant's particular circumstances. It follows that if the defendant uses money received from the claimant on normal living expenses this can still be considered to be extraordinary expenditure if the defendant would not have incurred the expense but for the receipt of the money from the claimant. A similar test is adopted in respect of the defence of estoppel, as was seen in *Avon County Council v Howlett*,[150] where the defence was established even though the defendant had spent money on everyday items, because he would not have purchased them if he had not received the money. That a similar approach can be adopted in respect of the defence of change of position is illustrated by the decision of the Newfoundland Court of Appeal in *RBC Dominion Securities Inc v Dawson*,[151] in which the defence applied to the extent that the defendant had used the money received from the claimant on clothes and furnishings which she had bought or refurbished only because she would not have done so if the money had not been received.

(e) Acquisition of a Cause of Action Against a Third Party

Where the consequence of the defendant's change of position is that he or she acquires a cause of action against a third party, can the defendant really be considered to have suffered detriment?[152] For example, if the claimant pays £1,000 to the defendant by mistake and this money is stolen by a thief, it might be concluded that the defendant's position has not changed because he or she has a restitutionary claim against the thief to recover the money. If the defendant has actually recovered the money from the thief it is obvious that the defendant's position has not detrimentally changed. But this is the easy case. What if the claimant sued the defendant for restitution before the defendant had sued the third party? Should the fact that the defendant has a potential claim against the third party mean that his or her position has not changed? Since the success of the defendant's claim is speculative, the preferable view is that the defendant should still be considered to have suffered a detrimental change of position, so that he or she will not be required to make restitution to the claimant.[153] The claimant may, however, seek the remedy of subrogation whereby the defendant's cause of action against the third party can be vested in the claimant.[154] If this remedy were not awarded the defendant could be unjustly enriched at the claimant's expense if the defendant did eventually recover the money from the third party. The consequence of this analysis is that the claimant ultimately bears the risk of the defendant losing the enrichment and being unable to recover it from the third party.

(2) The Detrimental Reliance Test of Causation

(a) The Basic Test

The alternative test of causation is satisfied where, even though the defendant has retained the particular benefit which he or she received from the claimant, the defendant relied on

---

[149] *Rural Municipality of Storthoaks v Mobil Oil Canada Ltd* (1975) 55 DLR (3d) 1, 13 (Martland J).
[150] [1983] 1 WLR 605. See p 670, above.   [151] (1994) 111 DLR (4th) 230.
[152] Nolan, 'Change of Position', 170–2.
[153] At least where there are significant practical or legal hurdles in pursuing the claim: Bant, *The Change of Position Defence*, 142.   [154] Nolan, 'Change of Position', 172. See p 20, above.

the validity of the receipt of the benefit and suffered detriment in other ways. For example, if the defendant received £1,000 by mistake and paid this money into a bank account, and, as a result of this receipt, sold some shares and used the proceeds to pay for a holiday, the defence should be available since, but for the receipt, the defendant's position would not have changed. Although the defendant will presumably have enjoyed the holiday, this can be considered to be a detrimental change of position because he or she has lost value by relying on the validity of the receipt and so can be considered to be no longer enriched to the extent of that value.

This test of causation has been recognized in some jurisdictions,[155] and it was effectively adopted in *Lipkin Gorman*,[156] where a thief had stolen money from the claimant and gambled with it at the defendant's casino. The defendant was considered to have changed its position by paying winnings to the thief. The detrimental reliance test of causation had been satisfied because, but for the defendant's belief that the thief was entitled to gamble with the money, it would not have paid the winnings to the thief.

In *Scottish Equitable plc v Derby*[157] Robert Walker LJ identified a number of situations where the necessary detriment could be identified. For example, where the defendant voluntarily gives up employment as a result of receiving a mistaken payment, at an age when it would not be easy to get new employment. Or where the defendant enters into a long-term financial commitment, such as a ten-year lease, which is not easy to dispose.

Usually the defendant's change of position will take the form of the defendant incurring expenditure as a result of the receipt of a benefit from the claimant. But the defendant's position may change in other ways. For example, the defendant may have received money from the claimant in the mistaken belief that the claimant owed him or her the money, whereas it was actually owed to the defendant by a third party. If the defendant relied on the validity of the receipt from the claimant and did not discover that the money was owed by the third party until the statutory limitation period had passed, the defendant's position will have changed, since he or she cannot recover the money from the third party. Consequently, if the claimant seeks restitution of the money from the defendant he or she should be able to rely on the defence of change of position.[158] In *Australian Financial Services and Leasing Pty Ltd v Hills Industries Ltd*[159] the High Court of Australia recognized that the defence was available where the defendant had relied on the receipt and suffered an irreversible detriment, which was established in that case where the defendant had decided not to pursue claims against the claimant following the receipt of a mistaken payment.

(b) General Hardship is Not Sufficient

It is not sufficient to satisfy this test of causation that the defendant suffered general hardship after receiving the benefit from the claimant, where the hardship does not relate to the receipt of that benefit. For example, if the defendant received £1,000 from

---

[155] See, for example, the New Zealand Judicature Act 1908, s 94B as amended. Proof of reliance on the validity of the receipt is also required in Canada (*Rural Municipality of Storthoaks v Mobil Oil Canada Ltd* (1975) 55 DLR (3d) 1, 13 (Martland J)), and Australia (*David Security Pty Ltd v Commonwealth Bank of Australia* (1992) 175 CLR 353, 385 and *Australian Financial Services and Leasing Pty Ltd v Hills Industries Ltd* [2014] HCA 14).

[156] [1991] 2 AC 548.   [157] [2001] 3 All ER 818, 827.

[158] Cf *Durrant v The Ecclesiastical Commissioners for England and Wales* (1880) 6 QBD 234 where the defence of change of position was rejected in such circumstances. If these facts arose today the defence should be available to the defendant.   [159] [2014] HCA 14.

the claimant by mistake and a month later the defendant was made redundant or was the victim of a burglary,[160] it will not be possible to establish change of position because the change in the defendant's circumstances is unrelated to the receipt of the enrichment from the claimant. There is no causal connection between the receipt of the benefit and the detriment suffered by the claimant.

(c) The Relevance of an Extraordinary Change of Position

Although Lord Goff suggested in *Lipkin Gorman*[161] that the defence could be established only where the defendant's change of position was extraordinary, this should be considered to be a requirement only where the defendant relies on the first test of causation. Where he or she relies on the detrimental reliance test of causation it should not be necessary to show that the defendant's change of position was extraordinary, simply because the defendant may be able to prove that he or she detrimentally relied on the validity of the receipt of the benefit even though the change was not extraordinary. Nevertheless, the fact that the change of position was extraordinary will make it much easier for the defendant to show that but for the receipt of the benefit the defendant's position would not have changed. It follows that the extraordinary nature of the defendant's change of position is a factor which suggests detrimental reliance, but should not be treated as a requirement in its own right.[162]

(d) Non-Pecuniary Change of Position

In *Commerzbank AG v Gareth Price-Jones*[163] the Court of Appeal recognized that a non-pecuniary change of position might be sufficient to establish the defence. In that case the defendant's change of position in staying in his job, rather than seeking more lucrative employment elsewhere, was not considered to be sufficient for it to be inequitable to require him to make restitution of £250,000 which his employer had paid by mistake. This was because there was no relevant connection between the anticipated receipt of money and the decision to stay in his job and that decision did not have a 'significant, precise or substantial adverse impact' on the defendant.[164] But the Court would have been willing to allow the defence to succeed if this connection could have been established on the facts. Although this conclusion might appear to undermine one of the essential characteristics of the defence, namely that it operates only to the extent that the defendant can be considered to have lost the value of the enrichment, this is not the case. A non-pecuniary change of position can only be taken into account if it can be valued in some way and so a non-pecuniary change of position can be converted into a pecuniary one. So, for example, if a defendant has turned down a firm offer of a better paid job elsewhere as a direct result of receiving a payment from his or her present employer, albeit a payment received by mistake, this is a detriment which can be valued and, to that extent, the defendant will have changed his or her position. In fact, this analysis is inevitable since a change of position can only be taken into account by identifying the value of a detriment and then using that value to reduce or negate the value of the enrichment received. It follows that if the 'non-pecuniary' change of position cannot be valued, it cannot be taken into account

---

[160] Where the £1,000 itself is stolen in the burglary the defendant will satisfy the first test of causation since he or she no longer has the benefit. See p 683, above.

[161] [1991] 2 AC 548, 580. See also *David Securities v Commonwealth Bank of Australia* (1992) 175 CLR 353, 386.   [162] Nolan, 'Change of Position', 62.

[163] [2003] EWCA Civ 1663, [2004] 1 P & CRD 15.   [164] Ibid, [44] (Mummery LJ).

as a sufficient detriment. So, if, for example, the defendant decides to start a family[165] as the result of receiving a mistaken payment of £100,000, the value of this 'detriment' is surely so speculative that it cannot be considered to be relevant.

(e) Anticipatory Expenditure

In *South Tyneside Metropolitan BC v Svenska International plc*[166] Clarke J held that, at least on the facts of that case, the defence was not available where the defendant had changed its position before receiving an enrichment. In *Svenska* the defendant bank had entered into an *ultra vires* swap transaction with the claimant local authority. The bank had also entered into hedging transactions to reduce substantially its potential liability to the local authority under the swap transactions. Since the swaps transactions were void the claimant sought restitution of its money and the defendant pleaded change of position on the ground that, in reliance on the validity of the swaps transactions, it had incurred losses by entering into the hedging transactions. Clarke J held[167] that the defence was not available because the swaps transaction was void. This was significant because, had the defendant received the enrichment before changing its position, it would be possible to conclude that the defendant had relied on the validity of the receipt. But where the change of position occurred before the enrichment had been received, the defendant could not rely on the validity of the receipt and could only rely on the validity of the transaction and, since the transaction was null and void, the defendant's reliance was a nullity.

It remained a matter of some controversy whether the decision in *Svenska* was confined to the peculiar facts of the case or was of general application. The Privy Council in *Dextra Bank and Trust Co v Bank of Jamaica*[168] subsequently concluded that, although the decision may be doubted, it is at the very least confined to its special facts, so that the defence of change of position may be applicable in respect of anticipated reliance. The Privy Council noted that the main justification for distinguishing between change of position before and after the receipt of a benefit is that 'whereas change of position on the faith of an actual receipt should be protected because of the importance of upholding the security of receipts, the same is not true of a change of position in reliance on an expected payment, which does not merit protection beyond that conferred by the law of contract (including promissory estoppel)'. Their Lordships did not, however, find such reasoning to be convincing. They said:[169]

> it is difficult to see what relevant distinction can be drawn between (1) a case in which the defendant expends on some extraordinary expenditure all or part of a sum of money which he has received from the plaintiff, and (2) one in which the defendant incurs such expenditure in the expectation that he will receive the sum of money from the plaintiff, which he does in fact receive. Since *ex hypothesi* the defendant will in fact have received the expected payment, there is no question of the defendant using the defence of change of position to enforce, directly or indirectly, a claim to that money. It is surely no abuse of language to say, in the second case as in the first, that the defendant has incurred the expenditure in reliance on the plaintiff's payment or, as is sometimes said, on the faith of the payment.

This approach has since been endorsed by the Court of Appeal in *Commerzbank AG v Gareth Price-Jones*.[170] The approach of the Privy Council is essentially consistent with that

---

[165] To use an example suggested by Birks, *Unjust Enrichment* (2nd edn), 260.
[166] [1995] 1 All ER 545.   [167] Ibid, 565.
[168] [2001] UKPC 50, [2002] 1 All ER (Comm) 193.   [169] Ibid, [38].
[170] [2003] EWCA Civ 1663, [2004] 1 P & CRD 15, [38] (Mummery LJ), and [64] (Munby J). See also *Charles Terence Estates Ltd v Cornwall County Council* [2011] EWHC 2542 (QB), [98] (Cranston J).

of the Court of Appeal in *Scottish Equitable plc v Derby*.[171] If the emphasis should now be placed on causation, it should make no difference whether the defendant's position changed either before or after the enrichment was received. If the position changed before the receipt, the defendant will need to establish that he or she relied on the possibility of a future receipt to change his or her position. True, such a defendant is taking a risk that he or she might not receive the enrichment, but, as the Privy Council acknowledged, the defence will only be available anyway where the enrichment has been received, for otherwise there will be no basis for the claimant to bring a restitutionary claim.[172]

(f) The Standard of Proof

In *Philip Collins Ltd v Davis*[173] Jonathan Parker J recognized that the evidential burden was placed on the defendant to establish the change of position, but he also recognized that the court should not apply too strict a standard of proof. In particular, it might not be appropriate to expect the defendant to produce conclusive evidence of his or her change of position, since the defendant would not have had any expectation of the need to prove this in court. In that case the claimant company had mistakenly overpaid royalties to the defendants, who were professional musicians. The question arose as to whether the defendants could rely on the defence of change of position. They were unable to show that any particular item of their expenditure was referable directly to the receipt of the royalties, but the judge did not consider this to be fatal on the facts of the case, because the approach of the defendants was to gear their outgoings to the income they received, and, because the royalties were received periodically, it was possible to conclude that the overpayments had caused a general change of position.

This was confirmed by the Court of Appeal in *Scottish Equitable plc v Derby*,[174] which emphasized that it was not appropriate to impose too demanding a standard of proof when an honest defendant stated that he or she had spent an overpayment on improving his or her lifestyle, but was unable to produce detailed accounts to establish how this lifestyle was improved.[175] The Court emphasized that the defence was not limited to specific identifiable items of expenditure.[176] In the context of claims for restitution against public authorities,[177] it has been recognized that, in respect of government expenditure, it is not necessary to show a precise link between particular receipt and particular items of expenditure.[178]

(ii) Whether it is Inequitable to Make Restitution

Once it has been shown that, but for the receipt of the benefit from the claimant the defendant's position would not have changed, it must then be shown that the particular circumstances of the change of position are such that it would be inequitable to require the defendant to make full, or even any, restitution to the claimant. Whilst equitable considerations of fairness and justice may appear to make the defence unnecessarily uncertain and unprincipled, and is inconsistent with Lord Goff's dictum that where restitution is denied 'it is denied on the basis of legal principles',[179] a number of factors can be identified

---

[171] [2001] 3 All ER 818.

[172] Bant, *The Change of Position Defence*, 156, defends anticipatory change of position by virtue of practice and policy.

[173] [2000] 3 All ER 808.   [174] [2001] 3 All ER 818.

[175] Ibid, 827 (Robert Walker LJ).   [176] Ibid.   [177] See p 410, above.

[178] *Bloomsbury International Ltd v Sea Fish Industry Authority* [2009] EWHC 1721 (QB), [2010] 1 CMLR 12, [137] (Hamblen J); *Test Claimants in the FII Group Litigation v HMRC (No 2)* [2014] EWHC 4302 (Ch), [356] (Henderson J).

[179] *Lipkin Gorman (a firm) v Karpnale Ltd* [1991] 2 AC 548, 578.

to assist in the determination of whether the defendant's change of position is such as to make restitution inequitable. It must be emphasized that the notion of what is equitable needs to be clearly ascertained. It is not acceptable for the defendant to argue that he or she should not make restitution simply because he or she suffered from some particular hardship, such as illness or disability. This is catered for by the requirement that the defence can only arise if the causation test is first satisfied. Notions of injustice then operate to restrict the application of the defence.

(1) Bad Faith

Lord Goff expressly recognized in *Lipkin Gorman* that a defendant will not be able to rely on the defence if he or she acted in bad faith.[180] It is clear that the defendant will have acted in bad faith where he or she changed his or her position knowing of the facts which entitle the claimant to restitution.[181] Similarly, the defence should be unavailable if the defendant knew that there was a risk, albeit small, that he or she was not entitled to the enrichment.[182] But it does not follow automatically that knowledge of the claim will disable the defendant from relying on the defence. Where the enrichment was lost or destroyed without conscious decision by the defendant, there is no obvious reason why the defence should be denied to him or her. Where, however, the defendant has received money and knows that the money has been paid by mistake, but still changes his or her position in reliance on the receipt, the defendant took the risk that he or she will be required to make restitution and should not be able to plead change of position. Indeed, the defendant cannot be said to have relied on the validity of the receipt in changing his or her position if the defendant knew that the payment has been received by mistake.[183]

It is also clear that bad faith does not include negligence.[184] Further clarification of the meaning of bad faith was provided by Moore-Bick J in *Niru Battery Manufacturing Co v Milestone Trading Ltd*[185] who held that it includes, but is not confined to, dishonesty. It also includes 'a failure to act in a commercially acceptable way and sharp practice that falls short of outright dishonesty'.[186] This embodies a notion of objective dishonesty,[187] since Moore-Bick J's reference to commercially acceptable conduct and sharp practice suggests an objective standard which does not have regard to the defendant's perceptions of what

---

[180] Ibid, 580. Bant, *The Change of Position Defence*, 151, considers that a test of reasonable reliance on the receipt of the enrichment embodies the notion of a good faith change of position, although she considers that, where the defendant's conduct is a factor in inducing the claimant's decision to transfer the enrichment, the defence should be barred: 184.

[181] See *McDonald v Coys of Kensington* [2004] EWCA Civ 47, [2004] 1 WLR 2775, 2792 (Mance LJ).

[182] *South Tyneside MBC v Svenska International plc* [1995] 1 All ER 545, 569 (Clark J). See also *Jones v Churcher* [2009] EWHC 722 (QB), [2009] 2 Lloyd's Rep 94; *Barclays Bank plc v Kalamohan* [2010] EWHC 1383 (Ch), [75] (Proudman J).

[183] J Palmer, 'Chasing a Will-o'-the-Wisp? Making Sense of Bad Faith and Wrongdoers in Change of Position' [2005] 13 RLR 53.

[184] *Dextra Bank & Trust Company Ltd v Bank of Jamaica* [2001] UKPC 50, [2002] 1 All ER (Comm) 193; *Niru Battery Manufacturing Co v Milestone Trading Ltd* [2002] EWHC 1425 (Comm), [2002] 2 All ER (Comm) 705, 738; *Papamichael v National Westminster Bank plc* [2003] 1 Lloyd's Rep 341, 368; *Maersk Air Ltd v Expeditors International (UK) Ltd* [2003] 1 Lloyd's Rep 491, 499; *Armstrong DLW GmbH v Winnington Networks Ltd* [2012] EWHC 10 (Ch), [2013] Ch 156, [110] (Stephen Morris QC); *Jeremy D Stone Consultants Ltd v National Westminster Bank* [2013] EWHC 208 (Ch), [247] (Sales J).

[185] [2002] EWHC 1425 (Comm), [2002] 2 All ER (Comm) 705.

[186] Ibid, 741. In *Challinor v Bellis* [2015] EWCA Civ 58, [116] Briggs LJ considered that conduct can only be considered to be commercially unacceptable as regards the claimant and cannot include conduct about which the claimant cannot complain.

[187] See Birks, *Unjust Enrichment* (2nd edn), 215.

that standard is. The Court of Appeal in *Niru Battery*[188] purported to approve the approach of the trial judge, but used the language of unconscionability instead. In the light of the developments concerning the interpretation of unconscionability for purposes of the claim for unconscionable receipt,[189] and because cases on bad faith in change of position have been applied by the courts when interpreting unconscionability for that claim and vice-versa,[190] the preferable interpretation of bad faith for the defence of change of position is whether the reasonable person would consider the defendant's conduct to be dishonest[191] with regard to the facts known or suspected by the defendant.[192] That would be consistent with the equitable restraint on the operation of change of position and how conscience and unconscionability is interpreted in Equity. This will include a defendant who changes his or her position in circumstances where he or she has good reason to believe that there are facts which enable the claimant to claim restitution, such as that money was paid by mistake, and does not make inquiries of the payer.[193] But it has been recognized that the defendant would not be acting in bad faith if he or she failed to make inquiries which a reasonable person would have realized should be made, if the defendant did not suspect that there were reasons why the claimant might have a claim for restitution.[194] A more objective interpretation of bad faith was, however, applied in *Harrison v Madesjski and Coys of Kensington*,[195] where it was held that the defence of change of position was not available when the defendant had paid £130,000 for a car which included a Cherished Mark which should not have been included in the sale, because no reasonable buyer would have concluded that the Mark was included in the sale. The purchaser was considered to have been blind to what should have been obvious to him. It followed that there was nothing inequitable about ordering the purchaser to make restitution of the unjust enrichment which had been received.

(2) Wrongdoing

In *Lipkin Gorman*[196] Lord Goff stated that 'it is commonly accepted that the defence should not be available to a wrongdoer'. It is not clear from this whether Lord Goff accepted this 'common' view, especially when this dictum was followed by the statement that such matters can 'be considered in depth in cases where they arise for consideration'. Is a wrongdoer anybody who commits a wrong, so that there is no scope for the application of the defence in any restitutionary claim brought against a wrongdoer, or can we distinguish between degrees of wrongdoing? If we can, perhaps the defence should

---

[188] *Niru Battery Manufacturing Co v Milestone Trading Ltd* [2003] EWCA 1446 (Civ), [2004] QB 985. See also *Abou-Rahmah v Abacha* [2006] EWCA Civ 1492, [2007] 1 All ER (Comm) 827.

[189] See p 648, above.

[190] *Abou-Rahmah v Abacha* [2006] EWCA Civ 1492, [2007] 1 All ER (Comm) 827. See also *Armstrong DLW GmbH v Winnington Networks Ltd* [2012] EWHC 10 (Ch), [2013] Ch 156, [132] (Stephen Morris QC).

[191] The language of dishonesty was preferred to that of unconscionability for the receipt-based claim by Lord Millett in *Dubai Aluminium Co Ltd v Salaam* [2002] UKHL 48, [2003] 2 AC 366, 391. See also *Williams v Central Bank of Nigeria* [2014] UKSC 10, [2014] AC 1189, [64] (Lord Neuberger).

[192] In *Papamichael v National Westminster Bank* [2003] Lloyd's Rep 341, 368 Judge Chambers QC described this as 'wilfully and recklessly failing to make such inquiries as an honest and reasonable person would make'. See also the test of dishonesty as now defined for the action of dishonestly assisting a breach of trust or fiduciary duty: see p 522, above.

[193] *Armstrong DLW GmbH v Winnington Networks Ltd* [2012] EWHC 10 (Ch), [2013] Ch 156, [108] (Stephen Morris QC).   [194] Ibid, [110].

[195] [2014] EWCA Civ 361, [61]. See p 71, above. See also *Jones v Churcher* [2009] EWHC 722 (QB), [2009] 2 Lloyd's Rep 94, [46] (Havelock Allan QC).

[196] *Lipkin Gorman (a firm) v Karpnale Ltd* [1991] 2 AC 548, 580.

be available for an innocent wrongdoer.[197] Perhaps, Lord Goff's explicit reliance on the notion of bad faith enables us to distinguish between different degrees of wrongdoer. Indeed, there is *obiter dicta* which indicates that the defence might be available to a claim grounded on the tort of conversion, which does not require proof of fault.[198] Further, in *Jeremy D Stone Consultants Ltd v National Westminster Bank*[199] Sales J recognized that the commission of a strict liability regulatory failure was insufficiently grave to debar a defendant from relying on the defence. In *Cavenagh Investment Pte Ltd v Rajiv*[200] Chan Seng Onn J of the Singapore High Court recognized that the defence should only be unavailable where the rationale of the defence cannot outweigh the policy for remedying the wrong. It was held as a consequence that the defence should be available where the restitutionary claim related to trespass to land.

Wrongdoing has also been interpreted in a much vaguer way in respect of claims for restitution from public authorities, where the defence of change of position has been held to be unavailable to a public authority if the claim is grounded on the public law *Woolwich* ground,[201] which is founded on the unlawful levying of tax. This has been considered to be a legal wrong so that the Revenue is a wrongdoer in receiving the tax. But it is not obvious that the receipt of tax in such circumstances necessarily involves the commission of a wrong, as has now been recognized by Henderson J in *Test Claimants in the FII Group Litigation v HMRC (No 2)*.[202] Rather, he considered that the defence of change of position is unavailable to a public authority where the *Woolwich* ground of restitution is engaged, because the policy in favour of restitution where the receipt is *ultra vires* the defendant public authority outweighs the policy against restitution where the defendant has changed its position.

The wrongdoing bar to the change of position defence was expanded in *Barros Mattos Jnr v MacDaniels*,[203] where Laddie J concluded (without explicitly acknowledging that he was elaborating Lord Goff's test in *Lipkin Gorman*) that the defence is barred where the change of position, albeit innocent, was illegal.[204] But this is not what Lord Goff said. His reference to wrongdoing was concerned with the characterization of the defendant as a wrongdoer, rather than the nature of the change of position as such.[205] But Laddie J's conclusion is consistent with the principle of public policy that it is not possible to found a cause of action on an immoral or illegal act.[206] Whilst that principle is usually employed to prevent the claimant from relying on an illegal act to establish a claim, as it is a principle of policy[207] there is no reason why that policy should not prevent the defendant from relying on a defence where the defendant needs to rely on an illegal act to establish it. The only

---

[197] See AS Burrows, 'Quadrating Restitution and Unjust Enrichment: A Matter of Principle?' [2000] RLR 257, 264. See also Nolan, 'Change of Position', 154.

[198] *Kuwait Airways Corpn v Iraqi Airways Co (Nos 4 and 5)* [2002] 2 AC 883, 1093 (Lord Nicholls).

[199] [2013] EWHC 208 (Ch), [251].   [200] [2013] SGHC 45, [2013] 2 SLR 543.

[201] *Test Claimants in the FII Group Litigation v HMRC* [2008] EWHC 2893 (Ch), [2009] STC 254, [339]. This point was not considered by the Court of Appeal: [2010] EWCA Civ 103, [2010] STC 1251, nor the Supreme Court: [2012] UKSC 19. See also *Littlewoods Retail Ltd v Commissioners for Her Majesty's Revenue and Customs* [2010] EWHC 1071 (Ch), [2010] STC 2072, [105] (Vos J).

[202] [2014] EWHC 4302 (Ch). See p 410, above.

[203] [2004] EWHC 1188 (Ch), [2005] 1 WLR 247. See also *O'Neil v Gale* [2013] EWCA Civ 1554.

[204] The question of illegality did not arise in *Lipkin Gorman* itself, because the change of position related to a gambling transaction which was unenforceable rather than illegal. In *Barros Mattos* the change of position arose from a foreign currency exchange which was illegal by Nigerian law.

[205] See *O'Neil v Gale* [2013] EWHC 644 (Ch), [68] (David Donaldson QC).

[206] See *Holman v Johnson* (1775) 1 Cowp 341, 343 (Lord Mansfield); *Tinsley v Milligan* [1994] 1 AC 340, 355 (Lord Goff). See p 709, below.   [207] *Tinsley v Milligan* [1994] 1 AC 340.

qualification to this policy will arise, as Laddie J recognized, where the nature of the illegality can be regarded as so minor that it can be dismissed.[208]

It seems, therefore, that wrongdoing should now be interpreted in two distinct ways. The first interpretation concerns the identification of the defendant as a wrongdoer. This should be interpreted restrictively by reference to a very clear policy that the wrongdoer should be prevented from relying on the defence. Secondly, where the circumstances of the change of position itself constitutes a wrong.

(3) Relative Fault of the Parties

In *Dextra Bank and Trust Co v Bank of Jamaica*[209] the Privy Council considered the relevance of both parties' fault to the operation of the defence. The defendant had argued that it was necessary to balance the respective fault of both parties because the object of the defence is to balance the equity of the party deprived of an enrichment with that of the party enriched. The Privy Council acknowledged that, if fault was to be taken into account at all, it would be unjust to take into account the fault of the defendant and ignore the fault of the claimant. Indeed, the relative fault of the parties can be considered in some jurisdictions.[210] But despite this, their Lordships concluded that the consideration of the relative fault of the parties was not relevant to the defence of change of position.[211] They confirmed that fault on the part of the recipient remained relevant, but the fault of the claimant was not. In reaching this conclusion they were clearly influenced by the fact that, for restitutionary claims involving mistake, the negligence of the claimant has not been considered to be a matter of significance for a very long time.[212]

The rejection of this notion of relative fault is a significant development. However, in *Commerzbank AG v Gareth Price-Jones*[213] Munby J, whilst acknowledging that relative fault was irrelevant, was clearly influenced by the fact that the defendant changed his position as a result of his own negligent mistake, which was not shared or induced by the claimant, in reaching his conclusion that it was not equitable to allow the defendant to rely on the defence.[214]

(4) Risk Allocation

The question of risk allocation may also be pertinent to the determination of the operation of the defence. If it can be concluded that the claimant should take the risk of any detrimental change in the defendant's position, this suggests that the defence should succeed. Alternatively, if the defendant can be considered to have taken the risk, this would suggest that the defence should fail.[215]

---

[208] *Barros Mattos Jnr v MacDaniels Ltd* [2004] EWHC 1188 (Ch), [2005] 1 WLR 247, [43].

[209] [2001] UKPC 50, [2002] 1 All ER (Comm) 193.

[210] In New Zealand, see the Judicature Act 1908, s 94B. This provision was considered in *Thomas v Houston Corbett and Co* [1969] NZLR 151. Now see *Saunders and Co (a firm) v Hague* [2004] 2 NZLR 475, 493 (Chisholm J). See also *Westdeutsche Landesbank Girozentrale v Islington LBC* [1994] 4 All ER 890, 905 (Hobhouse J).

[211] See the criticism of the weighing of the relative fault of the parties by PBH Birks, 'Change of Position and Surviving Enrichment' in WJ Swadling (ed), *The Limits of Restitutionary Claims: A Comparative Analysis* (London: UKNNCL, 1997), 41.

[212] *Kelly v Solari* (1841) 9 M and W 54, 59; 152 ER 24 (Parke B). See p 179, above.

[213] [2003] EWCA Civ 1663, [2004] 1 P & CRD 15.

[214] See also *Niru Battery Manufacturing Co v Milestone Trading Ltd (No 2)* [2004] EWCA Civ 487, [33] (Clarke LJ).

[215] *South Tyneside Metropolitan BC v Svenksa International plc* [1995] 1 All ER 545, 569 (Clarke J).

The importance of risk allocation is illustrated by *Goss v Chilcott*[216] where the defendants were held liable to repay a loan to the claimant on the ground of total failure of basis. When the defendants had first received the loan they lent it to a third party in a separate transaction and were unable subsequently to obtain repayment from that party. The defendants therefore pleaded the change of position defence to defeat the restitutionary claim. The Privy Council rejected this defence, primarily because the defendants knew throughout that they were liable to repay the loan and in lending the money to the third party they deliberately took a risk that he would be unable to repay them. Essentially what the defendants were doing was seeking to shift their loss to the claimant and, if they had been allowed to do this, it would have been unjust to the claimant, because the defendants had voluntarily taken the risk that they would lose their money.

Similarly, in *Haugesund Kommune v Depfa ACS Bank*[217] the claimant bank had lent money to Norwegian public authorities in circumstances where the authorities lacked the capacity to borrow the money. A claim in unjust enrichment was recognized on the ground of failure of basis.[218] The defendant public authorities pleaded change of position since they had suffered losses following investment of the money they had borrowed. The defence was held not to be available because the defendants knew at the time of receipt that the loans would need to be repaid, and they had taken the risk that they would not be able to do so. As all investors know, the value of investments may go down as well as up and the former cannot constitute a change of position.

(C) THE APPLICATION OF THE DEFENCE

In *Lipkin Gorman* Lord Goff recognized that it was not appropriate in that case 'to identify all those actions in restitution to which change of position may be a defence'.[219] Consequently, the application of the defence needs to be considered in respect of each part of the law of restitution.

(i) Claims Founded on the Reversal of the Defendant's Unjust Enrichment

Clearly the defence is applicable to founded on unjust enrichment.[220] The operation of the defence to particular types of claim may, however, differ. For example, some grounds of restitution depend on proof, either actual or presumed, of the defendant's unconscionable conduct and this may be sufficient to prevent the defendant from relying on the defence, since this will constitute evidence of bad faith.[221] Further, the defence will not be available in respect of many claims involving restitution from public authorities, particularly where the receipt of taxes was unlawful by EU law[222] or where the claim is grounded on the *Woolwich* principle.[223]

(ii) Restitution for Wrongs

Lord Goff in *Lipkin Gorman* specifically recognized that the defence was not open to a wrongdoer,[224] which might indicate that the defence is not available to any claim

---

[216] [1996] AC 788.   [217] [2010] EWCA Civ 579, [2012] QB 549.   [218] See p 375, above.

[219] *Lipkin Gorman (a firm) v Karpnale* [1991] 2 AC 548, 580.

[220] As recognized in *Lipkin Gorman (a firm) v Karpnale* [1991] 2 AC 548 itself.

[221] See M Chen-Wishart, 'Unjust Factors and the Restitutionary Response' (2000) OJLS 557.

[222] *Prudential Assurance Co Ltd v HMRC* [2013] EWHC 3249 (Ch), [2014] 2 CMLR 10, [188] (Henderson J). See further p 409, above.

[223] *Test Claimants in the FII Group Litigation v HMRC* [2014] EWHC 4302 (Ch), [2014] EWHC 4302 (Ch). See p 693, above.

[224] *Lipkin Gorman (a firm) v Karpnale* [1991] 2 AC 548, 580.

grounded on restitution for wrongs. But the defence should not automatically be denied to the defendant just because he or she committed a wrong, because the unlawfulness of wrongs varies a great deal.[225] The defence should be denied only where the defendant's wrongdoing can be treated as equivalent to acting in bad faith. Clearly, therefore, if the defendant is a thief or is a fiduciary who has accepted a bribe, the defence should be denied to him or her, particularly because such a wrongdoer was acting in bad faith. But on the other hand a confidant who unwittingly betrayed a confidence should not be treated as having acted in bad faith.[226] But what about a fiduciary who has profited from his or her breach of duty? Presumably the defence should not be available to such a wrongdoer who is liable to account for profits made from breach of duty, because of the high standards expected of them.[227] It would be inequitable for fiduciaries to rely on the defence, both because of the nature of their wrong and also because they can be considered to have acted in bad faith.

(iii) Restitutionary Claims Founded on the Vindication of Proprietary Rights

In *Lipkin Gorman* the House of Lords recognized that the defence of change of position should succeed on the facts of the case, where the defendant casino had received money belonging to the claimant firm of solicitors via a thief. If this case is treated as one involving the vindication of proprietary rights, rather than a claim founded on unjust enrichment,[228] it follows that the defence of change of position is applicable to such claims. Some of the leading cases involving tracing or claiming in which the proprietary claim has failed have been analysed with reference to the defence of change of position. So, in *Re Diplock's Estate*,[229] where money was used by a charity to improve property, the proprietary claim failed because it was not considered to be equitable for the claimant to obtain a proprietary remedy over a mixed asset to which an innocent volunteer had also contributed. In *Boscawen v Bajwa*[230] Millett LJ explained this result on the basis that the defendant charity had changed its position in good faith by spending the money.

In *Foskett v McKeown* there is an ambiguous dictum of Lord Millett that the defence of *bona fide* purchase[231] applied to claims to vindicate property rights, whereas the change of position defence applies to claims to unjust enrichment.[232] This is ambiguous, both because the issue was *obiter* since there was no evidence that the defendant children had changed their position, and because Lord Millett did not explicitly say that the change of position defence was unavailable to proprietary claims. However, he subsequently expanded on this extra-judicially[233] and confirmed that he did not consider that a claim for a proprietary remedy should be subject to the defence of change of position. This has been recognized in other decisions.[234]

Whether this is correct needs to be considered as a matter of principle and of policy. Where the claimant seeks to obtain a restitutionary remedy to vindicate proprietary rights, there are four different scenarios in which change of position might operate.

---

[225] See p 693, above.   [226] See p 514, above.   [227] See p 488, above.   [228] See p 560, above.
[229] [1948] Ch 465, 548.   [230] [1996] 1 WLR 328.   [231] See p 656, above.
[232] *Foskett v McKeown* [2001] 1 AC 102, 129.
[233] P Millett, 'Proprietary Restitution' in S Degeling and J Edelman (eds), *Equity in Commercial Law* (Sydney: Lawbook Co, 2005), 315 and 325.
[234] *Papamichael v National Westminster Bank* [2003] 1 Lloyd's Rep 341, 376 (Judge Chambers QC); *Armstrong DLW GmbH v Winnington Networks Ltd* [2012] EWHC 10 (Ch), [2013] Ch 156, [99]–[103] (Stephen Morris QC); *Test Claimants in the FII Group Litigation v HMRC* [2014] EWHC 4302 (Ch), [348] (Henderson J).

(1) Dissipation of the Property

If the claimant's property has been received by the defendant who then dissipates it in such a way that there is no traceable product or substitute, the restitutionary claim to recover the property will fail. But this is not because of the application of the defence of change of position, but simply because the defendant no longer has any property in his or her possession against which the claimant's property rights can be vindicated.

(2) Dissipation of Alternative Property

If the claimant's property has been received by the defendant who, in reliance on the validity of the receipt, dissipates other property, for example by selling some shares and spending the proceeds on a holiday, but retains the claimant's property, for example by crediting money received to the defendant's bank account, the elements of the change of position defence can be identified. For, in reliance on the validity of the receipt, the defendant's position has changed detrimentally and extraordinarily. This is the difficult case. It might be argued that it would not be fair for the claimant to recover the money credited to the defendant's bank account, since the defendant has suffered a detriment by selling the shares. If the defendant were also required to pay back to the claimant the money that had been credited to the bank account, the defendant would have suffered a net loss. But, against this, the claimant is able to show that the defendant has received and retained the value of the misappropriated money that is credited to the defendant's bank account. Should the claimant's proprietary right be defeated by the defendant's innocent change of position? This is a matter of judgment, but the better view is that the claimant's property rights should prevail and the defendant should not be able to plead the change of position defence. It follows that 'hard-nosed property rights'[235] should not be defeated by the defence of change of position.[236]

(3) Subrogation

Money in which the claimant has a proprietary interest might be used to discharge a debt owed by the defendant and the claimant might seek to be subrogated to the creditor's discharged security right. This is different from the other two scenarios because, although the property in which the claimant had an equitable proprietary interest has been dissipated through the discharge of the debt, the claimant is seeking a proprietary right to be created through the resurrection of the discharged security. This is the scenario in which Millett LJ in *Boscawen v Bajwa*[237] recognized that the claimant should have a defence of change of position. The operation of the defence in this context might be considered to be more defensible, because the claimant is not seeking to vindicate an existing property right. But the defence of change of position is not available in the law of unjust enrichment where the defendant has used money paid by mistake to discharge a liability,[238] since the defendant will not suffer any detriment if he or she is held liable to the claimant who paid the money by mistake. The same would be true were the claimant to seek the remedy of subrogation. Where the claimant's money has been used to discharge a secured debt, the resurrection of that debt in the claimant's favour will not cause any hardship to the defendant, because a secured liability to the claimant will simply be substituted for the liability owed to the original creditor.

---

[235] See *Foskett v McKeown* [2001] 1 AC 102, 108 (Lord Browne-Wilkinson).

[236] Cf Birks, *Unjust Enrichment* (2nd edn), 210, who wanted the defence to apply to proprietary restitutionary claims to substitute property which he analysed as involving the reversal of the defendant's unjust enrichment.

[237] [1996] 1 WLR 328, 341 (Millett LJ).   [238] See p 684, above.

(4) Personal Claims to Vindicate Property Rights

If the claimant's property has been received by the defendant who then dissipates it in circumstances where there is no surviving enrichment, then, although no proprietary remedy will be available, it may be possible to bring a claim for a personal remedy founded on the receipt of the claimant's property; at Common Law by means of the action for money had and received,[239] or in Equity by means of the action for unconscionable receipt.[240] Where the claimant seeks the restitution of value rather than the property itself, there may be scope for the application of the defence of change of position, as was the case in *Lipkin Gorman*, where a personal restitutionary remedy was sought at Law by means of the action for money had and received. Here the argument founded on hard-nosed property rights will not be relevant since there are no longer any rights over property. Consequently, at least at Law, it is appropriate for the defendant's innocent change of position to reduce or eliminate his or her liability to the claimant. This argument would not work, however, as regards the equivalent claim in Equity, at least in so far as that claim is presently defined. This is because the action for unconscionable receipt only applies where the defendant's receipt can be characterized as unconscionable and the definition of unconscionability has been influenced by the definition of bad faith in the context of the change of position defence.[241] It follows that, if the defendant's conduct can be characterized as unconscionable, then, by definition, the defence of change of position will not be available because the defendant will have acted in bad faith.

(D) THE RELATIONSHIP BETWEEN CHANGE OF POSITION AND OTHER DEFENCES

The change of position defence has a significant role to play in the modern law of restitution. But one of the most difficult questions following the recognition of the defence is what effect it will have on a number of the other defences which have been applied to restitutionary claims, particularly estoppel, the agent's defence and *bona fide* purchase.

(i) The Relationship Between Change of Position and Estoppel

Following the recognition of the defence of change of position the continued role of estoppel remains a matter of some controversy, even though Lord Goff did recognize in *Lipkin Gorman* that the defences were distinct.[242] It has been suggested in some cases that, with the recognition of change of position, there is no longer any place for the defence of estoppel by representation, at least in a restitutionary context.[243] Other cases have treated the defences as compatible.[244]

The question of the relationship between the two defences was considered by the Court of Appeal in *National Westminster Bank plc v Somer International (UK) Ltd*,[245] where it was emphasized that it was not for that court to conclude that, with the recognition of change of position, there is no longer any scope for relying on estoppel by representation; that being a decision for what is now the Supreme Court. But the Court of Appeal also

---

[239] See *Lipkin Gorman (a firm) v Karpnale Ltd* [1991] 2 AC 548. See p 642, above.

[240] *BCCI v Akindele* [2001] Ch 437. See p 645, above.   [241] See p 692, above.

[242] *Lipkin Gorman (a firm) v Karpnale Ltd* [1991] 2 AC 548, 578.

[243] *Dominion Securities Inc v Dawson* (1994) 111 DLR (4th) 230 (Newfoundland Court of Appeal); *Philip Collins Ltd v Davis* [2000] 3 All ER 808, 826 (Jonathan Parker J).

[244] *South Tyneside Metropolitan BC v Svenska International plc* [1995] 1 All ER 545; *Scottish Equitable plc v Derby* [2001] 3 All ER 818. See also Law Commission No 227 (1994), 48–9 and 141.

[245] [2002] 1 All ER 198, [2001] EWCA 970. See p 673, above.

recognized that the estoppel defence should be applied only to the extent by which the defendant's position had changed.[246] Although this would dramatically reduce the difference between the two defences, Potter LJ did identify certain remaining distinctions between them. For example, estoppel still requires proof of a representation and the fact that such a representation has been made may affect the court's view as to whether restitution should be ordered and, if so, by how much. He also recognized that change of position only protected actual reduction of the defendant's assets and did not cover somebody who has foregone a realistic and quantifiable opportunity to increase his or her assets. His Lordship did not, however, cite any authority for this proposition.[247] But surely, if the defendant foregoes an opportunity in reliance on the receipt of an enrichment and it can be shown that, but for the receipt of the enrichment, the defendant would have taken the opportunity, and, had he or she done so, a benefit would have been obtained, the test of causation will be satisfied since the defendant will be disenriched to the extent of that valuable benefit and the defence of change of position will be available. It might be thought that in such a case the defendant is better regarded as having taken a risk and it is not appropriate for the defence of change of position to be available, but if the change of position defence is not available in such a case then why should the defence of estoppel be available instead? Further, is the claimant's representation really of such significance to justify distinguishing between the two defences? A further difference between the two defences, not recognized by the Court of Appeal, is that, whereas change of position may not be available to a wrongdoer,[248] there is no similar bar on the defence of estoppel by representation. One way to justify such a distinction is that, in the context of estoppel, the claimant's representation, on which the defendant has relied, may negate the effects of the defendant's wrongdoing. There is, however, no authority on this point.

An alternative argument has been suggested, the effect of which is that the very recognition of the defence of change of position means that there is no longer any scope for a distinct defence of estoppel by representation. This argument was canvassed by Robert Walker LJ in *Scottish Equitable v Derby*;[249] an argument which he described as 'novel and ingenious' and which he found convincing. The essence of this argument is that, with the recognition of the defence of change of position, a detriment for the purposes of estoppel cannot be identified. The steps of the argument are as follows: first, to establish an estoppel a detriment must be suffered at the time when the person making the representation wishes to renege on it. Secondly, let us assume that, by the time the claimant wishes to renege on the representation, the defendant has suffered detriment by spending the money on a holiday. Thirdly, the claimant will say that the defendant did not in fact suffer a detriment, since the claimant cannot recover this sum back because it constitutes a defence of change of position. Consequently, the existence of change of position defeats the operation of estoppel by representation.

But this argument is not as convincing as Robert Walker LJ thought. First, as the law stands, it is presumably open to the defendant to choose on which defence he or she wishes to rely. If the defendant does wish to rely on estoppel, because a representation can be identified, is it really then open to the claimant effectively to plead a change of position in response? Why does not the very fact that the defendant has pleaded estoppel constitute

---

[246] See p 673, above.

[247] He only cited the note written by E Fung and L Ho, 'Change of Position and Estoppel' (2001) 117 LQR 14, 17, but they do not cite any authority for this proposition either. Now see *Commerzbank AG v Gareth Price-Jones* [2003] EWCA Civ 1663, [2005] 1 Lloyd's Rep 298 where the Court of Appeal recognized that a non-pecuniary change of position may be sufficient to establish the defence. See p 688, above.

[248] See p 692, above.   [249] [2001] 3 All ER 818, 830–1.

a waiver of the defence of change of position? Secondly, the success of the argument turns on what we mean by detriment for estoppel. Is it simply a factual detriment or does it encompass, as Robert Walker LJ appears to assume, detriment in a legal sense? Surely if the defendant has spent the money he or she has received on a holiday, so that the money has been dissipated, and even though the defendant presumably enjoyed the holiday, there is still a detriment since the defendant no longer has the money. Detriment equates with loss and it is possible to lose things in an enjoyable way and still suffer detriment.

The role of the defence of estoppel by representation clearly needs to be reviewed by the Supreme Court. The recognition by the Court of Appeal, albeit in *obiter dicta*,[250] that estoppel is a defence which operates as a matter of substance rather than evidence is to be welcomed, for it is clearly unacceptable for the defence to operate only as a complete bar to a restitutionary claim.[251] But is there a continued need for the estoppel defence? Surely not. The nature of the representation is not sufficient to justify the recognition of a distinct defence. Change of position should do the work. The defence of estoppel by representation should consequently be rejected.[252]

(ii) The Relationship Between Change of Position and the Agent's Defence

The recognition of the defence of change of position might mean that there is no longer any role for the agent's defence where the agent has received a benefit which is effectively transferred to the principal.[253] But, again, the differences between the two defences are such that the agent's defence continues to be relevant.[254] These difference include that, for the agent's defence, it is not necessary to show that the agent's circumstances have changed detrimentally, neither is it necessary to prove any extraordinary change of circumstances on the part of the agent, it being sufficient that he or she transferred the benefit to the principal because he or she was under a duty to do so.

Since the defences are compatible it follows that an agent could rely on both as defences to one restitutionary claim. So, for example, if the claimant paid the agent £1,000 by mistake, intending this sum to be paid to the principal, and the agent only paid £800 to the principal, the agent's defence will apply in respect of this amount. If the principal informed the agent that he or she could retain the remaining £200 as commission, and the agent donated this sum to charity, he or she could invoke the defence of change of position in respect of that amount.

(iii) *The Relationship Between Change of Position and* Bona Fide *Purchase*[255]

One consequence of the recognition of the defence of change of position is that the continuing existence of the defence of *bona fide* purchase has been called into question. It has been suggested that *bona fide* purchase is the paradigm example of change of

---

[250] *National Westminster Bank plc v Somer International (UK) Ltd* [2002] 2 All ER 198, 212 (Potter LJ) and 218 (Clarke LJ).

[251] Cf Hudson, 'Estoppel by Representation as a Defence to Unjust Enrichment—the Vine Has Not Withered Yet' who argues that the defence has a continued role as an absolute defence. See also Bant, *The Change of Position Defence*, 230.

[252] See also P Key, 'Excising Estoppel by Representation as a Defence to Restitution' [1995] CLJ 525.

[253] This is the view of Bant, *The Change of Position Defence*, 231.

[254] *Jeremy D Stone Consultants Ltd v National Westminster Bank* [2013] EWHC 208 (Ch), [244] (Sales J).

[255] For analysis of the bona fide purchase defence see Chapter 23. On the relationship between bona fide purchase and change of position see K Barker, 'After Change of Position: Good Faith Exchange in the Modern Law of Restitution' in PBH Birks (ed), Laundering and Tracing (Oxford: Clarendon Press, 1995), ch 7.

position[256] and that the two defences are founded on the same principle, namely that the defendant has changed his or her position in circumstances which make it inequitable to require the defendant to make restitution to the claimant. But, although Lord Goff recognized in *Lipkin Gorman* that change of position was akin to the defence of *bona fide* purchase, he did not regard the defences as identical.[257] This is the correct view.[258] There are enough differences between the two defences to justify their continued separate treatment.

(1) The *bona fide* purchase defence is a complete defence to the restitutionary claim, whereas change of position will only operate to the extent that the defendant's position has actually changed.

(2) The change of position defence will only apply where the defendant has detrimentally changed his or her position, whereas there is no need to show any detriment to establish the defence of *bona fide* purchase.

(3) Most importantly, whereas the change of position defence is a general defence which is potentially applicable to all restitutionary claims, the *bona fide* purchase defence is a specific defence which only applies where the restitutionary claim is founded on the vindication of property rights. This is because the rationale of the *bona fide* purchase defence is to give the defendant indefeasible title to property in which the claimant had a proprietary interest.

Since the requirements for establishing the two defences and the policies underlying them are so different, the recognition of change of position should not affect the continued existence of the defence of *bona fide* purchase.

---

[256] P Millett, 'Tracing the Proceeds of Fraud' (1991) 107 LQR 71, 82.

[257] *Lipkin Gorman (a firm) v Karpnale Ltd* [1991] 2 AC 548, 580–1.

[258] See P Key, '*Bona Fide* Purchase as a Defence in the Law of Restitution' [1994] LMCLQ 421 and Nolan, 'Change of Position', 186.

26

PASSING ON AND MITIGATION OF LOSS

Whereas the defences of estoppel, transfer by an agent to his or her principal and change of position are influenced by changes in the circumstances of the defendant, usually after he or she has received a benefit, the question which needs to be considered in this chapter is whether there are, and if not whether there should be, any defences in English law which operate by reference to changes in the circumstances of the claimant after the defendant's receipt of the benefit. There are two possible defences which, if they are recognized, would operate in this way, namely passing on and mitigation of loss.

1. PASSING ON

(A) THE GENERAL PRINCIPLE

If the defence of passing on[1] is recognized in English law it applies where the claimant has suffered loss by virtue of transferring a benefit to the defendant and the claimant has passed this loss on to a third party. It is in respect of restitutionary claims founded on the reversal of the defendant's unjust enrichment that the case for a defence of passing on is clearest. To establish such a claim the claimant must show that the defendant has been enriched at the claimant's expense. But, if the claimant has recouped his or her loss following the transfer of a benefit to the defendant by passing that loss on to a third party, the defendant's enrichment appears to have been at the expense of that third party and not the claimant. If the defendant made restitution in full to the claimant in such circumstances this would mean that the claimant becomes enriched at the expense of the third party by the receipt of a windfall gain. This can be illustrated by the following example. The defendant public authority demands the payment of a statutory duty from the claimant. The claimant pays this money to the defendant and then recoups it from its customers by increasing the price of its goods. The claimant later discovers that the defendant had no authority to demand the duty and so the claimant seeks restitution from the defendant. Since the claimant has not suffered any loss, because the initial loss was passed on to the customers, the defendant's enrichment does not appear to have been at the claimant's expense, but is instead at the expense of the customers, since they have ultimately borne the burden of the defendant's unauthorized demand.

In Chapter 5 the correspondence principle was recognized,[2] whereby the defendant is only required to make restitution to the claimant to the extent that the defendant's gain

---

[1] M Rush, *The Defence of Passing On* (Oxford; Hart Publishing, 2006). See also FD Rose, 'Passing On' in PBH Birks (ed), *Laundering and Tracing* (Oxford: Clarendon Press, 1995), ch 10 and M McInnes 'Passing On in the Law of Restitution: A Reconsideration' (1997) 19 Sydney LR 179.   [2] See p 116, above.

corresponds with the claimant's loss. This would appear to follow from the recognition of the principle of corrective justice as the fundamental principle which underpins unjust enrichment.[3] The key question, however, when determining whether passing on should be recognized as a defence is whether the law of restitution is only concerned with correcting the injustice as between the claimant and the defendant or whether other consequences external to their relationship should be taken into account.

(B) JUDICIAL EXAMINATION OF THE DEFENCE

(i) Recognition of the Defence

The defence of passing on has been recognized in some jurisdictions. For example, it was at one time recognized by the Supreme Court of Canada in *Air Canada v British Columbia*[4] and it has also been recognized by the European Court of Justice. In *Amministazione delle Finanze dello Stato v SpA San Giorgio*[5] it was held that Community law does not prevent Member States from 'disallowing repayment of charges which have been unduly levied where to do so would entail unjust enrichment of the recipients', as would occur where, for example, unduly levied charges have been incorporated into the price of goods and passed on to purchasers. However, the effect of Community law is that it simply 'does not prevent' Member States from adopting a passing-on defence. The *San Giorgio* case is not authority for the proposition that Member States must adopt such a defence.[6] Nevertheless, subsequent developments in EU law have recognized the defence as being available as regards claims for the recovery of overpaid tax paid in breach of EU law.[7]

The defence has been acknowledged in England as well. In *Marks and Spencer plc v Commissioners of Customs and Excise*[8] Lord Walker recognized that passing on is a possible defence to any restitutionary claim, although his Lordship cited *Roxborough v Rothmans of Pall Mall Australia Ltd*[9] in support of this conclusion, even though that decision expressly rejected the passing-on defence in Australia. Consequently, this dictum cannot be considered to be authoritative. Certain statutory provisions relating to the recovery of overpaid VAT and Car Tax effectively recognize the defence. For example, recovery of overpaid VAT is denied if repayment would unjustly enrich the person who paid the VAT.[10] This encompasses a defence of passing on, which would be applicable where, for example, the taxpayer had passed on the burden of the VAT to its customers.[11]

(ii) Rejection of the Defence

The passing-on defence has been expressly rejected in Australia[12] and Canada.[13] Whether the defence is recognized at common law in England has been a controversial matter. Although the point was left open by Lord Goff in *Woolwich Equitable Building Society v IRC*,[14] the

---

[3] See p 4, above.   [4] (1989) 59 DLR (4th) 161, 193–4 (La Forest J).   [5] [1983] ECR 3595.

[6] Ibid, 3636 (Mancini AG).

[7] Case C-398/09 *Lady and Kid v Skatteministeriet* [2012] STC 854, [20] and [25].

[8] [2005] UKHL 53, [25].   [9] (2002) 76 ALJR 203.

[10] Value Added Tax Act 1994, s 80(3). See GJ Virgo, 'Restitution of Overpaid VAT' [1998] BTR 582. See also Finance Act 1989, s 29(3) which contains a similar defence in respect of the recovery of overpaid car tax.

[11] This was recognized by Evans LJ in *Kleinwort Benson Ltd v Birmingham CC* [1997] QB 380, 389. See also *Customs and Excise Commissioners v McMaster Stores (Scotland) Ltd* [1995] STC 846; *Baines and Ernst Ltd v Commissioners of Customs and Excise* [2004] UKVAT V18769. See p 407, above.

[12] *Mason v New South Wales* (1959) 102 CLR 108; *Commissioner of State Revenue v Royal Insurance Australia Ltd* (1994) 126 ALR 1; *Roxborough v Rothmans of Pall Mall Australia Ltd* (2002) 76 ALJR 203.

[13] *Kingstreet Investments Ltd v New Brunswick (Finance)* [2007] 1 SCR 3.

[14] [1993] AC 70, 178.

defence was expressly rejected by the Court of Appeal in *Kleinwort Benson Ltd v Birmingham CC*.[15] This was one of the interest rate swap cases, where the defendant local authority argued that the claimant, a bank which was seeking restitution of money paid under a void interest rate swaps transaction to the defendant, had passed on the financial loss arising from the swap transaction by entering into hedging transactions to protect the claimant against the risks which are inherent in a swaps transaction. The Court of Appeal rejected this argument for two reasons.

First, if restitutionary remedies were concerned with what the claimant has lost, the passing-on defence would be highly relevant, because the fact that the claimant has passed on his or her loss would mean that he or she would require less compensation from the defendant. But, because the law of restitution is concerned with recovery of what the defendant has gained, it follows that the fact that the claimant has passed on his or her loss is an irrelevant defence to a restitutionary claim. This was well expressed by Saville LJ who said:

> [The defendant] does not cease to be unjustly enriched because the payer for one reason or another is not out of pocket. His obligation to return the money is not based on any loss the payer may have sustained, but on the simple ground that it is unjust that he should keep something to which he has no right.[16]

Secondly, Morritt LJ[17] relied on the question of what was just and equitable as a reason for rejecting the passing-on defence. He acknowledged that a consequence of rejecting the defence is that the claimant may be left with a windfall where he or she had been able to pass the loss on to a third party, but, crucially, he asserted that the claimant 'has a better title than the defendant to any "windfall" available, not least so as to be in a position to satisfy any claim made against him by those from whom the "windfall" was ultimately derived'.[18] Consequently, as between the claimant and the defendant it is the claimant who should benefit from the fact that a loss has been passed on to a third party.

Although the defence of passing on was rejected on the facts of the case, its availability was left open generally and particularly as regards claims for the recovery of tax and other duties.[19] Evans LJ did not consider these cases to be relevant to the swaps cases because they involved public law claims, but most of the swaps cases also involved a public law element since the restitutionary claim was brought against public authorities, albeit in respect of a private law claim. Indeed, *Kleinwort Benson* itself involved a claim brought against a public authority.

(C) SHOULD THE DEFENCE OF PASSING ON BE RECOGNIZED?

The state of English law is such that, save where specific provision has been made by statute or by EU law, the defence of passing on does not exist as a defence to restitutionary claims. But should such a defence be recognized? Although the defence is consistent with the correspondence principle, whereby the defendant's gain must correspond with the claimant's loss in order to establish unjust enrichment at the claimant's expense,[20] the reality is that invariably it will be impossible to prove that the claimant has actually passed on the

---

[15] [1997] QB 380. See also *Kleinwort Benson v South Tyneside MBC* [1994] 4 All ER 972 (Hobhouse J).

[16] *Kleinwort Benson Ltd v Birmingham CC* [1997] QB 380, 394. Evans LJ recognized, ibid, 393, that, even if the restitutionary claim was concerned with compensating the claimant for the loss it had suffered, the hedging transaction which the claimant had entered into was too remote and so need not be considered.

[17] Ibid, 401.   [18] Ibid.   [19] Ibid, 389 (Evans LJ).   [20] See p 116, above.

loss to a third party.[21] For example, if the claimant has paid money to the defendant and seeks to recoup this loss from his or her customers by increasing prices, it does not follow that the claimant will necessarily be able to recoup the loss. This was recognized by Advocate General Mancini in the *San Giorgio* case: '[The] passing on of charges is not generally relevant because of the innumerable variables which affect price formation in a free market and because of the consequent impossibility of definitively relating any part of the price exclusively to a certain cost.'[22] Consequently, even though the claimant may have increased the price of goods to recoup the enrichment which was transferred to the defendant, this may in turn have had an impact on sales volume resulting in an overall loss. It follows that the claimant would not have passed on the loss to his or her customers.

Further, from a theoretical perspective, the recognition of the correspondence principle as being founded on the principle of corrective justice, does not require the passing-on defence to be recognized. As Grantham and Rickett have noted,[23] the defence is inconsistent with the normative basis for recognizing restitutionary liability: 'the fundamentally correlative struc-ture of corrective justice is such that matters external to the relationship of claimant and defendant cannot bear on the issue of the normative equality of the parties and whether that equality has been disrupted'. In other words, the fact that, following the defendant's receipt of the enrichment, the claimant's position has changed through the passing on of the loss, is not relevant to the question of the imposition of liability as between the claimant and the defendant. A claim in unjust enrichment focuses on whether the claimant suffered an initial loss which corresponds with the defendant's gain at the time when the unjust enrichment claim crystalized.[24] The fact that the claimant's loss is subsequently reduced or dissipated does not affect whether the defendant's gain can be considered to have been obtained at the claimant's expense, because reduction or removal of the loss suffered by the claimant after the defendant has been enriched is not causatively linked to the defendant's enrichment.

There may, however, be circumstances where policy demands that events following the transfer of the enrichment to the defendant should be taken into account, which is why the passing-on defence is recognized in certain circumstances where the claim relates to the overpayment of tax to a public authority. In particular, the passing-on defence is the only defence recognized by EU law as regards claims for the recovery of overpaid tax paid in breach of EU law.[25] This is considered to be a justifiable defence because restitution should not be awarded where the claimant has not borne the burden of the unlawful tax. This also justifies the recognition of the defence by statute in claims for restitution of overpaid VAT. This argument might also be used to justify the recognition of the defence in any case where the claim for restitution is grounded on the *Woolwich* principle.[26]

2. MITIGATION OF LOSS

Even though the defence of passing has been rejected in English law as a general defence to restitutionary claims, it is still necessary to consider whether a similar but sufficiently

---

[21] See McInnes, 'Passing On in the Law of Restitution', 199 and Virgo, 'Restitution of Overpaid VAT', 588–9.

[22] [1983] ECR 3595, 3629. See also *Ministre du Budget, des Comptes Publics et de la Fonction Publique v Accor SA* Case C-310/09, [2012] STC 438, [74].

[23] RB Grantham and CEF Rickett, 'A Normative Account of Defences to Restitutionary Liability' (2008) CLJ 92, 118.					[24] See p 116, above.

[25] Case C-398/09 *Lady and Kid v Skatteministeriet* [2012] STC 854, [20] and [25].

[26] See p 298, above.

distinct defence should be recognized, namely the defence of mitigation of loss. If this defence were recognized it would mean that the claimant who has transferred a benefit to the defendant would be required to minimize his or her loss and, to the extent that this loss has been minimized, the defendant's obligation to make restitution should be reduced.

This defence was considered by the Court of Appeal in *Kleinwort Benson Ltd v Birmingham CC*,[27] where it was specifically rejected. In fact, the claimant's conduct in that case involved mitigation of loss rather than passing on the actual loss which the claimant had suffered, since the claimant had entered into a hedging transaction with a third party simply to minimize the risk of loss suffered by the claimant. The conclusion of the court that there was no duty on the claimant to mitigate his or her loss,[28] and that there was no defence of mitigation of loss,[29] is consistent with the rejection of the passing-on defence in the same case. But if the correspondence principle is recognized as part of the unjust enrichment principle, so that the defendant's gain must correspond with the claimant's loss,[30] should it follow that the claimant is under a *duty* to mitigate his or her loss? The preferable view is that this would be a step too far, since ultimately the unjust enrichment principle is concerned with the unjust enrichment of the defendant and depriving the defendant of a gain rather than with compensating the claimant for a loss suffered. Where the claimant has mitigated his or her loss it is appropriate for that to be taken into account, but the claimant should not be under any obligation to do so.

The only possible qualification to this rejection of the defence of mitigation of loss may arise where the restitutionary claim is founded on the commission of a wrong by the defendant, such as a tort. Where the claimant seeks a compensatory remedy from the defendant who has committed a tort, the claimant must mitigate his or her loss, and so it might be argued that the claimant is required to mitigate his or her loss even where he or she seeks a restitutionary remedy.[31] But this is a flawed argument. The claimant is only required to mitigate his or her loss where a compensatory remedy is sought since such a remedy is assessed only by reference to the claimant's loss. Where the claimant seeks a restitutionary remedy, albeit that the claim is founded on the commission of a tort, the remedy is only assessed by reference to the defendant's gain obtained from committing the tort. The fact that the claimant has or might have mitigated his or her loss is irrelevant. Where, however, the claimant is the victim of a wrong and he or she did mitigate his or her loss, it is unclear whether this should be taken into account in assessing the restitutionary remedy. If Edelman's[32] distinction between restitutionary damages and disgorgement damages for wrongs is taken into account, a case can be made for recognizing such factual mitigation. Where the remedy is concerned with restoring to the claimant what he or she lost as a result of the wrong, the award of restitution is founded on the principle of corrective justice, like the unjust enrichment principle, and, to the extent that the defendant's gain is not reflected by the claimant's loss because of actual mitigation of that loss, the defendant's liability should be reduced accordingly. Where, however, a disgorgement remedy is awarded there is no scope for mitigation of loss to operate, because the function of such a remedy is focused entirely on depriving the defendant of a gain rather than restoring to the claimant what he or she has lost.

---

[27] [1997] QB 380.   [28] Ibid, 393 (Evans LJ).   [29] Ibid, 394 (Saville LJ) and 399 (Morritt LJ).
[30] See p 116, above.
[31] A duty to mitigate loss in such circumstances was contemplated by Evans LJ in *Kleinwort Benson Ltd v Birmingham CC* [1997] QB 380, 393.
[32] J Edelman, *Gain-Based Damages: Contract, Tort, Equity and Intellectual Property* (Oxford: Hart Publishing, 2002). See p 419, above.

Where the restitutionary claim is founded on the vindication of property rights there is no scope for mitigation of loss to be considered, because such a claim is founded solely on depriving the defendant of actual property or the value of property and is not concerned with the nature of the loss suffered by the claimant. It is for this reason that where the property has increased in value the claimant can recover more than he or she actually lost.[33]

[33] See p 559, above.

27

ILLEGALITY

1. GENERAL PRINCIPLES

(A) PUBLIC POLICY AND JUSTICE

Most of the defences to restitutionary claims focus on the relationship between the claimant and the defendant, and are normatively related to the principle of corrective justice.[1] That is not the case with the defence of illegality, which is influenced by external considerations of public policy[2] rather than securing justice between the parties. It is for this reason that the illegality defence has such a bad reputation, being perceived as complex, capricious and unjust.[3] It is difficult even to identify an acceptable definition of illegality; to determine whether it should defeat restitutionary claims in all, some or any cases, and, if it applies, what might be the basis for determining its application. Further, where the defendant has obtained a benefit in circumstances where its transfer has been tainted by illegality, there is no *a priori* reason either why restitution should necessarily follow or be denied. As Wade[4] recognized:

> on one side the view that a court should not help a man who has engaged in an illegal transaction out of the predicament in which he has placed himself, and on the other the view that a court should not permit unjust enrichment of one person at the expense of another. Of these two arguments, each of which seems most nearly determinative upon its side of the question, neither takes precedence upon logical analysis.

Confusion about the role of the illegality defence runs throughout the law of obligations.[5] That confusion has been compounded by two decisions of the Supreme Court which, although not concerned with the law of restitution, betray a significant difference of approach about the role of illegality generally in private law which is of relevance to the analysis of the defence in unjust enrichment.

In *Les Laboratoires Servier v Apotex*,[6] in a case concerning a statutory tort, the Court of Appeal had approached the illegality defence on the basis that 'it required in each case ... an intense analysis of the particular facts and of the proper application of the various policy considerations underlying the illegality principle so as to produce a just and

---

[1] RB Grantham and CEF Rickett, 'A Normative Account of Defences to Restitutionary Liability' (2008) CLJ 92.

[2] *Hounga v Allen* [2014] UKSC 47, [2014] 1 WLR 2889, [42] (Lord Wilson), [55] (Lord Hughes); *Les Laboratoires Servier v Apotex* [2014] UKSC 55, [2015] AC 430, [13] (Lord Sumption).

[3] Lord Sumption, 'Reflections on the Law of Illegality' [2012] RLR 1, 12.

[4] JW Wade, 'Benefits Obtained Under Illegal Transactions—Reasons For and Against Allowing Restitution' (1946) Texas Law Review 31, 60.

[5] For tort see GJ Virgo, 'Illegality's Role in the Law of Tort' in M Dyson (ed), *Unravelling Tort and Crime* (Cambridge: Cambridge University Press, 2014), ch 7.

[6] [2014] UKSC 55, [2015] AC 430.

proportionate response to the illegality'.[7] This approach was specifically rejected by a majority of the Supreme Court. Lord Sumption emphasized that the defence was grounded on general rules of law and was not a mere discretionary power, involving fact-based evaluations of the effect of the rules in individual cases.[8] He considered the key issues to be only whether the relevant conduct involved sufficient turpitude and whether this was sufficiently related to the claim.[9] This strict approach to illegality can be contrasted with that of Lord Toulson, who refused to criticize the approach of the Court of Appeal and who considered that, when determining whether the illegality defence should apply, 'it is right to proceed carefully on a case by case basis, considering the policies which underlie the broad principle'.[10] This approach was also adopted by a differently constituted Supreme Court in the earlier decision of *Hounga v Allen*,[11] which concerned the tort of race discrimination following wrongful dismissal from employment. Lord Wilson[12] recognized that it was necessary 'first, to ask "What is the aspect of public policy which founds the defence?" and, second, to ask "But is there another aspect of public policy to which application of the defence would run counter?"'.

To the extent that there is division amongst the Justices of the Supreme Court, the strict approach of Lord Sumption would appear to prevail, being a judgment in the more recent case which had the explicit support of two Justices and the implicit support of another. But a larger number of Justices support the more flexible and fact-sensitive approach of Lord Toulson, with all the Justices in *Hounga* having adopted it. It follows that a fundamental difference of approach to dealing with illegality has emerged and it is necessary to consider carefully, in the light of this, how illegality should function in the law of restitution.

(B) THE *EX TURPI CAUSA* PRINCIPLE

All restitutionary claims, regardless of the underlying cause of action, are subject to a defence of illegality. This stems from the fundamental rule, known as *ex turpi causa non oritur actio* ('No action can arise from a base cause'[13]), meaning that the courts will not assist a claimant to obtain a remedy where the action is founded on illegal conduct. This rule was recognized by Lord Mansfield in *Holman v Johnson*:[14]

> The objection, that a contract is immoral or illegal as between the plaintiff and defendant, sounds at all times very ill in the mouth of the defendant. It is not for his sake, however, that the objection is ever allowed; but it is founded in general principles of policy, which the defendant has the advantage of, contrary to the real justice, as between him and the

---

[7] *Les Laboratoires Servier v Apotex* [2012] EWCA Civ 593, [2013] Bus LR 80, [75] (Etherton LJ).

[8] *Les Laboratoires Servier v Apotex* [2014] UKSC 55, [2014] 3 WLR 1257, [2015] AC 430, [13] and [22].

[9] Ibid, [22].

[10] Ibid, [57]. See also *Gray v Thames Trains Ltd* [2009] UKHL 33, [2009] 1 AC 1339, 1370, [30] (Lord Hoffmann); *Stone and Rolls Ltd v Moore Stephens* [2009] AC 1391, [25] (Lord Phillips).

[11] [2014] UKSC 47, [2014] 1 WLR 2889. See also *Parkingeye Ltd v Somerfield Stores Ltd* [2012] EWCA Civ 1338, [2013] QB 840, [40] (Sir Robin Jacob).

[12] *Hounga v Allen* [2014] UKSC 47, [2014] 1 WLR 2889, [42], with whom Baroness Hale and Lord Kerr agreed.

[13] Windeyer J in *Smith v Jenkins* (1969) 119 CLR 397, 411 considered that 'causa' did not refer to 'cause of action' but referred to illegal or immoral consideration, so the doctrine was only relevant to contractual claims. This was rejected by Dillon LJ in *Pitts v Hunt* [1991] 1 QB 24, 56.

[14] (1775) 1 Cowp 341, 343; 98 ER 1120, 1121. See also *Muckleston v Brown* (1801) 6 Ves Jun 52, 69; 31 ER 934, 942 (Lord Eldon LC).

plaintiff, by accident, if I may so. The principle of public policy is this; *ex dolo malo non oritur actio*. No Court will lend its aid to a man who founds his cause of action upon an immoral or illegal act. If, from the plaintiff's own stating or otherwise, the cause of action appears to arise *ex turpi causa*, or the transgression of a positive law of this country, there the Court says he has no right to be assisted.

This rule negating liability is explicitly founded on policy rather than justice. As Lord Goff said in *Tinsley v Milligan*:[15]

> it is a principle of policy, whose application is indiscriminate and so can lead to unfair consequences as between the parties to litigation. Moreover the principle allows no room for the exercise of any discretion by the court in favour of one party or the other.

(C) QUALIFYING *EX TURPI CAUSA*

The strict application of the *ex turpi causa* rule in denying a remedy to the claimant might be considered to produce unjust results where, for example, the illegality is minor or the defendant is more responsible than the claimant for participation in illegal conduct. The judiciary consequently sought to temper the strict rule to secure justice. For a few years in the 1980s this was achieved through the reformulation of the illegality rule by reference to the public conscience test, whereby the defence only applied where the public conscience would be affronted if relief was granted. This test originated in *Thackwell v Barclays Bank plc*,[16] where an action for conversion failed by virtue of the illegality defence, but only after the court had considered all the circumstances of the case, including the nature of the illegality, to determine whether, by granting a remedy to the claimant, it would be seen to be assisting or encouraging his criminal act. A remedy was eventually denied because the claimant had been a knowing party to a fraudulent transaction.

The public conscience test was rejected by the House of Lords in Equity, on the ground that it was inconsistent with the authorities and too uncertain.[17] The courts were surely right to do so. The public conscience test resulted in inconsistent decisions,[18] often turning on judicial outrage arising from the facts of the case.[19] Justice is dependent on a high degree of predictability, which is lacking under the public conscience test. But, even though subsequent cases have not resurrected the test, there remains a clear judicial desire to temper the rigidity of the *ex turpi causa* rule to avoid unjust results. But the *ex turpi causa* rule was never absolute; it has always been qualified. The flexibility of the *ex turpi causa* rule was recognized by Lord Mansfield in *Holman v Johnson*,[20] for his dictum continued as follows:

> It is on that ground the Court goes; not for the sake of the defendant, but because they will not lend their aid to such a plaintiff. So if the plaintiff and defendant were to change sides, and the defendant was to bring his action against the plaintiff, the latter would then have the advantage of it; for where both are equally in fault, *potior est conditio defendentis*.

It is the recognition of this other principle, known as the *in pari delicto est conditio defendentis* principle ('in the case of mutual fault, the position of the defendant is the

---

[15] [1994] 1 AC 340, 355. See also *Gray v Thames Trains Ltd* [2009] UKHL 33, [2009] 1 AC 1339, [30] (Lord Hoffmann).

[16] [1986] 1 All ER 676. See also *Saunders v Edwards* [1987] 1 WLR 1116; *Howard v Shirlstar Container Transport Ltd* [1990] 1 WLR 1292 and *Euro-Diam Ltd v Bathurst* [1990] 1 QB 1.

[17] *Tinsley v Milligan* [1994] 1 AC 340.   [18] Ibid, 363 (Lord Goff).

[19] *Hewison v Meridian Shipping Services Pte Ltd* [2002] EWCA Civ 1821, [2003] ICR 766, 788–9 (Ward LJ).

[20] (1775) 1 Cowp 341, 343; 98 ER 1120, 1121.

stronger one'), *in pari delicto* for short, that provides an important mechanism for qualifying the *ex turpi causa* defence, of particular relevance to the law of restitution. This *in pari delicto* principle enables the court to analyse the particular circumstances of the case to determine whether the claimant is less responsible for the illegality than the defendant, for then, as between the claimant and the defendant, the just result is that the claimant should not be denied relief, since the parties are not *in pari delicto*. But where the claimant is more responsible for the illegality or the parties are considered to be equally responsible, the *in pari delicto* principle applies and restitution will be denied.

That the illegality defence was always intended to be applied flexibly is reflected by *Holman v Johnson* itself,[21] which concerned an action to recover the price of tea supplied by the claimant to the defendant pursuant to a contract made in Dunkirk, which the defendant intended to smuggle into England. The claimant was aware of the defendant's intention, but was not part of the smuggling scheme. The defendant having failed to pay for the tea, the claimant sued for the price. The claim succeeded, both because mere knowledge of the smuggling was held not to be sufficient to bar the claim and because the claimant had not committed any crime. Although he knew of the smuggling, he was not concerned in the illegal transaction itself. It would have been different if the price would only have become due once the tea had landed in England, but the claimant's interest was considered to be at an end once the tea had been delivered in Dunkirk. In later cases the seller's claim failed where he both knew of the defendant's illegal purpose and assisted the defendant in that purpose. So, for example, in *Clugas v Penaluna*[22] the claimant assisted in the smuggling by packing the brandy and gin which was to be smuggled into England from Guernsey. Buller J distinguished *Holman v Johnson* on the ground that, 'if he takes part [in the transaction] it taints the whole of it'.[23]

A test stating that the court's assistance will be denied where the parties are *par delictum* is a test judged by reference to the comparative fault of the parties, or, perhaps preferably, the comparative taint of the illegality. Consequently, if the claimant is less responsible for the illegality than the defendant, relief should not be denied, because the illegality taints the defendant more than the claimant.

(D) PUBLIC POLICY AND THE LAW OF RESTITUTION

Where a restitutionary claim is tainted by illegality it will operate as a defence.[24] This is illustrated by *Parkinson v College of Ambulance*,[25] where the claimant had given a donation to a charity on the understanding that he would receive a knighthood as a result. When no knighthood was forthcoming, he sought restitution of the money on the ground of total failure of basis, but the claim failed because the contract was illegal as being contrary to public policy. Similarly, a defendant who has been tainted by illegality will not be able to rely on the defence of change of position.[26]

Although the illegality defence was intended to be applied flexibly, in the nineteenth and twentieth centuries the defence came to be applied more rigorously, so much so that it

---

[21] See also *Vita Food Products Inc v Unus Shipping Co Ltd* [1939] AC 277, 293 (Lord Wright).

[22] (1791) 4 Term Rep 466, 100 ER 1122.

[23] Ibid, 468; 1123. See also *Bernard v Reese* (1794) 1 Esp 91, 170 ER 290; *Waymell v Reed* (1794) 5 Term Rep 599, 600; 101 ER 335, 336 (Lord Kenyon CJ).

[24] *Muckleston v Brown* (1801) 6 Ves Jun 52, 69; 31 ER 934, 942 (Lord Eldon LC) and *Gordon v Chief Constable of Metropolitan Police* [1910] 2 KB 1080, 1090 (Vaughan Williams LJ).

[25] [1923] 2 KB 1. See also *Wacker* [2003] QB 1207, [32] (Kay LJ).

[26] *Barros Mattos Jnr v MacDaniels Ltd* [2004] EWHC 1188 (Ch), [2005] 1 WLR 247.

was used to bar the claim whenever the claimant had been tainted by illegality. For example, in *Wild v Simpson*[27] Atkin LJ gave the example of a taxi-driver, who was engaged to drive to a particular destination, and who was informed by his passenger halfway through the journey that he was going to perpetrate a burglary at the destination. Atkin LJ suggested that, if the driver proceeded with the journey, he would not be able to recover his fare or even half of it, since, assuming that the contract was void for illegality, the driver's restitutionary claim would have been tainted by the illegality. But surely the driver was much less responsible than the passenger for the illegality, so there is no reason why his claim for restitution should be defeated. The harshness of the existing law is also illustrated by the facts of *Wild v Simpson* itself, where a solicitor had entered into an illegal agreement with a client, whereby the client agreed to pay a percentage of whatever he recovered to the solicitor. The solicitor sought to recover his costs, but his action failed because the contract of service was illegal. This hardly seems fair. The solicitor had done work for the client but was unable to recover anything for this because of the illegal nature of the original agreement. It is right that the illegal agreement itself is not enforced, so the solicitor would not be allowed to sue for a percentage of what the client recovered, but why should this affect the restitutionary claim?

(E) ILLEGALITY IN EQUITY

A principle restricting recovery in cases of illegality also exists in Equity in the form of the maxim that the claimant who comes to Equity must come with clean hands.[28] This means that, if the claimant's conduct is regarded as improper, relief in Equity will be refused. In the leading case on this maxim, *Dering v Earl of Winchelsea*,[29] it was held that such improper conduct does not arise if there is merely moral impropriety; the impropriety must arise in a legal sense. Such impropriety does not, however, necessarily equate with illegality. Where there is illegality the transaction will be unenforceable both at Law and in Equity,[30] but where there is no illegality Equity may still deny relief by virtue of the unclean hands maxim.

The question of the operation of this equitable maxim was considered by Lord Goff in his dissenting judgment in *Tinsley v Milligan*,[31] where he concluded that it was not possible to vindicate proprietary rights in Equity where those rights had arisen under an illegal transaction, simply because the claimant must come to the court with clean hands. In fact, Lord Goff's interpretation of the clean hands maxim was mistaken because that maxim has a particular function which is very different to that of the illegality defence. This was recognized by Mummery LJ in *Dunbar v Plant*,[32] who emphasized that, whereas the *ex turpi causa* principle is a principle of public policy[33] which must be strictly applied by the court, the clean hands principle is a principle of justice which is designed to prevent those guilty of serious misconduct from securing an equitable remedy, such as specific performance[34] or an injunction.[35] The consequence of making this distinction between

---

[27] [1919] 2 KB 544, 566.
[28] See *Groves v Groves* (1829) 3 Y and J 163, 174; 148 ER 1136, 1141 (Lord Alexander CB); *Tinker v Tinker* [1970] P 136, 143 (Salmon LJ); *Tinsley v Milligan* [1994] 1 AC 340, 357 (Lord Goff) and *Nelson v Nelson* (1995) 70 ALJR 47, 68 (Dawson J).
[29] (1787) 1 Cox 318, 29 ER 1184.   [30] *Ayerst v Jenkins* (1873) LR 16 Eq 275.
[31] [1994] 1 AC 340.   [32] [1998] Ch 412, 422.
[33] As had been recognized by Lord Mansfield in *Holman v Johnson* (1775) 1 Cowp 341, 343; 98 ER 1120, 1121.
[34] See, for example, *Coatsworth v Johnson* (1886) 54 LT 520.
[35] See *Argyll (Duchess) v Argyll (Duke)* [1967] Ch 302, although the maxim did not apply on the facts because the claimant's unacceptable conduct was considered to be too remote.

principles of public policy and principles of justice is that the clean hands maxim only applies where the claimant seeks a discretionary equitable remedy and it does not apply where the claimant seeks equitable remedies as a matter of right, such as where he or she seeks to vindicate an equitable proprietary right.[36]

2. THE POLICIES UNDERPINNING THE ILLEGALITY DEFENCE

A number of policy reasons have been recognized for denying the claimant restitutionary remedies where he or she has been tainted by illegality.[37] Some of these policies had been identified by Etherton LJ in *Les Laboratoires Servier v Apotex Inc*,[38] although he emphasized that the defence does not necessarily apply simply because one of the policy rationales is relevant, but the defence 'must find its justification firmly in one or more of them'.

(A) CONSISTENCY

Where the illegality constitutes the commission of a crime, it is not for the law to undermine, or stultify,[39] the criminal law by providing a remedy. Consequently, consistency between the criminal law and private law is a legitimate policy aim,[40] which is furthered by the illegality defence. As Lord Hughes said in *Hounga v Allen*, the law 'cannot give with one hand what it takes away with another, nor condone when facing right what it condemns when facing left'.[41]

This policy assumes that there is a necessary inconsistency between criminal law and the law of restitution if a gain-based remedy is awarded, despite the claimant's participation in criminal conduct. But that does not necessarily follow, especially where the claimant is less responsible for the illegality than the defendant and where a literal restitutionary remedy, rather than disgorgement remedy, is awarded to restore to the claimant what had been received by the defendant at the claimant's expense. The inconsistency between the criminal law and the law of restitution would be much clearer if the award of a gain-based remedy enabled the claimant to profit from the commission of a crime, for it is a fundamental principle that a claimant should not be allowed to profit from his or her illegal conduct,[42] and it would not be appropriate for the law of restitution to enable the claimant to profit from the commission of a crime. This would apply where the claimant seeks an account of profits from the defendant where the profits arose from the commission of a crime.[43] But this will not occur where the claimant seeks a remedy to

---

[36] This is consistent with the approach of the majority in *Tinsley v Milligan* [1994] 1 AC 340, examined at p 590, above.

[37] See JK Grodecki, '*In Pari Delicto Potior est Conditio Defendentis*' (1955) 71 LQR 254, 265–73.

[38] [2012] EWCA Civ 593, [2013] Bus LR 80, [66]. This was based on the Law Commission's Consultation Paper No 189, *The Illegality Defence* (2009), para 3.142.

[39] E Weinrib, 'Illegality as a Tort Defence' (1976) 26 UTLJ 28, 52.

[40] See generally *Hall v Hebert* [1993] 2 SCR 159, 165 (McLachlan J); GJ Virgo, 'We Do This in the Criminal Law, and that in the Law of Tort: A New Fusion Debate' in E Chamberlain, J Neyers, and S Pitel (eds), *Challenging Orthodoxy in Tort Law* (Oxford: Hart Publishing, 2013).

[41] *Hounga v Allen* [2014] UKSC 47, [2014] 1 WLR 2889, [55].

[42] *Beresford v Royal Insurance Co Ltd* [1938] AC 586. See also *Hall v Hebert* [1993] 2 SCR 159, 169 (McLachlan J).

[43] Although those profits might be confiscated by the State. See Chapter 20.

reverse the defendant's unjust enrichment, since the defendant's gain will necessarily correspond with the claimant's loss.[44]

Further, the policy of consistency cannot generally operate where the illegality involves conduct which is not criminal,[45] although there may be circumstances where the principle should operate outside the criminal law where the claimant's conduct is considered only to be civilly unlawful, for the denial of a remedy might be consistent with the reason why the conduct was rendered unlawful in the first place. This was recognized by the High Court of Australia in *Equus Corp Pty Ltd v Haxton*,[46] where a restitutionary claim was defeated by a defence of statutory illegality, since the Court was concerned to prevent the common law from stultifying the statute's purpose.

(B) DETERRENCE

The deterrence policy is founded on the principle that the court should not assist or encourage the claimant in his or her illegal conduct or encourage others in similar acts.[47] But it is difficult to see how this policy justifies the denial of restitutionary relief to a claimant who has participated in illegal conduct.[48] Whether the denial of a remedy will actually deter participation in illegal activity depends on a variety of assumptions, particularly that the claimant knows or suspects that the conduct is illegal and is aware of the existence and effect of the illegality defence. In fact, if the defendant, who expects to receive a benefit from the claimant, is aware of the illegality and of the policy denying restitution, he or she is much more likely to participate in the transaction, knowing that any benefit which is received may be retained.[49] The policy of deterrence is just as likely to be fulfilled by allowing restitution to a claimant who has been tainted by illegality than by denying relief to such a person.[50] But this is a highly artificial argument, since it is unlikely that either party will be aware of the illegality defence and its implications.[51] Even if the parties were so aware, it would be very difficult for them to predict whether or not restitution would be denied because of the uncertain operation of the defence. Also, in those cases where the illegality is criminal, it is unlikely that the denial of a remedy will be a greater deterrent than that of the criminal law.[52]

(C) PUNISHMENT

It has been recognized that the denial of a remedy for illegality might be justified on the ground that it punishes the claimant.[53] But that is what the criminal law is for and, since the definition of illegality is not confined to criminal conduct, the punishment rationale cannot explain all cases where the defence has been applied. To the extent that illegality encompasses criminality and operates to bar the claim completely, then, if this is justified for reasons of punishment, it is not possible for the court to ensure that the punishment fits the crime, especially since the effect of the 'punishment' will depend on the value of the benefit which has been received by the defendant: the greater the value, the more severe

---

[44] See Chapter 5, above.   [45] See p 716, below.   [46] [2012] HCA 7.
[47] *Euro-Diam Ltd v Bathurst* [1990] QB 1, 35 (Kerr LJ).
[48] *Tinsley v Milligan* [1994] 1 AC 340, 368 (Lord Lowry).
[49] *Nelson v Nelson* (1995) 70 ALJR 47, 88 (McHugh J).
[50] *Smith v Bromley* (1760) 2 Doug 696n, 698; 99 ER 441, 443 (Lord Mansfield).
[51] See *Tribe v Tribe* [1996] Ch 107, 134 (Millett LJ).
[52] *Hewison v Meridian Shipping Pte Ltd* [2002] EWCA Civ 1821, [2003] ICR 766, [73] (Ward LJ).
[53] *Tinsley v Milligan* [1992] Ch 310, 334 (Ralph Gibson LJ).

the claimant's punishment. Further, there is a danger of double punishment, because the claimant might be punished through the imposition of a criminal sanction and also be denied a restitutionary remedy, the value of which might be much greater than any penalty which the criminal court might impose,[54] making the denial of relief disproportionate to the claimant's responsibility for the illegality. There may even be particular reasons why the criminal law will not impose liability, such as the age of the offender, which would not be recognized in the law of restitution. The punishment justification is consequently unconvincing.

(D) DIGNITY OF THE COURT

The court may be unwilling to award the claimant a remedy where he or she has been tainted by illegality, for fear of the court itself becoming tainted.[55] This is sometimes justified by a desire to preserve the court's credibility by its not appearing to condone illegal conduct.[56] For example, in *Everet v Williams*[57] the court refused to take an account between two highwaymen, because the claim was 'scandalous and impertinent'. As a consequence the claimant's solicitor was arrested and fined. Similarly, in *Parkinson v College of Ambulance Ltd*[58] Lush J considered that no court could award a remedy following breach of an illegal contract 'with any propriety or decency'.

But protecting the dignity of the court is an unsatisfactory justification for the illegality defence, because it suggests that the court is more concerned with its own dignity as a matter of policy rather than the need to secure justice between the parties. It appears to stem from a fundamental objection to assisting a person who has participated in criminal behaviour, involving a return to the medieval law of outlawry whereby an outlaw forfeited any rights to assistance from the courts. But, as Judge LJ recognized in *Cross v Kirby*:[59] 'today there are no outlaws. However abhorrent the crime, whatever the subsequent conviction, the protection of the law extends to the criminal who enjoys rights not only in theory but enforceable in practice.'

(E) SUMMARY

Analysis of these different justifications for the illegality defence suggests that there is no convincing policy reason in favour of denying restitution to a claimant who is tainted by illegality. Of all the suggested reasons, that which seeks to ensure the consistency, or integrity, of the legal system, is most persuasive, but there will be circumstances where this policy can be considered to be weak, or even non-existent, and so considerations of the demands of justice as between the parties should prevail.

Although the illegality defence as a function of public policy is applied strictly, at least as interpreted by the Supreme Court in *Les Laboratoires Servier v Apotex*,[60] the majority in that case did recognize that there were two questions which needed to be considered before the defence was engaged,[61] namely whether the claimant's conduct or purpose involves sufficient turpitude to engage the defence and whether the turpitude was sufficiently related to the claim. How these two questions are interpreted and answered will have an important effect on the ambit of the defence in the law of restitution.

---

[54] *St John Shipping Corp v Joseph Rank Ltd* [1957] 1 QB 267, 288 (Devlin J).
[55] *Collins v Blantern* (1767) 2 Wils 347, 350; 95 ER 850, 852 (Wilmot CJ).
[56] *Les Laboratoires Servier v Apotex* [2014] UKSC 55, [2015] AC 430, [23] (Lord Sumption).
[57] (1725) (unreported); see (1893) 9 LQR 197.   [58] [1925] 2 KB 1, 13.
[59] [2000] EWCA Civ 426.   [60] [2014] UKSC 55, [2015] AC 430.   [61] Ibid, [22] (Lord Sumption).

3. DEFINING TURPITUDE

There is no accepted definition of what constitutes illegality,[62] although it has been described as anything which is 'morally reprehensible'.[63] The word has often been used, not as a term of art, but simply to describe a state of affairs which is contrary to law; but mere unlawfulness does not necessarily equate with illegality, otherwise it would encompass a simple breach of contract.[64] A cognate principle is sometimes referred to, known as public policy, by virtue of which restitutionary claims may be defeated.[65] Reference to public policy creates uncertainty, because its requirements are uncertain and any notion of public policy is liable to change over time,[66] but also because this confuses the definition of illegality with the public policy principles which underpin the defence. It is preferable to focus on a distinct concept of illegality and to refer to public policy to explain its operation.

A number of categories of illegality can be identified. It clearly encompasses the commission of criminal conduct, save perhaps where the criminality is minor, as will sometimes be the case where the crime involves a strict liability offence,[67] at least where the claimant was unaware that his or her conduct was illegal.[68] It also includes conduct which is subject to civil penalties, such as breach of competition law,[69] involving payment to the claimant rather than the State, but where the relief still operates to punish the defendant rather than compensate the claimant for loss suffered. This has been described as 'quasi-criminal', because the interest of the State is engaged.[70]

Lawful conduct which is considered to be immoral may also be characterized as illegal. This was recognized by Hamblen J in *Nayyar v Denton Wilde Sapte*,[71] in holding that the receipt of a bribe was illegal because it evinced 'serious moral turpitude'.[72] Such immoral conduct has been held to include champertous agreements,[73] conduct relating to prostitution,[74] and agreements concerning the sale of offices and honours.[75] Illegality by virtue of immorality is illustrated by *Sutton v Mischon de Reya*,[76] where the claimant entered into what purported to be a cohabitation agreement with a third party. The relationship between the claimant and third party was one of master and slave and it was held that this made the contract illegal since it was a contract for sexual services. Although the expansion of the ambit of illegality to such immoral conduct has been justified on the ground that it too can be characterized as quasi-criminal,[77] this treatment of perceived immoral conduct as illegal is controversial.[78] It enables the law of restitution to be used to supplement the criminal law, through the denial of relief where the claimant's conduct is

---

[62] See H Beale (ed), *Chitty on Contracts* (31st edn, London: Sweet and Maxwell, 2012), paras 16-03 et seq.

[63] *Safeway Stores Ltd v Twigger* [2010] EWHC 11 (Comm), [2012] 2 Lloyd's Rep 39, [26] (Flaux J).

[64] *Les Laboratoires Servier v Apotex* [2014] UKSC 55, [2015] AC 430, [30] (Lord Sumption).

[65] See p 732, below.   [66] *Kellar v Williams* [2004] UKPC 30, [21] (Lord Carswell).

[67] *Gray v Thames Trains Ltd* [2009] UKHL 33, [2009] 1 AC 1339, [83] (Lord Rodger).

[68] *Stones and Rolls Ltd v Moore Stephens* [2009] 1 AC 1391, [24], [27] (Lord Phillips).

[69] *Safeway Stores Ltd v Twigger* [2010] EWHC 11 (Comm), [2012] 2 Lloyd's Rep 39 (price-fixing contrary to the Competition Act 1998). Although Flaux J justified the application of the illegality defence with reference to the claimant's immoral conduct rather than because it was unlawful.

[70] *Les Laboratoires Servier v Apotex* [2014] UKSC 55, [2015] AC 430, [25] (Lord Sumption).

[71] [2009] EWHC 3218 (QB), [92]. See also *Les Laboratoires Servier v Apotex* [2014] UKSC 55, [2015] AC 430, [13] (Lord Sumption).

[72] This may now be a crime: Bribery Act 2010.   [73] *Giles v Thompson* [1994] 1 AC 142.

[74] *Girardy v Richardson* (1793) 1 Esp 13, 170 ER 265.   [75] *Parkinson v College of Ambulance* [1923] 2 KB 1.

[76] [2003] EWHC 3166 (Ch).

[77] *Les Laboratoires Servier v Apotex* [2014] UKSC 55, [2015] AC 430, [25] (Lord Sumption).

[78] See J Goudkamp, 'Ex Turpi Causa and Immoral Behaviour in the Tort Context' (2011) LQR 354.

considered to be unacceptable in some way, even though it is lawful, which is difficult to defend convincingly.

Conduct which is characterized as involving wrongdoing under the civil law is generally not considered to constitute illegality. Crucially, in *Les Laboratoires Servier v Apotex*[79] the Supreme Court held that the infringement of a patent did not constitute a sufficient taint of illegality to engage the defence, because, although a patent is granted by the State, the public interest was not considered to be engaged by a breach of the patentee's rights.[80] Consequently, the infringement of private rights does not constitute illegality, although conduct which involves the commission of a tort has exceptionally been characterized as illegal where the tort requires proof of dishonesty,[81] presumably because this can also be considered to be quasi-criminal.[82] It follows that, generally, where private rights are wrongfully interfered with, there is no public interest in denying a remedy to the claimant, because, as Lord Sumption recognized, the 'public interest is sufficiently served by the availability of a system of corrective justice to regulate the consequences as between the parties affected'.[83]

Where the formation or performance of a transaction is prohibited by statute or the common law, the transaction is unenforceable by either party regardless of whether or not they knew of the illegality.[84] In other cases, whether the transaction is enforceable depends on the parties' intention or knowledge. So, for example, if both parties intend to commit an illegal act in the course of performing an otherwise legal transaction, or one party so intends and the other is aware of this illegal purpose, the transaction is unenforceable by both of them.[85] If just one of the parties had such a purpose which was unknown to the other, the party with illegal purpose would not be able to enforce the transaction, but this would have no effect on the other party's right of enforcement.[86] If one party has an illegal purpose and the other subsequently discovers it, the latter can refuse to take any further part in the transaction and will have a restitutionary action in respect of the work he or she had already lawfully done.[87]

In determining the correct definition of illegality, it is important to consider the consequences of concluding that the claimant is tainted by illegality. For, if the illegality defence is interpreted as applying absolutely without qualification, this will lead to a desire for the defence to be interpreted narrowly. But, if the defence is analysed as not being absolute in its application, it is not necessary to restrict the definition of illegality artificially, because the effect of the taint of illegality will be assessed separately, and more appropriately, with regard to identified principles. If the defence can be applied flexibly it follows that it is entirely appropriate to expand the definition of illegality to encompass certain types of civil wrongdoing and even immoral conduct.

4. MECHANISMS FOR EXCLUDING THE ILLEGALITY DEFENCE

It has been seen throughout this book that in a number of instances restitutionary remedies may be awarded despite the fact that the claimant has participated in an illegal

---

[79] [2014] UKSC 55, [2015] AC 430.   [80] Ibid, [30] (Lord Sumption).

[81] *Parkingeye Ltd v Somerfield Stores Ltd* [2012] EWCA Civ 593; [2013] Bus LR 80 (tort of deceit). See also *Brown Jenkinson and Co Ltd v Percy Dalton (London) Ltd* [1957] 2 QB 621.

[82] For example, the tort of deceit will typically, but not always, constitute a crime under the Fraud Act 2006.

[83] *Les Laboratoires Servier v Apotex* [2014] UKSC 55, [2015] AC 430, [28].

[84] *Re Mahmoud and Ispahani* [1921] 2 KB 716.   [85] *Pearce v Brooks* (1866) LR 1 Ex 213.

[86] *Archbolds (Freightage) Ltd v Spanglett Ltd* [1961] QB 374.

[87] *Clay v Yates* (1856) 1 H and N 73, 156 ER 1123.

transaction. In these cases illegality is not a ground of restitution itself,[88] but the claim will be founded on other grounds of restitution where the consequences of the illegality can be excluded on the ground that they are merely collateral to the claim.[89] Various mechanisms have been identified for establishing this. It is a matter of some controversy as to whether these mechanisms are considered to be rule-based, as the Supreme Court in *Les Laboratoires Servier v Apotex* indicated, or discretionary.[90] In the *Apotex* case Lord Sumption indicated that the mechanisms[91] were not dependent on 'a value judgment about the significance of the illegality or the consequences for the parties of barring the claim', and were not based on achieving proportionality between the claimant's misconduct and his or her loss.

(A) NO RELIANCE ON ILLEGALITY

Since the illegality defence is typically formulated in terms of the claimant being prevented from relying on the illegality to establish the claim,[92] it follows that a claim may succeed where its elements can be established without needing to rely on the illegality.[93] In *Tinsley v Milligan*[94] a majority of the House of Lords recognized that the claimant could vindicate proprietary rights even though she had participated in an illegal transaction, since it was not necessary to plead the illegality because the presumption of resulting trust was engaged.[95] But, if the claimant needs to refer to illegality to make good the claim, it will be defeated for reasons of public policy.[96] Consequently, where money has been paid to the defendant pursuant to a contract which is void for illegality, the claimant will not be able to recover it if he or she has to rely on the illegality to establish the claim. Since the claimant needs to establish that the contract is no longer operative before a claim in unjust enrichment can be brought,[97] typically it will be necessary to plead the illegality to show that the contract is void and that a failure of basis can be identified,[98] save if another reason for invalidity of the contract could be established, or another mechanism for avoiding the taint of illegality can be identified.[99] This is a potentially significant expansion of the illegality defence within the law of unjust enrichment. In *Patel v*

---

[88] Cf AS Burrows, *The Law of Restitution* (3rd edn, Oxford: Oxford University Press, 2011), 488.

[89] *Les Laboratoires Servier v Apotex* [2014] UKSC 55, [2015] AC 430, [18] (Lord Sumption).

[90] Rejected in *Les Laboratoires Servier v Apotex*, ibid, but consistent with the decision of the same court in *Hounga v Allen* [2014] UKSC 47, [2014] 1 WLR 2889. See also *Gray v Thames Trains Ltd* [2009] UKHL 33, [2009] AC 1339, [30] (Lord Hoffmann).

[91] Specifically, the no-reliance and close connection principles, see p 722, below.

[92] See Lord Mansfield in *Holman v Johnson* (1775) 1 Cowp 341, 343; 98 ER 1120, 1121; *Taylor v Chester* (1868–69) LR 4 QB 309; *Stone and Rolls v Moore Stephens* [2009] UKHL 39, [2009] 1 AC 1391, [86] (Lord Phillips).

[93] See *Bowmakers Ltd v Barnet Instruments Ltd* [1945] KB 65.

[94] [1994] 1 AC 340, 376 (Lord Browne-Wilkinson). See also *O'Kelly v Davies* [2014] EWCA Civ 1606, applying the same rule to the common intention constructive trust.

[95] See p 590, below.

[96] *Patel v Mirza* [2014] EWCA Civ 1047, [2015] 2 WLR 405, [20] (Rimer LJ), [102] (Vos LJ). See *Barrett v Barrett* [2008] EWHC 1061 (Ch), [2008] 2 P and CR 17.

[97] *Guinness plc v Saunders* [1990] 2 AC 663, 697–8 (Lord Goff); *Sandher v Pearson* [2013] EWCA Civ 1822. See Chapter 7.

[98] *Berg v Sadler and Moore* [1937] 2 KB 158, 163 (Lord Wright MR); *Patel v Mirza* [2014] EWCA Civ 1047, [2015] 2 WLR 405, [21] (Rimer LJ). Rimer LJ's assertion that allowing the claim would involve the enforcement of the illegal contract is plainly incorrect since it harks back to the discredited thinking of such claims being grounded on implied contracts.

[99] Such as withdrawal from the illegal purpose, which was engaged in *Patel v Mirza* [2014] EWCA Civ 1047, [2015] 2 WLR 405. See p 719, below.

Mirza[100] Gloster LJ, rather than considering whether the claimant needed to rely on the illegality, preferred to consider whether the illegality necessarily formed an essential element of the claimant's cause of action. But this simply repackages the rule and, anyway, in that case it was essential to the claim that the contract was void and this could only be established by reference to its illegal purpose.

Whether the claimant can establish the claim without relying on illegality is arbitrary and turns on chance. The Law Commission[101] concluded that such a principle 'produces complex and arbitrary results, depending on the detailed intricacies of trust law'.[102] For example, the result in *Tinsley v Milligan* would have been different had the presumption of advancement applied, for then the claimant would have needed to plead the illegal agreement to rebut the presumption. Even where the claimant needs to plead the illegality to establish the claim, it does not necessarily follow that the claim will be defeated.[103] Further, the illegality defence applies even if illegality has not been pleaded, since it may be raised by the judge.

In *Cross v Kirby* Beldam LJ said:[104] 'I do not believe that there is any general principle that the claimant must either plead, give evidence of or rely on his own illegality for the principle to apply. Such a technical approach is entirely absent from Lord Mansfield CJ's exposition of the principle.' Lord Phillips recognized in *Stone and Rolls Ltd v Moore Stephens*:[105]

> I do not believe ... that it is right to proceed on the basis that the reliance test can automatically be applied as a rule of thumb. It is necessary to give consideration to the policy underlying *ex turpi causa* in order to decide whether this defence is bound to defeat [the claimant's] claim.

Since there was no express reference in *Holman v Johnson* to the need to plead the illegality for the defence to be engaged, the preferable view is that this rule should be rejected for reasons of artifice and formalism. It follows that it should be possible for the claimant to refer to the illegality to establish, for example, that any contract does not provide a lawful basis for the defendant's receipt of an enrichment.

(B) WITHDRAWAL FROM AN ILLEGAL TRANSACTION

Where the claimant has effectively withdrawn[106] from an illegal transaction[107] before any part of it has been performed he or she may be considered no longer to be tainted by the illegality and restitution will be awarded. In *Patel v Mirza*[108] it was recognized that withdrawal does not require proof of repentance on the part of the claimant.[109] It is simply sufficient that the claimant has sought restitution before any part of the illegal agreement has been carried into effect to any extent, or the claimant has attempted to

---

[100] [2014] EWCA Civ 1047, [2015] 2 WLR 405, [79].

[101] *The Illegality Defence* (Law Com No 320, 2010).   [102] Ibid, 2.

[103] In *Silverwood v Silverwood* (1997) 74 P and CR 453, 457 Peter Gibson LJ accepted that the claimant could rely on the illegal purpose of the parties to rebut the defendant's defence that the transferor of the property had intended it to be a gift to the defendant. See p 590, above.

[104] *Cross v Kirby* [2000] EWCA Civ 426, [76].

[105] [2009] UKHL 39, [2009] 1 AC 1391, [25]. Affirmed by Lord Wilson in *Hounga v Allen* [2014] UKSC 47, [2014] 1 WLR 2889, [30].

[106] See *Taylor v Bowers* (1876) 1 QBD 291; *Tribe v Tribe* [1996] Ch 107. Cp *Kearley v Thomson* (1890) 24 QBD 742, where restitution was denied where the illegal agreement had been carried out.

[107] See p 353, above.   [108] [2014] EWCA Civ 1047, [2015] 2 WLR 405.

[109] This had also been recognized by Millett LJ in *Tribe v Tribe* [1996] Ch 107, 135.

carry it into effect,[110] even though the only reason for withdrawal is that it is impossible to carry out the agreement as originally envisaged for reasons outside the control of the claimant. In *Patel v Mirza* the claimant had paid money to the defendant pursuant to a contract which was illegal because it related to the crime of insider dealing.[111] The claimant was found to have withdrawn from the agreement even though the only reason for the withdrawal was that the illegal purpose was frustrated for reasons outside his control, namely that the expected inside information was not obtained. Consequently, withdrawal does not require any change of mind on the part of the claimant; it is simply sufficient that the illegal purpose was frustrated,[112] save, presumably, where the illegality is so grave that 'withdrawal' can never remove the taint of the illegality.[113] This is consequently a very significant restriction on the operation of the illegality defence, which enables the taint of illegality to be ignored so that the court can focus on correcting the injustice as between the claimant and defendant.

(C) THE PARTIES ARE NOT *IN PARI DELICTO*

The claimant's restitutionary claim will succeed even though the claim arises from participation in an illegal transaction, where the parties are not *in pari delicto*, which will usually be the case where the defendant is more responsible for participating in the illegal transaction than the claimant.

(i) Compulsion

The claimant will be able to bring a restitutionary claim by virtue of compulsion[114] despite the fact that he or she has been tainted by illegality.[115] This has also been recognized by the European Court of Justice in the context of a claimant who is not as responsible as the defendant for entering into an anti-competitive agreement which is illegal by EC law.[116]

(ii) Actual or Potential Exploitation

In certain circumstances the defendant will be deemed to be more responsible for participation in the illegal transaction than the claimant where the defendant occupied a position in which he or she could actually or potentially exploit the claimant's weaker position.[117] This will arise in two situations: first, where the defendant has acted oppressively;[118] secondly, where statute imposes an obligation on one party to ensure that the transaction complied with the law.[119]

---

[110] As occurred in *Alexander v Rayson* [1936] 1 KB 169; *Berg v Sadler and Moore* [1937] 2 KB 15; *Harry Parker Ltd v Mason* [1940] 2 KB 590; *Collier v Collier* [2002] EWCA Civ 1095.

[111] Contrary to s 52 of the Criminal Justice Act 1993.

[112] Cf *Bigos v Bousted* [1951] 1 All ER 92 where the withdrawal principle did not apply where the frustration of the illegal purpose resulted from the refusal of the other party to participate. This decision was described as 'dubious' by Millett LJ in *Tribe v Tribe* [1996] Ch 107, 135, although Rimer LJ in *Patel v Mirza* [2014] EWCA Civ 1047, [2015] 2 WLR 405, [41], considered it to be sound because there had been no 'voluntary withdrawal'. But there was no 'voluntary withdrawal' in *Patel* either, save that, once the agreement was frustrated, the claimant then sought restitution. Distinguishing between *Bigos v Bousted* and *Patel* with reference to the voluntariness of the withdrawal is unconvincing. See *Patel v Mirza*, [96] (Gloster LJ).

[113] See p 723, below.   [114] See p 205, above.   [115] *Astley v Reynolds* (1731) 2 Stra 915, 93 ER 939.

[116] Case C-453/99 *Courage Ltd v Crehan* [2002] QB 507.   [117] See p 286, above.

[118] See, for example, *Smith v Cuff* (1817) 6 M and S 160, 105 ER 1203.

[119] See, for example, *Kiriri Cotton Co Ltd v Dewani* [1960] AC 192.

(iii) Restitution for Wrongs

The principle that restitutionary relief will be available if the parties are not *in pari delicto* will also be relevant where the restitutionary claim is founded on wrongdoing. For, where the claimant is innocent of the wrong and it was the defendant who had acted illegally, the defendant cannot rely on the defence of illegality to retain an enrichment. [120]

(iv) Failure of Basis

Although it is a generally recognized rule that a restitutionary claim grounded on total failure of basis will be defeated if the claimant participated in an illegal transaction,[121] this will not be the case where the claimant is not as blameworthy as the defendant. This is illustrated by *Mohamed v Alaga and Co*,[122] where the claimant sued the defendant firm of solicitors for work done in preparing and presenting asylum claims. A contract between the claimant and the defendant concerning payment to the claimant for the introduction of clients to the defendant was illegal as it was an unlawful fee-sharing agreement, but the claimant's restitutionary claim succeeded as regards the professional work he had legitimately done. This work could be severed from the illegal fee-sharing part of the contract because the claimant was less responsible for the illegality than the defendant firm of solicitors, which was assumed to know the rules of the profession.[123]

(v) Summary

The not *in pari delicto* mechanism is very significant in restricting the ambit of the illegality defence as regards claims in unjust enrichment. Despite the taint of illegality, it enables the court to focus on the comparative responsibilities of the parties and enables the public policy of the illegality defence to be trumped by the need to secure justice between the parties.

(D) THE POLICY BEHIND THE ILLEGALITY

In Australia the operation of the illegality defence is determined by reference to the policy of the law by virtue of which the relevant transaction was found to have been illegal.[124] This was recognized by the High Court of Australia in *Nelson v Nelson*,[125] where Deane and Gummow JJ indicated that statutory policy might be less likely to defeat a claim where the claimant sought restitution to restore the claimant to his or her original position, rather than where the claimant sought to enforce a contract.[126]

This focus on the policy behind the law which renders a transaction illegal was considered further by the High Court in *Equus Corp Pty Ltd v Haxton*.[127] Money had been advanced under loan agreements which were made in furtherance of an illegal purpose to obtain tax deductions through an investment scheme in blueberry farms. The claimant sought restitution of the money transferred to the defendant, but it was held that the illegality which rendered the loan agreements unenforceable also denied the restitutionary claim, by reference to the scope and purpose of the statute which rendered the transaction illegal, particularly the purpose of protecting a class of persons from whom

---

[120] See, for example, Chapter 19.

[121] See *Parkinson v College of Ambulance* [1923] 2 KB 1, p 711, above. But note the interpretation of the withdrawal exception as embodying total failure of basis as a ground of restitution. See p 353, above.

[122] [2000] 1 WLR 1815.

[123] Cf *Awwad v Geraght and Co* [2001] QB 570 where the claimant was a partner in the firm of solicitors.

[124] See also PBH Birks, 'Recovering Value Transferred Under an Illegal Contract' (2001) 1 Theoretical Inquiries in Law 155.   [125] (1995) 184 CLR 538.

[126] Ibid, 552.   [127] [2012] HCA 7. See also *Miller v Miller* [2011] HCA 9, (2011) 242 CLR 446.

the claimant sought restitution. But the court also had regard to the responsibility of the claimant and whether it was innocent or was involved in the illegality,[128] which was specifically recognized as indicating that the parties were not *in pari delicto*.

Denying restitution where its award would stultify the purpose of the statute which rendered the relevant transaction illegal in the first place is clearly justified by the need to ensure coherence in the law, by avoiding stultification of the law.[129] This has been recognized by the American Law Institute's *Restatement of the Law, Third: Restitution and Unjust Enrichment*,[130] with reference to the need to ensure that the policy of the statute is not defeated or frustrated.

In England, whether it is possible to recover the value of a loan made pursuant to a void transaction has been held to depend on whether restitution would undermine the policy which rendered to transaction void. So, for example, in *Haugesund Kommune v Depfa ACS Bank*[131] the value of a loan could be recovered by means of a claim in unjust enrichment, albeit that in that case the loan was unenforceable by virtue of the defendant's incapacity to borrow the money, rather than because of illegality. But the Court of Appeal still emphasized that it was necessary to consider whether allowing restitution would be contrary to public policy with reference to the reason why the loan was void. It is likely that, where the loan transaction is illegal, the policy of the statute which renders the transaction void will deny restitution, especially where the policy is founded on the need to protect the defendant. Consequently, it is likely that *Equus Corp Ltd v Haxton* would be decided the same way in England.

(E) CLOSE CONNECTION OR INEXTRICABLE LINK

A further mechanism to limit the operation of the illegality defence is slowly emerging, namely whether there is a sufficiently close connection or inextricable link between the claim and the illegality that the court cannot permit the claimant to recover without appearing to condone the illegal conduct.[132] This has been recognized by the Law Commission,[133] which suggested that it would only be a proportionate response to deny the claimant a remedy where there was such a close connection. This also appears to have been recognized by the Supreme Court in *Les Laboratoires Servier v Apotex*,[134] in holding that the turpitude must be sufficiently related to the claim.

This test of close connection or inextricable link has proved to be especially important in the law of tort, where the defence will be engaged if the illegality is a proximate cause of the claimant's loss.[135] It follows that the claimant cannot recover for a loss arising from a punishment imposed for the commission of a crime,[136] by virtue of the policy to ensure consistency between the law of tort and the criminal law.[137] Further, the illegality defence

---

[128] *Equus Corp Pty Ltd v Haxton* [2012] HCA 7, [34] (French CJ, Krennan, and Kiefel JJ).

[129] *Boissevain v Weil* [1950] AC 327, 341.   [130] (2011) § 32(2), 505–6.

[131] [2010] EWCA Civ 579, [2012] QB 549. See p 375, above.

[132] *Cross v Kirby* [2000] EWCA Civ 426, [76] (Beldam LJ).

[133] Consultation Paper, No 189, *The Illegality Defence* (2009), 3.143.

[134] [2014] UKSC 55, [2015] AC 430, [22] (Lord Sumption).

[135] *Gray v Thames Trains Ltd* [2009] UKHL 33, [2009] 1 AC 1339 [32] (Lord Hoffmann). Lord Hoffmann preferred the language of causation to that of inextricable link: ibid, [53]. Some cases have focused on the language of remoteness, for example *21st Century Logistic Solutions Ltd v Madysen Ltd* [2004] EWHC 231 (QB), [2004] 2 Lloyd's Rep 92, [18] (Field J).

[136] *Askey v Golden Wine Co Ltd* [1948] 2 All ER 35, 38 (Denning J).

[137] *Gray v Thames Trains Ltd* [2009] UKHL 33, [2009] 1 AC 1339, [37] (Lord Hoffmann); *Delaney v Pickett* [2011] EWCA Civ 1532, [2012] 1 WLR 2149, [35] (Ward LJ).

prevents the claimant from recovering for loss which was a consequence of his or her own illegal act,[138] which has also been justified by the need to ensure consistency between tort and criminal law.[139]

This principle of close connection between the illegality and the claim was recognized by the dissenting minority in *Tinsley v Milligan*,[140] where Lords Keith and Goff, rather than focusing on whether the claimant needed to rely on the illegality to establish her claim, favoured a rule which would bar any claim tainted by a sufficiently close factual connection with the illegal purpose, and would consequently have dismissed the claim to an equitable proprietary interest for that reason.

The validity of this close connection test is, however, controversial, since it will often be unclear when the test is satisfied. Indeed, this might be considered to be a generic test for disapplying the illegality defence which will be met if any of the other mechanisms are established. So, for example, if allowing restitution is consistent with the policy of the statute which renders the conduct criminal, it would be appropriate to conclude that the illegality is then not sufficiently connected to the claim. Similarly, where the claimant has withdrawn from the illegal transaction or where the claimant is less responsible than the defendant for participation in the illegal transaction.

5. SERIOUS CRIMINAL CULPABILITY

Where the illegality involves particularly serious turpitude the policy behind the *ex turpi causa* defence should be regarded as absolute and should not be qualified.[141] Only in such circumstances should the public policies of protecting the dignity of the courts and seeking to deter illegal conduct take priority. Consequently, a court would never order restitution of money paid to the defendant to kill a third party, simply because the agreement would be too grossly immoral for the court to consider assisting the claimant,[142] even if the victim had died from natural causes, so frustrating the conspiracy.[143] Similarly, the court should not allow a claimant to vindicate his or her proprietary rights in respect of property which is held on resulting trust where the claimant had contributed to the purchase of a house which was vested in the sole name of the defendant, in circumstances in which the house was intended to be used as a base for terrorist activities.[144]

The decision of the Court of Appeal in *Taylor v Bhail*[145] can be justified on similar grounds. In that case the claimant builder had agreed with the defendant that he would submit an estimate for building work which was £1,000 above the actual cost of the estimated work, to enable the defendant to defraud his insurance company. The restitutionary claim that he should be paid for the work which he had actually done failed. This can be justified on the ground that the claimant and the defendant had committed the serious crime of conspiracy to defraud.[146] As Millett LJ recognized, such insurance fraud is a serious problem which needs to be deterred[147] and so restitutionary relief was denied

---

[138] *Gray v Thames Trains Ltd* [2009] UKHL 33, [2009] 1 AC 1339, [54] (Lord Hoffmann).

[139] Lord Sumption, 'Reflections on the Law of Illegality' [2012] RLR 1, 9.   [140] [1994] 1 AC 340.

[141] See *Bowmakers Ltd v Barnet Instruments Ltd* [1945] 1 KB 65, 72 (du Parcq LJ).

[142] *Tappenden v Randall* (1801) 2 Bos and Pul 467, 471; 126 ER 1388, 1390 (Heath J); *Kearley v Thomson* (1890) 24 QBD 742, 747 (Fry LJ).

[143] *Patel v Mirza* [2014] EWCA Civ 1047, [2015] 2 WLR 405, [117] (Vos LJ).

[144] See *Tinsley v Milligan* [1994] 1 AC 340, 362 (Lord Goff).

[145] [1996] CLC 377.   [146] Ibid, 381 (Russell LJ).   [147] Ibid, 384.

simply on the ground of public policy. This can, however, be contrasted with *Patel v Mirza*[148] where restitution was awarded even though money had been paid pursuant to a criminal conspiracy to commit insider dealing, which presumably should be deterred as well. It follows that it will be difficult to determine when the illegality is sufficiently grave. It has sometimes been suggested that it is not appropriate for the civil courts to grade illegality according to moral turpitude,[149] but that is something which the criminal courts do all the time as part of the sentencing exercise and there is no reason why the civil courts are unable to do so as well.

It has been suggested that the illegality defence should generally apply to any crime which is punishable with imprisonment,[150] but this has no regard to the circumstances in which the crime was committed. Factors which are relevant to the sentencing exercise in the criminal courts should also be relevant in the civil law, so it is not sufficient just to consider the maximum sentence available for the crime, but the circumstances in which the offence was committed and by whom should also be examined to determine whether the offender would have been imprisoned and for how long.[151]

6. THE PREFERRED APPROACH

The law on the defence of illegality is at a crossroads. There are three distinct routes which might be followed. The first is the purely public policy route, where illegality is treated as an absolute defence, and is constrained only by the adoption of a restricted definition of illegality and by the need to consider whether the illegality is sufficiently connected with the claim.[152] Such an approach has no regard to the justice of the case as between the parties or countervailing policy considerations. The second route focuses on the public policies which underpin the illegality defence, but seeks to ascertain whether the operation of the defence can be justified by virtue of those policies.[153] The legitimacy of this approach turns on the validity and acceptance of the underlying policies. There is a danger that this collapses from a principled exercise of judicial discretion into the exercise of arbitrary judicial discretion, potentially even returning to the old public conscience test. The third route adopts a middle way between the other two. It recognizes the public policy dimension of the illegality defence as a starting point for its application, but then moderates this by reference both to how illegality is defined and to various recognized mechanisms which can be analysed as involving both countervailing policy considerations and the need to consider the justice of the case as between the parties.

This middle way is preferable and should be adopted in the law of restitution. Consequently, where the claimant is no longer tainted by the illegality or can be considered to be less responsible for participation in the illegal transaction than the defendant, it is

---

[148] [2014] EWCA Civ 1047, [2015] 2 WLR 405.

[149] *Pitts v Hunt* [1991] 1 QB 24, 56 (Dillon LJ), what he called a 'graph of illegalities'.

[150] *Vellino v Chief Constable of Greater Manchester Police* [2001] EWCA Civ 1249, [2002] 1 WLR 218, [70] (Sir Murray Stuart-Smith).

[151] *Hewison v Meridian Shipping Services Pte Ltd* [2002] EWCA Civ 1821, [2003] ICR 766, [85] (Ward LJ).

[152] *Les Laboratoires Servier v Apotex* [2014] UKSC 55, [2015] AC 430.

[153] This was the approach adopted in *Stone and Rolls Ltd v Moore Stephens* [2009] UKHL 39, [2009] 1 AC 1391, [25] (Lord Phillips); *Hounga v Allen* [2014] UKSC 47, [2014] 1 WLR 2889; *Parkingeye Ltd v Somerfield Stores Ltd* [2012] EWCA Civ 1338, [2013] QB 840; and *Patel v Mirza* [2014] EWCA Civ 1047, [2015] 2 WLR 404, [62] (LJ). It was also adopted by the Court of Appeal in *Apotex*, which was rejected by the Supreme Court, and also by the Singapore Court of Appeal: *Ting Siew May v Boon Long Choo* [2014] SGCA 28.

appropriate for a restitutionary remedy to be awarded, save where the turpitude is especially serious.

In *Tinsley v Milligan*[154] Lord Goff said: 'I would be more than happy if a new system could be evolved which was both satisfactory in its effect and capable of avoiding the kind of result which flows from the established rules of law.' Subsequently, there have been demands for a statutory reform of the rule-based illegality defence,[155] along the lines of the law in New Zealand[156] and Israel,[157] to allow restitution despite the taint of illegality through the exercise of a structured judicial discretion. But there is no need for such statutory reform; the existing law can be rationalized in such a way as to avoid the perceived injustices identified by Lord Goff. The Law Commission has rejected statutory reform,[158] save where a trust has been created to conceal the beneficiary's interest in connection with a criminal purpose. It was right to do so.

The law can be summarized as follows: illegality should be recognized as a defence to restitutionary claims by virtue of public policy, primarily founded on the need for consistency between the criminal law and the law of restitution, but justice demands that the defence should not operate where the claimant is less responsible than the defendant for involvement in the illegal activity or cannot be considered to be tainted by the illegality anymore. Further, there may be countervailing policy reasons which trump the illegality defence, notably that the rule which makes the conduct illegal is not stultified by allowing restitution.

---

[154] [1994] 1 AC 340, 363.

[155] *The Illegality Defence* (Law Commission Consultation Paper No 189, 2009). See B Dickson, 'Restitution and Illegal Transactions' in AS Burrows (ed), *Essays on the Law of Restitution* (Oxford: Clarendon Press, 1991), 195; Lord Sumption 'Reflections on the Law of Illegality'.

[156] The Illegal Contracts Act 1970, s 7.   [157] Contract Law (General Part) 1973, s 31.

[158] *The Illegality Defence* (Law Com No 320, 2010).

28

INCAPACITY

1. QUESTIONS OF POLICY

It was seen in Chapter 14 that incapacity can operate as a ground of restitution in its own right, in that it enables the claimant who is incapacitated to secure restitution where the incapacity arises from mental disorder, minority or institutional incapacity. In each of these cases there is a strong policy of protection to ensure that the person who is incapacitated does not suffer from entering into foolish transactions. The question which needs to be considered in this chapter is whether the fact that the defendant was incapacitated in some way can operate as a defence to defeat a restitutionary claim, regardless of the nature of that claim. This raises two contradictory policy questions.

(A) DOES AN INCAPACITATED DEFENDANT DESERVE TO BE PROTECTED FROM RESTITUTIONARY CLAIMS?

The effect of recognizing a defence of incapacity is that the defendant would be able to retain benefits which he or she would otherwise be required to restore to the claimant. Does the fact that the defendant is incapacitated in itself require the defendant to be protected from restitutionary claims? Giving the incapacitated defendant a defence to a restitutionary claim is more difficult to justify than recognizing incapacity as a ground of restitution for a claimant who is incapacitated. This is because, where the defendant is incapacitated and is not prejudiced by being required to make restitution to the claimant, there is no obvious reason why the defendant's incapacity should bar the claim. Where the defendant would be prejudiced in making restitution this will usually be because the defendant's circumstances will have changed and he or she would usually be able to rely on the defence of change of position.[1]

(B) WOULD THE AWARD OF A RESTITUTIONARY REMEDY TO THE CLAIMANT SUBVERT THE LAW OF CONTRACT?

Usually the question of the defendant's incapacity will arise where the claimant and defendant have entered into a contract which has been vitiated by the defendant's incapacity. The claimant may have transferred a benefit to the defendant pursuant to the transaction which the claimant will then wish to recover. The consequent question of policy is whether the granting of a restitutionary remedy to the claimant against the incapacitated defendant can be considered to subvert the law of contract by virtue of which the contract was treated as vitiated in the first place. This is an important issue, since it is a fundamental principle of the law of restitution that the award of restitutionary

---

[1] See Chapter 25.

remedies must not subvert the law of contract.[2] If the contract was vitiated because of a policy of protecting the defendant from the consequences of his or her incapacity, perhaps this policy should be carried through to the law of restitution as well, so that the restitutionary claim should fail.

Both of these policy questions must be borne in mind when considering whether different types of incapacity should operate as defences to restitutionary claims.

2. MINORITY

(A) RESTITUTIONARY CLAIMS FOUNDED ON THE REVERSAL OF UNJUST ENRICHMENT

(i) The Supply of Necessaries

Where the claimant has supplied a minor, who is defined as anybody under the age of 18,[3] with necessary goods or services pursuant to a contract, the claimant is able to recover the reasonable value of these necessaries[4] even though the contract itself is unenforceable.[5] It is clear therefore that the restitutionary claim will succeed and the minor has no defence of incapacity.

(ii) The Supply of Non-Necessary Benefits

Where the claimant has transferred benefits to a minor which cannot be characterized as necessaries the claimant is unable to enforce the contract against the minor.[6] The traditional view is that the claimant will not be able to bring a restitutionary claim against the minor for the value of the benefit transferred because the defendant has a defence of minority. Although this defence has been recognized in a number of cases, careful analysis of them suggests that their conclusions are highly dubious in the light of later developments in the law of restitution.

(1) Decisions Which Recognize a Defence of Minority

The leading case which suggests that the defendant's minority is a defence to restitutionary claims is *Cowern v Nield*,[7] where the claimant paid the defendant, who was a minor, a sum of money for goods which the defendant subsequently failed to deliver. The claimant sued to recover the money on the ground of total failure of basis, but the claim failed because the court concluded that it was not possible to imply a contract between the minor and the claimant since this would result in the indirect enforcement of a contract which was void. Similarly, in *R Leslie Ltd v Shiell*[8] the claimant had lent money to the defendant minor, who had made a fraudulent misrepresentation as to his age. The claimant sought to recover this money but was unable to do so, again on the ground that the court would not indirectly enforce a contract which was void by reason of the defendant's incapacity.[9]

The problem with the reasoning in these cases is that it is founded on the fact that the court would not imply a contract to make restitution where that contract was void. But the

---

[2] See p 134, above. [3] Family Law Reform Act 1969, s 1.
[4] See the Sale of Goods Act 1979, s 3(2) which applies to the sale and delivery of goods which can be characterized as necessaries.
[5] See p 300, above. [6] See p 384, above.
[7] [1912] 2 KB 419. See also *Bristow v Eastman* (1794) 1 Esp 172, 170 ER 317.
[8] [1914] 3 KB 607. [9] Ibid, 612 (Lord Sumner).

implied contract theory of restitutionary claims was rejected by the House of Lords in *United Australia Ltd v Barclays Bank Ltd.*[10] It is now clear that the obligation to make restitution is imposed as a matter of law[11] and has nothing to do with the enforcement of any actual or implied contract between the parties. It follows that, if the claimant had been awarded restitutionary relief in these cases where the defendant was a minor, this would not have infringed the particular legal policy which stated that any contract made between the parties was unenforceable.

(2) Should a Defence of Minority Be Recognized?

Although the reasoning in the cases which have recognized a defence of minority can be rejected, it is still necessary to consider whether, as a matter of policy, the defendant's minority should operate as a defence to a restitutionary claim. Whilst it is true that minors require some protection against the consequences of entering into foolish transactions which they are not able to detect because of their immaturity, the minor should not be over-protected, since this may cause injustice to the party with full capacity. It follows that a restitutionary claim against a minor should only be defeated where there is a danger of the minor being unduly prejudiced by virtue of the obligation to make restitution. Such prejudice will not occur where the minor still has the benefit or its product which the claimant had transferred to him or her, since the minor can justifiably be expected to return that which he or she had no right to retain. Where, however, the minor has dissipated the benefit, he or she could be prejudiced if he or she was required to make restitution to the claimant, since the minor would need to find the value of the benefit from his or her own resources. But in circumstances such as this there is no need for the restitutionary claim to be defeated by a defence of incapacity, because the defence of change of position would presumably be applicable. Perhaps the defence of change of position should be interpreted more flexibly where the defendant is a minor, to give him or her greater protection against restitutionary claims than is available where the defend-ant is an adult. So where, for example, the minor has received a sum of money from the claimant to purchase necessaries and the minor wastes the money on extravagant parties, this might enable the defendant to rely on the defence of change of position even though the defence would not have been available had the defendant been an adult, because it would not have been equitable to allow the defence to succeed.[12] Consequently, the fact that the defendant was a minor should be taken into account when determining whether the change of position defence should succeed.

There was no obvious policy reason why the restitutionary claim should have failed in both *Cowern v Neild* and *R Leslie Ltd v Shiell*, because there was nothing to suggest that the award of a restitutionary remedy would have prejudiced the minor. In *Cowern v Nield* the minor had received money for goods which he had failed to deliver and, assuming that he had not changed his position, he should have been required to repay this money to the claimant. Equally, in *R Leslie Ltd v Shiell* if the minor had been obliged to repay the claimant the sum of money he had borrowed at a reasonable rate of interest the claimant could not be considered to have taken advantage of the defendant's minority in any way.

It follows that there is no role for a defence of minority where the restitutionary claim is founded on the defendant's unjust enrichment, since the defence of change of position, perhaps interpreted more liberally than normally, would give the defendant adequate protection against the restitutionary claim.

---

[10] [1941] AC 1.
[11] See *Westdeutsche Landesbank Girozentrale v Islington LBC* [1996] AC 669, 688 (Lord Goff).
[12] See p 690, above.

(B) RESTITUTIONARY CLAIMS FOUNDED ON WRONGDOING

(i) Tort

Where the defendant has obtained a benefit as a result of the commission of a wrong there is no reason why the fact that the defendant was a minor should defeat the restitutionary claim. A minor does not deserve particular protection against restitutionary claims where he or she has obtained a benefit as a result of wrongdoing. This has been recognized in a number of cases. For example, in *Bristow v Eastman*[13] the defendant was held liable for embezzling money from his employer. Here the underlying wrong was either the tort of conversion or of deceit. It was specifically held that minority was not a defence to this action, since the action was founded on the commission of a tort.

Where, however, the tort on which the claim is founded is connected with a contract made with a minor, it has been held that, because the contract is unenforceable, the action grounded on the tort will also be barred since if such a claim was allowed to succeed it would result in the indirect enforcement of the contract. This is illustrated by *Stocks v Wilson*[14] where the defendant, who was a minor, fraudulently misrepresented his age and consequently induced the claimant to sell and deliver to him furniture, paintings, and artefacts for £300. The defendant sold some of these items and used the rest as security for a loan. The defendant failed to pay the claimant the agreed contract price. The claimant unsuccessfully sued the defendant for breach of contract because the contract was unenforceable as a result of the defendant's minority. The claimant also sued the defendant for damages for deceit and this action also failed because the deceit related to the contract.

The reasoning of the judges in these cases is unconvincing because the remedy which the claimant sought was founded on tort and not contract. The fact that the tort related to the formation of the contract is irrelevant, particularly where the claimant seeks a restitutionary remedy, since the effect of this remedy is not to enforce any contract which was made as a result of the commission of the tort, but simply to deprive the defendant of any benefits obtained from the commission of the wrong.

(ii) Equitable Wrongdoing

Where the restitutionary claim is founded on an equitable wrong the fact that the defendant is a minor is no defence.[15]

(iii) Crime

Where the defendant has profited from the commission of a crime he or she should be required to disgorge any benefits derived from that crime by virtue of the principle that no criminal should be allowed to profit from a crime. This principle is so fundamental to the law of restitution that the defendant should be required to disgorge the profit even though he or she was a minor.

(iv) Breach of Contract

Where the restitutionary claim is founded on the defendant's breach of contract, the fact that the defendant is a minor will be a relevant consideration because the policy of the law of contract should prevail even though the claimant seeks a restitutionary remedy. Since a contract is unenforceable against a minor it should follow that, where the minor breaches the contract, he or she cannot be considered to have committed a wrong. Consequently, if

---

[13] (1794) 1 Esp 171, 170 ER 317.   [14] [1913] 2 KB 235. See also *R Leslie Ltd v Shiell* [1914] 3 KB 607.

[15] *Stocks v Wilson* [1913] 2 KB 235.

no wrong has been committed, there is no scope for the claimant to bring a restitutionary claim founded on restitution for wrongs. Here the defendant's minority does not operate as a defence to the claim; it simply prevents the claimant from establishing that claim in the first place.

(v) Conclusions

It follows that the defendant's minority should not operate as a defence to a restitutionary claim where that claim is founded on the commission of a wrong. But it is important to ensure that the award of a restitutionary remedy does not unduly prejudice the defendant. The mechanism for this is through the flexible application of the defence of change of position, through reduced emphasis on the fact that the defendant was a wrongdoer.

(C) RESTITUTIONARY CLAIMS FOUNDED ON THE VINDICATION OF PROPERTY RIGHTS

Although in principle if the claimant wishes to recover property from the defendant it should be irrelevant that the defendant was a minor when he or she received the property, the defendant's minority must be taken into account when the property has been transferred under a contract. This is because, by virtue of section 3(1) of the Minors' Contracts Act 1987, the court has discretion as to whether the claimant can recover his or her property from such a defendant where it considers it to be just and equitable that a restitutionary remedy should be available. It follows that the law contemplates that the claimant will be able to vindicate his or her proprietary rights against a minor, although the claimant does not have a right to a restitutionary remedy, since the award of the remedy lies in the discretion of the court.

3. MENTAL INCAPACITY

Mental incapacity may take a variety of forms.[16] It may be permanent, as where the defendant is insane, or temporary, as where the defendant was drunk at the time of entering a transaction with the claimant.[17] Whether mental incapacity can operate as a defence to restitutionary claims is something which has received little judicial attention. The leading case on the point is *Re Rhodes*[18] which, at first sight, might be interpreted as suggesting that such a defence is recognized because the restitutionary claim failed. The defendant was living in a mental asylum and the claimants, who were relatives of the defendant, had paid some of the charges which had arisen. The claimants sought to recover these charges from the defendant on the ground that they were necessaries, but this claim failed. This was not, however, because the defendant was incapacitated, but simply because the claimants were not able to show that they intended to be repaid by the defendant. In other words, the claimants had acted as volunteers. There was nothing in the case to indicate that the claim would otherwise have failed simply because the defendant was incapacitated.

---

[16] See p 381, above.

[17] An intoxicated defendant who has purchased necessaries and who was incompetent to contract because of the intoxication, is required to pay for them: Sale of Goods Act 1979, s 3(2). This provision used to extend to those who were mentally incapacitated, but this was revoked by the Mental Capacity Act 2005, Sch 6.

[18] (1890) 44 Ch D 94.

Since the defendant's minority does not operate as a defence to restitutionary claims, there is no reason why a defence of mental incapacity should be recognized, particularly because both forms of incapacity have a similar function, namely to protect the incapacitated person from the adverse consequences of entering into foolish transactions. Where a mentally incapacitated defendant has received a benefit from the claimant there is no reason why the defendant should retain that benefit simply because of the incapacity. The only significance of the defendant's incapacity is that, where his or her circumstances have changed since the benefit was received, the defence of change of position may be applied in a more flexible way than it would be if the defendant had full capacity.

4. INSTITUTIONAL INCAPACITY

The question of incapacity has been particularly important in the context of companies which have entered into transactions which they do not have capacity to make. Such *ultra vires* transactions are null and void.[19] In a number of cases the courts have had to consider whether the fact that the defendant company was incapacitated constituted a bar to a restitutionary claim. Although this is no longer a relevant question, because by virtue of section 39(1) of the Companies Act 2006 the claimant can enforce a transaction which is beyond the capacity of the company, the old cases remain relevant since they assist in determining what the position of the common law is as to the defence of incapacity generally. Also the question of incapacity remains highly relevant in respect of other institutions which remain subject to the *ultra vires* doctrine, most notably public authorities.[20]

(A) REJECTION OF A DEFENCE OF INSTITUTIONAL INCAPACITY

The general attitude of the common law has been that the fact that the defendant institution lacks capacity to enter into a transaction does not operate as a bar to a restitutionary claim. This is justifiable on policy grounds. The prime purpose of the *ultra vires* doctrine is to ensure that shareholders, taxpayers and creditors are protected from the consequences of the institution entering into speculative transactions. But this policy of protection is not furthered in any way by the defendant institution being able to retain benefits which would otherwise have had to be returned had the defendant not been acting *ultra vires*. This approach is reflected in *Re Phoenix Life Assurance Co*,[21] where a company issued marine insurance policies to the claimant which it lacked capacity to do. When the company was wound up, the claimant sought to enforce claims on these policies. Although the claims on the policies themselves were barred, because they were void as a result of the company's lack of capacity to issue them, the claimant was still able to recover the premiums in an action for money had and received, the ground of restitution being total failure of basis. The claim was not affected in any way by the defendant's incapacity. Similarly, in *National Bank of Egypt International Ltd v Oman Housing Bank SAOC*,[22] the

---

[19] *Ashbury Railway Carriage and Iron Co Ltd v Riche* (1875) LR 7 HL 653.
[20] See, in particular, *Woolwich Equitable Building Society v IRC* [1993] AC 70 and the litigation arising from interest rate swaps transactions.
[21] (1862) 2 J and H 441, 70 ER 1131. See also *Flood v Irish Provident Assurance Co* (1912) 46 ILT 214.
[22] [2002] EWHC 1760 (Comm); [2003] 1 All ER (Comm) 246.

claimant was able to recover money it had lent to a bank which lacked the capacity to borrow the money; the defendant's incapacity did not bar the restitutionary claim.

That institutional capacity should not be a defence to restitutionary claims at all is reflected in the litigation arising from public authorities entering into interest rate swap transactions. These transactions were null and void because the local authorities lacked capacity to enter into them.[23] Consequently, where a financial institution sought restitution from the local authorities a defence of institutional incapacity would have defeated the claim. But restitution was not denied in any of the swaps cases on the ground of incapacity. Indeed, restitutionary relief was awarded in many of them despite the defendant's incapacity.[24]

(B) IMPLICIT RECOGNITION OF A DEFENCE OF INSTITUTIONAL INCAPACITY

There are, however, certain cases where the defendant's incapacity has effectively operated as a defence to a restitutionary claim. The most important of these is the decision of the House of Lords in *Sinclair v Brougham*[25] where the claimants sought to recover money which they had lent to a building society which was carrying on a banking business even though it lacked capacity to do so. The House of Lords held that the claimants' personal claim for restitution failed, because the award of restitutionary relief would have indirectly contradicted the *ultra vires* bar, by enabling the claimants to recover their loan when the transaction was null and void. This did not, however, prevent the proprietary claim in Equity from succeeding, presumably because the award of a proprietary restitutionary remedy did not involve effective enforcement of the loan, since the claimants could only recover what the defendant had retained rather than what the defendant had received.

Although *Sinclair v Brougham* seems to deny personal restitutionary relief to the claimant, at least where he or she seeks restitution of money lent to the defendant, as a result of the defendant's incapacity making the transaction null and void, such a conclusion is no longer defensible. This was the conclusion of a majority of the House of Lords in *Westdeutsche Landesbank Girozentrale v Islington LBC*,[26] where it was recognized that, since the obligation to make restitution is imposed by law, the award of a restitutionary remedy does not effectively enforce the loan transaction. It follows that, where the claimant has lent money to the defendant in a transaction which is void because of the defendant's incapacity, that incapacity cannot bar the claim. This was subsequently confirmed in *Haugesund Kommune v Depfa ACS Bank*,[27] where a bank had lent money to Norwegian public authorities which lacked the capacity to borrow the money. It followed that the bank was unable to sue on the contract of loan, which was void, but it was recognized that the bank had a claim in unjust enrichment grounded on failure of basis.[28] The Court of Appeal did, however, recognize a specific defence grounded on public policy, whereby a claim for restitution will be defeated where the award of restitution is considered to be contrary to public policy, such as the objective of a statute which had rendered a contract void.[29] Although this claim was recognized in principle, the

---

[23] *Hazell v Hammersmith and Fulham LBC* [1992] 2 AC 1.

[24] See, in particular, *Westdeutsche Landesbank Girozentrale v Islington LBC* [1994] 1 WLR 938 (CA).

[25] [1914] AC 398.

[26] [1996] AC 669, 710 (Lord Browne-Wilkinson), 718 (Lord Slynn), and 738 (Lord Lloyd). Cf Lord Goff, ibid, 688.

[27] [2010] EWCA Civ 579, [2012] QB 549.   [28] See Chapter 13.

[29] See *Boissevain v Weil* [1950] AC 327; *Dimond v Lovell* [2002] 1 AC 384; *Wilson v First County Trust (No 2)* [2003] UKHL 40, [2004] 1 AC 816.

court went on to consider whether there was any policy which should defeat a claim for restitution involving money lent, either because restitution would have the effect of enforcing a void contract or because, in claims against public authorities, awarding a restitutionary remedy might undermine the policy of the *ultra vires* doctrine in protecting the public. Public policy was considered to be a distinct defence to restitutionary claims[30] and required consideration as to whether allowing restitution would be contrary to the policy underpinning the Norwegian statute which rendered the transaction void, even though English law was the applicable law, for reasons of comity. The relevance of Norwegian law is, however, dubious. It legitimately determined the capacity of the Kommunes to borrow money, but it was for English law, as the applicable law of the restitutionary claim, to determine whether restitution should be barred by English public policy. In the end it was held that the award of restitution would not infringe Norwegian public policy and so restitution was awarded.

5. SHOULD A DEFENCE OF INCAPACITY BE RECOGNIZED?

This analysis has shown that there is no justification for the law of restitution to recognize a distinct defence of incapacity. The failure even to consider such a defence in the swaps cases illustrates its unimportance. It is to be hoped that the modern developments in the law of restitution will mean that in future the question of incapacity as a defence can be stated simply: there is no such defence. Rather, restitution may sometimes be denied for reasons of public policy, where the award of restitution is considered to undermine the policy which renders a transaction void for lack of capacity.

---

[30] Although Etherton LJ in *Haugesund Komune* [2010] EWCA Civ 579, [2012] QB 549, [151], indicated that it would often form part of the change of position defence. See p 695, above.

29

LIMITATION PERIODS
AND LACHES

For reasons of public policy most civil actions are subject to a time bar, the effect of which is that, once a particular period of time has passed, the defendant can no longer be sued on that particular action. One of the main reasons for having time bars is to ensure that the threat of an action does not continually hang over the defendant, so that, once the limitation period has passed, he or she can be certain that the benefit has been validly received and will not need to be returned to the claimant. The existence of time bars also act as an incentive for claimants to bring claims as soon as possible. This is particularly advantageous since, as time passes, evidence may become less reliable and more difficult to obtain.

There are two distinct legal regimes relating to the barring of restitutionary claims by the passage of time. The first, and most significant, is contained in the Limitation Act 1980, which specifies particular limitation periods for different types of claim. Unfortunately the Act does not, with certain minor exceptions, contain any specific provision relating to restitutionary claims, so the question of what is the appropriate period of limitation is a matter which is not free from difficulty. The second regime is the equitable defence of laches, which determines whether an equitable action is time barred by reference to the justice of the case, having regard to all the surrounding circumstances. The Limitation Act applies to all Common Law claims and closely related equitable claims, whereas the defence of laches only applies where the claimant seeks equitable relief. Where the Limitation Act applies there is no scope for the application of the laches defence.[1]

1. LIMITATION PERIODS

The Limitation Act 1980 contains a variety of arbitrary limitation periods which apply to particular claims. Unlike the laches defence, these limitation periods are strictly applied without the court having any discretion to determine whether the conduct of the parties is such that the periods should or should not be enforced. Where claimants can sue under a number of different claims, such as unjust enrichment and equitable wrongdoing, the fact that one action is time barred does not prevent them from relying on the other one.[2] The question of the appropriate limitation period for restitutionary claims needs to be examined in respect of each type of claim.

---

[1] *Re Baker* (1881) 20 Ch D 230.   [2] *Nelson v Rye* [1996] 1 WLR 1378, 1389 (Laddie J).

(A) REVERSAL OF THE DEFENDANT'S UNJUST ENRICHMENT

(i) The Usual Limitation Period

No specific provision is made in the Limitation Act 1980 for restitutionary claims which are founded on the reversal of the defendant's unjust enrichment. Consequently, it might be argued that no limitation period should be applicable to such claims.[3] But, as a matter of policy, the claim should fail when sufficient time has lapsed to remove the injustice of the defendant retaining the benefit which was received from the claimant.[4] Therefore, some limitation period is necessary, bearing in mind that the equitable doctrine of laches is generally inapplicable to such claims since it only applies where the claimant seeks equitable relief. A limitation period must be identified therefore by analogy with one of the categories of claim for which the Limitation Act does make specific provision.

By section 5 of the Limitation Act 1980 actions which are founded on contract are barred after six years. The predecessor of this provision[5] was interpreted by the Court of Appeal in *Re Diplock*[6] as covering actions for money had and received, although 'the words used cannot be regarded as felicitous'. This conclusion was affirmed by Hobhouse J in *Westdeutsche Landesbank Girozentrale v Islington LBC*[7] on the ground that such actions should be treated as akin to ones relating to contract and so a limitation period of six years is applicable. This is artificial and harks back to the implied contract theory, but, since no specific provision is made for this type of restitutionary claim under the Limitation Act, it is the best solution available. It is certainly better than concluding that such restitutionary actions are subject to no limitation period at all. It is also consistent with the Limitation Act 1623, section 3 of which provided a limitation period of six years for all assumpsit claims and this provision continued to apply until 1939.

Specific provision is made in the Limitation Act 1980 for the recovery of money by virtue of any statute, where the limitation period is six years as well.[8] Consequently, restitutionary claims for money under the Law Reform (Frustrated Contracts) Act 1943 are subject to a limitation period of six years. Consistency demands that a similar limitation period should apply to all claims founded on the reversal of unjust enrichment, regardless of the ground of restitution on which the claimant relies.

(ii) Qualification of the General Limitation Period for Particular Restitutionary Claims

Even though the limitation period for restitutionary claims founded on the reversal of the defendant's unjust enrichment should usually be six years, it is clear that for particular types of claim different considerations may apply.

(1) Claims in Equity

Where the restitutionary relief which the claimant seeks is equitable, the Limitation Act 1980 is inapplicable[9] and so the equitable doctrine of laches applies.[10] Consequently, where the claimant seeks a restitutionary remedy on the ground of undue influence or the defendant's unconscionable conduct then, because such claims are equitable even though they are founded on the reversal of the defendant's unjust enrichment, it is the doctrine of laches rather than the Limitation Act which should be applicable.[11]

---

[3] Ibid, 1390.   [4] H McLean 'Limitation of Actions in Restitution' (1989) CLJ 472, 475.
[5] Limitation Act 1939, s 2(1)(a).   [6] [1948] Ch 465, 514.   [7] [1994] 4 All ER 890, 943.
[8] Limitation Act 1980, s 9.   [9] Ibid, s 36(1).   [10] See p 741, below.
[11] *Allcard v Skinner* (1887) 36 Ch D 145.

(2) Contribution

Where the claimant brings a contribution claim under the Civil Liability (Contribution) Act 1978[12] the claim is subject to a limitation period of two years from the date on which the statutory right of action accrues.[13]

(3) Salvage

The limitation period for salvage claims is two years from the date when the salvage services were rendered.[14]

(iii) The Determination of When Time Starts to Run

The limitation period begins to run from the date the cause of action accrues. For the purposes of a claim founded on the reversal of the defendant's unjust enrichment this is usually the point at which the defendant receives the enrichment.[15] Sometimes, however, the cause of action can only be established after the defendant has received the enrichment, as will be the case where the ground of restitution is total failure of basis. In such cases, time will only begin to run once the relevant ground of restitution can be established.[16] So, for example, it has been held that a restitutionary claim founded on frustration will only accrue once the contract is frustrated.[17] Similarly, in *Nu Line Construction Group Pty Ltd v Fowler*[18] it was held that an anticipated contract would be considered to have failed to materialize once the parties no longer share the common intention to make the contract, so that the basis will have failed at that point.

Despite certain dicta that a restitutionary cause of action will accrue only once the claimant has demanded the return of the enrichment,[19] the better view is that there is no such requirement, for otherwise the claimant would be able to postpone the date from which the limitation period begins to run until it suits him or her to inform the defendant of the restitutionary claim.[20]

There is, however an argument which can be run that claims for restitution of unjust enrichment, other than those which arise by virtue of statute, are not subject to any limitation period in practice, because the cause of action continuously accrues. It was recognized by Males J in *Equitas Ltd v Walsham Bros and Co Ltd*[21] that, where the defendant has received money which it was liable to pay the claimant in circumstances where there was a continuing duty to do so, the cause of action accrues each day the defendant failed to make remittance of the payment. Consequently where, for example, the claimant has paid money to the defendant by mistake, since the defendant is under a continuing duty to make restitution, the cause of action would arise anew each day after the payment had been made. It would follow that, if the claimant seeks restitution seven years later, this could be considered to be a new cause of action which had just arisen so that it is not time barred. Since, however, this would undermine the policy behind limitation periods, this idea of the cause of action arising each day should be rejected, at

---

[12] See p 248, above.

[13] Limitation Act 1980, s 10(1). To determine when the cause of action accrues see s 10(2)–(4).

[14] International Convention on Salvage 1989, art 23 (1) enacted by Maritime Shipping Act 1995, s 224, Sch 11. For an examination of salvage claims see p 305, above.

[15] *Kleinwort Benson v South Tyneside MBC* [1994] 4 All ER 972, 978 (Hobhouse J).

[16] *Guardian Ocean Cargoes Ltd v Banco de Brasil (No 2)* [1994] 2 Lloyd's Rep 152, 160 (Saville LJ).

[17] *BP Exploration Co (Libya) Ltd v Hunt* [1983] 2 AC 352, 373 (Lord Brandon of Oakbrook).

[18] [2014] NSWCA 51.

[19] See *Freeman v Jeffries* (1869) LR 4 Exch 189, 198 (Martin B) and 200 (Bramwell B).

[20] See *Baker v Courage and Co* [1910] 1 KB 56, 65 (Hamilton J); *Fuller v Happy Shopper Markets Ltd* [2001] 1 WLR 1681, 1689 (Lightman J).   [21] [2013] EWHC 3264 (Comm).

least in the context of a claim founded on the reversal of the defendant's unjust enrichment.

There are a number of specific rules relating to the time from which the limitation period begins to run in certain cases.

(1) Claimant Subject to Incapacity

Where the claimant is a minor or is suffering from mental incapacity[22] the limitation period will not begin to run until the claimant has ceased to be under a disability or has died, and it will then run for a period of six years.[23]

(2) Claim Founded on Spontaneous or Induced Mistake

Where the claim is founded upon the defendant's fraud,[24] or the defendant has deliberately concealed from the claimant any fact relating to the claimant's action,[25] or where the claim relates to mistake,[26] the limitation period will not begin to run until the claimant has discovered the fraud, concealment or mistake or could have discovered it with reasonable diligence. In determining what amounts to 'reasonable diligence' to make the relevant discovery of fraud, concealment or mistake, the court should have regard to what an ordinary prudent person would have done if he or she had carried on a business of the relevant kind with adequate, but not unlimited, staff and resources, and motivated with a reasonable, but not excessive, sense of urgency.[27]

In *Test Claimants in the FII Group Litigation v HMRC*[28] the Supreme Court held that, to gain the benefit of the extended limitation period, the mistake had to constitute an essential element of the cause of action and not simply form the context of the claim. It follows that, in a case where the claimant seeks restitution of overpaid taxes, the extended limitation period will only be available where mistake is pleaded as the ground of restitution and not where the public law *Woolwich* ground is pleaded, although it was acknowledged that, where both grounds of restitution are available, the claimant is free to choose the mistake ground to gain the benefit of the extended limitation period. The significance of this extended limitation period for mistake-based claims for the recovery of overpaid taxes has, however, been reduced in significance, particularly because the key statutory provisions for restitution, relating to overpaid income tax, capital gains tax, and VAT,[29] constitute an exclusive regime for restitution of those taxes paid by mistake, for which the limitation period is four years. Also the application of this extended limitation has been retrospectively abrogated by statute as regards claims for recovery of taxes,[30] although the retrospective nature of both provisions have been held to infringe EU law in respect of their application to restitution of taxes paid in breach of EU law,[31] in not providing transitional provisions.

---

[22] Limitation Act 1980, s 38(2).   [23] Ibid, s 28.   [24] Ibid, s 32(1)(a).   [25] Ibid, s 32(1)(b).

[26] Ibid, s 32(1)(c).

[27] *Paragon Finance v D B Thakerar & Co* [1999] 1 All ER 400, 418 (Millett LJ). See also *Peco Arts Inc v Hazlitt Gallery Ltd* [1999] 2 AC 349.

[28] [2012] UKSC 19, [2012] AC 337. See also *Hemming (trading as Simply Pleasure Ltd) v The Lord Mayor and Citizens of Westminster* [2013] EWCA Civ 591, [138] (Beatson LJ).

[29] See p 409, above.

[30] Finance Act 2004, s 320 for payments made before 8 September 2003 but where the claim was commenced after that date; Finance Act 2007, s 107 where the claim was commenced before that date.

[31] As recognized in *FII Group Litigation v HMRC* [2012] UKSC 19, [2012] AC 337 concerning Finance Act 2007, s 107; Case C-362/12 *Test Claimants in the FII Group Litigation v Commissioners of Inland Revenue and another* [2014] 2 CMLR 33 concerning Finance Act 2004, s 320.

The effect of the extended limitation period under the Limitation Act 1980 is that it is always necessary to identify with care what the ground of restitution is on which the claim is based. Provision is only made for fraud, mistake, and deliberate concealment. This is unfortunate. Where, for example, the claimant has been subjected to duress surely time should not begin to run until the duress has ceased, for the claimant who has succumbed to the defendant's threats cannot be expected to commence restitutionary proceedings until the threats have ceased to operate.[32]

(3) Recovery of Debts or Other Liquidated Pecuniary Claims

Where the claimant seeks to recover a debt or any other liquidated pecuniary claim and the defendant has acknowledged the claim or has made any payment in respect of it, time will only begin to run from the date of acknowledgement or payment.[33] The acknowledgement or payment by the defendant will only be relevant if it relates to the particular debt or other liquidated pecuniary claim which the claimant seeks to be paid.[34]

This provision should be applicable to all claims for money had and received and claims for money paid to the use of the defendant because these are liquidated pecuniary claims which are assessed by reference to the amount of money received by the defendant. In principle the provision could not be extended to cover claims for the reasonable value of services or goods because such remedies depend on the assessment of the court as to the value of the benefit received by the defendant and so do not constitute a liquidated claim. But in *Amontilla Ltd v Telefusion plc*[35] it was held that a *quantum meruit* claim for the reasonable value of building services constituted a liquidated pecuniary claim within section 29(5). This is a highly dubious decision.

(iv) Should a Different General Limitation Period Be Recognized?

Is six years an appropriate limitation period for most restitutionary claims founded on unjust enrichment? All limitation periods are arbitrary but, in the light of the recognition of the defence of change of position, a case can be made that the limitation period for restitutionary claims should be longer than for contract and tort claims, simply because the defence of change of position exists to give the defendant some security in his or her receipt. But, since that defence is generally interpreted restrictively, its potential application should not result in longer limitation periods for unjust enrichment claims. Consequently, it is entirely appropriate that the limitation period for restitutionary claims is consistent with that for other forms of civil liability.

(B) RESTITUTION FOR WRONGS

(i) Restitutionary Claims Founded on the Commission of Tort or Breach of Contract

By sections 2 and 5 of the 1980 Limitation Act, actions which are founded on tort and contract respectively are subject to a six-year limitation period. It follows that, where a restitutionary claim is founded on tort or breach of contract, the limitation period should be six years. This is because the underlying cause of action for the claim is the tort or the

---

[32] See McLean, 'Limitation of Actions in Restitution', 481. Cf the equitable doctrine of laches which will not apply in cases of undue influence until the claimant has ceased to be unduly influenced by the defendant. See p 742, below.   [33] Limitation Act 1980, s 29(5).

[34] *Kleinwort Benson v South Tyneside MBC* [1994] 4 All ER 972, 981 (Hobhouse J).

[35] (1987) 9 Constr LR 139.

breach of contract and so the limitation period for those causes of action should apply even where the claimant seeks a restitutionary remedy. If the wrong is statute-barred then there is no longer a cause of action on which the restitutionary claim can be based.[36]

Unfortunately, this simple analysis has not been reflected in the cases. The most important decision is *Chesworth v Farrar*,[37] where the claimant brought an action for money had and received to recover the proceeds of sale of converted goods. The question for the court was whether this was a cause of action in tort, for, if it was, a limitation period of six months was applicable, this being the limitation period in respect of tortious actions against the estate of a deceased tortfeasor.[38] The court adopted a purposive construction of the legislation to determine whether the tort limitation period applied to a restitutionary claim and concluded that it did not. Rather, because the claimant's action was analogous to a contractual action, a limitation period of six years applied, although the judge did recognize that it was crucial for the claimant's restitutionary claim that he established that the tort of conversion had been committed. But, if the claim depended on proof of the commission of a tort, surely the limitation period for that tort was applicable. This is because the purpose of a limitation period is to bar the cause of action rather than the remedy. If the cause of action is barred it follows that the claimant cannot obtain any remedy, regardless of the type of remedy which he or she seeks. The decision in *Chesworth v Farrar* must be wrong.

That this is the proper conclusion is supported by section 23 of the Limitation Act 1980 which states that, where the claimant seeks the remedy of account, the relevant limitation period is that of the underlying cause of action. In other words, this provision acknowledges that the limitation period is determined by the underlying cause of action and not the remedy sought. Consequently, if the claimant seeks an account of profits following the infringement of a copyright, the limitation period for the account is the same as that for the infringement of copyright.[39]

Where the claim is founded on tort or breach of contract the cause of action accrues from the date the wrong was committed. The date for the commencement of the limitation period will, however, be delayed if any of the particular statutory provisions under the Limitation Act are applicable. For example, where the claimant is the victim of fraud, as will be the case where the defendant has committed the tort of deceit, the limitation period is postponed until the claimant has discovered the fraud or could have discovered it with reasonable diligence.[40] Similarly, where the claim is dependent on proof of a mistake, as will be the case where the claimant sues in respect of a misrepresentation, the limitation period begins to run only once the claimant has or should reasonably have discovered the mistake.[41]

(ii) Restitutionary Claims Founded on Equitable Wrongs

Where the claim is founded on the commission of one of the equitable wrongs generally no specific provision for limitation periods is made in the statute. There are, however, particular statutory provisions in respect of certain claims founded on equitable wrong-doing. So, for example, where the claimant sues the defendant for non-fraudulent breach of trust, there is a six-year statutory limitation period,[42] although this will not apply where the claim is brought against a fraudulent trustee.[43] Outside of this, the usual six-year

---

[36] *Beaman v ARTS Ltd* [1948] 2 All ER 89, 92–3 (Denning J).   [37] [1967] 1 QB 407.
[38] Such a limitation period no longer exists.   [39] *Nelson v Rye* [1996] 1 WLR 1378, 1389 (Laddie J).
[40] Limitation Act 1980, s 32(1)(a).   [41] Ibid, s 32(1)(c).   [42] Ibid, s 21(3).
[43] Ibid, s 21(1)(a). 'Trustee' includes resulting and constructive trustees: Trustee Act 1925, s 68(17), incorporated by Limitation Act 1980, s 38.

limitation periods are not applicable as regards the granting of equitable relief save by analogy with the rules on contract and tort.[44] Where the Act is not applicable, the equitable doctrine of laches will apply instead. It has, however, been recognized that where a defendant is alleged to have breached his or her fiduciary duty, whether deliberately and dishonestly[45] or honestly,[46] the normal statutory limitation period of six years applies by analogy with the rules for breach of contract and tort. Similarly, where the defendant is liable for dishonestly assisting a breach of trust or fiduciary duty, the usual six-year limitation period is applicable.[47] Even though the assistant will have acted dishonestly, which might constitute fraudulent conduct, they are not trustees and are only subject to a personal liability to the claimant, so cannot be characterized as a fraudulent trustee to disapply the limitation period.

(C) VINDICATION OF PROPRIETARY RIGHTS

Determining the appropriate limitation period for restitutionary claims which are founded on the vindication of proprietary rights is a matter of some complexity, depending on the nature of the property in which the claimant has a proprietary interest and the nature of the restitutionary claim. The following principles will be particularly relevant to the determination of the appropriate limitation period for such claims.

(i) Land

Where the claimant brings an action to recover land, the claim is subject to a limitation period of 12 years.[48] Once the limitation period has passed the title of the owner of the land is automatically extinguished,[49] so the claimant ceases to have a proprietary base on which he or she can found a proprietary restitutionary claim.

(ii) Restitutionary Claims in Respect of Converted Goods

Where the claimant's property has been converted, his or her claim is subject to a six-year limitation period because conversion is a tort. Where, however, the property is converted again, before the claimant is able to recover it, there is no new limitation period for the second conversion.[50] So, for example, if D1 converts the claimant's property on 1 January 2011 and D2 converts the same property on 1 January 2016, the claimant only has one year to sue D2. Once the limitation period has passed in respect of any action relating to conversion the claimant's title to it is extinguished.[51]

(iii) Recovery of Stolen Property

Where the claimant brings a restitutionary claim in respect of stolen property the claim is not subject to a six-year limitation period.[52]

(iv) Equitable Proprietary Claims

Most equitable proprietary claims are not subject to a limitation period under the 1980 Act and will only be barred by virtue of the doctrine of laches. But the 1980 Act does make

---

[44] Trustee Act 1925, s 36(1).

[45] *Paragon Finance plc v DB Thakerar and Co (a firm)* [1999] 1 All ER 400; *Coulthard v Disco Mix Club Ltd* [2000] 1 WLR 707.

[46] *Cia de Seguros Imerio v Health (REBX) Ltd* [2001] 1 WLR 112.

[47] *Williams v Central Bank of Nigeria* [2014] UKSC 10, [2014] 1 AC 1189. See J Lee, 'Constructing and Limiting Liability in Equity' (2015) LQR 39.   [48] Limitation Act 1980, s 15.
[49] Ibid, s 17.   [50] Ibid, s 3(1).   [51] Ibid, s 3(2).   [52] Ibid, s 4(1).

specific provision for claims to recover trust property from anybody other than the trustee, such claims being subject to a limitation period of six years.[53] But there is no limitation period in respect of claims to recover trust property or the proceeds of trust property from a trustee.[54] This raises significant issues of characterization of trustees, since a trustee includes a constructive trustee,[55] and it therefore matters when a defendant can be characterized as such a trustee. Where a defendant holds property on constructive trust, this will be treated like an express trust, so that any claim to recover the property will not be time barred,[56] neither will any claim involving fraudulent breach of that trust.[57] Where the defendant has not been expressly appointed as a trustee, but has assumed the duties of one, the defendant is treated as a real trustee, albeit under a constructive trust, so a claim for the recovery of trust property would not be time barred. This includes a person who interferes with a trust as trustee *de son tort* or a fiduciary who misappropriates the property of the principal.[58] Where, however, the defendant is held liable for unconscionable receipt of property which has been transferred in breach of trust,[59] although the orthodox analysis has been that he or she is liable as if he or she was a constructive trustee, it has now been recognized that this is incorrect. The liability of the unconscionable recipient is simply a personal liability to account such that he or she does not hold any property on trust. Consequently, the normal six-year limitation period applies in respect of such claims.[60]

Claims to the personal estate of a deceased person are barred after 12 years from the date on which the right to receive the share or interest accrued,[61] though no limitation period applies where the trustee was fraudulent.[62]

2. LACHES

(A) THE FUNCTION OF THE LACHES DEFENCE

Laches[63] is an equitable doctrine[64] which defeats the claimant's equitable claim where there has been an unreasonable delay in the claimant suing the defendant.[65] The defence is potentially applicable whenever cases where the claimant seeks an equitable remedy, such as an account of profits, rescission for equitable grounds,[66] and equitable proprietary remedies. The rationale of the defence is that the claim should be defeated where there is such a delay in commencing proceedings that it would be unjust to the defendant to allow a claimant to enforce his or her rights. Laches can apply only where there is no statutory

---

[53] Ibid, s 21(3).   [54] Ibid, s 21(1)(b).   [55] Trustee Act 1925, s 68(7).

[56] By virtue of the Limitation Act 1980, s 21(1)(b). See *James v Williams* [2000] Ch 1.

[57] Limitation Act 1980, s 21(1)(a). See p 739, above.

[58] As recognized by Jonathan Parker J in *BCCI (overseas) v Jan* (unreported), 11 November 1999; *James v Williams* [2000] Ch 1.   [59] See p 645, above.

[60] *Williams v Central Bank of Nigeria* [2014] UKSC 10, [2014] 1 AC 1189.

[61] Limitation Act 1980, s 22(a). See *Re Diplock* [1948] Ch 465.

[62] Limitation Act 1980, s 21(1)(a). This provision will be applicable even where the trustee is not the defendant: *Baker Ltd v Medway Building and Supplies Ltd* [1958] 1 WLR 1216.

[63] See generally G Watt, 'Laches, Estoppel and Election' in PBH Birks and A Pretto (eds), *Breach of Trust* (Oxford: Hart Publishing, 2002), 353.

[64] The doctrine of laches is implicitly preserved by the Limitation Act 1980, s 36(2). See *Re Loftus (deceased)* [2006] EWCA Civ 1124, [2007] 1 WLR 591, [33] (Chadwick LJ).

[65] *Erlanger v New Sombrero Phosphate Co* (1878) 3 App Cas 1218, 1279 (Lord Blackburn).

[66] *Allcard v Skinner* (1887) 36 Ch D 145.

limitation period available in respect of the claim.[67] The doctrine will, however, be available where the Limitation Act states that there is no prescribed period of limitation under the Act, such as where the trustee is sued for a fraudulent breach of trust or where the claimant seeks to recover trust property.[68]

The function of the defence was identified by the Privy Council in *Lindsay Petroleum Co v Hurd*[69] in the following terms:

> the doctrine of laches in courts of equity is not an arbitrary or technical doctrine. Where it would be practically unjust to give a remedy, either because the party has, by his conduct, done that which might fairly be regarded as equivalent to a waiver of it, or where by his conduct and neglect he has . . . put the other party in a situation in which it would not be reasonable to place him if the remedy were afterwards to be asserted . . . lapse of time and delay are most material. But in every case, if an argument against relief, which otherwise would be just, is founded upon mere delay . . . the validity of that defence must be tried upon principles substantially equitable. Two circumstances, always important in such cases, are, the length of the delay and the nature of the acts done during the interval, which might affect either party and cause a balance of justice or injustice in taking the one course or the other, so far as relates to the remedy.

(B) ESTABLISHING LACHES

The key test for establishing laches is whether the lapse of time in commencing proceedings is such that it would be unconscionable for the claimant to assert his or her rights.[70] It was recognized in *Cattley v Pollard*[71] that establishing such unconscionability depended on all of the circumstances of the case, but usually required some unconscionable conduct on the part of the claimant. When deciding whether the laches defence should bar a restitutionary claim judges must exercise their discretion to decide where the balance of justice lies. A number of factors have been identified to assist in the exercise of this discretion. Particularly important factors are the extent of the delay, the degree of prejudice suffered by the defendant as a result of the delay, the extent to which this was caused by the claimant and whether the claimant knew that the defendant would suffer prejudice from the delay.[72] Lengthy delay will usually not be sufficient in itself to bar relief. Neither is it necessary to show that the prejudice suffered by the defendant was caused by the delay. Although laches is a separate defence from that involving limitation periods, the statutory limitation period is a useful indicator of what constitutes a reasonable time in which the action should be commenced.[73]

Where the claimant has been subject to undue influence time will start to run only once the claimant is free to exercise an independent choice, in other words once the undue influence has ceased to operate.[74] But, once the influence has been removed, the claimant has a reasonable time in which to bring proceedings.

Laches will only be established where the claimant knew of his or her claim, or was aware of the possibility that he or she might have such a claim.[75] So, for example, in

---

[67] *Re Loftus (deceased)* [2006] EWCA Civ 1124, [2007] 1 WLR 591, [37] (Chadwick LJ).

[68] Ibid, [41] (Chadwick LJ).   [69] (1874) LR 5 PC 221, 239–40.

[70] *Re Loftus (deceased)* [2006] EWCA Civ 1124, [2007] 1 WLR 591, [42] (Chadwick LJ). See also *Lindsay Petroleum Co v Hurd* (1874) LR 5 PC 221, 240 (Sir Barnes Peacock).

[71] [2006] EWHC 3130 (Ch), [2007] Ch 353, [1514] (Richard Sheldon QC).

[72] *Nelson v Rye* [1996] 1 WLR 1378, 1398 (Laddie J).

[73] *Allcard v Skinner* (1887) 36 Ch D 145 186 (Lindley LJ).

[74] Ibid, 187 (Lindley LJ).   [75] Ibid, 192 (Bowen LJ).

Lindsay Petroleum Co v Hurd[76] the claimant successfully rescinded a conveyance of land on the ground of fraudulent misrepresentation, even though he sought to rescind the conveyance 15 months after it had been made. This was because the claimant had acted promptly once he had discovered the fraudulent misrepresentation. In *Leaf v International Galleries*,[77] however, rescission on the ground of innocent misrepresentation was barred since five years had passed since the claimant had entered into the transaction. But the claimant had only discovered that the defendant had made an innocent misrepresentation shortly before he sought to rescind the contract and he could not reasonably have discovered this any earlier. Perhaps the stricter approach to the application of the doctrine which was adopted in this case can be justified on the ground that the misrepresentation was innocent rather than fraudulent, so that the balance of justice was not so much in the claimant's favour.

An important decision which illustrates how the judge determines whether the restitutionary claim should be defeated by the defence of laches is *Nelson v Rye*.[78] In this case the claimant was a professional musician who had appointed the defendant to manage his affairs. It was agreed that the defendant would pay the claimant annually the net profits which the claimant had earned. After 10 years the defendant terminated the relationship without having paid the claimant any of the profits which were due to him. Fourteen months later the claimant commenced proceedings to recover these profits on the ground of the defendant's breach of fiduciary duty. The claim was only partially successful since it was held that, in respect of the profits due from the first five years of the business relationship, the claimant's delay in bringing proceedings had caused the defendant substantial prejudice so that it would be unreasonable and unjust to allow the claimant to assert his right to an account for this period. This was because the judge found that the claimant had wilfully refused to involve himself in his own financial affairs. The judge concluded that the defendant had suffered prejudice as a result of the delay because the defendant's ability to give evidence as to what was actually due to the claimant, after the deduction of expenses, had been prejudiced by the delay, since the defendant had destroyed many invoices and receipts which were more than six years old and the defendant's memory would become less reliable over the passage of time.

3. REFORM OF THE LAW ON LIMITATION PERIODS

The Law Commission has recommended the reform of the law on limitation periods[79] so that a core regime should regulate limitation periods for claims, including restitutionary claims. According to this regime there would be an initial limitation period of three years from the date when the claimant knew or ought reasonably to have known of the existence of the cause of action. In addition, the claimant would not be able to bring a claim more than 10 years after the date of the act or omission which gave rise to his or her claim. The courts would not have a discretion to disapply this limitation period. If the law on limitation periods was reformed in this way it would bring much needed certainty to an area of the law which is of great practical importance but is unnecessarily complicated.

---

[76] (1873) LR 5 PC 221.   [77] [1950] 2 KB 86.

[78] [1996] 1 WLR 1378, subsequently overruled by *Paragon Finance v D B Thakerar & Co* [1999] 1 All ER 400, but on a different point, relating to statutory limitation periods, and the analysis of laches was not criticized.

[79] *Limitation of Actions* (Law Com No 270, 2001), para 4.78.

BIBLIOGRAPHY

AMERICAN LAW INSTITUTE, *Restatement of the Law of Restitution, Quasi-Contracts and Constructive Trusts* (St Paul, MN: American Law Institute Publishing, 1937)

AMERICAN LAW INSTITUTE, *Restatement Third: Restitution and Unjust Enrichment* (St Paul, MN: American Law Institute Publishing, 2011)

ANDREWS, N, 'Mistaken Settlements of Disputable Claims' [1989] LMCLQ 431

ANDREWS, N, and BEATSON, J, 'Common Law Tracing: Springboard or Swan-song?' (1997) 113 LQR 21

ANDREWS, N, and CLARKE, M, TETTENBORN, A, and VIRGO, G, *Contractual Duties: Performance, Breach, Termination and Remedies* (London: Sweet and Maxwell, 2012)

APLIN, T, BENTLEY, L, JOHNSON, P, and MALYNICZ, S (eds), *Gurry on Breach of Confidence: The Protection of Confidential Information* (2nd edn, Oxford: Oxford University Press, 2012)

ARISTOTLE, *Nichomachean Ethics* (D Ross ed, Oxford: Oxford University Press, 1984)

ARROWSMITH, S, 'Mistake and The Role of the "Submission to an Honest Claim"' in AS Burrows (ed), *Essays on the Law of Restitution* (Oxford: Clarendon Press, 1991), ch 2

ATIYAH, PS, *The Rise and Fall of Freedom of Contract* (Oxford: Clarendon Press, 1979)

ATIYAH, PS, 'Economic Duress and the "Overborne Will"' (1982) 98 LQR 197

AUSTEN-BAKER, R, 'Difficulties with Damages as a Ground for Specific Performance' (1999) KCLJ 1

BABAFEMI, FOB, 'Tracing Assets: A Case for the Fusion of Common Law and Equity in English Law' (1971) 34 MLR 12

BAKER, JH, 'The History of Quasi-Contract in English Law' in W Cornish, R Nolan, J O'Sullivan, and G Virgo (eds), *Restitution: Past, Present and Future* (Oxford: Hart Publishing, 1998), ch 3

BALOCH, T, 'The Unjust Enrichment Pyramid' (2007) LQR 636

BAMFORTH, N, 'Unconscionability as a Vitiating Factor' [1995] LMCLQ 538

BANT, E, *The Change of Position Defence* (Oxford: Hart Publishing, 2009)

BANT, E, 'Restitution from the Revenue and Change of Position' [2009] LMCLQ 166

BARKEHALL THOMAS, S, 'Thieves as Trustees: The Enduring Legacy of *Black v S Freedman and Co*' (2009) 3 J Eq 52

BARKER, K, 'After Change of Position: Good Faith Exchange in the Modern Law of Restitution' in PBH Birks (ed), *Laundering and Tracing* (Oxford: Clarendon Press, 1995), 191

BARKER, K, 'Restitution of Passenger Fare' [1995] LMCLQ 291

BARKER, K, 'Unjust Enrichment: Containing the Beast' (1995) OJLS 457

BARKER, K, 'Equitable Title and Common Law Conversion: The Limits of the Fusionist Ideal' [1998] 6 RLR 150

BARKER, K, 'Rescuing Remedialism in Unjust Enrichment Law: Why Remedies are Right' (1998) 57 CLJ 301

BARKER, K, 'Understanding the Unjust Enrichment Principle in Private Law: A Study of the Concept and its Reasons' in J Neyers, M McInnes, and S Pitel (eds), *Understanding Unjust Enrichment* (Oxford: Hart Publishing, 2004), 79

BARNETT, K, 'Deterrence and Disgorging Profits for Breach of Contract' [2009] RLR 79

BARNETT, K, *Accounting for Profit for Breach of Contract* (Oxford: Hart Publishing, 2012)

BARNETT, K, 'Distributive Justice and Proprietary Remedies over Bribes' (2015) 35 LS 302

BEALE, H, 'Points on Misrepresentation'
(1995) 111 LQR 385

BEALE, H (ed), *Chitty on Contracts* (31st edn,
London: Sweet and Maxwell, 2012)

BEATSON, J, 'Duress as a Vitiating Factor in
Contract' (1974) 33 CLJ 97

BEATSON, J, *The Use and Abuse of Unjust
Enrichment* (Oxford: Clarendon Press, 1991)

BEATSON, J, 'Restitution of Taxes, Levies and
Other Imposts: Defining the Extent of the
Woolwich Principle' (1993) 109 LQR 205

BEATSON, J, 'Restitution and Contract: Non-
Cumul?' (2000) 1 Theoretical Inquiries in
Law 83

BEATSON, J, 'Courts, Arbitrators and Restitutionary Liability for Breach of Contract'
(2002) 118 LQR 377

BEEVER, A, 'The Structure of Aggravated and
Exemplary Damages' (2003) 23 OJLS 87

BENTLEY, L, and MITCHELL, C, 'Combining
Money Awards for Patent Infringement'
[2003] 11 RLR 79

BERG, A, 'Permitting a Trustee to Retain a
Profit' (2001) 117 LQR 366

BIGWOOD, R, 'Undue Influence: "Implied
Consent" or "Wicked Exploitation"?'
(1996) 16 OJLS 503

BIRKS, PBH, '*Negotiorum Gestio* and the
Common Law' (1971) 24 CLP 110

BIRKS, PBH, 'The Recovery of Carelessly Mistaken Payments' (1972) 25 CLP 179

BIRKS, PBH, 'Restitution and Wrongs' (1982)
35 CLP 53

BIRKS, PBH, 'Restitutionary Damages for
Breach of Contract: *Snepp* and the Fusion
of Law and Equity' [1987] LMCLQ 421

BIRKS, PBH, *An Introduction to the Law of
Restitution* (rev edn, Oxford: Clarendon
Press, 1989)

BIRKS, PBH, 'The Remedies for Abuse of Confidential Information' [1990] LMCLQ 460

BIRKS, PBH, 'Restitution from the Executive:
A Tercentenary Footnote to the Bill of
Rights' in P Finn (ed), *Essays on Restitution*
(Sydney: The Law Book Co, 1990), 161

BIRKS, PBH, 'Restitution without Counter-
Restitution' [1990] LMCLQ 330

BIRKS, PBH, 'The Travails of Duress' [1990]
LMCLQ 342

BIRKS, PBH, 'In Defence of Free Acceptance' in
AS Burrows (ed), *Essays on the Law of Restitution* (Oxford: Clarendon Press, 1991), ch 5

BIRKS, PBH, 'The English Recognition of
Unjust Enrichment' [1991] LMCLQ 473

BIRKS, PBH, 'Civil Wrongs: A New World' in
PBH Birks, *Butterworth Lectures 1990-1991*
(London: Butterworths, 1992)

BIRKS, PBH, *Restitution—The Future* (Sydney:
The Federation Press, 1992)

BIRKS, PBH, 'The Fourth Part of the Principle'
in PBH Birks, *Restitution—The Future*
(Sydney: The Federation Press, 1992), ch 6

BIRKS, PBH, 'No Consideration: Restitution
after Void Contracts' (1993) 23 Univ
WALR 195

BIRKS, PBH, 'Equity in the Modern Law: An
Exercise in Taxonomy' (1996) 26 Univ
WALR 1

BIRKS, PBH, 'Failure of Consideration' in
F Rose (ed), *Consensus ad Idem—Essays in
the Law of Contract in Honour of Guenter
Treitel* (London: Sweet and Maxwell, 1996),
179

BIRKS, PBH, 'The Proceeds of Mortgage
Fraud' (1996) 10 TLI 2

BIRKS, PBH, 'Trusts Raised to Reverse Unjust
Enrichment: The *Westdeutsche* Case'
[1996] RLR 3

BIRKS, PBH, 'Change of Position and Surviving
Enrichment' in W Swadling (ed), *The Limits
of Restitutionary Claims: A Comparative
Analysis* (London: UKNNCL, 1997), 41

BIRKS, PBH, 'The Necessity of a Unitary Law
of Tracing' in R Cranston (ed), *Making Commercial Law, Essays in Honour of Roy Goode*
(Oxford: Oxford University Press, 1997), 239

BIRKS, PBH, 'On Taking Seriously the Difference Between Tracing and Claiming' (1997)
11 TLI 2

BIRKS, PBH, 'Property and Unjust Enrichment: Categorical Truths' [1997] NZ Law Rev 623

BIRKS, PBH, 'Unjust Factors and Wrongs: Pecuniary Rescission for Undue Influence' [1997] RLR 72

BIRKS, PBH, 'Misnomer' in W Cornish, R Nolan, J O'Sullivan, and G Virgo (eds), *Restitution: Past, Present and Future* (Oxford: Hart Publishing, 1998), ch 1

BIRKS, PBH, 'The Role of Fault in the Law of Unjust Enrichment' in GH Jones and WS Swadling (eds), *The Search for Principle* (Oxford: Oxford University Press, 1999), 235

BIRKS, PBH, 'Mistakes of Law' [2000] CLP 205

BIRKS, PBH, 'Rights, Wrongs and Remedies' (2000) OJLS 1

BIRKS, PBH, 'Property, Unjust Enrichment and Tracing' [2001] CLP 231

BIRKS, PBH, 'Recovering Value Transferred Under an Illegal Contract' (2001) 1 *Theoretical Inquiries in Law* 155

BIRKS, PBH, 'Undue Influence as Wrongful Exploitation' (2004) 120 LQR 34

BIRKS, PBH, *Unjust Enrichment* (2nd edn, Oxford: Oxford University Press, 2005)

BIRKS, PBH, and BEATSON, J, 'Unrequested Payment of Another's Debt' (1976) 92 LQR 188

BIRKS, PBH, and CHIN, NY, 'On the Nature of Undue Influence' in J Beatson and D Friedmann (eds), *Good Faith and Fault in Contract Law* (Oxford: Clarendon Press, 1995), 57

BRIGHT, S, and MCFARLANE, B, 'Proprietary Estoppel and Property Rights' (2005) 64 CLJ 449

BRYAN, M, 'Recovering Misdirected Money from Banks: Ministerial Receipt at Law and in Equity' in F Rose (ed), *Restitution and Banking Law* (Oxford: Mansfield Press, 1998), 182

BRYAN, M, 'Unjust Enrichment and Unconscionability in Australia: A False Dichotomy?' in JW Nyers, M McInnes, and SGA Pitel (eds), *Understanding Unjust Enrichment* (Oxford: Hart Publishing, 2004), ch 4

BRYAN, M, 'The Liability of the Recipient: Restitution at Common Law or Wrongdoing in Equity?' in S Degeling and J Edelman (eds), *Equity in Commercial Law* (Sydney: Lawbook Co, 2005), 339

BURNS, F, 'The Elderly and Undue Influence Inter Vivos' (2003) 23 LS 25

BURROWS, AS, 'Contact, Tort and Restitution—A Satisfactory Division or Not?' (1983) LQR 217

BURROWS, AS, 'Law Commission Report on Pecuniary Restitution on Breach of Contract' (1984) 47 MLR 76

BURROWS, AS, 'Free Acceptance and the Law of Restitution' (1988) 104 LQR 576

BURROWS, AS, 'Restitution from Assignees' [1994] RLR 52

BURROWS, AS, 'Swaps and the Friction Between Common Law and Equity' [1995] RLR 15

BURROWS, AS, 'Quadrating Restitution and Unjust Enrichment: A Matter of Principle?' [2000] RLR 257

BURROWS, AS, 'Proprietary Restitution: Unmasking Unjust Enrichment' (2001) 117 LQR 412

BURROWS, AS, *Hochelga Lectures, Fusing Common Law and Equity: Remedies, Restitution and Reform* (University of Hong Kong and Sweet and Maxwell Asia, 2002)

BURROWS, AS, 'We Do This At Common Law But That In Equity' (2002) 22 OJLS 1

BURROWS, AS, 'The English Law of Restitution: A Ten-Year Review' in JW Neyers, M McInnes, and SGA Pitel (eds), *Understanding Unjust Enrichment* (Oxford: Hart Publishing, 2004), 18

BURROWS, AS, *Remedies for Torts and Breach of Contract* (3rd edn, Oxford University Press, 2004)

BURROWS, AS, 'Absence of Basis: The New Birksian Scheme' in A Burrows and Lord Rodgers (eds), *Mapping the Law: Essays in*

Memory of Peter Birks (Oxford: Oxford University Press, 2006), ch 2

BURROWS, AS, *The Law of Restitution* (3rd edn, Oxford: Oxford University Press, 2011)

BURROWS, AS, *A Restatement of the English Law of Unjust Enrichment* (Oxford: Hart Publishing, 2012)

BURROWS, AS, and PEEL, E (eds), *Commercial Remedies: Current Issues and Policies* (Oxford: Oxford University Press, 2003)

BUTLER, PA, 'Mistaken Payments, Change of Position and Restitution' in P Finn (ed), *Essays on Restitution* (Sydney: The Law Book Co, 1990), 87

CAMPBELL, D, and HARRIS, D, 'In Defence of Breach: A Critique of Restitution and the Performance Interest' (2002) LS 208

CAMPBELL, ID, and WYLIE, OP, 'Ain't No Telling (Which Circumstances are Exceptional)' (2003) CLJ 605

CAPPER, D, 'Undue Influence and Unconscionability: A Rationalisation' (1998) 114 LQR 479

CAPPER, D, 'Unconscionable Bargains' (2010) LQR 403

CHADWICK, J, 'A Testator's Bounty to His Slayer' (1914) 30 LQR 211

CHAMBERS, R, *Resulting Trusts* (Oxford: Clarendon Press, 1997)

CHAMBERS, R, 'Tracing and Unjust Enrichment' in J Neyers, M McInnes, and S Pitel (eds), *Understanding Unjust Enrichment* (Oxford: Hart Publishing, 2004)

CHAMBERS, R, 'Resulting Trusts' in AS Burrows and Lord Rodger (eds), *Mapping the Law* (Oxford: Oxford University Press, 2006), ch 13

CHAMBERS, R, 'Two Kinds of Enrichment' in R Chambers, C Mitchell, and J Penner (eds), *Philosophical Foundations of the Law of Unjust Enrichment* (Oxford: Oxford University Press, 2009), ch 9

CHAMBERS, R, 'Trust and Theft' in E Bant and M Harding (eds), *Exploring Private Law* (Cambridge: Cambridge University Press, 2010), ch 10

CHEN-WISHART, M, 'Loss Sharing, Undue Influence and Manifest Disadvantage' (1994) 110 LQR 173

CHEN-WISHART, M, 'Unjust Factors and the Restitutionary Response' (2000) OJLS 557

CHOWDRY, M, and MITCHELL, C, 'Tax Legislation as a Justifying Factor' [2005] 13 RLR 1

CLARK, P, 'Frustration, Restitution and the Law Reform (Frustrated Contracts) Act 1943' [1996] LMCLQ 170

CLEARY, N, 'Property, Proportionality and the Change of Position Defence' in S Elliott, B Häcker, and C Mitchell (eds), *Restitution of Overpaid Tax* (Oxford: Hart Publishing, 2013), ch 5

COHEN, H, 'Change of Position in Quasi-Contracts' (1931–32) 45 Harv LR 1333

CONAGLEN, M, 'The Nature and Function of Fiduciary Loyalty' (2005) 121 LQR 452

CONAGLEN, M, 'A Re-Appraisal of the Fiduciary Self-Dealing and Fair-Dealing Rules' (2006) CLJ 366

CONAGLEN, M, 'Thinking about Proprietary Remedies for Breach of Confidence' [2008] IPQ 82

CONAGLEN, M, 'Fiduciary Regulation of Conflicts Between Duties' (2009) LQR 111

CONAGLEN, M, *Fiduciary Loyalty: Protecting the Due Performance of Non-Fiduciary Duties* (Oxford: Hart Publishing, 2010)

CONAGLEN, M, 'Difficulties with Tracing Backwards' (2011) LQR 432

CONAGLEN, M, 'The Extent of Fiduciary Accounting and the Importance of Authorisation Mechanisms' (2011) CLJ 548

CONAGLEN, M, 'Fiduciary Duties and Voluntary Undertakings' (2013) 7 Journal of Equity 105

COOKE, E, 'Trespass, Mesne Profits and Restitution' (1994) 110 LQR 420

COOKE, E, 'Estoppel and the Protection of Expectations' (1997) 17 LS 258

CORNISH, WR, 'Colour of Office: Restitutionary Redress Against Public Authority' [1987] JMCL 41

Cunnington, R, 'The Border Between Compensation, Restitution and Punishment' (2006) 122 LQR 382

Dagan, H, *The Law and Ethics of Restitution* (Cambridge University Press, 2004)

Davies, D, 'Restitution and Equitable Wrongs: An Australian Analogue' in F Rose (ed), *Consensus ad Idem—Essays in the Law of Contract in Honour of Guenter Treitel* (London: Sweet and Maxwell, 1996), 158

Davies, P, 'Contract and Unjust Enrichment: A Blurry Divide' (2010) LQR 175

Davies, P, 'Gain-Based Remedies for Dishonest Assistance' (2015) 131 LQR 173

Davies, P, and Virgo, G, 'Relieving Trustee's Mistakes' [2013] RLR 73

Dawson, JP, 'Economic Duress—An Essay in Perspective' (1947) 45 Mich LR 253

Dawson, JP, '*Negotiorum Gestio:* The Altruistic Intermeddler' (1961) 74 Harv LR 817

Day, W, 'An Application of *Wrotham Park Damages*' (2015) 131 LQR 218

Denning, A, 'The Recovery of Money' (1949) 65 LQR 37

Dickson, B, 'Restitution and Illegal Transactions' in AS Burrows (ed), *Essays on the Law of Restitution* (Oxford: Clarendon Press, 1991), ch 7

Dickson, B, 'An Action for Unjust Enrichment' (1993) 34 NILQ 106

Dietrich, J, *Restitution: A New Perspective* (Sydney: The Federation Press, 1998)

Dietrich, J, and Ridge, P, 'The Receipt of What? Questions Concerning Third Party Recipient Liability in Equity and Unjust Enrichment' (2007) 31 MULR 47

Du Plessis, J, 'Toward a Rational Structure of Liability for Unjustified Enrichment: Thoughts From Two Mixed Jurisdictions' (2005) 122 South African LJ 142

Dyson, M, and Greene, S, 'The Properties of the Law: Restoring Personal Property Through Crime and Tort' in M Dyson (ed), *Unravelling Tort and Crime* (Cambridge: Cambridge University Press, 2014), ch 14

Earnshaw, TK, and Pace, PJ, 'Let the Hand Receiving it Be Ever So Chaste' (1974) 37 MLR 481

Edelman, J, *Gain-Based Damages: Contract, Tort, Equity and Intellectual Property* (Oxford: Hart Publishing, 2002)

Edelman, J, 'Liability in Unjust Enrichment When a Contract Fails to Materialise' in AS Burrows and E Peel (eds), *Contract Formation and Parties* (Oxford: Oxford University Press, 2010), ch 9

Edelman, J, 'When Do Fiduciary Duties Arise?' (2010) LQR 302

Edelman, J, 'Change of Position: A Defence of Unjust Disenrichment' (2012) 92 Boston ULR 1009

Edelman, J, and Elliott, SB, 'Money Remedies Against Trustees' (2004) 18 TLI 116

Elliott, SB, 'Restitutionary Compensatory Damages' (1998) 6 RLR 135

Elliott, SB, and Mitchell, C, 'Remedies for Dishonest Assistance' (2004) 67 MLR 16

Enonchong, N, 'The Irrebuttable Presumption of Influence and the Relationship Between Fiancé and Fiancée' (2005) 121 LQR 567

Enonchong, N, 'Restitution from Public Authorities: Any Room for Duress?' in S Elliott, B Häcker, and C Mitchell (eds), *Restitution of Overpaid Tax* (Oxford: Hart Publishing, 2013), ch 4

Etherton, T, 'The Legitimacy of Proprietary Relief' (2014) 2 Birkbeck LR 59

Evans, S, 'Rethinking Tracing and the Law of Restitution' (1999) 115 LQR 469

Evans, W, 'An Essay on the Action for Money Had and Received' [1998] RLR 1

Farnsworth, FA, 'Your Loss or My Gain? The Dilemma of the Disgorgement Principle in Breach of Contract' (1985) 94 Yale LJ 1339

Farnsworth, FA, *Alleviating Mistakes* (Oxford: Clarendon Press, 2004)

Finch, V, and Worthington, S, 'The *Pari Passu* Principle and Ranking Restitutionary Rights' in FD Rose (ed), *Restitution and Insolvency* (Oxford: Mansfield Press, 2000), 1

FINN, PD, *Fiduciary Obligations* (Sydney: Law Book Co, 1977)

FINN, PD, 'Equitable Doctrine and Discretion in Remedies' in W Cornish, R Nolan, J O'Sullivan, and G Virgo (eds), *Restitution: Past, Present and Future* (Oxford: Hart Publishing, 1998), ch 17

FINNIS, J, 'The Fairy Tale's Moral' (1999) 115 LQR 170

FLANNIGAN, R, 'The Adulteration of Fiduciary Doctrine in Corporate Law' (2006) 122 LQR 449

FOX, D, '*Bona Fide* Purchase and the Currency of Money' (1996) 55 CLJ 547

FOX, D, 'The Transfer of Legal Title to Money' [1996] RLR 60

FOX, D, 'Legal Title as a Ground of Restitutionary Liability' [2000] RLR 465

FOX, D, 'Enforcing a Possessory Title to a Stolen Car' (2002) 61 CLJ 27

FOX, D, 'Overreaching' in PBH Birks and A Pretto (eds), *Breach of Trust* (Oxford: Hart Publishing, 2002), 95

FOX, D, *Property Rights in Money* (Oxford: Oxford University Press, 2008)

FREIBERG, A, 'Confiscating the Literary Proceeds of Crime' [1992] Crim LR 96

FRIEDMANN, D, 'Restitution of Benefits Obtained Through the Appropriation of Property or the Commission of a Wrong' (1980) 80 Columbia Law Rev 504

FRIEDMANN, D, 'Payment of Another's Debt' (1983) 99 LQR 534

FRIEDMANN, D, 'The Efficient Breach Fallacy' (1989) 18 JLS 1

FRIEDMANN, D, 'The Performance Interest in Contract Damages' (1995) 111 LQR 628

FRIEDMANN, D, 'Restitution for Wrongs: The Basis of Liability' in W Cornish, R Nolan, J O'Sullivan, and G Virgo (eds), *Restitution: Past, Present and Future* (Oxford: Hart Publishing, 1998), ch 7

FULLER, LL, and PERDUE WR, 'The Reliance Interest in Contract Damages' (1936–37) 46 Yale LJ 52

FUNG, E, and HO, L, 'Change of Position and Estoppel' (2001) 117 LQR 14

GARDNER, J, 'Ashworth on Principles' in L Zedner and J Roberts (eds), *Principles and Values in Criminal law and Criminal Justice: Essays in Honour of Andrew Ashworth* (Oxford: Oxford University Press, 2012), 25

GARDNER, S, 'Moment of Truth for Knowing Receipt?' (2009) 125 LQR 20

GARNER, M, 'The Role of Subjective Benefit in the Law of Unjust Enrichment' (1990) OJLS 42

GETZLER, J, 'Rumford Market and the Genesis of Fiduciary Obligations' in AS Burrows and Lord Rodger (eds), *Mapping the Law* (Oxford: Oxford University Press, 2006), ch 31

GIGLIO, F, 'A Systematic Approach to "Unjust" and "Unjustified" Enrichment' (2003) 23 OJLS 455

GIGLIO, F, 'Gain-Related Recovery' (2008) OJLS 501

GLEESON, S, 'The Involuntary Launderer: The Banker's Liability for Deposits of the Proceeds of Crime' in PBH Birks (ed), *Laundering and Tracing* (Oxford: Oxford University Press, 1995), 126

GLISTER, J, 'The Nature of *Quistclose* Trusts: Classification and Reconciliation' (2004) 63 CLJ 632

GLISTER, J, 'The Presumption of Advancement' in C Mitchell (ed), *Constructive and Resulting Trusts* (Oxford: Hart Publishing, 2010), ch 10

GOFF, R, 'Reform of the Law of Restitution' (1961) 24 MLR 85

GOODE, RM, 'The Right to Trace and Its Impact in Commercial Transactions' (1976) 92 LQR 360

GOODE, RM, 'Ownership and Obligation in Commercial Transactions' (1987) 103 LQR 433

GOODE, RM, 'Property and Unjust Enrichment' in AS Burrows (ed), *Essays on the Law of Restitution* (Oxford: Clarendon Press, 1991), ch 9

GOODWIN, J, 'Failure of Basis in the Contractual Context' [2013] RLR 24

GOUDKAMP, J, '*Ex Turpi Causa* and Immoral Behaviour in the Tort Context' (2011) LQR 354

GOYMOUR, A, 'A Contribution to Knowing Receipt Liability?' [2008] RLR 113

GRAHAM, M, 'Restitutionary Damages: The Anvil Struck' (2004) 120 LQR 26

GRANTHAM, RB, 'Doctrinal Bases for the Recognition of Proprietary Rights' (1996) 16 OJLS 561

GRANTHAM, RB, 'Absence of Juristic Reason in the Supreme Court of Canada' [2005] 13 RLR 102

GRANTHAM, RB, 'On the Subsidiarity of Unjust Enrichment' (2001) 117 LQR 273

GRANTHAM, RB, 'Disgorgement for Unjust Enrichment?' (2003) CLJ 159

GRANTHAM, RB, and RICKETT, CEF, 'Property and Unjust Enrichment: Categorical Truths or Unnecessary Complexity?' [1997] 2 NZ Law Rev 668

GRANTHAM, RB, and RICKETT, CEF, 'Restitution, Property and Mistaken Payments' [1997] RLR 83

GRANTHAM, RB, and RICKETT, CEF, 'Trust Money as an Unjust Enrichment: A Misconception' [1998] LMCLQ 514

GRANTHAM, RB, and RICKETT, CEF, 'Property Rights as a Legally Significant Event' (2003) CLJ 717

GRANTHAM, RB, and RICKETT, CEF, 'A Normative Account of Defences to Restitutionary Liability' (2008) CLJ 92

GRODECKI, JK, '*In Pari Delicto Potior est Conditio Defendentis*' (1955) 71 LQR 254

GULLEFER, L, 'Recovery of Misappropriated Assets; Orthodoxy Re-Established?' [1995] LMCLQ 446

GUMMOW, WMC, 'Unjust Enrichment, Restitution and Proprietary Remedies' in P Finn (ed), *Essays on Restitution* (Sydney: The Law Book Co, 1990), 47

GUMMOW, WMC, 'Bribes and Constructive Trusts' (2015) LQR 21

HÄCKER, B, 'Rescission and Third Party Rights' [2006] RLR 21

HÄCKER, B, 'Proprietary Restitution After Impaired Consent Transfers: A Generalized Power Model' (2009) 68 CLJ 324

HÄCKER, B, 'The Effect of Rescission on Bona Fide Purchase' (2012) LQR 493

HALLIWELL, M, 'Estoppel: Unconscionability as a Cause of Action' (1994) LS 15

HALSON, R, 'Opportunism, Economic Duress and Contractual Modifications' (1991) 107 LQR 649

HALSON, R, 'Rescission for Misrepresentation' [1997] RLR 89

HARDING, M, 'Justifying Fiduciary Allowances' in A Robertson and HW Tang (eds), *The Goals of Private Law* (Oxford: Hart Publishing, 2009), ch 14

HARDING, M, 'Constructive Trusts and Distributive Justice' in E Bant and M Bryan (eds), *Principles of Proprietary Remedies* (Australia: Thomson Reuters, 2013), ch 2

HARPUM, C, 'Fiduciary Obligations and Fiduciary Powers—Where Are We Going?' in PBH Birks (eds), *Privacy and Loyalty* (Oxford: Clarendon Press, 1997), 283

HART, HLA, 'Discretion' (2013) Harv Law Rev 652

HAVELOCK, R, 'Anticipated Contracts that Do Not Materialise' [2011] RLR 72

HAVELOCK, R, 'The Transformation of Knowing Receipt' [2014] RLR 1

HAYCROFT, AM, and WAKSMAN, DM, 'Restitution and Frustration' [1984] JBL 207

HAYTON, D, 'Fiduciaries in Context: An Overview' in PBH Birks (eds), *Privacy and Loyalty* (Oxford: Clarendon Press, 1997), 283

HEDLEY, S, 'The Myth of "Waiver of Tort"' (1984) 100 LQR 653

HEDLEY, S, 'Work Done in Anticipation of a Contract Which Does Not Materialise: A Response' in W Cornish, R Nolan, J O'Sullivan, and G Virgo (eds), *Restitution: Past, Present and Future* (Oxford: Hart Publishing, 1998), ch 12

HEDLEY, S, *Restitution: Its Division and Ordering* (London: Sweet and Maxwell, 2001)

HEDLEY, S, 'Implied Contract and Restitution' (2004) CLJ 435

HICKS, A, 'The Remedial Principle of *Keech v Sandford* Reconsidered' (2010) CLJ 287

HIGGINS, MJ, 'The Transfer of Property Under Illegal Transactions' (1962) 25 MLR 149

HILLIARD, J, 'A Case for Abolition of Legal Compulsion as a Ground of Restitution' (2002) 61 CLJ 551

HO, L, 'Bribes and the Constructive Trust as a Chameleon' (2012) LQR 486

HODKINSON, K, 'Tracing and Mixed Funds' [1983] Conv 135

HOPE, EW, 'Officiousness' (1929) Cornell LQ 25

HOPKINS, N, 'Conscience, Discretion and the Creation of Property Rights' (2006) 4 LS 475

HU, Y, 'Change of Position and the Revenue' [2011] RLR 112

HUDSON, J, 'Estoppel by Representation as a Defence to Unjust Enrichment—The Vine Has Not Withered Yet' [2014] RLR 19

HUNT, C, 'Rethinking Surreptitious Takings in the Law of Confidence' (2012) IPQ 66

IBBETSON, D, *A Historical Introduction to the Law of Obligations* (Oxford: Oxford University Press, 1999)

JACKMAN, IM, 'Restitution for Wrongs' (1989) 48 CLJ 302

JACKMAN, IM, *The Varieties of Restitution* (Sydney: The Federation Press, 1998)

JACKSON, RM, *The History of Quasi-Contract in English Law* (Cambridge: Cambridge University Press, 1936)

JAFFEY, P, *The Nature and Scope of Restitution* (Oxford: Hart Publishing, 2000)

JAFFEY, P, 'Efficiency, Disgorgement and Reliance in Contract: A Comment on Campbell and Harris' (2002) LS 570

JONES, G, 'Unjust Enrichment and the Fiduciary's Duty of Loyalty' (1968) 84 LQR 472

JONES, G, *Restitution in Public and Private Law* (London: Sweet and Maxwell, 1991)

KEY, P, '*Bona Fide* Purchase as a Defence in the Law of Restitution' [1994] LMCLQ 421

KEY, P, 'Excising Estoppel by Representation as a Defence to Restitution' [1995] CLJ 525

KHURSHID, S, and MATTHEWS, M, 'Tracing Confusion' (1979) 95 LQR 78

KING, C, 'Civil Forfeiture and Article 6 of the ECHR: Due Process Implications for England and Wales and Ireland' (2014) LS 371

KLIPPERT, GB, 'The Juridical Nature of Unjust Enrichment' (1980) 30 University of Toronto LJ 356

KORTMANN, J, *Altruism in Private Law: Liability for Nonfeasance and Negotiorum Gestio* (Oxford: Oxford University Press, 2005)

KREMER, B, 'Restitution and Unconscientiousness: Another View' (2003) 119 LQR 188

KULL, A, 'James Barr Ames and the Early Modern History of Unjust Enrichment' (2005) 25 OJLS 297

LANGBEIN, JJ, 'The Later History of Restitution' in W Cornish, R Nolan, J O'Sullivan, and G Virgo (eds), *Restitution: Past, Present and Future* (Oxford: Hart Publishing, 1998), 57

LANHAM, DJ, 'Duress and Void Contracts' (1966) 29 MLR 615

LAW COMMISSION, *Pecuniary Restitution on Breach of Contract* (Law Com No 121, 1983)

LAW COMMISSION, *Restitution: Mistakes of Law and Ultra Vires Public Authority Receipts and Payments* (Law Com No 227, 1994)

LAW COMMISSION, *Aggravated, Exemplary and Restitutionary Damages* (Law Com No 247, 1997)

LAW COMMISSION, *Limitation of Actions* (Law Com No 270, 2001)

LAW COMMISSION, *The Illegality Defence* (Consultation Paper No 189, 2009)

LAW COMMISSION, *The Illegality Defence* (Law Com No 320, 2010)

LEE, J, 'Changing Position on Change of Position' [2007] RLR 135

LEE, J, 'Constructing and Limiting Liability in Equity' (2015) LQR 39

LEOW, R, and LIAU, T, 'Resulting Trusts: A Victory for Unjust Enrichment'?' (2014) CLJ 500

LEWISON, K, 'Under the Influence' [2011] RLR 1

LODDER, AVM, *Enrichment in the Law of Restitution and Unjust Enrichment* (Oxford: Hart Publishing, 2012)

LOW, K, 'Recipient Liability in Equity: Resisting the Siren's Lure' [2008] RLR 96

MACDONALD, E, 'Duress by Threatened Breach of Contract' (1989) JBL 460

MASON, A, 'The Place of Equity and Equitable Remedies in the Contemporary Common Law World' (1994) 110 LQR 238

MATTHEWS, P, 'Money Paid Under Mistake of Fact' (1980) 130 NLJ 587

MATTHEWS, P, 'Stopped Cheques and Restitution' (1982) JBL 281

MAUDSLEY, RH, 'Proprietary Remedies for the Recovery of Money' (1959) 75 LQR 234

McCONVILLE, DA, 'Tracing and the Rule in *Clayton's Case*' (1963) 79 LQR 388

McFARLANE, B, 'Constructive Trusts Arising on a Receipt of Property *Sub Conditione*' (2004) 120 LQR 667

McFARLANE, B, *The Law of Proprietary Estoppel* (Oxford: Oxford University Press, 2013)

McFARLANE, B, and STEVENS, R, 'In Defence of *Sumpter v Hedges*' (2002) 118 LQR 569

McINNES, M, 'Passing On in the Law of Restitution: A Reconsideration' (1997) 19 Sydney LR 179

McINNES, M, 'At the Plaintiff's Expense— Quantifying Restitutionary Relief' (1998) 57 CLJ 472

McINNES, M, 'Interceptive Subtraction, Unjust Enrichment and Wrongs—A Reply to Professor Birks' (2003) CLJ 697

McKENDRICK, E, 'Frustration, Restitution and Loss Apportionment' in AS Burrows (ed), *Essays on the Law of Restitution* (Oxford: Clarendon Press, 1991), 147

McKENDRICK, E, 'Restitution, Misdirected Funds and Change of Position' (1992) 55 MLR 377

McKENDRICK, E, 'Restitution of Unlawfully Demanded Taxes' [1993] LMCLQ 88

McKENDRICK, E, 'Total Failure of Consideration and Counter-restitution: Two Issues or One?' in PBH Birks (ed), *Laundering and Tracing* (Oxford: Clarendon Press, 1995), 217

McKENDRICK, E, 'Work Done in Anticipation of a Contract which Does Not Materialise' in W Cornish, R Nolan, J O'Sullivan, and G Virgo (eds), *Restitution: Past, Present and Future* (Oxford: Hart Publishing, 1998), ch 11

McKENDRICK, E, 'The Further Travails of Duress' in A Burrows, and Lord Rodger (eds), *Mapping the Law: Essays in Memory of Peter Birks* (Oxford: Oxford University Press), ch 10

McLEAN, H, 'Limitation of Actions in Restitution' (1989) CLJ 472

MEAD, G, 'Free Acceptance: Some Further Considerations' (1989) 105 LQR 460

MEE, J, 'Presumed resulting trusts, intention and declaration' (2014) CLJ 86

MEIER, S, 'Restitution after Executed Void Contracts' in P Birks and F Rose (eds), *Lessons from the Swaps Litigation* (London: Informa Law, 2000), 168

MEIER, S, 'Unjust Factors and Legal Grounds' in D Johnston and R Zimmermann (eds), *Unjustified Enrichment: Key Issues in Comparative Perspective* (Cambridge: Cambridge University Press, 2002), 37

MEIER, S, and ZIMMERMANN, F, 'Judicial Development of the Law, Error Iuris and the Law of Unjust Enrichment' (1999) 115 LQR 556

MERKIN, R, 'Restitution by Withdrawal from Illegal Contracts' (1981) 97 LQR 420

MIDWINTER, S, '*The Great Pease* and Precedent' (2003) 119 LQR 180

MIDWINTER, S, 'Subrogation Finds Some "Well-Settled Principles"' [2003] LMCLQ 6

MILLETT, P, 'The *Quistclose* Trust: Who Can Enforce It?' (1985) 101 LQR 269

MILLETT, P, 'Tracing the Proceeds of Fraud' (1991) 107 LQR 71

MILLETT, P, 'Equity—The Road Ahead' (1995) 9 TLI 35

MILLETT, P, 'Equity's Place in the Law of Commerce' (1998) 114 LQR 214

MILLETT, P, 'Restitution and Constructive Trusts' (1998) 114 LQR 399

MILLETT, P, 'Restitution and Constructive Trusts' in W Cornish, R Nolan, J O'Sullivan, and G Virgo (eds), *Restitution: Past, Present and Future* (Oxford: Hart Publishing, 1998), ch 13

MILLETT, P, 'Foreword' to WJ Swadling (ed), *The Quistclose Trust: Critical Essays* (Oxford: Hart Publishing, 2004)

MILLETT, P, 'Proprietary Restitution' in S Degeling and J Edelman (eds), *Equity in Commercial Law* (Sydney: Lawbook Co, 2005)

MILLETT, P, '*Quistclose* Trusts: *Twinsectra v Yardley* Explained' (2011) 1 T&T 7

MILLETT, P, 'Bribes and Secret Commissions Again' (2012) CLJ 583

MITCHELL, AR, TAYLOR, SME, and TALBOT, KV, *Mitchell, Taylor and Talbot on Confiscation and the Proceeds of Crime* (3rd edn, London: Sweet and Maxwell)

MITCHELL, C, 'No Account of Profits for a Victim of Deceit' [1996] LMCLQ 314

MITCHELL, C, *The Law of Contribution and Reimbursement* (Oxford: Clarendon Press, 2003)

MITCHELL, C, 'The New Birksian Approach to Unjust Enrichment' [2004] RLR 265

MITCHELL, C, 'Liability Chains in Unjust Enrichment' in S Degeling and J Edelman (eds), *Unjust Enrichment in Commercial Law* (Sydney: Lawbook Co, 2008), ch 7

MITCHELL, C, MITCHELL, P, and WATTERSON, S (eds), *Goff and Jones: The Law of Unjust Enrichment* (8th edn, London: Sweet and Maxwell, 2010)

MITCHELL, C, 'Restitutionary Claims by Indirect Taxpayers' in S Elliott, B Häcker, and C Mitchell (eds), *Restitution of Overpaid Tax* (Oxford: Hart Publishing, 2013), ch 6

MITCHELL, C, and MITCHELL, C, '*Planché v Colburn* (1831)' in P Mitchell and C Mitchell (eds), *Landmark Cases in the Law of Restitution* (Oxford: Hart Publishing, 2006), ch 4

MITCHELL, C, and WATTERSON, S, *Subrogation: Law and Practice* (Oxford: Oxford University Press, 2007)

MITCHELL, C, and GOUDKAMP, J, 'Denials and Defences in the Law of Unjust Enrichment' in C Mitchell and W Swadling (eds), *The Restatement Third: Restitution and Unjust Enrichment* (Oxford: Hart Publishing, 2013), ch 6

MITCHELL, P, 'Artificiality of Failure of Consideration' (2010) 29 UQLJ 191

NADLER, JM, 'What Right does Unjust Enrichment Protect?' (2008) OJLS 245

NAHAN, NY, 'Rescission: A Case For Rejecting the Classical Model?' (1997) 27 Univ WALR 66

NEEDHAM, CA, 'Mistaken Payments: A New Look at an Old Theme' (1979) 12 Univ of Brit Col LR 159

NEUBERGER, D, 'The Remedial Constructive Trust—Fact or Fiction', Banking Services and Finance Law Association Conference, New Zealand (2014)

NICHOLLS, D, 'Knowing Receipt: The Need For A New Landmark' in W Cornish, R Nolan, J O'Sullivan, and G Virgo (eds), *Restitution: Past, Present and Future* (Oxford: Hart Publishing, 1998), ch 15

NOLAN, RC, 'Change of Position' in PBH Birks (ed), *Laundering and Tracing* (Oxford: Clarendon Press, 1995), 135

NOLAN, RC, 'Remedies for Breach of Contract: Specific Enforcement and Restitution' in F Rose (ed), *Failure of Contracts: Contractual, Restitutionary and Proprietary Consequences* (Oxford: Hart Publishing, 1997), 35

NOLAN, RC, 'Conflicts of Interest, Unjust Enrichment and Wrongdoing' in W Cornish, R Nolan, J O'Sullivan, and G Virgo (eds), *Restitution: Past, Present and Future* (Oxford: Hart Publishing, 1998), ch 7

NOLAN, RC, 'Property in a Fund' (2004) 120 LQR 108

O'DAIR, R, 'Restitutionary Damages for Breach of Contract and the Theory of Efficient Breach: Some Reflections' (1993) 46(2) CLP 113

O'DELL, E, 'Incapacity' in PBH Birks, and FD Rose (eds), *Lessons of the Swaps Litigation* (Oxford: Mansfield Press, 2000)

O'SULLIVAN, D, 'The Rule in *Phillips v Phillips*' (2002) 118 LQR 296

O'SULLIVAN, D, ELLIOTT, S, and ZAKRZEWSKI, R, *The Law of Rescission* (Oxford: Oxford University Press, 2007)

O'SULLIVAN, J, 'Undue Influence and Misrepresentation after *O'Brien*: Making Security Secure' in F Rose (ed), *Restitution and Banking Law* (Oxford: Mansfield Press, 1998), 42

O'SULLIVAN, J, 'Rescission as a Self-help Remedy: A Critical Analysis' (2000) 59 CLJ 509

O'SULLIVAN, J, 'Who Dares Whinges: Duress, Undue Influence and the SAS' (2003) 62 CLJ 554

OAKLEY, AJ, 'The Prerequisites of an Equitable Tracing Claim' (1975) CLP 64

OKUDA, S, 'Criminal Antiprofit Laws: Some Thoughts in Favor of Their Constitutionality' (1985) 76 Cal LR 1353

ORMEROD, D (ed), *Smith and Hogan, Criminal Law* (13th edn, Oxford: Oxford University Press, 2011)

PEARCE, R, 'A Tracing Paper' [1976] Conv 277

PHANG, A, 'Economic Duress: Recent Difficulties and Possible Alternatives' [1997] RLR 53

PALMER, J, 'Chasing a Will-o'-the-Wisp? Making Sense of Bad Faith and Wrongdoers in Change of Position' [2005] 13 RLR 53

POOLE, J, and KEYSER, A, 'Justifying Partial Rescission in English Law' (2005) 121 LQR 273

POSNER, R, 'Economic Analysis of Law' (7th edn, Boston, MA: Little Brown & Co, 2007)

PROKSCH, L, 'Rescission on Terms' [1996] RLR 71

REID, J, 'The Judge as Law Maker' (1972–73) 12 JSPTL (NS) 22

RICKETT, C, 'Equitable Compensation: The Giant Stirs' (1996) 112 LQR 27

ROSE, FD, 'Restitution for the Rescuer' (1989) 9 OJLS 167

ROSE, FD, 'Passing On' in PBH Birks (ed), *Laundering and Tracing* (Oxford: Clarendon Press, 1995), 261

ROSE, FD, 'General Average as Restitution' (1997) 113 LQR 569

ROSE, FD (ed), *Kennedy and Rose on The Law of Salvage* (8th edn, London: Sweet and Maxwell, 2013)

ROTHERHAM, C, *Proprietary Remedies in Context* (Oxford: Hart Publishing, 2002)

ROTHERHAM, C, 'Tracing Misconceptions in *Foskett v McKeown*' [2003] 11 RLR 57

ROWAN, S, 'For the Recognition of Remedial Terms Agreed *Inter Partes*' (2010) LQR 448

RUSH, M, *The Defence of Passing On* (Oxford: Hart Publishing, 2006)

SAMET, I, 'Guarding the Fiduciary's Conscience: A Justification of a Stringent Profit-Stripping Rule' (2008) OJLS 763

SAMET, I, '*Locus Poenitentiae*: Repentance, Withdrawal and Luck' in C Mitchell (ed), *Constructive and Resulting Trusts* (Oxford: Hart Publishing, 2010)

SCHLOTE, M, 'The Principle of Effectiveness and Restitution of Overpaid Tax' in S Elliott, B Häcker, and C Mitchell (ed), *Restitution of Overpaid Tax* (Oxford: Hart Publishing, 2013), ch 10

SEAH, W, 'Laspredictions, Mistakes and the Law of Unjust Enrichment' [2007] RLR 93

SHAND, J, 'Unblinkering the Unruly Horse: Public Policy in the Law of Contract' (1972) 30 CLJ 144

SHARPE, RS, and WADDAMS, SM, 'Damages for Lost Opportunity to Bargain' (1982) 2 OJLS 290

SHEEHAN, D, 'What is a Mistake?' (2000) 20 LS 538

SHEEHAN, D, 'Vitiation of Contracts for Mistake and Misrepresentation of Law' [2003] 11 RLR 26

SHEEHAN, D, 'Natural Obligations in English Law' [2004] LMCLQ 172

SHEEHAN, D, 'Information, Tracing Remedies and the Remedial Constructive Trust' [2005] 13 RLR 82

SHEEHAN, D, 'Disentangling Equitable Personal Liability for Receipt and Assistance' [2008] RLR 41

SHEEHAN, D, 'Unjust Factors or Restitution of Transfers *Sine Causa*' (2008) Oxford University Comparative Law Forum 1

SIMESTER, A, 'Unjust Free Acceptance' [1997] LMCLQ 103

SIMESTER, A, 'Correcting Unjust Enrichment' (2010) OJLS 579

SLOAN, B, 'Due Rewards of Undue Influence?—Property Transfers Benefiting Informal Carers' [2011] RLR 37

SMITH, LD, 'Three-Party Restitution: A Critique of Birks's Theory of Interceptive Subtraction' (1991) 11 OJLS 481

SMITH, LD, 'Disgorgement of the Profits of Breach of Contract: Property, Contract and "Efficient Breach"' (1992) 24 Canadian Business LJ 121

SMITH, LD, 'The Province of the Law of Restitution' (1992) 71 CBR 672

SMITH, LD, 'Tracing in *Taylor v Plumer*: Equity in the Court of King's Bench' [1995] LMCLQ 240

SMITH, LD, 'Tracing Into the Payment of a Debt' (1995) 54 CLJ 290

SMITH, LD, 'Constructive Fiduciaries' in PBH Birks (ed), *Privacy and Loyalty* (Oxford: Clarendon Press, 1997), 263

SMITH, LD, *The Law of Tracing*, (Oxford: Clarendon Press, 1997)

SMITH, LD, 'Unjust Enrichment, Property and the Structure of Trusts' (2000) 116 LQR 412

SMITH, LD, 'Restitution: The Heart of Corrective Justice' (2001) 79 Tex LR 2115

SMITH, LD, 'Simplifying Claims to Traceable Proceeds' (2009) 125 LQR 338

SMITH, LD, 'Constructive Trusts and the No-Profit Rule' (2013) CLJ 260

SMITH, S, 'Contracting Under Pressure: A Theory of Duress' (1997) 56 CLJ 343

SMITH, S, 'Concurrent Liability in Contract and Unjust Enrichment: The Fundamental Breach Requirement' (1999) 115 LQR 245

SMITH, S, 'Unjust Enrichment: Nearer to Tort Than Contract' in R Chambers, C Mitchell, and J Penner (eds), *Philosophical Foundations of the Law of Unjust Enrichment* (Oxford: Oxford University Press, 2009), ch 7

SMITH, S, 'A Duty to Make Restitution' (2013) 26 Canadian Journal of Law and Jurisprudence 157

SMITH, S, 'The Restatement of Liabilities in Restitution' in C Mitchell and W Swadling (eds), *The Restatement Third: Restitution and Unjust Enrichment—Critical and Comparative Essays* (Oxford: Hart Publishing, 2013), 227

STANLEY, P, *The Law of Confidentiality: A Restatement* (Oxford: Hart Publishing, 2008)

STEVENS, R, 'The New Birksian Approach to Unjust Enrichment' [2004] 12 RLR 270

STEVENS, R, 'Justified Enrichment' (2005) 5 OUCLJ 141

STEVENS, R, 'Why do Agents "Drop Out"?' [2005] LMCLQ 101

STEVENS, R, 'Three Enrichment Issues' in AS Burrows and Lord Rodger of Earlsferry (eds), *Mapping the Law* (Oxford: Oxford University Press, 2006), ch 3

STEVENS, R, *Torts and Rights* (Oxford: Oxford University Press, 2007)

STEWART, A, and CARTER, JW, 'Frustrated Contracts and Statutory Adjustment: The Case for a Reappraisal' (1992) CLJ 66

STOLJAR, SJ, 'The Doctrine of Failure of Consideration' (1959) 75 LQR 53

STOLJAR, SJ, 'Unjust Enrichment and Unjust Sacrifice' (1987) 50 MLR 603

STOLJAR, SJ, *The Law of Quasi-Contract* (2nd edn, Sydney: The Law Book Co, 1989)

STOLJAR, SJ, 'Restitutionary Relief for Breach of Contract' (1989) 2 JCL 1

SUMPTION, J, 'Reflections on the Law of Illegality' [2012] RLR 1

SUTTON, RJ, 'Payments of Debts Charged Upon Property' in AS Burrows (ed), *Essays on the Law of Restitution* (Oxford: Clarendon Press, 1991), ch 4

SUTTON, RJ, 'Mistake: Symbol, Metaphor and Unfolding' [2002] RLR 9

SWADLING, WJ, 'The Nature of Ministerial Receipt' in PBH Birks (ed), *Laundering and Tracing* (Oxford: Clarendon Press, 1995), 243

SWADLING, WJ, 'A Claim in Restitution?' [1996] 1 LMCLQ 63

SWADLING, WJ, 'A New Role for Resulting Trusts?' (1996) 16 LS 110

SWADLING, WJ, 'Restitution and *Bona Fide* Purchase' in WJ Swadling (ed), *The Limits of Restitutionary Claims: A Comparative Analysis* (London: UKNCCL, 1997), 79

SWADLING, WJ, 'The Myth of *Phillips* v. *Homfray*' in GH Jones and WH Swadling (eds) *The Search for Principle* (Oxford: Oxford University Press, 1999), 277

SWADLING, WJ (ed), *The Quistclose Trust: Critical Essays* (Oxford: Hart Publishing, 2004)

SWADLING, WJ, 'Rescission, Property and the Common Law' (2005) 121 LQR 123

SWADLING, WJ, 'Explaining Resulting Trusts' (2008) 124 LQR 72

SWADLING, WJ, 'Ignorance and Unjust Enrichment: the Problem of Title' (2008) OJLS 627

SWADLING, WJ, 'The Fiction of the Constructive Trust' (2011) CLP 1

SWAIN, W, 'Unjust Enrichment and the Role of Legal History in England and Australia' (2013) 36 UNSWLJ 1030

TANG, HW, 'Confidence and the Constructive Trust' (2003) 23 LS 135

TANG, HW, 'Restitution for Mistaken Gifts' (2004) 20 JCL 1

TANG, HW, 'Natural Obligations and the Common Law of Unjust Enrichment' [2006] OUCLJ 133

TARRANT, J 'Property Rights to Stolen Money' (2005) 32 UWALR 234

TARRANT, J 'Thieves as Trustees: In Defence of the Theft Principle' (2009) 3 J Eq 170

TAYLOR, J 'Total Failure of Consideration and *Roxborough v Rothmans*' (2004) 120 LQR 30

TETTENBORN, A, 'Lawful Receipt—A Justifying Factor?' (1997) 5 RLR 1

TETTENBORN, A, *The Law of Restitution in England and Wales* (3rd edn, London: Cavendish Publishing Ltd, 2002)

TOLHURST, G, 'Assignment, Equities, *The Trident Beauty* and Restitution' (1999) 58 CLJ 546

TRAKMAN, LE, and SHARMA, K, 'The Binding Force of Agreements to Negotiate in Good Faith' (2014) CLJ 598

TREITEL, GH, 'The Infants Relief Act 1874' (1957) 73 LQR 194

TREITEL, GH, *Frustration and Force Majeure* (3rd edn, London: Sweet and Maxwell, 2014)

ULPH, J, 'Confiscation Orders, Human Rights and Penal Measures' (2010) LQR 251

VERHAGEN, HLE, 'Absence of Basis and Unjustified Enrichment in Dutch Law' [2004] RLR 132

VERSE, DA, 'Improvements and Enrichments: A Comparative Analysis' [1998] RLR 85

VIRGO, GJ, 'The Law of Taxation is Not an Island—Overpaid Taxes and the Law of Restitution' [1993] BTR 442

VIRGO, GJ, 'Reconstructing the Law of Restitution' (1996) 10 TLI 20

VIRGO, GJ, 'The Effects of Illegality on Claims for Restitution in English Law' in WJ Swadling (ed), *The Limits of Restitutionary Claims: A Comparative Analysis* (London: UKNCCL, 1997), 141

VIRGO, GJ, 'The Law of Restitution and the Proceeds of Crime—A Survey of English Law' [1998] RLR 34

VIRGO, GJ, 'Restitution of Overpaid VAT' [1998] BTR 582

VIRGO, GJ, 'Undue Influence and Misrepresentation after *O'Brien*: Making Security Secure: A Commentary' in F Rose (ed), *Restitution and Banking Law* (Oxford: Mansfield Press, 1998), 77

VIRGO, GJ, 'What is the Law of Restitution About?' in W Cornish, R Nolan, J O'Sullivan, and G Virgo (eds), *Restitution: Past, Present and Future* (Oxford: Hart Publishing, 1998), 305

VIRGO, GJ, 'Restitution Through the Looking Glass: Restitution Within Equity and Equity Within Restitution' in J Getzler (ed), *Rationalizing Property, Equity and Trusts: Essays in Honour of Edward Burn* (London: Lexis Nexis, 2003), 106

VIRGO, GJ, 'Hypothetical Bargains: Compensation or Restitution?' (2006) 65 CLJ 272

VIRGO, GJ, 'The Role of Fault in the Law of Restitution' in AS Burrows (ed), *Mapping the Law of Obligations* (Oxford: Oxford University Press, 2006), ch 5

VIRGO, GJ, '*Deutsche Morgan Grenfell*: The Right to Restitution of Tax: Back to Basics' [2007] BTR 27

VIRGO, GJ, 'Causation and Remoteness in the Law of Restitution' in S Degeling and J Edelman (eds), *Unjust Enrichment in Commercial Law* (Sydney: Lawbook Co, 2008), ch 8

VIRGO, GJ, 'Crime and Restitution Revisited' [2009] RLR 29

VIRGO, GJ, 'Demolishing the Pyramid—the Presence of Basis and Risk-Taking in the Law of Unjust Enrichment' in A Robertson and HW Tang (eds), *The Goals of Private Law* (Oxford: Hart Publishing, 2009), 477

VIRGO, GJ, *Principles of Equity and Trusts* (Oxford: Oxford University Press, 2012)

VIRGO, GJ, '*Re Hallett's Estate*' in C Mitchell and P Mitchell (eds), *Landmark Cases in Equity* (Oxford: Hart Publishing, 2012), 389

VIRGO, GJ, 'We Do This in the Criminal Law, and that in the Law of Tort: A New Fusion Debate' in E Chamberlain, J Neyers, and S Pitel (eds), *Challenging Orthodoxy in Tort Law* (Oxford: Hart Publishing, 2013)

VIRGO, GJ, 'Illegality's Role in the Law of Tort' in M Dyson (ed), *Unravelling Tort and Crime* (Cambridge: Cambridge University Press, 2014), ch 7

VIRGO, GJ, 'Whose Conscience? Unconscionability in the Common Law of Obligations' in A Robertson and M Tilbury (eds), *The Common Law of Obligations: Divergence and Unity* (Oxford: Hart Publishing, 2015)

WADDAMS, SM, 'Restitution as Part of Contract Law' in AS Burrows (ed), *Essays on the Law of Restitution* (Oxford: Clarendon Press, 1991), ch 8

WADDAMS, SM, 'Gains Derived from Breach of Contract: Historical and Conceptual Perspectives' in D Saidov and R Cunnington (eds), *Contract Damages: Domestic and International Perspectives* (Oxford: Hart Publishing, 2008), 192

WADE, JW, 'Benefits Obtained Under Illegal Transactions—Reasons For and Against Allowing Restitution' (1946) Texas Law Review 31

WADE, JW, 'Restitution for Benefits Conferred Without Request' (1966) Vanderbilt LR 1183

WALKER, R, 'Tracing after *Foskett v McKeown*' [2000] 8 RLR 573

WALKER, R, 'Dishonesty and Unconscionable Conduct in Commercial Life—Some Reflections on Accessory Liability and Knowing Receipt' (2005) 27 Sydney LR 187

WATT, G, 'Laches, Estoppel and Election' in PBH Birks and A Pretto (eds), *Breach of Trust* (Oxford: Hart Publishing, 2002), 353

WATTERSON, S, 'Alternative and Cumulative Remedies: What is the Difference?' [2003] RLR 7

WATTERSON, S, 'An Account of Profits or Damages? The History of Orthodoxy' (2004) OJLS 471

WATTERSON, S, 'Direct Transfers in the Law of Unjust Enrichment' (2013) CLP 435

WATTERSON, S, and GOYMOUR, A, 'Testing the Boundaries of Conversion: Account-holders, Intangible Property and Economic Harm' [2012] LMCLQ 204

WATTS, P, 'The Limits of Profit-Stripping for Wrongs' (1996) 112 LQR 219

WATTS, P, 'Rescission of Guarantees for Misrepresentation and Actionable Damages' (2002) 61 CLJ 301

WEBB, C, 'Reasons for Restitution' in S Elliott, B Häcker, and C Mitchell (eds), *Restitution of Overpaid Tax* (Oxford: Hart Publishing, 2013), ch 5

WEINRIB, E, 'The Fiduciary Obligation' (1975) 24 UTLJ 1

WEINRIB, E, 'Illegality as a Tort Defence' (1976) 26 UTLJ 28

WEINRIB, E, *The Idea of Private Law* (London: Harvard University Press, 1995)

WEINRIB, E, 'Correctively Unjust Enrichment' in R Chambers, C Mitchell, and J Penner (eds), *Philosophical Foundations of the Law of Unjust Enrichment* (Oxford: Oxford University Press, 2009), ch 2

WILLIAMS, G, 'Mistake in the Law of Theft' (1977) 36 CLJ 62

WILLIAMS, R, *Unjust Enrichment and Public Law: A Comparative Study of England, France and the EU* (Oxford: Hart Publishing, 2010)

WILLIAMS, R, 'Overpaid Taxes: A Hybrid Public and Private Approach' in S Elliott, B Häcker, and C Mitchell (eds), *Restitution of Overpaid Tax* (Oxford: Hart Publishing, 2013), ch 2

WILMOT-SMITH, F, 'Replacing Risk-Taking Reasoning' (2011) LQR 610

WILMOT-SMITH, F, 'Reconsidering "Total" Failure' (2013) CLJ 414

WINFIELD, PH, 'Mistake of Law' (1943) 59 LQR 327

WINTERTON, D, and WILMOT-SMITH, F, 'Steering a Course on Contract Damages and Failure of Consideration' (2012) 128 LQR 23

WORTHINGTON, S, 'Proprietary Restitution—Void, Voidable and Uncompleted Contracts' (1995) 9 TLI 113

WORTHINGTON, S, 'Fiduciaries: When is Self-Denial Obligatory?' (1999) 58 CLJ 500

WORTHINGTON, S, 'Reconsidering Disgorgement for Wrongs' (1999) MLR 218

WRIGHT, RA, '*Sinclair v Brougham*' (1938) 6 CLJ 305

WRIGHT, RA, *Legal Essays and Addresses* (Cambridge: Cambridge University Press, 1939)

WRIGHT, RA, '*United Australia Ltd v Barclays Bank Ltd*' (1941) 57 LQR 184

YIP, M, 'The Use Value of Money in the Law of Unjust Enrichment' (2010) LS 586

YORK, KH, 'The Extension of Restitutional Remedies in the Tort Field' (1957) 4 UCLA Rev 499

YOUDAN, TG, 'Acquisition of Property by Killing' (1973) 89 LQR 235

ZIMMERMANN, F, 'Unjustified Enrichment: the Modern Civilian Approach' (1995) 15 OJLS 403

INDEX

absence of authority 369–370
absence of basis 127–132,
    371–378, 397, 399,
    578
account of profits 424–426,
    504–509
  breach of confidence 516–519
  definition 19
  equitable wrongdoing 275,
    486–487, 504–509,
    516–519
  limiting period for which
    account taken 426, 507
  trespass to land 459
action for unconscionable
    receipt *see*
    unconscionable receipt,
    action for
administration of
    estates 644–645
advance payments 337–338
advancement, presumption
    of 592
agency 111, 301–305 *see also*
    agent, defence of transfer
    of benefit by an
agent, defence of transfer of
    benefit by an 674–678,
    700
annuity cases 371
anticipated and incomplete
    contracts 343–350
anticipatory expenditure 79–81,
    689–690
assignment of right to
    restitution 111

bad faith 219–220, 691–692
basis *see also* failure of basis
  absence of basis 127–132,
    371–378, 397, 399, 578
  lawful bases 133–151
  mistake 189–191
  partial failure of
    basis 325–329, 355–367
  uncertainty as to
    basis 131–132
beneficial interests, recognition
    of 19
benefit
  agent, defence of transfer
    by 674–678

bona fide purchase
  defence 656–660
collateral benefits, receipt
    of 319–321
consequential
    benefits 115–116
definition 537
deprivation of benefits 10–11
earned benefit, defendant
    must not have 113–114
enrichment 62–63
entitlement, belief in 667–669
fall in value 684–685
forfeiture rule 543–554
incidental benefits 114–115
incontrovertible
    benefit 78–85
justice favouring
    retention 664
money, realizable and realized
    in 82–85
non-money 333–335,
    360–365
unjust benefits 62–63
wrongs 416–417
bona fide purchase, defence
    of 656–660
change of position 700–701
common law 657, 658
complete defence, as 659
conditions 658–659
function 656–657
good faith 648, 658–659
inapplicable, as being
    generally 657
money, proprietary claims
    to 657
not a *bona fide* purchase,
    where
    defendant 659–660
operation of defence 659–660
personal or proprietary
    remedies, application
    whether claimant
    seeks 660
purchase for value 659
rescission 660
resurrection of proprietary
    interest 660
breach of confidence 514–519
  abuse of
    relationships 275–278

account of profits 516–519
  choice of remedy 517–519
  constructive trusts 519
  gain-based remedies 516–519
  identification of duty 515–516
  negotiation damages 517
  privacy, breach of 464–465
  torts 471
breach of contract 312–313,
    332–343, 468–485
  Attorney-General v Blake,
    new approach
    in 473–481
  claimant, breach by 336–343
  cynical breach 482
  defendant, breach by 333–336
  denial of restitution 468–469
  deterrence 484
  fiduciary relationships,
    identification of 470
  gain-based remedies 469–473,
    481–485
  general availability of
    restitutionary
    remedies 481–485
  limitation periods 738–739
  minority 729–730
  part-performance 95
  price payable for interference
    with property
    rights 471–473
  profitable contract, defendant
    entering into more 483
  specifically enforceable
    contracts 483–485
  terms specifying restitutionary
    remedy 470
  torts 471
  total failure of basis 334–343
  wrongs 468–485, 729–730,
    738–739
breach of fiduciary
    duty 275–278, 488–514,
    521–525
breach of statutory
    duty 465–466
bribes or secret
    commissions 500–501
build and sell and contracts to
    sell, distinguishing
    between 318–319
burial 296–297

capacity *see* incapacity
causation
    but for test 175–176, 223–225
    change of position 682–690
    Commonwealth cases 173
    contributory cause
        test 175–176, 222–223,
        435
    criminal offences 530–532
    duress 208–210, 221–227
    estoppel by
        representation 670–671
    law, identification of mistakes
        of 183–186
    mistakes 170–186
    more than one
        victim 437–438
    negligence 178–180
    no reasonable alternative,
        where there is 225–227
    operating cause test, defining
        the 175–176
    recklessness 194–195
    remoteness of gain 435–437
    tracing 610
    voluntariness and risk-
        taking 176–181
    wrongs 434–438
change in
    circumstances 666–701
change of position 678–701
    agent, defence of transfer of
        benefit by an 700
    anticipatory
        expenditure 689–690
    bad faith 691–692
    bona fide purchase 700–701
    causation 682–690
    conditions for establishing
        defence 682–695
    detrimental reliance
        test 686–690
    estoppel by
        representation 698–700
    extraordinary
        changes 685–686, 688
    fault of parties, relative 694
    hardship not sufficient,
        general 687
    inequitable to make
        restitution, where it
        is 690–695
    loss of benefit test 683–686
    mistake 191
    non-pecuniary
        changes 688–689
    public authorities 409–411
    recognition of
        defence 678–680

relationship with other
    defences 698–701
risk allocation 694–695
standard of proof 690
third parties, acquisition of
    causes of action
    against 686
unjust enrichment, reversal
    of 695
value of benefit, fall
    in 684–685
vindication of proprietary
    rights 696–698
wrongs 692–694, 695–696
charges, equitable 20, 635–636
children *see* minority
civil recovery orders 542
claiming 612, 629–630
claims and remedies,
    distinguishing
    between 631
collateral benefits, receipt
    of 319–321
colore officii (colour of office),
    ground of 205, 395–396
common law and equity,
    relationship
    between 40–41, 612–613
compensation
    compensation
        principle 477–478
    equitable compensation 275
    gain-based remedies,
        relationship
        with 438–441
    inadequacy of compensatory
        remedies 424, 440–441
    torts 444–446, 448–449
compromise 143–144, 411–412
compulsion 203–254 *see also*
    duress; legal compulsion;
    undue influence; undue
    pressure
exploitation 255–256
grounds of
    restitution 204–205
illegality 205–206, 720
in pari delicto defences 720
necessity 205, 292–293
passing of title 577
threats to secure performance
    of statutory
    duty 253–254
time factor 204
vitiation of contracts 203–204
confidentiality *see* breach of
    confidence
confiscation regime following
    conviction 535–542

benefit, definition of 537
civil recovery orders 542
common law claims 542
couriers or custodians 540
criminal memoirs 541–542
joint receipt 539–540
money launderers 540–541
obtaining a benefit 537–538
tainted gifts 541
total value or profit 538–539
consideration *see* basis; failure of
    basis
constructive trusts 595–607
    common intention
        constructive trusts 597
    fault, degree of 601
    fiduciary duties, breach
        of 509–514, 519, 598,
        633–634
    forfeiture rule 549–552
    innocent volunteers 634
    institutional constructive
        trusts 595, 597–603
    legal title 600–601
    liability as a constructive
        trustees 596–597
    nature 595–607
    proportionate share 633–635
    proprietary remedies
        following
        recognition 509–514, 519
    recognition 509–514, 519,
        597–603
    remedial constructive
        trusts 595–596, 603–607,
        634–635
    rescission 602–603
    timing, question of 601–602
    transfer of property 633
    unconscionable
        retention 598–602
    wrongs 432–433
consumer credit 286
Consumer Rights Act 2015 367
contract *see also* breach of
    contract; frustration of
    contract
    anticipated and incomplete
        contracts 343–350
    build and sell and contracts to
        sell, distinguishing
        between 318–319
    collateral contracts 49
    compulsion 204
    continuing contractual
        regime 134–141
    discharge of a contractual
        obligation 134
    economic duress 213–215

entire obligations 95, 341–342
exclusion clauses and unfair
  contract terms 141
exploitation 257
express terms 81
implied contract
  theory 45–47, 445,
  655
lawful bases 133–134
losing contracts 335–336
minority 384–385
mistake 192–215
operative, contract must
  cease to be 314–315
part-performance 94–95
perform, defendant no longer
  ready, willing, and able
  to 315–316
pre-incorporation
  contracts 369
provision in contract 141–142
settlement and
  compromise 143–144
subject to contract 346–348
subrogation 20
subversion of contract
  law 726–727
third parties 142–143
unenforceable contracts 144,
  350–353
valuation of
  enrichment 99–103
void transactions 367–378
contribution 246–251
  causation 435
  Civil Liability (Contribution)
  Act 1978 248–251
  limitation periods 736
conversion 459–460, 641–642,
  740
copyright, breach of 460–461
corrective justice 4–7
correspondence of gain and
  loss 116–119
Court of Protection, powers
  of 381
criminal offences 526–554 see
  also confiscation regime
  following conviction;
  forfeiture rule
  causation 530–532
  crime itself, founding a claim
  on 528–534
  denial of benefits arising from
  commission of
  crimes 542–554
  fiduciary duty, breach
  of 527–528
  forfeiture rule 543–554

gain-based relied, nature
  of 530
Human Rights Act 1998 532
illegality defence, operation
  of 532
literary proceeds of crime,
  recovering the 533–534
minority 729
objections 528–529
obstacles to claims 530–532
recognition of
  claims 529–530,
  532–534
remoteness 530–532
serious culpability 723–724
State, restitutionary claims
  brought by 534–542
stolen property, recovery
  of 740
third parties, restitution
  from 534
threats to invoke criminal
  process 230–231
torts 527–528
unjust enrichment, claims
  founded on 527
victims, claims brought
  by 526–534
vindication of property rights,
  claims founded on 527
wrongs 527–534, 729

damages
  exemplary 432
  negotiation 429–432,
  448–449,
  455–457, 517
  nominal 448
  restitutionary damages 19,
  427–428, 457–459
  wasted expenditure
  336–343
  wrongful interference with
  same goods 245–246
debt
  action for debt 643
  determination when debt
  discharged 235–239
  discharge 144–146,
  235–252, 298
  failure to discharge 252
  legal compulsion 239–251
  limitation periods for
  recovery 738
deceit 462–464
defamation 466–467
defences see also change of
  position; illegality;
  incapacity; mistake

agent, transfer of benefit by
  an 674–678
bona fide purchase 656–660
change in
  circumstances 666–701
denials
  distinguished 663–664
enrichment-related,
  classification as 665
estoppel by
  representation 666–674
fundamental
  principles 663–665
justice favours the defendant
  retaining benefit,
  where 664
mitigation of loss 705–707
passing on 702–705
public authorities 408–412
security of receipt 664–665
unjust-related, classification
  as 665
wrongs, for 441–443
denials distinguished from
  defences 663–664
deposits 333
descriptive sense of unjust
  enrichment 8–9
deterrence 6, 423–424, 484, 714
discharge of a debt 144–146,
  235–252, 298
disclosure 200
discretion 41–42, 566–567
disgorgement 5–6
dishonest inducement or
  assistance in breach of
  trust or fiduciary
  duty 521–525
duress 206–208, 210–211,
  213–229
avoiding contracts
  for 213–215
bad faith 219–220
but for test 223–225
causation 208–210, 221–227
coercion of the will 227–229
economic duress 213–229
essential features 213–218
heads of duress 210
illegitimate threats and
  pressure 206–208,
  218–220, 222–223
kill or injure, threats to 211
lawful act duress 215–218
liberty, threats to interfere
  with 211
no reasonable alternative,
  where there is 225–227
person, duress of the 210–211

duress (cont.)
    property, duress of 212
    public authorities 394–395,
        399
    third parties 210
    threats not to contract with
        claimant 215–218

economic duress 213–229
election between inconsistent
    remedies 438–439
enrichment 62–103 see also
        valuation of enrichment
    defences classified as
        enrichment-
        classification 665
    direct enrichment 105–114
    discharge of debt 235–239,
        298
    essence of enrichment 64–72
    estoppel 90–93
    expense of claimant,
        at 104–119, 295–296
    forgoing a claim 78
    free acceptance 85–90
    grounds of restitution 83,
        125–126, 158–159, 203,
        256, 309
    identification of an
        enrichment 82–83,
        256, 295
    incontrovertible
        benefit 78–85
    indirect enrichment 107–114
    money 73–75, 79, 82–85
    necessary expenditure,
        anticipation of 79–81
    necessity 295
    non-money benefits 360–365
    objective test 65–69
    part-performance of
        contract 94–95
    performance, inadequacy
        of 102–103
    positive and negative
        enrichment 67–68
    receipt of enrichment 68–69
    release of obligations 77–78
    relevance of
        enrichment 62–72
    services 75–77, 319
    subjective devaluation,
        methods of
        defeating 66–90
    subjective test 69–72
    types of enrichment 73–78,
        158–159
    unjust sacrifice 93–94
    without enrichment 90–4

equitable charges 20, 635–636
equitable remedies see also
        constructive trusts
    charges 635–636
    equitable compensation 275
        487–488
    subrogation 636–641
    wrongs 275, 486–487,
        504–509, 516–519
equitable wrongdoing 275,
        486–525, 729,
        739–740
equity and common law,
        relationship
        between 40–41, 612–613
estoppel 520–525 see also
        estoppel by
        representation
    enrichment 90–93
    establishing the estoppel 91,
        520
    identification of appropriate
        relief 520–521
    promissory estoppel 350
    unconscionable
        conduct 520–521
    valuation of enrichment 99
estoppel by
        representation 666–674
    accuracy, duty of 668–669
    apportionment of
        payments 672
    burden of proof, shifting
        the 673
    causation 670–671
    change in
        circumstances 670–671
    change of position 698–700
    conditions for
        defence 667–671
    continuing role for estoppel,
        whether there is 674
    de minimis rule 672
    detriment 671
    entitled to benefit, defendant
        led to believe they
        are 667–669
    imposition of conditions 672
    justice of the case 671
    reliance by
        defendant 669–670
    representation of facts or
        law 667–668
    unconscionability 673–674
ethical standards 423–424
EU law 390–391
ex turpi causa principle 709–711
exclusion clauses and unfair
        contract terms 141

exemplary damages 432
expectant heirs, transactions
        with 284
expense of claimant, enrichment
        at the 104–119
exploitation 122, 255–288 see
        also unconscionable
        conduct; undue influence
    abuse of fiduciary
        relationships of
        confidence 275–278
    essence of exploitation 122,
        255
    identifying the
        enrichment 256
    illegality 286–288, 720
    in pari delicto
        defences 286–288,
        720–721
    mental incapacity 381–382
    minority 387
    passing of title 580
    principles, relationship with
        other 255–256
    trust and confidence,
        relationships of 497–500
    vitiation of
        transactions 256–257
    wrongs 257
express trusts 581–582

failure of basis 308–378 see also
        partial failure of basis;
        total failure of basis; void
        transactions and total
        failure of basis
    contingent condition, failure
        of a 310–311
    damages for breach of
        contract, relationship
        with 312–313
    definition 309–311
    good consideration, provision
        of 189–191
    grounds of restitution 309
    illegality 721
    in pari delicto
        defences 720–721
    minority 369
    mistake 189
    nature of
        enrichment 311–312
    passing of title 577–578
    perform bargain, failure of
        defendant to 310
    public authorities 397
    unauthorized receipt by public
        authority 397
fair-dealing rule 495–496

fault 34–35, 348–349, 601, 648–651, 694
fictions, principle against 39
fiduciary relationships
  abuse 274–278, 423
  account of profits 487, 504–509, 516–519
  breach of contract 470
  breach of duty 275–278, 488–514, 521–528, 598, 646
  categories 492–504
  confidence, abuse of relationship of 275–278, 501–502
  constructive trusts, proprietary remedies following recognition of 509–514, 519
  criminal offences 527–528
  dishonestly inducement or assistance in breach 521–525
  gain-based remedies 504–514
  identification 39, 276, 470, 488–491
  influence, relationship of 502–504
  innocent volunteers 634
  mixing 619–620, 623
  nature and ambit of relationship 39, 491–493
  proportionate share 633–634
  rescission 504
  tracing 617–620, 623
  trust and confidence, relationships of 492–501
  undue influence 275–278
following 607–608, 613 see also tracing
forfeiture rule 543–554
  allocation of benefits 551
  application 547–552
  caused by killing, entitlement must be 547–548
  constructive trusts 549–552
  Forfeiture Act 1982 552–554
  forfeiture principle 543–545
  illegality defence, relationship with 544–545
  joint tenancies 548–550
  life tenancies 550
  proof of guilt 547
  proprietary implications 551–552
  third parties 550–551
  triggering rule 545–547
  types of benefits 548

unlawful killing, types of 545–547
free acceptance 85–90, 99–100, 122–124
frustration of contract 355–367
  apportionment, arguments for and against 366
  benefits transferred before contract frustrated 355–367
  common law 356–357
  definition 356
  Law Reform (Frustrated Contracts) Act 1943 355–367
  money, restitution of 357–360
  non-money, restitution of 360–365
  part performance 95
  partial failure of basis 355–367
  reform, need for 365–367

general average 307
gifts 148–149, 181–183, 541
giving up rights and reinstatement of obligations 6
good consideration defence 189–191
good faith 658–659 see also bad faith
grounds of restitution 120–132
  absence of basis 127–132
  claimant-oriented grounds 121–122
  closed, grounds as not being 125
  compulsion 252–253
  defendant-oriented 122–124, 259
  enrichment 83, 125–126, 158–159, 203, 256, 309
  explanatory basis, no 128–129
  exploitation 122, 257–260
  free acceptance 122–124
  ignorance 152–153
  incapacity 380
  mistake 165–187
  over-simplification, danger of 125
  policy-oriented grounds 124–125
  public authorities 394–406
  qualified intention 121–122
  third parties 126–127
  type of enrichment 125–126, 158–159, 203, 256, 309

uncertainty as to basis 131–132, 367–368
unjust enrichment 120–132
vitiated intention 121

Human Rights Act 1998 532

ignorance 152–156
  direct recipients 572
  election between principles 155–156
  ground of restitution, whether 152–153
  indirect recipients 572–573
  interceptive subtraction 154–155
  mistake 159
  passing of title 572–573
  poor and ignorant, transactions with 283–284
  reliance on ignorance 153–155
  services provided in circumstances of ignorance 153–154
illegality 708–725
  close connection or inextricable link 722–723
  compulsion 205–206, 720
  consistency 713–714
  criminal offences 532, 723–724
  denial of restitution 330–332
  deterrence 714
  dignity of the court 715
  equity 712–713
  ex turpi causa principle 709–711
  exclusion, mechanisms for 717–723
  exploitation 286–288, 720
  failure of basis 330–332, 721
  forfeiture rule 544–545
  in pari delicto, parties not in 720–721
  justice 708–709
  mistake 186–197
  no reliance on illegality 718–719
  passing of title 579
  policies underlying defence 713–715
  policy behind the illegality 721–722
  preferred approach 724–725
  public policy 708–709, 711–712

illegality (*cont.*)
  punishment 714–715
  reform of law 725
  reliance, where there is
    no 718–719
  total failure of basis 353–355
  turpitude, defining 716–717
  withdrawal 353–355,
    719–720
  wrongs 423, 721
implied contract theory 45–47,
  445, 655
in pari delicto defence 286–288,
  720–721
incapacity 379–388, 726–733 *see*
  also mental incapacity;
  minority
  absence or vitiation of
    intent 379
  categories 381–388
  claimants 379–380
  contract law, subversion
    of 726–727
  defence, as a 380
  defendants 380
  general principles 379–380
  ground of restitution, as 380
  institutional incapacity 579,
    731–733
  intoxication 383
  limitation periods 737
  passing of title 579
  policy 389, 726–727
  protection, whether defendant
    deserves 726
  public authorities 379–380,
    387–388
  recognition of defence 733
  somnambulism 383–384
incomplete contracts 343–350
incontrovertible benefit 78–85
indirect enrichment 107–114
infancy *see* minority
injunctions 433
innocent volunteers 634
institutional constructive
  trusts 595, 597–603
institutional incapacity 579,
  731–733
intellectual property rights,
  interference
  with 460–462
interceptive
  subtraction 111–114,
  154–155
interest, award of 29–30, 406
intoxication 383

joint tenancy 548–550

laches 734, 741–743
land
  limitation periods 740
  trespass to 453–459
lawful bases 133–151
  contract 133–144
  discharge of a debt 144–146
  gifts 148–149
  natural obligations 147–148
  res judicata 147
  statutory authority 146
  voluntary transfers 149–151
legal compulsion 233–253
  contribution 246–251
  creditor, restitution from
    the 251–252
  debtor, restitution from
    the 239–251
  discharged, determining when
    a debt has been 235–239
  ground of restitution,
    as 252–253
life, health, and property,
  preservation of 298–301
life tenants 550
limitation periods 734–741
  breach of contract 738–739
  contribution 736
  conversion 740
  determination of when time
    starts to run 736–738
  different periods, recognition
    of 738
  equity, claims in 735, 739–740
  incapacity 737
  land 740
  mistake, spontaneous or
    induced 737–738
  public authorities 408–409
  qualification for particular
    claims 735–736
  recovery of debts or other
    liquidated pecuniary
    claims 738
  reform of law 743
  salvage 736
  stolen property, recovery
    of 740
  torts 738–739
  unjust enrichment, reversal
    of 735–738
  usual period 735
  vindication of proprietary
    rights 740–741
  wrongs 738–740
local authorities 378

maritime adventures, necessity in
  context of 305–307

medical treatment, provision
  of 297–298
mental incapacity 381–383,
  730–731
  Court of Protection, powers
    of 381
  exploitation 381–382
  knowledge of incapacity 382
  limitation periods 737
  non est factum 381, 383
  understand nature and effect
    of transaction, failure
    to 382
minority 384–387, 727–730
  contracts 384–385, 729–730
  criminal offences 729
  establishing that basis has
    failed, necessity of
    establishing 386–387
  exploitation 387
  failure of basis 369
  limitation periods 737
  necessaries, supply
    of 299–300, 727
  non-necessary benefits, supply
    of 727–728
  other transactions, effect
    on 385
  passing of title 579
  problems raised by
    minority 384
  recognition of
    defence 727–728
  relevance 385–386
  torts 729
  total failure of basis, need
    for 369, 385
  unjust enrichment, reversal
    of 727–728
  validity of contracts, effect
    on 384–385
  vindication of property
    rights 730
  wrongs 729–730
misprediction 162–164
misrepresentation 187, 197–200,
  576
mistake 157–202
  bars to restitution 189–192
  beliefs and
    assumptions 159–161
  causative mistakes 170–186
  change of position 191
  common mistakes 194–195
  completed invalid
    transactions 192
  compulsion 577
  concoction of claims 158
  consideration 189–191

contracts 192–215
defences 189–192
different types of
    claim 158–159
distinctions 159–165
fundamental
    mistakes 168–170
gifts 181–183
ground of restitution, as
    a 165–187
honest receipt 191–192
identity of property, mistake
    as to 574–575
identity of recipient, mistake
    as to 574
ignorance 159
illegality 186–197
induced mistakes 164, 187,
    737–738
justice for the defendant 158
knowledge 177
law, mistakes of 183–186,
    191–192
law and fact 161–162
legally effective basis 164–165
liability mistakes 165–168
limitation periods 737–738
misprediction 162–164
misrepresentation 187,
    197–200
mutual mistakes 195–196
non-disclosure 200
non est factum, doctrine
    of 196
passing of title 574–576
policies 157–158
public authorities 393–394,
    399
recognition as ground of
    restitution 157, 187–189
relief from transactions
    entered into under
    mistake 192–202
risk allocation 158
security of transaction 158
significance of mistake 158
spontaneous mistakes 164,
    165–187, 737–738
third parties 199–200
title not passing 574–577
total failure of basis 189
ultra vires payments 393–394
unilateral mistakes 195, 197
void/voidable
    transactions 193–202
voluntariness and risk-
    taking 176–181,
    200–202
mitigation of loss 705–707

mixed products/funds 618–623
money
    benefit realizable in
        money 84–5
    benefit realized in
        money 82–4
    enrichment 73–75, 82–85
    exchange value 73
    frustration 357–360
    incontrovertible benefit 79,
        82–85
    laundering 540–541
    money had and received 18,
        424, 642–643
    passive or active claims 83–84
    proprietary claims 657
    total failure of basis 333,
        337–339
    use value 73–75

natural obligations 147–148
nature of relationship between
    parties 38–39
nature of restitutionary
    remedies 3–33
    categories of remedy 3–4
    characteristics of
        remedies 4–6
    deprivation of benefits from a
        wrongdoer 10–11
    disgorgement 5–6
    giving up rights and
        reinstatement of
        obligations 6
    independent law of restitution,
        justification for
        recognition of 17–18
    limitation of remedies 296
    personal remedies 4
    proprietary claims and
        remedies 4, 558–559
    restoring what claimant has
        lost 4–5
    reversal of unjust
        enrichment 8–10
    types of remedy 18–33
    vindication of property rights
        interfered with 11–17
    when awarded 7–17
necessaries 299–300, 727
necessity 289–307
    agency 301–305
    circumstances of necessity,
        determining whether
        claimant acted
        in 293–295
    compulsion
        distinguished 205,
        292–293

expenditure, anticipation of
    necessary 295
expense of claimant,
    determining whether
    enrichment received
    at 295–296
free choice, interference with
    claimant's 291–292
general average 307
identifying the
    enrichment 295
intervention by
    stranger 296–301
limiting the restitutionary
    remedy 296
maritime adventures, context
    of 305–307
pre-existing legal
    relationships 301–305
public policy 291
salvage 305–307
valuation of enrichment 295
voluntariness, principle
    of 289–291
negligence 178–180, 466, 641
negotiation damages 429–432,
    448–449, 455–457, 517
no-conflict duty 493–494
no-profit duty 494–495
nominal damages 448
non est factum 196, 381, 383
non-disclosure 200
non-money benefits 333–335,
    360–365
nuisance 461–462

part-performance of
    contract 94–95
partial failure of basis
    arguments for and against
        recognition 325–327
    consequences of
        recognition 327–328
    Consumer Rights Act
        2015 367
    courts, recognition
        by 328–329
    frustration 355–367
    rejection of goods 367
    total failure of basis 325–329,
        355–367
passing of title 570–580
    absence of basis 578
    circumstances in which title
        will not pass 571–578
    circumstances in which title
        will pass 577–578
    exploitation 580
    failure of basis 577–578

passing of title (*cont.*)
  general rules 570–571
  ignorance 572–573
  illegality 579
  incapacity 579
  institutional incapacity 579
  misrepresentation 576
  mistake 574–576
  retention of equitable title 580
  revested in claimant,
      circumstances in which
      title will be 580
  total failure of basis 577–578
passing off 461
passing on defence 702–705
  correspondence
      principle 116–117
  judicial
      examination 118–119,
      411, 703–704
  public authorities 411
  recognition of
      defence 118–119, 703,
      704–705
  rejection 118–119, 703–704
patents, infringement of 461
perform, defendant no longer
      ready, willing, and able
      to 315–316
personal claims and remedies 4,
      641–655
  administration of
      estates 644–645
  bona fide purchase, defence
      of 660
  common law 641–643
  conversion 641–642
  debt, action for 643
  equity 644–655
  money had and received,
      action for 642–643
  proprietary claims 558–559,
      628–629
  rescission 24
  subrogation 655
  unconscionable receipt, action
      for 645–655
  vindication of proprietary
      rights 631, 641–655, 698
poor and ignorant, transactions
      with 283–284
powerlessness 576–577
price, relevance of 99–102
privacy, breach of 464–466
private information, receipt
      of 464–465
private nuisance 461–462
privity principle 104–116
promissory estoppel 350

property rights *see* proprietary
      claims; proprietary
      remedies
proportionate share 633–635
proprietary claims 4, 557–641 *see
      also* constructive trusts;
      following; passing of title;
      proprietary remedies;
      tracing; trusts; vindication
      of property rights
  bona fide purchase, defence
      of 656–660
  change of position
      defence 696–698
  common law 632
  compensation 448–449
  compulsion 577
  creation of proprietary
      interests 581–607
  criticisms of 15–16
  discretion, role of 566–567
  express trusts 581–582
  forfeiture rule 551–552
  framework for
      analysis 567–569
  identification of proprietary
      interests 569–607
  misrepresentation 576
  mistake 574–577
  money 657
  nature of claims 559–565
  nature of restitutionary
      remedy 558–559
  personal remedies 558–559,
      628–629
  policy issues 566–567
  powerlessness 576–577
  price payable for interference
      with property
      rights 471–473
  retention of equitable title 580
  retention of proprietary
      interest 570–580
  return property, failure
      to 81–82
  terminology 557
  unjust enrichment 11–17,
      559–565
  vindication of property
      rights 557–565
  wrongs 422–423, 565–566
proprietary remedies 4, 558–559,
      567–569, 628–641
  bona fide purchase, defence
      of 660
  breach of confidence 519
  claims and remedies,
      distinguishing
      between 631

  common law 632
  constructive trusts 509–514,
      519
  equitable wrongdoing 487,
      519
  personal remedies 631
public authorities 389–412
  absence of basis 397, 399
  change of
      position 409–411
  colore officii (colour of office),
      extortion by 395–396
  constitutional
      considerations 389–391
  defences 408–412
  definition 392
  duress 394–395, 399
  EU law 390–391
  failure of basis 397
  grounds of
      restitution 394–406
  implications for general
      community 391
  incapacity 379–380,
      387–388
  Law Commission 412–413
  limitation periods 408–409
  local authorities 378
  mistake 393–394, 399
  passing on 411
  pragmatism and
      policy 389–392
  public finances, disruption
      of 412
  reasons for different treatment
      from other
      defendants 389–392
  reform of law 412
  settlement 411–412
  total failure of basis 397
  ultra vires payment/
      receipt 393–394,
      398–408
  unjust enrichment,
      establishing 392–394
public finances, disruption
      of 412
public policy 39–40, 291,
      641, 708–709,
      711–712
publish information, threats
      to 231–232

quantum meruit 19
quantum valebat 19
Quistclose trusts 593–595

ratification 447
recklessness 194–195

rectification 21
reimbursement 239–246
reinstatement of obligations 6
rejection of goods 367
remedies *see* nature of
    restitutionary remedies;
    particular remedies
    (eg account of profits);
    personal claims and
    remedies; proprietary
    remedies; restitutionary
    remedies
remoteness 435–437, 530–532
representation, estoppel by *see*
    estoppel by
    representation
res judicata 147
rescission 21–33
  absolute, as 271–274
  affirmation 27–88
  bars 25–28
  bona fide purchase for
    value 660
  common law 23
  constructive trusts 602–603
  equity, in 23
  fiduciary relationships 504
  future of rescission 29–33
  impossible, where restoration
    is 25–27
  interest, award of 29–33
  lapse of time 28
  monetary remedies in lieu
    of 274–275
  partial rescission 28–29, 272
  personal 24
  proprietary interests 23–24
  restitution following
    rescission 23–24
  terms, rescission on 28–29,
    272–274
  third party rights 27
  undue influence 271–275
restitution, essence of 3–33
restitutionary damages 19,
    427–428
restitutionary remedies *see also*
    nature of restitutionary
    remedies; personal claims
    and remedies;
    proprietary remedies
  categories 3–4
  characteristics 4–6
  compensation
    principle 447–448
  disgorgement 5–6
  general principles 447–450
  identification of loss 449–450
  principal types 18–33

restoring what claimant
    lost 4–5
rights and reinstatement of
    obligations, giving up 6
torts 447–452
when awarded 7–17
resulting trusts 582–595
  absence of intent 583–588
  automatic resulting
    trusts 582–584, 592–593
  categories 584–588
  essence of resulting trusts 582
  positive intent 597
  presumed resulting
    trusts 582–584,
    588–592
  Quistclose trusts 593–595
  recognition 582–588
  theoretical foundations for
    recognition 582–588
return property, failure to 81–82
risk-taking 36–37, 176–181,
    346–348

sacrifice, unjust 93–94
salvage 284, 305–307, 736
secret commissions and
    bribes 500–501
security
  negligent failure to
    register 641
  receipt, of 664–665
  resurrection of
    discharged 638–639
  transactions, of 158
self-dealing rule 495
services
  contracts to provide
    services 319
  end product, resulting in
    an 76–77
  enrichment 75–77, 319
  ignorance 153–154
  pure services 77
  valuation 98–99
settlements 143–144, 411–412
somnambulism 383–384
State, restitutionary claims
    brought by 534–542
statutory authority 146
statutory duty, threats to secure
    performance of
    a 253–254
subject to contract 346–348
subrogation 20–1, 636–641
  contractual 20
  exclusion of remedy 640
  function 636–638
  intentional transfer 639–640

negligent failure to register
    security 641
no better position, putting
    in 640
operation of law, by 638
personal claims and
    remedies 655
public policy 641
restitutionary 20–1
security, resurrection of
    discharged 638–639
unintentional transfer 640
vindication of proprietary
    rights 698
substantive sense of unjust
    enrichment 9–10
sue, threats to 231
swaps litigation 372–373

tainted gifts 541
taxes, recovery of
    overpaid 401–402,
    406–408
third parties
  cause of action against third
    parties, acquisition
    of 686
  contract 142–143
  criminal offences 534
  duress 210
  forfeiture rule 550–551
  grounds for
    restitution 126–127
  misrepresentation 199–200,
    210
  mistake 199–200
  mixed funds 620–623
  necessity 296–301
  privity principle 104–116
  rescission 27
  total failure of basis 329–330
  tracing 620–623
  unconscionable
    conduct 282–283
  undue influence 269–271
time limits *see* limitation
    periods
title passing *see* passing of title
torts 444–467
  breach of contract 471
  breach of statutory
    duty 465–466
  compensation
    principle 447–448
  conversion 459–460
  criminal offences 527–528
  deceit 462–464
  defamation 466–467
  gain-based remedies 453–467

torts (*cont.*)
   identification of loss to
      establish the
      tort 449–450
   intellectual property
      rights 460–461
   limitation periods 738–739
   minority 729
   mistake 178–180
   negligence 178–180, 466,
      641
   negotiation damages 448–449
   nominal damages 448
   nuisance 461–462
   private information, receipt
      of 464–465
   private nuisance 461–462
   proprietary loss,
      compensation
      for 448–449
   remedies 453–466
   restitutionary
      remedies 447–452
   security, negligent failure to
      register 641
   trespass to land 453–459
   user principle 449
   waiver 444–447
total failure of basis 313–356 *see
   also* void transactions
   and total failure of basis
   absence of basis 371–378
   alternative claims 350
   anticipated and complete
      contracts 343–350
   apportionment 321–325,
      342–343
   breach of contract, discharge
      for 332–343
   build and sell and contracts to
      sell, distinguishing
      between 318–319
   collateral benefits, receipt
      of 319–321
   contracts
      breach, discharge
         for 332–343
      operative, contract must
         cease to be 314–315
      perform, defendant no
         longer ready, willing, and
         able to 315–316
      totally, basis must have
         failed 316–319, 325–329
   damages 336–343
   denial of restitution 330–332
   determining whether basis
      failed 316–317

entire obligations, part
      performance of contracts
      containing 341–342
   failure to discharge debt 252
   fault 348–349
   illegality 330–332, 353–355
   incomplete contracts 343–350
   losing contracts 335–336
   manipulating notion of total
      failure 319–325
   minority 385
   mistake 189
   money paid, restitution
      of 333, 337–339
   non-money benefits,
      restitution of 333–335,
      339–343
   operation of total failure of
      basis 332–355
   part performance of contracts
      with entire
      obligations 341–342
   partial failure 325–329,
      355–367
   passing of title 577–578
   perform, defendant no longer
      ready, willing, and able
      to 315–316
   prevention of
      performance 342
   problems in
      application 329–332
   services, contracts to
      provide 319
   subject to contract 346–348
   substantial performance 341
   third parties, restitution
      from 329–330
   totally, basis must have
      failed 316–319, 325–329
   unconscionability 349–350
   unenforceable
      contracts 350–353
   void transactions 367–378
   wasted expenditure,
      compensatory damages
      for 336–343
   withdrawal from illegal
      transaction 353–355
tracing 607–628 *see also*
      following
   attribution 610
   backward tracing 624–626
   causation 610
   claiming, distinguishing 612
   Clayton's Case, rule
      in 621–623
   common law 612–616

dissipation of assets or
      funds 623
   equity 612–613, 616–628
   essence 608–611
   fiduciary
      requirement 617–618
   fiduciary's money, mixing
      with 619–620, 623
   function 608–611
   future of rules 628–630
   identification of
      property 610–611
   lowest intermediate
      balance 624
   mixed products/
      funds 615–616,
      618–623
   pragmatic approach, move to
      more 627–628
   profits, into 614
   restrictions 623–627
   substitute assets and products,
      into 611–612, 613–614
   third parties 620–623
   unmixed funds 618
   value rather than identifying
      property,
      tracing 610–611
trademarks, infringement of 461
trespass to land 453–459
   account of profits 459
   capital value of land 454–455
   negotiation damages 455–457
   restitutionary
      damages 457–459
   use of land 455–459
   valuing defendant's
      benefit 454–455
trust and confidence,
      relationships of
   bribes or secret
      commissions 500–501
   exploitation of
      opportunities 497–500
   fair-dealing rule 495–496
   fiduciary, breach of duty
      of 492–501
   interference with people's
      property 496–497
   more than one principal,
      acting for 496
   no-conflict duty 493–494
   no-profit duty 494–495
   self-dealing rule 495
   wrongs 423
trusts *see also* constructive
      trusts; resulting trusts
   breach of trust 646–647

creation of proprietary
    interests 581–607
dishonestly inducement or
    assistance in breach of
    trust 521–525
express trusts 581–582

ultra vires payments/
    receipt 393–394,
    398–406
unauthorized transactions 393
unconscientious
    retention 53–55
unconscionability *see*
    unconscionable conduct
unconscionable
    conduct 278–286,
    520–521 *see also*
    unconscionable receipt,
    action for
anticipated and incomplete
    contracts 349–350
constructive trusts 598–602
consumer credit 286
definition 280
estoppel 520–521, 673–674
expectant heirs, transactions
    with 284
fair, just, and reasonable,
    whether transaction
    was 281
general principle 278–281
gross inequality of bargaining
    power 284–286
identification 281–282
inequality between
    parties 279–280, 283–286
poor and ignorant,
    transactions
    with 283–284
retention 53–55
salvage agreements 284
significant imbalance in
    substance of
    transactions 281
special disability 279–280,
    283–286
statutory regimes 286
third parties 282–283
total failure of basis 349–350
unconscionable, meaning
    of 280
unconscionable receipt, action
    for 645–655
beneficial receipt 647–648
breach of trust 646–647
conditions of
    liability 645–651
fault 648–651
fiduciary duty, breach
    of 646–647

future of the action 652–655
receipt of property 645–646
remedies 651–652
undue influence 257–275
actual undue
    influence 260–263
claimant- or defendant-
    oriented, whether 259
compulsion, distinguished
    from 205
equitable compensation 275
establishing undue
    influence 257–258,
    260–262
explanation, transaction
    requires 266–268
fiduciary relationships of
    confidence, abuse
    of 274–278
ground of restitution, essence
    as 257–260
identification 262
manifest and unfair
    disadvantage 262–263
monetary remedies in lieu of
    rescission 274–275
nature of relief 271–275
partial rescission 272
presumptions, use of 263–269
relationships of
    influence 264–266
rescission 271–275
third parties 269–271
types 257–258
undue pressure 205
wrongdoing, as form
    of 259–260
undue pressure 229–232
criminal process,
    threats to
    invoke 230–231
essence of undue
    pressure 229–230
general ground,
    whether 232–233
publish information, threats
    to 231–232
recognized heads 230–232
sue, threats to 231
threats 230–232
undue influence 205
unenforceable contracts and
    total failure of
    basis 350–353
United States, influence
    of 50–51
unjust enrichment 45–61 *see
    also* enrichment
    alternative theories 52–55
    anticipated and incomplete
    contracts 345–346

at the expense of the
    claimant 104–119
cause of action, identification
    of 60
correspondence
    principle 116–119
criminal offences 527
descriptive sense 8–9
English law approach 56
establishing claims 60–61,
    392–394
fiduciary relationships,
    identification of 39
formulaic function 55–56
function of principle 55–58
grounds of
    restitution 120–132
justification of
    principle 51–55
limitation periods 735–738
middle way 57–58
minority 727–728
normative function 56–57
obligations, place within the
    law of 51
possible functions 55–56
practice, role in 58–61
principle of 7–6, 17
privity principle *see* privity
    principle
proprietary restitutionary
    claims 11–17, 559–565
proprietary theory 52
recognition of law of unjust
    enrichment 61
recognition of
    principle 45–46
relationship between parties,
    nature of 38–39
reversal 8–10, 415–417,
    442–443, 559–565,
    695, 727–728, 735–738
substantive sense 9–10
unconscionable
    retention 53–55
unifying principle,
    lack of 53
United States, influence
    of 50–51
wrongs 415–421, 442–443
unjust sacrifice 93–94
user principle 449, 456, 479

valuation of enrichment 95–103,
    295, 360–362
contract, role of 99–103
estoppel 99
free acceptance 85–90
inadequate
    performance 102–103
land 454–455

valuation of enrichment (*cont.*)
  money 73–75
  necessity 295
  price, relevance of 99–102
  services, valuing 98–99
  subjective devaluation,
    methods of
    defeating 66–90
  subjective over-valuation 98
  test 97–99
  timing 96–97
  use value 73–75
VAT, recovery of
  overpaid 406–408
vindication of property
  rights 11–17, 631–655
  change of position 696–698
  claims and remedies,
    distinguishing
    between 631
  conversion 740
  criminal offences 527
  criticisms of
    principle 15–16
  dissipation of property 697
  equitable claims 740–741
  indirect enrichment 110
  justification of award of
    restitutionary
    remedies 16–17
  land 740
  limitation periods 740–741
  minority 730
  nature of restitutionary claims
    founded on
    vindication 11–12
  personal claims and
    remedies 631, 641–655
  personal remedies 631, 698
  proprietary remedies 631–641
  relationship with unjust
    enrichment 12–17
  stolen property, recovery
    of 740
  subrogation 697
  unjust enrichment 559–565
void transactions and
  total failure of
  basis 367–378
  absence of authority 369–370
  absence of basis 371–378
  annuity cases 371
  fully executed
    transactions 376–377
  infancy 369
  payments to discharge a liability
    which does not exist 371
  policy of invalidity 377–378

pre-incorporation
  contracts 369
swaps litigation 372–373
uncertainty as to ground for
  restitution 367–368
voluntariness 36, 232–234
  innocent volunteers 634
  necessity 289–291
  risk-taking 176–181
  selfishly rather than
    benevolently, claimant
    acting 290
  transfers 149–151, 243–246

waiver of tort 444–447
wasted expenditure 336–343
wrongs *see also* criminal
    offences; torts
  account of profits 424–426,
    487, 504–509
  advantage of treating
    restitution as not
    founded on unjust
    enrichment 417
  agents 676
  alternative analysis 417–418
  benefit, defendant must have
    obtained a 416–17
  breach of confidence 514–519
  breach of contract 468–485,
    729–730, 738–739
  categories 488–525
  causation 434–438
  change of
    position 692–694,
    695–696
  compensatory remedies
    gain-based remedies,
    relationship
    with 438–441
    inadequacy of 424,
    440–441
  constructive trusts 432–433
  criminal offences 527–534,
    729
  culpability of
    defendants 423–424
  defences 441–443
  deprivation of benefits 10–11
  deprivation of benefits from a
    wrongdoer 10–11
  deterrence 423–424
  dishonestly inducing or
    assisting breach of trust
    or fiduciary
    duty 521–525
  election between inconsistent
    remedies 438–439

equitable compensation 275,
  487–488
equitable wrongdoing 275,
  486–525, 729,
  739–740
essence of restitution for
  wrongs 415–422
estoppel 520–525
ethical standards 423–424
exemplary damages 432
fiduciary relationship, breach
  of 275–278, 488–514,
  521–525
gain-based remedies 416,
  422–433, 438–441
general principles 486–488
illegality 423, 721
in pari delicto defence 721
indirect enrichment 110–111
injunctions 433
interference with
  goods 245–246
law of restitution, restitution
  for wrongs as properly
  forming part of 418–419
limitation periods 738–740
minority 729–730
money had and received 424
nature of restitution for 9–10
negotiation damages 429–432
part of the law of restitution,
  whether forms 418–419
proof of action 416
property rights, interference
  with 422–423
proprietary claims 422–423,
  565–566
proprietary remedies 487, 519
ratification 447
reform, recommendations
  for 443
remedies 111, 275, 416,
  422–433, 438–441, 449,
  487–488, 519
restitutionary
  damages 427–428
restoration of property 433
torts 729, 738–739
trigger restitutionary
  wrongs, determining
  which wrongs
  will 422–424
trust and confidence, abuse of
  a relationship of 423
unconscionability 520–521
undue influence 259–260
unjust enrichment 415–421,
  442–443

Printed and bound by CPI Group (UK) Ltd, Croydon, CR0 4YY